The Palgrave Handbook of International Energy Economics

Manfred Hafner • Giacomo Luciani
Editors

The Palgrave Handbook of International Energy Economics

palgrave
macmillan

Editors
Manfred Hafner
SciencesPo PSIA
Johns Hopkins University SAIS-Europe
Oberägeri, Zug, Switzerland

Giacomo Luciani
Paris School of International Affairs
SciencesPo
Founex, Vaud, Switzerland

ISBN 978-3-030-86883-3 ISBN 978-3-030-86884-0 (eBook)
https://doi.org/10.1007/978-3-030-86884-0

Cover illustration: ART Collection / Alamy Stock Photo

This Palgrave Macmillan imprint is published by the registered company Springer Nature Switzerland AG.
The registered company address is: Gewerbestrasse 11, 6330 Cham, Switzerland

Foreword

The *Handbook of International Energy Economics* is an exhaustive compendium of the main economic issues related to the energy sector. In a constantly evolving world, our societies face unprecedented challenges, which will have to be tackled in the decades to come. Climate change ranks high among such challenges, and the transition to a low-carbon future will require deep changes to the way we produce, distribute and trade energy. This will have several implications on our economy, which need to be explained, understood and discussed.

It is therefore timely that we shed light on the complexities surrounding the energy transition, as well as on the ongoing transformations affecting the energy industry. This Handbook represents an important step in the right direction. The book provides a comprehensive and easily accessible reference on the structural economic aspects influencing energy policies and their outcomes. By gathering the contributions of leading experts in the field, it delves into some underlying economic factors that are unlikely to change in the short-to-medium term, emphasizing the economic consequences and trade-offs of the technological solutions currently available.

The analysis takes stock of all the technologies composing today's energy sector, avoiding an *a priori* selection between "old" and "new" sources. This all-inclusive approach allows for a thorough assessment of the economics of the different solutions, highlighting the advantages and disadvantages of alternative options against the backdrop of the United Nations Sustainable Development Goals (SDGs). It also offers a punctual analysis of energy markets, illustrating their organization and price discovery processes, as well as some global trends that may influence future supply and demand patterns.

Furthermore, the Handbook has the merit of showing the inherent tension between the global and local dimensions of the energy transition. On the one hand, it recognizes climate change as a global issue, calling for international cooperation and dialogue with a view to promoting a common response from the international community. On the other hand, it underlines the limitations of "one-size fits all"-type solutions.

The world we live in is marked by substantially different perspectives in the energy landscape at the inter-continental level, which influence the way countries and regions look at the transition. This reflects the different availability of primary sources across the globe, creating conflicting visions about which solutions should or should not be encouraged. The energy mix of the future can only stem from a combination of such visions. In this context, the role of the energy industry should be to provide multiple alternative technologies that can deliver abundant, decarbonized and affordable energy to all.

Towards this goal, it is crucial to promote an inclusive conversation about the energy transition, and yet one based on hard facts and realistic measures. Indeed, meeting the targets of the Paris Agreement will require concrete, rapid and economically sustainable solutions, coupled with a widespread understanding of the economic and technological aspects underpinning each and every energy option.

This Handbook should be regarded as an important contribution to improving access to relevant information for both professionals, politicians and the wider public. As Eni, we will continue to support academic efforts as part of our strong commitment to promote a just transition that creates long-term value and allows everyone to access reliable and clean energy.

Rome Eni

This book was published open access with the support of Eni.

Acknowledgements

We are grateful to all contributors to this volume, many of them fellow faculty members of the Master in International Energy of the Paris School of International Affairs of SciencesPo, for their enthusiasm and patience in the long gestation of the final product.

We owe special thanks to Pier Paolo Raimondi for his invaluable help in the editorial process and in collecting all authorizations and completing all the paperwork needed for publication.

Finally, we are most grateful to Eni for the generous grant that has permitted the publication of this work in open access, thus making it electronically accessible for free to all who might be interested and at a much-reduced price for all who may wish to purchase a hard copy. A special personal thanks to Dr. Lapo Pistelli who supported the initiative.

We hope that they will all be satisfied with the final product.

Manfred Hafner and Giacomo Luciani

Contents

Notes on Contributors

Marco Baroni is an energy expert, a consultant and a lecturer at the Institut d'études politiques de Paris (SciencesPo), France. Baroni has over 20 years of broadly varied work experience in the energy field, acquired in between a widely recognized international organization (the International Energy Agency, IEA), a very dynamic European electricity and gas utility, university and, more recently, energy consulting. He co-authored 11 editions of the *World Energy Outlook*, IEA's flagship publication, where he was in charge of managing the power and renewables team and responsible for the related analysis, modelling and write-up. He has also been co-responsible for scenario designing, climate, gas, subsidies and energy efficiency analysis. In the private sector, he worked as a senior market analyst in Essent Trading—a power and gas Dutch utility—responsible for coal and power markets in the mid- and long-term analysis. He holds a master's degree in Electrical Engineering from the University of Padova, Italy.

Dhruv Bhatnagar is a research engineer at Pacific Northwest National Laboratory, USA. He holds a bachelor's degree from the University of California and a master's degree from Carnegie Mellon University. His current areas of work involve techno-economic and regulatory analyses of energy technologies, including marine energy, offshore wind, electric vehicle, geothermal, hydropower and energy storage resources.

Eike Blume-Werry studied in the UK, Paris and Vienna. During his PhD in Energy Economics, he worked for Switzerland's largest electricity generation company Axpo Holding AG. He recently joined the Federation of German Industries in Berlin as a senior manager for climate and energy policy.

Andrea Bonzanni is an energy policy and regulation expert focusing on European electricity, gas and emissions markets. He has been employed by EDF Trading in London since 2013, where he has worked in the transmission, regulation, origination and compliance departments. Prior to joining EDF, he held roles at Statoil (now Equinor) in Brussels and at the United Nations

Economic Commission for Europe (UNECE) in Geneva. He is a visiting professor at SciencesPo—Paris School of International Affairs in Paris and the College of Europe in Natolin. In 2016, he was included in the 30 Under 30 Europe list by Forbes. He has degrees from the University of Pavia, Italy, and the Graduate Institute of International and Development Studies, Switzerland.

Liz Bossley is a trading consultant with 40 years' first-hand international trading experience. In April 1999, she founded a trading consultancy practice, the Consilience Energy Advisory Group Ltd. Consilience specializes in the physical oil and derivatives markets and associated activities, including oil transportation and refining. She provides consultancy advice to oil and gas companies, industrial firms, utilities, government entities, regulators and service providers on issues related to the operation of markets and contracts and on the pricing and risk management of crude oil, refined products and tankers. She appears regularly as an expert witness in courts and arbitrations within her areas of expertise. She is the author of several books and more than 100 articles in the energy press and academic journals.

Nadine Bret-Rouzaut is an associate professor at various universities. Previously, she was Director of the Center for Economics and Management of IFP School, a Graduate School for the energy and transport industries, where she managed five International Master's programmes in energy, some of which in partnership with American, Russian and European universities. Before joining IFP School, she had a variety of positions within the French Ministry of Industry, in the Oil and Gas division. She holds an engineering degree from IFP School, a master's degree in Theoretical Geophysics from the "Institut de Physique du Globe de Paris" and an MBA from the Sorbonne Graduate Business School. She lectures on economics and management in oil and gas exploration and production (strategy of the players, profitability studies). She is the coordinator and co-author of the book *Oil and Gas Exploration and Production—Reserves, Costs, Contracts.*

Mostyn Brown is a senior consultant at AFRY Management Consulting where he focuses on least-cost pathways to net-zero emissions. He leads AFRY's modelling of the world's largest carbon markets including the EU ETS and the voluntary offset market. He also specializes in the price, policy and regulatory risk governing the EU's renewable electricity markets and the role of digital technologies in transforming energy markets to reduce emissions. Prior to joining AFRY, Brown led a bionanotechnology research project investigating the properties of the world's smallest electric motor. He holds a DPhil in Biophysics from the University of Oxford.

Federico Cecchetti is a professional in the field of energy and environmental policies. He co-authored the chapter on "The Trading of Carbon" as junior researcher at the European Roundtable on Climate Change and Sustainable Transition (ERCST). Before joining ERCST, he completed traineeships at the European Parliament and the Dutch think-tank Clingendael International

Energy Programme (CIEP). He now works at Eni's Public Affairs Department in Rome, Italy. Cecchetti holds a bachelor's degree in Political Science from the University of Siena and master's degree in International Affairs from the Graduate Institute of International and Development Studies (IHIED) in Geneva, Switzerland.

Simonas Cerniauskas studied physics at the University of Leipzig and energy science and technology at the Technische Universität (TU) Darmstadt, Germany. Since 2017 he is working in the Techno-economic Systems Analysis (IEK-3) at the Research Center Jülich. Cerniauskas is working on his PhD thesis: "Introduction Strategies for a Hydrogen Infrastructure in Germany". His work focuses on hydrogen demand scenarios, hydrogen demand localization, infrastructure development and technology assessment.

Bertrand Château received his PhD in Energy Economics at Grenoble in 1977 and has graduated from the Engineering School "Ecole Centrale de Lyon" in 1971. He founded the energy intelligence bureau "Enerdata" in 1991 and remained its CEO until 2013, when he retired. Beforehand, he was the Director of the Economic Department of the French Agency for Energy Management (AFME) from 1988 to 1991, a professor at the Asian Institute of Technology and Consultant for the United Nations Development Programme (UNDP) from 1986 to 1988 and a researcher at the Institute for Energy Economics and Policy from 1973 to 1986, which he ruled for two years. Co-author, with B. Lapillonne, of the long-term energy demand forecasting methodology and models known as "MEDEE", Château has been involved in many studies and missions related to energy planning and demand forecasting for international institutions, energy companies and governments. He has been much involved in the development and application of decision-supporting tools referring to energy efficiency and climate change policies for the French Government and the European Commission mainly. He has also been deeply involved in various research programmes on sustainability, for the OECD, the European Commission and the French authorities.

Edward C. Chow is an international energy expert with more than 40 years of industry experience. He has developed government policy and business strategy while advising governments, international financial institutions, major oil companies and leading multinational corporations. He worked for 20 years at Chevron Corporation in headquarter and overseas assignments. He taught at Georgetown and George Washington Universities and served as visiting professor at Ohio University and Fudan University in Shanghai. He is a senior associate in the Center for Strategic and International Studies and affiliate faculty in George Mason University.

Philippe Copinschi is a specialist in political and socio-economic issues in the energy sector in Africa where he has been working on energy-related issues for nearly 20 years, both as an academic and as a consultant. He is a member of the SciencesPo—Paris School of International Affairs (PSIA) faculty, where he teaches several courses on political economy of sub-Saharan African and geopolitics of energy in Africa. His main topics of interest include the challenge of access to energy in Africa, governance and development strategies in African energy-producing countries and the economic and social impact of energy projects in Africa. He is the author of numerous scientific publications and articles for the layman on energy issues in Africa.

Anselm Eicke is a PhD candidate and research associate at Hertie School, Berlin, Germany. His research revolves around the regulation of electricity systems with high shares of renewable energy sources. Prior to his PhD, Eicke worked at Leibniz University Hannover, the German Corporation for International Cooperation (GIZ) in Mexico and the Bundesverband der Energie- und Wasserwirtschaft (BDEW) in Brussels. Eicke holds a master's degree in International Energy from SciencesPo Paris and a bachelor's degree in Energy Engineering from Technical University Berlin.

Laima Eicke is a research associate and PhD candidate at Institute for Advanced Sustainability Studies (IASS), Potsdam, Germany. Her work focuses on the international political economy of the global energy transition and she specialized in energy transition finance and the Global South. Prior to joining IASS, Eicke worked for the German Corporation for International Cooperation (GIZ), where she supported governments in the implementation of the Paris Agreement. Beforehand, Eicke worked at several research institutes, federal ministries, NGOs and consultancies. She studied international relations and socio-ecological economics and policy at Vienna University of Business and Economics, Technische Universität (TU) Dresden, in Buenos Aires and Lisbon.

Martin Everts is Head of Strategy & Transformation at Axpo. Before joining the energy sector, Everts was researching and teaching in monetary macroeconomics at the University of Bern, Switzerland, where he also completed his doctoral thesis in economics. During his master's studies in Business Administration from the University of St. Gallen, Everts was working in private equity, venture capital and private banking in Switzerland, Germany and the United States. Moreover, he co-founded several start-ups.

Giacomo Falchetta is a research fellow at the Fondazione Eni Enrico Mattei (FEEM) and a doctoral researcher at the Università Cattolica del Sacro Cuore, Italy. He holds a Master of Science from the London School of Economics. He has been a guest research scholar at the International Institute for Applied Systems Analysis (IIASA) and at the PBL Netherlands Environmental Assessment Agency. Falchetta carries out applied research in energy, economic and environmental systems analysis, with a strong regional focus on sub-Saharan Africa. He has extensive expertise in analysing the dynamics of electricity access and evaluating the climate-water-energy-food nexus. He has written numerous papers in high-impact peer-reviewed journals in the energy and environment fields and he contributed to internationally edited handbooks.

Arash Farnoosh holds graduate engineer's degrees (French *Grandes Ecoles*) from both INSA (Institut National des Sciences Appliquées) and ENSPM (Ecole Nationale Supérieure du Pétrole et des Moteurs IFP-School) in addition to a Research MSc in Energy and Transfer Engineering from the University of Toulouse, France. He received his PhD in Economics from the University of Montpellier. In parallel to his research activities within his Chair of "Electricity Economics and Digital Transition", he supervises two master's programmes and teaches courses on energy (oil, gas and electricity) economics and management at IFP School, SciencesPo. and École des Ponts ParisTech. Prior to joining IFP New Energies (a public research organization) as an economist and faculty member at IFP School, he worked in various entities such as Airbus France, Total E&P and BNP Paribas Investment Banking group as a techno-economic engineer and analyst.

Valerie Faudon is the Executive Officer of the French Nuclear Energy Society (SFEN), is the Vice-President of the European Nuclear Society (ENS) and teaches at SciencesPo—Paris School of International Affairs, France. Previously, from 2009 to 2012, she was the Marketing Director at AREVA after holding different executive positions at HP and Alcatel-Lucent in the USA and France. Faudon graduated from the École Polytechnique, the École Nationale des Ponts et Chaussées and the Institut d'études politiques de Paris. She also holds a Master of Sciences from Stanford University.

Jean-Pierre Favennec is an energy specialist, including energy economics, geopolitics and strategic aspects. He has also worked more specifically on the downstream sector of the hydrocarbons industry and has written a number of papers on these subjects. He is the author of several books: *Refining Economics and Management* (2001); *Research and Production of Oil and Gas: Reserves, Costs, Contracts* (2011); *The Energy Markets* (in French, 2013); *The Geopolitics of Energy* (2018) and *World Atlas of Energies* (in French, 2015). Favennec is a recognized expert for energy in Africa. He is the president of the Association for the Development of Energy in Africa. He wrote "Energy in Africa in 2050" (2015). He is the Director of the Energy Summit in Africa, held each year in Africa.

Carlos Fernández Alvarez joined the International Energy Agency (IEA) as a senior energy analyst in 2010. As such, he has contributed to many IEA publications, including the IEA's flagship publication the *World Energy Outlook*, the World Energy Investment report, the Global Energy Review and many others. He is responsible of the IEA Coal report. Alvarez has almost 30 years of experience in the energy sector. He started his career as an energy consultant for power plants, where he worked in a variety of projects: system modelling and safety assessments for nuclear power plants, control room design, radiological protection, licencing activities, research and development projects and bid assessments. In 2001, after ten years in the private sector, he joined the Spanish Government where he was for ten years. As Energy Adviser, he participated in the discussion of the Second Gas and Electricity Directives. In 2003, he was appointed Deputy Director for Mining in the Directorate of Energy Policy and Mining. From 2007 until he joined the IEA, he was Director of the Spanish Coal Agency, the body responsible for the coal sector and the alternative development of the coal mining areas in Spain.

Fabio Genoese is a German-Italian national, has been working in the energy sector for more than 12 years. He started his career in 2008 as a consultant to energy utilities and the German Government, playing a vital role in working out regulatory measures to avoid extreme negative electricity prices. From 2013 to 2016, he was in charge of electricity policy analysis at CEPS, a Brussels-based think tank, authoring numerous publications on electricity market design as well as engaging corporate and institutional stakeholders through CEPS Task Forces. In 2016/2017, he contributed to ENGIE's innovation strategy as Smart Energy Systems Expert in the fields of green gas and electric, autonomous mobility. He is Head of Strategy at Terna in Rome and has been a visiting professor at SciencesPo in Paris from 2014 to 2019. Genoese holds a Doctoral Degree in Energy Economics as well as a master's degree in Physics.

Manfred Hafner is Professor of International Energy Studies (Geopolitics and Economics of Energy), teaches as an adjunct professor at the Johns Hopkins University School of Advanced International Studies (SAIS Europe) and at SciencesPo—Paris School of International Affairs (PSIA) and is involved in many executive education programmes worldwide. Hafner is Programme Director of the "Geopolitics and Energy Transition" (previously "Future Energy") research programme at the Fondazione Eni Enrico Mattei (FEEM). He has over his more than 30-year professional career extensively consulted on international energy issues for governments, international organizations (European Commission [EC], World Bank [WB], International Energy Agency [IEA], International Renewable Energy Agency [IRENA], G7, G20, etc.) and industry, and has coordinated several major interdisciplinary research projects for the European Commission. Hafner holds master's degrees in Energy Engineering from the Technische Universität München, Germany; in Energy Economics and Business from the IFP-School of IFPEN, France, and the Université Paris2/Panthéon Assas, France; and in Energy Economics, Management and Policy from the University of Pennsylvania, USA. He also holds a PhD in Energy Studies from MINES ParisTech (Ecole des Mines de Paris). He has written several books on international energy issues.

Jerome Halbout is a Managing Partner of 4D Global Energy Advisors ("4D"), France, managing over US $450 million invested in small- and medium-sized private companies in the Oil and Gas sector and founder of a new 4DIGITAL investment platform. Prior to founding 4D in 2001, Halbout was Head of Project Finance at Lazard Frères & Cie and Head of Energy/Utilities at Crédit Lyonnais. A graduate of École Normale Supérieure, Paris, Halbout holds a PhD in Geochemistry and a Doctor of Science from Paris

University. Before working in the finance industry, he undertook ten years of scientific research at the CNRS in Paris and during his post-doctoral work at the Enrico Fermi Institute at the University of Chicago. A lecturer at SciencesPo—Paris School of International Affairs until 2015, Halbout served as a Director of EVOLEN, the association of French Oil Services companies, and is a member of the Paris Energy Club, a think tank founded by the Institut Français du Pétrole et des Energies Nouvelles. He has chaired and participated in numerous industry and investor panels, including for the International Energy Agency. He serves on the Board of Directors of several 4D portfolio companies.

Adi Imsirovic has over 30 years of experience in oil trading. He held a number of senior positions, including Global Head of Oil at Gazprom Marketing & Trading, Director of Petraco and the Head of their Singapore office and the Regional Manager of Texaco Oil Trading for Asia. Imsirovic also taught economics at University of Surrey, UK, for several years: energy economics as well as resource and environmental economics. He has written a number of papers and articles on the topics of oil and gas prices, benchmarks and energy security. He holds an honours degree (BSc) in Economics and a Master of Science (MSc) degree in Energy Economics from University of Surrey, UK. He is also a Fulbright Scholar and he studied at the Graduate School of Arts and Sciences, Harvard University.

Christina Kockel is a research associate at the Chair for Energy Resources and Innovation Economics, Rheinisch-Westfälische Technische Hochschule (RWTH) Aachen University, Germany. She graduated in Business Administration and Electrical Engineering from RWTH Aachen University. Her research focuses on the assessment of sustainability of energy systems from an environmental, social and economic perspective. For her research, she received the Best Paper Award at the International Conference on Energy, Ecology and the Environment (ICEEE) in 2019.

Elies Lahmar is Senior Market Designer at the European Power Exchange EPEX SPOT, France. Passionate about the energy transition and current challenges of the power sector, Lahmar holds a Degree in Mechanical Engineering from MINES ParisTech, where he also studied energy economics and power markets. As part of his curriculum, Lahmar worked at ArcelorMittal as an energy analyst, more specifically on the sourcing optimization of the steelmaker's European power and gas consumption portfolios. Furthermore, he worked at Danske Commodities, active on short-term European power and gas markets, where as a quantitative analyst, he designed and implemented automated trading strategies.

Giacomo Luciani created and is responsible for the scientific content of the Master in International Energy at the SciencesPo—Paris School of International Affairs, France. He also teaches at the Graduate Institute of International and Development Studies, Geneva, Switzerland, and in the Master of Science in

International Trading at the University of Geneva, Switzerland. In 2010–2013 he was a global scholar at Princeton University. His massive open online course (MOOC) "Politics and Economics of International Energy" is available on Coursera (https://www.coursera.org/learn/global-energy?).His work has focused on the political economy of MENA and global energy issues. His latest co-edited book, *When Can Oil Economies Be Deemed Sustainable?* (Palgrave Macmillan, 2020; available in open access at https://link.springer.com/book/10.1007/978-981-15-5728-6), discusses the meaning and challenges of sustainability for the GCC economies.

Reinhard Madlener is Full Professor of Energy Economics and Management at the School of Business and Economics, Rheinisch-Westfälische Technische Hochschule (RWTH) Aachen University, Germany; adjunct professor in the Department of Industrial Economics and Technology Management at Norwegian University of Science and Technology (NTNU), Norway; and co-director of the E.ON Energy Research Center (and as such founding and current director of the Institute for Future Energy Consumer Needs and Behavior, FCN). His main research interests, on which he has written extensively over the last 25 years, are in the fields of energy economics and policy; sustainable energy systems; energy efficiency and rebound; adoption, temporal and spatial diffusion of innovation; and investment in innovative energy technologies and portfolios under uncertainty. The main teaching activities of Madlener comprise energy economics, environmental & resource economics, economics of technological diffusion, behavioral energy and environmental economics, economics of technical change, smart grid economics and management and public choice. He acts as Vice-President of the Swiss Association for Energy Economics (SAEE), acts as a senior editor of the *Energy Policy* journal and serves on the editorial boards of numerous international scientific journals, including *Advances in Applied Energy*; *Applied Energy*; *Energy Efficiency*; *Energy Systems*; *Energy, Sustainability and Society*; *International Journal of Energy Sector Management* and the *Journal of Energy Storage*.

Andrei Marcu is the founder and Executive Director of the European Roundtable on Climate Change and Sustainable Transition (ERCST). He has vast experience in managing policy-focused organizations. His focus has been on sustainable development, climate change and energy. He has acted as a negotiator for developing countries, coordinator for the G-77 and China and representative of the international business community. He pioneered cooperation between the UN system and multinational corporations when serving as Manager of Private Sector Cooperation in the United Nations Development Programme. During his career, Marcu has performed at the highest managerial level, both in business organizations and in non-profit organizations. This includes Sr. Vice-President and Head of Regulatory and Policy Affairs at Mercuria Energy Group; CEO of BlueNext, a Paris-based exchange; Managing Director for Climate & Energy at the World Business Council for Sustainable Development (WBCSD) in charge of energy and climate and as Vice Chair of the Energy and Environment Commission of the International Chamber of Commerce in Paris; Senior Associate to the International Centre for Trade and Sustainable Development (ICTSD); Senior Advisor on Climate Change and Emissions Trading at Bennett Jones LLP in Canada; and Founder, President and CEO of the International Emissions Trading Association (IETA), a business association with offices in Geneva, Brussels, Washington and Toronto. Marcu founded the organization and made it into one of the leading global business NGOs and the voice of business in its field. Marcu initiated his career in Ontario Hydro, where among other responsibilities, he served as Chief of Staff for the Chairman and CEO.

Michal Meidan is Director of the China Energy Programme at the Oxford Institute for Energy Studies (OIES). Before joining OIES in July 2019, she headed cross-commodity China research at Energy Aspects. Prior to that, she headed China Matters, an independent research consultancy providing analysis on the politics of energy in China. Meidan also held senior analytical roles at Eurasia Group in New York and London and at Asia Centre-SciencesPo, Paris. She taught undergraduate courses on China's political economy at the Hebrew University in Jerusalem and has authored numerous academic articles. Meidan also regularly provides comments for a wide variety of media outlets and is featured as a speaker at industry conferences. She holds a PhD in Political Science and East Asian Studies from SciencesPo, Paris. She is fluent in Mandarin and French.

Tatiana Mitrova is Director, Energy Center, Moscow School of Management SKOLKOVO, Russia. She has more than 20 years of experience in the analyses of the global and Russian energy markets. She is a senior research fellow at the Oxford Institute for Energy Studies (OIES); scientific advisor at the Energy Research Institute of the Russian Academy of Sciences (ERI RAS); visiting fellow at the Center on Global Energy Policy, Columbia University; and distinguished research fellow at Institute of Energy Economics, Japan (IEEJ). She is also Non-Executive Director at Schlumberger NV and NOVATEK and a visiting professor at the Institut d'études politiques de Paris (SciencesPo), Paris School of International Affairs.

Tom Moerenhout teaches at Columbia University's School of International and Public Affairs and is a scholar at SIPA's Center on Global Energy Policy. He is involved as a practitioner on energy sector and structural reforms through his work as a consultant for the World Bank, International Institute for Sustainable Development and Bill & Melinda Gates Foundation, among others.

Gergely Molnar is a gas analyst at the International Energy Agency, within the Gas, Coal and Power Markets Division under the Directorate of Energy Markets and Security. Before joining the Agency, he held several positions in consulting and private research companies with a focus on European gas markets and gas infrastructure. He holds a master's degree in International Energy from the Paris Institute of Political Sciences and graduated in International Affairs from the Corvinus University of Budapest.

Eleanor J. Morrison is an energy and finance professional with over 25 years' experience working internationally in public and private sectors. She is a lecturer in the Master of International Energy programme at SciencesPo—Paris School of International Affairs in Paris, France.

Isabella Nardini is an International Transfer Manager at the Fraunhofer IEG (Institution for Energy Infrastructures and Geothermal Systems), Germany. She graduated in Geology in 1999 (BSc and MSc in Earth Science) and received her PhD in Geochemistry and Petrology from University of Pisa in 2004. She is an expert in international relations and an active leader of projects and programmes to support development and internationalization in the renewable energy sector. She is also a senior researcher in geochemistry and petrology. She has authored and co-authored many international scientific publications. She is a lecturer of a Hydro- and Geochemistry course for the MSc Programme "Geothermal Energy Systems" at the Bochum University of Applied Science.

Michel Noussan is senior research fellow at Fondazione Eni Enrico Mattei (FEEM), Italy, and Lecturer in Sustainable Mobility at SciencesPo—Paris School of International Affairs, France. His current research activities focus on the effect of decarbonization and digitalization trends on energy consumption, with a focus on the transport sector. He has previously worked several years as a research fellow in the Department of Energy at the Politecnico di Torino, Italy, where he developed strong skills in energy systems analysis and simulation, focusing on combined heat and power, renewable energy sources and district heating.

Rebecca O'Neil leads the Renewables team within the Electrical Infrastructure division at Pacific Northwest National Laboratory, USA. Her research interests focus on water power, market design, grid integration and energy storage. O'Neil has worked for over 20 years in the electric industry, administering utility energy efficiency programmes, rebalancing hydroelectric operations for environmental outcomes and overseeing clean energy programmes, including the state-wide renewable energy mandate, for the state of Oregon's energy office.

Aaron Praktiknjo is Heads of the Chair for Energy Resource and Innovation Economics at Rheinisch-Westfälische Technische Hochschule (RWTH) Aachen University, Germany. He is President of the German Association for Energy Sciences and Energy Policy (GEE), representative of the European Affiliates in the Council of the International Association for Energy Economics (IAEE) and spokesperson in the Research Network on Energy System Analysis of the German Ministry for Economic Affairs and Energy (BMWi). Together with Peter Zweifel and Georg Erdmann, he co-authored the textbook *Energy Economics—Theory and Application*.

Danielle Preziuso is an associate energy research scientist at the Pacific Northwest National Laboratory, USA. She holds a bachelor's degree in Mathematics from Bryn Mawr College and a master's degree from the Iceland School of Energy at Reykjavík University. Preziuso's current research focuses on the adoption and integration of distributed energy resources and renewable energy technologies.

Pier Paolo Raimondi is a researcher at the Fondazione Eni Enrico Mattei (FEEM) and the Istituto Affari Internazionali (IAI). His main research activity is related to energy geopolitics and geoeconomics in different geographical areas, mainly Europe, Africa, MENA region and Former Soviet Union area. He holds a master's degree in International Relations and a bachelor's degree in Political Science from Universita Cattolica del Sacro Cuore, Italy.

Marie-Noëlle Riboud-Seydoux has over 15 years' experience in Oil and Gas and Finance with a strong focus on emerging countries and has been advising small- and medium-sized energy companies as well as research groups since 2011. Prior to establishing her own advisory boutique in London, Riboud-Seydoux worked for Geoservices, a global Oil services company, and 4D Global Energy Advisors. A lecturer at SciencesPo—Paris School of International Affairs until 2015, Riboud-Seydoux graduated with honours from SciencesPo Paris (Economics and Finance) and holds postgraduate degrees in Business Law and Philosophy of Law. Riboud-Seydoux has advised the management teams of children charities and NGOs to help them expand their fundraising strategy.

Jorge-Andres Rincon-Romero is the Manager for Country Risk and Government Relations for Newmont Corporation, the world's leading gold producer. He leads the company's Country Risk Program and advises Newmont on key government relations' issues across the globe including political risk, social dynamics, economic trends and regulatory affairs. He holds undergraduate and advanced degrees from Georgetown University's School of Foreign Service.

Martin Robinius is Deputy Director and Head of the Department "Scenarios and Transformation Pathways" of the Institute of Energy and Climate Research (IEK-3). His research interests are the techno-economics of renewable energy and hydrogen-based systems, the need for detailed spatial and temporal models to account storage as well as infrastructure comparisons. Prior to taking up his current position, he wrote his PhD thesis at the same institute, and for which he won several awards. During that time, he was also a visiting researcher at the National Renewable Energy Laboratory (USA). He holds a Dr. Ing. from Rheinisch-Westfälische Technische Hochschule (RWTH) Aachen, a Master of Science from University of Kassel and a Bachelor of Engineering from the University of Applied Sciences and Arts in Hannover. Robinius has authored around 60 publications in journals such as *Applied Energy*, *Energies*,

International Journal of Hydrogen Energy and *Renewable Energy* and has been cited more than 2300 times.

Radia Sedaoui is the Chief of the Energy Section in the Climate Change and Natural Resource Sustainability Cluster of the United Nations Economic and Social Commission for Western Asia (ESCWA). She has an extensive experience in energy policy advice, renewable energy and energy efficiency, energy modelling, water-energy-food nexus, economic diversification and climate change policies and technologies, petroleum economics, oil and gas fiscal regimes and energy market developments. Sedaoui previously served as Head Statistics in the Gas Modeling Department at the Intergovernmental Organization of the Gas Exporting Countries Forum and previously held several senior positions in Algeria with "Sonatrach" as Director of Strategy and Corporate, Head Portfolio management and member of the Board of Directors of Sonatrach affiliates in Upstream, Midstream and Trading. She holds a bachelor's degree in Industrial Engineering and master's degrees in Petroleum Economics and Business Administration. Sedaoui is the President of the "Arab Energy Club" and a member of the "Algerian Association for Renewable Energies".

Detlef Stolten is the Director of the Techno-Economic Systems Analysis (IEK-3) at the Research Center Jülich, Germany, and has been holding the chair for fuel cells at the Rheinisch-Westfälische Technische Hochschule (RWTH) Aachen University since 2000. His research is focused on electrochemistry and process engineering for different types of fuel cells and electrolysers. Energy systems analysis and energy strategy form a new research topic taken up in 2010. It focuses on interconnecting the energy sectors and the role of storage encompassing gas and electric grid modelling, renewable power input, transportation energy requirements and storage via hydrogen, methane, liquid-organic hydrogen carrier (LOHC) and other options including renewable hydrogen production via electrolysis. For 12 years he worked in the industry with Bosch and Daimler Benz/Dornier. He is chairman of the Executive Committee of the Technology Collaboration Programme "Advanced Fuel Cells" of the International Energy Agency (IEA), Vice-President of the International Association of Hydrogen Energy (IAHE), member of the advisory board of the Society of Process and Chemical Engineering of the Association of German Engineers (VDI-GVC), member of the supervisory board of the Wuppertal Institute for Climate, Environment and Energy and member of the scientific advisory board of the Max Planck Institute for Dynamics of Complex Technical Systems. He wrote over 340 scientific articles and edited 6 books on the topics of hydrogen, fuel cells, carbon capture and the transition to renewable energy systems.

Simone Tagliapietra is a senior fellow at Bruegel. He is also Adjunct Professor of Energy, Climate and Environmental Policy at the Università Cattolica del Sacro Cuore and at the Johns Hopkins University—School of Advanced

International Studies (SAIS) Europe. His research focuses on the European Union climate and energy policy and on the political economy of global decarbonization. With a record of numerous policy and scientific publications, he is the author of *Global Energy Fundamentals* (2020), *L'Energia del Mondo* (Il Mulino, 2020) and *Energy Relations in the Euro-Mediterranean* (Palgrave Macmillan, 2017). Tagliapietra holds a PhD in Institutions and Policies from Università Cattolica del Sacro Cuore.

Philippe Vassilopoulos is Director of Product Design at EPEX SPOT, France, where he also served as Economist and Market Surveillance Officer. Before joining EPEX SPOT, Vassilopoulos was an Associate Director with IHS Cambridge Energy Research Associates (CERA). He specializes in the European wholesale power and gas markets. His expertise includes market design, price formation and price modelling, asset valuation and due diligence, regulations and market surveillance. Vassilopoulos also carried out applied research on price signals and investment incentives in the European electricity markets for the French Commission de Régulation de l'Energie. He holds a master's degree and a PhD from the University of Paris-Dauphine.

Stephen Woodhouse is Director at AFRY Management Consulting. Woodhouse has over 20 years' experience in design and evaluation of energy markets. He is an expert in market reform, from high-level policy design to adaptation by market participants. He contributes to the global debate on market design for renewable grid integration and is an inspirational conference speaker. Prior to joining AFRY, Woodhouse was an Economic Modeler for Ofgem. He holds an MA (Cantab) and a BA (Hons) in Economics from the University of Cambridge.

Abbreviations

AAU	Assigned amount unit
AC	Alternating current
ACQ	Annual contracted quantity
AEEP	Africa-European Union Energy Partnership
AEL	Alkaline electrolysis
AfDB	African Development Bank
AI	Artificial intelligence
API	American Petroleum Institute
API	Automated programming interface
APQ	Average program quantity
ASCM	Agreement on Subsidies and Countervailing Measure
b/d	Barrels per day
BAU	Business as usual
BCA	Border carbon adjustment
BEV	Battery-electric vehicle
Boe	Barrel oil equivalent
BOG	Boil off gas
BOS	Balance of system
BRP	Balance responsible party
BTU	British thermal unit
CAISO	California ISO
CAM	Capacity allocation mechanism
CAPEX	Capital expenditure
CAPP	Central African Power Pool
CBADM	Carbon border adjustment mechanism
CCGT	Combined cycle gas turbine
CCS	Carbon capture and storage
CCUS	Carbon capture, utilization and storage
CDM	Clean development mechanism
CER	Certified emission reduction

CFD	Contracts for difference
CFPP	Cold filter plugging point
CFR	Cost freight
CHP	Combined heat and power
CIF	Costs, insurance and freight
CME	Chicago mercantile exchange
CNG	Compressed natural gas
COB	California Oregon border
CPF	UK Carbon Price Floor
CRI	Coke reactivity index
CSP	Concentrated solar power
CSR	Coke strength after reaction
CTF	Cooking fuel and technology
CV	Calorific values
DC	Direct current
DCE	Discrete choice experiment
DER	Distributed energy resource
DES	Delivery ex ship
DFDE	Dual-fuel diesel electric
DFI	Development finance institution
DH	District heating network
DNO	Distribution network operator
DoD	Depth of discharge
DSM	Demand side management
DSO	Distribution system operator
E/P	Energy/power ratio
EAEC	European Atomic Energy Community
EC	European Commission
ECA	Export credit agency
ECSC	European Coal and Steel Community
EEG	Erneurbare Energien Gesetz
EEX	European energy exchange
EFP	Exchange for physical
EFS	Exchange for swap
EGS	Enhanced geothermal system
EI	Energy intensity
EIB	European Investment Bank
EII	Energy intensive industry
EMEC	European marine energy centre
EPAA	Emergency Petroleum and Allocation Act
EPC	Engineering, procurement, construction
ERCOT	Electricity Reliability Council of Texas
ERU	Emission reduction unit
ESP	Electronic sales platform
ESPP	East African Power Pool

ETS	Emission Trading System
EU	European Union
EU-27	European Union with 27 Member States (after 31.12.2020)
EU-28	European Union with 28 Member States (before 31.12.2020)
EV	Electric vehicle
FCC	Fluid catalytic cracking
FCEV	Fuel cell electric vehicle
FCFS	First-come-first-served
FEED	Front end engineering design
FERC	Federal Energy Regulatory Commission
FIEX	Financial expenditures
FIP	Feed-in premium
FIT	Feed-in tariff
FLNG	Floating liquefaction facilities
FOAK	First of a kind
FOB	Free on board
FPSO	Floating production storage and offloading
FSO	Storage and loading
FSRU	Floating storage and regasification units
FTR	Financial transmission right
FYP	Five-Year Plan
GAR	Gross as received
GDP	Gross domestic product
GHG	Greenhouse gas
GIS	Geographic information system
GPW	Gross product worth
GSA	Gas sales agreement
GT	Gas turbine
GTA	Gas Transportation Agreement
GTCC	Gas turbine combined cycle
GTL	Gas-to-liquids
GTS	Gas-to-solids
HAR	Harmonized allocation rule
HFO	Heavy fuel oil
IBRD	International Bank for Reconstruction and Development
ICE	Intercontinental exchange
IDC	Interest during construction
IEA	International Energy Agency
IFC	International Finance Corporation
IGU	International Gas Union
ILUC	Indirect land use change
IMO	International Maritime Organization
IOC	Independent oil company
IOC	International Oil Company
IOSCO	International Organization of Securities Commission

IPCC	Intergovernmental Panel on Climate Change
IPP	Independent power producer
IRENA	International Renewable Energy Agency
IRR	Internal rate of return
ISO	Independent system operator
ISO-NE	ISO New England
ISV	Independent software vendor
ITO	Independent transmission operator
JBIC	Japanese Bank for International Cooperation
JKM	Japan Korea Marker
JOA	Joint Operating Agreement
JSM	Japanese steel mill
JTF	EU Just Transition Fund
JV	Joint venture
KETS	Korean emissions trading system
KP	Kyoto Protocol
LCA	Lifecycle analysis
LCOE	Levelized cost of electricity
LCOS	Levelized cost of storage
LDC	Load duration curves
LLS	Louisiana light sweet
LMP	Locational marginal price
LNG	Liquefied natural gas
LNGC	LNG carrier
LOHC	Liquid-organic hydrogen carrier
LOLE	Loss of load expectation
LPG	Liquefied petroleum gas
LRF	Linear reduction factor
LSE	London Stock Exchange
LULUCF	Land use, land use change and forestry
MAOP	Maximum allowable operational pressure
MCP	Market clearing price
MCQ	Minimum contracted quantity
MDG	UN Millennium Development Goal
ME	Middle East
ME-GI	Electronically controlled, gas injection
MHV	Material handling vehicle
MIGA	Multilateral investment guarantee agency
MISO	Midwest ISO
MS	Member State
MSR	Market stability reserve
NA	North Africa
NAO	National Audit Office
NAP	National allocation plan
NAR	Net as received

NBP	National balancing point
NBS	China's National Bureau of Statistics
NDC	Nationally Determined Contribution
NEMO	Nominated electricity market operator
NOC	National Oil Company
NP	No price
NPV	Net present value
NREL	National Renewable Energy Lab
NS	North Sea
NYISO	New York ISO
NYMEX	New York Mercantile Exchange
O&M	Operation & maintenance costs
OFGEM	Office for the gas and electricity markets
OPEX	operating expenditures
ORC	Organic rankine cycle
OSP	Official selling price
OTC	Over-the-counter
OTEC	Ocean thermal energy conversion
P2G	Power-to-gas
P2H	Power-to-heat
P2L	Power-to-liquids
P2V	Power-to-vehicle
PA	Paris Agreement
PAYG	Pay-as-you-go
PCI	Pulverized coal injection
PE	Private equity
PEM	Proton-exchange membrane
PEMEL	Polymer electrolyte membrane electrolysis
PEMEX	Petroleos Mexicanos
PJM	Pennsylvania, Jersey and Maryland
PPA	Power purchase agreement
PPP	Public-private partnership
PPP	Purchasing power parity
PRA	Price reporting agency
PSA	Pressure swing adsorption
PSC	Production sharing contracts
PTR	Physical transmission right
PV	Solar photovoltaics
PVT	Pressure, volume and temperature
RAB	Regulated asset base model
RBL	Reserve-based lending
RCS	Regulated cost of service
RES	Renewable energy source
RGGI	Regional Greenhouse Gas Initiative
RLDC	Residual load duration curves

RMU	Removal unit
RoR	Run-of-river
ROW	Right-of-way
RPS	Renewable portfolio standard
RSP	Regulated social and political
RTO	Regional transmission operator
rTPA	Regulated third-party access
RVP	Reid vapour pressure
SAPP	South African Power Pool
SCADA	Supervisory control and data acquisition
SDG	Sustainable Development Goal
SDG 7	Sustainable Development Goal 7
SEC	Specific energy consumption
SECA	Sulphur emissions control areas
SEforALL	Sustainable Energy for All
SEM	Single electricity market
SMR	Small modular reactor
SMR	Steam methane reforming
SO	System operator
SOC	State-of-charge
SOEC	Solid oxide electrolysis cell
SOEL	Solid oxide electrolysis
SPA	Sale and purchase agreement
SPIMEX	Saint Petersburg International Mercantile Exchange
SPR	Strategic petroleum reserve
SPV	Special purpose vehicle
SRMC	Short-run marginal cost
SSA	Sub-Saharan Africa
T&D	Transmission and distribution application
TAN	Total acid number
TBP	True boiling point
TCO	Total cost of ownership
TFC	Total final energy consumption
TFDE	Tri-fuel diesel electric
TO	Transmission operator
TOP	Take-or-pay
TPES	Total primary energy supply
TRL	Technology readiness level
TSA	Temperature swing adsorption
TSO	Transmission system operator
TTF	Title transfer facility
UEC	Unit energy consumption
ULSD	Ultra-low sulphur diesel
UNFCCC	United Nations Framework Convention on Climate Change
UPS	Uninterruptible power supply

US	United States
USEC	US East Coast
USG	US Gulf
V2G	Vehicles-to-grid
VALCOE	value-Adjusted LCOE
VC	Venture capital
VGO	Vacuum gas oil
VIOC	Vertically integrated oil company
VoLL	Value of lost load
VPP	Virtual power plant
VRB	Vanadium redox battery
WACC	Weighted average cost of capital
WAF	West Africa
WAPP	West African Power Pool
WCI	Western Climate Initiative
WCS	Western Canada Select
WEC	Wave energy converter
WTI	Western Texas Intermediate
WTO	World Trade Organization
WTP	Willingness to pay
WTS	West Texas Sour
XDF	Low-pressure slow-speed dual-fuel

Energy Units

bcm	Billion cubic metres
bcma	Billion cubic metres annually
BTU	British thermal unit
gCO_2/kWh	Grams of carbon dioxide equivalent per kilowatt-hour
Gt	Gigatonne
Gtoe	Gigatonne of oil equivalent
GWe	Gigawatt electrical
GWh	Gigawatt-hours
GWth	Gigawatt thermal
kcal/kg	Kilocalorie per kilogramme
kg/min	Kilogramme per minute
kgH_2/h	Kilogramme of hydrogen per hour
kW	Kilowatt
kWel	Kilowatt electric
kWh	Kilowatt-hours
kWth	Kilowatt thermal
mmb/d	Million barrels per day
MMBtu	Million British thermal units
MMT	Million tonnes

Mt	Million tonnes
MT/y	Million tonnes per year
Mtoe	Million tonnes of oil equivalent
Mtpa	Million tonnes per annum
MW	Megawatt
MWe	Megawatt electric
MWh	Megawatt-hours
MWhu	Megawatt-hours useful energy for final users
PJ	Petajoule
tpa	Tonne per annum
TWh	Terawatt-hours
USD/kWh	US dollar per kilowatt-hour
$/boe	Dollar per barrel oil equivalent
€/kWel	Euro per kilowatt electric
€/kWP2L	Euro per kilowatt power-to-liquid
€/MWh	Euro per megawatt-hours
€/t	Euro per tonne

List of Figures

List of Tables

List of Boxes

Introduction

The future of energy has moved to centre stage in the political and economic debate at the national and international levels. Prompted by concerns for global warming, we have entered a phase of policy rather than solely market-driven energy transitions, which have turned energy from a mostly technological and occasionally geopolitical issue into a vital subject of economic policy and area of conflict between opposing interest groups. This book has the ambition to become a reference for readers who wish to be active in the debate and need basic understanding of the economics of energy in its international setting. Presenting a comprehensive overview of the issue, this book aims to be accessible to a wide readership of both academics and professionals working in the energy industry, as well as to graduate students and to general readers interested in the complexities of the economics of international energy.

The energy landscape changes frequently: multiple publications are available that monitor developments, either of the energy environment as a whole or of segments of the same, and these are continuously updated. We aim at complementing this abundant and frequently very professional literature with a reference book that will help readers understand the advantages and disadvantages, the opportunities and limits that characterize alternative solutions in the light of economic, and not just technological analysis. An economic approach and understanding is necessary, because technology offers multiple alternative solutions to our energy challenges (which, of course, is reassuring) but not all come at the same cost or promise the same economic reward. Furthermore, frequently the cost/reward profile of each technological solution is not intrinsic, but depends on circumstances—geographic, meteorological, demographic and social—as well as on the composition of the rest of the energy system, that is, on all other solutions that are adopted in parallel.

Energy is a complex system in which various sources interact and complement or contradict each other, generating end results in terms of availability and well-being for final consumers, or at least some of them. What may be appropriate in one country/region/economy may not fly in another. One needs to understand how the whole system works, that is, develop a holistic vision of energy and environment issues, to be able to identify feasible and appropriate solutions, depending on circumstances.

The reader will find in this volume competent and detailed discussions of the peculiarities of each major energy source, of the multiple energy markets and price formation processes, and of their interrelationships. The volume also covers a selection of the world's macro-regions to highlight how different conditions are in different geographical and meteorological situations.

Some major facts must be recalled to justify the structure of the volume and what it includes. Primary energy demand must be distinguished from final uses: the first includes original energy sources, which are then transformed into usable energy products to meet final uses. In 2019, fossil fuels accounted for 84 per cent of total primary sources: oil for 33 per cent, coal for 27 per cent and gas for 24 per cent. The share of fossil fuels in total primary energy has barely changed at all over the past three decades. Fossil fuels are transformed into usable final products through a process of refining or other chemical transformations. Alternatively, they are used to generate electricity. Electricity generation is also the predominant utilization of the remaining primary sources: hydro (6.5 per cent of total primary sources), renewables (5 per cent) and nuclear (4.5 per cent). The share of renewables has been growing and that of nuclear declining, so these two trends have roughly compensated each other.

Electricity covered 20 per cent of final uses in 2019, and the rest being accounted for by fuels for thermal or mobility purposes. It is widely expected that the share of final uses covered by electricity will increase thanks to greater convenience and improved efficiency. Electricity is expected to play a growing role across the spectrum, in mobility, thermal uses and industry. However, the increased penetration of electricity will perforce be a gradual process, so that the future of energy over several decades cannot coincide with the future of electricity.

Reliance on primary energy sources also varies greatly in different regions. The Middle East and North Africa region relies almost exclusively on oil and gas; other sources are marginal. In contrast, close to 50 per cent of energy consumed in Asia and the Pacific region is provided for by coal. The region with the highest contribution of hydroelectricity is South and Central America (22 per cent), while nuclear energy and renewables are most important in Europe (each accounting for 10 per cent of primary sources). Hence, the global energy landscape is the outcome of a mosaic of quite different tiles, responding to divergent endowments, opportunities and policies.

We know that the current energy system must evolve—it has constantly evolved since the invention of the steam engine and the dawn of commercial energy, but the pace of evolution must speed up, and the direction take a more decisive turn. In planning this Handbook, we have sought a compromise between the present and expectations for the future. Hence, the book does not attribute to "old" sources an attention proportional to their actual contribution, but neither ignores them. This results in relatively little attention to coal, whose importance is widely expected to decline rapidly, and large attention to energy sources which will continue to play a major role in international energy trade for decades (oil and gas) and those whose demand is expected to grow significantly in the future (electricity and renewables), while also addressing sources whose importance is at the moment almost non-existent, such as hydrogen, geothermal or tidal and waves, but which could also play an increasing role in the future.

Economics of Energy Production and Distribution

The book is divided in four main sections. The first is devoted to the economics of energy production and distribution and has separate chapters for all major sources of energy. Chapter 1 is devoted to oil and gas exploration and production, the so-called upstream section of the hydrocarbon industry. The chapter explains the different phases of an exploration-production project in order to highlight the cost structure and the nature of the risks related to each phase. It also discusses rent sharing according to the different taxation systems and points out the profitability problems of this capital-intensive industry.

As it is not possible to know in advance whether oil or gas (or neither) will be found, exploration is necessarily common. Furthermore, gas is frequently found in association with oil in fields containing predominantly oil, and liquids are frequently present in gas in predominantly gas fields; hence, the production of oil and gas is commonly joined. However, once brought to the surface, the paths of oil and gas diverge. The transportation of oil is relatively low cost: oil easily travels over long distances. Therefore, separate discussion of oil transportation was not considered necessary.

In contrast, gas transportation is expensive and has important implications on the industry. Gas tends to be utilized close to where it is produced to reduce the cost of transportation. Hence, the penetration of gas, or share of gas in total energy provision, varies very considerably between countries and regions, depending on whether gas is available (or historically was available) locally. This does not mean that gas is not transported over long distances—this is in fact an increasingly frequent occurrence. However, the high cost of transportation justifies significant differences in the price of gas in different parts of the world, which obviously also affects its relative competitiveness and which final uses it may be demanded for. Gas can be transported either in gaseous form by pipeline or in liquefied form by dedicated ships (LNG carriers). Chapter 2 provides a focus on the economics and commercial aspects of these large, often multibillion-dollar infrastructure projects, characterized by high upfront investment costs and requiring complex risk-sharing mechanisms between all parties involved.

Gas, once brought to the destination where it is demanded, normally does not require further treatment: the separation of higher molecules is made at the production site and what is transported is almost exclusively methane (CH_4). In contrast, oil must be refined in order to be transformed into usable products, depending on the technical characteristics required for each of its multiple uses, such as fuel (gasoline or diesel) in internal combustion engines, in aviation or shipping, in heating or the production of lubricants and so on. The process of refining is sensitive to the quality of the oil fed into the refinery, to the configuration of the refinery, that is, the number and quality of units (processes) available in it, and to the desired composition of the products slate. Refining is discussed in Chap. 3, where the key processes are explained together with their costs and siting issues. Historically, most oil has been refined in proximity of final markets, but this is no longer necessarily true, as producing countries are striving to integrate downstream into refining and petrochemicals to capture more of the value added than is allowed by the exportation of oil in its crude form only. Less demand in Europe and more demand in Asia have deeply changed the structure of the industry with closures of facilities in Europe and development of large, sophisticated plants in the Middle East and Asia.

Chapter 4 is devoted to hydrogen, which, in a sense, constitutes the bridge between the discussion of hydrocarbons and that of electricity that features in the following group of chapters. Hydrogen is not a primary source of energy because it is not found in isolation in nature and needs to be separated using energy: it is therefore an energy carrier rather than a source. At present, it is produced predominantly from hydrocarbons without carbon capture and sequestration, and is therefore a significant source of CO_2 emissions into the atmosphere. It is used predominantly for its chemical properties in refining and the chemical industry, rather than as carrier of energy. But the future is expected to be completely different, because hydrogen can be stored and offers a flexible source of both heat and electricity with no emissions of greenhouse gases. If produced from hydrocarbons with carbon capture and sequestration, it has the potential of "decarbonizing hydrocarbons", allowing the continued use of gas grids where they exist. It can also be produced from water through electrolysis, stored and turned to electricity again at some different time: it is therefore a form of electricity storage which is potentially crucial to facilitate the integration of non-dispatchable renewables into the grid.

We come therefore to the discussion of the electricity industry. Chapter 5 is devoted to the economics of power generation: this is a complex topic, due to the multiplicity of technologies available for power generation. The chapter introduces the major economic differences between the multiple power generation sources, highlighting the comparative advantages and disadvantages of each.

Chapter 6 is devoted to power generation from fossil fuels (coal, oil and gas) which constitute the bulk of global electricity generation (63 per cent of total—of which 36 per cent from coal, 23 per cent from gas and 3 per cent from oil). It covers the various technologies of power production and their key economics characteristics including CAPEX, OPEX, dispatchability, flexibility, location and expected service life.

Chapter 7 is devoted to nuclear energy (10 per cent of global power generation). It starts with the fundamentals of nuclear economics, with first the cost of nuclear operations, and also the revenue side, in both regulated and deregulated markets. Then it goes in depth into analysing the economics of two specific cases: long-term operations of existing nuclear plants and nuclear new build (covering potential for cost reductions and the case of Small Modular Reactors). The chapter concludes with a review of new research to understand the value of nuclear in future decarbonized electricity systems.

Chapter 8 is devoted to hydropower (16 per cent of global power generation), which is one of the oldest power generation technologies and the source of the largest power stations in the world. Despite a phenomenal rise of new renewable generation technologies, hydropower remains responsible for most of the renewable electricity generation around the globe. This chapter explores the economics of power generation from hydro and its advantages as well disadvantages. It describes the characteristics of the three hydropower generation types (run-of-river, hydro storage and pumped-storage) and provides an outlook on the future role of hydropower in modern energy systems.

The following two chapters deal with solar and wind (together accounting for 10 per cent of global electricity). Solar energy (Chap. 9) covers an increasing share of global energy demand. As a renewable source of energy, it will play a major role in decarbonizing electricity supply. The chapter provides an overview on the solar sector from an economic perspective. It describes the technical characteristics of photovoltaic and concentrated solar power and explains how these affect the economic competitiveness of solar energy. Wind power too plays a major role in decarbonizing electricity supply (Chap. 10). The chapter provides an overview on the economics of wind energy and highlights global trends in the wind sector. It describes the technical characteristics of onshore and offshore wind energy and explains how these affect the economic competitiveness of the technology. In both chapters, the authors describe how solar and wind power, as intermittent sources of energy, can be integrated into power systems. They also discuss how renewable energy support schemes contribute in fostering the deployment of solar and wind power.

The remaining two chapters are devoted to geothermal (Chap. 11) and tides and waves (Chap. 12), two renewable sources of electricity which presently play a very limited role, but are believed to offer considerable potential (geothermal in particular). Geothermal energy is emerging as one of the most reliable sources of renewable energy and gaining relevance over conventional and non-renewable sources of energy because of its constant availability and sustainable nature. Besides being a clean and renewable energy source with a low levelized cost of electricity, geothermal reservoirs have huge potential for power generation and thus may become the pillar of local grid systems, meeting baseload.

The above group of chapters deals with the economics of generating electricity, but that cannot be considered in isolation from the economics of electricity transmission and distribution, especially in view of the characteristics of the electricity grid, which requires instantaneous matching of demand and supply at all times. The following chapters deal with these issues from different angles.

Chapter 13 looks at the economics of energy networks (both electricity and gas) including from a regulatory point of view, that is, how the power and gas industries may be organized competitively and what challenges this entails. The chapter describes the physical and economic properties of energy networks, focusing on their monopolistic nature and the implications for electricity and gas systems. It goes onto review how energy networks are treated in competitive energy markets, how access to networks functions and what arrangements are established to ensure efficient economic outcomes and equal treatment of all market participants. Finally, it explains how access to energy networks is charged and how network users exchange energy within a network.

Chapter 14 deals with the challenges and opportunities of energy storage, with a specific focus on the economics of batteries for storing electricity. Storage technologies include a variety of solutions that have been used for different grid services, including frequency control, load following and uninterrupted power supply. Next, Chap. 15 provides an introduction to the main characteristics of sector coupling, which is often referred to as P2X, where "X" may stand for various applications, such as gas (G), heat (H), vehicles (V) or others. The common feature of these technologies is to provide additional flexibility to the power grid by the integration with other energy networks or sectors, through the conversion of electricity into other energy carriers.

In the light of the discussion in previous chapters, Chap. 16 deals with the integration of non-dispatchable renewables (i.e. solar and wind, whose availability cannot be controlled by the producer) into the electricity grid. At low levels of deployment, these technologies typically do not raise significant issues, but to reach high shares of generation within each power system, several measures are needed to integrate them in the overall electricity mix. The chapter reviews various potential approaches and discusses the challenge of reaching high levels of penetration of non-dispatchable renewables, while at the same time maintaining the stability of the grid and avoiding recurrent black-outs.

The last chapter in Part I (Chap. 17) is devoted to the financing of energy investment, which is closely related to the economics of each energy source. Energy projects can vary enormously in scale, risk and potential reward. Accordingly, different financial models need to be applied to optimally finance different typologies of projects. Also, different categories of investors, ranging from low risk to very high risk, must be tapped to succeed in financing projects. In the context of the substantial investments required to sustain the development of world's economies, this chapter reviews the key steps in the financing of an energy project, from the project viability analysis to the choice of financing instruments and structures. The authors highlight how the source of energy and the other characteristics of a specific project impact and shape its financing, using case studies from renewable and conventional energy alike, and conclude by drawing attention to the innovations taking place across all energy segments.

Economics of Energy Trading and Price Discovery

Part II of this Handbook is devoted to the economics of energy trading and price discovery. Energy markets, their organization and price discovery processes necessarily reflect technical features (elasticity of demand and supply, ease of transportation/transmission, potential for storage and intertemporal arbitrage, potential for substitution of one source/form of energy with another). On this basis, organizational and contractual structures are put in place which then shape the process of price discovery and eventually determine market prices.

Oil is by far the most widely internationally traded commodity in the world. Notwithstanding the decline in its price over the second half of the 2010s, crude oil alone still accounted for a significant share of international trade, and its weight has further increased with higher prices since 2021. The price of crude oil is a frequently referred to indicator for gauging global economic conditions. But the organization of the global oil market is very peculiar, as quality differences have significant bearing on the price of individual crudes, and trading takes place on the basis of reference to a limited number of physical benchmarks, whose availability and quality also evolve over time (Chap. 18). In addition, the logistics of trade delivery, whether seaborne by ship or overland by pipeline, also deeply influences the functioning of physical crude oil trading. The time dimension, which reflects delays needed to organize shipping or transit times, creates a demand for hedging instruments, which, in turn, motivates the establishment of a futures (or paper barrels) market that has grown enormously and has become the primary price discovery ground, with multiple ancillary markets linking different contracts and leading to advanced financialization. All of which means that the price of oil is not as straightforward as the price of potatoes in your local market: the complex structure and interrelationships must be understood to validly interpret the daily gyrations in the price of oil.

Oil product prices are discussed in Chap. 19. These obviously not only reflect the underlying price of crude oil, but also respond to the peculiarities of production and use of each product, keeping in mind that all are joint products from a refinery, whose configuration may differ significantly (as explained in Chap. 3) but cannot change in the short run, creating imbalances in the equilibrium of demand and supply of individual products at any moment in time. This chapter explains which hydrocarbons are mixed up inside a barrel of crude oil and how the refining process separates, treats and upgrades the composite to extract the usable products needed. It looks at whole crude properties and what these mean for handling and transporting the oil. It defines the different types of refinery process, from primary distillation to reforming right through to cracking and coking. It describes the range of products that result from refining crude oil and the use to which each product is put.

The pricing of internationally traded natural gas (discussed in Chap. 20) has fundamentally evolved over time, moving from predominant indexation to crude oil or oil products in accordance with various bespoke formulae peculiar to each long-term contract, to growing reliance on gas-to-gas competition and the emergence of gas trading hubs where both physical molecules and financial products are traded. The chapter explains why gas suppliers traditionally defended long-term oil-indexed contracts and analyses the main features of historical contracts. The old consensus on oil indexation, which had been a pillar of international gas trade for a decade, has been eroded in several regions. Beyond Europe and North America, Asia is also gradually moving towards a larger share of hub indexation, although it is still lagging behind in the process of establishing its own hubs. The chapter concludes that gas prices remain regional even if additional convergence is materializing thanks to the globalizing effect of flexible LNG.

The chapter devoted to international coal trading (Chap. 21) offers a view of coal production, consumption and trade at both global and regional levels. Given China's dominance of coal markets, the chapter describes the geography of Chinese coal supply chain in some detail. Some concepts of geology and mining are explained to facilitate a better understanding of the different coal qualities and grades, which play a more important role in coal trading and pricing than for other fossil fuels. The chapter offers a historical perspective of the evolution of the international coal market to describe the current market, very dynamic and liquid, with increasing variety of qualities.

The trading of electricity (Chap. 22) is conditioned by the need to constantly balance the grid, meaning that wholesale prices change almost continuously to reflect the changing balance of demand and supply. Therefore, in competitive markets electricity is traded in intervals that tend to be shorter and shorter (e.g. a new auction is conducted every 15 minutes, but in some markets every 5 minutes) as well as on a day-ahead basis. After a description of the functioning of wholesale electricity markets with a focus on the derivatives and the spot market, the authors analyse not only their main features such as trading venues, traded products, rules and the processes but also some key trends that can be observed. Going forward, electricity systems around the world are undergoing nascent but profound changes as market architecture and regulatory framework evolve to meet ambitious climate targets while maintaining efficient investment incentives and security of supply.

With the growing concern for climate change and based on the conviction that this is due to a market failure linked to the negative externality of emitting greenhouse gases (which the emitter is normally not requested to pay for), policies have been introduced to correct this and impose a monetary charge on emitters. This can be achieved either through the imposition of a carbon tax (i.e. a fixed price for each tonne of CO_2 emitted or equivalent) or through the creation of a market for emission allowances. Chapter 23 explores the concept of carbon pricing, with a specific focus on the trading of carbon via emissions trading systems (ETSs). The analysis starts with an overview of the main design options for a cap-and-trade system, presenting the experience of the European Union (EU) ETS as a real-world example of how such systems work. The history of the EU ETS is thoroughly examined, explaining what the main challenges and benefits of the system are and what lessons can be learnt from the world's biggest ETS. Using the European experience as a benchmark, other major ETS markets are also analysed, highlighting the potential for interconnection of different systems as well as the prospects for international cooperation mechanisms under Article 6 of the Paris Agreement.

The last chapter in Part II (Chap. 24) is devoted to the process of unbundling of vertically integrated industrial structures for the sake of enhancing competitive market relationships in lieu of market dominance on the part of one or few players. Energy market restructuring and liberalization have produced mixed results. While wholesale market design and competition have matured, retail competition has remained static. This chapter discusses the reasons that contribute to the success and failure of energy market unbundling with the use of global examples. The new trends and policies in energy markets are discussed from a regulatory perspective including active investor participation, technological innovation and the growth in renewable energy.

Global Energy Trends

Part III of the Handbook is devoted to the discussion of some global energy trends or transversal issues, which will play a key role in the shaping of the energy landscape in the coming decades.

Chapter 25 attempts at disentangling the multiple contrasting interactions between economic conditions and energy transitions. It goes without saying that the net effect, resulting from the balance of such multiple contrasting interactions, is extremely difficult or even impossible to predict. It very much depends on the specific characteristics of the economy facing the need to decarbonize, notably its current energy system, rate of growth of energy demand, available energy resources and opportunities for decarbonization. All of these parameters are extremely variable country by country. It also greatly depends on the specific transition path pursued and especially the intended speed of the transformation. The chapter lays special emphasis on the need to shift resources from consumption to investment and the consequent increase in the capital-output ratio, which has also consequences for the distribution of income.

Chapter 26 discusses the drivers of energy demand, which is one face of the relationship between the economy and energy (the flip face being how energy availability supports the generation of income). The chapter reviews all final uses of energy and discusses to what extent we may expect that the relationship between income availability or economic growth and energy demand may evolve. We know that energy demand grows less rapidly than GDP, but to what extent can the parameter linking the two be reduced? Is it conceivable that it may ever turn negative, that is, that income may increase while energy demand decreases?

Chapter 27 discusses energy subsidies, which are widespread among OECD and non-OECD countries alike and exist for all energy types. Governments often give noble and legitimate rationales for the introduction and continuation of various energy subsidies, but the reality of energy subsidy policies is nearly always more complex than the stated rationale. Governments have tried to balance the energy trilemma by implementing several types of energy subsidies at once. This has resulted in a complex political economy of pervasive subsidies across energy production and consumption. Even when some policy priorities clearly change, the phasing out of existing subsidies may prove politically challenging when powerful vested interest groups exercise their influence over governmental decision-making. The chapter goes in depth on the types, size, objectives and politics of subsidies to fossil fuel consumption and production and those to renewable electricity.

A closely related issue is that of energy access, which is dealt with in Chap. 28. Providing access to affordable modern energy services represents a key requirement for eradicating poverty and reducing inequalities. This is the reason why the United Nations included the achievement of universal access to affordable, reliable, sustainable and modern energy among the Sustainable Development Goals at the core of its 2030 Agenda for Sustainable Development. Several hundreds of million people especially in sub-Saharan Africa still lack access to modern energy for cooking (worldwide 2.9 billion people) or electricity (840 million), and what better income levels can they attain under these conditions? It is crucially important that energy transitions achieve the strategic goal of universal access to energy.

The remaining two chapters in Part III deal with technological advancement. Chapter 29 explores emerging technologies that may have a disruptive impact on the energy landscape. Disruption denotes an action that completely overhauls the traditional way an industry is working, for instance, by introducing a new technology or new standards. The shorter the transition, the more disruptive the event is considered. History shows that sudden disruptions are very rare in the energy industry, due to the relatively slow diffusion process of new technologies; nevertheless, the chapter argues that some disruption is possible especially in connection with electrification of passenger cars and increasing penetration of electricity in final uses.

Digitalization (Chap. 30) is another possible source of disruption. Previous energy transformations have largely been driven by the exploitation of a new energy source. In contrast, besides delivering cost reductions in the supply of both conventional and renewable energy, digitalization is transformational because it brings the demand-side into play, facilitating the move to a more integrated, highly flexible and customer-centric energy system which will ultimately unlock deep decarbonization of our societies. This transformation comes with risks: increased danger of cybersecurity attacks, threats to privacy especially in non-democratic political systems, increased use of energy and disruption of existing business relationships.

Energy and the Economy: Continental Perspectives

The last part (Part 4) of the Handbook features six chapters dedicated to major inter-continental differences and perspectives in the energy landscape, which profoundly influence the shape of energy transitions—justifying the necessity to speak of transitions in the plural rather than hypothesizing a uniform transition pattern applicable to the entire world.

There are striking differences in the availability of primary sources, with some regions/countries especially rich in coal or hydrocarbon resources, while others have favourable conditions for a major expansion of hydroelectricity or meteorological characteristics especially propitious for wind or solar energy. These differences cannot be ignored and determine vested interests in the existing global energy structures, on the one hand, as well as encouraging exploitation of innovative solutions, on the other.

History of course plays a huge role: energy structures have huge inertia and past decisions influence outcomes for very extended periods of time. Some forms of energy, like hydroelectricity or nuclear, have secular histories or have been profoundly influenced by political and military considerations.

The gap in income levels dividing continents has been narrowing since the end of the Second World War but remains very wide. The consumption of energy per capita in the Indian subcontinent or in sub-Saharan Africa remains at an order of magnitude smaller than in the advanced industrial countries. We have mentioned the importance of achieving universal energy access, but access per se is not sufficient. No bridging the huge remaining income gaps is possible if distances in energy availability per capita are not reduced. Priorities for countries where the population is energy poor cannot be the same as for countries that are major consumers and emitters of greenhouse gases and have been for centuries.

We have not pretended to offer an exhaustive geography of energy, opting rather for selecting a limited number of key cases. We begin with China (Chap. 31) for the simple reason that China is today the largest source of greenhouse gases and the country whose energy production and demand grow more rapidly in absolute terms. Despite large domestic resources of coal, oil and gas, the country has emerged as a key importer of oil and natural gas, exposing it to vulnerabilities associated with import dependence. Over the course of China's economic expansion, its energy policy has been geared towards ensuring adequate supplies at affordable prices to end-users, preferring to use administrative measures to regulate supply and demand rather than market mechanisms. Yet as the country's economic structure shifts away from heavy industry and towards consumer services, its energy needs and choices are changing, while the role of markets is expanding. And the negative environmental impact of China's energy choices has now become a social concern, as well as an industrial opportunity.

Russia (Chap. 32) deserves attention not only because it is the most important exporter of gas as well as one of the three most important producers of oil (with the United States and Saudi Arabia). Russia, ranking fourth in the world in the primary energy consumption and in the carbon dioxide emissions, adheres to the strategy of "business as usual" and relies on fossil fuels. Decarbonization of the energy sector is not yet on the agenda: a sceptical attitude to the problem of global climate change prevails among stakeholders. GDP energy intensity remains high, supported by relatively low energy prices and high cost of capital. The share of solar and wind energy in the energy balance is insignificant and is not expected to exceed 1 per cent by 2040. The challenge for Russia in the coming years is to develop a new strategy for the development of its energy sector, which enters the zone of high turbulence—even in the absence of the influence of the climate change agenda—due to the COVID-19, increasing global competition, growing technological isolation, financial constraints and, since February 2022, ostracism following the invasion of Ukraine.

The Middle East and North Africa (Chap. 33) is the region richest in hydrocarbon resources, but these are very unevenly distributed between countries. The region therefore displays great diversity in opportunities and perspectives. However, most countries remain exceptionally reliant on fossil fuels with a highly limited role played by clean energy alternatives; while the region also lags behind other region's progress in energy efficiency. In the Arab least developed countries (LDCs), energy access remains incomplete, severely obstructing socio-economic progress.

Sub-Saharan Africa (Chap. 34) embodies a paradox. Although the region is blessed with energy resources and has long attracted the oil and gas industry, the majority of its population lacks access to energy, especially electricity, which hinders their economic and social development. For decades the dominant discourse, from governments as well as international development agencies and economic actors, has considered that the exploitation of its energy resources would prompt the economic growth of the continent by giving the countries the financial means to undertake development strategies. Unfortunately, the reality seems much bleaker as most energy-producing countries in sub-Saharan Africa seem to underperform in terms of economic development, plagued by the so-called resource curse. Nigeria, the main oil-producing country on the continent, offers a dramatic illustration of this situation. However, a new approach has recently emerged which focuses on the development of access to energy for the population. As a consequence, all over the continent new initiatives have been put in place to boost the access to energy for the local population. This access has at last been acknowledged as a key driver for economic development.

The last two chapters are devoted, respectively, to North America (Chap. 35) and Europe (Chap. 36). North America is characterized by levels of energy consumption per capita which are double those in Europe or Japan; thus, issues of energy efficiency are extremely important. High energy consumption rates in United States and Canada challenge reaching climate policy goals, under heightened public pressure, and the search for alternatives to fossil fuels. Mexico will be more focused on economic development and energy access. The United States will continue to emphasize energy innovation, driven by public investment in research and development and private capital in commercial applications.

Finally, Europe has tended to occupy the moral high ground of decarbonization and energy transition, not without contradictions and with outcomes not exactly in line with expectations. Popular opinion plays a major role, and in contradictory directions, with simultaneous rise in green and populist political support, which results in hesitations and divergent priorities in individual countries. Progressively, a consensus on many important aspects has been emerging at least within the European Union, although divergences remain very strong on crucial items in the agenda, such as the future role of nuclear energy, carbon capture and sequestration and natural gas. The EU set an energy policy framework based on three pillars (security of supply, competitiveness and sustainability) with the goal to address three different priorities: competitiveness (affordable prices), security (of energy supply) and sustainability (clean energy). These three pillars appear to pursue contradictory goals, especially in the short term, but they are seen as converging in the longer term. This chapter aims to analyse how these different objectives have been key drivers of the European energy policy and economics. To illustrate this, the authors also present five case studies: the United Kingdom, Italy, France, Germany and Poland. Lastly, the chapter presents the "European Green Deal", whose ultimate goal is to reach carbon neutrality by 2050. The chapter analyses how a climate-neutrality goal requires a substantial transformation of the EU economy, which comes with some internal and external frictions.

In Conclusion

This book is the result of the collaboration of numerous authors from different institutions and with different backgrounds and perspectives. We have made no attempt to eliminate differences in opinions and conclusions because the future of energy is open to multiple solutions and the reader should be exposed to all points of view.

As stated at the beginning of this introduction, we have multiple alternative technological solutions that may deliver abundant and affordable energy for the future. The exact mix that will prevail is likely to be country- and region-specific because of structural differences as well as of different priorities and policies. In any case, the basis for rational decision-making is adequate knowledge and understanding of technical and economic opportunities and constraints. Energy is one of several areas in which a sometimes-difficult relationship exists between "experts", politicians and the wider public.

This handbook is the fruit of a lifelong hands-on experience by the editors working for the energy industry, international organizations, governments as well as in academia. We hope that this Handbook will give a modest contribution to improve access to relevant information for energy professionals, for politicians, for scholars and students as well as for a wider public and thus facilitate the adoption of sounder energy policies.

Manfred Hafner
Giacomo Luciani

PART I

Economics of Energy Production and Distribution

CHAPTER 1

Economics of Oil and Gas Production

Nadine Bret-Rouzaut

1 Introduction

Oil and Gas Exploration & Production involves exploring a sedimentary basin to discover a field, developing it to produce the oil or gas that can be extracted from it, and finally reclaiming the site at the end of production.

It is a very capital-intensive industry (the currency unit is one million US dollars, and the budget of many projects is over one billion), entailing multiple and varied risks but, in return, also the potential for high profitability.

Several actors, each with a well-defined role, are involved in enabling the quantities of hydrocarbons needed for consumption to be available on the market. The three main ones are:

- The State
- The oil companies
- The contractors.

To these main actors, one must add banks and insurance companies—to make financing possible—and professional organizations—to discuss and analyze challenges and find the best approaches to confront them.

In addition to these, the local population has gradually asserted itself and acquired influence, although even today in a number of countries the means at its disposal remain limited.

N. Bret-Rouzaut (✉)
IFP School, Paris, France

SciencesPo—Paris School of International Affairs, Paris, France

M. Hafner, G. Luciani (eds.), *The Palgrave Handbook of International Energy Economics*, https://doi.org/10.1007/978-3-030-86884-0_1

2 The Main Actors

2.1 *The State*

As a general rule (with the sole exception of privately owned land in the United States), the State is the owner of all underground natural resources, including hydrocarbons. It controls oil activities and acts as guarantor of the general interest, in particular when it authorizes companies to explore for and produce hydrocarbons or when it decides to introduce into the law an obligation of local content (through employment of local professionals, manufacturing of equipment in the country, or creation of local companies linked to the oil and gas sector).

Depending on the legal regime applicable to ownership of underground natural resources, there are two possible forms of intervention:

- direct: the holder of mining rights directly explores and produces hydrocarbon deposits either as owner of the land (for privately owned land of the United States) or as the State, through national companies, with or without a legal monopoly (such as it exists, e.g., in Saudi Arabia)
- indirect: in this case, the holder of the mining rights, as the State and by virtue of its power, designates who will carry out the exploration and exploitation of hydrocarbon fields within the framework of the legislation in force and the applicable patrimonial agreement and contractual regime (which can be either a concession, a production sharing contract or occasionally a service contract, as explained later).

In petroleum matters, the State is primarily represented by the Ministry in charge of hydrocarbons (Ministry of Petroleum, Ministry of Energy, Ministry of Mines and Subsoil, etc. depending on the country). But other ministries are also involved: the Ministry of Finance and Ministries in charge of security and environment, labor, and fisheries, if it is an offshore field. In some countries, specialized national agencies will support the Ministry in charge of oil affairs. For example, in Norway the Norwegian Petroleum Directorate provides high-level technical expertise to the Ministry.

2.2 *The Oil Companies*

We may distinguish several different categories of oil companies. A first distinction is usually made between integrated and non-integrated companies, also called independents. An integrated company has assets along the entire value chain from hydrocarbon exploration to the sale of petroleum products to the final consumer. Vertical integration is expected to enable the company to create more value, by adding downstream profits (from refining and distribution/marketing) to profits from the upstream (exploration and production). Vertical integration can also provide a balance when one of the segments of the value chain faces difficult market conditions, because chances are that in this case the other segments experience favorable conditions. For example, when the price of crude oil is high, upstream profits increase while the downstream activities, for which the price of crude oil is a cost, may be challenged.

In contrast, an independent company is only present in a single segment of the chain, that is, with respect to the discussion in this chapter, only in the upstream: its role ends when it sells the hydrocarbons it produces to buyers that are not linked to it. Independents are much smaller than integrated companies, and frequently quite risk-prone explorers.

Secondly, we may distinguish between national companies (NOCs), in which the State is the majority or sole shareholder, and international companies (IOCs) such as ExxonMobil, Shell, BP, Total, and others, which have their equity traded on stock exchanges and own assets in multiple countries.

These diverse companies must in the end work together. Indeed, it is very rare for a single company to be active in an oil field in the absence of any partner. Exploration risks are extremely high, and the probability of finding a commercial field low. The oil companies will therefore join forces in a Joint Venture (JV). Each individual company normally prefers to take a stake of variable importance in several licenses, rather than concentrate its investment on a few prospects, so as not to put "all its eggs in the same basket". Partners in the same project then sign an association agreement regulating their cooperation, called the Joint Operating Agreement (JOA). This agreement is signed by all the oil companies that come together to ensure the proper execution of the contract. The national company may be one of the partners of this JV when the State wishes to participate directly in operations, assuming the same rights and obligations as other companies, up to its share of participation.

The JOA defines the co-responsibility of the partners, the legal and fiscal transparency of each partner, the financing rules (procedure for calls for funds, invoicing methods, co-financing of expenses), and the sharing of results, as well as the rules for decision-making through a management committee. Operations are initiated, prepared, and directed by the company entrusted with the role of operator, whose responsibilities must be clearly spelled out in the JOA. The operator is also the representative, who communicates on behalf of the Association and represents it in all relations with the State. In the event of disagreement during the commitment period, it is usually the operator who decides. But sometimes some of the partners may decide to work on "sole risk", that is, to assume full responsibility for the work that the other partners do not want to do.

2.3 The Contractors

In the past, oil companies designed, planned, and carried out the engineering for oilfield exploration and development. This involved the possession of seismic and drilling equipment and the employment of the teams necessary for their operation. Then, in the 1980s, oil companies progressively decided to refocus on what they considered to be their core business, outsourcing activities not considered to be part of the core to oil service companies. The pendulum has repeatedly swung between internalization and outsourcing, but overall the trend has been to outsource more and more activities. The oil and gas contracting sector now carries out much of the work subcontracted by oil companies: geophysical activities (acquisition, processing, and interpretation of seismic data); drilling and related services; as well as engineering activities, such as underwater works (pipe laying) or platform construction (shipbuilding). In addition, there is a multitude of service providers including tool manufacturers (geophysics and drilling), metal construction, mechanical engineering, and engineering companies. The common point for all these companies is that they are service companies for the oil industry, first, second, or third tier providers.

In the past, the oil and gas contracting industry frequently developed in parallel with the exploitation of local hydrocarbon resources (the United States, the United Kingdom, Norway, etc.). In recent years, Chinese companies have entered this sector and have rapidly gained significant market shares. However, the United States is still the reference country for oil activity, which has led to the creation of a powerful oil-related industry, giving some companies a leading position today: examples are Schlumberger, a company that was originally French, or Halliburton. But exploration, development, and production operations involve multiple highly specialized competencies (driller, mud specialist, helicopter company, diver, etc.) so that oil companies must sign many contracts (one contract with each service company), which is a long and management-intensive process. To overcome these disadvantages, oil companies are increasingly opting to deal with only one company and sign integrated service contracts.

Faced with this demand, contractors embarked on a major industrial restructuring process in the early 1990s, mainly through external growth. Many mergers and acquisitions have thus taken place, and the industry has consolidated.

3 The Different Phases of Exploration-Production

3.1 *Exploration*

The purpose of exploration is to discover an oil and/or gas field. It involves three areas of expertise: geology, geophysics, and drilling.

3.1.1 Geology

The first step in the process is when geologists study the geology of large areas to define specific areas that may contain hydrocarbon accumulations. Then, geologists carry out geographical surface studies to verify the presence of the triplet essential for any conventional deposit:

- a source rock that generated hydrocarbons millions of years ago

- a reservoir rock which, due to its porosity characteristics, may have accumulated hydrocarbons in its pores
- an impermeable overburden rock that retained the hydrocarbon molecules trapped inside the reservoir rock.

Then they will study the topography and visible structures in order to deduce some characteristics of the formations and structures of the subsoil. When the region is mature (proven existence of hydrocarbons), they use many existing sources of information from databases of companies, public agencies, and so on. Geologists then synthesize all the information acquired in the form of subsurface maps at different scales. But knowledge of the characteristics of the surface terrain is not sufficient to extrapolate the properties of the subsoil. In addition, in submerged areas, nothing is visible. This is why geophysical exploration methods are used.

It is difficult to estimate the cost of geology, because geologists are present throughout the upstream chain and the related expenses are treated in association with other expenses.

3.1.2 Geophysics

Geophysics consists of making measurements of physical quantities of the subsoil and interpreting the results in geological terms. These geophysical methods are based on three approaches, two of which are marginal: magnetometry and gravimetry. The main approach is seismic reflection, which makes it possible to carry out a proper echography of the subsoil.

Seismic reflection consists in sending elastic waves into the subsoil, which propagate through the rock masses, then refract and reflect on certain geological discontinuities called mirrors. Like echoes, reflected waves then rise to the surface where they are recorded by sensors (geophones on land, hydrophones contained in a streamer at sea) that convert ground vibrations into electrical voltages transmitted to a recording laboratory. The seismic recordings collected by the geophysicist are then processed by powerful computers to increase the signal-to-noise ratio.

Seismic results provide a good idea of the underground structural formation—layer inclination, continuity, folding—that can make visible possible traps constituting potential target locations for drilling.

3.1.3 Seismic Cost

The cost of a seismic campaign can be broken down into:

- Cost for field data acquisition
- Cost for data processing (computer processing)
- Cost of interpretation (analysis and understanding of results to enable decision-making).

The acquisition of seismic data at sea is easier than on land, due to the ship's ease of movement in all directions. This allows covering a large area at lower cost.

As with acquisition, routine seismic processing is outsourced to service companies. Processing costs are usually significantly lower than acquisition costs. Once the seismic data has been acquired and processed, it must be transformed into information that can be used by decision-makers. The processing of data must be done under the control of specialists. This translates into personnel and IT costs that can range between a few hundred thousand and one million dollars per seismic campaign.

The total cost of a seismic campaign thus amounts to between a few million dollars and a few tens of millions of dollars, depending on the difficulty of access, the type of coverage desired, and the area covered (we can calculate a cost in $\$/km^2$). These costs are also related to the severe competition between service companies in local markets, with the award of seismic surveys being subject to competitive bidding in the countries concerned.

Thanks to geological and seismic data, it is possible to judge the prospect's interest and eventually make the decision to drill an exploration well, because only direct access to the subsoil, through drilling, can provide certainty that a field exists.

3.1.4 Drilling

The objective of drilling is to reach the target by perforating the geological layers over several thousand meters. A hydrocarbon field may be several kilometers from the surface, but never more than eight kilometers. If the hydrocarbon molecules have ventured into greater depths, they have been completely destroyed by the pressure and temperature at these depths. The most common drilling technique is to attack the rock with a rotating drilling tool, the drill bit. The driller must at all times ensure that there is a balance between the pressure inside the well and the pressure in the geological layers traversed. Drilling progresses at a rate of a few meters per hour, more and more slowly with increasing depth, punctuated by difficulties and regular replacement of the drill bit, which requires the entire drill string to be raised.

The main difference between onshore and offshore drilling is the support on which the rig must be installed at sea: platforms resting on the seabed (jack-up platforms used in shallow water), semi-submersible or floating structures (rather reserved for drilling in deeper waters). These devices are moved after each prospect drilled.

Whether the drilling leads to a discovery or not, it provides the geologist with important information in the form of cores, cuttings, and electrical records at the bottom of the well.

3.1.5 Cost of Drilling

Drilling of an exploration well generally lasts two to six months, depending mainly on the depth and hardness of the layers traversed, and 70 to 75% of the cost will be directly proportional to this duration. On the other hand, on average only one in five wells, or even only one in seven in poorly known areas, leads to the discovery of an economically exploitable reservoir, which means that the oil company must take into account the costs of all wells even if they have not led to a discovery.

The cost of drilling is higher than the cost of geology-geophysics and represents the bulk of the costs of an exploration program. The rental of the drilling rig from the contractor alone represents 20 to 40% of the total cost of drilling. The daily cost of renting a rig varies with its power, which depends on the depth of the well and, at sea, the depth of water in which the rig will be positioned. It also varies according to the rig utilization rate, that is, the ratio between the demand of oil companies and the supply of available drilling equipment, which varies with the price per barrel of crude oil.

To this cost must be added the costs of supervising the work, the cost of consumables (tubes, etc.), and the cost of other equipment and expertise required for drilling (logistics, mud, logging, etc.). In the end, a well will generally cost between a few million and a few tens of millions of dollars. An offshore well will often cost between 3 and 5 times more than an onshore well, even with a similar duration. Wells in extreme areas and/or at very great depths can cost several hundred million dollars.

3.1.6 Total Cost of Exploration

Exploration costs include seismic, geological, and geophysical interpretation and exploration drilling, including well testing.

Exploration expenses are, by definition, incurred before discovery and therefore have a direct impact on the company's accounts with two fundamental consequences:

- they will only be "refunded" if there is a commercial discovery; however, the probability of success of an exploration program is only 10 to 30%.
- they can only be financed from equity; given the high risk of failure, no bank will lend money to an oil company for exploration.

Exploration expenditures can vary over a very wide range. They may be limited to the cost of a seismic campaign and a dry well in the case of unsuccessful exploration. In this case, the oil company records a financial loss, even if this exploration campaign allowed the acquisition of additional information on the studied area. We express the cost in $/boe (barrel oil equivalent) by dividing the total amount of expenditures by the discovered reserves in barrels: depending on the region and time, this figure will generally range from $2 to $5 per boe.

3.2 Development

When exploration leads to a discovery, the next step is delineation (of the reservoir boundaries) and reservoir appraisal (e.g., homogeneous reservoir rock characteristics across the deposit). This provides additional information to confirm the discovery and assess with better accuracy the amount of reserves (quantity of hydrocarbons that can be extracted) and production conditions. Economic studies (crude oil/gas price, taxation, etc.) complement the technical studies to answer the essential questions: Is the field commercial? Should it be developed? If so, according to what scheme? Does it fit well into the company's strategy and its financial resources?

Once the decision to bring the field into production has been taken, the field must be developed, that is, all the equipment needed to exploit the field must be put in place: transport networks, production facilities, treatment and metering equipment, drilling of new wells, and so on.

3.2.1 *Production Drilling*

Unlike exploration drilling, production well drilling is a repetitive operation whose duration is easier to plan, and its costs are often better controlled. On average, production wells are drilled faster than exploration wells (learning curve).

In addition to drilling times, it is necessary to consider the completion times needed to connect the producing area to the borehole. The completion must ensure that the walls of the wellbore are secure. Today, while the vast majority of exploration or delineation wells remain vertical, production wells often use diverted or horizontal drilling techniques, particularly when the drilling area is inaccessible or urbanized or offshore, to limit the number of platforms or to exploit a deposit of low thickness or permeability (the latter being the case of shale oil and shale gas deposits). Multi-drain drilling can also be used when you want to produce several parts of the same reservoir simultaneously.

3.2.2 *Production Drilling Cost*

The cost of a production well is not very different from that of an exploration well. On the one hand, there is an additional cost due to the fact that the well must be equipped to be able to produce efficiently, but, on the other hand, thanks to experience, the well is drilled more quickly. In the case of a horizontal well, the cost is 20 to 30% higher than that of a vertical well, but in return, well productivity is increased by sometimes a factor of 3. Environmental constraints also can have an impact on well costs. These may be increased by the need to treat drilling waste, such as rock cuttings or various fluids, in order to comply with the country's environmental regulations.

3.2.3 *Floating Supports*

At sea, the equipment must be installed on floating supports. At shallow water depths, we can use a fixed structure (jacket), but for depths beyond a few hundred meters of water (currently, we are able to produce more than 3000 m of water, to which several thousand meters are added in the subsoil to reach the field), we then use one of three alternatives:

- A semi-submersible platform, anchored to the sea floor to be kept in place, and with a large and deep hull so as to have a low center of gravity and good stability
- A SPAR, a structure consisting of either a solid cylinder or a cylindrical part and a metal mesh with catenary anchor lines
- A Floating Production Storage and Offloading (FPSO): they were initially modified tankers used only for storage and loading of crude oil (FSO). Then, as the available tankers became scarce, new boats were built. By allowing autonomous production, the FPSO are more and more used in deep offshore areas where there are no export networks such as Brazil and West Africa.

Depending on the structure chosen, it will have to be built (or bought, or rented, if it is an existing structure) and installed during this development phase.

3.2.4 Total Development Costs

Development investments include the costs of development drilling (production wells and, where applicable, injection wells) and the costs of production facilities with separation and processing units, storage tanks, pumping and metering units, and discharge systems (pipelines and loading terminals).

Except for marginal cases such as small satellite fields whose development is very rapid, the development phase generally lasts 2 to 4 years.

In the development of an oil field, investments can reach several billion dollars. Identifying and evaluating the key parameters of a development are essential to the proper definition and profitability of the project. Some parameters, such as the situation of the field, the depth of the target, or the ocean-meteorological conditions, have strong influence on costs. Development costs represent between 40% and 60% of the total cost of the project.

Depending on the region, the cost of development varies considerably. In most cases the range will be between 7 and 15 \$/boe, but it can be much more for complex fields.

3.3 Production

It is impossible to recover all the hydrocarbons present in a reservoir because of the action of capillary forces. On average, around 80% of the gas and 30 to 40% of the oil originally in place can be recovered. The time profile of production is characterized by a build-up phase, followed by a plateau that can be maintained for a time comprised between a few months and 2–3 years (or longer for large deposits), and finally by a decline phase until the end of the deposit's life.

As production progresses, reservoir pressure drops, reducing the eruptive capacity of hydrocarbons, particularly of oil. Initially, the wells produce spontaneously (i.e. without stimulation), until the production of water becomes excessive. This so-called primary recovery ranges between 25 and 30% of oil in place and in the majority of cases does not allow economically sufficient volumes of oil to be extracted. This is why it is often financially interesting to implement methods of assisted recovery after a certain operating time, such as pressurized water injection (the most widely used) or gas injection. These methods allow higher recovery rates of up to 40 to 60%. To go even further, so-called tertiary recovery processes can be used, such as chemical or thermal methods, to improve spatial scanning and reduce capillary forces. Tertiary methods can provide an additional recovery of 5 to 10% of the oil in place. However, all these methods have a cost, and it will be necessary to verify that their implementation brings an improvement in profitability. This also depends on the characteristics of the company exploiting the field: large companies frequently face higher costs and may divest fields reaching the end of their life to smaller, more nimble companies.

In the particular case of shales (oil or gas), as these formations have low porosity and permeability, hydraulic fracturing will be required to create cracks in the reservoir using high hydraulic pressures and extract significant quantities of hydrocarbons. The introduction of retaining agents such as sand or small marbles keeps these fractures open. But as productivity declines very quickly in these formations, it will be necessary to constantly renew fracturing to maintain an acceptable level of production.

The sum of exploration and development costs constitute total capital expenditure (CAPEX).

3.3.1 Operating/Exploitation Costs

Operating costs (OPEX) are defined as all expenses related to the operation of a production facility. They can be classified as (Fig. 1.1):

- fixed (independent of production level) or variable (proportional to production level)
- direct (production, maintenance of wells, inspection, logistics, safety) or indirect (technical assistance, headquarters staff)
- according to their nature: personnel costs, consumption (fuel, energy, etc.), telecommunication costs, rentals, service, and maintenance contracts.
- according to their object (production, maintenance, security, etc.). This classification allows cost accounting closer to the operator's objectives.

One can find a great diversity of situations, depending on the field: OPEX will generally range widely, between 7 and 15 \$/boe, depending on the difficulty of extraction (gas, oil, heavy oil, etc.), field size, geographical location (land or sea), region (desert, jungle, far north, temperate zones, etc.).

As a general rule, the amount of operating costs in \$/boe is therefore of the same order of magnitude as development costs, but with one major difference: development costs must be financed at a time when there is still no cash inflow,

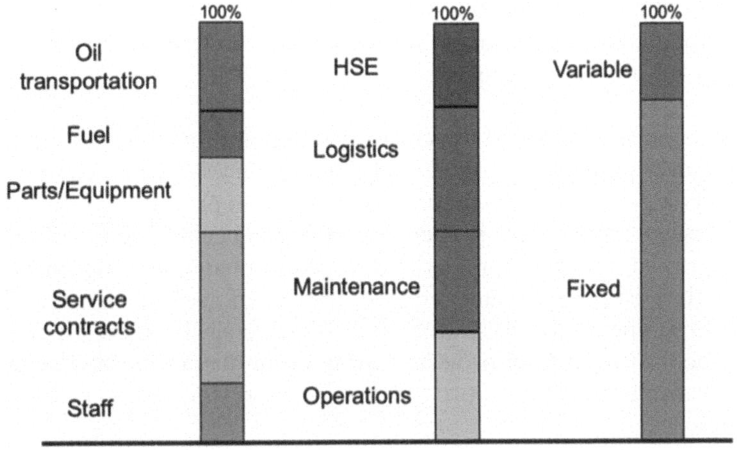

Fig. 1.1 Cost structure according to different types of breakdown by major cost families. (Source: Courtesy of Eric Descourtieux, Trident Energy)

since the field is not yet in production; while operating costs are funded from sales. Nevertheless, controlling operating costs is a daily concern for the operating teams, who must ensure an optimal level of production in complete safety and at the lowest cost.

3.4 *Dismantling—Site Restoration*

Finally, after a production period often of the order of 15 to 30 years, the limits of economic recovery of hydrocarbons are reached and the production structure is dismantled; if onshore, it is also necessary to rehabilitate the land. These operations can be very penalizing (the cost of dismantling an offshore platform is equal to that of its installation), especially since they occur at a time when the oil company no longer enjoys the cash flow from exploitation. It is therefore necessary to provision and take into account these costs in economic calculations from the start.

3.5 *Technical Cost*

Technical cost is defined as the total expenditure from exploration to decommissioning, that is, the sum of exploration and development investment, operating and maintenance costs of existing facilities, and decommissioning costs. The respective weights of these different categories of expenditure vary according to the project, but a few orders of magnitude can be given as a percentage of the overall cost of the project:

- 5 to 10% for exploration

- 35 to 45% for development
- 35 to 45% for operating and maintenance
- 5 to 10% for dismantling.

These costs are optimized to achieve the highest profitability. For example, it is sometimes preferable to reduce development investment and let operating costs increase accordingly, by renting the production platform rather than buying it. This will reduce expenses before production begins, and rental expenses will be charged annually during the production phase. Such optimization is aimed at the best possible value creation. In the end, technical costs are highly variable from one project to another, but will generally be in the range of $10 to $35/boe, with offshore projects costing more than onshore. The technological challenge of offshore production and more complex logistics explain this difference.

3.5.1 Cost Reduction

Companies must pursue two simultaneous objectives: increase production without endangering the production level of the reservoir and keeping costs as low as possible.

Two factors play a fundamental role in the evolution of costs:

- Technical and organizational innovation
- The level of economic activity, and more specifically the price of oil.

Regarding the first factor, the oil industry is relatively conservative in its technical choices, preferring to use proven methods to reduce the risks associated with the implementation of any new technology that could lead to a delay in the start of field production. However, some companies are ready to innovate, particularly when innovation allows significant gains or when the technical parameters of development require new solutions to reach new reserves. In terms of R & D, in response to the pattern of increasing outsourcing by oil companies, contractors have come to play a more important, and now even indispensable, role on the international oil scene.

Nowadays, a large part of innovation results from access to massive amounts of data, which makes it possible to have more reliable understanding and better forecasts (e.g., of oil prices) or optimize investment costs by managing the exploitation of a field remotely (the platform's size is reduced to a minimum to accommodate only a few people, the majority of the team remaining on land, with remote connections giving access to all the data necessary for the proper functioning of the exploitation).

But innovation is not limited to the technical sphere. Cost reductions can also result from organizational innovations, particularly in logistics. Rethinking the entire organization of a project to optimize each link, eliminating as much as possible redundancies without harming safety or the environment, using every possibility of connecting to existing installations, and finding associations that allow synergies are themes increasingly at the heart of the drive for optimization.

With respect to the influence of the oil price, costs will evolve according to the market situation (balance of demand and supply) of the sector in question (geophysics, drilling, construction, etc.). For example, the price of platforms will be sensitive to the costs of raw materials (steel in particular), the workload of platform-building companies, and the availability of construction sites. For the same type of platform, price differences of 20 to 30% can be observed, depending on the market situation. A construction site may be willing to accept a low price to just cover its operating costs and avoid closure if demand is low. On the contrary, in a situation of overheating, when the order books are close to full, suppliers and manufacturers have the power to negotiate and sign with the highest bidder. Maintaining, at each stage, effective competition between contractors when awarding work contracts helps reducing the final cost of a project. Consequently, there is a correlation between costs and oil prices: when the price of oil is high, companies have abundant cash from their producing fields and are therefore more willing to invest. Since they all have the same reaction at the same time, markets are quickly tightened. When the price of crude oil is low, we have the opposite reaction.

Cost control is now a priority for all companies, whether contractors or producers; they must set up procedures to ensure rigorous budget monitoring and permanent data exchange between the various entities involved in the project, whether with the client or the company's financial department.

4 The Patrimonial Agreement

The State, as responsible for the general interest, owns the natural resources of the subsoil (with the exception of private land in the United States), gives the authorization to explore for and exploit hydrocarbons, and controls oil activities. In each country, there is a law that provides the legal, financial, and fiscal framework for existing or potential exploration and production activity. It defines, inter alia, the applicable legal regime, the authority of the Minister responsible for Petroleum Affairs, the role of the national company (if there is one), and the tax regime.

Two modes of State intervention are possible:

- The State directly develops hydrocarbon fields through its national company, as in Saudi Arabia
- The State designates a company to carry out exploration and exploitation operations. It decides on the regime to which the chosen company will be subject, within the framework of the legislation in force (the regime can be a concession contract, a production sharing contract, or a service contract).

4.1 *Procedures for Awarding Mining Titles/Contract*

The granting of mining titles or oil contracts in available exploration areas can be decided through one of two alternatives:

- Negotiation process. In this case, companies are encouraged to submit an offer covering the terms and conditions of the proposed oil agreement. The State may then enter into negotiations with the proposing company, in order to reach a mutually acceptable agreement
- International call for tenders (also called "exploration round"). The State opens blocks and sets the conditions of the call for tenders (terms of submission, availability of data). It provides companies with a standard contract in which certain terms (work commitments, expenses, economic terms, participation rates, etc.) are left to the company to propose. After studying the offers, two cases are possible: either acceptance of the best offer, without negotiation (competitive bidding), or negotiation with the company having submitted the best offer, in order to improve the proposed terms and finalize a contract.

The tax system is defined by the State. There are two main alternative solutions: either a concession or a production sharing contract. The State can also offer only service contracts, but oil companies are reluctant to accept this solution, yet are sometimes forced to accept it if they want to work in the country.

5 Concession

In the concession regime, the legislation and regulations define the applicable framework in a detailed and non-discriminatory manner. A concession regime is the rule in Europe, the United States, Canada, Australia and Latin America, with few exceptions.

The concessionaire becomes the holder of an exploration license from the State, followed by an operating license (often called concession) in the event of a commercial discovery of hydrocarbons. The concessionaire exercises the exclusive right to explore for and exploit hydrocarbon fields over a defined area and for a limited period of time.

The concession contract is a document of about a hundred pages, whose various clauses can be grouped into three main categories:

- technical, operational and administrative clauses, covering the practical aspects of the conduct of operations during the various phases
- economic, fiscal, financial and commercial clauses, covering rent sharing between the parties, accounting for oil costs, valuation of production.

Subject to the fulfillment of all contractual obligations, the concession holder may withdraw at any time during the exploration phase or upon its expiry, if no commercial discovery has been made.

Under a concession contract, the oil company:

- owns the facilities until its mining rights expire
- exercises the exclusive right of exploration (in the form of an exploration permit or license).
- obtains a concession or operating permit (lease) to develop a commercial discovery.
- owns and freely disposes of all production at the wellhead, subject to certain obligations such as royalties and sales on the local market
- exercises this right for a limited period of time, at the end of which the exploited fields revert to the State.

Under the concession regime, government revenues are obtained through taxation and are therefore voted by Parliament, meaning that Parliament can decide to change the "rules of the game" at any time.

Government revenues fall into the following main categories:

- bonus: some concession agreements provide for the payment by the holder of an amount payable on the date of signature of the contract, called "exploration bonus". This can range from several million to hundreds of millions of dollars and constitutes a significant financial effort for the holder, especially since this bonus is paid before any discovery, and lost if there is no discovery. For the country, it represents a very attractive, immediate income source. In other cases, the bonus may be paid at the start of development or production. For the same country, there may be several bonuses paid at different times during the project.
- surface fees: the holder may be required to pay annually to the State a rent proportional to the area of his exploration/production permit. The amount of these rents is generally quite low (usually a few $\$/km^2$ per year)
- royalty on production, equal to a percentage of the value of the production paid to the State by the holder, either in cash or in kind. It can be considered as a tax directly proportional to the value of production, in the same way as a tax on turnover, regardless of profits. The calculation of the royalty depends first of all on the applicable rate. Royalty rates are generally different for crude oil and natural gas, and lower for the latter. In order to modulate the royalty according to the characteristics of the fields in exploitation, the contracts may provide for progressive rates according to production volumes.
- the holder's income tax. The holder is subject to a direct tax on the income resulting from his production activities, but also from the transport, refining or liquefaction of natural gas.
- possibly an additional tax on oil profits. The payment of a royalty on production and a direct tax on profits may be considered by the State to be insufficient in times of high crude oil prices. In this case, the State introduces a specific tax on the profits from hydrocarbon production.

6 Production Sharing Contracts

Under the production sharing regime, the relationship between the State and companies is governed by a contract signed after multiple negotiations. Therefore, each contract will to some extent be different.

In this regime, the contractor does not hold a mining title, as the contract with the State does not create such a title. It is often a national oil company that holds the mining title, and the contract is then concluded with this national company, as the representative of the State, in the form of a joint venture. The State's direct participation in the joint venture may be an option.

The oil company that signs the production sharing contract with the State is called a contractor. The company:

- is a simple service provider;
- bears the technical and financial risks of exploration;
- has the exclusive right to develop and exploit the field if there is a commercial discovery;
- does not own the facilities it has paid for, but has the exclusive right to use them free of charge for the duration of the contract. The transfer of ownership can take place either at the time of installation of the facilities, or after full recovery of petroleum costs;
- receives a remuneration limited to a certain fraction of the production and consisting of two parts:
- cost oil, which corresponds to reimbursements of expenses (CAPEX and OPEX) financed by the oil company, but with an annual limit, the "cost stop", equal to a percentage of the production valued. The balance of oil costs not yet recovered in one year is then recoverable in subsequent years. However, any reimbursement should only be made after the control of the ministry in charge, which may reject expenses that it considers illegitimate;
- and a share of the profit oil, the "Contractor profit oil". The other fraction paid to the state is called "State profit oil". Indeed, after deduction of the cost oil, the remaining part, called profit oil, is shared between the State and the oil company according to a percentage indicated in the contract;

It is increasingly common to also see the payment of a royalty envisaged in a PSC, in the form of a percentage of the production valued and deducted immediately from production. Sometimes, a PSC may even include a tax that will be deducted from the Contractor profit oil.

7 Comparison Between Concession and PSC

The Concession and the Production Sharing Contract regimes each have their advantages and disadvantages. Of course, oil companies cannot choose between one and the other: they have an obligation to accept the system in force in the country at the time they undertake exploration. In a nutshell, it can be said that the main advantages of the concession are:

- the oil company owns a mining title and the oil installations, and it becomes the owner of all production at the wellhead (less any quantities corresponding to the royalty, if it is paid in kind)
- it is generally possible to consolidate different mining titles in the same country, and positive with negative pre-tax results, thus minimizing the final tax payable.

The production sharing contract does not have these advantages, but on the other hand:

- it results from a negotiation between the company and the State, which gives the former more latitude to be flexible on points that are less important to it and, on the contrary, rigorous on what is non-negotiable from its point of view
- in most cases, the accounts are prepared in dollars, providing a more accurate view of the results, especially when the activity is located in a country with high inflation.

8 Service Contract

Service contracts are concluded by the national company of the producing country and enlist oil companies as contractors, with the task of carrying out exploration, development, and/or exploitation work on their behalf. Service contracts are mainly used in the Middle East and Latin America, but their spread remains limited because they are of little interest to oil companies, which get only a financial reward (no entitlement to oil or gas), with no possibility of substantial value creation.

Two categories of service contracts exist, depending on the level of risk taken by the oil company:

- risk service contracts (known as agency contracts), under which the contractor is only reimbursed for his financing in the event of production, and risks losing whatever sum investment if no production occurs;
- technical assistance or cooperation contracts, without risk, to carry out specific work in return for adequate remuneration.

9 Economic Studies

Throughout the project, economists will be required to carry out economic studies.

When you are in the prospecting phase, the purpose of the study is to evaluate the commercial interest of an exploration objective. The task begins with a geological study that defines the potential accumulation of hydrocarbons and the probability of success of an exploration well. Based on three geological scenarios, described as "mini", "mode", and "maxi", the team in charge will define, often by analogy with similar fields, the potential development architecture and the investment and operating costs associated. According to these data, an estimate of potential profitability is reached, to help decide whether to implement the proposed exploration program. The relevance of the analogies and extrapolations made in this type of approach will depend on the reliability of the available databases. Therefore, this method of analogy reasoning has limited validity when the assessment must include the use of new technologies. When there is a discovery, the sanctioning of a project will be based on a detailed economic study that integrates four types of data:

- the production profiles, established by the reservoir engineers based on the characteristics of the reservoir and the amount of reserves
- investment and operating costs, assessed by the experts in the estimation
- the valorization of hydrocarbons. Since it is impossible to predict the price of oil and gas over a horizon of several years, scenarios are used. In the past, the focus was on developing complex scenarios with different variations of price each year. Presently, companies rely on fixed price scenarios in constant or current currency and select two or three alternatives, between an optimistic vision (high crude oil price) and a pessimistic one (low crude oil price)
- the contractual and tax conditions that exist in the country in question.

Economic studies focus on studying the profitability of the project by calculating mainly the Net Present Value (NPV) and the Internal Rate of Return (IRR) of the project. The NPV is the sum of the annual and discounted net cash flows. If it is positive, the project is profitable since in this case, the cash flow generated reimburses investment and operating costs plus taxes, taking into account the cost of the capital invested and adding an extra value. The internal rate of return of a project is the value of the discount rate that cancels its NPV. If the project's IRR is higher than the applicable discount rate, the NPV is positive and therefore the project is profitable. The threshold discount rate chosen by the company is therefore a determining factor. In theory, this rate results from an estimate of the cost of capital used by the company, but in reality, it will depend on the management strategy: choosing a relatively high value leads to selecting only fewer very profitable projects and rejecting opportunities that could then be chosen by the competition. Choosing the lowest value compatible with the cost of capital will allow more numerous projects, but at the expense of profitability.

It is clear that the final decision will be based on many other elements, such as the company's overall strategy or the local strategy in the country in question: for example, if the company is negotiating to obtain new permits, it will be good practice to reach an agreement for fields already discovered. The search for an optimal portfolio requires a diversified portfolio that spreads risks: deep offshore in areas where the geological potential is high, projects in countries with high political risk but high profitability, projects with low profitability but in "safe" countries corresponding to a risk-free investment, and so on. This diversification will be all the more possible as oil companies are used to working in partnerships: multiplying the number of projects reduces the overall risk of the portfolio. However, the risk associated with a fall in the price of crude oil must never be forgotten, because the sensitivity to this parameter is very high, even if in some countries tax mechanisms can serve as shock absorbers (e.g., the royalty rate can be correlated with the price of crude oil).

Upstream Petroleum is a sector that faces many challenges. There are more than enough resources to meet the demand for hydrocarbons in the coming decades. But these resources will have to be developed at lower cost, especially when the price of crude oil is relatively low, which requires the discovery of new technologies, the implementation at all levels of the digital transformation, and the access to more efficient processes. Therefore, investment in R & D must be commensurate with the stakes involved.

Beyond these operational challenges, the main challenge is now the obligation for these companies to decarbonize in order to respond to the imperative need to reduce CO_2 emissions, as hydrocarbons represent a significant portion of these emissions. Depending on the distribution of their assets across the globe, their percentage of oil production versus gas production, the latter being less CO_2 emitting, and local environmental policies, the response will not be the same for all companies; for example, they can put in place procedures to reduce methane leaks (e.g., in maintenance), inject CO_2 into the subsoil, use electricity from renewable energies, and so on. Finally, most companies in this sector have started to diversify by developing their asset portfolio through equity investments or acquisitions of companies in the renewable energy sector. And for all of them, financial pressure is on the agenda of their top management: How to maintain profitability at a good level with an increasingly volatile crude oil price and equally volatile costs? Which niches should be invested in? How to retain the loyalty of current shareholders, some of whom wish to turn away from fossil fuels? How to attract new investors for risky projects in an uncertain environment? and so on.

This industry is undergoing a real transformation, and it will succeed only if the men and women who make it up show intelligence, curiosity, and responsibility.

Bibliography

Bret-Rouzaut, Nadine & Favennec, Jean-Pierre, Oil and Gas Exploration & Production, Reserves, Costs, Contracts, Editions Technip, 2011.

Darmois, Gilles, Sharing the oil rent, current situation and good practice, Editions Technip, 2014.

Inkpen, Andrew, Michael, Moffett, The Global Oil & Gas Industry, PennWell, 2011.

Johnston D & Johnston D, International Petroleum Fiscal System Analysis—State of Play, OGEL (Oil, Gas & Energy Law Intelligence), 2011.

Kasriel, Ken, Upstream Petroleum Fiscal and Valuation Modeling in Excel: A Worked Examples Approach, The Wiley Finance Series, 2013.

National Energy Technology Laboratory (NETL), US Department of Energy, Carbon Dioxide Enhanced Oil Recovery, March 2010.

CHAPTER 2

Economics of Gas Transportation by Pipeline and LNG

Gergely Molnar

The relatively low energy density of natural gas on a volumetric basis—almost 1000 times lower compared to crude oil—makes it one of the most challenging and expensive primary fuels to transport from the wellhead to the burner tip of end-consumers. Internationally traded natural gas is typically transported either in gaseous form via long-distance pipeline systems or in the form of liquefied natural gas on ships (LNG carriers).

The transport segment alone can account for over 50% of the costs occurring through the value chain of internationally traded natural gas. As a consequence, natural gas remained for a long time a local commodity, consumed relatively close to its production centres. Inter-regional natural gas trade emerged gradually with the start-up of the first commercial LNG export facilities and the construction of long-distance pipelines through the 1960s and 1970s.

The share of inter-regionally traded gas in total consumption rose gradually from below 5% in 1975 to 15% in the early 2000s and reached 21% in 2018. In comparison, around half of crude oil produced has been traded in 2018.

Whilst pipelines have dominated international gas trade for a long time, LNG exports more than tripled since the beginning of the century and accounted for just over half of international gas trade in 2018. This has been driven by a particularly strong gas demand growth in the markets of the Asia Pacific region, which have no or limited alternative supply options to LNG (such as Japan and Korea) (Fig. 2.1).

G. Molnar (✉)
International Energy Agency (IEA), Paris, France
e-mail: gergely.molnar@iea.org

M. Hafner, G. Luciani (eds.), *The Palgrave Handbook of International Energy Economics*, https://doi.org/10.1007/978-3-030-86884-0_2

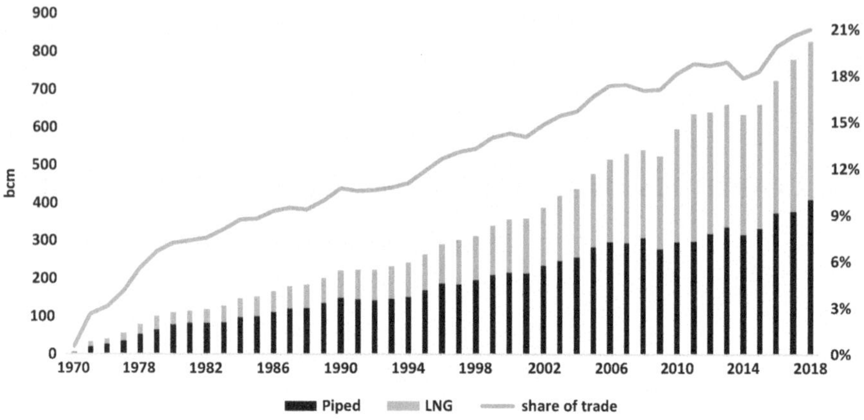

Fig. 2.1 International trade of natural gas (1970–2018). Total LNG exports and intercontinental pipeline trade, including Norway to the rest of Europe. (Source: International Energy Agency)

Besides pipelines and LNG, a number of alternative technologies and methods have been developed to monetize and transport natural gas; however, their utilization remains marginal and is typically serving local markets (see Box 2.1).

This chapter will focus of the economics of large infrastructure projects underpinning the international trade of natural gas, that is, long-distance pipelines and large-scale LNG.

Box 2.1 Alternative Gas-to-Market Transport Options

A number of methods have been developed to transport and monetize the energy value of methane.

This includes the transportation of compressed natural gas (**CNG**) containers and **small-scale LNG** ISO tanks via trucks and rail. These **"virtual pipelines"** can play a crucial role in meeting local natural gas demand in emerging markets with strong consumption growth and a still developing pipeline network. In China, LNG delivered via trucks accounted for over 10% of the national gas consumption in 2017.

Natural gas can also be **transformed into other forms of energy carriers** (gas-to-power, gas-to-liquids, gas-to-solids) close to the upstream source and transported as such to the end-consumers.

Gas-to-wire attracted considerable attention in emerging markets where natural gas is primarily used to meet rapidly growing electricity needs. The largest gas-to-wire project is currently developed in Brazil in the Açu port of Rio de Janeiro. The project consists of a 1.3GW combined cycle plant integrated to an LNG regasification terminal, a transmission line and a substation connected to the national grid.

(*continued*)

(continued)

Gas-to-liquids (GTL) is a refinery process transforming methane into a heavier hydrocarbon liquid (such as diesel or gasoline) most commonly using the Fischer-Tropsch (F-T) synthesis. First, methane is converted to syngas (a mixture of hydrogen, carbon dioxide and carbon monoxide). After impurities (such as sulphur, water and carbon dioxide) are removed, syngas is reacted in the presence of an iron catalyst in an environment of high pressure (40 atmospheres) and extremely high temperatures ranging from 260 to 450 °C. Whilst GTL is a technologically proven process, its commercial viability at a large still needs to be proven. There are currently five large GTL projects operating globally, with a total production capacity of close to 250,000 barrels per day (equating to ~0.2% of global liquids production).

Gas-to-solids (GTS) technology processes consist of transforming methane into a solid form called natural gas hydrates (NGH) by mixing natural gas with water at 80–100 bar and 2–10 °C. It is created when certain small molecules, particularly methane ethane and propane, stabilize the hydrogen bonds within water to form a three-dimensional structure able to trap the methane molecule. GTS technologies are still in the state of research and development and no project reached the state of commercial phase.

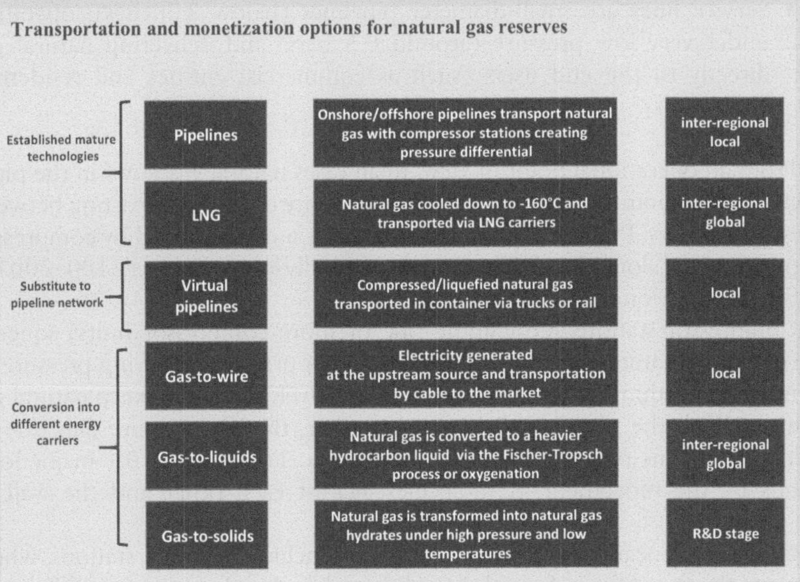

Transportation and monetization options for natural gas reserves

1 Long-Distance Pipelines

Pipelines have been the natural choice to transport methane in its gaseous form. First historical records of practical usage of natural gas date back to 500 BCE in China, where natural gas was transported via "bamboo pipes" and used to boil ocean water to separate salt and create drinkable water (effectively desalination).

Modern pipeline systems—most often built from steel—can transport natural gas through several thousands of kilometres from the wellhead to the burner tip of end-consumers. Four major types of pipelines can be distinguished along the transportation route:

- Gathering (or upstream) pipelines are typically low-pressure, small-diameter pipelines (4–12 inches) that transport raw natural gas from the wellhead to the processing plan.
- Transmission pipelines are large-diameter pipelines (16–56 inches) operating under high pressure (15–120 bar) and transporting cleaned, dry natural gas through long distances from the processing plant either directly to large end-consumers (such as power plants or industrial sites) or to the city gate where it connects to the distribution system.
- Distribution pipelines are small- to medium-size pipelines (2–28 inches) carrying odorized natural gas under a relatively low pressure (up to 14 bars) from the city gate to its connection with service lines.
- Service lines are small-diameter pipelines (below 2 inches), operating under very low pressure (around 0.5 bars) and delivering natural gas directly to the end users (such as commercial entities and residential consumers).

From an operational point of view, in all cases natural gas flows in the pipelines from one point to another due to the pressure differential existing between those two points. Pressure differential is created and maintained by compressor stations located along the pipeline system (typically located at every 100–200 km of the transmission pipelines).

Compressor stations (containing one or more compressor units) squeeze the incoming natural gas to push it out a higher pressure, allowing pressure to be increased within the pipeline, which is effectively needed to keep natural gas flowing. With the travelled distance increasing, the gas pressure falls due to friction and thus requires further compression. Friction loss (or major loss) results by the movement of molecules against each other and the wall of the pipe.

Other non-linear parts of a pipeline system include metering stations, which measure the flow of gas along the pipeline and enable the operator of the pipeline system to monitor natural gas flow along the pipeline. Operational information (such as flow rate, pressure, temperature and operational quality) from the compressor and metering stations is transmitted to a centralized control station via Supervisory Control and Data Acquisition (SCADA) systems. This allows a permanent monitoring of the pipeline system, ensuring its stable and safe functioning.

This chapter will focus on the large-diameter, long-distance transmission pipelines which enable international trade of natural gas by transiting methane through several countries and borders. The first part of the chapter will provide an overview of the underlying economics of pipeline projects (including CAPEX and OPEX), whilst the second part will focus on the commercial aspects (including contract structuring and tariff regimes).

1.1 Economics of Pipeline Projects

Natural gas pipeline projects are capital intensive by nature. High upfront investment costs typically account for over 90% of total costs occurring through the lifespan of a gas pipeline (~40 years), whilst operating expenses (e.g. fuel costs associated with gas compression, maintenance and repairs, staff, etc.) usually account for up to 5–10% of total costs. Consequently, the initial design of the project and the optimization of capital expenditures needs careful consideration as it has a disproportionate impact on the overall economics of the project.

1.1.1 CAPEX

The investment cost of a natural gas pipeline is ultimately determined by its (1) length, (2) capacity (diameter × operating pressure) and (3) unit investment costs.

The linear part of a pipeline system—commonly called the "line pipe"—accounts for the majority of the CAPEX, whilst the share of the investments into compressor and metering stations typically accounts between 15 and 30%.

Unit investment costs of international pipelines can vary in a wide range from \$30k to over \$200,000/km/inch, depending on a number of factors, including external conditions such as terrain and climatological context, labour and material costs, project management as well as the stringency of the regulatory framework(s) (primarily environmental and safety standards). The unit cost of compressor stations is typically in the range of \$2–\$4 million per MW of installed power.

Figure 2.2 shows the breakdown of the average unit investment costs for the line pipe and the compressor stations, respectively.

Unit investment costs can be broken down into four main categories:

- Material costs:
  - for the linear part of the pipeline system, it includes pipe sections (made usually from high carbon steel and fabricated in steel rolling mills), pipe coating and cathodic protection. It typically accounts for around one-third of total investments costs and is highly dependent of the evolution of steel prices;

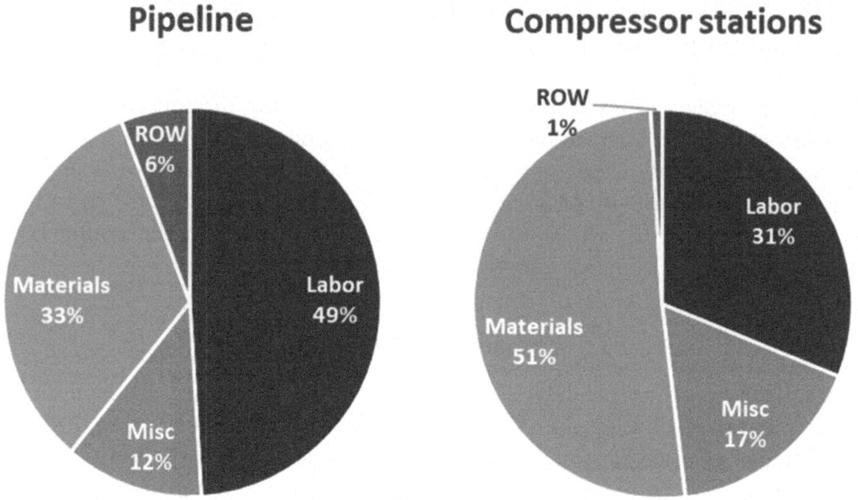

Fig. 2.2 Breakdown of average unit investment costs into pipelines and compressor stations. (Source: based on ACER (2015))

- for compressor stations, material costs are the most important cost component, accounting for about half of total investment. This includes the pre-fabricated modular functional units of a compressor station (such as gas scrubbing and liquid removal, compressor and driver units, gas coolers, pipes and valves).

- Labour costs:
  - are typically the most important cost component of the line pipe, accounting for over 40% of the unit investment cost. This includes the salaries and wages related to the preparation of the terrain (clearing, grading and trenching) and the construction of the pipeline (stringing, welding, coating pipeline segments, depositing the pipeline and backfilling);
  - the construction of compressor stations includes site preparation, construction of the compressor building(s) and assembling compressor units. It is a somewhat less labour-intensive process compared to pipe laying, with labour costs accounting to around one-quarter of unit investment costs of compressor stations.

- Miscellaneous costs generally cover surveying, engineering, supervision, contingencies, telecommunications equipment, administration and overheads, freight, regulatory filing fees as well as taxes. They typically account for over 10% of total unit investment costs in the case of both the pipelines and compressor stations.
- Right-of-way (ROW) costs include obtaining rights-of-way and allowing for damages.

It is important to highlight that the breakdown of average unit investment costs presented above is purely indicative.

Each pipeline system is unique and hence the cost breakdown will vary by pipeline. For instance, pipes built in more challenging external environments (such as mountainous terrain, rocky soil, wetlands or ultra-deep offshore) will usually have a higher proportion of costs associated with labour and logistics and will depend less on material expenditures. Pipelines crossing high population density areas have in general higher miscellaneous and right-of-way costs and need to abide to more stringent safety standards. Construction of offshore pipeline systems requires both specific line design (wall thickness up to 2 inches to support water pressure, insulation against low-temperature environment and ballasting to provide stability) and a specific set of logistics (including pipelaying vessels with day rates often at several $100k/day), which can increase significantly investment unit costs.

Figure 2.3 provides indicative additions to pipeline construction costs, depending on their respective external environment.

Worth to note that international pipelines—crossing several borders and countries—have to comply with various jurisdictions and regulatory frameworks—which can substantially increase their miscellaneous costs related to administration and regulatory filing fees.

In addition to the cost components related to technical CAPEX, the financial structure and the cost of capital can alter significantly the economics and the profitability of pipeline projects. External financing can account for up to 70% of financing in major international gas pipeline projects. Investors/lenders typically look for LIBOR +3–4% for pipeline investments, depending on the location, the project promoters and their risk appetite. Based on those assumptions, financial expenditures (FIEX) can add 10–15% to the initial technical CAPEX.

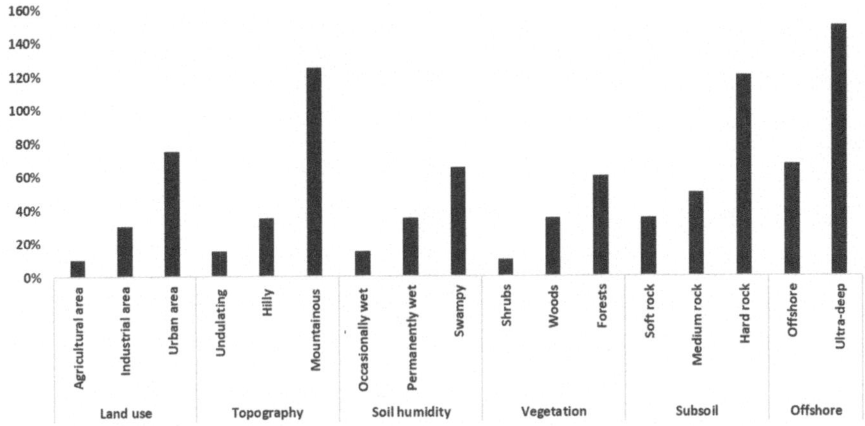

Fig. 2.3 Indicative additions to pipeline construction costs, per difficulty factor. (Sources: based on CEER (2019), Yamasaki (1980) and Author's estimates)

1.1.1.1 Economies of Scale

Natural gas transportation via pipelines naturally results in economies of scale. Whilst the throughput capacity of a pipeline is increasing following the $\pi r^2 L$ formula—where r stands for the radius (half of the diameter) and L for the length of the pipeline—the material costs required for the construction of the line pipe is increasing in line with the $2\pi rL$ formula. Consequently, unit transport costs for the same level of utilization are usually lower for pipelines with larger diameters and built in similar external environment.

Moreover, some of the costs associated with pipeline construction are fixed (design, permits) or increase insignificantly compared to a higher design and working capacity of the pipeline system.

Further, it should be noted that several smaller compressor units will have a higher cost per MW compared to a larger unit with same compressing power due to economies of scale (Fig. 2.4).

1.1.2 OPEX

Operating expenses represent a fraction of the overall costs occurring through the lifespan of a pipeline project, typically accounting for 5–10% of the total costs of natural gas transportation.

Figure 2.5 provides a purely illustrative example of the breakdown of operating expenses, based on the financial reporting of a major European gas transmission company.

Operating costs of a pipeline system can be broken down into four main categories:

- Fuel costs: primarily associated with the energy requirements of compressor stations running either on natural gas or on electricity (see Box 2.2). "Fuel gas" is either provided by the shippers themselves as "fuel gas in kind" or procured by the operator of the transmission system operator via

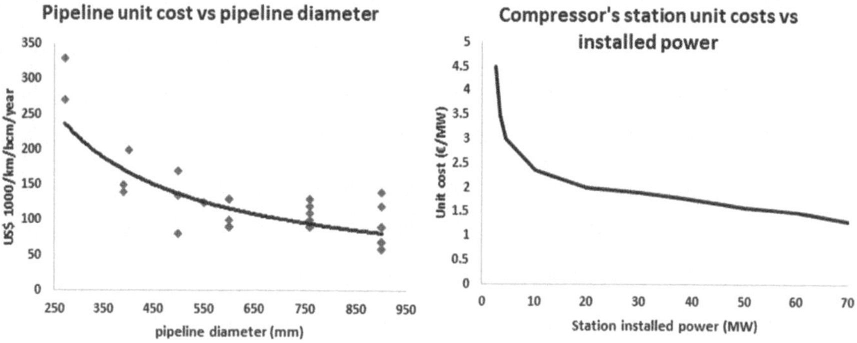

Fig. 2.4 Economies of scale in natural gas pipeline systems. Green dots indicating individual gas pipeline projects. (Sources: International Energy Agency (1994) and CEER (2019))

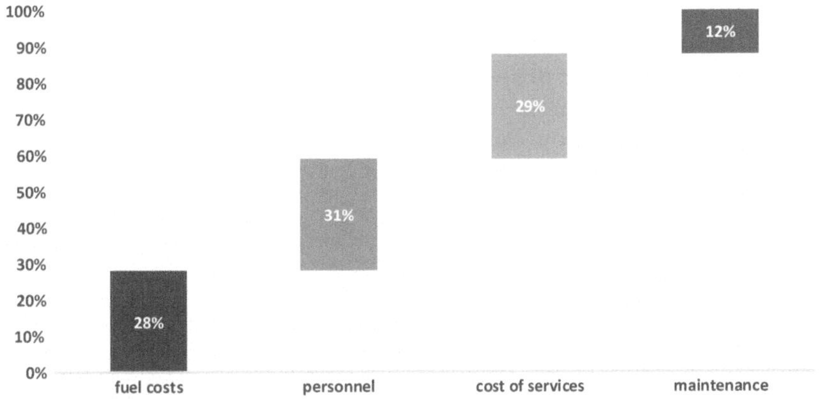

Fig. 2.5 OPEX of gas transmission company

Box 2.2 Compressor Stations

Compressor stations are at the heart of natural gas pipeline systems. The necessary operational pressure needed to transport ("make flow") natural gas is ensured at the starting point of the pipeline system by a **head compressor**.

Natural gas flow in the pipeline can be described with the **general flow equation**:

$$Q = \frac{7.574 \times 10^{-4}}{\sqrt{f}} \times \frac{Ts}{Ps} \times \sqrt{\frac{\left(P_1^2 - P_2^2\right) D^5}{SLZT}}$$

where Q stands for the gas flow rate (m³/h), f is a general friction factor for gas (determined from the Moody Diagram), T is the temperature in Kelvin, Ps is the standard pressure (in bar), P1 is the inlet pressure, P2 is the outlet pressure, D is the diameter of the pipeline in mm, S is the relative density (air/gas), L is the length of the pipeline (in m) and Z is the compressibility factor of gas (Nasr, Connor 2014).

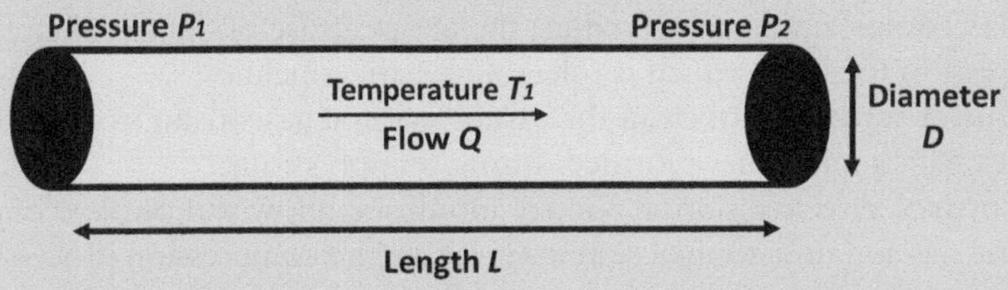

Steady gas flow in a pipeline

(*continued*)

(continued)

The initial **pressure drops** with the travelled distance due to the friction occurring between the molecules of methane and against the wall of the pipe. Pressure drop can be described from the **Darcy-Weisbach equation** as the following (Menon 2011):

$$H_f = f\frac{L}{D}\times\frac{V^2}{2g}$$

where H_f stands for the head loss due to friction, f is a general friction factor for gas, L is the length of the pipeline (m), D is the internal diameter of the pipeline (in mm), V is the velocity (in m/s) and g stands for the gravitational acceleration constant (9.81 m/s^2).

The loss of pressure requires the installation of so-called **intermediary compressor stations**, typically located at every 100–200 kms of the pipeline system.

The required **compression power** is given by the following equation (Menon 2011):

$$Power(kW) = 4.0639\left(\frac{y}{y-1}\right)QT_1\left(\frac{Z_1+Z_2}{2}\right)\left(\frac{1}{n_a}\right)\left[\left(\frac{P_2}{P_1}\right)^{\frac{y-1}{y}}-1\right]$$

where y stands for ratio of heat of gas (1.4), Q for gas flow rate (million m^3/d), T for temperature (in Kelvin), Z_1 compressibility of gas at suction conditions (when entering the compressor station), Z_2 compressibility of gas at discharge conditions (when leaving the compressor station), P_1 suction pressure of gas (kPa), P_2 discharge pressure of gas (kPa) and n_a is the compressor's isentropic efficiency (typically between 0.75 and 0.85).

A compressor station typically consists of the following facilities:

- **Inlet scrubber**: to clean up the entering natural gas stream from any impurities that may have formed during its voyage in the pipeline;
- One or several **compressor units**: each of which includes drivers and compressors;
- **Gas cooler**: necessary to reduce the temperature of the gas after compression to a level which is tolerable for the pipelines;
- **Outlet scrubber**: to clean the exiting natural gas stream from impurities which might have formed during compression;
- **Control systems**: station control monitors inflow and outflow of natural gas and unit control systems monitor the compression process. All data and information are reported to the central control station via SCADA.

(*continued*)

(continued)

Depending on the network configuration and throughput capacity of the pipeline system, aggregate capacity of compressor stations can range from less than 10 MW to several hundreds of MW. The world's largest compressor station is located in Portovaya, Russia, with an aggregate capacity of 366 MW.

Two main types of compressors can be distinguished:

- **Reciprocating compressors**: usually driven by either electric motors or gas engines with a reciprocating moving piston compressing natural gas;
- **Centrifugal compressors** are driven by gas turbines or electric motors, increasing the pressure of natural gas with mechanical rotating vanes.

Compressor stations are using either natural gas (typically taken from the transmission system) or electricity. Data from the International Energy Agency indicate that natural gas accounts for ~95% of energy consumed by natural gas pipelines.

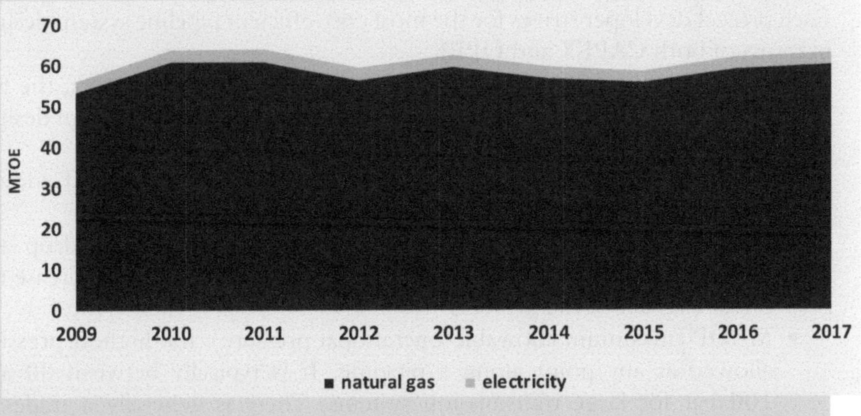

Energy consumption of pipelines per fuel (2009–2017). (Source: International Energy Agency)

Whilst the fuel efficiency of pipeline systems varies depending on their design and external environment, typically, fuel gas usage equates to less than 0.5% of the volume transported per 100 km, that is, less than 5000 cubic metre per 1 million cubic metre transported over 100 km. Pipelines with larger diameters tend to have a lower fuel requirement for the transportation of the same quantity of gas due to lower friction loss.

a competitive tendering process. In the case of vertically integrated companies, where the shipper and the transmission system operator are not separated, fuel costs are part of the company's internal costs.

- Personnel costs include salaries and wages of the employees of the company operating the transmission system, as well as social security contributions and other employee benefits.

- Services costs include all expenses related to services required to manage the pipeline system (such as information technology systems, telecommunication services) and the operating company itself (technical, legal, administrative, personnel-related services) as well as miscellaneous expenses (such as insurance, marketing and consulting).
- Maintenance costs are associated with the inspection, maintenance and repairs of the pipeline system in order to maintain its operational status without necessarily expanding its lifespan.

The breakdown of OPEX cost components can show a high degree of variation depending on technical features and general state of the pipeline system. For instance, an ageing pipeline system running through a challenging environment will naturally have higher maintenance and repair costs. Fuel costs will vary depending on the fuel procurement process, that is, inhouse, "gas in kind" or open tendering process.

1.1.3 Optimal Pipeline Design

Each project developer strives for the most cost-efficient pipeline system design, in terms of both CAPEX and OPEX.

Considering that length and terrain are external and fixed factors, the following considerations are usually taken into account for pipeline system design:

- Quantities to be transported: based on actual market demand and/or expectations, including seasonal variations and modelled peak;
- Internal pipeline diameter: larger diameters reduce pressure drop and hence lower the need for compression power, but necessarily increase the initial CAPEX of the project;
- MAOP (maximum allowable operational pressure): the highest pressure allowed at any point along a pipeline. It is typically between 80 and 100 bar for large transmission systems. There is generally a trade-off between MAOP and pipeline wall thickness. Generally, pipelines running through densely populated areas have a lower MAOP;
- Flow velocity: shall be kept below maximum allowable velocity to prevent pipe erosion (a maximum velocity of ~72 km/h is typically recommended);
- Compressor stations' capacity and spacing, which ultimately influence their fuel consumption (variable OPEX) and performance: a large pressure drop between stations results in a large compression ratio, typically leading to poor compressor station performance.

The techno-economic optimization of the pipeline system design should be based on the hydraulic calculation of the pipeline and followed by a series of NPV calculations (taking into consideration the cost of capital). Typically a software computer program is used for modelling purposes and cost computations before determining the optimal configuration of the pipeline

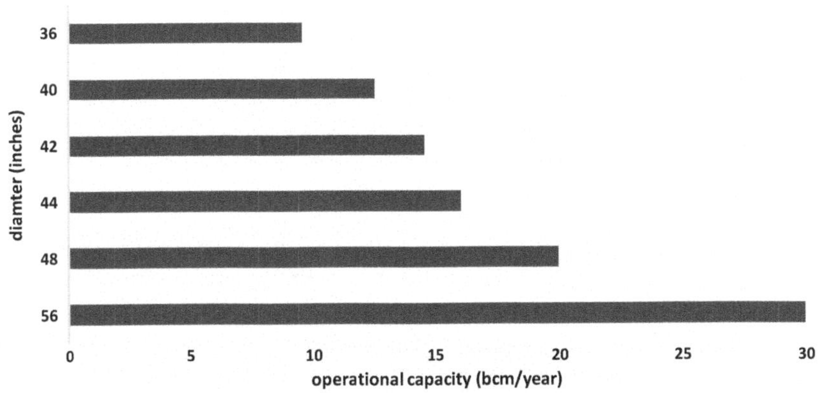

Fig. 2.6 Rule of thumb for optimal pipeline capacity in relation to internal pipe diameter. (Source: based on Brauer (2016))

system in relation to its throughput, diameter and operating pressure. Figure 2.6 provides typical throughput capacities associated with respective internal pipe diameters and assuming an operational pressure of 100 bar.

1.2 Commercial Implications: Contract Design and Tariff Structuring

Natural gas pipeline systems have high upfront investment costs, which become sunk as soon as the pipeline is laid down—due to the inflexible and durable nature of this infrastructure.

Consequently, project developers seek long-term and firm commitments from customers, in order to (1) mitigate investment risk (and hence lower the cost of capital) and (2) ensure a stable revenue flow to recoup capital investment.

Moreover, pipeline system owners have a strong incentive to maximize the utilization of the infrastructure, as it leads to a shorter payback period on capital and allows for a better optimization of fixed operating costs.

These basic considerations are typically reflected in the design and tariff structure of the Gas Transportation Agreements (GTA) concluded between the transporter (the operator of the pipeline system) and the shipper (the customer of the transporter—typically the owner of the natural gas being transported or an agent acting on its behalf).

In the case of the development of new, large gas pipeline systems, GTAs are usually signed before a final investment decision is taken, as they are seen as crucial to address the "capacity risk" of the pipeline project.

GTAs are often underpinned by Gas Sales Agreements (GSAs), between the seller (whose agent is the shipper) and its client(s) (located on the other end of the prospective pipeline). In these cases, GTAs often mimic the contractual arrangements of GSAs. For a detailed review of GSAs, please refer to Chap. 20 of the Handbook (*The trading and price discovery for natural gas*).

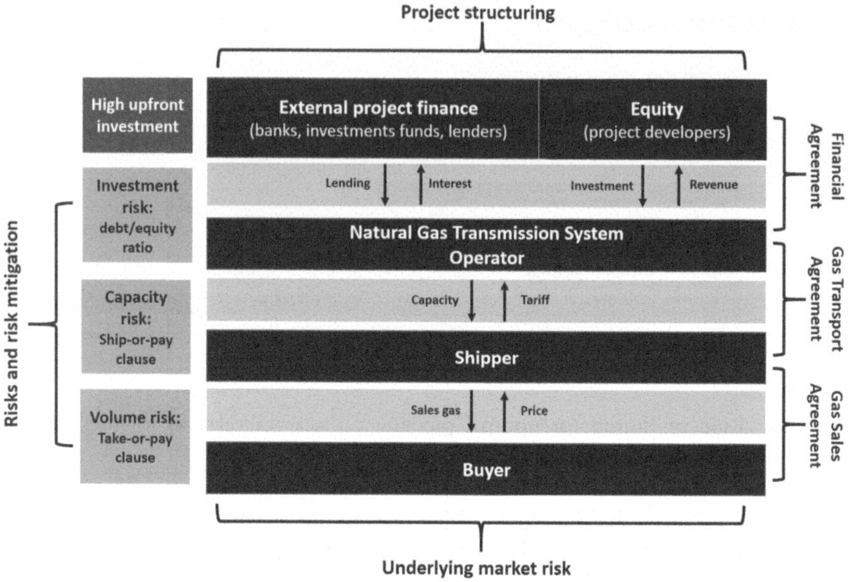

Fig. 2.7 Risk mitigation along the gas value chain. (Source: Author)

Figure 2.7 provides a simplified schematic representation of the interplay between financial arrangements, GTAs and GSAs in mitigating the investment risks associated with natural gas projects.

1.2.1 Characteristics of Gas Transportation Agreements

Under a Gas Transportation Agreement (GTA), the transporter provides a transportation service to the shipper between an input or entry point and one or multiple delivery points, in exchange for a payment made by the shipper and determined by the tariff structure (fixed in the GTA) and the volume transported and/or capacity contracted.

Capacities can be expressed either in volumetric terms (volume/time) or in reference to the energy value of the gas (energy/time).[1]

GTAs underpinning the development of new, large, international gas pipeline systems have typically the following characteristics:

1. Term commitment: GTAs are typically long-term contracts, with a duration of often over 20 years, necessary to recover the initial investment through the revenue from the transportation tariff paid by the shipper(s). The duration of the GTA is commonly aligned with the GSAs of the

[1] In SI units, volumetric capacity would be expressed as mcm/d and energy (thermal) capacity as MWh/d. In USCS, volumetric capacity can be expressed as mcf/d and energy capacity as mmbtu/d.

seller. Term commitments are usually shorter when concluded/renewed in relation to an existing gas transmission system.
2. Tariff commitment: the payments of the shipper for the used and/or reserved capacity will depend on the tariff fixed in the GTA. Tariffs should be non-discriminatory, cost-based and include a reasonable rate of return.
3. Capacity commitment: GTAs typically include a ship-or-pay commitment (often covering the entire firm technical capacity of the pipeline) from the shipper, in order to provide the transporter with a stable revenue stream through the lifespan of the contract. Two main types of GTAs can be distinguished in respect of capacity commitment:

    - Quantity-based: the transporter and shipper agree on the volumes of natural gas to be transported in the pipeline system under the fixed tariff structure. The shipper will typically take a ship-or-pay commitment in relation to the annual quantity (annual ship-or-pay quantity);
    - Capacity-based: the transporter and shipper agree on the capacity the transporter reserves for the shipper in the pipeline system (annual reserved capacity) and for which the shipper is obliged to pay irrespective of the volumes actually being transported. As such, capacity-based transportation agreements inherently have a ship-or-pay component.

In both cases, the shipper shall make a ship-or-pay payment, equating to: (ship-or-pay quantity—unused quantity) × tariff. Make-up provisions (for instance, allowing for a higher capacity usage during the next contract year in order to compensate for the previously unused capacity) might exist, but their occurrence in GTAs compared to GSAs is rare. Worth to mention, in liberalized gas markets the use-it-or-lose-it principle is prevailing: shippers are not allowed to hoard capacity, all unused capacity shall be made available to other, potentially interested shippers via auctions.

1.2.2 Tariff Structures

Alongside the duration of the contract and ship-or-pay commitments, the tariff structure fixed in the GTA is the most important factor underpinning the economic viability of a gas transmission system.

In essence, tariffs shall be structured in way to allow the recovery of the following three components:

- Capital costs related to the initial investment into the gas pipeline system;
- Operating costs occurring during the transportation services provided for the shipper (including fuel gas, personnel, etc.);
- Expected return: the profit element the owner of the transport system is expected to make on its investment.

The different cost elements can appear in a bundled way or separately, including a capacity component (fixed, reflecting the capacity booked) and a commodity charge (variable, reflecting the volumes actually transported). Similarly to capacities, tariffs can be either volume based (payment in relation to volume/time) or energy based (payment in relation to energy/time).

In liberalized gas markets, transport tariffs (1) have to be approved by the regulatory authorities; (2) have to be transparent; (3) should reflect actual costs incurred while including an appropriate return on investments and (4) should be applied in a non-discriminatory manner.

Two main types of tariff structures can be distinguished:

- Distance-based (point-to-point model): the transport tariff is set in relation to the distance between the input and delivery points.

$$C = TDV$$

where C stands for transport cost, T for tariff (€/100 km/1000 cubic metres), D for distance (km) and V for volume (cubic metres).

- Entry-exit system: the total transport costs for the shipper results from the addition of the entry and exit capacity charges it pays when entering and exiting the given transmission network.

$$C = E_n + E_x$$

where C stands for transport cost, E_n for entry fee (€/(m^3/h)/a) and E_x for exit fee (€/(m^3/h)/a).

In an entry-exit system, tariff setting can be based on a uniform approach where tariffs for different network points are set equally (postage stamp) or based on locational differentiation where the tariffs differ for every entry and exit point or zone (locational tariffs).

The tariff formula usually includes an inflation index to protect the investment value of the project (Fig. 2.8).

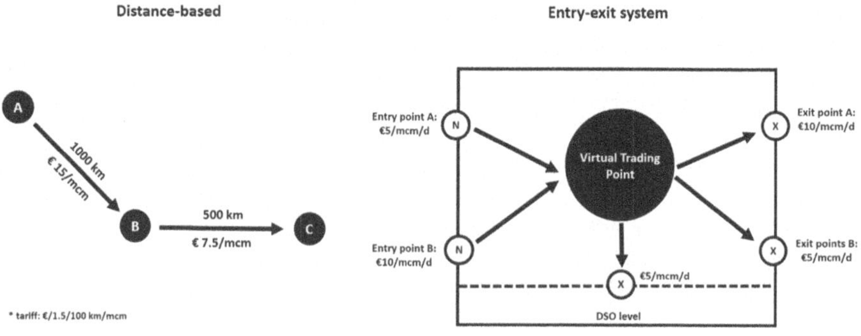

Fig. 2.8 Simplified scheme of tariff structures. (Source: Author)

Distance-based tariffs are typically used in the case of long-distance, inter-continental pipelines with a relatively simple point-to-point structure. Entry-exit models are commonly applied to more complex pipeline systems with multiple branches and interconnections.

The actual level of the pipeline tariff will ultimately depend on (1) initial unit investment cost; (2) expected rate of return and (3) additional transit payments in the case of transit.

Given that capital expenditure accounts usually for over 90% of total costs incurred through the lifespan of a gas pipeline system, tariff rates are intimately linked to the initial unit investment costs. Figure 2.9 illustrates this close interplay. Pipeline systems built in challenging environment (such as mountainous terrain or ultra-deep offshore) and/or with a suboptimal pipeline design will usually have high unit investment costs (over $80,000/km/inch), which in turn requires higher tariff rates to make the project financially viable. Pipelines with a relatively low unit investment cost (below $50/km/inch) can offer more competitive transport tariffs.

The transportation tariff is typically reflective of the expected return by the project developers (and lenders). This usually translates to the target return, used to calculate the target revenue. The target revenue will in turn determine the tariff, equating to total annual revenue/annual contracted capacity.

The transit fees paid by the operators of international pipelines crossing third-party countries will depend greatly on the bargaining power between the two countries, their (geo) political relationship and the potential (economic and political) benefits the transit country might receive from the transit pipeline. Transit fee payments can be paid either in cash or in kind. The Draft

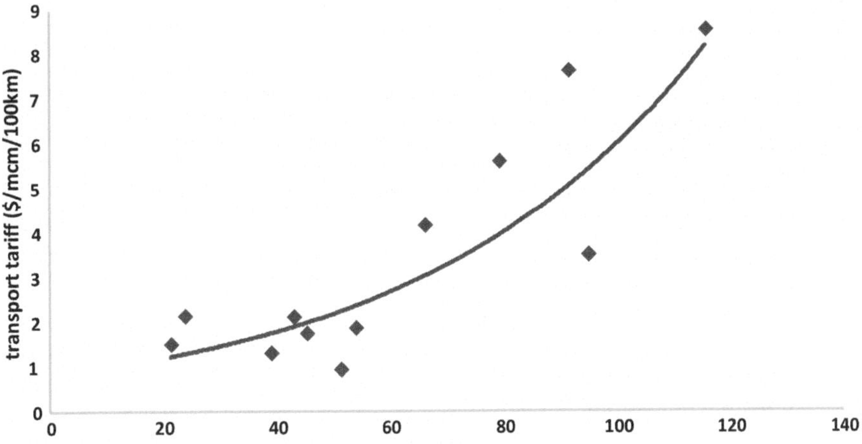

Fig. 2.9 Unit investment costs and transport tariffs of major international pipelines (2000–2020). (Source: Author based on publicly available information and industry estimates)

Transit Protocol of the Energy Charter requires that transit tariffs should be objective, reasonable, transparent and cost-based, "including a reasonable rate of return" (Energy Charter 2003).

Given the high variance of unit investment costs, transportation tariffs of international pipelines will vary in a wide range, from ~$1/mcm/100 km to over $10/mcm/100 km, translating into $0.5/mmbtu/1000 km at the lower end to over $2.5/mmbtu/1000 km for the most expensive pipeline routes.

2 LNG

Liquefied natural gas (LNG) is produced by cooling down methane to -162 °C. This effectively reduces its volume by ~600 times and as such allows for a more flexible way of transportation than through pipelines which have a fixed route by definition. Internationally traded LNG is transported via LNG carriers (LNGCs); however, smaller volumes of liquefied natural gas are also transported via trucks or railroad, typically serving local market as "virtual pipelines" (see Box 2.1).

First experiments with methane liquefaction date back to the beginning of the nineteenth century, when the British chemist Michael Faraday successfully chilled methane into liquefied form. The world's first liquefaction plant was built in 1912 in the United States in West Virginia for peak shaving.[2] An LNG facility was built in Cleveland, Ohio, in 1941. International LNG trade started in October 1964, with the first commercial shipment delivered by the LNG carrier Methane Princess from Algeria's Arzew GL4-Z liquefaction plant to Canvey Island in the United Kingdom (GIIGNL & SIGTTO 2014).

Global LNG trade grew from less than 50 bcm/year in 1970s to an average of 200 bcm/year through the 2000s and overpassed the 500 bcm mark in 2020, accounting for over 10% of global gas consumption and for over half of internationally traded gas.

The LNG value chain—not including upstream development—consists of three main components:

1. the liquefaction terminal: including pre-treatment and liquefaction units, storage tanks and an LNG loading jetty to load the LNG carrier via cryogenic pipes;
2. transportation via large LNG carries either by the buyer (free-on-board) or by the seller (delivery ex-ship);
3. a regasification terminal: including LNG unloading arms, storage tanks, vaporizers, odorization and metering stations and send-out to the transmission system.

[2] LNG peak shaving facilities store liquefied natural gas to meet short-term demand fluctuations.

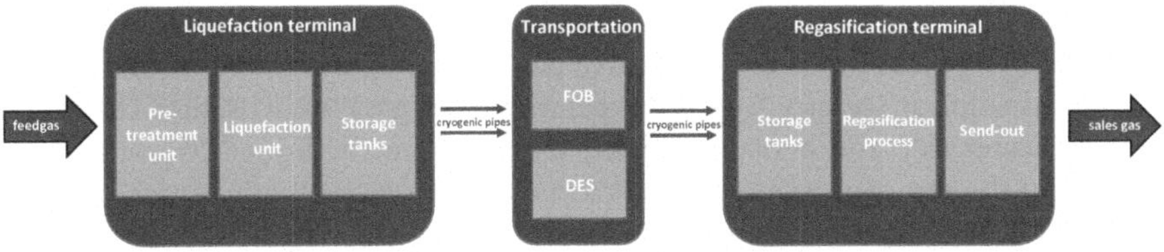

Fig. 2.10 Simplified scheme of the LNG value chain. (Source: Author)

Similarly to long-distance gas pipeline systems, the LNG value chain is characterized by high upfront investment costs and relatively small operating expenses. Consequently, the commercial contracts underpinning the development of LNG projects will show similar traits to the contractual arrangements necessary to mitigate the investment risks associated with pipeline systems (volume, term and tariff commitment) (Fig. 2.10).

Whilst this chapter will focus on the economics of the LNG value chain as described above, it is important to highlight that the costs associated with the upstream development of the reserve base supplying the liquefaction terminal (the cost of the feedgas) can significantly alter the overall economics of a project. The breakeven price of the feedgas can vary in a wide range, from below zero[3] to above \$5/mmbtu in the case of difficult-to-develop reserves (such as coal seam gas). Moreover, the distance between the upstream production facilities and the liquefaction terminal can contribute to the overall costs, in particular if it necessitates the build-up of an additional gas pipeline system.

2.1 *Liquefaction Terminals*

Liquefaction terminals are arguably the most complex and most costly components of the LNG value chain accounting for over half of total investment costs and operating expenses (when excluding upstream development). The following section provides an overview of their CAPEX structure, recent evolution of unit investment costs and description of typical operating expenses. This will be followed by the presentation of project structures and their contractual features.

2.1.1 CAPEX Structure

The CAPEX of an LNG project will ultimately depend on the liquefaction plant's production capacity (usually expressed in million ton per year, mtpa) and the unit investment cost (expressed in \$/ton per year, \$/tpa).

A liquefaction terminal typically consists of the following facilities, defining its CAPEX structure:

[3] A typical case is when the resource base is sufficiently rich in natural gas liquids (such as ethane, propane, butane, isobutene and pentane) to cover development costs of field.

1. Gas treatment unit: the incoming feedgas needs to be cleaned and purified to obtain pipeline-compatible gas. This includes the removal of CO_2 and sulphur (referred to as "sweetening" of gas), dehydration (to make it water free and hence avoid any icing during the liquefaction process) and the removal of mercury.
2. NGL and fractionation units: natural gas liquids (such as propane and butane) are separated from gas stream to obtain lean gas. Higher value NGLs (such as propane and butane) are separated into individual products for sale, generating additional revenue streams and hence improving project economics. The gas treatment and fractionation units usually account for 10–15% of the CAPEX.
3. Liquefaction unit: the lean, clean and dried gas is cooled down to -162°C through the application of a refrigeration technology, typically consisting of several consecutive cooling cycles (called an "LNG train"). The refrigeration and liquefaction units can account for 30–40% of the liquefaction plant's CAPEX.
4. Storage: liquefied natural gas is stored in large storage tanks before being unloaded via the product jetty through cryogenic pipelines. Besides optimizing production of the liquefaction unit, storage allows for enhanced LNG tanker scheduling flexibility and can serve as a back-up in the case of planned or unplanned maintenance. Most of LNG storage tanks are above ground with a double-walled design and insulated. Storage and unloading facilities account approximately for one-quarter of the CAPEX.
5. Utilities and offsites: due to their remoteness, liquefaction terminals usually rely on their own utilities for power generation, water supply, transport logistics and so on. These additional cost elements typically account for 20–25% of the project CAPEX.

Figure 2.11 provides an illustrative CAPEX breakdown, which could vary substantially depending on a number of factors, including external conditions, such as quality of feedgas, or remoteness of the terminal.

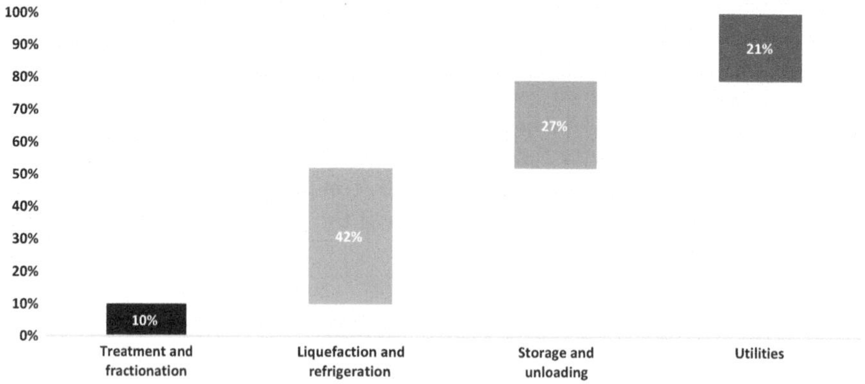

Fig. 2.11 Liquefaction terminal CAPEX breakdown. (Source: based on Songhurst (2018))

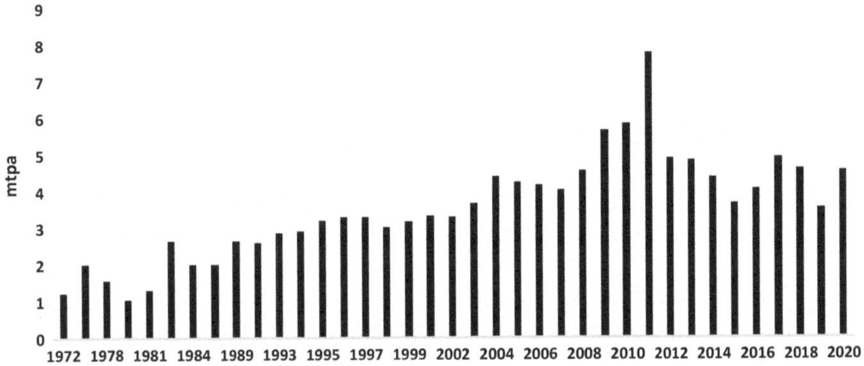

Fig. 2.12 Average nameplate capacity of liquefaction trains by commissioning year. (Source: based on ICIS LNG Edge)

2.1.2 Unit Investment Costs

The evolution of unit investment costs has been cyclical through the last couple of decades. Historical data suggest that the metric cost of liquefaction plants decreased from an average of $600/tpa during the 1970s and 1980s to below $400/tpa through the first half of 2000s. This has been partly driven by economies of scale: the average train size more than doubled over that period, from below 2 mtpa in the 1970–1980s to almost 4 mtpa in the first half of 2000s—and eventually reaching their peak of 7.8 mtpa with the commissioning of Qatar's mega-trains in 2009–2011 (Fig. 2.12).

However, liquefaction costs increased significantly over the last decade. According to the International Gas Union (IGU), the average unit cost of liquefaction plants more than doubled from $404/tonne in 2000–2008 to over $1000/tonne between 2009 and 2017 (IGU 2018).

This has been partly driven by the fact that a relatively high number of projects have been developed simultaneously, driving up demand for engineering, procurement and construction (EPC) services and the cost of labour. The cost inflation has been particularly felt by the developers of greenfield projects, for which unit cost practically tripled from $527/tonne to $1501/tonne over the same period. Projects in Australia (where unit costs went above $2000/tpa) have been confronted with availability of skilled labour, high logistic costs, exchange rate shifts and construction delays (IGU 2018).

In the case of brownfield projects, which usually benefit from existing infrastructure, unit costs have been increasing less significantly, by just over 40% from $320/tpa in 2000–2008 up to $458/tpa in 2019–2017. This includes LNG terminals in the United States (such as Cameron, Freeport or Sabine Pass), which have been originally developed as LNG regasification terminals. The addition of liquefaction plants on those sites required less important terrain preparation works, whilst further savings could be made on utilities and storage tanks development (IGU 2018).

The average metric cost of projects currently under construction is ~\$850/tpa. This is certainly lower than the highs experienced through the 2010s (mainly due to locational factors), but still considerably higher when compared to the unit investment costs of the early 2000s.

The efforts of project developers to reduce investment costs include:

- Modularization: an increasing number of project developers is choosing to use pre-fabricated modular units to offset some of the onsite construction expenses (where labour costs tend to be higher). Whilst the use of modular units has its own logistical challenges, it has been estimated by various consultancies that modularization can reduce the CAPEX of liquefaction plants built in remote areas by 5–10% (McKinsey 2019).
- **The return of large trains**: whilst mega-trains clearly demonstrated economies of scale through improved capital and process efficiency, they naturally require a larger reserve base and more capital at risk, which hindered their development since the commissioning of Qatar's mega-trains in the late 2000s. The average train size of projects under construction is about 25% higher compared to the ones commissioned between 2012 and 2018, mainly due to projects in Canada, Mozambique and Russia—which all have train sizes over 6.5 mtpa. Moreover, Qatar's announced expansion project (which would increase the country's liquefaction capacity from 77 mtpa in 2020 to 126 mtpa by 2027) will be based on mega-trains with a capacity of ~8 mtpa.
- **Floating liquefaction (FLNG) facilities** allow for a more cost-optimal development of stranded gas reserves. The first FLNG started operations in 2017 in Indonesia (Petronas' PFLNG Satu with a capacity of 1.2 mtpa), followed by Cameroon FLNG in 2018 (2.4 mtpa), Prelude FLNG in Australia (3.6 mtpa) and Tango FLNG in Argentina (0.5 mtpa) both in 2019. Whilst FLNG certainly can optimize upstream development costs, the average unit cost per liquefaction is relatively high (~\$1400/tpa) when compared to onshore liquefaction facilities. One should note that FLNG projects **based on vessel conversions** (such as Cameroon FLNG) can have substantially lower costs (~\$500–700/tpa) than greenfield, purpose-built FLNG vessels, further improving the overall project economics.

As presented in Fig. 2.13, LNG liquefaction costs can vary from ~\$200/tpa to well above \$2000/tpa, which naturally translates into a wide range of break-even costs (usually expressed in \$/mmbtu). On average, liquefaction break-even costs are in the range of \$2–3/mmbtu.

2.1.3 OPEX

As a thumb of rule, operating expenses of a liquefaction plant account between 3 and 5% per year of the initial capital investment. This is significantly higher when compared to the operating expenses of gas pipeline systems and is

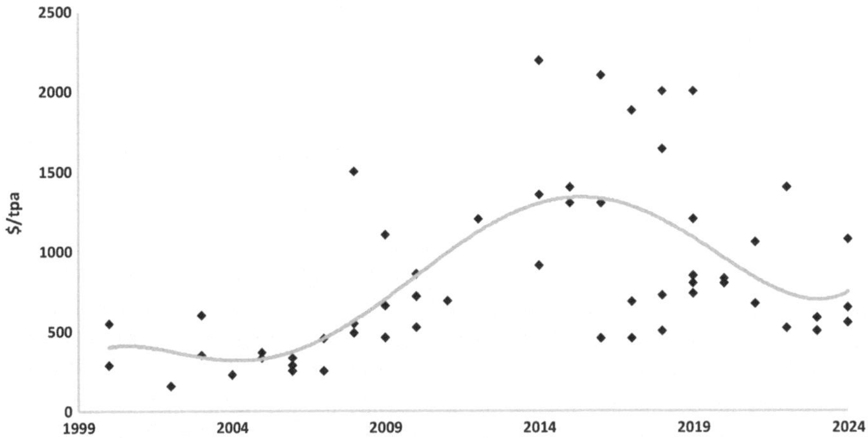

Fig. 2.13 Unit investment costs of LNG liquefaction projects (2000–2024). (Source: Author based on Songhurst (2018), publicly available information and various industry estimates)

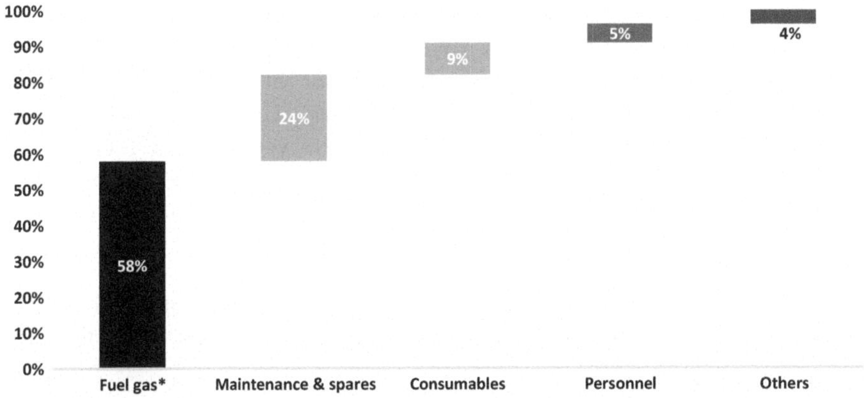

Fig. 2.14 Liquefaction plant OPEX breakdown. Assuming cost of fuel gas at $5/mmbtu. (Source: based on Songhurst (2018))

primarily due to the energy-intensive nature of the liquefaction process (Fig. 2.14).

Depending on the liquefaction process used, plant design and ambient temperatures, between 8 and 12% of the feedgas entering the liquefaction terminal is used to meet the energy requirements of the liquefaction plant (primarily to run the steam or gas turbine drivers powering refrigerant compressors). As such, fuel gas expenses can alone account for over half of the OPEX of a plant.

Other cost elements include expenses related to maintenance works, purchase of consumables (chemical products used for the refrigeration process), salaries of the personnel and insurance.

2.1.4 Project Structuring and Contract Design

Considering the high upfront investment costs of LNG liquefaction plants, project developers will seek to mitigate investment risks through risk sharing mechanisms incorporated in the project structure itself and the design of commercial contracts underpinning the procurement of feedgas on one hand and the market of sales gas/liquefaction capacity on the other hand.

Three basic types of commercial structures can be distinguished:

1. Vertical integration: the production of the feedgas, the ownership and operation of the liquefaction plant and the sale/export of the produced LNG are concentrated in one single commercial entity. The project revenues are derived from the sale of LNG via long-term sale and purchase agreements (SPAs).
2. Merchant model: the owner and operator of the liquefaction plant is a different commercial entity from the developer(s) of the upstream assets and supplier(s) of feedgas. This necessitates the conclusion of a gas sales agreement (GSA) between one or multiple upstream companies and the LNG project company. In essence, the GSA ensures the financial revenue stream of the upstream company on one hand and the supply of feedgas to the LNG project company on the other hand. The revenue stream of the LNG project company is derived from the sale of LNG via SPAs.
3. Tolling structure: the owner and operator of the liquefaction plant provides liquefaction services to its customers. The revenue stream of the LNG project is ensured by the tariff payments received from its customers under (typically) long-term liquefaction capacity agreements. The revenue stream of the customers of the LNG project company are usually ensured through long-term LNG SPAs (Fig. 2.15).

Furthermore, hybrid models can emerge. For instance, an LNG project company might offer in a bundled manner liquefaction capacity (for a fixed fee

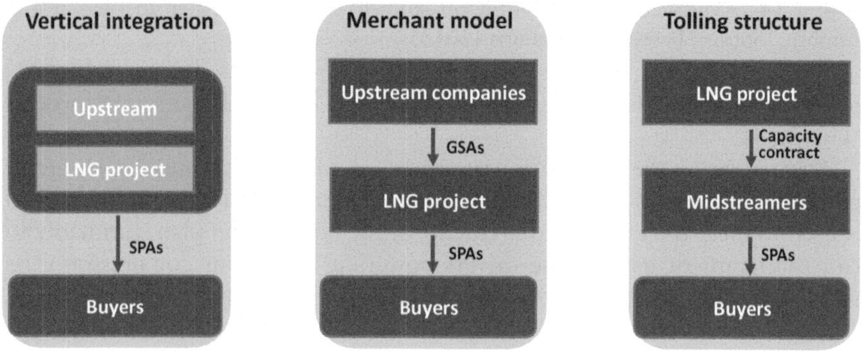

Fig. 2.15 LNG project structuring—basic models. (Source: Author)

indexed to inflation) and sourced feedgas supply (indexed to a given hub) to its customers (e.g. Cheniere's Sabine Pass or Corpus Christi projects)

Both LNG liquefaction capacity contracts and LNG SPAs have similar traits to gas transportation agreements:

- Term commitment: whilst the duration of SPAs went down, from an historical average of over 20 years to below 15 years for the contracts concluded between 2015 and 2019, liquefaction capacity agreements are typically signed for a duration of ~20 years;
- Volume/capacity commitment: both liquefaction capacity contracts and LNG SPAs underpinned by take-or-pay commitments (please refer to Chap. 20 of the Handbook) with limited volume flexibility;
- Price/tariff commitment: SPAs include a negotiated price formula applicable for the entire duration of the contract with eventual revision clauses (please refer to Chap. 20 of the Handbook). Liquefaction contracts are typically based on a fixed tariff (reflective of the breakeven cost of the project and expected margin of the developers) indexed to inflation;
- Destination commitment: historically LNG SPAs typically included destination restrictions (providing market segmentation influence to the seller). Whilst those clauses still exist in legacy contracts, they are becoming increasingly rare in new SPAs due to the resistance of buyers amidst an increasingly liquid and interconnected global gas market. The International Energy Agency's Global Gas Security Review 2019 shows that almost 90% of long-term contracts signed in 2019 had no fixed destination (Fig. 2.16).

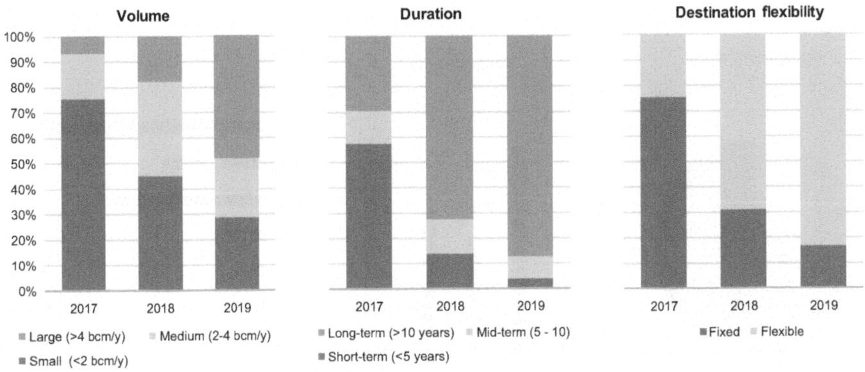

Fig. 2.16 Recent LNG contracting dynamics. (Source: International Energy Agency (2019))

2.2 LNG Shipping

Internationally traded LNG is transported via large, double-hulled vessels, with specifically designed cargo containment systems able to keep LNG at atmospheric pressure and at temperatures close to -162 °C.

The obligation of shipping LNG will depend on the contractual terms fixed between the seller and the buyer in the LNG SPAs and can take the following forms:

- Free-on-board (FOB): delivery takes place at the loading port and the buyer carries the obligation and costs of transportation;
- Delivery ex ship (DES): delivery takes place at the unloading port and the seller carries the obligation and costs of transportation;
- Costs, Insurance and Freight (CIF): the buyer takes title and risk of the LNG at the loading port, but the seller carries the obligation and costs of transportation.

The current section provides an overview of the recent trends in the LNG carriers' fleet, the contractual arrangement underpinning its development and the factors determining the unit cost of LNG transportation by vessels.

2.2.1 LNG Carriers

With a cost averaging at $200 million through the last decade, LNG carriers are fairly considered being amongst the most expensive vessels, second only to the large cruise ships.

By the end of 2019, there were just over 600 LNGCs in operation, including 37 FSRUs (Floating Storage and Regasification Units) and 46 vessels with a transportation capacity of less than 50,000 m³ (Fig. 2.17).

Two main types of cargo containment systems can be distinguished:

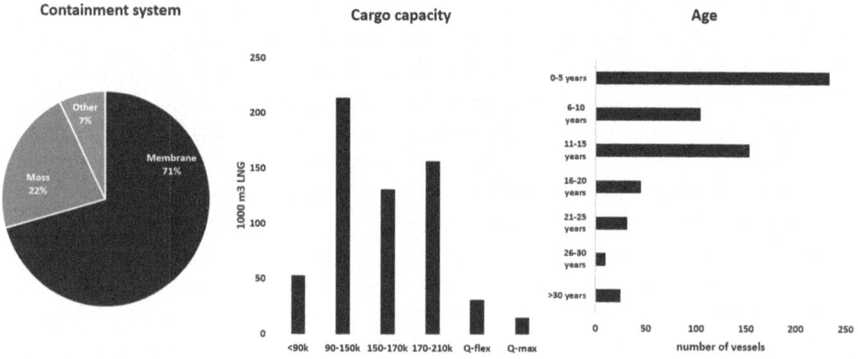

Fig. 2.17 The global LNG fleet. (Sources: based on GIIGNL (2020) and IGU (2020))

- Membrane are practically box-shaped tanks put into the vessel's holds. To cope with the cargo, holds are coated with a cryogenic lining that can withstand the load. Envelopes, known as membranes, contain the LNG at a temperature of -163 °C, sealing it with a totally impermeable layer between the liquid cargo and the vessel's hull, while also limiting cargo loss through evaporation. Membrane-type systems account today for over 70% of containment systems;
- Moss type consists of insulated independent spherical tanks constructed from aluminium alloy and designed to carry LNG at cryogenic temperatures and at a pressure close to atmospheric pressure. The tanks are encased within void spaces and situated in-line from forward to aft within the hull.

Both containment systems aim to minimize the evaporation of LNG (boil off gas, BOG). Typically, between 0.1 and 0.15% of the cargo evaporates per day during the voyage. Newer vessels are designed with lower BOG rates, with the best-in-class purporting rates as low as 0.08% (IGU 2018).

There has been a general trend towards larger cargo capacity, increasing by almost 30% from an average of 125,000 m^3 through the 1970s and 1980s to over 160,000 m^3 since the mid-2000s. The largest LNGCs (Q-max, with a capacity of over 260,000 m^3) were commissioned between 2008 and 2011 in line with the start-up of Qatar's mega-trains. According to the International Maritime Organization (IMO) safety requirements, the tanks can be filled up to maximum 98% of their capacity.

The relatively young age of the LNG fleet—with over half of the LNGCs under 10 years of age—is primarily the reflection of the strong growth LNG trade underwent through the last decade, increasing by almost twofold. LNGCs are typically retired/reconverted after reaching an age of 30–35 years.

In terms of propulsion systems, the following main types can be distinguished (IGU 2020):

- Steam turbines: boilers generate steam to run the propulsion turbines and auxiliary engines. The boilers typically use boil-off-gas and can be partially (or in some cases fully) fuelled with heavy fuel oil. They have been the dominating type of propulsion systems in the past, however are gradually losing their market share due to their relatively low thermal efficiency (resulting in high variable operating expenses). They still account for over 40% of propulsion systems under use in 2020.
- DFDE (Dual-Fuel Diesel Electric) are electric propulsion systems powered by dual-fuel, medium-speed diesel engines, which can run both on diesel and on BOG. They are typically 25–30% more efficient than steam turbines.
- TFDE (Tri-Fuel Diesel Electric) are electric propulsion systems which can be powered by diesel, heavy-oil and BOG. Altogether with DFDE, they represent one-third of propulsion systems in use.

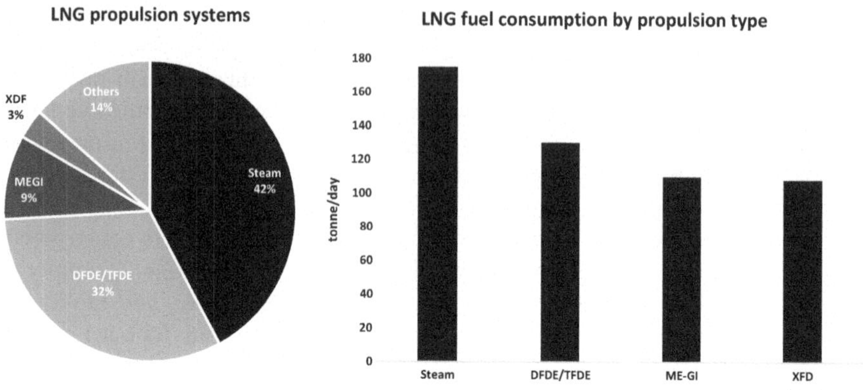

Fig. 2.18 Propulsion systems in use by market share and respective fuel efficiency. (Sources: based on ICIS LNG Edge and IGU (2018))

- ME-GI (Electronically Controlled, Gas Injection) propulsion systems pressurize boil-off gas and burn it with a small amount of injected diesel fuel. They can reach an efficiency 15–20% higher compared to DFDE and currently account for ~10% of propulsion systems in use.
- XDF (Low-Pressure Slow-Speed Dual-Fuel) represents the latest generation of propulsion systems. It burns fuel and air, mixed at a high air-to-fuel ratio, injected at a low pressure. When burning gas, a small amount of fuel oil is used as a pilot fuel. It has a fuel efficiency comparable to ME-GI propulsion systems. Currently, XDF systems account for only a fraction of propulsion systems in use, however they represent almost two-thirds of the vessel orderbook beginning in 2020 (Fig. 2.18).

2.2.2 LNG Chartering

The majority is LNGCs are owned by independent shipowners (with a share of ~70%), who charter LNGCs to market players (including sellers, buyers, aggregators, traders) typically under long-term lease agreements.

The average length of term charter contracts has significantly decreased in recent years, from over 20 years to below 10 years for the contracts concluded between 2008 and 2017. This partly reflects the changing flexibility requirements of LNG players and the shorter duration of LNG SPAs (Fig. 2.19).

Two basic types of long-term charter agreements can be distinguished:

- Time charter: the shipowner provides the LNG carrier and operating services (including the crew, management, maintenance, insurance, etc.). The tariff ("hire rate") hence has two components: a fixed CAPEX-based and a variable OPEX-based. The charterer pays for the voyage-related expenses, including fuel and port costs;
- Bareboat charter: the shipowner simply provides the LNG carrier for which it receives a usually fixed CAPEX-based tariff.

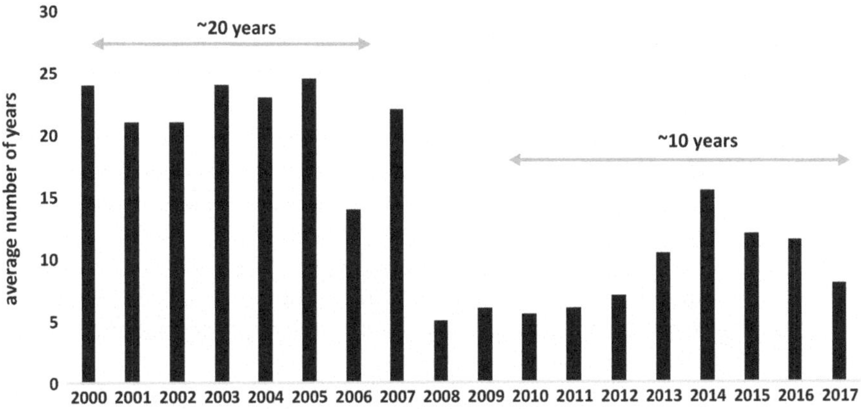

Fig. 2.19 Average length of term charter contracts, per year of contract signing. (Source: based on Adede (2019))

Long-term charter rates remain opaque. Based on the estimates of various price reporting agencies, long-term rates for LNGCs with steam turbine propulsion systems averaged at ~$50,000/day and ~80,000/day for TFDE LNGCs between 2018 and 2019.

Besides long-term charters, there is an increasing number of LNG vessels available (~10% of the global fleet) for short and spot charter deals, supporting further the development of short-term LNG trading. It should be noted that spot charter rates naturally display greater volatility, with charter rates fluctuating between $30,000/day and $200,000/day in 2018.

2.2.3 *Unit Cost of LNG Transportation*

The unit cost of LNG transportation between a given liquefaction and regasification terminal will depend on a number of factors, including:

- Distance and voyage time: the distance (expressed in nautical miles) typically refers to the length of the entire roundtrip. The voyage time is important given that charter rates are paid per diem and will depend on the speed (expressed in knots=nautical miles[4]/hour) of the vessel. Typically the vessel spends one day at the export terminal and one day at the import terminal with loading and unloading operations, respectively;
- Charter rates typically account for over half of the total transport unit cost. They will vary accordingly to the vessel's size, age, propulsion system and BOG rate, and in the case of spot charters will be largely determined by the prevailing market conditions;
- BOG: will depend on the vessel's BOG rate, the distance and the speed of the vessel;

[4] Nautical miles equate to 1.15 miles and to 1.852 kms.

- Fuel cost is directly proportional to the distance and speed of the vessel. Higher speeds (~19 knots) will naturally translate into higher fuel and/or BOG consumption (vs a vessel running at 14–15 knots can rely purely on natural BOG), whilst lowering the voyage time could reduce chartering costs. The fuel price will depend on market prices for bunker fuel (typically HFO/MDO) and the charterer's procurement strategy. Inclusive of BOG, fuel costs are usually the second most important component of total unit transport costs (over 25% for ST vessels);
- Heel gas requirements of the LNG vessel refer to the minimum inventory level to keep the tanks cool after unloading and potentially necessary for unladen voyages if running on boil-off. It is typically assumed to be ~2–4% of the initial cargo;
- Canal costs has to be paid when transiting through the Suez and Panama canals. They are set by Canal Authorities and are typically in the range of \$300–500,000/transit;
- Port costs: paid per diem during the loading and unloading operations and are usually assumed ~\$100,000/day;
- Brokerage fee: spot charters are typically arranged through specialist brokers, usually attracting 1–2% of the total charter cost;
- Insurance: typically covers the vessel and the cargo, either separately or bundled.

Illustrative LNG shipping costs are provided in Fig. 2.20, for major transport routes. Altogether, the approximative unit transport cost in the case of a DFDE vessel with a cargo capacity of 160,000 m^3, chartered for \$80,000/day and sailing at 18 knots, without the need to transit via canals, would be \$0.04/mmbtu/1000—significantly cheaper than transportation via pipelines (with tariffs ranging between \$0.5 and 2/mmbtu/1000).

2.3 *Regasification Terminals*

Regasification terminals can be located onshore (representing almost 90% of global regasification capacity in the beginning of 2020) or offshore on Floating

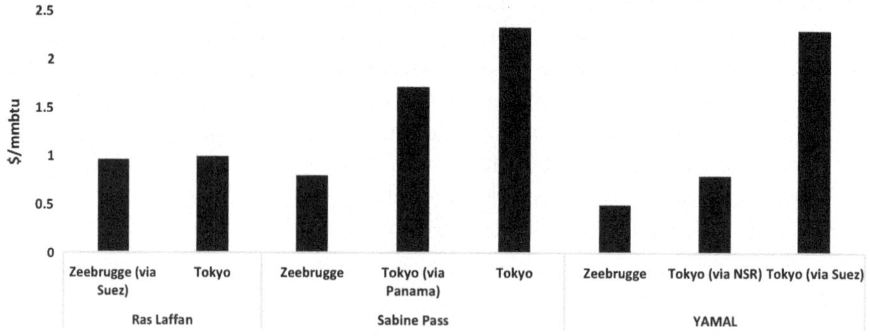

Fig. 2.20 LNG shipping costs for major transport routes for a DFDE vessel. (Source: based on ICIS LNG Edge)

Storage and Regasification Units (FRSUs or FRUs—in the absence of storage capabilities).

A regasification terminal consists typically of the following facilities:

- Unloading arms: LNG is delivered from the LNG carrier via unloading arms, establishing the connection between the vessel's manifold system (piping connection) and the terminal. There are usually several unloading arms and one vapour return arm. It is necessary to send back vapour to the LNG carrier to avoid vacuum conditions. Unloading typically takes 12–16 hours, and the carrier stays about one day in the port.
- Storage: once unloaded, LNG is transported via cryogenic pipelines to storage tanks. Storage tanks allow for tanker scheduling flexibility and optimization of send-out to the downstream market. They have similar design to the ones located at liquefaction terminals and primarily serve tanker scheduling flexibility and optimization of send-out (and hence sales). It is worth to note that in markets with no significant underground storage capacities, LNG storage can enhance security of supply.
- Vaporizers: the LNG sent from the storage tanks is regasified with vaporizers. Four basic types can be distinguished: (1) open rack vaporizers using seawater for the heat necessary to vaporize LNG; (2) submerged combustion vaporizers using natural gas produced by the terminal and pass the hot gases into a water bath containing a tubular heat exchanger where LNG flows; (3) intermediate fluid vaporizer has two levels of thermal heat exchange, first between LNG and an intermediate fluid such as propane and between the intermediate and a heat source (typically seawater); (4) ambient air vaporizers using the heat from the air (usually applied at smaller regasification terminals).
- Send-out: once regasified, natural gas flows to the pressure-regulating and metering station, before being sent-out to the national gas transmission system. Depending on the configuration of the LNG regasification terminal, natural gas can be odorized in an odorizing station before leaving the terminal.

Onshore regasification terminals have significantly lower unit investments costs compared to liquefaction terminals, averaging at ~\$250/tpa between 2013 and 2017. However, one should note that this represents a significant cost-escalation compared to the projects commissioned between 2006 and 2012, with an average unit investment cost of \$115/tpa. The rise in unit costs has been driven by higher expenses associated with EPC contracts and by the general trend towards larger storage tanks.

Offshore regasification terminals have usually lower metric costs (~\$100/tpa), as they require less terrain preparation and ground work. FSRUs are often reconverted LNG carriers, which tend to lower their unit costs as well. They typically have shorter lead times (e.g. Egypt's second FSRU project has been implemented in a record time of 5 months) compared to conventional onshore

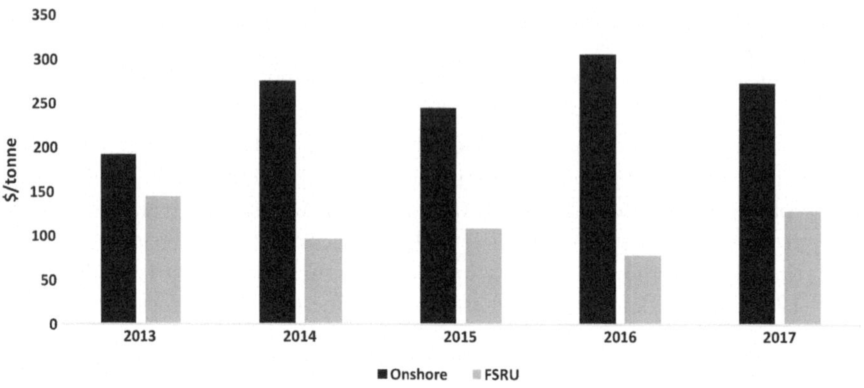

Fig. 2.21 Regasification unit investment costs (2013–2017). (Source: based on IGU (2013–18))

regasification terminals. This can be of particular interest in markets which experience near-term gas demand growth or potential supply-demand imbalances. On the flipside, they tend to have higher operating expenses (as the vessel is most commonly leased), lower storage capability and no option for future expansions. Since the first FSRU has been commissioned in 2005, offshore regasification has been growing considerably to over 100 mtpa by the beginning of 2020 (Fig. 2.21).

Regasification capacity is usually booked under long-term capacity contracts. In liberalized markets, under the principle of use-it-or-lose it, unused capacity has to be offered on the secondary market, for instance, via auctions. Regasification fees typically range between $0.3 and $1/mmbtu.

3 Conclusion

Transportation typically accounts for over half of total costs occurring through the value chain of internationally traded natural gas and hence greatly influences its cost competitiveness.

Both long-distance pipeline systems and LNG have high upfront investment costs, requiring risk sharing mechanisms being incorporated either in the project structure itself (primarily via vertical integration) and/or into the design of commercial contracts between the project developers and their customers.

Risk sharing typically translates by the buyers' long-term commitment to pay a fixed tariff (reflective of the breakeven cost of the project and expected margin of the project developers) for the liquefaction/transportation capacity purchased on a firm basis and underpinned with ship-or-pay clause. Whilst gas sales contract structuring has been evolving towards a greater commercial flexibility (allowing for shorter term deals with less firm commitments and more diverse price formulae), transportation contracts—especially when underpinning the development of new infrastructure—have largely retained their conservative design, allowing project developers (and their lenders) to recover the initial high upfront investment cost through a stable revenue stream.

When comparing transportation costs via LNG vs long-distance pipeline systems, one should note that in the case of LNG the majority of costs—both initial investment and operational expenses—occur upfront, at the stage of liquefaction and then increase relatively slowly (less than $0.05/mmbtu/1000 km) during the transportation phase via LNGCs. In contrast, in pipeline systems transportation costs increase more swiftly ($0.5–2.5/mmbtu/1000 km) with the travelled distance.

Consequently, LNG becomes cost competitive with pipeline transportation only on long distances, typically beyond several thousand kms. This is illustrated in Fig. 2.22, comparing the delivery costs of LNG (assuming an average ~$2.4/mmbtu liquefaction and 0.4/mmbtu regasification fee) transported via an LNGC with a typical long-term hire of $80,000/day versus pipelines operating under a relatively low tariff rate of $0.5/mmbtu/1000 km and a higher tariff of $1/mmbtu/1000 km.

Considering the above-described assumptions, LNG becomes cost competitive with pipeline transportation for distances above 3000–7000 kms. However, as discussed through the chapter each pipeline and each LNG project is unique and unit investment costs vary in a wide range for both type of infrastructure, which can significantly alter the "breakeven distance" between LNG and long-distance pipeline systems.

The high transportation costs of natural gas compared to other primary fuels (such as coal or crude oil) is severely weighing on the cost competitiveness of methane molecules. The gas industry will need to continue to work on optimizing transportation costs.

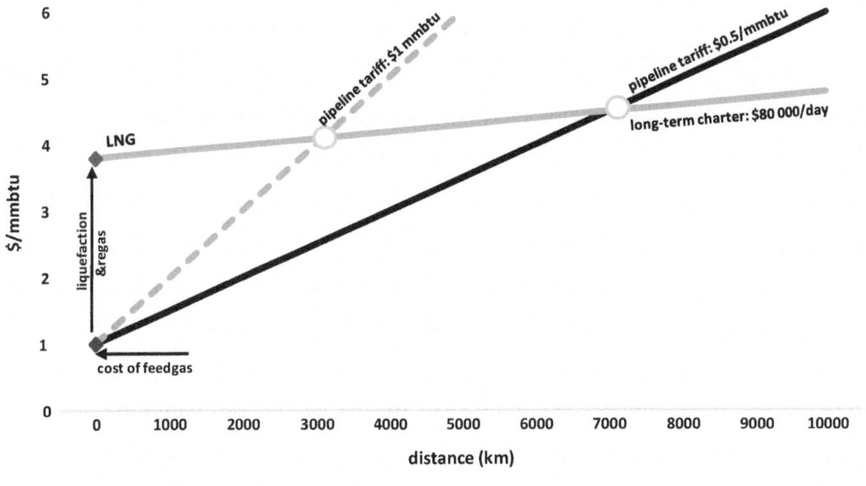

Fig. 2.22 LNG versus pipeline transportation costs. (Source: Author)

The unit investment cost of liquefaction plants has been decreasing since the highs (over $2000/tpa) reached in the early 2010s. However, the average metric cost of projects currently under construction (~$850/tpa) is still approximately twice the unit investment cost of projects commissioned between 2000 and 2008. This highlights the potential cost reductions which might be reached through improved project management, plant design optimization and usage of innovative construction approaches (e.g. modularization, vessel conversions to FLNG).

Given the maturity of technology, the cost reduction potential in gas pipeline systems is considered to be rather limited. The design of newly built pipelines will increasingly need to take into account the requirement of improved compatibility with low-carbon gases, including hydrogen (see Chap. 4 of the Handbook, *Economics of hydrogen*), biomethane and synthetic gas.

References

ACER (2015), Agency for the Cooperation of Energy Regulators, Gas Infrastructure Unit Investment Costs Report, Ljubljana.

Adede (2019), Amokoye Adede, Evolution of Flexibility/Liquidity in the LNG Shipping Market, 19th International Conference & Exhibition on Liquefied Natural Gas, Shanghai.

Brauer (2016), Ansgar Brauer, Techno-economic optimisation of large natural gas transmission systems, Gas for Energy.

CEER (2019), Council of European Energy Regulators, Pan-European cost-efficiency benchmark for gas transmission system operators, Brussels.

Energy Charter Secretariat (2003), Final Act of the Energy Charter Conference with respect to the Energy Charter Protocol on Transir (Draft), Brussels.

GIIGNL (2020), International Group of Liquefied Natural Gas Importers, GIIGNL 2020 Annual Report, Neuilly-sur-Seine.

GIIGNL & SIGTTO (2014), International Group of Liquefied Natural Gas Importers and Society of International Gas Tanker and Terminal Operators Ltd, LNG Shipping at 50: A commemorative SIGTTO/GIIGNL publication, Riviera Maritime Media Ltd, Enfield.

ICIS (2020), Independent Commodity Information Service, LNG Edge.

International Energy Agency (1994), Natural Gas Transportation: Organisation and Regulation, OECD, Paris.

International Energy Agency (2019), Global Gas Security Review 2019, OECD, Paris.

IGU (2013), International Gas Union, World LNG Report -2013 Edition, Barcelona.

IGU (2014), International Gas Union, World LNG Report -2014 Edition, Barcelona.

IGU (2015), International Gas Union, World LNG Report -2015 Edition, Barcelona.

IGU (2016), International Gas Union, 2016 World LNG Report, Barcelona.

IGU (2017), International Gas Union, 2017 World LNG Report, Barcelona.

IGU (2018), International Gas Union, 2018 World LNG Report, Barcelona.

IGU (2019), International Gas Union, 2019 World LNG Report, Barcelona.

IGU (2020), International Gas Union, 2020 World LNG Report, Barcelona.

McKinsey (2019), Setting the bar for global LNG cost competitiveness.

Menon (2011), E. Shashi Menon, Pipeline Planning and Construction Field Manuel, Gulf Professional Publishing, Elsevier, United States of America.

Nasr, Connor (2014), G.G. Nasr and N.E. Connor, Natural Gas Engineering and Safety Challenges: Downstream Process, Analysis, Utilization and Safety, Springer, Switzerland.

Songhurst (2018), Brian Songhurst, LNG Plant Cost Reduction 2014–18, Oxford Institute for Energy Studies, Oxford.

Yamasaki (1980), Robert M. Yamasaki, Proposed Oil and Gas Transportation Scenarios of Proposed OCS Sale No. 53 Offshore Central and Northern California, Bureau of Land Management. Pacific Outer Continental Shelf Office, United States of America.

CHAPTER 3

Economics of Oil Refining

Jean-Pierre Favennec

1 Introduction

Refining is a key step in the oil industry, as we do not directly consume crude oil. A petroleum refinery is a set of installations intended to transform crude oil, generally unusable as such, into petroleum products: motor gasoline, jet fuel, diesel fuel, fuel oil, lubricants, liquefied petroleum gases, naphtha, and so on.

The products consumed in largest volumes are motor gasoline, motor diesel, and heavy fuel oil. The products with the fastest growing consumption are jet fuel and diesel fuel (Table 3.1).

1.1 Crude Oil

Crude oil is composed mainly of hydrocarbon molecules formed from carbon and hydrogen atoms. Impurities, particularly sulfur and metals, are also found in oil. Sulfur is found in the products and gives SO_2 by combustion, which is dangerous for the environment. Metals are present in very small quantities (a few parts per million—ppm), but, even in very low concentrations, their presence in petroleum products can be harmful to the processes that use them (especially catalysts).

There are probably more than 400 different crude oils in the world. While the annual production of Arabian Light, a crude oil extracted mainly from the Ghawar field in Saudi Arabia, exceeds 250 million tons per year (Ghawar, from where it is produced, originally contained more than 10 billion tons of crude oil), many crude oils are produced in very small quantities. Only about a hundred crude oils are traded on a significant international scale.

J.-P. Favennec (✉)
WDCOOPERATION, Paris, France
e-mail: jpfavennec@yahoo.fr

M. Hafner, G. Luciani (eds.), *The Palgrave Handbook of International Energy Economics*, https://doi.org/10.1007/978-3-030-86884-0_3

Table 3.1 Global consumption of refined products (million tons)

	1973	*2017*	*2017 vs 1973*
LPG/Naphtha	199	517	260%
Gasoline	559	1112	199%
Jet	114	371	325%
Diesel oil	592	1422	240%
Fuel oil	747	371	50%
Others	196	605	309%
Total	2407	4337	180%

Source: Adapted from International Energy Agency

So many deposits, so many raw materials. Each crude oil is characterized in particular by its density, which is commonly measured in American Petroleum Institute (API) degrees.[1] The current crudes have a density between 0.8 (about 45° API) and 1 (10° API). A light, low-density crude oil will produce relatively high levels of gasoline and diesel fuel and low levels of fuel oil. On the other hand, a heavy crude oil will give a lot of heavy fuel oil.

1.2 The Main Steps of Refining

The refining of petroleum, that is, the transformation of crude oil into finished products, requires several operations that can be grouped as follows:

- the separation of crude oil into different fractions, which are the basis for the manufacturing of finished products
- the improvement of the quality of some cuts
- the transformation of heavy cuts into light cuts
- the final preparation of the finished products by blending

A refinery consists of several distinct parts:

- the process units where oil is separated into fractions or cuts; some cuts undergo additional processing for improvement in order to reach commercial requirements; heavy fractions can be converted into light fractions,
- utilities, that is, all units of production of fuel, electricity, steam, and so on, necessary for refining processes
- storage facilities
- reception and shipping facilities,
- blending facilities.

[1]The formula for API gravity is: (141.5/Specific Gravity)-131.5. Hence water, which has a specific gravity of 1, has an API degree of 10. All crude oil is lighter than water, and the lighter it is, the higher is the API degree.

The area covered by a refinery can reach several tens of hectares, but a large part of this area is covered by storage facilities

2 History and Evolution of Refining

The use of oil goes back to the earliest times. The Mesopotamian king Sargon refers to bitumen in the cuneiform texts that have come down to us. Reference is also made to the bitumen in the Bible, whether it is the caulking of Noah's Ark or the coating of Moses' cradle to allow it to float on the Nile.

Very early on, the Chinese refined crude oil. Many texts mention the use of petroleum-based products as lubricants.

More than one thousand years ago, oil fields were already being exploited in the Baku region (which was the main oil production region at the beginning of the intensive exploitation era, during the Russian Tsar's empire in 1900).

Around the year 1000 Arab chemists used the distillation of oil to make different products, like lubricants.

Oil was also widely used as a weapon of war. The famous "Greek fire" spread terror in many naval fleets from the beginning of our era in the Mediterranean area. Arab and Persian chemists, then Chinese chemists, also used highly flammable products in the same way.

However, the modern history of the oil industry is said to have begun with the production of kerosene for illumination. For many years, the use of lamp oil (mostly whale oil) was the best way to illuminate a room, until the whale population decreased rapidly. In 1846, Abraham Gessner of Nova Scotia, Canada, developed a process to produce kerosene from coal. Shortly afterwards, in 1854, Ignacy Łukasiewicz began producing kerosene from hand-dug oil wells in Poland.

In the United States, the indigenous Indians used seepages of oil in different ways, including lighting. Some specialists considered that probably oil could be found in the ground, and the oil industry began in 1859, when Edwin Drake discovered oil near Titusville, Pennsylvania, by digging a 20-meter deep well. Very rapidly, John D. Rockefeller, a young smart accountant, built several refineries to produce mainly kerosene and took monopolistic control of the oil refining and marketing industry in the United States. He created Standard Oil, a company capable of manufacturing kerosene of standard—that is, constant—quality, from different crude oils with different characteristics. The company was an association of several corporations, more or less one per US state. However, in 1911, Standard Oil was taken to court because it was a monopoly, prohibited under the newly approved Sherman Act, and was broken up into 34 companies including Standard Oil of New Jersey, now Exxon, part of Exxon Mobil; Standard Oil of New York, now Mobil, the other part of Exxon Mobil; Standard Oil of California, today's Chevron, and so on. At the beginning of the twentieth century, the introduction of the internal combustion engine and its use in automobiles created the gasoline market, which became the driving force behind the relatively rapid growth of the oil industry. Early oil discoveries, such as those in Ontario and Pennsylvania, were quickly overtaken by large oil "booms" in Oklahoma, Texas, and California.

From a technical point of view, the refining industry really began in 1863 with the construction of the first distillation unit in Boston, USA. Certainly, this unit has nothing to do with the refineries we know today. Still, it made possible to extract from crude oil the kerosene or lamp oil consumed at the time. The development of electricity by Thomas Edison introduced a competitor to kerosene, but the development of electricity consumption was very slow. Shortly afterwards, the appearance of the automobile led to an increase in the consumption of petrol and diesel. Then fuel oil found an outlet in the navy, just before the First World War.

The refining industry was booming, and on the eve of the Second World War, distillation capacity reached 364 MT/y—Million Tons per year—worldwide, two-thirds of which in the United States and only 4% (16 Mt./year) in Europe.

More distillation units, but also more so-called secondary treatment units were built. First of all, thermal reforming was developed to increase the production of gasoline. Then came thermal cracking to reduce the production of heavy fuel oil and increase the production of light products, especially gasoline and diesel. Finally, after Second World War, catalytic reforming was introduced to improve the quality of gasoline. Many other processes developed in parallel, but the refining industry can now be considered a mature industry.

Rockefeller initially focused on crude oil processing and product distribution operations, leaving oil production, which he considered too risky, to other players. But gradually, within the major oil companies, refining has become integrated with oil exploration and production on the one hand, and distribution on the other. Integration provides the company with its sources of crude oil and its outlets, thus promoting the smooth physical operation of the oil chain. Gradually, however, and in particular because of nationalization of the oil fields in several counties in the 1970s (Algeria, Libya, Iraq first, Venezuela, Kuwait, Saudi Arabia some years later), international companies became mainly refining and distribution companies, with crude oil production being largely in the hands of the national companies of producing countries. This trend has been partially reversed: some producing countries opened their oil exploration and production in order to attract the large international oil companies (the Majors), which can bring expertise and financing. Very often this has been carried out through associations (joint ventures) between the national oil company and the foreign companies.

On the other hand, some OPEC countries now play a key role in refining. The countries of the Persian Arab Gulf and Venezuela have developed significant capacities, which are largely export-oriented. For strategic reasons, some of them (Saudi Arabia and Venezuela) have also taken control of important capacities abroad (especially in the United States).

3 Refining Capacities Around the World

Refining capacity, measured by atmospheric distillation capacity, increased from just over 1 billion tons per year in 1950 to over 4 billion tons per year in 1980. It declined to less than 3.60 billion tons in 1985, following the second oil crisis. After the fall in oil prices in 1986, capacity increased again and is currently of the order of 5 billion tons per year, or 100 million barrels per day.

- *Asia* (from Pakistan to Japan, and including Australia and New Zealand) is now the world's largest refining area, with a distillation capacity of 1.7 billion tons per year. Japan and China have the largest facilities, but South Korea and India also have a significant tool. Capacity has increased very rapidly in recent years due to the very strong growth in demand, especially in China and India.
- *North America* (the United States, Canada, and Mexico) also has a very large refining base, representing more than 20% of the world's capacity. The United States has more than 80% of the capacity in this region. It should be noted that the number of US refineries has fallen from 320 to 135 in 40 years, while total capacity increased. Small refineries in the middle of the United States have been closed for lack of crude oil at the time, while large refineries developed on the coast.
- *Western Europe and Turkey*, with 17% of the world's capacity, remains a major refining area, despite the very sharp capacity reductions in the early 1980s. The number of refineries has decreased from 160 to about 100, with a 30% reduction in total capacity. Capacity in Eastern Europe is around 13% of global total. Most (80%) of this capacity is located in the former USSR, but these figures should not be misleading: facilities in this region are generally old, unsophisticated, and currently much underutilized.
- *Central and South America* is well equipped with refineries, with Brazil and Venezuela having the largest capacities. Large-scale refineries are located in the Caribbean and Venezuela: they are often export-oriented and the United States is a privileged market for refineries in this subregion. However, it should be stressed that at the time of writing US sanctions on Venezuela are impacting the refining industry there.
- *The Middle East* is also an important refining center with several large refineries for export, particularly to Asia. The largest exporters are Kuwait, Saudi Arabia, and Abu Dhabi. The strong growth in demand, driven by economic growth and rather low product prices, requires a rapid increase in capacity. In addition, large new refineries have recently been built in Saudi Arabia, for example, SATORP, a 20 million tons very sophisticated refinery built by Total and Aramco. Sinopec and Aramco are building a similar refinery.
- Finally, *Africa* has only limited capacity. Four countries (Algeria, Egypt, Nigeria, and South Africa) represent more than 60% of the continent's

> capacity. Apart from Algeria, Libya, and Egypt, which export finished products to Europe and the United States, refineries in this area are mainly used to supply local markets. In many sub-Saharan countries, there are small refineries (of about 1 to 3 million tons) to supply local markets of the same size. The profitability of these refineries is precarious, but they give autonomy in terms of products, which can be precious, to the countries where they are located.

However, many of these refineries have closed more or less recently (Mauritania, Sierra Leone, Liberia, Togo on the West Coast; Mombasa, Dar Es Salaam, and Maputo on the East Coast). These refineries are finding it increasingly difficult to compete with products that arrive in large quantities from large refineries built in the Persian Gulf or in India.

In total, there are currently approximately 700 refineries worldwide with a total processing capacity of approximately 100 million barrels per day. The average capacity of a refinery is therefore around 150,000 b/d or nearly 8 Mt./year.

The Jamnagar refinery is the largest oil refinery in the world since 2008, with a processing capacity of 1.24 million barrels per day (more than 60 million tons per year, almost equivalent to the capacity of a major European country!). Located in Gujarat, India, it is owned by Reliance Industries.

Among other very large facilities, we find the Paraguana refinery in Venezuela, which is the result of the merger of the Amuay and Cardon refineries (pipe connections have been established between the two refineries). Its capacity totals 980,000 barrels per day. There are also the South Korean refineries in Ulsan (two refineries) and Yeosu, whose combined size exceeds 2 million barrels per day. Other very large refineries are found in Saudi Arabia and the United States.

On the other hand, there also are small refineries adapted to small and isolated markets. Inland countries (Mali, Niger, Chad, Uganda, Rwanda, and so on) are very difficult to supply with finished products from the African coast, which can be more than a thousand kilometers away. In Chad and Niger, which have domestic oil resources, two similar 20,000 barrel per day refineries were built by Chinese companies just after 2010.

4 Refining Structure and Evolution of Demand by Product

As we have seen, the strong growth in the consumption of oil (and therefore petroleum products) dates back to the 1950s and 1960s. At that time, the switch from coal to liquid fuels led to an impressive increase in demand for heavy fuel oil and heating oil. Until the early 1970s, a simple refinery (composed of Distillation + Catalytic Reforming + Desulfurization Units), which processed a medium crude oil of the Arabian Light type, was perfectly adapted to demand, producing 40 to 50% heavy fuel oil, used in the industry and for electricity production, in line with the demand.

The 1973 and 1979 oil shocks, by increasing the price of oil tenfold, led to a sharp drop in demand for heavy fuel oil, replaced by coal, gas, or nuclear power. On the other hand, demand for gasoline, diesel oil, and jet fuel, for which there were no substitutes, continued to grow. To cope with this change in the structure of demand, it was necessary to build many conversion units, which are capable of transforming heavy distillation fractions into lighter fractions, petrol or diesel components. Most of the units built were of the FCC type (fluid catalytic cracking) because they have the dual advantage of very high fuel efficiency and a "moderate" investment cost compared to that of alternative solutions, such as a hydrocracker. The conversion rate, measured by the ratio of the weighted sum of a refinery's conversion capacity to its distillation capacity, increased in all regions of the world. The development of conversion has been significant in Western Europe, where the conversion rate of around 5% in 1975 increased to more than 50%. In 1977, Western Europe had 143 refineries, but only one-third of them had FCCs. Ninety percent of the remaining 100 refineries are now equipped with FCCs (or equivalent process units).

Similar trends have been observed in other regions of the world. The latest refineries built in Asia and recent extensions in the Middle East include many cracking units.

4.1 Recent Developments

Refineries must constantly adapt to major changes, for example, switch to unleaded petrol around 1990; general reduction in the sulfur content of fuels; and reduction in sulfur dioxide emissions from ships, which requires the installation of scrubbers or switching to LNG.

Thus, we have witnessed the construction of units capable of supplying gasoline components with increased octane number (regenerative catalytic reforming, isomerization, alkylation, etc.) to meet the demand for unleaded petrol and remodeling—rather than new construction—of desulfurization units to cope with the mandated reduction in the sulfur content of products, and in particular diesel fuel.

The decrease in heavy fuel oil production—which is imperative given market trends—is being achieved through improvements to existing FCC-type units capable of handling "heavier" loads and recent or future projects in deep conversion units, and remains a major challenge for refiners. The construction of very expensive deep conversion units (residue hydrocracking, coking with coke gasification) requires a considerable spread between the prices of diesel oil and that of heavy fuel oil. The changes to the FCCs also allow heavier loads to be handled. The transformation of residues into electricity via gasification is also an interesting option.

The refining industry in the United States is characterized by a particularly high conversion rate. Traditionally, the American refining industry has had to face very strong demand for motor gasoline. US demand for gasoline is in the order of 400 million tons per year, or about 45% of total US demand for petroleum products and 40% of total world demand for gasoline. The size of the car fleet, the high unit consumption of cars in the United States, and the fact that part of the commercial vehicle fleet is equipped with gasoline engines explain the strong demand for this product. On the other hand, abundant gas and coal resources have reduced the market for heating and heavy fuel oil. As a result, American refineries—or at least the largest ones—are equipped not only with FCC units but also with cokers. Eighty percent of cokers in the world are located in the United States. The average gasoline yield of US refineries exceeds 55%.

5 Refining Investment Costs

The investment cost of a completely new refinery depends on its size, complexity, and location. It is generally estimated that a 160,000 b/d (8 million tons per year) refinery, equipped with catalytic cracking, visbreaking, and gasoline units and built in Europe, would currently cost more than $6 billion. This cost can be significantly increased in the event of extremely stringent emission regulations, in terms of both the refinery's environment and the product quality.

A simple refinery (atmospheric distillation and catalytic reforming, plus distillate hydrodesulfurization) of a smaller size (100,000 b/d or 5 million tons per year) would cost half of this amount, or $3 billion. But the construction of such small refineries, which are no more profitable because they produce too much heavy fuel oil, is no longer on the agenda. Conversely, the investment required for a very large refinery, equipped with a deep conversion unit in order to reduce the production of heavy fuel oil to very small quantities, would cost more than $10 billion.

The analysis of investment costs shows the very high proportion of "offsites" (production of utilities, storage, receiving and shipping facilities), which can represent more than half of the cost for simple refineries. All other things being equal, the degree of autonomy of the refinery in electricity (whether or not it is purchased externally), the size of the tank farm, the size of the reception and shipping facilities are, among many others, important parameters in the total amount of the investment.

Two characteristics are essential in determining the investment cost:

- *Size*: The volume of a vessel (which determines its production capacity) is a function of the cube of the radius, while the surface (which determines its cost) is a function of the square of the radius. As the size of the vessel increases, its production capacity therefore increases faster than its cost. There are therefore significant economies of scale in a refinery. These savings are limited by the maximum size of some units. Thus, an atmospheric distillation unit will usually not exceed a dozen million tons per year of capacity. A larger refinery will therefore have at least two atmospheric distillation columns.

- *Location*: The cost of transporting the equipment and the cost of assembly are significant elements of the construction cost. A refinery located at a site far from the manufacturing plants for the main components (columns, reactors, etc.) will therefore be more expensive than the same refinery located near suppliers (North America, Europe, and Southeast Asia). The scarcity of local labor, forcing the movement of specialized teams, also has a significant impact on investment. Finally, particular climatic conditions can also have an impact on the price of the equipment.

6 Refining Costs

For ease of analysis, a distinction is made between variable costs (proportional to the quantities of crude processed), fixed costs (independent of the quantity of crude oil processed: personnel, maintenance, overheads) and capital costs (or depreciation).

6.1 Variable Refining Costs

These are proportional to the quantities of crude oil processed: they are mainly related to chemicals and catalysts.

Chemicals: A large number of chemicals are used in refining processes, but the costs involved remain limited. For a long time, the main focus was on lead additives (tetra-ethyl lead) to improve the octane number of gasoline. The gradual disappearance of these additives led to a reduction of the total cost for "chemicals". However, the increasing use of other additives (cetane improvers, additives improving cold resistance for diesel fuel, "pour depressants", etc.) slightly increases costs.

Catalysts: Most refineries—with the exception of refineries which have just a single distillation column—include catalytic process units: reforming, cracking, isomerization, alkylation, hydrodesulfurization, catalytic cracking, hydrocracking, and so on. The catalysts used are very diverse. The reforming process uses noble metal catalysts, whose cost exceeds several hundred dollars per kilo. However, these catalysts are regenerated (continuously in recent units, periodically in older units): at the end of the use cycle, the noble metals are recovered and reused.

For catalytic cracking, catalyst losses are continuously compensated by an injection of new catalyst. The cost of the catalyst is limited.

In total, the cost of chemicals and catalysts, per barrel of crude oil processed, is in the order of one dollar.

6.2 Fixed Costs

These costs include personnel, maintenance, insurance, local taxes, overheads, and so on, which are almost independent of the quantity of crude processed. Indeed, whether the refinery operates at 60% or 100% of its nominal capacity, personnel costs, for example, are the same.

Staff: The number of people working in a refinery varies greatly. It is at least about 200 to 250 people for a simple refinery. It can be much higher for a complex refinery, equipped with several atmospheric distillation units and cracking. For example, a large refinery (with two atmospheric distillations, two reformers, one catalytic cracker, one hydrocracker, one visbreaking unit, but also hydrodesulfurization units and an oil chain) directly employs more than 1000 people. The staff numbers therefore depend very little on size, but mainly on complexity. Personnel costs range from about \$15 million/year for a simple refinery to \$40 million/year for a refinery equipped with deep conversion. As a reminder, it should be noted that some refineries, particularly in the former Soviet Union countries, had a very large number of employees, several times higher than the number of employees in a Western European refinery. This is due to both the multiplication of small units in the same refinery and the existence of highly developed ancillary services (some factories even had spare parts manufacturing workshops, health services, and agricultural production cooperatives).

Maintenance: Maintenance is more or less proportional to the initial investment cost. A rule of thumb considers that the annual maintenance cost represents approximately 1 or 2% of the initial investment, that is, between about \$50 million/year (simple refinery) and \$100 million/year (deep conversion refinery). In Western refineries, most of the maintenance services, which are not considered part of the core business, are now outsourced.

General costs: These cover taxes, insurance, miscellaneous operating costs, overheads.

Total fixed costs are in the order of \$2 to \$3 per barrel processed (if the refinery operates at or close to capacity).

6.3 *Recovery of Capital Costs*

Capital, whether it is the cost of initial capital investment for a new refinery or the cost of new units in an existing refinery, must be recovered as depreciation. For a 160,000 barrel per day refinery equipped with conventional conversion, the initial investment, as we have seen, is about \$6 billion. If this unit is new, the incidence of capital depreciation (which can be interpreted as the sum of interest and repayments assuming the money needed to build the refinery is fully borrowed) will be in the range of \$8 to \$9 per barrel of crude processed (again, if the refinery operates at or close to capacity).

6.4 *Total Refining Cost*

In total, the costs and charges (excluding utilities) for a new conventional conversion refinery operating at full capacity would amount to just over \$10 per barrel. But the majority of refineries in operation is largely amortized and therefore operates with lower refining costs, in the order of \$3 to \$5 per barrel of crude oil processed.

6.5 *Factors That Influence Refining Costs and Profitability*

As we have seen, fixed costs (personnel, maintenance, and overheads) and capital costs represent the bulk of the total cost of processing crude oil. This has a very significant impact on the economics of refining.

(a) *Operating Rate*

This is the most important parameter. It is essential for a refinery to operate at a rate close to the maximum. This is of course true not only for atmospheric distillation but also for other units. A running rate of 66% translates, compared to full capacity operation, into a 50% increase in fixed costs per ton of crude oil processed.

This reasoning can be tempered by the fact that the full capacity operation of all refineries in an area where distillation capacities exceed overall product demand can result (and generally results) in a collapse of prices and therefore margins. This is why some refiners in such circumstances sometimes decide to decrease the quantity of crude oil processed. These measures are generally of short duration because a strengthening of margins immediately translates into a return to full capacity.

(b) *Size*

For a given utilization rate, the refining cost per ton of crude decreases as the size of the refinery increases. Indeed:

- Personnel and overhead costs are almost independent of the size of the refinery.
- Maintenance costs and capital charges increase less quickly than size.

For this reason, refineries with a size of less than about 5 million tons of distillation per year are no longer built, except in very special cases. Only geographical reasons (proximity to crude oil, e.g., in the United States; proximity to isolated markets, e.g., in Africa) can justify the existence of small refineries.

(c) *Complexity*

The degree of complexity of a refinery naturally increases the cost of processing a ton of crude oil. This is mainly due to higher cost of capital and maintenance. Two important remarks, however:

- a complex refinery will generate a higher margin than a simple refinery, all other things being equal (size, location, market, etc.) due to higher yields of light products

- a complex refinery will effectively generate a higher margin than a simple refinery if the crude oil is adapted to the processing in the conversion units. In other words, it will have to deal with heavier loads allowing it to fully utilize its crackers.

(d) *Location*

A refinery whose investment cost was increased by the distance from equipment suppliers, the scarcity of labor and extreme climatic conditions will of course have a higher operating cost per ton of crude oil.

(e) *Synergy with Petrochemicals*

The juxtaposition of refining with other activities, in particular, production of petrochemicals, is a very important asset, not only for the direct provision of charges for the steam cracker (the main process unit to make olefins which are the basis for the manufacturing of plastics, synthetic fibers, and synthetic rubber), but also because of the potential for common support services (maintenance, laboratory, general services, shipments, etc.) for all the site's activities.

7 Costs and Margins

The refining (gross) margin is the difference between the value of products (excluding taxes and distribution costs) leaving the refinery and the cost of crude oil entering the refinery. The net margin is equal to the gross margin less variable costs. The refining margin depends on many parameters and in particular on the refining scheme. We will thus speak of a TRCV margin for a refinery equipped with Topping, Reforming, Cracking (catalytic) and Visbreaking. Refining margins also depend on the region in which the refinery is located. A good geographical location translates into increased product value and therefore a better margin. In the United States, for example, refining margins in the interior of the continent are higher than those on the coast.

As previously discussed, total, refining costs for a newly built conventional refinery with 160,000 barrels per day of capacity and standard conversion units would be about $10 per barrel of crude processed, taking into account capital costs (interest and loan repayments). But most refineries, at least in North America and Europe, were built more than 20 years ago and are now depreciated. Their operating costs are in the order of $3 per barrel.

While production costs are relatively stable, margins are highly variable. They will depend on the market situation. Refining margins were very low until around 2000. They have improved over the past few years due to rationalization of capacity, which has involved many closures. Current margins, without generally allowing full cost coverage, make it possible to cover the limited cash costs and depreciation of recent investments. Indeed, most of the refineries in operation were built before the first oil crisis. In most Western countries, the most recent refineries date back to the 1970s. The initial installations are therefore largely amortized. Of course, new investments are constantly being made in refineries. But the economic depreciation associated with these new investments is only a small fraction of that that would result from the construction of a new refinery.

7.1 *Margins by Region*

Margins in the United States vary widely from one region to another. Around the Gulf of Mexico, the refining margins of the large, sophisticated refineries built to maximize gasoline production are fair. Margins in this area, which is very open to imports, are affected by product arrivals, particularly from Europe and Latin America. On the other hand, margins are much higher in the Midwest and even more so in California due to a better supply-demand balance on the one hand, and higher product prices on the other. Higher quality standards for products are reflected in prices. We should stress that the price of crude oil in the center of the United States is referred to the quotation of WTI (West Texas Intermediate crude) in Cushing, Oklahoma. Cushing is a place supplied with crude oil from many different origins (including synthetic crude from Canada) and equipped with large storage facilities. The price of WTI, which is a reference for other US crude oils, is normally low compared to Brent because of the large inflow of crude and limited pipeline facilities to transfer the crude. This is the main reason for better margins in the United States.

Refining margins in Asia were relatively high before the Asian crisis of 1997. Margins in this region were then more favorable than elsewhere due to continued growth in demand and the protection of certain markets. Margins collapsed in mid-1997 due to the region's economic problems, which slowed demand growth just while very large capacities were built. They rebounded in 2000, but remain relatively low if calculated on the basis of spot prices. However, we should remember that product prices are controlled by the government in many countries, allowing some profitability of the industry.

In Europe, the margins of a complex reference refinery located in Rotterdam were in the order of $1 to $2 per barrel in the 1990s, before recovering in 2000. Rapid variations in crude oil prices can also lead to very significant variations in the level of the margin.

7.2 *Future Margins and Costs*

Margins published by oil companies or trade journals are typical margins for fictitious refineries. This is called a margin indicator. In Europe, margin indicators generally correspond to the case of a refinery located in Rotterdam and operating in a highly competitive environment. These "Rotterdam calculated" margins do not cover the full costs of a new refinery.

A number of factors improve the economic situation of refining:

- Very significant productivity progress has been made in terms of costs: a few years ago, a large French company announced that it would lower its refining "break-even point" by around $1 per ton of crude oil processed per year. This trend continues: improvement in operating rates, efforts on the various items, reduction of inventories, and strict selection of investments are among the elements that explain this improvement;
- The generally published margins only take into account major products (gasoline, jet fuel, diesel, fuel oil). The so-called specialties products (lubricants, bitumen, LPG, or even petrochemical products) are not taken into account. However, these products often generate positive results that contribute to improved refining margins;
- The prices at which some refineries can actually sell their products are often higher than those taken into account in the calculation of margin indicators, because of a possibly more favorable geographical situation: a refinery located in Europe inland in an importing area will sell its products at a much higher price than Rotterdam, the difference reflecting transport costs;
- In a number of countries, refiners offset low refining margins with their presence in the distribution sector
- In order to better cope with competition and poor market conditions, restructuring is taking place in cooperation between operators.

Capacity restructuring in the face of a market that is likely to continue to grow for a few years suggests a good situation for global refining.

8 Oil Demand for Tomorrow

In a base scenario, the International Energy Agency (IEA) forecasts that oil demand—100 Million b/d in 2018—could exceed 110 Mb/d (5.5 Gtoe) in 2030, with most of the increase in demand coming from emerging countries, which will account for more than 60% of world consumption in 2030 compared to slightly more than 50% today. The share of motor fuels in oil consumption will continue to rise to more than 60%. Of course, in this baseline scenario, global carbon dioxide emissions will increase in contradiction with the Paris agreements of 2015.

However, the IEA proposes a second scenario, reflecting the impact of proactive energy policies and measures by governments and leading to a modest demand reduction of 10% in 2030 compared to the baseline scenario. In the latter scenario, oil consumption is therefore reduced to 99 Mb/d and the share of biofuels in total fuels increases from 4 to 7%, which seems unambitious but can be explained, at least in Europe, by the difficulties encountered in harmonizing the actions of the 27 Member States.

The increase in oil-related carbon dioxide emissions will greatly increase pressure on governments to limit demand growth, but the implementation of measures with a significant impact will require real political will.

Oil will increasingly be used for fuels and petrochemical bases, to the detriment of uses for heating and power generation.

The development of oil substitutes: agro fuels, synthetic fuels obtained by the Coal to Liquids (CTL), and Gas to Liquids (GTL) processes will be limited because they are expensive in energy and the improvements of the catalysts make it possible to manufacture products of excellent quality in refineries. The only GTL units recently built were in Qatar but no new units are planned.

9 The Future of Refining

The steady increase in the consumption of petroleum products requires increased refining capacity. Given the disappearance of refineries, often of small size, because unprofitable, the construction of new capacities is inevitable. These capacities will be built mainly in Asia, to cope with growing demand, and in the Middle East, where the availability of crude oil is a major factor. The refineries to be built will have to take into account the constant decrease in the demand for heavy products, because of price and the need to reduce pollution. The shift of ships to use of low sulfur fuels, which became mandatory in 2020, illustrates this perspective. New refineries will also face increasingly stringent specifications for light products.

Refineries will benefit from a favorable factor, rarely anticipated by forecasters. While in the 70s and 80s it seemed inevitable that the oils to be discovered would be increasingly heavy and sulfurous, this trend never materialized. For example, the crude oils found in Saudi Arabia after the discoveries of the large deposits around the Second World War were lighter than the oils of the first discoveries. Of course, the massive production of shale oil, called Light Tight Oil because their density (API degree between 40 and 45) is very low, goes in the same direction. The development of refining will no doubt be limited by the uncertain future of demand for petroleum products. Why build a refinery today if demand is to decline in 20 or 30 years?

The economic situation of refining is however better today than it was 30 years ago. The recurring weakness of margins—and profits—in the 1980s led to restructurings that paid off. We can therefore expect a slow but certain evolution toward refineries on average larger and more sophisticated, with a fair profitability.

Bibliography

Favennec, J-P. (2003) *Petroleum Refining—Vol 5: Refinery Operation and Management* IFPEN Rueil Malmaison.

Leffler, W.L. (2008) *Petroleum Refining in Nontechnical Language, Fourth Edition* Pennwell Tulsa Oklahoma.

Leprince, P. (ed.) (2001) *Petroleum Refining—Volume 3 : Conversion Processes* IFPEN Rueil Malmaison.

Trambouze, P. (2000) *Petroleum Refining—Volume 4 : Materials and Equipment* IFPEN Rueil Malmaison.

Wauquier, J-P. (1995) *Petroleum refining—Volume 1: Crude Oil, Petroleum Products, Process Flowsheets.*

Wauquier, J-P. (2000) *Petroleum refining—Volume 2: Separation Processes* IFPEN Rueil Malmaison.

CHAPTER 4

Economics of Hydrogen

Martin Robinius, Simonas Cerniauskas, Reinhard Madlener, Christina Kockel, Aaron Praktiknjo, and Detlef Stolten

1 Introduction

Concerns about the growing greenhouse gas emissions and associated anthropogenic climate change call for new solutions for developing a decarbonized and more sustainable energy system. Hydrogen can be a versatile non-fossil energy carrier and has substantial potential to enable such a

M. Robinius (✉)
Institute of Energy and Climate Research, Techno-economic Systems Analysis (IEK-3), Forschungszentrum Jülich GmbH, Jülich, Germany

JARA-ENERGY, Jülich, Germany

umlaut energy GmbH, Aachen, Germany
e-mail: martin.robinius@umlaut.com

S. Cerniauskas
Institute of Energy and Climate Research, Techno-economic Systems Analysis (IEK-3), Forschungszentrum Jülich GmbH, Jülich, Germany

RWTH Aachen University, c/o Institute of Electrochemical Process Engineering (IEK-3), Forschungszentrum Jülich GmbH, Jülich, Germany

R. Madlener
School of Business and Economics / E.ON Energy Research Center, Institute for Future Energy Consumer Needs and Behavior (FCN), RWTH Aachen University, Aachen, Germany

Department of Industrial Economics and Technology Management, Norwegian University of Science and Technology (NTNU), Trondheim, Norway

JARA-ENERGY, Aachen, Germany

M. Hafner, G. Luciani (eds.), *The Palgrave Handbook of International Energy Economics*, https://doi.org/10.1007/978-3-030-86884-0_4

transition. This chapter provides an extensive overview of the technical and economic characteristics of hydrogen and outlines the necessary background to foster the discussion of the role of hydrogen in a decarbonized energy system. First, we review potential applications of hydrogen and estimate its market potential in a typical industrialized nation in the year 2050. Subsequently, hydrogen-related policies and regulations are discussed. Then, we describe the most important facets of hydrogen supply, including its production, storage, processing and conditioning, delivery, and refueling. Then, the public acceptance and security aspects of hydrogen fuel supply chains and use are addressed. Finally, we analyze consumer willingness to pay for hydrogen technologies.

2 Hydrogen Use and Markets

Hydrogen can be used in many different sectors, including transportation, households, commerce and trade, chemical and heavy industry, and power sectors (Fig. 4.1). Therefore, hydrogen is increasingly considered a highly promising energy carrier necessary to achieving a fully decarbonized energy system (Robinius et al. 2017a; Henning and Palzer 2013; Knor et al. 2014). To provide a brief overview of hydrogen applications and related market potentials, anticipated hydrogen utilization in different sectors of the energy system will be described. More than 99% of the current worldwide hydrogen demand of 74 million tons arises from the heavy and chemical industry sector (SRI 2007; IEA 2019). Thus, hydrogen already plays today a vital role in this sector.

C. Kockel
School of Business and Economics / E.ON Energy Research Center, Institute for Future Energy Consumer Needs and Behavior (FCN), RWTH Aachen University, Aachen, Germany

A. Praktiknjo
School of Business and Economics / E.ON Energy Research Center, Institute for Future Energy Consumer Needs and Behavior (FCN), RWTH Aachen University, Aachen, Germany

JARA-ENERGY, Aachen, Germany

D. Stolten
Institute of Energy and Climate Research, Techno-economic Systems Analysis (IEK-3), Forschungszentrum Jülich GmbH, Jülich, Germany

JARA-ENERGY, Jülich, Germany

RWTH Aachen University, c/o Institute of Electrochemical Process Engineering (IEK-3), Forschungszentrum Jülich GmbH, Jülich, Germany

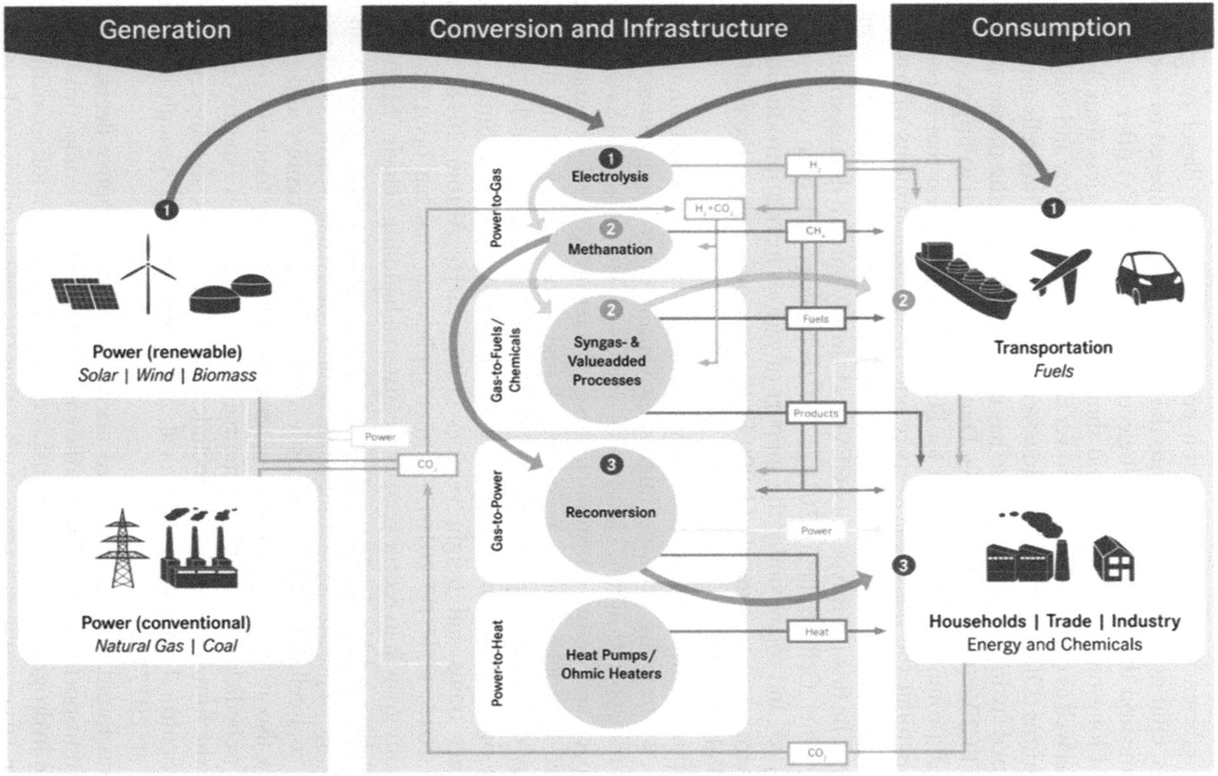

Fig. 4.1 Overview of hydrogen's potential role in the energy system (Robinius et al. 2017b)

2.1 *Transport*

In the transportation sector, hydrogen can be utilized in conventional combustion engines or, more prominently, to supply fuel cells, which have significantly higher efficiencies than combustion engines and, unlike diesel or gasoline engines, emit no CO_2 and NOx into the atmosphere. Compared to alternative zero emission drivetrains, fuel cell-electric vehicles (FCEVs) offer the advantages of long range (>500 km) and short refueling times (less than 3–5 minutes), as well as comparably high power capacity for heavy duty and commercial applications (Offer et al. 2010). However, the high cost of fuel cells and underdeveloped hydrogen infrastructure has until now limited the market penetration of FCEVs (Gnann et al. 2015). Due to its size and high willingness to pay, the most prominent target market for FCEVs historically was that of passenger cars. To fulfill the high vehicle space and design requirements of passenger vehicles, FCEV cars are generally equipped with 700 bar of onboard hydrogen storage. The first prototypes of FCEVs had already entered development in the 1960s (Fuel Cells Bulletin 2016). The technology has been continuously developed, and today, under the support of various market introduction policies, there are approximately 11,000 FCEV passenger cars on the road worldwide (Fukui 2019).

Despite the slow progress of FCEVs in the passenger car segment, the technology is attracting growing interest in various other applications, such as public transportation and commercial vehicles (Wulf et al. 2018a). Due to their space and design constraints, these vehicles are generally operated with onboard hydrogen storage at 350 bar. Range constraints, limiting the functionality of battery-electric vehicles (BEVs) for commercial vehicles, create a market opportunity for the introduction of fuel cells in local buses, smaller passenger trains and freight vehicles (Ritter 2016; Alstom 2018; Roland Berger 2015; FCH JU 2016). Another application that has been exhibiting significant growth in recent years is the material handling vehicle (MHV) market (Micheli and Hanke 2015). Fast refueling, emission-free operation, and a wide range of possible operating temperatures (i.e., harsh weather conditions) enable fuel cell MHVs to save costly space in logistics centers and operate indoors also at low temperatures as, for example, typically found in cold storages (Fischedick 2017). Other potential FCEV applications expected to play a role in the future energy system include motorbikes, ships, airplanes, railways, and agricultural machinery (Hart et al. 2015; New Holland Agriculture 2014; Hof et al. 2017).

It was found that the associated market potential of captive fleets, such as public transport and forklifts, is sufficient to provide a cost-competitive, countrywide hydrogen supply (Cerniauskas et al. 2019a). From infrastructure perspective, larger mobility markets, such as those for freight vehicles and passenger cars, require a public hydrogen refueling station network, and therefore, these markets are more challenging to enter. Finally, green hydrogen could play a key role in the future production of synthetic fuels, such as synthetic gasoline, synthetic kerosene, and so on, which are among the main options for decarbonizing air travel and high-power vehicles such as locomotives.

2.2 *Private Households and Heat*

Hydrogen can be flexibly used in the heating sector to achieve various inlet temperature levels, thus giving it a broad range of applications (e.g., space heating, hot water preparation), from single-family houses to large, multi-storey commercial and residential buildings. Existing natural gas boilers can be retrofitted to use hydrogen, as it has a similar Wobbe index as natural gas (Hodges et al. 2015). Given sufficient hydrogen supply infrastructure, this approach would allow rapid decarbonization of the heating sector, as a successful large-scale retrofit of heating appliances has already been demonstrated during the shift from town gas to natural gas in the first half of the twentieth century and during the still ongoing shift from low- to high-calorific natural gas (Dorrington et al. 2016; Fernleitungsnetzbetreiber 2017). Nevertheless, the blending of hydrogen with natural gas is currently limited by natural gas quality requirements, which vary significantly among countries, from 0.01 to 12%vol. (ITM Power PLC 2013; Dolci et al. 2019). The thermal use of admixed hydrogen and the cost-competitiveness of natural gas make this market more difficult to penetrate than is the case of mobility applications.

In fact, due to its low exergetic efficiency, the combustion of hydrogen is the less preferred utilization option. Alternatively, hydrogen can be used to operate combined heat and power units (CHPs), which are increasing in importance in decentralized energy systems (Weidner et al. 2019). Fuel cell CHPs enable an even higher overall efficiency (equivalent to a coefficient of performance (COP) of >5) than an all-electric solution, which combines the highest efficiency combined-cycle gas turbine (efficiency of >50%) with the highest efficiency heat pump (COP 3–4) (Staffell 2015). In Rigas and Amyote (2013), the effectiveness of support schemes for micro fuel cells in Germany is analyzed against the latest market conditions, support schemes, and legislative changes. The study shows that the technology is still far removed from competitiveness in domestic applications in Germany and that PEMFC system costs must be halved for the representative system considered (viz. from €19,500 to €10,500), including all auxiliary devices, before the technology can compete on the market without any form of subsidy.

2.3 *Chemical and Heavy Industry*

Hydrogen already plays a vital role in the heavy and chemical industry sector. However, instead of being used as an energy carrier, hydrogen is mostly utilized as a chemical feedstock for ammonia and methanol production and in the refining of oil (SRI 2007). Smaller hydrogen demand can also be found in the food-processing sector and in glass manufacturing (Schenuit et al. 2016).

Furthermore, hydrogen can be used for the direct reduction of iron ore and thus foster the decarbonization of the still very GHG-intensive steel industry (Otto et al. 2017).

However, the penetration of green hydrogen in the chemical and heavy industry sector, which encompasses the use in current chemical processes as well as novel applications such as the direct reduction of iron (Power-to-Steel) and the production of synthetic fuels (Power-to-Fuel), is more difficult than in transport. The high cost-competitiveness of the global commodity markets, as well as technological and market development uncertainties, significantly diminish the willingness of industrial consumers to shift to green hydrogen in the short- to medium-term perspective. Therefore, the large-scale adoption of green hydrogen in the industry is generally anticipated during the later stages of the hydrogen market development (Fraunhofer ISI and Öko-Institute 2015; Hydrogen Council 2017). Finally, green hydrogen could play a key role in the future production of synthetic fuels, such as synthetic gasoline, synthetic kerosene, and so on, which are among the main options for decarbonizing air travel and high-power vehicles such as long-haul trucks.

2.4 *Power Sector*

The growing capacity of variable renewable energy sources, such as wind and solar PV, increases the need for storage systems to buffer energy production fluctuations and provide sufficient flexibility to meet current supply security requirements. Short-period hourly and daily fluctuations can be absorbed by conventional pumped hydro power and more novel solutions, such as state-of-the-art compressed air and battery storage technology. However, the seasonal variation of renewable energy technologies requires long-term storage spanning weeks to months, which can be provided by underground chemical storage by means of hydrogen or synthetic methane (Welder et al. 2018). The stored energy can be shifted to transportation, heat, and heavy industry sectors or converted back into electricity with dedicated open-cycle gas turbines. However, the higher electrochemical conversion efficiency of fuel cells (60%) than of gas turbines (40%) favors coupling with other sectors over repowering. On this, various studies have suggested that hydrogen electrification would play a pivotal role in the power sector with a high degree of renewable power penetration (Henning and Palzer 2013, 2015; Knor et al. 2014). The economic feasibility of power-to-gas (P2G) systems in combination with hydrogen (and renewable methane), as well as underground storage used for load-balancing, is analyzed in Roche et al. (2010) employing a techno-economic model. The authors found that in none of the cases investigated (i.e., base case; storage and arbitrage; storage and balancing) was the P2G system economically viable under present market conditions, and so it requires substantial financial policy support.

3 Potential Applications of Hydrogen

3.1 Hydrogen Policy and Regulation

The literature on hydrogen policy and regulation has been growing in recent years, especially regarding green (Fig. 4.2) hydrogen in transport (Ajanovic and Haas 2018; Bleischwitz and Bader 2010; Collantes 2008; Rodrígueza et al. 2019; Pique et al. 2017). The economic prospects and necessary policy framework for green hydrogen used in passenger car transport are investigated by Ajanovic and Haas (2018), taking into account hydrogen production costs from variable renewable energy technologies and learning curve effects concerning fuel cell vehicles. The authors conclude that the prospects for hydrogen, apart from the need to become economically viable, depend a lot on the prevailing policy framework (to foster low-emission vehicles), for example, in terms of vehicle taxation/subsidization (purchase and use), non-monetary measures (entry to city centers, use of bus lanes, the free use of public parking spaces, etc.), and fuel economy standards. Bleischwitz and Bader (2010) review the current EU policy and regulatory framework for the transition toward a hydrogen economy, with a particular focus on prevailing barriers and inconsistencies. The authors conclude that the present policy framework does not hinder hydrogen development but that it does not forcefully compel it either. The most substantial impact is on hydrogen and fuel cell research and development. Regulatory policies are found to have a weak but positive impact on hydrogen, whereas EU funding policies show some inconsistencies. In their view, the large-scale market diffusion of hydrogen and fuel cells will require a new, technology-specific support approach, with a supportive policy framework that takes the regional dimension explicitly into account. However, recent changes in the EU Renewable Energy Directive, which includes green hydrogen

Brown	Coal gasification
Grey	Water electrolysis using power from fossil fuels
	Reforming of natural gas
White	By-product of industrial processes
Blue	Coal gasification with CCS
	Reforming of natural gas with CCS
Turquoise	Methane pyrolysis
Yellow	Water electrolysis using nuclear power
Green	Reforming of biogas
	Gasification and fermentation of biomass
	Water electrolysis using regenerative power sources

Fig. 4.2 Color coding for origins of hydrogen

as a feedstock switch in refineries, indicates the increasing consistency of EU policy (European Parliament and Council 2018).

The manifold dimensions of the policy debate over transportation fuels, with a particular focus on hydrogen, are analyzed in Collantes et al. (Collantes 2008) for the US, based on a web-based survey involving 502 individuals from 323 different stakeholder organizations. Policy beliefs and policy preferences of stakeholders are collected in order to identify, and obtain measures of, the main dimensions of the policy debate related to the use of hydrogen as a transportation fuel in the US, thus greatly reducing the complexity of the policy picture. Three policy preferences found are (i) command-and-control approaches; (ii) addressing externalities with technology-neutral approaches; and (iii) facilitating technological progress and innovation. Another effort to translate the potential contributions of hydrogen technology into public policy schemes was undertaken in Rodrigueza et al. (Rodrígueza et al. 2019) in the case of the legal framework for hydrogen regulation in Mexico. The study found that the lack of hydrogen storage, lack of regulation on the use of hydrogen in final applications, and lack of safety regulation are essential barriers that must be overcome before the hydrogen economy can unfold. Finally, Pique et al. (2017) report on a comparative study on regulations, codes, standards, and practices on hydrogen fueling stations in nine different countries, namely, the US (California), the UK, Italy, Germany, Canada, Sweden, Norway, Denmark, and Spain. The authors find that countries often have no national regulation specific to hydrogen fueling, have no specific regulations other than their own technical guidelines, and that international standards (such as ISO 17268 or ISO 20100) are the references applied in almost all countries.

Leibowicz (2018) develops policy recommendations for the transition to sustainable mobility and transport system by investigating the historical dynamics of this sector, and in particular, regularities concerning the relative timing of infrastructure, vehicle, and travel diffusion processes across systems. In doing so, he analyzes technological lock-ins, techno-institutional complexes, technology transitions, barriers to adoption, and the historical diffusion of transport systems.

4 Hydrogen Infrastructure

4.1 Production

Hydrogen can be separated from water or hydrocarbon compounds found in various fossil fuels and biomass. The element hydrogen is colorless, but due to the broad spectrum of possible production alternatives, there exist different names to classify the hydrogen according to its CO_2 emissions, like gray, blue, and green hydrogen (IEA 2019) (see Fig. 4.2). In general, the term gray hydrogen refers to hydrogen production via fossil fuels, with the most common process being the steam methane reforming (SMR). Depending on the CO_2 intensity of the electricity mix, production via electrolysis from the grid electricity may also be called gray hydrogen due to the high associated CO_2 emissions. Nonetheless, additional sub-classes to the CO_2 intensive production, such as brown and white hydrogen, have been proposed. Brown hydrogen stands for hydrogen production from coal and is the most CO_2 intensive among the production sources. By-product hydrogen that is not used as feedstock but is exploited thermally near its source was proposed to be referred to as white hydrogen. In the case of other use cases, the thermal utilization on-site can be substituted by the combustion of natural gas, thus leading to a smaller CO_2 intensity than in the case of the gray hydrogen. Blue hydrogen generally refers to non-renewable hydrogen production meeting low CO_2 intensity criteria. Application of carbon capture and storage (CCS) to coal gasification and SMR enables these processes to sufficiently reduce the associated emissions to meet this criterion. However, additional classes of the turquoise and yellow hydrogen have been proposed. Turquoise hydrogen is produced by methane pyrolysis, in which methane is split in a thermochemical process into solid carbon and hydrogen, and if the heat supply of the high-temperature reactor is provided by renewable energy sources, the process yields low CO_2 emission intensity, whereas hydrogen production via electrolysis from nuclear power is called yellow hydrogen. Green hydrogen is produced exclusively from renewable energy sources. Typically, green hydrogen is produced by water electrolysis. Further possibilities are the gasification and fermentation of biomass and the reformation of biogas. The following sections will explore the key features of the essential hydrogen production processes defining the described classification.

Currently, the most widely utilized options to retrieve hydrogen from hydrocarbons are SMR, partial oxidation, and gasification (gray hydrogen) (SRI 2007). SMR comprises a high-yield endothermic reaction of natural gas and steam to allow high-purity hydrogen production (Gupta 2008). The partial oxidation of hydrocarbons has lower material efficiency and hydrogen purity but can utilize a larger variety of fuels, including oil residues (Gupta 2008). Gasification has the lowest material efficiency and hydrogen purity; however, it allows the use of more widely accessible fuels, such as coal (brown hydrogen) and biomass (Gupta 2008) [43]. Against the background of CO_2 emissions reduction policies, these processes can be extended with subsequent CCS (blue hydrogen), thus enabling to diminish the CO_2 footprint of hydrogen production, which is expected to be the key bridge technology to the widespread low-emission hydrogen production (IEA 2019). Another possibility of providing hydrogen while avoiding CO_2 emissions is methane pyrolysis (turquoise hydrogen), which uses the thermal non-catalytic splitting of methane into hydrogen and carbon at high temperatures. However, despite up-and-coming applications, due to its low technology readiness level (TRL), methane pyrolysis is not expected to become commercially available within the next 10–20 years (Geres et al. 2019). To put the state of technology's development into perspective, the latest pilot project aims to reach a production capacity of up to 12 kg_{H2}/h (ARENA 2019) which is approximately equivalent to production of an electrolyzer with 600 kW_{el} capacity with running on full load

SMR

Property	Low	High
$\eta_{LHV,CH4}$ %	70	78
Cost €/kg_{H2}	1.0	2.2

TRL: 9

Advantages:
Low cost H_2 production
Established technology
Scalable process

Disadvantages:
High CO_2 emissions

Selected projects:
Corpus Christi (USA)
Ludwigshafen (GER)

SMR+CCS

Property	Low	High
$\eta_{LHV,CH4}$ %	70	78
Cost €/kg_{H2}	1.2	2.8

TRL: 8

Advantages:
Intermediate CO_2 emissions
Medium cost H_2 production
Scalable process

Disadvantages:
Intermediate CO_2 emissions
Requires CO_2 infrastructure

Selected projects:
H21 (GBR)
H2 Magnum (NLD)

Methane Pyrolysis

Property	Low	High
$\eta_{LHV,CH4}$ %	55	75
Cost €/kg_{H2}	1.0	2.5

TRL: 5

Advantages:
No CO_2 emissions
Black carbon as byproduct
Low cost H_2 production

Disadvantages:
Tradeoff of H_2 and carbon quality
No clearly preferred process

Selected projects:
Hazer (AUS)
Monolith (USA)

SMR: Steam Methane Reformer **CCS**: Carbon Capture and Storage **LHV**: Lower Heating Value
TRL: Technology Readiness Level

Fig. 4.3 Comparison of natural gas-based hydrogen production methods (Geres et al. 2019; ARENA 2019; Monolith Materials 2018; Parkinson et al. 2019; Sarsfield-Hall and Unger 2019; Eikaas 2019; Machhammer et al. 2016; Abánades et al. 2013)

at all hours in a year. Figure 4.3 provides an overview of the most promising low CO_2 intensity production options from natural gas.

Alternatively, with expanding decarbonization of electricity production (green and yellow hydrogen), by using electrolysis hydrogen can be retrieved from water. The main electrolysis processes currently being discussed are alkaline (AEL), polymer electrolyte membrane (PEMEL), and solid oxide (SOEL) electrolysis. AEL is the most mature technology and is already implemented on an industrial scale of several MW and is used for 4% of current hydrogen production (SRI 2007). Due to its typical application for chlorine production instead of variable renewable energy integration, AEL has important constraints on the operating range, requiring a minimal load of 20% and relatively slow dynamics between operating points of <30 s (Schmidt et al. 2017a; Brinner et al. 2018). Alternatively, PEMEL has a wider operating range of 0%–150% and dynamic operation between operating points of <2 s, thus enabling the coupling of PEMEL with highly intermittent power sources such as solar PV and wind (ITM Power 2018; Bayer et al. 2016; Kopp et al. 2017) [55–57]. Another alternative is SOEL, which operates at high temperatures (700–1000 °C with ZrO_2 ceramic as electrolyte) that allow higher efficiency than in the case of other electrolyzer systems (Brinner et al. 2018). However, the high operating temperature also increases the thermal inertia and thus feasible size of the cells, which poses significant challenge for larger scale SOEL deployment and integration with variable renewable energy technologies. Furthermore, current SOEL must overcome important deficiencies, such as

PEM Electrolysis

Property	Today	Future
$\eta_{LHV,el}$ %	63	70
CAPEX €/kW$_{el}$	1500	500

TRL: 7-8

Advantages:
High gas purity
High load flexibility
High power density

Disadvantages:
Rare metals in catalysts

Selected projects:
Energy Park Mainz (DE)
Energy Valley (NL)

Alkaline Electrolysis

Property	Today	Future
$\eta_{LHV,el}$ %	65	70
CAPEX €/kW$_{el}$	1000	580

TRL: 9

Advantages:
No rare metals in catalysts
Low specific cost
Established technology

Disadvantages:
Requires purification
Limited flexibility

Selected projects:
George Olah (ISL)
Audi e-gas (DE)

Solid Oxide Electrolysis

Property	Today	Future
$\eta_{LHV,el}$ %	75	83
CAPEX €/kW$_{el}$	2500	500

TRL: 4-5

Advantages:
Potentially high efficiency
Utilization of exhaust heat
Reversibility of the process

Disadvantages:
High material stress
Short lifetime

Selected projects:
Dresden (DE)

PEM: Polymer Electrolyte Membrane **LHV**: Lower Heating Value **TRL**: Technology Readiness Level
CAPEX: Capital Expenditure

Fig. 4.4 Comparison of electrolytic hydrogen production methods (Wulf et al. 2018a; Brinner et al. 2018; Schmidt et al. 2017b; Saba et al. 2018; Glenk and Reichelstein 2019; Smolinka et al. 2018)

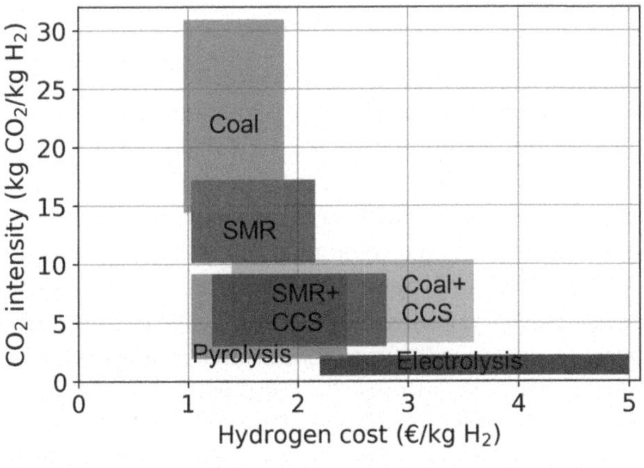

Fig. 4.5 Hydrogen production cost and intensity (adapted from the literature (Parkinson et al. 2019; Heuser et al. 2019))

short lifetimes and material degradation (Schmidt et al. 2017a). Figure 4.4 provides an overview of the most important features of electrolytic hydrogen production technologies.

Figure 4.5 summarizes the literature review of the CO_2 intensity and the cost of hydrogen production for a selection of the most promising technologies. The results consider estimates of life-cycle emissions of the production and primary energy sources. In the case of coal-based processes, underground mined coal, and in the case of electrolysis, renewable electricity is considered in the analysis. Furthermore, emissions occurring in the natural gas supply chain are additionally considered for SMR and SMR+CCS (Munnings and Krupnick 2018). The respective technologies are displayed as areas encompassing underlying uncertainties and variations of the data in the literature. The displayed variation of fossil fuel-based production is mainly affected by efficiency and the costs of primary energy and CCS where applicable, whereas in the case of electrolysis, the uncertainty appears primarily due to different renewable energy availability and anticipated future technological development of electrolysis and renewable energy generation technologies. It can be observed that moving from top to bottom along the y-axis, these technologies display a Pareto frontier of both hydrogen production cost and associated CO_2 intensity. Whereas, on the one hand, coal and SMR lead to not only lowest cost but also highest CO_2 emissions, on the other hand, green electrolytic hydrogen enables the lowest CO_2 emissions at the cost of higher production costs. In between, one can observe pyrolysis and coal as well as natural gas-based hydrogen production with CCS. Nevertheless, as mentioned above, pyrolysis is still at an early stage of development. Thus, the initial transition to less CO_2 intensive production will potentially not be able to rely on this technology.

4.2 *Storage*

Seasonal variations of renewable energy sources such as wind and solar PV require long-term storage solutions to cope with intermittent power production. The long-term storage requirements of renewable energy integration can be fulfilled with hydrogen. Hydrogen storage can be facilitated by the storage of pure hydrogen or by using hydrogen carriers (Reuß et al. 2017). Pure hydrogen can be stored in specialized steel containers in a compressed, liquid state or, alternatively, compressed hydrogen can be stored in underground facilities. The high storage capacity and relatively low costs of underground storage make it an especially attractive solution for seasonal renewable energy variations. Gaseous and liquid storage options, by contrast, are more suitable as buffer systems at hydrogen refueling stations. Since the 1960s, the utilization of underground storage in industrial facilities has proven the technical feasibility of GWh-scale underground hydrogen storage (Crotogino et al. 2010). However, despite large potential in Europe and some other regions, the geological limitations of the required rock formations for salt caverns and porous rock diminish the global availability of hydrogen underground storage (and multiple media may compete for underground storage, such as compressed air, CO_2, and hydrogen itself). Alternatively, hydrogen can be stored in the form of synthetic fuels or by making use of specialized energy carriers. While the use of synthetic fuels would allow the existing infrastructure to be used, drawbacks include high energy losses during the conversion and the cost of CO_2 separation from the air, as it is anticipated to decarbonize the energy

Salt Cavern[1]

Property	Today	Future
Density GJ/m³	1,44	1,44
CAPEX €/kg_{H2}	21	21

TRL: 8-9

Advantages:
Long term storage
Low space demand
Low specific cost

Disadvantages:
Geological constraints

Selected projects:
Clemens Dome (US)
Tesside (UK)

Gaseous H_2 Bundle

Property	Today[2]	Future[3]
Density GJ/m³	2,88	3,84
CAPEX €/kg_{H2}	800	600

TRL[2]: 8-9

Advantages:
Long cyclic lifetime
Established technology[2]
No geological constraints

Disadvantages:
High specific cost

Selected projects:
London (UK)
Oslo (NOR)

Liquid H_2 Tank

Property	Today	Future
Density GJ/m³	8,5	8,5
CAPEX €/kg_{H2}	25	25

TRL: 9

Advantages:
Long cyclic lifetime
Established technology
No geological constraints

Disadvantages:
Requires liquefaction

Selected projects:
Vancouver (CAN)
London (UK)

TRL: Technology Readiness Level
CAPEX: Capital Expenditure
1: Cavern V = 500.000 m³, P = 150 bar
2: Bundle pressure = 350 bar
3: Bundle pressure = 500 bar

Fig. 4.6 Features of hydrogen storage (Wulf et al. 2018a; FCH JU 2016; Brinner et al. 2018; Reuß et al. 2017; Hua et al. 2014; Acht 2013; Yang and Odgen 2007)

system by 2050. Specialized energy carriers, such as hydrides and liquid organic energy carriers, can offer advantageous energy density properties under low pressure, thus mitigating potential hydrogen risks (Reuß et al. 2017). However, these technologies also feature drawbacks in terms of efficient energy discharge and must still be proven in day-to-day operation to demonstrate the technology's readiness for commercialization (Fig. 4.6).

4.3 *Hydrogen Processing and Conditioning*

The varying technical characteristics of the components along the hydrogen supply chain with respect to the hydrogen's state, purity, and pressure necessitates conversion steps, such as compression, liquefaction, and purification. In the case that energy carriers are used for the storage and transport of hydrogen, charging and discharging units must be taken into consideration.

Electrolytic hydrogen production output is typically conducted between 1 and 20 bar, while to accommodate sufficient quantities of hydrogen and to save space, mobile hydrogen fuel cell applications operate at 350–700 bar. This creates a significant pressure increase that must be maintained and operated along the supply chain. Furthermore, hydrogen supply chain components, such as high-pressure pipelines and 500-bar trailers, have additional hydrogen pressure constraints. To fulfill the aforementioned hydrogen pressure requirements, the compression can be facilitated via mechanical, electrochemical, hybrid, and ionic means. However, only the former is an established technology with proven operational viability. Alternatively, for the gradual pressure increase along the supply chain, hydrogen can be liquefied at the production point and subsequently evaporated and compressed to the required pressure level at the refueling station.

As with the pressure, hydrogen purity is defined by the hydrogen quality requirements of the final consumer; for example, PEMFCs have a 99.97% purity requirement (ISO 2012). However, depending on the hydrogen supply chain pathway used, additional hydrogen purity constraints can arise when SMR and by-product hydrogen or hydrogen liquefaction are considered (Berstad 2018; Zhu et al. 2018). The most widely adopted hydrogen purification methods encompass temperature swing adsorption (TSA) and pressure swing adsorption (PSA). Special membranes also are promising for smaller throughput applications.

4.4 Hydrogen Delivery

The three main routes of hydrogen distribution are gaseous hydrogen trailers and pipelines, as well as liquid hydrogen trailers. The choice of the most effective delivery method depends on the chosen means of storage, as changes in the state of hydrogen increase energy losses, delivery distance, and throughput (Reuß et al. 2017; Yang and Odgen 2007).

Gaseous hydrogen trailers offer a cost-effective solution during the introduction phase, marked by low and sparsely distributed demand. They become less economical in the later market stages when hydrogen demand increases. Nevertheless, even with significant hydrogen demand, the last mile distribution from the hydrogen pipeline to the refueling station remains a cost-effective option (Reuß et al. 2019). Alternatively, hydrogen can be liquefied or transported in the form of liquid organic hydrogen carriers. Both options enable cost-efficient, long-distance hydrogen transportation, which is especially interesting for overseas hydrogen trade (Heuser et al. 2019). Challenges related to the transport of liquified hydrogen are comparable to those of LNG, which requires high insulation to avoid boil-off losses. Therefore, as with LNG transport, LH_2-transporting ships and trucks can be operated on the boil-off losses of hydrogen. In the case of liquid organic hydrogen carriers (LOHCs), transportation is very similar to liquid fuels, and therefore, few modifications to current fossil fuel pipelines and trailers would be necessary. However, studies have shown that economic viability of LOHCs delivery depend strongly on the availability of low-cost heat energy (Reuss 2019), constraining LOHCs to more specific environments (Fig. 4.7).

Hydrogen pipelines are often considered as the most cost-efficient and environmentally favorable means of delivering large volumes of hydrogen over medium to large distances (Wulf et al. 2018a; Tlili et al. 2020; Emonts et al. 2019). This makes it especially attractive for a transmission network and the connection of industrial sites. Currently, there are already several insulated hydrogen pipeline networks supplying industrial sites with a total length of 3000 km in Europe and the US. The risk of low pipeline utilization and

H_2 Pipeline

Property	Today[1]	Future[2]
Capacity t_{H2}/h	2,4	245
CAPEX €/m	500	3400

TRL: 8-9
Advantages:
High throughput capactiy
Low space demand
Low specific cost

Disadvantages:
High upfront cost

Selected projects:
Leuna (DE)
Texas (US)

Gaseous H_2 Trailer

Property	Today[3]	Future[4]
Capacity kg_{H2}	400	1100
CAPEX €/kg_{H2}	500	600

TRL[3]: 9
Advantages:
No liquefaction required
Low investment cost
Established technology[3]

Disadvantages:
Low transport capacity

Selected projects:
London (UK)
Oslo (NOR)

Liquid H_2 Trailer

Property	Today	Future
Capacity kg_{H2}	4300	4300
CAPEX €/kg_{H2}	200	200

TRL: 9
Advantages:
Low investment cost
High transport capactiy
Established technology

Disadvantages:
Requires liquefaction

Selected projects:
Vancouver (CAN)
London (UK)

TRL: Technology Readiness Level
CAPEX: Capital Expenditure

Fig. 4.7 Features of hydrogen delivery methods (Wulf et al. 2018a; FCH JU 2016; Brinner et al. 2018; Reuß et al. 2017; Hua et al. 2014; Tractebel and Hinicio 2017; Krieg 2012)

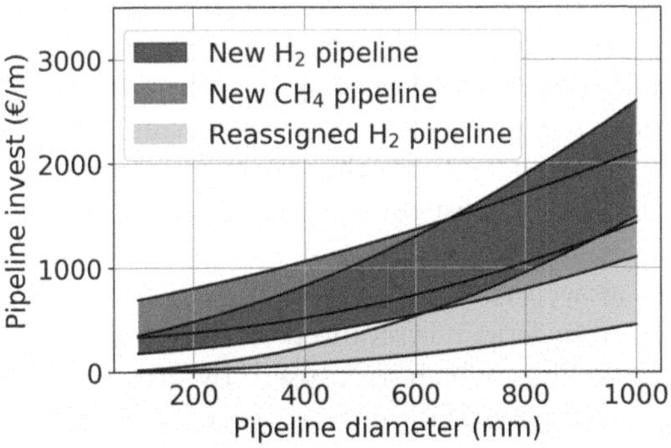

Fig. 4.8 Pipeline investment cost overview (Robinius et al. 2017a; Fernleitungsnetzbetreiber 2017; Krieg 2012; Cerniauskas et al. 2019a; Mischner et al. 2011)

elevated initial investment in the steel pipelines (Fig. 4.8) challenges the implementation of hydrogen pipelines during the market introduction phase. However, pipeline costs can be alleviated through the reassignment of existing natural gas pipelines, which, with the increasing electrification of the heating sector and the shift from low- to high-caloric natural gas, will increasingly become available. Initial investigation of the German natural gas transmission grid has shown that, despite additional measures for handling hydrogen-related material embrittlement, pipeline reassignment can reduce yearly pipeline expenditures by up to 80% in comparison to a new, dedicated hydrogen pipeline (Cerniauskas et al. 2019a). Another option to use hydrogen in the natural gas grid is to blend hydrogen with natural gas. Historically, there have been many cases of utilizing hydrogen-rich town gas (50–60% of H_2), which were abandoned in favor of natural gas in the 1960s (Williams 1981). Currently, different countries make use of hydrogen gas admixtures with natural gas of up to 10% w\m (ITM Power PLC 2013), which can be further increased if heating devices and natural gas turbines and CNG vehicles, which currently allow 2%vol max, are adapted for higher hydrogen concentrations (DVGW 2019). Comparable large-scale change in consumer devices was already observed during the transition from town gas to natural gas in the 1960s, as well as during the ongoing shift from low- to high-caloric natural gas (Fernleitungsnetzbetreiber 2017; Williams 1981). Nevertheless, despite the apparent benefits of the widespread availability of natural gas infrastructure and the avoidance of new infrastructure implementation, hydrogen blending might lock in hydrogen to thermal use, as any other hydrogen applications would require subsequent hydrogen purification (ISO 2012).

4.5 Hydrogen Refueling

Currently, all hydrogen-powered vehicles prefer gaseous over liquid onboard hydrogen storage, as the latter would inevitably lead to boil-off losses in the vehicle. For use in passenger cars, the current state of the art is a gauge pressure of 700 bar, while 350 bar is the prevailing pressure for hydrogen use in buses and other commercial applications. The underlying structure of hydrogen refueling stations is comparable to that of current fossil fuel refueling and consists of a buffer storage, dispenser, cooling unit, and fuel-processing unit that creates the necessary pressure gradient to facilitate refueling. This principle holds for gaseous as well as liquid and LOHC delivery (Pratt et al. 2015). Additional cooling of hydrogen is required to compensate for the temperature increase during refueling, which is caused by the Joule-Thomson effect. Detailed hydrogen refueling station designs generally differ concerning the form of hydrogen delivery and the chosen method for creating the required pressure gradient. For the 700-bar hydrogen refueling of passenger cars, the pressure is increased to 875 bar to enable rapid refueling rates of 1.8–3.6 kg/min (FCH JU 2016; SAE 2014). To achieve this, hydrogen is generally either stored in high-pressure vessels that facilitate the refueling process or medium pressure vessels, with a small additional compressor, which covers the highest pressure-gradient requirements, being installed. In the case of liquid or LOHC hydrogen delivery, hydrogen is evaporated or discharged from the hydrogen carrier and compressed to the required pressure. In the case of 350-bar vehicles, rapid refueling requires a lower pressure gradient, and therefore, 500-bar trailers can be employed as high-pressure hydrogen storage media for vehicle refueling (Elgowainy et al. 2014; Reddi et al. 2017).

5 Hydrogen Safety

In general, concerns about hydrogen safety are different but not more demanding than those pertaining to fossil fuels such as natural gas, gasoline, or diesel (Rigas and Amyote 2013). Most hydrogen hazards relate to the fact that, like methane, hydrogen gas cannot be detected with human senses (Rigas and Amyote 2013). In the case of methane, gas leakage detectability increased with the addition of odorants to the methane gas. However, the current high hydrogen purity requirements of fuel cells preclude the use of odorants (Rigas and Amyote 2013). Nevertheless, hydrogen-related material degradation is a well-understood and -managed hazard, as it is among the main causes of equipment failures in the oil and gas industry (Popov et al. 2018; Shehata et al. 2008). Hydrogen also has positive features when compared to fossil fuels. In contrast to methane and gasoline, hydrogen rapidly disperses to incombustible concentrations and has less explosive energy (Hess Corp 2007; Linde AG 2018; Air Liquide AS 2018). Furthermore, unlike gasoline, hydrogen is neither toxic nor carcinogenic (Hess Corp 2007; Linde AG 2018).

Hydrogen-related incidents are constantly tracked and analyzed to improve the safety of hydrogen system operation. The major causes of hydrogen-related incidents can be classified into the following categories (Federal Institute for Materials Research and Testing 2002):

- Mechanical and material failure
- Corrosion and embrittlement
- Incidents of over-pressurization
- Incidents of expanding liquid hydrogen boil-off
- Hydrogen-unrelated incidents
- Human error

An overview of more than 240 historical incidents revealed that 95% of these were not associated with any fatalities, while 34% did not result in any damage (Rigas and Amyote 2013; Weiner and Fassbender 2011). It could also be identified that most of the accidents occurred as a result of simple equipment, such as valves and fittings, which often relates to human error during assembly and maintenance (H2 Tools 2019). Therefore, despite the fact that most of the accidents were directly caused by equipment failure, the most frequent direct and indirect cause of the accidents was a lack of situational awareness and human error (Rigas and Amyote 2013; H2 Tools 2019).

Markerta et al. (2017) advocate the use of a holistic approach for analyzing the risk and sustainability of hydrogen infrastructures, proposing the use of the "functional modeling" method and combining this with life-cycle analysis (LCA) and geographic information systems (GIS). They consider risk assessment as part of a more general decision plan needed to design and establish sustainable supply chains that are economical, efficient, reliable, safe, and secure. By using functional decomposition (from an early design stage onward), it is possible to analyze and compare alternative supply chain solutions that provide the required system functions with regard to safety, reliability, environmental impact, and costs.

5.1 *The Public Acceptance of Hydrogen*

The public acceptance of hydrogen technologies has been the subject of research for several decades. Varying levels of acceptance were examined in broad, methodological studies. The following comments highlight only a few selected criteria that relate predominantly to the perception of the general population in Germany (Zimmer 2013a; Spillet and IFOK 2016). An overall positive basic attitude toward hydrogen transportation is often found due to its tailpipe emission-free nature and status as a futuristic technology. One exception was civil society actors surveyed who were reasonably skeptical about hydrogen transportation applications. Citizen surveys focused in particular on expectations of the technology in terms of vehicle usability, health and noise, climate and environmental protection, and safety sensitivity (Zimmer 2013a; Spillet and IFOK 2016). With regard to usability, the interviewees largely assumed current conditions with regard to range, performance, vehicle size, and filling station availability (Zimmer 2013a).

According to the report for Germany, noise abatement played a minor role in the assessment (Zimmer 2013a). The most important added value was considered the technology's contribution to environmental protection. The often critical issue of safety perception due to the chemical-physical properties of hydrogen played hardly any role in the study. The report noted that this was demonstrated by the fact that the hazardous nature of hydrogen was not once addressed. Also, in a citizen conference, after an initial discussion of safety concerns on the part of citizens, the assessment was expressed that hydrogen vehicles are safe. Furthermore, a representative survey was carried out in which approximately 1000 people were asked about their view of the statement, "I would be more afraid to live next to a hydrogen filling station than next to a conventional filling station," with 6% replying that this would be "fully applicable," 17% that it would be "rather applicable," 43% that it would be "rather not applicable," and 34% that it would be "not applicable at all." An overwhelming majority of 77%, therefore, rejected the statement. Zaunbrecher et al. interviewed 182 people about their attitude and acceptance of hydrogen storage in Germany (Zaunbrecher et al. 2016). Of the 141 answers supplied, it could be concluded that hydrogen, in contrast to other currently discussed technologies of the energy system transformation, is generally viewed positively in terms of social acceptance. The construction of necessary facilities is also supported in principle, although there are uncertainties about the risks if hydrogen is stored near residential areas.

Studies on similar questions have also been carried out in other nations. Despite this study's focus on Germany, the results of studies in other countries will be presented briefly, as hydrogen-based passenger car transport can only be successful if it can be implemented worldwide. Iribarren et al. investigated the social acceptance of hydrogen in Spain as a fuel for road traffic (Iribarren et al. 2016). Some central questions included the public perception of hydrogen itself, hydrogen as a fuel in public transport, and its environmental friendliness. All three questions were answered in the affirmative, in some cases at more than 70%. On the question of the acceptance of hydrogen fueling stations, it is striking that more than 50% of those questioned had no objections to these but preferred that they be built away from residential areas. Only about 3% of the respondents were against hydrogen fueling stations. The aspect of supporting the market introduction of hydrogen was examined on the basis of the question of an appropriate ("affordable") tax. A total of 74% responded positively, but around 60% felt that this transition should not be undertaken with the help of a direct tax. Similar findings were found in a trans-European study on hydrogen acceptance as well, thus indicating the underlying societal acceptability and support for hydrogen and fuel cell technology applications (HYACINTH 2013).

A study by Bögela et al. (2018) investigates the implications of prior attitudes for public-facing communication campaigns related to hydrogen technologies in seven European countries, finding low attitude strength and low stability of attitudes with regard to hydrogen fuel cells for both stationary and mobile applications. The implications of these findings are that information campaigns in early stages can help increase awareness among those with no or low prior knowledge about hydrogen technologies and positively influence attitudes toward the technology. At a later stage, when public knowledge and awareness increase, psychological research on prior attitudes becomes more relevant and should address the context-specificity and empirical testing of the theoretical models used.

An interesting question is whether the provision of quantitative risk information on hydrogen infrastructure increases or decreases acceptance (behavior toward the technologies) and acceptability (attitudes). In a repeated Japanese online survey (Ono and Tsunemi 2017; Ono et al. 2019) regarding the scenario of constructing a hydrogen fueling facility at the gas station in the vicinity to the home of the respondents, the public acceptance of hydrogen fueling was investigated on the basis of risk perception scales. The provision of quantitative risk information and risk acceptance criteria increased the acceptability of hydrogen refueling stations in proximity to the homes of respondents but decreased acceptability at the nearest gas station.

Roche et al. (2010) review the various conceptual frameworks and methodologies used for studying public attitudes toward new transport technologies. They review the findings of recent literature on acceptance, attitudes, and preferences for hydrogen and fuel cell end-use technologies from a vehicle perspective. The authors recommend using approaches that build knowledge and familiarity with the technology prior to the exploration of attitudes. They advocate further studies that take a whole-system perspective on hydrogen technologies, looking at (green) hydrogen in the context of other competing CO_2-free fuel technologies, and which aim to identify the early signs of possible social acceptance barriers (to be prepared if opposition arises in the course of increasing the penetration of hydrogen, and in particular concerning growing numbers of hydrogen refueling stations).

5.2 *Willingness to Pay*

For the broad adoption of hydrogen-based transportation, in addition to the right conditions for supply with FCEVs and hydrogen, the question arises of whether or not consumers are willing to opt for hydrogen-based transport by purchasing an FCEV. According to economic theory, a customer purchases a product or service if (a) the utility it provides exceeds the so-called total cost of ownership (TCO), that is, its net utility is positive, and (b) if its net utility is the highest among all available alternatives (Zweifel et al. 2017). While utility itself is subjective and dependent on the personal preferences of consumers, its influencing factors are measurable. In the case of hydrogen-based transportation, primary drivers certainly take mobility itself (e.g., distances one can travel in a specific timeframe) into account. However, as Hackbarth and Madlener show, there are other factors, such as a reduction of CO_2 emissions, that might add to a consumer's perceived utility of hydrogen-based transportation (Hackbarth and Madlener 2016). With respect to TCO, one can differentiate between fixed and variable costs for consumers. In terms of fixed cost, the most substantial impact is the cost of the vehicle itself. Other fixed costs might include expenditures for taxes or insurance. With variable cost, the most significant factor is the cost of hydrogen as a fuel. Additionally, the maintenance costs depend on the use of FCEVs.

The monetary value of consumers' willingness to pay (WTP) can be quantified using different analytical methods. In general, these approaches can be divided into the actual (revealed) or hypothetical (stated) market behavior of the consumers. On the one hand, the preferences of customers can be revealed through their actual purchasing behavior in the markets. Using observations of actual market transactions, highly reliable and valid data on consumer preferences can be obtained (Schmidt and Bijmolt 2019). From volumes purchased as a function of market prices, one can derive the WTP of the consumers. However, such revealed preference methods require sufficiently liquid markets for the good or service in question in order to obtain the necessary data on actual consumer behavior. In the case of hydrogen-based transportation, markets with sufficient liquidity for such analyses are yet to be formed. On the other hand, analysts can use stated preference-based methods to study WTP. Particularly for goods or services where liquid markets are yet to be formed, as in this instance, such methods are the most frequently used. Among these methods are the so-called discrete choice experiments (DCE). Here, surveys are used where respondents chose their favorite option out of a set of alternative choices where different attributes (e.g., CO_2 emissions, refueling time, etc.) vary. Of these choices, analysts can derive the WTP for the good or service in question through the choices of the respondents.

For consumers to choose hydrogen-based transportation services over the available alternatives (i.e., fossil-fueled ones), its individual net utility must be the higher of the two. Currently, the TCO of hydrogen-based transportation exceeds the TCO of alternatives employing other fuels. In this case, either the WTP for hydrogen-based transportation must substantially exceed the WTP for fossil-based forms (i.e., because consumers are willing to pay more for environmentally friendlier transportation) or the TCO of hydrogen-based transportation must be substantially decreased until it is about on par with fossil-based alternatives. In either case, state regulation could lead to a situation in which the net utility of hydrogen-based transportation is maximal either by increasing net utility for hydrogen-based transportation (e.g., through subsidies) or by decreasing the net utility of fossil-fueled alternatives (e.g., through taxes). In accordance with the aforementioned observations (see Hydrogen Policy and Regulation section), a successful reduction in CO_2 emissions will require a balanced mix of these two measures.

A representative survey by Zimmer (2013a) for Germany indicates that about 83% of the population would be willing to spend about 5000 EUR more for environmentally friendlier alternatives. Translating the results of this study into TCO, environmentally friendlier mobility can exceed the TCO of fossil-fueled transportation but only by about 5000 EUR in the German case. Figure 4.9 illustrates some further results from studies on WTP for transportation. It indicates that WTP may vary greatly depending on location (country) and other characteristics (e.g., environmental concerns, refueling time, and the

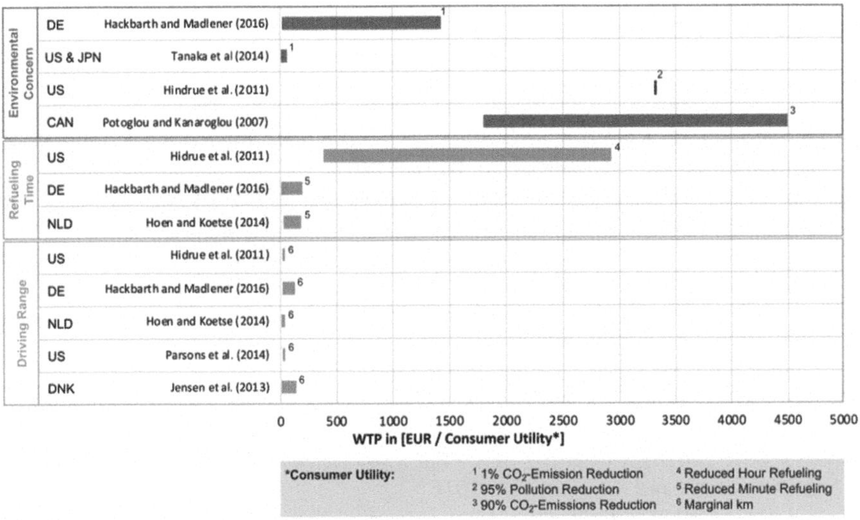

Fig. 4.9 Study results of the willingness to pay for different user aspects (Hackbarth and Madlener 2016; Tanaka et al. 2014; Hidrue et al. 2011; Hoen and Koetse 2014; Parsons et al. 2014; Jensen et al. 2013; Potoglou and Kanaroglou 2007)

driving range). According to the results, customers are willing to pay more for an alternative-fueled vehicle with reduced CO_2 emissions. Both FCEVs and BEVs might meet these requirements. However, compared to BEVs, FCEVs can offer the customer a higher degree of pain flexibility through a faster refueling process of only a few minutes, resulting in a driving range of several hundred kilometers. Although most average daily journeys are well below the range of BEVs, this flexibility remains an important criterion for vehicle purchases. Figure 4.9 shows that this directly translates into a higher WTP.

6 Conclusions

Hydrogen is a versatile energy carrier that offers numerous possibilities to decarbonize various sectors of the economy. To date, hydrogen has been used on an industrial scale worldwide but has been produced almost entirely from natural gas or coal. Hydrogen production from low-carbon energy resources is still costly, but its costs are expected to decline rapidly due to the falling costs of renewable energy and to realizing economies of scale and economies of mass production for electrolyzers (Dodds 2015). Green hydrogen is favorably received by the public and is less hazardous than fossil fuels, thus providing beneficial conditions for the technology's acceptance. Furthermore, many prospective consumers express a positive willingness-to-pay for green hydrogen services, which further reduces the utility gap for the adoption of hydrogen technologies. For these reasons, green hydrogen market entry and commercialization is receiving increasing attention from policymakers and businesses alike.

References

Abánades A., Rubbia C. and Salmieri D. (2013), *Thermal cracking of methane into Hydrogen for a CO2-free utilization of natural gas.* International Journal of Hydrogen Energy, 2013. 38(20): p. 8491–8496

Acht A. (2013), *Salzkavernen zur Wasserstoffspeicherung.* 2013: RWTH Aachen

Air Liquide AS (2018), *Safety data sheet: methane.* 2018, Air Liquide AS

Ajanovic A. and Haas R. (2018), *Economic prospects and policy framework for hydrogen as fuel in the transport sector.* Energy Policy, 2018. 123: p. 280–288

Alstom (2018), *Coradia iLint regional train.* 2018 accessed on 11.12.2017]; Available from: http://www.alstom.com/products-services/product-catalogue/rail-systems/trains/products/coradia-ilint-regional-train-/

ARENA (2019), *World-first project to turn biogas from sewage into hydrogen and graphite.* 2019, Australian Renewable Energy Agency (ARENA): ARENA media

Bayer A. et al. (2016), *Compact 1 MW PEM water electrolysis system—renewable hydrogen for mobility and energy storage.* 2016

Berstad D. (2018), *Technologies for hydrogen liquefaction*, in *Proceedings of Gasskonferansen.* 2018: Trondheim, Norway

Bleischwitz R. and Bader N. (2010), *Policies for the transition towards a hydrogen economy: the EU case.* Energy Policy, 2010. 38(10): p. 5388–5398

Bögela P. et al. (2018), *The role of attitudes in technology acceptance management: Reflections on the case of hydrogen fuel cells in Europe.* Journal of Cleaner Production, 2018. 188: p. 125–135

Brinner A. et al. (2018), *Technologiebericht 4.1 Power-to-gas (Wasserstoff)*, in *Technologien für die Energiewende. Teilbericht 2 an das Bundesministerium für Wirtschaft und Energie (BMWi).* 2018, Wuppertal Institut, ISI, IZES: Wuppertal, Karlsruhe, Saarbrücken

Cerniauskas S. et al. (2019a), *Future Hydrogen Markets for Transportation and Industry—The Impact of CO2 Taxes.* Eneriges, 2019. (Submitted)

Cerniauskas S. et al. (2019b), *Options of Natural Gas Pipeline Reassignment for Hydrogen: Cost Assessment for a Germany Case Study.* International Journal of Hydrogen Energy, 2019. (Submitted).

Collantes G. (2008), *The dimensions of the policy debate over transportation energy: The case of hydrogen in the United States.* Energy Policy, 2008. 36(3): p. 1059–1073

Crotogino F. et al. (2010), *Large-scale hydrogen underground storage for securing future energy supplies.* in *18th World Hydrogen Energy Conference (WHEC2010).* 2010. Essen, Germany

DECHEMA Gesellschaft für Chemische Technik und Biotechnologie e.V

Dodds P.E. (2015), *3—Economics of hydrogen production*, in *Compendium of Hydrogen Energy*, V. Subramani, A. Basile, and T.N. Veziroğlu, Editors. 2015, Woodhead Publishing: Oxford. p. 63–79

Dolci F. et al. (2019), *Incentives and legal barriers for power-to-hydrogen pathways: An international snapshot.* International Journal of Hydrogen Energy, 2019. 44(23): p. 11394–11401

Dorrington M. et al. (2016), *Desk study on the development of a hydrogen-fired appliance supply chain.* 2016, Kiwa, E4Tech

DVGW (2019), *Mehr Wasserstoff technisch sicher verankern*, in *DVGW-Regeln für klimafreundliche Energieinfrastruktur.* 2019, DVGW

Eikaas S. (2019), *Low carbon solutions*, in *Energirike Konferansen.* 2019

Elgowainy A. et al. (2014), *Tube-trailer consolidation strategy for reducing hydrogen refueling station costs.* International Journal of Hydrogen Energy, 2014. 39(35): p. 20197–20206

Emonts B. et al. (2019), *Flexible sector coupling with hydrogen: A climate-friendly fuel supply for road transport.* International Journal of Hydrogen Energy, 2019. 44(26): p. 12918–12930

European Parliament and Council (2018), *Directive (EU) 2018/2001 of the European Parliament and of the Council on the Promotion of the Use of Energy from Renewable Sources*, The European Parliament and T.C.o.t.E. Union, Editors. 2018

FCH JU (2016), *Clean Hydrogen in European Cities 2010–2016, Fuel Cell electric buses: A proven Zero-Emission Solution key facts, results, recommendations.* 2016, Fuel Cell Joint Undertanking (FCH JU).

Federal Institute for Materials Research and Testing (2002), *Hydrogen Safety.* Federal Institute for Materials Research and Testing, 2002, Brussels

Fernleitungsnetzbetreiber F.G.-D. (2017), *Netzentwicklungsplan Gas 2016–2026.* 2017

Fischedick M. (2017), *Energie der Zukunft?: Nachhaltige Mobilität durch Brennstoffzelle und H2.* 2017, Wuppertal Institut: Hamburg. p. 37

Fraunhofer ISI and Öko-Institute (2015), *Klimaschutzszenario 2050.* 2015, Fraunhofer ISI, Öko-Institut: Berlin

Fuel Cells Bulletin (2016), *GM marks 50 years of FCEV development, from Electrovan to Chevrolet Colorado ZH2.* Fuel Cells Bulletin, 2016. 2016(11): p. 14–15.

Fukui H. (2019), *Tracking Clean Energy Progress.* Hydrogen 2019 [08.11.2019]; Available from: https://www.iea.org/tcep/energyintegration/hydrogen/

Geres R. et al. (2019), *ROADMAP CHEMIE 2050.* 2019, FutureCamp Climate GmbH

Glenk G. and Reichelstein S. (2019), *Economics of converting renewable power to hydrogen.* Nature Energy, 2019. 4(3): p. 216–222.

Gnann T. et al. (2015), *Modelling market diffusion of electric vehicles with real world driving data—German market and policy options.* Transportation Research Part A: Policy and Practice, 2015. 77: p. 95–112.

Gupta R.B. (2008), *Hydrogen Fuel, Production, Transport and Storage.* 2008: CRC Press

H2 Tools (2019), *Contributing Factors.* Available from: https://h2tools.org/lessons

Hackbarth A. and Madlener R. (2016), *Willingness-to-pay for alternative fuel vehicle characteristics: A stated choice study for Germany.* Transportation Research Part A: Policy and Practice, 2016. 85: pp. 89–111

Hart D. et al. (2015), *Scenarios for deployment of hydrogen in contributing to meeting carbon budgets and the 2050 target.* 2015, E4tech, UCL Energy Institute, Kiwa Gastec.

Henning H.M. and Palzer (2015), *Was kostet die Energiewende? Wege zur Transformation des deutschen Energiesystems bis 2050.* Fraunhofer ISE, 2015: p. 89

Henning H.-M. and Palzer A. (2013), *Energiesystem Deutschland 2050.* 2013, Fraunhofer ISE: Freiburg.

Hess Corp (2007), *Material safety data sheet: gasoline.* 2007, Hess Corp

Heuser P.M. et al. (2019), *Techno-economic analysis of a potential energy trading link between Patagonia and Japan based on CO2 free hydrogen.* International Journal of Hydrogen Energy, 2019. 44(25): p. 12733–12747

Hidrue M.K. et al. (2011), *Willingness to pay for electric vehicles and their attributes.* Resource and Energy Economics, 2011. 33(3): p. 686–705

Hodges J. et al. (2015), *Injecting hydrogen into the gas network—a literature search.* 2015, Health and Safety Laboratory: Buxton

Hoen A. and Koetse M.J. (2014), *A choice experiment on alternative fuel vehicle preferences of private car owners in the Netherlands.* Transportation Research Part A: Policy and Practice, 2014. 61: p. 199–215

Hof E., Madlener R. and Kukla P. (2017) *Power-to-Gas for Rail Transport: Economic Evaluation and Concept for the Cost-Optimal Hydrogen Supply.* 2017, Institute for Future Energy Consumer Needs and Behavior, RWTH Aachen University: Aachen

Hua T. et al. (2014), *Status of hydrogen fuel cell electric buses worldwide.* Journal of Power Sources, 2014. 269: p. 975–993

HYACINTH (2013), *Hydrogen acceptance in the transition phase (HYACINTH).* 2013

Hydrogen Council (2017), *Hydrogen scaling up: A sustainable pathway for the global energy transition.* 2017, Hydrogen Council

IEA (2019), *The Future of Hydrogen. Seizing today's opportunities*, IEA, Paris.

Iribarren D. et al. (2016), *Assessing the social acceptance of hydrogen for transportation in Spain: An unintentional focus on target population for a potential hydrogen economy.* International Journal of Hydrogen Energy, 2016. 41(10): p. 5203–5208

ISO (2012), *ISO 14687-2: 2012: Hydrogen fuel—product specification—Part 2: Proton exchange membranes (PEM) fuel cell applications for road vehicles.* 2012

ITM Power GmbH (2018), *Wasserstoff als Nutzungsoption für Windparks.* 2018, ITM Power GmbH

ITM Power PLC (2013), *Power-to-gas A UK feasibility study*. 2013, ITM Power PLC: Sheffield

Jensen A.F., Cherchi E. and Mabit S.L. (2013), *On the stability of preferences and attitudes before and after experiencing an electric vehicle*. Transportation Research Part D: Transport and Environment, 2013. 25: p. 24–32.

Knor K. et al. (2014), *Kombikraftwerk 2*. 2014, Fraunhofer IWES, Siemens AG, University Hannover, CUBE Engineering GmbH.

Kopp M. et al. (2017), *Energiepark Mainz: Technical and economic analysis of the worldwide largest Power-to-Gas plant with PEM electrolysis*. International Journal of Hydrogen Energy, 2017. 42(19): p. 13311–13320

Krieg D. (2012), *Konzept und Kosten eines Pipelinesystems zur Versorgung des deutschen Straßenverkehrs mit Wasserstoff*. Schriften des Forschungszentrums Jülich: Reihe Energie & Umwelt. 2012, Jülich: Forschungszentrum Jülich, Zentralbibliothek. 228 Seiten

Leibowicz B.D. (2018), *Policy recommendations for a transition to sustainable mobility based on historical diffusion dynamics of transport systems*. Energy Policy, 2018. 119: p. 357–366

Linde AG (2018), *Safety data sheet: hydrogen (compressed)*. 2018, Linde AG

Machhammer O., Bode A. and Hormuth W. (2016), *Financial and Ecological Evaluation of Hydrogen Production Processes on Large Scale*. Chemical Engineering & Technology, 2016. 39(6): p. 1185–1193.

Markerta F. et al. (2017), *Risk and sustainability analysis of complex hydrogen infrastructures*. International Journal of Hydrogen Energy, 2017. 42(11): p. 7698–7706

Micheli R. and Hanke M. (2015), *Einsatz einer wasserstoffberiebenen Flurförderzeugflotte unter Produktionsbedingungen: Herausforderungen, Wirtschaftlichkeit, Nachhaltigkeit. 18.VDI-Flurförderzeugtagung 2015*, R. Micheli M.Sc., Lehrstuhl fml Dipl.-Ing. M. Hanke, Linde Material Handling AG, *22.09.2015.*, 2015.

Mischner J., Fasold H.-G. and Kadner K. (2011), *Systemplanung in der Gasversorgung Gaswirtschaftliche Grundlagen*. 2011, Munich, Germany: Oldenbourg Industrieverlag GmbH

Monolith Materials (2018), *Monolith's Seaport Plant*. [04.02.2018]; Available from: https://monolithmaterials.com/pilot-plant/

Munnings C. and Krupnick A. (2018), *Comparing Policies to Reduce Methane Emissions in the Natural Gas Sector*. 2018

New Holland Agriculture (2014), *New Holland NH2 Hydrogen Powered Tractor*. 2014, New Holland Agriculture

Offer G.J. et al. (2010), *Comparative analysis of battery electric, hydrogen fuel cell and hybrid vehicles in a future sustainable road transport system*. Energy Policy, 2010. 38(1): p. 24–29.

Ono K. and Tsunemi K. (2017), *Identification of public acceptance factors with risk perception scales on hydrogen fueling stations in Japan*. International Journal of Hydrogen Energy, 2017. 42(16): p. 10697–10707

Ono K., Kato E. and Tsunemi K. (2019), *Does risk information change the acceptance of hydrogen refueling stations in the general Japanese population?* International Journal of Hydrogen Energy, 2019. 44(31): p. 16038–16047

Otto A. et al. (2017), *Power-to-Steel: Reducing CO2 through the Integration of Renewable Energy and Hydrogen into the German Steel Industry*. Energies, 2017. 10(4): p. 451.

Parkinson B. et al. (2019), *Levelized cost of CO2 mitigation from hydrogen production routes*. Energy & Environmental Science, 2019. 12(1): p. 19–40

Parsons G.R. et al. (2014), *Willingness to pay for vehicle-to-grid (V2G) electric vehicles and their contract terms.* Energy Economics, 2014. 42: p. 313–324

Pique S. et al. (2017), *Comparative study of regulations, codes and standards and practices on hydrogen fuelling stations.* International Journal of Hydrogen Energy, 2017. 42(11): p. 7429–7439

Popov B.N., Lee J.-W. and Djukic M.B. (2018), *Chapter 7—Hydrogen Permeation and Hydrogen-Induced Cracking*, in *Handbook of Environmental Degradation of Materials (Third Edition)*, M. Kutz, Editor. 2018, William Andrew Publishing. p. 133–162

Potoglou D. and Kanaroglou P.S. (2007), *Household demand and willingness to pay for clean vehicles.* Transportation Research Part D: Transport and Environment, 2007. 12(4): p. 264–274

Pratt J. et al. (2015), *H2FIRST Reference Station Design Task.* 2015, NERL: USA

Reddi K. et al. (2017), *Impact of hydrogen SAE J2601 fueling methods on fueling time of light-duty fuel cell electric vehicles.* International Journal of Hydrogen Energy, 2017. 42(26): p. 16675–16685

Reuß M. et al. (2017), *Seasonal storage and alternative carriers: A flexible hydrogen supply chain model.* Applied Energy, 2017. 200: p. 290–302

Reuß M. et al. (2019), *A hydrogen supply chain with spatial resolution: Comparative analysis of infrastructure technologies in Germany.* Applied Energy, 2019. 247: p. 438–453

Reuss M.E. (2019), *Techno-ökonomische Analyse alternativer Wasserstoffinfrastruktur.* Schriften des Forschungszentrums Jülich Reihe Energie & Umwelt / Energy & Environment. 2019, Jülich: Forschungszentrum Jülich

Rigas F. and Amyote P. (2013), *Hydrogen Safety.* Green Chemistry and Chemical Engineering, ed. S. Lee. 2013, USA: CRS Press.

Ritter M. (2016), *Wasserstoff und Brennstoffzelle im Schienenverkehr.* 2016.

Robinius M. et al. (2017a), *Linking the Power and Transport Sectors—Part 2: Modelling a Sector Coupling Scenario for Germany.* Energies, 2017. 10(7): p. 957

Robinius M. et al. (2017b), *Linking the Power and Transport Sectors—Part 1: The Principle of Sector Coupling.* Energies, 2017. 10(7): p. 956

Roche M.Y. et al. (2010), *Public attitudes towards and demand for hydrogen and fuel cell vehicles: A review of the evidence and methodological implications.* Energy Policy, 2010. 38(10): p. 5301–5310

Rodrígueza, M.L.Á., et al. (2019), *The legal regulation of the H2 as a strategy for public policy in Mexico from the consolidation of the National Council of the hydrogen.* International Journal of Hydrogen Energy, 2019. 44(24): p. 12303–1230

Roland Berger (2015), *Fuel Cell Electric Buses—Potential for Sustainable Public Transport in Europe.* 2015, Fuel Cells and hydrogen joint undertaking (FCHJU).

Saba S. M. et al. (2018), *The investment costs of electrolysis—A comparison of cost studies from the past 30 years.* International Journal of Hydrogen Energy, 2018. 43(3): p. 1209–1223

SAE (2014), *SAE J2601, Fueling Protocols for Light Duty Gaseous Hydrogen Surface Vehicles.* 2014, SAE

Sarsfield-Hall R. and Unger B. (2019), *Hydrogen from natural gas—The key to deep decarbonisation.* 2019, Zukunft ERDGAS.

Schenuit C., Heuke R. and Paschke J. (2016), *Potenzialatlas Power to Gas.* 2016, Deutsche Energie-Agentur GmbH (dena)

Schmidt J. and Bijmolt T.H.A. (2019), *Accurately measuring willingness to pay for consumer goods: a meta-analysis of the hypothetical bias.* Journal of the Academy of Marketing Science, 2019

Schmidt O. et al. (2017a), *Future cost and performance of water electrolysis: An expert elicitation study.* International Journal of Hydrogen Energy, 2017. 42(52): p. 30470–30492

Schmidt O. et al. (2017b), *The future cost of electrical energy storage based on experience rates.* Nature Energy, 2017. 2.

Shehata M.T., Elboujdaini M. and Revie R.W. (2008), *Initiation of stress corrosion cracking and hydrogen-induced cracking in oil and gas line-pipe*, in *Safety, Reliability and Risks Associated with Water, Oil and Gas Pipelines* G. Pluvinage and M.H. Elwany, Editors. 2008

Smolinka T. et al. (2018), *Study IndWEDe—Brief Overview.* 2018, NOW GmbH

Spillet and IFOK (2016), *HyTrustPlus.* 2016, NOW GmbH: Berlin

SRI (2007), *Industrial Gases*, in: Chemical Economics Handbook.

Staffell I. (2015), *Zero carbon infinite COP heat from fuel cell CHP.* Applied Energy, 2015. 147: p. 373–385.

Tanaka M. et al. (2014), *Consumers' willingness to pay for alternative fuel vehicles: A comparative discrete choice analysis between the US and Japan.* Transportation Research Part A: Policy and Practice, 2014. 70: p. 194–209

Tlili O. et al. (2020), *Geospatial modelling of the hydrogen infrastructure in France in order to identify the most suited supply chains.* International Journal of Hydrogen Energy, 2020. 45(4): p. 3053–3072.

Tractebel and Hinicio (2017), *Study of early business cases for H2 in energy storage and more broadly power to H2 applications.* 2017, Fuel Cells and Hydrogen Joint Undertaking (FCH JU)

Weidner E., Ortiz Cebolla R. and Davies J. (2019), *Global deployment of large capacity stationary fuel cells*, in *JRC Technical Reports.* 2019, Joint Research Centre (JRC)

Weiner S.C. and Fassbender L.L. (2011), *Lessons Learned from Safety Events*, in *International Conference on Hydrogen Safety (ICHS2011).* 2011

Welder L. et al. (2018), *Spatio-temporal optimization of a future energy system for power-to-hydrogen applications in Germany.* Energy, 2018. 158: p. 1130–1149

Williams T.I. (1981), *A History of British Gas Industry.* 1981, Oxford, UK: Oxford University Press

Wulf C. et al. (2018a), *Life Cycle Assessment of hydrogen transport and distribution options.* Journal of Cleaner Production, 2018. 199: p. 431–443

Wulf C., Linßen J. and Zapp P. (2018b), *Review of Power-to-Gas Projects in Europe.* Energy Procedia, 2018. 155: p. 367–378.

Yang C. and Odgen J.M. (2007), *Determining the lowest-cost hydrogen delivery mode.* International Journal of Hydrogen Energy, 2007. 32(2): p. 268–286

Zaunbrecher B.S. et al. (2016), *What is Stored, Why, and How? Mental Models, Knowledge, and Public Acceptance of Hydrogen Storage.* Energy Procedia, 2016. 99: p. 108–119

Zhu X. et al. (2018), *Two-train elevated-temperature pressure swing adsorption for high-purity hydrogen production.* Applied Energy, 2018. 229: p. 1061–1071

Zimmer D.R. (2013a), *Auf dem Weg in die Wasserstoffgesellschaft*, 2013

Zimmer R. (2013b), *HyTrust Auf dem Weg in die Wasserstoffgesellschaft.* 2013, Unabhängiges Institut für Umweltfragen e.V.

Zweifel P., Praktiknjo A. and Erdmann G. (2017), *Energy economics.* 2017, New York, NY: Springer Science+Business Media

CHAPTER 5

Economics of Power Generation

Manfred Hafner and Giacomo Luciani

Electricity can be generated either chemically (as in photovoltaic panels) or, more frequently, mechanically, through the rotary movement of a generator (a magnet moving within a net of cables). The needed rotary movement can be obtained by the force of steam expanding at high temperature, water flowing, or wind blowing in a turbine; or even by using a regular internal combustion engine. The high temperature needed to raise steam can be derived from burning coal, oil, gas, waste and biomass; from controlled fission in a nuclear reactor; by concentrating solar radiation; or by extracting heat from the earth crust. The bottom line is that there are numerous solutions to generate electricity, and each of them has specific characteristics that render it more adapted to the specific conditions and circumstances where and when electricity is required.

In order to provide a satisfactory treatment of power generation technology and economics, a single chapter would have expanded beyond a practical dimension: accordingly the discussion has been divided into a general

M. Hafner (✉)
SciencesPo—Paris School of International Affairs, Paris, France

Johns Hopkins University SAIS Europe, Bologna, Italy

Fondazione Eni Enrico Mattei (FEEM), Milan, Italy
e-mail: Manfred.hafner@sciencespo.fr

G. Luciani
SciencesPo—Paris School of International Affairs, Paris, France

Graduate Institute of International and Development Studies, Geneva, Switzerland
e-mail: giacomo.luciani@sciencespo.fr

M. Hafner, G. Luciani (eds.), *The Palgrave Handbook of International Energy Economics*, https://doi.org/10.1007/978-3-030-86884-0_5

introduction and a sequence of specific chapters each devoted to a different generation solution: thermal power based on fossil fuels (coal, oil, and gas)—Chap. 6; thermal power based on nuclear fission—Chap. 7; hydroelectricity—Chap. 8; solar power—Chap. 9; wind power—Chap. 10; geothermal power—Chap. 11; and power from tides and waves—Chap. 12. In this introductory chapter, we touch upon the major economic differences between these multiple solutions, highlighting the comparative advantages and disadvantages of each. In the end, a well-functioning electricity system will always necessitate a combination of different technologies assorted in an appropriate way to satisfy a range of situations that are expected to arise in time.

When discussing electricity and comparing different power generation technologies and their properties, the reader must first and foremost keep in mind the distinction between *capacity* (or power) and *energy (or electricity generated* or consumed). Capacity (or power) is the electricity that a generation plant produces (or an electricity device consumes) instantaneously. It is measured in watts, kilowatts (1 kW = 1000 watts), megawatts (MW: 1 MW = 1000 kW), and gigawatts (1 GW = 1000 MW). The installed (or nominal) capacity of a power plant is (generally) the maximum capacity of a power plant. The amount of electricity a power plant produces (or an electricity device consumes) over a given time is measured in kilowatt-hours (kWh). Kilowatt-hours are determined by multiplying the number of kW produced (required) by the number of hours of production (use). Energy is thus the amount of electricity generated (consumed) over time and is measured in watt-hour, kilowatt-hour (kWh), megawatt-hour (MWh), gigawatt-hour (GWh), and terawatt-hour (TWh).

Unlike coal, oil, or gas, electricity cannot be stored easily. It must thus be generated and delivered at the precise moment it is needed. The most important element to be considered when addressing power generation is the *demand load curve*. A load curve shows the variation of load (in kW or MW) over time (in hours). The load curve can be plotted for 24 hours a day, it is then called a daily load curve; if one year is considered, it is called annual load curve. The load curve is important because the electricity capacity demanded by consumers (industry, residential, and commercial) varies over time. Typically, industrial activities are the highest during the day, commercial activities are high during the day and the early evening hours, and residential activities are high mainly in the evening when everybody is at home and turns on the lights, watches television, and uses other electric devices.

The resulting daily load curve of a country is one with a low level during the night and a higher level during the day with some peaks either during the day or in the evening hours. Moreover, the load curve differs from day to day (on weekends and festivities when industrial activities are reduced, the load curve is generally lower) and across seasons (in cold climates, electricity load is higher during the winter months due to heating, while in hot climates, it may be highest in summer months due to cooling). Some high-income countries with a relatively temperate climate may nowadays have two seasonal peaks: a winter peak due to heating and a summer peak due to cooling. The load curve thus differs from country to country due to cultural and meteorological differences. The integral (surface) below the load curve represents the electricity demand (electricity demand = capacity × time = kW × h = kWh).

All of this is of utmost importance because the load curve will define the amount of the electricity demand which is *base load* (load needed all year), *peak load* (load needed only a few hours a day), and *intermediate load (or mid-load)* for operating hours between base load and peak load. Different power plants with their different repartition of capital cost and operating cost will be used to satisfy different load segments.

All power generation plants are relatively capital-intensive, in the sense that the initial investment costs are a significant and frequently dominant component of total cost; however, the *ratio of capital vs. operating costs* varies significantly: it is highest for nuclear, wind, solar, large coal-fired, and some hydropower plants and smallest for gas turbines or plants based on internal combustion engines. Nuclear, coal-fired, and hydropower plants with large reservoirs are available for many hours, and it is convenient to keep them in use for as many hours as possible, in order to amortize the very high capital cost over the maximum number of hours and reduce the unit cost of producing each kilowatt-hour. The same would be true for solar and wind, except that these plants are non-dispatchable; therefore, the operator cannot control the extent of their use. Consequently, nuclear, coal-fired, and some hydropower plants are optimal to meet base load demand. In contrast, gas turbine power plants or generators based on internal combustion engines are typically preferred for meeting demand peaks or dealing for emergency situations, for example, in islands or other isolated tourist destinations during the high season, or in hospitals in case electricity from the grid is no longer available. Hydroelectric plants with small storage will be used during peak hours due to the high opportunity cost of these plants.

A further distinction of importance is between *indirect* and *direct* operating costs. Indirect costs are related to the upkeep of the plant independently of how much the plant is being used and are typically incurred on a yearly basis. In contrast, direct costs are directly related to the utilization of the plant, for example, the cost of fuel in a coal- or oil-fired thermal plant or in a gas turbine plant. Indirect costs are fixed and fundamentally unavoidable, while direct costs are directly related to the production of power. Hence, both capital and indirect costs are not part of *marginal* cost, which is the cost of producing one additional KWh of power, and exclusively reflects direct costs. Hence, some technologies, notably solar, wind, and most hydropower plants, have zero marginal costs, and nuclear has low marginal costs because the cost of fuel per kWh produced is very small. To the opposite extreme, gas turbines or internal combustion engine-based plants have significant marginal costs and will only be started if demand justifies it.

A generation plant will not always generate at full capacity: there will be times when it generates at less than full capacity, and times when it is not in use and does not generate at all. This may be due to the load curve or intrinsic non-availability by some plants (the most obvious are solar and wind availability for plants relying on these energy sources).

How much electricity will be produced by a plant of a given installed (or nominal) capacity depends on the number of hours that the plant is available for production (***availability***) and the number of available hours that the plant is actually in use.

There are 8760 hours in a year, and no power plant can be available throughout the year. Some plants may be available most of the time in a year (coal-fired, nuclear, biomass, geothermal, run-of-river hydroelectric plants, or hydroelectric plants with a very large reservoir of water) and may be relied upon for close to 8000 hours (due to maintenance and other outages they cannot operate all hours of the year).

Other plants, in contrast, are necessarily limited in their availability: for example, solar photovoltaic panels only produce electricity during the day and will produce very little when the sun is low over the horizon or it is covered by clouds, meaning that even in the best imaginable conditions, a photovoltaic panel cannot possibly reach 3000 hours of availability, and in many locations may be available for as little as 1000 hours. Similarly, a hydropower plant with a small reservoir (e.g. in the Alps) may only be able to produce electricity at nominal capacity for 2–3000 hours in the year.

The difference between the last two cases is that in the case of a hydropower plant the operator may normally decide when to use the plant using an opportunity cost approach (i.e. to decide when to "spend" the limited plant's hours of availability in order to maximize revenues), while in the case of solar photovoltaic the operator has no control at all on the availability, and electricity may be produced when it is needed, but possibly also when it is not needed. Hence a further key difference between various technologies is ***dispatchability***. Some technologies (notably thermal power plants, independently of the source of heat, and hydropower plants with large reservoirs) are fully dispatchable, in the sense that the operator decides when the plant is in operation. At the opposite extreme, some technologies are not dispatchable at all (wind, solar, and hydro run-of-the-river, i.e. with no reservoir), and electricity is produced when the appropriate natural conditions exist, and not at other times.

This distinction is important because, as already mentioned, the demand and supply of electricity in a grid must be balanced at all times in real time. The power producer (or the manager of the grid, called a Transmission System Operator or TSO) has little or no control over demand and must adjust supply to demand—a task made considerably more difficult if power is produced from non-dispatchable technologies. The details of this are discussed in Chap. 13 on the economics of networks, and the integration of non-dispatchable renewables is discussed in Chap. 15. The issue of non-coincidence of demand and supply highlights the importance of electricity storage, which is limited and expensive: this is discussed in Chap. 14 as far as battery storage is concerned and in Chap. 8 as far as pumped storage is concerned (so far the only way to store electricity by converting it to potential energy).

Producing peak load electricity is more expensive than producing base load electricity; in the first case, an equipment needs to be built which only runs a few hours a day, and in the latter case, investments can be amortized producing electricity almost all year. Even though in physics a kWh is equal to a kWh regardless when and where it is consumed, in economic terms a kWh is not equal to a kWh. The cost of producing a kWh depends on the moment when it is consumed and thus when it needs to be produced since it cannot be easily and cheaply stored.

This time element of demand (and thus production) is relevant not only for *power plant dispatching*, but also for *future capacity planning*. If overall demand of electricity in a country increases by a certain amount of TWh but most demand increase is expected to happen during peak hours, the required power plant investments will be fundamentally different compared to the case where the demand increase happens mainly during low load hours thus increasing base load.

A distinction needs to be made between capacity investment planning in order to satisfy future electricity demand evolutions and dispatching existing and available power plants for the hour or day ahead. For future capacity planning, a full cost (or *long-run marginal cost*) approach needs to be taken (including investment cost, operating and maintenance cost, fuel costs, and possibly the cost of carbon emissions—as well as possibly other costs aimed at internalizing environmental and other externalities), while for dispatching purposes, only the short-run marginal costs (fuel costs and other unit-based environmental costs) are taken into account. The choice of power generation technology (and thus energy) being used on a given moment of the day depends thus on the merit order (marginal costs) of the different power plants to satisfy demand. For dispatching purposes, all fixed costs are to be considered sunk cost.

With increasingly large shares of non-dispatchable power generation sources in electricity producing systems, flexibility mechanisms become of utmost importance. Non-dispatchable power generation means (e.g. wind and solar) are always first in the merit order, thanks to their zero short-run marginal cost, but they are largely not reliable in the sense that whenever the sun shines and the wind blows, you will use them, but whenever the sun does not shine and the wind does not blow, they are not available. In fact, dispatchable power plants no longer need to follow the "demand load curve" as defined by consumers, but the so-called net load curve, that is, the difference between the load curve as demanded by consumers and the electricity produced by non-dispatchable zero marginal cost electricity (mainly solar and wind). The net load curve is much less predictable and has much higher ramp up and ramp down requirements compared to the load curve of consumers. Needed *flexibility* mechanisms include (i) the capability of power plants to ramp up and ramp down quickly (storage hydroelectric and, to a slightly lesser extent, gas turbine power plants can ramp down/up very quickly, while steam turbine-based power plants [in particular large coal and even more so nuclear plants] are not well suited for fast ramp up/down of power output), (ii) interconnections to neighboring electricity systems, (iii) storage (so far mainly pump-storage, but in the future possibly to some extent also batteries), (iv) electricity demand side management (in particular demand response), and (v) sector coupling (e.g. power to heat, power to gas, power to vehicles).

A further differentiating characteristic is *size*, as measured by the plant's capacity. For some technologies, notably coal-fired and nuclear plants, economies of scale are potentially very important, favoring the construction of very large power plants (in excess of 1 GW of capacity). However, nuclear power plants can also be medium or small size (including less than 100 MW), and in fact, there is growing interest toward such smaller nuclear alternatives. Gas turbine-based plants can be small (gas turbines—GT) or medium size (combined cycle power plants—GTCC). Individual wind turbines are small (today up to 10 MW) and individual photovoltaic panels very small. Hydropower plants can be of all sizes: the largest power plants in the world are hydroelectric, but hydro solutions are available also for very small applications in locations where the grid does not reach.

Another relevant dimension of size is *space occupation* and the physical impact on the immediate environment. Hydropower plants with large reservoirs may entail the flooding of vast surfaces and the need to relocate large numbers of people, an obvious drawback. Large solar power plants also occupy very large surfaces for relatively limited capacity, an obstacle to their deployment in cultivated, forested, or inhabited spaces that are in demand for other purposes. This is one of the reasons why large solar power plants tend to be proposed for desert regions, where space has limited alternative potential use (the other reason is that in dry desert areas solar radiation is very high). To the opposite extreme, nuclear power plants are very small relatively to the very large capacity that they can reach, especially where several plants are grouped in a single location, as is frequently the case.

A final important characteristic is *locational constraints*. Some technologies are available only in specific locations, this being most evidently the case of hydro, but conditions for wind and solar are also greatly variable depending on latitude, meteorology, and orography. This is important because electricity is expensive and difficult to transport over long distances, and plants must be sized in view of the total demand that they can effectively reach and satisfy economically. Thus, some very promising locations for hydro, wind, and solar remain underexploited or unexploited because no demand is geographically close enough to justify creating transmission capacity and a generation plant.

In contrast, thermal power plants are extremely flexible from the point of view of their localization, as they basically only need proximity to a body of water for cooling purposes. Historically, this has allowed industry to be localized in the proximity of markets, or where other factors of production, notably labor, are present at low cost; while in past centuries, when energy was predominantly available in kinetic form, industry clustered in the proximity of energy sources (mostly flowing water). With increased reliance on renewable sources (solar, wind, and hydro) the pendulum may, at least to some extent, swing back to localizing industry close to the source of energy, with potentially momentous consequences on the international distribution of industrial production, especially in sectors that are highly energy-intensive.

CHAPTER 6

Power Generation from Coal, Oil, Gas, and Biofuels

Arash Farnoosh

1 Introduction

This chapter provides an introduction to the economics of electricity generation based on four different energy sources: coal, oil, natural gas, and biofuel. It covers the various technologies of power production and their key economics characteristics including CAPEX, OPEX, dispatchability, flexibility, location, and expected service life. The formula and calculations are provided for further analysis of power generation projects in view of optimizing the choice of technology. Some conclusions are drawn from comparative analysis of coal-, oil-, gas-, and biofuel-fired power generation units.

Thermal power has always accounted for a large proportion of the world's power generation. It has been above 60% since the 1990s. Since 1875, when the world's first thermal power plant was built at the *Gare du Nord* station in Paris, which supplied the lighting nearby, the world's power industry has gradually evolved toward better performances and larger capacities.

Currently, the world's largest coal-fired power plant by installed capacity is the Toketo power plant in China, the largest gas-fired power plant is Russia's Surgut plant, and finally, the largest oil-fired power plant is Saudi Arabia's Shoaiba power station (Table 6.1).

Coal, oil, and natural gas have always been the main energy sources to produce electricity (Fig. 6.1). Although with the increase of environmental

A. Farnoosh (✉)
IFPEN, IFP School, Paris, France

SciencesPo—Paris School of International Affairs, Paris, France
e-mail: arash.farnoosh@ifpen.fr

M. Hafner, G. Luciani (eds.), *The Palgrave Handbook of International Energy Economics*, https://doi.org/10.1007/978-3-030-86884-0_6

Table 6.1 The world's top 10 thermal power plants

Power station	*Fuel*	*Installed capacity (MW)*
Toketo, Inner Mongolia, China	Coal	6720
Taian power station, South Korea	Coal	6100
Tanjin power station, South Korea	Coal	6000
Taichung power station, China	Coal	5700
Shoaiba, Saudi Arabia	Oil	5600
Surgut-2 power station, Russia	Natural Gas	5597
Belchiatov, Poland	Coal	5300
Jebel Ali Power and Desalination Plant, UAE	Natural Gas	5163
Higashi-Niigata power station, Japan	Natural Gas	5149
Jiaxing power plant, China	Coal	5120

http://dy.163.com/v2/article/detail/EEM9SO3F05484WS6.html

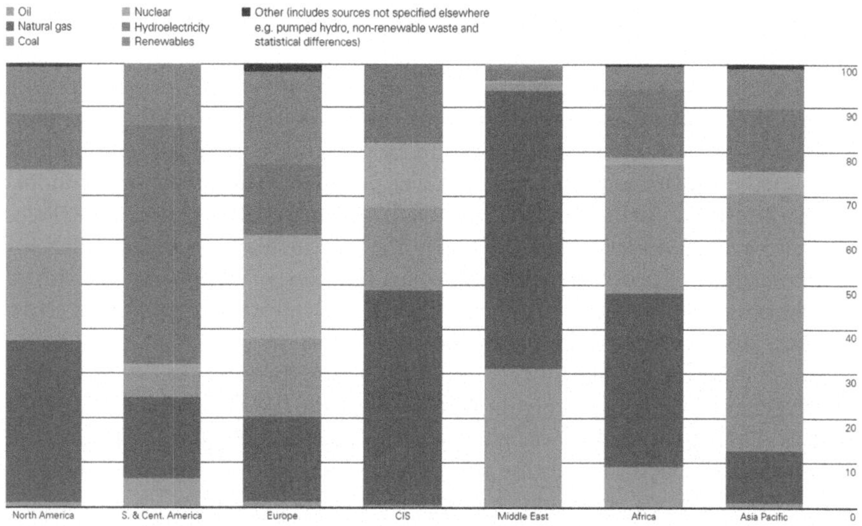

Fig. 6.1 Regional electricity generation by fuel (in percentage) in 2019. BP Statistical Review of World Energy 2020

protection awareness, renewable energy has gradually come into play, the position of fossil energy sources in producing electricity is still unshakable.

Coal accounts for around 40% of electricity production globally, making it the most important power generation fuel in the world, and is a major source of carbon dioxide emissions. It has achieved its pre-eminence because it is cheap and widely available. Coal has been used as a source of energy for over 4000 years, but electricity production from coal only began at the end of the nineteenth century. Initially, it was based on steam engines, but with the development of the steam turbine, coal became the major means of electricity generation during the twentieth century. Many nations have built their prosperity based on coal. The largest users of domestic coal for power generation are China, the United States, and India.

Currently, natural gas power accounts for 23.23% of total electricity generation and is forecasted to grow constantly. Due to the growth of global carbon emissions and the intensification of greenhouse effects around the world, several countries are actively taking measures to abate emissions. These have frequently used natural gas to replace coal, as its associated carbon dioxide emissions are 54% of those originating from coal-fired plants on average.

In a gas-fired power station, air goes through a compressor, is mixed with natural gas in the combustion chamber, and burned. The hot combustion gases expand, driving the gas turbines and turning the generators to produce electricity. The waste gases are emitted to the atmosphere through the stack but can also be recycled in a steam generation unit so as to run a steam turbine in parallel. (This is called a combined cycle gas turbine plant, or CCGT.)

Oil can be used for power generation in a plant very similar to a natural gas one.

Whether it is coal, natural gas, oil, or biomass energy, they all have a common feature, that is, they turn the turbine through combustion so that thermal energy can be converted into mechanical energy and then further converted into electric energy, thus realizing the transition from primary to secondary energy. Natural gas can be recycled through air cycling and condensation.

From the environmental protection point of view, natural gas and biomass are cleaner than coal concerning CO_2 emission. However, from the perspective of the total cost of electricity produced, a coal plant is the cheapest, and a gas-fired plant comes just after, because gas is more expensive to produce, transport, and store, even though it is the most efficient among all other types of power plants.

In the following, we discuss the power generation process of these different types of power plants in details.

2 Alternative Electricity Generation Options

2.1 Coal Power Plants

2.1.1 The History of Coal-Fired Power Generation

The use of coal for power generation began in the United States in the 1880s, based on the same technology that was then used to create mechanical power from the steam engine. Coal was burned to raise steam and the steam used to drive an engine, which in turn drove a dynamo or alternator, which produced electricity. The first fully commercial electric power station was the Pearl Street station in New York, which was built by Thomas Edison and started operating in 1882. The Pearl Street plant used a Porter Allen reciprocating steam engine and dynamo to produce a direct current, which supplied power only for lighting.

The next major advancement was the steam turbine, which was invented by Charles Parsons in 1884. Steam turbines allowed more efficient energy conversion and higher outputs. During the twentieth century, coal-fired power stations using steam turbines became the most important source of electricity across the globe. They remain the single most important source of electricity in the second decade of the twenty-first century.

2.1.2 Global Coal-Fired Electricity Generation

World coal production increased in 2018 by 250 Mt., an increase of 3.3%, driven by increases in steam and coking coal production.

Global coal production increased by 4.3% in 2018, significantly above the 10-year average of 1.3% (Fig. 6.2). Production growth was concentrated in Asia Pacific (163 Mtoe) with China accounting for half of global growth and Indonesian production up by 51 Mtoe. China has been the world's leading coal producer since 1985 and retained the top spot in 2018, producing 3550 Mt. of coal in total, 4.5% higher than in 2017. Production in the United States decreased by 2.5% in 2018, continuing the long-term trend that has seen it fall by more than one-third since 2008.

Coal consumption increased by 1.4% in 2018, the fastest growth since 2013. Growth was again driven by Asia Pacific (71 Mtoe), and particularly by India (36 Mtoe). This region now accounts for over three-quarters of global consumption, while 10 years ago it represented two-thirds.

At a global level, coal still accounts for 38% of power generation, the same share as two decades ago. Coal continues to be primarily used, at 66.5%, for electricity production and commercial heat. However, in OECD countries, the share of electricity and heat produced from primary coal as a fuel fell to 25.2% in 2018, down from 44.4% in 1985.

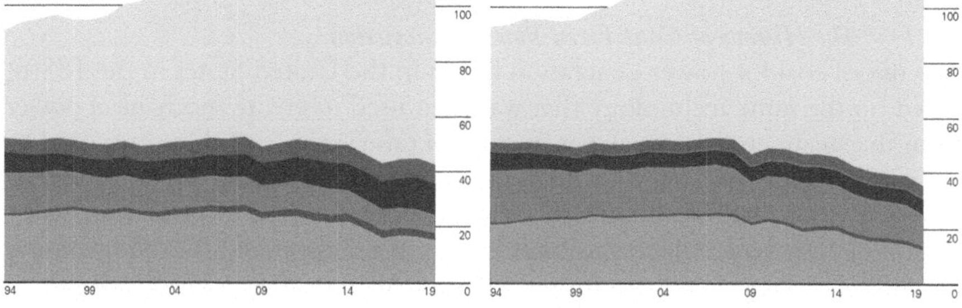

Fig. 6.2 Coal: Production (left) and Consumption (right) by region (Million tonnes oil equivalent). BP Statistical Review of World Energy 2020

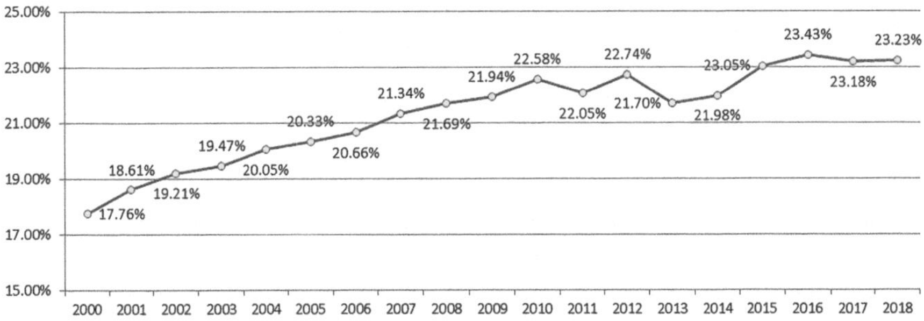

Fig. 6.3 The share of natural gas power generation in global total electricity generation. BP Statistical Review of World Energy 2020

2.2 *Global Gas Power Generation*

2.2.1 Status Quo

It can be seen from the line chart (Fig. 6.3) that the share of natural gas compared to other power generation sources globally has shown a gradual upward trend in the past two decades. Due to the growth of carbon emissions and intensification of the greenhouse effect around the world, several countries have used natural gas to replace coal.

The shale gas revolution in the United States has led to a sharp increase in natural gas supply and drop in prices, thus significantly reducing the cost of natural gas; this, coupled with the fact that natural gas power plants are easier and lower cost to build than coal-fired power plants and have less pollution emissions, resulted in a sharp increase in the proportion of natural gas power generation. In 2019, the United States gas power generation accounted for 27% of the world's total generation from gas, and for 6% of world's total power generation.

Russia is also rich in natural gas resources and suitable for gas power generation but ranks second in the world. Ranked third, Japan uses imported liquefied natural gas to boost its gas power generation, which itself has stimulated the development of the global LNG industry. However, Japan has the largest number of gas-fired power stations, which began using imported liquefied natural gas to generate electricity as early as the 1970s. Seven of the world's top 10 gas power stations are situated in Japan.

There are great differences in the share of natural gas power generation in the energy mix in different regions of the world (Table 6.2). The share of natural gas in power generation is the highest in the Middle East (around 63%) followed by the CIS countries (mainly Russia and Ukraine). Due to the great differences in oil and natural gas reserves among different countries, the proportion of natural gas power generation in each country is also quite different (Table 6.3). In 2019, natural gas power generation accounted for 3%

Table 6.2 Share of natural gas power generation in total power generation in the world in 2019

	North America	*S. & Cent. America*	*Europe*	*CIS*	*Middle East*	*Africa*	*Asia Pacific*
Total power generation (terawatt-hours)	5426	1329	3993	1431	1264	870	12,691
Gas power generation (terawatt-hours)	1976	245	768	693	793	340	1483
Percentage	36%	18%	18%	48%	63%	40%	12%

BP Statistical Review of World Energy 2020

Table 6.3 Share of natural gas power generation in the total power generation in 2019 (in selected countries)

	US	*Canada*	*Germany*	*UK*	*Russia*	*Iran*	*South Africa*	*China*	*Japan*	*India*
Total power generation (terawatt-hours)	4401	660	612	324	1118	319	253	7503	1037	1559
Gas power generation (terawatt-hours)	1701	69	91	133	520	200	2	236	362	71
Percentage	38%	10%	15%	40%	47%	63%	1%	3%	35%	5%

BP Statistical Review of World Energy 2020

of China's domestic electricity generation, compared with 38%, 47%, and 35% in the United States, Russia, and Japan, respectively.

This is also related to domestic resources and energy policies. For example, in countries such as Turkmenistan, Qatar, and Malaysia, natural gas production is quite high, while coal and water resources are limited, and natural gas power generation accounts for more than 70% of total electricity production. Countries such as Argentina and the Netherlands, despite their high natural gas production, have other sources of electricity, and around 50% of their electricity is produced by gas. Countries with 20% to 40% of power production from gas are the United Kingdom, Japan, and Italy, while countries such as South Korea and Hungary account for 10% to 20%.

2.2.2 *Future Plans*

The trend of global natural gas power generation in the future may depend on the policy adjustment of countries to deal with global climate change and the flexibility of natural gas power generation required by the instability of new renewable sources (wind and solar), but the price of natural gas is high and discourages its larger application to power generation.

On the whole, natural gas power generation has many advantages, such as energy saving and emission reduction, improving power supply security, cutting peaks and filling valleys of power and gas supply, and promoting the development of a circular economy, which is an irreversible trend in the field of modern energy. With the growth of global power consumption in the future, the absolute amount of natural gas consumption for power generation is bound to grow further. Although the growth rate has slowed, it will still account for the largest share of added power generation capacity in the world in the next decade or so.

According to multiple scenarios, the overall rise in global electricity demand drives the rise in natural gas demand; notwithstanding the fact that the proportion of natural gas in the power industry is likely relatively flat at about 20%.

2.3 Biofuel-Based Power Generation

2.3.1 Current Situation

Biomass, which is a renewable energy source that has the potential of being CO_2 neutral, is normally used for power generation in association with other fuels in so-called co-firing systems.

There are several successful co-firing projects in many parts of the world, particularly in Europe and North America. However, despite their remarkable commercial success in Europe, most of the biomass co-firing in North America is limited to demonstration levels.

Biofuels can be divided into four categories. First-generation biofuels can be produced from rapeseed, grains, potatoes, sugar beets, and canes. These biofuels are made from oil-based plants, starch crops, and sugar. The fuel industry has to compete with the nutrition and fodder industries for these products. On the other hand, the production of second-generation biofuel is essential for limiting food versus fuel competition by using non-edible oil feedstock such as agricultural waste and residues. Second-generation biofuels are produced from non-nutrition products, mainly from straw, miscanthus, sedges, and energetic plantations, mostly from agriculture and forestry residues. The third-generation biofuels derived from oleaginous microorganisms have also gained attraction recently as the potential feedstock in generating fuel for energy production. They do not compete with food crops on arable land. Algae can be cultivated in wastewater and other residual water. Finally, fourth-generation biofuels are produced from genetically modified (GM) algae to enhance biofuel production. Although GM algae biofuel is a well-known alternative to fossil fuels, the potential environmental and health-related risks are still of great concern.

2.3.2 *Process and Technology Status*

Co-firing is regarded as the most attractive short-term option for power generation from biomass. It is defined as the blending and simultaneous combustion of biomass with other fuels, such as coal or natural gas, to raise steam and generate electricity. Biomass co-firing in coal power plants is by far more widespread and extensively proven than in gas-fired plants. Co-firing can play an important role in increasing the share of biomass and renewable sources in the global energy mix and reducing greenhouse gas (GHG) emissions. It also creates opportunities in industries like forestry, agriculture, construction, manufacturing, food processing, and transportation to better manage large quantities of agricultural and wood waste. The cost of adapting an existing coal power plant to co-fire biomass is significantly lower than the cost of building new systems relying only on biomass. Although a biomass dedicated plant offers significant environmental benefits, relying solely on biomass is risky due to unpredictable feedstock supply. Other constraints of generating power solely from biomass are the low heating values and the fuel's low bulk densities, which create the need to transport large volumes of biomass.

Co-firing includes three major technologies: direct, indirect, and parallel. The approaches differ in terms of the boiler system design as well as the percentage of biomass to be co-fired.

Direct co-firing is the simplest, cheapest, and commonest option. Biomass can either be milled jointly with the coal (i.e. typically less than 5% in terms of energy content) or pre-milled and then fed separately into the same boiler. Common or separate burners can be used, with the second option enabling more flexibility with regard to biomass type and quantity. Figure 6.4 shows that in direct co-firing technology, biomass is fed directly into the furnace after being milled either together with the base fuel or separately.

Indirect co-firing is a less common process in which a gasifier converts the solid biomass into a fuel gas that is then burned with coal in the same boiler. Though more expensive because of the additional technical equipment (i.e. the gasifier), this option allows for a greater variety and higher percentages of biomass to be used. Gas cleaning and filtering is needed to remove impurities before burning, and the ashes of the two fuels remain separate.

Finally, parallel co-firing requires a separate biomass-fired boiler that supplies steam to the same steam cycle. This method allows for high biomass percentages and is frequently used in pulp and paper industrial facilities to make use of by-products from paper production, such as bark and waste wood. In parallel, biomass co-firing technology, as shown in Fig. 6.5, biomass

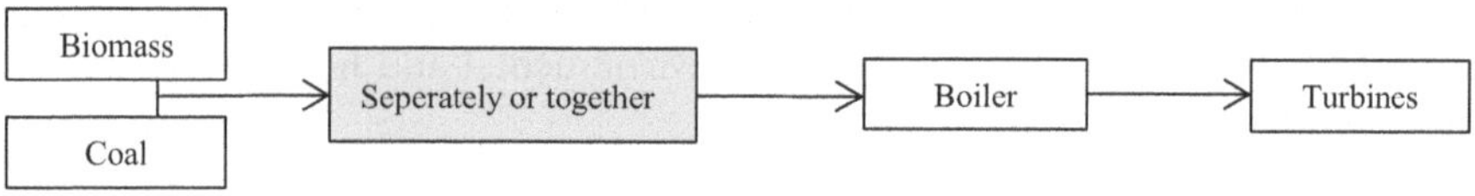

Fig. 6.4 Direct biomass co-firing technologies

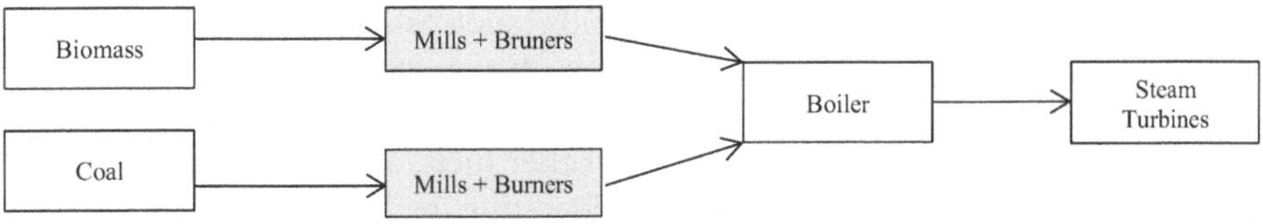

Fig. 6.5 Parallel biomass co-firing technologies

pre-processing, feeding, and combustion activities are carried out in separate biomass burners. Parallel co-firing involves the installation of a completely separate external biomass-fired boiler in order to produce steam used to generate electricity in the power plant.

2.4 Oil-Fired Power Stations

2.4.1 Role at Present

Similar to natural gas, oil is burned at power plants to create heat, which is then used to raise steam and turn turbines and create electricity. There are three kinds of oil products mostly used as power plant fuel: crude oil, diesel oil, and heavy fuel oil.

Crude oil is extracted directly from the oil well in the purest condition. It forms the basis of all petroleum products, and it has more than 500 components. According to its sulfur content, crude oil can be "sweet" (low sulfur content) or "sour" (high sulfur content).

Diesel oil is a blend of different middle distillates derived from the crude oil refining process. It is usually composed of light and heavy gas oil, light and heavy cycle oil, as well as vacuum gas oil.

Heavy fuel oil (HFO), also known as "residual fuel oil", is based on the high viscosity, tar-like mass, which remains after the distillation and subsequent cracking of crude oil in the refining process. As a residual product, HFO is relatively inexpensive—it typically costs 30% less than distillate fuels and less than crude oil.

Oil-fired power plants commonly emit nitrous and sulfur oxides, methane, mercury compounds, and significant amounts of carbon dioxide. Similar to gas-fired and coal-fired plants, oil-fired plants require large quantities of water for the production of steam and for cooling. The use of oil at power plants also results in residues called sludge that are not completely burned and therefore require disposal in landfills.

Roughly, 70% of oil-fired electric generating capacity that still exists today was constructed prior to 1980. Utility-scale generators that reported petroleum as their primary fuel comprised only 3% of total electric generating capacity at the end of 2018 and produced less than 1% of total electricity generation.

Power plants that burn petroleum liquids (such as distillate or residual fuel oils) are generally used for short periods during peak electricity demand. Otherwise, oil-fired power plants operate mostly at low capacity factors because of the high price of petroleum relative to other fuels, air pollution restrictions, and lower efficiencies of their aging generating technology. Most oil-fired generators are either turbines or internal combustion engines used to supply power only at peak electric power demand or when natural gas prices rise due to local natural gas demand.

2.4.2 Oil-Fired Plants in Different Countries

In the United States, more than 68% of the 36.4 GW of domestic oil-fired generating capacity is located in 10 states, primarily in coastal states with access to marine ports. When these plants were built around the 1970s, coal-fired generators were the main sources of electricity. However, coastal states (e.g. Florida) are relatively far from coal production areas. Since coal is primarily transported by rail, the cost of long-haul coal transport may not be competitive in these areas compared with oil delivered by marine modes. A fundamental shift in the perception of oil as a utility fuel occurred not only in the United States but in the whole world during the 1970s, when world oil markets experienced sharp price increases. Supply shortages during the main oil shocks (Arab Oil Embargo, the Iranian Revolution, and the Iran-Iraq war) also discouraged oil-fired electricity generating capacity additions globally.

However, in Saudi Arabia, the Shoaiba oil-fired power facility, located on the Red Sea coast, is the largest oil-fired power plant and second largest thermal power plant in the world. The Shoaiba project is a distinctive Saudi Arabian one. As a matter of fact, currently, very few countries are building oil-fired power plants, in part because of environmental concerns as oil burning is a significant contributor to greenhouse gas emissions. They are also unpopular because of price and supply uncertainty, which is not at all the case of Saudi Arabia, with huge domestic oil supplies.

Iran, possessing significant fossil fuel resources, has also consequently invested in utilization of thermal systems for electricity generation. Almost 90% of the required electric energy is produced via thermal power plants. Natural gas (66%) is the largest source of fuel for electricity generation (which is also the case in most other Persian Gulf countries) followed by heavy oil (17.4%) and gas oil (6.6%) (Table 6.4).

Last but not the least, Japan is also among the large users of oil-fired power plants mainly due to its geographical situation. For example, the Kashima Power Station located on Japanese coast, about 50 miles north-east of Tokyo, is the world's second largest oil-fired (and gas-fired) thermal power station with 5204 MW of installed capacity.

Table 6.4 The world's largest oil-fired power plants

No.	*Power station name*	*Countries*	*Installed capacity (MW)*	*Fuel*	*The company of affiliation*
1.	Shoaiba oil-fired CCGT power plant	Saudi Arabia	5600	Crude oil	Saudi Electricity Company
2.	Kashima Power Station	Japan	4400	Fuel oil, natural gas	Tokyo Electric Power Company
3.	Anegasaki Power Station	Japan	3600	Crude oil, fuel oil, natural gas	Tokyo Electric Power Company
4.	Hirono Power Station	Japan	3200	Crude oil, fuel oil, coal	Tokyo Electric Power Company
5.	Yokosuka Thermal Power Station	Japan	2276	Light oil, natural gas	Tokyo Electric Power Company

http://dy.163.com/v2/article/detail/EEM9SO3F05484WS6.html

Source: https://www.power-technology.com/features/feature-giga-projects-the-worlds-biggest-thermal-power-plants/

3 Economic Characteristics

3.1 Economic Analysis

3.1.1 Fixed and Variable Costs

The fixed costs of an electricity plant project consist of capital expenditure (CAPEX) and fixed operating and maintenance cost (OPEX).

1. **CAPEX**

Capital expenditure occurs during the construction phase of the project before its commissioning and is expressed in monetary units (Euro, US dollar, or whatever currency is selected) per kW of installed or nominal capacity. Capital expenditure must be broken down by its components based on various technical life durations and equity investors (e.g. utility company, private equity holder, consumer...).

CAPEX varies for different projects and technologies. As it can be seen in Table 6.5, capital expenditures for coal and biofuels plants are far greater than those for other traditional fossil fuel power plants, and among all technologies, natural gas power generation is the most competitive.

2. **OPEX**

Operating expenses (OPEX) are cash expenditure that occur every year and may be either fixed (if independent of production) or variable (if linked to production). They are expressed in monetary unit per annum and per kW of installed or nominal capacity for fixed OPEX and per kWh of produced power for variable OPEX.

Table 6.5 Range of CAPEX for mid-scale generation projects

		Coal	*Natural gas*	*Biomass combustion electricity plant*	*Biogas digester and electricity generator*	*Diesel generator*
CAPEX ($/kW)	Min	3600	900	2500	3000	1000
	Max	5000	1300	4500	6500	1300

Source: Sustainable Energy Handbook, simplified financial models module 6.1, 2016

Table 6.6 Range of OPEX for mid-scale projects

		Coal	*Natural gas*	*Biomass*	*Biogas*	*Diesel*
Fixed OPEX(% of CAPEX)	Min	1.0%	0.5%	4.0%	5.0%	2.0%
	Max	1.5%	1.6%	6.0%	8.0%	4.0%
Variable non-fuel OPEX ($/kWh)	Min	–	–	0.002	0.020	0.014
	Max	–	–	0.004	0.030	0.028
Variable fuel OPEX ($/kWh)	Min	0.004	0.002	0.005	0.014	0.300
	Max	0.007	0.006	0.022	0.058	0.500

Source: Sustainable Energy Handbook, simplified financial models module 6.1, 2016

It is clear in Table 6.6 that both fixed and variable OPEX is higher for a biofuels plant than for a fossil fuel plant, and again natural gas plant is most advantageous. Part of the OPEX cost is variable (per kWh of output) as it is linked to the consumption of basic commodities such as cooling water, chemicals, lubricants, replacement of wearing parts and of course fossil fuel. Due to fixed operating cost, if the plant's output is lower than expected, the project owner/operator is exposed to the risk of a higher average cost per kWh; the latter may exceed the revenue from the power purchase agreement that is usually strictly proportional to the kWh output. For a new project, the OPEX is the full operational cost of the project. For a rehabilitation/strengthening or an expansion/extension project, the OPEX is the marginal operational cost incurred by the project.

3. **Total Cost**

The total cost of production of an installed technology (€/MWh) includes fixed and variable costs:

$$C_{total} = \frac{C_f}{\eta} + [\frac{P_{CO2}}{\eta} * \frac{1}{E}] + VCOM + \frac{FCOM}{U} + \frac{aI}{U.}$$

where

C_f is the fuel cost given in €/MWh,

η is the total thermal efficiency,[1]

[1] Efficiency of thermal power plants are different for various technologies and could be also different within the same technology as it depends on the design and engineering of the thermal

P_{CO2} is the emitted CO_2 price in €/t, in jurisdictions where a carbon tax or emission trading system is in force,

1/E is the emission factor of the considered fuel in t/MWh,

VCOM is the variable cost of operation and maintenance in €/MWh and *FCOM* is the fixed part,

a is the annuity corresponding to the *i* (interest rate), and *I* is the unit investment cost in €/MW,

U is the utilization ratio in hours/year.

We understand easily from the formula that the total cost of a power unit with heavy investment cost is much more sensitive to the utilization time compared to that of a unit with lower initial investment cost, even if the latter's fuel cost is more expensive.

It is the same for the sensitivity to the interest rate *i*, or the number of years over which the power unit is amortized.

3.1.2 *Life Duration and Revenue*

For some technologies, capital expenditure (CAPEX) may be a recurrent expense as reinvestment has to be factored periodically (e.g. every 5 or 10 years), in order to replace specific components that have a shorter life than the useful life of the project. This is the reason why CAPEX is broken down by components with shorter technical life duration than the economic life of the project. It may also be useful to separate components that receive a performance guarantee from the manufacturer for a shorter period than the economic lifetime of the project. In this latter case, it is assumed that the component must be replaced at the extinction of the guarantee period.

The revenue generated by the project is calculated on an annual basis and starts at the commercial commissioning of the project. This revenue will offset the project costs and is usually calculated as a physical quantity of energy generated by the project (or off-taken by a paying consumer) multiplied by a unit price.

3.1.3 *Basic Economic Indicators*

1. Pay-Back Period

The pay-back period calculates how many years are necessary to cover the CAPEX with the net annual revenue that consists of the annual income minus the annual OPEX charges. The economic sustainability of a project is subject to the pay-back period being shorter than the project economic life.

units. On average, it is between 40% and 44% for coal plants, 20% to 25% for biofuel/gas plants, 35% to 40% for single gas turbines (oil or gas-fired), and from 55% up to even 63% for combined cycles which are the most efficient thermal power plants. (IEA 2018).

2. Internal Rate of Return

The internal rate of return calculates the interest rate that makes equal to zero the net present value of all cash flows, both negative (costs) and positive (revenue), over the period of revenue certainty.

$$\sum_{t=1}^{n} \frac{(R_t - C_t)}{(1+i)^t} = I_0$$

where R_t is the revenue in year t; C_t is the total cost in year t; i equals to internal rate of return, and I_0 is the initial investment (or overnight cost in the electricity jargon).

In the first year, the cash flow consists of the CAPEX and is negative. From the second year until the end of the time series, the cash flow consists of the revenue minus the OPEX (minus the reinvestment cost if applicable). To be financially viable, the investment should have an internal rate of return exceeding the weighted average cost of capital (WACC).

3. Net Present Value (NPV)

The last, but absolutely not the least, criteria is the Net Present Value (NPV) of the project over its economic lifetime. The cash flow schedule is the same as for the calculation of the internal rate of return from second year onward.

$$NPV = \sum_{t=1}^{n} \frac{(R_t - C_t)}{(1+i)^t} - I_0$$

where R_t, revenue in year t; C_t, costs in year t; i, discount rate; I_0, initial investment. For the project to be economically viable, the NPV must be positive.

3.2 *Financial Analysis*

The total amount to be financed includes the capital investment cost as described in the economic analysis section plus the specific financing cost that occurs during the construction period, which is called interest during construction (IDC). During the construction period, the project cannot reimburse financial charges from revenue. Therefore, this cost has to be factored in the project cost used to calculate the funding requirements.

There are three types of sources for funding: equity, loans, and in some cases grants. Equity is the money committed by the owners of the project from their own sources or through an equity partner. Loans are funds committed by banks against a predetermined repayment schedule. Grants are funds provided by a donor with no obligation of repayment (assuming that such a donor is available).

1. Weighted Average Cost of Capital (WACC)

The Weighted Average Cost of Capital (WACC) is the equivalent discount rate applicable to the project cost that will be sufficient to repay the loans and generate the expected return on equity. The WACC is calculated over the loan duration as follows:

$$\text{Share of loan} \times \text{loan interest rate} + \text{share of equity} \times \text{duration of loan} \times \text{expected return on equity} + \text{share of grant} \times 0$$

In the above formula, the higher is the share of grant, the lower will be the WACC (as a result of a lower share of loan + equity).

2. Levelized Cost of Electricity (LCOE)

The Levelized Cost of Electricity (LCOE) is calculated by adding the annuitized capital cost to the annual operating expense, and dividing by the quantity of electricity generated. The LCOE should be inferior to the electricity price—otherwise, the project will generate a loss.

$$PV\,of\,Total\,Costs = \sum_{n} \frac{total\,capex\,and\,opex\,costs}{(1+i)^n}$$

$$PV\,of\,Electricity\,Generation = \sum_{n} \frac{total\,net\,electricity\,generation}{(1+i)^n}$$

$$LCOE = \frac{PV\,of\,Total\,Costs}{PV\,of\,Electricity\,Generation}$$

where i is the discount rate and n the lifetime of the power plant.

3.3 *Dispatchability and Flexibility*

There are two main types of power station in the world: base-load generator units and peaking stations. Base-load generators (the majority of coal power plants) are useful where there is a steady demand and a stable source of fuel, such as coal or gas, to power the generators. Electricity peaking stations (Table 6.5), also called peak-lopping plants, are power plants designed to help balancing the fluctuating power requirements of the electricity grid. Peaking stations typically operate in standby mode, and when there is a peak in demand for power from the electricity grid, they receive a signal to commence operation. Due to their flexibility and robustness, they are able to provide a rapid response to fluctuating demand. They are then turned off as demand declines.

For example, oil-fired generators tend to be used to meet electricity demand during peak hours, and they generally have lower capacity factors and higher heat rates than most other types of power plants. They are installed in places where there is no easy access to alternative power sources and are mainly used as backup for uninterrupted power supply whenever there are outages. Moreover, these plants require only a small area to be installed and offer higher thermal efficiency compared to coal-fired power plants.

In general, liquid fuel power plants have great dispatchability to supply electricity to the grid within seconds and can reach full capacity in minutes. Additionally, they have tremendous fuel flexibility, with the possibility of running with heavy fuel oil, light fuel oil, crude oil, emulsified fuels, or liquid biofuel. Some oil-fired power plants are capable of switching between fuels, potentially complicating the calculation of capacity factors. For instance, plants that normally burn natural gas may choose to burn oil (or oil products) during times of high natural gas demand.

Natural gas power stations are also very flexible and their ramping time (from zero to full capacity) is short. The operation of single cycle mode, in which only one gas turbine is running, takes only about 10 minutes from start-up to full load and the combined cycle (running simultaneously both gas and steam turbines) takes 40–50 minutes. A natural gas power plant has good regulation performance and can operate in the range of 25% to 100% output without any problem. For example, a GE HA class gas combined cycle plant with an installed capacity of 570 megawatts can start in less than 30 minutes and increase or reduce the load at a rate of 60 megawatts per minute. Under some load conditions, provided that the load is at least 200 MW, it can still meet the emissions standard and stabilize the power supply and can also form a reliable backup with intermittent sources (e.g. wind & solar) to promote the rapid growth of renewable energy. Besides, it can operate as flexibly as a liquid fuel power plant. It is also available in multi-fuel versions. When the gas supply is uncertain, or prices are volatile, it is possible to switch from gas to liquid fuel, and vice versa, even during operation.

It is worth to mention that at present, gas power generation has some unique advantages compared to all other source of electricity. An example is the world's first battery-gas turbine hybrid power generation system deployed by GE and Southern California Edison. It integrates a 10-megawatt lithium-ion battery energy storage system and a LM6000 aviation gas turbine, as well as the corresponding control system, allowing the gas turbine to be in rotating standby mode without using fuel and responding immediately to changing power dispatching requirements. When peak shaving is not needed, the gas turbine is in a rotating standby state (connected to the battery), and when the peak shaving is required, the gas turbine is immediately awakened from the rotating standby state through the advanced control system, and the gas turbine is quickly started with load, and the power is immediately transmitted to the power grid.

3.4 Location

Coal power generation location is more restrictive compared to other technologies because coal is a solid and its transport cost is high, while its combustion efficiency is lower than for other technologies. Usually coal plants are located near coal mines and the choice of different means of transport will affect the location of the plant area as well as the size and form of the required land plot, especially for a large power plant. The transportation mode should allow for large volume, low freight, high speed, and flexibility, which will make the location of coal plant all the more difficult.

On the contrary, oil is easy to transport with multiple transportation options including by pipeline and by ship; therefore, oil-fired plants are usually located in coastal areas. A gas-fired power plant is characterized by little land occupation and is very suitable for countries and areas with dense population and scarce land resources. Compared with coal-fired power plants, gas power generation equipment is more compact and does not occupy a large area. Besides, it consumes one-third of the water needed for a coal-fired power plant.

3.5 Expected Service Life

Thermal power plants are designed for an economic lifetime of 30 to 40 years, but some plants have been also used beyond their design life in certain areas. The critical components are the boiler and the turbine. The operation of thermal power generation is faced with both tangible and intangible aging processes. Tangible or physical aging refers to the equipment operating under high pressure and temperature, and bearing mechanical stress, resulting in physical and chemical changes, such as wear, creep, corrosion, and so on, gradually making the equipment unable to continue operating safely under the required design parameters. Invisible aging refers to technological progress. The advent of more efficient or less labor-intensive production equipment means that older equipment will operate under less and less economic conditions. The physical aging of some equipment (such as condenser copper pipes, heater pipes, boiler heating surface pipes, turbine blades, furnace walls, etc.) can be removed during overhaul. However, it is often the aging of these important equipment components that determines the technical and consequently economic lifetime of thermal power plants. Operating experience shows that the service life of equipment operating under 450 °C is between 40 and 50 years. For equipment operating at temperatures above 450 °C, the operating hours could even be reduced to 100,000 hours.

Both gas and steam turbines are devices that drive the rotor to rotate at high speed through high-pressure gas with high temperature and humidity.

The difference is that the pressure and temperature of gas in the gas turbine is higher than in the steam turbine. Taking the GE PG9351FA Class F gas turbine as an example, the gas temperature entering the turbine from the combustion chamber is 1327 °C and the exhaust gas temperature is 609 °C. This working environment at such high temperature and thermal stress aggravates the periodic damage to gas turbines. The material of thermal parts is deformed due to low cycle fatigue[2] and thermal stress, which increases the failure probability of different components and seriously affects the service life of the equipment. Moreover, for two-shaft peak shaving generators, frequent start-up and shut-down is also one of the main causes of shorter life. For gas-steam combined units, the life of the gas turbine, waste heat boiler, and steam turbine could be seriously affected by peak shaving operation. Finally, we should mention that the reliable operation and reasonable maintenance of gas turbine affects not only the safety but also the economy of the whole unit.

4 Conclusion

This chapter illustrated the fundamentals of power generation economics from different fossil sources. It started with the largest fossil-fuel-fired power plants in the world followed by introduction and technology performance of each source (coal, natural gas, biofuels, and oil) of electricity generation. Then economic analysis is introduced and discussed regarding the CAPEX, OPEX, indicators like NPV, IRR, and LCOE in addition to other techno-economic characteristics like dispatchability, flexibility, and expected life service of each technology. The conclusion that can be drawn from the above discussions and the related recommendation is as follows:

While general technology cost assessments can provide rough estimates, the actual cost of each technology is highly dependent on project-specific factors. Power sector planners should not underestimate the level of uncertainty when it comes to technology costs or future operating costs. Country-level analysis can provide a more accurate picture of the relative costs of each technology, but even then any forecast should be treated with care. Rather than attempting to pick the "best" technology, they should instead determine which technologies and fuels are well suited to their particular circumstances and then seek to create a diversified portfolio of options. Doing so can protect against major disruptions in any technology or fuel and help to balance capital and operational costs while mitigating environmental impacts.

Acknowledgment I would like to take the opportunity to thank those people who have provided helpful suggestions and data for this chapter, particularly my graduate students, Di Peng, Yao Xuebing, and Zou Zhiqin.

[2] Low-cycle fatigue is the regime associated with a load amplitude high enough to cause the fracture of a part after a limited number of cycles (typically less than 10^5 cycles).

Bibliography

Valdemaras, M., Astrida, M., Tatiana, S., Natalia, T., Tadas, S. The impact of biofuels production development in the European Union. Agricultural Economics (Zemědělská ekonomika). 2018,64(No. 4):170–185.

Agbor, E., Zhang, X., Kumar, A. A review of biomass co-firing in North America. Renewable and Sustainable Energy Reviews. 2014,40:930–943.

Washburn, C., Pablo-Romero, M. Measures to promote renewable energies for electricity generation in Latin American countries. Energy Policy. 2019,128:212–222.

Freitas, F.F., De Souza, S.S., Ferreira, L.R.A., Otto, R.B., Alessio, F.J., De Souza, S.N.M., Venturini, O.J., Ando Junior, O.H. The Brazilian market of distributed biogas generation: Overview, technological development and case study. Renewable and Sustainable Energy Reviews. 2019,101:146–157.

Bórawski, P., Bełdycka-Bórawska, A., Szymańska, E.J., Jankowski, K.J., Dubis, B., Dunn, J.W. Development of renewable energy sources market and biofuels in The European Union. Journal of Cleaner Production. 2019,228:467–484.

Borychowski, M. Journal of Agribusiness and Rural Development. 2017,16(2):263–275.

Fantin, V., Giuliano, A., Manfredi, M., Ottaviano, G., Stefanova, M., Masoni, P. Environmental assessment of electricity generation from an Italian anaerobic digestion plant. Biomass and Bioenergy. 2015,83:422–435.

Loução, P.O., Ribau, J.P., Ferreira, A.F. Life cycle and decision analysis of electricity production from biomass—Portugal case study. Renewable and Sustainable Energy Reviews. 2019,108:452–480.

Gómez, A., Rodrigues, M., Montañés, C., Dopazo, C., Fueyo, N. The potential for electricity generation from crop and forestry residues in Spain. Biomass and Bioenergy. 2010,34(5):703–719.

Topcu, I., Ülengin, F., Kabak, Ö., Isik, M., Unver, B., Onsel Ekici, S. The evaluation of electricity generation resources: The case of Turkey. Energy. 2019,167:417–427.

Arifin, Y., Tanudjaja, E., Dimyati, A., Pinontoan, R. A Second Generation Biofuel from Cellulosic Agricultural By-product Fermentation Using Clostridium Species for Electricity Generation. Energy Procedia. 2014,47:310–315.

Leong, W.-H., Lim, J.-W., Lam, M.-K., Uemura, Y., Ho, Y.-C. Third generation biofuels: A nutritional perspective in enhancing microbial lipid production. Renewable and Sustainable Energy Reviews. 2018,91:950–961.

Abdullah, B., Syed Muhammad, S.A.F.A, Shokravi, Z., Ismail, S., Kassim, K.A., Mahmood, A.N., Aziz, M.M.A. Fourth generation biofuel: A review on risks and mitigation strategies. Renewable and Sustainable Energy Reviews. 2019,107:37–50.

Zhou, Q., Cai, W., Zhang, Y., Liu, J., Yuan, L., Yu, F., Wang, X., Liu, M. Electricity generation from corn cob char though a direct carbon solid oxide fuel cell. Biomass and Bioenergy. 2016,91:250–258.

Hassan, S.H.A., el Nasser A. Zohri, A., Kassim, R.M.F. Electricity generation from sugarcane molasses using microbial fuel cell technologies. Energy. 2019,178:538–543.

Adeniyi, O.M., Azimov, U., Burluka, A. Algae biofuel: Current status and future applications. Renewable and Sustainable Energy Reviews. 2018,90:316–335.

Jin, E., Sutherland, J.W. An integrated sustainability model for a bioenergy system: Forest residues for electricity generation. Biomass and Bioenergy. 2018,119:10–21.

Sagani, A., Hagidimitriou, M., Dedoussis, V. Perennial tree pruning biomass waste exploitation for electricity generation: The perspective of Greece. Sustainable Energy Technologies and Assessments. 2019,31:77–85.

Biomass Co-firing Technology Brief. IEA-ETSAP and IRENA Technology Brief E21. 2013.
Chiodo, V., Zafarana, G., Maisano, S., Freni, S., Galvagno, A., Urbani, F. Molten carbonate fuel cell system fed with biofuels for electricity production. International Journal of Hydrogen Energy. 2016,41(41):18815–18821.
Nazari, S., Shahhoseini, O., Sohrabi-Kashani, A., Davari, S., Sahabi, H., Rezaeian, A. SO2 pollution of heavy oil-fired steam power plants in Iran. Energy Policy. 2012,43:456–465.
Park, J.-K., Park, S., Kim, M., Ryu, C., Baek, S.H., Kim, Y.J., Kim, H.H., Park, H.Y. CFD analysis of combustion characteristics for fuel switching to bioliquid in oil-fired power plant. Fuel. 2015,159:324–333.
Kharbach, M., Chfadi, T. Oil prices and electricity production in Morocco. Energy Strategy Reviews. 2018,22:320–324.
Wu, T.Y.-W., Rai, V. Quantifying diversity of electricity generation in the U.S. The Electricity Journal. 2017,30(7):55–66.
Sustainable Energy Handbook. Simplified Financial Models. Module 6.1.2016.
Jed Bailey. Inter-fuel Competition in Electricity Generation. A Latin American & Caribbean Experience. Inter-American Development Bank. 2012.
BP Statistical Review of World Energy 2020.

CHAPTER 7

Power Generation from Nuclear Energy

Valerie Faudon

Nuclear is recognized by the Intergovernmental Panel on Climate Change (IPCC) as a low-carbon energy source, along with renewables and fossil fuels with carbon capture and sequestration (CCS). As of today, it is available in more than 30 countries and deployable on a large scale. Public opinion toward nuclear varies a lot from one country to another, with strong influence on energy policies: some countries, like the United Kingdom, are developing nuclear to meet their climate goals and insure security of supply, while others, like Germany, have decided to phase it out.

At a 2019 conference, the IPCC Chairman pointed out that "there is considerable potential, as well as considerable uncertainty for nuclear power" (Lee 2019). He added that, beyond public opinion, the real challenge in the years to come for nuclear power was "to be cost competitive with other non-fossil fuel technologies and to deploy nuclear power much faster than in the past". He addressed the representatives of the nuclear community: "I wish you success in meeting these challenges because climate needs all the help it can get".

This chapter discusses the economics of nuclear. It covers the fundamentals of nuclear economics and reviews the cost drivers for the long-term operation

This chapter leverages a lot of recent work done with my colleagues at SFEN and OECD-NEA, with special thanks to Michel Berthélémy.

V. Faudon (✉)
European Nuclear Society, Brussels, Belgium

SFEN, Paris, France

SciencesPo—Paris School of International Affairs, Paris, France
e-mail: valerie.faudon@sfen.org

M. Hafner, G. Luciani (eds.), *The Palgrave Handbook of International Energy Economics*, https://doi.org/10.1007/978-3-030-86884-0_7

of the existing fleet and new nuclear projects. It then reviews the latest research related to the value that nuclear can bring to the overall electricity system and in wholesale price formation in deregulated markets.

1 Reminder: Current and Expected Role of Nuclear in Decabonization Scenarios

Today, nuclear makes a significant contribution to low-carbon global electricity supply:

- As of 2020, about 450 nuclear reactors operate in the world (IAEA n.d.), with a combined capacity of more than 400 GWe. Nuclear energy accounts for more than 10% of worldwide gross electricity production (OECD-IEA 2019) and 25% in the European Union.

- Thanks to nuclear, more than 60 Gt of CO_2 emissions have been avoided since 1970 (OECD-IEA 2019), equivalent to five years' worth of CO_2 emissions from the electricity sector. Nuclear is the second largest source of low-carbon energy in the world behind hydropower and the number one source in the OECD.

International institutions have stated that all low-carbon technologies, including nuclear, will be needed to achieve carbon neutrality by 2050.

- According to the IPPC, "the strategy for reducing energy related CO_2 emissions are robust and well-known: very ambitious efficiency improvement, increased electrification, and decarbonization of electricity supply" (Lee 2019). The SR1.5 report describes four "1.5C" trajectories in its "Summary for policymakers", envisaging nuclear production two to six times higher by 2050, compared to today.
  - According to the IEA, to meet climate goals, the expansion of clean electricity would need to be three times faster than at present (OECD-IEA 2019). Along with massive investments in efficiency and renewable energies, the trajectory should deliver an 80% increase in global energy power production by 2040.
  - The latest reference scenarios from the European Commission confirm that the combination of nuclear and renewables will be the basis of a carbon-free energy mix in 2050 (European Commission 2018). By this time, nuclear would represent about 18% of the total.

2 Fundamentals of Nuclear Economics

2.1 Cost of Production

The cost of nuclear power production, as for any other energy source, includes generally three different components:

- *Capital costs*: These have a very high contribution to the LCOE of new plants, as they include the initial investment in building the plant. Nuclear, like wind and solar, is a highly capital-intensive industry. The share of capital costs decreases after the initial depreciation period, specifically in the case of long-term operation of nuclear plants.
- *Plant operating costs*: These include the fuel costs and operation and maintenance costs (O&M). The share of fuel costs, which is usually high for fossil fuel and biomass, and zero for wind and solar, is considered low for nuclear, with uranium estimated on average at 5% of total nuclear production cost. As a result, nuclear plants are less subject to fuel price volatility than fossil fuel plants: a 50% rise in the fuel cost would only result in a 5% increase in the overall generation cost (Cour des Comptes 2014).
- *External costs*: As opposed to coal or gas plants, nuclear is a low-carbon technology and provides little to no air pollution. Also, as it is highly regulated, it must include costs provisions for funding the plant decommissioning and the management and disposal of used fuel and wastes. External costs could however include the costs of dealing with a serious accident that are beyond the insurance limit: in practice, this type of risk (high potential cost with very low probability) is picked up by governments.

2.2 Revenues from Nuclear Plants

The cost of power generation is one of the three components of the retail price of electricity, together with the cost of the transmission and distribution infrastructures, and taxes.

In so-called regulated markets, revenues from power generation are determined through a regulatory process, under the supervision of a Public Utility Authority. In "deregulated" markets, the electricity produced is traded in a wholesale market, where prices are set, on an instant basis, by the "merit order" (economic precedence) logic: as electricity cannot be stored on a large scale, to meet a given level of demand, the various power generation units are called according to their increasing marginal cost.

Nuclear power plants, as we have seen, have low fuel costs, and therefore low marginal costs: they are usually called second after the units with zero to no fuel costs, such as hydro, wind, and solar. Nuclear is called before thermal power plants (coal or gas). The wholesale price for electricity, which will determine the nuclear plant revenue, will be given by the variable cost of the marginal plant, usually a thermal one.

3 Economics of Nuclear Long-Term Operations

In advanced economies, most of the nuclear power plants now in operations were built before 1990, and the average age of nuclear capacity stands at 35 years (OECD-IEA 2019). Most existing nuclear plants have been built with an initial design lifetime of 40 years, but engineering assessments have established that they can operate much longer (60 or even 80 years in the United States). One of the fastest and cheapest ways for these countries to support low-carbon production capacity is to undergo "long-time operation" programs (Fig. 7.1).

In the past years, operators of many older nuclear plants have been investing in such programs, in some cases increasing capacity at the same time (so-called uprates). In the United States, 95 nuclear reactors are currently in operations (IAEA n.d.). They account for 20% of the nation's total electric energy generation and about 50% of US low-carbon generation. About 88 have already renewed their operating license once, extending their lifetimes from 40 to 60 years (Patel 2019). However, since the majority of these will be nearing the end of that 20-year extension by 2029, it is expected that many will seek to renew their license a second time for another 20-year period. In December 2019, the US Nuclear Regulatory Commission (NRC) has for the first time issued license renewals that authorize nuclear reactor operation beyond 60 years and up to 80 years for 2 units in Florida.[1]

3.1 Cost Drivers for Long-Term Operation of Nuclear Plants

Cost estimates are impacted by reactor type, plant situation, and regulatory requirements (IAEA 2018). Most of the costs are related to plant refurbishment and, in particular, replacement of major components to mitigate aging or

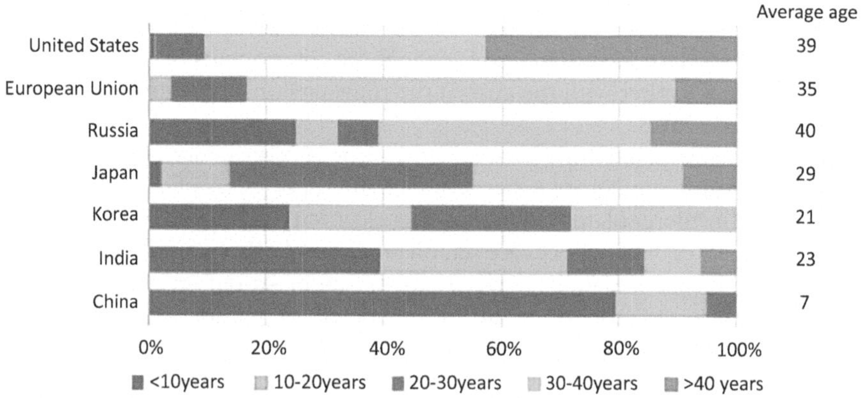

Fig. 7.1 Age profile of nuclear power capacity in selected countries/regions. (Source: OECD-IEA [2019])

[1] Units 3 and 4 at Florida Power & Light's Turkey Point Nuclear Generating plant.

obsolescence. But they also come from safety enhancements to meet the changes in national licensing requirements: these come, for instance, in response to lessons learned from operating experience, changes in industry practices and operating experience feed-back, or studies and lessons learned from accidents (such as Fukushima Daichi). Many new plant systems or systems configuration that were not considered at the time of plant commissioning may be added. In some cases, refurbishments and safety enhancements will come with power uprates, which include new licensing costs, changes in the fuel cycle, and replacement of some other components.

3.2 *Competitiveness of Long-Time Operations of Nuclear Power Plants*

According to OECD-IEA (2019), nuclear lifetime extensions are "one of the most cost-effective ways of providing low-carbon sources of electricity through to 2040". The capital costs of extending the operational lifetime of light water nuclear power plants generally range from USD 500 million per GW to USD 1.1 billon per GW, for a duration between 10 and 20 years. The levelized cost of electricity (LCOE) associated with a nuclear long-time operations project generally falls into the range of USD 40–60 per MWh.[2] The competitiveness of nuclear plant extensions is even more favorable when the full value of nuclear power as a dispatchable, high-availability (on average the capacity factor for nuclear has consistently been between 78 and 83% over the last 20 years), low-carbon source of electricity is taken into account, as we will see in part IV. In the graph below, the "value adjusted LCOE (VALCOE)" is a new IEA metric which combines a technology's costs with estimates of these values (Fig. 7.2).

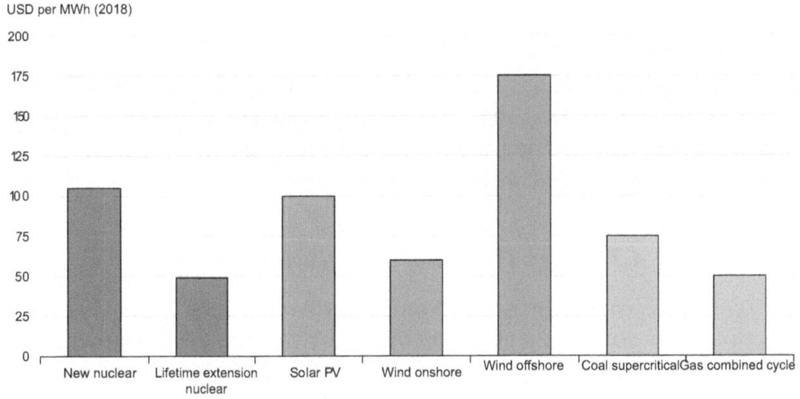

Fig. 7.2 LCOE by technology in the United States, 2018. (Source: IEA, LCOE by technology in the United States, 2018, IEA, Paris https://www.iea.org/data-and-statistics/charts/lcoe-by-technology-in-the-united-states-2018)

[2] Based on investment of USD 500 M-1.1 Bn and an extension of 10–20 years, assuming an 8% WACC.

4 Economics of New Nuclear Projects

The number of nuclear reactors in construction worldwide is 54 (OECD-IEA 2019), the majority of them in Asia, with some in Europe and America.

4.1 Challenges Associated with Delays and Cost Overruns in Recent Projects

Over the last decade, as mentioned by William Magwood, Director General of OECD's Nuclear Energy Agency (NEA), "significant cost overruns and delays in a number of OECD countries have challenged the competitiveness of nuclear power and are driving the risk perception on future projects" (OECD-NEA 2020). As the industry transitioned from "generation 2" reactors to "generation 3" reactors, which present an increased level of safety but are more complex to build, most "First of a Kind" (FOAK) projects worldwide have shown significant delays compared to initial estimates, as shown by Table 7.1:

This situation is quite common for the delivery of large complex infrastructure projects, specifically FOAK projects, and is well documented in the economic literature. A well-known example is the construction of the Channel Tunnel, whose initial budget doubled by completion. Many studies (McKinsey 2013; Merrow et al. 1981; Yemm et al. 2012) have also highlighted the "optimism bias" upstream of these projects, as well as the "rapid learning" phases on the subsequent projects.

Delays for nuclear projects vary according to two country profiles. On one side, there are countries which have been building new reactors in a continuous manner over time, either because they are still in the process of building their initial fleet (China) or because they have begun renewing part of their fleet (Russia). It is symptomatic that the first of third-generation reactors put into service was in Russia and that the first European Pressurized Reactor (EPR) to start was in China. On the other side, there are countries (France, Finland, the United States) which had stopped building for 10 to 15 years: these countries not only have had to face the challenges associated with the first projects (FOAK), but also had to bring their skills and supply chain back again up to the standards required for the construction of nuclear reactors.

4.2 Cost Drivers of New Nuclear Projects

As for renewable energy projects (wind, photovoltaic, and hydraulic) nuclear production costs are very largely dominated by the cost of investment during the construction phase. In an average case (see Fig. 7.3), it is estimated that the cost of investment will make about two-thirds of the production cost. More than half of the investment cost will be the construction cost. Furthermore, the cash flow structure of nuclear projects requires large amount of capital to be mobilized upfront. Construction lead times and costs, together with the cost of capital, determine a plant's economic performance. Once a plant is built, its O&M and fuel costs are low and predictable.

Table 7.1 Construction costs of recent FOAK Gen-III/III+I projects

Type	*Country*	*Unit*	*Construction start*	*Initial announced construction time*	*Ex-post construction time*	*Power (MW_e)*	*Initial announced budget ($\$/kM_e$)*	*Ex-post construction cost ($\$/kM_e$)*
AP 1000	China	Sanmen 1,2	2009	5	9	2 × 1000	2044	3154
	USA	Vogtle 3,4	2013	4	8/9	2 × 1117	4300	8600
APR 1400	Korea	Shin Kori 3,4	2012	5	8/10	2 × 1340	1828	2410
EPR	Finland	Olkiluoto 3	2005	5	16	1 × 1630	2020	>5723
	France	Flamanville 3	2007	5	15	1 × 1600	1886	8620
	China	Taishan 1,2	2009	4,5	9	1 × 1660	1960	3222
VVER 1200	Russia	Novovoronezh II-1 & 2	2008	4	8/10	2 × 1114	2244	No data available

Source: Author's elaboration on NEA

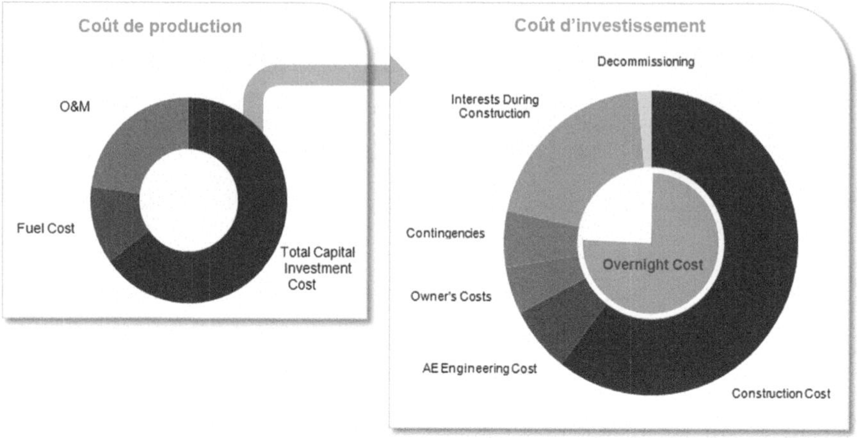

Fig. 7.3 Production and Investment Cost. (Source: OECD, SFEN)

When evaluating the cost of a new nuclear project, the discount rate, which varies a lot depending on whether the borrower is the government or a private party, has a major impact on LCOE. A sensitivity analysis by the OECD-NEA (2015) shows that average plant construction expenses would account for 45€/MWh with a 7% discount rate, but only 20€/MWh with a 3% discount rate.

4.3 Potential for Reduction in the Cost of New Nuclear Projects

Several reports and studies (OECD-NEA 2020; SFEN 2018), in recent years, have looked at lessons learned from projects as well as cost reduction drivers to reduce construction and capital costs on new nuclear projects. We will draw from them in this section.

The most important lesson learned, and cost driver, from FOAK projects has been that detailed designs must be complete and ready before the construction starts, in order to translate design specifications into detailed supply chain requirements and plans for each construction stage. For example, for the EPR construction in Finland, where anticipation of a nuclear renaissance and hopes to benefit from a first mover advantage had led Areva-Siemens to bid with an unfinished design, reveals the need for numerous adjustments which, given the complexity of the project, were responsible for the major part of the delays and cost overruns. Conversely, the construction of the EPR in Taishan benefited from the design and first level of lessons learned from Flamanville: according to the Folz report (2019), while the final cost of construction of Flamanville 3 in France is estimated at 12.4 Bn€, the total cost for the two EPRs in Taishan are estimated at 12.3 Bn€, that is 6 Bn€ per unit.

Besides this key lesson, recent studies have identified numerous cost reduction opportunities, as described in Fig. 7.4:

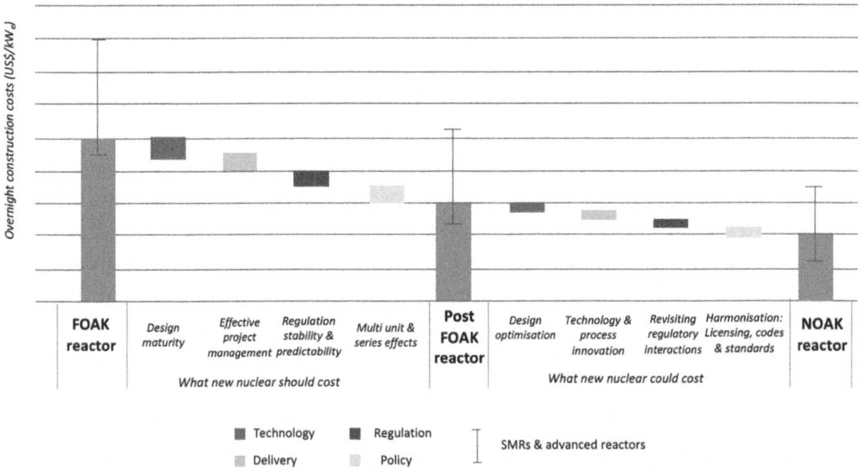

Fig. 7.4 Nuclear cost and risk reduction drivers. (Source: Author's elaboration on OECD-NEA 2020)

In the FOAK stage, the interplay between plant design and effective project management presents a range of cost reduction opportunities: one key example is the engagement in the supply chain early in the design process to integrate all requirements necessary for construction. In the post-FOAK stage, continuous improvement and innovation can yield additional opportunities: one example is the expected introduction into the nuclear industry of the "system engineering" and "project life management" methods, which have been successfully implemented in aeronautics and allow all players involved in a given project to share the same data, from design to construction.

In the longer term, as in any other kind of project, product, or service, the main driver for cost reduction in construction is the series effect. When adequate design maturity has been achieved, the design configuration should be frozen and systematically replicated as many times as possible. We can see then first a program effect (studies, qualifications, and testing work are shared across several units) and productivity effects in the supply chain: thanks to the visibility obtained from a guaranteed order, suppliers can plan and optimize their resources and production tools. Feedback from the construction of the French nuclear fleet in the 80s showed that the maximum series effect can be reached by building reactors in pairs (15% of cost reduction for one pair on a single site), with a 30% reduction for a series of a minimum of three pairs (Cour des Comptes 2014; SFEN 2018). The recent Barakah 4-unit project in the United Arab Emirates, whose first unit achieved first criticality in July 2020, is reported to have achieved more than 50% cost reduction between the first and the fourth unit (Gogan 2019). Probably drawing from these conclusions, India recently confirmed the construction of a total of 16 identical 700 MW reactors (IANS 2020), with, after the first units being built, a "set up in fleet mode" for the units to be completed progressively by 2031.

Finally, we have seen above how sensitive the LCOE is to the discount rate. In the case of the Hinkley Point C project in the United Kingdom, the National Audit Office (NAO) has shown the potential for very significant savings on financial costs, via a better distribution of risks between the various stakeholders (NAO 2017). For example, should the required return on capital (after tax) drop from 9% (value close to the rate used by EDF Energy for the project) to 6% (considering the project as a public infrastructure with the associated investment framework), this would result in a reduction by one-third of the cost per kilowatt hour for consumers. Further studies must be carried out to determine the best project governance allowing the distribution of risks between the various actors. In 2019, the UK government launched a consultation on a so-called regulated asset base model (RAB)—used for other forms of infrastructure such as energy networks. This would lower the cost of capital of the scheme because consumers would have a surcharge added to their energy bills before the plant was completed (FT 2020). However, some have suggested that direct government funding would be a more logical and effective solution (Ford 2020).

The EDF CEO has declared that his company's objectives for future nuclear projects in France, through leveraging all the cost drivers, should be in the 50–70€/MWh range, far below the recently announced Flamanville 3 latest estimate of 110–120€/MWh (Cour des Comptes 2020).

4.4 A Case for Disruptive Innovation: Small Modular Reactors (SMRs)

The delays and cost overruns in large Gen3 projects generated increased interest for a new, disruptive concept of smaller units with simpler designs. Defined as reactors of 300 MWe equivalent or less, Small Modular Reactors (SMRs) would not necessitate as large upfront capital costs per reactor and would be designed for serial construction. In fact, they could potentially be manufactured in an offsite dedicated facility to improve the level of construction quality and efficiency, and then later be installed independently on site or assembled module by module to form a large nuclear power plan.

In addition to traditional baseload power, SMRs would be able to address new markets and applications: their small size and passive safety features would be better suited for countries with smaller grids and less experience of nuclear power. In large countries, they could power islands (e.g., in Indonesia), isolated sites (mines), and remote areas (Northern Canada or Siberia). In the United States, they could target the brownfield sites to replace decommissioned coal plants. Finally, they could be used as well as an alternative to storage, to load follow on grids with a high share of variable renewable energies, to produce heat and decarbonize local district systems (China or Finland), to desalinate water (Saudi Arabia), or to provide low-carbon industrial heat and decarbonize complex industrial processes.

Several projects of SMRs, with different sizes and designs, are underway worldwide. The most advanced is probably the Nuscale project in the United

States, which is supported by the US Department of Energy, has reached several licensing milestones, and is currently preparing for its FOAK project in Idaho.

For SMRs to be a credible option by the early 2030s, successful prototypes must be developed in the 2020s to demonstrate the announced benefits. Specially, they will need to deliver on the ambition with regards to the series effect, as well as simplification and standardization, all the more so because they will need to counterbalance some diseconomies of scale, for instance, on safety systems. Having access to a global market is necessary to foster series-production economies, but this will be possible only with regulatory and industrial harmonization.

5 New Research on the Value of Nuclear in the Future Low-Carbon Mix

To maintain a constant balance of electricity supply and demand, in face of constant demand changes and uncertainties, conventional electricity systems have relied on dispatchable generation such as thermal power plants and hydro power, that in some cases provide a lot of flexibility, as they can ramp up and down on short notice.

According to all decarbonization scenarios, future systems will need to integrate more and more variable capacity—essentially wind and solar power—to meet climate objectives. However, at the same time they will need to shut down traditional dispatchable coal and gas plants, to achieve net zero emissions in the electricity sector. This is a true paradigm shift that will have a major impact on how electricity systems are managed, and how much they cost.

5.1 Beyond the Cost of Power Generation, the Notion of "System Costs"

When shares of variable renewables (wind and solar) are low, the variability can be easily absorbed by the system. However, as their share increase, the introduction of variable renewable energies (wind, solar photovoltaic) will require additional back-up (such as storage) and adjustment capacities (such as demand flexibility) in order to guarantee the quality of electricity and the supply-demand balance. It will also involve strengthening the electricity networks. These effects lead to additional costs for the power system to be integrated when comparing the production costs of different technologies. A recent OECD-NEA study (2019) shows that these "system costs" can increase from €7/MWh to almost € 45/MWh when the share of variable renewables increases from 10 to 75% of the electricity mix.

In this new paradigm, the question of the competitiveness of each means of production can no longer be asked without consideration of the characteristics of the system where it operates: we will have to take into account the interdependencies within the electricity system (share of non-dispatchable sources, limits of storage facilities, and other sources of flexibility) and the structure of the electricity market. New nuclear power, a low-carbon source that can be controlled 24/7 and offers great flexibility (possible variation of 5% of nominal power/min), must in fact be compared, with respect to the services it provides to the system, to other controllable means such as hydroelectricity or to fossil means (coal, gas) equipped with carbon capture and sequestration.

5.2 *MIT Study Shows That the Least-Cost Carbon-Neutral Portfolio Includes a Share of Nuclear*

A recent MIT study (2018) explored in detail how imposing a carbon constraint affects the optimal electricity generation mix in different regions of the world (the United States, the United Kingdom, China). Should the carbon constraint not be a determinant factor, fossil fuels, whether coal or natural gas, are generally a lower cost alternative for electricity generation. Under a modest carbon emission constraint, renewable generation usually offers a lower cost alternative. However, as the world seeks deeper reductions in electricity sector carbon emissions, the cost of incremental power from renewables increases dramatically.

The study concludes that the least-cost portfolios include a significant share for nuclear, the magnitude of which significantly grows as the cost of nuclear drops. The levels of 'deep decarbonization'—meaning emissions target for the electric sector that is well below 50 gCO_2/kWh—including nuclear in the mix of low-carbon solutions, help to minimize rising system costs, which makes attaining stringent emissions goals more realistic (in comparison, worldwide, electricity sector emissions currently average approximately 500 gCO_2/kWh). Lowering the cost of nuclear technology can help reduce the cost of meeting even more modest decarbonization targets (such as a 100 gCO_2/kWh emissions target).

5.3 *Toward Major Changes in the Regulation of Electricity Markets*

Several studies (OECD-NEA 2019; SFEN 2020) have shown that, as a consequence of the increased share of variable renewables in the electricity mix, the volatility of electricity prices will increase substantially with periods of very high production of solar and wind (with episodes of very low and sometimes negative prices) alternating with very low production (with episodes of very high prices). As a result, the studies conclude that, as their deployment increases, the value of variable resources for the system decreases: this has important implications on their ability to be financed in energy-only markets.

In this environment, a recent SFEN study in France shows that a significant share of nuclear in the low-carbon mix plays an important role in stabilizing electricity prices; as its marginal cost is not zero, it is dispatchable and capable of load-following to support the integration of solar and wind production. It also provides frequency services to the network and operates in the long-term (60 years at least).

In general, as most generation technologies would have to rely on a limited number of hours with high market prices to recover their investment costs, it will make it even more difficult for investors to predict future revenues from their investment and will require changes in the regulation of electricity markets.

6 Conclusion

In its 2019 report, the OECD-IEA makes a few major recommendations directed at countries that intend to retain the option of nuclear power. The first one is to keep the nuclear option open and authorize lifetime extensions of existing nuclear plants as long as safely possible. The second one is to value dispatchability and design the electricity market in a way that properly values the system services needed to maintain electricity security, including capacity availability and frequency control services. In general, the Agency recommends to value non-market benefits and remunerates them accordingly.

References

Cour des Comptes (2014) Le coût de production de l'énergie nucléaire, actualisation 2014, Paris, mai. https://www.ccomptes.fr/sites/default/files/EzPublish/20140527_rapport_cout_production_electricite_nucleaire.pdf

Cour des Comptes (2020) La filière EPR, Paris, Juillet https://www.ccomptes.fr/fr/publications/la-filiere-epr

European Commission (2018): The Commission calls for a climate neutral Europe by 2050, November 28 https://ec.europa.eu/clima/news/commission-calls-climate-neutral-europe-2050_en

Folz, J.-M. (2019) La construction de l'EPR de Flamanville—Rapport au President Directeur Général d'EDF https://www.vie-publique.fr/sites/default/files/rapport/pdf/271429.pdf

Ford, J. (2020) Britain needs new nuclear, and the government should fund it, Financial Times June 1, 2020.

FT (2020) Cost of new Sizewell C nuclear plant put at £20bn, June 26.

Gogan, K. (2019), "The potential for nuclear cost reduction", presentation at IAEA Atoms 4 Climate Conference, Vienna, 7–11 October 2019.

IAEA (2018) Economic Assessment of the Long-Term Operation of Nuclear Power Plants: Approaches and Experience, IAEA Nuclear Energy Series NP-T-3.25 https://www.iaea.org/publications/11162/economic-assessment-of-the-long-term-operation-of-nuclear-power-plants-approaches-and-experience

Lee, H. (2019) speech at IAEA's International Conference on Climate Change and the Role of Nuclear Power; video available at http://streaming.iaea.org/21230; transcript available at https://ideesrecuessurlenergie.wordpress.com/2019/10/19/hoesung-leespeech-ipcc-president-from-the-iaea-conference/

IAEA (n.d.) Power Reactor Information System (PRIS) https://pris.iaea.org/PRIS/home.aspx

IANS (2020) Four More Nuclear Power Units with Total Capacity of 3400 MW to Be Built In Haryana, Tamil Nadu. Swarajya magazine July 29, 2020 https://swarajyamag.com/news-brief/four-more-nuclear-power-units-with-total-capacity-of-3400-mw-to-be-built-in-haryana-tamil-nadu

McKinsey and Co. (2013) A risk-management approach to a successful infrastructure project, Working Paper on Risks n° 52, https://www.mckinsey.com/industries/capital-projects-and-infrastructure/our-insights/a-risk-management-approach-to-a-successful-infrastructure-project

Merrow, E. M. et al. (1981) Understanding Cost Growth and Performance Shortfalls in Pioneer Process Plants, Santa Monica, CA: Rand Corporation.

MIT (2018) The Future of Nuclear Energy in a Carbon Constrained World https://energy.mit.edu/wp-content/uploads/2018/09/The-Future-of-Nuclear-Energy-in-a-Carbon-Constrained-World.pdf

NAO (2017) Hinkley Point C—Report by the Comptroller and Auditor General https://www.nao.org.uk/wp-content/uploads/2017/06/Hinkley-Point-C.pdf

OECD-IEA (2019) Nuclear Power in a Clean Energy System May 2019 https://www.iea.org/reports/nuclear-power-in-a-clean-energy-system

OECD-NEA (2015) Projected Costs of Generating Electricity https://www.oecd-nea.org/ndd/pubs/2015/7057-proj-costs-electricity-2015.pdf

OECD-NEA (2019) The Cost of Decarbonization: Systems Costs with High Shares of Nuclear and Renewables https://www.oecd-nea.org/ndd/pubs/2019/7299-system-costs.pdf

OECD-NEA (2020) Unlocking reductions in the construction costs of nuclear http://www.oecd-nea.org/ndd/pubs/2020/7530-reducing-cost-nuclear-construction.pdf

Patel, S (2019) NRC Issues First Subsequent License Renewals, Extends Nuclear Reactor Life to 80 Years, Power Magazine December 11, 2019 https://www.powermag.com/nrc-issues-first-subsequent-license-renewals-extends-nuclear-reactor-life-to-80-years/

SFEN (2018) Les coûts de production du nouveau nucléaire français https://new.sfen.org/note-technique/les-couts-de-production-du-nouveau-nucleaire-francais/

SFEN-CL (2020) Peut-on prendre le risque de ne pas renouveler le parc nucléaire français? https://new.sfen.org/note-technique/peut-on-prendre-le-risque-de-ne-pas-renouveler-le-parc-nucleaire-francais/

Yemm, R. et al. (2012) Pelamis: experience from concept to connection, Phil. Trans. R. Soc. A (2012) 370, 365–380 https://royalsocietypublishing.org/doi/pdf/10.1098/rsta.2011.0312

CHAPTER 8

Hydropower

Eike Blume-Werry and Martin Everts

1 Introduction

Hydropower has been used by mankind for centuries, with early references dating back to the Han Dynasty in China and the ancient Greeks. Whilst it was then predominately used to grind grains, it later became a source of power for spinning frames to spin cotton during the industrial revolution.

Turbine technology innovations in the nineteenth century paved the way for modern uses of hydropower. In 1827, the French engineer Benoît Fourneyron developed the first waterwheel that is referred to as turbine, capable of producing approximately 6 horse powers or 4.5 kW. Later versions of his turbines spread across Europe and the United States. The most commonly used turbine, the Francis turbine, was developed shortly after, in 1849, by British-American engineer James Francis. In the late 1870s, American inventor Lester Allen Pelton invented an impulse water wheel, the Pelton turbine.

These innovations enabled to utilise hydropower for electricity generation whereby the first installation lit a single light bulb in 1878 in Northumberland, England. Many more followed, first in Europe and North America and by the turn of the century also elsewhere around the globe. During the twentieth century, increasingly larger hydropower stations were developed, and some projects' purposes extended from electricity generation to flood control and irrigation. In 1936, in the middle of the Great Depression, the Hoover Dam started production with an initial capacity of 1345 MW.

E. Blume-Werry (✉)
Bundesverband der Deutschen Industrie e.V., Berlin, Germany

M. Everts
AMAG Group AG, Cham, Switzerland

M. Hafner, G. Luciani (eds.), *The Palgrave Handbook of International Energy Economics*, https://doi.org/10.1007/978-3-030-86884-0_8

Today, hydropower is the source of the largest power stations in the world, the Three Georges Dam in China, with a capacity of 22.5 GW, and the Itaipu Dam at the border of Brazil and Paraguay, with a capacity of 14 GW. Globally, with over 4000 TWh generated in 2018, hydropower accounts for approximately 16.3 per cent of electricity generation and installed capacities exceed 1000 GW (International Energy Agency 2018). This makes it, at the time of writing, by far the most important renewable energy source, providing approximately 67 per cent of all electricity generated from all renewable sources (International Energy Agency 2018). Hydropower stations are located all over the world and in all climate zones as Table 8.1 illustrates. However, hydropower stations are predominantly installed in regions with favourable topographies.

Whilst in the developed world the best and most suitable sites for hydropower generation have long been exploited, there remain significant hydropower potentials in the developing world, in particular in Africa. There has been substantial hydropower growth in the last decades in East Asia, almost exclusively due to growth in China, which has the highest installed capacity and production of any country. Altogether, hydropower has been a competitive source of electricity generation for over a century, yet it requires certain geographical features, which will be explored in more detail later. As a result, suitable locations in the developed world have mostly been exploited, and during the last decades, growth has taken place primarily in the industrialising economies.

One can differentiate between three hydropower generation types: run-of-river, hydro storage and pumped storage. The following chapters describe the characteristics of the three technologies. The generation in all three types follows the same principle, as water is used to turn one or multiple turbines. One can calculate the power output of a hydroelectric turbine with the following formula:

$$P = \eta \times \rho \times q \times g \times h$$

Table 8.1 Installed hydropower capacity by regions (2016)

Region	*Installed hydropower capacity (in GW)*	*Share of total*
Africa	22.3	2.1%
Middle East & North Africa	18.1	1.7%
Latin America & The Caribbean	140.4	13.2%
North America	171.3	16.1%
Europe	259.6	24.4%
South & Central Asia	63.8	6.0%
East Asia	336.2	31.6%
South East Asia & Pacific	51.1	4.8%
Total	1064	100%

Source: World Energy Council

where P is the power output, η the efficiency of the turbine (generally between 0.8 and 0.95), ρ the density (approximately 1000 kg/m^3 for water), q the site-specific water flow in m^3 per second, g the gravity (9.81 m/s^2) and h stands for the hydraulic head, that is, the falling height in metres.

2 Run-of-River

Run-of-river hydroelectricity describes hydro generation plants using the water stream of a river to generate electricity without any, or only limited storage, referred to as pondage. The volume of water flowing down the river and the drop of the riverbed level determine the amount of electricity that can be generated. The larger the drop of the riverbed level and the volume of water, the greater the potential energy that can be converted into electricity. Run-of-river power plants usually divert water from the river into a canal or pipe that directs the water to the powerhouse. The so-called penstocks lead the water through turbines which generate electricity. Afterwards the water flows downstream through pipes or canals referred to as tail race back into the river.

Due to the fact that run-of-river power plants do not store water in a reservoir, they are somewhat limited in their scalability and flexibility. Capacities range from micro installations with a capacity of only a few kilowatt (kW) to large-scale plants, which may have a capacity of up to several hundred megawatt (MW). Typically, plants with a capacity of 100 kW up to 1 MW classify as mini installations, with plants up to 10 MW (or up to 50 MW depending on national jurisdiction) are labelled as small and anything larger as large-scale plants. Generally speaking, large-scale plants between 10 and 1000 MW capacity dominate global installed capacities and production volumes.

The lack of water storage makes run-of-river power plants dependent on river flows that can have significant daily and seasonal fluctuations. Plants by alpine rivers, for instance, experience considerable larger production volumes in spring and summer months following the snow melt (see Fig. 8.1). In other parts of the world, freshets, monsoon seasons or other weather phenomena such as El Niño can cause similar production fluctuations in other months. Run-of-river power plants are therefore an intermittent power generation technology that is only partially dispatchable and cannot always adjust its power output according to the demand, as, for instance, hydro storage plants.

Since run-of-river power plants do not require large dams that store water, construction is simpler and avoids accompanying issues that are associated with the construction of dams (see next section).

The environmental impact of any hydropower plant ought to be regarded on an individual basis as it depends on the location as well as the type and size of the plant. Generally speaking, run-of-river power plants have a lower environmental impact on human and aquatic life than hydro reservoirs or pumped-storage plants, given that no dam construction and flooding of land areas is required. Nevertheless, run-of-river power plants still have a negative impact

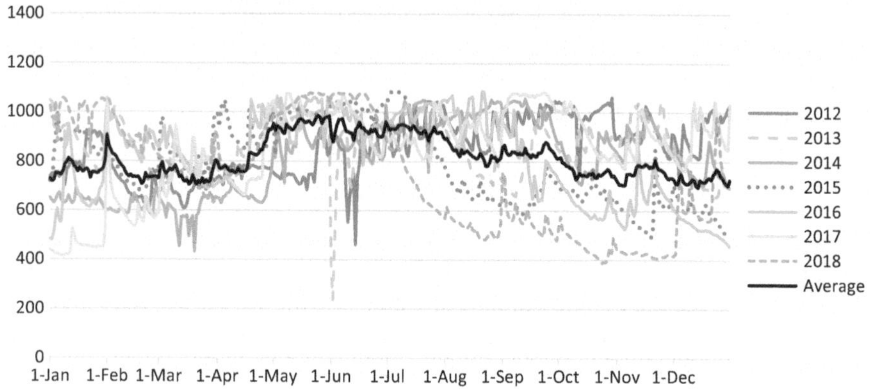

Fig. 8.1 Production profile (daily average produced megawatt hours) of a run-of-river power plant in Switzerland shows yearly and seasonal variations. (Source: Authors' elaboration on Axpo Holding AG data)

on (often fragile) river ecosystems. The plant represents a physical barrier for fish populations, especially migratory fish, and depending on turbine design and operating mode, passage can often be lethal or sublethal for the fish.[1] In recent decades, improvements have been made in terms of turbine designs and bypassing options such as fish ladders, yet legislative requirements vary significantly by country or jurisdiction.

Run-of-river power plants have very long lifetimes. Some key equipment such as turbines last about 25 years before they are replaced, yet the power plant typically has a long lifetime of approximately 80 years. Often power plants approaching the end of their lifetime are modernised rather than dismantled, since suitable locations are limited and hydropower is still an economic source of renewable energy today. Some of the older hydropower plants, especially in Europe, are listed buildings of cultural heritage.

3 Hydro Storage

Hydro storage power plants typically use a dam to store water in a reservoir. The reservoir acts as energy storage, using the gravitational potential energy of water at higher elevation. To generate electricity, gates let water flow into penstocks, which in turn lead the water to one or multiple turbines in the powerhouse. Afterwards the water flows downstream into a basin and/or river. In essence, the general concept works like in a run-of-river power plant with the key difference that the water flow is controlled by the plant operator. This means that hydro storage is—unlike run-of-river hydro—a dispatchable source

[1] See Anderson et al. (2015) for a detailed analysis of run-of-river hydropower's impact on ecological conditions of rivers.

of energy. Operators can choose the quantity and timing of electricity to be generated within given regulatory restrictions.

Hydro storage power plants and dams can be colossal in size and capacity and form some of the largest man-made structures on earth. The Three Gorges Dam in China, for instance, is the largest power station in the world with an installed capacity of 22,500 MW. In terms of electricity production, only the Itaipu Dam on the border of Brazil and Paraguay surpasses the Three Gorges Dam (depending on hydrological conditions) with recorded production volumes of over 96 TWh annually in the late 2010s. Aside those enormous-sized hydro storage plants, there are also comparably small hydro storage installations of only a few MW. Micro or mini hydropower plants, however, usually do not classify as hydro storage but as run-of-river.

The operational nature of hydro storage power plants differs significantly. Some, such as the two named above, produce baseload power and have comparably high capacity factors. Others are peak-load power stations with much lower capacity factors and operate only in times of high demand or high prices. The size of reservoir, the water flow into the reservoir and the turbine capacity are factors that determine how a hydro storage power plant operates. Depending on the site, further factors such as legally required minimal water flows and reservoir levels also play a role.

Most hydro storage power plants in liberalised European power markets function as peak-load plants. During spring and summer months, following the snow melt, the reservoirs fill up. Peak demand, and with it high prices, usually occurs in Europe during winter months, which is why operators of hydro storage power plants discharge the majority of water then (see Fig. 8.2: Weekly water levels of Swiss hydro reservoirs (in per cent) illustrate the seasonal usage of hydro storage plants in the Alps. Source: Authors' elaboration on Swiss Federal Office of Energy data). Given that each unit of stored water can only

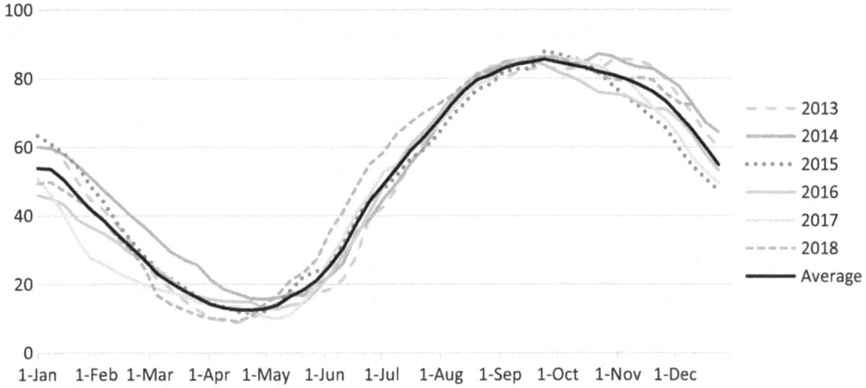

Fig. 8.2 Weekly water levels of Swiss hydro reservoirs (in per cent) illustrate the seasonal usage of hydro storage plants in the Alps. (Source: Authors' elaboration on Swiss Federal Office of Energy data (2019))

be discharged once, the discharging, that is, selling of hydro storage, reflects a bet against higher prices in the future. A certain amount of water (site-specific, see formula mentioned earlier) in an upper reservoir is equal to a call option of generating a unit of electricity. The opportunity costs of releasing water are equal to the expected future value of electricity. Hydro storage power plant operators use modern option pricing theories to optimise the dispatch of their plants. Put simply, operators try to serve the highest priced hours a year with the limited amount of water available in their reservoirs. Unlike other generators who bid with their marginal costs on energy-only markets, the dispatch of hydro storage power plants is not marginal cost based. Instead, operators use shadow prices—reflecting the marginal costs of additional alternative (thermal) power plants—to place their bids on the market.

Hydro storage power plants require certain geographical and geological features. Usually they are located in mountainous areas where elevation levels of river drop sharply, and the topography enables storing water in a reservoir. The reservoirs of hydropower plants often cover vast areas of formerly dry land. The construction of dams and creation of reservoirs thus have far-reaching consequences for river ecosystems and surrounding areas. Reservoirs do not only flood large areas of land, converting valleys into lakes, but also alter the river ecosystem further downstream. Natural seasonal floods no longer occur and altered flow rates lead to losses in biodiversity as well as changes in sedimentation, as dams may hinder the flow of sediments downstream. There is also an ongoing academic debate on the greenhouse gas emissions (first and foremost methane) of reservoirs, especially in tropical climates, due to microbial decomposition of organic material in the water under anaerobic conditions.[2]

It is important to note at this point that the construction of (large) dams and reservoirs has an impact on not only the natural environment but also the people living there. At the turn of the century the 'World Commission on Dams', a global governance forum researching controversial issues of large dams under patronage of Nelson Mandela presented a final report (World Commission on Dams 2000). A key motivation was to solve and prevent human conflict associated with the construction and use of dams especially in developing countries. The final report highlights inter alia that in too many cases an unacceptable price in social and environmental terms has been paid for the considerable benefits of dams by communities downstream and by people displaced, whose number is estimated at 40–80 million (World Commission on Dams 2000).

Just like run-of-river power plants, hydro storage power plants have very long lifetimes of approximately 80 years. Hydromechanical elements usually have shorter life spans and are replaced accordingly, whilst the structure of the dam can have a longer lifetime than 80 years, depending on the design. Regular assessments of the structural safety of dams are essential, given catastrophic consequences of a dam failure. In Europe, a governing body grants operators

[2] See Prairie et al. (2018) for a detailed discussion on greenhouse gas emissions from reservoirs.

concessions that typically cover a period of 25–75 years (Glachant et al. 2014, p. 21). Once a hydro storage power plant with dam and reservoir is built, it is usually there to stay. Dismantling a hydroelectric dam with a reservoir is a complex and costly task. In Europe, dams approaching the end of their lifetime undergo a modernisation in most cases and only comparably small dams have been removed thus far. Hydropower dam removal has been more significant in North America, yet no dams with considerable large power productions have been dismantled to date.

4 Pumped-Storage Hydroelectricity

Pumped-storage hydropower plants use two or more reservoirs at different elevation levels to store electricity in form of gravitational potential energy of water. During low-priced hours, water is pumped to a reservoir with a higher elevation level, and in times of high prices, it is discharged to generate electricity. The power generation process is the same as for hydro storage power plants, the only difference being that discharged water is collected in a reservoir at lower elevation.

Since the pumping process consumes electricity, pumped-storage hydropower plants both consume and produce electricity. Pumped hydro is to date the only (grid scale) economically viable and mature form of storing electricity, yet significant progress has been made in different battery technologies in recent years. The round-trip efficiency (pumping up water and discharging it to generate electricity) of pumped-storage hydropower is typically between 70 and 80 per cent (Rehman et al. 2015).

In general, pumped-storage hydropower plant reservoirs tend to be smaller than those of hydro storage power plants without a pumping component. This is due to different use cases. Whereas many hydro storage power plants serve as seasonal storage with reservoirs filling up during spring and summer months, pumped-storage plants function first and foremost as daily or weekly storage units. There are, however, also pumped-storage plants with comparably large reservoirs and conventional hydro storage plants that have had a pumping component and lower-elevation reservoirs added. Economies of scale apply to pumped-storage hydropower plants, which are why installations are commonly large scale, with typical capacities between 1000 and 1500 MW, the largest installation being the 3003 MW Bath County Pumped Storage Station in the United States. Globally, installed pumped-storage hydro capacity reached approximately 160 GW at the end of 2018, accounting for over 94 per cent of installed energy storage capacity (Henley 2019).

The aforementioned location constraints of hydro storage power plants apply also to pumped-storage installations, yet reservoirs tend to be smaller. Consequently, pumped-storage hydropower plants are typically located in mountainous areas and have an elevation difference between reservoirs of a few hundred metres. The first pumped-storage hydropower station was developed

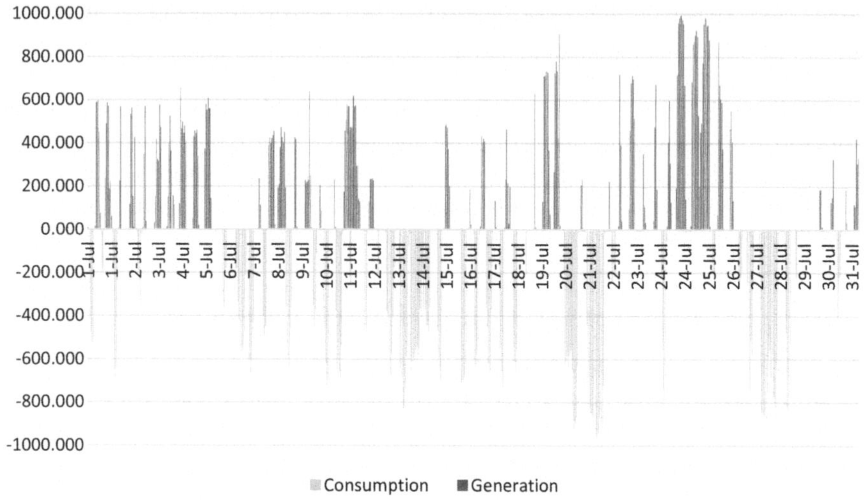

Fig. 8.3 Monthly pump/generation profile of a pumped-storage hydropower plant in MWh. (Source: Authors' elaboration on Axpo Holding AG data)

in the Swiss Alps over 100 years ago. Today, China, Japan and the United States are the countries with the highest installed capacities of pumped storage.

Economically, pumped-storage hydropower plants use price spreads on electricity markets. During low-priced hours (e.g. during night-time, weekends or at times of excess supply), water is pumped up in the upper reservoir, and during high-priced hours, it is discharged to generate electricity (see Fig. 8.3). The greater the price spreads on a given market, the higher the profitability of pumped-storage power plants. This operating nature contributes to balance markets, especially at high penetration rates of intermittent renewable energies, which is a matter that will be explored in more detail in the following section.

Given the similarities of conventional hydro storage and pumped-storage power plants, environmental concerns of conventional hydro storage (see above) apply also to pumped-storage installations. In addition, pumped-storage power plants have been criticised for the fact that they consume more electricity than they generate (unless there is a considerable natural inflow). This criticism neglects the fact that pumped-storage plants generate electricity during times of peak demand that would otherwise be covered by dispatchable conventional fossil fuel-based generation sources. Indeed, operators of pump-storage power plants use shadow prices of additional conventional fossil fuel-based power plants in the merit order for their dispatch strategy and bids on power markets. There is little doubt amongst experts that energy systems with (very) high penetration of intermittent renewables require storage solutions such as pumped storage and batteries, highlighting the importance of pumped-storage hydropower plants for decarbonising power systems.

5 Role of Hydropower in Generation Portfolios and Flexibility

Hydropower has been an economically viable generation technology for over a century. The role of hydropower in countries' generation portfolios has therefore developed slowly over time without the radical changes observed in other renewable energy capacities. Wherever the natural environment enabled the use of hydropower in the industrialised world, then hydropower capacities were often deployed. Today, hydropower benefits from the fact that it is a renewable and emission-free power generation technology, something that was not deemed particularly relevant in the early days of hydropower development. The role of hydropower in countries' generation portfolios is therefore typically set by how well a given country is suited for hydropower. Some countries such as Norway, Albania or Paraguay cover virtually all or even more than their domestic electricity needs by hydropower sources.

It is fair to note that the role of hydro in a generation mix is more a result of the natural environment than of policy decision, as hydropower typically offers an economically viable and sustainable source of power if suitable waterways with considerable elevation drops are available. As a result, hydropower potentials in developed nations are largely exploited, and global hydropower growth is less substantial than that of other renewable energies such as wind and solar photovoltaics (PV). China accounts for most of the global growth of hydropower and has a share of approximately 19 per cent in its generation mix (International Energy Agency 2018). In the United States, around 7 per cent of the power generation comes from hydropower sources, and in the European Union (EU-28), it is approximately 10 per cent with considerable differences between member states (Eurostat 2019; International Energy Agency 2018).

As aforementioned, hydropower plants can be used to meet near baseload demands with high capacity factors. They can also be designed to cover peak demand with high installed capacities and lower capacity factors and everything in between. Be that as it may, even when the share of hydropower is small in any given country, the flexibility of hydro storage and pumped-hydro is often crucial for the stabilisation and balancing of the power grid. Hydro storage and pumped-storage plants can ramp up production within seconds to react to market signals and grid demands. In other words, the flexible plants help to keep the frequency stable at sudden changes of supply or demand, by adjusting the power output accordingly. In a decarbonising world with increasing penetration of variable renewables in power grids, this flexibility is critical for security of supply. Pumped-hydro flexibility is twofold and comes handy, as it not only can provide additional generation capacity during times of high demand but also acts as a consumer to store surplus electricity. Whilst pumped hydro functions as a daily storage unit in most cases, conventional hydro storage plants typically serve as seasonal storage units. The use case therefore differs from the one of grid-scale batteries, which have been experiencing significant cost reductions over the last years, but are adapted only for shorter flexibility. Aside batteries, hydro storage is currently the most flexible generation technology that can follow the load without the efficiency losses of conventional thermal power plants at lower loads. Power systems with considerable shares of flexible hydro units can therefore integrate variable renewable production more efficiently.

6 Hydropower Costs and the Financing of Hydropower Plants

Construction costs for hydropower plants are very site-specific. Large and small-scale plants can differ significantly in their costs per unit of installed capacity and per unit of electricity generated. Yet not just the size of the power plant but also the legal/regulatory requirements (e.g. fish passages) and the location (e.g. remote mountainous areas) are key factors that determine the costs of a specific plant and may vary drastically from site to site. Anyhow, compared with other power generation technologies hydropower plants are typically characterised by high to very high capital expenditures (capex). The International Renewable Energy Agency (IRENA) sets the installation cost range for large hydropower at 1050 to 7650 USD_{2010} per installed kW and slightly higher for smaller plants as they are less likely to profit from economies of scale (IRENA 2012).

In contrast to the high capex, the operating expenditures (opex) of hydropower plants are very low, since the fuel, that is, the water, is usually free. The operating costs of hydropower plants stem primarily from maintenance costs of mechanical equipment and labour costs for operating the plant resulting in very low overall opex.[3] IRENA describes the annual operation and maintenance costs of large hydropower projects as 2 to 2.5 per cent of investment costs per installed kilowatt and slightly more for smaller installations (IRENA 2012). Put together, hydropower can be a very economic source of electricity when analysing the costs over a lifetime. In this context, scholars refer to the so-called levelised costs of electricity (LCOE) that describe the average lifetime costs of electricity generation. Following IRENA's hydropower installation and operating costs, the agency gives large hydropower an LCOE range of 0.02 to 0.19 USD_{2010} per kilowatt hour (and up to 0.27 USD_{2010}/kWh for small hydropower) assuming a 10 per cent cost of capital (IRENA 2012).

The relatively high capital expenditures (capex) combined with a typically rather long lifetime of hydropower plants make investments in hydro power difficult. During the first wave of hydropower, in the first half of the twentieth century, many hydropower plants were built by state owned companies or quasi monopolies. Nowadays most hydropower plants have to be financed by privately owned companies with no or very limited subsidies or securities from governments or states. However, financing infrastructure investments with

[3] It should be noted that this is subject to varying national jurisdictions that may increase operational expenditure, for instance, by charging hydropower plant operators for the use of the water.

high capital expenditures, long lifetimes and uncertain future revenues can be challenging.

Other renewable energy sources such as wind and photovoltaic also have high capex compared to their operating expenditures. But similar to hydropower plants, many governments and states helped building the first wave of wind and photovoltaic plants with subsidies such as fixed tariffs or with other forms of securities for future revenues. Over the last decade, most governments and states reduced securities they offer for new wind and photovoltaic plants. With this reduction of subsidies and securities, the market developed new instruments for financing renewable plants, first and foremost power purchase agreements. However, these power purchase agreements typically have a duration of only 10 years. For power plants with lifetimes of approximately 20 years, a security for the first half of their duration is typically enough to enable private financing. But for hydropower stations with significantly longer lifetimes, power purchase agreements with a duration of 10 years do not cover enough uncertainties regarding future revenues to allow for significant private investments.

7 Outlook for Hydropower

As a renewable and clean generation technology, hydropower should continue to play an important role in future low carbon power systems. Even though further sites for hydropower deployment are limited in the developed world, there are significant untapped technical potentials in the developing world, especially in Africa (Henley 2019).

Unlike other renewable energy technologies such as wind and PV that experienced substantial technical innovation during the last two decades, no such drastic innovations or cost reductions can be expected for hydropower. However, it can be expected that the benefits of flexible hydropower technologies will be challenged by other storage technologies such as batteries. Moreover, one can assume that the benefits of renewable run-of-river plants will be challenged by other renewable technologies.

However, at a broader picture one can assume that geography will always be a driving factor behind renewable energy sources. In windy regions, some form of wind power plants will be used (as it was already used for at least two centuries), sunny regions will try to harvest the power of the sun, and in wet and mountainous regions, some form of hydropower will continue to play an important role in the power generation.

References

Anderson, D., Moggridge, H., Warren, P., Shucksmith, J., 2015. *The impacts of 'run-of-river' hydropower on the physical and ecological condition of rivers.* Water and Environment Journal 29, 268–276. https://doi.org/10.1111/wej.12101

Eurostat, 2019. *Electricity production, consumption and market overview.* https://ec.europa.eu/eurostat/statistics-explained/index.php/Electricity_production,_consumption_and_market_overview#Electricity_generation (accessed 5.09.19).

Glachant, J.-M., Saguan, M., Rious, V., Douguet, S., Gentzoglanis, E., European University Institute Florence, I., 2014. *Regimes for granting right to use hydropower in Europe.* EUI, San Domenico di Fiesole.

Henley, W., 2019. *2019 Hydropower Status Report.* International Hydropower Association, London.

International Energy Agency, 2018. *Key World Energy Statistics 2018.* International Energy Agency, Paris.

IRENA, 2012. *Renewable Energy Technologies: Cost Analysis Series—Hydropower (No. 3/5)*, Renewable Energy Technologies. International Renewable Energy Agency (IRENA), Bonn.

Prairie, Y.T., Alm, J., Beaulieu, J., Barros, N., Battin, T., Cole, J., del Giorgio, P., DelSontro, T., Guérin, F., Harby, A., Harrison, J., Mercier-Blais, S., Serça, D., Sobek, S., Vachon, D., 2018. *Greenhouse Gas Emissions from Freshwater Reservoirs: What Does the Atmosphere See?* Ecosystems 21, 1058–1071. https://doi.org/10.1007/s10021-017-0198-9

Rehman, S., Al-Hadhrami, L.M., Alam, Md.M., 2015. *Pumped hydro energy storage system: A technological review.* Renewable and Sustainable Energy Reviews 44, 586–598. https://doi.org/10.1016/j.rser.2014.12.040

Swiss Federal Office of Energy, 2019. *Electricity statistics.* https://www.bfe.admin.ch/bfe/en/home/versorgung/statistik-und-geodaten/energiestatistiken/elektrizitaetsstatistik.html (accessed 30.09.19).

World Commission on Dams (Ed.), 2000. *Dams and development: a new framework for decision-making.* Earthscan, London.

CHAPTER 9

Solar Power Generation

Laima Eicke, Anselm Eicke, and Manfred Hafner

1 Introduction

In less than two hours, enough sunlight strikes the earth to satisfy the world economies' annual energy demand. Despite this abundance of solar energy, the conversion of sunlight into usable energy forms only represents a tiny fraction of today's global energy supply. Yet, the share of solar energy in global energy supply, especially in the electricity sector, is rising rapidly. Unprecedented deployment has taken place in the last decade, stimulated by efforts to improve energy access, security of supply and mitigate climate change. Between 2010 and 2017, the global installed capacity of solar generation increased more than

L. Eicke (✉)
Harvard Kennedy School, Harvard University, Boston, MA, USA

Institute for Advanced Sustainability Studies (IASS), Potsdam, Germany

Universität Erfurt, Erfurt, Germany
e-mail: Laima.Eicke@iass-potsdam.de

A. Eicke
Hertie School, Berlin, Germany
e-mail: anselm.eicke@daad-alumni.de

M. Hafner
SciencesPo—Paris School of International Affairs, Paris, France

Johns Hopkins University SAIS Europe, Bologna, Italy

Fondazione Eni Enrico Mattei (FEEM), Milan, Italy
e-mail: mhafner@johnshopkins.it

M. Hafner, G. Luciani (eds.), *The Palgrave Handbook of International Energy Economics*, https://doi.org/10.1007/978-3-030-86884-0_9

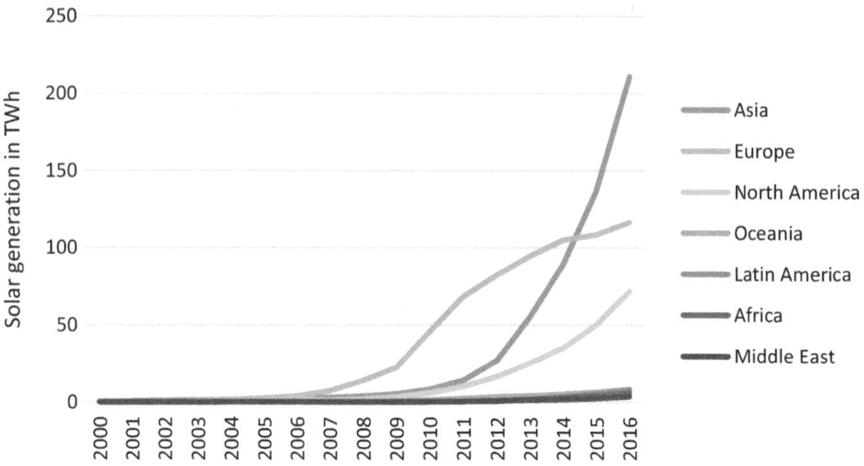

Fig. 9.1 Power generation from solar energy by region (in TWh). (Authors' own elaboration, data from IRENA 2020)

tenfold from 34 GW to 437 GW (IRENA 2020). Steep learning curves and the economies of scale enabled technological improvements and, in consequence, have led to massive cost reductions.

Solar photovoltaics (PV), the conversion of light into electricity using semiconducting materials, were one of the most expensive electricity-generating technologies when first employed in astronautics in the late 1950s. By 2020, it has become an economically viable energy source for many applications. An alternative technical process to generate electricity from solar radiation is concentrated solar power (CSP). Yet, the latter, accounted for less than 3% of all solar power in global electricity generation in 2017 (IRENA 2020).

PV is the third most important renewable energy source in terms of global capacity after hydro and wind power. Globally, solar energy is mostly used in Asia, Europe and North America with the strongest rise in Asia, mostly driven by China and India (Fig. 9.1). According the World Energy Outlook of the International Energy Agency, solar PV may become the largest technology in terms of global installed capacity in the Stated Policies Scenario by 2035 (IEA 2019).

2 Technical Characteristics of Solar Energy

A brief introduction to the technical characteristics of solar energy provides the necessary background information to better understand its economics.

2.1 Solar PV

The main components of photovoltaic cells are semiconducting materials such as silicon and germanium. In these materials, sunlight releases charge carriers (electrons), which create an electrical field. As source of electricity generation, this field induces a direct electrical current. This process is known as the photovoltaic effect. Electricity generation exploiting this effect is not only possible from direct sunlight, but also from its diffuse components, implying that PV cells also generate electricity with cloudy skies.

Photovoltaic cells are integrated in solar arrays. Inverters (to invert DC current from solar panels into AC), transformers, electrical protection devices, wiring and monitoring equipment are summarized as balance of system (BOS). In some cases, BOS also includes sun-tracking systems, which increase the yield by positioning the panels towards the sun.

The three major types of solar PV technology are monocrystalline cells, polycrystalline cells and thin firm cells, of which the first two make up more than 95% of global module production (Fraunhofer ISE 2019).

Monocrystalline solar cells have the highest efficiency rates, typically 15–20% but the highest quality panels can reach up to 23% efficiency. As for all solar panels, the efficiency of monocrystalline panels depends on ambient temperature. On average, efficiency declines by about 10% when the ambient temperature rises by 25 °C (Quaschning 2019). Featuring high efficiencies, monocrystalline solar panels are space efficient, i.e. they require smaller ground areas to generate the same amount of electricity compared to other technologies. They also live the longest with most manufacturers putting a 25-year warranty on monocrystalline solar panels. Their main disadvantage is the high cost, because manufacturing requires the highest-grade silicon.

Polycrystalline silicon cells are cheaper because of a simpler production process and the amount of waste silicon is less compared to monocrystalline cells. The efficiency of these panels is typically lower (13–16%). They also have a slightly lower heat tolerance, which means that polycrystalline perform slightly worse in high temperatures than monocrystalline panels.

Thin film solar cells deposit one or several thin layers of photovoltaic material onto a substrate. Most thin-film modules have efficiencies of around 9–11%. Their mass production makes them cheaper than crystalline based solar cells. Thin film solar panels are mostly used in applications where panel sizes are not an issue. Another advantage is that they can be more easily integrated into facades and roofs.

When comparing efficiencies, it is important to differentiate between efficiencies of single cells, of panels and of the entire installation including converter and transformer. In the last 10 years, the efficiency of average commercial silicon modules increased from about 12% to 17% (Fraunhofer ISE 2019). Lab cell efficiencies of close to 50% when concentrating light rays and applying new materials demonstrate the potential for further efficiency increases at the production level (Geisz et al. 2020).

2.2 *Concentrated Solar Power*

Concentrated solar power (CSP) does not exploit the photovoltaic effect. Instead, mirrors are used to focus solar rays to heat a fluid. Similar to

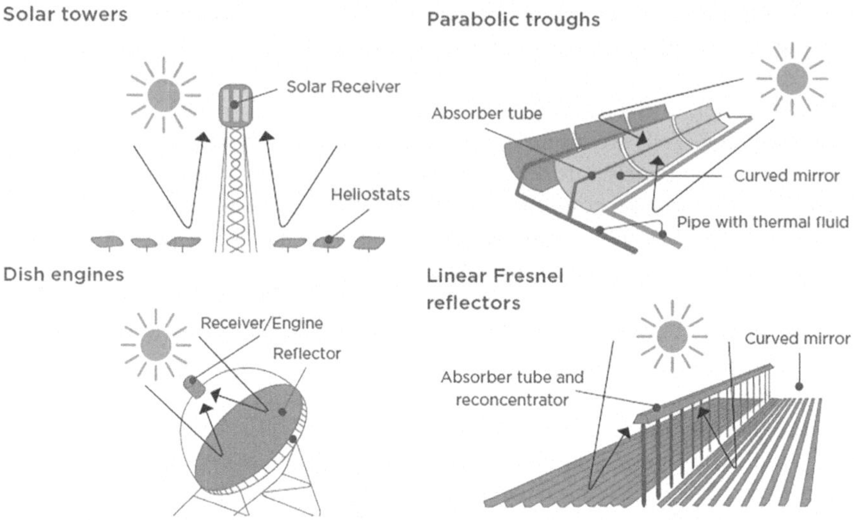

Fig. 9.2 Concentrated solar power technologies. (Source: Qader and Stückrad 2016)

conventional power plants, the thermal energy then drives a turbine to generate electricity. A downside of the CSP technology is that direct radiation is required for the process, because diffuse radiation cannot be focused. CSP plans are therefore mostly sited in countries with high direct radiation and a dry climate (see section on solar potential), for example, in northern Africa and the Middle East.

One major advantage of the CSP technology compared to solar PV is that heat can be stored at comparatively low cost. Equipped with molten salt vessels as thermal energy storage, most CSP plants have a steadier generation profile during the day and extend electricity generation long beyond sunset.

The four main construction types of CSP plants are solar towers, parabolic troughs, linear Fresnel reflectors and small-scale dish engines (Fig. 9.2). Parabolic trough and solar tower CSP plants are the most mature CSP technologies and lead new installations by far (REN21 2019).

CSP technologies can be grouped into point concentration systems (solar towers and dish engines), and linear concentration systems (parabolic troughs and linear Fresnel reflectors). Technologies based on point concentration systems achieve higher temperatures (up to 1200 °C) than linear concentration technologies (300–550 °C), and thus yield higher thermal efficiencies. However, focusing a large number of mirrors on a single point is highly complex and leads to high construction and maintenance costs. By contrast, linear concentration technologies require less land than point concentration systems.

Parabolic troughs and tower systems have first been built commercially in the 1980s. Whereas learning potentials in well-developed, mature steam processes, such as steam turbines, condensers and generators have been exhausted, further technological improvements are expected in other components. For example, higher storage potentials could be reached by using new fluids or particles that enable transfer and storage of sun energy at higher temperatures; enhanced mirror materials could reduce costs and increase reflectivity; and information technology can be used to detect system failures, reducing operation and maintenance costs, in particular of complex point concentration systems; such technological innovations could further improve the technology's efficiency and further reduce costs (Desai and Bandyopadhyay 2017; Islam et al. 2018).

3 Applications of Solar Energy

Photovoltaic systems have long been used in specialized applications as stand-alone installations (island systems). Grid-connected PV systems were first constructed in the 1990s. Nowadays, solar energy for electricity generation is applied on the wide range between small roof-top PV systems and large utility scale solar parks. In contrast to the modular solar PV, CSP is mostly deployed in large-scale power plants.

PV and CSP in large-scale solar parks, directly connected to the high voltage grid, are used to generate electricity on a commercial-scale. The largest solar power plants around the world are PV parks with installed peak capacities of up to 2 GW per site, the order of magnitude of a large nuclear power plant. The largest solar PV parks are located in India, China and the Middle East.

The modularity of solar PV (and dish engine CSP plants) also allows small-scale deployment. Roof-top PV systems have increased significantly, fostered by falling costs and governmental support policies. On a small-scale, roof-top PV serves self-consumption or supplies local mini-grids. In most countries, distributed residential systems already have generation costs below (the energy portion of) retail electricity prices, making the deployment of solar PV for self-consumption economically attractive (IEA 2020b). Behind-the-metre business models, increasingly comprising battery storage, allow to self-consume electricity generated by roof-top PV. In remote off-grid rural areas, particularly in developing countries with good solar resources, decentralized solar power feeding into local mini-grids may provide electricity access in places where a connection to the national grid is too expensive. In urban areas, roof-top PV could provide a back-up for an unreliable grid supply. In these applications, roof-top PV does not compete against large-scale power plants but against other small-scale generation units such as diesel generators. Often, solar is not only the most sustainable alternative but also economically viable. This increasing economic attractiveness of small-scale PV systems could lead to rapid expansion of decentralized PV capacity.

Aside from power generation, CSP can also generate steam, which can be used in other sectors, for example, in enhanced oil recovery or steam-using industry processes. Thus, CSP technologies could be elements of sector coupling to enable further decarbonization of economies.

4 Costs of Solar Energy

Investment costs are by far the highest cost component of solar energy. Variable operation costs of solar energy are close to zero because it uses no fuel other than solar radiation, which is free of charge. This cost structure is structurally different compared to conventional generation technologies. In this section, we discuss the development of investment and maintenance costs.

4.1 Declining Investment Costs of Solar Energy

Between 2010 and 2018, the average total installation costs of solar PV declined by 74% (Fig. 9.3). These exceptional cost reductions were made possible by extraordinarily high growth rates of PV capacity. The compound annual growth rate of PV installations was 36.8% between 2010 and 2018 (Fraunhofer ISE 2019). The learning curve (or experience curve) is another indicator of cost reduction. It describes how prices decline when the number of manufactured goods increases. Learning curves of solar PV modules were particularly steep: they have followed a 20–22% cost reduction for each doubling of capacity during the last four decades (Fraunhofer ISE 2019). Within the module, PV cells

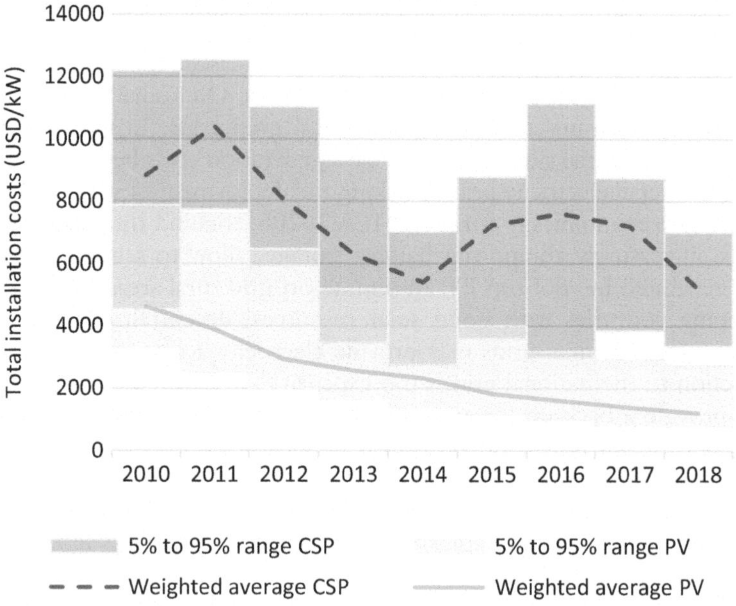

Fig. 9.3 Development of installation costs for solar PV and CSP. (Authors' own elaboration, data from IRENA 2020)

account for the highest cost shares. The three main factors driving the cost reductions of PV cells were (i) increasing sizes of manufacturing plants (economies of scale), (ii) improved module efficiency (technological advances), and (iii) a decline in costs of purified silicon. A high share of the recent cost reductions can be traced back to the rapid expansion of cell manufacturing in China, where about 70% of all PV modules are produced (Fraunhofer ISE 2019). Due to the modularity of PV panels, long distance transportation of the panels is easier than for most other generation technologies, such as, for example, blades and towers of wind turbines, which are usually manufactured locally. The market for solar panels is therefore a global market, characterized by large-scale manufacturing sites and high competition with cost-cutting effects.

The decline in balancing of system costs was led by inverter cost reductions. While PV modules historically had the largest share in total cost, in 2020 the overall BOS costs account for up to 40–60% of total PV investment costs (IEA 2020b).

Similar to solar PV, high upfront capital investment costs are also a major barrier for CSP technologies. They account for almost four fifth of the total costs. Throughout the past decade, average installation costs of CSP plants have been falling from 8800 USD/kWh in 2010 to 5,200 USD/kWh in 2018 (Fig. 9.3), albeit less constantly than they have been for solar PV. The uneven trajectory can be explained by a much lower number of new installations and an uneven buildout among countries. Until 2013, most capacity additions occurred in Spain and the United States, incentivized by generous past incentive schemes. But no new capacity has entered commercial operation in Spain since 2013 and in the United States since 2015. Current capacity extensions are led by China and Morocco (REN21 2019).

4.2 *Operation and Maintenance Costs of Solar Energy*

A second relevant cost driver of solar energy is the operation and maintenance (O&M) costs. To ensure high levels of technical performance of the solar system, it is necessary to identify and replace broken modules of a PV plant, or receivers and mirrors of a CSP plant. Particularly dusty areas (e.g. deserts) require regular cleaning of mirrors and modules. Both tasks make up for significant costs (IRENA 2020). Large-scale solar plants benefit from significant economies of scale in these O&M costs.

The development of large-scale power plants has increased the demand for tools for inspection and monitoring. Drones are often used in the solar industry due to their wide range of surveillance and monitoring capabilities. The formerly manual process of monitoring is increasingly replaced by data driven monitoring solutions. With sensing elements, drones capture the necessary data in less time and a more accurate form, which is then digitally processed. This enables long range inspection and easy control of plants and thereby reduces operation and maintenance costs significantly.

4.3 LCOE of Solar Energy

The levelized cost of electricity (LCOE) combines investment and operation costs. It is defined as the average cost of electricity per unit of electricity output. The LCOE is a good metric to measure cost reductions and technological improvements of a technology. However, this indicator should not be used to compare different technologies. It is highly sensitive to the number of full load hours of a technology and it neglects the value of electricity, i.e. how much electricity is valued at the time when generated (see Chap. 15 on system integration).

In 2018, the LCOEs of Solar PV ranged from 60 to 210 USD/MWh with a global average of 85 USD/MWh (IRENA 2019c). Further cost declines are expected to reach 20–80 USD/MWh in 2030 and 14–50 USD/MWh in 2050 (IRENA 2019a). The LCOEs of CSP technologies have also been falling throughout the last decade. In the US, the LCOE of CSP halved from 340 USD/MWh in 2010 to 190 USD/MWh in 2018 (IRENA 2019c), and is even expected to fall to 50 USD by 2030 (US Department of Energy 2020).

LCOEs decline when costs are reduced but also when the electricity output increases. Such increase is reflected in rising capacity factors (also utilization rates or load factors), describing the ratio of generated electricity to installed capacity. A capacity factor of 20% implies that the electricity generation is equivalent to this generator operating 20% all hours in the year at full capacity. As we will discuss in the following sections, capacity factors strongly depend on the location of solar energy installations and the natural resources.

5 Generation Pattern of Solar Energy

Solar generation is highly variable. Power generation with solar energy is limited to daytime given that the sun does not shine at night. Consequently, capacity factors of solar power plants (without storage) are lower compared to other technologies and typically range between 10% and 20% in most regions, reaching up to 25% at the best spots in desert locations. Since 2010, the global weighted average capacity factor of utility scale PV systems has been constantly increasing (Fig. 9.4). Three major drivers explain rising capacity factors (IRENA 2019c). First, solar PV is increasingly deployed in regions with higher irradiation levels. Second, tracking systems that follow the movement of the sun are increasingly employed, which increases the yield. And third, system losses have been reduced, for example through improvements in the efficiency of inverters.

Figure 9.4 shows that the capacity factors of CSP experienced a significantly stronger increase compared to PV. The main reason for this development is the increasing combination of CSP plants with thermal storage. This helps shifting generation into hours without sunlight, thereby allowing capacity factors exceeding 30–40%. Storage and turbine dimensioning allow to theoretically achieve capacity factors of over 90%, which is however not economical. The

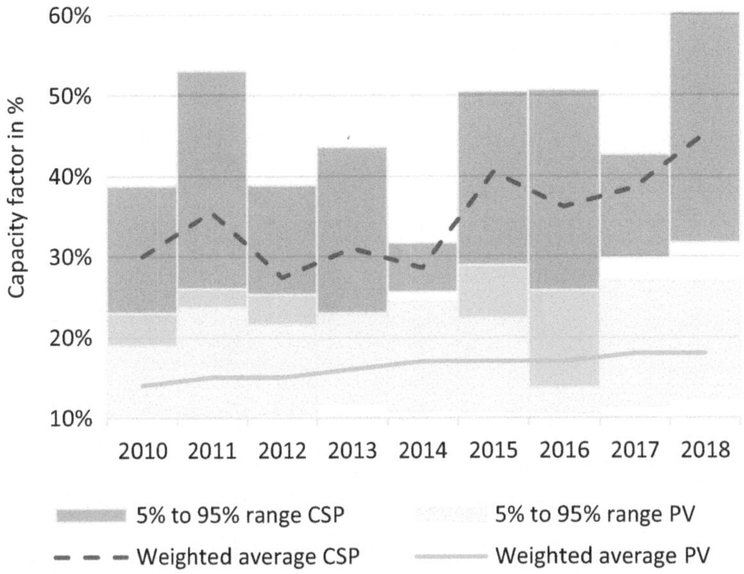

Fig. 9.4 Capacity factors of solar PV and CSP. (Authors' own elaboration, data from IRENA 2020)

high fluid temperatures of solar power CSP plants are best suited for storage. This technology has therefore the highest realized capacity factors of up to 70% (IRENA 2020). Due to the extension with thermal storage, generation patterns of CSP plants differ from solar PV. This flexibility provides an additional value compared to the non-dispatchable solar PV (Pfenninger et al. 2014).

Because of its comparatively low capacity factors, the share of solar energy in the generation mix of a country is usually lower than its share in terms of total installed capacity. A second relevant effect resulting from its generation pattern is the high concentration of solar energy generation in few hours of the day. In these hours, most PV plants of an area generate electricity. The high simultaneous electricity supply of solar generation has a depressing effect on electricity wholesale prices. In countries with high shares of solar energy, solar market values are significantly lower than for other technologies, implying that revenues from selling electricity from solar generation are, on average, lower than average wholesale electricity prices (Hirth 2013). This effect is known as merit order effect and it applies in particular to solar PV because its generation is most concentrated in time.

6 Potential of Solar Energy

The potential of solar energy varies strongly across the globe (Fig. 9.5). Depending on solar irradiance levels, solar capacity factors are highest close to the equator and decline towards the poles. The highest potential for solar

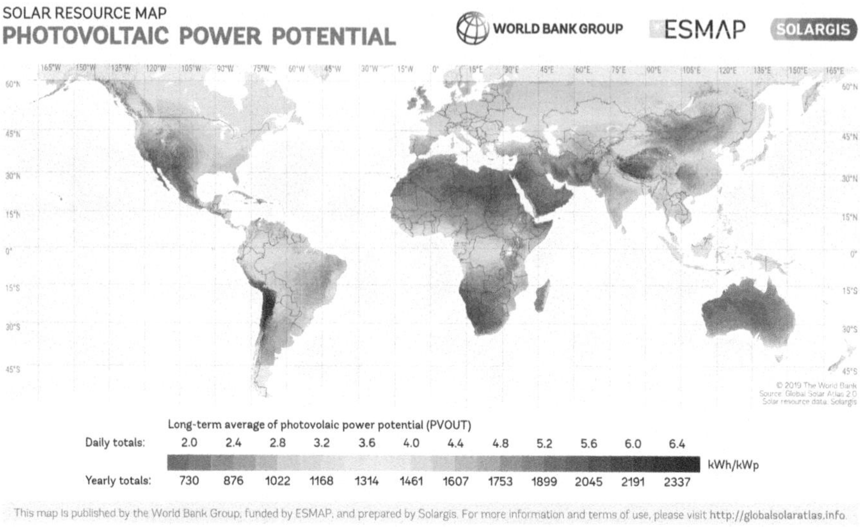

Fig. 9.5 The geographical potential of solar energy. (Source: Global Solar Energy Atlas 2019)

energy lies in the Atacama Desert in South America, the Sahara region, in the Middle East, the Gobi desert in western China, Australia and the western part of the United States. Solar irradiation in these areas is more than twice as strong as in eastern China and most northern European countries where large parts of global solar energy installations are located. Consequently, the electricity output, and with it the electricity generation costs, varies by a factor of up to two depending on the location.

CSP technologies are even more dependent on direct solar radiation than Solar PV plants and need direct normal irradiance values of at least 1800 kilowatt-hours per square meter per year. Their applicability is thus much more limited. However, well suited conditions can be found on all continents, including regions in south-western United States, the Middle East and North Africa, South Africa, Australia, Mexico, Chile and Southern Europe.

In addition to daily patterns, solar generation features seasonal patterns, especially at higher degrees of latitude, i.e. towards the poles. Close to the equator, solar irradiance increases but also cloud cover tends to be higher. In these areas, solar energy output remains relatively stable throughout the year; the position of the sun varies less and the time of sunrise and sundown remain similar.

7 Policy Instruments and Support Schemes

The strong increase in solar buildout would not have been possible without enabling government policies. These include research and development funding and development policies, which led to the development of a solar industry. This development was in particular driven by guaranteed feed-in tariffs which were first implemented in Germany in 2000.

The design of effective support schemes for solar energy needs to take into account the cost and finance structure of solar generation: as discussed in previous sections, solar plants are very capital intensive. Most expenses of solar power generation occur during construction, early in the project's lifetime. Higher cost of capital, for example due to high interest rates, strongly affects the project's profitability because expenditures in these years are recovered a decade later. The economic viability of solar therefore strongly declines with increasing cost of capital. Gas-fired power plants, in comparison, have comparatively low construction costs and a significant share of the expenses, fuel costs and emission costs, are settled when revenues from power generation accrue.

One main target of support schemes is thus to reduce the cost of capital, for example by lowering risks for project developers. Initially, feed-in tariffs were the primary support scheme for solar energy, which was mostly built on a small-scale by private households. By guaranteeing fixed feed-in tariffs, uncertainty about future revenues declined. Also, the risk of electricity price variations is mitigated for investors. With these support schemes, solar projects became profitable. Starting in 2010, many countries began to determine the level of feed-in tariffs for large-scale projects in auctions. In these auctions, projects compete for a predefined amount of supported capacity and only the most cost-efficient ones get financial support. Since the late 2010s, a shift from subsidy driven development to a competitive pricing model becomes visible in many markets. This also includes bilateral Power Purchase Agreements (PPA) between producers and off-takers, such as utilities and industry, absent of governmental support.

The less mature CSP technologies are still dependent on policy support in order to be economically viable. Due to their higher LCOE compared to solar PV, support schemes would need to reflect better the system benefits provided by CSP's dispatchability to foster a further development of CSP technologies. System stabilizing effects such as the ability to generate electricity during demand peaks will become increasingly important as energy systems decarbonize and move towards high shares of renewable energy sources.

8 Outlook

Unleashing the huge potential of solar energy will be key to achieve global climate targets and to limit global warming (IRENA 2019a). Continuous policy support is thus granted in many countries around the globe. In addition to support schemes, further cost declines and innovations drive the rapid expansion of solar energy. As in many other markets, digitalization drives cost reductions in the solar sector. Predictive algorithms based on big data and artificial intelligence enable an optimized adjustment of solar PV modules and CSP mirrors to the sun's position in order to maximize the power output. New monitoring and control systems reduce maintenance costs. Further improvements in terms of sustainability and cost reductions could be achieved by recycling materials, for example, silicon.

Driven by increasing cost competitiveness and policy support, solar energy is highly dynamic. Between 2019 and 2024, the IEA predicts solar to be the fastest growing energy source worldwide with an increase in total installed capacity of around 700 GW (IEA 2020a), more than doubling the 2018 level of 490 GW (IRENA 2019b). China, the European Union, the United States, India and Japan are expected to drive this development (IEA 2020b). By 2050, IRENA expects the total installed capacity of Solar PV to exceed 8000 GW—equalling 16 times the 2018 level (IRENA 2019b). The solar industry needs to prepare for this rising global demand—scaling up investments is therefore key in the next decade.

Literature

Desai, N. B., & Bandyopadhyay, S. (2017). Line-focusing concentrating solar collector-based power plants: a review. *Clean Technologies and Environmental Policy*, 19(1), 9–35.

ESMAP. 2019. Global Solar Atlas 2.0 Technical Report. Washington, DC: World Bank.

Fraunhofer ISE. 2019. "Photovoltaics Report." Freiburg. https://www.ise.fraunhofer.de/en/publications/studies/photovoltaics-report.html.

Geisz, John F., Ryan M. France, Kevin L. Schulte, Myles A. Steiner, Andrew G. Norman, Harvey L. Guthrey, Matthew R. Young, Tao Song, and Thomas Moriarty. 2020. "Six-Junction III–V Solar Cells with 47.1% Conversion Efficiency under 143 Suns Concentration." *Nature Energy* 5 (4): 326–35. https://doi.org/10.1038/s41560-020-0598-5.

Hirth, Lion. 2013. "The Market Value of Variable Renewables: The Effect of Solar Wind Power Variability on Their Relative Price." *Energy Economics* 38: 218–236.

IEA. 2019. "World Energy Outlook 2019." 2019. https://www.iea.org/reports/world-energy-outlook-2019.

———. 2020a. "Solar—Fuels & Technologies." 2020. https://www.iea.org/fuels-and-technologies/solar.

———. 2020b. "Solar PV—Tracking Power—Analysis." 2020. https://www.iea.org/reports/tracking-power-2019/solar-pv.

IRENA. 2019a. "Future of Solar Photovoltaics: Deployment, Investment, Technology, Grid Integration and Socio-Economic Aspects (A Global Energy Transformation: Paper)."

———. 2019b. "Renewable Capacity Highlights." Renewable Capacity Statistics 2019. 2019. https://www.irena.org/-/media/Files/IRENA/Agency/Publication/2019/.

———. 2019c. "Renewable Power Generation Costs in 2018." https://www.irena.org/publications/2019/May/Renewable-power-generation-costs-in-2018.

———. 2020. "Solar Energy." 2020. https://www.irena.org/solar.

Islam, M. T., Huda, N., Abdullah, A. B., & Saidur, R. (2018). A comprehensive review of state-of-the-art concentrating solar power (CSP) technologies: Current status and research trends. *Renewable and Sustainable Energy Reviews*, 91, 987–1018.

Pfenninger, Stefan, Paul Gauché, Johan Lilliestam, Kerstin Damerau, Fabian Wagner, and Anthony Patt. 2014. "Potential for Concentrating Solar Power to Provide Baseload and Dispatchable Power." *Nature Climate Change* 4 (8): 689–92. https://doi.org/10.1038/nclimate2276.

Qader, M., & Stückrad, S. (2016). Concentrated Solar Power. IASS Fact Sheet, 2016(2). https://doi.org/10.2312/iass.2016.029.

Quaschning, Volker. 2019. *Regenerative Energie systeme Technologie—Berechnung—Klimaschutz*. Carl Hanser Verlag.

REN21. 2019. "Renewables 2019 Global Status Report." 2019. https://www.ren21.net/gsr-2019.

US Department of Energy. 2020. "Concentrating Solar Power." https://www.energy.gov/eere/solar/concentrating-solar-power.

CHAPTER 10

Wind Power Generation

Anselm Eicke, Laima Eicke, and Manfred Hafner

1 Introduction

Wind energy has been deployed for several thousand years. The kinetic energy of moving air was driving propeller boats in ancient Egypt, pumping water in ancient Persia and later employed to grind grains across the Eurasian continent. The first windmill for electricity production was built in Scotland in 1887. Pioneer projects followed in the US and several European countries. Wind turbines as known today were only developed in the second half of the twentieth century.

Since the early 2000's, global wind energy installations have experienced high growth rates. Globally installed wind capacity grew more than six-fold in the past decade from 100 GW in 2008 to more than 620 GW in 2019. Worldwide, wind power is the second largest deployed renewable energy

A. Eicke (✉)
Hertie School, Berlin, Germany
e-mail: anselm.eicke@daad-alumni.de

L. Eicke
Institute for Advanced Sustainability Studies (IASS), Potsdam, Germany

Harvard University - Harvard Kennedy School, Boston, MA, USA
e-mail: Laima.Eicke@iass-potsdam.de

M. Hafner
SciencesPo—Paris School of International Affairs, Paris, France

Johns Hopkins University SAIS Europe, Bologna, Italy

Fondazione Eni Enrico Mattei (FEEM), Milan, Italy
e-mail: mhafner@johnshopkins.it

M. Hafner, G. Luciani (eds.), *The Palgrave Handbook of International Energy Economics*, https://doi.org/10.1007/978-3-030-86884-0_10

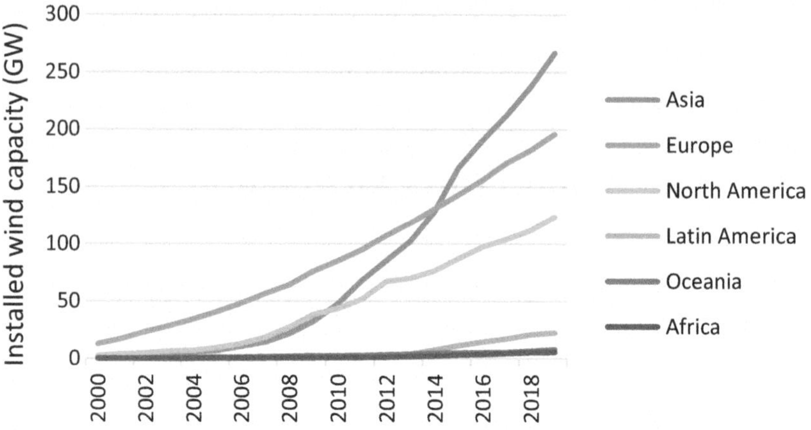

Fig. 10.1 Installed wind capacity per region (onshore and offshore combined). (Authors' own elaboration, data from IRENA 2020)

technology after hydropower, and is placed second in terms of capacity additions with 51 GW added in 2018, only surpased by solar energy (IEA 2020). Wind energy is distinguished between onshore and offshore depending on the location of turbines. Yet, as of 2018, offshore wind accounts for only 4.1% (24 GW) of the total installed wind capacity (IEA 2019).

The global wind energy market is dominated by Asia, where 41% of the global capacity is installed (Fig. 10.1). Asia overtook Europe in 2014, which was previouosly driving the expansion of wind power and accounted for 75% of global capacity in the early 2000's. North America ranks third with 112 GW installed in 2018. Despite huge potential, wind energy currently plays only a minor role in other continents (IRENA 2020). Wind energy makes up merely 6% of the world's electricity generation in 2018; yet, the international renewable energy agency (IRENA 2020) expects wind power to become the largest source of power generation in 2050, when about 35% of electricity supply may stem from wind energy (IRENA 2019).

Compared to onshore wind, offshore wind energy technologies had their technological break-through significantly later. The first larger-scale wind parks were installed along the coast lines of the North Sea and the Atlantic Ocean only in 2010. These two areas still encompass 90% of installed offshore wind capacity (IRENA 2020). Between 2010 and 2018, the global offshore wind market grew nearly 30% per year and it is expected to expand significantly in the upcoming years, with most capacity additions in 2018 located in China, North America, and Oceania (IEA 2019). IRENA projects the strongest growth of wind power in Asia where more than 50% of global wind energy capacity will be located in 2050. According to these projections, 23% of total installed onshore capacity will be located in North America and about 10% in Europe (IRENA 2019). For the offshore wind sector, projections also see Asia at the forefront in 2050, accounting for 60% of total installed capacity, followed by Europe (22%) and North America (16%).

2 Technical Characteristics

Wind turbines convert the kinetic energy of moving air into electricity. As the blades of a wind turbine are set in motion, their rotation turns a turbine. This rotational energy moves the shaft connected to the generator, producing electrical energy.

Modern wind turbines consist of three key components: the tower, the nacelle, and the rotor blades. The nacelle serves as the heart of the turbine. It encompasses the machine set, which includes the rotor hub, a generator, and the gearbox. The rotor blades are connected to the gearbox, or sometimes also directly to the generator, via a shaft. Electrical equipment allows adjusting the angle of the blades to limit electricity generation at high wind speeds and to optimize the output at changing wind speeds.

Abstracting from technical details, the power output of wind turbines mostly depends on two parameters: the wind speed and the length of the rotor blades. Because the electricity output of wind turbines is proportional to the swept area of the rotor blades, a doubling of the blade length squares the wind power potential. The energy output also raises proportionally to the third power of the wind speed. Doubling the wind speed thus leads to an increase in power potential by a factor of eight. This indicates that the hub height, that is, the length of the tower, is a crucial design parameter of wind turbines because wind speeds usually increase with height from the ground. In general, higher towers therefore improve the yield of wind turbines. Aside from height above the ground, wind speed also varies strongly across regions. The location of the installation is thus of key importance for the economics of wind energy. In general, coastal areas benefit from higher wind speeds compared to landlocked regions. This drives the deployment of offshore wind turbines despite the significantly higher technical complexity and costs. Offshore wind turbines are mostly fixed, and still rarely floating. Fixed turbines have their foundation on the ocean ground and they are therefore only deployed in shallow coastal areas. Floating offshore turbines are a less mature technology based on experiences made in the oil and gas sector. They allow harvesting wind energy farther offshore in deep waters. Only in 2017, the world's first commercial floating wind farm started operating in Scotland.

Technological improvements focus on increasing rotor diameters and the hub height to increase the power output of wind turbines. Yet, there is a trade-off between these two parameters: the higher the tower, the less weight it can hold due to turbulences caused by higher wind speeds. The firmness of construction materials sets limits to these efforts. The efforts to increase efficiency have been guiding technological development and led to significant cost reductions during the past decades: tower heights vary between 50 and 200 m, and average rotor diameters have more than doubled from 50 m in 2000 to 110 m in 2018. These improvements led to an increase in the average capacity by 250% (IRENA 2019). This trend is expected to continue: in the early 2020s, the largest windmills are expected to reach capacities of 12.5 MW and rotor diameters of up to 220 m. Nameplate capacities of future wind turbines are expected to further increase (GE Renewable Energy 2020).

The development of wind energy markets started in windy countries, including Denmark, Germany, and the UK. While the windiest locations are gradually filled by wind farms, renewable energy developers increasingly focus on locations with medium and low wind speeds (see below, the section on technical potential). Manufacturers have started developing new turbine designs specifically for these lower wind-speed sites. This is mostly achieved by increasing the height of towers. But the size of the generator also yields trade-offs: combining a small generator (with low rated capacity) with large blades, leads to a higher capacity utilization at low wind speeds, resulting in a more constant generation profile. This facilitates the integration of wind energy into the power system (see Sect. 10.5). The downside of such low wind-speed turbines is that not all the kinetic energy of wind is converted into electricity at high wind speeds. In turn, bigger (and more costly) generators produce significantly more electricity in times of high wind speeds, but are oftentimes underused. By now, wind turbine manufacturers offer a wide range of turbine sets, optimized for specific wind conditions.

Trends going beyond rising average tower heights and rotor diameters include new, aerodynamic profiles of blades and new materials, in order to increase durability and reduce maintenance costs also in demanding locations such as deserts or high seas (IRENA 2019). Digitalization drives predictive algorithms based on big data. These optimize the positioning of turbines in the wind and improve monitoring and control systems, further reducing maintenance costs (Wood Mackenzie 2019). Improvements in terms of sustainability and cost reductions could be achieved by recycling various materials. Pioneer projects have shown promising results for example, by recycling expensive fiberglass components of wind turbines (IRENA 2019).

3 Technical Potential of Wind Energy

Wind energy potential, often expressed as the mean wind speed of a location, is unequally distributed around the globe (Fig. 10.2). The power output of wind turbines thus varies strongly between locations. Generally, wind resources of higher quality for energy production are close to the poles; the lowest potential is close to the equator. The most promising areas in Europe are in the north, for example, in the North and Baltic Seas; the coasts of South America and New Zealand equally bear large potentials (Fig. 10.2).

Today's wind installations are far from tapping this huge theoretical potential. In theory, the most lucrative sites could provide more than today's total electricity consumption worldwide (IEA 2019). In practice, land usage conflicts, citizens' opposition, and environmental regulations limit deployable

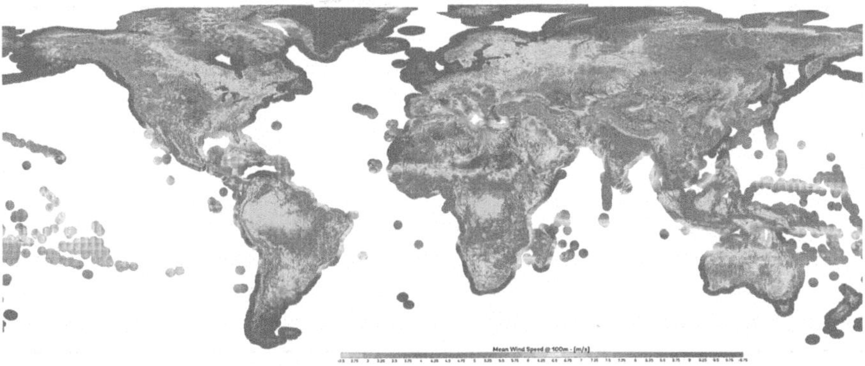

Fig. 10.2 The global wind energy potential shown as mean wind speeds 100 m above ground. (Source: Global Wind Energy Atlas 2019)

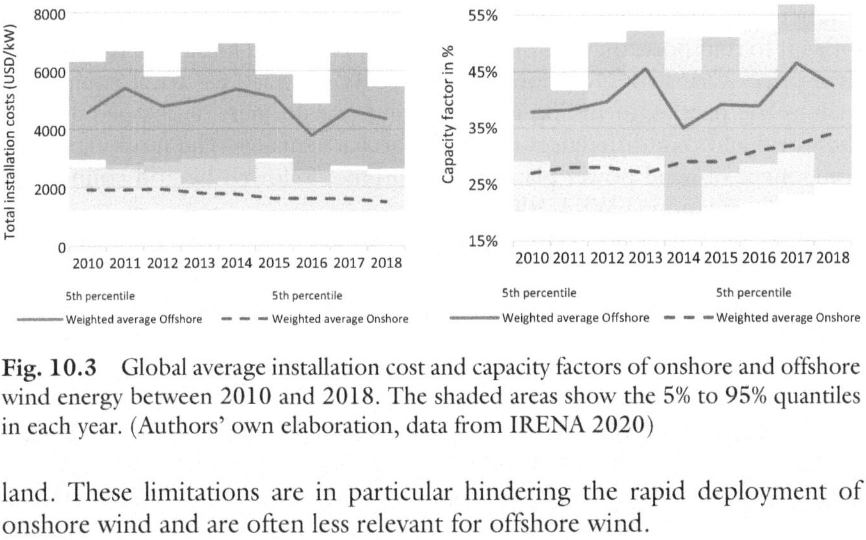

Fig. 10.3 Global average installation cost and capacity factors of onshore and offshore wind energy between 2010 and 2018. The shaded areas show the 5% to 95% quantiles in each year. (Authors' own elaboration, data from IRENA 2020)

land. These limitations are in particular hindering the rapid deployment of onshore wind and are often less relevant for offshore wind.

Wind speeds vary not only by region but also over time. Most of the time, wind farms do not generate electricity at full capacity. The capacity factor indicates how much electricity a wind turbine generates on average per year. It is defined as the actual electricity generation divided by the maximum theoretical electricity generation, that is, the power output if the turbine always generated at nameplate capacity. The higher the capacity factor, the more electricity a wind turbine produces. Typical capacity factors of onshore wind power range between 30% and 40%, with an average of 34% in 2018 (Fig. 10.3). The highest values are achieved in favorable sites and with newer wind turbine designs. In particular, coastal areas feature higher levels of wind speeds than landlocked regions, and offshore wind power's electricity generation is usually significantly higher per unit of capacity installed. Capacity factors of offshore wind farms range between 35% and 65% with an average of 43% in 2018. Some of the highest levels are reached in the North and Baltic seas in Europe (IEA 2019). Next to sites, also the turbine's design affects the capacity factor as we have discussed in the previous subsection.

4 Costs of Wind Energy

In comparison to electricity generation from fossil fuels, wind power is much more capital-intensive. Because wind power has no fuel cost and has comparatively low cost for operation and maintenance, the largest cost-components of wind turbines are investment and finance costs. This makes wind power plants particularly dependent on good financing conditions and low cost of capital.

The installation cost of wind energy varies strongly between countries. For example, the average total installation costs for onshore wind farms ranged between USD 1170 per kW in China and USD 2030 kW in the UK in 2018 (IRENA 2019). The main reason for this difference is the market structure of wind energy components. Blades and towers of wind turbines are bulky and difficult to transport; they are therefore usually produced locally. Consequently, their prices vary strongly among countries. By contrast, electrical equipment such as the nacelle, including generator and transformers, is shipped around the world and cost differences for these parts are smaller. The most expensive component of wind power plants is the turbine, followed by grid connection and the foundation (EWEA 2009).

On average, installation costs of onshore wind projects have been falling by 22% between 2010 and 2018 (Fig. 10.3, left) and are expected to further decline. The cost decline for onshore wind was mainly driven by technological advancement in turbine technologies, measured by high learning rates (IRENA 2017; Williams et al. 2017). These were fostered by public investment in research, development, and demonstration in several key markets (Klaassen et al. 2005; Zhou and GU 2019). Especially larger generators and longer blades increased power output and led to a decline in the specific (per capacity) costs. At the same time, average capacity factors of onshore wind turbines increased from 27% to 34% (Fig. 10.3, right). This is due to better-informed selection of sites and to developments of new turbine designs, better adapted to lower wind speeds.

Offshore wind parks are much more costly to construct than onshore installations. Grounding wind turbines on the sea requires expensive equipment, including for example specialized ships. Similarly, maintenance throughout the turbine's lifetime is more complex than for onshore installations due to the challenging accessibility. In terms of installation costs, the average cost of offshore energy is about three times higher than for onshore energy (USD 4360 per kW compared to USD 1500 per kW, Fig. 10.3, left panel) (IRENA 2019). But the costs of offshore wind projects have also been decreasing in recent years, for reasons similar to onshore wind. Particularly strong improvements were achieved in reducing operation and maintenance costs. Further cost decreases of offshore wind energy are expected due to high investment plans in China, likely to result in further technological improvements.

The levelized cost of electricity (LCOE) is a metric for the average cost of power generation. The LCOE is the ratio of all costs divided by the generated electricity produced over the lifetime of the plant. It therefore captures declines in costs and also technological improvements in the form of higher capacity factors. Note that LCOE is a useful metric for the cost improvements within a technology, but it should not be used to compare different generation technologies because it neglects the time-value of electricity, that is, the value that wind power offers to the electricity sector in terms of offsetting other electricity costs. LCOE of wind energy declined as technological improvements had a decreasing effect on cost (in the denominator) and increasing capacity factors improved the electricity yield (in the nominator). IRENA expects a continued decline of onshore LCOE from USD 60 per MWh in 2018 to USD 40 per MWh by 2030 (IRENA 2019). Due to the different generation profiles, a cost-benefit comparison between the two technologies exceeds the comparison of LCOE, which are significantly lower for onshore than for offshore wind (55 USD/MWh compared to 186 USD/MWh, IRENA (2020)). As discussed in the previous section, offshore wind power has significantly higher capacity factors than onshore (Fig. 10.3, right) and thereby, steadier generation profiles. This implies offshore wind also generates electricity when onshore wind does not. Because wind generation often has a depressing effect on wholesale prices, their steadier generation profile allows offshore wind to produce electricity when the wholesale electricity price is higher, which generally leads to higher market values.

As more and more wind parks that have been installed 20 to 30 years ago reach their technical lifetime, repowering old wind farms entails further cost-saving potential. Full repowering describes the replacement of entire wind parks whereas partial repowering implies that single components, such as rotors or gearboxes, are replaced while foundations and towers remain in place. The replacement or upgrading of older components with more advanced technologies can enhance the power output of wind parks and increase their operating time. This strategy allows installing the most advanced technologies at locations with best wind resources, which often had already been covered by installations. Higher rates of social acceptance by local communities, already accustomed to wind power, and existing environmental assessments decrease risks and costs in comparison to new sites. Repowering may also require grid extension due to more powerful turbines (IRENA 2019).

The installation costs of onshore and offshore wind projects are expected to continue their past decline during the next decades (IRENA 2019). Further technological advancement, more competitive supply chains, and economies of scale in production are the main drivers of these developments. Limitations to further reductions in cost are cost of materials, transportation, and the costs deriving from regulatory processes.

5 System Integration

The rapid expansion of wind power imposes new challenges on power systems. The four main characteristics of wind power hindering its system integration are the temporal variability, rapid changes in generation, difficult predictability, and regionally diverging wind energy potentials. These characteristics impose additional costs on the power system.

Changing wind speeds cause wind generation to vary over time. The replacement of dispatchable energy sources with variable wind energy raises the question of generation adequacy. Will there always be sufficient generation capacity to meet electricity demand? The contribution of wind energy to the system's generation adequacy is called "capacity value", that is, the amount of dispatchable generation capacity that it can replace without reducing security of supply. The capacity value of wind energy depends on how much wind resource is available during times of peak loads. As a rule of thumb, the capacity value is close to the average power produced by wind power when the share of wind power in the system is small (Milligan et al. 2017). This implies that offshore wind power tends to have higher capacity values than onshore wind due to its higher capacity factors. With an increasing share of wind in the system, its capacity value declines. The capacity factor can become higher if wind conditions systematically correlate with electricity demand, for example, when high wind speeds in winter time cause higher electricity consumption for heating.

High shares of wind power may cause rapid changes in electricity generation, for example, due to a weather front rapidly changing wind speed. This requires dispatchable generators to quickly adapt power output, and it imposes steep ramping gradients. Most conventional generators in today's power systems are not designed and optimized for such operational mode, in particular nuclear and coal plants. But simultaneity in wind generation is also a problem for wind power plant operators. An oversupply of electricity leads to a declining value of wind energy, reflected in low prices in liberalized markets (known as merit order effect).

The difficult predictability of wind generation has raised concerns about increasing balancing costs due to the deployment of wind energy. Yet, practical experience has shown decreasing balancing costs despite growing shares of wind power (e.g. Hirth and Ziegenhagen 2015). In several countries in Europe and the United States, wind power provides frequency support services (IEA Wind Task 25 2017). Measures to enhance flexibility with high shares of wind power include the introduction of new electricity markets, demand-side flexibility, and storage. Electricity markets that have cross-border trades of intraday and balancing resources and emerging ancillary services markets are supporting the integration of wind power.

All three issues (variability, rapid changes, and difficult predictability of wind power) are strongly reduced through interconnecting multiple power systems. Such geographical smoothing reduces extreme variations. For example, all wind plants in Europe generated less than 5% of their installed capacity in 2017 only in two consecutive hours. The maximum duration of less than 10% of capacity was 38 hours (IEA Wind Task 25 2017).

The fourth major challenge for integrating wind power into power systems are regionally diverging wind energy potentials. Wind farms, usually in remote lowly populated areas or offshore, require a grid connection to load centers. Aggravating the challenge, wind turbines are typically built in large wind farms to benefit from economies of scales. A large wind farm may consist of several hundred individual wind turbines, ranging up to a total of 1.5 GW, equivalent to a large conventional power plant. The construction of additional transmission infrastructure is a time-consuming process in many countries. A lack of grid infrastructure implies that electricity from wind cannot be transmitted and is consequently curtailed. The required network reinforcement for wind power significantly varies between regions, depending on where wind power plants are located relative to load and existing grid infrastructure. Grid connection is often a major component of the integration cost of wind energy. Yet, in most countries, these costs are usually not paid by wind plant operators (Eicke et al. 2020), also because the network costs are difficult to attribute to individual assets.

6 Policies Supporting Wind Energy

In this chapter, we have discussed various barriers hindering wind energy. Technological challenges include harsh environmental conditions, variability, and uncertainty of generation and infrastructure needs. Economic barriers are the high upfront capital costs and long payback periods which impede the access to finance in many countries. In addition, wind turbines are often confronted with limited social acceptance, increasing investment risks and prolonged installation processes. To address these challenges and to advance the deployment of renewable and domestic energy sources, countries around the world introduced support policies for wind energy, which can be grouped into deployment policies, integration policies, and enabling policies (IRENA 2019).

Deployment policies address economic barriers. They are based on fiscal and financial/economic instruments: in Europe, several countries introduced feed-in tariffs in the early 2000s, while the US and India deployed renewable portfolio standards, and introduced tax incentives. Since the late 2010s, renewable auctions have been increasingly introduced across the globe (IRENA 2019). Competitive auctions brought down installation costs and are meant to create incentives for technological advancements. This even led to extremely low auction results with bids for offshore wind energy without guaranteed feed-in tariffs in the Netherlands, Germany, and the UK (IRENA 2019). In technology neutral auction designs, wind energy often won; many countries therefore started using technology specific auction designs (Steinhilber 2016; Mitchell and Connor 2004). Furthermore, the deployment of offshore wind energy is often supported through financing grid connections and redeveloping sites.

Technical integration policies for wind energy tackle technological challenges by improving the flexibility of power systems. These comprise the enhancement of existing grid infrastructure, and promoting research and development of sector coupling and electricity storage. Several countries with high shares of wind energy generation, including Denmark and Germany, encourage the transformation into hydrogen of electricity at peak wind generation. The EU is supporting the strategic build-up of battery cells and hydrogen solutions within its Green Deal (Eicke and Petri 2020). Social integration policies improve public acceptance for wind energy. They include participatory processes in the planning stage of projects, and the engagement of local communities via ownership models or the provision of local services. Policies fostering local co-ownership or financial benefits for nearby communities have been shown to increase the acceptance of wind parks in the population (Wolf 2019).

Enabling policies address several of the above-mentioned challenges in an integrated manner, taking the whole economy into account. Examples are climate targets and industrial strategies that provide medium and long-term guidance and investment security. They foster the development of wind projects and the build-up of domestic wind industries. Such industrial policies for the wind energy sector have been part of recovery packages in response to the COVID-19 pandemic, for example in China and Germany (Weko et al. 2020). These measures are based on strong economic growth prospects and job creation potentials (Helgenberger et al. 2019). Enabling policies also encompass labor market measures, research programs and education policies to build up well-trained and skilled personnel for wind energy. Economic/financial policies might change the cost of electricity from wind generation in relation to fossil fuels significantly, for example, by introducing carbon pricing (IRENA 2019).

The design of supporting policies differs significantly by country context and policy objectives. In combination, development, integration, and enabling policies aim to tackle the technological, economic, and social challenges we discussed in this chapter. This helps further improving wind energy technologies and taping their huge potentials across the globe.

Literature

Eicke, A., Khanna, T. & Hirth, L. (2020). Locational Investment Signals: How to Steer the Siting of New Generation Capacity in Power Systems?. *The Energy Journal, 41*(6), 281–304.

Eicke L., Petri F. (2020) The EU in Global Energy Governance. In: Knodt M., Kemmerzell J. (eds) Handbook of Energy Governance in Europe. Springer, Cham.

EWEA (2009) The Economics of Wind Energy. Available online at: http://www.ewea.org/fileadmin/files/library/publications/reports/Economics_of_Wind_Energy.pdf. Last Accessed: 20.06.2020

GE Renewable Energy (2020): Driving efficiency and decreasing the cost of offshore wind energy. Available online at: https://www.ge.com/renewableenergy/wind-energy/offshore-wind/haliade-x-offshore-turbine Last Accessed: 20.06.2020

Global Wind Energy Atlas 2019. Map obtained from the “Global Wind Atlas 3.0, a free, web-based application developed, owned and operated by the Technical University of Denmark (DTU). The Global Wind Atlas 3.0 is released in partnership with the World Bank Group, utilizing data provided by Vortex, using funding provided by the Energy Sector Management Assistance Program (ESMAP).URL: https://globalwindatlas.info/download/high-resolution-maps/World

Helgenberger, S., Jänicke, M., & Gürtler, K. (2019). Co-benefits of Climate Change Mitigation. In W. Leal Filho, A. M. Azul, L. Brandli, P. G. Özuyar, & T. Wall (Eds.), Climate Action: Encyclopedia of the UN Sustainable Development Goals. Cham: Springer International Publishing.

Hirth, L., and Ziegenhagen, I., (2015). Balancing power and variable renewables: Three links, Renewable and Sustainable Energy Reviews, Volume 50, Pages 1035–1051, https://doi.org/10.1016/j.rser.2015.04.180.

IEA (2020): Wind. Available online at: https://www.iea.org/fuels-and-technologies/wind Last Accessed: 20.06.2020

IEA (2019) Offshore Wind Outlook. Available online at: https://www.iea.org/reports/offshore-wind-outlook-2019 Last Accessed: 20.06.2020

IEA Wind Task 25 (2017): Design and operation of power systems with large amounts of wind power. Final summary report, Phase four 2015–2017. Available online at: https://www.vttresearch.com/sites/default/files/pdf/technology/2019/T350.pdf Last Accessed: 20.06.2020.

IRENA (2017): Onshore Wind Industry Learning Fast. Available online at: https://www.irena.org/newsroom/articles/2017/Mar/Onshore-Wind-Industry-Learning-Fast Last Accessed: 20.06.2020

IRENA (2020): Statistics. Available online at: https://www.irena.org/Statistics/View-Data-by-Topic/Capacity-and-Generation/Regional-Trends Last Accessed: 20.06.2020

IRENA (2019): Future of wind. Available online at: https://www.irena.org/-/media/Files/IRENA/Agency/Publication/2019/Oct/IRENA_Future_of_wind_2019.pdf Last Accessed: 20.06.2020

Klaassen, G., Miketa, A., Larsen, K., & Sundqvist, T. (2005). The impact of R&D on innovation for wind energy in Denmark, Germany and the United Kingdom. Ecological economics, 54(2–3), 227–240.

Milligan, M., Frew, B., Ibanez, E., Kiviluoma, J., Holttinen, H., and Söder L., 2017. “Capacity value assessments of wind power,” Wiley Interdisciplinary Reviews: Energy and Environment, Wiley Blackwell, vol. 6(1), January.

Mitchell, C., and Connor, P. (2004): Renewable energy policy in the UK 1990–2003. *Energy Policy*, vol. 32, no. 17, pp. 1935–1947.

Steinhilber, S. (2016): Auctions for Renewable Energy Support in the Ireland: Instruments and lessons learnt. *Aures Report D4.1-IE.*

Weko, S., Eicke, L., Quitzow, R.,Bersalli, G., Lira, F., Marian, A., Süsser, D., Thapar, S., and Xue, B. (2020). Covid-19 and Carbon Lock-In: Impacts on the Energy transition. IASS Study. https://doi.org/10.2312/iass.2020.027

Williams, E., Hittinger, E., Carvalho, R., & Williams, R. (2017). Wind power costs expected to decrease due to technological progress. Energy Policy, 106, 427–435.

Wolf, I. (2019): Soziales Nachhaltigkeitsbarometer der Energiewende 2019. *IASS Study.*

Worldbank (2019): Global Wind Atlas. Available online at: www.Globalwindatlas.info Last Accessed: 20.06.2020

Wood Mackenzie (2019): Unplanned wind turbine repairs to cost industry $8 billion+ in 2019. Available online at: www.woodmac.com/press-releases/unplanned-wind-turbine-repairs-to-cost-industry-$8-billion-in-2019 Last Accessed: 20.06.2020

Zhou, Y., & Gu, A. (2019). Learning Curve Analysis of Wind Power and Photovoltaics Technology in US: Cost Reduction and the Importance of Research, Development and Demonstration. Sustainability, 11(8), 2310.

CHAPTER 11

Geothermal Power Generation

Isabella Nardini

1 Introduction

The word *geothermal* comes from the Greek *gê* and *thermòs*, which literally means *Heat of the Earth.*

Geothermal energy derives from thermal energy that is contained within the Earth. The main sources of this energy are the radiogenic heat produced by the radioactive decay of isotopes (atoms of a given element, in this case potassium, thorium and uranium, with the same number of protons but different numbers of neutrons) in the mantle and crust, and the primordial heat left over from the formation of the Earth. This heat is constantly transferred from the interior of the Earth to its surface: due to this heat flow, the rock temperature increases by about 30 °C for each km of depth (geothermal gradient). Rainwater circulating underground through porous, fractured, permeable rocks is heated up. The hot water (or steam), rising through faults and fractures, can reach the surface and form hot springs, fumaroles and geysers but most of it, instead, remains underground, trapped in fractures and porous layers of rock between impermeable surfaces. Drilling wells connect the geothermal resource with the surface for using the thermal energy contained in the fluid.

The total estimated thermal energy of the Earth is immense but only a fraction can be recovered and utilised by humankind.

Geothermal energy from natural pools and hot springs was known since ancient times. More than 10,000 years ago, Native Americans used geothermal energy for cooking, bathing and warming. The beneficial effects of baths

I. Nardini (✉)
Fraunhofer IEG, Institution for Energy Infrastructures and Geothermal Systems, Bochum, Germany
e-mail: isabella.nardini@ieg.fraunhofer.de

M. Hafner, G. Luciani (eds.), *The Palgrave Handbook of International Energy Economics*, https://doi.org/10.1007/978-3-030-86884-0_11

heated by hot springs and thermal waters were considered sacred gifts by Egyptians, Israelites, Hindus. Also Greeks and Romans used the water for bathing, cooking and curative purposes and one of the best-preserved evidence is the Roman city of Pompeii during the first century CE, where the water supply and the heating system were constantly updated with the most advanced techniques of that time. Such uses of geothermal energy were initially limited to sites where hot water and steam were accessible.

The world's pioneer district heating system was installed at Chaudes-Aigues (France) at the beginning of the fourteenth century, but only in the late nineteenth century, it was commercially introduced in several cities of USA and industry began to realize the economic potential of geothermal resources. Today the world's largest geothermal district heating system is in Reykjavik (Iceland), which has utilized natural hot water to heat its buildings and houses since 1930. Early industrial applications included the extraction of boric acid from geothermal fluids in Larderello (Italy) during the early nineteenth century. The first attempt at geothermal electric power generation took place in Larderello, with the successful development of an experimental plant in 1904. The first geothermal well was drilled in Japan in 1919, and at the Geysers in northern California in 1921. Geothermal power plants were then commissioned in New Zealand in 1958, in Mexico in 1959, in the USA in 1960, and later in many other countries.

2 Geothermal Energy Technology and Utilization

Geothermal energy can be found around the globe and is not conditioned by external conditions (whereas e.g. solar and wind energy present higher variability and intermittence) but upon the depth to the resource and economic convenience to produce it. Growing awareness and interest in renewable resources has raised the need to homogenize the reporting requirements for geothermal resources so that they can be applied worldwide. As no internationally agreed standards, guidelines or codes exist, the ambiguity inherent in the definition of geothermal assessments leads to increased resource uncertainty, more investment risk and less confidence in development Beyond the fact that the classification of a geothermal resource is strongly dependent on different approaches (i.e. by temperature, use, type and status, accessibility, electric power generation, stored heat, specific energy, recoverable volume, recoverable heat, recoverable power, net profit) (Falcone et al. 2013), it can be used to generated clean electricity, for heating and cooling or for industrial purposes. However, for electricity generation, medium- to high-temperature resources, which are usually close to volcanically active regions, are needed. A simplified scheme based on reservoir temperature, fluid type (water or steam), applications and technology is shown in Fig. 11.1.

Geothermal energy utilization is commonly divided into two categories: electric energy generation and direct uses. Deep geothermal technologies generally take advantage of a much deeper (commonly more than 2 km depth),

RESERVOIR TEMPERATURE	FLUID TYPE	APPLICATION	TECHNOLOGY
HIGH -T >150°C	water, vapour	electricity generation direct heat use	▪ DRY STEAM TURBINE ▪ SINGLE/DOUBLE/TRIPLE FLASH ❖ HEAT EXCHANGER
MEDIUM-T 90-150°C	water	electricity generation direct heat use	▪ BINARY CYCLE ❖ HEAT EXCHANGER ❖ GEOTHERMAL HEAT PUMP
LOW-T <90°C	water	direct heat use	❖ HEAT EXCHANGER ❖ GEOTHERMAL HEAT PUMP ❖ DIRECT HEAT USE

Fig. 11.1 Simplified scheme of geothermal resources, application and technology

higher temperature geothermal resource to generate electricity, while ground source heat pumps and direct use geothermal technologies utilize shallower, lower temperature geothermal resource for heating, cooling and industrial applications.

2.1 Dry Steam Power Plants

These plants draw from underground resources of steam. The conversion device is a steam turbine designed to directly use the low-pressure, high-volume fluid produced in the steam field. The steam is piped directly from underground wells to the power plant, where it is directed into a turbine/generator unit. Dry steam plants commonly use condensing turbines. The condensate is re-injected (closed cycle) or evaporated in wet cooling towers. This type of geothermal power plant uses steam of 150 °C or higher. Direct dry steam plants range in size from 8 MW to 140 MW (S&P Global Platts 2016).

2.2 Flash Steam Power Plants

These conversion facilities are the most common type of geothermal electricity plants in operation today. They are similar to dry steam plants; however, the steam is obtained from a separation process called flashing. They use geothermal reservoirs of very hot water that flows up through wells in the ground under its own pressure. As it flows upward, the pressure decreases and some of the hot water boils into steam. The steam is then separated from the water and directed to the turbines. The fluid fraction exiting the separators, as well as the steam condensate (except for condensate evaporated in a wet cooling system), is usually re-injected. The temperature of the fluid drops if the pressure is lowered, so flash power plants work best with well temperatures greater than 180 °C. Flash plants vary in size depending on whether they are single- (0.2–80 MW), double—(2–110 MW) or triple-flash (60–150 MW) plants (S&P Global Platts 2016).

2.3 *Binary Cycle Power Plants*

These plants operate on water at lower temperatures. The primary resource fluid is used, via heat exchangers, to heat a secondary working fluid, usually an organic compound with a low boiling point (i.e. ammonia/water mixtures used in Kalina cycles or hydrocarbons in Organic Rankine Cycles—ORC), in a closed loop. Typically, binary plants are used for resource temperature between 100 °C and 170 °C. Although it is possible to work with temperatures lower than 100 °C. Binary plants range in size from less than 1 MW to 50 MW (S&P Global Platts 2016).

2.4 *Combined-Cycle or Hybrid Plants*

Some geothermal plants use a combined cycle, which adds a traditional Rankine cycle to produce electricity from what otherwise would become waste heat from a binary cycle (ORMAT 2017). The typical size of combined-cycle plants ranges from a few MW to 10 MWe. Hybrid geothermal power plants use the same basics as a stand-alone geothermal power plant but combine a different heat source into the process; for example, heat from a concentrating solar power (CSP) plant. This heat is added to the geothermal brine, increasing the temperature and power output.

Geothermal electricity generation relies mainly on technologies that exploit conventional geothermal resources, such as: dry steam plants, flash plants, binary plants, and combined-cycle or hybrid plants. However, as high-quality conventional resources become harder to access, deeper resources may become accessible in the future through the development of Enhanced Geothermal System (EGS).

2.5 *Enhanced Geothermal System (EGS)*

A large part of the geothermal potential is heat stored at depths greater than commonly drilled.

The principle of the EGS is to create artificial fractures to connect production and injection wells by hydraulic or chemical stimulation. Stimulation is accomplished by injecting water (natural water flow is absent) and a small amount of chemicals at high pressure to create or reopen fractures in the deep rock. The EGS uses binary plants to produce power from the hot brine, which needs then to be totally re-injected in order to keep the pressure and production stable. During EGS reservoir creation and stimulation, rocks may slip along pre-existing fractures and produce micro-seismic events, which is one of the major controversial issues for the development of these systems.

2.6 *Heat Pump and Direct Use Systems*

A ground source heat pump utilizes the naturally occurring difference between the subsurface ground temperature (average temperature at depth of 20–100 m is 14 °C depending on the site) and the subsurface ambient air temperature. Geothermal hot water can be used for many applications that require heat. In these systems, a well is drilled into a geothermal reservoir to provide a steady stream of hot water. The water is brought up through the well (horizontally or vertically drilled), and a mechanical system (piping, heat exchanger and controls) delivers the heat directly for its intended use. A disposal system then either injects the cooled water underground or disposes of it on the surface. The heat pump can also operate in reverse, moving heat from the ambient air in a building into the ground, in effect cooling the building. A supplementary advantage of this system is that hot water can also be supplied to the building using the same loop. During the heat exchange, the excess heat from the building is transferred to its hot water system before reaching the ground loop. No additional energy is required to heat the water and no gases are released as everything is in a closed loop.

Beyond the heat pump systems for heating and cooling buildings and district heating, direct use systems have a wide range of applications such as greenhouse operations, heating the sidewalks and roads to melt snow, hot water supply, aquaculture and other industrial uses like laundries, drying, biological processes, waste management, resorts and spas in tourism industry. With some applications, researchers are exploring ways to effectively use the geothermal fluid for generating electricity as well.

3 Geothermal Power Generation Worldwide and Market Overview

The renewable power capacity data shown in the tables and figures below represent the maximum net generating capacity of power plants and other conversion facilities that use renewable energy sources to produce electricity. For most countries and technologies, the data reflect the capacity installed and connected at a given year. The capacity data are presented in megawatts (MW) and the generation data are presented in gigawatt-hours (GWh).

Geothermal installed capacity worldwide has continued to grow in the last decade (Fig. 11.2). In 2020, global geothermal installed capacity has increased up to 14,013 MW, representing approximately 0.5% of renewable power capacity worldwide. Tables 11.1 and 11.2 and Figs. 11.3 and 11.4 show data of the total installed geothermal capacity respectively per region and per country. The Asian regions share 32.4% of the total geothermal installed capacity due to the remarkable contribution of Indonesia (2131 MW) and the Philippines (1928 MW) followed by Japan (481 MW). North America shares 24.9% of the total with the highest contribution per country given by the USA (2587 MW). Europe shares 11.8% of the total and the major contribution is given by Italy

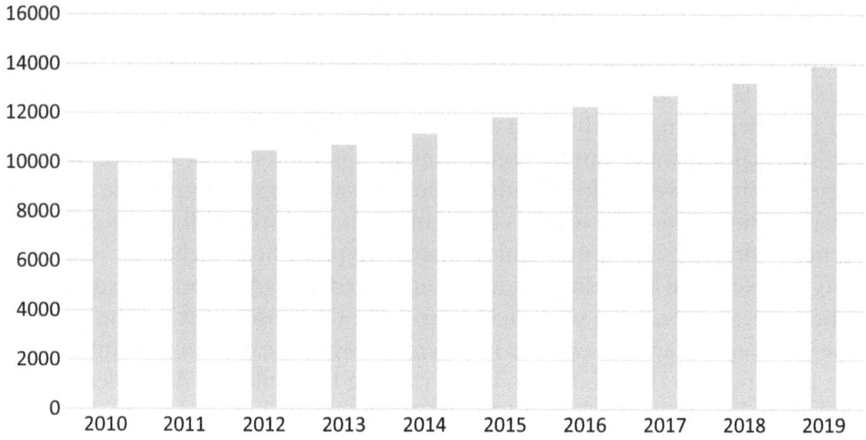

Fig. 11.2 Total Geothermal Installed Capacity (MW). (Source: IRENA_Renewable_Energy_Statistics_2021)

Table 11.1 Geothermal installed capacity by region

Region	*Geothermal Installed Capacity (MW)*	*Share of Total*
Asia	4540	32.4%
N America	3492	24.9%
Europe	1652	11.8%
Eurasia	1695	12.1%
Oceania	1040	7.4%
Africa	831	5.9%
C America + Carib	723	5.2%
S America	40	0.3%
Total	14013	100.0%

Data Source: IRENA_Renewable_Energy_Statistics_2021. The data refer to 2020 obtained from a variety of sources, including: the IRENA questionnaire; official statistics; industry association reports; and other reports and news articles

(797 MW) and Iceland (756 MW). Eurasia (Russian Federation and Turkey) shares 12.1%, almost all in Turkey (1613 MW), with only a minor estimated contribution by the Russian Federation (81 MW). In Oceania, a major contribution is given by New Zealand (984 MW). The African countries share 5.9% of the total, basically concentrated in Kenya (824 MW) and Ethiopia (7 MW). Central America and the Caribbean are mainly represented by Costa Rica (262 MW), El Salvador (204 MW) and Nicaragua (153 MW). The geothermal installed capacity in South America is completely concentrated in Chile (40 MW).

Table 11.2 Geothermal Installed Capacity by country in 2020

Country	*Geothermal Installed Capacity (in MW)*	*Share of Total*
United States	2587	18.5%
Indonesia	2131	15.2%
Philippines	1928	13.8%
Turkey	1613	11.5%
New Zealand	984	7.0%
Mexico	906	6.5%
[a]Kenya	824	5.9%
Italy	797	5.7%
Iceland	756	5.4%
Japan	481	3.4%
Other	1006	7.2%
Total	14,013	100.0%

Data Source: IRENA_Renewable_Energy_Statistics_2021. Data obtained from a variety of sources, including: the IRENA questionnaire; official statistics; industry association reports; and other reports and news articles

[a] Data estimated by IRENA from a variety of different data sources

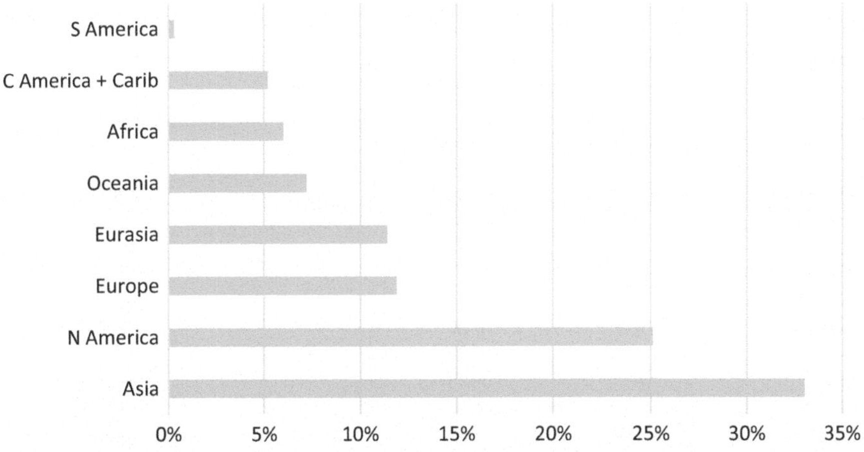

Fig. 11.3 Share of Total Geothermal Installed Capacity by region in 2020. (Source: IRENA_Renewable_Energy_Statistics_ 2021)

Coherently also the electricity generation from geothermal has grown from 69,856 GWh in 2011 to 92,047 GWh in 2019. The top ten countries are listed below in Table 11.3 and shown in Fig. 11.5.

At the end of 2020, there were 139 geothermal power plants with 3.5 GWe of geothermal electricity capacity across Europe. In 2020, Turkey has become the most active geothermal power market in the world with 8 new plants which added 165 MWe of geothermal electricity installed capacity. Moreover, a profitable development is driven by the confirmation from the Turkish government on the extension of the feed in tariff program applicable to plants entering in

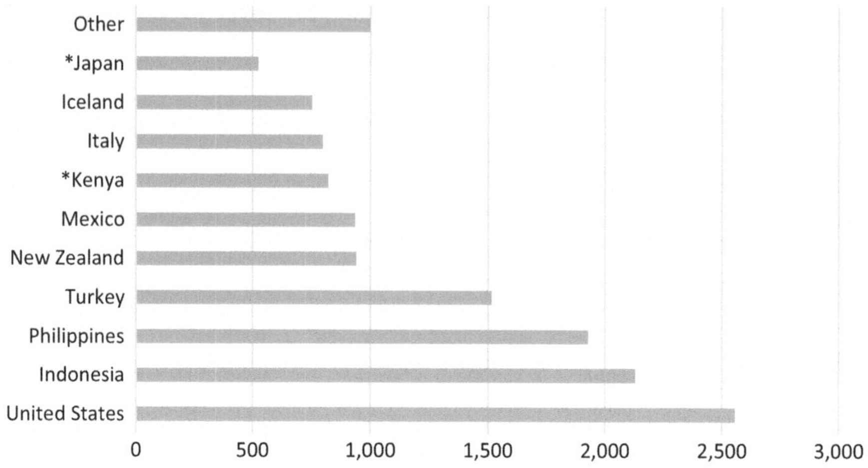

Fig. 11.4 Installed Geothermal Capacity by country in 2020 (MW). (Source: IRENA_Renewable_Energy_Statistics_ 2021)

Table 11.3 Geothermal electricity production by country in 2019

Country	*Electricity Production (GWh)*	*Share of Total*
United States	18,364	20.0%
Indonesia	14,100	15.3%
Philippines	10,691	11.6%
Turkey	8952	9.7%
New Zealand	8041	8.7%
Mexico	5330	5.8%
[a]Kenya	5384	5.8%
Italy	6075	6.6%
Iceland	6018	6.55%
Japan	2830	3.1%
Other	6262	6.8%
Total	92,047	100.0%

Data Source: IRENA_Renewable_Energy_Statistics_2021. Data obtained from a variety of sources, including: the IRENA questionnaire; official statistics; industry association reports; and other reports and news articles

[a] Data estimated by IRENA from a variety of different data sources

operation by 2025 (EGEC 2020). The European geothermal electricity market remains highly dominated by Italy and Iceland. The geothermal power potential is large and could cover, or exceed, the actual electricity demand in many countries. The EU Member States' National Energy and Climate Plans (NECPs) indicate as their target to reach the electricity production of 8 TWhe by 2030.

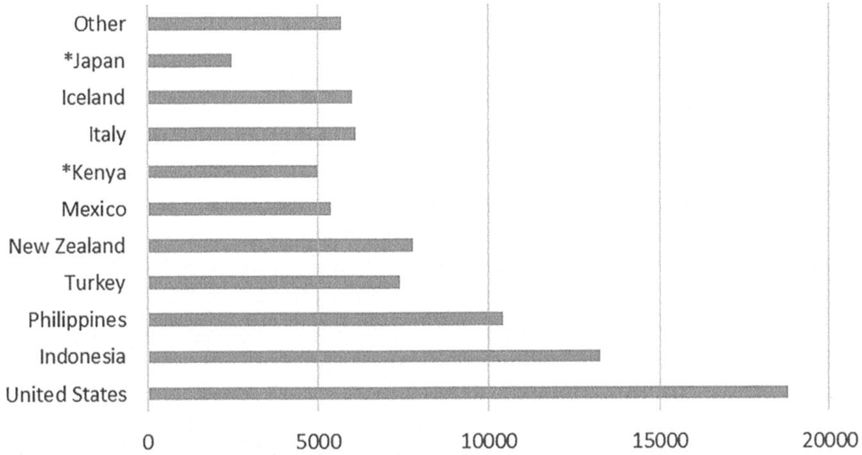

Fig. 11.5 Geothermal Electricity Production by country in 2019 (GWh) (Source: IRENA_Renewable_Energy_Statistics_2021)

Europe is a principal global market for geothermal district heating and cooling for buildings, industry and other services. In 2019, there were 5.5 GWht of installed geothermal district heating and cooling capacity in 25 European countries, corresponding to 327 systems. In 2020 a total of 350 geothermal district heating and cooling systems in operation plus 232 under development ready to be operational by 2025 (EGEC 2020). The status of geothermal district heating and cooling in Europe reflects a strong interest for this renewable resource and the possibility to implement it almost everywhere in Europe. The Netherlands continues to be the driving European market for deep geothermal heating and cooling.

The European geothermal heat pump market reached the milestone of 2 million units installed, as it is becoming a major heating and cooling solution in some regional or national markets because of its high efficiency and decreased costs due to the distribution of bigger systems in large edifices. Mature market for geothermal heat pumps in Europe include Germany, France and Switzerland. In colder climate countries, geothermal heat pumps are closer to market maturity and Sweden is the only country qualified as a mature market.

4 Geothermal Energy Costs and the Financing of Geothermal Power Plants

The overall cost of a geothermal project is extremely site-sensitive in the broadest sense, depending not only upon the geological setting but also, to a large extent, on market and policy from national to local scale. There are however, economic factors common to all projects such as provision of fuel (resource type), conversion technology, revenue generation and financing. The investment cost is basically divided into the cost of surface infrastructures and operations and the cost of subsurface activity. The surface costs include the cost of surface exploration and resource assessment and the cost of conversion technology (design and construction of the conversion facility and related surface equipment, such as electrical generation plant with required transformers and transmission lines, roads, buildings), while the cost of subsurface investment is that of drilling (exploration drilling, drilling of production and injection wells). While surface costs can be predicted with a certain degree of accuracy, higher uncertainty is represented by the drilling cost. The drilling cost for a low-temperature geothermal development typically is 10–20% of the total cost, and that for a high-temperature field is usually 20–50% of the total cost. Although drilling costs have a strong influence on the overall cost, the uncertainty driving the geothermal development cannot be exclusively attributed to them.

Typical costs for geothermal power plants range from 2000 USD/kW to 6000 USD/kW (depending on the site, if installing additional capacity at existing brown field or new green field). The data for recent projects shows that global weighted-average total installed costs were USD 4468/kW in 2020, slightly lower than in 2019, but broadly in line with values seen over the last four years.

The LCOE from a geothermal power plant is generally calculated by using the installed costs, operations and maintenance (O&M) costs, economic lifetime, and weighted average cost of capital. The global levelized cost of electricity (LCOE) of geothermal power of commissioned plants in 2020 was USD 0,071/kWh, having slightly declined from previous years (IRENA 2021, Renewable Power Generation Costs in 2020). O&M costs are high for geothermal projects, because of the need to work over production wells on a periodic basis to maintain fluid flow and hence production.

Capacity factors for geothermal plants, are the highest with respect to all other renewables, typically expected in the range of 70–90%, but lifetime capacity factors, considering a 25-year economic life, will depend heavily on well performance and ongoing investment to maintain production wells or drill new ones as the reservoir responds to the extraction and reinjection of fluids.

Costs for geothermal technologies are expected to continue to drop through 2050 (Sigfusson and Uihlein 2015). The economics of geothermal power plants may be improved by exploiting by-products such as silica, carbon dioxide and other chemicals.

Geothermal power plant development is capital-intensive due to exploration and drilling costs, for which it can be difficult to obtain bank loans. Since geothermal exploration is considered high risk, developers generally need to obtain some type of public financing. This risk is derived from the fact that capital is required before confirmation of the presence of the resource and therefore before project profitability can be determined. Policy makers can surely contribute to decrease the risk and the capital cost for private developers by deploying economic and financial instruments for example, by cost-sharing for drilling and by the activation of public-private risk insurance schemes; by data sharing with developers (including seismic events/fractures and deep drilling data owned by national or local governments).

5 Outlook for Geothermal Energy

The transition from current fossil-fuel energy system towards a sustainable one-based requires renewable energy technology. The potential of geothermal energy is huge and can be used globally. Given the somewhat unique nature of geothermal resources, geothermal power generation is very different to other renewable power generation technologies. Geothermal is a mature, commercially proven technology and with advances in technology and processes, it can become increasingly competitive as expected by 2050. Moreover, advantages of geothermal energy are not only the generation of electricity in different plant configurations but also the direct application of heat in industry, the heating and cooling. It is well positioned to play an important role in mitigating global climate change, increasing national energy security, and making the economy more competitive.

There are significant risks involved with initial exploration and drilling, but favourable regulatory environments (including tax incentives and land permitting and licensing legal framework) can do much to facilitate further developments in the sector. Besides, from being a clean and renewable energy source, geothermal power is also suitable for base load electricity generation and thus has the potential to become the backbone of local grid systems.

Cited References and Consulted Official Report and Scientific Publications

EGEC (2020) - EGEC Geothermal Market Report 2020

Falcone, G., Gnoni, A., Bob Harrison, B., Alimonti, C. (2013). Classification and Reporting Requirements for Geothermal Resources. European Geothermal Congress 2013, Pisa, Italy, 3–7 June 2013.

IRENA (2021), Renewable Energy Statistics 2021 The International Renewable Energy Agency, Abu Dhabi.

IRENA (2021), Renewable Power Generation Costs in 2020, International Renewable Energy Agency, Abu Dhabi.

ORMAT, (2017). *Combined Cycle Units Geothermal Power Plants*, ORMAT.

S&P Global Platts (2016). "UDI World Electric Power Plants Data Base", https://www.platts.com/products/world-electric-power-plants-database

Sigfusson, B., Uihlein, A., (2015). 2015 JRC Geothermal Energy Status Report, EUR 27623 EN; https://doi.org/10.2790/757652.

CHAPTER 12

Power Generation from Tides and Waves

Dhruv Bhatnagar, Danielle Preziuso, and Rebecca O'Neil with contribution by Jan Alam, Saptarshi Bhattacharya and Sarmad Hanif

1 Introduction

Ocean waves and tides have the potential to supply a significant portion of the world's energy needs. Water is denser than air, ocean forces are powerful, and significant population density and corresponding electricity loads occur near ocean environments around the world. Yet commercial development of energy capture technologies from marine resources has been limited to date, generating only 1.2 TWh of electricity across the globe in 2018 while global electricity demand was 23,000 TWh (International Energy Agency 2019a, b).

Currently, cost and technology uncertainty of marine energy devices remain the primary barrier to expansion. However, as renewable energy technologies mature and become more viable through policy intervention, economic development, generation incentives, and robust research and development programs, marine technologies increasingly hold promise of commercialization.

This chapter discusses the development of marine energy projects to date, economic factors for deployment and operations, and commercialization pathways for the future. While marine renewable technologies include a range of devices such as ocean thermal conversion technologies and ocean current devices, the chapter focuses on the wave and tidal energy sectors.

D. Bhatnagar • D. Preziuso • R. O'Neil (✉)
Pacific Northwest National Laboratory, Richland, WA, USA
e-mail: Rebecca.ONeil@pnnl.gov; https://www.pnnl.gov/marine-energy; https://www.pnnl.gov/projects/marine-energy-grid-value

M. Hafner, G. Luciani (eds.), *The Palgrave Handbook of International Energy Economics*, https://doi.org/10.1007/978-3-030-86884-0_12

2 Resources, Technologies, Deployments

Tidal current energy capture devices and wave energy converters (WECs) can vary greatly in design, scale, stage of development, and technology readiness level. Given this range, the most useful common references for economic potential are tidal and wave energy resource characteristics and occurrence.

2.1 *Tidal Current Devices*

Tidal current is generally driven by the Earth's rotation, the relative positions of celestial bodies to the Earth, and local bathymetry (i.e., ocean depth and topography). Tidal currents are bi-directional but generally one-dimensional, as a given tide typically ebbs and flows along one vector. Tidal devices may be mounted to the ocean floor and elevated to the current or may be suspended from the surface. Ultimately, the amount of energy that can be harnessed is dictated by the velocity of the tidal current.

The simplest and most dominant form of a tidal current device is the horizontal axial-flow turbine, which roughly resembles a horizontal axis wind turbine and operates in a similar manner. A variety of other device types are being developed, including tidal kites, oscillating hydrofoils, ducted turbines and screw turbines (Roberts et al. 2016; U.S. Department of Energy 2015). All of these technologies differ from tidal barrages, which are configured to extract energy from changes in tidal elevation rather than the horizontal current of tides, and have been in commercial use for decades.

Due to the nature of the resource, tidal energy is considered variable but highly predictable in its variability, unlike other renewable resources (e.g., wind and solar), which require extensive short-term forecasting and energy reserves to compensate for weather conditions. Tidal patterns are generally sinusoidal but can show great variation in intensity and pattern within short distances. Less than 20 miles apart, the maximum velocity at Admiralty Inlet, Washington (Northwest USA) can be more than double the maximum velocity at Sequim Bay, Washington over the course of a day and display significantly different resource patterns over time as shown in Fig. 12.1.

2.2 *Tidal Current Device Deployment*

Although tidal devices have not been deployed at utility scale, there have been successful grid-connected deployments and prototype tests. The most developed tidal stream turbine installation to date, SIMEC Atlantis Energy's SeaGen device, was installed in Strangford Lough, Northern Ireland, United Kingdom and connected to the grid in 2008 (MacEnri et al. 2013). Over the course of its lifetime, the 1.2 MW system produced over 11.6 GWh of electricity, which ESB Independent Energy bought through a power purchase agreement before the device was fully decommissioned in 2019 (SIMEC Atlantis Energy 2019; Renewable Technology 2017).

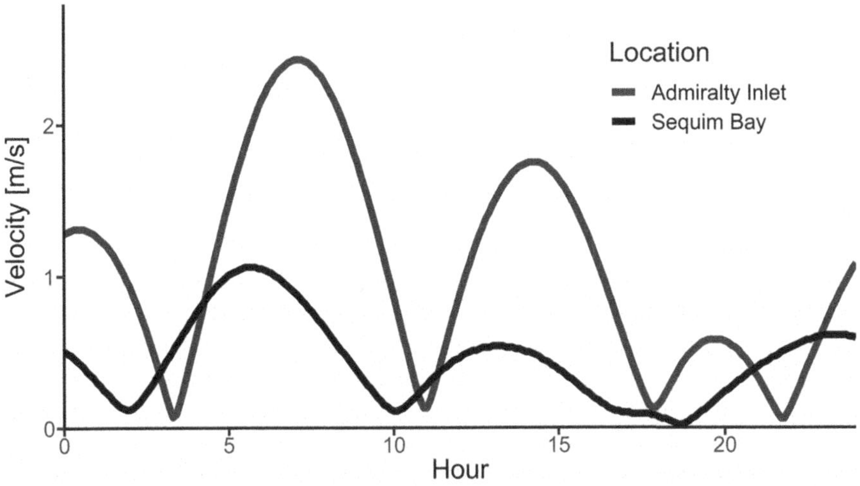

Fig. 12.1 Tidal current velocity [m/s] at Admiralty Inlet and Sequim Bay in Washington, USA. Data are from the Assessment of Energy Production Potential from Tidal Streams in the United States (Haas et al. 2011)

The European Marine Energy Centre (EMEC) has hosted and tested several prototypes in recent years, including Orbital Marine Power's SR2000 tidal turbine, which was launched at the facility in 2016. During its first 12 months of operation at EMEC, the 2 MW floating twin-turbine system produced over 3 GWh of electricity (Orbital Marine Power 2020). Pilot projects have also taken place in North America, with Sustainable Marine Energy testing its 280 kW PLAT-I tidal energy platform in Grand Passage, Nova Scotia in February of 2019. The project has successfully generated electricity with no noticeable negative marine wildlife impacts to date. It is however not connected to the grid (Sustainable Marine Energy 2019a).

In September 2019, Sustainable Marine Energy announced that it had been awarded a license by the Nova Scotia Department of Energy and Mines to sell power via a power purchase agreement to Nova Scotia Power. The company anticipates the development of 9 MW of tidal capacity in the Bay of Fundy in a joint venture with Minas Tidal LP (Sustainable Marine Energy 2019b). The Faroe Islands' electric utility, SEV, awarded a power purchase contract to Minesto in November 2018 to deploy two installations of its tidal kite devices. The European Commission's SME Instrument Programme in June 2019 issued a €2.5 million grant to Minesto and SEV to support the installation of the devices (Minesto). As of April 2020, all siting permits have been approved for the two tidal kites in Vestmannasund as part of the Deep Green Island Mode Project (Minesto 2020a).

2.3 Wave Energy Converters

Waves are a fundamentally fluctuating energy source. Ocean surface waves are created by the movement of wind over the ocean. Once produced, they can travel large distances. When they arrive at a location far from the area of production, they are called swells. While waves express high variation between their peak intensity and average intensity, they also display seasonal patterns. The behavior of ocean waves is classified by amplitude, phase, and directionality.

Unlike tidal energy devices, there is a variety of WEC designs (Falcão 2010; Drew et al. 2009). Point absorbers, oscillating wave surge devices, attenuators, and oscillating water columns are among the most common device classifications, with the first three technology types often consisting of one or more bodies that generate power from the wave-induced relative translation motion and/or rotational motion between the body and a reference frame (e.g., seabed). Oscillating water columns differ from these devices in that they instead consist of a column of air trapped on top of a column of water; the rise and fall of the water column due to incident waves pushes the air through a turbine, thus generating power. Most devices are wave-to-wire, generating power within an individual device, then aggregating within an array and sending power to shore via an export cable. Other hydraulic devices are designed for near-shore environments and they pump water to onshore power generation equipment.

2.4 Wave Energy Converter (WEC) Deployment

As with tidal current devices, WECs have not yet reached commercial development, yet a variety of WECs have been deployed and tested around the world, many of which have been connected to local grids. In 2011, the Spanish utility Ente Vasco de la Energía supported the deployment of a 300 kW oscillating water column system integrated with the breakwater of the harbor in Mutriku, Spain. The system was also the first multi-turbine WEC system tested in the world (International Energy Agency—Ocean Energy Systems 2016). In Australia, Carnegie Clean Energy has deployed several successful pilots. The Perth project off Garden Island included three fully submerged buoys that were connected to the grid and operated continuously for 12 months. The project incorporated a desalination plant to produce freshwater (Carnegie Clean Energy), and the Australian Department of Defence contracted for the electricity generation under a power purchase agreement (Sawyer 2017). North America has also seen grid-connected WEC deployments. The first grid-connected device in the United States was an 18 kW Azura technology deployed by Northwest Energy Innovations at the U.S. Navy's Wave Energy Test Site in Hawaii in 2015 (Whitlock 2015).

3 Cost Drivers

3.1 *Technology Cost Drivers*

Anticipated deployment costs for wave and tidal devices are relatively high to other existing generation technologies. As described above, deployments have consisted of small-scale projects or pilots intended to test technologies in the water, their electricity production, interaction with the marine environment and integration into power systems. Device development for projects is a custom process, introducing construction costs and delays without manufacturing standardization, supply chain alignment, or cross-over with maritime sector applications for economies of scale and availability.

The marine operating environment introduces specialized hazards, which accordingly introduces novel and unavoidable costs. Saltwater contains minerals that can corrode materials and coatings. Aquatic life will interact with the deployment, raising environmental concerns and triggering regulatory requirements. Wave energy devices are intentionally mobile with exposed mechanics and changing levels of submersion. Tidal and wave devices will require special protections with advanced coatings, corrosive resistant materials, or protective casings. Deployment in the ocean can be limited due to customized supply chain, specialized vessels and equipment, and limited operational windows. Technology developers must design devices to withstand strong and multi-directional forces. Research and development programs across the world have promoted strategic investments to drive down these costs (U.S. Department of Energy 2019b; International Energy Agency 2019b). Individual wave energy conversion devices must be built for a significantly higher power output capacity than their average power output to handle the natural fluctuation in wave intensity (Yu et al. 2018).

3.2 *System Costs: Levelized Cost of Electricity*

The levelized cost of electricity (LCOE) is the most common metric for comparing the cost-benefit of different energy generation technologies. For example, the often-cited Lazard estimates compare technologies on an LCOE basis (Lazard 2019). Compared to simple representations like installation cost per unit of rated power, LCOE offers a more holistic representation of an energy project by considering actual generation.

The LCOE metric creates a ratio between the present value of a project's lifetime costs and the amount of energy that the project will produce throughout the project's lifetime. LCOE is in units of currency per amount of energy, or in the United States, dollars per kilowatt hour. It is calculated as (Fig. 12.2):

The metric recognizes that project costs vary over time and that the siting of renewable energy projects dictates resource strength and energy available. The differences in energy production impact the denominator of the LCOE equation: the more energy the project can produce each year, the lower the cost of

$$LCOE = \frac{cost\ to\ generate\ (capital\ and\ O\&M\ over\ project\ lifetime)}{total\ amount\ of\ energy\ generated}.$$

Fig. 12.2 Simple formula for Levelized Cost of Energy

electricity becomes. LCOE has largely been the metric of choice when governments consider incentivizing new technologies and it is a primary screen for gauging which innovative technologies are nearing commercial viability and if they can be considered for out-year investment.

LCOE estimates for small and early developments of tidal current and wave energy projects are within the range of \$400/MWh to \$800/MWh for tidal (Jenne et al. 2015; IEA-OES 2015) and \$250/MWh to \$2000/MWh for wave (IEA-OES 2015). This can be compared to \$49/MWh for solar, \$57/MWh for wind and \$119/MWh for combined cycle natural gas power plants sited in California (Neff 2019).

The highly variable range of wave and tidal LCOE values is mirrored in the estimates used by the electric utility sector in planning documents. From a review of U.S. utility integrated resource plans (IRPs), with values escalated to 2019\$ U.S., tidal and wave sectors both have over 6-to-1 cost ratios from the lowest to the highest. The range for offshore wind is lower at 5-to-1. This range is still expressed with very few data points: tidal values only have 4 observations from which to generalize, while there are 8 observations for offshore wind and for wave energy. See Fig. 12.3.

Estimated LCOE for tidal and wave devices is higher by an order of magnitude relative to other generating resources. As tidal and wave devices are not yet commercially available, and as evidenced by the broad range in value, these cost estimates remain guesswork and are not considered reliable comparators or gages for future levelized costs. Both solar panels and wind turbines in the early stages of development had similarly high levelized costs. In 2010, the global weighted average LCOE of utility-scale solar photovoltaic (PV) was approximately \$370/MWh. Since that time, the levelized cost has dropped by 77% (IRENA).

Research has shown potential for wave energy devices to be co-located with offshore wind plants, as the generating resources can be complementary and co-location reduces the cost per energy generation for both resources (Reikard et al. 2015; Chozas et al. 2012). Similarly, energy storage is particularly well suited for pairing with tidal energy projects. Tidal energy's inherent predictability and periodicity lend itself well to coupling devices with a limited amount of storage. Hybridization with energy storage has the potential to change the competitiveness of a tidal project by decreasing the fluctuation in power output over time; however, introducing storage increases project costs and slightly reduces the net energy produced onsite due to round-trip efficiencies (Zhou et al. 2013; Ben Elghali et al. 2019).

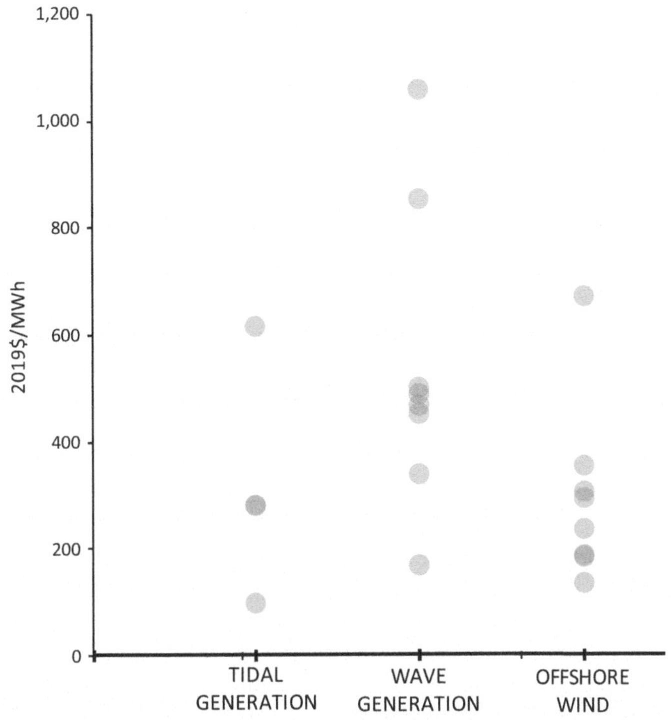

Fig. 12.3 LCOE (converted to $2019) for tidal generation, wave generation, and offshore wind as reported in U.S. utility integrated resource plans (IRPs). Points are partially transparent such that darker points represent more than one IRP reporting an LCOE of the indicated value. (Cooke et al. 2020)

While LCOE is widely used and covers a renewable energy project's economic lifetime, it represents an incomplete picture of the *value* of a particular energy project. LCOE fails to capture a range of other potential value streams that generators supply, most notably services critical to the operation of the grid (The University of Texas at Austin Energy Institute 2020; Ueckerdt et al. 2013). In the past, when the energy system was composed of entirely dispatchable resources—where output could be modulated to meet load and technology attributes varied little (i.e., large central scale power plants that operated for decades and required similar amounts of land and fuel supplies)—LCOE was an appropriate metric to directly compare across technologies. Today, there is an increased recognition of the range of technology attributes and differentiators, as well as contributions to grid reliability beyond simple energy that need to be measured and accounted for.

On a simple cost basis, an energy project in the ocean will always be challenged to appear competitive with a land-based energy project. The economic competitiveness of tidal and wave energy resources to future electric grid conditions is better evaluated, then, by these resources' unique values and attributes rather than its costs alone. In order to review potential future development markets and economic opportunities, the remainder of this chapter discusses unique or competitive value that tidal and wave energy devices can provide to global energy systems.

4 Economic Value: Relevant Markets and Applications

While operation in a marine environment has cost implications, in certain markets this attribute of wave and tidal resources may provide a competitive edge. Opportunities for development may exist in a wide variety of markets, particularly remote and island communities, military bases, and constrained grids and grids with high contributions from renewable energy sources. Further, maritime applications, may also provide market opportunities.

4.1 *Remote and Island Communities*

Tidal and wave development are more promising in locations where the cost of electricity is high and access to a consistent fuel supply (e.g. diesel fuel) is challenging. These are often remote and island communities with small grids.

Island and coastal communities are often at the forefront of climate impacts and have a strong driver to move to cleaner energy sources (Dornan and Shah 2016). Beyond providing clean energy, the development of renewable resources in remote communities can have benefits in job creation, economic development, and emissions reductions (Shirley and Kammen 2013). Tidal and wave resources can help avoid the impacts of fossil fuel use and address challenges associated with other renewable technology integration (i.e., solar or wind variability, intermittency and a lack of predictability). Research suggests that marine energy resources can avoid transmission investments to remote, coastal locations (Robertson 2010; Moazzen et al. 2016); that as a predictable resource, marine energy would require a fraction of associated integration costs and support the integration of other resources; and that to achieve high physical penetration levels of renewable energy, winter peaking resources with seasonal variation such as marine energy could be valuable. The use of marine energy in a portfolio increases resource diversity, reducing vulnerability to grid and fuel supply disruptions and exposure to fuel price volatility.

The following examples highlight the unique value associated with tidal and wave devices and illustrate broader potential market opportunities.

4.2 *Faroe Islands (Resource Complementarity)*

The utility in the Faroe Islands, SEV, has evaluated the use of tidal energy as part of its approach to achieve a 100% renewable energy generating portfolio. SEV finds that tidal energy can provide a consistent and predictable output, complementing other seasonally variable resources of wind, hydroelectric generation, and solar photovoltaic. These resources, in combination with pumped storage and batteries, SEV predicts, can enable it to successfully and reliably achieve a 100% clean generation portfolio. Doing so otherwise would require a significant overbuild of wind and solar resources (Katsaprakakis et al. 2019). The utility is presently working on the pilot project previously mentioned to showcase the use of tidal energy, and if successful, intends to expand this effort with larger tidal turbine units (Minesto 2020b).

4.3 Alaska (Fuel Supply and Resource Availability)

The U.S. state of Alaska has several remote communities. Many of these communities are not connected to a large electric grid and are self-sufficient for their energy, reliant mostly or entirely upon diesel generation for electricity (Beatty et al. 2010). There is significant interest in the use of renewables to provide reliable and fuel-independent electricity to these communities in order to lessen the high costs of using diesel generation that result from high fuel costs (due to transportation) and supply chain uncertainty. Shipped diesel fuel may be disrupted due to weather or other factors, creating a potential resilience benefit from the use of local, reliable, and available resources. The community of Igiugig in Alaska has deployed a river current device, similar to tidal energy, and the community of Yukatat is evaluating the potential for a wave energy converter to test the provision of electricity from these resources and reduce their use and dependence on fossil generation (Alaska Center for Energy and Power 2016; ORPC 2020).

4.4 Caribbean & Indian Ocean Islands (Land Use)

Another advantage of wave and tidal devices is their small terrestrial footprint, which is limited to an electric cable and auxiliary on-shore equipment for interconnection. Land is a scarce commodity on islands and subject to competing uses. With the expectation that renewable resources will need to be significantly increased to meet climate goals, there is increasing benefit to siting renewable energy resources offshore in areas where available land is scarce. In its 2017 Integrated Resource Plan for the Caribbean Utilities Company, Pace Global found an advantage in utilizing marine energy, specifically ocean thermal energy conversion (OTEC), as significantly less land was required for its development relative to other resources (Pace Global 2017). Similarly, the Seychelles Energy Commission approved a 25-year power purchase agreement for a 4 MW floating solar development in a lagoon off Mahé island, with the African Legal Support Facility citing that the plant provides clean energy generation while avoiding the challenge of land constraints on the island (Bellini 2020).

4.5 *Military Bases*

There are several remote military bases around the world: remote outposts within a nation's mainland borders that are not grid-connected, or remote outposts on islands or another nation's territory. Energy is a critical need for military operations and these bases must have reliable power at all times, especially during severe weather events and military conflicts, which is problematic when these bases are heavily reliant on imported diesel (Defense Science Board 2016). Similarly, there are numerous grid-connected bases that are reliant upon grid-delivered electricity that is susceptible to interruption in contingency events (Samaras et al. 2019). For example, in April 2011, a tornado left the U.S. Army's Redstone Arsenal base in Huntsville, Alabama without power for eight days, leading to a base closure and a reliance on diesel backup generators for critical activities. By the end of the outage, the generators had almost emptied their fuel reserves (Marqusee et al. 2017).

Recently militaries have explored the use of alternative resources, particularly renewable resources with energy storage, to reduce reliance on diesel, which not only avoids costs and emissions but also achieves their primary goal of ensuring continued operations if diesel supplies are no longer available (Samaras et al. 2019). Tidal and wave energy devices can act as a replacement to fossil generation as a result of their improved predictability and periodicity, supporting load when implemented in conjunction with intermittent renewable technologies and energy storage, in a microgrid, for example. Further, tidal and wave devices can provide resilience by offering an improved level of uninterrupted generation relative to solar or wind (Newman 2020). Figure 12.4 below highlights this value using the output of a microgrid dispatch model. The box and whisker plot indicates the percentage reduction in renewable energy capacity, battery capacity, diesel generator capacity, and diesel fuel consumption for a microgrid ensuring the delivery of energy during different electric grid outage lengths using the addition of a tidal energy resource instead of a solar PV resource across 100 simulations.

4.6 *Constrained Grids and Grids with High Renewable Energy Contributions*

Electric generation sources can be located at great distances from both large and remote coastal electric loads, which means that transmission infrastructure is needed to assure reliable electric delivery over these long distances. Transmission services can be capacity constrained along the coasts, making it difficult to add new electric loads to the system, inhibiting economic growth. Installing new transmission infrastructure is an expensive and spatially constrained proposition (ScottMadden 2020). Further, coastal transmission and distribution lines may be single points of failure, providing no redundancy for these communities if a line is suddenly unavailable (Hasan et al. 2013).We see examples of this in coastal cities of North Carolina, USA, where extreme

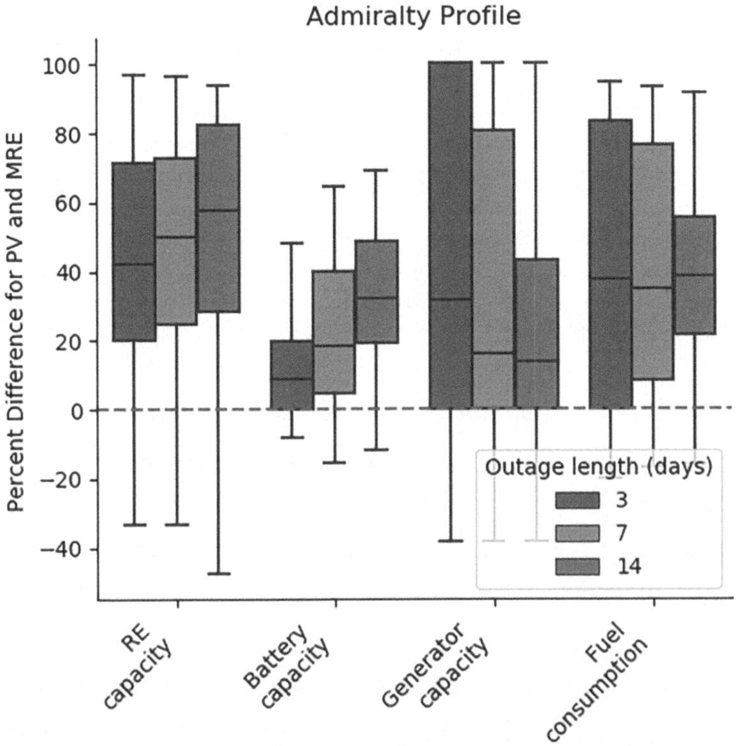

Fig. 12.4 Percent reduction in the required RE capacity, battery capacity, generator capacity, and fuel use resulting from adding additional MRE instead of PV capacity to meet 100% uptime during different outage lengths, across 100 simulations for a hypothetical load served by a microgrid with a diesel generator, battery, solar PV and tidal energy. (Newman 2020)

weather events, like hurricanes, and unforeseeable contingencies result in widespread power outages in major tourist locations (Bohatch 2017; Dalesio 2014).

Siting tidal and wave energy devices in such constrained areas could provide both clean renewable energy and unique benefits to the system, such as a deferral or reduction of investments in the distribution and transmission system, provision of ancillary services (e.g., frequency and voltage support), and local power quality benefits. Another benefit could be supporting economic development in otherwise energy constrained areas (Oregon Department of Energy 2012). Finally, the infrastructure build-out required to meet renewable energy goals, especially when policy includes a resource proximity requirement, such as direct interconnection to a state or particular utility's electric system, may have unacceptable demands on available land, creating another opportunity for tidal and wave resources (ScottMadden 2020).

Wave and tidal device output will be more predictable than their solar or wind renewable counterparts. This advantage enables tidal and wave resources to provide benefits to the grid in several other ways, including accommodating optimal amounts of complementary resources, distribution and transmission system management, and reduced costs in holding fewer operating reserves. Wave and tidal energy have electricity generation profiles that complement wind and solar resource availability over annual, seasonal, and daily periods. These resources fill critical resource timing gaps in grids with increasingly high levels of renewable energy generation. A wider portfolio of diverse contributing renewable energy brings geographic diversity, supports resource adequacy, and reduces reliability risks.

4.7 *Scotland (Energy Storage Integration)*

In 2018, Nova Innovation integrated a Tesla battery storage system with the Shetland Tidal Array in Scotland and expanded the generating capacity at the site (Renewable Energy Magazine 2018). The system allows for storage of excess tidal energy during energy production peaks and then discharges stored tidal energy during low to no device output periods. The facility is claimed as the world's first "baseload" tidal power facility (Nova Innovation 2019) due to its relatively flat net production.

By coupling with storage, tidal or wave facilities could achieve better controllability and offer a scaled version of dispatchable generation. Researchers have explored the coupling of non-battery storage solutions with marine energy. Though of relatively small scale, an electrolyzer, which splits water using electricity to generate hydrogen gas (H_2), with a generation capacity of 220 kg of H_2/day was developed using tidal current device prototypes for its electric input (ITM Power 2017). The resulting hydrogen from this system could be used to generate electricity when demand increases, potentially for much longer timeframes than the typical four-hour limitations that standard commercial battery technologies currently allow. Such a system could also be used to supply fuel cell-based vehicles and additional transportation systems (U.S. Department of Energy 2019a). These developments suggest that coupling marine energy devices with various types of energy storage can enable new value streams.

4.8 *Australia (Renewables Integration)*

As Australia deploys more renewable resources on its electric system, the country has recognized a need for supporting technologies and resource diversity to help integrate this renewable energy. Wave and tidal energy use could reduce system capacity and balancing requirements by reducing the overall variability of the energy generation profile. The diversity could also provide a natural resiliency effect: the more geographic diversity of the overall generation profile, the less likely it is to be interrupted by contingency events. As renewable resources reach higher levels of deployment, seasonal and daily ramps of generation will cause significant reliability management challenges. In contrast, wave energy will maintain consistent production over seasonal periods and could fill the production gaps to provide reliable electric service. Australia's Commonwealth Scientific and Industrial Research Organization has evaluated Australia's wave energy potential and finds that the southern coastline of the country has a wave resource that could contribute up to 11% of Australia's total energy needs (CSIRO 2020).

4.9 Powering the Blue Economy

One strategy to advance commercialization of wave and tidal energy technologies in the near-term is to develop these technologies for electric demands within existing and emerging maritime sectors, called the "blue economy." Meeting the electricity needs of maritime sectors requires targeted technology development at small scales with specialized characteristics to fit the demands of the maritime environment. These markets include ocean observation, desalination, seawater mining, and aquaculture (LiVecchi et al. 2019). While this approach may advance commercialization of marine energy technologies, the largest economic opportunity still remains in serving traditional electric grids under the circumstances described above.

5 Conclusion

Considering the magnitude of tidal and wave resources and the policy drive toward a cleaner, decarbonized electricity system, it is reasonable to anticipate that tidal and wave energy will be able to commercialize and deploy around the world. This may be especially true in environments where there are limited clean energy resource options, the marine nature of these deployments provides additional value, or grid conditions require the unique attributes of tidal and wave energy resources.

Acknowledgments Research described in this article was sponsored directly by the U.S. Department of Energy's Water Power Technologies Office.

References

Alaska Center for Energy and Power. 2016. "Yakutat Wave Energy Resource Assessment." Alaska Center for Energy and Power. Accessed May 18. http://acep.uaf.edu/projects-(collection)/yakutat-wave-energy-resource-assessment.aspx.

Azzellino, Arianna, Vincenzo Ferrante, Jens Peter Kofoed, Caterina Lanfredi, and Diego Vicinanza. 2013. "Optimal siting of offshore wind-power combined with wave energy through a marine spatial planning approach." *International Journal of Marine* Energy 3–4: e11-e25. https://doi.org/10.1016/j.ijome.2013.11.008, http://www.sciencedirect.com/science/article/pii/S2214166913000349.

Beatty, Scott J., Peter Wild, and Bradley J. Buckham. 2010. "Integration of a wave energy converter into the electricity supply of a remote Alaskan island." Renewable

Energy 35 (6): 1203–1213. https://doi.org/10.1016/j.renene.2009.11.040, http://www.sciencedirect.com/science/article/pii/S096014810900528X.

Bellini, Emiliano. 2020. "Quadran International wins Seychelles tender for large-scale floating PV with bid of $0.095/kWh." PV Magazine. Last Modified January 10 2020. Accessed May 18. https://www.pv-magazine.com/2020/01/10/quadran-wins-seychelles-tender-for-large-scale-floating-pv-with-bid-of-0-095-kwh/.

Ben Elghali, Seifeddine, Rachid Outbib, and Mohamed Benbouzid. 2019. "Selecting and optimal sizing of hybridized energy storage systems for tidal energy integration into power grid." Journal of Modern Power Systems and Clean Energy 7 (1): 113–122. https://doi.org/10.1007/s40565-018-0442-0.

Bohatch, Emily. 2017. "No light in sight: North Carolina barrier islands could be without power for weeks." USA Today. Last Modified July 28, 2017. Accessed September 23. https://www.usatoday.com/story/news/2017/07/28/north-carolina-barrier-islands-without-power-no-timeline-restoration/519972001/.

Bryden, I. G., and D. M. Macfarlane. 2000. "The utilisation of short term energy storage with tidal current generation systems." Energy 25 (9): 893–907. https://doi.org/10.1016/S0360-5442(00)00020-7, http://www.sciencedirect.com/science/article/pii/S0360544200000207.

Carnegie Clean Energy. "CETO 5—Perth Wave Energy Project." Carnegie Clean Energy. Accessed June 17. https://www.carnegiece.com/project/ceto-5-perth-wave-energy-project/.

Chozas, Julia Fernandez, H. C. Sørensen, and N. E. Helstrup Jensen. 2012. Economic Benefit of Combining Wave and Wind Power Productions in Day-Ahead Electricity Markets.

Cooke, A.L., R.S. O'Neil, and D.C. Preziuso. 2020. Review of Marine Renewable Energy in Integrated Resource Plans. PNNL-29862. Richland, WA: Pacific Northwest National Laboratory. (Anticipated.)

CSIRO. 2020. "Wave Energy in Australia." CSIRO. Last Modified April 29 2020. Accessed May 18. https://www.csiro.au/en/Research/OandA/Areas/Marine-technologies/Ocean-energy/Wave-energy.

Dalesio, Emery. 2014. "Arthur hits North Carolina coast just before holiday." Associated Press. Accessed September 23. https://krcgtv.com/news/local/arthur-hits-north-carolina-coast-just-before-holiday-08-14-2015.

Defense Science Board. August 2016. *Task Force on Energy Systems for Forward/Remote Operating Bases: Final Report.* Defense Science Board (Washington, D.C.: Defense Science Board). https://dsb.cto.mil/reports.htm.

Dornan, M., and K. U. Shah. 2016. "Energy policy, aid, and the development of renewable energy resources in Small Island Developing States." Energy Policy 98: 759–767. https://doi.org/10.1016/j.enpol.2016.05.035. <Go to ISI>://WOS:000387300300073.

Drew, B., A. R. Plummer, and M. N. Sahinkaya. 2009. "A review of wave energy converter technology." Proceedings of the Institution of Mechanical Engineers, Part A: Journal of Power and Energy 223 (8): 887–902. https://doi.org/10.1243/09576509JPE782.

Falcão, António F. de O. 2010. "Wave energy utilization: A review of the technologies." Renewable and Sustainable Energy Reviews 14 (3): 899–918. https://doi.org/10.1016/j.rser.2009.11.003, http://www.sciencedirect.com/science/article/pii/S1364032109002652.

Fernandez, JC, HC Sorensen, and NE Helstrup. 2012. *Economic benefit of combining wave and wind power productions in day-ahead electricity markets.* (International Conference on Ocean Energy). https://www.icoeconference.com/publication/economic_benefit_of_combining_wave_and_wind_power_productions_in_day_ahead_electricity_markets/.

Fraunhofer ISE. 2020. Recent Facts about Photovoltaics in Germany. Fraunhofer ISE (Fraunhofer ISE). https://www.ise.fraunhofer.de/content/dam/ise/en/documents/publications/studies/recent-facts-about-photovoltaics-in-germany.pdf.

Haas, K.A., Fritz, H.M., French, S.P., Smith, B.T., and Neary, V. 2011. Assessment of Energy Production Potential from Tidal Streams in the United States. Georgia: Georgia Tech Research Corporation.

Hasan, Kazi Nazmul, Tapan Kumar Saha, Mehdi Eghbal, and Deb Chattopadhyay. 2013. "Review of transmission schemes and case studies for renewable power integration into the remote grid." Renewable and Sustainable Energy Reviews 18: 568–582. https://doi.org/10.1016/j.rser.2012.10.045, http://www.sciencedirect.com/science/article/pii/S1364032112005965.

International Energy Agency—Ocean Energy Systems (IEA-OES). 2015. *International Levelised Cost of Energy for Ocean Energy Technologies: An analysis of the development pathway and Levelised Cost of Energy trajectories of wave, tidal and OTEC technologies.* IEA Technology Collaboration Programme for Ocean Energy Systems (OES) (IEA Technology Collaboration Programme for Ocean Energy Systems (OES)).

———. 2016. *Ocean Energy Systems Annual Report.* (International Energy Agency The Executive Committee of Ocean Energy Systems). https://report2016.ocean-energy-systems.org/.

International Energy Agency. 2019a. "Global energy demand rose by 2.3% in 2018, its fastest pace in the last decade." International Energy Agency,. Last Modified 28 March 2019. https://www.iea.org/news/global-energy-demand-rose-by-23-in-2018-its-fastest-pace-in-the-last-decade.

———. 2019b. Tracking Power. (Paris, France: International Energy Agency). https://www.iea.org/reports/tracking-power-2019.

IRENA. 2019. Future of Solar Photovoltaic: Deployment, investment, technology, grid integration and socio-economic aspects (A Global Energy Transformation: paper), International Renewable Energy Agency, Abu Dhabi. https://irena.org/-/media/Files/IRENA/Agency/Publication/2019/Nov/IRENA_Future_of_Solar_PV_2019.pdf.

ITM Power. 2017. "World's first tidal-powered hydrogen generated at EMEC." Accessed May 2. http://www.itm-power.com/news-item/worlds-first-tidal-powered-hydrogen-generated-at-emec.

Jenne, D.S., Y.-H Yu, and V. Neary. 2015. "Levelized Cost of Energy Analysis of Marine and Hydrokinetic Reference Models." 3rd Marine Energy Technology Symposium, Washington, D.C. NREL/CP-5000-64013.

John, Jeff St. 2020. "Transmission Emerging as Major Stumbling Block for State Renewable Targets." Greentech Media. Last Modified January 15 2020. Accessed May 19. https://www.greentechmedia.com/articles/read/transmission-emerging-as-major-stumbling-block-for-state-renewable-targets.

Katsaprakakis, Dimitris Al, Bjarti Thomsen, Irini Dakanali, and Kostas Tzirakis. 2019. "Faroe Islands: Towards 100% R.E.S. penetration." Renewable Energy 135: 473–484. https://doi.org/10.1016/j.renene.2018.12.042, http://www.sciencedirect.com/science/article/pii/S0960148118314733.

Lazard. 2019. "Levelized Cost of Energy and Levelized Cost of Storage 2019." Lazard. Last Modified November 7 2019. Accessed May 18. https://www.lazard.com/perspective/lcoe2019.

Lehmann, Marcus, Farid Karimpour, Clifford A. Goudey, Paul T. Jacobson, and Mohammad-Reza Alam. 2017. "Ocean wave energy in the United States: Current status and future perspectives." Renewable and Sustainable Energy Reviews 74: 1300–1313. https://doi.org/10.1016/j.rser.2016.11.101, http://www.sciencedirect.com/science/article/pii/S1364032116308164.

LiVecchi, A., A. Copping, D. Jenne, A. Gorton, R. Preus, G. Gill, R. Robichaud, R. Green, S. Geerlofs, S. Gore, D. Hume, W. McShane, C. Schmaus, and H. Spence. 2019. *Powering the Blue Economy; Exploring Opportunities for Marine Renewable Energy in Maritime Markets.* U.S. Department of Energy (Washington, D.C.: Office of Energy Efficiency and Renewable Energy U.S. Department of Energy). https://www.energy.gov/sites/prod/files/2019/03/f61/73355.pdf.

MacEnri, J, M Reed, and T Thiringer. 2013. "Influence of tidal parameters on SeaGen flicker performance." *Philosophical Transactions of the Royal Society A.* https://doi.org/20120247, https://royalsocietypublishing.org/doi/10.1098/rsta.2012.0247.

Magagna, Davide, and Andreas Uihlein. 2015. "Ocean energy development in Europe: Current status and future perspectives." International Journal of Marine Energy 11: 84–104. https://doi.org/10.1016/j.ijome.2015.05.001, http://www.sciencedirect.com/science/article/pii/S2214166915000181.

Marqusee, Jeffrey, Craig Schultz, and Dorothy Robyn. 2017. Power Begins at Home: Assured Energy for U.S. Military Bases. Reston, VA: Noblis. https://www.pewtrusts.org/~/media/assets/2017/01/ce_power_begins_at_home_assured_energy_for_us_military_bases.pdf

Minesto. "Faroe Islands—tidal energy to reach 100% renewable by 2030." Minesto. https://minesto.com/projects/faroe-islands.

———. "Faroe Islands—tidal energy to reach 100% renewable by 2020a. "Minesto secures all permits for Faroe Islands' installations." Minesto. Last Modified April 1 2020a. Accessed May 18. https://minesto.com/news-media/minesto-secures-all-permits-faroe-islands%E2%80%99-installations.

———. "Faroe Islands—tidal energy to reach 100% renewable by 2020b. "Minesto signs PPA with electric utility SEV for utility-scale tidal energy installations." Minesto. Last Modified February 19 2020. https://minesto.com/news-media/minesto-signs-ppa-electric-utility-sev-utility-scale-tidal-energy-installations.

Moazzen, I., B. Robertson, P. Wild, A. Rowe, and B. Buckham. 2016. "Impacts of large-scale wave integration into a transmission-constrained grid." Renewable Energy 88: 408–417. https://doi.org/10.1016/j.renene.2015.11.049. <Go to ISI>://WOS:000368563900039.

Neff, Bryan. 2019. Estimated Cost of New Utility-Scale Generation in California: 2018 Update. (California Energy Commission). https://ww2.energy.ca.gov/2019publications/CEC-200-2019-005/CEC-200-2019-005.pdf.

Newman, S. 2020. "Marine Renewable Energy Meta-Analysis with the Microgrid Component and Optimization for Resilience (MCOR) Tool." Richland, WA: Pacific Northwest National Laboratory. (Anticipated.)

Nova Innovation. 2019. "Bluemull Sound, Shetland." Nova Innovation Ltd. Accessed September 10. https://www.novainnovation.com/bluemull-sound.

Orbital Marine Power. 2020. "Orbital Marine Power Takes Final Lessons from SR2000 Tidal Turbine and Brings Prototype Programme to a Close." August 12, 2020.

https://orbitalmarine.com/orbital-marine-power-takes-final-lessons-from-sr2000-tidal-turbine-and-brings-prototype-programme-to-a-close/.

Oregon Department of Energy. 2012. "Why Wave Energy?: Why wave energy is good for Oregon's energy systems" https://digital.osl.state.or.us/islandora/object/osl%3A12964/datastream/OBJ/view

ORPC. 2020. "RivGen® Power System." ORPC Inc. Accessed May 18. https://www.orpc.co/our-solutions/scalable-grid-integrated-systems/rivgen-power-system.

Pace Global. 2017. 2017 Integrated Resource Plan Report Prepared for: Caribbean Utilities Company. (Pace Global).

Reikard, Gordon, Bryson Robertson, and Jean-Raymond Bidlot. 2015. "Combining wave energy with wind and solar: Short-term forecasting." Renewable Energy 81: 442–456. https://doi.org/10.1016/j.renene.2015.03.032, http://www.sciencedirect.com/science/article/pii/S0960148115002141.

Renewable Technology. 2017. "Strangford Lough Tidal Turbine, Northern Ireland." https://www.renewable-technology.com/projects/strangford-lough-tidal-turbine-northern-ireland/.

Renewable Energy Magazine. 2018. "Tesla Battery Storage Successfully Integrated with Tidal Energy Array." Accessed November 6. https://www.renewableenergymagazine.com/ocean_energy/tesla-battery-storage-successfully-integrated-with-tidal-20181031.

Roberts, A; Thomas, B; Sewell, P; Khan, Z; Balmain, S; Gillman, J. 2016. "Current tidal power technologies and their suitability for applications in coastal and marine areas." Ocean Engineering and Marine Energy. https://link.springer.com/content/pdf/10.1007%2Fs40722-016-0044-8.pdf.

Robertson, Bryson. 2010. *Ocean Wave Energy Generation on the West Coast of Vancouver Island and the Queen Charlotte Islands*. Vol. 3.

Samaras, Constantine, William J. Nuttall, and Morgan Bazilian. 2019. "Energy and the military: Convergence of security, economic, and environmental decision-making." Energy Strategy Reviews 26: 100409. https://doi.org/10.1016/j.esr.2019.100409, http://www.sciencedirect.com/science/article/pii/S2211467X19301026.

Sawyer, Tim. 2017. "Perth Wave Energy Project." Tethys. Last Modified January 24 2017. Accessed May 18. https://tethys.pnnl.gov/project-sites/perth-wave-energy-project.

ScottMadden. 2020. Informing the Transmission Discussion. WIRES (WIRES). https://wiresgroup.com/wp-content/uploads/2020/01/ScottMadden_WIRES_Informing-the-Transmission-Discussion_2020_0113_FINAL.pdf

Shirley, R., and D. Kammen. 2013. "Renewable energy sector development in the Caribbean: Current trends and lessons from history." Energy Policy 57: 244–252. https://doi.org/10.1016/j.enpol.2013.01.049. <Go to ISI>://WOS:000318530300029.

SIMEC Atlantis Energy, 26 July 2019. "Atlantis Successfully Decommissions 1.2 MW SeaGen Tidal System in Industry First," https://simecatlantis.com/2019/07/26/meygen-operational-update-3-2/.

Stoutenburg, E. D., N. Jenkins, and M. Z. Jacobson. 2010. "Power output variations of co-located offshore wind turbines and wave energy converters in California." Renewable Energy 35 (12): 2781–2791. https://doi.org/10.1016/j.renene.2010.04.033. <Go to ISI>://WOS:000280379400020.

Sustainable Marine Energy. 2019a. "Results of First Phase PLAT-I Testing at Grand Passage." Sustainable Marine Energy Ltd. Last Modified June 6th, 2019. https://sustainablemarine.com/news/plat-i-testing-1-1.

———. 2019b. "SME reveals plans for 9MW Pempa'q Tidal Energy Project." Sustainable Marine Energy Ltd. Last Modified September 30th, 2019. https://sustainablemarine.com/news/pempaq-project.

The University of Texas at Austin Energy Institute. 2020. "The Full Cost of Electricity." The University of Texas at Austin. Accessed May 19. https://energy.utexas.edu/policy/fce.

U.S. Department of Energy. 2015. "Advancing Clean Electric Power Technologies: Technology Assessments." In *Quadrennial Technology Review 2015.*

———. 2019a. *H2@Scale: Enabling Affordable, Reliable, Clean, and Secure Energy across Sectors.* U.S. Department of Energy, Office of Energy Efficiency and Renewable Energy (Washington, D.C.). https://www.energy.gov/sites/prod/files/2019/09/f67/fcto-h2-at-scale-handout-2019.pdf.

———. 2019b. *Water Power Technologies Office 2019 Peer Review Final Report.* U.S. Department of Energy, Office of Energy Efficiency and Renewable Energy (Washington, D.C.). https://www.energy.gov/eere/water/2019-water-power-program-peer-review-report-and-presentations.

Ueckerdt, Falko, Lion Hirth, Gunnar Luderer, and Ottmar Edenhofer. 2013. "System LCOE: What are the costs of variable renewables?" Energy 63: 61–75. https://doi.org/10.1016/j.energy.2013.10.072, http://www.sciencedirect.com/science/article/pii/S0360544213009390.

Whitlock, Robin. 2015. "Azura wave energy device deployed at US Navy test site." Renewable Energy Magazine. Last Modified 18 June 2015. Accessed May 19. https://www.renewableenergymagazine.com/ocean_energy/azura-wave-energy-device-deployed-at-us-20150618.

Yu, Yi-Hsiang, Nathan Tom, and Dale Jenne. 2018. "Numerical Analysis on Hydraulic Power Take-Off for Wave Energy Converter and Power Smoothing Methods." ASME 2018 37th International Conference on Ocean, Offshore and Arctic Engineering.

Zhou, Zhibin, Mohamed Benbouzid, Jean Frédéric Charpentier, Franck Scuiller, and Tianhao Tang. 2013. "A review of energy storage technologies for marine current energy systems." Renewable and Sustainable Energy Reviews 18: 390–400. https://doi.org/10.1016/j.rser.2012.10.006, http://www.sciencedirect.com/science/article/pii/S1364032112005485.

CHAPTER 13

The Economics of Energy Networks

Andrea Bonzanni

1 Wires and Pipes: Electricity and Gas as Network-based Energy Sources

In spite of their many differences and specificities, electricity and gas are two energy carriers unequivocally associated with the existence of large and complex transportation networks to move energy from production to consumption points. While long-distance transportation is common for other energy sources (see, for instance, the global seaborne coal trade) and networks to connect producers to consumers are not unusual (see, for instance, the extensive pipeline systems for crude oil and refined products), only electricity and gas display networks as a fundamental feature, without which they would be rendered almost worthless and unable to play a role in modern energy systems. Electricity and gas are network energies par excellence. For this reason, in this chapter we will simply refer to 'energy networks' to indicate the infrastructure to transport electricity and gas.

This chapter will provide an overview of the economics of transporting electricity and gas through networks. In Sect. 2, we will describe what energy networks are, with a focus on their physical and economic properties. In Sect. 3, we will discuss the monopolistic nature of energy networks and the implications for electricity and gas systems. In Sects. 4, 5 and 6, we will review how energy networks are treated in competitive energy markets, how access to networks functions and what arrangements are established to ensure efficient economic outcomes and equal treatment of all market participants. In Sect. 7, we will explain how access to energy networks is charged and how network users exchange energy within a network.

A. Bonzanni (✉)
IETA, Geneva, Switzerland

SciencesPo—Paris School of International Affairs, Paris, France
e-mail: Andrea.bonzanni@sciencespo.fr

M. Hafner, G. Luciani (eds.), *The Palgrave Handbook of International Energy Economics*, https://doi.org/10.1007/978-3-030-86884-0_13

2 Physical and Economic Properties of Energy Networks

The movement of electricity and gas through networks are very different phenomena from a physical perspective.

Electricity networks are made up of *electrical conductors* (most commonly aluminium wires wrapped around a steel core) through which electrons flow as a result of a difference in electric potential between two points (called *voltage*), creating an electric current. Modern networks are based on *alternating current (AC)* with variable voltage oscillating with a frequency of 50 or 60 cycles per second (Hertz). *Direct current (DC)* elements are sometimes used to flow electricity between separate AC networks. Rectifiers are used to covert AC into DC and inverters are used to covert DC into AC. The amount of electricity a set of wires (referred to as a *line*) can transport over a given distance is a function of its thermal capacity (measured in Watts) and peak voltage (measured in Volts). Lines are usually placed above ground on steel towers, wood H-frames, wood or concrete single poles of differing structures and heights depending on their voltage and external environmental conditions. Lines can be buried underground and even submerged in water in areas where overhead lines are technically unfeasible or unacceptable for environmental reasons. The complex physics of electricity requires electricity networks to be equipped with numerous instruments and devices that control and regulate the system. *Switching stations* and sub-stations housing *transformers* are disseminated through the networks to ensure that the voltage of the current flowing through the lines is always appropriate. *Circuit breakers* are necessary so that flows can be rapidly disconnected from networks to avoid disruptions and equipment damage.

Gas networks consist of pipelines (usually buried underground), valves, compressor and metering stations. *Pipelines* can be made of carbon steel, high strength plastic or composite material depending on their diameter and the pressure level at which they are operated. *Compressor stations* (fired by turbines, electric motors or engines) pressurise the gas to reduce its volume and propel it through the pipelines by creating a pressure differential so that gas will flow from the high- to the low-pressure points in the network. They are installed at regular intervals of 50 to 160 km to ensure the right level of pressure and a constant flow rate are maintained. The speed at which gas moves within the network ranges from 15 to 32 km per hour. *Valves* work like gateways, blocking the flow of gas and directing it where required. *Metering stations* are used to monitor, manage and account for the gas flowing through the pipelines. They are often associated with other control components such as filters and odorisation equipment.

A vital element of both electricity and gas networks is the *control room*, or control centre. It is a physical central location where staffs operating 24 hours a day and 365 days a year monitor the functioning of networks and makes the necessary decisions to ensure its stability and safety. Advancements in data technologies have led to an increased importance of the control room in energy networks as information availability and quality have improved and more elements and processes can be managed remotely.

In spite of these key fundamental differences, electricity and gas networks are structured and classified in a similar manner. We conventionally divide energy networks into transmission and distribution networks. *Transmission* refers to the movement of electricity and gas over long distances, through high-voltage lines in electricity and large diameter high-pressure pipelines in gas. *Distribution* refers to the networks connecting transmission systems to end users through low-voltage lines and low-pressure pipelines. There is no conventional dividing line between transmission and distribution. In electricity, most distribution networks operate below 50 kV, but some are operated at up to 132 kV and some transmission lines are operated as low as 66 kV. Likewise, in gas, parts of transmission and distribution networks operate at similar pressure levels around 200 psi, but some transmission pipelines operate at above 1000 psi and pipelines connected to end users operate at below 10 psi. The connection points between transmission and distribution networks, however, are well identified and are usually called *city gates*. In both electricity and gas, some large consumers (such as industrial sites and gas-fired power stations) are able to connect directly to the transmission network, bypassing the distribution stage.

Energy networks have been planned to accommodate flows from a few dozens of large injection points (thermal or nuclear power plants, import pipelines, gathering pipelines connecting gas production fields) to a few dozens of large withdrawal points (distribution networks, large consumption sites) and most transmission lines and pipelines have operated on a one-way basis. However, the evolution of energy systems has increased the need to have energy networks that can accommodate *bi-directional* flows. In electricity, especially, the rapidly growing output from distributed renewable energy sources (DERs) connected to distribution grids is increasing the instances in which electricity flows from low-voltage to high-voltage lines. In gas, energy security and diversification objectives have prompted investment to enable some networks to operate more flexibly.

Networks are a complex and costly undertakings. Several estimates of the cost of gas pipelines and electric lines per kilometre or per unit of energy transported have been made but they are reliant on a huge number of assumptions that render these calculations of little general use. It is, however, possible to identify some key features about the cost of energy networks:

- Construction costs are highly variable and dependent on external factors, such as the cost of land, environmental conditions and constraints, the complexity of the permitting process;
- Fixed costs are much higher than variable costs, so the total cost of a network is largely independent of the amount of energy that flows through it;

- Capital costs are much higher than operations and maintenance (O & M) costs, so the largest share of costs is incurred during the planning and development stage of a network, rather than during its operation;
- The costs of ensuring orderly flows through the networks are heavily dependent on the rules governing the behaviour of network users but, as a general principle, are much greater for electricity than for gas.

3 Natural Monopoly and Vertical Integration

A remarkable consequence of the economic properties described above is the ability to generate a rare consensus within the economics profession—energy networks are unanimously considered natural monopolies. The concept of *natural monopoly* has been discussed in economics since the nineteenth century and is formally defined as a particular activity in which a firm can serve the market at a lower cost than any combination of two or more firms.[1] In essence, the economies of scale of energy networks are so large that, whatever the level of output, the long-run average cost of transporting electricity and gas is continuously decreasing (and is always above the long-run marginal cost). This creates a decisive prime mover advantage and an insurmountable barrier to entry for latecomers. Any attempts to introduce competition in natural monopolies would result in a wasteful duplication of assets and the failure of the new entrant, unless it is continuously subsidised. Competition in energy networks is therefore neither sustainable nor desirable (Fig. 13.1).

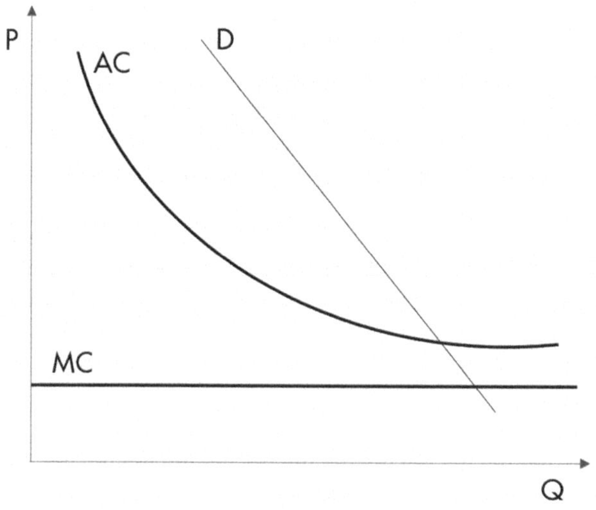

Fig. 13.1 Natural monopoly. (Source: Author's elaboration)

[1] OECD (2003).

Some exceptions to this general principle are represented by relatively simple DC lines and long-haul pipelines in which multiple competing providers can serve the market profitably if demand is sufficiently high. These are commonly called *merchant transmission investment*. Successful examples are very rare in practice.[2] Many of the merchant transmission lines in Australia in the early 2000s and the IUK and BBL pipelines connecting the UK with mainland Europe have subsequently applied for regulated status following changes in market conditions and the expiration of the long-term contracts that initially triggered the investment.

The ownership of energy networks, if unchecked, provides exorbitant *market power* and gives rise to opportunities to foreclose markets to competitors and discriminate between firms engaging in activities for which network usage is necessary, such as gas production, electricity generation, gas and electricity supply. While economic theory has shown that long-term contracts can be used to govern the unequal relationship between network owners and network users,[3] in practice, this enormous advantage has discouraged investment and market entry, resulting in the establishment of monopolistic market structures beyond transmission and distribution. Since the early days of energy networks, *vertical integration* along supply chains emerged as the dominant industry structure and the provision of electricity and gas rapidly became the prerogative of vertically integrated local or national monopolies (Fig. 13.2).

When acting purely on the basis of profit-maximising considerations, monopolists inevitably take advantage of their market power and hike prices to

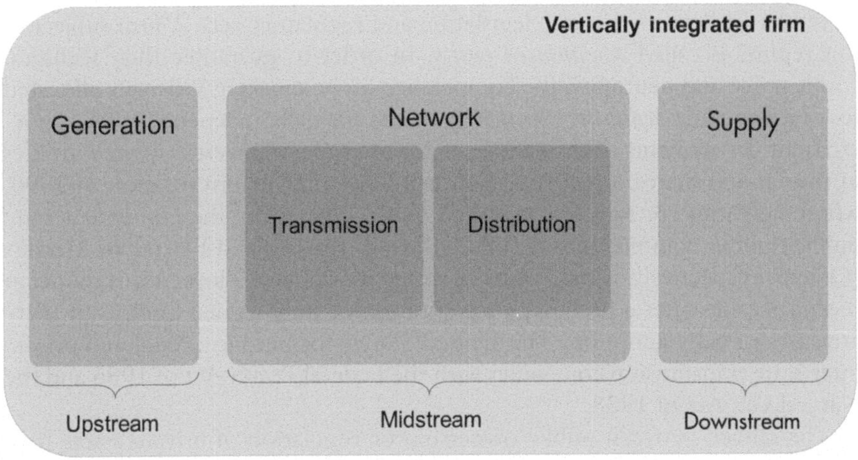

Fig. 13.2 Vertical integration in network energies. (Source: Author's elaboration)

[2] For a theoretical discussion of the merchant model and its practical shortcomings, see Joskow and Tirole (2005).

[3] Joskow (1984).

a level significantly above marginal cost. The impact of such a decision is particularly severe in the energy sector given the very low price elasticity of energy demand and the large spill-overs energy costs have on other economic sectors and society at large. Hence, public intervention is warranted and it can take the form of changes in ownership or regulation. While conceptually very different, the impact of the two models is very similar. In both cases, public authorities ensure that the monopolist no longer acts as a profit maximiser but sets its prices and makes key decisions taking broader welfare impacts into account.

Public ownership is the simplest and crudest measure that can be taken to avoid abuse of market power by a monopolist. It has been the preferred options for governments across the world for much of the twentieth century. Public ownership of energy assets, including but not limited to energy networks, has long been the norm, either as the result of acts of nationalisation (such as in France in 1946 or in the United Kingdom between 1947 and 1949) or due to the direct involvement of central or local governments in the establishment of these industries (as in the cases of Eni in the Italian gas sector or the *stadtwerke*, or municipal utilities, in Germany). A variant of public ownership is co-operative ownership, whereby network owners are fully or partially private actors but their interest is not profit maximisation from the natural monopoly activity. Cooperatives (such as agricultural or industrial consortia) were very common in the early days of the energy industry and are experiencing a revival with the proliferation of DERs and microgrids.

Regulation is an alternative model in which assets continue being owned by private firms but their pricing policies, revenue requirements, terms of service as well as any other key decisions around operations and investment are defined by public authorities through legislation and regulatory acts. A firm subject to this regime is called a *regulated entity*. In order to guarantee their technical competence and neutrality, the competence for rulemaking is usually allocated to a technocratic *regulatory authority* that is formally independent from government departments. This is the case, for example, of investor-owned utilities in the United States or the UK National Grid after its privatisation in 1990, whose activities are tightly monitored and regulated by the competent state public utilities commissions and the Office for the Gas and Electricity Markets (Ofgem) respectively. Most countries in the world have adopted this model in recent decades after a process of privatisation of state-owned assets, but there are cases of early adoption. The United States, for instance, regulated private inter-state transmission companies with the Federal Power Act of 1935 and the Natural Gas Act of 1938.

The choice between public ownership or regulation of private assets have often been determined by ideology, with nationalisations commonly implemented as part of a programme of sweeping economic reforms by left-leaning or socialist governments and more conservative administrations favouring regulation without impinging on existing property rights. The level of capability within public agencies also plays a role. Governments with limited know-how tend to favour public ownership due to its simplicity—once the nationalisation process is completed, they will have full control over decision-making processes in the industry. On the other hand, regulation of private assets requires constant monitoring and a deep understanding of industry functioning to ensure rules are always fit for purpose and keep pace with change.[4] For these two reasons, the pendulum has decidedly swung from public ownership to regulation from the late 1980s to the 2000s as free-market doctrines imposed themselves as the mainstream ideology in economic policy and governments had built up more sophisticated expertise. Even in countries where government ownership was retained, vertically integrated firms were incorporated as limited companies and independent regulatory authorities were created to regulate and oversee them. More recently, with state intervention experiencing new-found intellectual popularity and decarbonisation policy objectives posing unprecedented challenges to energy systems, calls for public ownership have resurfaced.

4 The Unbundling of Energy Networks

Perceived shortcomings of vertically integrated firms, either government-owned or regulated, led to attempts by policymakers to introduce competition in the electricity and gas sectors. This process has conventionally been termed *liberalisation*, restructuring, reform or, with a misnomer, deregulation. A prerequisite for effective competition is the separation of the natural monopoly element from the other segments of the value chain where competition can exist. Such a vertical de-integration is termed *unbundling* and it consists of the creation of separate network companies that cannot engage in other activities along the electricity and gas value chain. These network companies continue to be regulated entities, whereas firms active in other segment of the value chain are left free to operate as profit-maximising entities. The rationale for unbundling is to avoid conflicts of interest and ensure that both operational and long-term strategic decisions regarding networks are taken in an independent and transparent manner treating all firms active in the sector in a non-discriminatory fashion. With no dominant player benefitting from the enormous advantage provided by the control over networks, firms could compete on an equal footing and, the theory goes, invest and provide consumers with better services and cheaper prices.

After unbundling, ownership and operation of networks usually coincide, even though there are cases in which the two functions are performed by separate entities. Unbundled firms are conventionally called *Transmission System Operators (TSOs)* or *Distribution System Operators (DSOs)* in Europe. The use of the term Distribution Network Operators (DNOs) is also common,

[4] The extensive academic literature and anecdotal evidence on regulatory capture, a process whereby regulatory authorities become unable to perform their tasks due to a disproportion in financial and cognitive means between them and the industries they should regulate, are indicative of how difficult it is to deliver effective regulation, even in the most advanced economies.

especially in the United Kingdom. In the United States, gas TSOs are simply called pipeline companies, whereas in electricity we distinguish between Independent System Operators (ISOs), which are company that operate networks they do not own, and Regional Transmission Organizations (RTOs), which are multi-state network operators. In this chapter, we will use the generic term 'network operator' to indicate the companies operating an energy network, regardless of ownership arrangements.

Conceptually, four types of unbundling can be distinguished (Table 13.1):

- *Ownership unbundling*. The network is transferred to a newly created company, which becomes the owner and operator of the network. This is the purest form of unbundling. The new company retains no links to the previously vertically integrated undertaking it belonged to and it is forbidden from engaging activities other than the transmission and distribution of energy. This is the case of the United Kingdom, where National Grid plc. has been created as an independent TSO for electricity and gas.
- *Legal (or functional) unbundling*. Network ownership and operation is transferred to a separate subsidiary of the vertically integrated undertaking. If implemented correctly, it should guarantee operational and managerial independence, but it is seen as a shallower form of unbundling. This is the model adopted in France, where the electricity and gas networks have been transferred to RTE and GRTgaz respectively, but the sole shareholders of these companies remain the former vertically integrated monopolists EDF and Engie (formerly GDF).
- *Operational unbundling*. Network ownership and operation are separated, with the former usually remaining with the former vertically integrated undertaking and the latter performed by an independent entity, which is usually called Independent System Operator (ISO). This is another shallow form of unbundling. It is common in electricity markets, especially in North America where nine ISOs and RTOs operate large parts of the electricity networks in the United States and Canada. It is very rare in gas, even though there are no fundamental reasons that make this form of unbundling unsuitable for the gas industry.
- *Accounting unbundling*. Network ownership and operation remain within a vertically integrated firm but separate financial statements are

Table 13.1 Unbundling models

	Network owner	*Network operator*	*Legal separation*
Ownership	Separate company	Separate company	Full
Legal	Separate subsidiary	Separate subsidiary	Shallow
Operational	Vertically integrated firm	Separate company or separate subsidiary	Shallow
Accounting	Vertically integrated firm	Vertically integrated firm	None

Source: Author's elaboration

produced for the activities of transmission and distribution. This is a very mild form of unbundling, which does not deliver independent decision-making but at least provides regulators with sufficient information to monitor the behaviour of vertically integrated firms and intervene if deemed necessary. It is the model adopted for distribution networks in several European countries.

Attempts to liberalise energy markets and unbundle networks have often, but not always, coincided with the ***privatisation*** of energy assets. The two processes, however, are conceptually distinct and do not need to go hand in hand. A case in point is Poland, which fully unbundled its electricity and gas TSOs PSE and OGP Gaz-System and from PSE and PGNiG respectively, even though all four companies remain under state control.

The first country to pioneer unbundling was Chile in 1981,[5] followed by the United Kingdom between 1986 (for gas) and 1989 (for electricity). Unbundling has subsequently been the cornerstone of the liberalisation of European energy markets promoted by the European Commission in the 1990s and 2000s. International financial institutions routinely include unbundling in their set of recommendations and make support conditional to its implementation. The separation of Ukrtransgaz from Naftogaz completed on 1 January 2020 in the Ukraine following pressure from the IMF, the European Bank for Reconstruction and Development (EBRD) and the European Commission is the most recent example. Some form of unbundling has now been implemented in most of Europe and Latin America but vertical integration still dominates in Africa, much of Asia as well as, somewhat surprisingly, North America.

Numerous studies have attempted to demonstrate the effectiveness of unbundling using econometric techniques, but evidence has been inconclusive, and often contradictory.[6] In most of these studies, end user prices are used as the metric of success for unbundling with a very simple logic—if prices in the period following unbundling are lower than in the period preceding it, unbundling is considered successful; if prices are higher, it is a failure. In reality, too many intervening variables are at play, reducing the explanatory power of these analyses. First, low end user prices cannot be reliably used as a proxy for functioning markets as too many factors contribute to their formation. Electricity and gas prices are highly dependent on global commodity cycles, which in turn depend on industry specific and macroeconomic trends. Moreover, the period following unbundling have coincided, at least in Europe, with early attempts to decarbonise energy systems, which resulted in direct support for renewable energy sources and higher system costs, most of which have been passed on to end users. Second, unbundling in isolation cannot be used to define the success of market liberalisation. Even after the separation of networks from the rest of the value chain, one or a handful of dominant firms can still have tools to

[5] Pollitt (2004).

[6] For an overview of empirical studies, see Growitsch and Stonzik (2011, pp. 6–7).

exercise market power, collude and restrict market entry. If this happens, additional policy measures are necessary, either through horizontal de-integration (breaking up large generation and supply companies) or direct support and facilitations for new entrants.

When these elements are taken into consideration, the debate over the effectiveness and benefits of unbundling blends into the broader debate about the effectiveness of liberalisation and competition in network energies.[7] The separation of networks from the rest of the value chain is a necessary element for the creation of functioning competitive energy markets, but it is not sufficient alone. On the other hand, it is difficult to envisage competitive energy markets without some form of network unbundling.

5 Third-party Access to Unbundled Networks

As a result of unbundling, gas producers, electricity generators and suppliers have to become customers of transmission and distribution networks, or network users, to continue operating their businesses. Access to unbundled energy networks and all interactions between the networks and their users are governed by a set of detailed rules that ensures that all network users are treated equally. These rules, usually called *network codes*, are reviewed and approved (if not drafted) by regulatory authorities. This is the principle of *regulated third-party access (rTPA)*.

A key element covered by rTPA is *network connection*. Gas producers, electricity generators and consumers (either directly for large users or through a supplier for households and small businesses) must be connected to networks to partake in energy systems. The connection process is managed by the network operator, which performs all the necessary actions to physically connect the new network point in exchange for a fee, which is usually cost reflective. The network connection cost would depend on elements such as the capacity of the requested connection, its distance from the existing network and the cost of any upgrade to the rest of the network that it may trigger. rTPA rules ensure that this process is well-defined and prevents the network operator from discriminating between network users. Network connection is a much more complex process in electricity than in gas given that the additional injections or withdrawals at the newly connected point are deemed to have a greater impact on the rest of the network. Under rTPA systems, network operators have usually been under an obligation to grant a connection to all network users who request it. However, some electricity systems are increasingly under pressure due to an excess of connection requests for DERs which the network operator

[7] While the benefits of competition are widely discussed, a fair assessment should recognise some of unquestionable advantages that a vertically integrated monopolistic market structure provides, such as better coordination of operational and investment decisions (which in turn can improve system reliability and security of supply), limited allocation of capital to marketing activities, lower financing costs due to capital availability and better creditworthiness of vertically integrated undertakings.

struggles to manage, so alternative models are being evaluated. In Spain, for instance, a proposal to set a maximum threshold to connections of new generators and allocate them to the highest bidders through an auction mechanism is under discussion.

Another key element governed by rTPA is the ability to dispatch energy to various points within the network. This is done through the reservation of the right to transport a defined amount of energy through a pipeline or a transmission line over a specified period of time. Reserved network capacity is called a ***transmission right*** in electricity, whereas in gas the phrase ***capacity booking*** is preferred. The two concepts, however, are not fundamentally different. rTPA rules ensure that all prequalified parties can reserve network capacity and become network users.

Network capacity is allocated in the form of standardised products allowing to transport a fixed amount of energy over a period of a year, a month, a day or an hour. Half-yearly and quarterly products are also allocated by some electricity networks. Multi-annual capacity bookings (up to 15 or 20 years ahead) were once common, especially in gas, but their use is now increasingly rare.

Network users book in advance the amount of capacity they need based on their estimated peak demand over the relevant period. If their capacity needs are predictable, they can try to profile their bookings through a combination of products of different durations (Fig. 13.3).

The process through which network users can obtain transmission rights or capacity bookings is termed ***capacity allocation***. It can take several forms:

- *First-come-first-served (FCFS)*. Capacity is allocated to the first user who formally requests it (and pays the corresponding fee). This is the simplest and most rudimentary form of allocation. It has gradually been abandoned as rTPA systems have become more sophisticated. However, it is

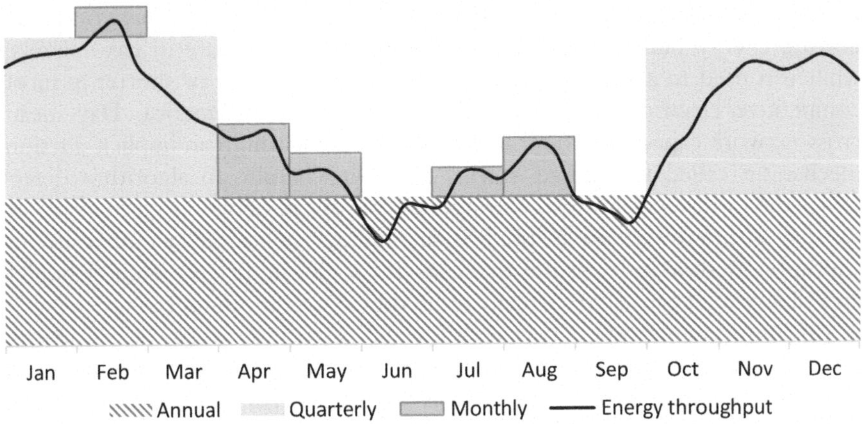

Fig. 13.3 Illustrative profiled capacity booking. (Source: Author's elaboration)

sometimes still used. For instance, within-day transmission capacity in most European electricity markets is still allocated on a FCFS basis.

- *Pro-rata*. It is a process in which the network operator collects binding requests from all interested parties. If the total amount of requests does not exceed available capacity, all requests are fulfilled. If they exceed available capacity, all requests are rebased so that each network user receives an amount of capacity equal to its request reduced by a fixed percentage. Such a mechanism is seen as fairer than FCFS as it does not grant excessive first mover advantages. However, it is prone to gaming and may lead to inefficient outcomes.
- *Auctioning*. Capacity is allocated to the highest bidder after an auction is held. Auctions can take various forms. Auctioning is the standard mechanism to allocate capacity in European electricity and gas markets following the implementation of the EU network codes on Capacity Allocation Mechanism (CAM) and Harmonised Allocation Rules (HAR).
- *Open seasons*. This method is used to allocate capacity that does not yet exist. Network users bid for prospective capacity, which is then realised if sufficient bookings are guaranteed to underpin the necessary investment. Open seasons are by nature used to allocate long-term capacity (from a minimum of 5 years to 20 years or more) and are iterative processes, normally including an initial non-binding phase and a binding phase in which users commit to book (and pay for) the new capacity.

Capacity allocation can be either explicit or implicit. *Explicit allocation* is the most intuitive process, whereby the network operator first allocates the capacity, then requests the holder of the capacity booking to communicate the amount of energy it intends to flow through that capacity. Such a communication is called *nomination*, or scheduling. Explicit allocation is used almost universally in gas markets and is common in electricity markets for timeframes of one month or longer. On the other hand, when an *implicit allocation* mechanism is in place, network capacity is assigned automatically to the network users flowing energy between two network points. It is very rare in gas markets, while it is used to allocate capacity for timeframes of a day or shorter in most competitive electricity markets in Europe and North America. Day-ahead cross-network capacity within the EU is allocated through an implicit auction mechanism called flow-based *market coupling* whereby an algorithm determines the most efficient flows through the European networks given available capacity within the networks. Implicit auctioning is considered a more efficient allocation method as it ensures that capacity is allocated to the highest bidder and all allocated capacity is actually utilised by the network user.

An important feature of network capacity is their *firmness*. Firm capacity gives the user that books it a firm right to flow energy through it. However, this cannot be guaranteed in practice as flows of energy through the network are not always reliably predicted and *network congestion* may occur. In these situations, network operators can prevent holders of capacity from using it and block any scheduled flow of energy. Such an action by the network operator is called *curtailment*. The problem is obviously more acute in electricity given the greater complexity of managing flows for this energy carrier, but it is not uncommon in gas, especially in case of exceptional events such as unplanned maintenance or unseasonal cold snaps. Holders of firm capacity that is curtailed are entitled to receive compensation from the network operator. Rules around curtailments and compensations are amongst the most controversial aspects of rTPA regimes. A common practice in gas networks is to allocate *interruptible capacity*. Holders of this type of capacity do not have a firm right, so network operators can curtail their flows without compensation. Such capacity products are very rare in electricity.

Another important distinction between types of capacity products is the one between physical and financial transmission rights. *Physical transmission rights (PTRs)* give their holder the right to physically dispatch energy between two locations. On the other hand, *financial transmission rights (FTR)* are financial options that replicate the economic outcome of holding actual network capacity. In practice, a holder of an FTR between two locations will sell energy in one location, buy energy in the other location and receive the difference (spread) between the two market prices, if positive, from the network operator that allocated the FTR. While PTRs cannot guarantee full firmness for the reasons described in the previous paragraph, FTR are financially firm, meaning that the network operator is obliged to correspond the price spread under all circumstances, irrespective of whether the flow of energy was physically possible. The allocation of FTR is therefore very complex for network operators and requires a deep understanding of network flows and high computational abilities to allocate the right amount of FTRs at the right price. All capacity bookings in gas are PTRs. FTRs are common in electricity markets in North America and are gradually being introduced in Europe.

Allocation of network capacity in derogation to the principle of rTPA is exceptional but commonly foreseen for new infrastructure projects that would otherwise not be realised. The rationale behind *TPA-exempted* capacity allocation is that network users would not commit to the level of capacity bookings necessary to make the project viable unless they are granted the privilege of exclusive access to the new infrastructure. TPA exemptions are usually approved by regulatory authorities with strict conditions attached and for a limited period of time (Fig. 13.4).

6 Revenue Regulation in Energy Networks

As regulated monopolies, energy networks are subject to stringent *revenue regulation*. The basic principle of revenue regulation is that the remuneration that can be accrued by a network operator (usually called *allowed revenue*) is constrained by rules and parameters set by the regulatory authority. In order to provide stability to both network operators and network users, allowed revenues are set and held stable for a period of several years (usually five), which is

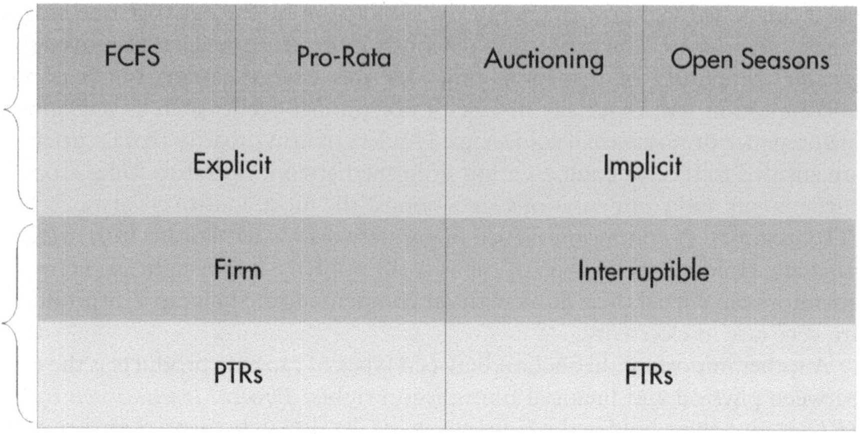

Fig. 13.4 Features of capacity allocation by network operator. (Source: Author's elaboration)

called *regulatory period*. Significant changes can only take place between different regulatory periods. Revenue regulation is arguably the most crucial and complex task energy regulatory authorities have to perform in a liberalised market.

No two revenue regulation regimes are alike, but the methodologies used by regulatory authorities can be classified into two broad families: rate-of-return (also called cost-of-service) regulation and incentive regulation, in which we distinguish between price-cap regulation and revenue-cap regulation. In a *rate-of-return regulation* regime, the regulatory authority sets a target rate of return the network operator is entitled to receive on the capital invested. The revenue of the network R will be equal to:

$$R = (\mathrm{RAB} \times r) + E + d + T$$

where:

- RAB is the regulatory asset base, or the total amount of capital and assets the network operator employs to perform its activities;
- r is the permitted rate of return set by the regulatory authority;
- E is the operating expenses incurred by the network operator to perform its activities;
- d is the expenses incurred to account for the depreciation of capital assets; and
- T is the tax paid by the network operator.

The crucial variable in the formula above is r, which must be set at a level that is sufficient to attract the necessary level of investment. In accounting terms, it is said that r must be above the network's weighted average cost of capital (WACC), that is the firm's cost of servicing its debt and making its equity investable.[8] Rate-of-return regulation is effectively a form of *cost-plus pricing*, as the network operator is guaranteed a fixed margin (in this case a fixed percentage of the RAB), irrespective of the level of its costs. Whilst this system guarantees stable long-term returns to investors, which in turn tends to lower financing costs, it provides the network operator with no incentive to reduce its operating expenses. Moreover, given that the remuneration is directly proportional to the level of the RAB, it incentivises networks to over-invest in capital assets, a phenomenon that is pejoratively referred to as gold-plating. In spite of these shortcomings, rate-of-return regulation has been the standard methodology to regulate monopolies in the energy sector for most of the twentieth century and its use to regulate energy networks is still widespread, especially in the United States.

Price-cap regulation was developed in the United Kingdom in the 1980s in response to the above-mentioned inefficiencies of rate-of-return regulation. Its origin is conventionally traced back to a 1983 report for the UK Department of Industry on the recently privatised telecommunication industry.[9] As the name suggests, this methodology is aimed at directly capping the prices the network operator can charge, by limiting the increase Δ P by the following formula:

$$\Delta P = \text{RPI} - X$$

where:

- RPI stands for Retail Price Index, a measure of inflation published by the UK Office for National Statistics; and
- X is a parameter intended to capture the efficiency gains the network operator was expected to achieve over the relevant period.

The objective of price-cap regulation (often simply referred to as 'RPI minus X') is to incentivise the network operator to operate more efficiently by letting the firm keep the additional revenue generated in case the efficiency gains it achieves are greater than the parameter X. The implicit assumption behind this idea is that, due to information asymmetries, the regulatory authority is unlikely to correctly assess the value of the network's asset base and its operating costs (which are key parameters in determining the network's remuneration in a rate-of-return regime). By adopting price-cap regulation, one could expect that the network operator's full efficiency capabilities would be revealed and

[8] It is worth noting that in case the network owner is a government entity, r could, at least in theory, be set at a level below the firm's WACC due to government policy favouring a less efficient allocation of public capital in exchange for lower energy costs.

[9] Littlechild (1983).

the regulatory authority could eventually set regulated prices at a lower level by adjusting the parameter X in the following regulatory periods. Due to its theoretical attractiveness and simplicity, the uptake of price-cap regulation across the world was rapid. Price-cap regulation proved particularly popular in Latin America and Asia during the privatisation wave of the 1990s and early 2000s. However, empirical evidence of the superiority of price-cap regulation is limited and the extra-profits it allows network operators to retain have frequently triggered political backlashes. Even in the United Kingdom, the pure RPI minus X system was rapidly abandoned in favour of hybrid regimes that monitored the behaviour of network operators more intrusively.

Revenue-cap regulation shares many of the elements of a price-cap regime, with the exception that, as the name suggests, the variable on which a cap is imposed is the total revenue the network operator is entitled to earn. In a stylised representation, the revenue R_1 a network operator can accrue over a period is equal to:

$$R_1 = (R_0 \times \pi) + I_1 + d \pm A_0$$

where:

- R_0 is the allowed revenue over the preceding period;
- π is a measure of inflation;
- I_1 is the expenses to be incurred for investment the network operator has committed to make over the period;
- d is the expenses incurred to account for the depreciation of capital assets; and
- A_0 is the discrepancy between the allowed revenue R_0 and the actual accrued revenue, which can be positive (over-recovery) or negative (under-recovery).

While conceptually very similar to price-cap regulation, one crucial feature of revenue-cap regulation is that it decouples the network's revenue from the amount of services sold.[10] As such, this regime insulates network operators from demand fluctuation, making it particularly apt for activities whose costs are overwhelmingly fixed and in which public policy objectives often favour lower network utilisation (see, for instance, the promotion of energy efficiency, self-consumption and demand response). The majority of networks in Europe are currently subject to some form of revenue-cap regulation.

In practice, incentive regulation is accompanied by additional rules and mechanisms attempting to make them fairer and fit for purpose, albeit ever more complex. Detailed reporting obligations on business plans and investment, tight monitoring of costs and mechanisms providing network operators

[10] Jamison (2007).

with incentives or penalties depending on the performance against certain targets (including those related to transparency and conduct) are common features of modern revenue regulation regimes. *Benchmarking* remuneration against the performance of a best-in-class operator (a regulatory practice referred to as yardstick competition) is also used.

As much as accumulation of experience and improvements in computational ability will continue refining the capabilities of regulatory authorities, revenue regulation is deemed to remain an area prone to errors and controversy. On the one hand, network operators tend to have better insight than the regulatory authority over some of the key parameters and may be tempted to game the process. On the other hand, the inherent uncertainty of other input factors does not depend on information asymmetries. For instance, neither the network operator nor the regulatory authority is able to forecast with precision demand trends and interest rates, which significantly affect network utilisation and the viability of investment. Under these circumstances, the accuracy of revenue and cost forecasts for several years ahead is inevitably low, prompting the occurrence of situations in which the network gets either overcompensated, thus undermining the credibility of the regulatory authority, or gets undercompensated, resulting in harmful under-investment or even endangering the financial viability of the network operator.

7 Network Tariffs and Market Structures

In accordance to the principles of revenue regulation and rTPA discussed in the previous sections, the fee a network operator can charge network users for each service it provides (such as a network connection or the booking of capacity at a network point) must be set at an equal level for all network users, called *regulated network tariffs*. In case a service is allocated through an auction, the regulated tariff will be the auction starting price. The calculation or approval of network tariffs, which result from the application of a predefined methodology (also called *charging regime*), is another key task of energy regulatory authorities. Tariffs are a politically sensitive topic as they determine the allocation of network costs among different categories of network users, which in turn significantly influences the energy costs paid by different end users.

Like revenue regulation regimes, network tariffs methodologies vary greatly from one to another. The main distinction that can be observed is between zonal and nodal tariff systems. In a *zonal tariff system*, network users pay fees to the network operator when they book capacity to enter and exit the network, while they are not charged for moving energy within it. For this reason, they are also called *entry-exit* systems. From a practical perspective, a network user injecting energy at network point A and withdrawing it at network point B will book entry capacity at point A and exit capacity at point B, pay the corresponding tariffs, then schedule energy flows at these two points. The movement of energy between point A and point B is solely managed by the network operator. Zonal tariff systems are divided into *postage-stamp* regimes and methodologies that take into account *locational signals*. In the former, like in traditional postal systems, tariffs at all entry and exit points are the same regardless of the costs incurred to move the electrons or gas molecules between network points. In the latter, such costs (which are usually driven by the distance between points) are taken into account when determining the tariffs. The majority of electricity transmission networks and the near totality of gas transmission networks apply a zonal tariff system. Distribution networks, both in electricity and gas, usually charge according to a zonal postage-stamp system.

A *nodal tariff system* is a more complex regime in which network operators charge users a tariff for each movement of energy between two nodes of the network. Such a granular charging of network capacity can potentially lead to the emergence of a different price for energy at each point of the network. For this reason, these systems are also called *locational marginal pricing (LMP)* systems. In practice, in a nodal tariff system capacity between any two network nodes is usually auctioned with a reserve price of zero, so there will be a positive price for capacity between two nodes only if there is more demand than capacity available, or network congestion. The difference of price between two locations is therefore called *congestion revenue*. There is a broad academic consensus on the benefits of nodal systems over zonal ones because they allow for more efficient pricing of energy within networks and, consequently, more efficient network utilisation.[11] However, zonal systems are still more common as they are generally simpler to operate and less politically controversial.[12] Nodal tariffs have been adopted in several electricity transmission networks in the United States over the 1990s and 2000s, but their uptake outside North America has been slow.

Network tariff methodologies also influence how network users exchange energy between themselves. In zonal tariff systems, it is common for the network operator to manage *virtual trading points* (also called virtual hubs), either directly or through an appointed third-party provider, at which transactions notionally take place. The alternative for network users would be to trade at the interconnection between two networks (called flange trading). Across Europe, for instance, all networks (or cluster of networks) have their own virtual trading point, which tends to be given a specific name in gas (for instance, TTF, NBP, NCG, PSV), while is simply called with the name of the network in electricity. Flange trading has been actively discouraged by policymakers since the early 2000s and has almost disappeared. In nodal systems, on the other hand, market participants can in theory buy and sell energy at each node of the network. In practice, trading coalesces at some key locations, or *physical hubs*, either because they are key infrastructural interconnections or because trading activity has conventionally focused there over time. In the United States, most

[11] Hogan (1999).

[12] The application of locational marginal pricing (LMP) and the resulting differences in the energy price paid by consumers on the basis of their location, while economically efficient, has proved to be politically unacceptable in most countries.

exchanges of electricity take place at approximately ten major physical hubs. Likewise, the North American gas market is based on trading at Henry Hub (a physical location in Louisiana) and several satellite regional hubs.

8 Conclusion: The Future of Energy Networks

This chapter has provided an overview of the structure and functioning of energy networks. Many of the key concepts outlined, such as unbundling, rTPA and revenue regulation, are currently at the core of the energy policy debate. Established wisdom in the field of the economics of energy networks is being revisited by academics and practitioners in the attempt to devise appropriate solutions and organisational models for the unprecedented policy and environmental challenges energy networks need to tackle. Current trends only superficially appear to be impacting electricity and gas networks in different manners. Instead, both share a future where rapid transformation and massive investment are necessary. Electricity networks are expected to cope with large increases in throughput due to the electrification of many energy uses (primarily road transport), while being able to manage more volatile and unpredictable energy flows resulting from the replacement of dispatchable thermal generators with non-dispatchable renewable installations. On the other hand, the gradual phase-out of fossil gas in power generation, industry and heating puts gas networks at risk of demise unless they promote a conversion of their infrastructure to low-carbon gases, such as biomethane and hydrogen. Closer interaction between electricity and gas networks (including joint infrastructure planning and operation) is also likely to take place.[13]

In spite of a much-publicised push to off-grid solutions made possible by rapid improvements in DERs and digitalisation, it is difficult to envisage a future in which networks do not continue to play a fundamental role in modern energy systems. Even in the plans of the most enthusiastic proponents of self-generation, continued reliance on network connection, either to supply energy or to evacuate excess on-site production, remains essential. Energy networks are therefore likely to be going through a rapid but incremental evolution of their role and functioning, rather than a full-blown revolution. Despite the radical uncertainty crippling the energy sector, we can confidently state that energy networks are here to stay.

Acknowledgements The author is thankful to Linda Rotasperti for her helpful comments on earlier drafts of this chapter and her invaluable support with graphs and figures.

[13]A full integration of electricity and gas networks is a distinct possibility in a scenario where electrolysers turning electricity into hydrogen (which would provide both electricity storage and low-carbon gas) become a significant feature of energy systems.

Bibliography & Further Readings

Biggar, Darryl R. and Hesamzadeh, Mohammad Reza (2014), The Economics of Electricity Markets. Chichester: IEEE Press/Wiley.

Brunekreft, Gert, Neuhoff, Carsten and Newbery, David (2005), Electricity transmission: An overview of the current debate. Utilities Policy, 13(2), 73–93.

Chawla, Mallika and Pollitt, Michael (2013), Global Trends in Electricity Transmission System Operation: Where Does the Future Lie? The Electricity Journal, 26(5), 65–71.

Council of European Energy Regulators (2019), Implementation of TSO and DSO Unbundling Provisions. CEER Status Review.

Council of European Energy Regulators (2020), Report on Regulatory Frameworks for European Energy Networks. CEER Report.

Dahl, Carol A. (2014), International Energy Markets: Understanding Pricing, Policies, and Profits—2nd edition. Tulsa: PennWell.

Folga, Stephen M. (2007), Natural Gas Pipeline Technology Overview. Argonne National Laboratory Report.

Glachant, Jean-Michel et al. (2013), Incentives for investments: Comparing EU electricity TSO regulatory regimes. Florence: European University Institute.

Greenblatt, Jeffrey B. (2015), Opportunities for Efficiency Improvements in the U.S. Natural Gas Transmission, Storage and Distribution System. Ernest Orland Lawrence Berkeley National Laboratory Report.

Growitsch, Christian and Stronzik, Marcus (2011), Ownership Unbundling of Gas Transmission Networks—Empirical Evidence. EWI Working Paper, No. 11/07.

Henriot, Arthur (2013), Financing investment in the European electricity transmission network: Consequences on long-term sustainability of the TSOs financial structure. Energy Policy, Elsevier, vol. 62(3), 821–829.

Hogan, William W. (1999), Transmission Congestion: The Nodal-Zonal Debate Revisited. Harvard University, John F. Kennedy School of Government, https://scholar.harvard.edu/whogan/files/nezn0227.pdf (retrieved on 02/07/2020).

Jamison, Mark A. (2007), Regulation: Price Cap and Revenue Cap, in Encyclopaedia of Energy Engineering and Technology, Vol. 3. New York: CRC Press, Taylor and Francis.

Joskow, Paul L. (1984), Vertical Integration and Long Term Contracts: The Case of Coal Burning Electric Generating Plants. Journal of Law Economics and Organization, 1(361), 33–80.

Joskow, Paul L. (2008), Lessons Learned from Electricity Market Liberalization. The Energy Journal, 29(2), 9–42.

Joskow, Paul L. (2014), Incentive Regulation in Theory and Practice: Electricity Distribution and Transmission Networks, in Rose, Nancy L. (ed.), Economic Regulation and Its Reform: What Have We Learned? Chicago: Chicago University Press.

Joskow, Paul L. and Tirole, Jean (2005), Merchant Transmission Investment. The Journal of Industrial Economics, 53(2), 233–264.

Laffont, Jean-Jacques and Tirole, Jean (1993), A Theory of Incentives in Procurement and Regulation. Cambridge: MIT Press.

Littlechild, Stephen C. (1983), Regulation of British Telecommunications' Profitability—Report to the Secretary of State. London: UK Department of Industry.

Newbery, David M. (1998), Rate-of-return regulation versus price regulation for public utilities, in Newman, Peter (ed.), The New Palgrave Dictionary of Economics and the Law. London: Macmillan.

OECD (2003), Glossary of Statistical Terms—Natural Monopoly. OECD, https://stats.oecd.org/glossary/detail.asp?ID=3267 (Retrieved: 29/05/2020)

Pipeline Safety Trust (2015), Pipeline Basics and Specifics About Natural Gas Pipelines. Pipeline Briefing Paper, No. 2.

Pollitt, Michael (2004), Electricity Reform in Chile Lessons for Developing Countries. Centre for Energy and Environmental Policy Research (CEEPR), Working Paper, 04-016.

Stern, Jon (2003), What the Littlechild Report Actually Said. Regulation Initiative Working Paper, No. 55.

U.S. Department of Energy (2015), Quadrennial Technology Review 2015—Technology Assessment 3F: Transmission and Distribution Component. Washington, DC: U.S. Department of Energy.

Vagliasindi, Maria and Besant-Jones, John (2013), Power Market Structure: Revisiting Policy Options. Washington, DC: The World Bank.

World Energy Council (2020), Performing while transforming: The role of transmission companies in the energy transition. World Energy Council Innovation Insights Brief.

CHAPTER 14

Economics of Electricity Battery Storage

Michel Noussan

1 Introduction

The energy consumption related to human activities always involved a specific energy supply chain, which provided to the final users the exact amount of energy required at a specific time. Since it is not always possible to match the energy supply with the user's demand, there is a need for storing energy to compensate this mismatch. The storage may be required with a large diversity of durations, ranging from fraction of seconds to months or even years. Different energy carriers involve multiple storage solutions, based on limits and opportunities related to the form of energy that is stored (chemical, potential, kinetic, electro-static, etc.), as well as on technical and economic features of the available storage technologies.

The easiest energy storage usually happens with fuels, especially solid and liquid, which can be generally stored in their normal form without the need of specific solutions. While attention must be paid in avoiding potential self-combustion, chemical degradation, or phase change, solid and liquid fuels are usually stored in simple tanks (eventually cooled or heated in particular climate conditions).

Additional requirements are usually needed for gaseous fuels, mainly natural gas. Due to its low volumetric density, its transportation and storage are usually performed either by compressing it at high pressures or by liquefying it with the need of providing continuous cooling. Natural gas storage is usually

M. Noussan (✉)
Fondazione Eni Enrico Mattei (FEEM), Milan, Italy

Decisio s.r.l., Turin, Italy

SciencesPo—Paris School of International Affairs, Paris, France
e-mail: michel.noussan@sciencespo.fr

M. Hafner, G. Luciani (eds.), *The Palgrave Handbook of International Energy Economics*, https://doi.org/10.1007/978-3-030-86884-0_14

performed on a seasonal basis, to match the continuous supply with the fluctuating demand driven by different weather conditions throughout the years. Such storage strategies usually involve large-scale underground formations, either depleted reservoirs or saline formations. The low energy and fuel losses are generally compensated by the significant economic savings that can be obtained with continuous upstream operations for natural gas.

Another energy carrier that is commonly stored is heat, usually in the form of warm or hot water, either in large-scale facilities connected to district heating networks or industrial users or at small-scale heat storage systems for domestic users. Heat storage is mostly used to exploit the better efficiency related to heat generators operating at constant load, especially biomass boilers and heat pumps. However, large seasonal underground systems are being used in some countries to store solar energy in summer and supply district heating in winter. Some systems exploit the ground as storage medium, while others rely on very large water volumes (Bott et al. 2019). For small-scale storage, alternative technologies based on phase-changing materials are the objective of multiple research efforts, although commercial applications are still limited.

Electricity stands out among the most difficult energy vectors to be stored. Electricity storage solutions are usually relying on its conversion to another form of energy. With the exception of superconductivity, other current technological solutions rely on chemical, mechanical, gravitational, or electro-static forms of energy. Nevertheless, electricity storage systems are strongly needed to guarantee the continuous balance of the power grid and provide reliable and effective service to the final users. For this task, a wide range of services is required, which are usually categorized with respect to storage duration: from few seconds or minutes for frequency control; to energy transfers across weeks, days, or day-night (also called arbitrage); and to the need of providing UPS (Uninterrupted Power Supply) for industrial consumers connected to the grid (Crampes and Trochet 2019).

Each available storage technology is usually tailored to a preferred application, based on technical limitations, design choices, and economic features. Today, most electricity storage worldwide is performed by pumped hydro systems, which rely on a mature technology with lower costs in comparison with the alternatives. Although pumped storage may be used also for frequency regulation, the flexibility provided by its potentially long discharge time (up to a few dozens of hundred hours) is usually exploited for arbitrage. Frequency control is provided through flywheels but more often by backup power generators. Batteries are somewhat in between, since they have discharge times that usually reach some hours, but at the same time they are responsive enough to provide frequency regulation services. Compressed-air storage systems have similar applications than pumped hydro, but due to limited available sites few applications exist.

While most storage systems are mature technologies, there is currently an interesting potential in the deployment of electric batteries, especially based on lithium-ion. The two leading drivers are the additional flexibility required by non-dispatchable renewable sources (mainly solar and wind) and the strongly decreasing cost expected by massive upscaling of battery manufacturing for electric vehicles. Although other chemistries may prove to be disruptive in the future, the current choice appears to be firmly oriented toward Li-ion, which is the preferred choice of numerous large-scale factories worldwide (so-called gigafactories). Their modularity also allows a large range of applications, from utility-scale grid storage to beyond-the-meter batteries for final users, usually coupled with distributed PV generation.

For these reasons, this chapter focuses on Li-ion batteries, given their expected central role in the future power systems. Alternative chemistries will be briefly mentioned, with the aim of highlighting the potential advantages they may provide. Section 2 provides a technological perspective to highlight the main aspects that are involved in battery design, deployment, and operation. Section 3 focuses on battery economics, with attention on the manufacturing supply chain and on the sizing and operational logics. Finally, Sect. 4 closes the analysis by recapping the main take-aways, together with some policy implications.

2 Battery Technologies

Different technologies exist for electric batteries, based on alternative chemistries for anode, cathode, and electrolyte. Each combination leads to different design and operational parameters, over a wide range of aspects, and the choice is often driven by the most important requirements of each application (e.g. high energy density for electric vehicles, low cost for stationary storage, etc.). The current rise in battery manufacturing capacity worldwide is associated with Li-ion batteries, which are meeting the requirements of the electric vehicles (EVs) industry and offer a viable solution also for stationary storage applications, both for utility-scale batteries and behind-the-meter distributed storage.

The historical trend of global stationary storage capacity (see Fig. 14.1) shows an increase in recent years, from around 0.6 GWh in 2010 up to 3.5 GWh in 2017. While up to 2010 most of the capacity was relying on sodium batteries, in 2017 almost 60% of the total capacity is made up of Li-ion batteries (figures may slightly differ when considering output power, since the energy/power ratio is usually different from one technology to another). This rise is due to different factors, but the most important is surely declining costs driven by manufacturing upscaling of this technology for use in EVs, as is further explained later.

Figure 14.1 is limited to utility-scale capacity, while there is also a growing, although much more difficult to quantify, amount of behind-the-meter storage.[1] Estimates for 2016 range from 0.5 to 2.4 GWh, depending on the source, limited to distributed storage operated by residential, industrial, and

[1] Behind-the-meter storage refers to the distributed battery storage installed by private users, mostly residential. It is often coupled to distributed generation systems, such as photovoltaics.

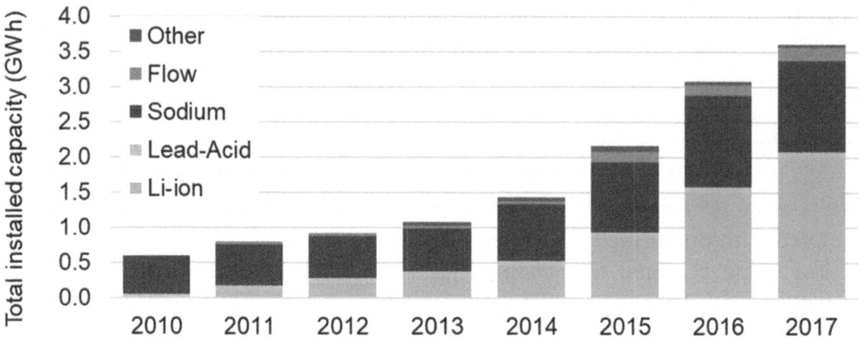

Fig. 14.1 Evolution of installed capacity for stationary storage (utility scale), per technology. (Source: Author's elaboration on (Tsiropoulos et al. 2018))

commercial users. This capacity is made up of a large number of storage systems with small capacity, usually coupled with local generation from RES (mostly solar). While utility-scale batteries are usually managed centrally, an optimized operation of the distributed energy systems requires the operation of smart grids and networks supported by digital platforms (such as virtual aggregators[2]).

It is important to highlight that stationary storage may refer to different services for the power network, at both the transmission and the distribution levels, which differ based on the response time of the batteries, the discharge duration, and the size of the system. The applications may include services for the transmission grid (arbitrage, frequency regulation, peak shaving, black start, and ramping[3]) or for the distribution grid and users (voltage support, balance management, uninterruptible power supply (UPS), and support to self-consumption from PV generation[4]).

[2] Virtual aggregators are digital platforms that coordinate the operation of multiple systems, including generation units, energy storage systems, and demand response, with the aim of reaching the minimum threshold of power required to participate to wholesale markets (usually higher than 1 MW).

[3] Arbitrage is the practice of purchasing electricity from the grid when it has a low price and storing it for later use when the price increases. Frequency regulation is a service provided to the grid that ensures that alternate electric current is maintained within the required tolerance bounds by synchronizing the power generators. Peak shaving is the practice of using available storage capacity to limit the maximum power demand during peak hours, to optimize the generation units and avoid excessive variations. Black start is the process of restoring the operation of an electric grid after a partial or total shutdown, while ramping is the operation of increasing or decreasing the output power of a generation unit.

[4] Voltage support and balance management are flexibility services provided to the distribution grid that allow a proper operation of all the network within the tolerance boundaries. UPS units guarantee that in the case of a network failure the electricity supply is not interrupted, and it is usually required by expensive machineries that may be sensitive to power shortages. Support to self-consumption from PV generation may be required to maximize the local use of electricity to improve the energy efficiency of the system and/or decrease costs for the users.

Table 14.1 Main characteristics of different battery technologies

	Unit	*Li-ion*	*Pb-A*	*Na-S*	*V-R flow*
Cycle life	(cycles @ % SOC variation)[a]	3000 to 10,000 @ 80%	200 to 1800 @ 80%	4500 @ 80%, 2500 @ 100%	10,000 to 12,000+ @ 100%
Specific energy	Wh/kg	75 to 200	30 to 50	150 to 250	10 to 30
E/P ratio	kWh/kW	0.025 to 0.6	0.13 to 0.5	6	1.5 to 6+
Cycle efficiency	–	80% to 98%	63% to 90%	75% to 90%	75% to 80%
Daily self-discharge	–	0.1% to 0.3%	< 0.5%	20% (thermal)	Negligible

Source: Author's elaboration from Leadbetter and Swan (2012)

[a]SOC—State of charge. Cycle life is often measured considering the number of cycles that can be performed with respect to a specific variation of the state-of-charge of the battery

The following section will describe the main characteristics of the most significant available technologies, not only with a strong emphasis on Li-ion batteries but also with a discussion of the main alternatives: lead-acid (Pb-A) batteries, sodium-sulfur (Na-S) batteries, and vanadium redox (V-R) flow batteries. The main characteristics of different technologies are summarized in Table 14.1.

As already anticipated, each battery shows peculiar parameters that are tailored to specific applications. Particularly, the energy/power (E/P) ratio is crucial for the choice of the application, and while there is some room for adjustment by considering specific design parameters (such as electrodes thickness in Li-ion batteries), each technology usually fits best in a specific application as presented hereafter.

2.1 Li-Ion Batteries

Li-ion batteries are a recent technology, initially developed at Bells labs in the 1960s and first commercialized by Sony in 1990. The Nobel prize in Chemistry in 2019 has been awarded to J. B. Goodenough, M. S. Whittingham, and A. Yoshino for their crucial role in the development of Li-ion batteries at different steps (Nobel Media AB 2019). Their success for portable electronics has been mainly triggered by high cycle life, high energy density, and high efficiency, although at a higher price in comparison with other solutions.

Li-ion batteries were mostly applied to portable electronics (including laptops, phones, etc.), until the rising interest in EVs triggered a significant deployment of batteries, whose price decreases also helped their increased sales for stationary energy storage and other applications (including medical devices, gardening tools, and electric bikes) (Fig. 14.2).

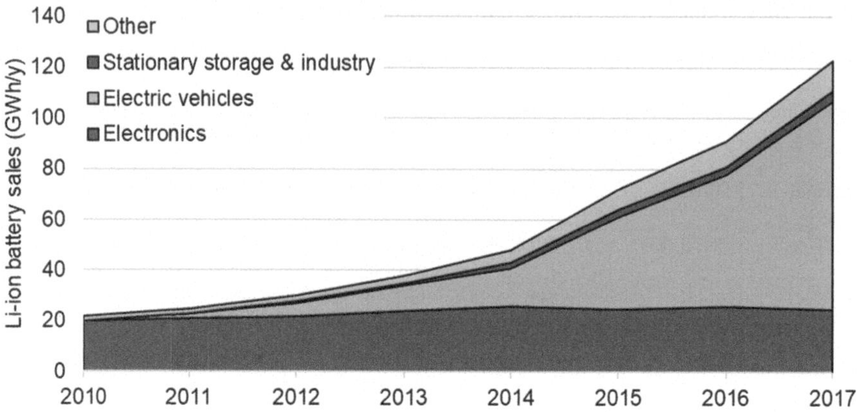

Fig. 14.2 Evolution of Li-ion battery sales worldwide. (Source: Author's elaboration on (Tsiropoulos et al. 2018))

Thanks to their superior performance, they represent the most interesting technology for research and development. In particular, most research is focusing on alternative cathode chemistries to improve energy density and safety or reduce cost through limited use of specific materials (especially cobalt). Other areas of research include anode and electrolyte materials and manufacturing processes.

2.2 *Other Battery Technologies*

2.2.1 *Lead Batteries*

Pb-A batteries are the most mature and diffused battery technology in the world, with their first applications dating back to the 1860s. The extensive research that has been made on many different aspects now guarantees low costs, although with limited life cycles and energy density. Specific additives are available to reach specific objectives, such as reducing the self-discharge or decreasing corrosion issues (Leadbetter and Swan 2012). Lead batteries are seldom used for heavy cycling applications, but they are generally suitable for infrequent cycle applications such as peak shaving or uninterruptible power supplies. Large batteries have been installed as case studies in different countries, up to 20 MW and 40 MWh, demonstrating good performance over several cycles, although requiring appropriate energy management methods. Notwithstanding the technology maturity, research is still active in different domains with the aim of decreasing costs and addressing specific challenges, such as longer lifecycles or more accurate determination of the state of charge (SOC).

2.2.2 *Sodium-Sulfur Batteries*

Na-S batteries are another relatively new technology, having been developed from the 1960s to the 1990s. While they were initially investigated for electric vehicles without much success, they eventually became among the lowest-cost options for grid storage and renewable applications. The operation of Na-S batteries involves peculiar aspects, including the need of high temperature operation for liquid sodium (300–350°C) and the potential very high reactivity of sodium with air in case of containment losses. While the inefficiency during the operation is generally enough to keep the sodium at the right temperature without the need of an external energy supply, in case of non-operation the battery records up to 20% of daily capacity losses due to heat dissipation. Existing installations have grown rapidly in the last decades, with the largest system for stationary storage reaching to date a capacity of 34 MW and 245 MWh coupled with a 51-MW wind farm to stabilize its power output (Leadbetter and Swan 2012).

2.2.3 Flow Batteries

The most diffused technology for flow batteries is the vanadium redox battery (VRB), whose development began in the early 1980s. Its peculiar features include a very long life cycle, the possibility of independently designing the required power and energy output, very low self-discharge losses, and moderate efficiency and costs. In a flow battery, two electrolytes are stored in two separate tanks, and an electrical current is created through a redox reaction by circulating H^+ ions through a membrane. Storage capacity can be raised by increasing the size of the tanks, at constant power output, while increasing the membrane area has the only effect of expanding the power output (i.e. with constant storage capacity). A significant issue is the limited temperature operational range (10–35°C), which usually requires the installation of a temperature control system, although additions to the electrolytes can increase this range. VRB batteries are at a lower technology readiness level in comparison with other solutions, and there are few and small commercial applications to date. An example of application is a 500 kW/1 MWh VRB installed in a wind power research and testing center in Zhangbei, China (IRENA 2015). Its main objective is to support wind generation by storing excess production and delivering it to the grid in hours with higher demand, and the battery can also provide services over a shorter timeframe, such as load following and voltage support. However, experts warn that significant cost reductions would be required to compete with Li-ion or advanced Pb-A technologies, which in turn would require increasing manufacturing and development funding, which may not be the case without increasing revenues (Fisher et al. 2019).

3 Economics of Li-Ion Batteries

Batteries are still an emerging technology in the framework of power systems management and face high upfront costs and regulatory constraints due to lack of technical know-how in governments and public authorities. The investment costs include the battery pack, balance-of-system (BOS) costs and engineering, and procurement and construction (EPC) costs. Battery pack prices are strongly decreasing, driven by economies of scale related to EVs deployment, and the remaining costs are also expected to decrease sharply, thanks to increased standardization of storage modules and increased competition on the market.

The economics of Li-ion batteries can be quantified by defining a levelized cost of storage (LCOS), in analogy to the well-known definition of the levelized cost of electricity (LCOE), with the aim of accounting for all technical and economic parameters affecting the lifetime cost of discharging stored electricity (Schmidt et al. 2019). This metric has been defined to improve the limitations of considering only the investment cost, which is often the only indicator that is analyzed, by including replacement and disposal costs, maintenance and operation costs, as well as performance parameters such as capacity degradation over time. LCOS is thus defined as the total lifetime cost of the investment in an electricity storage technology, divided by its cumulative delivered electricity (Schmidt et al. 2019); the calculation involves a more in-depth analysis on the expected performance of the unit.

A general formulation of the LCOS is represented in Eq. (14.1), defining the discounted cost per unit of electricity delivered by the batteries, in line with the most recent publications on the subject (Jülch 2016; Lazard 2018; Schmidt et al. 2019). The main aspects included in this formulation are the investment cost, the operation and maintenance cost, the charging cost, and the end-of-life cost, all divided by the sum of the electricity discharged by the storage system over the entire economic lifetime (N), discounted by the discount rate (i).

$$LCOS\left[\frac{\$}{MWh}\right] = \frac{INV_{cost} + \sum_{n=1}^{N}\frac{O\&M_{cost}}{(1+i)^n} + \sum_{n=1}^{N}\frac{Charging_{cost}}{(1+i)^n} + \frac{EOL_{cost}}{(1+i)^{N+1}}}{\sum_{n=1}^{N}\frac{E_{discharged}}{(1+i)^n}} \tag{14.1}$$

The LCOS is generally defined with respect to the energy discharged, but for specific applications that focus on services related to active power, a more suitable definition would consider the available output power rather than the energy delivered. Some literature works evaluate also an LCOS based on power, by considering the net power capacity that can be provided each year (Schmidt et al. 2019).

The investment cost is usually parameterized on both power output and energy capacity of the battery, and some components need to be replaced in the lifetime of the battery. The replacement costs may be included in the investment cost, properly discounted based on the estimated year of replacement, or they may be considered part of the maintenance costs, without any difference on the final calculation of the LCOS.

Annual costs include O&M costs and charging costs, both affected by the annual number of cycles of the battery. Charging costs are also related to the specific price of electricity, which can show large variations, and the round-trip efficiency, for which a degradation over time should be considered. End-of-life costs are usually calculated as a fraction of investment costs, but the evolution of recycling procedures (and dedicated regulations) may have a significant impact.

The following sections will focus on the main economic aspects involved with investment, operational, and maintenance costs, as well as on the performance parameters that affect the LCOS both on the annual charging cost and on the electricity discharged.

3.1 *Investment Cost*

The investment cost of Li-ion batteries significantly declined in recent years, and the trend is expected to continue in the future. As already discussed, the most important trend is currently the strong demand of batteries for the EV sector, which is leading to factory capacity expansion in different regions of the world. While this trend is pushing toward a decrease of battery packs cost, Li-ion batteries for stationary storage also include additional components, such as balance of system, power conversion system, energy management system,[5] engineering, procurement, and construction. Some of these additional components may face similar cost decreases in the future thanks to potential synergies with other industries (e.g. inverter costs decrease thanks to their application in the PV deployment).

Detailed information on the investment cost breakdowns is usually not available, due to confidentiality restrictions. Moreover, due to the high variability of both technologies and battery configurations related to specific applications, it is difficult to draw conclusions related to the weight of each component of investment costs. Material-related costs analyzed in different literature studies range from one-third to almost two-thirds of the total system costs, depending on the source, as illustrated in Fig. 14.3 (IRENA 2017).

However, when considering the breakdown of material costs, the figures show less variability: electrode materials (anode, cathode, and electrolyte) constitute roughly half of the cost, with the main contribution related to cathode (between 31% and 39% of the total cost of materials). Notwithstanding the variable impact of materials in the total investment cost of batteries, the increase of the energy density driven by technology innovation will eventually lead to cost savings, thanks to the lower material input required for the same output capacity.

[5] The balance of system includes the components that monitor the battery operation to avoid that specific parameters reach values outside the acceptable range, including the calculation and reporting of indicators. The power conversion system includes the components that allow to convert electricity from one form to another, such as from direct current to alternate current, and modifying voltage or frequency. The energy management system includes the software and operational logics that guarantee the interaction between the battery and the power grid, to support the charging and discharging phases and ensure an efficient operation of the energy storage system.

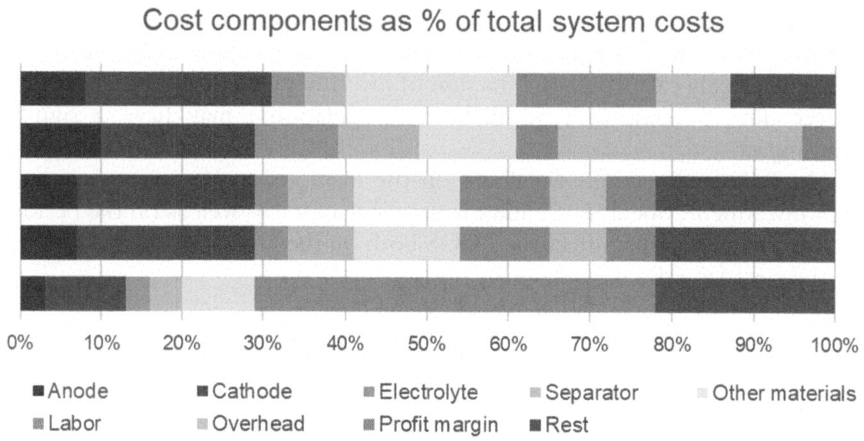

Fig. 14.3 Investment cost breakdowns from five different sources. (Source: Author's elaboration on (IRENA 2017))

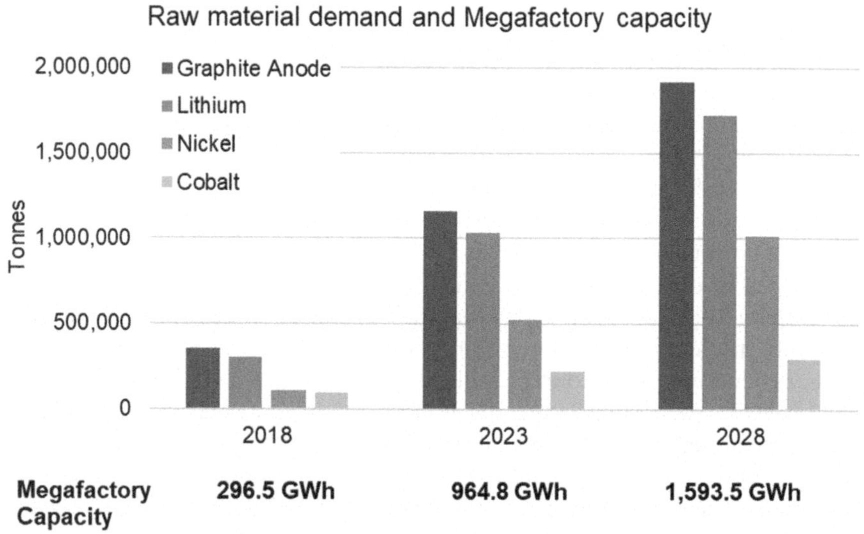

Fig. 14.4 Expected increase in raw material demand for global Li-ion batteries manufacturing. (Source: Author's elaboration on (Benchmark Mineral Intelligence 2018))

Many authors calculate learning curves based on the historical trend, assuming that the cost decrease has no significant limitations related to external constraints (Berckmans et al. 2017; Kittner et al. 2017; Schmidt et al. 2017). However, other works highlight the fact that the cost of active materials, especially under rising global demand, may act as a strong constraint to further reduce battery costs and may slow down the learning curves (Hsieh et al. 2019).

The rise of battery demand will translate to fast-increasing raw materials requirements, as estimated in the chart of Fig. 14.4 with reference to the expected increase of Li-ion battery production capacity worldwide. In particular, cobalt demand could roughly triple in the period 2018–2028, lithium and graphite demand would grow by 5.5 times, and nickel demand may increase ninefold. Although there has been much debate on the possible lack of materials to support such an expansion, the most critical bottlenecks are expected in the short term, due to the need of adequate planning to upscale the mining industry and the downstream supply chain. Particular issues are related to cobalt, both for the spatial concentration of the resources (more than two-thirds of global cobalt in 2018 have been mined in the Democratic Republic of Congo) and for the fact that is usually obtained as a by-product of nickel and copper mining, making a production upscale more difficult. Moreover, the market concentration of raw materials processing is even more critical, with China representing the largest part of products manufacturing for lithium (51%), refined cobalt (62%), and spherical graphite (100%) worldwide in 2018 (Colbourn 2019). Industry concentration also limits market opportunities, since the lack of diverse perspectives may result in conservative supply expansion plans from existing players (IRENA 2017).

The increase of materials demand may be partly compensated by a development of recycling procedures for the depleted batteries, which will need to demonstrate their effectiveness in the coming years, when the first Li-ion batteries used in EVs will start to approach their technical lifetime.

3.2 O&M and Charging Costs

Operational costs of stationary storage are mainly related to electricity cost for charging and maintenance procedures, and the latter may include the replacement costs for components with durability lower than the lifetime of the battery. O&M costs vary depending on the application, but their share on the total LCOS shows limited variation, in the range of 16%–24% for current installations (Lazard 2018). Higher costs are related to wholesale and transmission and distribution (T&D) applications (22%–24%), while utility-scale or behind-the-meter applications coupled with PV usually have a lower impact of O&M costs (16%–19%).

The electricity cost for charging is an important aspect, and its variability is related not only to the application, with large differences in electricity prices for T&D and behind-the-meter systems, but also to the location of these systems, as electricity price has very large variations from country to country. Moreover, all the applications coupled to variable RES generation are usually considering a null cost for charging, although a part of the investment cost of generation plants should somehow be factored in.

Charging costs in LCOS studies generally consider a fixed average price (and in some cases some increment over the lifetime of the system), usually around 50$/MWh for T&D applications and 100$/MWh for behind-the-meter applications (Schmidt et al. 2019). However, while it is difficult to forecast more accurate values on such a long interval, it is important to remind that this cost often shows significant variability over time, and for some applications (e.g. energy arbitrage), it is the main driver of the frequency and duration of battery charge/discharge cycles. Behind-the-meter applications usually face rather constant electricity prices, albeit higher.

3.3 *End of Life: Decommissioning and Recycling*

The end of life of Li-ion batteries may include different pathways: reusing or repurposing for other applications, recycling of materials, and disposal. While current research is strongly focused on potential recycling procedures, it is estimated that the large majority of batteries is currently disposed, and recycling of Li-ion batteries has not yet emerged as a competitive solution on the market (Pellow et al. 2019). However, other more mature battery technologies, especially lead-acid, have already established recycling pathways, but establishing clear policy targets is a key component in the development of adequate technological solutions.

As discussed for battery manufacturing, also in recycling the larger share of EV batteries will probably drive the market for recycling processes. However, end-of-life conditions of these two applications may broadly differ. Research studies suggest the possibility of reusing EV batteries as stationary storage for residential and industrial applications (Mirzaei Omrani and Jannesari 2019). While a certain level of performance degradation of battery packs may not be acceptable for transport requirements, they could be repurposed for stationary applications thanks to their very low cost. If this option gains interest, the direct material recycling of EV batteries may remain limited, thanks to their extended lifetime through this potential second life.

Few studies currently estimate the potential recycling cost of Li-ion batteries, and the very different assumptions across research works lead to very low comparability of the results. Recovery rates of specific materials are very highly variable, and it is difficult to compare academic studies with the few real applications. There is still a lack of consensus on the sustainability of the end-of-life of Li-ion batteries, both concerning specific energy consumption and environmental impacts (Pellow et al. 2019).

3.4 *Performance Parameters*

While it is important to focus on the total costs over the life cycle of a battery, its performance is another relevant aspect for the comparison of different solutions, since it directly affects the available electricity that can be supplied by the battery for a given electricity input. Batteries are usually compared based on their energy capacity, although their nominal charge/discharge rate, the maximum depth of discharge (DoD), and their cycle efficiency[6] are just as impor-

[6]The discharge rate measures the speed at which a battery is designed to be charged or discharged, giving the information on the average duration of these processes. The maximum DoD is

tant. An additional aspect is the potential degradation rate of these parameters over time, which can lead to total life-cycle performances lower than the nominal conditions for a new battery. Some aspects are related to the specific technological solution, while others can be adjusted by an accurate choice of design parameters, often based on the specific application that is of interest.

An additional aspect that has an impact on Li-ion batteries performance is the operation temperature, which can affect efficiency, safety, and lifetime. High temperatures accelerate the rate of unwanted chemical reactions that degrade the battery cells, reducing the total lifetime up to 50% for each 10°C of difference with respect to design temperature (IRENA 2017). The longest lifetime is usually achieved in the range 20°C–30°C, resulting in the need of cooling systems in hot climates. On the other hand, operation at extremely low temperatures leads to significant power loss, resulting in significant limitations for electric transport systems in some locations.

Therefore, attention should be paid on the discrepancies for actual operational performance in comparison with expected ratings from manufacturers or testing results, especially considering the different cycling hypotheses and their effect on battery degradation. Multiple circumstances occurring during the operation may lead to degradation of the batteries, including overcharging/discharging, high currents, and mechanical stresses, such as electrode material expansion[7] (Li et al. 2019).

3.5 *Comparison of Different LCOS Studies*

As discussed in the previous sections, the hypotheses required to calculate the LCOS are abundant, resulting in a low comparability of different studies. Nonetheless, some information can be retrieved from the most recent literature available on the subject, to represent the range of variability of LCOS results related to Li-ion applications. Figure 14.5 reports the average values of LCOS for Li-ion batteries calculated in different studies (Comello and Reichelstein 2019; Jülch 2016; Lazard 2018; Schmidt et al. 2019).

While many analyses exist for current LCOS, few studies extend the analysis to the future evolution of LCOS values for storage. Since Schmidt et al. (2019) is the only study providing detailed projections of future trends, as well as a differentiation of results for large batteries and behind-the-meter batteries, it

the share of usable amount of energy with respect to the nominal energy capacity of the battery that can be safely used without compromising the battery performance, due to the fact that some battery chemistries need to guarantee a minimum state of charge. The cycle efficiency is usually calculated as the ratio between the energy supplied by the battery during the discharging phase and the energy consumption of the charging phase, and this ratio is lower than 100% due to the energy losses of these processes.

[7] The operation of the battery in conditions that go beyond the designed values may induce different problems. An excessive charging of the battery and/or excessive electric currents may degrade its chemical components, and due to the volume changes that are associated with charging and discharging processes, additional mechanical stresses can be induced into the materials.

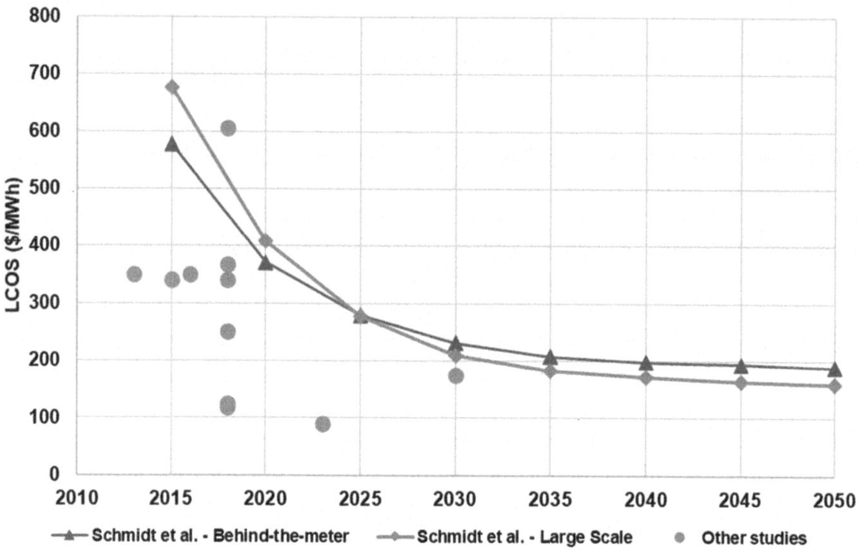

Fig. 14.5 Comparison of average values of LCOS for Li-ion batteries from selected studies. (Source: Author's elaboration)

has been given more relevance in the chart. It is important to underline that these numbers are strongly affected by the high uncertainty associated both to investment costs of the technology and to the market conditions for the electricity supply. For this reason, the values reported in Fig. 14.5 should only be considered as a potential future indication based on the most recent available literature, but since the commercial deployment of Li-ion batteries for stationary storage is only beginning, these numbers may be subject to significant revisions in the years to come. Additionally, just like any other comparison of literature results, it is important to highlight the caveat that the calculation of the LCOS requires multiple assumptions, which may differ across multiple research works.

3.6 *External Context and Revenue Opportunities*

While much attention is generally paid to energy storage costs, since this aspect is often the more limiting factor, a brief analysis of the potential revenue opportunities can provide additional insights on the economics of Li-ion batteries. The opportunities for any storage technology are related to the variable value that a commodity can have over time, and electricity storage is thus most required when there is a larger mismatch between the electricity demand and supply.

Such mismatch was generally tackled through bids and offers in capacity markets at the transmission level, whose participation was usually limited to dispatchable power plants such as thermoelectric and pumped hydro storage.

However, such mechanisms may not be enough in the current transition toward higher shares of RES and distributed generation. In this transition phase, virtual power plants are being deployed: a virtual aggregation of several small units of different nature (i.e. electricity producers, storage units, demand-side management) thanks to the use of digital technologies. In the context of this transition, energy storage can fit at different levels thanks to the possible scalability of system size and the flexibility of operation.

The involvement of different stakeholders may be tightly related to the specific policies and regulations that will be implemented, but the flexibility requirements of a low-carbon energy system will necessarily include storage among other different solutions. While transmission and distribution systems operators are evaluating batteries for a wide range of network services, they are also being considered by large-scale variable RES producers to increase their capacity of dispatching electricity and the associated value and market opportunities (IRENA 2019a). A similar driver exists at residential level, where households equipped with a PV system try to maximize their self-consumption if they face high electricity prices (IRENA 2019b). Final users are generally more affected by stringent regulations, and the profitability of behind-the-meter storage may exhibit strong differences across countries.

Current opportunities are emerging with an uneven distribution at global scale, since countries with favorable regulations are already seeing deployment of battery storage systems at different levels, including Germany, Australia, South Korea, and the United States (IRENA 2019a).

3.7 Future Deployment of Stationary Li-Ion Batteries

In parallel to the economic analysis that has been presented before, it is important to discuss the expected scenarios for stationary battery deployments. While these numbers are continuously being updated based on the evolution of the energy systems and energy markets, the comparison of the current scenarios of different international organizations underlines the strong momentum and the high potential of stationary storage.

Figure 14.6 reports a comparison of the future trends expected by some of the most influential energy organizations, that is, the International Renewable Energy Agency (IRENA 2017), the International Energy Agency (IEA 2019), and Bloomberg New Energy Finance (BNEF 2019). These scenarios differ for the final capacity deployed, and it is not always clear which kind of applications are included in the forecast, in particular as far as behind-the-meter applications are concerned. Nevertheless, in all the cases the expected battery storage capacity reaches a considerable total volume, although stationary storage will likely remain a minor market in comparison with Li-ion batteries used in electric vehicles.

To give some context to these volumes, the current energy storage capacity of pumped hydro storage, as of 2017, sum up to 4.5 TWh worldwide (IRENA 2017). However, it is important to highlight that batteries and pumped storage

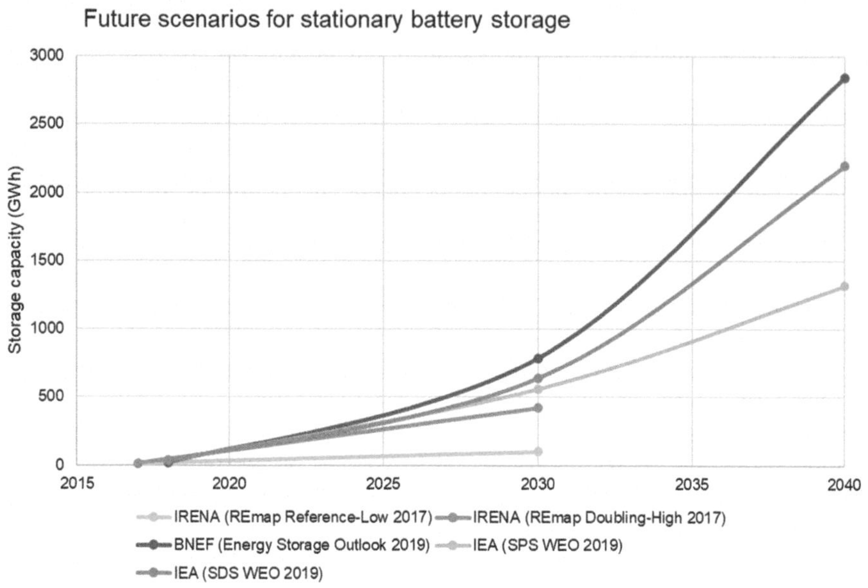

Fig. 14.6 Comparison of future scenarios for stationary batteries deployment. (Source: Author's elaboration)

are not in competition but rather provide complementary services, since electric batteries will mostly be used for short-term services (up to some hours or in some cases few days), while pumped hydro storage is characterized by longer charging and discharging times (in the order of weeks or months).

4 Conclusions

This chapter described the main aspects of the economics of battery storage systems and provided a qualitative discussion of battery technology and potential. Due to the high momentum of Li-ion batteries, especially in connection to the expected strong manufacturing capacity increase for electric vehicles applications, updated figures may exhibit strong variations from a year to another. On the other hand, underlying trends related to the main cost drivers and revenue opportunities will likely show lower variations and maintain their importance.

Li-ion batteries for stationary storage have recorded massive upfront cost decrease in the last years, and this trend is expected to continue in the coming decade. The reason is the expected increase of batteries supply capacity at a global level, driven by rising demand of electric vehicles, which is benefitting from economies of scale as well as technological improvements related to both battery performance and manufacturing efficiency. A secondary effect of large deployment of EVs may be the availability of cheap second-life batteries, whose remaining performance level not suitable for transport could be acceptable for stationary storage requirements.

While much emphasis is usually put on Li-ion batteries investment costs, there are other factors that affect the real total cost of batteries operation, which can be evaluated through the levelized cost of storage (LCOS). Such factors include not only the O&M costs, the electricity costs for charging, and the end-of life costs, but also a number of technical parameters that affect the performance of the battery and thus the electricity output that can be achieved. They include the energy/power ratio (usually resulting from design choices), the round-trip efficiency, the calendar and cycling lifetimes, the degradation over time, as well as the operation logic of the battery in terms of number of cycles per year and the average discharge duration. An understanding of these parameters is essential to have a complete picture on the economics of Li-ion batteries operation for electricity storage, since the results of available research studies are strongly dependent on underlying hypotheses.

Current applications of Li-ion batteries for stationary storage, both as utility-scale and behind-the-meter systems, demonstrate the crucial importance of policies and regulations in fostering the adoption of such technologies and improving their maturity. While upfront costs remain the main barrier to widespread adoption, existing regulations are often limiting the development and deployment of batteries for different applications and network services. Moreover, key stakeholders are not always aware of the potential of this technology and the results from existing case studies.

If the current trend of declining costs will continue in the future, without being hindered by issues related to the lack of raw materials or bottlenecks in the supply chain, Li-ion batteries are expected to play a crucial role in providing the required flexibility for low-carbon electricity systems. A crucial aspect will be the competition with the EVs market, since its expansion may lead to either positive or negative impacts on stationary storage applications.

References

Benchmark Mineral Intelligence, 2018. Lithium ion battery megafactory assessment.

Berckmans, G., Messagie, M., Smekens, J., Omar, N., Vanhaverbeke, L., Van Mierlo, J., 2017. Cost Projection of State of the Art Lithium-Ion Batteries for Electric Vehicles Up to 2030. Energies 10. https://doi.org/10.3390/en10091314

BNEF, 2019. Energy Storage Outlook 2019.

Bott, C., Dressel, I., Bayer, P., 2019. State-of-technology review of water-based closed seasonal thermal energy storage systems. Renew. Sustain. Energy Rev. 113, 109241. https://doi.org/10.1016/J.RSER.2019.06.048

Colbourn, R., 2019. Europe's Role in the Battery Megafactory Supply Chain.

Comello, S., Reichelstein, S., 2019. The emergence of cost effective battery storage. Nat. Commun. 10, 2038. https://doi.org/10.1038/s41467-019-09988-z

Crampes, C., Trochet, J.-M., 2019. Economics of stationary electricity storage with various charge and discharge durations. J. Energy Storage 24, 100746. https://doi.org/10.1016/J.EST.2019.04.020

Fisher, M., Apt, J., Whitacre, J.F., 2019. Can flow batteries scale in the behind-the-meter commercial and industrial market? A techno-economic comparison of storage technologies in California. J. Power Sources 420, 1–8. https://doi.org/10.1016/J.JPOWSOUR.2019.02.051

Hsieh, I.-Y.L., Pan, M.S., Chiang, Y.-M., Green, W.H., 2019. Learning only buys you so much: Practical limits on battery price reduction. Appl. Energy 239, 218–224. https://doi.org/10.1016/J.APENERGY.2019.01.138

IEA, 2019. World Energy Outlook 2019. https://doi.org/DOE/EIA-0383(2012) U.S.

IRENA, 2019a. Utility-scale Batteries—Innovation Landscape Brief.

IRENA, 2019b. Behind-the-meter Batteries—Innovation Landscape Brief.

IRENA, 2017. Electricity storage and renewables: Costs and markets to 2030, Electricity-storage-and-renewables-costs-and-markets.

IRENA, 2015. Battery storage case studies.

Jülch, V., 2016. Comparison of electricity storage options using levelized cost of storage (LCOS) method. Appl. Energy 183, 1594–1606. https://doi.org/10.1016/J.APENERGY.2016.08.165

Kittner, N., Lill, F., Kammen, D.M., 2017. Energy storage deployment and innovation for the clean energy transition. Nat. Energy 2, 17125.

Lazard, 2018. Lazard's Levelized Cost of Storage Analysis—v 4.0.

Leadbetter, J., Swan, L.G., 2012. Selection of battery technology to support grid-integrated renewable electricity. J. Power Sources 216, 376–386. https://doi.org/10.1016/J.JPOWSOUR.2012.05.081

Li, Y., Liu, K., Foley, A.M., Zülke, A., Berecibar, M., Nanini-Maury, E., Van Mierlo, J., Hoster, H.E., 2019. Data-driven health estimation and lifetime prediction of lithium-ion batteries: A review. Renew. Sustain. Energy Rev. 113, 109254. https://doi.org/10.1016/J.RSER.2019.109254

Mirzaei Omrani, M., Jannesari, H., 2019. Economic and environmental assessment of reusing electric vehicle lithium-ion batteries for load leveling in the residential, industrial and photovoltaic power plants sectors. Renew. Sustain. Energy Rev. 116, 109413. https://doi.org/10.1016/J.RSER.2019.109413

Nobel Media AB, 2019. Press release: The Nobel Prize in Chemistry 2019.

Pellow, M.A., Ambrose, H., Mulvaney, D., Betita, R., Shaw, S., 2019. Research gaps in environmental life cycle assessments of lithium ion batteries for grid-scale stationary energy storage systems: End-of-life options and other issues. Sustain. Mater. Technol. e00120. https://doi.org/10.1016/J.SUSMAT.2019.E00120

Schmidt, O., Hawkes, A., Gambhir, A., Staffell, I., 2017. The future cost of electrical energy storage based on experience rates. Nat. Energy 2, 17110. https://doi.org/10.1038/nenergy.2017.110

Schmidt, O., Melchior, S., Hawkes, A., Staffell, I., 2019. Projecting the Future Levelized Cost of Electricity Storage Technologies. Joule 3, 81–100. https://doi.org/10.1016/J.JOULE.2018.12.008

Tsiropoulos, I., Tarvydas, D., Lebedeva, N., 2018. Li-ion batteries for mobility and stationary storage applications, JRC Science for Policy Report, EU Commission., Publications Office of the European Union. https://doi.org/10.2760/87175

CHAPTER 15

Economics of Sector Coupling

Michel Noussan

1 Introduction

The integration of increasing shares of non-dispatchable variable renewable energy sources in power systems requires additional flexibility options, to ensure the continuous matching between demand and supply required to operate the power grids. Traditional technologies to provide energy balance services include electricity storage, transmission networks, fossil-based dispatched energy, and demand response and/or management programs.

In this framework, an alternative solution that is emerging is sector coupling, also called "P2X", where "X" may stand for various applications, such as gas (G), heat (H), vehicles (V), liquids (L) or others. The idea of sector coupling is to convert the excess available electricity into another energy carrier which is required or can be more easily stored than electricity. In some cases, the transformation is reversible, that is, electricity can be generated again, although generally with low roundtrip efficiency.

However, in some cases sector coupling applications can lead to significant benefits in long-term storage, especially for power-to-gas (P2G) or power-to-liquids (P2L). In some current applications, sector coupling is exploited to avoid curtailing of renewable energy sources (RES) in specific hours when production exceeds demand, by exploiting available power at no cost. However, in most cases the limited number of annual operational hours does not allow

M. Noussan (✉)
Fondazione Eni Enrico Mattei (FEEM), Milan, Italy

Decisio s.r.l., Torino, Italy

SciencesPo—Paris School of International Affairs, Paris, France
e-mail: michel.noussan@sciencespo.fr

M. Hafner, G. Luciani (eds.), *The Palgrave Handbook of International Energy Economics*, https://doi.org/10.1007/978-3-030-86884-0_15

acceptable pay-back times, also due to the relatively high investment costs for some technologies. Some applications, including hydrogen and synthetic fuels, may need dedicated RES supply to reach annual load factors that justify current investment costs.

P2X is expected to play a significant role in the energy transition, in parallel with the direct use of renewable energy or the clean power generation from renewable energy sources (RES). However, to unlock the full potential of sector coupling technologies three main aspects need to be tackled: scaling up technologies, defining markets and demand structures, building up favorable investment frameworks to secure supply (Perner and Bothe 2018). While the required cost decrease may be obtained through a scale-up of technology driven by demand, this would require customers to buy and pay for a cleaner alternative to the current use of fossil fuels. Policy-driven incentives or CO_2 emissions markets may support future business models for P2X technologies.

The following sections will present the most promising applications of sector coupling: power-to-gas (P2G), power-to-heat (P2H), power-to-vehicles (P2V), and power-to-liquids (P2L).

2 Power-to-Gas

P2G is probably the most common application when talking about P2X, and although it usually refers to hydrogen production through electrolysis, it may also include a further methanation step to produce synthetic methane. The additional complexity and energy consumption required by methanation may be justified by the opportunity of exploiting existing assets operating with natural gas (e.g. pipelines or turbines). In this case, methane production requires as additional input a carbon dioxide stream, which could be obtained from carbon capture or direct air capture to close the CO_2 cycle and avoid net emissions during the use of synthetic methane. A scheme of the main P2G supply chains is illustrated in Fig. 15.1.

The current energy efficiency of electrolyzers lays in the range 60% to 81%, with variations related to technology type and load factor. The role of electrolysis in the current global production of hydrogen (69 MtH_2) is below 0.1%. A shift to 100% would result in an electricity consumption of 3600 TWh, which is more than the total annual electricity generation in the European Union (IEA 2019a). Thus, a significant role of hydrogen in future energy systems would require massive deployment of electricity generation from RES. An additional side effect is the need of freshwater as input resource, which could be a problem in water-stressed areas. The use of seawater would require an additional desalination process, which could be done through reverse-osmosis technologies, whose costs are in the range from 1 to 2 € per cubic meter (Caldera et al. 2018). Thus, desalination costs are likely to represent a marginal share of total P2G costs, since a cubic meter of water allows the production of more than 110 kg of hydrogen.

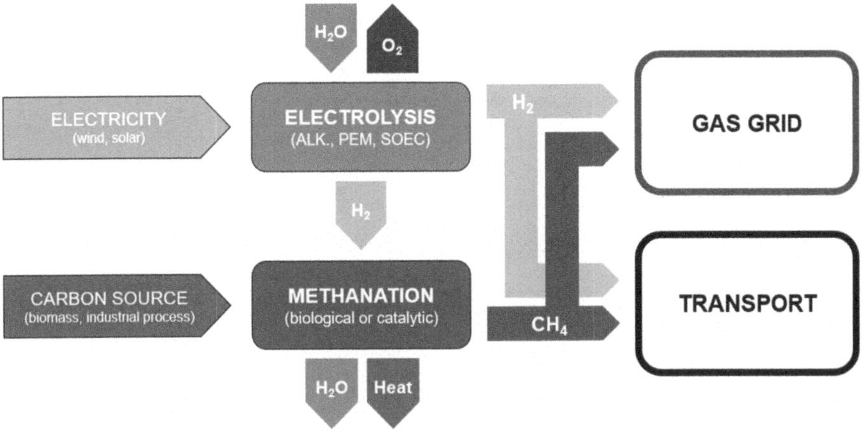

Fig. 15.1 Example of P2G supply chains. (Author's elaboration from: (Götz et al. 2016))

Alternative electrolysis technologies exist, with different performance, operating pressure and temperature, as well as lifetime stack, load range flexibility, and investment cost. The most mature technologies are alkaline electrolysis, proton-exchange membrane (PEM) electrolysis and solid oxide electrolysis cells (SOECs), whose main operational parameters are reported in Table 15.1. The most diffused technology worldwide for energy purposes has shifted in the last years from alkaline to PEM, with almost 90% of the 95 MW of capacity additions in the years 2015–2019.

The production cost for hydrogen based on hydrolysis depends on multiple assumptions, with the most significant parameters being the investment cost, the electricity cost, and the annual hours of operation. Based on the estimation of (IEA 2019a), the production of hydrogen by 2030 in Europe could cost 2–4 €/kg if based on dedicated RES plants, or 3.2–6.5 €/kg when considering grid electricity. Still, these costs are expected to remain higher than the production pathways from fossil fuels (both natural gas and coal), either with or without carbon capture, use and storage (CCUS) facilities.

However, other world regions may experience lower costs related to higher RES potentials, especially for solar energy, although with limited annual operational hours. Wind plants, especially offshore, may lead to higher load factors, representing more interesting options when they are coupled with electrolyzers.

It is important to notice that hydrogen may have a number of applications where it is used directly, but often it involves a further conversion into electricity. In this perspective, P2G (combined with the subsequent process "G2P") can be considered as an electricity storage solution, which is particularly effective for long-term storage (from days to months). Today, hydrogen is already the most effective storage solution for seasonal storage, excluding pumped

Table 15.1 Main electrolysis technologies, operation parameters

	Alkaline electrolyzer			*PEM electrolyzer*			*SOEC electrolyzer*		
	Today	*2030*	*Long term*	*Today*	*2030*	*Long Term*	*Today*	*2030*	*Long Term*
Electric efficiency (%, LHV)	63–70	65–71	70–80	56–60	63–68	67–74	74–81	77–84	77–90
Pressure (bar)	1–30			30–80			1		
Temperature (°C)	60–80			50–80			650–1000		
Operation (thousand hours)	60–90	90–100	100–150	30–90	60–90	100–150	10–30	40–60	75–100
CAPEX (USD/kWel)	500–1400	400–850	200–700	1100–1800	650–1500	200–900	2800–5600	800–2800	500–1000

Source: IEA (2019a)

hydro and compressed-air storage (Schmidt et al. 2019), and on the long term it is expected to provide better performances.

In last years, P2G projects with methanation seems to catch up with simple hydrogen generation, and they show higher potential for energy efficiency improvement from current levels, especially by strengthening the exploitation of by-products, oxygen and heat, an aspect that is seldom considered in existing projects. Current figures for capital expenditure (CAPEX) costs related to CO_2-methanation, referred to the input power consumed by the upstream electrolyzer, is around 800 €/kW_{el} for chemical methanation and 1200 €/kW_{el} for biological methanation (both values excluding the cost of the electrolyzer). These values are expected to fall by 2030 to 500 €/kW_{el} and 700 €/kW_{el} respectively (Thema et al. 2019). These cost evolutions are expected to rely on production upscaling, although technological development may have an influence.

3 Power-to-Heat

Power-to-heat (P2H) aims at exploiting the potential synergies between power and heating sectors, either through the coupling with existing district heating (DH) networks or with distributed heat generation for single users. The applications in DH networks are currently more diffused, thanks to the fact that in large centralized plants any potential economic advantage is of particular interest. Thus, also due to the common practice of including multiple generation technologies in the same system, low electricity prices can be exploited to generate heat through electric boilers or large-scale heat pumps. In comparison with other sector coupling applications, P2H shows relatively low investment costs, relying on components that are already broadly used for various applications and have high technological maturity (heat pumps and even more electric boilers). However, again, the trade-off of such additional investment is related to the amount of annual operational hours, which in turn are related to the volatility of the price of electricity, and in some cases of alternative fuels (notably of natural gas when bought with hourly prices). These solutions are often most profitable for large customers, such as DH generation plants or large commercial users, which can have multiple generation options to supply the required heat demand. P2H is currently a reality in limited markets, due to its generally higher cost in comparison with traditional technologies, but it shows an interesting potential, especially through heat pumps, in a future perspective of stronger decarbonization measures and lower electricity prices.

P2H has already a suitable maturity in DH networks applications, especially in some countries in northern Europe, such as Denmark, Sweden and Norway, but there is still a significant unexploited potential (Schweiger et al. 2017). Using electric boilers, which have generally low investment costs, DH network managers exploit the low electricity market prices in specific hours of RES surplus to obtain a lower marginal cost in comparison with alternative generation technologies. The trade-off market prices vary from a country to another, mainly due to different power mixes and to the taxation levels on electricity consumption.

A study on 2014–2015 market data in Denmark, Sweden and Norway (Rosenlund Soysal and Sandberg 2016) analyzed electric boilers in DH systems. Results showed that electric boilers had lower marginal costs than natural gas combined heat and power (CHP) units for 26% of the DH operating hours in Denmark and 46% in Sweden. However, only in Norway they were able to compete with biomass CHP units, showing lower marginal costs in 14% of the annual hours. The trade-off heat prices against gas-powered CHP were 22.7 €/MWh in Denmark and 26.5 €/MWh in Sweden, and in Norway 14.4 €/MWh in competition with biomass CHP units. Although with similar electricity purchase prices, these countries showed very different electric boilers fixed marginal prices (i.e. excluding electricity purchase but including taxes): 51.6 €/MWh in Denmark, 38.9 in Sweden and 12.8 in Norway.

Figure 15.2 shows the comparison of different generation technologies in Sweden and Denmark (data from (Rosenlund Soysal and Sandberg 2016)), comparing the variation of the heat price based on the electricity price. The cost of heat generated from electric boilers increases with the electricity price, while in CHP technologies increased revenues from high-cost electricity lead to a lower price of the produced heat. It is important to remark that this chart is based on the wholesale electricity price, and additional taxes are considered to calculate the marginal price, thus resulting in a positive value for electric boilers even at a null cost of electricity.

A broader application of P2H is the progressive electrification of heating and cooling sector to support higher levels of RES penetrations. This trend is supported by decarbonization policies at different levels, and heat pumps are generally preferred against electric boilers thanks to their higher energy efficiency, although with significantly higher investment costs. However, in countries with high electricity prices for final customers, the total cost over the lifetime of the appliance may justify the choice of a heat pump. However, in

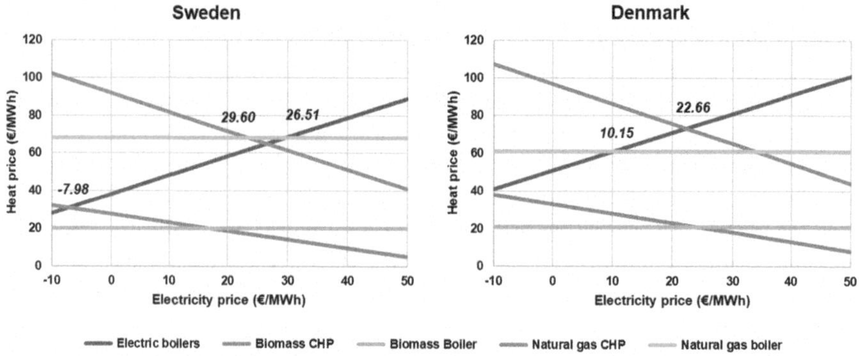

Fig. 15.2 Marginal costs of different heat generation technologies in Sweden, based on electricity price. (Source: Author's elaboration on: (Rosenlund Soysal and Sandberg 2016))

most countries, the total cost remains significantly higher in comparison with traditional fossil-powered boilers, and incentives are often in place to support the users in transitioning toward cleaner fuels.

The current operation of small-size heat pumps is generally bound to fixed electricity tariffs, and there is a limited application of time-of-use tariffs that can follow the wholesale market price. However, there is an interesting potential for power aggregators that may exploit large pools of small-size heat pumps, especially when coupled with local thermal storage, to provide services to the power system. The participation to balancing markets is among the most interesting applications for aggregators, although with the need of fast reaction times, a bi-directional communication and generally a minimum pool size of few MW (Spreitzhofer 2018). Some undergoing projects of P2H through heat pumps are available in different countries, including Austria (BMVIT and FFG 2019), Switzerland, Germany, and the United States (IEA HPT 2017).

4 Power-to-Vehicles

Another sector that may face a significant increase of electricity penetration in next decades is transport, in particular with the deployment of electric vehicles (EVs) in the market of private cars. The need for recharging car batteries will unlock additional electricity demand, but also flexibility options through the management of the charging timing and profiles of a large number of distributed batteries. There are basically two distinct levels of integration, from delayed charging (also called smart charging, or P2V) to bi-directional sector coupling, often referred to as vehicles-to-grid (V2G). The latter requires a specific battery design, due to the need of discharging toward the power grid upon request, which is seldom available in the current generation of electric cars.

The future deployment of P2V schemes is tightly related to the market share of electric vehicles, whose sales are showing exponential increases in last years, with 2018 sales reaching 2 million units at global scale, roughly doubling the previous year (IEA 2019b). Future scenarios show high variability from one source to another, and they have often been revised upwards each year. Figures from IEA 2019b estimate annual global EV sales between 23 and 43 million by 2030, with electric car stocks in the range 130–250 million.

A crucial aspect will be the number of available charging points, and the share between public and private charging points, and between slow and fast charging. The interaction between power grid and a pool of EVs will require them to be continuously connected through dedicated charged points, especially during daytime, when electricity balance needs are higher. Thus, high numbers of publicly accessible charging points will be required, since private charging points in households are mostly used overnight. The current global ratio of publicly accessible charging points per electric car has decreased from 0.14 in 2017 to 0.11 at the end of 2018 (IEA 2019b). Figures show a wide variation from one country to another, from one public charger every 20 electric cars in Norway or in the United States to one charger every four to eight electric cars in Denmark or in the Netherlands.

P2V is based on EVs smart charging strategies, with the aim of shifting the additional power demand from peak hours to off-peak hours. Researchers found that most current EV users are charging their vehicles in the early evening, when electricity demand is high, thus a shift toward the night hours may lead to better power network operation. P2V may require either time-of-use tariffs, or a third-party player that directly controls the charging process (based on the specific requests from the final user). Customers should be able to set some charging targets based on their needs, that is, the amount of charge required at a specific hour, while at the same time keep some room for unpredicted early need to use their cars. A dedicated research work in UK found that user-managed charging was preferred over supplier-managed charging, because of perceived personal control and lower perceived risk that a vehicle might not be fully charged at the required time (Delmonte et al. 2020). On the contrary, preference for third-party charging of users was based mainly on perceived advantages to society. At a system level, different research studies analyzed the effect of smart charging strategies to support an increased use of RES share in power generation, with favorable results in different countries (Daina et al. 2017; Jian et al. 2018).

V2G goes beyond the simple schedule of EV charging, by exploiting the vehicle as a battery when the grid needs balancing services. In comparison with P2V, further aspects are involved. EV batteries should be technically allowed to operate in discharge mode toward the grid, charging points should have higher average power, battery state-of-charge should be carefully monitored (and stay in restricted ranges) to meet the required levels when the users need it, and there may be potential issues related to battery quality depletion over time due to additional cycles. Dedicated algorithms will be needed to optimize the charge/discharge strategies, and ideally, large EV pools would provide more flexibility to the aggregator, considering the multiple constraints. Results from a test study on the behavior of a real pool of EVs showed that the ratio of available battery capacity over the nominal capacity of the pool at specific times of the day could fall to very low values (Irie 2017). The worst case happened for daytime charging, when only 2.1%–3.9% of capacity was available, due to few connected vehicles and remaining state-of-charge levels. Nighttime charge and peak-hours discharge reached up to 30% of available capacity, but in some days resulted in shares as low as 14% and 8% respectively.

5 Power-to-Liquids

P2L applications can prove to be a necessary solution in the decarbonization of some sectors that lacks other alternatives, such as long-haul aviation, international shipping and specific high-temperature industrial processes (Perner and Bothe 2018). Synthetic fuels may become a complementary solution to biofuels in these key sectors, and like biofuels they can often exploit existing appliances and infrastructures (e.g. gasoline, diesel, and kerosene), with the possibility of an immediate shift in some existing applications without the upfront costs associated to convert the appliances of the final users or the different components in the supply chain.

P2L applications include a variety of processes, of which the most mature are methanol synthesis and Fischer-Tropsch synthesis. Methanol can be used directly (with some limitations) or it can be further converted to other fuels, such as petrol, diesel, or kerosene. In comparison with hydrogen, methanol has some advantages, including the lower safety procedures related to its liquid state under normal conditions, requiring no further actions in terms of high-pressure (or low-temperature) storage. Moreover, methanol synthesis is a well-known industrial process, and so are further processes to convert it to other fuels for specific sectors (Varone and Ferrari 2015). Fischer-Tropsch synthesis requires carbon monoxide and hydrogen to produce a raw liquid fuel that is then upgraded toward a traditional fuel by different processes. It is a relatively established technology, which has also been applied to obtain synthetic fuels from coal and natural gas.

Few studies address P2L costs in comparison with available literature on hydrolysis or methanation. Synthetic liquid fuels production relies on more mature technologies, with a smaller potential of further cost reductions related to process improvements. However, investment costs could decrease in the next decades thanks to standardization effects driven by large-scale plants deployment. Current specific investment costs related to the output production lay in the range 800–900 €/kW_{P2L} for both processes, depending if they are coupled with high-temperature or low-temperature electrolysis (which in turn have different costs). Future developments are expected to lower the costs to 544–828 €/kW_{P2L} by 2030 and 300–800 €/kW_{P2L} by 2050, depending on different scenarios (Agora Verkehrswende et al. 2018). These values do not include CO_2 capture, which may have a significant impact on the total cost, especially when relying on direct air capture. The cost associated to CO_2 direct air capture coupled with P2L applications is currently as high as 2200 €/kW_{P2L}, and also with an expected decrease to 1600 €/kW_{P2L} by 2050 it would remain the most expensive part of the process.

The total supply chain costs of producing synthetic fuels are always higher than for P2G, both due to the additional required components and the lower supply chain efficiency, with current values in the range 46%–64% depending on the hydrolysis temperature (Blanco et al. 2018). The higher costs may be justified considering the energy system with a broader perspective, with potential benefits such as the use of existing infrastructures and the easier storage procedures. For some applications, especially aviation, the energy density of the fuel will be another key aspect in the choice between available alternatives. It is important to highlight the need of dedicated CO_2 streams from carbon capture technologies in order to close the cycle and allow for carbon-free synthetic fuels, which is the main driver in comparison with fossil-based alternatives. In the long term, direct air capture may be preferred, thanks to the possibility of using it anywhere (i.e. without the need of the proximity of a CO_2 generating system, or a dedicated CO_2 supply chain), although with additional electricity consumption as well as higher investment costs.

6 Economic Comparison of Sector Coupling Options

An economic comparison of sector coupling alternatives is not straightforward, since multiple parameters are affecting the operation and the business models of these technologies. As already mentioned, the first applications of P2X rose from the opportunity of exploiting the excess of electricity from RES, especially in the cases where low CAPEX investments did not require high annual operational hours. These applications were particularly successful in some niche markets, such as P2H in district heating networks in Nordic European countries. However, for many applications the operational hours remain a critical issue, due to the high prevalence of CAPEX over operational expenditure (OPEX). In these cases, P2X technologies could provide some degree of flexibility to exploit an available excess of electricity from RES, but they could not rely solely on that excess.

While the availability of excess electricity in some hours of the year, which may even be considered with a null cost, can be a significant advantage, such a limited operation would not be compatible with the high CAPEX of multiple P2X applications. Similarly, on-site generation from RES shows promising levelized costs of electricity (LCOE), but annual load factors of wind and solar resources are limited.

A simplified economic comparison of the P2X technologies presented in this work is reported in Fig. 15.3, where an average economic margin is calculated as the difference between the revenues and the generation costs of different solutions, which are compared on the basis of a unit of available electricity. The revenues are estimated as the avoided cost of generation by a reference

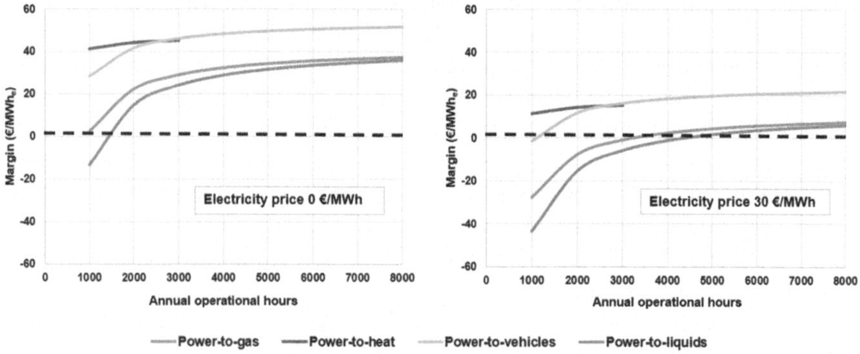

Fig. 15.3 Economic comparison of different P2X technologies with variable electricity cost and hours of operation (estimated values for 2040). (Source: Author's elaboration)

Table 15.2 Hypotheses for economic comparison of P2X technologies (year 2040)

Parameter	*Unit*	*P2G*	*P2H*	*P2V*	*P2L*
CAPEX	*€/kW$_e$*	600	90	400	850
Efficiency	*MWh$_u$/ MWh$_e$*	0.75	0.99	1	0.65
Alternative solution	–	Hydrogen via SMR	Heat from natural gas boiler	EV charging from power grid	Gasoline
Alternative solution cost (incl. Emissions)	*€/MWh$_u$*	56.4	47.6	55.0	66.3
Alternative emissions	*t/MWh$_u$*	0.30	0.21	0.05	0.26
Alternative emission costs[a]	*€/MWh$_u$*	29.6	21.3	5.0	25.9

Source: author's elaboration

[a]Based on a carbon price of 100 €/t_{CO2}.

alternative technology (see Table 15.2 for further details). Given the different contexts in which these technologies are operating, there are not only different CAPEX and OPEX costs and logics, but also different benefits depending on the energy carrier or service that needs to be supplied.

This simplified analysis highlights the role of the electricity cost and the annual operational hours on the profitability of some P2X solutions in the long term. The results suggest that the applications with higher conversion efficiency show the higher margins, but at the same time, it may be more difficult to ensure a high number of operational hours due to demand constraints. The lower conversion efficiencies of P2G and P2L, which are also part of the cause of their higher CAPEX, may be compensated by the flexibility value associated with the possibility of long-term storage for their products. However, such an evaluation would require a detailed analysis taking into account daily and seasonal demand profiles.

The main hypotheses used in this analysis are listed in 2, which is based on figures on a 2040 time horizon, obtained from different literature sources integrated with expert opinions. All the P2X technologies are considered on a 15-years lifetime, and the revenues are estimated as the avoided costs of a corresponding traditional solution for the production of the very same service (including a CO_2 cost of 100 €/t, where appropriate). The alternative solutions are presented in the table on the basis of the useful energy that is made available for the final users (expressed in MWh_u).

It is important to remark that the objective of this exercise is to provide the readers with a qualitative comparison of the effects of different drivers, since the uncertainty of estimating these parameters may lead to huge variations in the results.

7 Conclusions

This chapter provided a description of the main aspects involved with the potential profitability of sector coupling applications. While each application has the peculiar features that have been described in the previous sections, some common patterns are worth mentioning.

For all P2X application, the two main drivers are the decreasing electricity price and the policy push toward decarbonization, through an increased penetration in different sectors of clean electricity. As a result, each P2X solution will most probably be deployed firstly in regions with favorable renewable potential, with high annual capacity factors from either wind or solar plants. As a result, applications that lead to the production of a storable fuel will benefit from the implementation of an international market, with specific agreements that are based on the advantages of synthetic fuels over traditional ones, with particular emphasis on the benefits related to their contribution in decarbonization strategies (Perner and Bothe 2018).

Such an international market would benefit from a distributed potential for solar and wind on many countries, in contrast with the current strong concentration of fossil fuels reserves in a limited number of areas on a global scale. Different countries in various continents could play complementary roles in the deployment of various P2X technologies, depending on their resource potentials, existing infrastructures, and national policy trajectories.

P2X may also operate as a storage alternative, especially for long-term storage, and therefore it has some similarities with batteries (see Chap. 14), including the need of upscaling technology deployment to decrease investment costs, and ensure an acceptable amount of operational hours to guarantee fair returns to investors.

While some applications have already proven their economic sustainability in specific markets under current conditions, a broader policy support is required to trigger the further development of these technologies, which are often in competition with incumbent fossil-based alternatives. In this perspective, carbon pricing models or similar policies to factor in the climate externalities may prove to be a key aspect to unlock the potential of P2X technologies in contributing to the decarbonization of the energy system.

Bibliography

Agora Verkehrswende, Agora Energiewende, Frontier Economics, 2018. The Future Cost of Electricity-Based Synthetic Fuels.

Blanco, H., Nijs, W., Ruf, J., Faaij, A., 2018. Potential for hydrogen and Power-to-Liquid in a low-carbon EU energy system using cost optimization. Appl. Energy 232, 617–639. https://doi.org/10.1016/J.APENERGY.2018.09.216.

BMVIT, FFG, 2019. fit4power2heat research project [WWW Document]. URL https://nachhaltigwirtschaften.at/en/sdz/projects/fit4power2heat.php (accessed 11.21.19).

Caldera, U., Bogdanov, D., Afanasyeva, S., Breyer, C., 2018. Role of seawater desalination in the management of an integrated water and 100% renewable energy based power sector in Saudi Arabia. Water (Switzerland) 10. https://doi.org/10.3390/w10010003.

Daina, N., Sivakumar, A., Polak, J.W., 2017. Electric vehicle charging choices: Modelling and implications for smart charging services. Transp. Res. Part C Emerg. Technol. 81, 36–56. https://doi.org/10.1016/J.TRC.2017.05.006.

Delmonte, E., Kinnear, N., Jenkins, B., Skippon, S., 2020. What do consumers think of smart charging? Perceptions among actual and potential plug-in electric vehicle adopters in the United Kingdom. Energy Res. Soc. Sci. 60, 101318. https://doi.org/10.1016/J.ERSS.2019.101318.

Götz, M., Lefebvre, J., Mörs, F., McDaniel Koch, A., Graf, F., Bajohr, S., Reimert, R., Kolb, T., 2016. Renewable Power-to-Gas: A technological and economic review. Renew. Energy 85, 1371–1390. https://doi.org/10.1016/J.RENENE.2015.07.066.

IEA, 2019a. The Future of Hydrogen, The Future of Hydrogen. https://doi.org/10.1787/1e0514c4-en.

IEA, 2019b. Global EV Outlook 2019.

IEA HPT, 2017. Annex 42 -Heat Pumps in Smart Grids—Market status summary per country.

Irie, H., 2017. NEDO Smart Community Case Study.

Jian, L., Yongqiang, Z., Hyoungmi, K., 2018. The potential and economics of EV smart charging: A case study in Shanghai. Energy Policy 119, 206–214. https://doi.org/10.1016/J.ENPOL.2018.04.037.

Perner, J., Bothe, D., 2018. International aspects of a power-to-X roadmap.

Rosenlund Soysal, E., Sandberg, E., 2016. Electric boilers in district heating systems—A comparative study of the Scandinavian market conditions, in: SAEE-Conference, Luleå.

Schmidt, O., Melchior, S., Hawkes, A., Staffell, I., 2019. Projecting the Future Levelized Cost of Electricity Storage Technologies. Joule 3, 81–100. https://doi.org/10.1016/J.JOULE.2018.12.008.

Schweiger, G., Rantzer, J., Ericsson, K., Lauenburg, P., 2017. The potential of power-to-heat in Swedish district heating systems. Energy. https://doi.org/10.1016/j.energy.2017.02.075.

Spreitzhofer, J., 2018. Electricity-market participation of heat pumps in single family houses and district heating networks, in: Workshop—Energy Sector Coupling: Electric-Thermal Interaction through Heat Pumps.

Thema, M., Bauer, F., Sterner, M., 2019. Power-to-Gas: Electrolysis and methanation status review. Renew. Sustain. Energy Rev. 112, 775–787. https://doi.org/10.1016/J.RSER.2019.06.030.

Varone, A., Ferrari, M., 2015. Power to liquid and power to gas: An option for the German Energiewende. Renew. Sustain. Energy Rev. 45, 207–218. https://doi.org/10.1016/J.RSER.2015.01.049.

CHAPTER 16

The Integration of Non-dispatchable Renewables

Marco Baroni

1 Introduction

The energy world is undergoing a profound transformation, driven by a combination of technological, economic and environmental factors, with changing costs and ways for producing energy, and new and more efficient means to consume it. This transformation is often referred to as the "clean energy transition". The power sector is the largest CO_2 emitting energy sector and is therefore central to any decarbonisation strategy. It also plays a pivotal role in reducing the carbon footprint of final uses by increasing their electrification.

The last two decades have seen a spectacular growth of wind (initially onshore and, more recently, also offshore) and solar (mostly photovoltaics) technologies, pushed by policies put in place by governments around the world to support their deployment. The continued deployment led to a strong decrease of investment costs of these technologies, which triggered more ambitious goals and more countries to support them. This created a virtuous

The author wishes to thank Manuel Baritaud, Marco Cometto, Karolina Daszkiewicz, David Wilkinson and Matthew Wittenstein for their comments, views and support. The views and opinions expressed are solely the views of the author and do not represent a statement of the views of any other person or entity.
Lecturer at Institut d'études politiques de Paris (SciencesPo), energy consultant in Baroni Energy Consulting and former Head of Power Sector Analysis in the World Energy Outlook team of the International Energy Agency.

M. Baroni (✉)
SciencesPo—Paris School of International Affairs, Paris, France
e-mail: marco.baroni@sciencespo.fr; marco.baroni@baronienergy.com

M. Hafner, G. Luciani (eds.), *The Palgrave Handbook of International Energy Economics*, https://doi.org/10.1007/978-3-030-86884-0_16

snow-ball effect between policy support, increased targets, development and cost reductions.

In the last 20 years, global electricity generation of wind and solar PV combined increased more than 110-fold in absolute terms, increasing from a mere 0.1% of global electricity generation in 1998 to 7% in 2018 (IEA Statistics 2020), and reaching much higher levels in some countries. This level of deployment is set to increase in all countries and in all scenarios developed by all major institutions—with an ever-growing role in decarbonisation scenarios coherent with the goals agreed during UNFCCC's Conference of Parties 21 (COP 21) held in Paris.

Despite the encouraging recent trends, the continued expansion of these technologies cannot be taken for granted, and it is the duty of all actors involved—policymakers, industry, financial institutions, academia—to anticipate the challenges ahead and to provide early solutions. The aim of this chapter is not to provide optimal deployment levels of wind and solar technologies in the power mix, but rather to provide a guide of the characteristics of these technologies and of the major challenges faced by the power sector in reaching such high level of deployment.

2 Characteristics of Non-dispatchable[1] Renewable Energy Sources

The availability of renewable energy sources varies widely across the globe and the technologies exploiting them have different history and levels of maturity. Hydropower was the first renewable source to be used, with its early steps dating back to the late nineteenth century. By 2018, there were almost 1300 GW of hydropower installed capacity globally (IRENA 2019a), generating over 60% of total renewable power production.

As electricity systems developed, it increasingly became clear that flexibility (i.e. being readily dispatchable) was a fundamental characteristic for matching electricity demand and supply. With hydropower exhibiting this characteristic in addition to being a relatively cheap source, reservoirs and pumped storage plants were developed and deployed worldwide. Other important dispatchable renewable technologies include geothermal and bioenergy.

Over the last two decades, two newer renewable technologies with different characteristics than conventional technologies, and in particular with a limited flexibility, have made sizable inroads into the electricity mix: wind and solar photovoltaics (PV). These are the focus of this chapter. There are several other non-dispatchable renewables-based technologies (such as marine energy),

[1] Non-dispatchable generation refers to the electricity generation from technologies that cannot (or have limited ability to) adjust their power output to match electricity demand, as their source is weather-dependent. Downward adjustments are still possible by curtailing generation, as well as upward ramping is possible if pre-curtailment had previously been envisaged. But no generation is possible if the resource is unavailable.

Table 16.1 Non-dispatchable technologies

Technology	*Typical capacity factor (%)*	*Global capacity at end-2018 (GW)*	*Level of maturity*
Wind onshore	15–50	543	High
Wind offshore	35–60	23	Mid
Solar PV	10–25	495	High
Solar CSP (without storage)	15–25	3	Low
Hydropower run-of-river	20–80	>100[a]	High
Marine	15–25	0.5	Low

Sources: IEA (2019b) and IRENA (2019a)

[a] Comprehensive data on the total global capacity of run-of-river hydropower are not available, but can be estimated in the order of 100 GW or more

which also may play a role in the future power mix but for now are still in relatively early stages of development.

2.1 *Technologies and Their Characteristics*

Several renewables-based technologies can be classified as non-dispatchable. These include wind onshore, wind offshore, solar PV, concentrating solar power (CSP) without storage, hydropower run-of-river[2] (RoR), and marine (tide and wave) energy (Table 16.1). The main common characteristic is that their electricity generation changes with the variations of the related natural source (wind, sun, rainfall patterns, moon attraction) and cannot be increased or decreased at will to match the variations in electricity demand. The costs, level of maturity and global diffusion varies significantly for each of these technologies.

Wind, solar PV and hydropower RoR have reached the highest level of maturity and deployment among non-dispatchable renewables, while solar concentrating solar panel (CSP) and marine energy can still be considered at their infancy stage, with low deployment rates and high electricity generation costs. Furthermore, the future deployment of solar CSP is expected to be associated with thermal storage, therefore bringing this technology out of the non-dispatchable renewable group.

Hydropower potential is still very large globally, with the strongest deployment in future years likely to come from developing countries and regions such as China, Latin America, India, Southeast Asia and Africa. In advanced economies, the hydropower remaining potential, as well as environmental and social issues, limit greatly the possible further exploitation of medium and large

[2] Run-of-river hydropower indicates a power station with no or very small reservoir capacity. Its electricity generation is therefore dependent on the variability of the water stream. As water cannot be stored (except in some cases for small quantities), excess supply of water is lost.

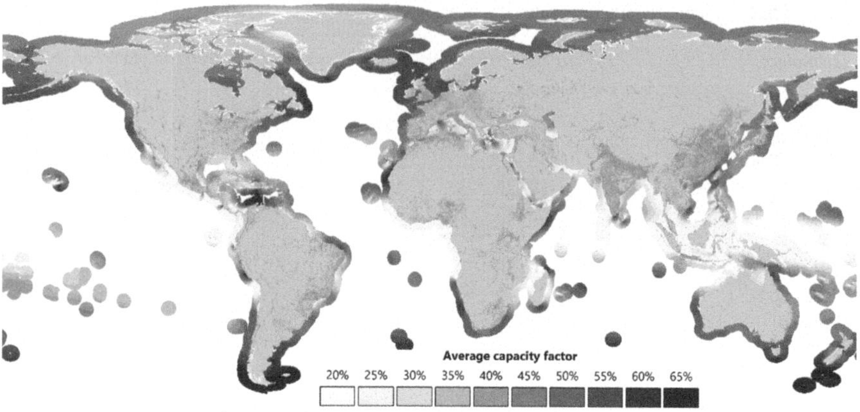

Fig. 16.1 Average simulated capacity factors for offshore wind worldwide. (Source: IEA 2019a)

hydro sites (i.e. sites that support capacities greater than 10 MW[3]), but further deployment of small, mini or micro run-of-river systems may be expected. Solar and wind potentials are vast (see related chapters), but nonetheless with strong variations from region to region. A differentiation between technical and realisable potential needs to be introduced to fully understand the feasibility of tapping into these vast potentials.

An important element to take into consideration is the quality of each resource. The solar irradiance,[4] the speed and variation of wind or the seasonality of water inflows are often translated in power station terms through capacity factors. This measures the ratio (expressed in percentage terms) between the electricity generated by the power station and the maximum theoretical output[5] that could be produced over a given period (typically one year).

Capacity factors of non-dispatchable renewables can differ significantly across regions and technologies. Typically, the capacity factors of offshore wind farms can reach the highest levels, in the range of 35% to 65%, with some of the highest levels being reached in the North and Baltic seas in Europe (IEA 2019a) (Fig. 16.1). Onshore wind and hydropower RoR can also reach very high levels in the best sites (up to around 60% and 80% respectively), for example in Brazil, while the other non-dispatchable technologies usually are limited to a 10–25% range. Solar PV often oscillates in the lower side of the non-dispatchable technologies range, mainly due to the inability to generate during night. Due to the nature of solar irradiance, solar capacity factors are highest towards the equator and lowest towards the poles.

[3] Small hydropower can be defined as having a capacity smaller than 10 MW, medium hydropower from 10 to 100 MW and large hydropower plants for capacities larger than 100 MW.

[4] The solar irradiance is often expressed through indicators such as direct normal irradiance (DNI), diffuse horizontal irradiance (DHI) or global horizontal irradiance (GHI).

[5] Obtained multiplying the installed (maximum) capacity by the number of hours in the period considered (8760 hours in the case of one year).

Over the last two decades, solar PV and onshore wind technologies have seen impressive capacity growth—each adding over 500 GW globally. Economies of scale led to a sharp decrease in costs for both technologies. The decrease of onshore wind costs was due to two main factors: the improvements in manufacturing and installation costs on one side and the increase of average capacity factors on the other. These two factors brought the weighted-average global levelised cost of electricity (LCOE)[6] to drop by 35% in less than 10 years (IRENA 2019b). Similar factors to onshore wind formed the basis of the cost decrease for offshore wind, but this was also coupled with improved operating and maintenance costs. The increase in size of wind turbines played a key role in increasing capacity factors, with larger generators, and longer blades (resulting in larger swept areas and increased power output) leading to lower costs per kilowatt.

Generation cost decreases have been the sharpest and most successful than any other technology for solar PV systems, driven by PV module cost reductions, together with falling costs for the entire balance of system costs (BoS), that were in turn led by inverter cost reductions. The observed prices for solar PV systems and the actual costs of its components can differ significantly depending on eventual subsidies provided by some governments to manufacturers. All these elements have led solar PV module prices to follow a 20–22% experience curve (i.e. the price reduction for each doubling of capacity) (Fig. 16.2), with a decrease of over 90% in less than a decade.

2.2 *Key Properties*

The electricity generation of non-dispatchable renewables (sometimes called intermittent or variable renewables in other publications) cannot be adjusted with respect to the variations of electricity demand unless curtailment takes place (if the generation is in excess) or if prior curtailment has been foreseen (to be able to ramp up). In any case, no generation is possible when the resource is not available (e.g. during night for solar PV or when wind does not blow).

The hourly (or sub-hourly) electricity-generation profile of the non-dispatchable renewables technologies and the way that they match (or not) the hourly electricity demand is critical with larger shares of deployment. An illustrative profile of onshore wind and solar PV is shown in Fig. 16.3. The variability of generation from different projects may be smoothed if the geographical area is sufficiently large, provided that enough grid transmission capacity is available in the considered area. Conversely, the situation may be compounded if the generation profiles of the different projects are similar, with peaks and valleys appearing during the same hours. However, the combination of

[6] The levelized cost of electricity (LCOE) is an indicator of the average cost per unit of electricity generated by a power plant. Under the standard formulation, LCOE is the minimum average price at which electricity must be sold for a project to "break-even", providing for the recovery of all related costs over the economic lifetime of the project (IEA 2016a).

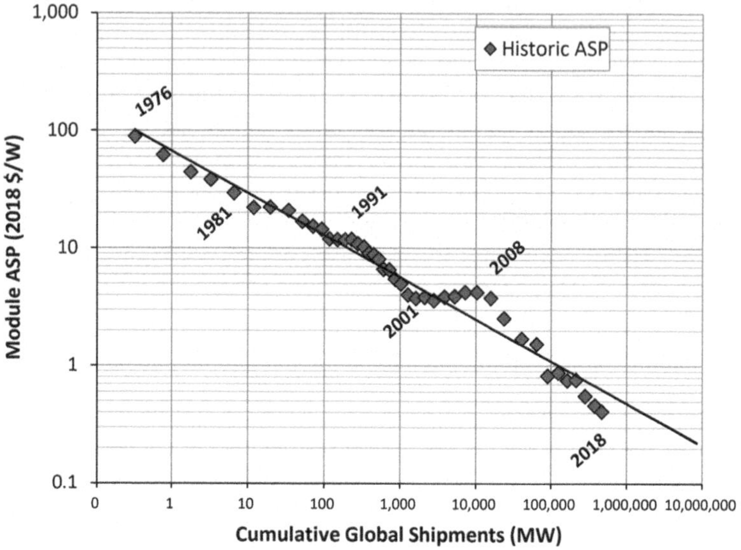

Fig. 16.2 Decreasing investment prices for solar photovoltaics modules. (Source: Paula Mints 2019)

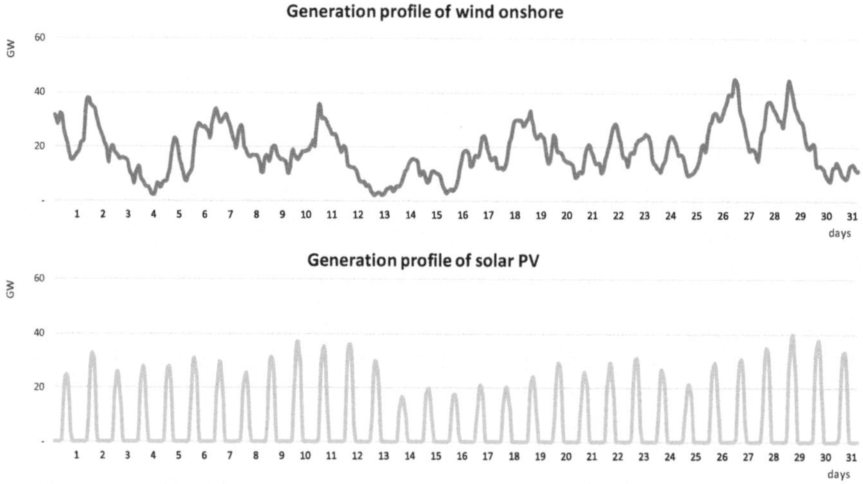

Fig. 16.3 Illustrative generation profile of onshore wind and solar PV for a given month. (Source: Synthetic data, not based on specific systems)

different non-dispatchable technologies may offset and somewhat complement each other to reduce the overall variability of the total, for example in places where onshore wind generation is stronger in winter, but quite low in calm summer days with generation from solar PV that is generally stronger in summer months and can be much lower in winter ones.

The challenge of integrating these sources in power systems has been summarised in the International Energy Agency's World Energy Outlook 2016 (IEA 2016a) through three key properties:

1. *Scarcity*. This situation happens when the generation from non-dispatchable renewable resources is insufficient to meet electricity demand at its highest levels, requiring other types of installed capacity or solutions to meet demand. This issue is strictly linked to the system adequacy issue discussed in the next section.
2. *Variability*. The rapid change of electricity generation from non-dispatchable sources requires the ramping up or down (or the start and stop) of generation from dispatchable sources in the given time. The time required by these generators to react, in particular for ramping up generation, is dependent on the type of technology and on whether the plant needs to start or was already generating. Forecasting methodologies to accurately estimate the future wind and solar PV generation can therefore play a very important role.
3. *Abundance*. At high levels of penetrations of wind and solar PV in power systems, periods of excess generation can occur, in particular in periods of low demand. This issue is linked to curtailment, with important implication on system stability and electricity pricing (see Sect. 3.4).

3 The Changing Structure of Power Systems

The introduction of growing shares of non-dispatchable generation sources is set to change the way power system are structured and operated. Following the properties discussed in the previous section, several changes to power systems must be considered: the type and amount of the capacity installed, the way that electricity demand is going to be satisfied, the impact on the electricity dispatching mechanism and its consequences on power prices.

3.1 Impact on System Adequacy

Power systems can be schematically characterised by three elements: The generation facilities, the demand centres and the grids that allow to transport the energy from the first to the second. Electricity demand fluctuates every moment (for the sake of simplicity, we will approximate it to "every hour") and its profile over time changes depending on the use (e.g. industrial use, lighting or cooking have very different hourly patterns). Typically, demand at night is lower than during the day, summer demand is higher where air conditioning systems dominate, while winter demand is higher where electric space heating in cold temperature regions is strong.

Throughout the history of deployment of power systems, reliability and security of supply have been a central concern. The ability of meeting demand

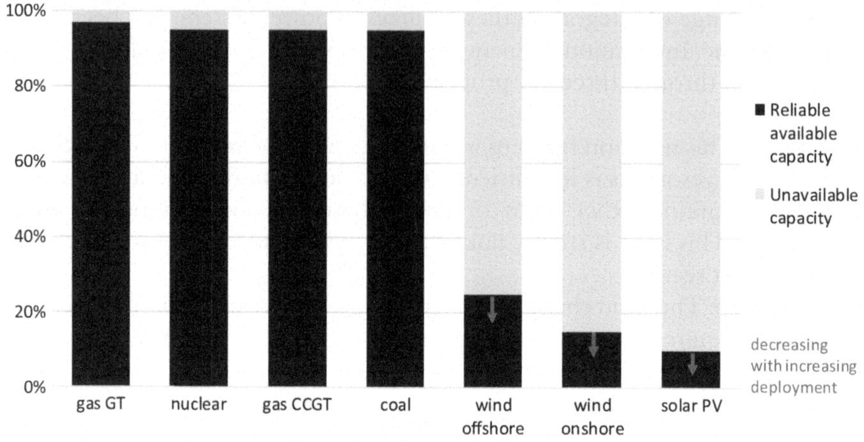

Fig. 16.4 Indicative availability of capacity at peak demand by selected technology. (Source: author's elaboration)

at its highest levels (peak demand) has been a fundamental characteristic of power system and markets. The *system adequacy* of a power system measures if enough generation and transmission capacity is present in the system in order to meet demand at all times (ENTSO-E 2015).

To be able to meet peak demand, enough capacity needs to be present in the system, once all unavailable capacity has been excluded and a security margin has been accounted for. A loss of load expectation (LOLE)[7] indicator can be calculated to measure the adequacy of the system. This margin is often called reserve margin or capacity margin. The unavailable capacity takes into account unexpected outages, services reserve, maintenance and non-usable capacity. The last component is particularly linked to the deployment of wind and solar PV technologies and is linked to their *capacity credit*, which indicates the portion of wind and solar PV capacity that can be reliably expected to generate electricity during times of peak demand in the network to which it is connected.

Indicative availability of capacity at peak demand for selected technologies as a share of installed capacity is shown in Fig. 16.4, where an average rate of unexpected outages has been considered for dispatchable fossil fuel and nuclear plants, and an indicative capacity credit for wind and solar PV technologies. It should be noted that generally the capacity credit of non-dispatchable technologies depends on several factors, and primarily on the resource, the generation profile and the match or mismatch with the demand profile.[8]

The contribution (capacity credit) of non-dispatchable technologies to system adequacy tends to become progressively lower as their share of total

[7] Loss of load expectation (LOLE) is the number of hours in a given period (generally one year) in which the available generation plus import cannot cover the load in an area (ENTSO-E 2015).

[8] In systems where the production of non-dispatchable renewables coincides well with peak demand, the capacity credit at low penetration rates can be higher than in the figure.

generation increases, while the capacity credit can increase when different areas with different profiles are better interconnected. An important implication of the low capacity credit of wind and solar PV technologies is that with increasing installed capacity of these technologies, the total installed capacity in a system increases significantly, as other types of capacity are needed for the system adequacy. For example, if in a system with 100 GW of dispatchable plants we add an equal amount of onshore wind and of solar PV (100 GW each, with a capacity credit of 10%), the total capacity in the system will be roughly around 280 GW, after retiring 20 GW of the existing dispatchable plants.

The consequences of this increase of capacity in the system on electricity generation and electricity pricing are explored in the following sections.

3.2 Impact on the Mix, Type and Operations of Plants in the System

The fluctuations of electricity demand require different power plants types to operate in varied ways. Load duration curves[9] (LDC) have long been used to represent in a simple way electricity demand and the type of power plants needed in a system by their utilisation rate or capacity factor. A classical way to classify them is by decreasing utilisation rate into baseload (with a typical capacity factor of 75–90%), mid-load (with a typical capacity factor of 40–60%) and peak-load plants (with a typical capacity factor of 0–15%). Linked to load duration curves, screening curves represent fixed and variable costs of thermal power plants over all the 8760 hours of generation in a given year, allowing to identify the cost-optimal thermal generation mix given a set of investment, operating and maintenance (O&M) and fuel cost data. The utilisation of these curves, while allowing to simplify the representation of hourly electricity demand, loses the temporal continuity of each hour, limiting its use to evaluate flexibility needs, such as ramping of power plants or charging and discharging of storage devices.

The deployment of non-dispatchable energy technologies requires the introduction of an intermediate step in order to keep using these two useful approaches (the load duration curve and the screening curve). *Residual* load duration curves (RLDC) are obtained by subtracting the hourly generation of non-dispatchable technologies from the hourly electricity demand, and then applying the same re-ordering from highest to lowest level as for the LDCs. An example is shown in Fig. 16.5 for different levels of solar PV capacity penetration into a fictitious power system.

Residual load duration curves are often very close to load duration curve at peak levels, while they become steeper along the curve, the more wind and solar technologies are added into the system. This change of the steepness of the RLDC has the effect to increase the need for peak- and mid-load plants,

[9] Load duration curves are obtained by reorganizing the hourly electricity demand from the highest value to the lowest throughout all the 8760 hours in a year (i.e. 365 days by 24 hours).

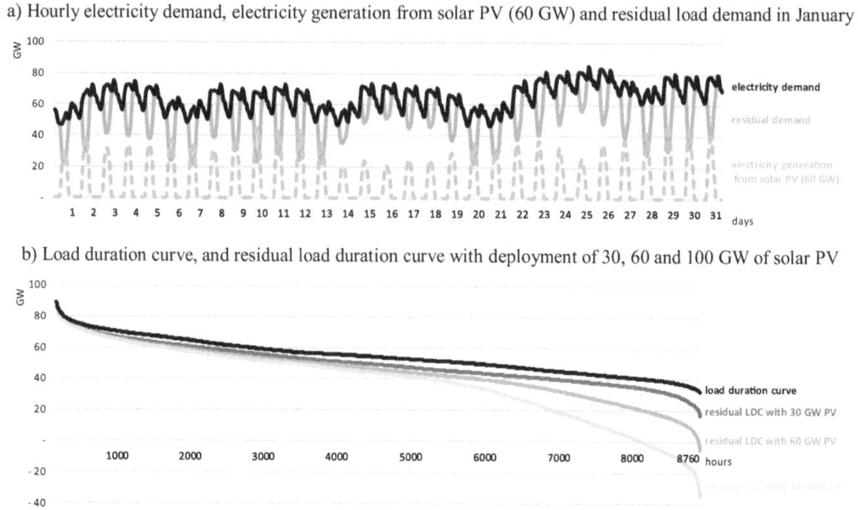

Fig. 16.5 Example of residual load duration curve. (**a**) Hourly electricity demand, electricity generation from solar PV (60 GW) and residual load demand in January. (**b**) Load duration curve, and residual load duration curve with deployment of 30, 60 and 100 GW of solar PV. (Source: author's elaboration)

and to reduce the need for baseload ones.[10] Negative values of the RLDC indicate excess generation that, in absence of integration measures, would be curtailed.

The low capacity credit of wind and solar PV plants (as seen in Sect. 3.1) brings a second important implication for the dispatchable power plants. As capacity in the system is higher and generation from wind and solar PV gets dispatched first in the merit order due to their near-zero variable cost, the utilisation factor of dispatchable plants is decreased.

A third effect—that, as mentioned, cannot be captured by the RLDC—is linked to the variability of the generation of wind and solar technologies and how it relates to electricity demand from hour to hour. As can be seen in the example of California ((Source: CAISO Fig. 16.6), where peak demand occurs in the evening, a growing share of solar PV in the mix keeps reducing the residual electricity demand around midday. This leads to a strong call on dispatchable generators in the late hours of the afternoon (from around 17:00 to around 20:00), requiring ramping of dispatchable plants two-to-three times higher than in the case without solar PV. Consequently, there is a growing call for greater flexibility of dispatchable generators. The increase of ramping services (up and down) of dispatchable generators can increase the costs linked to standby and lead to faster wear and tear of the plants, eventually decreasing their efficiency and lifetime, unless adequate retrofit for such operations is foreseen.

[10] The optimal mix of low-carbon technologies depends on several factors and is not the object of this chapter.

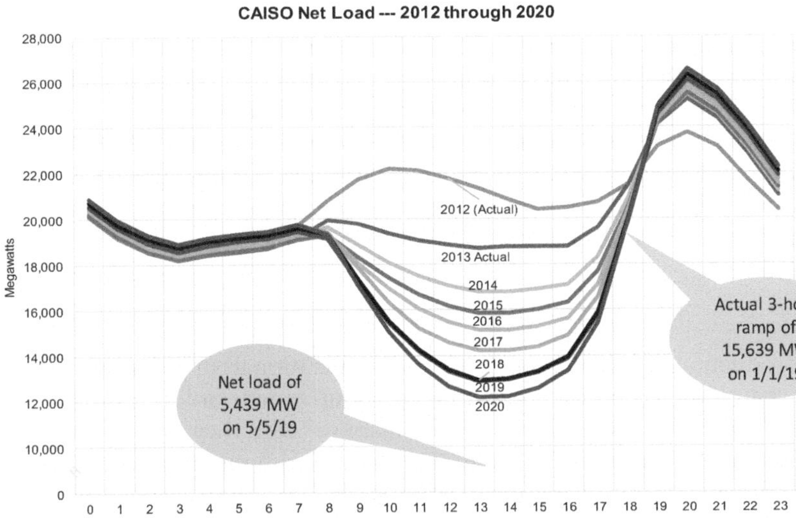

Fig. 16.6 Residual hourly demand in a typical spring day in California. (Source: CAISO 2019)

3.3 *The Rise of Distributed Generation*

Wind and solar PV projects can have very different sizes, ranging from few kilowatts to several hundreds of megawatts (currently up to 1200 MW for offshore wind and solar PV projects and several thousands of megawatts for onshore wind farms). For this reason, they can be broadly separated into utilities-scale and buildings-scale, with the latter often divided between commercial and residential scales. While the utility-scale projects tend to have similar size to conventional plants (that can range from 50–400 MW for gas plants up to 500–1600 MW for coal or nuclear plants and to more than 10,000 MW for the largest hydropower plants) in terms of location and connection to the grids, the building-scale ones are much more numerous, more distributed over geographical areas and generally connected to lower-voltage grids.

Power systems saw a major change over the last few decades as markets moved from monopolies to liberalised markets, increasing the number of generators and generally of actors on the market. While the new wind and solar PV utility-scale projects fit more into this path, the deployment of commercial and residential scale plants are increasing substantially the number of power producers from few dozens to thousands or millions.

These producers are often connected to mid- or low-voltage levels grids (distribution grids), generally closer to demand centres, and are often consumers of electricity themselves. This new category of "prosumers" (producers and consumers of electricity) is actually not new. Autoproducers of electricity have existed for decades in many countries (UN Statistics 2020), but this role was predominantly linked to enterprises which produced their own electricity for their own business/activity needs (e.g. heavy industry) and sold the excess.

The main change introduced by prosumers is their number, scale and diffusion. This is already having an important impact on transmission and distribution grids, and is expected to change the way that transmission system operators (TSO) and distribution system operators (DSO) function and interact, including the possibility for DSOs to provide flexibility services to the system through the aggregation of small active actors (TSO–DSO 2019).

3.4 *The Merit Order Effect*

The introduction of high quantities of power generation from non-dispatchable sources can have a significant effect on the hourly merit order dispatch.[11] As wind and solar PV have usually near-zero marginal cost, they are positioned at the beginning of the merit order and they usually push more expensive generating technologies out of the merit order stack. This effect changes hour by hour and can be very pronounced, limited or null depending if their generation is high, moderate or near zero. For example, in the case of solar PV, this can correspond to pronounced periods of generation around midday during summer days, limited during winter days, or no impact at night.

The overall merit order effect on annual electricity prices depends on several factors, including the level of deployment, the type, mix and geo-localisation of wind and solar PV technologies, their generation profile, the match or mismatch with the hourly electricity demand, the eventual bottlenecks in transmission and distribution grids, and the mix and marginal cost of the dispatchable plants.

An additional important element that can affect the merit order is represented by the level of capacity adequacy (e.g. if the system is in a situation of overcapacity or conversely lack of capacity) and the speed with which wind and solar PV capacity are being added to the system. In the case of lack of capacity in the system, the additional non-dispatchable capacity is likely to help the adequacy, but have limited effect in term of impact on the average wholesale electricity prices.[12] In the case of overcapacity coupled with very high deployment rate of non-dispatchable technologies, the reduction of average wholesale prices is likely to be more pronounced.

[11] The merit order dispatch is a commonly used method to rank electricity generators according to their increasing marginal cost (or variable cost), reporting the amount of electricity generated by each plant on the x-axis and the corresponding variable cost on the y-axis. It is usually built for each hour (or sub-hour period, depending on the market) to determine which plants will generate for a given level of demand. The highest marginal cost of the plants that are brought online determines the price in each hour. As demand changes every hour along with the availability of the different plants, so will the hourly electricity price. The annual electricity price is given by the average of the 8760 hourly prices, weighted by the hourly generation.

[12] Depending on how the shortage is priced, the hourly and the average wholesale prices could potentially be reduced too.

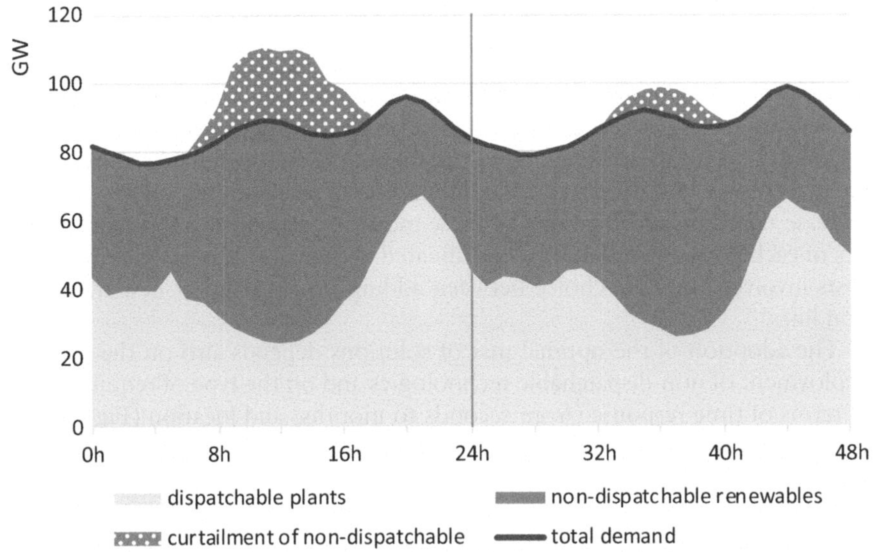

Fig. 16.7 Example of curtailment of non-dispatchable sources. (Source: author's elaboration)

Increasing levels of non-dispatchable generation have the effect of making the residual load duration steeper and steeper—as illustrated in Fig. 16.5b—with increasingly lower prices corresponding to the low end of the curve. When the levels of wind and solar PV generation are such that too much generation is present in the system, and that the dispatchable plants cannot reduce further due to physical constraints, curtailment of non-dispatchable generation occurs (Fig. 16.7). In these situations of electricity oversupply, the electricity prices are typically at zero or near-zero.[13]

The addition of any type of plant to a power system usually reduces the average electricity price—even if by a small amount—as it replaces some more expensive plant in the merit order (except for cases of replacement of capacity) that would otherwise be utilised. This can have a significant impact on the revenues perceived by individual electricity generators. In the case of non-dispatchable renewables, the price reduction often occurs during the hours of highest generation (e.g. solar PV), therefore exacerbating the reduction of revenues that can be perceived from the market. Ensuring that market mechanisms can provide the right type of price signals and that these are sufficient for the necessary investments to be forthcoming is a key issue of any market design, as it will be discussed later in this chapter (see Sect. 5.2).

[13]The phenomenon of negative electricity prices observed in some markets is voluntarily excluded from this chapter, as this can be only a transitory phenomenon and not a long-term one. Should this prove not to be the case, "near zero" prices should be substituted with "near-zero or negative prices".

4 Main Integration Options

Low levels of wind and solar PV in the power mix can usually be integrated in power systems without major challenges and without adopting integration measures on a large scale, unless specific bottlenecks appear, often due to sub-regional concentrations. The higher the share of non-dispatchable sources, the more there will be a need to use a combination of integration measures, and to increase them in scale. The mix of these measures depends on the characteristics of each power system, and a coordinated approach is needed to reduce the costs involved (e.g. the choice between adding new storage or new transmission lines).

The adoption of the optimal mix of solutions depends also on the level of deployment of non-dispatchable technologies and on the type of requirements in terms of time response (from seconds to months) and location (Fig. 16.8). Four main integration options can be identified and will be discussed in this section:

- Flexibility of power plants
- Energy Storage
- Demand-side response
- Transmission and distribution grids and interconnections

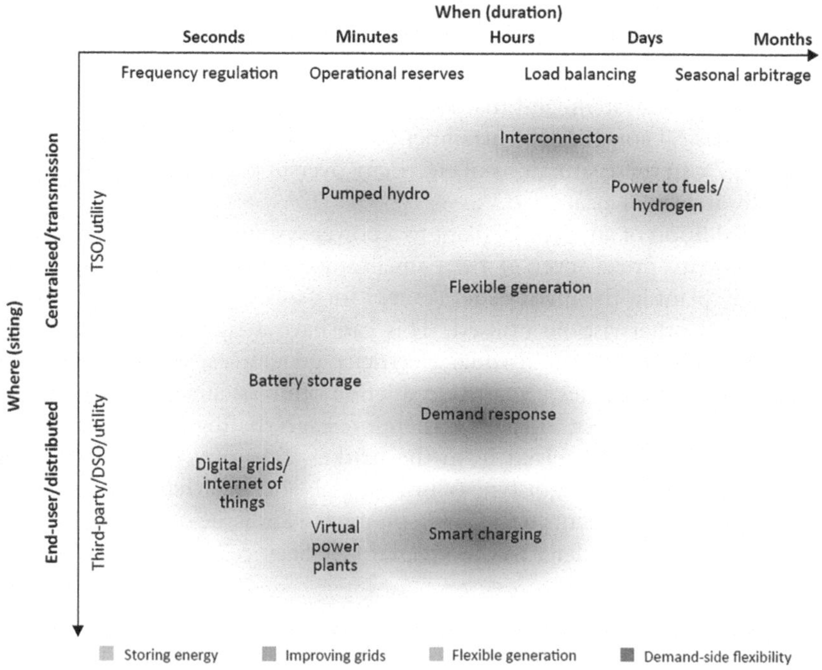

Fig. 16.8 Range of options for integration. (Source: IEA 2018)

Wind and solar technologies can also contribute themselves to their own integration, through careful choice of siting, using technological advancements (e.g. new wind turbines that reduce fluctuations of wind, inverter size lower than peak capacity of the PV module, changing the orientation of PV modules to allow to produce more during "shoulder hours"), or allowing for pre-curtailment to be able to ramp up production during a forecasted need. The pre-curtailment, though, must show a clear economic case, as it requires to limit production during a period to be able to increase it at a later stage.

The highest share of combined generation of wind and solar PV in the world on average in 2018 was reached in Denmark, where about 50% of total annual generation came from non-dispatchable sources, primarily wind (IEA Statistics 2020). This high level was reached thanks to several factors, with high levels of interconnection with the neighbouring countries playing a primary role.

While solar PV is still limited as a share of total generation, with only California passing the double-digit share (at around 14%) and Italy ranking second in the world at around 8%, several countries have surpassed the 15% threshold of wind share in their power mix, with some even exceeding the 30% threshold. This is the case for several States in the centre of the United States (EIA 2020) (with a high quality of wind resources), while several countries in Europe produced more than 20% of their mix from wind and solar PV combined (e.g. Ireland, Germany, Spain, the United Kingdom), and a similar level is being approached in other areas in Asia, such as in the Inner Mongolia province in China.

4.1 *Increasing Flexibility of Power Plants*

Flexibility in power systems is not new, nor is it linked to the deployment of non-dispatchable sources. Electricity supply has been matching the variations of electricity demand for decades, and the flexibility of power plants was central to achieve this goal. The novelty introduced by non-dispatchable renewable sources is primarily represented by the scale of the hour-to-hour variations of wind and solar electricity production that are present in few systems today and are expected to appear and increase in scale in many power systems in the coming future (Fig. 16.9).

Today, the flexibility of power systems is mostly provided by power plants, with a smaller role for interconnectors. At global level, battery and interruptible industrial customers still play a marginal role (IEA 2018). Hydropower plants with reservoir storage often provide the greatest flexibility at least cost—but this resource is limited in many countries—while gas-fired plants are typically the most flexible albeit pricier alternative. In some countries, such as France, nuclear power can contribute significantly to the flexibility of the system. The flexibility requirements depend on the mix of power plants present in a system and can vary significantly over the year. For example, in the United States, with combined high penetration of wind and solar PV, high levels of flexibility can be expected to be needed during spring (NREL 2013).

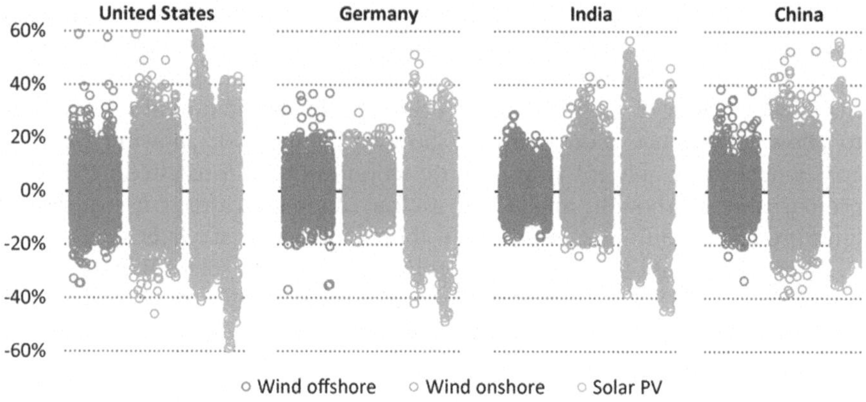

Fig. 16.9 Range of simulated hour-to-hour variations in output for new projects by technology, 2018. (Source: IEA 2019a)

Greater flexibility can come from existing plants, but many of these plants (e.g. older plants designed originally for baseload operation) might require retrofit or refurbishment to increase ramping capabilities, minimum level of sustainable output and accelerated timing for shut down and start up. An example can be provided by the case of China, where high levels of curtailment of wind generation have been registered, in particular in the north-western provinces. One of the main causes[14] of the curtailment has been identified in the lack of flexibility of fossil-fuelled plants, and of combined heat and power (CHP) plants in particular. Providing these plants with higher flexibility has allowed to decrease the curtailment levels (CEM 2018).

4.2 *Energy Storage*[15]

Electricity cannot be easily stored in large quantities, contrary to the case of fossil fuels (see chapter on Energy Storage), and it needs to be stored through some other form of energy means. Gravitational, mechanical, chemical and thermal are the most common forms. An important difference to consider between these forms of storage is whether they can shift the use of electricity over time (like in the case of hydro storage or batteries) or they convert it to another energy form (like in the case of thermal storage).

The main technology that allows electricity storage today is pumped storage hydropower (PSH) that stores electricity in the form of gravitational potential energy. In 2018, 155 GW of hydropower pumped storage capacity was installed

[14] Another important cause was the lack of transmission capacity.

[15] "Energy storage in the electricity system means the deferring of an amount of the energy that was generated to the moment of use, either as final energy or converted into another energy carrier" (EC 2017).

globally (IEA 2019b), representing over 90% of power storage capacity worldwide. Compressed-air, flywheel and other storage technologies, while promising, are still quite limited. Hydrogen production and storage hold very interesting potential, but cost and development of infrastructure could delay ambitions and deployment (IEA 2019c).

Storage in form of heat is being considered in several countries. Denmark and Sweden, for example, have robust district heating networks and an extensive use of CHP plants. Excess generation from non-dispatchable sources can be used in electric boilers (DTU 2019), therefore allowing for heat storage and reducing the need for fossil fuels. Further projects are being explored to store high temperature heat for use in industrial applications. In China, the use of heat storage and pumped hydro storage is being considered to reduce the curtailment of wind electricity generation (Zhang et al. 2016).

Battery storage—the majority of which are lithium-ion—has been soaring over the last few years, to reach about 8 GW in 2018. About 60% of the total installed capacity has been added in the last two years, showing how a combination of policies (targets and subsidy schemes) and costs reductions can support technology deployment. Over 60% of the 3 GW added in 2018 were for batteries behind the meter, and the rest for utility-scale (IEA 2019d). These two market segments hold very large potential for further development.

In the case of the residential segment, one of the main drivers for battery deployment is expected to come from the increase of self-consumption, in particular as the selling price to the grid of the electricity produced by distributed wind and solar PV will become more reflective of market price and not determined by support policies. In the case of utility-scale, batteries can provide different system and ancillary services, with duration ranging from seconds to hours. Frequency regulation has been an important factor for deployment.

Electrical storage (such as batteries) can play a very important role in the integration of non-dispatchable renewable technologies, in particular if excess generation (and curtailment) is present in the system (Fig. 16.10). In this case, the charging of the battery happens at near-zero cost, and most of the discharging can take place in the following hours when the generation from dispatchable plants is highest and correspondingly the electricity price received or potentially saved (if it reduces own needs when exposed to high price signals) by the storage operator.

The electricity price differential between charging and discharging is a fundamental parameter for the economic viability of battery storage, as the investment cost and the number of cycles that the battery is called upon in a year (which generally renders storage uneconomical for seasonal storage). As can be seen in the figure, storage capacity reduces the call on other dispatchable plants, and consequently is likely to reduce the overall electricity price in those hours. This operation can be repeated for growing amounts of battery capacity, until the selling electricity price that is achieved reduces the profits to a level that makes economically unprofitable adding further capacity into the system.

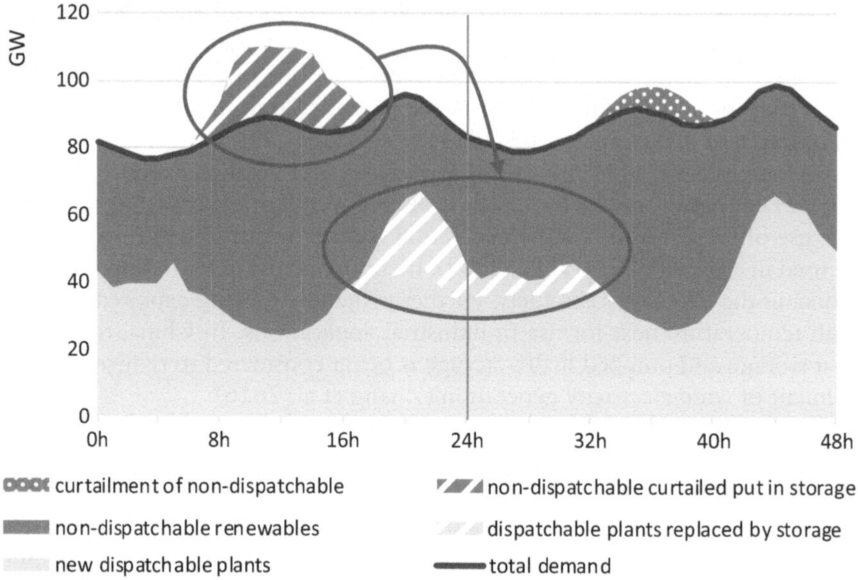

Fig. 16.10 Reduction of curtailment of non-dispatchable renewables and of dispatchable plants' generation through storage. (Source: author's elaboration)

4.3 Demand-Side Response

Electricity demand must be matched in every moment by corresponding electricity generation. Historically, electricity generation has been adjusted to match the fluctuations of electricity demand, as the majority of the generators present in the system were dispatchable units, and demand was relatively inflexible. The more non-dispatchable generators will be added into the system, the more this paradigm will change. Electricity demand can—and is set to—contribute to the flexibility of the system, adjusting to the availability of low cost non-dispatchable generation.

While storage shifts electricity production of non-dispatchable technologies to periods when it is needed, demand-side measures can help the integration of wind and solar PV by shifting demand to the moments in which the generation of these technologies is highest (Fig. 16.11). Demand-side measures are aimed at lowering electricity consumption in moments when generation from dispatchable source (and consequently the electricity price) is higher, and shifting demand to moments of high non-dispatchable generation. An example is provided by delaying the use of appliances in the residential sector.

Deferring (or anticipating) consumption by few hours can increase electricity demand during the hours when the production of non-dispatchable renewables would have been otherwise lost or difficult to use. The economic incentive of this action is given by the electricity price differential between the avoided consumption and the actual consumption. The higher this differential is, the

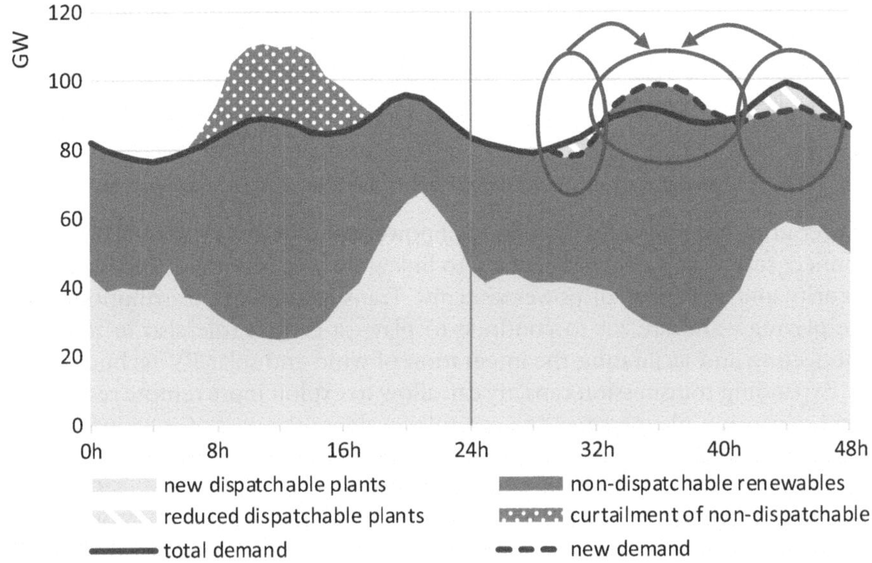

Fig. 16.11 Reduction of curtailment of non-dispatchable renewables and of dispatchable plants' generation through demand-side management. (Source: author's elaboration)

higher the potential that can be achieved with different measures in different sectors.

Demand response is not new to power systems, but until recently, it was limited only to large industrial or commercial customers (mainly for load shedding) and, in some cases, enabled by night and day tariffs. Digitalisation, the deployment of smart appliances and internet of things, the surge of distributed prosumers, the diffusion of smart meters, the increase of electric vehicles and smart charging, all contribute to increase the accessibility of a much greater number of actors to participate and to increase the flexibility of electricity demand.

Regulation, time-of-use and real-time tariffs[16] can play a key role in the effective realisation of the demand-side potential. The potential of demand-side response is huge, and has been estimated at 4000 TWh worldwide for the year 2017 (IEA 2018). Most measures shift the consumption for a duration that spans typically from 1 hour up to 8 hours, with upfront and operating costs that are quite limited for a range of options.

The sectors with the highest potential are the commercial and residential ones, but industry and transport (especially with the multiplication of electric

[16] In time-of-use tariffs, retail prices typically change in pre-determined sets of hours, regardless of system conditions, while in real-time tariffs retail prices change dynamically according to system conditions. Smart meters are needed for the latter.

vehicles) can have a significant impact too. The potential varies significantly by country or region, with significant differences over the different periods of the year, making the realisable potential much more limited than the theoretical one. Policies and regulation will be key to unlock this potential.

4.4 Transmission and Distribution Grids and Interconnections

Power grids have been the backbone of power systems for decades, allowing to connect supply and demand centres, to link and share resources, and to sustain security and reliability of power systems. Transmission and distribution grids are playing—and are set to continue to play—a central role also in terms of connecting and facilitating the integration of wind and solar PV technologies.

Expanding transmission capacity can allow to exploit more remote resources. Grid-expansion planners need to carefully evaluate the cost of such infrastructure against the value and quality of the resource and whether the grid expansion is needed for the overall power system needs. For example, in China, a significant expansion of HVDC lines is planned to connect the north-west provinces to the load centres in the south-east provinces, which will allow to exploit the wind and solar resources in those provinces and export towards high-demand centres. Expanding transmission capacity can also allow to connect and develop additional resources, as in the case of offshore wind through submarine extensions, connecting new farms, creating new power hubs, and eventually allowing to create meshed networks to increase security and reaching better integration throughout different regions.

Interconnections across different areas can have a double value for the integration of non-dispatchable renewables. On one side, they contribute to smooth the fluctuations of generation of different wind and solar PV plants (Fig. 16.12), and on the other they allow to even out different regional electricity demand profiles. Increased interconnection across different areas also

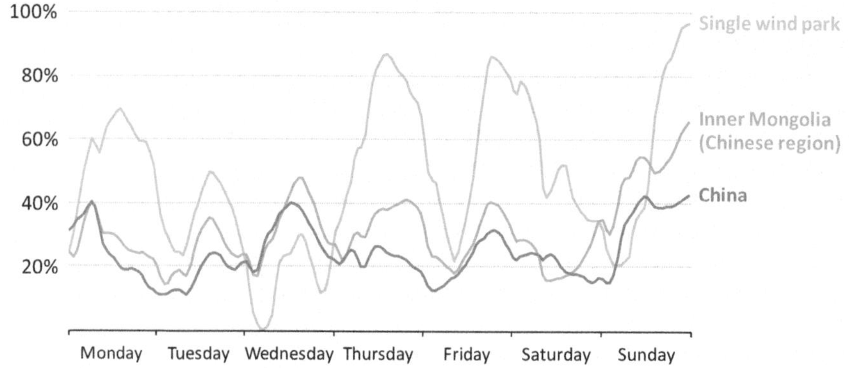

Fig. 16.12 Impact of increasing interconnection on hourly capacity factors of wind power in selected regions, 2014. (Source: IEA 2016a)

allows to better integrate electricity markets and decrease price differences across regions. The Clean Energy for All Europeans Package adopted by the European Union in 2019 (EC 2019) has among its targets to "allow at least 70% of trade capacity to cross borders freely, making it easier to trade renewable energy across EU borders and hence support efforts to reach the EU's binding goal of 32 % renewables by 2030". Grid codes can play a crucial role to reach this goal (IRENA 2016).

The diffusion of distributed generators is likely to change the relative role of transmission system operators and distribution system operators, as discussed earlier in this chapter, and will call for increased interaction and coordination. The level of deployment of the different integration means is going to affect each other. Economics and policy support are at the basis of the different choices of the mix of integration measures, but also the type and scale of the solutions will be an influencing factor. The impact of the deployment of battery storage and demand response on electricity grids can be very different depending on if they increase auto-consumption at the sites where they are deployed. In this case, the call on the grids is likely to decrease. If, instead, their deployment allows for higher consumption in neighbouring areas, the call on distribution grids is likely to increase. If the deployment of storage or demand-side measures takes place at utility scale or in places geographically distant, the call on both transmission and distribution grids is likely to increase.

5 Economic Implications

5.1 Economic Value of System Flexibility

Flexibility is set to play a central role in future power systems. Nonetheless, it has been a key feature also of past systems. All flexibility options were already present in power systems: interconnections to share adequacy reserves (and therefore lower costs), interruptible loads, storage (mainly in the forms of pumped storage hydropower plants) and—mainly—flexibility from existing power plants.

The value of flexibility was often expressed by the higher value and remuneration of plants operating during peaking hours. These plants were typically low-investment, high-fuel cost plants, running for only few dozen or hundreds of hours per year. The other flexibility measures were often aimed at reducing peak demand and move load towards increased utilisation of cheaper baseload plants (e.g. in the case of night and day tariffs).

In these systems, there was a very good correspondence between base, mid and peak demand with base, mid and peak prices, as ensured by the use of merit-order dispatching—once constraints and bottlenecks in a balancing area had been taken into account. The increase of non-dispatchable renewable capacity in power systems is set to change this correspondence, moving the hours with the highest electricity prices away from peak demand periods, but rather to correspond with the peak hours of *residual* electricity demand (see

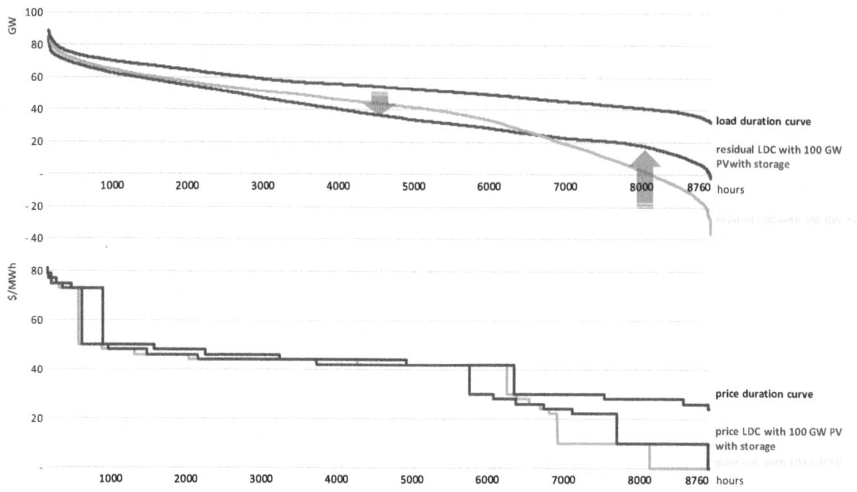

Fig. 16.13 Indicative impact of integration measures on residual load duration curve and prices. (Source: author's elaboration)

Sect. 3.2). Similarly, the lowest prices are likely to happen at times of high production from non-dispatchable sources, which in some systems may no longer correspond to the periods of lowest demand. For example, in systems with high shares of solar PV, peak residual demand tends to occur in early morning or late afternoon, while the lowest residual demand occurs in summer midday times. Significant variations of electricity prices can then arise with increasing hour-to-hour variation of wind and solar PV electricity production.

The value of increased system flexibility reflects the value of exploiting the highest possible volumes (its entirety might not be always economically viable) of available non-dispatchable generation. In other words, the introduction of growing shares of wind and solar PV generation in the system tend to make the residual curve steeper, while the introduction of growing amounts of integration measures (such as demand- side measures or battery storage) tend to turn the residual curve flatter again, avoiding (or reducing the amount of hours) for it to go negative, and for the related prices to reach near-zero levels (Fig. 16.13). Moreover, the value of flexibility is also important on the intraday, balancing and system services markets (e.g. frequency regulation).

The mix of generating technologies and of integration measures depends on a variety of factors. It is mostly affected by economics and by policy, decisions and can change significantly across countries or power balancing areas. The level of decarbonisation that is aimed for and the targeted speed of transformation of the system, the eventual introduction of carbon pricing, the availability of renewable resources (e.g. how much hydropower can still be added in the system, or the type, quality and distance of wind and solar resources from demand centres), the ban or introduction of technologies (e.g. nuclear or

CCUS) and the power market rules, all play a fundamental role in determining the mix.

The value of an additional plant in a given system depends on its impact on the other technologies and measures and on the overall system costs. The introduction of growing shares of wind and solar PV has an impact on their own competitiveness and ability to recoup their investment costs. The next two sections discuss the decreasing value of the electricity generated by non-dispatchable sources, and the limitations of the use of LCOEs for the evaluation of competitiveness and possible ways to overcome these limitations.

5.1.1 *Changing Value of Wind and Solar PV Electricity Production*

The increase of overall installed capacity in power systems following the increase of wind and solar PV capacity and the related effects on the merit order can have—as discussed above—a significant impact on the wholesale electricity prices. The hourly power prices are set to change only marginally in hours of low generation from non-dispatchable renewable sources. Conversely, they decrease substantially during the hours of very high generation from non-dispatchable sources.

At high levels of penetration of non-dispatchable renewables sources in the overall power mix, during the hours of highest generation, the hourly wholesale prices can reach zero or near-zero levels. The hours in which wind and solar PV generate the most will therefore register the lowest levels of prices. The value of the generation from an additional plant in those hours will therefore be minimal, bringing the overall value to decrease at growing levels of penetration in the mix (Hirth 2013).

This effect—often referred to as the "auto-cannibalisation" effect—has important implications on the evaluation of competitiveness (see below the section on LCOEs), on the system value of each technology, on the evaluation of eventual subsidies and on the mechanisms to put in place for these plants to recover their investments. If wind and solar PV plants recover their investments through out-of-power market mechanisms (such as subsidy mechanisms or long-term power purchase agreements), the evaluation of the market value is important to assess the extent of subsidies and the possibility and timing for an eventual phase-out. If these plants are going to participate more and more in electricity markets, this evaluation is key to assess their possible future deployment. If the deployment of capacity is centrally planned, this evaluation can provide very important information to evaluate the optimal low-carbon capacity mix.

5.1.2 *Competitiveness, LCOE and System Costs*

Wind and solar PV technologies have been deployed fast thanks to support policies and to falling costs. As their cost decreases, they are approaching competitiveness with other sources and the need to have a proper evaluation method is more and more concrete. Nonetheless, the evaluation of competitiveness of different power generating sources can be very complex, as several parameters need to be taken into account. A first step in this process is to assess the cost of production of different generation technologies. These include the fixed costs (investment and operating and maintenance), the cost of capital, the variable costs (fuel, operating and maintenance, eventual CO_2 pricing), efficiency, construction time, lifetime (or cost recovery period), the amount of electricity generated, and (in some cases) the decommissioning costs.

An indicator that is often used and that combines all these elements together is the Levelised Cost of Electricity (LCOE) (see footnote 53). This indicator has the advantage to be practical and easy to calculate, at least in its simplified version. It does present, though, several limitations, among which: it is most often based on a fixed amount of operating hours over the entire lifetime (at least in the simplified formula); it doesn't include externalities (if not priced, such as CO_2 emissions); it doesn't show the value of specific technologies to the power system; it doesn't include information about grid costs or integration costs; it considers the costs but not the value of the electricity produced.

Overall, the LCOE is a flawed indicator to evaluate competitiveness (Joskow 2011), in particular when comparing plants used for different uses (e.g. peak vs. baseload plants) and even more to compare dispatchable and non-dispatchable technologies. As the generating technologies cannot be considered in isolation one from another, the overall system costs should be considered (NEA 2012), including balancing costs, adequacy costs, grid costs, the cost of integration measures.

To properly allow the evaluation of competitiveness across technologies, several studies and institutions have developed indicators to complement or surpass the LCOE limitations. Among these: the Levelized Avoided Cost of Electricity developed by the United States' Energy Information Administration (EIA 2019), System Costs developed by the OECD's Nuclear Energy Agency (NEA 2019), System LCOE (Ueckerdt et al. 2013) and the Value Adjusted LCOE (VALCOE) developed by the International Energy Agency (IEA 2018).

The indicator (VALCOE) developed by the International Energy Agency, for example, includes three main components of adjustment—energy, capacity and flexibility—respectively to account for the value of electricity produced, the contribution to system adequacy and to the flexibility of the system (Fig. 16.14). Many indicators—including the IEA's—while recognising the need to include grid costs (in particular the effect on distribution grids) and electricity security considerations, still do not include them, often due to the difficulties linked to their evaluation.

5.2 *Impact on Power Markets and Attractiveness to Invest in New Plants*

The introduction of large shares of non-dispatchable renewables in power systems has, as discussed above, an impact on the amount and type of capacity installed, and the way that power plants operate. Overall, this leads to a

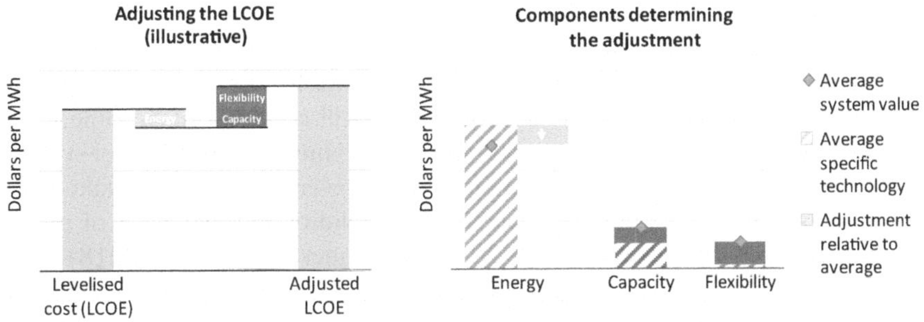

Source: IEA, 2018.

Fig. 16.14 Levelised cost of electricity (LCOE) vs. value adjusted LCOE (VALCOE). (Source: IEA 2018)

significant increase of the installed capacity in a determined power balancing area, a decrease of the utilisation factors of dispatchable plants and a decrease of wholesale power prices (at least in the short term).

Power markets have been designed to provide appropriate price signals for the efficient dispatching in the short term, and to incentivise adequate investment in the long term. While the merit order dispatch continues to be the most efficient way in the short term to select the power plants that will run each hour, the changes introduced by wind and solar PV in power systems raise the question whether the market signals will be sufficient in the long term to stimulate enough investments in new power plants to ensure capacity adequacy and to achieve low-carbon power systems. This impact can be very different if a plant seeks to recover the majority of its revenues through power market mechanisms or through support mechanisms (IEA 2016b).

Power plants that traditionally look for revenues through power markets have seen their profits decrease through a combined effect of lower amounts of running hours and decreased power prices. The issue of revenues being insufficient to stimulate new investment is not new, in particular for peak-load plants, and has been present well before the large increase of wind and solar PV. This has been and is leading to changes in some countries from the originally designed "energy-only" markets to include growing remuneration for capacity, flexibility and ancillary services mechanisms. While the role of these components may be limited now, it can be expected to grow following the increasing shares of non-dispatchable renewables.

Nonetheless, many power plants nowadays do not receive the bulk of their revenues from the power market. Several types of support measures are in place across many countries. Feed-in-tariffs (FiTs), Contracts for Difference (CfD), premiums, tax exemptions or credits and long-term power purchase agreements (PPAs) (with or without auctions to award them) are some of the most common forms (Hafner et al. 2020). Mostly designed for supporting the take-off of renewable sources, these mechanisms are now frequently adopted for nuclear power plants, carbon capture, utilisation and storage (CCUS) demonstration plants, and in some cases also for fossil fuel-fired capacity.

The support measures for renewable sources have been evolving throughout the last 15 years, and it is very likely that they will continue to become more sophisticated and adapted to the needs and requirements of each power system. However, if the majority of investment in new power plants is set to take place through non-power market mechanisms, the validity and existence of power markets for long-term signals could be put into question (Joskow 2018).

While the decreasing costs of wind and solar PV technologies has brought them closer to competitiveness, the "auto-cannibalisation effect" (i.e. the reduction of possible revenues on the power markets for wind and solar PV) discussed above puts in question the ability of these plants to sustain the current (or even an accelerated) pace of deployment without a continuation of some form of support measures.

A key and common characteristic among most low-carbon technologies is given by the importance of the weighted average cost of capital (WACC) in their overall generating cost. Wind and solar PV, like most of these technologies, are capital-intensive, with little or no fuel cost. The different types of risks associated to the project are reflected in the WACC, making it a crucial element for the viability of new investments. Private investors usually can successfully handle market risks (such as those linked to commodities fluctuation), but can be wary of uncertainties surrounding political and regulatory risks. Conversely, adequate policy measures can moderate financing risks and costs of low-carbon projects, therefore playing a central role in their competitiveness and in reducing overall system costs.

Facilitated by the decrease of storage and demand-side technology costs and by the increasing digitalisation of appliances and information systems, the power sector is also seeing the emergence of new actors. A growing role could be played by aggregators such as virtual power plants (VPPs) that pull together decentralised producers and consumers, storage owners, flexible load, and are enabled by smart meters and smart grids.

5.3 *Impact on Electricity Prices and Affordability*

The way electricity prices are formed depends on several factors and on the market rules of each power system. End-user electricity prices typically include (IEA 2012):

- Wholesale electricity generation costs: capital costs of power plants, fuel and eventual CO_2 costs, operating and maintenance costs;
- Adequacy and balancing costs;
- Transmission and distribution costs: capital costs of network infrastructure and operation and maintenance costs;
- Metering, billing and other commercial costs; and,

- Taxes and subsidies such as Value-added taxes, subsidies (such as renewable source specific ones) and other taxes and subsidies.

Wind and solar PV technologies have been deployed thanks to subsidies, which are often paid by consumers through an additional component on the end-user tariffs (such as the Erneuerbare Energien Gesetz (EEG) component in Germany). Conversely, as previously discussed, the introduction of growing amounts of wind and solar capacities in power systems has the effect of reducing wholesale prices to at least partially compensate the increase of end-user prices due to subsidies (Cludius et al. 2013).

The anticipated continuing reduction of investment costs of wind and solar PV technologies is expected to contribute to moderate or reduce the overall system costs. Whether this decrease will be compensated by the cost of adequacy and balancing cost, and of integration measures (e.g. investments in transmission and distribution grids, dispatchable low carbon sources, storage or demand-side technologies), is the object of several studies.

The overall power system costs will also depend on additional solutions and interactions with other sectors such as with the transport sector (smart charging of electric vehicles), the heat sector (possibly using excess of non-dispatchable renewables in water-heater boilers), or with other energy vectors (such as hydrogen).

The evaluation of the relative economics and the integration with policies in other sectors is set to play a fundamental role. In particular, the coordination of renewable policies with energy efficiency ones can be very important to reduce (or mitigate the increase) of electricity (and energy, at large) bills for end-use consumers. The affordability of the transformation towards a low-carbon power sector for end users will critically hinge on the ability of minimising the costs involved, without forgetting the need for dedicated policies aimed at removing inequalities and supporting the poorest part of population.

6 Conclusions

Non-dispatchable renewable energy sources are set to play a key role in the decarbonisation of electricity generation and are set to increase in the power mix in all countries. Their particular properties—scarcity, variability and abundance depending on the time of production (within a day, month or season)—are changing the way power systems have been operated till now. Low shares of these technologies in the power mix do not pose significant challenges, while the impact increases with growing shares.

The change in system adequacy calculations, the much higher amounts of capacity present in the systems, lower capacity factors of dispatchable plants, the need for greater system flexibility, the changes in the merit order and the electricity pricing mechanisms, and a greater number of actors on the producing side are the main challenges identified in this chapter.

Several solutions already exist: improving the flexibility of existing power systems and making this a requirement for future capacity additions, expanding the role and interconnection of electricity grids (with an evolving interaction between TSOs and DSOs), enhancing and enabling the development of storage capacity and demand-side management technologies.

The ability to tap into all these options will hinge critically on adequate policies being put in place for these technologies to be deployed and to participate in power markets. The minimisation of the overall system costs may require to coordinate the deployment of some of the integration measures—e.g. the choice between adding new storage or new transmission or distribution lines—as the value of each choice depends on its relative economics with all other choices.

The economic impact is uncertain, and efforts need to be made in particular from policymakers making this transformation affordable to consumers, and ensuring that businesses are not at a disadvantage with their competitors. The mix of low-carbon technologies to achieve the decarbonisation of the power sector is set to depend on relative economics, but policies will play a key role to make sure that the different integration options are deployed to their full potential.

References

California Independent System Operator (CAISO) (2019) Accessed in April 2020. https://www.caiso.com/Documents/FlexibleResourcesHelpRenewables_FastFacts.pdf

CEM (2018) Thermal Power Plant Flexibility, a Publication Under the Clean Energy Ministerial Campaign. https://www.cleanenergyministerial.org/sites/default/files/2018-06/APPF%20Campaign_2018%20Thermal%20Power%20Plant%20Flexibility%20Report_cleanenergyministerial.org__0.pdf

Cludius, J., Hermann, H., and Matthes, F. (2013, May) The Merit Order Effect of Wind and Photovoltaic Electricity Generation in Germany 2008–2012. CEEM Working Paper 3-2013 (PDF). Sydney, Australia: Centre for Energy and Environmental Markets (CEEM), The University of New South Wales (UNSW). http://ceem.unsw.edu.au/sites/default/files/documents/CEEM%20(2013)%2-%20MeritOrderEffect_GER_20082012_FINAL.pdf

DTU (2019) Whitebook Energy Storage Technologies in a Danish and International Perspective, DTU Energy, Department of Energy Conversion and Storage, Roskilde, Denmark.

European Commission (EC) (2017, February) European Commission Staff Working Document, Energy Storage—The Role of Electricity, European Commission, SWD (2017) 61 final. https://ec.europa.eu/energy/sites/ener/files/documents/swd2017_61_document_travail_service_part1_v6.pdf

ENTSO-E (2015) ENTSO-E Scenario Outlook and Adequacy Forecast 2015, Brussels. https://eepublicdownloads.blob.core.windows.net/public-cdn-container/clean-documents/sdc-documents/SOAF/150630_SOAF_2015_publication_wcover.pdf

European Commission (EC) (2019) Clean Energy for All Europeans Package, Brussels. https://ec.europa.eu/energy/en/topics/energy-strategy-and-energy-union/clean-energy-all-europeans

Hafner, Manfred et al. (2020) The Geopolitics of the Global Energy Transition, Policy and Regulation of Energy Transition Chapter, Springer Nature, Volume 73. https://link.springer.com/content/pdf/10.1007%2F978-3-030-39066-2.pdf

Hirth, Lion (2013) The Market Value of Variable Renewables. Energy Policy, 38: 218–236. https://www.neon-energie.de/Hirth-2013-Market-Value-Renewables-Solar-Wind-Power-Variability-Price.pdf

IEA Statistics (2020) International Energy Agency, Paris, Web Page Accessed in July 2020. https://www.iea.org/data-and-statistics/data-tables

International Energy Agency (IEA) (2012) World Energy Outlook 2012, Paris. https://www.iea.org/reports/world-energy-outlook-2012

International Energy Agency (IEA) (2016a) World Energy Outlook 2016, Paris. https://www.iea.org/reports/world-energy-outlook-2016

International Energy Agency (IEA) (2016b) Re-Powering Markets, Paris. https://www.iea.org/reports/re-powering-markets

International Energy Agency (IEA) (2018) World Energy Outlook 2018, Paris. https://www.iea.org/reports/world-energy-outlook-2018

International Energy Agency (IEA) (2019a) Offshore Wind Outlook 2019, Paris. https://www.iea.org/reports/offshore-wind-outlook-2019

International Energy Agency (IEA) (2019b) Renewables 2019 Market Report, Paris. https://www.iea.org/reports/renewables-2019

International Energy Agency (IEA) (2019c) The Future of Hydrogen, Paris. https://www.iea.org/reports/the-future-of-hydrogen

International Energy Agency (IEA) (2019d) Annual Storage Deployment, 2013–2018, Paris, Accessed in December 2019. https://www.iea.org/data-and-statistics/charts/annual-storage-deployment-2013-2018

International Renewables Energy Agency (IRENA) (2016) Scaling Up Variable Renewable Power: The Role of Grid Codes, 2016, Abu Dhabi. https://www.irena.org/publications/2016/May/Scaling-up-Variable-Renewable-Power-The-Role-of-Grid-Codes

International Renewables Energy Agency (IRENA) (2019a) Renewables Capacity Statistics 2019, Abu Dhabi. https://www.irena.org/-/media/Files/IRENA/Agency/Publication/2019/Mar/IRENA_RE_Capacity_Statistics_2019.pdf

International Renewables Energy Agency (IRENA) (2019b) Renewable Power Generation Costs in 2018, Abu Dhabi. https://www.irena.org/publications/2019/May/Renewable-power-generation-costs-in-2018

Joskow, Paul L. (2011) Comparing the Costs of Intermittent and Dispatchable Electricity Generating Technologies. American Economic Review, 101(3): 238–241. https://www.aeaweb.org/articles?id=10.1257/aer.101.3.238

Joskow, P. (2018) Challenges for Wholesale Electricity Markets with Intermittent Renewable Generation at Scale: The U.S. Experience, MIT CEEPR Working Paper, Dec 2018. https://economics.mit.edu/files/16650

Nuclear Energy Agency (NEA/OECD) (2012) Nuclear Energy and Renewables. System Effects in Low-carbon Electricity Systems, Paris. https://www.oecd-nea.org/ndd/pubs/2012/7056-system-effects.pdf

Nuclear Energy Agency (NEA/OECD) (2019) The Costs of Decarbonisation: System Costs with High Shares of Nuclear and Renewables, Paris. https://www.oecd-nea.org/ndd/pubs/2019/7299-system-costs.pdf

National Renewable Energy Laboratory (NREL) (2013) The Western Wind and Solar Integration Study Phase 2, Golden, Colorado. https://www.nrel.gov/docs/fy13osti/55588.pdf

Paula Mints (2019, April) Photovoltaic Manufacturer Capacity, Shipments, Price & Revenues 2018/2019, SPV Market Research. Report SPV-Supply6.

TSO–DSO (2019) TSO–DSO Report, An Integrated Approach to Active System Management, Brussels. https://www.edsoforsmartgrids.eu/wp-content/uploads/2019/04/TSO-DSO_ASM_2019_190304.pdf

Ueckerdt, F., Hirth L., Luderer G., and Edenhofer, O. (2013, December 15) System LCOE: What Are the Costs of Variable Renewables? Energy, 63: 61–75. https://www.neon-energie.de/Ueckerdt-Hirth-Luderer-Edenhofer-2013-System-LCOE-Costs-Renewables.pdf

UN Statistics (2020) United Nations Statistics Division, Accessed in April 2020. https://unstats.un.org/unsd/energy/Eprofiles/2015/03.pdf

United States Energy Information Administration (EIA) (2019) Levelized Cost and Levelized Avoided Cost of New Generation Resources in the Annual Energy Outlook 2019, Accessed in April 2020. https://www.eia.gov/outlooks/aeo/pdf/electricity_generation.pdf

United States Energy Information Administration (EIA) (2020) Accessed in April 2020. https://www.eia.gov/electricity/data.php

Zhang, N, et al. (2016) Reducing Curtailment of Wind Electricity in China by Employing Electric Boilers for Heat and Pumped Hydro for Energy Storage. Applied Energy. https://www.sciencedirect.com/science/article/pii/S0306261915013896

CHAPTER 17

Financing of Energy Investment

Jérôme Halbout and Marie-Noëlle Riboud-Seydoux

The future landscape of Energy projects is likely to be a mix of fossil fuel and renewable Energy investments, some completed years ago and still operating or in need of a technical upgrade, and some others that are currently under development or at their commissioning phase. Even in a conservative scenario (moderate Energy consumption growth combined with improvements in efficiency), the investment required in the very near future to sustain the development of world's economies is still enormous.

In that context, the financing of any Energy investment poses at least three different challenges.

The first is the amount of bank loans available to develop or refinance Energy projects since the 2008 financial crisis. The subsequent credit market contraction directly impacted projects meant to be closed in 2009 and 2010 but also projects initially completed in the mid1990s and reaching their refinancing stage in 2008–2010. Indirectly, it also reshaped the financing landscape for all Energy projects in the 2010s, forcing project sponsors to seek for new sources of monies and provide additional reassurance to investors, who in turn have responded with innovative financial instruments and structuring packages.

The second is the competition to attract funds. In the context of an investment gap, investors have now, more than ever, a wide choice when it comes to where and how they may allocate their funds. The profitability of Energy projects is being highly scrutinised with particular attention paid to the volatility of cash flows and the cost of financing. Investors, notably those with previous experience in the Energy sector, will also thoroughly conduct due diligence covering the non-financial benefits of a potential investment, such as a stepping

J. Halbout (✉) • M.-N. Riboud-Seydoux
4D Global Energy Advisors, Paris, France
e-mail: jerome.halbout@4dgea.com

M. Hafner, G. Luciani (eds.), *The Palgrave Handbook of International Energy Economics*, https://doi.org/10.1007/978-3-030-86884-0_17

into a new country or sub-market, establishing a joint-venture with a desirable partner, or building or reshaping their asset portfolio.

Finally, when it comes to financing Energy projects, there is little room for replication. A small-scale solar project in a developing country faces different challenges, carries different risks and attracts different potential investors than a liquefied natural gas (LNG) plant in the USA. With lower-income countries needing more Energy to sustain the development of their economy and the necessary shift towards renewable sources, there cannot be a "one fits all" financing structure.

With these challenges in mind, this chapter describes and discusses the main steps in the financing of any Energy project, then focuses on the respective characteristics of projects depending on the Energy source at stake.

The first step in financing an Energy project is to assess the size and the nature of the funds needed to sustain its development (Sect. 1). The structuring itself requires to identify the most efficient financial model and to source funds from relevant investors (Sect. 2). Although various mechanisms and policies have encouraged investment in all segments of the renewable Energy sector, there is still a huge diversity of financing opportunities among individual renewable Energy sources (Sect. 3). Meanwhile, the well-established financing models for oil and gas projects, which still represent a significant share of the Energy mix, have been able to adapt and innovate (Sect. 4).

1 Identifying the Volume and the Nature of the Funds Needed

1.1 *Project Viability Analysis*

The analysis of a project's financial viability involves the calculation of the Internal Return Rate (IRR) that investors can reasonably expect to remunerate the risk/return, the opportunity cost plus their own funding cost to mobilise their money into that project. The project IRR depends on the project's costs, its revenues and the risks attached to both. Financing an Energy project therefore starts with a thorough risk assessment in addition to its economics projections.

1.1.1 Revenues

Depending on the Energy sector and technology, investors might gain various levels of comfort on the project's future revenues. In the upstream oil and gas sector there is generally no specific government regulated price or support, and the project revenues will mostly depend on the production profile of the asset and the price of the extracted commodities. If the production output is sold to a specific buyer, such as a refiner or a long-term purchaser of LNG, then investors will expect the price and volume of production sold to follow the conditions set forth in a Sales and Purchase Agreement (SPA) recording the undertakings of both parties. When the production is exported to a global commodity market, it is sold at the international market price (including on futures markets—which may be used to hedge the price volatility) taking into account the transportation cost. While an international market price has always existed for oil, LNG has historically been a point-to-point, producer-to-buyer market and there was no single international price *per se*. But, as the LNG markets gain in maturity and availability both in producer and receiver facilities globally, spot LNG and forward gas markets develop and progressively replace long-term, fixed- or indexed-price SPAs.

For renewable power generation, governmental support through various mechanisms has constantly underpinned the development of the sector and its attractiveness for investors. Feed-In-Tariff (FIT) policy, a long-term (15 to 20 year on average) contract setting a fixed price for the generated electricity and a guaranteed grid connection, is the most widely implemented renewable Energy policy instrument, adopted by more than 100 jurisdictions at the national, state or provincial levels in 2018 (REN21 2019). Some FIT policies even adjust the tariff depending on the phase of the projects. Coupled with the possibility for developers to enter a Power Purchase Agreement (PPA) this scheme offers potential investors a high level of assurance on the future revenues stream, provided the governmental support and the FIT are preserved for the duration (or at least for the payback time) of the project. A PPA requires the power producer to supply to the purchaser (the "off-taker", usually a state-owned electricity utility) a certain amount of power at a specified price throughout the life of the agreement, in exchange of which the purchaser accepts to pay a capacity price, linked to the availability of the producing plant, in addition to the Energy price per KWh. A PPA reduces cash flow uncertainty, making the investment similar to an annuity bond which is the type of security and return that institutional investors typically look for. A rating can be assigned to this debt, taking into account the risk profile of the project, including the creditworthiness of the off-taker.

In developing countries where the off-taker is often a national utility (which may be subject to financial stress), the rating of the project can be improved by several credit enhancement or insurance mechanisms provided by international financial institutions or private insurers. Investors can also benefit from tax credit mechanisms where a tax credit originated by their investment can be used to offset tax liabilities in other segments of their businesses. This is called 'Tax Equity' and it has been used to encourage investment into renewable Energy in the USA. Many substantial wind and/or solar projects have been developed thanks to the Production Tax Credit for wind and the Investment Tax Credit for Solar.

1.1.2 Costs

Financing a project in a high-risk, capital-intensive industry can expose the investors to major cost uncertainties, in particular when unforeseen events or cost- or time- overruns impact the project and jeopardise its financial viability, or because the cost of alleviating these risks negatively impacts the project economics. Depending on the sector, the size of the project, its location, and the stage at which the financing is required, the risk profile is obviously different.

However, most Energy projects carry the same three types of risks. First is the legal environment: Are there rights allowing the project to be built and to operate in place? Are there any sovereign guarantees? What are the relationships with the host government? The TNK-BP project is a "worst case" example of a political and country risk in the Energy sector. In 2003, UK-based oil major BP entered into a joint-venture agreement with AAR, a Russian consortium, establishing a new structure, TNK-BP, which at the time accounted for about one quarter of BP's then global oil production. Although it proved to be a rather successful investment, at the end, mainly because of the rise in Energy prices, BP had to face severe setbacks such as back-tax claims adding up to US$936mn and various expropriation attempts.

Secondly, Energy projects carry environmental risks, each type of project to a different extent. While this seems obvious for nuclear plants and oil exploration and production, it is also the case, for instance, for wind farms especially offshore as regards the decommissioning phase.

Last but not least, the project's operational risks *stricto sensu*, which includes construction risk and operation risk, is probably the type of risks that experienced industrial sponsors and developers can more easily anticipate and hence mitigate.

Costs incurred at the construction phase and the operation and maintenance (O & M) phase are allocated differently depending on whether the Energy technology requires the purchase, import and transport of fuel (Frankfurt School 2018). While circa 85% to 90% of total project costs of solar, wind and hydropower projects in developed countries are consumed by equipment and construction costs, that percentage drops to circa 65% for coal projects and down to circa 30% for gas projects (CPI 2014).

Capital costs for renewable Energy projects have been decreasing over the past few years (Swiss Re/BNEF 2013) and projects which would have not been viable in the past can now deliver a return deemed attractive by investors (Frankfurt School 2018). Thanks to a combination of improvements in manufacturing processes (notably due to new entrants often pushing prices down), economies of scale and technological innovations, wind turbine prices have decreased by about 30% between 2013 and 2016 (World Economic Forum 2017). As a result, onshore wind has now become one the cheapest sources of electricity in many countries. Solar photovoltaic (PV) modules costs have also been reduced dramatically, by more than 75% between 2009 and 2016 (IRENA 2016). These trends are reflected in the strong reduction of renewable energies' Levelized Cost of Energy (LCOE), an economic assessment of all the costs of an Energy generating system over its lifetime, including initial capital investment, O & M costs, cost of fuel and cost of financing (the latter is discussed further in the next section).

Unforeseen events can incur exceptional costs, even after the construction and completion stage. One of the most common cases is a substantial damage to the producing asset, which is why investors often require that developers buy an insurance cover for operational risk. Other exceptional events include delay and overruns, especially in mega projects such as oil refineries, nuclear or LNG plants. To mitigate that risk, potential investors will be willing to see that selected contractors and suppliers have a strong track record in that specific Energy segment. Two contracts will focus the attention of the fund providers: the Front End Engineering Design (FEED) contract, identifying the technical requirements and a rough cost estimate for the project, and the Engineering, Procurement, Construction (EPC) contract for the procurement of equipment and material and the construction and commissioning of a fully functioning facility.

1.2 *The Nature and the Cost of Funds*

1.2.1 Financing Instruments

The three main instruments which can be used to fund an Energy project are equity, debt and hybrid instruments. For each of these, the risk level and hence the expected return vary as described in the figure below (Fig. 17.1). Bank debt ranks ahead of equity, which means that when a project is no longer financially viable, invested equity is used to cover losses, and monies recovered are paid to the bank first. For the higher level of risk they take, equity investors consequently expect a higher IRR, ranking typically between 15% for infrastructure funds to 30–35% for Private Equity funds (see Section 2).

Hybrid instruments combine characteristics of equity and debt. They offer more flexibility to investors and can be an entry point for those not familiar with Energy projects, or wishing to limit their contribution to a very specific stage of the project. One hybrid instrument, mezzanine finance, has been

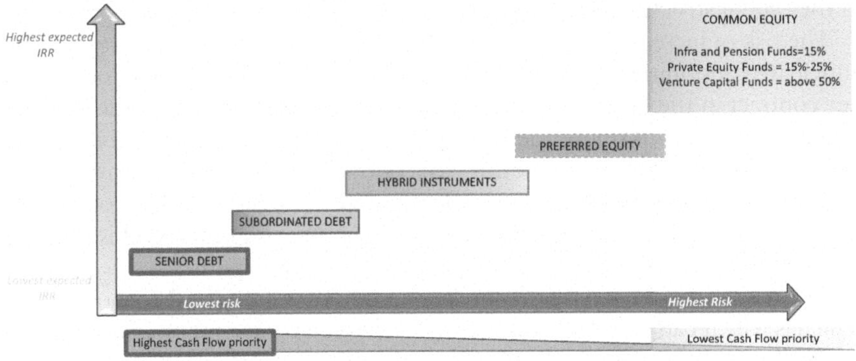

Fig. 17.1 Risk and return of different financing instruments. (Source: Authors' elaboration)

increasingly used in the financing of Energy projects over the last two decades, especially for projects where most of the costs are incurred at the construction phase. Mezzanine is more expensive than traditional bank loans, but cheaper than equity, and does not take control away from project sponsors, as it is not dilutive. Another argument in favour of mezzanine is that it puts less pressure on the project's cash flows, as regular payments of a mezzanine loan are made after those of a senior debt.

Mezzanine offers a higher return and a longer tenor than senior debt. Energy project sponsors may typically seek mezzanine loan if equity is perceived as too risky (country risk) or too expensive, and/or if the amount of senior bank debt available is insufficient.

The distinction between equity and debt is blurred by definition with a hybrid instrument, but it can also be so in case equity is funded by debt. When sponsors such as large oil and gas companies or state-owned utility companies finance their equity contribution, they might need to borrow funds from one or several financial institutions, the latter making the loans against the creditworthiness of the sponsor.

1.2.2 Cost of Financing

One of the primary criteria for equity and debt investors is the minimum rate of return that they expect from the project into which they would channel their money. It is measured through the Weighted Average Cost of Capital (WACC), which reflects the overall cost of financing, taking into account the respective weight of equity and debt in the financing structure. Any scheme or instrument that lowers the cost of additional equity or gives investors a higher level of reassurance on their future revenue stream, such as FIT policies or power purchase agreements, lowers the cost of capital. Conversely, the end of previously existing subsidies or the lack of government support mechanisms means that banks will require to see a higher share of equity in the project. Notably for these reasons, the cost of capital for oil and gas companies is traditionally higher than for power companies, with a higher cost of equity and a higher share of equity in the capital structure (IEA 2019).

The risk of increased cost of capital due to construction cost overrun can be anticipated and mitigated with the introduction of an EPC contract or a turnkey contract in the financing package. Both are designed to satisfy the lenders' requirement for bankability and to provide a single point of responsibility (one single contractor coordinates other subcontractors and service providers), a fixed contract price and a fixed completion date. The fact that the contractor, and not the owners, bears most of the construction risk in the end is the sort of guarantee that investors now almost systematically require.

The cost of capital also reflects the perception of political and economic risk, which is why it can vary quite dramatically between projects. For solar PV projects in Europe for example, WACC in Germany is on average 4%, while it can reach up to double digit figures in Greece (DiaCore 2016). In many developing countries, the cost of financing can be even higher, as debt is structurally more expensive. This is due to the limited supply of capital available for long-term investment and also to currency exchange risk, that is, a potential devaluation of the currency in which the investment was initially made (CPI 2014). Smaller projects are even less attractive for private investors than large-scale projects, as in addition to expensive debt there is often a lack of equity sponsors (which in turn increases the need for debt financing) and potential grid connection issues. This is why greenfield Energy projects in developing countries rely heavily on public finance institutions, such as multilateral and bilateral agencies acting as facilitators for other investors.

Since the 2008 financial crisis and the subsequent coming into force of Basel III regulations, commercial banks are extremely reluctant to offer debt for longer than seven to eight years (compared with the 15-year loans available before the crisis). Project developers having to refinance the project before it is completed now turn more easily to project bonds, an instrument which was traditionally used only to refinance completed (hence less risky) projects but is now increasingly popular in the earlier stages of the investment. When the capacity of the bank market contracted in 2008, interest in the project bond market was reignited, and 2009 saw a string of project bond issuances, notably for LNG facilities or gas pipelines, competing with comparable bank loans (Latham and Watkins 2009). Arranging project bonds to finance projects in their construction phase requires various tools of risk mitigation such as fixed-price turnkey contracts—but investors are now familiar with these.

One relatively new form of bond financing is "Green Bonds" which can finance projects tackling climate change or encouraging Energy transition and Energy efficiency. More attractive than comparable taxable bonds as they come with tax incentives, these bonds are often used as a refinancing tool once the construction has been completed. Issuers of Green Bonds include development banks (such as the World Bank), commercial banks, public sector agencies and corporations.

2 Structuring the Financing of an Energy Project

2.1 Financing Models Used for Energy Projects

2.1.1 "Corporate Finance" and "Project Finance"

Although there is a huge variety of financing structures in the Energy sector, all projects fall into two large categories, depending on which investor or stakeholder is eventually liable for the project's upfront costs. In an "on-balance sheet" financing, the sponsor, either a large Energy company or the host government, uses its own balance sheet to fund the project. The choice of "Corporate Finance" is without the prejudice to the origin of the funds, as the project sponsor might need itself to borrow funds to finance an Energy investment. In the case of host government financing, the financial contribution is made to the off-taker which then uses the funds to develop the project. Here again, the choice of "on-balance sheet" financing does not dictate the form of the contribution, which can be a loan or equity.

The second type of financing structure is "Project Finance", when a special purpose vehicle (SPV) is created "off-balance sheet" of the developers, with the sole purpose of developing and operating a specific Energy project. The SPV receives equity contribution from its shareholders and borrows funds from commercial banks and other sources. Loans are then secured by all the assets and the commercial rights of the SPV, but only by these assets. It means that if the SPV was not generating enough cash for the service of the debt, the lenders, left with no recourse against the shareholders, would become the owners of the project. Project Financing requires more complex transactions than Corporate Financing and it is usually more expensive, as it incurs transaction costs and costs incurred by potential delays due to the coordination of multiple parties involved. However, it has been and is still widely used in the Energy sector as it gives the option for investors to participate to only a slice of a bigger project, depending on the level of IRR they are seeking. Because of the in-built transaction costs, Project Finance is usually only a viable option for projects large enough to justify these additional costs. Generally speaking, lenders take some reassurance from a larger amount of equity invested by the project sponsors and developers as it reflects their commitment and incentive to see the project through to completion. Over the last two decades, Project Financing has evolved under the increasing scrutiny of rating agencies (which now include off-balance sheet debt in their analysis of the company) and of course under the Basel III regulations. While leverage ratios in the 70% to 80% range were not uncommon, they are now more than often closer to 60% to 70%.

2.1.2 The Choice of the Financing Structure

Most of the segments in the Energy sector see a co-existence of projects funded through non-recourse finance (Project Finance) and projects funded through on-balance sheet finance. Although it is almost impossible to assess how many projects per Energy segment exactly have historically been financed on or off the balance sheets of sponsors, the International Energy Agency has gathered data on newly developed projects. In 2018, more than 80% of power investments were financed on the balance sheets of utilities, independent power producers and consumers (IEA 2019).

The nuclear sector has always been an exception in the Energy industry, as all nuclear plants are financed through Corporate Finance. The developer, usually a large utility (sometimes partnering with other utilities) raises financing from its own resources, and loans are taken against all its existing assets. Given the specificities of the asset, Project Financing is not an option for lenders, as in a scenario of no repayment of the debt (probably resulting from an incomplete construction), they would be left indeed with de facto little recourse or even no recourse at all (NEA 2009).

Generally speaking, if the Energy project value is less than US$30–40 m, Project Financing is probably too costly a route. A developer with a reasonably

Table 17.1 Characteristics of Corporate Finance and Project Finance

	Corporate financing "On-Balance Sheet"	*Project Financing "Off-Balance Sheet"*
Specificity	• None compared to other Corporate transactions	• Creating of a SPV for the sole purpose of financing the development of an Energy Project
Recourse	• Resource against the Sponsors' Balance Sheets • Use of Corporate debt capacity	• Resource is limited to the Project's (SPV) Balance Sheet • No claim against the Sponsors' Balance Sheet
Debt service	• On Corporate Balance Sheets	• On Cash Flows generated by the Project
Debt maturity	• Repayment periods are usually shorter than in Project Finance	• Longer repayment periods can be agreed
Gearing	• Lower gearing is possible	• High gearing level
Complexity	• Low to medium—similar to other Corporate transactions	• High coordination of different external teams
Natural candidates	• Companies with very strong Balance Sheets (large-scale utilities) • Project with limited or no recourse (Nuclear Projects) • Small Companies (transaction costs of Project Finance unaffordable)	• Projects too big compared to the Sponsors' Balance Sheets • Projects in high-risk countries • JV with partners perceived as "weaker"

Source: Authors' elaboration

strong balance sheet is likely to consider borrowing some funds through corporate finance in the first instance, unless the project, because of its risk profile, can be managed more safely through a SPV (Table 17.1).

2.2 *Investors in Energy Projects*

Most Energy projects, especially the large-scale ones, are financed thanks to the contribution of several types of equity providers and debt providers.

2.2.1 *Debt Lenders*

Commercial banks are traditionally the main source of debt for Energy corporations. According to IEA (2019), debt represents up to half of the capital structure of top listed Energy companies (25% for oil and gas and 50% for power companies). Commercial banks also traditionally finance around 70% of Energy SPVs, de facto reducing the need for a more costly equity financing. In the immediate aftermath of the 2008 financial crisis, the banks' need to reduce their own leverage and exposure to illiquid situations created a relative lack of finance for Energy projects. Now that risks and costs have significantly decreased for many Energy technologies, commercial banks are more likely again to look favourably at this category of projects. Banks can do so either within a syndicate (a group of up to 20 banks for the largest projects, led by one or several banks acting as "arrangers"), or through a "club deal" for smaller projects (and in this case, which is more widely used since the financial crisis, all banks participate on equal terms). Some commercial banks which used to be focused on their regional markets are now more likely to fund projects internationally. Japanese banks have been funding an increasing number of wind projects in Europe; and Chinese banks' involvement in Africa, be it in fossil fuel or in renewable Energy projects, is now widespread.

The urgent need to provide access to Energy sources for communities and businesses in developing countries justifies the increasing involvement of public finance actors into the financing of Energy projects. While development finance institutions (DFIs) have traditionally focused on grants and concessional lending to fund projects in countries where there is limited access to private finance, they now act as private finance facilitators by offering a wide range of instruments, funds and guarantees. Their intervention de facto lowers the project's risk profile and attracts local banks lacking the experience or the balance sheet to lend funds outside a syndication. Multilateral development banks, such as the World Bank, the European Investment Bank (EIB) or the African Development Bank (AfDB) use their own capital to provide funds and risk mitigation instruments. Since 2008, the World Bank and its entities have provided almost US$50bn for Energy projects, either to Government entities or to private companies under the form of loan or equity, offering potential investors a higher level of reassurance. Three World Bank institutions are particularly active in the Energy sector: the International Bank for Reconstruction and Development (IBRD), the Multilateral Investment Guarantee Agency (MIGA) and the International Finance Corporation (IFC). The IFC lends to and makes equity investment in private companies, offers syndicated loans and underwrites securities issues by companies in developing countries. The European Investment Bank, which raises its own resources on capital markets, set up a series of renewable Energy equity funds with private entities, and lends mid-term and long-term funds. At the United Nations level, the Multi-donor trust funds, a pooled financing mechanism, promotes renewable Energy and Energy efficiency in developing countries through small- to medium-sized projects. Alongside development banks, bilateral agencies from developed countries, such as US Aid, Proparco (France) and Saudi Fund, provide highly concessional loans to developing countries.

Export Credit agencies (ECA) also play a significant role in Energy financing especially when it comes to large-scale projects. The initial role of the ECAs was to help project sponsors attract commercial bank debt by providing political risk cover in emerging markets. As the need for alternative sources of finance has increased, notably following the 2008 financial crisis, the products offered by ECAs have evolved and now encompass loan guarantee, export credit insurance and direct lending to the purchaser of the project equipment and goods, more than often on competitive terms. ECAs are now mainstream project investors which can finance a significant portion of mega-large projects, as illustrated by the record direct tied lending of US$2.5bn (10% of the total project costs) by the Korean ECA, K-Exim, to the Barakah nuclear power project in Abu Dhabi in 2016 (Irwin et al. 2019).

2.2.2 *Equity Investors*

While banks provide the majority of the funding, the project itself is primarily initiated and developed by sponsors and developers, which bear the costs of the earliest phases (such as feasibility studies) on their balance sheet. The project's shareholders can be either the developers themselves (oil and gas companies, power companies) or investment companies such as Private Equity (PE) or Venture Capital (VC) funds, but also host governments through a state-backed utility company or a National Oil Company (NOC).

While both VC and PE funds provide equity to Energy projects, they intervene at different stages of a project's life. VC funds focus on early stage, smaller-sized companies such as Energy efficiency start-ups. PE funds can invest as early as the latest phase of the development of the project, provided there is a proven technology, and throughout the construction phase or manufacturing scale-up. They seek undervalued companies and projects, under-performing listed companies, or companies ready to consider a listing. Energy-focused funds have the ability to work in partnership with an existing management team. They can invest either alongside project sponsors and/or with other co-investing PE funds bringing to the table either a regional expertise or previous experience in the project's specific sub-segment.

Infrastructure funds and institutional investors, such as pension funds or sovereign wealth funds, take a growing interest in long-lived physical assets that would match their long-term, low risk liabilities and offer a bond-type IRR. Institutional investors look favourably at insurance products lowering the project risks, and more generally at projects with substantially reduced construction costs or at their refinancing stage. After a few years of operations, once the Energy project enters a lower risk phase, institutional investors have indeed the opportunity to negotiate more favourable debt terms or enter into a power purchase agreement.

Public markets are both an investment category and a source of funds for Energy projects and Energy assets. They offer a high level of liquidity for investors and different forms of entry points, notably equity shares of publicly listed Energy companies or quoted project funds. Energy companies raise funds through stock markets once they have reached certain milestones, although some markets dedicated to smaller growing companies have been used in the past to finance early stage projects. Once listed, the value of the company and hence its refinancing capacity mostly depend on its share price.

3 Financing Renewable Energy Projects

Despite the undeniable attractiveness of renewable Energy sources over the last couple of decades, some projects are still struggling to close financing. In developed countries and China, where governments have supported the Energy transition, renewable Energy has now become a "mature sector increasingly dominated by big industrial players, utilities, and institutional investors" (Frankfurt School 2018) able to fund Greenfield projects on their balance sheets. In developing countries, though, the situation can be dramatically different.

3.1 Financing Solar Photovoltaic (PV) Projects

Although solar PV generation is still more expensive than onshore wind, it is less risky as it relies on fewer moving parts that can be replaced easily (Swiss Re/BNEF 2013). The financing of a solar project notably depends on its size and location.

For a large project (above US$50 m) based in the USA, equity can represent between 15% of the project funding (high capital cost scenario) to 35% (low capital cost scenario) (Feldman and Schwabe/NREL 2018). Small-scale solar (less than 1 MW) is mainly a mix of residential and commercial rooftop systems, with two main financing options for the host companies going solar. Either the system is rented in return of regular fixed payments, or a classic PPA is entered where the host company pays a pre-determined rate to a third-party investor. Installers are turning away from the leasing model to more conventional debt financing (Frankfurt School 2018), with the option to access solar equipment loans for residential PV systems. One of the biggest markets for small-scale solar developments, the USA see the emergence of innovative financing instruments with Green Bonds now being available to residential solar systems. There are also new investor categories, such as Tax Equity investor syndicates, Canadian independent power producers and regional banks. The US solar market has matured notably thanks to the Investment Tax Credit for Solar, which is the basis for a popular financing structure, the partnership "flip" (see Fig. 17.2). Under this structure, the partnership allocates 99% of tax credits, income and losses to the Tax Equity investor, until it reaches a target yield. Once this yield is reached, there is a "flip" in allocation and the Tax investors' share drops. When this scheme expires in 2023, the US solar market is likely to become more competitive and vendors are likely to react by cutting costs.

In developing countries, structuring the financing of a small-scale solar project is a quite different process. Financing of solar lighting or rooftop solar plants can be made through off-grid Pay-as-you-go (PAYG) scheme, where companies sell home system products for a low down-payment followed by regular small payments made by mobile phone services. The users get to own the systems after less than a year for the most successful schemes (Frankfurt

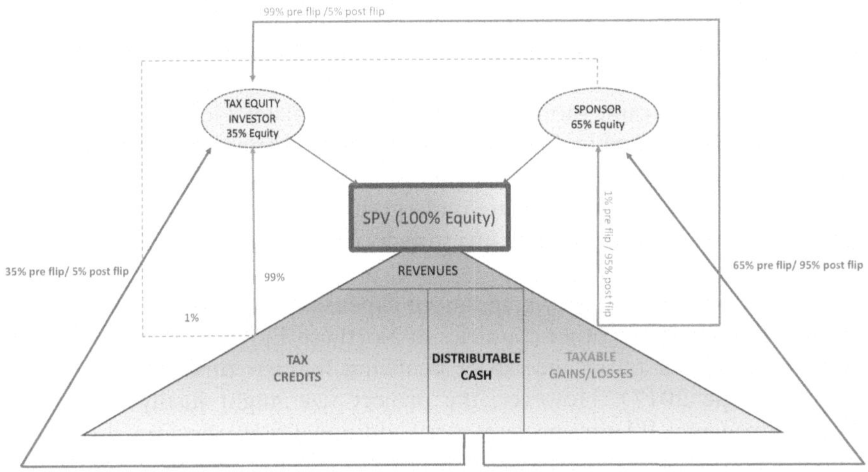

Fig. 17.2 Partnership "flip" structure. (Source: Authors' elaboration [based on Feldman and Schwabe / NREL 2018])

School 2018). These companies themselves are typically funded by VC and PE funds, "impact" investors and multi-donor programmes, and try to replicate the US model of securitising residential solar panels. Off-grid solar systems can be funded by banks, which receive funds from development institutions to reduce the interest rate they will be charging to users.

Some solar projects can be dropped if investors deem the country risk too high for the project economics. If the host State fails to sign power purchase agreements for projects contracted in auctions, or if the tender evaluation process is unclear, investors simply decide not to commit. In South Africa, the repeated refusal of Eskom, the local utility company, to enter into PPAs with renewable Energy developers wiped out the record investment figures from the early 2010s (investments fell to US$100 m in 2017, vs. US$5.6bn in 2012 according to Frankfurt School 2018 report). In India, one of the biggest markets for solar power, some projects were dropped between 2015 and 2018 because their size exposed them to multiple country risks. Some large deals have been secured with robust independent power producers (often teamed up with PE funds and a World Bank participation), but for mid-size projects the environment was significantly different. In some Indian states, repeated cancellations of auctions doubled with the upcoming elections and the subsequent risk of having to cohabit with local public funding pushed private sponsors and commercial banks away.

3.2 Financing Wind Projects

Project Finance has traditionally been the predominant model for onshore wind in Europe, with debt levels of around 70% (Wind Europe 2017). Debt used in Project Finance is traditionally senior debt, and the equity is preferably paid upfront. Yet, the earliest phases of the project (before the permits are obtained) are funded by the developers and the utilities on their own balance sheets. The 2008 financial crisis naturally hit the financing of onshore wind projects as banks became more risk averse, but multilateral lending institutions such as the EIB stepped in. The involvement of multilateral banks made some projects attractive for PE firms and infrastructure funds. Now that onshore wind markets have matured and are undergoing an aggregation phase, attracting large players like institutional investors looking for low risk portfolio companies has become easier.

Offshore wind is still on average more expensive and riskier than onshore. In the UK, contrary to other countries in Northern Europe, power producers traditionally favour on-balance sheet financing for new offshore wind farms (Wind Europe 2017). However, the project size might justify opting for Project Financing. If larger projects carry additional risks, they can also afford transaction costs incurred by off-balance sheet financing. The biggest offshore wind farm in the world since its extension in 2018, the Walney Offshore Wind Farm, was financed through Project Financing, with the backing of many diverse investors (Table 17.2).

3.3 *Financing Grid*

One of the challenges ahead for financing renewable power generation is grid investment.

While onshore and offshore wind farms can be constructed and operational within 3 to 5 years, grid improvement, extension or interconnection can take much longer. Uncertainty about the evacuation of the power to the national

Table 17.2 Walney Offshore Wind Farm financing

Type of investment	*Organisation*	*Amount*
EQUITY	DONG Energy Group	50.1% majority stake (estimated at GBP 646 million)
	Scottish Southern Energy (SSE)	25.1% minority stake (estimated at GBP 324 million)
	OPW Hold CO UK Ltd. (dedicated investment vehicle for PGGM and Ampère Equity)	24.8% minority stake (estimated at GBP 320 million)
DEBT (relates only to OPW minority stake) 70%	UK Green Investment Bank Royal Bank of Scotland plc Siemens Santander Lloyds Bank	Estimated at GBP 224 million

Source: IRENA (2016)

grid means that onshore wind, despite a generally lower risk profile, cannot always be easily financed.

In the case of Africa's largest wind power project to date, the Lake Turkana Wind Power Farm in Kenya, investors were concerned that the construction of the transmission line would be delayed, as it was funded by Kenya's state-owned utility. After a few years of uncertainty, developers asked the World Bank to provide a partial risk guarantee, but the World Bank declined to do so as long as the Kenyan government would not issue a counter-guarantee. MIGA also declined, uncertain whether the off-taker could buy the electricity. Eventually, the Africa Development Bank issued a partial risk guarantee to ensure the off-taker payments for the first 6 months of power generation.

Grid investment is highly needed in many emerging countries, either as an initial development or as an extension and interconnection in countries where governments already undertook grid programmes in the 1960s. Upper-middle income countries might also require grid investment to enable Energy transition. In Germany, where Energy produced in the north has to be transported to the country's industrial heartlands in the south and west, the estimated capital spending needed to upgrade the grid and distribution networks by 2020 reaches EUR52bn (Zank 2019). This is supported by the transmission system operators, which, although they will claw back the investment through higher tariffs, will need to mobilise external funding beyond their balance sheet.

3.4 Financing Hydropower

With a technical lifespan of 50 to 60 years, high civil work costs due to site specificities of each project and high construction and environmental risks, hydropower plant financing has traditionally relied on public funds. However, years of electricity market deregulation prompted developers to eventually raise funds from private investors. Project Financing was a natural option, especially under Public-Private Partnerships (PPP). As per Fig. 17.3, financing is dependent on the project's future cash flows, set out in a power purchase agreement. Under a PPP, a public administration delegates for a fixed period to a private company the development and the construction of a new hydropower plant. At the end of this period, the facility and its revenue are transferred to the public sector.

A variety of investors and financial instruments contribute to the financing of a new hydropower plant. The host government does not necessarily take an equity share but can provide various forms of guarantees. The developer can issue bonds, and domestic commercial banks, if their balance sheets allow it, can provide a range of loans alongside development banks. The biggest challenge in the financing of hydropower is the gap between the maturity of loans, the debt service obligations and the much longer technical lifespan of the plant. To address this gap, tariffs are usually increased during the first years of operations, making privately funded hydro projects less competitive than other generation sources (and conversely much more competitive once the debt has been

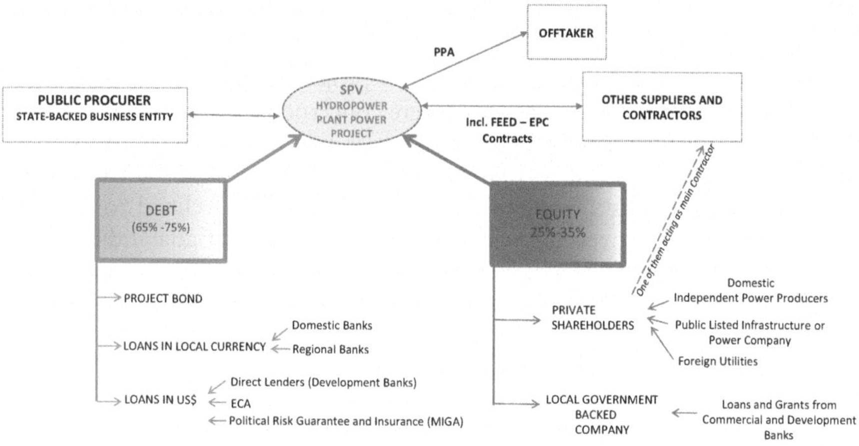

Fig. 17.3 Typical financing of a hydropower plant in a developing country. (Source: Authors' elaboration)

fully serviced). In developing countries, the World Bank's IFC is extremely active to help finance hydropower plants and has developed innovative financing structures to lower the project risk and attract co-investors. IFC has been acting as a developer while offering a political risk coverage through MIGA and has also pooled investments in different renewable Energy sources, creating a platform SPV that will raise Project Finance from IFC and other investors.

Small hydropower projects (under US$100 m of capital investment) are structurally less profitable than large hydro and highly cost sensitive, as the cost of the feasibility studies are almost fixed costs. These small projects can only access non-recourse finance if they are under a feed-in-policy or a power purchase agreement (IFC/Fichtner 2017).

4 Financing Oil and Gas Projects

4.1 Financing Upstream Oil and Gas Projects

Upstream oil and gas projects are among the riskiest investments in the Energy industry. The vast majority of the geological surveys do not lead to the appraisal stage. Even when sites potentially containing viable reserves have been identified, the investigations carried out at the appraisal phase might indicate that these reserves are not sufficient to justify the size of the investment required to extract them. These first two stages are entirely funded on the balance sheet of the oil and gas companies, using traditional corporate finance instruments. At the development and the production stages, when the project's cash flows become more predictable, developers can tap into a wider range of funds (Fig. 17.4).

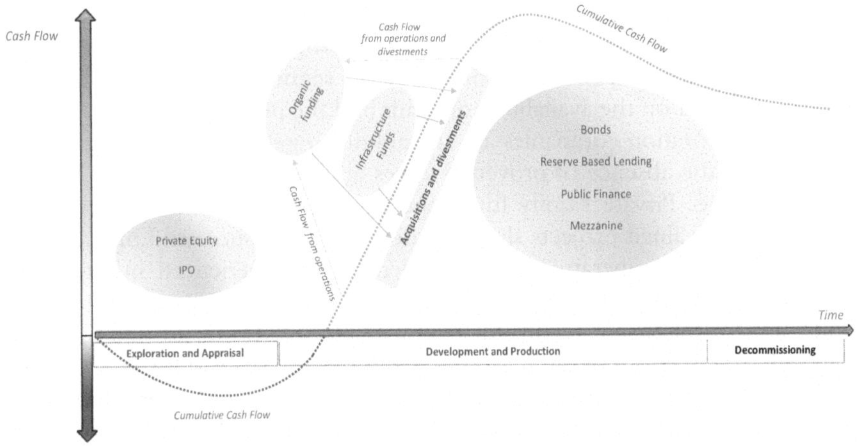

Fig. 17.4 Upstream Oil and Gas—Different funding sources over the life of a project. (Source: Authors' elaboration)

Large Independent Oil Companies (IOC) can finance their pre-producing assets through the reserve-based lending (RBL) model. Commercial banks lend funds on the basis of the net present value of cash flows generated by the underlying reserves. The loan facility is repaid using the proceeds from sales of the asset's output and the amount of the facility is adjusted from time to time during the loan life to reflect changes in the estimated project value. The share price of a listed IOC is driven by the level of production of its producing wells and by its ability to discover, appraise and develop new sites. Careful attention is then paid by investors to the IOC's ability to manage its asset portfolio, as it encapsulates the company's future value.

IOCs looking for funds are regularly in competition with National Oil Companies (NOCs) which increasingly act like private corporations. Both types of companies are looking to tap into local and international debt markets. NOCs from developing countries in Asia and Africa now also use pre-payment transactions to obtain immediate funding in exchange for future oil supply (E & Y 2014).

For upstream projects exposed to a specific country risk, investors will also carefully assess whether and how to partner with the host government. Any change in the country's legal or fiscal environment might impact the value, if not the existence, of the investment. For gas projects, which quite often have a high local content, currency risk should not be underestimated. Private Equity funds considering financing projects in developing countries, especially in Africa, might be concerned about the potential lack of exit, as there is almost no option for a public listing on a local capital market.

Project Finance is mainly used in the upstream sector either by smaller IOCs with insufficient balance sheets or, at the other end of the spectrum, by major oil companies whenever the project risk profile requires it (e.g. country risk).

The use of Project Finance is less popular than in other segments of the oil and gas industry, as the revenues of an upstream project still mostly depend on market commodity prices. Like in other Energy segments, the size of the project has an impact on the availability of funds and the profile of investors. Small, pure-play exploration companies are struggling to get support from commercial banks in the absence of proved reserves and cash flow, and often turn to equity issuance. Private Equity funds specialising in oil and gas are likely to consider undervalued projects showing an evidence of successful operation of similar or adjacent operating wells and led by an experienced management team. Following the 2014 oil crash there was a rebound in interest by PE funds, with an estimated record fundraising of US$39bn by around 50 funds (Senchal 2015). PE funds have also been active in the shale industry, especially in the USA, a natural investment environment for large funds. While Energy majors were able to use their balance sheets to obtain access to shale reserves, small independent players had to look for external financing (new debt and issuance of new equity). As the industry matures, they can now increasingly rely on cash flow generated by their own activities.

4.2 Financing Mid and Downstream Oil and Gas Projects

LNG projects were traditionally ideal candidates for Project Finance, with highly capital-intensive development and construction phases, and creditworthy off-takers (oil and gas companies). Debt would usually not exceed 70% of the total project costs, and equity was provided by sponsors such as large oil and gas companies or sovereign-owned oil and gas entities.

In 1996, the Project Financing of RasGas, a JV between Qatar Petroleum and ExxonMobil, launched a new fully integrated structure, under which the SPV had a stake in every stage of the project (liquefaction, storage and upstream assets). A fully integrated project required the support of extremely robust equity sponsors such as oil and gas state-owned companies and conglomerates, able to assess and mitigate the pure reserve risk, but also allowed higher leverage ratios (Czarniak and Howling 2019).

In the 2000s, LNG financing evolved to a tolling model, where the scope of the SPV is reduced to the liquefaction plant only. Under that structure, the LNG is sold by the upstream companies that tolled through the liquefaction plant. More recently a new financing model has emerged, under which the project company shareholders fund the liquefaction plant through their own equity and subsequently take the LNG into their own portfolios (Fig. 17.5).

The very robust US LNG market has seen an increasingly popular use of alternative sources of financing, as lenders are not willing to extend the part of senior debt in the total project costs. Mezzanine offers sponsors some flexibility to help cover potential cost overruns without any dilution of their equity. ECAs, which have always contributed to the financing of LNG projects due to the need to procure highly specialised equipment and materials, are now very active players in the US LNG export projects, especially K-Exim (Korea), the

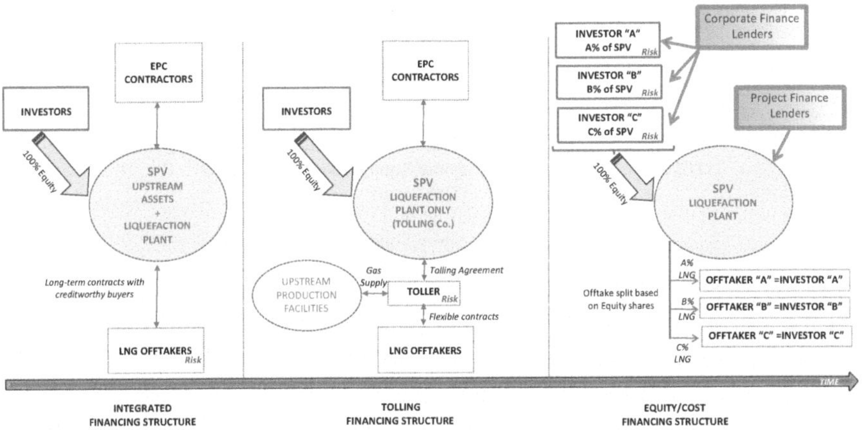

Fig. 17.5 LNG Financing structures—Evolution and innovation. (Source: Authors' elaboration)

Japanese Bank for International Cooperation (JBIC) and US Eximbank (Czarniak and Howling 2019).

A newly built (Greenfield) refinery project has a different risk profile than the upgrade or expansion of an existing asset. A Greenfield project carries pure construction risk coupled with potential country and currency risk, while the upgrade or expansion of a refinery is almost similar to refinancing as it can be mostly funded through traditional loans.

The upgrading of refineries in developing countries, notably to meet European or US standards, can appeal development investors such as World Bank's IFC. The construction of Satorp (Saudi Aramco Total Refining and Petrochemical Company) refinery in Jubail in the early 2010s is a case in point of the variety of financing sources and the complexity of the financial package (Table 17.3). It was the first Project Financing in Saudi Arabia to feature an Islamic bond. Circa 60% of the US$14bn project was financed through debt, a lower level than what was seen before the financial crisis (back in 2004, around 90% of the construction of the Sohar refinery through Project Financing was financed through direct loans of several banks and ECAs). A syndicate of commercial banks agreed to lend US$4.5bn of senior debt at a competitive rate, and several ECAs, together with Saudi Arabia's Public Investment Fund invested another US$4bn. The remaining part of the SPV was financed by the project sponsors, Aramco (62.5% of the SPV) and Total (37.5% of the SPV).

5 Conclusion

As already noted in the introduction of this chapter, the ways to finance Energy projects is not one but many. Depending on the size, the location, the technology, the level of reassurance that investors can get on future revenues, the

Table 17.3 Complexity of a greenfield refinery financing—Satorp refinery in Jubail (based on Petroleum Economist 2010)

Nature of funds	*Source of funds*	*Amount Invested (Estimated in US$ bn)*	*Notes*
Equity <40% of total Project Costs	ARAMCO TOTAL	62.5% of Satorp Equity (US$3.5bn) 37.5% of Satorp Equity (US$3.5bn)	Structure of Satorp JV follows Islamic Finance principles
Debt >60% of total Project Costs	**7 ECAs** Korea Export Insurance Corporation K-ExIm (Korea) Japan Bank for International Co. operation Nippon Export and Investment Insurance CESCE (Spain) COFACE (France) Euler Hermes (Germany)	US$2.7bn	Direct loans and debt cover
	12 LOCAL COMMERCIAL BANKS	US$1.4bn of both US$ and SAR 16-year sharia compliant debt US$0.5bn equivalent of conventional 16 years RAS debt	Conventional position of the SAR denominated debt is priced below banks' cost of funds Local banks are in a club deal
	19 INTERNATIONAL COMMERCIAL BANKS Credit Agricole Societe Generale KFW Bank Deutsche Bank EDC Sumitomo Mitsui Banking Corporation Bank of Tokyo Mizuho Corporate Bank Standard Chartered Bank Barclays Citibank JPMorgan RBS APICORP Gulf International Bank Riyadh Bank Banque Saudi Fransi HSBC Arab Bank	US$1.6bn of 16-year US$ debt	International banks in a club deal Lending not far above cost of funds
	PUBLIC INVESTMENT FUND	US$1.3bn	Saudi Arabia sovereign wealth fund
	SPONSOR LOAN/ ISLAMIC BOND	US$1bn	This US$1bn was initially to be funded through the first ever Islamic Bond ("Sukuk") but its structuring was not completed when the construction started. Aramco and Total agreed to provide each a senior shareholder loan of almost US$0.5bn to cover first stages of construction. Once finally arranged, the bond carried the same tenor as the rest of the financial package.

Source: Authors' elaboration based on Petroleum Economist 2010

financing of some projects will be finalised and implemented, while others will be dropped.

Beyond the specificities of each financing, there are however a few facts and trends which are true for most Energy projects.

First, to quote the International Energy Agency in its World Energy Investment 2019 report, current investment in Energy is "poorly aligned with future needs and challenges". This is very likely to translate into an increased competition between projects to attract funds in the very near future. Growing investment needs, especially for renewable Energy projects but not only, will require new sources of capital, such as institutional investors. This category of investors is attracted by bond-type investments and stable cash flows, which can be delivered for example through insurance products, the development of which is then likely to flourish in the coming years.

Second, except maybe for nuclear plant projects, there have been significant cost reductions in all Energy projects over the last decade, together with a shift towards shorter construction time (IEA 2019). Here again, this could lead to increased interest from institutional investors, as it lowers the projects' risk level. We could add that development finance institutions have not only played a facilitating role, but have now become key financing actors across all Energy segments.

Finally, most Energy investments are now facing new financing challenges. If the rise in interest rates was to continue, most of the projects could be adversely impacted and sponsors would have to replace the funding traditionally provided by commercial loans with new sources.

Would governmental support to renewable Energy stop, as it seems to be the case in the USA in the coming years, projects would then depend on power purchase agreements or simply merchant power prices. A new source of financing could come from corporate PPAs, currently only accounting for 5% of solar PV and wind investment. Global oil and gas companies are also increasingly active in financing renewable Energy assets, either by investing directly into renewable Energy projects through dedicated subsidiaries or by taking equity participations into renewable Energy companies such as research and development companies focusing on Energy efficiency. In the context of a necessary Energy transition and increasing investment into renewable Energy sources, it will be imperative to understand where new funds are originally stemming from.

References

CPI—Climate Policy Initiative, David Nelson and Gireesh Shrimali (2014). Finance Mechanisms for Lowering the Cost of Renewable Energy in Rapidly Developing Countries. Retrieved from https://climatepolicyinitiative.org/wp-content/uploads/2014/01/Finance-Mechanisms-for-Lowering-the-Cost-of-Clean-Energy-in-Rapidly-Developing-Countries.pdf

Czarniak, J.A., & Howling, G.D. (2019). Current Trends in LNG Development and Construction. The International Comparative Legal Guide to: Project Finance

2019. 8th edition. Global Legal Group Ltd., London. Retrieved from https://www.skadden.com/insights/publications/2019/05/iclg-project-finance

DiaCore Project. (2016). Assessing Renewables policy in the EU. Key findings from the DiaCore project. Retrieved from http://diacore.eu/images/files2/DIA-CORE_Final_Brochure.pdf

E & Y—ERNST & YOUNG. (2014). Funding challenges in the oil and gas sector. Innovative financing solutions for oil and gas companies. Retrieved from https://www.ey.com/Publication/vwLUAssets/EY-Funding-challenges-in-the-oil-and-gas-sector/$FILE/EY-Funding-challenges-in-the-oil-and-gas-sector.pdf

Feldman, David, and Paul SCHWABE / NREL. 2018. *Terms, Trends, and Insights on PV Project Finance in the United States, 2018*. Golden, CO: National Renewable Energy Laboratory. NREL/TP-6A20-72037. Retrieved from https://www.nrel.gov/docs/fy19osti/72037.pdf

Frankfurt School—UNEP Centre & BNEF. (2018). Global Trends in Renewable Energy investment 2018. Retrieved from http://www.iberglobal.com/files/2018/renewable_trends.pdf

IEA—International Energy Agency. (2019). World Energy Investment 2019. Retrieved after download from https://www.iea.org/wei2019/

IFC / Fichtner—International Finance Corporation / Fichtner. (2017). Hydroelectric power. A Guide for Developers and Investors. Retrieved from https://www.ifc.org/wps/wcm/connect/906fa13c-2f47-4476-9476-75320e08e5f3/Hydropower_Report.pdf?MOD=AJPERES&CVID=kJQl35z

IRENA—International Renewable Energy Agency. (2016). Unlocking Renewable Energy Investment: the role of risk mitigation and structured finance. Retrieved after download from https://www.irena.org/publications/2016/Jun/Unlocking-Renewable-Energy-Investment-The-role-of-risk-mitigation-and-structured-finance

Irwin, O., Pridgeon, B., & Knox, G. (2019). Growing Complexity of ECA Financing. Bracewell LLP. Retrieved from https://bracewell.com/sites/default/files/news-files/PFI%20Global%202019%20-%20Growing%20Complexity%20of%20ECA%20Financing.pdf

Latham and Watkins. (2009). Why Project Bonds Now? Client Alert, Number 914. Retrieved from https://www.lw.com/thoughtLeadership/why-project-bonds-now

NEA—Nuclear Energy Agency. (2009). The Financing of Nuclear Power Plants. Retrieved from https://www.oecd-nea.org/ndd/reports/2009/financing-plants.pdf

Petroleum Economist. (2010, July 15). Aramco, Total sign Jubail refinery financing. Retrieved from https://www.petroleum-economist.com/articles/markets/trends/2010/aramco-total-sign-jubail-refinery-financing

Ren21. (2019). Renewables 2019. Global Status Report. Retrieved after download from https://www.ren21.net/reports/global-status-report/

Senchal, O. (2015). Preqin Industry News. Retrieved from https://docs.preqin.com/newsletters/pe/PESL-March-15-Industry-News.pdf

SWISS RE./BNEF (Bloomberg New Energy Finance). (2013). Profiling the risks in solar and wind. A case for new risk management approaches in the renewable energy sector. Retrieved after download from https://www.bnef.com

Wind Europe. (2017). Financing and investment trends. The European Wind industry in 2016. Retrieved after download from https://windeurope.org/about-wind/reports/financing-investment-trends-2016/

World Economic Forum. (2017). Renewable Infrastructure Investment Handbook: A Guide for Institutional Investors. Retrieved from http://www3.weforum.org/docs/WEF_Renewable_Infrastructure_Investment_Handbook.pdf

Zank, S. (2019)—Scope Ratings. "Germany's grid operators face growing multi-billion euro investment challenge". Retrieved from https://www.scoperatings.com/ScopeRatingsApi/api/downloadstudy?id=79fb4e35-2a1c-4e07-95d4-f3ae8d0ca6fe

Recommended Readings

African Development Bank. (2019, August 01). African Development Bank helps power wind of change in Kenya. Retrieved from https://www.afdb.org/en/news-and-events/african-development-bank-helps-power-wind-change-kenya-28239

Baker and Mckenzie. (2014). Global update and Africa Focus. Export Credit and Development Finance. Retrieved from https://www.bakermckenzie.com/-/media/files/insight/publications/2014/09/global-update-and-africa-focus-export-credit-and__/files/read-publication/fileattachment/arfc_bf_exportcreditreport_sep14.pdf

BP. (2019a). Statistical Review of World Energy 2019, 68th Edition. Retrieved fromhttps://www.bp.com/content/dam/bp/business-sites/en/global/corporate/pdfs/energy-economics/statistical-review/bp-stats-review-2019-full-report.pdf

BP. (2019b). BP Energy Outlook: 2019 edition. Retrieved from https://www.bp.com/content/dam/bp/business-sites/en/global/corporate/pdfs/energy-economics/energy-outlook/bp-energy-outlook-2019.pdf

Eckert, V. (2019, February 4). German Grid Firms see extra costs to meet renewable power target. Retrieved from https://www.reuters.com/article/us-germany-powergrids-plan/german-grid-firms-see-extra-costs-to-meet-renewable-power-target-idUSKCN1PT1LS

IGU—International Gas Union. (2018). 2018 World LNG Report—27th World Gas Conference Edition. Retrieved from https://www.igu.org/sites/default/files/node-document-field_file/IGU_LNG_2018_0.pdf

Lazard. (2018). Levelized Cost of Energy and Levelized Cost of Storage 2018. Retrieved from https://www.lazard.com/media/450784/lazards-levelized-cost-of-energy-version-120-vfinal.pdf

Marks, E.L., & Nicolaides, C.M. (2014). Understanding Basel III. Retrieved from https://www.lw.com/presentations/understanding-basel-III-2014

Razavi, H. (2007). Financing Energy projects in developing countries (2nd ed.). USA. PennWell Books.

UKERC—UK Energy Research Centre. (2014). UKERC Energy Strategy under uncertainties. Financing the Power Sector: Is the Money Available? Retrieved from https://ukerc.rl.ac.uk/UCAT/PUBLICATIONS/Financing_the_Power_Sector_-Is_the_Money_Available.pdf

World Bank. (2014). Sustainable Energy for all: Sector Results profile. Retrieved from https://www.worldbank.org/en/results/2013/04/10/sustainable-energy-for-all-results-profile

PART II

Economics of Energy Trading and Price Discovery

CHAPTER 18

The Trading and Price Discovery for Crude Oils

Adi Imsirovic

1 Introduction: Global Oil Markets

The oil market is by far the biggest commodity market in the world. Several billion dollars of physical oil is bought and sold every day. However, this is only tip of the iceberg. Not only are some cargoes often traded more than once, but a whole array of forward, futures, swaps, options and other derivative products have developed around physical exchanges. On August 16, 2019, in a single day, the two main oil exchanges traded, in two crude oil futures contracts alone, an equivalent of well over two months of global oil production.[1] This was an exceptional day, following an attack on Saudi oil facilities. However, this did not stop traders in the US, Europe or anywhere else in the world from buying US light sweet crude oil or North Sea Brent futures contracts, thousands of miles away from the areas affected by the conflict. Oil markets are linked by these commonly traded types of oil (or 'benchmarks'), creating one global pool. This is oil markets' most interesting feature: oil derivatives trade in far greater volumes than physical oil, and a majority of the physical barrels are not traded at all: they are supplied on long-term contracts at the price set by one of the global benchmarks. Thanks to the derivatives associated with these benchmarks, oil can seamlessly flow around the globe with relatively little risk. As we shall show, the world oil markets are all about benchmarks and their working.

[1] NYMEX saw 3.68 million WTI futures and options change hands. ICE had 3.12 million contracts of Brent futures and options traded. Each contract is 1000 barrels (bbls) equation to almost 7 billion barrels! It was an exceptional day, following drone attacks on Saudi oil facilities.

A. Imsirovic (✉)
Oxford Institute of Energy Studies, Oxford, UK
e-mail: adi.imsirovic@oxfordenergy.org

M. Hafner, G. Luciani (eds.), *The Palgrave Handbook of International Energy Economics*, https://doi.org/10.1007/978-3-030-86884-0_18

It helps that oil is relatively easily transported and stored, so that factors influencing prices in one market very quickly spread and resonate in all other oil markets. However, global oil markets, prices and their interactions have taken decades to develop. The first section of this chapter will give a historical perspective and understanding of how and why oil markets developed, why they are so volatile and why they have their current form.

There are hundreds of different types of crude oil which can substantially differ in quality.[2] Over time, their prices evolved as differentials to most commonly traded benchmarks. Benchmarks are well accepted, commonly used, types of crude oil that have many buyers and sellers with prices which are very liquid and transparent.[3] The main global benchmarks are West Texas Intermediate (WTI) in the US, Brent in Europe and Dubai and Oman in Asia. Their prices reflect their quality and fundamental factors prevailing in the regions in which they trade. We shall discuss the main regional benchmarks, how they work and all the main derivative markets associated with them. Benchmarks have their own dynamics and they change as markets change. They evolve over time and new, competing benchmarks emerge. All of this will be discussed in the second half of this chapter.

Global oil markets are linked by arbitrage. If gasoline rich oil from Vietnam becomes scarce and dear, similar quality of oil from Libya, Norway or the US will soon find its way to Asia. This is possible to do in a relatively riskless manner, thanks to well developed and mature 'paper' markets around the benchmarks in each region, with layers of associated derivative products designed to mitigate specific risks. For example, moving oil from Norway to Asia does not only involve buying and selling physical oil and shipping it. The whole process takes at least a couple of months and price risk over this period is enormous. Managing the risk between the purchase and sale is likely to involve 'locking in' the Brent—Dubai arbitrage[4] (through a 'swap spread' or exchange for swaps—EFS[5]), hedging with forwards or futures and 'contracts for differences' (CFDs),[6] exchange for physicals (EFPs),[7] 'rolling' some contracts (through spreads) and so on. Interactions between the benchmarks, derivative instruments associated with them, arbitrage and global oil flows will be discussed in the last section.

[2] It is probably impossible to count them. Most grades of oil are themselves blends of oil from different fields. The most important differences are in specific gravity (often expressed as AP index) and sulphur content. But this is just a tip of an iceberg as yield of particular products, product qualities, acidity and so on are important.

[3] For discussion on actors involve in assessing oil benchmarks, see Owain Johnson: 'The Price Reporters: A Guide to PRAs and Commodity Benchmarks', Routledge 2018.

[4] North Sea crude trades on Brent Dated basis, while Asian grades may trade on Dubai basis.

[5] EFS for December for example is a spread between December Brent futures contract and Dubai swaps for December.

[6] CFD in oil market usually refers to a spread between Dated and forward Brent.

[7] EFP is a swap of futures for cash or physical barrels.

Over time, market participants have evolved into two primary groups: 'Price takers' accept market prices as given and use them to manage risk. Usually, they are producing, or 'upstream' companies, refiners and other commercial entities involved in physical oil, and their primary focus is to reduce the price risk. 'Price makers' are companies actively involved in the price-making process by trading benchmarks and in the process, taking some price risk. In most cases, they are 'buyers of risk' and comprise of trading companies, banks, investment funds and the like. Of course, the picture is not clear-cut, and many major oil companies involve production, transport, refining as well as trading. The role of 'risk takers' or speculators in shaping the oil market and oil prices is discussed. Key market players will be discussed in detail.

Oil has become and asset class in its own right. High oil prices tend to be negatively correlated with a number of assets such as bonds and equities.[8] This makes oil derivatives potentially attractive assets in any portfolio. 'Financializaton' of oil has introduced new actors into the oil markets and changed dynamics of trading and oil prices. 'Financialization' of oil markets, new methods of trading such as algorithmic trading (often referred to as 'black box' trading) and artificial intelligence (AI) and their impact will be discussed in the final section. The concluding remarks will summarise the main points of the chapter and hint at possible future development of the oil markets (Fig. 18.1).

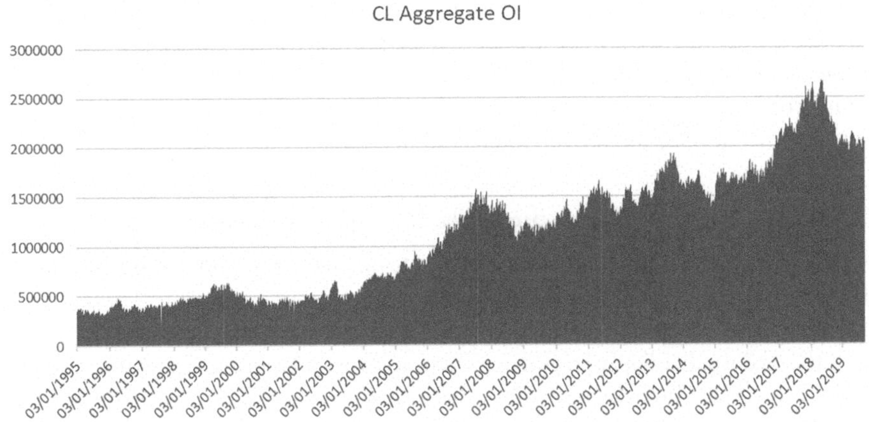

Fig. 18.1 WTI Open Interest (OI) on CME Exchange (Number of contracts, each 1000 barrels) indicating a relentless growth in oil trading over time. Data from CME. (Source: Author's elaboration)

[8] In a nutshell, high oil prices may lead to inflation, eroding bond yield. Higher interest rates (to combat inflation resulting from higher oil prices) undermine equity valuations. There is a huge amount of literature on effects of oil prices on trade and economy.

2 Oil Industry and Markets: A Brief Historical Introduction

History of oil markets is a history of natural monopoly, booms and busts.

Natural monopoly can emerge in perfectly competitive markets. Economists define it by presence of both economies of scale and 'sub-additivity'. The latter simply means that it is more efficient (cheaper) to have one provider than two or more. Oil projects tend to be big, capital intensive with long gestation periods, with assets specific that can be used for very specific purposes and usually, for very long-time periods. Capital spending tends to be front-loaded, with returns on investments enjoyed many years later. After the capital has been sunk, the operating costs are relatively small, making it harder to reduce or stop the use of assets. Drilling rigs, pipelines and refineries are only a few good examples. This makes energy projects sensitive to prices, interest rates and politics. They are risky.

Large energy investments usually come in discrete, indivisible 'chunks' to achieve economies of scale. Refineries, ships, pipelines and other assets are designed and built to an optimal size that is difficult to adjust and change quickly. Economies of scale make one larger project cheaper than several small ones for the same purpose. Natural monopolies are generally resolved either by breaking the integrated structures (caused by new technologies, entrants, supplies etc.) or by government regulation.

Breaking monopolies has generally led to emergence of competitive markets, lower prices and technological improvements. Competition can lead to extreme volatility and even waste while monopoly can give energy markets predictability and stability. Of course, on the downside, monopoly normally leads to higher prices and barriers to entry and change. For this reason, examining the market structure and the way it changes over time can give us an insight into development of markets and prices.

2.1 *Beginnings of the Oil Industry in the US*

In the early days of the industry in Pennsylvania in 1860s and 1870s, discoveries led to a rush for drilling and intense competition to produce, refine and transport the commodity. But the 'boom' soon led to overproduction, waste and the eventual collapse in prices. Then, as now, producers made attempts to reduce output,[9] but cheating and free-riding was common, with disastrous results. Between 1860 and 1862, oil prices fell from $20 to $0.20 per barrel (McNally 2019).[10] These booms and bust cycles went on well into the end of the century. It was the railroads, another 'natural monopoly', that helped Rockefeller tame and ultimately control the oil industry (Tarbell 1904).[11] This

[9] For example, the Oil Creek Association formed in Pennsylvania in 1861.

[10] Robert McNally: 'Crude Volatility' page 15.

[11] See Ida Tarbell: 'The History of the Standard Oil Company'

kind of control of the industry from drilling to marketing of products (and everything in between) is called 'vertical integration'. It protected monopoly and prices by creating 'barriers to entry'.[12] But during the Rockefeller monopoly, price volatility fell by about a half (McNally 2019).[13] Although his Standard oil company was broken up in 1911 by the Roosevelt administration, its legacy will live on in companies that inherited it: ExxonMobil, Chevron and others and will dominate the oil markets in the 1950s and in some ways, ever since. Government intervention in the oil industry not only continued but also intensified from the British government's purchase of 51% of British Petroleum (Anglo-Persian Oil company) in 1913, 'Texas Railroad Commission' in the 1930s, nationalisations and the birth of OPEC in 1960 to the lifting of the US oil exports ban in the 2015. Strategic importance of oil in the transportation sector facilitated the World War I and was probably one of the ultimate goals (or 'The Prize')[14] (Yergin 1991) in the Second one.

2.2 The 'Majors'

In the 1950s and 1960s, international oil markets were largely controlled by large oil companies or oligopoly of oil 'Majors' (Yergin 1991).[15] Aside from being vertically integrated, the industry was also integrated 'horizontally'; oil was carefully supplied from various geographic areas to ensure that supply and demand were balanced at lowest possible cost. Such integration enabled the supply of oil to be fine-tuned to the prevailing demand for end products, thus ensuring price stability.

Horizontal integration was done through joint ownership of several operating companies throughout the Middle East (ARAMCO, Anglo-Persian—later to become British Petroleum, Kuwait Oil Company etc.). These joint ventures continued historical and old colonial links involving the British, American, French and other governments. Companies worked with and closely followed the strategic interest of their governments. They operated through mutual agreements, preventing 'harmful' competition.[16] The share of each Major oil company in any of the markets was to remain 'As-Is'[17] (in line with the prevailing market shares in 1928). Also, the world oil markets were to be supplied without 'disruptive price competition' (Yergin 1991).[18]

[12] Producers without transportation would face higher costs, refiners without petrol stations would be forced to sell cheaper and so on; soon, they would be driven out of business.

[13] R. McNally, page 32.

[14] Hence the name of the book by D. Yergin: 'The Prize', Simon & Schuster 1991.

[15] Ibid. pp. 475.

[16] In the international scene, oil production from Baku, now Azerbaijan, Dutch East Indies, now Indonesia as well as large discoveries in Texas and Oklahoma (Spindletop in 1901, for example) also caused an oversupply. This led to fierce price wars in the early 1900 involving Standard Oil and Shell. Agreements were designed to prevent this.

[17] 'As was' might have been a better name.

[18] D. Yergin, pp. 264.

Mechanisms for controlling these large petroleum reserves were ingenious, generally based on various 'rules' such as Average Program Quantity (APQ) in Iran, the 'Five Sevenths' rule in Iraq and the 'Dividend Squeeze' in Saudi Arabia (Sampson 1988).[19] Monopoly prices were charged using 'Gulf Plus System'; all delivered oil prices included freight cost from the US Gulf regardless of its origin.[20] By 1950, the 'Seven Sisters'[21] owned 70% of the world refining capacity outside the Communist block and North America, almost 100% of the pipeline networks and over 60% of the world's privately owned tanker fleet. They priced crude oil using 'posted prices' to maximise they own revenues within their vertically integrated systems. The producing countries were receiving royalties on percentage basis and posted prices were kept low to minimise this cost. They had done so through collusion while it was possible[22] and through joint ventures which provided them with information to control the market and avoid competition. As Fig. 18.2 below illustrates, during this 'golden period' of their reign, oil prices were low and very stable.

2.3 The 'Independents'

Towards the end of the 1950s, cracks were appearing in this structure. Existing oil producers such as Venezuela and Iran were pushing for higher production and revenues. Large profits of the oil 'Majors' were attracting 'newcomers' in terms of smaller 'independent'[23] oil companies. These newcomers, such as

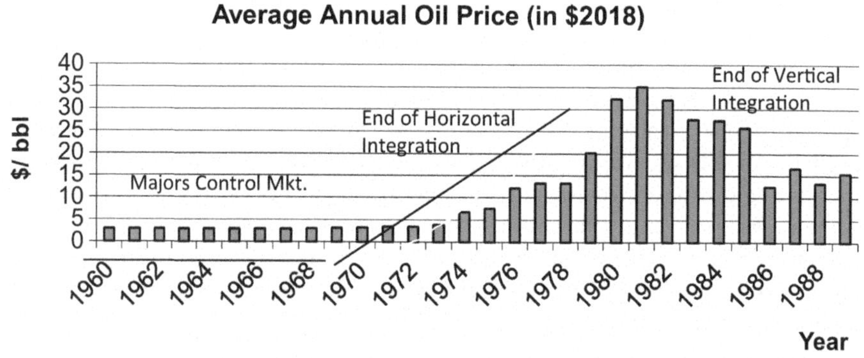

Fig. 18.2 Major oil companies control of the market and prices. Author, prices, BP Statistical Review. (Source: Author's elaboration)

[19] 'Seven Sisters' A. Sampson 1988 pp. 145.

[20] For example, if BP supplied Iranian oil to Italy, they would charge much higher freight, from the US Gulf to Italy, even though they never incurred that cost. See A. Sampson, pp. 90.

[21] 'Seven Sisters' were Exxon, Shell, BP, Chevron and Texaco (now Chevron), Gulf and Mobil (now both Exxon).

[22] Although illegal in most jurisdictions.

[23] The term loosely means companies 'other than Majors'. In USA, these were Amoco, Sohio, Conoco, Atlantic Richfield (Arco), Occidental and some others. By and large, they emerged from

J.P. Getty paid producing countries more for concessions and offered higher royalties (Sampson 1988).[24] Despite paying a lot more, Getty still made a fortune. It did not go unnoticed among the producers. In 1956, a French State oil company Elf[25] discovered oil in Algeria. In Libya, the 1955 Petroleum Law offered many smaller concessions and stricter terms for exploration than the existing producers did (Yergin 1991).[26] In 1956, BP and Shell found oil in Nigeria. More than half of the Libyan production ended up in the hands of companies which had no integrated systems in Europe (such as Conoco, Marathon and Amerada Hess) and hence no outlets for the oil. In 1959, ENI started importing cheap Russian oil from the Urals region into Italy, undercutting prices set by the Majors. By the end of 1950s, the USSR became the second largest producer in the world, after the US. It produced a volume of oil that could compete with the Middle East (Yergin 1991).[27] At the same time, the US had an import quota system, designed to protect the domestic oil producers (Sampson 1988).[28] This legislation left the independents 'stranded' with the oil which had to find markets elsewhere, in the world markets and put further pressure on prices. These newcomers, not unlike the shale producers now, were keen to get the oil out of the ground quickly and secure a return to their investment. Despite growing demand in this period (Yergin 1991),[29] the excess supply was becoming obvious. Oil had to be offered at a discount to the posted prices. This was making the royalties paid to the producing countries effectively higher than the 'usual' 50% prevalent at the time. The Majors were losing not only money and market share, but also the ability to balance the supply and demand and thus prices.

The integrated structure of the industry was crumbling. In 1946, nine oil companies operated in the Middle East. By 1970, this number reached 81 (Yergin 1991)[30]! By 1966, very little crude was traded at posted prices. In the 1960–1965 period, Majors' share of the European refining capacity fell from 67% to 54%. This intensified competition in the products markets reducing the refinery margin and putting further pressure on the oil prices. The growing

Texas, which, in 1960 produced some 39% of US oil. Libya was a stepping stone for Amerada (Hess), Continental and Marathon. Occidental took off in Russia and Getty in S. Arabia and later Iran. In Europe, 'independents' included French Total (CFP) and Elf, Italian Agip (ENI), Belgian Petrofina and others. For an excellent narrative, see A. Sampson, chapter 7, 'The Intruders'.

[24] A. Sampson pp. 157. In Saud Arabia, Getty made a $9.5 m down payment and offered higher royalties for exploration and production in the Neutral Zone, between S. Arabia and Kuwait. Getty was later bought by Texaco, which in turn, was bought or 'merged' with Chevron.

[25] Later to merge with and become 'Total'.

[26] D. Yergin pp. 528.

[27] D. Yergin pp. 515.

[28] A. Sampson 1988 pp. 161.

[29] Between 1948 and 1972, the US consumption tripled, European demand increased fifteen times, and in Japan, it increased 137 times over! D. Yergin pp. 541.

[30] D. Yergin pp. 531.

competition[31] for oil concessions between the Majors and the 'independent oil companies', coupled with the falling oil prices (Yergin 1991)[32] put increasing pressure on the relationships between the oil producing countries and the Majors.

2.4 The Oil Cartel

In 1950s, a new breed of populist leaders emerged in some of the producing countries Nasser in Egypt, Muammar al-Qaddafi in Libya, Boumediene in Algiers, Abdullah Tariki in Saudi Arabia and Perez Alfonso in Venezuela. Apart from being better educated, they sheared strong anti-colonial feelings. The Algerian President argued for the producing countries to lead the 'Third World' towards a more equitable and just global world order (Sampson 1988).[33] Better terms offered to producers by the 'newcomers' made it very clear that the 'old' terms agreed with the Majors were a bad deal. On 9th of August 1969, Exxon, the largest Major and a price leader, announced a posted price cut of up to 14 cents per barrel without warning or consulting the governments of the producing countries. Other Majors in the M. East followed suit. The producing countries were outraged and swiftly arranged a meeting on September 10th in Baghdad.[34] Four days later, OPEC was born. Its major objective was to defend the price of oil (Bhattacharyya 2011).[35] OPEC was coloured by political ideas of the time. Nationalisation echoed from the OPEC Caracas meeting in December 1970 and Qaddafi implemented it after the Beirut meeting of the cartel in 1971.[36]

The early 70s ended an era of the control of the crude oil industry by the Major oil companies. The control of production decisions shifted from these companies to the national governments of oil producing countries, usually through their national monopolies. The idea was that the national oil companies (NOCs) would give them power to decide output and hence influence the oil prices. Since NOCs had few assets such as ships, refineries and distribution networks, the distinction between buyers and sellers of oil in the international markets became obvious. As the market control by the Majors broke up, oil price (as illustrated in Fig. 18.2 below) became highly volatile.[37]

[31] For example, the auction in Venezuela in 1956 attracted generous bids. Also, the bidding for the Iranian offshore areas attracted 33 companies.

[32] Between 1960 and 1969, the oil price fell by 22% and in real terms by 40% D. Yergin pp. 529.

[33] A. Sampson 1988 pp. 20.

[34] S. Arabia, Venezuela, Kuwait, Iraq and Iran.

[35] For an excellent summary of various economic models of OPEC behaviour, see Bhattacharyya (2011) pp. 344.

[36] The process of nationalisation started in March 1938 in Mexico and 1951 in Iran.

[37] It is well summarised in: 'Crude Volatility' by Robert McNally, Columbia University Press 2017. Between October 1973 and January 1974, the price of Arab Light jumped from \$2.8 to \$10.84/ barrel and from \$18 to \$30/ barrel between October 1979 and October 1980.

3 'Spot' Market and Prices

Following the collapse of the horizontal integration in the early 70s, the vertical integration of the industry ended with the fall of Shah of Iran in 1979. After the revolution, the Majors were forced to cancel the third-party oil deliveries from the country, which drove buyers of oil into the spot market (Treat 1990).[38] With no vertically integrated market tightly controlled by the companies, discrepancies between nomination dates, quantities, types and location of crude oil purchased by refiners became an issue.[39] To remedy these problems, long-term contract holders had to swap and trade different types of oil among themselves. The result was a massive growth of the volume of spot trades from some 3–5% in January 1979 to about 15–20% (Treat 1990)[40] by March of the same year.

Throughout its history, OPEC has had a fair share of infighting in their ranks, mainly over pricing policy and the fundamental long-term strategy. This was particularly obvious in the 1980 conference in Algiers where a lack of agreement led to a 'free for all' policy. By adhering to the system of 'Official Prices' which most of OPEC was abandoning (due to competition and oversupply, they were too high), Saudi Arabia was forced to reduce the volumes and take on the role of a 'swing producer'.[41] But the rigid official prices were falling out of line with the 'real' spot market. The House of Saud rejected a continuous decline in the volume of their exports (exports fell from about 10 mbd to just 3 mbd between 1980 and 1986!). They opted to recover their share of the world market by selling their oil at 'netback' prices.[42] A year later, the oil prices fell to $8/ barrel (World Bank 1995).[43] With OPEC unable to control the supply, the industry resembled the early days of intense competition, booms and

[38] Although this process accelerated following the Iranian revolution, it had its roots in the early 70s. In ten years following the Arab embargo in 1973, the oil available to the Majors fell by nearly 50%. Equity volumes fell even more, by about 75%. Overall fall in their share of the internationally traded oil was from 62% to 37%. Source: 'Energy Futures' ed. J E Treat, PennWell Publishing 1990 pp. 11.

[39] When an oil refinery is designed and built, it is done with a particular supply of oil in mind. When that supply is lost, refineries have to look for similar alternatives which may well be more expensive or simply hard to find on regular basis.

[40] Ibid.

[41] Saudi Arabia was forced to take on a role of a 'swing' producer, absorbing the impact of changes in supply and demand. Ever since the last Iraqi war, the Saudis have used their large excess capacity to balance the market and regain its leadership status within the cartel.

[42] The price is set to be equal to the value of the products derived from the given crude. In effect, it guaranteed a refinery margin which, in periods of excess refining capacity which prevailed at the time, resulted in falling products prices. This, in turn, led to a collapse of the oil prices.

[43] This was due to a fall in demand that responded to the 1979 peaks as well to an increase in supplies due to the same reason. In the 1979 to 1985 period, oil's share of primary energy demand fell from 48% to 40%. World Bank Discussion Papers no. 3011995. pp. 1. A similar event will happen later, at the end of 2014, in response to the growing US shale output.

busts. With growing volatility,[44] the price risk had to be managed. This was especially the case as the term supplies from OPEC countries were generally of a long-haul nature.[45] In a volatile market, the price could significantly change between the time of purchase and delivery, exposing both seller and buyer to a large financial risk. The risk could be 'hedged' by selling relatively liquid forward Brent crude at the time of purchase and buying it back around the time of delivery. To make this risk management easier, the International Petroleum Exchange was launched in 1980, soon followed by an oil contract underpinned by the largest single grade in the North Sea, the Brent Blend.[46]

Given that neither the official OPEC prices nor the 'netback' prices were acceptable any longer, a system of 'spot' related formulae prices was gradually adopted.[47] By 1987, over 60% of the oil prices were tied to the spot market prices.[48] This marked the birth of the modern oil market. This principle of setting prices for individual grades of oil against a published benchmark[49] has not changed to this day.

4 Oil Price Benchmarks

In all energy markets, government policy is critical, and oil is no exception. In response to the Arab oil embargo of 1973, US government imposed price controls through the Emergency Petroleum and Allocation Act (EPAA). In a well-supplied market of 1981, the US government lifted these controls, opening the markets to competition, trading and transparency. This 'liberalisation' of the market was instrumental for the success of the new, 'paper' contract for the domestic light sweet crude, West Texas Intermediate (WTI) with a delivery point in Cushing, Oklahoma. The contract was listed by the New York Mercantile Exchange (NYMEX) in March 1983, alongside then existing heating oil and gasoline contracts. It was a physical oil delivery contract, designed to mimic well established, physical trading around the Cushing hub.

[44] The official Saudi (and other OPEC) prices were not changed frequently enough to follow the volatility of prices in the spot market. For example, in the 1979 Geneva OPEC meeting, the Arab Light price was increased from \$18 to \$24/ barrel as the spot price rocketed to \$45/ barrel.

[45] A very large crude carrier (VLCC) would take about six weeks to arrive to NWE from the Arab Gulf.

[46] Ninian crude was added in 1990, all still loaded at the Sullom Voe terminal in the Shetland Islands, Scotland.

[47] The national Oil Company Pemex of Mexico pioneered it. It involves setting 'official' discounts relative to oil frequently traded in spot markets and called benchmarks such as Brent or WTI. These discounts (or premiums) are usually set once per month and reflect relative quality difference as measured by value of end product which they yield in the refinery. The 'absolute' price level is set on daily basis by the Benchmark crude.

[48] OPEC Bulletin Nov/Dec 1988 pp. 18.

[49] For example, Saudi official selling price (OSP) to Asia in November 2019 would be the average of Dubai and Oman prices +\$3.00. In a similar fashion, it would be set against WTI for sales to the US and against Brent for sales to Europe. Since the Saudis have no influence on Dated Brent itself, they are price takers.

OPEC pricing arrangements were also challenged by large discoveries outside the cartel members, particularly in the North Sea. The Ekofisk oilfield was discovered in 1969 in Norway by Amoco, the Forties field in 1970 by BP and the Brent field in 1971 by Shell (McGrandle 1975).[50] By 1980, the North Sea production was 2 million barrels per day (mbd), making the region an important supplier of non-OPEC crude oil. Underpinned by English law, standardised contracts,[51] no destination restrictions and tax advantages in 'spinning' or 'churning' the cargoes, North Sea Brent market developed as the prime, transparent and liquid spot market (Mabro and Horsnell 1993; Fattouh 2010).[52] Price reporting agencies (PRAs) Argus and Platts added to transparency of the market.[53] The benchmarks were set by participants in the spot and paper markets ('price makers') while the producers became 'price takers'.[54] Oil price became the price of one of these grades. All the risk management involved derivative markets which grew alongside Brent, WTI and Dubai. These benchmarks became the backbone of oil trading.

4.1 West Texas Intermediate (WTI)

Throughout the modern history, the US has been the world single largest regional market.[55] Cushing, Oklahoma is at the crossroads of the US pipelines linking production in Oklahoma and West Texas (Midland), and the refining centres of Midwest, Midcontinent and US Gulf (see Fig. 18.3 below) in the country. Together with a massive storage capacity in tens of millions of barrels[56] and a large number of participants, the hub ensures unprecedented liquidity in trading light sweet crude oil,[57] surpassed at times only by Intercontinental Exchange (ICE)[58] Brent oil contract.

Interaction between the oil gathering centres, pipelines, refining and import/ export facilities is the key to understanding development and dynamics of the WTI benchmark. As domestic production and refining changed, so

[50] Leith McGrandle: The Story of North Sea Oil, Wayland 1975.

[51] Such as Brent 'SUKO 1990' (Shell UK 1990) contract.

[52] For a comprehensive introduction, see Mabro and Horsnell (1993); and Fattouh (2010) R. Mabro and P. Horsnell: *Oil Markets and Prices, The Brent market and the Formation of World Oil Prices*, OUP/OIES 1993. See also, B. Fattouh (2010) 'An Anatomy of the Crude Oil Pricing System', OIES Paper WPM 40.

[53] Platts started publishing its 'Crude Oil Market Wire' in 1978 and in the same year, Argus started first daily reporting on the emerging spot crude market in the 'Argus Telex'.

[54] For detailed discussion on the subject, see the last section in the chapter as well as footnote #121.

[55] At the time of writing, US demand is close to 20 mbd and production about 12.5 mbd.

[56] At the time of writing in 2019, about 77 million barrels of storage was available in Cushing.

[57] To be delivered as WTI, oil has to meet the following specifications: Sulphur: 0.42% or less; Gravity: Not less than 37 degrees API, nor more than 42 degrees API Viscosity: Maximum 60 Saybolt Universal Seconds at 100 degrees Fahrenheit; Reid vapor pressure: Less than 9.5 pounds per square inch at 100 degrees Fahrenheit; Basic Sediment, water and other impurities: Less than 1%; Pour Point: Not to exceed 50 degrees Fahrenheit. Source: NYMEX/ CME.

[58] In 2001, ICE bought IPE for $130 million, making the Brent trading fully electronic.

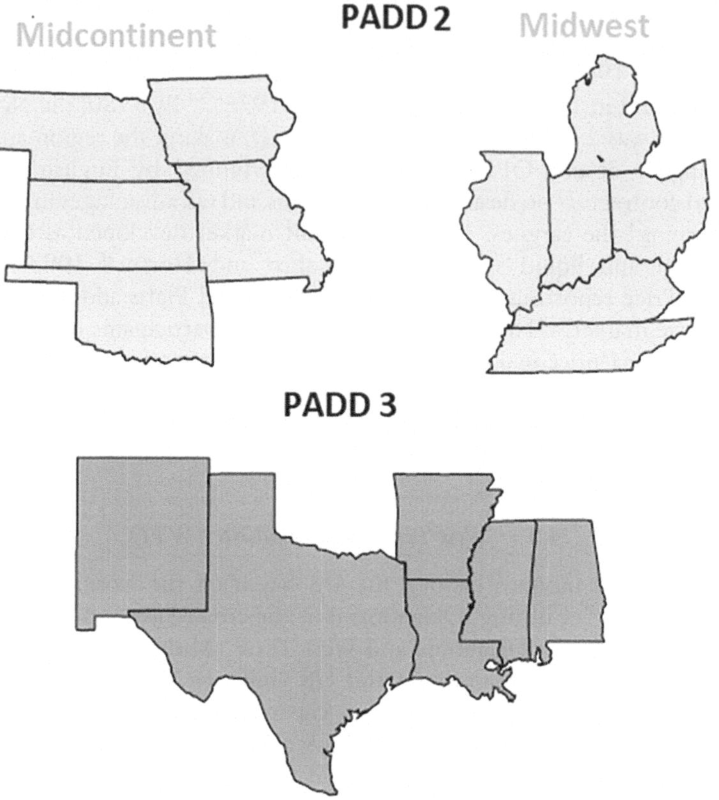

Fig. 18.3 US Petroleum Administration for Defence Districts or PADDs; The figure presents the key PADD 2 & PADD3 districts for WTI Benchmark formation. (Source: Author's elaboration)

did the infrastructure linked to Cushing. The pipeline links to the US Gulf (USG) are essential in keeping the benchmark linked to the rest of the world. When domestic production fell in the mid-1980s, it was the imports of foreign sweet barrels that set the price of WTI.

Even though the US imposed a ban on oil exports between 1977 and 2015, the sheer size of the US market provided the trading liquidity, making WTI one of the two most important oil benchmarks. The key events leading to the birth of the benchmark happened in 1980s: Lifting of the price controls in 1981; Setting up of the WTI futures contract on the New York Mercantile Exchange (NYMEX) in March 1983 and the oil price collapse in 1986. Following 'decontrol' of prices in 1981, spot trade quickly grew and the price reporting agency (PRA) Platt's started surveying and publishing prices for WTI as well as the sour grades, Louisiana Light Sweet (LLS) and West Texas

Sour (WTS) (Purvin & Gertz 2010).[59] The NYMEX WTI contract had a good and well established underpinning in the physical trades (Purvin & Gertz 2010).[60]

Being land-locked, oil balances in Cushing are subject to changes in flows and infrastructure in and around the hub. For this reason, the oil price crash in 1986 led to a fall in domestic production by over 1.5 mbd[61] and change in flows around the hub (Purvin & Gertz 2010).[62] Starved of the local crude oil, inland refineries had to import oil from the Gulf (USG) using reversed pipeline flows.[63] Given the 'price war' in the international markets at the time, foreign imports became competitive and soon the WTI introduced an 'alternative delivery procedure' which allowed for the foreign sweet crudes to be delivered into the contract.[64] This increased the 'depth' of the market; there was more oil to be delivered into the contract and more new players to do so. Open interest took off in 1986 and grew steadily from about 100,000 contracts then, to about half a million contracts in 1990s (see Fig. 18.1—each contract is one thousand barrels).

The following decade and a half saw relative price stability around $20 per barrel. Iraq war in 1991 was followed by a large release of oil from the US Strategic Petroleum Reserve (SPR) and eventually the price stabilised. Another market event in this period was the 1997–1999 Asian Financial Crisis when the prices fell from the peak of about $25 to $10, but eventually recovered and picked up in 2000. However, it was geopolitical events—the '9/11' terrorist attack and the subsequent invasion of Iraq in March 2003—that rattled the market and increased demand for 'paper barrels' for mitigating this volatility. By the end of 2004, WTI had crossed $50 mark. The market was entering a new period of dizzyingly high economic growth in Asia and particularly China. Thus, began a period of 'financialisaton' of the oil market with price action being dominated by new players such as funds and other financial institution. This is an important development in the history of the oil markets and will be discussed separately, later in the chapter.

Like most benchmarks, WTI benchmark has faced some difficult times. Perhaps the most serious one was in the 2005–2015 period. It started somewhat

[59] For a historical overview see: Purvin & Gertz: The role of WTI as a crude oil benchmark, Jan. 2010.

[60] Ibid. 'The Cushing location not only represented a gathering hub for the local crudes for refiners in Oklahoma, Kansas and Missouri, but it also was the central gathering point for terminus of pipelines originating in Texas and Oklahoma with onward distribution to the main refining centres in the central and eastern Midwest markets in Indiana, Illinois and Ohio.'

[61] The fall was much greater for the inland refineries because the 1.5 fall was cushioned by the 1978 discovery and then production from Alaska.

[62] Ibid. WTI dropped to near $10/Bbl at the lows in 1986. ' 25,000 producing wells were lost in 1986 and by 1990 that drop had approached 45,000 wells versus the peak number in 1985.'

[63] Seaway pipeline was converted (again) from gas to oil and started importing USG oil in 1996.

[64] In 2020, Platts and Argus are considering inclusion of WTI into the 'Brent' contract. How times have changed.

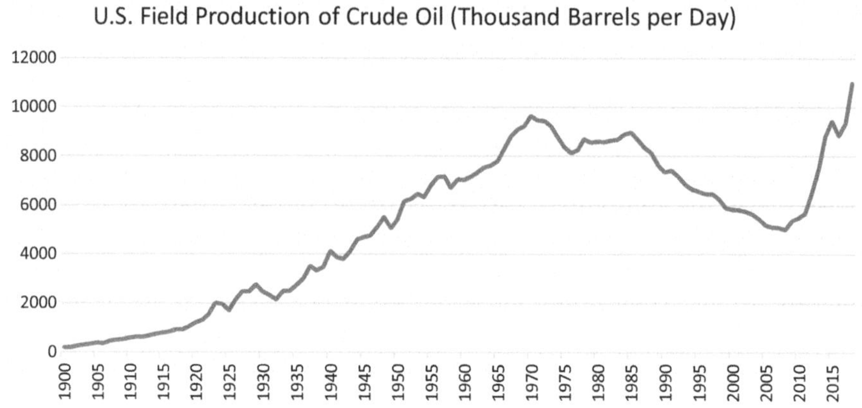

Fig. 18.4 US Crude Oil Production, EIA Data. (Source: Author's elaboration)

earlier, in the mid-1990s with increasing Canadian oil sands production,[65] which found its main outlet in the US. These cheap barrels had a natural outlet in the Midwest and Midcontinent refineries which invested in upgrading their facilities to take advantage of them.[66] The greatest changes in the WTI benchmark came from explosion in the US shale production and the eventual lifting of the oil export ban in 2015. It can be seen in the Fig. 18.4 below that oil production picked up substantially after 2011, choking up international imports and resulting in domestic oversupply of oil. As there was a ban on US oil exports[67] at the time, it created an excess supply of oil and resulted in the price of WTI falling relative to other benchmarks. Figure 18.5 clearly shows this decoupling of WTI not only relative to Dated Brent but also relative to LLS. Oversupplied and banned from exports, WTI started trading at deep discounts to Brent as well as LLS. It decoupled from the international markets, and USG refineries as well as exporters of sweet crude from Europe and West Africa relied primarily on LLS as an indicator of market fundamentals in the USG refining hub. Unhappy with the state of affairs, Saudi Aramco switched from Platts WTI benchmark to The Argus Sour Crude Index ("ASCI")[68] in 2009, followed by Kuwait and Iraq later.

The isolation of WTI eased off with a reversal (yet again) of the Seaway pipeline from Cushing to USG in 2012.[69] However, as can be seen in Fig. 18.1, the open interest of WTI contract did not fall as much as one would expect.

[65] Conventional production in Canada peaked at over 1.5 mbd in 1970; however, 'oil sands' production took off sharply in 2000s supported by high oil price, making total production at well over 3.5 mbd in 2018, most of it exported to the US.

[66] Due to geography and environmental reasons, Canadian production is 'landlocked' and confined to a monopsony buyer.

[67] There were few exemptions:

[68] The ASCI differential index is a daily volume-weighted average of deals done for the component crude trades of US sour grades of oil: Mars, Poseidon and Southern Green Canyon. However, it is expressed as a differential to WTI.

[69] Reuters Business news May 19, 2012 / 9:13 PM with plans to increase the capacity to 850 kbd.

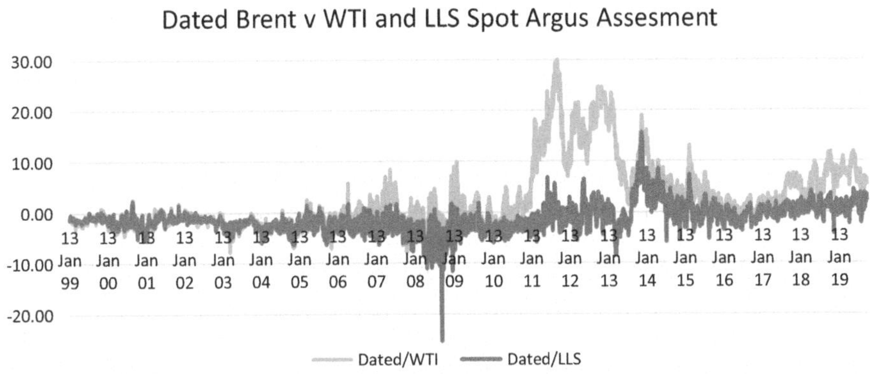

Fig. 18.5 Dated Brent vs. WTI and LLS (Argus spot assessments data). (Source: Author's elaboration)

This proves one very important point regarding benchmarks in general: liquidity of the contract and the confidence that traders get from it is often far more important than the basis risk[70] involved. Traders value the ability to enter and exit contracts without fear of being 'squeezed' long or short. A contract that provides this assurance will be more successful than an illiquid contract which provides less basis risk (Williams 1986).[71] This 'rule' will be confirmed in the case of Dubai, Oman, Murban and many other aspiring oil benchmarks.

Eventually, the US oil export ban was lifted in December 2015, relieving the pressure at Cushing, and WTI connected again with the international markets, increasing and eventually achieving record volumes of volume of open interest.[72]

4.2 Dated Brent

Arguably, 'Dated Brent' is the world's most important oil benchmark. It dominates as a pricing reference for the Atlantic basin (North Sea, Mediterranean and Africa) and for most 'sweet' (low sulphur) crude in Asia (Australia, Malaysia, Vietnam and others).[73] It is generally accepted that Dubai, the main benchmark in Asia, or more generally, 'East of Suez', is essentially (as discussed in the next section), a spread to Brent.

The Brent field was discovered in 1971 north of British Shetland Islands in the North Sea and the first 'Bravo' platform started production in 1976. In the

[70] Basis risk is correlation between the contract and underlying commodity being hedged. The higher the coefficient, the less basis risk there is in using the contract.

[71] A great read on the subject is Jeffrey Williams' 'The economic function of futures markets' Cambridge University Press 1986.

[72] This was not a smooth process. With shale output increasing by over 1 mbd on annual basis, the offtake pipeline capacity was lagging behind at least until 2020.

[73] According to the Intercontinental Exchange (ICE) website (https://www.theice.com/brent-crude), 'Brent is the price barometer for 70% of global crude, with accessibility as a waterborne supply that is easily transported around the world'.

1980s, it was producing between 400,000 and 500,000 barrels or roughly just short of one cargo per day (one cargo = 600,000 barrels). It loads at Sullom Voe terminal in the Shetlands. Brent 'paper' has evolved from being a 'forward'[74] market in physical cargoes in the 1980s, to become the most complex oil market in the world (Mabro and Horsnell 1993; Fattouh 2010).[75] 'Brent' is a brand name of a benchmark that has reinvented itself many times since 1980s. Due to falling production, other sweet North Sea grades were gradually introduced into the Brent delivery mechanism forming what we now call a Brent or 'BFOET basket' comprising and named after Brent, Forties, Oseberg, Ekofisk and Troll[76] crude oils. Physical volumes of oil in the 'Brent basket' have increased over time by widening the 'window' of cargo loadings which qualify for the price assessment of Dated Brent. From the beginning, in 1987, to 2002, this 'window' was up to 15 days ahead of the date of assessment (often referred to as 15-day Brent); in 2002, the window was expanded to 10–21 days ahead; in 2012 it was expanded to 10–25 days ahead; finally, in 2015, it was extended yet again to a 10 days–one calendar month forward 'window'. Each of these changes added to the volume of oil trade included in the assessment. As we can see in Fig. 18.6 below, this has stabilised the volume of reported deals in the 'Brent basket'.

While Brent trading started as 'forward' physical or 'cash' market where oil was 'churned' for tax optimisation reasons (Mabro and Horsnell 1993),[77] Dated Brent is simply Brent with loading dates,[78] often referred to as 'wet' (as opposed to 'paper' Brent with no loading dates, in the forward markets). Dated Brent being a price of actual physical oil is generally used as a benchmark for physical trades of other types of crude oil. To understand what the actual Dated Brent benchmark price is, it is necessary to understand how its price is assessed. In a nutshell, it is based on four pillars:

- Physical assessment of the value of the BFOET ('Brent')[79] grades.
- A forward curve based on the Dated swaps market.

[74] Forward Brent is simply physical cargo sold 'forward' or in advance of the issue of the loading programme for that month, indicating loading dates.

[75] For a historical overview, see R. Mabro and P. Horsnell: *Oil Markets and Prices, The Brent market and the Formation of World Oil Prices*, OUP/OIES 1993. See also, B. Fattouh (2010) 'An Anatomy of the Crude Oil Pricing System', OIES Paper WPM 40.

[76] The physical oil underpinning the benchmark has been maintained by adding alternative delivered grades: Forties (introduced in 2002, with Buzzard field entering production in 2007), Oseberg (2002), Ekofisk (2007) and most recently Troll (2018). What is left of Brent blend crude oil, loading at Sullom Voe terminal, is now just a brand name.

[77] Seminal work on Brent, explaining details of the original forward market is: Horsnell, P. and Mabro, R. (1993) Oil Markets and Prices: The Brent Market and the Formation of World Oil Prices. Oxford: OIES.

[78] It means that the nomination procedure has been completed and a three-day laycan or loading window is known.

[79] Brent and BFOET will be used interchangeably, both having the same meaning: the Brent benchmark basket.

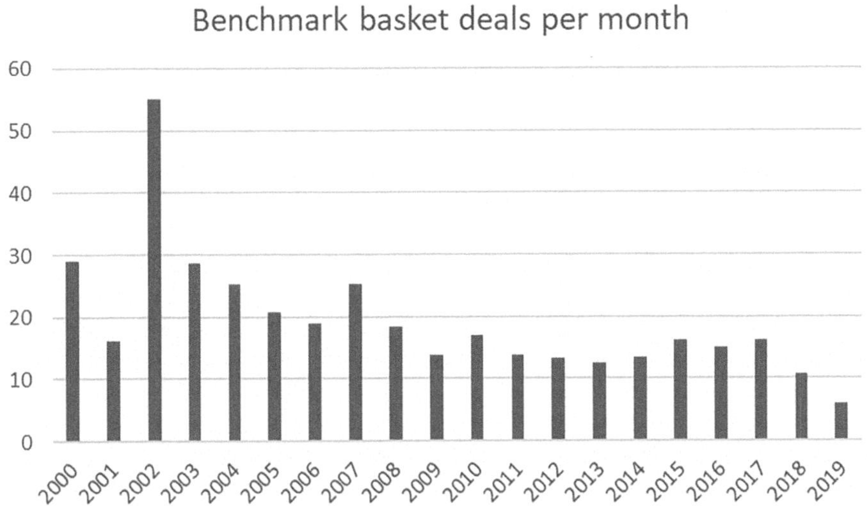

Fig. 18.6 Number of physical BFOET or 'Brent Basket' deals (cargoes, 600 kbd each, including all the BFOET grades; Argus data). (Source: Author's elaboration)

- The fixed price of the forward or futures 'Brent' contract.
- Quality differentials or premiums (QP) of crudes other than Brent or Forties.[80]

Assessment of the Dated Brent curve allows for a wide range of crudes to be priced off this single benchmark. PRAs such as Platts and Argus report a wide variety of price differentials (for instance, Urals, West African, Mediterranean, North Sea and even many Asia-Pacific crudes) vis-à-vis the Forward Dated Brent (Argus refers to this as Anticipated North Sea Dated). This allows the refineries to compare the relative value of the different crudes and assess which crudes are being valued competitively relative to a single benchmark.

The most peculiar feature of the physical BFOET market is that it is generally traded as a differential to Dated Brent. Therefore, the PRAs are challenged to assess the Dated Brent price based on physical trades which are themselves differentials to Dated Brent! Fortunately, the expected assessments for Dated Brent are traded in a liquid derivatives market as weekly swaps,[81] called Contracts for Difference or CFDs.[82] Historically, CFDs developed from a need to convert an outright Forward Brent price into a Dated Brent price plus a differential (and vice versa). In the 1980s, most of the Forward Brent contracts

[80] Forties has a sulphur de-escalator (see endnote #70). This and quality premiums are discussed in the next section.

[81] It is assessed on a weekly basis, because oil in Europe traditionally prices over a five-day range, usually around the 'bill of lading'.

[82] CFD is a differential between physical or Dated Brent v forward (usually first) Brent. The swap is usually traded over one week period, mimicking a five-day pricing normally used for North Sea cargoes.

were traded on an outright price basis. As alternative grades of oil used Dated Brent pricing around the Bill of Lading as a reference price (normally a five-day period taken two days before loading date and two days after the loading date), there was a need to value them using a common denominator. Given that CFDs trade at least six to eight weeks forward, they are used to construct the Brent Dated forward curve. The example below will help illustrate this.

CFD Brent swaps are differentials between Dated and forward Brent values. For example, 1–5 April CFD swaps may trade at June forward Brent, minus 50 cents per barrel (-$0.50). The following week (8–12 April), they may trade at -$0.30, and so on. PRAs need to establish these values (forward curve) as they are the key to resolving the circular problem where physical or Dated Brent normally trades as a differential to Dated Brent! Let's take an example of a cargo of Forties crude (one of the grades in the 'Brent basket), loading 2–4 April, traded at Dated+$0.50/bbl and another cargo of the same grade loading 9–11 April traded at Dated+$0.30/bbl. Given the above CFD values, they have both effectively traded at the same absolute price, equal to June forward Brent[83] (-$0.50 + $0.50 = 0 and -$0.30 + $0.30 = 0). The actual value for June forward Brent is established at the end of a 'window' at 16.30 London time (S&P Global Platts 2019; Argus Media 2019)[84] and the above differentials are added or subtracted from it.

The higher quality grades in the BFOET basket such as Ekofisk, Oseberg, and Troll have a quality premium (QP) applied[85] to 'normalize' the differentials for the assessment process. Brent's most representative grade is usually Forties—due to its relatively, but not exclusively, high sulphur levels—and it commonly establishes the value of Dated Brent. The quality of Forties crude may sometimes vary depending on the contribution of the Buzzard field,[86] and a sulphur de-escalator is applied later, to compensate buyers when the level of sulphur is above 0.6%.[87] This whole process happens in the London 'window'

[83] Mathematically, it is irrelevant what that June forward Brent price is; $50 or $100 will make no difference.

[84] For exact specification see: 'Platts Methodology and specifications guide Crude oil', S&P Global Platts, January 2019: https://www.spglobal.com/platts/en/our-methodology/methodology-specifications/oil/crude-oil-methodology and 'Argus Methodology and Reference Lists': https://www.argusmedia.com/en/methodology/methodology-listing?page=1

[85] It is applied at 60% of an established premium between Oseberg and Ekofisk and the cheapest grade. Troll QP was introduced in March 2019; see 'Platts Methodology and specifications guide Crude oil', January 2019.

[86] Introduction of Buzzard field into the Forties and therefore Brent basked caused a lot of controversy at the time, given its high sulphur content of 1.42% and lover API gravity. For example, with zero Buzzard added to it, Forties crude would be API 44 and 0.27% S. With 'normal', about 30% Buzzard in the blend, Forties crude is much lower API 39.6 and much higher 0.68%S.

[87] To compensate the buyers for sulphur levels over 0.6%. See: 'Methodology and specifications guide North Sea sulphur de-escalator', S&P Global Platts: 'https://www.spglobal.com/platts/plattscontent/_assets/_files/en/our-methodology/methodology-specifications/northseadeescalator.pdf

between 16.00 and 16.30 BST, with most trades being done during the last minute of the 'window'. This is a somewhat simplified rendition of the process.[88]

What is clear is that derivatives markets, namely CFD swaps play a key role in establishing the value of Dated Brent. Hence, sometimes the criticism that 'the (derivatives) tail is wagging the (physical crude oil value) dog' is heard.[89]

Brent has been trading as a futures contract since 1983 and it is listed on both ICE and CME exchanges. It is normally financially settled on the last day of trading based on an index[90] calculated based on the physical trades on the last day of the contract. Traders with a futures position in Brent can easily turn it into a physical delivery contract through an 'EFP' (Exchange for Physicals) trade, usually through a broker, in one simple transaction. This establishes a pretty seamless link between futures and physical oil, making Brent one of the most robust benchmarks in the world and it serves as a basis for another regional benchmark used 'East of Suez', Dubai. What is more, the most common grade setting the Brent benchmark, Forties, is popular in the Far East. With falling energy demand in Europe and growing Asian thirst for the commodity, after about 2010, the North Sea oil has depended on Asian demand to balance the market. This can be clearly seen on Fig. 18.7 below, as more and more Forties ended up being refined East.

4.3 Dubai: Brent's Asian Cousin

Dubai crude oil has been the main Asian benchmark since the mid-1980s (Fattouh 2012).[91] It is responsible for the pricing of almost 30 million barrels per day (million b/d) of crude oil currently exported to Asia. Since its introduction, Dubai production has diminished substantially. Dubai does not release figures for its crude oil production but, from the loading data and sales, it can be deduced that production has fallen below 70,000 b/d in 2019 from a peak of about 400,000 b/d in 1991.[92] However, just like Brent, the benchmark has evolved into a 'brand name', allowing for the delivery of Oman, Upper Zakum, Al Shahen and Murban grades of oil in into the 'Dubai basket' during the so called

[88] For now, we avoid discussing the issue of EFP in Platt's methodology. Traders hedging their physical oil with futures and CFDs take additional EFP risk as CFDs are based on the Dated and forward Brent differential and not on the Dated and futures Brent differential!

[89] The author does not share this view; see Imsirovic (2013) 'Do not blame PRAs for oil industry structural failures', *Financial Times*, 20 May 2013.

[90] The ICE Brent Index represents the average price of trading in the BFOE (Brent-Forties-Oseberg-Ekofisk) 'cash' or forward ('BFOE Cash') market in the relevant delivery month as reported and confirmed by industry media. Only published full cargo size (600,000 barrels) trades and assessments are taken into consideration in the calculation. The ICE Brent Index is published by ICE Futures Europe on the day after expiry of the front month ICE Brent futures contract and used by the Exchange as the final cash settlement price. CME Brent Index is calculated in similar fashion.

[91] See Fattouh, Bassam. (2012), 'The Dubai Benchmark and Its Role in the International Oil Pricing System', Oxford Energy Comment.

[92] At the time of writing, there are about 3 cargoes of Dubai available for loading each month.

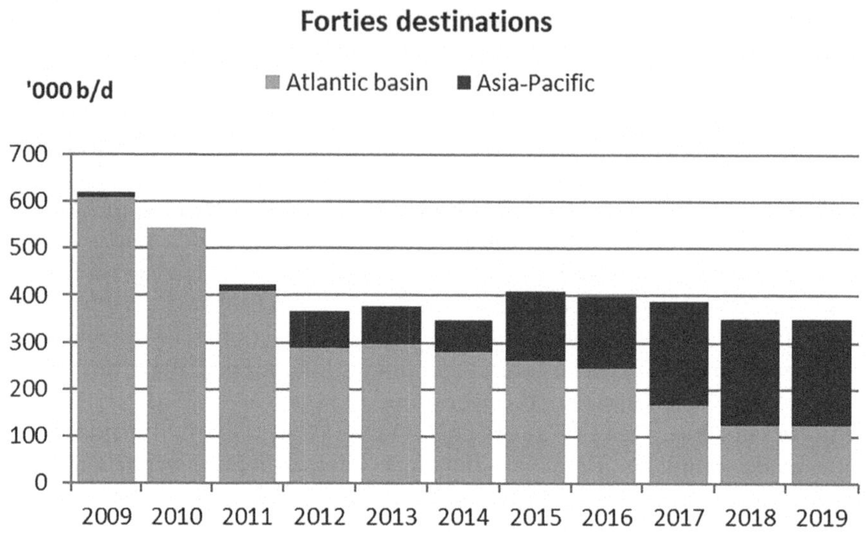

Fig. 18.7 Destination for the North Sea Forties crude over time. Argus data. (Source: Author's elaboration)

'Platts Dubai window', between 16.00 and 16.30 Singapore time.[93] Dubai partials trade (on a fixed price basis, in dollars per barrel) only during this half hour window. For the remainder of the trading day, all Dubai trades are still differentials to Brent (EFS) or spreads to other Dubai swap months (swap spreads). A large derivatives market has grown around the Dubai 'brand name', feeding back into the price discovery of the benchmark itself (Fattouh 2012).[94]

As discussed earlier, the 1990s and early 2000s have witnessed two main themes in the world oil markets. The first is a shift in demand from the developed to the developing world, particularly towards Asia and the Middle East (ME). The second is a large increase in light oil and gas production in the Americas (Imsirovic 2014).[95] The consequences for the crude oil and

[93] Platts uses the Market On Close (MOC) to assess prices for crude oil, petroleum products and related swaps. The MOC is a structured process in which bids, offers and transactions are submitted by participants to Platts' editors. Following the close, Platts' editors examine the data gathered through the day and develop price assessments that reflect an end-of-day value. The Platts 'window' is the term market participants use to refer to the 30 to 45-minute period before the close of the market, when Platts no longer accepts new bids or offers in the price assessment process. More on this in footnote 7 below, as well as inhttp://www.platts.com/IM.Platts.Content/MethodologyReferences/MethodologySpecs/Crude-oil-methodology.pdf. Oman was introduced in January 2002 and Upper Zakum in February 2006. According to Platts, this should provide the contract with over one million b/d of deliverable physical oil.

[94] Fatouh, Bassam. (2012), 'The Dubai Benchmark', p. 4.

[95] For a more detailed discussion see: Imsirovic (2014) 'Asian Oil Market in Transition' Journal of Energy Security, April 2014 (http://www.ensec.org/index.php?option=com_content&view=article&id=520:asian-oil-markets-in-transition&catid=143:issue-content&Itemid=435)

petroleum product flows to Asia, as well as main price benchmarks, have been profound.

United States East Coast (USEC) and Canadian refiners, traditional buyers of high gasoline yield crude oil from the North Sea (NS), West Africa (WAF) and North Africa (NA), have essentially stopped importing, given the availability of locally produced, light sweet shale crude oil. Sweet barrels from the Atlantic basin, which mainly trade on spot basis and have no destination restrictions (unlike most OPEC crude oil), have become 'swing' barrels for the Asian refiners looking for cheaper feedstock (Fattouh and Sen 2014).[96]

Given weak European demand and poor margins, European refineries have been closing during this period.[97] Most of the new and more sophisticated refinery capacity was being built in the ME and Asia at the expense of Europe. This was exacerbated by the Russian tax incentives to increase product exports at the expense of the traditional crude oil, in order to maximise revenue.[98] Despite the slowing Chinese economy, the main demand drivers in the oil markets continued to be China and the ME.[99] Therefore, the oil flows shifted towards Asia from almost all the producing areas. Since the oil prices are set by the 'marginal' barrels and the region is a main buyer of these barrels, Asia was the main driver of global oil prices. Hence, delivered price of oil in Asia was the key signal for the world oil markets. At the same time, ME producers became more dependent on Asian buyers. This resulted in increased market power of the Asian consumers and the demise of the so called 'Asian premium' (Doshi and Imsirovic 2013).[100]

The growing importance of Asia as a destination for oil from all over the world has profoundly impacted the Dubai market. 'Arbitrage' barrels that normally trade against Brent and WTI benchmarks are generally being evaluated by end users (refiners) and sold on Dubai-related prices.[101] This means somewhere

[96] See Fattouh, Bassam and Sen, Amrita. (August 2014), 'New swings for West African crudes', Oxford Energy Comment.

[97] Europe lost a nominal refinery capacity of just short of 2 million b/d since 2009. It is estimated that another 1–1.5 million b/d of capacity needs to be shut before 2018. Chinese new greenfield refinery projects between now and 2016 amount to an additional capacity of 2.3 million b/d. Planned ME refinery projects excluding Iraq between 2014 and 2018 amount to almost 3 million b/d. (All calculated from various Platts announcements).

[98] In spite of this, Russians have been able to increase their crude oil sales to Asia through the ESPO pipeline.

[99] According to the IEA 'Oil Market Report' May 2014, the bulk of the increase in the global oil demand will come from China (0.39 million b/d), ME (0.31 million b/d) and Latin America (0.19 million b/d).

[100] See Doshi, T.K. and Imsirovic, A. (2013) 'The Asian Premium in crude oil markets: fact or fiction? Chapter 2 in 'Managing Regional Energy Vulnerabilities in East Asia' edited by Zha Daoijong, USA: Routledge.

[101] There are clearly exceptions to this. Most Angolan barrels sold to China are probably priced on Brent Dtd basis. India buys WAF on the same basis. It is impossible to know internal benchmarking for each refiner, but it is generally accepted that Dubai is the prevalent benchmark in Asia. This large Brent/Dubai exposure may be too large for the Asian paper markets to bear, resulting in refiners either internalising the exposure within their trading arms (such as Unipec being a trad-

in the supply chain, prices may need to be converted from other benchmarks to Dubai prices. The process of arbitrage involves buying the benchmark other than Dubai (Brent, WTI)[102] and selling Dubai swaps, in order to 'lock in' the differential that makes oil competitive in Asia. As Brent is the dominant international benchmark, Brent futures versus the Dubai swaps differential is also the dominant trading link between the two benchmarks.[103] It is known as EFS (exchange for swaps since Brent futures are 'exchanged' for Dubai swaps). For example, importing Brent-related barrels loading in the month of December to Asia and converting its price into a Dubai-related one, would normally involve a purchase of December EFS (buying December Brent futures and selling December Dubai swaps can be done as one trade by buying the December EFS). Then, as the cargo has 'priced in', usually during the loading period, December Brent futures are sold rateably. Since the cargo is placed with an end user at a Dubai-related price, the swap would be simply left to 'price out'.

To understand what the 'Dubai' benchmark price actually is, it is worth briefly revisiting the process of assessing of the Dubai benchmark. Firstly, Asian refiners normally buy oil over a calendar month of loading.[104] Secondly, most physical crude trades as a differential to Platts Dubai assessment during a calendar month of loading, the value of which equates to the Dubai[105] swap for that month. Refinery Linear Programming models use Dubai swap values (normally based on an estimated forward curve) as a common denominator for comparing different grades of crude oil.[106]

Unlike Brent and WTI, Dubai has no liquid functioning futures markets.[107] However, the over-the-counter (OTC)[108] markets for EFS,

ing arm of China Petroleum & Chemical Corporation, or Sinopec) or demanding Brent exposure which is easier to manage.

[102] Often it is both in sequence: Wti/ Brent, then Brent/ Dubai.

[103] As the Atlantic basin crude oil is normally purchased on pricing period a few days around or after the bill of lading, Brent futures are the common way to hedge such price. On the other hand, there is no liquid futures market for Dubai. Given that the ME producers and Asian refiners have traditionally been using the whole month of loading for the pricing period, making Dubai swaps a more convenient method of hedging Dubai price.

[104] This is for historical reasons, going back to OPEC 'formulas' or benchmark-related prices.

[105] For example, December Dubai swap is an average of all the mean daily Dubai quotations during the month of December. Note that Platts and Argus would assess the value of February (M+2) loading Dubai during this period.

[106] Retroactive OSPs such as Abu Dhabi and Qatari reflect already known Dubai averages. For example, July OSP for the Upper Zakum grade, published in early August at $66.80 is the equivalent of July Dubai + $0.65 since, during July, Dubai averaged at $ 66.15. A notable exception (and a bit of a mind-twister) is Dubai OSP which is set as a differential to an average of the monthly settlements for Oman crude on DME.

[107] Dubai swaps, swap spreads and Brent—Dubai swap spread and EFS do trade on ICE and CME. These are normally based on Platts assessments (for Dubai). But there is no futures contract for the actual Dubai crude oil contract.

[108] These are direct markets between two counterparties, largely unregulated and not always reported. However, since 2008 economic troubles, most of the OTC deals are either traded or cleared on one of the exchanges.

Brent-Dubai[109] swap spread and Dubai spreads frequently trade. Therefore, the way to establish a value of a Dubai swap is to use Brent and apply the prevailing EFS value to it. This is best illustrated by an example. Physical Dubai cargoes traditionally trade as a differential to Dubai assessments (equal to swap value during the month of loading). For example, physical Dubai loading in the month of October will trade as a premium or a discount to October Dubai, and would normally trade about two months earlier, during August. Also, in August, the most liquid EFS market will be October (October Brent futures and Dubai swaps). By applying October EFS to October Brent futures, a trader can obtain the October Dubai swap value. During August, when October Dubai normally trades, its value is equal to the calculated October swap, plus some differential (positive or negative), depending on the fundamentals of the market (Horsnell 1997).[110]

Like Dated Brent, The Platts window is dominated by a small elite of self-selected 'price makers' (Fattouh 2012),[111] with Shell, Glencore and Vitol accounting for about a half of all cash Market On Close (MOC) activity in 2019 (Fig. 18.8). Half a dozen players account for almost all the deals. Few, if any, of the NOCs are involved.[112] Of course, significant participation of one or more large producers could also produce a biased benchmark.

As already mentioned, other grades of oil are deliverable into the Dubai contract. As these two grades have higher net worth for most refiners, it is presumed they will be delivered at Dubai prices only when the Dubai price is above its 'true market value', providing the liquidity in the pricing 'window' and putting a 'cap' on the Dubai price, avoiding a possible 'squeeze'.[113]

[109] As opposed to EFS, which is Brent futures to Dubai swaps spread, BD swaps spread is a spread between the Brent swaps and Dubai swaps on average month basis (e.g. December Brent swaps v December Dubai swaps).

[110] The conclusion that Dubai is a benchmark derived from Brent and not a centre of absolute price discovery remains valid: Horsnell, P. (1997) 'Oil in Asia: Markets, Trading, Refining and Deregulation', Oxford: Oxford Institute for Energy Studies.

[111] See Fattouh, Bassam (2012), 'The Dubai Benchmark'. Of course, participation of one or more large producers could also produce a biased benchmark. It should be said that the Brent market also involves a small 'self-appointed elite' of participants. However, unlike Dubai, Brent has a hugely liquid futures market working in tandem with the PRA assessment process in providing the price discovery.

[112] One should note that it is becoming increasingly hard to distinguish 'oil traders' from other market participants. For many years now, most majors have had trading arms (Stasco, a trading arm of Shell, is possibly the biggest trading company in the world). However, more and more refiners (Unipec, China Oil, Reliance and others) have their own trading companies. Even producers such as Oman have a trading company (OTI) in a joint venture with Vitol. Finally, trading houses such as Glencore, Vitol and others have had both upstream and downstream assets for quite some time.

[113] Squeeze is usually defined as a situation in which a buyer buys all the available crude produced. When futures and forward markets are traded, the actual pricing exposure may exceed total production. For grades physically delivered in the Platts Dubai contract, see Fig. 18.4.

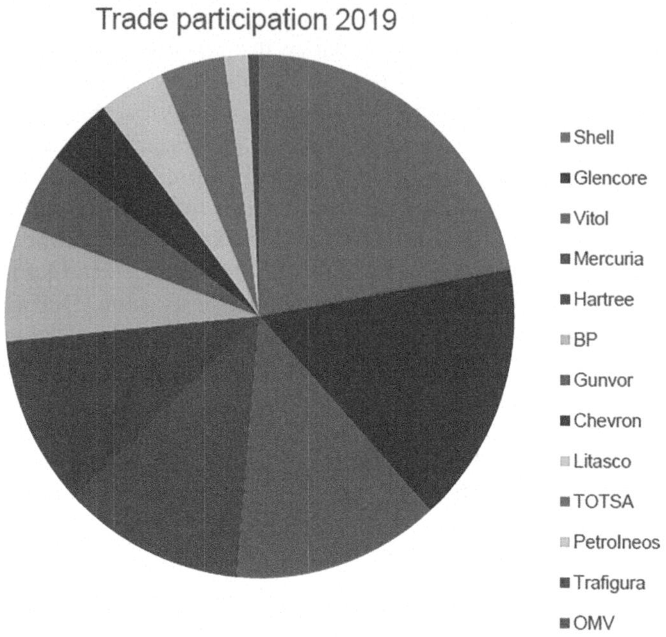

Fig. 18.8 Cash BFOE MOC Participation. Source: Platts. (Source: Author's elaboration)

4.4 Oman: Dubai's Neglected Sibling

A number of OPEC producers base their pricing formula on both Dubai and Oman.[114] Oman is lighter with lower sulphur content, making it a higher value grade of oil and it normally trades at a premium to Dubai. It is also well accepted by most Asian refiners that it has no destination restrictions and it is frequently traded. With at least 50 physical cargoes produced every month and loaded outside the Strait of Hormuz, it has many characteristics of a good benchmark. It is a part of the 'Dubai basket' as it is deliverable into the Dubai contract.

Figure 18.9 below shows that Oman and Dubai prices, or a spread, can diverge by a dollar per barrel, and often more. While this difference can be significant, historically Asian refiners have not done much to hedge it. The evidence for this is a relatively low volume of Oman trading on the Dubai Merchantile Exchange (DME) outside the 'pricing window' and pure physical delivery. The DME Oman futures contracts settle daily, based on a weighted average of trades between 16.25 and 16.30 Singapore time (Exactly the same time as the 'Singapore Dubai window'). In line with the usual timing of Asian oil purchases, this contract trades two months before the actual month of

[114] They are Saudi Arabia, Kuwait and Iraq. They use 50% Dubai and 50% Oman based on Platts quotations. In 2018, Saudis changed from Platts Oman to DME futures Oman.

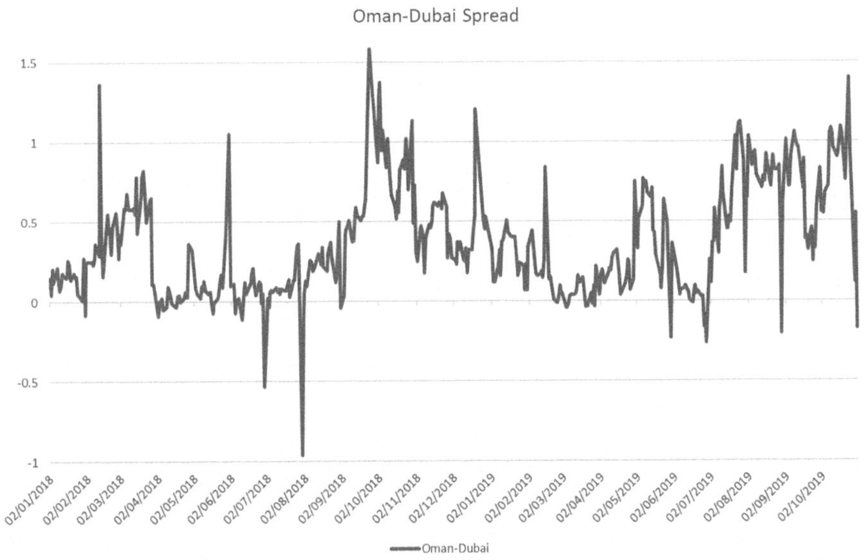

Fig. 18.9 Oman vs. Dubai differential. Platts data for Dubai and DME Oman \$/bbl. (Source: Author's elaboration)

loading. So, during November 2019, the front month contract is January 2020. The Oman official selling price (OSP) is set using the monthly average of the DME Oman daily settlements. Physical Oman is generally traded as a differential to this OSP.[115]

Even though Oman is used as a pricing basis by some of the most important producers in the world and is widely traded, it has remained a minor benchmark overshadowed by Dubai. This is partly to do with a difference in philosophy between some Middle East (ME) producers and Platts. For Platts, there is only one ME benchmark with Dubai 'brand' that currently encompasses the five grades of ME oil[116] including Oman. But given the Saudis and the other ME producers' preference to the 'Oman/Dubai' formula, Platts had no choice but to continue publishing the 'Oman' assessment as well.[117] Indeed, the Oman assessment is not even included in the 'Key Benchmarks' section of their flagship publication, Crude Oil Marketwire.

[115] If the contract has already 'priced in' most of the OSP (say in the middle of December for February loaded cargoes, Oman will trade on Dubai swap basis—calendar January Dubai swap plus a differential or discount. This is one of those curiosities of the Asian benchmarks—Dubai OSP is actually set base on the DME Oman settlements!

[116] Dubai, Oman, Upper Zakum, Al Shaheen and Murban. This is like Platts 'Brent' with delivery of Brent, Forties, Oseberg, Ekofisk and Troll (BFOET). Warning to the reader is that these baskets can change.

[117] Historically, physical Oman used to be traded extensively and hence the origins of the Platts Oman assessment and its inclusion into the Saudi pricing formula.

In October 2018 Saudi Aramco switched to DME Oman daily settlement price (instead of Platts Oman assessment), in its pricing formula for Asian customers. However, the decision made little, if any, impact on the volumes of Oman traded. This seems to confirm the 'rule' about benchmarks in general (as discussed in the section about WTI) that traders prefer liquidity over basis risk. In other words, they are prepared to take some risk (pay some risk premium) and use an imperfect, but liquid instrument rather than eliminate this risk by trading an illiquid contract (which carries its own risks and possibly costs).

So far, we can conclude that the whole global oil market revolves around three (some would argue two: WTI and Brent, as Dubai is generally traded as a spread to Brent) main benchmarks. There is also a plethora of 'quality' or 'regional' benchmarks. Examples of these are Russian Urals, Kazakhstani CPC Blend, Nigerian Qua Iboe, UAE Murban, Indonesian Minas and many others. What they all have in common is that, while their price provides good signal regarding demand and supply of that particular quality and the market in which they trade, they all trade as a differential to Brent, WTI or Dubai. Strictly speaking, they are not benchmarks. True benchmarks trade at fixed price, in Dollars per barrel and thus set the 'absolute price level' for all other oil to trade against.

It should be clear from the discussion so far that the world oil market is dynamic and changing all the time. As demand and supply in different regions change, so do price benchmarks, sending signals to the market and thus facilitating global oil flows. Over time, these flows change and so do benchmarks. When the supply of oil in Cushing dried up following the 1986 price crash, 'an alternative delivery procedure' was introduced into the WTI contract incorporating many imported grades of oil. With the Asian boom of the early 2000s and 'centre of gravity' of the oil market moving East, Dubai benchmark needed major adjustments incorporating new types of crude such as Oman, Upper Zakum and later Al Shaheen and Murban. The same was true for Brent, especially as one of its main 'basket' crude, Forties started to move East, making it vulnerable to 'squeezes'.[118] Following the shale boom, the US exports swamped the European market and often exceeded the whole North Sea production. If the Brent benchmark did not change, it could become irrelevant (Imsirovic 2019).[119] For the same reasons, the price of WTI in Cushing is less important for international buyers of the US crude. They are more concerned about the price of WTI in the USG area, where they load the oil. For this reason, all major PRAs and exchanges have launched some form of new WTI contract based there (Imsirovic 2019).[120] Finally, the Middle Eastern producers have

[118] Squeeze happens when one or more player buys the whole (or even more!) than the whole benchmark production for a particular month.

[119] See A. Imsirovic: Changes to the 'Dated Brent' benchmark: More to come', OIES March 2019.

[120] Ibid.

long wanted more control over their export prices. While Oman has had some traction, there is a fair chance that Murban could emerge as a new benchmark in this region. This will require a lot of changes in the way this grade of oil is sold and traded, but rewards may well be worth it (Mehdi et al. 2019).[121]

5 Global Oil Markets: Benchmarks in Action

While benchmarks are the backbone of the global oil prices, not all market participants are involved in setting those prices. As briefly mentioned, the oil industry can be divided between those actively involved in setting up the benchmark prices and trading them and those who simply use those set prices for pricing of physical crude and hedging (Luciani 2015).[122] It is important because prices of benchmarks are eventually set through participation in the market place, wether through exchanges, PRA 'windows' or any other way. In an ideal world, benchmarks should be set by all the market players participating in the price setting process; but this is not the case. This is a problem as it is sometimes suggested that the benchmark price is 'too high' or 'too low'; but if the 'too high' prices are not sold into, and 'too low' prices are not bought by the market, there is no mechanism to 'correct' the benchmark price (Imsirovic 2013).[123] What is more, markets are not 'perfect' in the economic-theory sense: Like most other markets, oil is dominated by a handful of very large players and setting benchmark prices is often left to large traders or trading arms of large oil companies.[124] As a result, there is no perfect oil price benchmark.

However imperfect, benchmarks and their associated derivatives—futures, forwards, swaps, spreads, options and other instruments have created a market ecosystem facilitating smooth global movement of crude oil with relatively little price risk. Regional benchmarks such as Dubai in Asia clearly indicate the value of oil in that part of the world, set by local fundamentals of demand and supply. It is the function of the market to use this price signal and allocate the cheapest way to satisfy demand in Asia. It can be done with oil from the North Sea, West Africa, US shale regions or elsewhere, depending on the price of oil in those regions and the cost of moving oil to Asia. This is set by the spreads between benchmarks such as WTI/ Brent and Brent/Dubai. So, a tight Asian market will result in strong Dubai prices (and narrow WTI/ Dubai and Brent/ Dubai spreads). Narrow arbitrage spreads are akin to open doors. Once it is decided to move oil from one region to the other, spreads will be purchased to hedge risk. This will widen the spreads and 'close the door' for further

[121] See A. Mehdi et al.: 'Murban: A benchmark for the Middle East?' OIES, October 2019.

[122] For great arguments on how the Saudis could bridge the gap from a price taker to a price maker, see Luciani (2015): 'From Price taker to Price maker: Saudi Arabia and the World Oil markets' in 'Saudi Arabia in Transition' ed. B. Haykel et al. Cambridge University Press 2015.

[123] See A. Imsirovic: 'Don't blame PRAs for oil industry's structural failures', the FT Letter May 21, 2013.

[124] See examples and Fig. 18.3 in Imsirovic (2014): 'Oil Markets in Transition and the Dubai Benchmark, OIES October 2014.

arbitrage. Hence, these benchmark spreads are the key indicators of the relative oil market strengths around the globe. This requires the 'paper' oil to be traded many times the volume of the actual physical barrels being moved.[125]

Of course, trading does not only involve the movement of oil through space. It also involves movement of oil in time and it this reflected in time-spreads. This is normally referred to as the 'time structure' of prices. Demand for oil is derived from the demand for products and it is highly seasonal. People drive more in the summer and heat houses more in the winter. Weak spot prices relative to delivery of oil in future is referred to as 'contango', and it is a signal to the market that cheap prompt oil can be purchased and stored profitably, as long as the 'contango' is greater than the overall cost of storage. Then it can be delivered later, when there is more demand for it. On the other hand, strong prompt price relative to future delivery, referred to in industry speak as 'backwardation', is a signal to the market that oil is needed and that it should come out of storage. In reality, trading involves movement of oil both in space and time. Contango in WTI and Brent are ideal for oil shipments over long distances such as Asia as the time spread is paying for at least a part of the shipping cost.

While oil benchmarks and spreads between them give a good signal where oil is most needed and offer instruments for moving it with little risk, there is no guarantee that the demand and supply of these 'paper' instruments are well matched (Imsirovic 2014).[126] This is because not every buyer and seller of oil mitigates risk through hedging. If they all had same internal measures and risk profiles, 'paper' markets would be ideally matched in terms of supply and demand. Unfortunately, this is not the case. So, a new class of market participants is necessary to take the excess risk: speculators. When returns on the commodity are high, speculators (investors) are attracted to the market and thus they provide the additional liquidity needed for the smooth functioning of the market.

6 Speculation and Financialization: Price Makers and Price Takers

It is generally accepted in virtually all the markets that speculators (Fattouh et al. 2012; Medlock 2013; Vansteenkiste 2011)[127] add liquidity, at a price. However, they may also add volatility (Einloth 2009),[128] especially in the global

[125] Hedging commonly involves not only Brent or WTI futures, and time spreads, but also CFDs, EFS, EFPs and other instruments.

[126] For an example of possible 'market failure', see Imsirovic (2014): 'Oil Markets in Transition and the Dubai Benchmark, OIES October 2014.

[127] For excellent reviews of the literature on influence of speculation on prices, see: 'The Role of Speculation in the Oil Markets' by Fattouh, Killian and Mahadeva, OIES, March 2012; and K.B. Medlock III: 'Speculation, Fundamentals, and the price of crude oil', James A. baker III Institute for Public Policy, Rice University, August 2013; Isabel Vansteenkiste: 'What is Driving Oil Futures prices: Fundamentals v Speculation', European Central Bank, Working Paper Series No 1371 / August 2011.

[128] See: James Einloth: 'Speculation and Recent Volatility in the Price of Oil', October 2009; FDIC Center for Financial Research, Working Paper, No. 2009–08.

oil market with relatively low elasticity of demand and supply and high geopolitical risk. This was a particularly hot topic during the 2000s commodity boom when oil prices well exceeded $100 per barrel and ideas of 'peak oil' came back to vogue.[129]

The commodity boom coincided with the growth in other financial markets. Large funds were shifting significant amounts of money into oil 'paper' markets looking for hedge against inflation as well as higher yields. The share of 'non-commercial'[130] participants who are generally seen as 'speculators' increased from about 20% in 2001 to about 50% in 2006 and kept on growing until the financial crisis of 2008 (Medlock 2013).[131] Some producers and OPEC in particular, were often deflecting the blame of high oil prices on 'speculation'. However, the causality of the events is hard to establish: Did the 'speculators' and 'financialization' of the oil market cause the high oil prices or were they simply attracted by bullish market fundamentals and high returns? A large body of literature has been dedicated to this problem and their results widely wary. However, the general consensus seems to be that the prices were primarily driven by market fundamentals while speculation might have had influence in certain periods.[132]

However, terms such as 'financialization', commoditization' and innovation continue to dominate oil markets. Artificial Intelligence (AI), algorithms, 'data mining', 'black box' trading and so on are just some terms applied to various computerised trading strategies that increasingly dominate oil markets. It is impossible to read the future, but just like any other human activity, oil trading will be more and more dominated by the information technology.

7 Concluding Remarks

Oil markets, like most energy markets, are shaped by 'natural monopolies'. These monopolies bring stability but also lack of transparency and lead to higher prices. They are usually broken when there is excess supply or by government intervention. Modern oil market has emerged following the collapse

[129] In 1956, Hubbert proposed that fossil fuel production in a given region over time would follow a roughly bell-shaped curve. In other words, it would inevitably 'peak' and decline. In 1972, The Club of Rome published similar ideas in the 'The Limits to Growth'. In 2005, Matthew R. Simmons published 'Twilight in the Desert: The Coming Saudi Oil Shock and the World Economy' which brought these incorrect ideas back in vogue.

[130] Commercial participants such as oil producers and refiners primarily hedge their physical positions. Non-commercials tend to be funds, asset managers and so on and are generally seen as 'speculators'. For definitions, see: https://www.cftc.gov/MarketReports/CommitmentsofTraders/index.htm

[131] K.B. Medlock (2013) page 23.

[132] For example, following the literature in endnote no. 122, The 2011 ECB paper finds that prior to 2004, market was largely fundamental, but post-2004 speculators dominate; Kilian and Murphy (2012) find no pre-2008 speculation driving the market; Juvenal and Petrella (2012) look at 2008 and find that the price was largely driven by demand, but speculation was significant too; Finally, Fattouh et al. (2012) find no evidence of any significant role of speculation.

of the integrated structures of the oil 'Majors' in 1960 and the failure of OPEC to effectively control it.[133] The result has been more competition, spot trading, transparency, lower prices, but also higher volatility. The way markets deal with risk and volatility is by developing 'paper' or derivatives instruments which enable risk mitigation far into the future. In this respect, oil market is perhaps the most developed and sophisticated commodity market in the world. To facilitate trading in hundreds of different grades of oil, three dominant benchmarks have emerged—WTI, Brent and Dubai—representing the three major trading regions: US, Europe and ME/Asia. When we talk about the price of oil, we normally talk about the price of one of these three, especially Brent and WTI. All other types of crude oil are traded, one way or the other, using one of these three price markers. In order to manage price risk, market participants have developed a plethora of derivatives contracts to such an extent that futures, swaps, options and other contracts often far exceed the total global oil production many times over. With maturity, they have added to the complexity of the market. As we have shown, derivatives are often essential for the establishment of the physical benchmark prices themselves. Benchmarks have substantially changed over time, following changes in the underlying fundamentals of supply and demand. They are constantly being challenged by new potential benchmarks such as WTI in the USG, LLS, ASCI index, Oman, Murban and others. Adaptation and Schumpeterian 'creative destruction' are the way oil markets work, and this process will enable it to continue to function smoothly for as long as there is oil trading.

Bibliography

Argus Media (2019), Argus Methodology and specifications guide Crude Oil, available at: https://www.argusmedia.com/en/methodology/methodology-listing?page=1

Bhattacharyya, S. C. (2011). Energy economics: Concepts, Issues, Markets and Governance, Springer.

Doshi, T. K., and Imsirovic, A. (2013). 'The Asian Premium in crude oil markets: fact or fiction? Chapter 2 in 'Managing Regional Energy Vulnerabilities in East Asia' edited by Zha Daoijong, USA: Routledge.

Einloth J. (2009), Speculation and Recent Volatility in the Price of Oil, FDIC Center for Financial Research, Working Paper, No. 2009-008, October 2009.

Fattouh B. (2012), The Dubai Benchmark and Its Role in the International Oil Pricing System, OIES, Comment, 2012.

Fattouh B. (2010), An Anatomy of the Crude Oil Pricing System, OIES, Paper WPM 40, 2010.

Fattouh B., Killian N. and Mahadeva N. (2012), the role of Speculation in the Oil Markets, OIES, Comment, 2012.

Fattouh B. and Sen A. (2014), New swings for West African crudes, OIES, Comment, 2014.

Horsnell P. (1997), Oil in Asia: Markets, Trading, Refining and Deregulation, OIES.

[133] This is not saying that OPEC had no influence on the market and prices.

Imsirovic A. (2019), Changes to the 'Dated Brent' benchmark: More to come, OIES, March 2019

Imsirovic A. (2014), Asian Oil Market in Transition, Journal of Energy Security, April 2014. Available at: http://www.ensec.org/index.php?option=com_content&view=article&id=520:asian-oil-markets-in-transition&catid=143:issue-content&Itemid=435

Imsirovic A. (2013), Do not blame PRAs for oil industry structural failures, Financial Times, 20 May 2013.

Luciani G. (2015), From Price taker to Price maker: Saudi Arabia and the World Oil markets: in Haykel B. et al. (2015) Saudi Arabia in Transition, Cambridge University Press, 2015.

Mabro R. and Horsnell P. (1993), Oil Markets and Prices, the Brent market and the Formation of World Oil Prices, OUP/OIES 1993.

McGrandle L. (1975), The Story of North Sea Oil, Wayland, 1975

McNally R. (2019), Crude Volatility, Columbia University Press

Medlock K.B. III (2013), Speculation, Fundamentals, and the price of crude oil, James A. Baker III Institute for Public Policy, Rice University, August 2013

Mehdi A. et al. (2019), Murban: A benchmark for the Middle East?, OIES, October 2019

OPEC (1988), Bulletin Nov/Dec 1988

Purvin & Gertz (2010), The Role of WTI as a Crude Oil Benchmark, January 2010.

Sampson A. (1988), Seven Sisters,

S&P Global Platts (2019), Platts Methodology and specifications guide Crude Oil, January 2019. Available at: https://www.spglobal.com/platts/en/our-methodology/methodology-specifications/oil/crude-oil-methodology

Tarbell I. (1904), The History of the Standard Oil Company, McClure, Phillips and Co.

Treat J.E. (1990), Energy Futures, PennWell Publishing

Vansteenkiste I. (2011), What is driving oil futures prices: fundamentals v speculation, European Central Bank, Working Paper Series No. 1371, August 2011.

Yergin D. (1991), The Prize, Simon & Schuster

Williams J. (1986), The Economic function of futures markets, Cambridge University Press, 1986.

World Bank (1995), Review and Outlook for the World Oil Market, World Bank, Discussion Papers no. 301, Shane S. Streifel, September 1995.

CHAPTER 19

The Trading and Price Discovery of Oil Products

Liz Bossley

1 Introduction

It may seem obvious to say that crude oil is, by-and-large,[1] only useful because of the products that can be extracted from it by the refining process. But the knowledge silos that exist in the oil industry often mean that the upstream industry does not know what is happening downstream at the refining end of the supply chain, let alone what retailers are up to at the consumer end.

Fortunately, although historically many crude oil traders were completely divorced from what their refined product trading colleagues were doing, today the division between crude and products trading is less like separate knowledge silos and more like two sides of a louvre door. There is still a division, but more exchange of knowledge and information between the two disciplines.

It is the purpose of this chapter to examine:

1. what is crude oil and the range of different types of crude oil that exist;
2. the most common types of refinery processes;
3. the quality and quantity of different products that can be extracted from crude by refining;
4. the purpose to which those refined products are put by the consumer; and
5. the inter-relationship between crude oil and refined product prices.

[1] The exception that proves that rule is the handful of countries, including Saudi Arabia, who burn crude oil directly in power stations to generate electricity.

L. Bossley (✉)
Consilience Energy Advisory Group Ltd., London, UK
e-mail: LizBossley@ceag.org

M. Hafner, G. Luciani (eds.), *The Palgrave Handbook of International Energy Economics*, https://doi.org/10.1007/978-3-030-86884-0_19

2 Some Very Basic Carbon Chemistry

Crude oil as it comes out of the ground is a complex mixture of hydrocarbons, which as the name suggests are compounds containing, among other things, carbon and hydrogen atoms and some of which contain oxygen. This differentiates them from the carbohydrates, which *all* contain oxygen atoms, that are more familiar outside the oil industry.

For those who did not pay attention at school, or for whom school is a dim and distant memory, an atom is made up of a positively charged nucleus surrounded by negatively charged electrons. The number of positive charges in the nucleus determines how many electrons are needed to stabilise, or neutralise, the atom. The atom will tend to gain or lose electrons in order to neutralise the charge of its nucleus.

The valence of an element is related to its ability to combine with hydrogen ('H'), which has a valence of 1, to achieve neutrality. Hydrogen is an atom containing a single positively charged proton in the nucleus orbited by a single negatively charged electron. This electron is available for sharing with other atoms to form compounds.

For example, one oxygen atom combines with two hydrogen atoms to form water and, since the valence of each hydrogen is 1, the valence of oxygen can thus be deduced to be 2. An atom of carbon ('C') is capable of combining with up to four other atoms, that is, it has a valence number of 4.

So, one familiar basic hydrocarbon molecule is CH_4, that is, methane. This represents one C, with a valence of 4, combined with 4 H, each with a valence of 1.

```
   H
   |
H—C—H   i.e. Methane =CH4
   |
   H
```

But carbon atoms can combine not only with atoms of other elements, like hydrogen, but with other carbon atoms. This means that carbon atoms can form chains and rings onto which other atoms can be attached. Carbon compounds are classified according to how the carbon atoms are arranged and what other groups of atoms are attached.

2.1 PONA

'PONA' indicates how these carbon chains or rings are organised in crude oil. It stands for Paraffins, Olefins, Naphthenes and Aromatics. These four types of hydrocarbons will sum to 100%, so the lower the paraffin content, the higher the naphthenes and aromatics. Olefins are not found in crude oil for reasons explained later.

Paraffins, also known as alkanes, are straight ('normal') or branch ('iso-') chained hydrocarbons 'saturated' with hydrogen. In other words, the valence number of 4 of the carbon has been neutralised by the attachment of sufficient 1 valence hydrogen atoms to use up all the valence of the carbon.

Paraffinic material is used in the petrochemical industry for making ethylene and propylene, which are the building blocks to make polythene and polypropylene. Paraffins occur in all crude oils, especially in so-called paraffinic crude in the lightest distilled fractions.

i.e. normal or n-pentane $=C_5H_{12}$

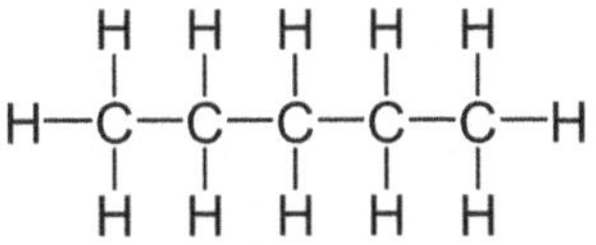

By referring to alkanes, or paraffins, as 'saturated' we mean that there are no double or triple bonds between the carbon atoms, that is, the valency is 'neutralised' because each 4 valency carbon atom is attached to four other atoms.

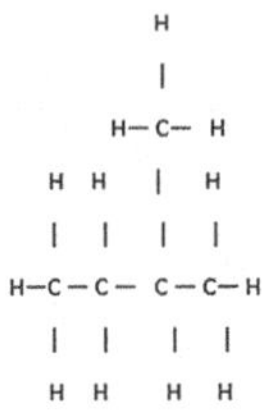

i.e. branched or iso-pentane = C_5H_{12}

Olefins, also known as alkenes, are unsaturated and are made up of hydrocarbons containing carbon double bonds. When there are insufficient hydrogen or other atoms available, the 4 valency of carbon atom is 'unsatisfied'. The carbon will attempt to acquire a spare electron from another carbon atom. The carbon atoms are depicted as sharing the available short supply of electrons amongst themselves and forming double bonds.

Olefins tend not to occur naturally in hydrocarbons because the double bonds are highly reactive and the olefins are quickly converted to more complex molecules where all the carbon's appetite for electrons is satisfied.

However, when large carbon molecules are broken up in the refining process, such as in a catalytic or FCC cracker as explained below, olefins tend to be more prevalent, that is, carbon to carbon bonds are broken and valency needs to be satisfied by saturation with hydrogen. If there is insufficient hydrogen available double bonds or even less stable triple carbon bonds ('alkynes') will form. For this same reason olefins tend to poison catalysts in catalytic crackers because they are so reactive and build up a residue of molecules on the catalyst surface.

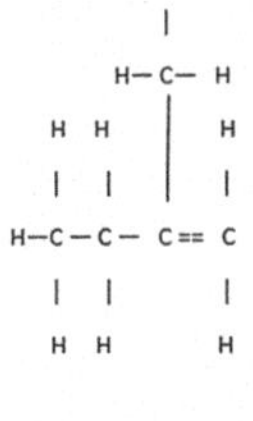

i.e. branched or iso-pentene = C_5H_{10}

Naphthenes, also known as cyclo-paraffins or C-alkanes, are saturated cyclical chains of more than 4 carbon atoms, such as cyclopentane or cyclohexane, the latter depicted below.

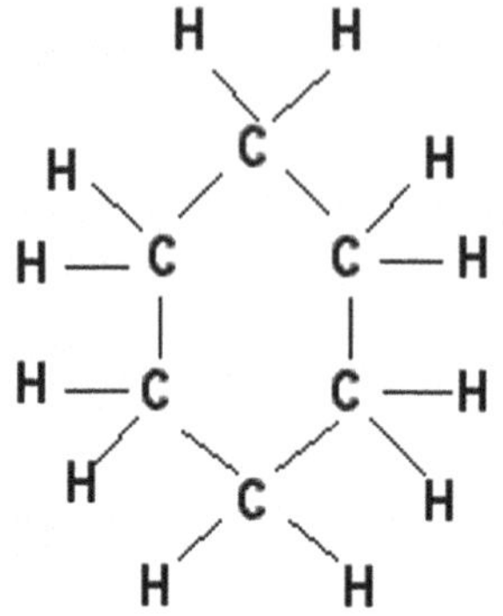

i.e. cyclohexane $=C_5H_{12}$.

Unsaturated cyclo-alkenes also exist such as cyclopentadiene, depicted below.

That is, cyclopentadiene = C_5H_6

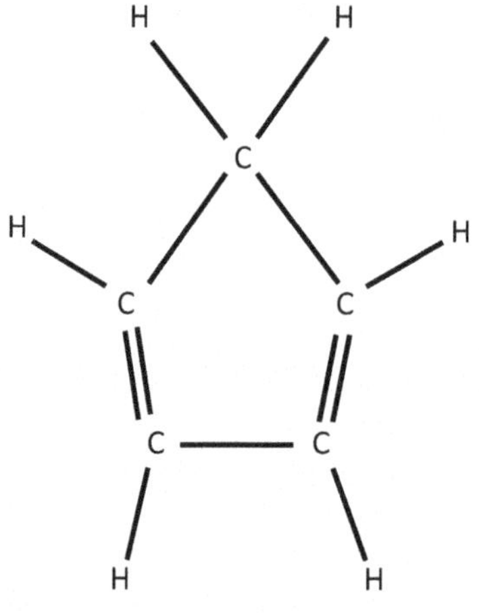

i.e. cyclopentadiene $=C_5H_6$

A key specification in the distilled product, naphtha, is its paraffin content compared with olefins, naphthenes and aromatics ('PONA'), as mentioned above. These four types of hydrocarbons will sum to 100%, so the lower the paraffin content, the higher the naphthenes and aromatics. This will dictate if the naphtha is naphthenic and will go on to a reformer to produce gasoline or is paraffinic and will be used as a petrochemical feedstock.

Aromatics are cyclical unsaturated molecules such as benzene, toluene and xylene.

The simplest aromatic, benzene, is depicted below, represented simply as a carbon ring with a cloud of electrons in the middle shared amongst the six carbons.

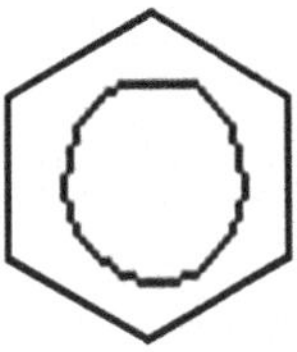

i.e. C_6H_6 benzene.

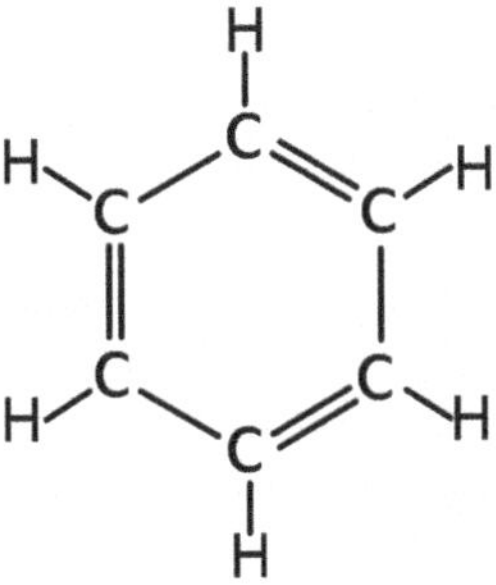

Aromatics differ from cyclo-alkenes in that they have an uninterrupted cyclic electron cloud. N+A ring structures are typically used in gasoline production and aromatics are used in making polystyrene, paint, solvents and so on. Right, enough chemistry.

3 The Crude Oil Assay

There are two different kinds of crude oil assay that are used in the oil industry:

1. the PVT assay; and
2. the refining assay.

PVT stands for pressure, volume and temperature and is an analysis of how the crude oil will flow in the reservoir and the well from which the oil is produced. This is upstream data used by reservoir engineers. Frequently oil field project managers will present their oil traders with a PVT assay and expect the trader to come back with an estimate of the value of their particular crude oil in the market.

Unfortunately, consumers in the market are not interested in the reservoir characteristics of crude oil. They are interested in what type and quantity of oil products can be extracted from the crude by refining. So, in order to value a particular type of crude oil, the trader needs to see a refining assay. This can only be obtained from a sample of the crude that is produced from the well, which is then sent to a laboratory to simulate passing it through various refinery processes of increasing complexity.

The resulting refining assay is usually provided in tabular form and contains data concerning:

- The whole crude properties of the unrefined crude, which give important information about how the crude oil should be handled, stored and transported;
- A True Boiling Point ('TBP') distillation curve, which plots the cumulative volume and weight of the crude oil that has boiled off at increasing temperatures;
- A basic PONA breakdown, as described above, of the refined products, usually the lighter ends. The olefin content should be at or close to zero in crude oil. The presence of olefins may mean the crude volume has been bulked out by adding some cracked material that has already been through the refining process. The presence of olefins should be questioned by a buyer;
- The quantity and quality of the different products that are derived from the crude oil are arranged into different temperature ranges or cut-off points, usually just called 'cut points'. For example, everything that boils off between say 165°C and 235°C might be categorised as kerosene.

4 Whole Crude Properties

4.1 Density

Every assay will contain information about the density of the crude as one of the prime characteristics defining the crude. Density is defined as the mass per unit of volume and may be expressed as kilograms per cubic metre or kilograms per litre. Since the volume of materials change with temperature, density is referenced at an exact temperature, typically 15°C.

Density is often expressed relative to the density of water, that is, the specific gravity, with both substances at the same temperature. Specific gravity is a ratio and is not a particularly user-friendly number. It may be a number such as 0.8536, with the specific gravity of water being 1. So, in the oil industry, we have our own measure of density, namely API gravity.

The higher the API gravity, the lighter the crude. For crude oil the API gravity ranges from less than 10° for some of the very heavy, dense Venezuelan crudes, to up to about 45–50°, which are very light and are often categorised as condensate. The API gravity of water is 10°. Most crude floats on water because the oil is usually lighter or greater than 10° API.

4.2 Sulphur Content

Sulphur is a contaminant, which is present to a greater or lesser extent in all crude oil. The desire to burn 'cleaner' fuels means that sulphur compounds need to be removed from the crude before the end products are sold to the consumer. There are different kinds of sulphur compounds of varying corrosiveness and toxicity increasing from disulphides, sulphides, thiols, also known as mercaptans, and, the most toxic, hydrogen sulphide ('H_2S'). This last compound is strictly limited by pipeline operators usually to less than 10 parts per million ('ppm'). Beyond 100 ppm it is considered to be potentially fatal.

Mercaptans too can be limited because of their characteristic 'rotten eggs' odour, which can be detected down to 0.5 ppm. This makes them useful when added to the gas supply to help detect leaks. But tankers will often reject high mercaptan crudes because the odour is not only unpleasant, but persistent. Some ports will not admit tankers that have carried a high mercaptan crude oil as one of its previous five cargoes.

4.3 *Pour Point*

As the name suggests the pour point is the temperature below which the oil cannot be poured, or pumped. If the pour point is too high then it may need to be shipped in a tanker with heating coils, depending on the time of year and climate at the destination port. There have been cases when vessels carrying high pour point crude oil have been arrested, for reasons connected to previous voyages, at northern ports in the summer and, by the time the dispute was resolved and the vessel was released in the winter, the oil had solidified and had to be dug out of the tanker.

The pour point is associated with the wax content and the kinematic viscosity of the crude oil. Highly paraffinic crudes may have a high content of complex wax molecules that begin to crystallise at low temperatures, as measured by their 'cloud point'. But this is not a hard and fast rule as some highly naphthenic crudes, such as some Venezuelan grades, also have high viscosity. The cloud point is the temperature at which these crystals first appear. Kinematic viscosity records the time taken for a given volume of oil to flow a known distance through a pipe at a controlled temperature, subject only to the force of gravity.

4.4 *Acid, Salt and Metals*

The Total Acid Number ('TAN') is the amount of potassium hydroxide in milligrams required to neutralise a gram of crude oil, and it is therefore a measure of the acidity of the whole crude. A TAN of more than 0.3 can present difficulties for refineries that do not have acid-resistant metallurgy and indicates that the refinery may need to blend the crude oil with a low acid grade or avoid that grade altogether.

High salt content can also be corrosive and requires treatment in a desalter before being introduced into the distillation column. Most refineries have such desalters. The presence of metals, such as vanadium and nickel, can cause problems for refineries that use catalysts because the trace metals can deposit on the catalyst surface slowing down the rate of chemical conversion reactions.

An analysis of these whole crude properties gives an initial indication of the type of crude that is being analysed and what type of refinery is most likely to squeeze the last cent of value out of the oil in question.

More detail is contained in the product cuts described by the refining assay. We will return to these after a discussion of the refining process.

5 Refining Processes

Refining processes can be classified into three basic types:

- *Separation*, which divides the crude oil into different categories of products like LPG, naphtha, kerosene, gas oil and heavy fuel oil. This does not make any changes to the crude at the molecular level. Recombining the products would, in theory, restore the crude oil;
- *Treatment*, which does not change the yield of individual products, but changes the characteristics of the product to remove contaminants, often sulphur. Treatment may involve blending the products with other material or including additives to enable the product in question to meet the quality specifications that the market, or government regulation, demand; and
- *Upgrading/conversion*, which changes the yield, breaking down less valuable heavy products into lighter, more valuable products.

5.1 Primary or Atmospheric Distillation

Primary distillation is carried out at atmospheric pressure and is the most common separation process employed in the oil refining sector. It is the starting point of crude oil's journey towards the refined products that the end-user demands.

The crude oil is heated up in a furnace so that a large proportion is vapourised and the liquid/vapour mixture is introduced into the distillation column. Any liquid that has not been vapourised falls to the bottom of the column. This is known as long residue. The vapour rises up the column where it passes through a number of perforated trays. Each tray contains liquid and, as the vapour bubbles through the liquid, it cools down. Some of the vapour will revert to liquid at this cooler temperature, and can be drawn off from the side of the tray. The lighter components remain as vapour and rise higher to the next tray where the process continues. The lowest tray will extract the heavier fractions and the higher trays will extract progressively lighter fractions. The end result is LPG, naphtha, kerosene, gas oil and long residue. The last of these can be used to make heavy fuel oil, but is more often processed further to generate more of the lighter products needed by the end-user.

Depending on the placement and the temperature of the trays, the refiner can produce a bit more or less naphtha and a bit less or more kerosene, or a bit less kerosene and a bit more gas oil.

Historically, a number of refineries ceased processing the crude at that point. These were referred to as 'topping' refineries. Very few simple topping refineries remain and those that do tend to sell their product on to more complex refineries as semi-finished product for treatment and upgrading.

The highest boiling point compounds are not acceptable for upgrading by the cracking process, described below. So, it is necessary to separate further the fractions suitable for upgrading by additional distillation.

The residue produced from primary distillation will disintegrate or crack up into lighter products in an uncontrolled and undesirable manner if it is subjected to higher temperatures. So, to extract the residue without it breaking up, a secondary distillation is carried out on the atmospheric residue, this time under a vacuum. This reduces the boiling points needed to separate the fractions and the vacuum gas oil ('VGO') can be separated out and used for selective cracking. The vacuum residue, or short residue, which is left over from this process is a heavy, viscous, tar-like material, which can be used as bitumen or for fuel oil, or which can be upgraded through processes such as coking or long residue hydrocracking. These are explained below.

Separation of products in crude oil by temperature, with or without a vacuum, is not the only separation process. Separation can also be achieved by freeze point and solvency in different chemicals. But primary distillation is the predominant methodology in commercial use.

5.2 *Hydrodesulphurisation and Reforming-Hydroskimming*

Treatment processes are primarily involved with treating or removing sulphur compounds contained in the products. There are two main techniques:

1. *Hydrodesulphurisation*, in which sulphur is removed, by first converting the sulphur compounds to H_2S, which, as a gas, can be separated easily from liquid products. Elemental sulphur can be recovered from the gas.
2. *Merox* treatment involves converting mercaptans by oxidising them to disulphides, which are sweeter and non-corrosive.

The hydrodesulphurisation process requires supplies of hydrogen gas to stimulate the removal of sulphur contained in the products. This is why hydrodesulphurisation tends to go hand in hand with reforming.

A reformer converts the naphtha from the primary distillation column into gasoline. The naphtha is heated over a platinum catalyst and its octane number is improved. As discussed below octane number is a measure of a fuel's ability to burn evenly. A number of chemical reactions take place in the reformer and hydrogen is generated as a by-product. This hydrogen can be used in the hydrodesulphurisation process and so the 'hydroskimming' refinery was developed, combining reforming with hydrotreating.

The end result of the processes in a hydroskimming refinery is LPG, gasoline, kerosene or aviation turbine oil, gas oil and long residue in broadly the same proportions as seen in primary distillation. There will also be elemental sulphur recovered from the hydrotreater.

5.3 *Upgrading/Conversion*

The third type of process encountered in oil refineries is upgrading or conversion. These processes are employed to change the yield of products and generally consist of converting the unwanted high boiling point, long chain hydrocarbons to shorter molecules. This is achieved through application of heat and catalysis to 'crack' the molecules.

Cracking processes employ a catalyst to promote thermal decomposition of the long hydrocarbon chains. Cracking is an endothermic reaction, that is, it needs the input of heat. It also produces carbon, which can be used to generate heat and re-energise the process. Cracking processes include Fluid Cat Cracking ('FCC') and hydrocracking, which also consumes hydrogen to saturate the olefins produced.

5.4 *Other Refining Processes*

Other upgrading processes include:

Alkylation—combines light, gaseous hydrocarbons such as propylene, butylene and isobutane to make gasoline components;

Visbreaking—thermal cracking to produce more middle distillate from residual fuel oil;

Coking—converts the residual oil from the vacuum distillation column into low molecular weight hydrocarbon gases, naphtha, light and heavy gas oils and petroleum coke;

Zero Fuel—the continued drive to reduce greenhouse gas emissions has meant that oil refiners have had to employ more upgrading processes to produce proportionally greater yields of clean transportation fuels. Refiners have been required to employ more than one form of cracking and 'zero fuel oil' refineries have started to be sought out by refiners. Generally, a coking plant is employed with a cracking unit to completely destroy fuel oil fractions.

After the treating and upgrading process, the products that emerge differ from those that result from primary distillation and hydroskimming: they will comprise more LPG, more gasoline, about the same amount of aviation turbine oil or jet fuel, more ultra-low sulphur diesel ('ULSD') or gas oil and much less heavy fuel oil. How much more or less depends on the specific crude or blend of crudes put through the refining system and the nature of that crude, as identified by the refining assay.

As mentioned above, the quantity and quality of the different products that are derived from the crude oil are arranged in the assay into different temperature range cut points. There are no absolute rules about where these cut points should be because there can be considerable overlap in the refining process between the different categories.

	TBP ranges (°C)
Light naphtha	C5[a]–85
Heavy naphtha	85–165
Kerosene	165–235
Middle distillates	235–350
Vacuum gas oil	350–550
Long residue	350+
Short residue	550+

[a]C_5 refers to pentane, which has 5 carbon atoms and 12 hydrogen atoms (C_5H_{12}). The shorter chained hydrocarbons, methane (CH_4), ethane (C_2H_6), propane (C_3H_8) and butane (C_4H_{10}), occur naturally as gases at atmospheric temperature and pressure.

6 Refined Products

When crude oil traders and refined product traders switch disciplines the first and most obvious difference apparent to them is the definition of the quality of what is being bought and sold.

Crude oil traders are used to buying a crude oil identified by its 'brand name' alone. This might be something like Bonny Light of the quality available at the time and place of delivery, Nigeria, or Lula of the quality as available at the time and place of delivery, Brazil.

This is particularly problematic when the crude oil is a blended stream of production from a number of different oil fields of varying quality. The quality of the blend can vary, sometimes quite substantially, depending on the production rates of the various contributing fields, for example during maintenance. Certain blended crudes that have a reputation for highly variable quality are sold with price adjustment mechanisms in the sales contracts to compensate the buyer if the quality actually delivered on the day is outside a pre-defined range.

The buyer typically does not have the right to reject the cargo if the quality delivered is not as expected. In such circumstances the refiner may have to subject the cargo to a different type of refinery process or to blend it with some other grade of crude oil or semi-finished product.

In the case of refined products, the buyer is much more specific about the quality of the product that is to be delivered and much less concerned about the crude oil from which it originated. The products have to be fit for the purpose for which they are being purchased and the buyer will reject any cargo that does not meet the specifications contained in the contract.

The refined products, or distillates, that are produced in the refining process can be separated into two categories: the major products that are burned and the specialty products that are not burned. The major products are LPG, gasoline, kerosene/jet fuel, gas oil/diesel and fuel oil. The specialty products are naphtha, bitumen, lube oils, waxes and coke.

6.1 LPG

Liquefied petroleum gases are mixtures of propane and butane. These are used for heating/cooking and as motor fuel, but additionally can be used as chemical plant feedstock or propellant.

Because propane and butane are pure compounds, it is generally only necessary to specify the chemical composition of the mixture to define the requisite quality. Other important qualities specified are the sulphur levels and other hydrocarbon contaminants.

6.2 Naphtha

Naphtha is used either as a precursor for gasoline or for petrochemical manufacturing. It can also be used directly as a solvent. As mentioned above, its chemical composition, that is, its N + 2A, will determine whether it is suitable for reforming into gasoline or whether it should be used as petrochemical feedstock. N + 2A can be calculated as the volume or weight per cent of naphthenes in the naphtha plus twice its volume or weight of aromatics.

The higher N + 2A naphtha the higher the octane of the output when the naphtha is fed through a reformer to produce gasoline. A low N + 2A percentage means that the naphtha is likely to be sold to the petrochemical industry.

Light naphtha, in particular straight-chain pentane and hexane, known as 'normal' pentane and hexane, or n-pentane and n-hexane, together with n-butane can be passed through an isomerisation unit to convert them into their branched chain equivalents. These have a higher octane number than their straight-chain incarnations and are used in gasoline blending. Iso-butane provides additional feedstock for an alkylation unit, as described above.

The boiling range of the naphtha is specified in the contract as a key component in determining the yield of the naphtha in a reformer. The sulphur content is also relevant because it is a potentially toxic contaminant.

6.3 Gasoline

As mentioned above, the burning qualities of gasoline are defined by the octane number. This is an index against iso-octane, which is defined to be 100 octane, and heptane, which is defined to be 0 octane. Octane number is a measure of a fuel's ability to burn smoothly without engine knock. Engine knock is heard when multiple flame locations occur within a piston.

The Reid Vapour Pressure ('RVP') of the gasoline is measured in pounds per square inch ('psi') and indicates the volatility of the fuel, or the extent to which it vapourises at a given temperature. This is important because the fuel must be capable of vapourising and igniting at low temperatures to ensure that cars start on cold mornings. Sulphur content and chemical composition are also regulated for ever-tightening environmental reasons.

Gasoline blending is the most complex of refinery operations and is often performed at specialist blending terminals. The objective is to source cheap, poor quality components to blend them with more expensive, better quality components in pursuit of the whole being greater than the sum of the parts. Gasoline is a highly seasonal product and the differences between winter and summer specifications are significant, particularly in cold climates.

6.4 *Kerosene/Jet Fuel*

Kerosene is still used for heating and lighting in many countries. Kerosene and jet fuel are essentially the same product, but jet fuel has more extensive specifications.

The burning characteristic of both these products is defined by the smoke point, measured in millimetres. This is the maximum flame height at which the flame will burn without smoking. Paraffins have a high smoke point, while naphthenes and aromatics have progressively lower flame heights.

For jet fuel, the volatility and freeze point are particularly important because of the low temperature and pressure at high altitudes, as are stability, boiling range and acidity. Jet fuel is the only internationally specified product, because airplanes need to be able to fuel up with confidence at any airport in the world.

Interestingly jet fuel is permitted the highest sulphur content of all transportation fuels. Because it is burned at high altitude it is considered to be less of a threat to humans.

6.5 *Gas Oil/Diesel Fuel*

Gas oil and diesel fuel are essentially the same product, but diesel fuel has more extensive specifications for use in diesel car engines. Gas oil is most commonly used in agricultural and construction machinery. Marine quality gas oil is increasingly used in the bunker fuel industry as described below.

The burning characteristics of these products are defined by the Cetane Number, or Index. This measures the time between the start of ignition and combustion. The lower the Cetane Number the longer the ignition delay and the less suitable is the fuel for automotive diesel engines.

The cold flow properties are particularly important for diesel fuel and are measured by the Cold Filter Plugging Point ('CFPP'). It is measured in degrees centigrade and is the lowest temperature at which a given volume of diesel can be drawn through a standard filter in 60 seconds under controlled temperature and pressure conditions. The sulphur levels for both diesel and gas oil are strictly controlled and the boiling range and density are also specified.

6.6 *Fuel Oil and Bunkers*

Fuel oil is a term used to cover the higher boiling point fuels used in heavy power plants, furnaces and slow speed diesel engines. Density and cold flow properties, as measured by viscosity and pour points, are important specifications for heavy fuels. Metal content and sulphur levels are strictly controlled for environmental reasons because the product is burned often in the proximity of humans.

Bunker fuel used to be the pool into which cracked fuel oil and other low-quality residual fuel could be dumped for burning in engines onboard tankers and other sea-going vessels. Environmental concerns have changed this attitude to bunkers. Consequently, increasingly the bunker pool is taking material from the gas oil pool to provide higher quality marine gas oil.

In 2016 the International Maritime Organisation ('IMO') announced a global sulphur cap of 0.5% on marine fuels starting from 1st January 2020, down from 3.5% in one fell swoop. This limit applies outside Sulphur Emissions Control Areas ('SECAs'). Inside SECAs the limit is even lower at 0.10% sulphur. At the time of writing the list of IMO SECAs is:

- Pacific coasts of North America;
- Atlantic coasts of the United States, Canada and France and the Gulf of Mexico;
- Hawaiian Islands;
- US Caribbean sea;
- The Baltic; and
- The North Sea.

China introduced its own ECAs on 1 January 2019. This is gradually tightening over time.

From 1 March 2020 it is prohibited to even carry non-compliant bunkers unless the ship has exhaust gas cleaning systems, or scrubbers, which can be retrofitted, but which are expensive.

Sulphur is not the only environmental target for bunker fuels. The IMO introduced a mandatory marine fuel consumption data regulation for global shipping from 2019, with a view to make the future fleet more fuel efficient and reducing greenhouse gas emissions from burning bunkers.

6.7 *Lubes*

Crude oil that is approved for the production of lubricating oil contains a small economic jackpot because it is one of the highest value-added products in the barrel. The additional margin usually accrues to the refiner of lube manufacturer rather than the upstream producer. Because of the use to which lubes are put, viscosity, cold flow properties and wax content are significant specifications.

There are two main types of lubricants: Paraffinic and Naphthenic. Paraffinic lubes are used in situations where there is a significant change in operating temperatures. The Viscosity Index is used to measure the change in the viscosity of the lubricant at different temperatures. Naphthenic lubes are used in situations where temperature will be virtually constant and therefore the absolute viscosity is more relevant.

It takes a long time to get a grade of crude oil approved for lubes production. This is because the lube oil has to be tested to destruction in an engine, which can take over a year in a laboratory.

Lubes are made largely from vacuum gas oil and is subjected to further processing and improvement with chemical additives.

6.8 Bitumen

Bitumen is used in the paving and road industry. The relevant properties are the softening point and penetration, which describe the ability of the material to maintain its integrity with changes in ambient temperature. Since bitumen is not burnt, its sulphur content is not as important as it is for other products.

6.9 Coke

Petroleum coke is a by-product from the thermal destruction of high boiling components of crude oil, such as from a coker, as mentioned above. High-quality coke can be used as electrical anodes for metal electrolysis processes, but typically the product is used for burning in furnaces.

As stated earlier, petroleum products have a significant degree of overlap between their boiling point ranges. For example, heavy naphtha can become part of the gasoline, kerosene or even the gas oil pool. A refiner can choose to eliminate the kerosene yield and instead maximise gasoline and gas oil production. It is important to recognise the overlap of product yields as this can have an impact on determining crude values.

7 Gross Product Worth and the Value of Crude Oil

We said at the outset that crude oil is only useful because of the products that can be extracted from it by the refining process. We have looked at the chemical analysis of crude oil as expressed by an assay. We have looked at different refinery processes and how they are used to extract and treat usable products from the crude oil in the quantities and of the qualities demanded by the market. We have also looked at the applications in which these refined products are employed by end-users.

It is time to look at what all the foregoing means for the value of crude oil. One of the basic tools used for this task is the Gross Product Worth ('GPW').

A GPW is established by considering the physical and chemical analysis of the grade of crude oil involved, that is, the assay. The assay can be evaluated in the context of how that particular quality of oil will perform in different types of refineries of varying complexity. This will produce an assessment of the amount and quality of refined products that can be extracted from that grade of crude, if sold to the right refiner.

For example, the crude seller will not get the best price by selling a very high API gravity light crude to a refinery with coking capability. The coker would be much better off buying cheaper, low gravity heavy crude and extracting more valuable light ends from short residual fuel from the vacuum distillation unit, as explained above. Similarly, a refinery with stainless steel metallurgy is not going to maximise its margin by buying low TAN crude. It would be better off buying cheap, high TAN crude that it can run when others cannot.

Taking the assay together with the optimum type of refinery model for the crude in question allows the calculation of the GPW of the crude.

The GPW takes the price of each of the products that can be derived from a specific crude oil in a specific refinery configuration, multiplies the yield of each product by its price and adds these up to give an estimate of the likely value of the crude oil in the market. It is the sum of the quantities of each product multiplied by the prices of each of those products. Obviously, the right product prices have to be used. There is no point trying to value a crude that you are trying to sell to a refinery in Singapore using product prices in Rotterdam.

In reality, the actual traded price in the market may be very different from the GPW, because there is more to the price of crude oil than its quality. For example, the refiner will not just be influenced by the GPW of the crude. It will also take into account the cost of freight to get the oil to its refinery. The refiner may favour a grade of crude oil that gives it a lower GPW, but which is located on its doorstep and gives it a minimal freight cost. The buyer may take into consideration any factors that in its sole opinion it considers relevant. For example, if it buys FOB from a loading terminal where there are persistent delays and where demurrage claims are not settled promptly, or at all, it may mark down the price it will pay for that crude.

The GPW is not an exact proxy for the absolute value of a barrel of crude. But it is a useful tool for assessing the likely market price of a grade of crude oil where there is not much data available on trades, by comparing it with the GPW of a grade of oil where there is active trading and transparent price information. Comparing the GPWs of two different grades of crude oil is the normal starting point for assessing the likely relative price of the two grades of crude oil in the market, that is, the price differential between the two.

8 Leads and Lags in Petroleum Prices

One of the perennial conundrums within the oil trading community is whether refined product prices lead crude oil prices up or down, or whether the opposite is true and crude price movements precede a rise or fall in product prices. There is no single correct answer as both statements can be true at different times.

For example, back in the mid-1980s when OPEC decided to maintain its market share in the face of rising oil production from newcomer producers such as the North Sea, the OPEC producers undertook to guarantee their buyers a positive refining margin, or 'netback'. With an assured margin, refiners started producing flat out and churned out more refined products that the market needed or wanted. Product prices fell and, to honour the promise of positive refining margins, the OPEC producers had to cut their crude prices. Crude oil prices chased product prices down to less than $10/bbl before OPEC 'blinked' in August 1986 and abandoned the netback policy.

As another example, the crude oil price collapse at the end of 2014 makes a classic case study in market economics at work. Crude oil prices, driven up by burgeoning demand for refined products in China, India and other emerging economies, led to a rapid increase in crude oil supply from oil fields that had hitherto been uneconomic, including US oil production from shale. This increased production had a moderating effect on oil crude prices, while the high refined product prices choked off demand and the emerging economies faced a recession. This is 'Economics 101'.

The old maxim that 'when China sneezes the rest of the world catches a cold' seems cruelly prophetic when the impact of the 2020 COVID-19 virus on oil prices is considered. The collapse in demand for refined products as China went into quarantine, followed by the rest of the world, cratered demand for products and would have inevitably dragged crude oil prices down after them, absent any other factors.

But another compounding factor in 2020 was the oil production war led by Saudi Arabia on one side and Russia on the other. The 'OPEC+' cooperation pact amongst 24 oil-producing nations to moderate production, which had been in existence since 2017, broke down at a meeting in March 2020 and the floodgates of crude supply were opened, accelerating the race to the bottom of the whole crude and product price complex.

The relationship amongst and between crude oil and refined product prices is heavily influenced by the process of arbitrage. If oil prices are high in one region and low in another, traders will buy the lower priced oil and transport it to the higher priced region up to the point where the cost of freight and the time value of money no longer make it economic to do so.

Similarly, if the price of oil for delivery today is lower than the price of oil for delivery next month, traders will buy oil for delivery now and store it for delivery later when prices are higher. They will do this until the cost of storage and the time value of money no longer make it economic to do so.

Lastly, if the demand for a particular specification or quantity of refined product differs between regions, whether for climatic, seasonal or regulatory reasons, traders will respond by transporting and/or storing and/or blending the oil to iron out the anomalous discrepancy in prices between regions.

Refiners respond to such price anomalies by changing the types of crude oil they put through their refineries, that is, their 'crude slate', to meet the quality specifications demanded by end-users up to the point where they no longer have a positive refining margin. At which point the anomaly is likely to have been eliminated by the combination of responses referred to above.

Bibliography

"Trading Crude Oil: The Consilience Guide", by Liz Bossley, published by The Write Approach Limited, 2013.
"Trading Refined Oil Products: The Consilience Guide", by Liz Bossley and Catherine Jago, published by The Write Approach Limited, 2014.
"Petroleum Refining for the Non-Technical Person", by William L. Leffler, published by Pen Well Publishing Company, Second Edition 1985.
"Oil Markets and Prices" by Paul Horsnell and Robert Mabro, published by The Oxford Institute for Energy Studies, 1993.
"Demand, Prices and the Refining Industry", by Robert Bacon, Margaret Chadwick, Joyce Dargay, David Long and Rober Mabro, published by The Oxford Institute for Energy Studies, 1990.

CHAPTER 20

The Trading and Price Discovery for Natural Gas

Manfred Hafner and Giacomo Luciani

Pricing mechanisms are crucial elements in gas trade. In the last decade, they have been increasingly under the spotlight as disagreements between suppliers and buyers increased. This happened first in Europe, particularly in the first half of the 2010s, and subsequently in Asia, towards the end of the decade. A wave of renegotiations and arbitrations of long-term supply contracts shook the pillars of the gas industry, with pricing being the core issue. This chapter aims to briefly discuss general notions of pricing, reflect on the importance of pricing mechanisms, analyse different pricing mechanisms across time and space, and account for the most important recent transformations, some of which are still unfolding.

M. Hafner (✉)
SciencesPo—Paris School of International Affairs, Paris, France

Johns Hopkins University SAIS Europe, Bologna, Italy

Fondazione Eni Enrico Mattei (FEEM), Milan, Italy
e-mail: manfred.hafner@sciencespo.fr

G. Luciani
SciencesPo—Paris School of International Affairs, Paris, France

Graduate Institute of International and Development Studies, Geneva, Switzerland
e-mail: giacomo.luciani@sciencespo.fr

M. Hafner, G. Luciani (eds.), *The Palgrave Handbook of International Energy Economics*, https://doi.org/10.1007/978-3-030-86884-0_20

1 Pricing and Prices—General Remarks on Their Functions

One could argue that what ultimately matters for both suppliers and buyers are price levels. In this sense, pricing mechanisms are important insofar as they are one of the key factors that influence price levels. As a matter of fact, pricing mechanisms are instruments that determine how changes in the supply and demand balance (market fundamentals) for a commodity are translated into price levels. In other cases, pricing mechanisms do not take into account market fundamentals. In any case, while price levels are probably the most important outcome of pricing mechanisms, suppliers and buyers might nurture other long-term and/or strategic interests with regard to pricing mechanisms that go beyond the prices that such mechanisms deliver in a specific moment in time. These interests might relate for instance to stability (lack of volatility) and transparency. There are cases in which short-term interests might clash with long-term interests. For instance, a supplier might support a pricing mechanism over another even if this delivered a relatively low price initially, because it might hold expectations of delivering higher prices over the long term.

The importance of the function played by prices (and pricing) in the gas business cannot be overestimated. First of all, price levels (and pricing mechanisms) are key ingredients to adjust demand and supply. Moreover, they are a fundamental component of any risk management strategy, for both buyers and producers. They also play an important role in signalling investment opportunities and investment needs. For example, if a region pays a substantial price premium relative to a bordering region, there will be a signal to invest in cross-border trade capacity. Also, pricing and prices are decisive factors determining the competitiveness of gas with respect to alternative energy carriers. They also influence the competitiveness of certain gas sources with other gas sources. Pricing and prices will influence sales levels and thus revenues—provided that buyers are not captive and are able to switch to an alternative supplier. Finally, gas pricing and prices are an important factor to look at when analysing the competitiveness of products for which gas is an important input and a key cost component (e.g. fertilisers).

2 Variety of Pricing Mechanisms Along the Gas Value Chain

It is intuitive that gas prices change over time and it is quite well known that they also change across geographies. What is less known is that they also change along the gas value chain. Upstream, a wellhead price will be charged. This is essentially the wholesale price of gas at its point of production. As gas is transported, stored and distributed, new price components will be added to reflect additional costs incurred (keeping in mind that it is paramount to analytically distinguish prices and costs). For instance, prices will tend to reflect entry fees, storage fees and exit fees. First of all, supply transportation costs will have to be covered (international pipeline fees or shipping in case of LNG). Market import prices (border or beach prices) are not yet the final prices that end-users in a country will end up paying. In fact, prices will also need to reflect costs of transmission in the destination market area and merchant selling costs (including taxes and excises, as well as a margin for the merchant). Some large users are directly connected to the transmission network. But customers further downstream will pay a price that is also reflective of storage and distribution costs, once again including taxes and excises as well as a margin for the distributors. Another important concept is that of 'citygate price': this is usually the price charged at the entry of the distribution network, where gas is transferred to a local utility. Retail prices differ significantly from wholesale prices and import prices.

Gas is also traded differently at various levels of the value chain. For pricing purposes, it is particularly relevant to make a distinction between trade that takes place between a producer and an importing company, for example, Gazprom and Eni, and domestic sales by an importing company, that is, Eni's deliveries to its Italian customers, including industrial users, power plants and retail users. Traditionally, the more one moves towards the downstream segment, the more gas tends to be traded under short-term arrangements. International trade, on the other hand, used to be dominated by long-term contracts. While these are still the dominant arrangement governing internationally traded gas (for both piped gas and LNG), short-term trade has made substantial inroads in recent years. Short-term trade refers to both contracts with a duration of 3–4 years or lower and spot transactions[1]—which can in turn take many different forms (Over-the-Counter, Exchange, etc.).

3 A Taxonomy of Pricing Mechanisms

Generalising considerations about pricing mechanisms beyond this point is very difficult, because gas prices and pricing are very much subject to geographical variables. Unlike oil, gas markets still retain marked regional characteristics. This has to do with the fact that transporting gas is relatively more expensive than oil. This is in turn explained by the different nature of gas molecules (gaseous) and oil molecules (liquid)—which makes the energy density of gas lower than that of oil. Given the larger impact of transportation on final gas delivery/procurement costs, gas trade has traditionally tended to be (at best) regional rather than intercontinental. Actually, the vast majority of gas produced in the world is consumed in the same country where it is produced.

LNG trade is changing this. Price convergence across regions is increasing. However, differences between the gas market and the oil market remain, and a full gas price convergence at the global level is unlikely. While Asian and European prices might very well become more structurally and closely

[1]According to the classification by GIIGNL (International Group of Liquefied Natural Gas Importers).

correlated as LNG trade progresses towards full commoditization, the gap between prices in producing/net exporting regions and consuming/net importing regions is going to remain. It is going to be very difficult for Europe to achieve Henry Hub parity, simply because domestic production in Europe is declining and European prices depend on international trade and availability of flexible volumes. Conversely, in the US, local hub prices are set by domestic supply and demand dynamics. Albeit to a lesser extent than today, regional pricing and price spreads are thus expected to persist.

The most widely followed taxonomy for pricing mechanisms is provided by the International Gas Union (IGU) (IGU 2019). This taxonomy makes a first distinction between oil price escalation and gas-to-gas competition, a dichotomy at the heart of the renegotiations and arbitrations that shook the gas business in the 2000s (and are likely to continue shaking the gas business in Asia). The main difference between oil price escalation (oil indexation) and gas-to-gas competition (hub indexation) is that under the former scheme, the price of gas is indexed to that of another commodity (oil), while under the latter, the price of gas is determined by gas supply and demand. The debate on whether oil indexation is still acceptable is very fierce. Oil indexation has been called a 'barbarity' and an anachronism by some (Pirrong 2018). Others are almost emotionally attached to long-term oil-indexed contracts, defending their merit and historical role in providing stability and consensus and in mobilising essential capital-intensive investment (Komlev 2016).

In oil indexation, the gas price is indexed, typically through a base price and an escalation clause, to the price of crude oil (notably in Asia) or a basket of oil products such as fuel oil, gasoil and gasoline (more frequent in Europe). Theoretically, gas prices could very well be indexed to prices of other energy carriers. Instead of oil, the price of electricity could be used as benchmark, or the price of coal. This has been done only in isolated cases. Actually, it might make more sense to index gas prices to coal prices because gas and coal still compete directly in the power sector, while gas and oil do not compete much at the moment.

In gas-to-gas competition, the price is determined by supply and demand. The trading activity that sets prices can take place over different periods: every day, every month, ever year and so on. Day-ahead, month-ahead, year-ahead prices reflect these different trading horizons. Trading can happen at physical or virtual hubs. It is important to highlight that gas can be exchanged in term contracts with an *indexation* to hub prices or directly through spot transactions that take place on hubs. Long-term contracts and hub prices are therefore perfectly compatible: clearly, hub prices need some spot and short-term trading activity to take place in order to exist (and in order to be reliable: the more trading activity and the more traders, the more the hub price will be set transparently and the more it will be a trusted, representative benchmark). But nothing prevents parties from adopting hub pricing mechanisms in long-term supply contracts.

Besides oil and hub indexation, a third pricing mechanism included in the IGU taxonomy is bilateral monopoly. This refers to a price that is set in bilateral negotiations between seller and buyer. The price can be set using a variety of criteria. It cannot be excluded that some of these criteria might be market related, but often there will be a mix of cost-related considerations, considerations on what a 'fair price' might be, and political considerations. After an agreement is struck, it will remain in force for a fixed period, typically one year. The agreement is often high level, involving governments or state-owned incumbents. With respect to internationally traded gas, it is a mechanism that has been mostly used in the Former Soviet Union and in the Middle East, but seldom in the Western world.

Oil indexation, hub indexation and bilateral monopoly are the three broad categories of pricing mechanisms used in internationally traded gas. For domestic sales, there are some additional possibilities. The first one identified by the IGU taxonomy is called 'netback from final product'. This essentially means that the gas supplier will receive a price that is a function of the price received by the buyer of gas for the product (e.g. a fertiliser) that the buyer of gas produces. This typically happens when gas is a major variable cost in a production and there is the intention to maintain the buyer of gas (and producer of the final product) afloat financially.

Besides, gas prices are often regulated. This however usually applies to domestic gas rather than internationally traded gas (Fig. 20.1).

Fossil fuels are still heavily subsidised in a number of jurisdictions. This is often grounded on sound social and political motivations, even if it is under increasing attack from the climate agenda perspective, and the International Energy Agency (IEA) consistently calls for an end of fossil fuel subsidies.[2] In fact, a significant share of population in a number of low-income countries would not be able to pay international market prices for energy. Low-income countries also need to promote manufacturing for economic diversification purposes, and it is often by offering low energy prices to national industries that governments ensure their international competitiveness. In very cold countries, gas heating also performs key humanitarian functions. However, regulated prices have a number of distortive effects. One of them is that consumers will not perceive gas as a scarce resource. This encourages wasteful use of the commodity, decreasing energy efficiency. Over time, this can put processes in motion that result in booming domestic demand, which can get out of control if combined with massive demographic and economic growth. Some countries in North Africa, for example, have been struggling and are still struggling to honour their gas export contracts because their domestic demand is growing in an uncontrolled way, also due to regulated prices at home. This example is also useful to illustrate that while regulated prices refer to national gas consumption, there are links with international gas trade as well. The large gap often found between the price of gas in developing countries and global

[2] https://www.iea.org/topics/energy-subsidies.

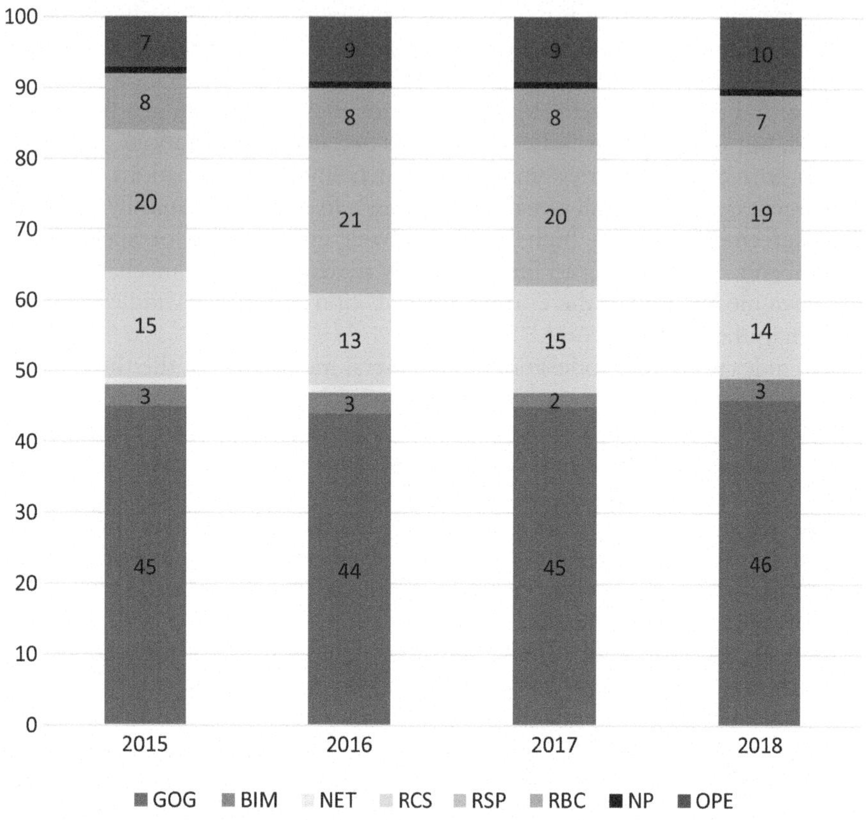

Fig. 20.1 Evolution in pricing mechanisms of domestically consumed gas (IGU 2019). *GOG* gas to gas competition, *BIM* bilateral monopoly, *NET* netback, *RCS* regulated cost of service, *RSP* regulated social and political, *RBC* regulated below cost, *NP* no price, *OPE* oil price escalation. Source: IGU 2019

gas markets is also at the basis of international oil and gas companies' reluctance to commit to substantial sales to local markets. They tend to prefer selling to global markets. However, host countries will often want some local gas development programmes to industrialise and reduce poverty. IOC-host country negotiations on pricing, prices and share of domestic sales are often complex and drawn-out.

In regulated prices, a first broad, important distinction can be made between prices set above cost and prices set below cost. In fact, prices are sometimes lower than market prices but nevertheless allow for the recovery of costs of production (and sometimes also of transmission and other activities throughout the gas value chain). In other, more extreme cases of subsidisation, prices are so low that production (or other activities in the value chain) is performed at a loss. The government will have to step in, with the result that the costs are socialised. Sometimes there is also cross-subsidisation, that is, some users are charged more than others and allow to cover the gap left by non-paying customers or protected customers. The IGU further distinguishes between 'regulated cost of service' (RCS), when the price is determined by a government agency or regulatory authority and the price is designed deliberately to cover costs and a minimum rate of return, and 'regulated social and political' (RSP), when a price is set at irregular time intervals on a markedly political or social basis, in response to specific needs or to raise revenue. The last category identified by the IGU is 'No Price' (NP). Gas is provided for free in a number of cases, either to military users or to domestic industries, particularly in settings where there is a lot of associated gas production and no other clear or evident uses for the gas, which would otherwise be flared.

4 The Rationale of Oil Indexation

As mentioned, in international gas trade transactions, oil indexation and hub indexation are the prevailing price mechanisms, and a transition is underway from long-term oil-indexed contracts to shorter term trade and hub pricing.

One might wonder why gas has been (and still is) indexed to another commodity. The short explanation is that gas markets have been limited in size and participation, while the oil market has been a truly global, liquid market for decades. The physical characteristics of the two commodities—as described above—largely accounted for these differences. Because gas markets were immature, they were not considered able to express reliable benchmarks. The potential for price manipulation is high in a market that is primarily local and dominated by a monopoly (or a cartel). Another overarching reason why oil indexation survived for so long is that, in general, there is inertia to changing pricing mechanisms. Once trust in a system is established, it is not easy to deviate from it without shocks.

When long-term oil-indexed contracts were conceived, the rationale was strong. Gas suppliers had to allocate substantial investment in production and transportation, and gas buyers often had to invest a lot in distribution networks. Appliances geared towards gas had to be adopted downstream by industrial residential and commercial users, often with the help of the State. The gasification of entire countries carried hefty costs. Strong guarantees were thus needed by both suppliers and buyers, and oil—by virtue of its liquid, global, traded nature—offered stronger guarantees than a nascent commodity.

The discipline of Transaction Cost Economics—and particularly the work by its founder Oliver Williamson (1979)—helps explaining why long-term contracts, rather than spot transactions, are adopted to govern certain types of exchanges. Under perfect market conditions, as described by neoclassical economics, there are no transaction costs. With zero transaction costs, Williamson argues, there would be no need for economic organisation. However, in real-world economic exchanges, information is never perfect and transaction costs exist. Special governance structures will have to replace standard market exchanges when transaction-specific value is high. According to Williamson, transaction-specific governance structures have to be created to govern transactions that are recurrent, entail 'idiosyncratic' investment and are conducted in a context of uncertainty. Let us review these concepts below.

Frequency is important because problems related to imperfect information (and the parties' ability to project future costs and benefits) begin to matter when an interaction is repeated or continuing, while they are not relevant in one-time transactions.

Secondly, Williamson argues that goods that are not specialised do not pose significant hazards because buyers can easily fall back on alternative suppliers and vice versa. However, in cases when the individuality of the parties affects costs significantly, conditions of 'non-marketability' can arise. Transactions involving this type of goods are called 'idiosyncratic'. In this respect, it is important to emphasise the higher specificity of investments in pipelines than in LNG (when the LNG market starts being global and mature): while LNG flows can be rerouted in case a customer is lost (or LNG can be sourced from another location if a supplier is lost), a pipeline cannot be moved, thus creating situations where buyers and suppliers are captive.

Contracts covering idiosyncratic activities have to solve problems arising from bounded rationality and opportunism. Once an investment is made on assets that have no alternative use to the one for which they were earmarked, such investment will be 'sunk'. In default of special governance structures offering guarantees and reassurances, marked asset specificity leads to what Klein et al. (1978) described as a 'hold-up' situation: perceiving a high risk of not being able to recoup the benefits of its investment, the investing party will be reluctant to invest, which can lead to endemic underinvestment. When there are idiosyncratic activities, spot exchanges will fail to provide the right investment incentives, and the assurance of a long-lasting relation is necessary as a ground for investing.

Uncertainty also plays an important role. Long-term contracts implemented in uncertain conditions make comprehensive contracting ('presentation') pricey if not impossible. Not all future eventualities for which revisions are needed can be anticipated at the beginning. Flexibility is thus key. In contracts whose future payoffs depend on future states of the world ('state-contingent claims'), disputes are likely to arise and, given that parties are assumed as opportunistic, it is difficult to establish whose claims should be believed. Mechanisms for dispute settlement are thus also needed.

Long-term gas supply contracts reflect all of these features. While it was said earlier that, conceptually, oil indexation and long-term contracting are different, the two were part of an 'inseparable package' at the beginning of gas trade between, for instance, Europe and the Soviet Union, on the one hand, and Japan and South-east Asian LNG exporters, on the other.

They can be regarded as 'inseparable packages' in the sense that they were complex risk allocation schemes, that is, arrangements where volume, duration and price clauses were all essential components for making it acceptable for both buyers and sellers to embark on a gas trade adventure that would last for decades. For this reason, even if this chapter focusses on pricing, a number of key non-pricing contract clauses must be discussed.

The schemes that were adopted, namely, in Euro-Soviet contracts, conferred greater price risk to exporters and greater volume risk to importers. Exporters were exposed to (higher) price risk in the sense that they were committed to providing contracted volumes regardless of the contract price. Fluctuations of oil prices trickled down to contract prices, and there was no guarantee that these would not be low for protracted periods of time. To limit price volatility, contract prices were calculated on the basis of the average price of a basket of oil products over several months (typically the 12 previous months) and applied for a shorter period (typically the 6 following months). It would however be incorrect to state that price risk was entirely taken by exporters. Importers were in fact also exposed to price fluctuations but with a limited risk—as they could pass through (higher) sourcing costs to their end-users, which were captive (in a pre-liberalisation environment). Instead, the main risk for importers was to be unable to sell the contracted gas volumes in case of lower-than-expected demand (volume risk).

Oil indexation was chosen because, as a liquid gas market did not exist, contracting parties found it necessary to peg contract prices to a more deeply traded commodity. Oil indexation was also chosen because companies in importing countries already had experience with it, and international oil market dynamics were well known to operators in the energy sector. Furthermore, oil indexation made sense because gas and oil were deeply interwoven at the time, not only in the upstream (with sizeable associated gas production) but also in the downstream—since gas was competing with oil products in heating and industry and to a lesser extent in power generation (Stern 2012). As mentioned, unlike Asian contracts, indexed to crude oil, contracts between Russia and Europe were indexed to oil products, especially heavy fuel oil—competing with gas in industry—and gasoil—competing with gas in the residential sector. A typical oil-indexed formula used in European import contracts could be simplified as follows:

$$\mathbf{P_t = P_0 + \alpha \times a_1 \times b_1 (Go_t - Go_0) + (1 - \alpha) \times a_2 \times b_2 (HFO_t - HFO_0)}$$

with P_t representing the contract price, P_0 the base price, α and $1-\alpha$ the weight of different market segments (in this example, the residential and industrial sectors); a_1 and a_2 the factors to convert oil product units to natural gas units; b_1 and b_2 the pass-through factors to transform oil product price changes into gas price changes (usually applying an 80–90 percent discount rate vis-à-vis oil products); and Go_0 and HFO_0 the values of gasoil and heavy fuel oil at a time t_0, calculated on an average of several months.[3]

[3] Cf. also L. Franza, *Long-Term Gas Import Contracts in Europe: The Evolution in Pricing Mechanisms*, Clingendael International Energy Programme, 2014.

Asian price formulae were designed differently. Apart from indexation to crude oil rather than products, one of the most distinctive features in Asian long-term contracts has been the presence of an oil slope with a gradient equal to 14.85 percent (derived from the historical 'benchmark' contract between Indonesia's Pertamina and Japan's Western Buyers consortium) (Flower and Liao 2012). The slope was changed over time and across contracts, but it typically remained in the range of 10–17 percent. The slope essentially determined the indexation ratio (taking into account the calorific difference between the two commodities). In the early days of LNG trade, there was a linear relationship between LNG and crude oil prices (in addition, the formula included a proxy for inflation). Typically, the original Asian formula of the type described above delivered a price of gas that was higher than crude oil in a low-price environment and potentially lower in a high-oil-price environment. S-curves (softening the relationship between gas and oil prices when the latter ones were either very low or very high) were intermittently applied when pricing became unsustainable for one of the parties (Flower and Liao 2012).

A fundamental property conferred to long-term contracts and pricing mechanisms was indeed flexibility. As the payback time of transmission pipelines was projected to extend over decades, contracting parties anticipated that market conditions would change along the lifespan of contracts, requiring dynamic adaptations. As has just been mentioned relative to Asian contracts, and as was certainly the case with European-Russian contracts (*below*), pricing mechanisms could be adjusted by one of the parties if the situation became unsustainable.

With hindsight, long-term import contracts proved extremely flexible: in spite of deep geopolitical transformations and fundamental changes in energy use, they sure have been bent—yet never broken—in decades of trade.[4]

First of all, volumetric flexibility was provided, entailing that when demand was falling, buyers could purchase volumes below the Annual Contracted Quantity (ACQ—with the possibility of compensating in the following years). Clearly, there were downward thresholds that the buyer had to respect. The buyer could still buy lower physical volumes, but, under a certain threshold, it would have still had to pay the equivalent price of gas not purchased (whereby the expression 'take or pay', which could be reformulated more clearly as 'whether you take it or not, you still have to pay for it'). This lower threshold is referred to as Minimum Contracted Quantity (MCQ) of take-or-pay (TOP) threshold, and it is usually somewhere between 75 and 85 percent of the ACQ. In addition to this downward flexibility, there is also upward flexibility, allowing sellers to ship volumes above the ACQ. Russia in particular

[4] Cf. Gustafson, "recent gas negotiations have shown flexibility and adaptation between Russian sellers and European buyers, and commercial logic has driven significant compromises—particularly on the Russian side, as Gazprom has responded to commercial and regulatory pressures", T. Gustafson, *The Bridge: Natural Gas in a Redivided Europe* (Cambridge, MA, 2020): Harvard University Press.

committed to make available larger volumes if requested, thanks to its spare production capacity.

The second element of flexibility related to pricing. Review clauses allowed the parties to ask for amendments to pricing mechanisms in certain time intervals (originally every three years) if justified by changes in the market. This was done to avoid that pricing formulae would deliver price levels that were entirely unprofitable for either the buyer or the seller (including opportunity cost considerations). In Eurasian gas trade, for instance, given the asset specificity of the investments and the need for market access, Gazprom was interested in extracting profits from gas sales as much as it was in keeping its European buyers satisfied (to avoid switching to other energy sources or gas suppliers) or at least financially solvent.

In sum, long-term contracts were sophisticated governance structures designed to allocate commercial risk between contracting parties involved in schemes that also had geopolitical objectives. Given the prominent ambition of *détente* as a catalyst for the Euro-Soviet contracts, and the characteristics of the underlying transactions, long-term contracts were given a relational character. Their provisions were designed to minimise disputes or at least to manage them. Contracts between Japan and South-east Asian countries were also strengthened by high-level political coordination. Japan chose to pursue robust LNG imports and internal gasification for security of supply reasons, namely, to reduce its dependency on oil (and the Middle East) after the 1973 price shock. A *rapprochement* with Indonesia and Malaysia—two countries that Japan had occupied during WWII—was favoured by the necessity to sign gas deals.

This political digression is important to highlight that, historically, pricing mechanisms have been part of a broader 'inseparable package' that served long-term strategic purposes both commercial and geopolitical. To be sure, the schemes also had to make commercial sense. This, together with their flexibility, made them resilient for decades. To use Williamsonian jargon, the mechanisms described in this section were intended to limit ex-post opportunism by the parties in presence of highly asset-specific investment, recurrent transactions and remarkable uncertainty.

5 Oil Indexation Comes Under Pressure: Gas-to-Gas Competition

For quite some time, the US has been an exception in the global landscape when it came to gas pricing. In fact, the US, a major producer of gas, did important pioneering work in establishing hub pricing as an industry norm. The important price-setting role of Henry Hub is not a simple given, but rather the result of painstaking regulatory work.

In the US, removal of wellhead price controls was one of the first key steps in the liberalisation of gas markets, followed by the introduction of competition in the wholesale market through unbundling of transmission infrastructure and third-party access. The first steps in deregulating the US gas market were made in the 1978 Natural Gas Policy Act, which contained rules for the gradual removal of price ceilings at the wellhead. Complete deregulation of wellhead prices was carried out later, by the 1989 Natural Gas Wellhead Decontrol Act. The New York Mercantile Exchange (NYMEX) opted for Henry Hub as a location for contracts in 1989, as full deregulation of wellhead prices took place. Henry Hub was chosen because of the great concentration of supply and infrastructure in that part of Louisiana. Indeed, one of the advantages of the US, greatly helping liquidity, is the fact that the country is itself a major producer.

Since then, Henry Hub has provided the basis for price formation in the US. Regional hubs also exist, but they are usually following Henry Hub except for cases where bottlenecks exist. Henry Hub prices have seen important variations throughout the decades, but for the last 10 years and until 2021, they have been at very low levels (often below 3$/MMBtu) as a result of the shale revolution.

In the 1990s and 2000s, the gas business changed radically also outside of the US, and traditional pricing mechanisms started to also come under increased pressure elsewhere.

The asset specificity of the gas investment stock diminished, particularly in mature markets. Transmission and distribution infrastructure started to become amortised, and LNG became subject to significant reductions in capital intensity thanks to technological progress and upscaling (Cornot-Gandolphe 2003; Jensen 2003). Lower capital intensiveness leads to lower risks and limits the 'hold-up' problem (Chyong 2015), thus softening the requirement of backing investments with long-term contracts.

The growth in LNG trade relative to pipeline trade also contributed to these dynamics. Since LNG trade is less asset-specific than pipeline trade—owing to its liquid nature—it brought more flexibility to both sides of the market (Chyong 2015). Access to flexible LNG and an increasing number of players contributed to changing the underlying structural conditions under which long-term oil-indexed contracts had thrived.

Gas trade became more 'impersonal' and less relational, and the pressure for market-based pricing mechanisms increased accordingly. Long-term strategic considerations gradually started to give way to shorter term, profit-oriented motivations. As gas markets (and hubs) matured—thus increasing trust that gas-to-gas competition itself could offer reliable price discovery—and direct competition between gas and oil weakened, oil indexation lost a lot of its attractiveness and original rationale.

Exogenous factors also played a fundamental role in changing the approach to pricing. The most important factor is gas market liberalisation, which started in the US and then extended to the UK and Continental Europe. More recently, countries outside of the West also started to liberalise their gas markets. Japan has enforced third-party access to infrastructure, and even China is now unbundling its gas pipelines. Liberalisation is important for pricing because one of its main effects is that of breaking the strong ties between incumbents and end-users. In a liberalised market, end-users stop being captive. They are able to switch to an alternative supplier and procure gas directly on the hub. This has the key implication that incumbents (mid-streamers, i.e. the importing companies) lose the ability to pass through additional procurement costs. Liberalisation also sets a virtuous circle in motion whereby the larger volumes are made available on hubs, the more hubs become benchmarks, attracting more trade and so on. Provided of course that physical volumes are available.

In a liberalised market, prices are set on hubs, which are marketplaces where gas is exchanged, either virtually or physically. Henry Hub in the US, the National Balancing Point (NBP) in the UK and the Title Transfer Facility (TTF) in The Netherlands are the most liquid hubs in the world at the moment. In Asia, where the process of hub creation is not as advanced as in the West, a key market marker is the Japan Korea Marker (JKM), a proxy calculated by Platts on the basis of trading activity. Producing countries, after opposing hub-based pricing and defending oil indexation as much as they could, are starting to experiment with hub trade. Since they have seemingly acknowledged that oil indexation belongs to the past and that the most modern pricing mechanism is hub pricing, they are now trying to at least establish their own hubs, so that their revenues are not completely determined by a hub in the export market, over which they have no control whatsoever. Notably, Russia has recently established an exchange, the Saint Petersburg Mercantile Exchange (SPIMEX), and in 2018, it has started selling gas volumes to Europe through an Electronic Sales Platform (ESP).

The possibility for end-users to procure gas directly on hubs was revolutionary and brought old business models under pressure. Pressure reached a breaking point when the gap between oil-indexed supplies and hub prices widened so much that it became unsustainable for mid-streamers. In 2008–2009, a situation of global gas oversupply emerged. Qatari LNG volumes originally destined for the North American market could not be sold there because in the meantime the US had gained the ability to produce domestically all the gas that it needed. Qatari LNG was thus looking for new outlets and was directed towards Europe. The economic and financial crisis of 2008–2009 depressed gas demand, aggravating the mismatch between supply and demand. Hub prices in Europe collapsed. At the same time, mid-streamers (importing companies) had long-term commitments to purchase oil-indexed gas from Russia, Algeria and other suppliers. Because, unlike in the past, they could not fully pass through the increased procurement cost to their end-users, they found themselves in an unsustainable situation. On the one hand, they had to buy expensive oil-indexed gas; on the other, they had to sell at a major discount in order to be able to market it.

For this reason, in the first half of the 2000s, European mid-streamers started to ask for renegotiations of their long-term contracts. Their key demand was to bring contract prices in line with market prices. Gazprom, Sonatrach and Qatar initially refused to overhaul pricing mechanisms, but with time they all gave in, due to the threat of adverse arbitration rulings, Gazprom in particular initially tried to tweak the components of traditional formulae, such as the P_0 or the conversion factors, so that these formulae would deliver prices more in line with market prices—thereby offering relief to European mid-streamers, without structurally changing the formula. However, over time, and starting in Northwest Europe, Gazprom and other suppliers were forced to more structurally adopt hub indexation. Hub indexation is now prevalent in European import contracts. In Asia, a similar pressure to renegotiate emerged in 2018–2019, with the key difference that Asia lacks fully liberalised market with gas-to-gas competition and national hubs (except for a somewhat artificial, albeit widely followed benchmark such as the JKM).

6 Gas Pricing in the 2020s

Gas pricing undertook significant transformations as a result of the trends described above. According to the 2019 IGU Wholesale Pricing Survey (IGU 2019), hub indexation expanded by 16 percent between 2005 and 2018, while oil indexation declined by 5 percent. The reason for this mismatch is that while in some regions (notably Europe) hub indexation replaced oil indexation, in others, namely in emerging markets, oil indexation substituted more obsolete pricing practices, at least introducing a market component (albeit an exogenous one). Bilateral monopoly, which was already a marginal price-setting mechanism, further shrunk by 2.5 percent. Regulated pricing at cost of service increased by 9 percent, and social and political regulation increased by 3 percent. Finally, regulated pricing below cost declined by almost 20 percentage points, reflecting a phaseout of the most extreme, loss-making subsidy schemes (Fig. 20.2).

In Europe, as a result of developments described in the previous section, three quarters of gas are now hub-indexed. Oil indexation is confined to one-quarter of consumption and regions such as the Iberian Peninsula, North-eastern and South-eastern Europe. Hub indexation is not only prevalent in North-western Europe but also in Italy and Central-Eastern Europe. It is important to highlight that these are only approximate estimates, as many import contracts actually feature hybrid formulae combining oil indexation and hub indexation. Whether one or the other is applied also depends on the price level, as pricing corridors have been introduced in which contract prices follow hub or oil indexation depending on price levels. As a result of the European Commission DG Competition's decisions concerning Gazprom's activities in Europe, Gazprom committed to adapt pricing in Eastern Europe to market markers. Customers in those regions can now request that contract prices are calculated using an average of Western European hub prices. Pressure to move further away from oil indexation has decreased together with the fall in oil prices in 2014 and 2020.

In Asia, as mentioned, oil indexation has increased substantially because it substituted non-market pricing mechanisms. In terms of domestically produced gas, the expansion of oil indexation is explained by wider adoption in

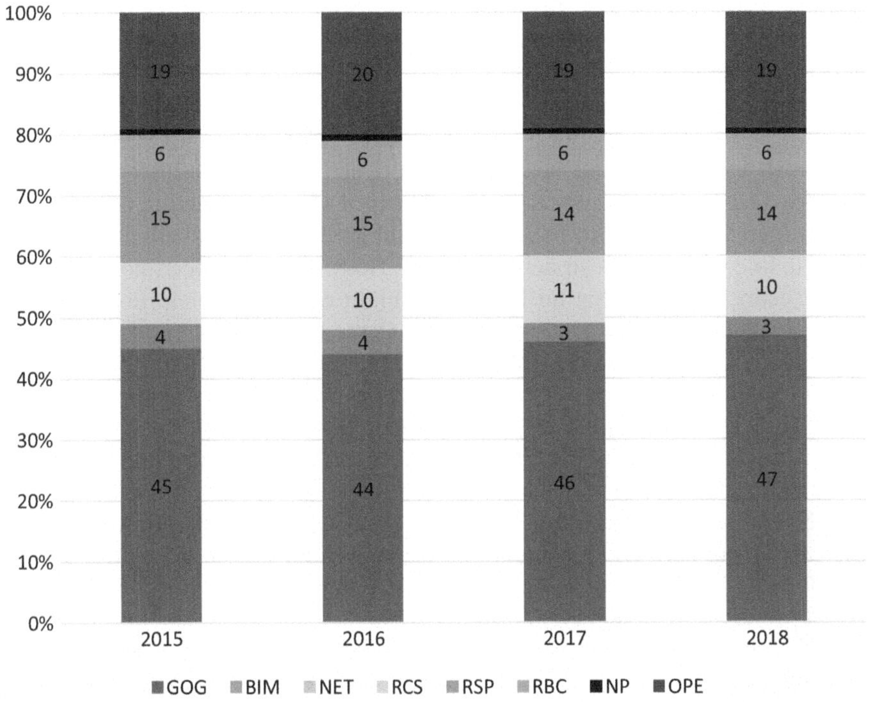

Fig. 20.2 Evolution in pricing mechanisms—global consumption (IGU 2019), %. *GOG* gas to gas competition, *BIM* bilateral monopoly, *NET* netback, *RCS* regulated cost of service, *RSP* regulated social and political, *RBC* regulated below cost, *NP* no price, *OPE* oil price escalation. Source: IGU 2019

China, Indonesia and Malaysia, where it has replaced regulated prices. Moreover, oil indexation increased because it was chosen as a pricing mechanism in new Turkmenistan-China gas contracts, which are very large from a volumetric perspective.

North America has not witnessed any transformation because it had already achieved full hub indexation (see above).

Africa has also seen limited changes in pricing mechanisms. Regulated pricing remains dominant although there has been a transition from regulation below cost to regulation at cost of service.

The Middle East remains dominated by regulated prices, particularly social and political regulation (76 percent). Subsidies are however being reduced, and there has been a particularly strong decrease in regulation below cost. The figure for regulated pricing is so high because this is the pricing mechanism adopted for domestic sales in gas heavyweights like Iran, Saudi Arabia and United Arab Emirates. Bilateral monopoly has been increasing between 2005 and 2018, reflecting a larger relative share of piped gas exports from Qatar to the United Arab Emirates and Oman.

Africa has seen limited changes in pricing mechanisms. Regulated pricing remains dominant although there has been a transition from regulated below cost to regulated cost of service.

In Russia, there was a move from regulation below cost in domestic production to gas-to-gas competition, as independent gas producers started to compete with each other and with Gazprom. Furthermore, Gazprom switched from regulation below cost to regulated cost of service, reflecting the Russian government's ambition to increase domestic prices and gradually bring them more in line with European netback parity. This process has been slowed down by the economic crisis that hit Russia but might resume in the future. Another transformation has been the switch from bilateral monopoly to oil indexation in Russia-Ukraine contracts, followed by the adoption of hub indexation in Ukraine import contracts as Ukraine started to import from Europe.

In Latin America, hub indexation has increased from 4 percent to 17 percent between 2005 and 2018 thanks to reforms in Argentina and Colombia and rising LNG imports, while social and political regulation declined from 52 percent to 16 percent and, against the global trend, regulation below cost increased from zero to 13 percent because of its adoption in Venezuela.

Globally, hub indexation is prevalent in piped gas trade while oil indexation is still prevalent in LNG (Fig. 20.3).

This might sound counterintuitive, because oil indexation is seen as 'old' (relative to hub indexation) while LNG is seen as 'new' (relative to pipeline

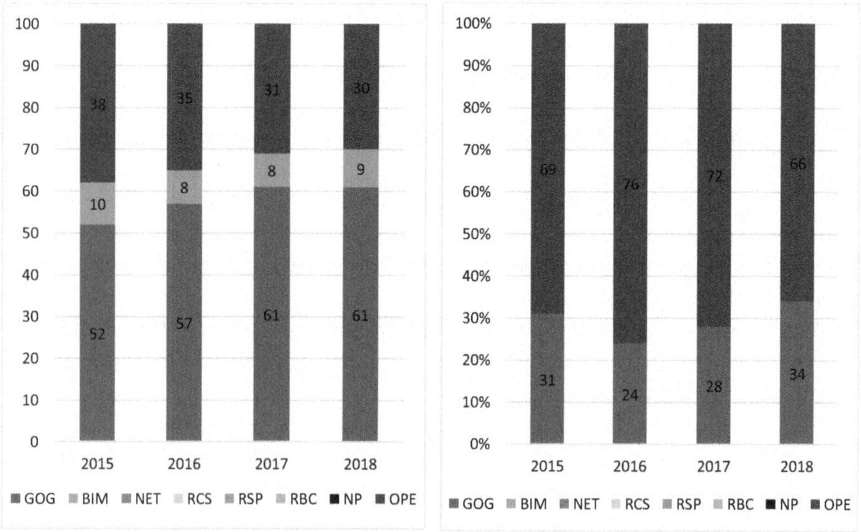

Fig. 20.3 Evolution in pricing mechanisms in pipeline and LNG trade (IGU 2019). *GOG* gas to gas competition, *BIM* bilateral monopoly, *NET* netback, *RCS* regulated cost of service, *RSP* regulated social and political, *RBC* regulated below cost, *NP* no price, *OPE* oil price escalation. Source: IGU 2019

trade). Also, we discussed how LNG has revolutionised gas trade and reduced asset specificity, paving the way for a transition away from point-to-point trade towards commoditization. The contradiction is however only apparent: the fact that LNG is predominantly oil indexed reflects the fact that three-quarters of global LNG flows target Asia, a region where oil indexation is still prevalent. Conversely, Europe represents a high share of piped gas imports. Oil indexation has not prevented LNG from revolutionising gas trade thanks to its destination flexibility.

7 Conclusion

Pricing mechanisms are a key element of gas trade as they are a decisive factor that concurs to determine price levels, namely, how prices respond to variations in supply and demand. The choice of a pricing mechanism also influences the strategic room for manoeuvre that suppliers and buyers have in opting for volume or value maximisation. Traditionally, gas suppliers defended long-term oil-indexed contracts. However, the old consensus on oil indexation, which had been a pillar of international gas trade for a decade, has been eroded in the last decade—particularly in Europe. More impersonal market exchange now prevails, whereas relational contracting had been essential to build the gas industry.

Gas markets are maturing and trading activity is increasing, creating an incentive to adopt hub indexation in a larger number of countries. North America has been a pioneer in deregulating wellhead prices and embracing gas-to-gas competition. Hubs offer better price discovery than in the past also in Europe because they are supported by more efficient financial services and more players are active on hubs, reducing volatility and opportunities for manipulation. Regulation played and continues to play a key role in facilitating the emergence of well-functioning, liquid trade hubs. The vast majority of gas sold to Europe is now hub-indexed. Asia is also gradually moving towards a larger share of hub indexation, although it is still lagging far behind in the process of establishing its own hubs. It now mostly relies on a proxy, the Japan Korea Marker by Platts, which has started to decorrelate from oil in 2018–2019. Elsewhere, regulated prices remain the norm. The weight of regulated pricing in total gas consumption is also explained by the large share of gas that is produced and consumed domestically.

Overall, gas prices remain regional. Additional convergence is materialising thanks to the globalising effect of flexible LNG, a commodity traded by parties that look for arbitrage opportunities. However, infrastructural bottlenecks, responsiveness to location-specific regulation and market fundamentals and lately the growing risk of politicisation (for instance, the introduction of tariffs on LNG as a result of US-China trade wars) limit the scope for further convergence.

References

Chyong, C.K. (2015), Markets and Long-term Contracts: The Case of Russian Gas Supplies to Europe (Cambridge, 2015): Energy Policy Research Group, University of Cambridge

Cornot-Gandolphe, S. (2003), *The Challenges of Further Cost Reductions for New Supply Options* (2003), Paper for the 22nd World Gas Conference

Flower, A. and Liao, L. (2012), LNG Pricing in Asia, in: Stern, J. (ed.), 'The Pricing of Internationally Traded Gas', Oxford Institute for Energy Studies (OIES), 2012.

Franza, L. (2014). *Long-term Gas Import Contracts in Europe: The Evolution in Pricing Mechanisms*, Clingendael International Energy Programme, 2014.

Gustafson, T. (2020), *The Bridge: Natural Gas in a Redivided Europe* (Cambridge, MA, 2020): Harvard University Press.

IGU (2019) Wholesale Gas Pricing Survey, International Gas Union, 2019.

Jensen, J. (2003), 'The LNG Revolution', *The Energy Journal*, 24:2 (2003), 1–45.

Klein, B. et al (1978), 'Vertical Integration, Appropriate Rents and the Competitive Contracting Process', *Journal of Law and Economics*, 21:2 (1978), 297–326.

Komlev, S. (2016), Oil Indexation: The Best Remedy for Market Failure in the Natural Gas Industry, Demian Literary Agency, 2016.

Pirrong, C. (2018), Liquefying a Market: The Transition of LNG to a Traded Commodity, University of Houston, Presentation, 2018.

Stern, J. (2012), 'The Pricing of Gas in International Trade—an Historical Survey' in: Stern, J. (ed.), The Pricing of Internationally Traded Gas (Oxford, 2012): The Oxford Institute for Energy Studies.

Williamson, O. (1979) 'Transaction Cost Economics: the Governance of Contractual Relations', *Journal of Law and Economics*, 22:2 (1979), 233–261.

CHAPTER 21

The Trading and Price Discovery for Coal

Carlos Fernández Alvarez

1 Major Producers, Importers and Exporters of Coal: Main Trends

Coal is the second largest source of primary energy in the world (26% in 2019), after oil. Coal is the main source of electricity worldwide (36% in 2019) and also the largest source of energy for steel and cement production, two essential materials for the modern world. Around two-thirds of coal is used for power generation, around 15% is used by the iron and steel industry, 6% by the cement industry and the balance is used in residential heating and various industrial applications.

The world's largest producer is China (3550 Mt. in 2018), which represents 45% of the global production (7813 Mt), followed by India (771 Mt), United States (685 Mt), Indonesia (549 Mt) and Australia (483 Mt). Russia, South Africa, Germany, Poland and Kazakhstan complete the list of the ten largest producers. The world's largest consumer is also China (3756 Mt. in 2018), representing 49% of the global consumption (7721 Mt), followed by India (985 Mt), United States (615 Mt), Russia (232 Mt) and Germany (215 Mt). South Africa, Japan, Korea, Poland and Turkey complete the list of the ten largest producers.

This chapter should be authored to Carlos Fernández Alvarez, Senior Coal Analyst of the International Energy Agency (IEA). Any acknowledgement should mention the International Energy Agency.

C. Fernández Alvarez (✉)
International Energy Agency (IEA), Paris, France
e-mail: Carlos.FERNANDEZALVAREZ@iea.org

M. Hafner, G. Luciani (eds.), *The Palgrave Handbook of International Energy Economics*, https://doi.org/10.1007/978-3-030-86884-0_21

Those lists and figures require two important caveats. Regarding the geographical breakdown, there are two different trends in the world: in Europe and United States, coal use is collapsing through a combination of sluggish electricity demand, climate and environmental policies, lower gas prices and direct coal phase out policies in some countries. In 1990, the United States and the EU represented 40% of the global coal demand. In 2019, it was 12%. By contrast, in Asia there is no indication of coal demand declining, while in many Asian countries, coal consumption is growing steadily. Germany, for example, the fifth largest consumer in 2018, might disappear from the top ten list very soon. The second caveat refers to the unit used to measure coal. Owing to the wide range of calorific values for different coals (CV), that is, the energy contained in the fuel per mass unit of coal, the volumes of coal measured by mass (tonnes) and measured by energy (tonne coal equivalent) can be very different if different qualities are involved. Using energy terms, China's share in the global consumption is well over 50% and Germany's coal consumption falls behind South Africa, Japan and Korea. While the energy basis is more relevant than mass, especially when compared with other sources, most people in the industry use mass, and this is the criteria followed in this chapter.

Looking at the country breakdown, it is evident that the most distinctive characteristic of the global coal market, compared with other fossil fuels, is the full dominance of one country, China. United States, the world's largest oil and gas producer in 2018, represented 13% of global oil production and 20% of gas, very far from China's 45%. On the demand side, United States, also the largest oil and gas consumer, has a share in the global consumption around 20% for both oil and gas, again far from China's 49% in coal. Another unique feature of China's dominance is that the Chinese domestic market is three times bigger than the global international coal trade, in which China is the largest importer. This has major implications for trade and price setting across the world.

Despite internationally traded coal is gradually increasing its share in global coal use for some years, coal is the most common domestic fossil fuel, as 82% of global coal is consumed in the country where it is mined, compared with 68% for gas and 42% for oil. Lower energy density or calorific value, as traded coal has typically a CV of 20–30 GJ/t compared with oil (over 40 GJ/t) or gas (over 50 GJ/t), is one of the main reasons for it, since transportation costs increase with lower energy density. Less than 20GJ/t CV coal is mostly consumed at mine-mouth.

Out of 1.4 bt of coal internationally traded in 2018, 1060 Mt. were thermal coal (including small volumes of anthracite and lignite) and the balance was coking coal (including hard coking coal, semi-soft coking coal and pulverised coal injection (PCI)). Seaborne coal trade volume of 1280 Mt. (of which 1 bt of thermal and 280Mt of coking coal) represents the second largest bulk traded commodity globally by mass after iron ore. International coal trade represented revenues over $140 billion in 2018. Indeed, this amount largely depends on prevalent prices, which change substantially from year to year. In 2019, trade revenues were around \$100 billion, owing to lower prices compared with 2018.

The largest exporters of thermal coal are Indonesia (456 Mt in 2019, including 85 Mt of lignite), Australia (212 Mt), Russia (193 Mt, including 25 Mt of anthracite and 12 Mt of lignite), South Africa (79 Mt), Colombia (76 Mt) and United States (34 Mt). The largest exporter of metallurgical coal by far is Australia (183 Mt in 2019), followed by United States (50 Mt), Mongolia (34 Mt), Canada (31 Mt) and Russia (25 Mt). Mongolia plays a different role than the others in the international market, as it is a landlocked country, and the destination of all its coking coal exports is China. By revenue, owing to its dominance in the more expensive metallurgical coal market, Australia is the largest exporter by far.

The largest importers of thermal coal are China (225 Mt in 2019, including around 10 Mt of anthracite and 100 Mt of lignite), India (187 Mt), Japan (143 Mt), Republic of Korea (123 Mt) and Chinese Taipei (65 Mt). The largest importers of metallurgical coal are China (75 Mt in 2019), India (61 Mt), Japan (43 Mt) and Korea (25 Mt). Whereas coal exports are dominated by six countries in the thermal space and by five in the coking coal space, imports are more widely distributed, as most countries in the world import coal either for power generation or for industrial applications.

Given the dominance of big domestic markets (China, India or United States) in the global coal consumption, the largest coal-producing companies dedicate their production to serve domestic markets. Among the world's eight largest producers, Coal India is a state-owned company serving the domestic Indian market, Peabody Energy is a US company focused on the domestic market and the other six are state-owned Chinese companies serving mostly the domestic Chinese market (Chinese exports represent 0.2% of its production). Glencore, the largest coal exporter in the world, is only the ninth largest producer. An important trend in the last years is that the big diversified companies are leaving the coal business. Rio Tinto sold its last coal mining assets in Australia in 2018. BHP spun off most of its thermal assets into a new company, South 32, and now is almost exclusively a coking coal producer. Anglo American has announced the spin-off of its South African export-oriented thermal assets in the coming years after having sold domestic-oriented mines few years ago. In short, among the big diversified miners, only Glencore has maintained its position on coal, although in 2019 it committed to keep coal production below 150 Mt, which limits future potential growth. Pure coal players, like SUEK, Adaro, Peabody Energy, Bumi, Yancoal Australia, Drummond, Whitehaven, are experiencing growing pressure from investors due to climate change concerns. Interestingly, there has not been shortage of buyers when coal assets have been put on sale.

Traditionally, international coal trade has taken place in two main markets, with different dynamics, although interconnected: the Atlantic Basin and the Pacific Basin. In the Atlantic, Europe was the main destination, and United States, South Africa and, to a lesser extent, Colombia were the main exporters.

In the Pacific, Japan was the main destination, with Korea and Taiwan also playing a relevant role. Australia was the main supplier, complemented by Indonesia. In the last decade, coal markets have changed dramatically. China, which was in 2003 the world's second largest coal exporter behind only Australia, shifted to a net import position in 2009. Two years later, it became the world's largest importer surpassing Japan. This shift, together with the perspective that Chinese imports could continue such strong growth for some years, was paramount to explaining the dynamics of coal over the last decade, including the oversupply and lower prices of the 2012–2016 period.

China's unrivalled dominance on coal markets means that understanding how Chinese domestic market works is key to understanding how global coal markets work. In particular, it is important to understand the geography of coal production and consumption in China. The three largest coal-producing provinces in Northwest China, Inner Mongolia (976 Mt. in 2018), Shanxi (893 Mt) and Shaanxi (623 Mt), account for almost three quarters of total Chinese production, and the majority of the coal exported to Chinese provinces. Coal from these provinces is transported to the northern ports by rail, as all the seven major ports in the north, the so-called N7 ports (Qinhuangdao, Tianjin, Jingtang, Huanghua, Qingdao, Rizhao and Lianyungang), are connected to, at least, one major rail line. Then coal is shipped to the consumption centres throughout the coast, mostly East China (Shanghai and Zhejiang) and Southeast China (Guangdong and Fujian), with smaller volumes shipped to Guangxi and Shandong. The volume shipped from the northern ports to the coastal regions is around 750 Mt, per year. If we now add 300 Mt of coal imported in China, it results that the seaborne coal trade in coastal China (both domestic and international) is larger than the seaborne coal trade outside China. The arbitrage between domestic and international supply in coastal China is pivotal to set prices across the world. The Chinese government, while using coal imports to balance the domestic markets, also tries to rein in imports to protect Chinese producers, through a variety of policies, not always implemented in a fully transparent way. In 2014, it seems that the government sent Directives to the utilities to recommend reducing coal imports. In 2015, quality control of trace elements gave rise to delays and rejection of imports. In 2016, the 256 working day policy triggered prices in China and elsewhere. In 2018, import quotas were established. Those changing policies, given China's dominance, have a deep impact on the global coal market.

Another country where domestic and international markets interact is the United States, unlike the other major exporting countries, where domestic and international markets are largely disconnected for quality, geography and contractual reasons. There are five main producing areas with different qualities, costs and prices: Central Appalachia, Northern Appalachia, Illinois Basin, Uinta Basin and Powder River Basin. Whereas domestic prices are much lower than international prices, when transportation costs, including domestic transportation, are included, most US coal is hardly competitive in the international markets. This is the reason why United States is a swing supplier of thermal coal in the Atlantic Coast. As delivery costs of US producers are generally higher than Russian, South African or Colombian, when markets are tight and prices go up, US coal jumps in. On the contrary, when the market is eased and prices go down, US producers refrain. An exception is Illinois coal, but its sulphur content obliges to sell at a discount or to blend it with low sulphur coal.

2 Different Coal Qualities and Price Discovery Tools

2.1 *Quality*

Coal is a sedimentary rock, made up of old phytomass, that is, trees and plants, which has been buried under high pressure and temperature in the absence of oxygen, in a process lasting from tens of millions of years for young lignite up to hundreds of millions of years for old anthracite. During this transformation, moisture in the original phytomass has been gradually disappearing, while carbon is preserved. Given the different origins, ages and circumstances involved in the process of coal formation, coal presents a much wider variation than the other fossil fuels, that is, oil and gas, as the range of the different parameters defining coal quality changes in a very broad range. Moisture, for example, which can be less than 5% in some anthracites, can reach 50% in some lignites. Ash content, volatile matter, sulphur and other impurities also present a wide variation throughout different coals. In fact, reflecting the wide variety of coal, there are also many different classifications across the world. The most common way for classifying coal refers to the ranking of coal, that is, how advanced has been the transformation from the original phytomass into coal, also called coalification. From more to less coalification, which is almost equal to say from more to less carbon, and from less to more moisture, coal is classified as anthracite, bituminous coal, subbituminous coal and lignite. In general this classification also places coal from more to less calorific value, with two important caveats. Firstly, some bituminous coal can have higher CV than anthracite owning to higher hydrogen content. Secondly, ash has no energy content, and therefore, the more ash the lower CV for each rank. However, although this is the most used classification for coal, for commercial purposes a more consumption-oriented classification is used. At global level, most of coal (around 80%) is burned to produce heat to be used either directly or mostly to generate steam to move a turbine as part of the Balance of the Plant to produce electricity. Around 15% of coal is not burned, but subject to a pyrolysis to produce coke, a very carbon-intensive fuel, of which around 90% is used to produce iron in the blast furnace. Less than 5% of coal is used in various applications, the main one being gasification, in which coal is blown with air, steam, oxygen or a combination of them to obtain syngas, which can be used to produce fertilisers, hydrogen, chemicals or electricity. There are also a variety of coal products and by-products used for very specific purposes. Therefore, in practical terms, along this chapter we will refer to a more market-based classification, distinguishing between thermal coal—including anthracite and lignite—and metallurgical coal. For thermal coal, for which energy is the main output, CV is the main determinant, and the content of sulphur, ash and other impurities is penalised. Anthracite, which represents only a fraction of bituminous and sub-bituminous coal, is used for different purposes depending on its quality. Pricing of anthracite depends on its quality and use. Lignite, due to high moisture content, that is, low calorific value and high transportation costs, is mostly used mine-mouth or transformed nearby. The volumes of lignite internationally traded are small, and generally follow thermal coal practices. For coking coal, its behaviour in the blast furnace is the most important characteristic, and hence, coke strength after reaction (CSR) and coke reactivity index (CRI) are the main parameters when pricing. Like thermal coal, the content of impurities such as ash, sulphur and phosphorus is penalised. PCI, coal injected in the blast furnace to save coke, is included in the metallurgical coal category. It represents only a fraction of coking coal and it is usually priced at a discount to coking coal.

2.2 *Some Concepts on Coal Mining*

Coal price, like so many other goods, is derived from supply and demand conditions. However, thermal coal prices—coking coal volatility is exacerbated by geographical concentration—are less volatile than oil and gas prices. Coal mining, although capital-intensive, is less capital-intensive than oil and gas production, so variable costs for coal mining and inland transportation—the so-called FOB cash costs—make up a higher share of full costs than for oil and gas. Therefore, FOB cash costs drive coal prices more than in gas and oil, especially in a situation of oversupply, when most analysts work under the assumption, supported by experience, that market prices find the floor once they reach the FOB cash-costs of 90% of producers. Indeed, take-or-pay contracts with rails and ports operators are used very frequently in some exporting countries, and this has to be taken into account. If FOB cash cost of producer A is \$70/t, of which \$20/t is take-or-pay contract with the rail, it will incur in a loss of \$10/t selling coal at \$60/t, but it is saving \$10/t as the rail cost is sunk, so the effective FOB cash cost is \$50/t. In addition, coal storage is much simpler/cheaper than oil or gas storage, which limits the potential for prices plummeting. Lack of storage is very much related to price spikes both upside and downside. For example, negative prices in the wholesale electricity markets can occur, as electricity storage is very expensive. Negative prices in some gas hubs can also occur, and even in April 2020 for the first time ever US oil prices were into the red zone, due to lack of storage capacity during a supply-demand imbalance.

2.3 *Price Discovery*

Coal price discovery takes place in both the physical and the derivative markets, which currently operate with enough liquidity in many segments. From around 2011 on, there has been a growing segmentation by quality of the thermal coal market, with an increasing share of off-spec coal trade. Although the prices of different qualities are usually correlated, the spread can change dramatically. The gap between Newcastle FOB prices for 6000 kcal/kg and 5500 kcal/kg was $9/t (11% discount) in March 2017 and $51/t (45% discount) in August 2018. In the short term, issues in the supply side, like disruptions in mining production, freight bottlenecks, restrictions in port capacity, will have a bullish impact on prices. Likewise, speculation in the financial market in some particular segment can have an impact on the short-term prices, but in the long term, it is believed that fundamentals will prevail. Price discovery is completed with other tools, like broker sheets, trade publications and supply cash-cost information. Given the relevance of cash cost at determining coal price, most of the market players use commercial companies to assess the supply cash cost curve, including the impact of relative movements of currency exchanges and oil price, as the cost of delivered coal depends on oil price. Coal mining, in particular open pit mining, is diesel fuel-intensive, and transportation costs—which indeed depend on oil price—are an important share of coal delivery cost. Whereas coking coal faces only weak competition (Electric Arc Furnace can compete with Basic Oxygen Furnace only up to a point, depending on scrap availability), coal for power generation has to compete directly with gas, and in the longer term, with other generation sources, that is, nuclear and renewables. Therefore, coking coal prices move more driven by a direct supply-demand balance, whereas thermal coal is also impacted by gas and CO_2 prices, electricity policies and so on.

For thermal coal, given the great variety existing, there are as many different qualities as anyone can define. As already discussed, the volatile content and amount of impurities contained in coal (sulphur is the main one, but also ash is relevant) are used for defining coal quality, with relevance for price, but of course CV is the main parameter.

There are many different international commercial terms (incoterms), which define the allocation of costs between buyer and seller, but in this section only FOB, CIF and CFR will be used. FOB (Free on Board) typically used for pricing coal in the exporting ports refers to the price paid once coal is loaded in the ship. CIF (cost, insurance, freight) refers to the price including cost of coal, insurance and freight and it is typically used for imported coal in receiving ports. CFR (cost, freight) is also used for coal received in imported coal, but it does not include insurance costs. As CIF and CFR (in $/t) include freight, ship's size is usually included in the price assessment. For thermal coal, specifications of calorific value can refer to high calorific value (GAR, gross as received) or to low calorific value (NAR, net as received). NAR is typically around 5%

lower than GAR (the exact relation depends on moisture and hydrogen content).

In the physical market, the price markers assessed by Price Reporting Agencies (PRAs) play a pivotal role in price discovery. PRAs are private organisations without vested interest on the level of the price they report, which compete between them to offer the best assessment and which follow the principles set up by the International Organisation of Securities Commissions (IOSCO). The main PRAs operating in the international coal market are Argus, S&P Global Platts and IHS Markit (formerly McCloskey).

2.4 *Thermal Coal Qualities*

Traditionally, standard traded coal CV has been 6000 kcal/kg NAR, with sulphur content limited to less than 1%, with three main price markers for coal of that quality—API2, API4, API6—produced jointly by Argus and IHS Markit/McCloskey. API2 is a weekly assessment of CIF price for coal imported in ARA (Amsterdam-Rotterdam-Antwerp) hub. API4 is a weekly assessment of FOB price for coal exported from Richards Bay port in South Africa, and API6 is a weekly assessment of FOB price for coal exported from Newcastle port in New South Wales, Australia. In the last decade, both the demand and the supply side experienced substantial changes. Firstly, the emergence of new major importers, that is, China and India, which valued costs as much as quality or security. Secondly, the ramp up of Indonesian exports, which became the largest thermal coal exporter by far, doubling thermal coal exports from Australia, the second largest. Most of coal exported by Indonesia is out of the 6000 kcal/kg specification and low or very low sulphur, suitable for blending with high sulphur Chinese coal, and hence, a good deal for utilities in coastal China. Given the increasing off-spec demand, traditional 6000 kcal/kg exporters like Australia and South Africa have also increased their high-ash coal exports to some degree. In short, the market has changed dramatically, and currently, coal out of API2/API4 specifications represents the bulk of the seaborne coal trade, accounting for almost two thirds of the volumes. Answering the need for new markers for new coal flows, the PRAs have created price markers for them. In the early 2010s Argus and IHS Markit launched API8 assessing CFR price of 5500 kcal/kg coal imported in South China (Guangzhou), API3 assessing FOB price of exported 5500 kcal/kg coal from Richards Bay and API5, assessing FOB price of 5500 kcal/kg coal exported from Newcastle. For Indonesian coal, for example, Argus/CoalIndo offer price markers called ICI1, ICI2, ICI3, ICI4 and ICI5, assessing coal of 6500 kcal/kg GAR (6200 NAR), 5800 kcal/kg GAR (5500 NAR), 5000 kcal/g GAR (4600 NAR), 4200 kcal/kg GAR (3800 NAR) and 3400 kcal/kg GAR (3000 NAR), respectively. ICI4 is the most relevant and liquid index. Poorer quality involves a price discount reflecting higher logistics costs, as it is necessary to deal with more mass for the same energy, and lower efficiencies during the final consumption, associated with high moisture (in the case of Indonesia), high ash and so on. As a very rough rule of thumb, 3000 kcal/kg coal price can be one third of 6000 kcal/kg.

Given China's global impact, price markers in China are very relevant across the world. There are assessments for a great variety of coal trade in China, especially in terms of CVs, for which 5500 kcal/kg is the most relevant. Regarding the geography, for FOB prices Qinhuangdao is the most relevant origin, and for CFR is South China (Guangzhou). Bohai Rim Steam-Coal price Index—a benchmark for a basket of products in northern ports of China—has been traditionally the most relevant price assessment, as it is often used by the government to set policies, but for commercial traders CCI5500, published by Fenwei, also a composite index assessing spot and contract prices, is the main reference.

3 Major International Contracts

3.1 Thermal Coal

In 1996, the *Directive 96/92/EC of the European Parliament and of the Council of 19 December 1996 concerning common rules for the internal market of electricity* was adopted, obliging all the EC (now EU) countries to de-regulate their electricity markets. Liberalisation of European markets changed the market dramatically. With liquid markets for power, gas, CO_2 and coal, spot trade combined with hedging strategies dominate the trade in Europe, and contracts have virtually disappeared. There are still few countries in the Atlantic procuring coal through term contracts, but both length of the contracts and volumes are shrinking.

By contrast, in the Pacific Basin long-term contracts (typically one year long) still play an important role, especially in the trade between Australia and Japan, Korea and Chinese Taipei, in which approximately half of the trade is made through long-term contracts, also shrinking as it used to be 90% one decade ago. Security of supply is highly valued by Japanese Power Utilities (JPUs), and so too, the quality and consistency of Australian coal. Therefore, JPUs prefer to ensure some volumes at fixed price, although liberalisation of Japanese electricity market has pushed JPUs to diversify sources and to increase spot purchases. The most important contract is the one that Glencore and Tohoku sign for the Japanese fiscal year (April to March), as it is the benchmark for the industry. Whereas frequent in the domestic market, Chinese and Indian buyers are more reluctant to sign long-term contracts on imports.

3.2 Coking Coal

Since the 1960s until the end of the twentieth century, coking coal trade was very stable. On the demand side, the Japanese Steel Mills (JSMs), as Japan was the largest importer of coking coal, led the negotiations with the suppliers, and the other steel mills in the region, that is, Korea and Chinese Taipei followed agreements similar to the JSM ones, which procured their coking coal through long-term contracts. Japanese companies were pioneers investing in the producing regions, that is, Queensland in Australia and Elk Valley in Canada in the 1960s, and British Columbia in the 1970s. Long-term contracts and Japanese investment guaranteed supply and the power exerted by JSMs ensured that negotiated prices were as low as reasonably profitable for producers. In the 1990s, after some years of low prices, the supply side faced a dramatic change. Some companies left, the major miners entered and by the early 2000s BHP Billiton (currently BHP), Teck Resources, Xstrata (currently Glencore), Anglo American and Rio Tinto controlled more than half of the international trade, which shifted the balance of negotiation power from the buyers to the sellers. At the same time, new entrants from China and India with a different, more spot-oriented approach were also eroding the old system. By 2011, China was already importing almost as much coking coal (45 Mt) as Japan (50.6 Mt) and India (35 Mt) had surpassed Korea (32 Mt). In the fourth quarter of 2010, Queensland suffered heavy rains, which flooded mines, railways and ports, and strongly disrupted coal exports during the first quarter of 2011 from that region, the origin of more than half of the global coking coal exports. This, together with strong demand from China, gave rise to a spike price over $300/t in 2011. At that time, BHP, which had pushed contracts from annual to quarterly and then monthly benchmark against heavy resistance from JSMs, decided to go a step further and sell a great part of its production through index-linked spot sales. This movement shook the market, which has developed considerably since then. Currently the estimates are that more than 50% of Australian coking coal is sold in the spot market, with the rest through index-linked term contracts, which means that the long-standing benchmark set through bilateral negotiations between Australian producers and JSMs has vanished. The change in coking coal market has been very fast, considering that the first coking coal index was launched in 2010, but volatility of coking coal, which has been key for that movement, seems unavoidable. In the supply side, Queensland's dominance plays an important role, as any disruption—usually weather-related—leads to an important price spike. In the demand side, China dominates coking coal demand—with more than half of the global demand—and imports are only a small fraction of its domestic consumption, and therefore, policy changes in China have strong implications for the international markets.

4 Derivatives and Market Liquidity

Due to the wide range of coal quality and properties, coal commoditisation was traditionally considered more difficult than other commodities. However, the liberalisation of the electricity markets in Europe and the search of hedging tools by the utilities triggered the development of paper markets. The first coal swaps emerged in 1998, and given the interest of European utilities, API2 and API4 were the underlying asset. In 2002, Central Appalachian's first coal futures were traded in NYMEX. Others followed, based on API5, API8 and

ICI4. It took some years to develop a liquid derivative market, but the volume probably crossed the 1 bt threshold in 2006, and one year later, the API2-based trade. Most of that trade was in OTCs until 2010, and therefore, volumes are difficult to estimate with accuracy. API2-based swaps and futures have concentrated the majority of the paper trade, around 80%, despite physical volumes in ARA hub have a much lower share. Owing to its higher liquidity, API2 derivatives have been used as a proxy for other coals. With some ups and downs due to the financial conditions, coal derivatives were growing for more than 15 years. In 2016, more than 4 bt of coal derivatives were traded. The unexpected reverse of the market during 2016 put many into red. Some large trading houses left coal trade, and coal paper trade is declining since then. Given the expected collapse of European coal demand, how liquidity on API2-based derivatives will evolve is an open question.

By contrast, in China the paper market continues to grow. The first swaps based on Chinese coal emerged in 2011. In September 2013, the Zhenghou Commodity Exchange launched the first derivatives in China based on thermal coal. In August 2014, the Shanghai Commodity Exchange launched its first thermal coal swaps. Since then, volumes have continuously increased and now paper trade in China is larger than the paper trade in the rest of the world combined.

In the coking coal market, the increasing use of index-linked spot and contract trades has encouraged development of hedging strategies. First coking coal derivatives were launched in 2011, and after some years of muted activity, volumes grew dramatically, probably also boosted by cyclone Debbie-induced volatility, in 2016. In March 2013, the Dalian Commodity Exchange launched the first derivatives for coking coal in China, and the market has been growing since then, trading billions tonnes per year.

5 Notes

All the data and information have been obtained from IEA publications, in particular the Medium-term Coal Market report 2011–2019 (re-branded as Coal Report in 2018), and IEA databases.

The data in this chapter generally refer to 2019. In the cases in which 2019 data are not available, 2018 data have been used instead.

CHAPTER 22

The Trading of Electricity

Philippe Vassilopoulos and Elies Lahmar

1 Introduction

1.1 The Electricity Industry and Its Value Chain

Electricity is defined as a set of physical phenomena corresponding to the presence and flow of electric charge. Since the discovery of electricity in the nineteenth century, electricity has become an essential good to our society that has played an immense role for mankind's economic development, enabling a widespread and cheap energy production and transportation that is used to power our economy and daily lives.

Electricity is an energy source like no other, in the sense that it is immaterial. Other energy sources like wood, gas or oil are material, can be contained and quantified with a volume or a weight and are storable on a large scale, unlike electricity. Moreover, electricity is not freely available in large amounts naturally and must be generated from a primary energy source. Electricity can be produced on a large scale from:

- Thermal power plants: A fluid (most often water) is heated by the combustion of a fuel (gas, coal, oil) or by a nuclear reaction (nuclear reactor). This energy in the form of heat is then converted to electric power. In most designs, the water is turned into steam and spins a turbine driving an electrical generator;
- Hydro power plants: The water flow coming from a reservoir or in a river spins a turbine driving an electrical generator;

P. Vassilopoulos (✉) • E. Lahmar
EPEX SPOT, Paris, France
e-mail: p.vassilopoulos@epexspot.com

M. Hafner, G. Luciani (eds.), *The Palgrave Handbook of International Energy Economics*, https://doi.org/10.1007/978-3-030-86884-0_22

- Wind turbines: The wind flow spins a turbine driving an electrical generator;
- Solar photovoltaic installations: Electricity is generated through the conversion of light into an electric current using the photovoltaic effect.

In this chapter, electricity is referred to as either *power*—expressed in megawatts (MW)—that corresponds to instantaneous 'work' or *energy*—expressed in megawatt-hours (MWh)—which represent work over a period of time.

Once produced, the electricity is transported to the end-consumers through the power grid, that can be divided in two parts:

- The transmission grid, that serves for the transportation of electricity over long distances, mostly through high-voltage overhead power lines;
- The distribution grid, that represents the last stage of the grid before the consumer. It is a low-voltage grid and consists of cables and lines connected to the consumers.

The value chain of the electricity industry can therefore be summarized into the four elements in Fig. 22.1.

1.2 The Emergence of Electricity Markets

When the electricity sector first developed in the nineteenth and twentieth centuries, electricity was not traded or commercialized through markets. The initially decentralized electricity grids were increasingly interconnected, and publicly owned vertically integrated utility companies were created to manage the whole value chain of the electricity system across large geographical areas: electricity generation, transmission, distribution and sale to end consumers. The price of electricity was regulated and determined by regulatory and government bodies. Such an organization worked well in many countries worldwide and has enabled a wide development of the electricity systems, grids and generation capabilities. It is in the late twentieth century that first concepts for the introduction of electricity markets were formulated and implemented.

- In 1990, the United Kingdom privatized the electricity supply industry, followed by the deregulation in several countries of the Commonwealth, notably giving rise to the National Electricity markets of Australia and New Zealand and the Alberta Electricity market in Canada.

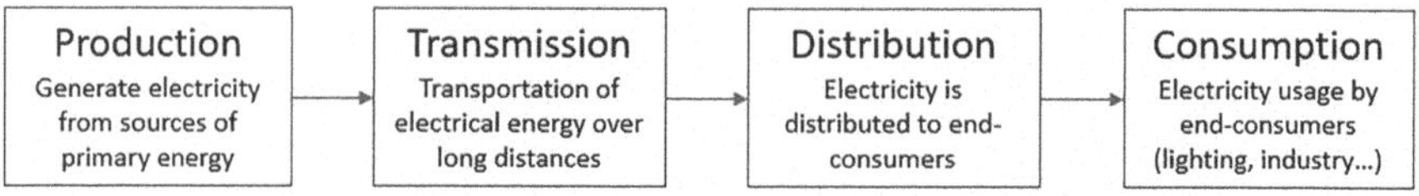

Fig. 22.1 Value chain of the electricity sector. (Source: Authors' elaboration)

- In 1991, the Norwegian electricity market is deregulated.
- In California, the market is deregulated in 1996, followed by many other states in the USA.
- In Europe, a European Union directive dating back to 1996 creates the framework for a liberalized European electricity market, which prompted the implementation of electricity markets throughout Europe in the early 2000s.

Essentially, the deregulation—or liberalization—of the electricity market corresponds to the introduction of (1) competition to sell electricity production with the creation of *a wholesale electricity market*, and in most cases (2) competition for electricity sale to consumers with the creation of *a retail market*. In practical terms, this means that formerly vertically integrated monopolies must be unbundled or disintegrated: electricity production and retail activities are competing in markets, whereas grid operations for the transmission and in most countries the distribution of electricity which are natural monopolies are managed within separate independent and regulated entities. The liberalization therefore sees the emergence of new types of companies (as illustrated in Fig. 22.2):

- **Electricity generation companies:**
  These are companies owning electricity generation assets that are competing to sell their production on the wholesale market. They make investment decisions to build new power plants in the hopes of making returns from the sale of the electricity production on wholesale markets.

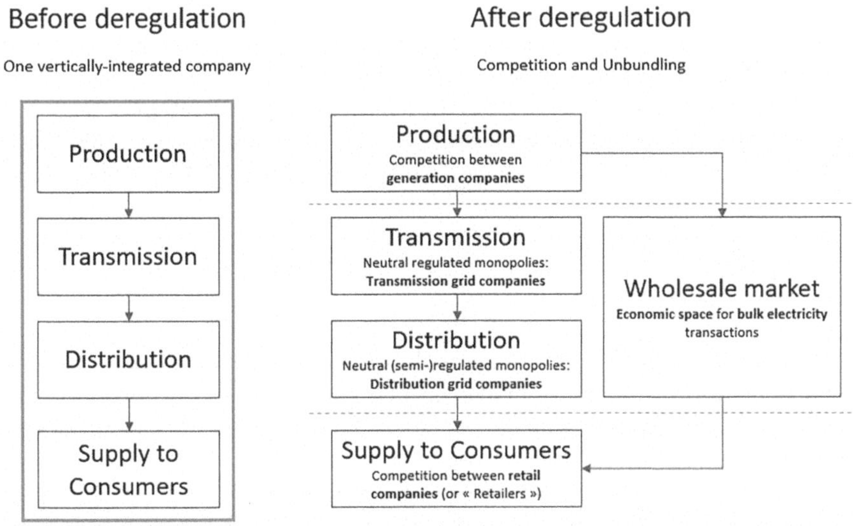

Fig. 22.2 Diagram showing the structure of the electricity value chain before and after the deregulation of the market. (Source: Authors' elaboration)

- **Transmission grid companies:**
  They operate the high-voltage transmission grid and are responsible for grid stability and security of supply. They are regulated monopolies, and offer a neutral non-discriminatory grid access to all potential grid users (generators and consumers).
- **Distribution grid companies:**
  They operate the distribution grids and offer non-discriminatory access to the distribution grid. They are (semi-)regulated monopolies and, in some countries, are not unbundled from retail or generation activities. In this case, there might be no competition in the retail market, as the only possible retailer in a given area is the local distribution grid company. Most European countries and American states have now implemented retail competition.
- **Electricity retail companies:**
  They are commercial companies procuring electricity on the wholesale market in large amounts (or producing it with their own generation capabilities) and selling it to end-consumers on the retail market.

2 Theoretical Foundation and Design of Wholesale Electricity Markets

The main ground for the introduction of electricity markets was to increase the social welfare over the electricity value chain and enable long-term benefits to consumers compared to the regulated monopoly structure, by means of reduced electricity prices and improved security of supply. Indeed, the competitive organization of the sector would (Joskow 2003):

- Provide incentives to improve capital investments and operating costs of existing and new generation assets
- Encourage technological innovation in electricity generation
- Shift the risk of technology choice, construction cost and operating "mistakes" from consumers (through public monopolies) to suppliers (and their private shareholders)
- Create better incentives for transmission and distribution monopolies, that would reduce associated costs for consumers and enable more efficient wholesale and retail markets

In Europe, there was also a second argument—a political one—for the implementation of electricity markets. Such markets would *de facto* be integrated into one common European market that would increase the cooperation and political ties between European countries.

The implementation of an electricity market is however no easy task on a technical level. Indeed, the electricity system relies on the electricity grid to function. When an electricity quantity is produced, it is injected at one location—or node—of the grid and withdrawn at the same or another node of the grid, where the consumer is. This physical system is bound by the laws of physics, that make electricity a very special commodity. Here are its main characteristics:

1. **Grid balance:** electricity cannot be stored on a large scale. Therefore, the grid must be balanced at all times between electricity generation and consumption;
2. **Transmission constraints:** each line or cable in the electricity grid has a maximum amount of power that can flow through it at any given time. This figure is called the transmission capacity. If a flow exceeds this limit, it creates a congestion that can lead, in the worst case, to a blackout;
3. **Grid losses:** the transportation of electricity through the power grid induces thermal energy losses, as the electric current heats the lines and this energy—in the form of heat—is dissipated into the atmosphere. On average, between 3% and 5% of the energy injected in the grid is lost through grid losses;
4. **Electricity flows:** electricity flows follow several paths in the grid from injection to withdrawal (as per Kirchhoff's laws) with complex interactions between flow paths and generation or injection points, sometimes resulting in so-called loop flows which are unintended flows that can cause congestions on certain paths.

2.1 How to Define the Price of Electricity?

2.1.1 Marginal Pricing of Electricity

One of the most fundamental questions in the field of electricity system economics, even before the introduction of electricity markets, is the question of the price of electricity: at which price should electricity be sold in order to maximize economic welfare?[1]

Long before the introduction of electricity markets, foundational work by the French engineer, economist Marcel Boiteux, published in 1949 (Boiteux 1949), paved the way to answer this question. His research has shown that electricity should be priced at its marginal cost.

In the case of an electricity system with several generation technologies, all electricity generation plants are sorted in the ascending order of their short-run marginal costs,[2] forming a step-wise curve called "merit-order." The cheapest generation plants to meet a given electricity demand volume are dispatched to produce electricity. Finally, a unique electricity price is set *for all consumers and*

[1] Level of prosperity in the society.

[2] The short-run marginal cost of electricity production is defined as the cost of generating one more Megawatt-hour of electricity, which encompasses power plant fuel, operational costs (and nowadays CO_2 emissions costs) but not investment or fixed maintenance costs, that must be paid regardless of the actual electricity generation.

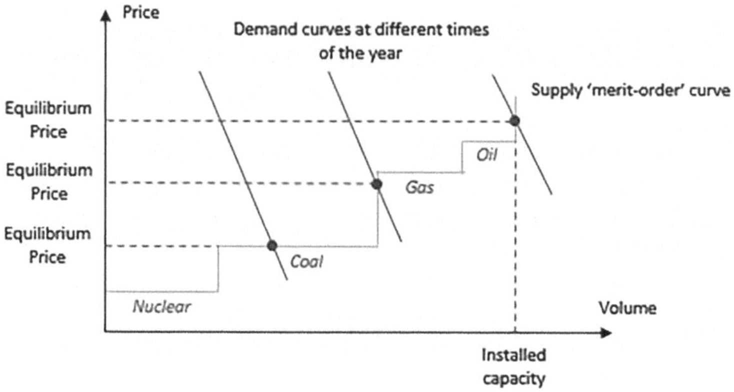

Fig. 22.3 Graph illustrating the concepts of marginal price, merit-order curve and short-run supply-demand equilibrium (as demand varies in time, several demand marginal benefit curves are shown in the graph). (Source: Authors' elaboration)

all producers, as the (1) the short-run marginal cost (SRMC) of the most expensive power plant dispatched to produce electricity or (2) the demand marginal benefit[3] when the demand equals the generation capacity of a given technology. In all cases, it is the price at the equilibrium of supply and demand marginal costs and benefits. As the volumes and costs of supply and demand vary in time, the electricity price varies accordingly, but always remains at the equilibrium, as illustrated in Fig. 22.3.

Micro-economics theory shows that this price is generating the most economic welfare for a given demand-supply situation. This result is intuitive: if the prices were arbitrarily set any higher or lower, some value-generating consumption or production would not take place (or take place at a loss).

The energy rent earned by electricity generators is the difference between the electricity price and their short-run marginal cost of production. This rent must reimburse sunk investment costs and fixed maintenance costs for a power plant investment to be profitable. The electricity system reaches its long-term investment equilibrium when the annual energy rent of the system marginal power plant equals its annual fixed costs (capital annuities and maintenance). This concept is illustrated in Fig. 22.4.

In Fig. 22.4, the annual energy rent of a power plant decreases as the ratio of installed generation capacity versus peak demand in the system increases, because electricity prices decrease as the offer to produce electricity relative to peak demand increases. Let us review two cases to illustrate the investment equilibrium:

[3] Also called demand marginal utility, it is the maximum amount a consumer is willing to pay for the electricity.

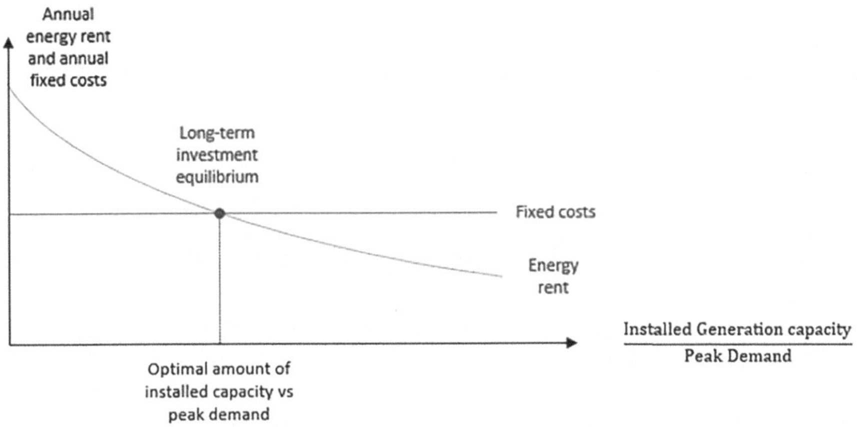

Fig. 22.4 Graph illustrating the concept of long-term investment equilibrium. (Source: Authors' elaboration)

- If the energy rent earned by existing generators is consistently higher or expected to be higher in the future than their annual fixed costs—for instance because of a wholesale price increase—this indicates economic viability in investing in new generation capacity;
- On the contrary, if the energy rent is (or is expected to be) consistently lower than the fixed costs, some built power plants are not or will not be making positive returns on investment from their electricity sale, and it is a signal that new power plants would not be economically viable.

The long-term investment equilibrium is therefore reached when the energy rent of the least-earning generation plants equals their annual fixed costs, and it sets the optimal amount of generation capacity in the system relative to a given peak demand.

In the short term, because many consumers do not observe prices and cannot respond to prices in real time (the demand is inelastic), when the system load reaches the maximum capacity in the system prices can spike spectacularly to reflect the need for additional capacity (that will not be built overnight).

2.1.2 Spatial Distribution of Electricity Prices

As explained in the introduction of this theoretical section, there are grid limitations to the amount of electrical power that can be transferred from a grid node to another (the transmission constraints) and costs associated with electricity transmission (the grid losses), making the location an important factor for electricity price determination. In 1988, the spatial distribution of electricity prices was theorized by the American engineer Fred Schweppe and his colleagues (Schweppe et al. 1988) and later complemented by Hogan (1992) in 1992, with the emergence of the concept of Locational Marginal Pricing. The underlying idea is that one optimal electricity price—the Locational Marginal Price (LMP)—is determined at each node of the grid, as the price equilibrium between supply and demand at the node, that is to say the cost of delivering one extra megawatt-hour at the node, taking into account grid losses, loop flows and congestion costs. The marginal transmission cost (cost of transferring power) between two nodes is the difference in the cost of generation at these nodes. With such prices, a generator will produce if its SRMC plus the transmission price is lower than the cost of generation at the destination node. If the transmission capacity was unlimited between all grid nodes and there were no grid losses, the price would be equal for all nodes.

A simple two-node LMP example is described in Fig. 22.5 in two cases, with and without congestion.

In case 1 without congestion, the generation source at node A is used to meet all the demand at nodes A and B, and their respective LMPs are equal to the cost of meeting an extra megawatt-hour of electricity. At node A, it is at the SRMC of the generation, equal to 30 €/MWh. At node B, it is the SRMC at node A plus the 5% grid loss cost, in total equal to 30*(1/0.95) ≈ 31.6 €/MWh.

In case 2 with congestion, the transmission capacity from node A to node B is fully used and the more expensive generator at node B is dispatched to supply 81 MW of demand at node B (as only 19 MW arrive from node A due to grid losses). The LMPs at nodes A and B—in other words the costs of meeting an extra megawatt-hour of demand at nodes A and B—are respectively equal to 30€/MWh and 40€/MWh.

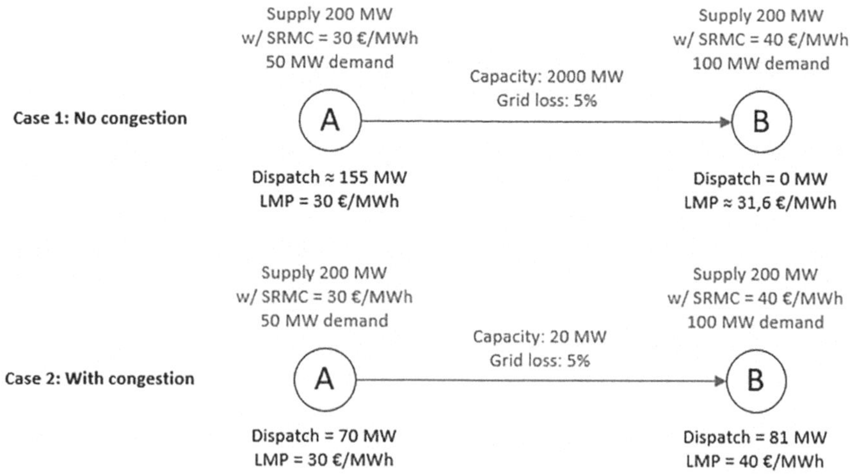

Fig. 22.5 Simple two-node example illustrating the concept of LMP. (Source: Authors' elaboration)

2.2 *The Emergence of Different Wholesale Market Designs*

The aforementioned principles for the electricity price determination were formulated before the implementation of electricity markets and were originally meant to optimize electricity systems under the vertically integrated monopoly regime. They were however fundamental economic principles for the electricity price determination, that allowed the emergence of electricity markets. The SRMC of generation units and marginal demand benefit are replaced by market offers from generation and retail companies and the regulated investment in generation capacity by monopolies is replaced with private investment.

Regardless of the market design, the wholesale electricity markets are always divided into several timeframes:

- A long-term market allows for the trading of derivative products indexed on the short-term spot price of electricity. Market participants can manage their long-term price risk based on their future consumption needs or production capabilities;
- In the short term, a spot market allows for the physical dispatch of power plants, starting on the day-ahead of delivery down to the real time. This dispatch exercise is first done on the day-ahead of delivery as many large power plants have long start-up and ramping times. The spot market sets a spot price for electricity used to determine the dispatch of power plants in the short term and as a price reference for longer term derivative products.
- In real time, the electricity system is steered by system operators to ensure security of supply as all system constraints must be respected to ensure security of supply.

2.2.1 *Nodal and Zonal Market Designs*

Several wholesale electricity market designs have been studied and are currently implemented around the world. They differ with regards to how grid constraints are considered, how prices are calculated and information on production and consumption capabilities is centralized. This has consequences on the determination of the spot price and on the form and type of transactions that take place. The two general market designs that have emerged are the ***nodal*** design (currently implemented in several US states) and ***zonal*** market design (currently implemented in the European Union).

As its name suggests, the nodal market design corresponds to the determination of an LMP at each node of the electricity transmission grid (see Sect. 2.1), whereas in the zonal market design, zonal Market Clearing Prices (MCPs) are calculated for large geographical area, called Bidding Zones, as illustrated in Fig. 22.6. Biddings zones consist of many transmission nodes between which capacity limits are neglected under the so-called copper-plate assumption. For the price determination, each bidding zone in the zonal model is equivalent to

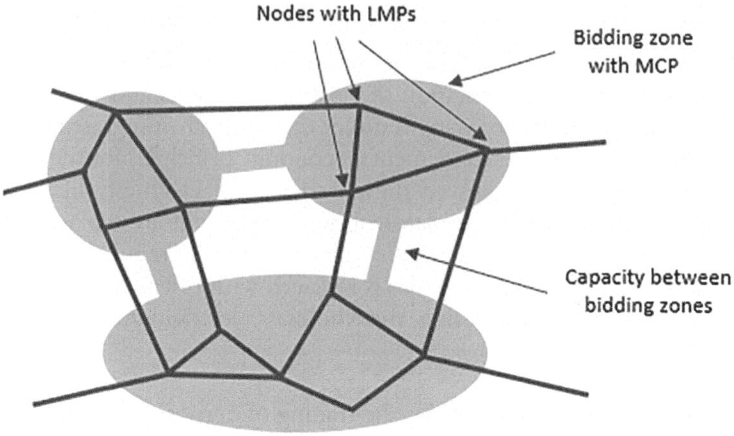

Fig. 22.6 Illustration of the notion of bidding zone, node, and capacity between bidding zones. (Source: Authors' elaboration)

a node in the nodal model as only transmission capacities between bidding zones are considered for the MCP calculation. This leads to different paradigms for congestion management.

In the nodal model, all potential congestions are considered "by design" for price determination leading to LMP differences between nodes in case of congestion. In the zonal model, only constraints between bidding zones are considered for the MCP calculation. Potential "intra-zonal" congestions are alleviated by Transmission System Operators (TSOs) outside of the wholesale market after the MCP has been determined, in several ways:

- **Topological changes:** changes to the grid topology to re-route electricity flows and alleviate the congestions.
- **Re-dispatching measures:** changes to the schedules of specific power plants to change the electricity flows throughout the grid and alleviate congestions.

The costs of these congestion-management measures are not reflected in the zonal MCPs and are borne by all grid users within the bidding zone. In nodal markets, such congestion-management measures can also be taken by Independent System Operators (ISOs) in case congestions appear due to an unforeseen event (power plant or transmission outages, forecast errors, etc.).

2.2.2 Centralized and Decentralized Market Organizations

One important characteristic of a market design is whether the market is *centrally* or *decentrally* organized. The real-time system steering is necessarily centralized and managed by system operators regardless of the design. However, the spot markets can either be centrally organized (e.g. US nodal markets) or decentrally organized (EU zonal markets).

In the US nodal markets, the short-term spot market algorithm sets the dispatch of power plants based on their technical constraints and marginal cost, submitted at a unit level to the market algorithm. These schedules are binding for power generators and can only be changed in the real-time market. The market bidding is therefore referred to as "centrally dispatched unit bidding." Each unit has an individual commitment and a tailor-made contract (Ahlqvist et al. 2019). In some ways such markets reflect some procedures from national monopolies and regional power pools that existed before the deregulation (Wilson 2002). New England, PJM, Midwest, New York and California nodal markets are all in central-dispatch. In Europe, the UK England and Wales pool and the Single Electricity Market (SEM) in Ireland were examples of centralized markets, most other markets being decentrally organized. Britain and Ireland both changed to decentralized markets in 2001 and 2018 respectively.

In EU's zonal spot market, market participants have the responsibility to optimize their assets themselves. They provide aggregated portfolio bids in accordance with the technical characteristics of their assets or with their consumption needs. Accepted bids create a physical delivery responsibility that can be adjusted in a continuous intraday market running until real time. This way of functioning is called the "self-dispatch with portfolio bidding". Market players have an implicit responsibility to balance the electricity system; the Balance Responsible Parties (BRPs) are financially responsible for keeping their own position (sum of injections, withdrawals and transactions) balanced over given delivery periods, called the imbalance settlement periods. Depending on the state of the system, an imbalance charge is imposed per imbalance settlement period on the BRPs that are not in balance.

2.2.3 Ancillary Services

Under liberalized—or deregulated—electricity markets, the responsibility of the security of supply and grid stability is taken by system operation companies—the ISO in a nodal model and the TSO in a zonal model. As a complement to the wholesale electricity market, and in order to guarantee the security of supply throughout the interconnected electricity grid, there are ancillary services—or system services—managed by these system operating companies. These ancillary services correspond to a large set of operations going beyond the commercial operation of electricity generation, transmission and consumption activities. Historically, ancillary services were procured by system operators from large power plants, but they are nowadays increasingly more open to consumption and storage capacities as well as smaller scale generation. The main services covered by ancillary services are the following:

- **Balancing and frequency control:** the balancing of the grid to maintain the physical balance between supply and demand at every instant. The frequency of the grid is a value that can be monitored and reflects the real-time demand-supply balance. System operators typically contract flexible generation or storage that form "reserves" that are able to quickly react to frequency variations to keep it within a given range, around 50 Hz in Europe and 60 Hz in the US.
- **Voltage control:** the voltage in the electricity grid must be maintained within a given range and this is done by system operators through active and reactive power control on some generation assets.
- **Black start:** this system service guarantees the ability of the electricity grid to get back in operation after a black-out event. Power plants providing this service must be able to start their operations without relying on the electricity from the grid.
- **Congestion management:** system operators have the ability to steer some power plants and change their scheduled generation in order to solve expected grid congestions.

Ancillary services, although answering the same general objectives—as the laws of physics are the same everywhere—are organized differently from one market to another and are usually specific to given system operators. In the nodal market designs as implemented in some US states, the procurement of several ancillary services, such as the operating reserves for balancing, is co-optimized within the day-ahead wholesale market optimization, whereas in the zonal market design as applied in the EU, ancillary services are procured by TSOs in separate mechanisms and markets outside the wholesale market framework.

Table 22.1 summarizes the main characteristics of nodal and zonal market designs.

Table 22.1 Summary of the main characteristics of nodal and zonal market models

	Nodal market	*Zonal market*
Day-ahead spot price	Locational marginal price	Zonal market clearing price
Market bidding	Centrally dispatched unit bidding including technical constraints	Free portfolio-based bidding with self-dispatch
Market operation	ISOs	Power exchange and TSOs
Real-time balancing	Through real-time market with virtual bidding between DA and RT	Balancing organized by TSOs independently of wholesale market
Congestion management	Included in the day-ahead optimization algorithm for all transmission lines	1. Included in the day-ahead optimization for inter-zonal congestions 2. Solved through out-of-market redispatch for intra-zonal congestions

2.3 *The Problem of System Adequacy: Capacity Mechanisms*

The adequacy or reliability of the electricity system corresponds to the system's ability to adequately supply the demand for electricity at any given time, and especially in times of peak demand. It relates to system planning (by TSOs or ISOs) and more specifically to the amount of available generation capacity available in the system with regards to the level of electricity demand. Reliability can be quantified with criteria such as the Loss-Of-Load Expectation (LOLE).[4]

In a liberalized electricity market, the amount of electricity generators present in the system depends on the price of electricity and on the generators' revenues from wholesale markets and ancillary services. This rent must reimburse sunk investment costs paid to build a power plant (capital cost annuities) and fixed operations and maintenance costs (fixed O&M costs) to make a power plant investment profitable.

In an "energy-only" market,[5] the installed generation capacity relative to peak demand—and therefore the system adequacy—is set by market forces through investment in generation capacity (see the long-term investment equilibrium described in Sect. 2.1).

In some wholesale electricity market setups, the energy-only remuneration of generators is not enough to guarantee the adequacy of the electricity system. The American economist S. Stoft (2002) is the first to have highlighted this issue in energy-only markets. For him, "The missing money problem is not that the market pays too little, but that it pays too little when we have the required level of reliability." Such a situation can arise for different reasons:

- The market design and regulation do not allow generators to earn enough money to cover their fixed costs. For instance, electricity prices should be able to reach very high levels in times of supply scarcity, up to the level of Value of Lost Load[6] (VoLL), which is rarely allowed;
- A reliability criterion arbitrarily set for the electricity system[7] is conservative and maintains many generators in the system, increasing competition and bringing the market price and generation rents down.

[4] Number of loss-of-load hours in a year. A loss-of-load event corresponds to a market situation in which the demand exceeds the supply, the price reaches the maximum market price and some consumers must be curtailed.

[5] A market in which the only revenue of generators comes from their electricity sales on the wholesale market (and payments for ancillary services).

[6] The VoLL represents the maximum price that consumers are willing to pay to be supplied with energy, and at that price they will be indifferent between, on the one hand, being supplied and paying the price and, on the other hand, not being supplied (and pay nothing) [source: https://www.emissions-euets.com/internal-electricity-market-glossary/966-value-of-lost-load-voll].

It is often estimated in the tens of thousands of euros or dollars per MWh.

[7] In the US, one common reliability criterion is one day of loss of load every 10 years (2.4 hours per year). In France (EU), the criteria are set at 3 hours per year by the authorities.

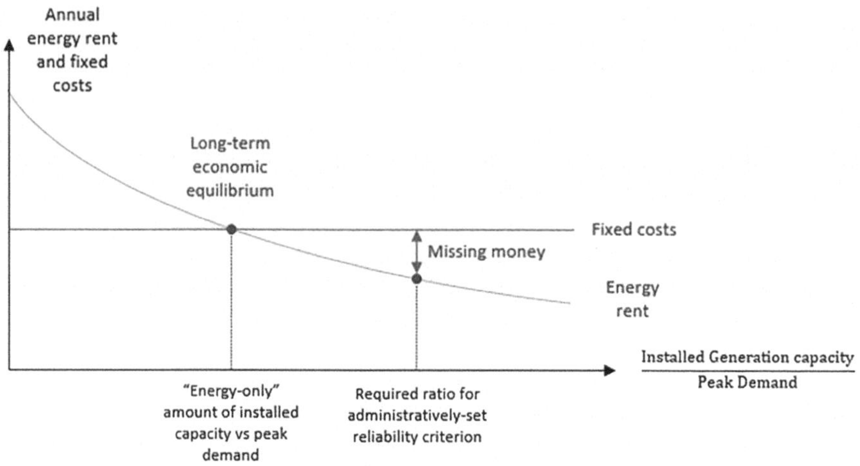

Fig. 22.7 Graph illustrating the "Missing" Money problem. (Source: Authors' elaboration inspired by The Brattle Group)

The "missing money" is the difference between the generators' annual fixed costs and their energy rent from the sale of electricity in the wholesale market and ancillary services in a medium- to long-term perspective (the market could be over-supplied in the short term).

The energy-only markets are therefore sometimes complemented with capacity mechanisms or capacity markets, remunerating installed generation capacity for being available in order to compensate the generators' missing money and ensure a given level of reliability in the system. In the case of a capacity market, market forces adjust the capacity price to compensate the missing money and ensure needed investments in generation capacity to meet the defined reliability criterion. The graph in Fig. 22.7 illustrates the notion of missing money with a comparison to the long-term "energy-only" investment equilibrium.

3 Electricity Trading in Practice

After having introduced the theoretical foundations of electricity markets, and some of the main design features, this section shows how they function in practice. We start by a description of the functioning of wholesale electricity markets where we focus on the derivatives and the spot market to analyse their main features, the traded products, the trading venues, the rules, processes and some of the challenges going forward.

3.1 Wholesale Electricity Trading

Since liberalization started, it is not the vertically integrated monopoly that decides which are the least-cost assets to start and stop in order to meet electricity demand. Nor where, when and what to invest. In a decentralized manner, market participants take these decisions based on the long- or short-term power prices.

3.1.1 Electricity Transactions

For various reasons that we will detail going forward, market participants trade before electricity is delivered to end-consumers (residential, businesses or industry) via the grid. A transaction is a contractual agreement made between a buyer and a seller to exchange a given volume of electricity in megawatt-hour during a given delivery period, at a given location for a given price.

3.1.2 Market Participants

Like in markets for other commodities, there are two general categories of actors active in the wholesale electricity markets: *fundamental* participants and *speculative* players:

- Fundamental market participants are active to value and optimize physical assets in the market. They carry their "buyer" or "seller" positions until delivery, based on their specific portfolio of assets, be it consumption, generation or both;
- Speculative market players do not have a fundamental need to buy or sell electricity. They participate in the market in hope of making a profit from buying low and selling high. Their activity has a zero-sum volume effect on the market as they do not carry positions to delivery.

In practice, the fundamental market participants are either electricity generators, who trade and sell the output from their power plants, or electricity retailers who trade and source electricity to sell it to their end-consumers. For companies that own generation assets and sell directly to end-consumers, part of the electricity injected into the network is not directly traded in the markets but delivered directly to end-consumers. A utility that produces more energy than its customers' needs can sell the excess power on the wholesale market (net seller). Symmetrically, a retailer that doesn't produce enough energy to cover the needs of its customers can buy it from the wholesale market (net buyer). In addition to these traditional actors, a new type of fundamental participant has been emerging over the last decade: aggregators for Demand Side Management (DSM) or small-scale renewables. They act on behalf of a group of producers and/or consumers, aggregating assets they can steer and market at the wholesale level. In Europe, Transmission System Operators are also active participants on the wholesale market although their activity is regulated.

They intervene on the spot markets to compensate the transmission system's grid losses.[8] In Germany, they are also in charge of marketing green electricity subsidized under the feed-in tariff regulatory scheme.

Trading companies, hedge funds and banks have also entered wholesale electricity markets since the first days of liberalization. They usually perform speculative trading or trade for the account of customers. These financial participants take positions on either the long-term derivatives market or on the spot market and provide market access services to other counterparties (i.e. hedge funds).

3.1.3 *Trading Venues*

Electricity can be traded on "organized markets" (managed by power exchanges) or "Over-The-Counter" (OTC) bilaterally or through intermediaries called brokers. Power exchanges run auctions and continuous double-sided markets. Brokers usually offer phone and continuous screen trading coverage to their customers.

OTC transactions are bilateral, non-anonymous transactions between a buyer and a seller with the counterparty risk[9] managed bilaterally between them, even if a broker is involved. On their end, power exchanges give access to anonymous markets creating a level playing field between all exchange members. This is possible as the counterparty risk is centralized by a clearing house that guarantees the fulfilment of all financial obligations of the trading participants through a daily settlement of profits and losses and a margining and collateralization system. OTC transactions can be recorded for clearing at power exchanges as a way of eliminating counterparty risk.

In both the US and EU, dedicated large commodity exchanges, such as European Energy Exchange (EEX), Intercontinental Exchange (ICE), Chicago Mercantile Exchange (CME) or Nasdaq operate power derivatives exchanges. In Europe, a model of exchange alliance has emerged in recent years. Established stock exchanges acquire majority (together with minority TSO shareholders) and integrate power spot and/or derivatives with their commodity businesses. Examples are Nasdaq OMX Commodities, ICE and Endex, EPEX SPOT and EEX, IDEX and London Stock Exchange (LSE), Nord Pool and Euronext.

3.1.4 *Liquidity*

Liquidity is a desirable characteristic of a competitive market. It can be defined as the ability to transact quickly with little price impact. Liquidity is materialized by a high level of trading activity and a high number of active market participants. It can be measured by price resiliency for an auction and bid-ask spread and market depth for a continuous market:

[8] In the US grid losses are not compensated by the ISOs and need to be taken into account by the traders when performing their trades.

[9] Risk of a party defaulting on its contractual obligations (e.g. non-payment or non-delivery).

- As a measure of overall market activity, the Churn ratio is the ratio between domestic consumption of electricity (considered an indicator of fundamental trading needs) and the volumes traded on the wholesale market. In Germany, the largest EU power market for spot and derivatives, the Churn reached 12 times the total consumption (European Commission 2017).
- For an auction, price resiliency can be defined as the sensitivity of the market clearing price to the submission of a price-independent bid of 500 and 1000 MW for a given delivery hour on either the buy or sell side.
- For a continuous market, the bid-ask spread is the spread between the best buy and best sell prices in the order book. The lower the bid-ask spread, the higher the chances are the prices on which buyers and sellers agree reflect the fair value of the good.

Liquidity has traditionally been greater in less concentrated markets with high number of participants.

A trading member can act as a market maker—or liquidity provider. The aim of market makers' service is to provide liquidity to a continuous market. Market makers in power exchanges provide liquidity for a given product by standing ready to purchase or sell a given amount of power, for instance by providing a continuous bid-ask spread. The specific price range for market makers' orders is contractually set in advance with the power exchange or broker. Market makers earn the bid-ask spread (when their buy and sell transactions compensate each other) but they can also benefit from fee rebates when they fulfil their bidding requirements based on the size of the spread and its duration.

3.1.5 *The Trading Sequence*

As first described in Sect. 2.2, electricity markets cover several timeframes, ranging from years ahead of delivery until real time. Market participants use longer term derivatives markets to hedge sales or purchases and manage their electricity price risk. The short-term spot market lets participants schedule their assets close to real time and manage their volume risk (i.e. forecast errors), as described in Fig. 22.8.

The following sections explain in more details how the derivatives and spot markets work, how they interact and what the listed products are.

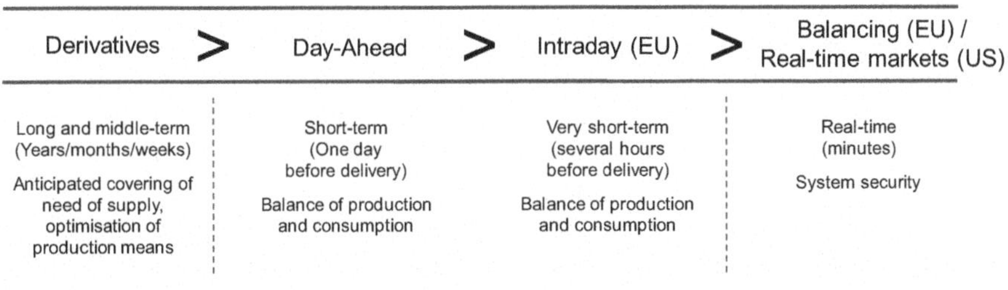

Fig. 22.8 Trading sequence from long term to real time. (Source: Authors' elaboration)

3.2 Power Derivatives

Power derivatives correspond to traded contracts that are indexed on an underlying price of electricity, most often the short-term spot price. Most common exchange-based derivatives are futures and options, competing with OTC-traded forwards, options and swaps.

3.2.1 Hedging, Sourcing and Arbitraging

Fundamental market participants are exposed to price variations in different ways:

- Retailers most often offer fixed-price contracts to their clients and their margins are exposed to electricity price variations;
- Generators' margins directly depend on the price at which they sell electricity and they are exposed to market price variations.

The basic idea behind a hedge is the limitation of the price risk associated with the electricity price variations. Hedging allows consumers, retailers and generators to take a known fixed price now rather than to accept the risk of this price changing. Long-term derivatives markets allow this risk to be shared among market participants through transactions over derivative contracts (e.g. Futures, Forwards, Options, Swaps).

In long-term derivative markets, market players trade for the future supply or demand of electricity for long delivery periods such as weeks, months, quarters or years, at a price negotiated on the contract date. To make trading easier and reinforce liquidity, these derivative contracts apply to standardized products, for example, the supply of 1 MW of baseload electricity (constant power during all hours of the delivery period) or peak load electricity (between 8 am and 8 pm, Monday to Friday during the delivery period). Financial Futures contracts are cash-settled against the spot price, and therefore represent the average of the expected spot prices over a longer period. They are generally used as a basis for determining the prices paid by end-consumers. When retailers enter into contracts with customers, they generally purchase the derivatives products required to cover most of the electricity they will need to supply. As the delivery time approaches the remaining variations around the forecast and finer granularity variations (hourly and sub-hourly) are handled in the day-ahead and intraday timeframes in Europe and in day-ahead and real-time markets in the US.

The very limited storability of electricity explains the lack of a well-defined relationship between spot and long-term power prices. According to the storage theory (Kaldor 1939), companies trading commodities keep stocks to respond to unanticipated demand variations. This exposes them to storage costs but makes possible the selling of retained stocks later when the commodity is valued more (the convenience yield). The non-storability of electricity limits the standard no-arbitrage approach in modelling electricity futures prices. The relationship between spot and futures electricity prices "only" reflects expectations about future supply and demand characteristics for electricity (that determine the spot price) and risk aversion (Shawky et al. 2003).

Allowing participants the opportunity to hedge against locational price differences is an important aspect of a power market. Long-term transmission rights such as Physical and Financial Transmission Rights (PTRs and FTRs) enable market participants to cover the risks of changing conditions between the contracting and delivery of contracts and to hedge short-term price differentials between two bidding zones (EU) or nodes (US). PTRs entitle their holder to physically transfer a certain volume of electricity in a certain period between two zones in a specific direction. FTRs are a mechanism for market participants to hedge against the volatility of transmission congestion between two points on the network. In the US only FTRs are used for the nodal markets. There are long term, yearly and monthly auctions for FTRs organized by ISOs. In Europe, depending on the borders, both Physical Transmission Rights and Financial Transmission Rights are used.

3.2.2 Power Derivatives in Europe and the US

Electricity is traded in Europe and the US on the "curve" several years ahead of delivery through either OTC (bilaterally or through inter-dealer brokers) or exchange-based[10] until the day-ahead of delivery when the "physical" market starts. Traded futures are financially cash-settled against a reference price of the underlying asset (the daily spot settlement price), but in Europe physical futures can also be traded and give rise to a delivery of power (i.e. schedule to the relevant TSO). In the EU, Futures with maturities of up to 10 years can be found on the most liquid hubs but they are less liquid. However, most of the liquidity is concentrated on the next three years ahead of delivery, next three months, next three quarters.

In Europe, Nord Pool, the Nordic Power exchange was the first power market for spot and derivatives in the Scandinavian countries in 1993, followed by EEX and all major stock exchanges (e.g. ICE, Nasdaq, CME). Two standardized products are traded on Futures and Options: quotation is made with a tick size of 0.01 €/MWh and a minimum size of 1 MW. The nominal of the contract is expressed in megawatt-hours. The futures price is denominated in Eur/MWh, and the contract is financially settled against the average hourly spot price (base and peak load contracts). The daily settlement price is used as a reference for the clearing house[11] to value on a daily basis a position and to close a position in case of a defaulting buyer or seller. European power options are financially settled on the futures index with monthly, quarterly and yearly delivery periods.

[10] In Europe Financial products can only be offered by regulated Exchanges in the MIFID sense.

[11] To ensure the financial and physical settlement of transactions as well as "collateralization" of transactions to remove the counterparty/default risk exchanges use clearing houses for the futures and spot transactions.

In the US, Futures (Forwards and Swaps on the OTC) contracts listed at exchanges have also been created to cover specific geographic regions or hubs (electricity products can be traded at several dozen hubs and delivery points in North America). After the COB (California Oregon Border) and PV (Palo Verde, Arizona) contracts introduced in 1996, the NYMEX allowed trading the Cinergy contract (covering the Midwestern region), Entergy contract (Louisiana region) and PJM contract, whose delivery point is the border intersect of Pennsylvania, New Jersey and Maryland (Eydeland and Wolyniec 2003). Major hubs have developed around the Regional Transmission Operator (RTO) markets:[12] ISO New England (ISO-NE), New York ISO (NYISO), PJM Interconnection (PJM), Midwest ISO (MISO), Electric Reliability Council of Texas (ERCOT), two locations in the California ISO (CAISO), Louisiana (into Entergy), Southwest (Palo Verde) and Northwest (Mid-Columbia) (Table 22.2).

With the expansion of the Nodal Pricing implemented in most competitive power markets states, Nodal Futures can be traded allowing to decrease basis risk management with futures contracts traded at the Nodal Exchange. Nodal futures are financially settled using the monthly average of the appropriate hourly Locational Marginal Prices (LMPs) for the location(s) specified in the contract as published by the organized power markets, which are overseen by the Federal Energy Regulatory Commission (FERC) (Fig. 22.9).

Although for derivatives both EU and US share similar arrangements, in the case of spot markets there are major differences.

Table 22.2 Contract examples for US and EU

Exchange	*Type of contract*	*Granularity*	*Traded maturities*	*Physical vs. financial*
European Energy Exchange	Futures	Bidding zone (Germany)	Days, weeks, months, quarters, years	Cash settled
European Energy Exchange	Options	Bidding zone (Germany)	Days, weeks, months, quarters, years	Cash settled
Nasdaq	Futures	Bidding zone (Nordics)	Months, quarters, years	Cash settled
Intercontinental Exchange PJM Real-Time Western Hub	Futures	Hub (PJM)	Days, weeks, months, quarters, years	Cash settled
Nodal exchange Cash Settled Financial Off-Peak Power, CAISO SP15, Day Ahead	Futures	Transmission node/hub (CAISO)	Days, weeks, months, quarters, years	Cash settled

Source: Authors' elaboration

[12] In the US, the large ISOs have expanded geographically and have been renamed Regional Transmission Organizations (RTOs).

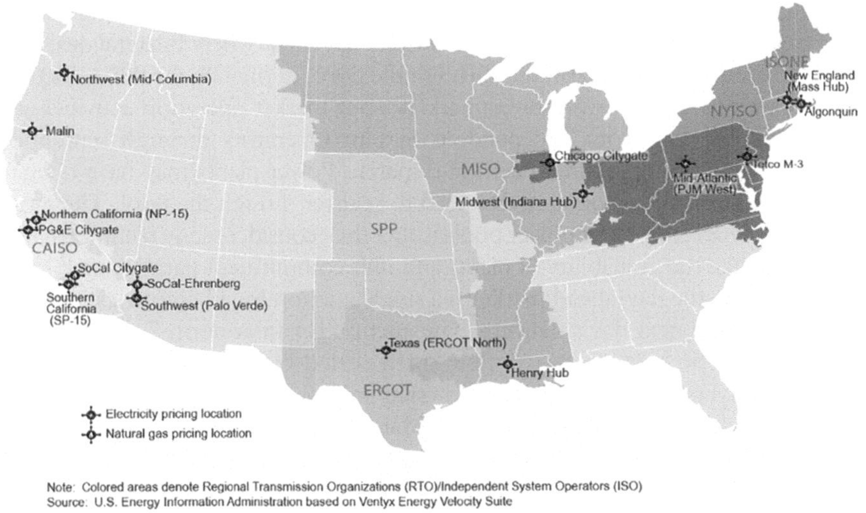

Fig. 22.9 Selected price hub for wholesale electricity and natural gas reported by Intercontinental Exchange. (Source: US Energy Information Administration)

3.3 *Spot Electricity Markets*

Market structures in both continents differ by the nature and role of the stakeholders. Day-ahead markets are operated in the US by Independent Systems Operators (e.g. PJM, MISO, ERCOT, etc.) which are non-profit federally regulated organizations, while such markets are organized in the European Union (EU) by power exchanges which are for-profit companies that are designated as Nominated Electricity Market Operators (NEMO) in the European legislation.[13] In both the US and the EU the main physical market is the auction that takes place the day-ahead of delivery for all the hourly delivery periods of the next day. Such a "physical dispatch" market on the day-ahead of delivery is necessary considering that some power plants have long ramp-rates.

3.3.1 The Day-Ahead Spot Market

Power Exchanges can be either based on the "pool" or "exchange" models. Most European countries have adopted an exchange model with bilateral contracts and a voluntary electricity trading (self-scheduling model) and the pools running centralized dispatch with often some mandatory features. A power pool is often the result of a public initiative, that is, a government wants to implement competition at the wholesale level, and participation is mandatory, that is, no

[13] The Capacity Allocation and Congestion Management (CACM) guidelines released by the European Commission describe the legal framework in which these NEMOs (e.g. EPEX Spot, OMIE, GME, Nord Pool, etc.) operate. In particular, non-monopoly NEMOs can compete for spot market services throughout Europe.

trade is allowed outside the pool.[14] Currently in Europe a semi-mandatory solution has been applied in Iberian OMIE and Italian GME where bilateral deals are possible but need to be registered through the pool. In the US, for the states that have moved to competitive power markets, spot market operation activities are performed by non-profit Independent System Operators through semi-pool type arrangements operating a central dispatch. Power plants may have obligations to bid in the pool or all trades need to register though the pool. The most important characteristic of power pools is that they consider many technical characteristics, like the availability of plants and unit commitment parameters.[15]

In Europe, the day-ahead market is a single auction for all countries[16] and all 24 hours of the next day's delivery. The auction is run at noon 7 days a week, year-round. The auction is a double-sided sealed-bid uniform-price auction where all buyers and sellers make offers that are not visible to the other market participants and pay/receive the same Market Clearing Price (MCP) respectively. All cross-border interconnectors are considered in the market clearing algorithm through a process called "market coupling" that implicitly allocates the interconnection capacity between bidding zones together with the energy and optimizes its usage. If enough transmission capacity is available, then a common market clearing price is determined. If transmission capacity is saturated, separate clearing prices are determined across the border. Market participants send their orders to their respective power exchange. All orders are collected and submitted to the market coupling algorithm that decides which orders are to be executed and which orders are to be rejected such that the social welfare[17] generated is maximal and the power does not exceed the capacity of the relevant network elements.

In the US, ISOs run a nodal day-ahead auction taking into account a full topology of the transmission grid. A second auction is performed for the real-time market with the same grid topology but updated bids.[18] In the Day-ahead Market hourly clearing prices are calculated for each hour of the next operating day based on generation offers, demand bids at the node level. Moreover, there is a simultaneous clearing of energy and reserves (co-optimization). Market participants bid technical/cost data by unit (unit-bidding) and the ISO solves a co-optimization based on market participants bids and bilateral transaction schedules submitted in the Day-ahead Market.

[14] The England and Wales's pool, as it existed before the New Electricity Trading Arrangements (NETA), was a typical example of this model. The reader can refer to Newbery (1997).

[15] Often costs of capacity can be considered in pool system, too.

[16] Integrated in Multi-Regional Coupling encompasses Germany/Luxemburg, Austria, France, Belgium, the Netherlands, Great Britain, the Nordics and Baltics, Spain, Portugal, Italy and Slovenia. This geographical scope is set to be expanded to more countries in the years to come according to the European target model.

[17] Social welfare is the sum of the consumer surplus, producer surplus and the congestion rent across the countries which corresponds to the price differential when a congestion occurs.

[18] This is known as a two-settlement (multi-settlement) system design. In a multi-settlement system, two successive runs of LMP are cleared with the first run occurring the day prior to the operating day, appropriately named the Day-Ahead energy market.

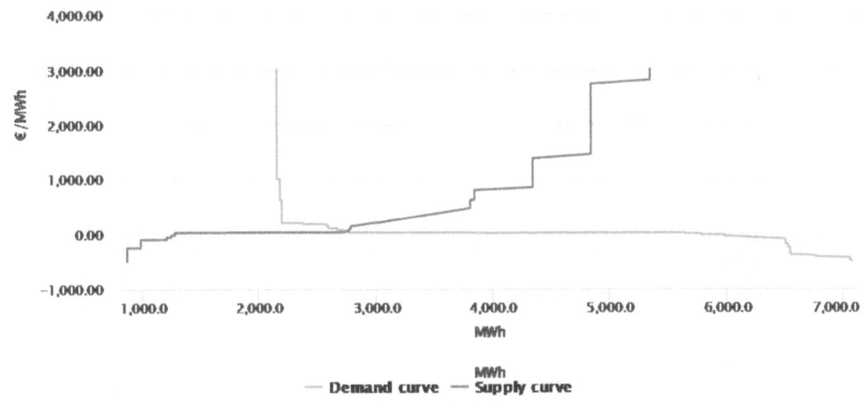

Fig. 22.10 Aggregated curves, Austria 2/06/2020, hour 19–20. (Source: Authors' elaboration on EPEX Spot data)

In both the US and EU, price caps have been set on the energy market prices for technical reasons but also to avoid extreme prices that would result from the abuse of market power. Price-limits are set quite arbitrarily today in the 000 EUR/MWh or 000 $/MWh level, due to the difficulty to define a market-wide Value of Loss of Load and the difficulty of consumers to express their real willingness to pay. Across Europe there are single day-ahead harmonized price caps at (-500; +3000 €/MWh) (EPEX Spot 2020) with an obligation set by the authorities to increase the price-cap every time it is reached (ACER 2017). Figure 22.10 shows an example of supply and demand aggregated curves.

As an example of a US-based nodal design, the PJM market offers are capped at 2000 $/MWh and need to justify cost-basis but during scarcity conditions the price can rise to 3700 $/MWh (PJM 2018). Usually, offer caps on units are imposed when the local market structure is non-competitive. Offer capping is a means of addressing local market power. The market rules require that offers in the energy market be competitive, where competitive is defined to be the short-run marginal cost of the units. The short-run marginal cost can and should also reflect opportunity costs.

Because generators face non-convex cost functions due to technical constraints such as startup costs, minimum up and down times, ramp rates (depicted in Fig. 22.11), in Europe, the market coupling algorithm allows for "block orders" of a given amount of electric energy in multiple consecutive hours, as an addition to simpler hourly orders.

Block orders "link" several hours and allow a better modelling and optimization of power plants in the day-ahead auction. The uniform price auction rule means that the same price applies to all and there are no side-payments (make-whole payments) linked with non-uniform pricing rules.

In the US, producers typically use three-part bids specifying start-up costs, no-load costs and marginal costs (Sioshansi et al. 2009). Centralized markets have a non-linear pricing scheme with make-whole or uplift payments to ensure

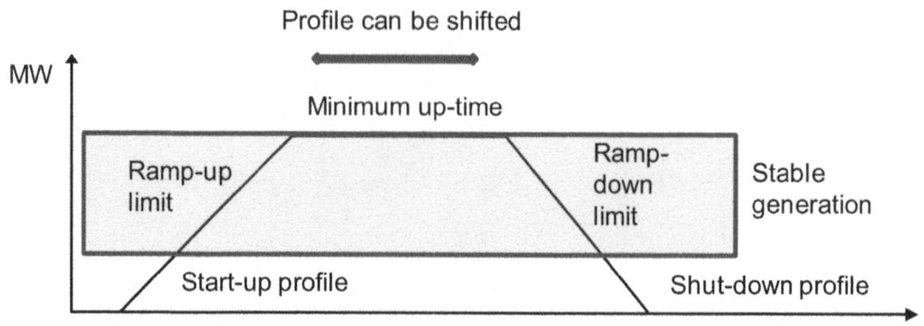

Fig. 22.11 Technical constraints of a thermal power plant. (Source: Authors' elaboration)

that a unit does not make a loss. Uplift payments are made to market participants for operating a unit under specific conditions as directed by ISOs to ensure that they recover their total offered costs when market revenues are insufficient or when their dispatch instructions diverge from their dispatch schedule.

Spot power markets are very computation-intensive and hard to scale up, especially if they include complex network topologies or complex bid structures (Ahlqvist et al. 2019). This is true for the US with nodal pricing and in the case of Europe for the Day-ahead algorithm complexity with the integration of all borders, national requirements (i.e. Italian single national price Prezzo Unico Nazionale (PUN)) and block order complexity in the market coupling algorithm. This is a potential problem as the global trend is to increase the geographical size of electricity markets, to introduce finer granularity products and integrate millions of assets, including storage which creates dynamic time dependencies and high algorithmic complexity.

3.3.2 The Intraday and Real-Time Markets

As day-ahead auctions are based on a prediction of the next day's required load or generation, the actual demand or supply for power is not known when the auctions are run. Intraday markets are the last opportunity for market participants to adapt their offers and assets before real time. These variations can occur for several reasons, but traditionally the intraday and real-time markets have been used to balance volume risk as a result of:

- Forced outages of generation units;
- Forecast errors of demand. A drop in the temperature or a rise in cloud coverage might require additional generation resources to meet load in real time;
- Forecast errors of intermittent Renewable Energy Sources (RES) such as wind and solar.

In the US a real-time market is used to correct deviations very close to real time. In the Real-Time Market the product is procured for immediate delivery. The locational marginal prices are calculated for every five-minute step on the actual system operations security-constrained economic dispatch. The real-time market acts as a balancing market where day-ahead commitments are balanced against actual demand and system constraints. The generation offers are updated and used to make real-time dispatching decisions. A higher amount of price volatility can occur in the real-time market as dispatching is adjusted to the real-time system load and outages. When the two-auction settlement system is performing well and the day-ahead forecasts were accurate, the real-time price will clear similar to the day-ahead. Virtual bids can be placed in both markets (in opposite directions) to arbitrage the price differences between the day-ahead and real-time markets (Jha and Wolak 2016).

In the EU, the aforementioned forecast errors can be rebalanced on the cross-border continuous intraday 24 hours a day, 7 days a week, year-round. From 3 pm on the day ahead of delivery until 5 minutes before delivery with a gradual opening of 15, 30 and 60-minute granularity products. In 2015, an additional uniform-price auction for 15-minute time slots was introduced in Germany at the beginning of the intraday trading session at 3 pm to help the market participants market their solar ramps (Fig. 22.12).

The continuous trading implements a pay-as-bid continuous matching algorithm which implies that market participants must anticipate the market price. Figure 22.13 shows an example of the evolution of the bid-ask spread and market depth during a trading session.

Since their introduction in 2007, the intraday market volumes have increased a lot reflecting the higher needs to re-balance supply and demand between day-ahead and real-time as a result of ever-growing renewable capacities of wind and solar. Figure 22.14 shows the evolution of intraday volumes in Germany for the period 2010–2018 during which they have been multiplied by ten.

Other trends that have been observed following the integration of massive amounts of renewables are trading in more granular products and closer to real time:

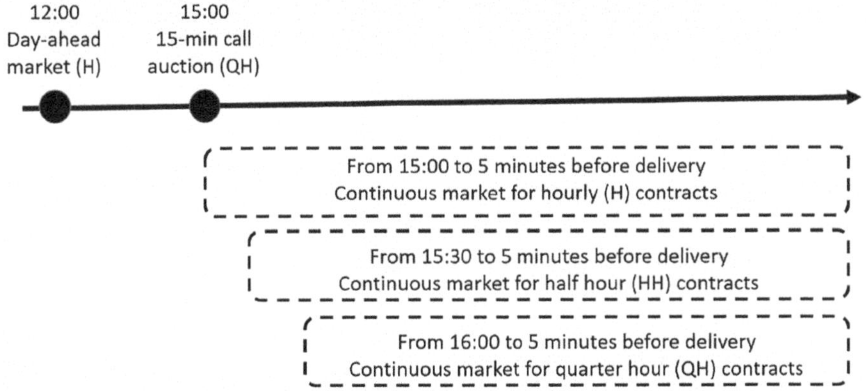

Fig. 22.12 The “Spot” trading process. (Source: Authors’ elaboration)

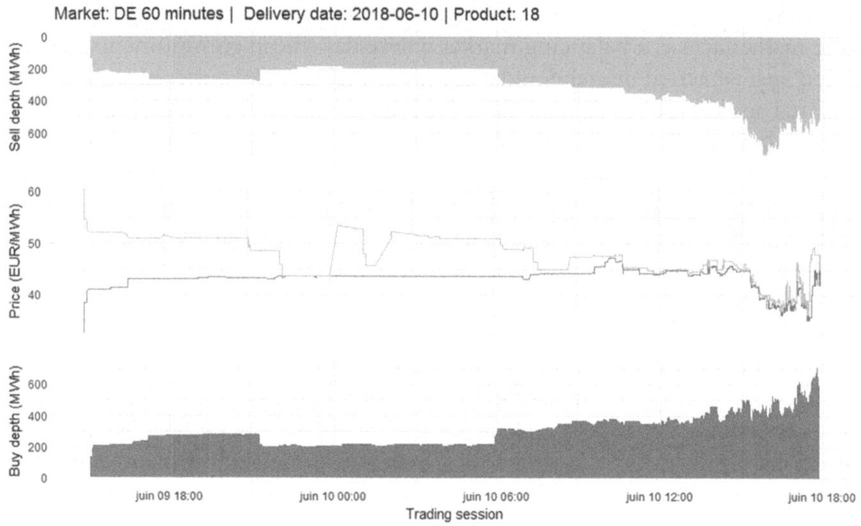

Fig. 22.13 Bid-ask spread and market depth of the continuous intraday market. (Source: Authors' elaboration on EPEX Spot data)

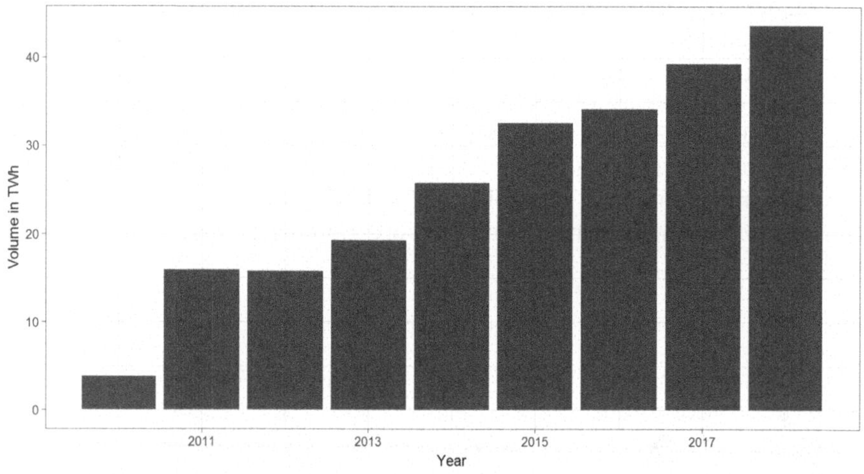

Fig. 22.14 Continuous intraday volumes in Germany 2010 to 2018. (Source: Authors' elaboration on EPEX spot data)

- The finer granularity products allow market participants to match generation and demand for each 15-minute time step to satisfy their balancing obligations. They represent roughly 20% of the total traded volumes of the intraday continuous market;
- The trading activity in the last 30 minutes before real-time has increased over the last years as participants benefit from trading opportunities until the last minutes. On the German Intraday 15% of intraday continuous volumes are traded in the last 30 minutes before real time (Fig. 22.15).

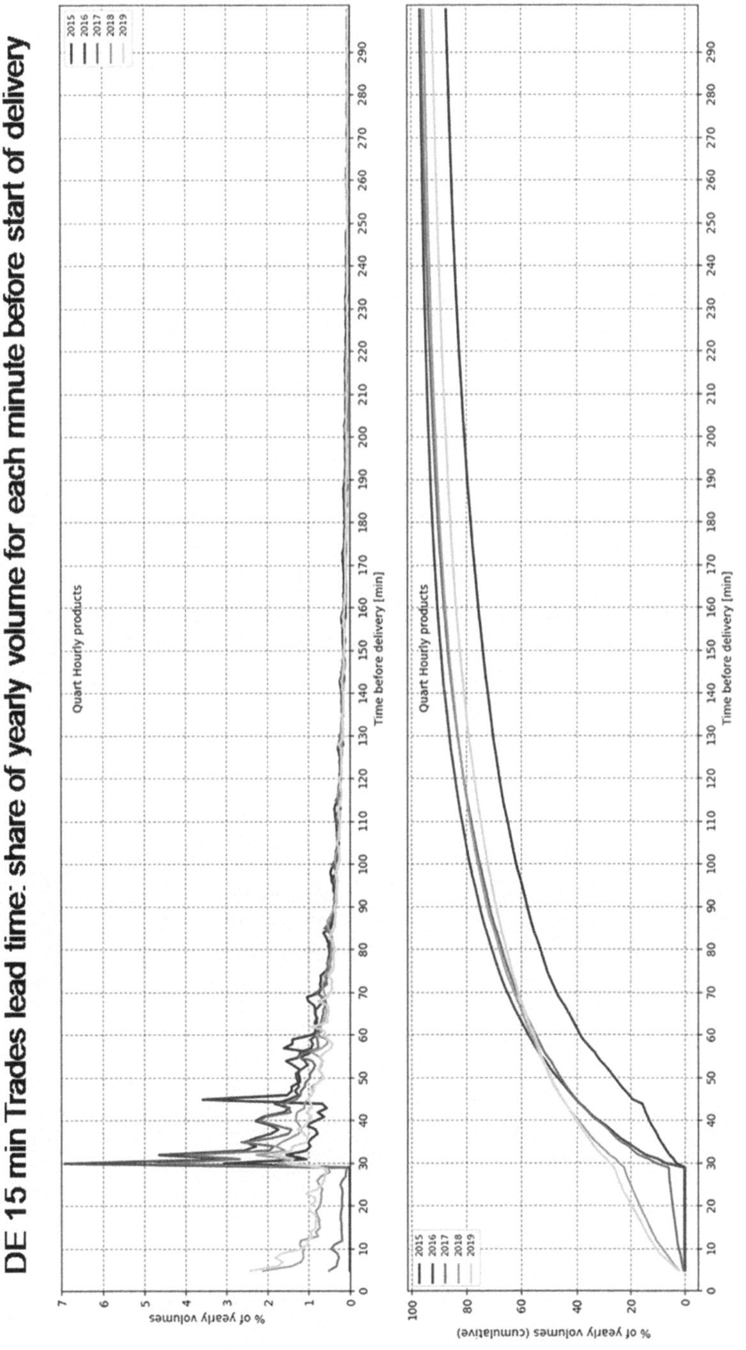

Fig. 22.15 Lead time to delivery in minutes in the intraday market (% of yearly volumes). (Source: Authors' elaboration on EPEX Spot data)

- Automated trading applications are developed either in-house or by Independent Software Vendors (ISVs) and automate power trading on the basis of algorithms. The applications are connected 24/7 through APIs (Automated Programming Interfaces). This enables market participants to react quickly to fluctuations in power production and demand.

4 Looking Ahead, New Challenges for the Power Markets

Electricity systems around the world have been undergoing nascent but profound changes in recent years, that are expected to further progress in the years to come. These intertwined trends are sometimes referred to as the 3 Ds: Decarbonation, Decentralization and Digitalization.

Global awareness around climate change makes the decarbonation of the electricity sector one of the important stakes to curb global warming. Along emerging carbon pricing initiatives creating an economic signal for CO_2 emissions (by "internalizing" their negative externalities), many governments and policymakers have implemented renewable energy sources (RES) support schemes and subsidies to promote clean energy sources. As a result, there has been a strong development of solar and wind RES worldwide. In Germany alone, a pioneering country in this field, there is more than 110 GW of wind and solar capacity installed with more than 36% of domestic electricity consumption covered by RES in 2016 (BMWi 2017) (from only 6% in 2000). In California, the famous "duck" curve illustrates the gradual penetration of solar PV in the market (CALISO 2012) (Fig. 22.16).

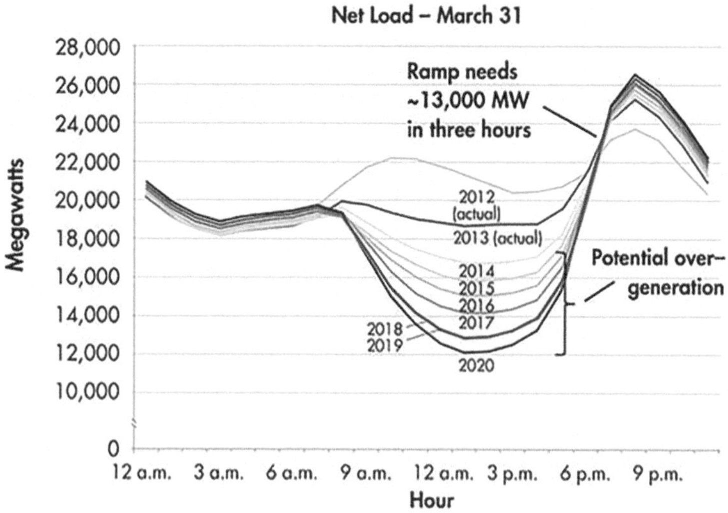

Fig. 22.16 Duck-shaped curve of load at the California ISO. (Source: CAL ISO)

This RES development trend is expected to continue, as illustrated by ambitious policy objectives. The EU aims to be climate-neutral by 2050 (EU Commission 2019). Such a shift in the electricity generation mix, towards more renewables, mostly intermittent electricity production, induces new challenges for cost-efficiency, resource adequacy and security of supply:

- **Increased missing money:** RES having an SRMC close to 0 €/MWh (as there are no fuel and emission costs, and little O&M variable costs), they have a bearish effect on wholesale spot electricity prices[19] and tend to increase the "missing money" problem (first introduced in Sect. 2.3). Indeed, they cannot fully replace dispatchable generation for system adequacy, as the need for available dispatchable generation remains high to cover peak demand events with no wind nor sun;
- **Need for flexibility:** furthermore, with rising RES penetration, resource adequacy and system reliability do not only depend on peak demand anymore. Production flexibility is also increasingly needed to compensate for large and short-term RES-induced production variations. Capacity mechanisms can contribute to solving the intermittency backup problem although their primary purpose is not to increase flexibility. Efficient measures, in market design and regulatory fields, will be needed to further enhance flexibility incentives in the market. Paradoxically, to further develop RES going forward, there is a need for flexibility that can currently mainly come from fossil fuels (e.g. flexible gas power plants), as demand-response and batteries remain respectively not fully exploited or too expensive on a large scale, but could emerge as a result of decentralization and digitalization trends.

Decentralization corresponds to the growing development of smaller scale assets (RES, storage, demand-response) in the distribution grids, slowly shifting the traditional paradigm of the electricity sector from a centralized electricity supply from large power plants to a more distributed supply. In this context, digitalization acts as a catalyst with the deployment of smart metering, energy management systems and new communication technologies, paving the way for a more precise, data-intensive and coordinated power system management and enabling the development of smaller scale flexibility. New opportunities can emerge for consumers, suppliers and aggregators to adapt their load or production profiles, provided that the right price signals are in place to foster their development. It will be needed to combine the largest number of players in the market with a better ability to react to prices to manage the electrical system at a lower cost.

Going forward, it seems essential to identify the future needs of the power system and align them with global policy objectives in order to adapt and enhance the way electricity markets generate social welfare. It is a continuous

[19] But not necessarily on total electricity costs, as RES in most regions worldwide is not economically viable at market prices without subsidies.

process that is becoming increasingly complex: how should the market architecture and regulatory framework evolve to meet ambitious climate targets while maintaining efficient investment incentives and security of supply? The answer probably lies in more temporal and spatial market granularity, the emergence of the right price signals and incentives along with the proper integration of new opportunities stemming from technological breakthroughs.

Bibliography

ACER (2017) Decision of the Agency for the Cooperation of Energy Regulators No 04/2017 of 14 November 2017 on the Nominated Electricity Market Operators Proposal for Harmonized Maximum and Minimum Clearing Prices for Single Day-Ahead Coupling, http://www.acer.europa.eu/Official_documents/Public_consultations/PC_2017_E_02/PC_2017_E_02%20on%20maximum%20and%20minimum%20prices.pdf

Ahlqvist, Holmberg, Holmberg, P., and Tangerå, T. (2019) Central- versus Self-Dispatch in Electricity Markets

BMWi (2017) Renewable Energy Sources in Figures, Germany Federal Ministry of Economic Affairs and Energy

Boiteux, M. (1949) La tarification des demandes en pointe: application de la théorie de la vente au cout marginal, Revue Générale de l'Electricité

California independent System Operator (2012) What the Duck Curve Tells Us About Managing a Green Grid. https://www.caiso.com/Documents/FlexibleResources HelpRenewables_FastFacts.pdf

EPEX Spot (2020) Rules and Regulations, https://www.epexspot.com/en/downloads#rules-fees-processes

European Commission (2017) Quarterly Report on European Electricity Markets, Market Observatory for Energy DG Energy Volume 10 (issue 4; fourth quarter of 2017)

European Commission (2019) The European Green Deal

Eydeland, A., and Wolyniec, K. (2003) Energy and Power Risk Management, Wiley

Hogan, W.W. (1992), Contract Networks for Electric Power Transmission: Technical Reference

Jha, A., and Wolak, F.A. (2016) Testing for Market Efficiency with Transactions Costs: An Application to Convergence Bidding in Wholesale Electricity Markets. 2013

Joskow, P.L. (2003) The Difficult Transition to Competitive Electricity Markets in the U.S.

Kaldor, N. (1939) Speculation and Economic Stability, The Review of Economic Studies, 7(1), 1–27

Newbery, D.M. (1997) Pool Reform and Competition in Electricity

PJM (2018) Day-Ahead-Energy-Market, https://www.pjm.com/-/media/training/nerc-certifications/markets-exam-materials/generation-itp/day-ahead-energy-market.ashx?la=en

Schweppe, F.C., et al. (1988) Spot Pricing of Electricity, Kluwer

Shawky, A.H., Marathe, A., and Barrett, C.L. (2003) A First Look at the Empirical Relation between Spot and Futures Electricity Prices in the Unites States. The Journal of Futures Markets, 23(10), 931–955

Sioshansi, R., et al. (2009) Three-Part Auctions Versus Self-Commitment in Day-Ahead Electricity Markets, Utilities Policy, Elsevier
Stoft, S. (2002) Power System Economics, Wiley
Wilson, R. (2002) Architecture of Power Markets, Journal of the Econometric Society, 70(4), 1299–1340

CHAPTER 23

The Trading of Carbon

Andrei Marcu and Federico Cecchetti

1 Introduction

The rationale for establishing carbon markets is based on the economic theory of market externalities. This theory was initiated by the work of R. H. Coase in 1960, thanks to an article titled 'The Problem of Social Cost', which highlighted the inefficiencies caused by market externalities (Coase 1960). Since then, the theory of externalities has analysed circumstances when actions of one economic agent make another economic agent worse or better off, yet the first agent neither bears the costs nor receives the benefits of doing so (Saez 2007). When one's actions have harmful effects on the others, this is called a 'negative externality' as opposed to a 'positive externality'.

One case in point of negative externalities is carbon emissions, as the emitter can 'externalise' the cost associated with its emissions by passing it on to society. This negative externality is a market failure, because the emitter does not bear the true costs of emitting.

To respond to the market failure of carbon emissions, two types of approaches can be envisioned, the two not being mutually exclusive:

- Command and control measures
- Economic instruments

Andrei Marcu is the Executive Director of the European Roundtable on Climate Change and Sustainable Transition (ERCST), Federico Cecchetti is a Junior Researcher at ERCST.

A. Marcu (✉) • F. Cecchetti
European Roundtable on Climate Change and Sustainable Transition (ERCST), Brussels, Belgium
e-mail: acmarcu@ercst.org

M. Hafner, G. Luciani (eds.), *The Palgrave Handbook of International Energy Economics*, https://doi.org/10.1007/978-3-030-86884-0_23

A command and control approach means that a host of rules and restrictions are imposed on producers and consumers, with the aim of constraining emissions. Accordingly, certain behaviours or production methods might be disincentivised, or prohibited altogether.[1]

On the other hand, approaching carbon emissions through economic instruments means that a price signal is associated with GHG emissions. This signal could be either positive, incentivising certain activities or behaviours (e.g. by granting subsidies), or negative, imposing a cost on emissions.

The idea that polluters should be charged for their emissions according to the corresponding cost caused to society by their actions reflects the so-called polluter pays principle (LSEPS 2018a). This principle translates in applying a cost to carbon pollution, giving an economic signal to emitters who will decide for themselves whether to reduce the amount of greenhouse gases they emit or continue polluting yet pay for it (World Bank 2019). In essence, emitters will be forced to 'internalise' the cost of pollution, ending the 'negative externality' of carbon emissions.

Countries have applied both command and control and economic approaches to the issue of climate change. In the quest to limit global warming well below 2°C above pre-industrial levels, in line with the Paris Agreement, the two methods should be seen as complementary.

Looking at the potential economic approaches to carbon emissions, economists widely agree that introducing a carbon price allows to achieve environmental goals in the most flexible and cost-effective way to society (LSEPS 2018b).

This chapter will explore the concept of carbon pricing, with a specific focus on carbon trading via emissions trading systems (ETSs). The first section will analyse the rationale for ETSs as opposed to carbon taxes, looking at the main differences between these two approaches to carbon pricing. The second section will highlight the main design options for a cap-and-trade system.

The third section will focus on the experience of the European Union (EU) ETS, being the world's first international ETS and still today the biggest one. The history of the EU ETS will be examined, explaining what the main challenges and benefits of the system are, and what lessons can be learnt from this ongoing experience.

The fourth section will broaden the analysis to other existing ETSs worldwide, while also trying to shed light on the potential for international cooperation in the area of carbon trading. Using the EU ETS as a benchmark, other major ETSs will be briefly described, highlighting the potential for interconnection of different systems, as well as analysing the outlook for the emergence of a reference global carbon price.

[1] This was the case of the Montreal Protocol, which was created to eliminate the production of chlorofluorocarbons (CFCs) that were found to contribute to a hole in the earth's ozone layer. To clarify further, see: Heskett (2018).

2 Pricing Carbon: Carbon Taxes Versus Emissions Trading Systems

Carbon pricing is gaining momentum worldwide. As of 2019, 57 carbon pricing initiatives have been implemented or are scheduled for implementation, with 46 national and 28 subnational jurisdictions placing a price on carbon emissions through a combination of ETSs and taxes. This equals to roughly 20% of global emissions, up from 13% in 2016 (ICEVE 2019).

Against this backdrop, studying how carbon pricing works is becoming increasingly important. There are two main alternatives to deliver an explicit price on carbon:

- Carbon tax
- Emissions trading system

In broad terms, a carbon tax implies that the price for carbon emissions is fixed by regulatory authorities. An emissions trading system fixes the total amount of emissions allowed under the system (i.e. a cap), and leaves it to the market to find the price needed to constrain emissions within that limit.

The key difference between these two alternatives is which variable the regulator chooses to make predictable: the carbon price or the total emissions under the scheme (Stenegren 2018). In the case of a carbon tax, there is certainty on the carbon price as set by the government, whereas the quantity of emissions is not controlled. Entities are allowed to emit as long as they pay for their emissions, with the carbon tax acting as an economic disincentive towards emitting emissions.

Conversely, an ETS creates certainty on the environmental outcome by fixing a cap on the quantity of emissions.[2] However, the price is determined by the market according to the supply-demand balance of emission 'allowances' (i.e. emissions permits). Therefore, the price of carbon is not fixed, in principle, but fluctuates according to market conditions.

Hybrid systems, combining elements of both approaches, also exist in different forms. One example is an ETS with a price floor and/or ceiling (ICAP 2016).

Both approaches share several advantages over alternative policies (Kaufman et al. 2016). Firstly, both carbon taxes and ETSs reduce emissions by encouraging the lowest cost emissions reductions, without dictating where and when the emissions reduction should take place. Secondly, they both represent an economic incentive to low-carbon investments and can therefore help driving technological innovations. Third, both policies generate revenues for the

[2] Unless the legislator chooses an intensity cap for the ETS, which would guarantee the achievement of an intensity target but not of an absolute emissions reduction target. This is the case of the Low Carbon Fuel Standard in California. To clarify further, see: https://ww3.arb.ca.gov/fuels/lcfs/background/basics-notes.pdf

government, provided that allowances under an ETS are auctioned and not handed out for free.

At the same time, any ETS or carbon tax at the sub-global level runs the risk of harming the competitiveness of the economic actors covered. This is usually referred to as the risk of 'carbon leakage'. Companies in countries without or with less stringent emissions constraints could be advantaged over the regulated entities to a 'tight' ETS or a 'high' carbon tax, as the latter will be required to bear higher carbon costs.

This loss of competitiveness could lead to the perverse effect of reducing emissions in one jurisdiction yet increasing them somewhere else, with total global emissions potentially increasing. Indeed, production could shift to countries with laxer emissions constraints, through businesses moving or being outcompeted by foreign competitors not facing similar climate-related costs (European Commission 2019a). This is especially the case for 'trade-exposed' products (Tiche et al. 2014).

Another common challenge for both approaches lies in the complex administrative structure they require, as monitoring (M), reporting (R), and verifying (V) emissions can be particularly challenging, especially in the context of countries with limited administrative capacities.

Carbon taxes and ETSs also come with specific positive and negative sides. As mentioned before, by not putting a limit on emissions, a carbon tax runs the risk of not reaching environmental targets. Setting a carbon tax might require adjustments according to the elasticity of demand of companies.

Furthermore, carbon taxes are oftentimes associated with the negative 'stigma' of being an additional tax for taxpayers, making it usually difficult to secure public support—unless a carbon tax is directly linked to tax rebates or revenue recycling. On the positive side, the design of a carbon tax is generally easier than a cap-and-trade system, and it provides investors with a stable price signal.[3]

Ensuring a long-term, explicit carbon price is particularly important, as it guarantees a long-term signal for investments in low-carbon practices and technologies, even at times when emissions reductions might become cheaper than expected or are caused by other causes—as in the case of an economic downturn causing emissions to temporary fall, regardless of the actual emission abatement efforts.

On the other hand, a cap-and-trade system has the advantage of ensuring delivery of a predetermined emissions target, providing a reasonable confidence about the future level of emissions. This emissions reduction will take place progressively, given that an ETS typically decreases the supply of allowances over time by lowering the cap.

[3] The design of a carbon tax could lead to an equally complex system, according to how benchmarks and threshold for applying the tax are designed, but an ETS is generally perceived as being more complex given that it also includes trading operations.

ETSs also offer the great advantage of a higher degree of flexibility compared to a carbon tax in terms of abatement opportunities, as it allows actors to pay others to reduce their emissions first, if they have more cost-effective alternatives to decarbonise—or, put differently, actors with lower abatement costs have the possibility to get rewarded by others for reducing their emissions first (Eden et al. 2016).

One key downside of an ETS without a price floor is that it cannot guarantee a long-term, explicit price signal the way a carbon tax would do, considering that the price of carbon will be determined by supply-demand trends.

Leaving aside any specific consideration about the pros and cons of the two alternatives, it is worth highlighting how both can deliver positive environmental results, as long as they are well designed. The following section analyses in more depth what are some of the main design options for an emissions trading system.

3 Design Options for Emissions Trading Systems

There are many design options that can be considered for an ETS, including provisions mimicking the behaviour of a market with flexibility on both supply and demand sides. This section will focus on the following seven points, given their relevance for an ETS functioning[4]:

- Cap setting
- Scope and coverage
- Supply of allowances to the market
- Flexibility provisions
- MRV, enforcement and market oversight
- Price and quantity management mechanisms
- Use of revenues

3.1 Cap Setting

The cap represents one of the most important design characteristics of an ETS, as it defines the upper limit of GHG emissions allowed under the system. If an ETS aims at reaching a given environmental target of cutting emissions by X% over a set period of time, the legislator will set a ceiling on emissions (so-called emissions budget) equal to the total number of allowances available to covered entities over that period (European Commission 2015). This cap has to be translated into units with a face value, which are used by covered installations for trade and compliance—usually referred to as emissions allowances or emissions permits.

[4] Section 3 is by and large based on: Laing and Mehling (2013), Newell et al. (2012), Prag et al. (2012), Neuhoff (2008), ICAP (2019a)

The cap should reflect the mitigation opportunities available, the economic and technological feasibility of meeting the target for covered entities, but primarily the jurisdiction's overall mitigation objectives. In this sense, having a robust foundation of both historical data and counterfactual projections is a key pre-requisite to the cap setting.

When setting the cap, the legislator should seek to balance the reasons for emissions reduction with the economic implication of a 'tighter' cap for covered entities. All else being equal, the more ambitious the cap the lower the amount of allowances issued is, and thus the greater the scarcity in the market, which will translate into higher compliance costs.

Two types of cap can be set:

- an absolute cap, setting the maximum quantity of emissions allowances over a given period of time;
- an intensity cap, setting the number of allowances issued per unit of output or input (e.g. emissions per unit of GDP, kilowatt-hour of electricity, tonne of raw material, etc.).

An absolute cap has the benefit of providing upfront certainty to both regulators and market participants, being an independent variable that does not change according to other factors. On the contrary, under an intensity approach, the absolute amount of emissions allowed under the cap will increase or decrease as a function of the input or output chosen. In both cases, the legislator will need to choose a reference point for emissions.

Another distinction is the time period considered for the cap, which can be annual or on a multiyear basis. This typically means choosing a starting date and an end date.

In practice, the cap period usually corresponds to a commitment period or 'ETS phase', during which other programme design features are also specified. Decisions on the duration of the ETS phase(s) will influence the flexibility given to stakeholders to decreasing their emissions throughout time.

Ultimately, two approaches are available when deciding on the ambition of an ETS cap: top-down and bottom-up. In the case of the former, the legislator will set the cap in line with the underlying environmental target to be met, ideally reflecting a high-level assessment of the mitigation potential and costs across all capped sectors.

For the latter, a bottom-up approach will translate in a more detailed assessment of the mitigation potential of the different sectors, subsectors or even individual participants, and aggregating that into an overall cap. A bottom-up approach has the advantage of reflecting the specificities of all or most entities that are part of an ETS. However, it requires high-quality, disaggregated data, and might still result in the cap not being aligned with the broader mitigation target of the jurisdiction.

3.2 *Scope and Coverage*

The scope and coverage of an ETS refer to the geographical area, sectors, emissions sources and gases that are covered under an ETS. It defines the boundaries of the policy, and will have critical repercussions on the administrative efforts and transaction costs for regulated entities. A broad number of sectors and gases covered would, in theory, increase the opportunities for low-cost abatement, reducing the overall marginal costs for emission reductions while increasing liquidity in the regulatory market created.

On the other hand, limiting the scope and coverage lowers the bureaucratic costs related to an ETS, both for the legislator and for the regulated entities. Of course, this is to be balanced against the costs of covering sectors/entities outside of the ETS with other climate regulations. The ability and cost for the legislator of monitoring and regulating a large number of actors and emissions sources should not be dismissed as marginal in the decision of an ETS scope, especially if alternative policies might also be envisioned.

The legislator should seek to limit compliance costs for all covered entities. This is especially true for those small entities who would not be able to bear high administrative costs, and who might suffer a competitive disadvantage when asked to cover similar fixed administrative burdens to that of major emitters. For these reasons, ETSs will usually aim at covering major emitters, creating some thresholds under which smaller entities will be exempted from compliance. These thresholds can reflect both economic and environmental considerations, such as production levels or GHG emissions per year.

Similar considerations apply to the decision of which sectors should be included in an ETS. Covering sectors representing a big share of a jurisdiction's emissions will be seen as more beneficial towards achieving the ETS environmental goal, whereas covering less pollutant sectors could sometimes be considered not worth the administrative costs, if, an alternative policy could be implemented.

Similarly, sectors dominated by a small number of large emitters can provide high benefits as well as limit administrative efforts, whereas covering sectors composed of many small entities may involve disproportionately high costs relative to benefits.

Every decision on the scope of an ETS might have repercussions on market liquidity and market power, as well as on the competitiveness of different actors. Creating exemptions for entities or sectors always has the potential for these repercussions.

An additional design feature concerns the point at which those emissions are regulated. For a number of emissions sources, especially those involving fossil fuel use, the main 'points of regulation' are:

- upstream, that is, where the source of emissions is first commercialised, or where non-energy process emissions are generated from industrial activities;
- downstream, that is, where GHG emissions are physically released into the atmosphere.[5]

Regulating emissions upstream has the advantage of lowering the administrative costs, considering that there are usually fewer entities involved in extraction and commercialisation of carbon-intensive resources, as opposed to the number of actors using those resources as final consumers. Furthermore, the coverage across sectors tends to be higher with an upstream regulation: regulating emissions upstream reduces the need for sectoral thresholds compared to downstream systems, where thresholds are usually required to avoid high transaction costs.

On the other hand, downstream regulation might be preferred if installation-level data of downstream users already exists, limiting the administrative burden of regulating emissions at the point where they are actually released (ICAP 2016). Many existing ETSs, including the largest EU ETS, have a downstream point of regulation.

In terms of the gases covered, all the existing ETSs include carbon dioxide as a minimum. Some ETSs include other gases, such as methane, N_2O, PFCs, and so on. If an ETS covers GHGs other than CO_2, their emissions are typically expressed as carbon dioxide equivalent (CO2e), to facilitate the measuring and trading of allowances.

3.3 Supply of Allowances to the Market

Allocation is the process of distributing emission allowances to covered entities in an ETS. Given that these allowances have an associated value, the way they are distributed should reflect considerations of fairness and cost distribution across the society.

Allowances can be either sold through auctions or distributed for free according to pre-set rules (so-called free allocation). For auctioned allowances, their selling generates an income stream for the state, and the price at which allowances are sold reflects their perceived scarcity in the market, presumably connected to secondary market price.

Apart from generating revenues, selling allowances through auctions has the advantage of reflecting the actual demand on the ETS. This facilitates price discovery and market liquidity. Furthermore, auctioning clearly reflects the 'polluter pays' principle.

However, auctioning also has disadvantages, particularly as it does not offer protection against the risk of carbon leakage and of loss competitiveness. To

[5] This also includes non-energy process emissions generated from industrial activities.

avoid such risks—especially carbon leakage—free allocation of allowances has oftentimes been seen as necessary in a period of transition.

There are two main methods for handing out allowances for free:

- grandfathering
- benchmarking

Through grandfathering, regulated entities receive permits according to historical emissions during a given period of time. This approach limits initial costs for covered sectors but runs the risk of benefiting historically high emitters with windfall profits, as allocation is not linked to the actual performance or production during the ETS periods. New entrants will also be disadvantaged, unless specific provisions are put in place.

When using benchmarking regulated entities receive free allocation according to some performance indicators. This can translate in sector benchmarks or output-based allocation (OBA), aiming to reward efficient installations and early movers that actively embark in emissions reduction strategies.

The calculation of benchmarks will depend on the availability of reliable and robust data collection. Only perfectly accurate data will ensure the same economic efficiency as auctioning allowances. Otherwise, any type of free allocation will, in practice, be less economically efficient than auctioning, with risks of over- or under-allocation. This risk is also dependent on production levels.

3.4 Flexibility Provisions

In the analysis of the cap setting it was mentioned how the decision on the time period for setting the ETS phase(s) has implications on the temporal flexibility provided to stakeholders. In essence, temporal flexibility refers to when or how quickly regulated entities need to achieve their emissions reductions.

Some provisions can be designed to increase an ETS temporal flexibility, including:

- banking of allowances from the current compliance period for use in future periods;
- borrowing of allowances from future compliance periods to the current period.

The banking of allowances allows regulated entities to build a buffer against future high prices, if they consider early-on mitigation options as less expensive than in future compliance periods. Borrowing provisions provides entities with higher flexibility in the determination of their compliance strategy, particularly in those sectors where abatement opportunities take longer to bear fruits.

Both borrowing and banking provisions, however, might have negative effects on the functioning of an ETS. Unlimited banking, for instance, could carry forward the effects of an oversupply of permits, whereas allowing very generous borrowing could give companies an incentive to delay emissions reduction indefinitely (ICAP 2017).

A different set of flexibility provisions includes the use of mitigation offsets and/or allowances from a baseline and credit system. In addition, linking with other carbon markets is also a potential source of flexibility for covered entities. These are usually referred to as 'geographical flexibility' (ICAP 2017).

The main reason for opening up an ETS to domestic and/or international offsets, or linking an ETS with other cap-and-trade systems, is to reduce the overall costs for compliance and increase liquidity. Theoretically, by expanding the compliance opportunities, regulated entities should be able to seek the most cost-effective abatement option across a wider range of opportunities.

Domestic offsets provide credits for emissions reductions taking place in sectors non-covered by an ETS, yet within the same jurisdiction. International offsets give credits for mitigation actions taking place outside the ETS-jurisdiction, provided that these actions comply with some pre-set standards of environmental integrity.[6]

Additional flexibility can be provided through the 'linking' of two or more ETSs. If two systems mutually recognise their respective allowances for domestic compliance (full linking), this should offer participants with a larger carbon market within which to operate. As an alternative, a unilateral direct linking implies that a given ETS A explicitly recognises allowances from ETS B as eligible for compliance, but not vice versa (Borghesi et al. 2016).

As in the case of domestic and international offsets, linking should increase the compliance flexibility for the stakeholders of an ETS, by expanding the range of abatement options available and, likely, lowering the average cost of allowances of both ETSs.

At the same time, any kind of 'geographical flexibility' mechanism might also cause problems to an ETS, notably in terms of supply-demand balance and potential for carbon lock-ins. Jurisdictions usually limit the number of offsets that may be used, to ensure that most of the abatement efforts take place within the domestic ETS (Borghesi et al. 2016).

3.5 MRV, Enforcement and Market Oversight

For any ETS to function properly, control and enforcement measures are very important. There has to be a high level of trust that emissions are accurately monitored (M), reported to regulators (R), and verified (V); that market oversight is guaranteed; and that non-compliance is effectively sanctioned.

Most ETSs have established legal MRV frameworks to track compliance and guarantee the principle that a 'ton is always a ton'.[7] Accordingly, emissions are

[6] Historically, examples of international credits are credits generated by Joint Implementation projects and Clean Development Mechanism project activities under the Kyoto Protocol.

[7] This principle implies that a claimed emissions reduction of X tonnes of CO2 reflects an equivalent atmospheric reduction.

measured either via direct monitoring (real-time emissions) or using emission factors of fuels or chemical processes.

Measured emissions are reported to the relevant authority—usually government inspectors or third-party experts—which will be responsible for the auditing and verification of the compliance of regulated entities (Wettestad and Gulbrandsen 2017). Registries—databases that record and monitor the creation, trading, and surrender of all units within a system—also need to be developed and verified (ICAP 2016).

The impartiality and fairness of the verification mechanisms are key to guarantee the trustworthiness of the system. In cases of non-compliance, enforcement provisions have to identify penalties. Enforcement provisions can include monetary sanctions as well as criminal penalties.

Finally, a cap-and-trade system should ensure that the trade of permits is not vulnerable to fraud and manipulation. Market oversight provisions are therefore needed, in order to safeguard the integrity of the trading activities. Such provisions should seek to facilitate price discovery by increasing transparency, containing risk, maximising liquidity, and ensuring fair competition (Kachi and Frerk 2013). Market oversight should apply equally to primary and secondary markets, as well as to derivatives contracts.

3.6 *Price/Quantity Management Mechanisms*

ETSs are regulatory markets and, as any other market, can incur in supply-demand imbalances for a multiplicity of reasons. Endogenous or exogenous shocks, regulatory uncertainty, and the existence of flaws in the design of the market are just a few examples of reasons for a carbon market to not live up to its expected performance.

In this context, the legislator may want to intervene in the market to avoid excessive price variability, ensure cost containment, and/or improve the resilience of an ETS from the effects of different types of shocks (e.g. economic events, policy overlaps, etc.). Two market interventions that can be envisioned include:

- price management mechanisms
- quantity management mechanisms

Price mechanisms usually aim at limiting excessive price volatility, while ensuring medium- to long-term stability of the price signal to the market. Approaches in this sense include the creation of a price ceiling to avoid excessively high prices, a price floor to guarantee that prices do not fall below a certain threshold, or a price corridor having both a floor and a ceiling.

The rationale for quantity-based mechanism is similar, in the sense that they are implemented to improve the supply-demand balance of an ETS. However, quantity-based mechanisms act on the allowance volumes, avoiding lengthy political debates on the establishment of price thresholds. Approaches to quantity management mechanisms include the creation of a quantity-triggered reserve, adjusting the supply of allowances of an ETS according to some predefined triggers. These triggers do, however, need a political agreement determining their functioning, including what thresholds trigger the quantity-based mechanisms.

Both price and quantity management mechanisms should be carefully designed, keeping in mind that market interventions can also lead to market distortions. Furthermore, any legislative intervention has the potential to increase regulatory uncertainty, thus decreasing the overall confidence in the system.

3.7 Use of Revenues

Governments can use ETS-revenues in multiple ways, from adding those revenues to the general budget, to earmarking carbon revenues for specific purposes. In evaluating options, there are several key principles a jurisdiction should consider, including: potential economic and environmental gains, efficiency, interaction of spending with the carbon price itself (Carbon Pricing Leadership Coalition 2016).

One possible approach is to use revenues for public spending, as part of a jurisdiction's general budget. This could translate in financing other tax reductions, cutting the public debt and/or deficit, or, more broadly, using carbon revenues for expenditures not related to the ETS. This is perfectly justifiable from an economic standpoint, as economists often consider earmarking as being inefficient (Carbon Pricing Leadership Coalition 2016).

However, empirical evidence shows that ETS-revenues are often channelled to further climate action or to compensate particularly vulnerable groups. The main rationale for this is to increase the political and social acceptability of putting a price on carbon, and increase the environmental delivery of an ETS—thus managing the transition (Santikarn et al. 2019).

Actions to compensate vulnerable groups include addressing fairness and competitiveness concerns arising from the ETS, for example by directing revenues to low-income households suffering the effects of ETS prices or supporting industries at risk of carbon leakage.

Examples of earmarking ETS-revenues for climate action include supporting investments in low-carbon technologies and innovation, financing climate and energy programmes, and/or incentivising adaptation strategies to limit climate change impacts (Santikarn et al. 2019).

4 The Experience of the EU ETS and its Ongoing Evolution

4.1 The Early Years of the EU ETS

Since 2005, the EU ETS has been a core element of the EU's policy to combat climate change, and, according to the European Commission, a 'key tool for reducing greenhouse gas emissions cost-effectively' (European Commission 2019b).

In more than ten years of operations, the system had to overcome ad-hoc challenges, and went through different reforms and changes. Analysing the history and learning process of first major ETS can be very useful to understand some of the key lessons that can be extrapolated from the European experience. These lessons could help others in developing their respective ETSs.

Starting from the beginning, it is important to appreciate that the advent of the EU ETS came as a result of the failure to achieve a political agreement on the implementation of a carbon tax in Europe during the 1990s. In the aftermath of the adoption of the 1992 United Nations Framework Convention on Climate Change (UNFCCC), the European Commission (EC) started an internal debate to promote an EU-wide carbon tax to tackle Europe's GHG emissions (Andersen and Ekins 2009).

However, this proposition found the opposition of many industrial players and a group of EU Member States (MS) led by the United Kingdom, who portrayed the idea of a CO_2/energy tax as largely detrimental for Europe's international competitiveness (Dupont and Moore 2019). This opposition also stemmed from political considerations, with some MS being unwilling to give away legislative powers to the EC on taxation measures, considering that taxation is a core competence of EU MS (Climate Policy Info Hub 2019a).

It was only after the introduction of the Kyoto Protocol in 1997 that the idea of pricing carbon came back at the centre of the EU policy-making debate. The Kyoto Protocol acted as the enabling framework within which the EU ETS came to life. Article 17 mentioned that the parties to the Protocol may engage in emissions trading to achieve their emissions reduction targets, adding that any such trading should be 'supplemental to domestic actions' (UNFCCC 1998).

Article 17 helped the creation of the EU ETS in two ways. First, it created a new commodity which could be traded internationally, shaping the idea that countries could 'trade carbon' in the form of assigned amount units (AAUs), that is, the unit used to define the Kyoto Protocol GHG emission targets.

Second, it promoted a discussion on the 'supplementarity' of international emissions trading. This debate discouraged the idea that rich countries could just buy off allowances without engaging in domestic mitigation actions (Albrecht 2002). Facing with the perspective that the EU would have to reduce its domestic emissions one way or another, the suspicions of the European business community towards a EU-wide carbon market started to fade away (Mäenpää 2016).

Moreover, the idea of implementing an ETS in Europe had the political advantage of it not being a tax. The EC managed to present the EU ETS as an environmental measure, which would not need a unanimity vote within the European Council. This helped alleviate the opposition of those MS who had opposed to a carbon tax in the early 1990s (Climate Policy Info Hub 2019b).

Furthermore, at that point in time there was already one pioneering example of a cap-and-trade system in the field of environmental regulation: the sulphur dioxide (SO_2) emissions trading system in the United States. This market was engineered by Richard L. Sandor, and addressed the threat of acid rain as part of the Clean Air Act Amendments of 1990 (Chan et al. 2012). The SO_2 market proved to be very successful in reducing emissions in a timely and cost-effective manner, showing in practice that market mechanisms could help achieving environmental goals (Sandor 2016). The design and experience of the SO_2 market became a reference for policy-makers and researchers in favour of cap-and-trade systems for decades to come.

It was in this context that in the late 1990s the EC started elaborating a proposal for an EU ETS addressing emissions from key economic sectors, presenting it as a key measure to reach the Kyoto Protocol targets. The legitimacy the EU ETS was given through the Kyoto Protocol was important in securing the support of the European environmental community, which was initially sceptical about the proposal, but wanted the Kyoto Protocol to succeed. The support of the EU environmental groups was further reinforced by the idea that the EU ETS would contain a binding cap, and the cap would decrease throughout time.

The first two phases of the EU ETS were agreed upon by the EU institutions in 2003. This first phase was designed as a pilot phase for the period 2005–2007, with the idea that regulated entities could use it as a 'learning by doing', yet not creating any continuity with the following trading periods through mechanisms of intertemporal flexibility (e.g. borrowing, banking).

The allocation of European Union Allowances (EUAs) was done through national allocation plans (NAPs) via free allocation based on grandfathering.[8] The main rationale for NAPs was to secure MS support towards the system, leaving them with the task to set their own cap and determine the distribution of allowances to affected facilities, subject to a review by the EC. As a result of this, the EU-wide cap was in practice the sum of MS caps (Ellerman et al. 2015).

The point of regulation was set downstream. In Phase 1, the scope of the EU ETS included both the power sector and large industrial installations (Zetterberg et al. 2014). This meant that over two billions tCO2e emissions were covered in 2005, amounting to ca. 37.6% of total EU emissions (EEA 2019).

However, the allocation of EUAs was too generous to ensure the supply-demand balance in the market. By grandfathering allowances based on historic production levels, the allocation did not reflect actual emissions of the covered

[8] The fact that MS were left with the task of distributing allowances during the EU ETS Phase 1 and 2 helped securing political support towards the system.

installations. Moreover, MS did not want to risk jeopardising the competitiveness of their national businesses, and tended to over-allocate allowances through NAPs.

As soon as it became evident that the Phase 1 supply would outstrip demand, prices started decreasing, to end up at zero by the end of Phase 1, reflecting the absence of borrowing/banking mechanisms.

Nevertheless, Phase 1 was still beneficial on many aspects:

- first, it built a framework for MRV;
- second, it encouraged data collection for installations' emissions, which would later be used as a baseline;
- third, it made stakeholders trade carbon for the first time, creating a price for carbon in Europe.

During the first three years of the EU ETS operations, around 200 million tonnes of CO_2, or 3% of total verified emissions, were abated (IETA 2011).

4.2 Challenges and Reforms: EU ETS Phase 2 and Phase 3

The second phase of the EU ETS corresponded to the first commitment period under the Kyoto Protocol (2008–2012) and saw the EU adopting the goal of reducing emissions under the EU ETS cap by 6.5% compared to 2005 levels. Some of the initial key design elements included (Delbeke and Vis 2016):

- a binding, enforceable and decreasing cap placed on absolute GHG emissions;
- a percentage of allowances to be auctioned for the first time (up to 10%);
- continuation of the national allocation plans (NAPs), the sum of which established the overall cap of the system (European Commission 2019c, 2019d);
- introduction of both borrowing and banking mechanisms;
- acceptance of international credits from the Kyoto Protocol's clean development mechanism (CDM) and joint implementation (JI) projects, which could be used for compliance on top of the EU ETS cap (up to 1.4 billion tonnes of CO2e).
- introduction of intra-EU flights into the system, as of January 1, 2012;
- penalty for non-compliance rising from 40 to 100 €/tCO2e, compared to Phase 1.

Furthermore, from the beginning of Phase 2, Iceland, Norway and Liechtenstein also linked their domestic ETSs with the EU ETS (European Commission 2007).

Phase 2 marked the actual start of the European carbon market, but it took less than one year of operations for the system to suffer its first major crisis. Indeed, as soon as the 2008 economic crisis hit the European economy, the demand for allowances dropped, leading to the price of EUAs going from

30€/tCO2e in June 2008 to less than ca. 9€/tCO2e in February 2009 (Sandbag 2019). This revealed the fundamental weakness of the EU ETS design, putting the system's credibility in serious jeopardy (Climate Policy Info Hub 2019a).

The combination of decreasing EUAs demand and stable supply based on grandfathering on production levels led to the built-up of a significant surplus of allowances, with companies receiving more EUAs than the amount they needed for compliance. The creation of the surplus was further exacerbated by the availability of cheap international credits coming to the market on top of the EU ETS cap, which contributed to maintaining prices well below 10€/tCO2e for several consecutive years.

To make things worse, MS had a perverse incentive to allocate EUAs as generously as possible to their industries via NAPs, as failing to do so would put neighbouring countries' actors at a competitive advantage, particularly in the context of a concurrent macroeconomic recession (Stenegren 2018).

The system design had a lack of flexibility of supply, both in free allocation and auctioning. The EU ETS was not able to react to supply and/or demand shocks. On the supply side, the low cost of international credits led to high imports of credits—increasing supply as the number of EUAs allocated and auctioned was not adjustable. On the demand side, the 2008 economic crisis on the demand side led to significant reductions to GHG emissions through slowing economic activity—including GHG emitting ones. Carbon prices ended dropping, and becoming too low to drive investments in emissions abatement. Additionally, the effects of other EU-wide overlapping policies (e.g. legislations aiming to promote energy efficiency and renewable energy sources) also contributed to further decrease the demand for EUAs.

In order to address the supply-demand imbalance and restore confidence in the system, the EC promoted a first reform of the EU ETS in 2009, the effects of which would unfold in the EU ETS Phase 3 (2013–2020) (European Parliament and Council 2009).

Compared to Phase 2, an EU-wide cap on emissions was set centrally replacing the system of NAPs. This cap reflected the EU's ambition to cut emissions in EU ETS sectors by 21% by 2020. To achieve this target, the cap was designed to decrease each year by a linear reduction factor (LRF) of 1.74% of the average total quantity of allowances issued annually in 2008–2012 (European Commission 2019e). Other new features of Phase 3 were:

- a longer commitment period of 7 years;
- auctioning partially replaced free allocation, and sectoral benchmarks were used for the remaining free allocation, instead of grandfathering (European Commission 2019f)[9];

[9] Generally speaking, a product benchmark under the EU ETS is based on the average GHG emissions of the best performing 10% of the installations producing that product in the EU.

- more stringent qualitative and quantitative limits on the imports of international credits[10];
- increase of scope;
- requirement for MS to spend at least 50% of the ETS-revenues in support of the achievement of specific climate and energy activities;
- establishment of the NER300, a funding programme financed through ETS-revenues, supporting innovative low-carbon energy demonstration projects.

Under the Phase 3 reform, the power sector was entirely moved to auctioning (with the exception of some solidarity clauses for lower income MS), while industrial installations considered at significant risk of carbon leakage continued to receive free allocation through benchmarks (Stenegren 2018). This was done to limit windfall profits, as the electricity sector is able to pass ETS additional costs through to customers, as it is not subject to international competition.

However, these reforms did not address the main problem of the EU ETS, namely the accumulated surplus carried on from the early years of the EU ETS, which continued to hamper the EU ETS supply-demand balance.

The short-term legislative response to addressing the surplus was to reduce the quantity of allowances available for auctioning in the years 2014 to 2016 by 900 million allowances, and re-inject them into the market in the year 2019–2020 (Delbeke and Vis 2016). This 'back-loading' measure was agreed on by the European institutions in 2011 as a stop-gap measure and helped containing the oversupply of EUAs at least in the short term (EU Commission Regulation 2011).

However, the reform did not eliminate the surplus in the medium to long run, as all the backloaded allowances were expected to come back to the market in 2019–2020. This would have caused a rebound of the surplus, albeit a few years later.

Facing with this situation, the EU institutions were left with the task of adopting a more comprehensive reform to the system, which took place via two separate legislations:

- the Market Stability Reserve (MSR) Decision, adopted in 2015 (European Parliament and Council 2015);
- the revised EU ETS Directive for Phase 4 (2021–2030), entered into force in April 2018 (European Parliament and Council 2018).

4.3 *EU ETS Fit for Life? Phase 4 Reform*

With the adoption of the MSR Decision and the revised EU ETS Directive for Phase 4, the European institutions have tried to tackle a number of issues. The

[10] To clarify what qualitative and quantitative restrictions were imposed, see: European Commission (2015).

two reforms aimed at addressing the historical surplus of EUAs, and making the EU ETS supply more responsive to changes in demand and able to deal with future oversupply.

Furthermore, the legislators sought to create a stronger link between free allocation and the actual production levels, as well as increasing the funds available for innovation and modernisation, to be financed through ETS-revenues (Marcu et al. 2018).

Some of the more significant measures taken are:

- increase of the LRF from 1.74 to 2.2% starting from 2021;
- alignment of the cap with a 43% GHG emissions reduction target by 2030, compared to a 2005 baseline;
- creation of a Market Stability Reserve to tackle the historical surplus of allowances on the market, while improving the EU ETS responsiveness to future shocks;
- phase-out of free allocation for those sectors not deemed at high risk of carbon leakage by the end of Phase 4;
- establishment of innovation and modernisation funds to support the energy transition;
- more flexible rules to better align the level of free allocation with actual production levels;
- benchmarks for free allocation to be updated twice during Phase 4, to avoid windfall profits and better reflect technological innovations (European Commission 2019g).

The introduction of a quantity management mechanism as the MSR deserves particular attention. Indeed, the MSR acts on the EU ETS through adjustments to the supply of auctioned allowances, increasing or reducing the supply of EUAs according to some pre-set threshold that reflect the total number of allowances in circulation. Starting from 2023, the MSR will invalidate the allowances held in the reserve at that point in time, if these exceed the previous year's auction volume.

This instrument is designed to eliminate the built-up surplus while improving the overall resilience of the EU ETS to market future imbalances. The key rationale for having an MSR is to prevent the formation of new surpluses on the market, as happened during the EU ETS Phase 2 and Phase 3 (ICAP 2019a).

4.4 *Lessons Learnt and Way Forward*

All in all, the recent reforms of the EU ETS framework follow almost 15 years of changes and adjustments to the European carbon market. The EU institutions have repeatedly tried to improve the functioning of the system, seeking solutions to the different challenges that emerged throughout the years.

Looking forward, it remains to be seen whether the Phase 4 reform and the MSR will bear the expected fruits, and if the EU ETS will continue representing a core element in the EU's environmental strategy towards 2030 and beyond.

Since the start of the EU ETS in 2005, many important lessons were learnt, especially with regard to the allocation of allowances and the risk of overcompensation. To fix these issues, different legislative reforms put increasing emphasis on auctioning as opposed to free allocation, with the latter moving from grandfathering to the use of benchmarks in order to reflect more closely the carbon intensity levels and efficiency of covered installations, while also rewarding early action, flexibility, and level of production.

Another key innovation was the recent introduction of the MSR, which should be welcomed as a positive attempt to shield the EU ETS from the effects of old and new sources of imbalance. The increasing attention to mobilising funding for innovation and modernisation is also an interesting development that could further encourage decarbonisation.

To evaluate the experience of the European carbon market, it is worth noting that the EU ETS was never a standalone policy: it operates in a highly interconnected environment and is affected by climate change and other policies at the global, EU, and EU MS levels (Marcu et al. 2019). Its performance should be analysed against this background, and not compared to an ideal world.

At the time when the EU ETS was launched, there was a widespread perception that other countries and jurisdictions would follow suit, and that there would be opportunities for international collaboration under the umbrella of the Kyoto Protocol. The EU ETS was crafted with the ambition of becoming a reference model for emissions trading, in a world where carbon trading would be broadly adopted as a leading solution to tackle climate change.

These expectations were partially frustrated. Internationally, the failure of adopting a new global climate agreement until the Paris Agreement in 2015 led to competitiveness concerns taking a central stage in the discussion on climate policy for many years (Stenegren 2018). At the same time, other ETSs emerged in different jurisdictions, proposing new models and different approaches to the trading of carbon.

At the EU-level, the domestic problems of the EU ETS supply-demand balance limited its function as the main driver of the EU's decarbonisation strategy. The weakened price signal in the market contributed to the EU ETS not playing a central role in the decarbonisation of ETS-sectors, as initially intended. The recent price increase of 2018–2019 seems to indicate a reversal of this trend, but it remains unclear whether this reflects a structural change or just a temporary trend.

With the urgency of tackling climate change becoming increasingly evident, the EU ETS will have to face new challenges in the future. In its 1.5 C report, the Intergovernmental Panel on Climate Change (IPCC) warned the international community about the impacts of climate change, urging countries to cut their emissions to net-zero by 2050 (IPCC 2018).

The EU followed this call and decided to embrace a carbon neutrality goal for 2050. The EU ETS 2030 target was significantly revised to reach an overall reduction of 55%. This translated into the adoption of an emissions cap of 61% by 2030 in the ETS sector, and a LRF of 4.2%. Expanding the scope of the system to include the transport and buildings sectors is envisaged (von der Leyen 2019).

5 Other Major ETS Markets and Potential for Interconnection

5.1 Emissions Trading Systems: Examples from Around the World

The EU ETS is not the only living example of an emissions trading system. Other ETSs have been in place for a number of years, each with specific design characteristics and different stories of successes and setbacks. This section will present an overview of the most significant experiences with the trading of carbon outside Europe, paving the way for a discussion on the potential for interconnecting different ETSs, also taking into account Article 6 of the Paris Agreement.

National or sub-national ETSs are already operating in many parts of the world. The focus will be on the examples of Canada, China, South Korea, and the United States.

At the time of writing, three out of four of these ETSs only apply at the sub-national level:

- Québec and Nova Scotia in Canada;
- Chinese city and provincial pilot projects in Beijing, Chongqing, Fujian, Guangdong, Hubei, Shanghai, Shenzhen, and Tianjin;
- In the United States the Regional Greenhouse Gas Initiative (RGGI)[11] and California.[12]

The different systems will be analysed using as a metric the main design options of an ETS, as outlined in Sect. 3 of this chapter.

5.1.1 Western Climate Initiative (WCI): California and Québec

Since 2014, the ETSs of California and Québec are linked under the umbrella of the Western Climate Initiative (WCI). We will therefore analyse them together.

[11] The states involved are Connecticut, Delaware, Maine, Maryland, Massachusetts, New Hampshire, New Jersey, New York, Rhode Island, and Vermont. Since 2018, Massachusetts also complements the RGGI to help ensure it achieves its mandatory mitigation targets.

[12] Other ETSs in force or scheduled for implementation: Switzerland, New Zealand, Mexico, Colombia, Kazakhstan, Ukraine, Japan (city-level systems in Tokyo and Saitama). Jurisdictions considering the implementation of an ETS: Brazil, Chile, Russia, Turkey, Taiwan, Vietnam, Thailand, Indonesia, Japan. To clarify further, see: ICAP (2019c), 'Emissions Trading Worldwide—Status Report 2019'.

Compared to other existing ETSs, the WCI has the largest coverage, accounting for approximately 80% of the two jurisdictions' GHG emissions.[13]

California's cap-and-trade programme was launched in 2012, with compliance obligations starting from 2013. The programme has a mixed point of regulation for emissions above a certain threshold, which applies both downstream to electric power plants and industrial installations, as well as upstream by targeting fuel distributors. The inclusion of fuels distributors allows to incorporate more sectors into the system, such as transportation and building energy use (Hausfather 2017).

The allocation of allowances takes place through both auctioning and free allocation, roughly in equal shares (ICAP 2019c). Free allocation is based on benchmarking, in an attempt to reward efficient facilities while protecting them from the risks of carbon leakage. However, investor-owned utilities receiving free allocation are required to use the value of allowances to benefit ratepayers and achieve GHG emissions reductions (Center for Climate and Energy Solutions 2019a).

The overall GHG reduction target is set at 40% by 2030, from 1990 levels. To meet this target, the yearly cap declines at 4.1% between 2021 and 2030. In terms of flexibility mechanisms, banking is allowed under certain rules, borrowing is prohibited, and domestic offsets for projects in the US territory are allowed up to 8% of a facility's compliance obligation (California Environmental Protection Agency 2015).

Covered entities must report emissions annually, which are then submitted to an independent third-party evaluation. To avoid excessive price volatility, the Californian ETS has both a price floor and price ceiling. This means that the price of allowances cannot go below a pre-determined minimum. The state will sell an unlimited amount of emission permits if the price of carbon would reach the ceiling (Hausfather 2017).

Being linked to the Californian ETS, Québec's system has very similar design characteristics. Both systems cover the same greenhouse gases and sectors, set the same emissions thresholds and point of regulation, and have similar environmental targets (Kroft and Drance 2015). The allocation methods are also comparable in terms of the use of benchmarks and combination of free allocation and auctioning. However, Québec auctions a higher share of allowances than California, up to 70% in 2017 (ICAP 2019c). Price control mechanisms are identical under the WCI (Purdon et al. 2014).

5.1.2 Regional Greenhouse Gas Initiative (RGGI)

The RGGI was the first mandatory cap-and-trade programme in the United States. The system was first established in 2005, and became operational in 2008. It aims at limiting emissions from the power sector, and requires fossil

[13] Ontario has also been part of the WCI but has decided to termite its commitment in 2018. On the contrary, Nova Scotia entered the WCI since the beginning of 2019. The case of Nova Scotia will not be analysed, given that the ETS has been in place for only a few months.

fuel power plants with capacity greater than 25 megawatts to surrender an allowance for each ton of CO_2 emitted annually (Center for Climate and Energy Solutions 2019b).

Compared to the WCI, it only covers CO_2, and applies only to the electricity sector, with a downstream point of regulation. This translates in a coverage of less than 20% of the overall GHG emissions in those jurisdictions.

RGGI allocates 100% of the allowances via full auctioning, making it in theory the most economically efficient system (Narassimhan et al. 2018). A low marginal abatement cost, however, might also show that the system is tackling emissions from a sector where abatement opportunities exist and are available, not addressing other sectors where cutting emissions might be more challenging.

The system was reviewed in 2017. The new rules establish that between 2021 and 2030 the cap will reduce by 30% from a 2020 base year (ICAP 2019c).

Similarly to the WCI, the RGGI has price management mechanisms in place. The system has a price floor as well as a cost containment reserve, which releases allowances to the market when certain price triggers are reached.

Finally, RGGI states have been investing their auction revenues in programmes which benefit consumers: energy efficiency, renewable energy, direct energy bill assistance, and other greenhouse gas reduction programmes (ICAP 2019d). This has helped increasing the social acceptability of the system.

5.1.3 Korean Emissions Trading System (KETS)

The KETS has been operational since 2015 and represents East Asia's first nationwide mandatory ETS. The ETS covers almost 600 of the country's largest emitters, accounting for approximately 68% of the national GHG emissions (ICAP 2019c). Its coverage and scope include several gases and sectors, and emissions are regulated downstream.

One notable characteristic of the KETS compared to other ETSs is that it includes not only the power generation sector, but also indirect emissions from electricity use. The reason for this is that the electricity price in Korea is rigid and controlled by the government, so it would not automatically provide carbon cost pass-through. Therefore, the efficient use of electricity is encouraged by including electricity consumption in the ETS, thereby providing a direct price signal to consumers (Asian Development Bank 2018a).

The KETS cap reflects an environmental target of cutting emissions by 37% by 2030 compared to a business as usual (BAU) scenario, that is, a 22% reduction below 2012 GHG levels (NDC) (ICAP 2019e). This cap was set through a bottom-up approach. This has attracted the criticism of some analysts, considering the heavy reliance on reported data from manufacturers (ICAP 2019c).

To meet the KETS target, up to 38 million international credits may be used for compliance, including international credits through the KETS, as well as alternative options as land use, land use change and forestry (LULUCF) and other international credits (i.e. under Article 6 under the Paris Agreement) (ICAP 2019c). The positive approach of Korea towards the use of international credits can be explained by one issue which has represented a problem for the KETS since the beginning of its operations: a general lack of market liquidity.

Indeed, being the Korean market fairly limited in terms of market participants, it has suffered from the unwillingness of its participants to sell unused allowances, as they preferred to bank for future compliance periods (Lee and Yu 2017). Connecting the KETS with other ETSs through linking or expanding the acceptance of international credits is perceived as a way to increase liquidity and increase the trading volumes.

Opposite to the example of the RGGI, allocation under the KETS takes place through free allocation for 97% of the total allowances put on the market. This has helped the initial public backing for the system, yet to the detriment of price discovery due to low liquidity in the secondary market, and no revenue generation for the government. Similarly to the RGGI and the WCI, the KETS has market stability provisions that adjust the supply of allowances according to some pre-set price thresholds.

5.1.4 China

The prospect for China to introduce a nation-wide ETS has long been discussed, attracting a lot of attention given China's role as the world's largest GHG emitter. In 2013, China initiated pilot ETSs in seven regions, aiming at the future creation of a national system. In 2016, an eighth pilot ETS was launched in the province of Fujian (Zhang et al. 2019).

Since 2017, the Chinese national ETS was politically launched, and the first trading operations started in July 2021. As soon as trading began, the Chinese ETSs became the world's largest carbon market, almost doubling the size of the EU ETS, although it only includes the power sector initially, but the scope should be gradually expanded to other industries (ICAP 2019f).

The analysis of the pilot projects can give us some guidance on how a Chinese ETS might look like, and what design characteristics would the system have. For all of them, the decision was to set absolute-based caps (with the exception of Shenzhen, which adopted both an absolute and intensity cap), with different degrees of stringency and linear reduction factors. The programmes account for ca. 30% of China's GDP and 17% of the country's CO_2 emissions (ICAP 2019c).

Most pilots focus on CO_2 emissions, whereas they all include both power installations and some industrial sectors. The vast majority of the pilots adopt free allocation as the main allocation method, though several are also opening up to auctioning allowances. In terms of the way allowances are freely allocated, grandfathering seems to emerge as the default option, with only the Shenzhen ETS using benchmarking for allocation (ICAP 2019c).

So far, carbon prices have been relatively low, affected primarily by generous levels of allocation. Furthermore, the credibility of the system has been put into question due to limited market transparency and access to data. On the other hand, the pilot programmes are having the positive implication of legitimising the concept of carbon trading in China, training local governments officials and making MRV standards mainstream. This is preparing the way for the potential adoption of a national system (Timperley 2018).

5.2 *Carbon Trading and Potential for International Cooperation Mechanism*

Section 3.4 highlighted that ETSs can increase flexibility and increase economic efficiency, effectively lowering costs for abatement by:

(a) accepting domestic offsets for compliance;
(b) accepting international offsets for compliance;
(c) linking different ETSs—that is, participants in one system can use a compliance instrument issued by another ETS for domestic compliance.

The idea of interconnecting different systems through the international trading of carbon has been at the centre of the international debate on climate change since the adoption of the Kyoto Protocol.

Article 17 of the Kyoto Protocol (KP) states:

> *The Conference of the Parties shall define the relevant principles, modalities, rules and guidelines, in particular for verification, reporting and accountability for emissions trading. The Parties included in Annex B may participate in emissions trading for the purposes of fulfilling their commitments under Article 3. Any such trading shall be supplemental to domestic actions for the purpose of meeting quantified emission limitation and reduction commitments under that Article.*

Art. 17 has represented the umbrella for the creation of an international carbon market, including the trade of international offsets, and linking of different ETSs.

When discussing the potential for linking, it was mentioned that creating a bilateral link has the main benefit of reducing the total cost of achieving the combined emissions target of the linked ETSs (Partnership for Market Readiness 2014). Additionally, linking could prove particularly beneficial for small jurisdictions, where setting up an independent ETS could lead to high technical and compliance costs, with likely problems of market liquidity.[14]

At the same time, linking can also cause problems, as it changes the distribution of costs in each system. This leads to price convergence, benefitting buyers with the higher pre-link price and sellers with the lower pre-link price (ICAP 2019c).

To limit these issues, the linking of different systems should be carefully designed, and both jurisdictions will need to abide by similar, if not identical,

[14]This was one of the main drivers behind the agreement between the EU and Switzerland to link their respective ETSs. To clarify further, see: ICAP (2019g).

standards. Indeed, the experience of the California-Québec linking suggests that linking is easier if certain design features are aligned. The same can be said also of the EU ETS, where the distribution of allowances and operation of the registry have been gradually centralised, following initial years when the EU Member States were in charge of these operations even if this was one ETS.

Overall, different jurisdictions will be open to the possibility of linking for as long as they have reasonable certainty that the system they are linking to has similar design and objectives. Besides the technical considerations, linking also relies on the political will to cooperate with a foreign jurisdiction on climate change policy, as it implies partially losing control over the ETS. Domestic support for emissions trading and linking is therefore a crucial pre-requisite to the decision to linking different ETSs (Beuermann et al. 2017).

The other possibility for the international trading of carbon is via international carbon offsets. According to the United Nations, *offsetting is a climate action that enables individuals and organizations to compensate for the emissions they cannot avoid, by supporting worthy projects that reduce emissions somewhere else* (UN 2019). Historically, in the context of the UNFCCC, offsetting could be done by industrialised nations, mentioned in Annex I of the KP, as they were the only ones who had committed to caps under Kyoto. The KP created three main categories of offset credits: emission reduction unit (ERU) generated by joint implementation (JI) projects; certified emission reduction (CER) generated from clean development mechanism (CDM) project activities; and removal unit (RMU) generated by LULUCF activities.

Offset credits can also be produced outside the UNFCCC. These include voluntary offset programmes (e.g. Verified Carbon Standard), national offset programmes (e.g. Australia's Carbon Farming Initiative), bilateral offset mechanisms (e.g. Japans' Joint Crediting Mechanism), and regional offset programmes (e.g. Climate Action Reserve offsets allowed under California's cap and trade scheme) (Carbon Market Watch 2013).

Primarily, international offsets must ensure environmental integrity in order to be effective. To this end, it has long been recognised that offset credits should be 'real, permanent, additional and verified'. Indeed, environmental integrity of offset credits is guaranteed for as long as:

- emissions reductions have actually occurred, and are not merely artefacts or incomplete/inaccurate accounting—'real';
- reductions are permanently removed from the atmosphere and/or are backed by replacement mechanisms if they are re-emitted to the atmosphere—'permanent';
- the emissions reduction that underpin the credit would not have occurred in the absence of the activity that generates the credit—'additional';
- reductions result from projects that can accurately be monitored and verified—'verified' (Gero 2009).

Failure on one or more of these dimensions would risk undermining the credibility and effectiveness of an offset. Notably, credits under the KP were sometimes criticised by campaigners who claimed that credits under the KP suffered from shortfalls in terms of environmental integrity, accounting, and contribution to sustainable development.

A new system for the international trade of carbon is now being developed as part of the negotiations for the Rulebook of Article 6 of the Paris Agreement (PA), which were successfully concluded at COP 26 in Glasgow (Marcu 2021).

Article 6 provides a framework for general cooperation in the implementation of the Paris Agreement and the nationally determined contributions (NDCs), including provisions to create a framework that will enable the creation of an international carbon market.

One key difference between the PA and the KP is that under the PA all countries, both developing and developed countries, have to submit NDCs as part of the joint effort to reach the overall objective of the Agreement. This implies that potentially all countries might be interested in the international trading of carbon, as both buyers and sellers.

As a consequence, before engaging in the international trading of carbon under Art. 6, countries will need to agree on how to ensure environmental integrity, how credits might or might not account towards the achievement of a country's domestic NDC, and how double counting can be avoided on the basis of corresponding adjustments (Asian Development Bank 2018b).

More broadly, the open question for the future is whether carbon markets will play a central role in the fight to climate change, and if there is room for the emergence of a global carbon price. Developments of new ETSs and the outcome of the negotiations on Article 6 of the PA will reflect the attitude of the international community towards the use of market-based approaches to climate policy.

If anything, the emergence of a global carbon price would have the undisputable benefit of alleviating carbon leakage concerns.

The ongoing development of new ETSs in high-emitting countries like China could be seen as a step in the right direction, as having more jurisdictions effectively pricing carbon decreases the potential for unfair competition. However, it remains to be seen if the new emerging ETSs will apply high standards of environmental integrity, triggering ambitious decarbonisation strategies in their respective jurisdictions.

As for international cooperation mechanisms under Art.6 of the PA, this could represent a steppingstone for a resurgence of the trading of international carbon credits, potentially helping the international harmonisation of carbon pricing (Asia Society Policy Institute 2018).

Finding an agreement on the operationalisation of Art. 6 is therefore extremely important, provided that such agreement shapes a system that works for the environment and helps countries achieving the objectives of the PA. All in all, while markets do adapt to many circumstances, they will be attractive only if they have clear objectives, have governance that ensure predictability, are liquid and transparent, and participants are re-assured that they have clear ownership of the assets (Marcu 2019).

Bibliography

Aki Kachi and Michel Frerk (2013), 'Carbon Market Oversight Primer', ICAP.

Alexander Eden, Charlotte Unger, William Acworth, Kristian Wilkening and Constanze Haug (2016), 'Benefits of Emissions Trading', ICAP.

Andrei Calin Marcu (2019), 'Reflections on Art 6 Post- Katowice', ERCST. Retrieved from: https://ercst.org/wp-content/uploads/2019/03/20190318-Reflections-post-Katowice-vFW-1.pdf.

Andrei Calin Marcu (2021), 'Article 6 rule book: a post COP26 assessment', ERCST. Retrieved from: https://ercst.org/wp-content/uploads/2021/11/20211122-COP26-Art6-final.pdf

Andrei Calin Marcu and Mandy Rambharos (2019), 'Rulebook for Article 6 in the Paris Agreement: takeaway from the COP24 outcome', ERCST. Retrieved from: https://ercst.org/wp-content/uploads/2019/02/Rulebook-for-Article-6-in-the-Paris-Agreement-Takeaway-from-the-COP-24-outcome.pdf.

Andrei Calin Marcu, Emilie Alberola, Jean-Yevs Caneill, Matteo Mazzoni, Stefan Schleicher, Wijnand Stoefs, Charlotte Vailles, Domien Vangenechten and Federico Cecchetti (2019), '2019 State of the EU ETS Report', ERCST. Retrieved from: https://ercst.org/wp-content/uploads/2019/05/2019-State-of-the-EU-ETS-Report-1.pdf.

Andrei Calin Marcu, Emilie Alberola, Jean-Yevs Caneill, Matteo Mazzoni, Stefan P. Schleicher, Wijnand Stoefs, Charlotte Vailles, Domien Vangenechten (2018), '2018 State of the EU ETS Report', ERCST. Retrieved from: https://ercst.org/wp-content/uploads/2019/03/20180416-2018-State-of-EU-ETS-Report-Final-all-logos-.pdf

Andrew Prag, Gregory Briner, and Christina Hood (2012), 'Making Markets: Unpacking Design and Governance of Carbon Market Mechanisms', OECD.

Asia Society Policy Institute (2018), 'Northeast Asia Carbon Markets and Trade Connections'. Retrieved from: https://ercst.org/wp-content/uploads/2018/12/1cs6m7r3o_298044.pdf.

Asian Development Bank (2018a), 'The Korea Emissions Trading Scheme Challenges and Emerging Opportunities'.

Asian Development Bank (2018b), 'Decoding Article 6 of the Paris Agreement'. Retrieved from: https://ercst.org/wp-content/uploads/2018/12/article6-paris-agreement.pdf.

California Air Resources Board (2019), 'Low Carbon Fuel Standard in California'. Retrieved from: https://ww3.arb.ca.gov/fuels/lcfs/background/basics-notes.pdf.

California Environmental Protection Agency (2015), 'ARB Emissions Trading Program', retrieved from: https://ww3.arb.ca.gov/cc/capandtrade/guidance/cap_trade_overview.pdf.

Carbon Market Watch (2013), 'Briefing Note for ICAO: Carbon Offsetting—Do's and Don'ts'.

Carbon Pricing Leadership Coalition (2016), 'What Are the Options for Using Carbon Pricing Revenues?', World Bank.

Center for Climate and Energy Solutions (2019a), 'California Cap and Trade', retrieved from: https://www.c2es.org/content/california-cap-and-trade/.

Center for Climate and Energy Solutions (2019b), 'Regional Greenhouse Gas Initiative (RGGI)', retrieved from: https://www.c2es.org/content/regional-greenhouse-gas-initiative-rggi/.

Christiane Beuermann, Julia Bingler, Marissa Santikarn, Dennis Tänzler, Johannes Thema (2017), 'Considering the Effects of Linking Emissions Trading Schemes', Adelphi.

Claire Dupont and Brendan Moore (2019), 'Brexit and the EU in Global Climate Governance', Politics and Governance (Volume 7, Issue 3), Cogitatio.

Climate Policy Info Hub (2019a), 'European Climate Policy—History and State of Play', European Union.

Climate Policy Info Hub (2019b), 'The EU Emissions Trading System: an Introduction', European Union.

Crispin Mäenpää (2016), 'Something Worth Fighting For: The Evolution of Lobbying Coalitions in the Emissions Trading System', College of Europe.

Denny Ellerman, Claudio Marcantonini, Aleksandar Zaklan (2015), 'The European Union Emissions Trading System: Ten Years and Counting', Review of Environmental Economics and Policy (Volume 10, Issue 1), Oxford.

DW (2019), 'Net-zero by 2050: What does it mean?'. Retrieved from: https://www.dw.com/en/net-zero-by-2050-what-does-it-mean/a-48958487.

Easwaran Narassimhan, Kelly S. Gallagher, Stefan Koester, and Julio Rivera Alejo (2018), 'Carbon pricing in practice: a review of existing emissions trading systems', Climate Policy (volume 18 issue 8), 967–991..

Emmanuel Saez (2007), 'Externalities: Problems and Solutions', in: Jonathan Gruber (2007), 'Public Finance and Public Policy', Worth Publishers.

EU Commission Regulation (2011), No 1210/2011 of 23 November 2011, retrieved from: https://eur-lex.europa.eu/legal-content/EN/TXT/PDF/?uri=CELEX:32011R1210&from=EN.

European Commission (2019a), Carbon Leakage, European Commission website. https://ec.europa.eu/clima/policies/ets/allowances/leakage_en.

European Commission (2019b), EU Emissions Trading System (EU ETS), European Commission website, retrieved from: https://ec.europa.eu/clima/policies/ets_en

European Commission (2019c), National Allocation Plans, European Commission website, retrieved from: https://ec.europa.eu/clima/policies/ets/pre2013/nap_en.

European Commission (2019d), Phase 1 and 2 (2005–2012), European Commission website, retrieved from: https://ec.europa.eu/clima/policies/ets/pre2013_en.

European Commission (2019e), Emission Cap and Allowances, European Commission website, retrieved from: https://ec.europa.eu/clima/policies/ets/cap_en

European Commission (2019f), Allocation to industrial installations, European Commission website, retrieved from https://ec.europa.eu/clima/policies/ets/allowances/industrial_en.

European Commission (2019g), Revision for Phase 4 (2021–2030), European Commission website, retrieved from: https://ec.europa.eu/clima/policies/ets/revision_en.

European Commission (2015), 'EU ETS Handbook'. Retrieved from: https://ec.europa.eu/clima/sites/clima/files/docs/ets_handbook_en.pdf.

European Commission (2007), 'Emissions trading: Commission announces linkage EU ETS with Norway, Iceland and Liechtenstein', Press release.
European Environment Agency website (2019), retrieved from: https://www.eea.europa.eu/data-and-maps/dashboards/emissions-trading-viewer-1.
European Parliament and Council (2018) Directive (EU) 2018/410 of the European Parliament and of the Council of 14 March 2018, retrieved from: https://eur-lex.europa.eu/legal-content/EN/TXT/PDF/?uri=CELEX:32018L0410&from=EN.
European Parliament and Council (2015), Decision (EU) 2015/1814 of the European Parliament and of the Council of 6 October 2015, retrieved from: https://eur-lex.europa.eu/legal-content/EN/TXT/PDF/?uri=CELEX:32015D1814&from=EN.
European Parliament and Council (2009), Directive 2009/29/EC of the European Parliament and of the Council. Retrieved from: https://eur-lex.europa.eu/LexUriServ/LexUriServ.do?uri=OJ:L:2009:140:0063:0087:EN:PDF
Fitsum Tiche, Stefan Weishaar, and Oscar Couwenberg (2014), 'Carbon Leakage, Free Allocation and Linking Emissions Trading Schemes', Carbon & Climate Law Review 8, 97–105.
Gabriel Chan, Robert Stavins, Robert Stowe, and Richard Sweeney (2012), 'The SO2 Allowance Trading System and the Clean Air Act Amendments of 1990', Resources for the Future.
Gary Gero (2009), 'The Role of Carbon Offsets in Cap-and-Trade', Climate Action Reserve.
Hanna Stenegren (2018), 'Fighting climate change with the market', Fores. Retrieved from: https://www.liberalforum.eu/wp-content/uploads/2018/11/Emissions-trading_online_final_version.pdf.
ICAP (2019a), 'An Introduction to Emissions Trading Schemes', retrieved from: https://icapcarbonaction.com/en/partnership/about-emissions-trading/introduction.
ICAP (2019b), 'EU Emissions Trading System (EU ETS)'.
ICAP (2019c), 'Emissions Trading Worldwide—Status Report 2019'.
ICAP (2019d), 'Canada—Québec Cap-and-Trade System'.
ICAP (2019e), 'USA—Regional Greenhouse Gas Initiative (RGGI)'.
ICAP (2019f), 'Korea Emissions Trading Scheme'.
ICAP (2019g), 'China National ETS'.
ICAP (2019h), 'Swiss ETS'.
ICAP (2017), 'Flexibility in Emissions Trading'. Retrieved from: https://icapcarbonaction.com/en/?option=com_attach&task=download&id=494
ICAP (2016), 'Emissions Trading in Practice: a handbook on design and implementation', World Bank.
IETA (2011), 'The EU's Emissions Trading System' Retrieved from: https://www.ieta.org/resources/Resources/3_Minute_Briefings/phase%203%20eu%20ets_final.pdf.
Institute for Climate Economics and Vivid Economics (2019), 'Using Carbon Revenues', Partnership for Market Readiness, World Bank.
IPCC (2018), 'Global Warming of 1.5°C. An IPCC Special Report on the impacts of global warming of 1.5°C above pre-industrial levels and related global greenhouse gas emission pathways, in the context of strengthening the global response to the threat of climate change, sustainable development, and efforts to eradicate poverty'.
Jaeseok Lee and Jongmin Yu (2017), 'Market Analysis during the First Year of Korea Emission Trading Scheme', Energies.

James Heskett (2018), 'What's the Best Administrative Approach to Climate Change?', Harvard Business School.

Jason Kroft, Jonathan Drance (2015), 'Examining California and Quebec's cap-and-trade systems', Knowledge Hub.

Jocelyn Timperley (2018), 'How will China's new carbon trading scheme work?', Carbon Brief.

Johan Albrecht (2002), 'Instruments for Climate Policy: Limited Versus Unlimited Flexibility', Edward Elgar Publishing.

Jørgen Wettestad, Lars Gulbrandsen (2017), 'The Evolution of Carbon Markets: Design and Diffusion', Routledge.

Jos Delbeke and Peter Vis (2016), 'EU Climate Policy Explained', European Union. Retrieved from: https://ec.europa.eu/clima/sites/clima/files/eu_climate_policy_explained_en.pdf

Karsten Neuhoff (2008) 'Tackling Carbon, How to Price Carbon for Climate Policy', Climate Strategies.

Kyoto Protocol to the United Nations Framework Convention on Climate Change (1998), United Nations. Retrieved from: https://unfccc.int/resource/docs/convkp/kpeng.pdf.

Lars Zetterberg, Dallas Burtraw, Daniel Engström Stensson, Charlotte Paulie, Susanna Roth (2014), 'Europe's choice—Facts and function of the EU emissions trading system', IVL Swedish Environmental Research Institute.

London School of Economics and Political Science (2018a), 'What is the polluter pays principle?'. Retrieved from: http://www.lse.ac.uk/GranthamInstitute/faqs/what-is-the-polluter-pays-principle/.

London School of Economics and Political Science (2018b), 'What is a carbon price and why do we need one?'. Retrieved from: http://www.lse.ac.uk/GranthamInstitute/faqs/what-is-a-carbon-price-and-why-do-we-need-one/.

Lu Zhang, Yi Zeng, Dayuan Li (2019), 'China's Emissions Trading Scheme: First Evidence on Pilot Stage', Polish Journal of Environmental Studies, 28, 543–551.

Marissa Santikarn, Christopher Kardish, Johannes Ackva, and Constanze Haug (2019), 'The Use of Auction Revenue From Emissions Trading Systems', ICAP.

Mark Purdon, David Houle, and Erick Lachapelle (2014), 'The Political Economy of California and Québec's Cap-and-Trade Systems', University of Ottawa.

Mikael Skou Andersen and Paul Ekins (2009), 'Carbon-Energy Taxation: Lessons from Europe', Oxford.

Noah Kaufman, Michael Obeiter, and Eleanor Krause (2016), 'Putting a price on carbon: reducing emissions', World Resources Institute.

Partnership for Market Readiness (2014), 'Lessons Learned from Linking Emissions Trading Systems: General Principles and Applications'.

Richard Newell, William Pizer, and Daniel Raimi (2012), 'Carbon Markets: Past, Present, and Future', Resources For the Future.

Richard Sandor (2016), 'SO2 emissions allowances—anatomy of a mature market', in: R. L. Sandor (2016), 'How I Saw It: Analysis and Commentary on Environmental Finance (1999–2005)', World Scientific Publishing Company.

Ronald Coase (1960), 'The problem of social cost', Journal of Law and Economics (volume 3), University of Chicago.

Sandbag (2019), 'Carbon Price Viewer', retrieved from: https://sandbag.org.uk/carbon-price-viewer/.

Simone Borghesi, Massimiliano Montini, Alessandra Barreca (2016), 'The European Emission Trading System and Its Followers: Comparative Analysis and Linking Perspectives', Springer.

Tim Laing and Michael Mehling (2013), 'International Experience with Emissions Trading', Climate Strategies

United Nations website (2019), Retrieved from: https://offset.climateneutralnow.org/aboutoffsetting.

Ursula von der Leyen (2019), 'A Union that strives for more My agenda for Europe', Retrieved from: https://ec.europa.eu/commission/sites/beta-political/files/political-guidelines-next-commission_en.pdf.

World Bank (2019), 'What is Carbon Pricing'. Retrieved from: https://www.worldbank.org/en/programs/pricing-carbon

Zeke Hausfather (2017), 'Explainer: California's new 'cap-and-trade' scheme to cut emissions', Carbon Brief.

CHAPTER 24

Unbundling, Markets, and Regulation

Eleanor J. Morrison

1 Introduction

Energy market restructuring and liberalisation over the past thirty years has produced mixed results. Wholesale market design and competition has expanded and matured, while retail competition has remained static. Industrialised countries have observed both positive outcomes and market failures, while developing countries have had limited success in restructuring energy systems. Forming a global picture of the liberalisation progress is difficult, as countries launched from differing starting points, and advance at different speeds, with continuous changes introduced due to political unrest and financial crises. Energy policies tend to be multi-dimensional which, in turn, makes benchmarking and evaluating success of unbundling and liberalisation a challenging endeavour.

Energy policies are translated into regulatory frameworks to support policy goals. These goals include, but are not limited to, security of supply, increased competition by encouraging new participants through open transparent market structures, and environmental sustainability programmes. In order to analyse the results of liberalisation, an understanding of the extent to which stages of liberalisation have actually been implemented in the energy sector and remain in place is needed. The three stages in effective liberalisation include unbundling, launch of a wholesale market, and support for a retail market.

Liberalisation has evolved from different frameworks. The United States took an approach of cautious relaxation of regulatory control over prices and close observation of the potential problems inherent in participant market

E. J. Morrison (✉)
SciencesPo—Paris School of International Affairs, Paris, France
e-mail: eleanor.morrison@sciencespo.fr

M. Hafner, G. Luciani (eds.), *The Palgrave Handbook of International Energy Economics*, https://doi.org/10.1007/978-3-030-86884-0_24

power. Europe, on the other hand, created markets under a new competitive framework that crosses member state boundaries. Most other countries approached liberalisation in a stepwise fashion by observing the performance of each stage of market restructuring. OECD countries have been reforming energy product market regulations, improving and adapting regulatory techniques to changing market and technological conditions. This is crucial to management of the competitive and non-competitive market segments that exist in the natural gas and electricity markets.

Government energy policies pushed for deregulation to improve sector efficiencies, while large energy consumers, such as industrial and commercial sectors, pushed to access cheaper pricing. In liberalising policy, states intended to encourage the competition needed to reduce costs by unbundling vertically integrated monopolies, effectively separating generation from transmission and distribution. To pass these expected savings on to consumers requires a sufficient number of competitors that have access to an open wholesale market. Eliminating guaranteed fixed price contracts should encourage private investment to participate in an efficient manner to add generation capacity based on market signals. However, private investment financing depends not just on an expected revenue stream but also on the degree of confidence that can be attached to those revenues. Increased renewable energy participation in electricity generation and change in price formation patterns have increased investors' uncertainty in the past decade. In most countries, the existing wholesale market structures were designed to suit the technical, cost, and operating characteristics of fossil fuel plants. Thus, the advent of large volumes of zero marginal cost generation, a significant part of which may be intermittent or inflexible or have other characteristics very different from conventional thermal plants, will require substantial revisions of existing marketing structure to ensure system stability and to encourage private investment (Sioshansi 2013).

Regulators have worked hard to transfer efficiency gains in transmission and distribution into lower consumer prices (Newberry 2002) and some markets that initially offered lower retail prices. But most retail consumer costs increased. This was due to ongoing infrastructure costs in the delivery of energy and for electricity consumers specifically, because end-user energy billing absorbed the costs of renewable generation incentives, to encourage private investment, promised by governments. Germany is a prime example of the success of regulation in supporting renewable development, but the ultimate costs for these developer incentives were socialised into retail infrastructure bills. In a frustrating dichotomy, average wholesale prices have fallen and retail prices have risen (Hannesson 2019) (Fig. 24.1).

The past two decades have seen an increased frequency of electric power shortages in both the developing and developed world. Power shortages seldom have a single or the same cause. However, a typical pattern begins with underinvestment or very rapid demand growth that degrades reserve margins below acceptable reliability levels, and then unusual combinations of market fundamentals, such as adverse weather, fuel supply, or plant availability, will

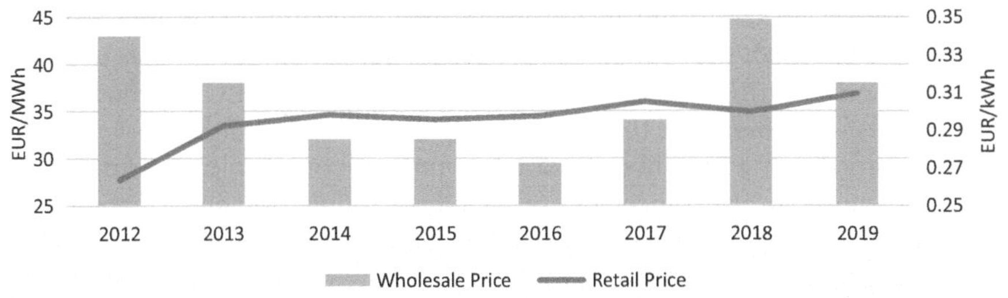

Fig. 24.1 Historical German retail price and wholesale market prices. (Source: Author's graph, retail prices include taxes, levies, and fees. Data from Federal Statistical Office and European Energy Exchange)

create a crisis (Heffner et al. 2010). These shortages have occurred in both liberalised market structures and traditional regulated monopolistic regimes. While liberalisation of energy markets and the resulting new regulatory structure have not delivered the results economic policy makers expected, market efficiencies and product delivery seem no worse than prior to liberalisation.

This chapter will focus on a comprehensive review of the alternative restructuring approaches used to break up vertically integrated monopolies and is presented along with the effects of generation deregulation on competition, the efficiency of system operations, and the impact on wholesale and consumer prices. It will highlight key historical moments in policy liberalisation. The chapter will concentrate on the electricity sector with brief reference to the natural gas experience and the importance of natural gas market liberalisation for electricity markets. Price risk resulting from unbundling and opportunities for hedging in the physical and financial markets will be discussed. The California energy crisis will be used to highlight the intersection of market failures in the state's first attempt at liberalisation and establishment of a new regulatory framework. Structural economic factors of the energy sector relating to policy and regulation will be discussed. Both developed and developing countries have achieved success of policies for renewable energy investment and more mixed results through environmental cap-and-trade programmes. The chapter will conclude by describing expected future challenges to regulatory market structure in the form of increasingly intermittent supply, decentralised generation, and changing consumer demand patterns.

2 Energy as a Network Industry

Network industry privatisation commenced with the first wave of neoliberalism, under the political stewardship of Ronald Reagan and Margaret Thatcher during the 1980s. The European Commission (EC) took up Thatcher's privatisation programme at the end of the 1980s, introducing mandated deregulation and privatisation to remove state control and eliminate the concept of the public good. The norm in the United States model is to have private ownership of unbundled network utilities combined with regulation oversight. OECD countries other than the United States have liberalised energy utilities without the use of privatisation (Ugur 2007). The EC along with OECD governments had successfully liberalised the telecommunications and air transport sectors, offering proof that a fully liberalised environment would unleash competitive forces. Technological advancement provided the foundation and capability for market unbundling and vertical separation. New governance and regulatory techniques and an increase in openness to international challenges and competition accelerated liberalisation and privatisation (Belloc and Nicita 2011).

Electricity and natural gas are network industries and have similar characteristics to other network industries such as telecom and rail transport. Network industries are traditionally characterised as natural monopolies that were originally under the control of public ownership. Natural monopolies exist when economies of scale are significant in that a single firm can produce total business output at a lower unit cost and thus more efficiently than multiple firms. This situation gives rise to a potential conflict between cost efficiency and competition. Energy markets typically exhibit structural characteristics that allow incumbent firms to exercise market domination, which restricts competition and potentially generates higher prices and reduced consumer protection. Thus, competition cannot be relied upon to provide the socially optimal outcome. Some form of government intervention in these network industries is required to support quality of service and price protections for consumers (Gonenc et al. 2000).

Energy industry unbundling has resulted in generation, transmission, and distribution as independent segments. History has shown that generation is an excellent candidate for liberalisation and privatisation. Technology through investment channels have delivered more efficient and smaller scale energy production to an open transparent competitive market. Much like the energy industry generally, energy transmission and transportation infrastructure is considered a natural monopoly. There has never been a serious attempt to liberalise this segment through the enticement of private investment. These networks have high fixed costs, long approval processes and construction timelines, and little opportunity for long-term contracts, which provides little attraction to private investors. Thus, transmission assets are either public or privately owned with regulatory oversight to ensure system reliability and fair market pricing to participants.

3 Unbundling Vertical Monopolies and Enforcing Competition Through Regulation

Regulation is driven not only by normative considerations, such as reducing and controlling rent-seeking behaviour, but also by the impetus to determine the optimal organisation of the system it regulates. This positive theory of regulation treats the existence and forms of regulation as a response to demands of politicians and interest groups. Government ideology significantly influences energy regulation (Chang and Berdiev 2011). A government's degree of fragmentation, political strength, and authority determine its ability to implement regulation of the energy sector. Private investors lack confidence that changes in rules will not affect their investment if the sustainability of the regulation design is not clear, and thus they are wary of investing in energy in countries with signs of institutional weakness.

In OECD countries, network industry liberalisation in the 1990s resulted in the emergence of national- and subnational-level regulators to advocate for unbundling, open access, and the creation of market-driven signals to encourage competition. Competing regulatory bodies at differing levels of government as well as competitive and monopolistic design frameworks for generation, transportation, and distribution systems created confusion for potential investors. Although these regulatory groups were intended to coordinate and harmonise rules, inefficiencies in competing regulatory strategies emerged.

For mature network sectors, liberalisation policy started with unbundling the value chain into separate components and then determined which ones are potentially competitive or monopolistic. The competitive activities were liberalised via reduction of the state's role and the introduction of a competition framework to produce economic efficiencies. Competition improved the focus on consumer experience and added consumer choice, which drove new product and service innovation.

Unbundling creates price risk. Producers and generators need to sell their commodity at market prices. Regulators did not fully understand the consequences of the market price risks or the application of forward contracts for hedging. The volume and complexity of linear and non-linear derivatives have increased as energy trading markets have matured making market monitoring challenging. Regulators need to maintain currency in trading strategies, to identify opportunities for further market efficiencies, and to monitor and punish market manipulation behaviours.

Public response to environmental degradation contributed to government intervention and climate change regulations in the energy sector. Global climate change may well be the environmental externality governments had the most difficulty regulating (Bazilian et al. 2011). The only proven means of boosting environmental protection, in an efficient manner, is economic incentives. The introduction of quantity-based mechanisms, such as tradable permits, has created market-harnessing controls aimed at policy goals (Stavins 2010). The largest market for tradable permits is the European Emissions Trading Scheme (ETS) for carbon emissions, which covers all medium- and large-scale industries within the EU borders.

States have embraced several approaches to regulation to ensure fair pricing in the energy sector: direct command and control, incentive based (which includes cost of service), rate of return and price caps, and market-based controls (which provide a structural form in the market to influence competition). Public ownership was historically run as a cost of service regulation, but both consumers and politicians criticised it because of the lack of incentives to reduce costs or address operating inefficiencies. Rate of return regulation has also been criticised for having poor incentives to develop efficiencies for lower costs to the end consumer. Price cap mechanisms have had more support and perceived efficiencies, since the energy producer will only improve financial performance, by lowering their costs.

Energy regulation evolved to protect both consumer and investor interests by setting prices or rates that were considered 'just and reasonable'.[1] Prices were set at levels in response to consumer and political pressures and provided acceptable returns on investment for private and public integrated utilities. The US Federal Energy Regulatory Commission (FERC) relies on market forces, rather than regulation, to support competition and to achieve just and reasonable wholesale prices. While this avoids a host of distortions and inefficiencies, FERC's record suggests the mere possibility of a market failure is insufficient to ensure good outcomes for consumers.

Comparing the outcomes of observed regulatory regimes provides information as to what policies are superior. Four model frameworks for the energy sector exist, three of which represent stages of liberalisation. These four illustrate the choices that governments make in deciding how to run the energy industry (Table 24.1).

The first model is franchise monopolies, the traditional regulated utility scenario, where no competition exists at the generation or transmission levels. One company, which can be a public or private entity, is allowed to produce energy and deliver it to end consumers. Franchise monopolies have no liberalisation.

The second model is the single buyer structure. In this model, generation is fragmented into multiple legally separated companies to ensure none dominates the market and competition is possible. The transmission grid is not deregulated, meaning companies do not have open access, because the purchasing agent designated to represent all consumers is the only possible user of the grid. The companies have long-term contracts so that they have revenue

Table 24.1 Energy sector paradigms and competition

Model paradigm	*Level of competition*	*Private investment*	*Multiple producers*	*Multiple buyers*	*Network access*
Monopoly	No	X	X	X	X
Single purchase agent	Generation only	✓	✓	X	X
Wholesale market	Generation, trading	✓	✓	✓	✓
Wholesale + retail market	Generation, trading	✓	✓	✓	✓

[1] For historical application of just and reasonable terminology in the energy sector, refer to working paper: Isser, S.N., 2015. Just and Reasonable: The Cornerstone of Energy Regulation.

certainty to obtain and support generator financing arrangements. This approach is considered an interim step in the road to full liberalisation, with unbundling of only generation, as the government deregulates generation and acts as an agent to provide stability while the generation market structure changes take place.

The third model is the efficient launch of wholesale energy competition with open access to pipeline and transmission systems. As with the single buyer structure, there are multiple competing energy-independent producers, but in this structure, there are also multiple competing buyers. No market power exists for the producer or consumer side of the market. Transmission has been unbundled from distribution, allowing for the design of an open access platform for all participants with an energy market structure in place, either by a bilateral trading market or by a centralised pool. This market structure is commonplace in the United States, the UK, and Europe.

The final model is complete liberalisation, which extends wholesale market and transmission access to include retail competition. It provides an effective retail market, where a retail market framework is implemented and where customers can choose their service providers. Implementation of this model involves a delay in the benefit to the end consumer in the wholesale and retail markets, since competition takes time to develop. The concept relies on consumer choices which increase transaction costs involved in managing the improvement of metering and the wide assortment of consumer contract structures.

Unbundling of a vertically integrated monopoly involves the functional and structural separation of different segments of the energy production and transmission systems (Sen et al. 2016). A simple approach to unbundling focuses on functional unbundling, which entails creating a separate legal business unit with separate accounting. Structural unbundling is more complex and requires separation of ownership of the grid from the generation and the designation of an independent system operator (ISO) or independent transmission operator (ITO). The ISO structure involves ownership unbundling of the system operator (SO), who runs the grid, from the transmission operator (TO), while the TO owns the transmission assets. In jurisdictions that have an ITO structure, regulators have left some flexibility for incumbent utilities such that transmission assets remain within the vertically integrated utility (Nardi 2012).

The energy sector is not fully liberalised in any country in the world, although most regions where unbundling has occurred have seen the wholesale market migration to an open competitive framework. Regulation in the gas market, particularly in continental Europe, has taken time to find an acceptable equilibrium that tackles import security and competitive concerns. Thus, electricity provides the best evidence on the consequences of unbundling and the sharpest test for regulatory frameworks.

4 Natural Gas Unbundling and Liberalisation

Unbundling of the natural gas industry decentralises the industry along horizontal and vertical lines, lowering barriers to entry, which resulted in the arrival of new participants to the market. Natural gas liberalisation not only benefits the wholesale natural gas market, but also opens access to transportation pipelines and storage for buyers. Regulators do not set natural gas prices directly. Instead, they support fair natural gas pricing by increasing competition using two types of market trading models: bilateral trading, which is popular in the United States, and centralised pool coordination, present in the UK. Both models provide a platform for streamlined trading and promote efficient wholesale pricing and minimise transaction costs.

The speed of natural gas market liberalisation has varied across the globe due to political forces and incumbent market structure. National energy policy for natural gas generally has three objectives: enable competition, security of supply, and environmental sustainability. Natural gas regulations were not initially designed with the expectation of a static supply-demand equilibrium, but instead with knowledge that a mature, growing electricity market is increasingly dependent upon gas-based generation.

Countries have taken two different approaches to the unbundling of natural gas utilities. The simple approach requires a separate legal entity and the structural approach involves ownership unbundling. The UK and Portugal have adopted ownership unbundling, while France and Germany have employed lighter legal unbundling rules (Growitsch and Stronzik 2014). In the United States, most states have legal unbundling of distribution in the natural gas chain and transmission remains tied to distribution (Ascari 2011). The standard argument about ownership unbundling indicates that, because it leads to a large number of independent producers, market discrimination is unlikely, while higher transaction costs could lead to a loss of economics of scope and lower efficiency. It may lead to forestalled investment and therefore security issues (Brandão et al. 2016). Recent research on the European Internal Energy Market have found that liberalisation of natural gas markets has produced only negligible reduction in wholesale and retail gas prices and that ownership unbundling had no impact on natural gas end-user prices (Growitsch and Stronzik 2014). Historically, gas suppliers, particularly outside the United States, hold long-term importing contracts, which are sometimes linked to oil pricing mechanisms, with take-or-pay clauses resulting in liberalisation policies for entry and market segmentation without benefits for consumers. In order to foster gas-to-gas competition, the development of liquid, transparent wholesale exchanges at market hubs is necessary to allow for development of short-term market transactions.

After the production segment liberalisation, regulation of the natural gas industry focused on pipeline transportation and distribution, segments that have monopolistic characteristics (Juris 1998). Although the market power of pipeline companies affects the transportation market, resale of transportation contracts introduces competition in this market and facilitates the efficient allocation of these contracts. In markets with transportation constraints, namely, gas importing countries such as Italy and Portugal, regulatory reforms have not helped foster competition. New investments are both subsidised and exempted from third-party access regulation for financial reasons, but importantly history has shown that a lack of ownership unbundling can negatively affect the incentive to invest (Cavaliere 2007).

Evidence has shown that during the deregulation of the electricity sector, liberalised coal generators benefited from lower costs as they were able to shop around for better coal prices. Natural gas-fired generators did not see a similar cost savings. Liberalised natural gas market trading already has liquid, transparent price signals that provide the best price availability to all wholesale buyers, such as natural gas-fired generators. Coal markets were at that time and continue today to be more opaque.

5 Electricity Market Liberalisation

Electricity market design aims to define rules and incentives that lead to an efficient functioning competitive market. For the past decade, market success has been achieved in OECD countries as wholesale pricing is near marginal cost. Power plants are more fuel efficient and system operators are able to optimally dispatch power plants to lower costs over larger geographic areas. Economists and policy makers use these and other factors to evaluate success and obstacles in electricity market unbundling: restructuring impact on wholesale competition, system operations, generation investment, retail competition, and environmental performance.

Competition in wholesale electricity markets can be described as somewhat competitive with mature systems around trading and price settlement. Wholesale prices in the UK, Australia, Norway (Nordpool), and, despite notable isolated failures of competition, US electricity markets (e.g. the Electricity Reliability Council of Texas (ERCOT) and the Pennsylvania, Jersey, and Maryland (PJM) Regional Transmission Operator (RTO)) are now reasonably competitive in the short run (Newberry 2002). A primary driver of this competitive performance has been the extent and magnitude of forward commitments, through contracts and vertical integration, between generation firms and retail providers.

California's market liberalisation experience (2000–2001) was an unquestioned failure and most of the original initiatives were ultimately reversed (Carmona et al. 2012). The debacle showed that poor market design and circular regulatory and political intervention produce unsatisfactory outcomes when generation capacity is tight, particularly if energy shortages are unexpected. California had both inadequate legal frameworks and inadequate production capacity. Illustrating the importance of forward commitments, utilities were prevented from establishing proper risk management programmes, all in the name of encouraging participation in short-term markets. Price caps intended to protect energy buyers from egregiousness behaviour actually resulted in energy delivery out of state during critical in-state shortages.

California Electricity Crisis (2000–2001)
California's first foray into liberalisation began in March 1998 with the launch of the wholesale power market along with consumer choice. Starting in 2000, the power exchange experienced high wholesale electricity settlement prices and intermittent power shortages. The three investor-owned utilities (PG&E, Socal Edison, SDG&E) began to have severe financial problems. By February 2001, after a series of rolling blackouts, the state government stepped in and purchased electricity on behalf of PG&E and Socal Edison, effectively ending market deregulation.

In order to support market growth and benefit from expected lower wholesale prices, utilities were not permitted to sign long-term contracts, instead were required to purchase electricity for end customers through the short-term power market exchange. This resulted in unhedged customer sales exposed to higher short-term price volatility. Chronic underinvestment in generation meant that supply did not keep pace with a robust, price inelastic, demand pattern in the years leading up to liberalisation. Imports from out of state were restricted in 2000 and 2001 due to very dry hydro conditions in the region. Complicating matters, electricity was being exported out of California to realise higher prices than in-state price cap limitations. State power shortage emergencies escalated through 2000, and there were thirty-eight Stage 3 levels in the first three months of 2001, which indicated that less than 1.5% reserve margin available and resulted in several rolling blackouts during the winter of 2001. Wholesale prices increased to price cap levels for prolonged periods, resulting in average daily prices of almost 400 USD/MWh in December 2000 compared to approximately 30 USD/MWh average in December 1999. Independent and out-of-state generators stopped selling to the three utilities from fear of non-payment. In order to stabilise the market, retail prices were reluctantly increased, which impacted end consumers. PG&E ultimately filed for bankruptcy in April 2001.

(Data sourced from US Energy Information Administration website, Subsequent Events California Energy Crisis Report)

The market for transmission and the market for energy are inherently intertwined in electricity system operations. The RTO should not be separated from the ISO or power pool (Hogan 1995). The ISO is responsible for grid stability through congestion management, balancing, ancillary services, and transmission usage. Integration of these functions with wholesale transmission leads to market success. The market has not facilitated transmission investment (De La Torre et al. 2008). This is in part because forward-looking congestion rents are an inadequate means of cost recovery for lumpy transmission investments. Efficient new transmission lines often eliminate the congestion rents that would otherwise motivate the investment. One way regulators can create market mechanisms to value transmission is to provide financial transmission rights (FTR) contracts. It is difficult to forecast future value of FTRs over long periods because of the challenges in accounting for changes to the generation resources and transmission system over time.

The attention to system reliability is not necessarily at odds with increasing competition and the improved economic efficiency it brings to wholesale power markets. Reliability and economic efficiency can be compatible if regulators, policy makers, and industry leaders work together to strengthen and maintain the institutions and rules that will protect these goals. In recent years, efforts at the grid level have largely been focused on dealing with issues such as renewable intermittency, congestion, load shifting, and bidirectional flow in distribution networks. In the future, technological innovation at the grid edge will facilitate the development of markets for distributed resources, service-oriented business models, and active distribution grid management (IRENA 2019). Regulators should emphasise investment incentives and innovation, not short-run operational efficiencies.

Generation investment from private sources has been robust for renewable energies where a subsidy mechanism is present. Growth in thermal dispatch generation has limited success because forward energy markets do not provide profitable price signals to entice investment and construction. Capacity markets in the long term are still uncertain as revenues from short-term energy and ancillary service markets have, most of the time, been insufficient to recover the full average cost of power plant construction and operations. The day-ahead, intra-day, and occasionally the forward market show negative prices because of production and transmission congestion dynamics. While negative prices accelerate system operations quickly in order to realign supply-demand equilibrium in the generation stack, in the long run they do not aid generation investment analysis.

While wholesale markets have clearly benefited from unbundling, retail electricity prices have remained static, or in many cases have increased, due to higher costs to support renewable energy development and integration. Retail electricity prices are more tightly linked to natural gas wholesale prices in regions that have restructured generation away from monopoly frameworks. Residential customers exhibit choice frictions, leaving most residential customers purchasing energy from distribution providers of last resort.

Emission cap-and-trade programmes are most effective when combined with competitive electricity markets. Well-connected wholesale markets have the potential to exacerbate the potential of pollution leakage in settings where pollution regulations only apply to a subset of the generators in the market. Regulated utilities and independent power producer (IPPs) respond to pollution cap-and-trade programmes differently; regulated firms invest in capital-intensive abatement technologies, while IPPs pursue lower cost abatement options. The European Union Emission Trading Scheme launched in January 2005 is preparing to enter the fourth phase, in January 2021, representing further reductions to industrial emission levels. This programme experienced growing pains, including market theft, tax evasion, and lack of coordination by member states (Stern 2009). Another example of an environmental regulation cap-and-trade programme using tradable permits was the successful reduction of SO_x and NO_x levels from coal-fired generation plants in the Los Angeles basin during the 1990s.

Electricity market manipulation enforcement actions have moved from the conventional analysis of generator market power abuse in day-ahead and real-time physical markets to material allegations of sustained cross-product price manipulation in forward financial markets. Electricity forwards and associated derivative product pricing with complex embedded optionality, occasionally with limited market transparency, and high expected implied volatility term structures, are challenging to price. Therefore, it is difficult to develop and apply forward market analytical frameworks and models for comparison to market price action. States have begun to use an adaptation of cross-product manipulation models from cash-settled financial markets, which provides a real demonstration under uncertainty and asymmetric information (Prete et al. 2019).

6 Unbundling Markets in Developing Countries

The foremost objective of governments of developing countries in utility reform differs from that of governments of developed countries. While the latter focus on improving existing energy structure efficiencies, developing countries have insufficient public funding to address high growth demand and weak infrastructure and, therefore, chronic supply shortages. Financing of energy infrastructure investment can, then, be considered fundamentally a macroeconomic problem. As a result, reforms prioritise the attraction of investment for generation capacity expansion. One financial implication of this is that funding through external capital channels by means of loans or debt adds to the country's foreign liabilities and complicates its debt management. Consequently, in developing countries, motivation for privatisation has been driven to expand central systems, develop decentralised solutions for remote populations, and choose an energy growth trajectory that avoids the fossil fuel trap. Public-private partnerships (PPPs) that include development banks and institutional investors are not unusual in project financing. Such arrangements place development banks, which are local and regional in nature, on a participating partnership footing with a proactive agency role as initiators and coordinators (Arezki et al. 2017).

Selecting and applying the most appropriate institutional framework of regulation is a major challenge for developing and transition economies. Developing countries tend to take a stepwise approach to unbundling in order to determine foreign investor interest at each stage of change. With little financial support or expected private investment, countries such as Vietnam, Thailand, and Malaysia have been reluctant to open a full liberalisation process, instead maintaining unbundled generation model paradigm with IPP participation (Hall and Nguyen 2017). Brazil and the Philippines are the only developing countries that have followed the liberalisation process through from unbundling generation to the creation of a retail market with strong and ongoing government regulatory direction (Santiago and Roxas 2010).

Countries with limited regulatory capacity rely on multisector agencies that consolidate scarce regulatory resources (Estache 1997). Suboptimal energy network services can impede growth. This raises the question as to whether an unregulated private monopoly will make the investments necessary to offer the quality of service appropriate to a country's changing needs over time. Implementation of regulatory reforms must occur upfront and prior to privatisation and should be as unambiguous as possible to ensure optimal transparency. History has shown that investor response is stronger under government guarantees. Establishing strong rules securitised in law can open channels of foreign investment for governments with low creditability and an inadequate track records, which is common in countries in sub-Sahara Africa. This can provide stability for foreign investors, although it compromises regulatory flexibility to fine-tune market support mechanisms.

Developing countries struggle to provide the regulator the independence that domestic and foreign investors seek. Most struggle with weak regulatory institutions and changing government ideology. In actual practice, they have little ability to ensure independence of the energy regulator. Hungary's experience highlights the problems that arise when regulatory agencies change the rules or renege on pre-privatisation promises that guaranteed foreigners fixed real return on investments (Slay and Capelik 1998).

Latin America does provide liberalisation and privatisation success stories. Chile was the first to reorganise its electricity market, embarking on deregulation and privatising its national power system in the early 1980s. It focused, first, on vertical unbundling of the electricity supply chain. Cross-ownership and conflicts of interest initially hindered the development of a more competitive generation market. However, its well-designed regulatory structure that included power generation paid on a cost-based formula, unit dispatch order based on marginal costs, a power trading system between generators to manage customer contracts, and separation of large customers to allow them to freely transact in the wholesale market produced success. Transmission and distribution systems were maintained as monopoly entities with regulated price cap mechanisms. Government regulators were hands-on at the right times, supporting construction of critical interconnectors between the thermal-based generation region in the north and the renewable energy-dominated south region, to support energy transition (Pollitt 2008). Chile also avoided any significant changes in government policy over an extended period of time, and this allowed the market to stabilise and mature (Pollitt 2004). Argentina and Columbia liberalised their markets soon after Chile did, fragmenting generation capacity into many companies, allowing for divestitures and inflow of international capital, to alleviate stress on the governments' financing of outstanding debt (Joskow 1998; Lalor and García 1996).

Brazil, the Philippines, and South Africa have not fared as well. Energy crises in these countries have resulted in frequent brownouts or blackouts due to unanticipated demand growth, and a failure to meet that demand indicated a lack of effective regulatory oversight, forecast planning, and lack of incentives for public or private sector expansion of capacity. In South Africa, the regulatory framework failed to motivate private sector participation (Castellano et al. 2015). In South Africa, as in California, market deregulation of the vertically integrated system led to a market failure and energy crisis, in this case in 2008. Regulators took a stepwise approach to deregulation which resulted in a miscalculation of the structure and size of the market.

India witnessed failure of market development coordination between national- and state-level natural gas and electricity sectors. In keeping with the global trend shifting from coal to natural gas thermal systems, India has experienced strong growth in natural gas-fired generation and hence demand for the natural gas commodity. The market structure for natural gas did not develop at a parallel speed with expected electricity generation demand, resulting in a shortage of natural gas for power generation. With the expected arrival of further natural gas pipeline capacity set for several years from now, many investors have reclassified generation plants as stranded assets. Regulators did not understand that liquefied natural gas, which is traded in a global market, would not be suitable for the country's power generators due to the delivery cost structures (Worrall et al. 2018). This case highlights the importance of harmonised interaction between policy and regulations of the intertwined natural gas and electricity markets.

Africa as a continent is only beginning to liberalise. Several countries are pursuing the creation of renewable technologies connected to localised, rather than centralised grids to obtain high electrification rates (Clark et al. 2017). Fee-for-service methods of financing decentralised supplies rest on business models where local agents, operating concessions granted by a central authority, supply installations and maintenance and recover costs from subsidies and fee-for-service customer payments. Since the long-run financial sustainability of this model is not yet known, it is too early to say that it can be successful and have a significant positive impact on electrification rates. Botswana recently opened its market to private generation investment, while the incumbent utility remains a vertically integrated monopoly. It and other countries in Africa may move directly to an agile energy system.

As a group, few developing economies have functioning energy markets. Those that do have both government capacity and policy conviction. Unbundling of state-owned enterprises with an eye to privatisation has resulted in improved system performance, but a lack of planning for competitive markets remains (Sen et al. 2016). In fact, energy sector liberalisation and market design in developing economies have largely failed over the last fifteen years. Most rural populations in developing countries remain without electrification (Marandu et al. 2010). While the push to liberalise energy sectors continues in policy discussions, many countries are not moving forward with unbundling and liberalisation, as they have seen the developed world's struggles and minimal success.

7 Energy Market Transition and Innovation

The process of globalisation which integrates world economies into a single system has supported environmental and climate change regulation of the energy industry. Two of the United Nations Sustainability Development Goals make direct reference to energy: access to clean energy sources for all populations and energy sector initiatives to further drive low-carbon development investment. The 2015 UN Climate Change conference, held in Paris, was the inflection point for nations agreeing on targets to reduce carbon intensity in support of climate change directives. Government support via research investment and incentive programmes, such as subsidies or tax benefits for renewable energy technology development, had started to pay off. We are now in the midst of an accelerating energy transition. Public policies to encourage the development and adoption of renewable energy technologies are essential, because low-carbon performance is not visible to most consumers and carbon is not priced in the broader global market. A wide range of factors, including volatile fossil fuel costs, falling renewable energy capital costs, energy security, climate change mitigation, and the avoidance of externalities attributed to fossil fuel energy, drive the trend to renewables. Governments spend relatively modest amounts on renewable energy research, compared to other government-sponsored programmes, but these government incentives are essential for continued market growth.

Renewable energy growth is a policy and regulatory success story that does not necessarily require unbundling of incumbent utilities or the presence of a retail or wholesale market structure. Policy which focuses on renewable energy has led to an increase in IPP investment. This growth has directly correlated to availability of government subsidies, such as feed-in tariffs or guaranteed long-term power purchase agreements (PPAs), not a competitive market sending price signals to encourage new renewable generation investment. If a country or region cannot liberalise its market, it can employ competitive bidding for supplying renewable generation resources under PPAs in an auction. This adds important renewable resources to the network, but there is little price competition in the wholesale market afterwards. This pattern is changing as the levelised cost of wind and solar technologies has decreased. Policy makers and regulators are encouraging private investors to take the wholesale market price risk, which may make it difficult to secure financing, as there is no guaranteed fixed-price revenue stream. Institutional investor participation in low-carbon energy projects may increase their attractiveness to a growing class of potential savers who value environmental benefits and act as a hedge against the climate change risk, such as stranded fossil fuel assets to which other investments in their portfolio may be exposed (Shishlov et al. 2016).

Regulatory structures in place today were designed for the initiation of market unbundling and liberalisation, an era characterised by centralised resources, unidirectional power flows, and inelastic price demand. The transition to an increasingly higher percentage of renewable resources in the generation stack, combined with a recent emergence of distributed energy resources (DERs), is challenging the status quo of today's regulatory market structure. In the longer term, it is important that the measures introduced to encourage low-carbon investment are flexible enough to accommodate future market changes and new technologies. In light of the decentralisation of the power sector, regulators and policy makers must be technology agnostic and carefully reconsider how industry structures at the distribution level affect system planning, coordination, and operation as well as competition, market development, and cost efficiency.

The speed of energy technology innovation is only just coming to light as long-term historical data sets become available. The support of renewable energies through regulatory incentives over the past two decades has proven successful in reducing carbon intensity of energy portfolios. The growth of modern renewable energies, which include wind, solar, geothermal, and modern biofuel technologies, has increased global renewable electricity supply from 18% in 2000 to 26% in 2018, according to the International Energy Agency. In tandem with the positive news on renewable energy growth, the unique properties of variable generation bring new benefits to the system in addition to new challenges. There is concern that intermittent energy delivery, which contributes to increased market clearing price volatility, has created obstacles for efficient market operations. Most modern wind and solar photovoltaic plants have fast and precise control capability, typically exceeding that of most thermal generators (Milligan and Kirby 2010). These additional benefits of variable generation may not be accessible under existing market rules, but suitable adjustment of market designs could make it possible for generators and system operators to harness these benefits.

Lower wholesale prices of electricity have been routinely observed due to structural changes of supply with the low operating costs of primarily wind power. These lower wholesale prices are not translating into lower pricing for the retail end consumers. Subsidies are the most likely reason the price of retail electricity has risen, as the percentage of wind and solar generation has increased. There are two reasons for this retail price dynamic. First, there is often a gap between the feed-in tariff rate and the market-clearing price, such that the renewable generator receives a higher price than the market-clearing level. Second, electricity distributors are purchasing renewable electricity at a high price via direct long-term contracts under mandatory portfolio standard programmes. Renewable portfolio standard (RPS) programmes are largest and perhaps the most popular climate policy in the United States. Between 2009 and 2019, renewables' share from RPS programmes increased by 4.2%, such that the energy component of unbundled retail pricing increased by 17% (Greenstone et al. 2019). These cost estimates significantly exceed the marginal operational costs of renewables and likely reflect costs that renewables impose on the generation system, including those associated with their intermittency, higher transmission costs, and any stranded asset costs assigned to ratepayers.

Interestingly, the price of coal- and natural gas-derived electricity, ceteris paribus, has risen during low-production periods for renewables. This situation has been observed in both the United States and Europe, and more recently in the UK, and appears because fossil fuel generators have seen a reduction in revenue opportunities. Bid prices to cover variable costs and an attempt to cover some portion of fixed costs have arisen to match the change in plant operating dynamics (Greenstone et al. 2019). In some countries, Germany in particular, taxes and retail costs to support renewable energy have increased substantially (Morey and Kirsch 2014).

Transforming an electricity grid to a cleaner, smarter, and more flexible system means capturing the value from resources at the distribution edge of the network. DERs are directly connected to low- or medium-voltage distribution systems. They include both distributed generation units (e.g. fuel cells, micro-turbines, and small-scale photovoltaic) and storage units (such as batteries and electric vehicles; Akorede et al. 2010). Building regulatory models to accommodate higher levels of renewable energy means DERs must be able to seamlessly integrate with utility-scale resources and wholesale markets. Policy makers and regulators face a complex challenge to price DERs (the current approach is net metering) and incorporate them into multi-party market transactions. The implications of DER ownership and aggregation in the market competition model are complex. Market mechanisms for coordinating vertically and horizontally disaggregated participants require updating and improving distribution-level price signals. Electricity tariff structures need to evolve to capture marginal costs and benefits of DER participants to the end consumers.

Energy regulators must take into consideration the fast-changing combination of different forms of energy, which are increasingly derived from low-carbon sources, on diverse scales and from distinct business models. Proper incentives via effective regulatory frameworks to measure progress towards low-carbon goals will be required, so that analysts and policy makers can identify top-performing technologies and policies. In this way, the carbon intensity of technologies can be compared and evaluated against performance targets, depending on particular global or regional concerns such as emissions. Energy regulation is entering uncharted territory with the new requirements for data privacy and security as demand management programmes, such as smart grids, are disseminated.

8 Conclusion

Technology failures, short-lived market participants, and imperfect policy choices with misalignment of regulatory instruments have complicated energy transformations throughout history. There have been successes with unbundling of energy utility monopolies, which included active investor participation, maturing of wholesale markets with a tendency to lower prices, and high level growth in renewable energy.

There remain several challenges for study and improvement. So far, benefit to the retail consumer has been elusive. Large energy consumers can access lower prices through wholesale market participation, but retail consumers' energy bills continue to climb. While the arrival of renewable energies to the electricity grid has been lauded, system operation finds managing grid stability challenging with large swings in intermittent energy availability. Approaches to wholesale price formation and short-term system optimisation that the industry have employed for the past two decades appear unsustainable beyond the next decade. Emerging market countries continue to struggle with access to the private capital needed to succeed in market liberalisation and the ability to increase consumer access to energy services.

Regulation requires robustness to manage complications that arise from changes in market structure, such as the potential shift from the utility, as the traditional supplier of last resort model. The challenge is to establish a stable and politically sustainable regulatory toolbox that would combine the efficient benefits of competition, taking into account management of risks and the necessary sustained investment. Regulators must be actively engaged in all aspects of the market via monitoring progress to ensure regulatory design of market structure remains relevant and acts efficiently by taking a greater role in risk monitoring to avoid market manipulation.

Governments need to recognise the explosion in low-carbon energy technology development and support initiatives with targeted programmes. Should the current momentum with renewables continue, it may well be enough to establish serious in-roads with decarbonising global energy supply within the timelines of the UN sustainable development goals.

References

Akorede MF, Hizam H and Pouresmaeil E (2010) Distributed energy resources and benefits to the environment. *Renewable and Sustainable Energy Reviews* 14: 724–734.

Arezki R, Bolton P, Peters S, Samama F and Stiglitz J (2017) From global savings glut to financing infrastructure. *Economic Policy* 32: 221–261.

Ascari S (2011) An American model for the EU gas market? Working Paper, EUI RSCAS, 2011/39, Florence School of Regulation.

Bazilian M, Hobbs BF, Blyth W, MacGill I and Howells M (2011). Interactions between energy security and climate change: A focus on developing countries. *Energy Policy* 39: 3750–3756.

Belloc F and Nicita A (2011) Liberalization-privatization paths: Policies and politics. Report, Università di Siena.

Brandão A, Pinho J, Resende J, Sarmento P and Soares I (2016) Welfare effects of unbundling under different regulatory regimes in natural gas markets. *Portuguese Economic Journal* 15: 99–127.

Carmona R, Coulon M and Schwarz D (2012) The valuation of clean spread options: Linking electricity, emissions and fuels. *Quantitative Finance* 12: 1951–1965.

Castellano A, Kendall A, Nikomarov M and Swemmer T (2015) Brighter Africa: The growth potential of the sub-Saharan electricity sector. Report, Infrastructure Consortium for Africa.

Cavaliere A (2007) The liberalization of natural gas markets: Regulatory reform and competition failures in Italy. Report, Oxford Institute for Energy Studies.

Chang CP and Berdiev AN (2011) The political economy of energy regulation in OECD countries. *Energy Economics* 33: 816–825.

Clark WW II, Zipkin T, Bobo S and Rong M (2017). Global Changes in Energy Systems: Central Power and On-Site Distributed. Agile Energy Systems: Global Distributed On-Site and Central Grid Power 61.

De La Torre S, Conejo AJ and Contreras J (2008) Transmission expansion planning in electricity markets. *IEEE Transactions on Power Systems* 23: 238–248.

Estache A (1997) *Designing Regulatory Institutions for Infrastructure: Lessons from Argentina*. Washington, DC: World Bank.

Gonenc R, Maher M and Nicoletti G (2000) The implementation and the effects of regulatory reform: Past experience and current issues. *SSRN Electronic Journal* 2001(1): 3–3.

Greenstone M, McDowell R and Nath I (2019) Do renewable portfolio standards deliver? University of Chicago, Becker Friedman Institute for Economics Working Paper.

Growitsch C and Stronzik M (2014) Ownership unbundling of natural gas transmission networks: Empirical evidence. *Journal of Regulatory Economics* 46: 207–225.

Hall D and Nguyen TA (2017) Electricity liberalisation in developing countries. *Progress in Development Studies* 17: 99–115.

Hannesson R (2019) How much do European households pay for green energy? *Energy Policy* 131: 235–239.

Heffner G, Maurer L, Sarkar A and Wang X (2010) Minding the gap: World Bank's assistance to power shortage mitigation in the developing world. *Energy* 35: 1584–1591.

Hogan WW (1995) Electricity transmission and emerging competition. *Public Utilities Fortnightly* 133: 32–36.

IRENA (2019) Innovation landscape for a renewable-powered future: Solutions to integrate variable renewables. International Renewable Energy Agency, Abu Dhabi.

Joskow P (1998) Regulatory priorities for infrastructure sector reform in developing countries. Presented at the Annual World Bank Conference on Development Economics. Washington, DC. 20–21 April.

Juris A (1998) *The Emergence of Markets in the Natural Gas Industry*. Washington, DC: World Bank.

Lalor RP and García H (1996) Reshaping power markets-lessons from Chile and Argentina. *Public Policy for the Private Sector*. Note No. 85. Washington, DC: World Bank.

Marandu EE, Moeti N and Joseph H (2010). Predicting residential water conservation using the Theory of Reasoned Action. *Journal of Communication* 1: 87–100.

Milligan M and Kirby B (2010) *Market Characteristics for Efficient Integration of Variable Generation in the Western Interconnection*. Golden, CO: National Renewable Energy Lab.

Morey M and Kirsch L 2014. Germany's renewable energy experiment: A made-to-order catastrophe. *The Electricity Journal* 27(5): 6–20.

Nardi P (2012) Transmission network unbundling and grid investments: Evidence from the UCTE countries. *Utilities Policy* 23: 50–58.

Newberry DM (2002) *Privatization, Restructuring, and Regulation of Network Utilities.* Cambridge, MA: MIT Press.

Pollitt M (2004) Electricity reform in Chile: Lessons for developing countries. *Journal of Network Industries* 5: 221–262.

Pollitt M (2008) Electricity reform in Argentina: Lessons for developing countries. *Energy Economics* 30: 1536–1567.

Prete CL, Hogan WW, Liu B and Wang J (2019) Cross-product manipulation in electricity markets, microstructure models and asymmetric information. *Energy Journal* 40: 221–246.

Santiago A and Roxas F (2010) Understanding electricity market reforms and the case of Philippine deregulation. *Electricity Journal* 23: 48–57.

Sen A, Nepal R and Jamasb T (2016) *Reforming Electricity Reforms? Empirical Evidence from Asian Economies.* Oxford: Oxford Institute for Energy Studies.

Shishlov I, Morel R and Cochran I (2016) Beyond transparency: Unlocking the full potential of green bonds. Institute for Climate Economics Working Paper.

Sioshansi FP (2013) *Evolution of Global Electricity Markets: New Paradigms, New Challenges, New Approaches.* Cambridge, MA: Academic Press.

Slay B and Capelik V (1998) Natural monopoly regulation and competition policy in Russia. *Antitrust Bulletin* 43: 229–260.

Stavins RN (2010) Market-based environmental policies. In: Portney PR and Stavins RN (eds) *Public Policies for Environmental Protection.* Abingdon-on-Thames: Routledge, pp. 41–86.

Stern N (2009) Deciding our future in Copenhagen: Will the world rise to the challenge of climate change? Policy brief. Available at: www.lse.ac.uk/GranthamInstitute/wp-content/uploads/2014/02/PBStern_copenhagen_Dec09.pdf.

Ugur M (2007) Liberalisation of Network Industries in the European Union: Evidence on Market Integration and Performance. Available at: http://aei.pitt.edu/8053/.

Worrall L, Whitley S, Garg V, Krishnaswamy S and Beato C (2018) India's stranded assets: How government interventions are propping up coal power. Working Paper 538. London: Overseas Development Institute. Available at: https://www.odi.org/publications/11185-india-s-stranded-assets-how-government-interventions-are-propping-coal-power.

PART III

Global Energy Trends

CHAPTER 25

Macroeconomics of the Energy Transition

Giacomo Luciani

1 Introduction

Two conflicting narratives are frequently heard in connection with the economic impact of energy transitions. The first maintains that energy transitions are a great opportunity to revitalize economic growth and increase employment. The second, in contrast, estimates that objectives like reaching carbon neutrality by 2050, as pledged by the European Union, would be "too expensive." Which is right?

In the following pages, we attempt at disentangling the multiple contrasting interactions between economic conditions and energy transitions. It goes without saying that the net effect, resulting from the balance of such multiple contrasting interactions, is extremely difficult, or even impossible to predict. It will surely very much depend on the specific characteristics of the economy facing the need to decarbonize, notably its current energy system, rate of growth of energy demand, available energy resources, and opportunities for decarbonization. All of these parameters are extremely variable country by country. It will also greatly depend on the specific transition path pursued, and especially the intended speed of the transformation.

This chapter expands and modifies an earlier similar essay of mine entitled "The Impacts of the Energy Transition on Economic Growth and Income Distribution" (Luciani 2020); some passages are reproduced, but the thrust of the argument is completely different.

G. Luciani (✉)
SciencesPo—Paris School of International Affairs, Paris, France

Graduate Institute of International and Development Studies, Geneva, Switzerland
e-mail: giacomo.luciani@sciencespo.fr

M. Hafner, G. Luciani (eds.), *The Palgrave Handbook of International Energy Economics*, https://doi.org/10.1007/978-3-030-86884-0_25

2 Energy: In Transition

Energy, its qualitative characteristics and relative cost, is very closely interrelated with the economy:

- Energy availability is a condition for economic growth (quantitative expansion) and development (qualitative evolution).
- Technological progress opens up new sources or opportunities to harness energy; and the availability of energy in new forms allows for further new technology development and uptake.
- Economic growth and development, in turn, are the main determinants of the volume and quality of energy demand.

The energy industry entered in a phase of constant evolution and permanent transition already at the beginning of the nineteenth century, in parallel with the industrial revolution; we have witnessed an "energy permanent revolution" ever since.

Until recently, this permanent revolution has been driven mainly by market forces. New sources/forms of energy grew in importance because they were cheaper or more convenient or both. Yet, older sources of energy, while accounting for a progressively diminishing share of a rapidly growing total primary energy demand, were not abandoned—indeed they hardly declined in absolute terms at all.

Major changes in relative prices, and/or in the composition of final demand, did impact the total demand for energy as well as the demand from specific energy sources (e.g., mobility drove the demand for oil; appliances and electronics drove the demand for electricity). The increase of oil prices in the 1970s did create a discontinuity in the trend of oil demand, which slowed down markedly thereafter (e.g., losing the power generation market almost completely).

Demand for immaterial services has gradually gained importance in the composition of gross national product (GNP) over material goods from agriculture or industry. It is often assumed that services are less energy intensive than material products, although this is not necessarily the case (e.g., financial or information services and/or international travel and tourism can be highly energy intensive). In addition, technological progress has to some extent also allowed for more energy-efficient production of material goods. In consequence, the elasticity of energy demand relative to GDP growth has been declining and is below 1 (meaning that for a given percentage increase in GDP, energy demand will register a smaller increase). Yet, in a crucially important list of energy-intensive industries (chemicals, metals, glass, paper, cement, etc.) energy efficiency has not improved very much. In some industries/services, energy intensity has even tended to increase, for example, in agriculture and in the retail trade of food products (chilling, packaging, etc.). It is therefore not possible to conclude with certainty that the elasticity of energy demand relative to GDP is bound to decline further: it depends on the nature of future technology and composition of future demand.

In discussing the economic impact of the energy transition, we need to keep the other side of the coin, that is, the impact of economic "transitions" on energy, in mind. Demographic, health, financial, political, and security developments can massively impact the demand for energy, either directly or indirectly through economic growth (or lack of it). The COVID-19 crisis has been a very clear illustration of how exogenous shocks (in this case health-related) can impact the economy and the energy industry very profoundly.

Vice-versa, since the invention of the steam engine, energy developments never were the cause of a major economic crisis. Rather, it is arguably the case that historically the abundant availability of cheap energy greatly facilitated the extended period of rapid growth that began after the Second World War—and may have ended in the first decade of the current century. The impact of other factors on economic growth has been much more important and in turn has conditioned the evolution of the energy landscape. If we conceive of economic growth as a bounded optimization exercise, energy very rarely was an active boundary responsible for limiting growth. It did so only occasionally and for very short periods of time.

The need for a new, different phase in the process of continuous energy evolution is directly related to the impact that the use of fossil fuels has had on the concentration of greenhouse gases (GHGs) in the atmosphere, and the consequent warming of global climate. The assertion that there must be an energy transition is, per se, nothing more than an extrapolation of existing trends, because energy has been in a transition for the past two hundred years. What is new is the belief that we face a market failure: the market does not take into account the cost of global warming, therefore a continuing energy transition based purely on spontaneous market forces would be heading in the wrong direction. We must intervene to change this course, and somehow interfere with market forces to drive down emissions, and at a rapid pace. The pace is important, because there is considerable inertia in energy structures: most installations are expected to have economic lives of several decades, and turnover is slow.

What is new is not the fact that we are in an energy transition. What is new is the conviction that the transition must now be guided by policies aimed at remedying a market failure.

3 Imposing a Price on Carbon

Global warming is a market failure due to the fact that the cost of emitting CO_2 and other greenhouse gases (GHGs) into the atmosphere is not borne by the emitter (Nordhaus 2013). No one has to pay for using the atmosphere, and rules for preventing corporations and individuals from emitting pollutants are mostly concerned with local or, at most, national atmospheric conditions.

Until very recently, the emission of GHGs has not involved a cost for the emitter, thus creating a negative externality.

This interpretation assumes that in the absence of a cost for emissions, carbon-intensive technologies will be more attractive than clean alternatives. According to a point of view which is more and more frequently expressed, some clean alternatives—notably non dispatchable renewables—are becoming cheaper and cheaper, and soon will be, or are already, competitive with, or even absolutely preferable to carbon-intensive technologies, even in the absence of the imposition of a cost for emissions. These expectations mostly do not account for systemic costs arising from growing penetration of non-dispatchable renewables beyond a certain threshold (variously estimated at 35–50%). But even ignoring the issue of systemic costs, if it is verified that clean sources become cheaper than fossil ones, the market would be vindicated, and policies to promote clean technologies would not be needed, because the latter would prevail out of their own greater competitiveness. At most, the energy transition might be a matter of speeding up (at a cost) a process that is taking place anyhow.

Internalizing the cost of emissions requires that a price be imposed on them, subjecting emitters to a carbon tax or the obligation to buy emission allowances from an emission trading system (ETS). By definition, the emergence of a new cost associated with the production of goods reduces the value added which the economy generates. Other things being equal, the new cost increases the total cost of production. As energy enters in the production of all goods, this means that all productive activities will be faced with an increase in production costs—the energy-intensive ones more so.

What happens next depends on the market power of producers: if they have market power and can pass on the increased cost, they will be able to defend their value added. Given the wage bill, passing on the increased cost to sale prices may allow to defend the revenue accruing to capital. However, the subsequent increase in the general level of prices (inflation) erodes the purchasing power of salaries; in constant prices, salaries will be reduced. Therefore, even if producers have market power, some reduction of value added in constant prices seems inevitable.

If, on the other hand, producers have no market power and cannot pass the increased cost on to sale prices, the revenue accruing to capital is reduced. So, we cannot say for sure whether the decrease in value added will manifest itself through lower real wages or lower enterprise revenue, but in either case value added is decreased. As the definition of GDP is the sum total of value added generated in all activities in an economy, imposing a price on carbon decreases GDP.

Furthermore, imposing a price on carbon emissions will affect different industries differently, depending on their respective carbon intensity. The result will be a realignment of relative prices, with carbon-intensive goods becoming relatively more expensive. Value added will be more significantly reduced in carbon-intensive industries. If these lack market power (which might well be the case if they are exposed to international competition) then enterprise revenue may be significantly eroded and the very viability of the industry may be challenged. If the affected productive activities are closed down, GDP will be further negatively affected. At the same time, it is of course possible that other productive activities specifically functional to the reduction of carbon emissions may be able to increase their revenue and be encouraged to expand by growing demand for their products; but this is a successive development, requiring additional investment.

We conclude that a first, static effect of imposing a price on carbon is some decline of GDP.

It may be argued that the downsizing of GDP when the cost of carbon emissions is made explicit is the consequence of the failure of acknowledging this cost in earlier years, since the beginning of the industrial era. In this view, past estimates of GDP, that do not include externalities, are exaggerated, and the introduction of an explicit cost for carbon emissions is just a remedy to past miscalculation. Following this line of thinking, the World Bank has proposed a concept of adjusted national income, which estimates environmental depletion associated with value added generation, and not included as production cost; and corrects national income accordingly (Lange 2018). The weakness in this approach is the difficulty in estimating the negative value of environmental depletion, and the suggested approach has remained of specialist interest only.

The matter is further complicated by the time lag between damage to the environment and the emergence of the economic cost of such damage. We suffer today from emissions released by past generations over longer than a century; and future generations will suffer because of our emissions. The economic damage that emitting a ton of CO_2 today entails will only be visible in the future, and depends on how much CO_2 has been emitted in the past. Therefore, in fact we cannot internalize the externality by imputing as cost the present value of the future economic damage caused by an additional unit of emissions, because we have no precise idea of what this cost might be. We are, rather, imposing a price on carbon emissions in order to solicit a market response and achieve a reduction or elimination of emissions. This price then represents the opportunity value to the potential emitter of emitting one additional unit (ton of CO_2 or other): he will stop emitting only if the price is higher or equal to the benefit that he may derive from emitting one additional GHG unit.

An alternative way to look at a price for carbon is to consider the cost of abating or eliminating a given weight of CO_2 emissions. In other words, CO_2 emissions may still happen but may be captured and sequestered, or compensated by CO_2-absorbing activities at a cost. The target price for carbon should then be that which incentivizes enough CO_2-absorbing activities so that overall net emissions are zero.

The explicit addition of a previously hidden cost is the reason that most governments are reluctant to introduce carbon pricing, whether under the form of a carbon tax or of a price generated by an emission trading system. Governments frequently prefer to resort to regulation and administrative measures, whose cost is non transparent and not immediately predictable by those on whose shoulders it will fall. But some additional cost is created anyhow: it may manifest itself as a shift from a preferred technology to a less commercially attractive one, or as accelerated obsolescence of the existing capital stock, and will lead to a decline in value added, hence of GDP.

4 Carbon Prices Are a Tax

But how is a price imposed on carbon? It is out of acts of government introducing an emission trading system or a carbon tax (or a combination of the two). In one way or another, the imposition of a price for carbon emissions translates into revenue for the government, that is, higher taxation.

As any tax, a carbon price has an immediate recessionary effect. For this reason, it is rarely proposed without some form of compensatory measure, which can be either a parallel reduction of other taxes, or a parallel increase in expenditure. Historically, energy products have been taxed in many jurisdictions, at relative levels that mostly do not reflect the carbon content, but rather various social or policy considerations. Thus, for example, gasoline may be taxed more heavily than diesel, and the latter may be taxed more when used for road vehicles than when it is used in agriculture or fishing, or for heating homes. In contrast, in numerous countries energy products have been subsidized more or less indiscriminately, with negative consequences on the fiscal equilibrium of the respective states. Attempts at eliminating such subsidies have frequently led to protests and political instability, indicating how politically difficult it might be to impose a price on carbon.

If expenditure is increased in parallel with imposing a price on carbon, the recessionary effect can be compensated. In this case, we should note that not all expenditure is the same: investment expenditure has a higher multiplier effect than expenditure on consumption; and support to low-income households more likely translates into consumption rather than savings, thus again a higher multiplier effect than other forms of redistribution. Thus, if the imposition of a carbon price is fully compensated by an increase in expenditure focused specifically on supporting investment, the net result may be expansionary, especially if the volume of investment set in motion exceeds the government expenditure itself. If the revenue from the carbon price is destined to supporting the income of the poorer segments of the population the net effect may also be expansionary, because low-income households are less inclined to save. In contrast, if the revenue from imposing a price on carbon is not entirely spent, then some recessionary effect may be inevitable.

More broadly, the effect of the imposition of a price on carbon should be discussed in the context of the overall fiscal balance of the country in question. It may not be appropriate to tie specific expenditure to a specific source of revenue, although this is frequently done in the political debate. In the end what matters is the total fiscal position of the government, which may be expansionary or contractionary depending on circumstances and considerations that may be totally unrelated to the objective of imposing an explicit price on carbon.

It is therefore not a very sensible approach to discuss the *net* effect of imposing a price of carbon, because in the end whatever may be the net effect of this disposition narrowly defined, it will be compensated or exacerbated by the overall context of the country's fiscal policy.

5 Effects on the Destination of Income

Policies for decarbonization will also affect the allocation of income to investment as opposed to consumption. From this point of view, the needed outcome is a decline in consumption, and increase in investment.

All consumption of goods and services entails some demand for energy. Energy saving is unanimously identified as a key component of the necessary decarbonization process: we need to drive less, fly less, heat or air condition less, and so on. We may shift to more efficient machines (requiring additional investment) in order to maintain the same level of net service while reducing energy consumption (increasing energy efficiency), but very likely reduced net service is part of the deal.

At the same time, there is no progress possible toward decarbonization that does not require some form of investment. True, the energy sector always stood out as relatively capital intensive, meaning that investment would in any case be necessary to satisfy growing demand or improve efficiency, even if we were to continue with emitting GHGs into the atmosphere; however, the decarbonization agenda entails even higher investment.

If an economy is operating below full employment of its resources of labor and/or capital, measures aiming at supporting investment, in general or specifically targeted to clean energy and reduced emissions, may be expected to result in improved economic conditions. Any increase in expenditure, be it for consumption or investment, will generate an increase in income higher than the initial expenditure (Keynes's multiplier), but investment expenditure will have a higher multiplier than consumption because it helps bridging the gap between propensity to save and propensity to invest. The less than full employment equilibrium is caused by an excess of savings over investment: increasing investment will tend to eliminate this excess and fully absorb available savings. Energy transitions require large increases in investment, thus are commonly presented as being favorable to economic expansion.

However, this preliminary conclusion must be mitigated by consideration of the effect on the economy's average capital-output ratio as well as rate of capital obsolescence. Energy in general is a sector characterized by high capital intensity and capital/output ratios, but clean energy tends to be even more capital intensive (see text box). In all forms of clean energy—hydro, solar wind, and even nuclear—the bulk of the production cost is in the initial investment, direct costs are small, and marginal cost close to zero. Hence if investment in energy, and specifically in clean energy, increases as a share of total investment, the overall capital-output ratio of the economy may be expected to increase. The productivity of capital, which is the inverse of the capital-output ratio, will decrease.

The capital-output ratio governs the speed at which an economy can grow. Given the propensities to save and invest, a higher capital-output ratio means that the economy can only grow more slowly. This is simply because the total investment will generate a smaller increase in income in successive periods, hence also less growth in further investment. Of course, one can hypothesize that the propensities to save and invest will both increase, that is, that consumption will decrease, and more resources will be made available for investment. This assumption highlights how energy transitions are much more problematic in poorer countries, where the level of consumption is hardly compressible, than in richer ones—a point that will be further explored.

At the same time, the goal of abating GHG emissions will also accelerate the obsolescence of capital. Most energy-related capital equipment is characterized by long economic lives. Power plants, refineries, pipelines, transmission networks: these are all installations expected to last several decades. If we had the time to let an energy transition take place at a pace that does not force early retirement of existing productive capacities, accelerated obsolescence would not be a problem. But this is not the case: we know that existing installations, if allowed to continue in production without any remedial action, would exhaust the remaining carbon budget that we have if we want to achieve the objective of the Paris agreement (IEA 2020). Therefore, we need to speed up the process, and retire some productive capacity ahead of the end of its economic life, or engage in further investment to reduce the emissions that it generates.

In the first case, early retirement of "stranded" assets, new investment will largely simply substitute for retired capacity, and the net effect might be little or no capacity addition. In this case, marginal capital productivity would be zero. Another way to look at this is to refer to the distinction between gross and net fixed capital formation, of which only the latter is proper net investment. Accelerated obsolescence widens the gap between these two measures, reducing the importance of net over total investment.

Are Low-Carbon Sectors Less Capital and More Labor Intensive?

Some sources assert that low-carbon sectors are less capital and more labor intensive than high-carbon sectors. Thus, for example the IMF (2020) writes:

High-carbon sectors (such as fossil fuel energy and heavy manufacturing) are typically more capital intensive, whereas low-carbon sectors (such as renewable energy and many services) are more labor intensive. (page 92)

The expanding low-carbon sectors (renewables, services) are also less capital intensive than the contracting sectors (fossil fuel energy, manufacturing), further reducing demand for capital investment. (page 99)

(*continued*)

(continued)

A graph shows a very high "job multiplier" especially for solar photovoltaic, and a note explains "Each bar shows the total number of job-years generated per gigawatt-hour of capacity. This includes both direct and indirect jobs...." This is puzzling because capacity is measured in gigawatt rather than gigawatt-hour (which measures energy produced). It seems that jobs generated by the creation of capacity (the investment process) are conflated with jobs in production proper (the process of generating electricity from existing capacity). The latter are minimal, as demonstrated by the fact that renewables are normally characterized by zero marginal cost of production, the latter involving no added labor at all.

When this chapter asserts that renewable sources are highly capital intensive and have low capital-output ratios, reference is made to production proper. In other words, most of the cost is in the investment phase (the creation of capacity) and direct costs are minimal. That the investment phase may be labor intensive is another matter, unless we want to abolish the distinction between the creation of capital (i.e. capacity) and the output from it (electricity generated). This would be a very unusual approach.

All energy production is highly capital intensive relative to other sectors, but within the energy sector production of electricity from renewables is comparatively more capital intensive than its production from other sources, as well as of production of other forms of energy, such as fossil fuels.

In the second case—investment aiming at abating emissions from existing power plants—we may even encounter examples of investment projects that reduce net output, rather than increasing it. For example, retrofitting an existing coal power plant with carbon capture and sequestration may reduce the net output of electricity from the plant by 30-35%. If a high enough price for carbon is imposed, a project of this kind may earn a net positive return for the plant owners, but in material terms it would still be a destructive project—if we look at the primary goal of the plant itself, that is, making electricity available.

Or consider the expected transformation of the mobility industry from internal combustion to electric engines (whether alimented by batteries or fuel cells) or alternative fuels such as clean hydrogen: this requires huge investment on the part of the vehicle manufacturers for the introduction of new models; on the part of distributors or municipalities for the installation of recharging stations; and on the part of final consumers for buying new vehicles—and the end result is a mobility service which is somewhat more limited (because of range limitations or recharging times) or at most equivalent to what they enjoyed previously. Thus, statistically GDP may increase because changes in relative prices, taxes and subsidies, or regulation may create an economic incentive to achieve this transition, but the utility of the final consumer is not improved.

We conclude that in case of an economy that finds itself in an equilibrium of less than full employment of available resources an increase in investment driven by the objective of decarbonization may have an expansionary effect, but this is potentially less important than if investment were directed to sectors with a lower capital-output ratio, or if it were geared to add capacity rather than just replace existing capacity whose obsolescence is accelerated.

This takes us back to the difference between rich and poor countries. In the latter, investment is frequently limited by the lack of an investable surplus, that is, insufficient rather than redundant savings. In fact, these countries normally depend on finance from abroad to support their investment requirements. These are also frequently countries where energy supply falls short of demand: the lack of access to modern energy, especially electricity, is a potent obstacle to their economic growth; meaning that additional energy availability may have a much larger impact on productivity and growth, well beyond the increased output of energy itself. Furthermore, demand for energy is normally rapidly increasing, thus energy investment is more likely to be for adding capacity, rather than just in substitution of existing capacity made obsolescent ahead of time.

We conclude that clean energy investment is much more likely to have a positive impact on economic growth in emerging countries where the main obstacle to growth is the lack of investable surplus (and modern energy supply) than in advanced industrial countries. Furthermore, in the context of insufficient finance for clean energy projects, emerging countries may opt for more carbon-intensive but cheaper or more easily financed solutions.[1] Hence, we see clearly that the idea of turning decarbonization into a tool for promoting economic growth is best pursued by promoting clean energy projects in emerging countries, rather than in advanced industrial ones, where the net benefit may be more limited than sometimes proposed.

6 How to Encourage Investment?

The needed shift in the destination of income from consumption to investment is unlikely to be achieved easily. In our capitalist economies, investment is justified by the expectation of profit, which ultimately is supported by consumer demand. In the past half-century at least, economic growth has been driven by consumer spending and international trade. The latter has increased competition, lowered prices of consumer products, and opened wider markets to

[1] Both China and Japan have been criticized for offering cheap export finance to their national companies selling new coal-fired power plants in emerging countries. Large-scale hydro projects also attract export finance, but smaller, distributed solar and wind projects may be more difficult to fund.

producers, thus facilitating the introduction and success of new products. Looking ahead, it is likely that globalization will be at least partially reversed, and consumer spending must be compressed to allow for increased investment. In the context of the decarbonization drive, not just enterprises, also households are requested to invest more: in improving the energy efficiency of their homes and appliances, or buying new mobility tools (perhaps just an e-bike rather than a new electric car). This will leave less money available for other forms of consumption, and consumers may not be willing to accept the shift. In most cases, the time needed for recovering the initial investment on the part of households runs into several years or even decades, meaning that the required parallel decrease in consumption may be long-lasting.

Supporting investment in an economy facing slower consumption growth, or even decline, is a major policy challenge. It entails departing from consumerism, which has been the engine of modern capitalism. Shifts in relative prices such as would be brought about by the imposition of a hefty price on carbon may render investment in clean energy projects potentially profitable, but this is not enough to guarantee that private entrepreneurs will engage in them. The profitability of investment in clean energy solutions must be clearly established and consistently supported for investors to take the plunge.

Governments can encourage investment by limiting the risk for enterprises. This can be accomplished through availability of debt finance at low interest rates, through participation in the equity, through price/demand guarantees such as long-term purchase agreement or contracts for difference. All of the above are widely used instruments for supporting investment especially in the decarbonization of electricity. Then there are also subsidies for the purchase of specific products, such as electric cars, or tax rebates offered to enterprises and households that engage in decarbonization-related investment. In other words, the state must step in and devote resources in ways that may be more or less effective, but in all cases represent a departure from the prevailing liberal credo.

The task is to simultaneously increase the propensity to save (reduce consumption) and increase the propensity to invest even more, so as to move in the direction of fuller employment of resources. It is not clear that financial intermediaries may be able to deliver this major redirection of our economies. The active engagement of the state is needed, but it is limited by fiscal constraints. The state may need to reduce other expenditure or increase taxation to be able to pay for the added burden; only a relatively few governments are in a position to increase their debt, and doing so may push interest rates upwards, which would negatively affect capital-intensive projects.

Such considerations apply even more cogently if we move from the national to the global level. Globally, many investment opportunities in cleaner energy sources are to be found in countries with dubious or precarious governance, presenting a risk profile, which few investors are willing to underwrite. Global decarbonization ideally entails a massive shift of financial resources from the industrial to the emerging countries, because there demand for energy is growing faster, and the deployment of renewable energy sources would in many cases be easier.

7 Income Distribution

It is generally accepted that an increasing cost of energy has a regressive impact on income distribution, because energy expenditure is a larger share of the budget of poorer households. In addition, households are expected to invest to minimize the added cost, for example, in insulation of their homes or buying new electric vehicles, but the vast majority of households have no net savings and no borrowing power. Thus, richer households can contain the added cost by engaging in investment, but poorer citizens simply must bear the brunt of the decarbonization agenda.

In order to palliate the negative effect of higher energy cost brought about by charging a price on carbon, it has been proposed that the revenue from the latter measure should be returned to all citizens in equal installments (CLC 2019; EC 2019). In this way, the poor would receive more than the increase in their energy expenditure, that is, would be net beneficiaries; while the rich would be net contributors. This may certainly facilitate the popular acceptance of imposing a price on carbon, although similar proposals aimed at introducing some form of universal basic income have not found majority support where they have been put to the test of the electorate.

But there is a more systemic reason for expecting a deterioration in income distribution, and this is that the energy transition entails an increase in the capital/output ratio, which in turn automatically results in an increasing share of income accruing to capital, unless investors are ready to accept falling returns on industrial investment or lower interest rates on borrowed capital. We do live in a world of historically low interest rates, but this is creating multiple dislocations and is not accepted as normal in the longer run. Furthermore, there is no evidence that corporations are ready to accept lower returns: in fact, the opposite is true, as the perception of risk has widely increased, and in the energy industry the perspective of decarbonization further increases risk. Thus, the increase in the capital/output ratio associated with the energy transition may be expected to also determine (or require) a shift of income from labor to capital—that is, a widening of inequality in income and wealth distribution.

In this respect, the energy transition simply reinforces a trend that has been underway ever since the end of the Second World War (Piketty 2013). Thus, while we certainly cannot attribute exclusive responsibility for growing inequality to the energy transition, the fact that it adds to an unwelcome existing trend further complicates things. Yet, the simple idea of devoting the revenue from a higher price on carbon to the creation of some form of citizens' income is unlikely to be optimal. Why should the introduction of a citizens' income be funded in particular by the carbon tax? These two measures are logically separate and the only reason for coupling them is to facilitate the swallowing of the bitter pill—the carbon tax—with sugar coating—citizens' income. Furthermore, devoting the revenue from a carbon tax to redistribution, rather than in particular supporting investment functional to the transition, would reduce the effectiveness of the policy with respect to its environmental goal.

In perspective, the carbon tax has the ambition of eventually generating no revenue at all, when decarbonization will have succeeded; in other words, to the extent that the tax is successful, the revenue it generates will progressively shrink, and the citizens' income will need funding from other sources; the tax is therefore not an appropriate fiscal tool for addressing a problem (inequality) that will remain long after decarbonization has succeeded.

Rather, what is needed is acceptance of lower rates of return for industrial and financial investment—that is, as earlier indicated, an increase in the propensities to save and invest. But the transition from an economy driven by consumption and encouraging consumer debt, to an economy encouraging frugality and investment is not achieved easily.

8 Employment

Another effect commonly associated with accelerated decarbonization is employment creation. This expectation is commonly supported with estimates of the number of people potentially employed in the manufacturing and deployment of renewable energy systems. It is not difficult to see that this approach is highly simplistic, because it does not take into account the parallel potential destruction of employment in industries that will be negatively affected by the process. It is difficult to argue in abstract whether the net employment effect of the decarbonization drive will be positive or negative, as the conclusion depends on many circumstances and assumptions. It is nevertheless interesting to explore the implication and significance of the possibility that the net effect is in fact positive, that is, that more jobs are created than destroyed.

The point is that, although employment creation is a constant preoccupation for governments, labor is a cost, which enterprises strive to minimize. There is constant tension between increasing labor productivity and full employment: the former should be maximized, preferably with no detriment to the latter; but this is only possible if total production is growing in line with productivity. The energy transition is expected to lead to an increase in the capital/output ratio, that is, a decrease in the productivity of capital (output per unit of capital is the inverse of capital/output). Assuming that, other things being equal, employment will also grow for a given output is tantamount to saying that the productivity of labor (which is the ratio of output to employment, or output per worker) will also decrease. In other words, we are envisaging a decline in both the productivity of capital and of labor, that is, a poorer world.

This seeming paradox can be partly explained by noting that the production of decarbonized energy is capital intensive, but the manufacturing and installation of the fixed capital required may be labor intensive. In fact, most of the expected employment creation is not linked to the utilization of clean energy production capacity, but to the creation of it (see text box above). With respect to the improvement of energy efficiency, much of what needs to be done for buildings will translate into support to construction jobs. This may mean that the employment creation effect is purely temporary; if it is not, because of the need for frequent replacement or expanding capacity, then the previous conclusion remains valid, and the economy will record a decline of productivity of both capital and labor.

9 Conclusions

Although the economic implications of energy transitions very much depend on the specific circumstances of each economy, some broad generalizations are possible.

Firstly, internalizing the cost of emissions in order to address the market failure that generated the threat of climate change adds a cost to most production activities, which inevitably leads to some reduction of aggregate value added, that is, GDP.

Secondly, as a price for carbon is akin to a tax, it may have a recessionary or expansionary effect depending on the prevailing equilibrium in government finance in the country concerned. If it leads to less deficit spending, it will be recessionary. In this respect, a carbon price is not different from any other indirect tax.

Thirdly, clean energy solutions are almost invariably more capital intensive than those that the market would support in the absence of a price for carbon. Thus, mitigating climate change entails an increase in the average capital-output ratio in the economy, which in turn tends to slow down growth. To avoid this effect, it would be necessary to increase the propensity to invest given available savings; and if the economy does not suffer from excess savings, also increase the propensity to save and compress consumption accordingly.

Therefore, there is an intrinsic link between the clean energy agenda and the overcoming of the consumerist growth model that has prevailed for longer than half century. How a shift from this model toward an alternative model based on frugality and more investment can be obtained is not clear. It is a question that touches the respective roles of the state, the market and financial intermediaries, and may require important institutional and policy adaptation.

It is also to be expected that the increasing capital-output ratio will tend to shift income from labor to capital, and widen inequality. This can only be prevented if the expected return on capital is permanently lowered, which is possible, but has cascading effects on the stability of important financial institutions, as experienced in recent years because of negative interest rates.

Finally, while there may be a positive effect on employment, the reverse side of the coin is that labor productivity would decline, and this while the productivity of capital would also decline.

With respect to all of the above, the importance of the effect is crucially linked to the desired speed of the transformation. If transitions are allowed to stretch out in time and accommodate the high inertia of energy systems, the difficulty would be greatly reduced. But we increasingly are convinced that there is no time, and changes must take place within close deadlines.

Besides their sheer cost, which may be bearable, the challenge of energy transitions is in the required change in the growth model. Energy transitions are not the only development necessitating a change in the growth model: the aging of our societies and almost universal increase of capital-output ratios in most industries point to the same direction. The way in which the economics of energy transitions will play out will have much broader implications than for the energy industry alone.

Bibliography

CLC 2019 *Economists' Statement on Carbon Dividends* Wall Street Journal January 17.

EC 2019 *Commission Decision of 3.7.2019 on the proposed citizens' initiative entitled 'A price for carbon to fight climate change'* Brussels C (2019) 4973 final.

IEA 2020 *World Energy Outlook 2020* Paris.

IMF 2020 *World Economic Outlook: A Long and Difficult Ascent* Washington October.

Lange 2018 Glenn-Marie, Quentin Wodon and Kevin Carey eds. *The Changing Wealth of Nations 2018* World Bank Group, Washington DC.

Luciani 2020 Giacomo "The Impact of the Energy Transition on Economic Growth and Income Distribution" in Manfred Hafner and Simone Tagliapietra eds. *The Geopolitics of the Global Energy Transition, Springer,* Cham (Switzerland).

Nordhaus 2013 William *The Climate Casino* Yale University Press New York and London.

Piketty 2013 Thomas *Le capital au XXI siècle* Seuil Paris.

CHAPTER 26

Energy Demand Drivers

Bertrand Château

1 Introduction

Energy demand is usually associated with economic development (Gross Domestic Product per capita—GDP/cap) and energy prices. Climate, endowment in natural resources and geography explain differences in energy/cap between countries with similar GDP/cap and energy prices and differences in the dynamics of energy demand in relation to GDP. To better understand the drivers of energy demand and how they are connected to GDP and energy prices, this chapter first proposes an overview of the issue and then discusses in greater depth the critical aspects of energy demand in the three consuming macro-sectors: industry, transport and buildings. Finally, the determinants of increasing electrification are discussed.[1]

[1] All data used in this chapter come from Enerdata's databases (www.enerdata.net), which are constituted from many international sources, among which the most important for this chapter are: the International Energy Agency (AIE), the ODYSSEE project (European Union) and national sources.

The methodology and the scientific background of this chapter are taken from the research works carried out by the author on this subject since 1975. These are listed in the bibliography at the end of this chapter.

B. Château (✉)
Enerdata, Grenoble, France
e-mail: bcarcadia@wanadoo.fr

M. Hafner, G. Luciani (eds.), *The Palgrave Handbook of International Energy Economics*, https://doi.org/10.1007/978-3-030-86884-0_26

2 Assessing Energy Demand Drivers: Overview

2.1 Energy Demand: What Is Behind?[2]

Energy "demand" refers to the energy quantities that people are willing to purchase (or to pick-up for free in nature). In the countries with supply availability constraints, potential demand may be higher than actual consumption. In this case, energy consumption can increase for the sole reason that more energy is made available (e.g. through electrification). Energy demand results from the fulfilment of energy needs in a given energy prices context. But no one "needs" energy for itself, rather for the services that energy provides. The same service can be provided by different energy quantities, depending on equipment used: moving over one kilometre with a bicycle or a car does not require the same amount of energy. Therefore, the dynamics of the "need" for energy services can be different from that of the energy "demand," just because technology changes. To sum up, the drivers of energy demand are, first, the socio-economic drivers of the needs for energy services,[3] and, second, the technology drivers that convert these needs into energy demand.

This applies to final energy consumers, industries, buildings, transport modes, agriculture, and to standardized energy products elaborated and distributed by the energy sector (refineries, power plants, etc.). From a statistical viewpoint, this is captured by the "final energy consumption"[4] metric. In order to elaborate and distribute these energy products, the energy sector itself consumes various primary energy resources (crude oil, natural gas, uranium, wind power, solar power, hydropower, etc.); imports and exports of all kinds of standardized energy products; and uses/loses part of these products in the transformation/distribution process (electricity transport/distribution losses for instance). Statistically, this reality is captured by the "primary energy consumption" metric: consumption of primary resources plus imports minus exports. The more important the losses in the energy transformation/distribution sector, the bigger the gap between primary and final energy consumption. One of the main determinants of the difference between primary and final energy consumption is the share of electricity in final energy demand, and how this electricity is generated: thermal power plants burning fossil fuels or uranium experience high transformation losses, ranging from 50% to 70% of the primary energy input. Therefore, the drivers of primary energy demand include the composition of the electricity generation mix. In this chapter, we focus mostly on final energy demand drivers, and give a brief overview of the contribution of the electricity sector to primary energy demand.

[2] For methodology and further details, B. Château and B. Lapillonne (1977).

[3] For further development on "needs," B Château (2015).

[4] For all definitions and units used in energy statistics, and adopted in this chapter, see AIE (2011).

2.2 Time Issues

Energy demand drivers do not change over time at the same speed, and their relative contribution to the change of energy demand is very different whether we look at the short term (up to two years), the medium term (two to five years), the long term (up to 30 years) or the very long term beyond 30 years.

In the *short term*, all the drivers related to social change, structural change of the economy and technology change are almost constant, and their contribution to energy demand variations is negligible. On the contrary, cyclic climatic conditions, energy prices and GDP may change significantly, and cause significant variations in energy demand.

In the *medium term*, social changes remain almost negligible as regards energy demand. Same for average climatic conditions. Economic structures and the technology heritage are likely to change a little, but their impact on energy demand remains minor compared to that of economic growth (aggregate demand) and prices.

However, in the *long term*, everything is likely to change. Changes in average climatic conditions remain almost negligible compared to other forces affecting energy demand. Social changes may become significant, in particular in emerging countries. Changes in economic structures and technology background can be more and more dramatic as time flows, with increasingly severe impacts on energy demand, whatever the country. These impacts can become more important than those directly driven by economic growth or relative prices after 15 to 20 years.

In the *very long term*, changes in average climatic conditions may become not negligible, in particular if global warming keeps worsening. Progressively, social changes become the first driving force of energy demand, either directly (changes in needs) or through their impact on the overall economy. Technology change remains a key driving force, but is increasingly difficult to forecast, since it results at least partly from scientific discoveries in the future; only the part of today's technology heritage (buildings, transport infrastructures, machinery, etc.) that will still be there in the distant future, and new technologies that can emerge from today's scientific knowledge can be properly considered (Château and Alii 2002).

2.3 Role of Main Actors

Apart from those related to the physical and macro-economic environment, all the drivers of energy demand change over time according to decisions made by final consumers, either in their budget allocation or in their investment choices. These decisions depend obviously on the overall physical and macro-economic context, but also on incentives, regulations and equipment/technology offer, which frame the possibilities of choice.

Incentives are of two natures: psychological and economic. *Psychological incentives* are highly related to the cultural environment, and driven by two main forces: imitation and citizenship. Imitation is one of the strongest engines of consumerism, responsible for the spread of new consumer goods and services. Citizenship expresses the adequation, in anyone's decisions, to commonly shared global objectives (like reducing CO_2 emissions for instance) proposed by various actors (public authorities, NGOs, etc.). *Economic incentives* include taxes, subventions and tax reductions. They contribute to change the relative prices of equipment goods and energy carriers in order to orient the investment decisions of the final consumers.

Norms and regulations frame the technology background of a country and the technical characteristics of each particular piece of equipment (in particular its energy yield). Investment decisions made by final consumers are therefore conditioned by them. These are elaborated primarily at the national level, but increasingly also at the international level: European Union, OECD, UN.

The *technology/equipment offer* is in the hands of industrial producers. Because of international trade, scale economies in production and globalization, there has been a movement towards the harmonization of this offer worldwide, accompanied by concentration in the hands of few very large industrial producers. This means that this offer may become less and less dependent on the specific economic and industrial conditions of each individual country. The dynamics of the equipment/technology offer is driven first by RD & D, which is concentrated in a limited number of countries worldwide (USA, China, EU, etc.) and dominated by the political, socio-economic and industrial context and priorities of these few countries.

2.4 Social Forces and Behaviour

Individual needs drive directly the energy demand of households and workers in buildings, offices and factories; but also, indirectly, the energy demand for producing, transporting and delivering the goods and services required to satisfy these needs.

Social forces drive demographic changes within countries. Besides overall population growth (or decline), in emerging countries migration from traditional rural to urban areas also has an impact on energy demand.

Income distribution and behaviour are the main driving forces of change in the intensity of needs. All behavioural drivers are likely to change over time, because of global changes in cultural habits, or in the physical environment, or finally in the sensitivity to environmental or social issues (citizenship).

3 Energy Demand Drivers in Industry

Industry refers to the production of manufactured goods. From a final energy demand viewpoint, industrial energy demand does not include the energy transformation sector (from primary to final) nor small-scale producers, which are included in the commercial sector; it is limited to production facilities and does not include energy used for transporting products or for office buildings outside the factory.

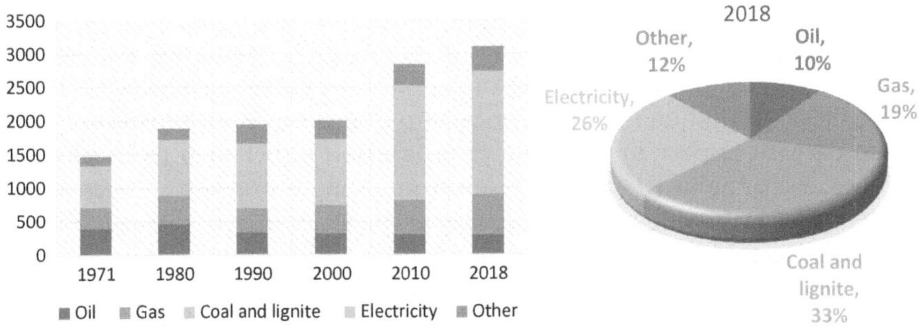

Fig. 26.1 World energy consumption of industry, by energy carrier, Mtoe. (Source: Own elaboration on www.enerdata.net)

3.1 Outlook of Energy Demand in Industry

At world level, industry consumes around 3100 Mtoe[5] (2018), that is, 31% of total final energy consumption. Industrial energy demand has roughly doubled over the last 50 years, and increased by 50% since 2000 (see Fig. 26.1).

Coal and lignite remain the main energy sources used in industry. Their share, which slowly decreased from 1971 to 2000 (from 28% down to 26%), has dramatically increased since then (reaching 33% in 2018). At the opposite extreme, the share of oil has fallen continuously, from 27% in 1971, down to 16% in 2000 and 10% in 2018. That of natural gas has kept increasing rather slowly, from 19% in 1971 to 21% in 2000 and 22% in 2020. Electricity is obviously the winner in the evolution of the energy mix of industry: 14% of the total consumption in 1971, 23% in 2000 and 26% in 2018. Such electrification of energy consumption in industry is mostly the result of its structural evolution towards higher value-added activities.

Altogether, the steel and the non-metallic minerals industries, which are very big coal consumers, account for 35% of the total energy consumption of world industry (2017), and this share keeps increasing since 1990 (28% in 1990, 30% in 2000). This explains the high and increasing coal share in the energy mix of the industrial sector. Together with the chemical industry, whose share is rather constant around at 16%, these energy-intensive industries account in 2017 for more than half of total energy consumption (51%). In the remaining 49%, mining and construction only account for 4%.

3.2 Overview of Energy Demand Drivers in Industry

The energy intensity (EI) of Gross Domestic Product (energy consumption per unit of value-added) is normally taken to capture the technology driver of the energy demand. From a purely technological viewpoint, it is final energy

[5] Mtoe: Million tons of oil equivalent. This is the current energy unit used in the energy balances and statistics. A ton of oil equivalent corresponds to 41.8 GJ. For more details see AIE (2011).

consumption per unit of physical output that drives energy demand. For thermal end-uses, this means the specific useful energy consumption per unit of physical output and the average performance of the energy products. Changes in specific consumption indeed contribute to changes in EI. But, because EI is measured with respect to the value of production rather than to its physical measure, a change in EI can also result from changes in relative prices, independently of technology. Thus, assessing technology drivers through EI can sometimes be misleading.

The other technology driver, the overall performance of energy products, is captured by the ratio between useful energy and final energy. This depends on the contribution of the various energy products to useful energy (energy mix) and their relative yields.

This brief outlook suggests separating the discussion of energy-intensive industries, for which the drivers can be related directly to physical outputs, from general manufacturing.

3.3 *Insights in Energy-Intensive Industries*

Energy-intensive industries (EII) are mostly engaged in primary transformation and their output are intermediate products. They are characterized by high demand of process energy, frequently low value-added per ton of output and high concentration of production in relatively few, large plants. Worldwide, EII account for the bulk of coal, lignite and petroleum coke consumed in industry (77% of coal and lignite, 100% of petroleum coke). The most important energy-intensive industries are crude steel, cement and lime, primary aluminium and other non-ferrous metals, paper and pulp, glass, petrochemicals, chlorine and nitrogen production. See Fig. 26.2.

At the level of each *individual factory*, physical output determines directly one part of energy demand, and production capacity drives the other part, related to the management of the factory. For instance, a glass factory must

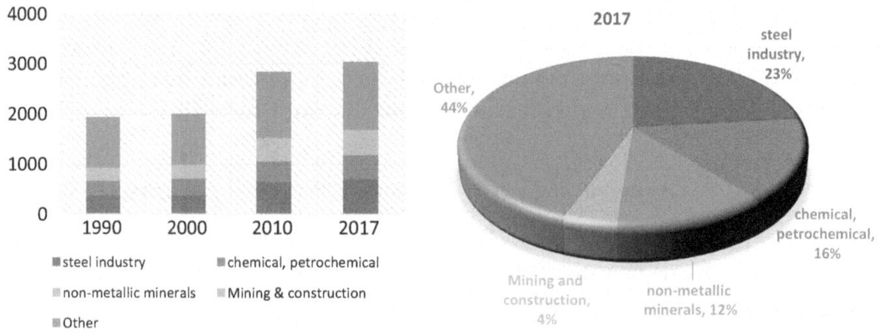

Fig. 26.2 Energy-intensive industries in final energy demand, world. (Source: Own elaboration on www.enerdata.net)

keep the furnaces at an appropriate temperature all the time, whatever the quantity of glass actually produced. The lower the capacity utilization of the factory, the higher the energy requirement per ton of output.

Intermediate products are relatively homogeneous as they must fit well-established parameters. It is therefore possible to aggregate physical production and load factors as energy demand drivers in a fairly meaningful way. Productions and prices of energy-intensive products in each country may be influenced by global competition, partly disconnecting value-added from physical output, and national production from national aggregate demand; hence the necessity to consider physical outputs.

For many products of EII, a limited number of production processes are available and used. In some cases, the production process requires a particular energy product also due to its chemical composition: for example coke in blast furnaces, naphtha in steam-cracking or petroleum coke in clinker furnaces.

The unit energy consumption (UEC) can change over time because of changes in the process energy performance or changes in the EII structure. In time, less efficient plants are replaced by more efficient ones,[6] driving a change in the average UEC of the whole EII. This structural movement is mostly driven by the obsolescence of existing plants and the speed of production growth. The level of obsolescence is the result of the industrial development history of the country. The speed of growth, as a driving force of UEC, shows interdependence between economic and technology drivers: competitiveness, which is a condition for production increase, is driven by energy performance (decrease in UEC), while production increase drives the change in UEC. This is illustrated in Fig. 26.3 for the steel industry.[7]

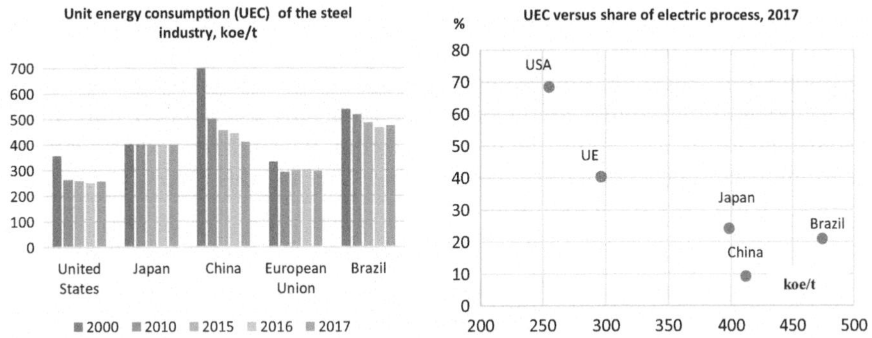

Fig. 26.3 Specific energy consumption of the steel industry according to time and processes. (Source: Own elaboration on www.enerdata.net)

[6] For details, see Château and Lapillonne (1982), Enerdata (2019a).
[7] Other examples can be found in Enerdata (2019b).

3.4 Insights in Other Sub-sectors

Physical outputs can still be aggregated for well-focussed homogeneous sub-sectors (automobiles, sugar, etc.). But in most cases, the remaining sub-sectors are rather heterogeneous, producing a large variety of different products, with very different energy demand per product. Physical outputs can no longer be aggregated, and energy demand must be assessed through value added and energy intensity (EI). Since they aggregate many different productions with rather different EIs, the overall EI of the sub-sector can change only because the relative weight of the various products changes, without any relation with technology.

In these sub-sectors, the share of energy in production costs is generally rather small. This explains why changes in energy prices have limited direct consequences on their energy demand.

3.5 Some Critical Issues

Globalization affects industrial production levels in all countries, by disconnecting industrial production from internal demand, also thanks to the greatly reduced cost of long-distance sea transport. Labour-intensive industries tend to locate where labour force is cheap, energy-intensive industries where energy is cheap and high value-added industries where highly skilled labour is available.

The industrial infrastructure heritage, in particular in energy-intensive industries, weighs heavily on energy demand in industry. When the investment cost in capacity development or in capacity renewal is very large, requiring a long period of time to be paid back, it is convenient to use existing plants as much as possible, in particular when they have already been amortized. This weakens significantly the impact of energy prices on new technology uptake.

At the same time, globalization increases competition worldwide, and accelerates the obsolescence of existing processes in operating factories, in particular in countries with higher production costs.

Energy efficiency and environment policies set up regulatory frameworks, incentives and economic instruments that frame the decisions of industrial companies, either to commit themselves to required standards and regulation, or to improve their competitiveness. In general terms, this drives downwards the energy intensity of all industries.

3.6 National Versus Global Vision of Energy Demand in Industry/Regional Issues

3.6.1 How Energy Consumption for Industry is Distributed Among World Regions?

Altogether, the industrialized countries of Europe, North America and CIS, which accounted for the bulk of the world energy consumption in the early 1970s (72% in 1971), now account for only 28% (2018). At the opposite

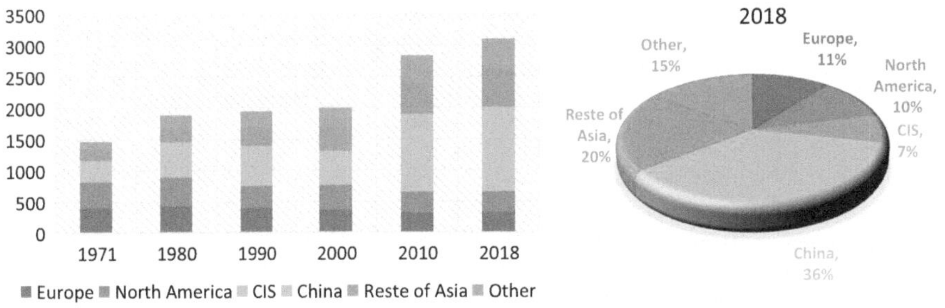

Fig. 26.4 World energy consumption of industry by regions, Mtoe. (Source: Own elaboration on www.enerdata.net)

extreme, the share of China more than doubled from 1971 to 2000 (from 8% to 17%), and again from 2000 to 2018 (up to 36%). The Asian continent accounts today for 56% of the world energy consumption in industry. This evolution is due first to the rapid economic growth of emerging countries (so-called BRICs), in particular in China, since the early 1980s; and, second, to the delocalization of many industries from the Western world to these emerging countries. See Fig. 26.4.

3.6.2 Energy Versus Industrial GDP and Share of Energy-Intensive Industries

When comparing the energy intensity of industry across regions/countries and time, the first observation is that the energy intensity of industry is globally inversely proportional to GDP/cap: the higher the GDP/cap, the lower the energy intensity of industry: this is true almost everywhere except in Middle East, where the petrochemical industry, which is highly energy intensive, developed rapidly during the last 20 years. This inverse relationship is due to the growing specialization in higher value-added industry in countries with high GDP/cap. Another reason is because, in most cases, the industry value-added grows with the extension of the value-chains towards higher value-added and less energy intense products. A last reason is because of the continuous progress in intelligence and information control and processing, which contributes to electrification of the energy demand and better energy performance of industry technology.

Nevertheless, for similarly low levels of GDP/cap, large discrepancies exist between countries, according to the weight of energy-intensive industries in energy consumption: 68% in China in 2018, 60% in the CIS, 47% in the rest of Asia. See Fig. 26.5.

The main discriminating factors among countries, when assessing energy demand drivers of industry, are the endowment in natural resources and the heritage in energy-intensive industries, in particular primary metals, primary chemicals, fertilizers or paper and pulp.

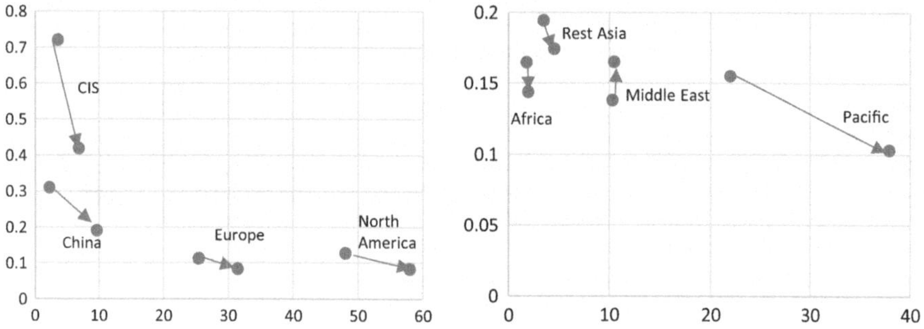

Fig. 26.5 Energy intensity of industry versus GDP/cap, from 2000 to 2018. (Source: Own elaboration on www.enerdata.net)

4 Transport

From an energy viewpoint, the transport sector includes all means of transportation of passengers and freight, whatever the owner and whatever the purpose. This is different from the economic definition of the transport sector, in particular in national accounts, where it includes only the value added of transport companies. In the energy balances, a distinction is made between the final energy demand of domestic[8] transport (so-called transport sector in the final consumption section) and that of international air and sea transport, included under the label "bunkers" in the primary section of the balance. Except for the world, the final energy demand of the transport sector corresponds only to the domestic transport. For the world, it accounts for both.

Geography, transport infrastructure heritage and GDP/cap are the key factors differentiating transport energy consumption between countries. The bigger the size of the country, the more important high-speed trains and air transport to accommodate the demand for increased speed. The smaller the size, the higher the population density, the more cost-effective is public transport of passengers by road or rail and the less attractive are private vehicles.

Natural waterways have been used and fitted out everywhere for centuries. Rail transport emerged in the second half of the nineteenth century, well before motorized road transport, and, in many countries, rail infrastructures were developed on a large scale before roads started to be paved. The development of road infrastructure in the twentieth century contributed to the obsolescence of part of the rail and waterways infrastructure already in place. But the remaining part, maintained and modernized, constitutes a heritage that strongly influences the modal structure of the movement of passengers and freight. In countries which do not benefit from this heritage, the development of modern rail and waterways is very often hampered by the very high investment costs involved.

[8] "Domestic" means "inside the country's boundaries." It includes all the energy purchased inside the country, whatever the origin and destination of the transport.

Energy prices have a relatively low impact on transport energy demand in the short-medium term, for two reasons: the high share of mandatory or highly constrained passenger travel and freight movement and the rigidity in modal switch for both passengers and freight. In the long term, energy prices influence changes in technology and modal competition.

4.1 *Outlook of Energy Demand in Transport: Historical Evolution, Structural Aspects*

At the global level, transport accounts for around 2800 Mtoe (2018), that is, 28% of total final energy consumption. This consumption has been multiplied by 3 over the last 50 years and increased further by 47% since 2000. Domestic transport alone consumes 2400 Mtoe (2018), and experienced a similar evolution. Road accounts for the bulk of transport energy consumption (76% in 2018), followed by air and waterways (12% and 10% respectively). With 2%, rail is almost marginal. See Fig. 26.6.

Transport relies almost entirely on oil: 98% in 2000, 94% in 2018. Road transport accounts for 80% of this total oil consumption of transport (94% of its final oil consumption), while air transport (jet fuels) and sea transport (heavy fuel oil or bunkers) account for 18% (2018). Almost all the remaining oil (mostly diesel oil) is consumed by railways and internal waterways. Road transport relies almost entirely on gasoline and diesel oil, with a little LPG (butane and propane) and, recently, increasing quantities of natural gas and bio-additives (ethanol and biodiesel).

Sea bunkers have doubled over the last 50 years (220 Mtoe in 2018), and jet fuels for international air transport multiplied by 3.5 (194 Mtoe in 2018). Altogether, the energy consumption of international transport has grown a little slower than that of the domestic transport over the last 50 years (multiplied by 2.5), but more rapidly since 2000 (53%). See Fig. 26.7.

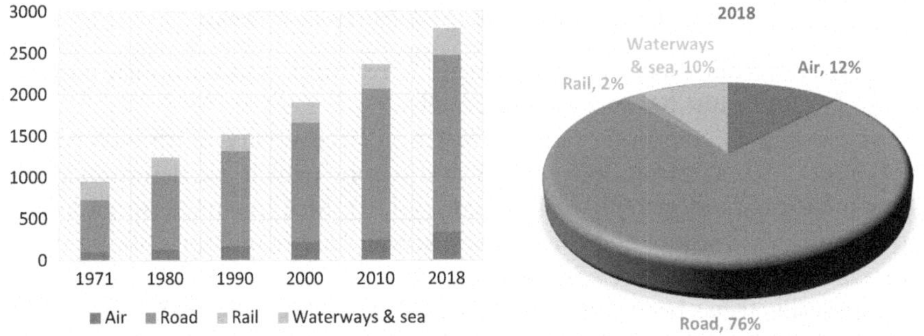

Fig. 26.6 World transport energy per mode, Mtoe. (Source: Own elaboration on www.enerdata.net)

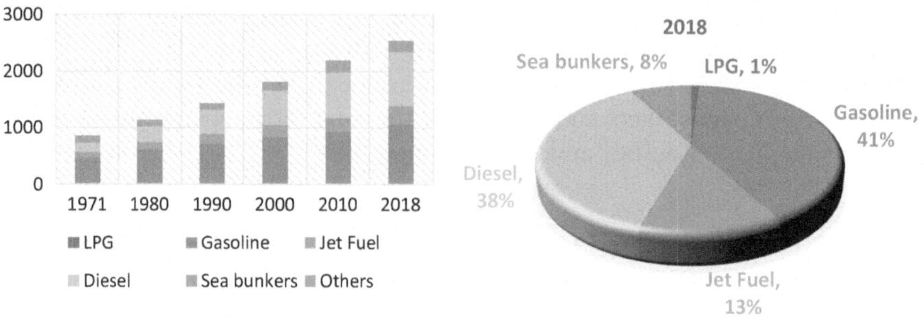

Fig. 26.7 World transport oil consumption per product, Mtoe. (Source: Own elaboration on www.enerdata.net)

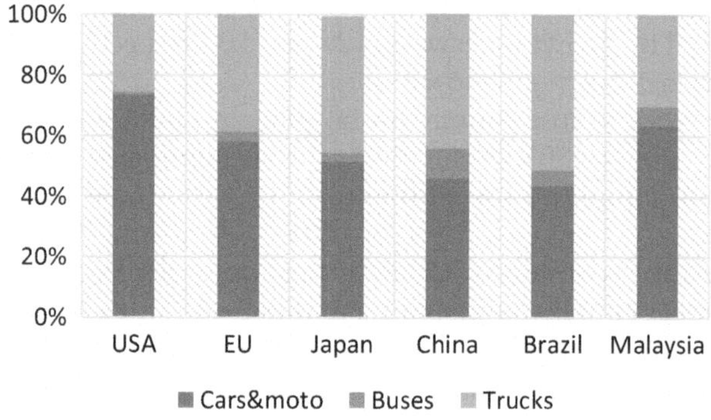

Fig. 26.8 Road transport by vehicles types, selected countries, 2018. (Source: Own elaboration on www.enerdata.net)

Private vehicles, that is, cars and motorcycles, account for 40% to 70% of the oil consumption for road transport in industrialized countries and BRICs, and freight for 30% to 50% (2018). See Fig. 26.8.

4.2 *Drivers Related to Mobility and Trade*

As regards determinants of energy demand consumption in transport, passengers and freight must be discussed separately.

For passengers, energy is required to meet accessibility needs—to access work places, shops, community spaces and so on—which are determined by either the formation or the use of income (GDP). Movements between home and workplace or school and for business services are mandatory; shopping is constrained at least to some extent, while leisure is not.

Empirically, it has been observed that everywhere in the world, and for the last two centuries at least, the average time an individual spends for mobility is roughly the same, around 1 hour per day (Zahavi 1974). This implies that the distance that each individual covers on average depends on the speed of movement, which has proved to be highly correlated to GDP.[9]

Technically, speed and accessible distances depend on the transport means. Walking, horse riding and bicycling are slow, the accessible distances are short, but they do not require commercial energy. Using motorized vehicles increases speed a lot, and allows for access over much greater distances, creating new accessibility opportunities, but requiring commercial energy. The speed of motorized vehicles differs according to the various modes and infrastructure: rail, road, waterways, air. To a certain extent, any increase in average speed can only occur through modal switch towards faster modes. Therefore, because of differences in energy demand per distance/speed across transport modes, the change of average speed drives passenger transport energy demand.[10]

Private vehicles (motor-cycles, motor-cars) can respond to almost all kinds of accessibility needs, while public motorized transport modes (buses, trains, planes, boats) respond to only part of them, those located on their dedicated routes. As a result, the average yearly mobility (kilometres travelled each year) of individuals having a private mode at their disposal is usually much higher than that of those who don't. Therefore, to assess properly energy demand drivers for passenger transport, private vehicles must be considered separately.

4.2.1 Passenger Transport in Private Vehicles

For those using private vehicles (cars and motorcycles), mobility is first a matter of equipment. The mobility needs covered by these vehicles are determined by the *number of vehicles* used, the *average distance* they travel and the average number of persons travelling together in the same vehicle (*load factor*).

Income and vehicles' prices are the two main drivers of the changes in the *number of vehicles* in use. However, beyond a certain level the market may become saturated and the increase in the number of vehicles in circulation will slow down.

Distances travelled yearly by private vehicles are determined by their use according to travel purposes, inside the time-budget constraint, and by the quality of road infrastructure. The distribution of car and motorcycles use among travel purposes changes very slowly in time. The same is true for road transport infrastructure. Ownership appears to be the main driver of the average yearly distance travelled by private vehicles in the medium-long term.[11] Consequently, in general, income growth is accompanied by a decrease of the

[9] The reason is because the value of time increases with the average hourly labour earnings, while the time-budget for transport remains mostly constant. (Bagard 2005)

[10] For further insight on this matter, and its consequences for the long distance future, see Château and Alii (2012).

[11] In most countries over the world, it has been observed over the last 50 years that the annual distance travelled in average was decreasing when the car stock was increasing. The reason behind is quite simple: private vehicles are purchased first by those having big accessibility and mobility needs, and increasingly by those having lower needs. Multi-ownership obeys to the same rule.

average distance travelled over the medium-long term, which slows down the growth of the energy demand.

Energy prices influence the distance travelled by private vehicles, partly through substitution with public modes, partly through financial constraints on discretional movement. But the price elasticity of the energy demand of private vehicles in the short term is very low (Labandeira et al. 2017).

Load factors of private vehicles (number of persons per vehicle on average) are rather specific to travel purposes and closely related to the size of households and to ownership level: the higher the ownership, the lower the load factors. So, income is indirectly a driver of the average load factor, through the size of households in countries experiencing a demographic transition, and through ownership. The lower the load factor, the higher the energy demand per passenger-km.

4.2.2 Passenger Transport in Public Modes

For public transport modes, as for private vehicles, total travel determines energy consumption. Load factors are very high at peak times and rather low otherwise, but energy consumption does not change much.

The offer of public transport is likely to drive changes in both the private vehicles stock and yearly distance travelled in the medium-long term. When people can choose among different modes to fulfil their accessibility needs, relative prices, comfort and relative speed determine their choice. The higher the speed, the more appealing the mode.[12] In congested urban areas where car traffic is very slow, offering rapid public transport (tramways, urban trains, metro, buses on dedicated lanes) drives people away from private vehicles, decreasing their yearly distance travelled by car. The same is true also for long distances, with a new offer of fast trains or domestic air transport. For people living in big urban areas, this may decrease significantly the desire for multi-vehicle ownership, and in some cases (very big conurbations) even the desire to own a car at all, hence the size of the car stock.

Altogether, the structure of public transport services and private vehicles ownership drive the change of average load factors of alternative modes, that is, the energy demand per passenger-km.

4.2.3 Freight Transport

The final energy demand of the transport sector includes only movements over land (including from/to borders), while international bunkers cover international sea and air trade.

Energy demand for freight is determined by the travel of the freight transport modes (vehicle-km) in response to the freight transport demand, that is, the tons which need to be transported over distances (ton-kilometres).

[12] The reason behind is rather simple: the transport time-budget being constrained (around one hour a day per person on average, see supra), the higher the speed, the more the accessibility needs that can be fulfilled, the wider the activity programme.

Domestic freight transport demand is highly correlated with GDP. But GDP growth also brings changes in the structure of the domestic and international trade. This impacts the mix of products transported, usually towards higher value/lower density products, which favours road transport. Because of the much higher energy demand per ton-kilometre of road transport as compared to rail and waterways (see Fig. 26.9), this evolution contributes to making freight transport more and more energy intensive as GDP expands. As a consequence, road transport accounts today for the bulk (above 85%) of the freight transport energy demand everywhere: 87% in Canada where road accounts only for 39% of freight traffic, up to 93% in the European Union, where it accounts for 77% of freight traffic (Enerdata 2019c).

Historically, international sea transport was driven by primary commodities (oil, coal, ores, primary metals). These accounted for the bulk of sea transport until the end of the 1980s. Since then, globalization, in relation to the dramatic fall of the sea transport costs, has boosted the international long-distance trade of all kinds of products, and became the main driver of international sea transport. As a consequence, world oil bunkers demand, which had slowly decreased between 1970 and 1990 (-10%), almost doubled between 1990 and 2010, and has roughly stabilized since then. See Fig. 26.9.

4.3 *Drivers Related to Technology*

Technology-related drivers must be appraised at two levels: transport modes infrastructures and vehicles within each mode.

4.3.1 Transport Modes Infrastructures

Passengers and freight traffic are distributed among infrastructures, which have specific characteristics as regards loading capacity (passengers and freight) and speed, and therefore energy demand per traffic unit. In general terms, the higher the loading capacity, the lower the energy required; and the higher the speed, the higher the energy required. Thus, the modal split drives energy demand for both passengers and freight transport.

Fig. 26.10 compares average unit consumption of various modes/vehicles, that is, statistical records of energy consumed per passenger-km or ton-km, in actual traffic conditions.

Fig. 26.9 World oil bunkers, Mtoe. (Source: Own elaboration)

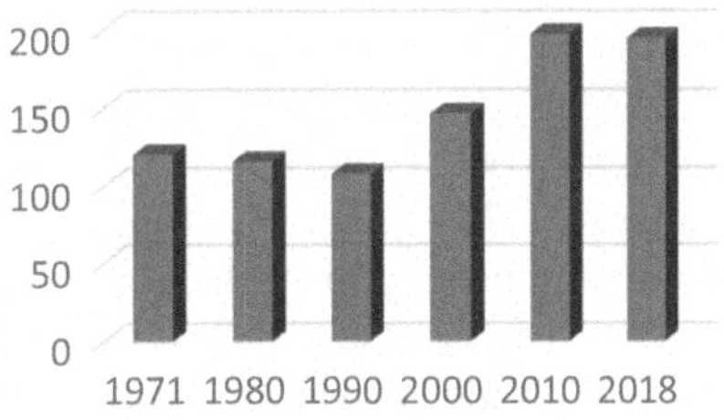

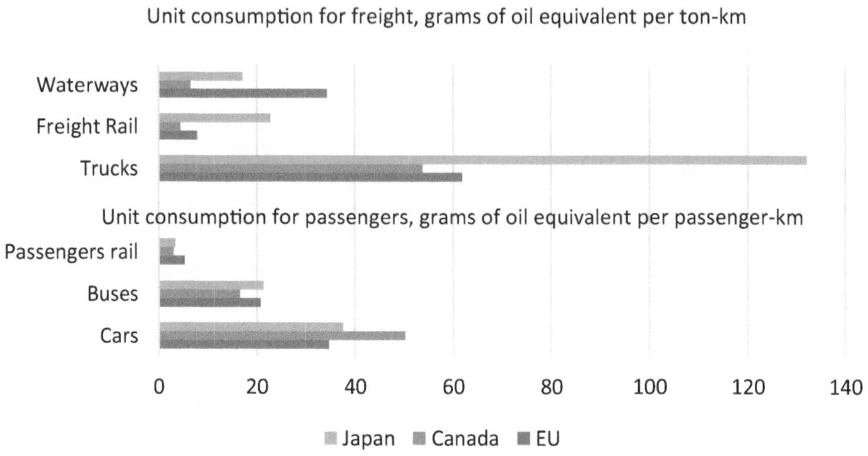

Fig. 26.10 Unit energy consumption per transport mode, 2018. (Source: Own elaboration on www.enerdata.net, ODYSSEE)

Transport infrastructure changes rather slowly. It takes 5 to 10 years, sometimes more, to build a new motorway, rail track or canal. Therefore, infrastructure's influence on overall average unit energy consumption per passenger-km or ton-km is very small in the short-medium term, but increases with time, and becomes critical in the very long term. Infrastructure changes are driven by two main forces: cost-effectiveness and demand for higher speed. Over time, low-speed infrastructure tends to disappear and new fast-speed infrastructure to expand. This usually drives the overall average unit energy consumption per ton-km or passenger-km upwards for most transport services, except those in congested urban areas.

4.3.2 Vehicles Technology

The other main driving force of the UECs is the specific energy consumption (SEC) per vehicle-km of the vehicles in circulation. The SECs of existing vehicles almost do not change over time, but the SECs of new vehicles are often lower than those of existing ones. Which means that, for each category of vehicles, their average SEC is driven by the stock and the life time span of the vehicles: the faster the stock increase, the higher the proportion of new vehicles, the faster the change in average SEC; the shorter the lifetime span, the faster the replacement of old vehicles by new ones, the faster the change of average SEC.

The lifetimes of vehicles depend on the mode and type of service: quite short for road trailers and buses (<7–10 years), longer for private cars and planes (15–25 years), even longer for rail and waterways vehicles (up to 30–40 years). Lifetimes almost do not change over time, or very slowly.

The SEC of new vehicles is driven by two forces: energy prices and energy efficiency and environment policies. Because energy accounts usually for a big

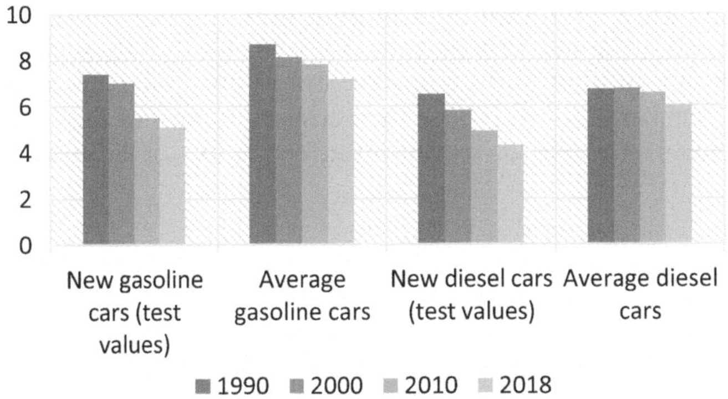

Fig. 26.11 Specific energy consumption of cars in France, l/100 km. (Source: Own elaboration on www.enerdata.net, ODYSSEE)

share of the operating cost of the vehicles, whatever the mode, energy prices drive the competition among vehicles manufacturers towards lower SECs. This is particularly true for road, air and waterways, less for rail. The higher the energy price expectations, the lower the SEC targeted for each category of vehicles. Energy efficiency and environment policies influence SEC evolution in two ways. Economic incentives/penalties (taxes, bonus/malus, subsidies) influence consumer choices when purchasing a new vehicle, and then give appropriate signals to manufacturers as regard SEC. Regulation and norms set on exhaust gas emissions can be fulfilled in two different ways: adapting the motorization to reduce NOx, particles and so on per vehicle-km, or limiting the CO_2 emission per vehicle-km. Both ways impact the SEC of new vehicles: often upwards in the first case, and downwards in the second. See Fig. 26.11.

The speed of replacement of old vehicles is influenced by the evolution of energy prices (including taxes) and incentives to purchase new vehicles (e.g. to promote electric cars, as in many countries nowadays).

4.3.3 Main Issues

When assessing the technology drivers of transport energy demand, three main issues must be kept in mind: the transport infrastructure heritage, worldwide competition in the automotive industry and the policy context for energy efficiency and the environment.

Transport infrastructure has very long lifetimes, over 50 years in general, and changes very slowly over time. Since part of the energy demand drivers is directly linked to the availability and performances of the transport infrastructure, heritage drives the speed of change of transport energy demand in the future.

The vehicles manufacturing industry is highly concentrated, with few, very large companies located in a limited number of countries worldwide. Their technological innovations spread rapidly in all countries of the world, whatever the specific economic or geographic conditions of these countries.

Energy efficiency and environment policies set up regulatory frameworks, incentives and economic instruments. These frame the decisions of vehicles purchasers and manufacturers, either to commit themselves to required standards and regulation, or to reduce their costs and improve their competitiveness. In general terms, this drives downwards the UECs of the various transport services.

4.4 *National Versus Global Vision of Energy Demand in Transport*

4.4.1 *How Energy for Transport Is Distributed Worldwide?*

The distribution worldwide of domestic transport energy consumption has changed a lot during the last 50 years. The share of the industrialized countries of Europe, North America and CIS, which was up to 80% in the early 1970s, decreased to 64% in 2000, and, even more rapidly, to 49% in 2018. At the opposite extreme, China's share surged from 2% in 1971 to 5% in 2000 and 14% in 2018, pulling the share of Asia as a whole from 11% to 20% and 34% for the same years. See Fig. 26.12.

4.4.2 *Transport Energy and GDP According to World Regions, and Motor Fuel Prices*

Transport energy demand is correlated to GDP almost everywhere in the world. Indeed, GDP drives almost all direct determinants of energy demand: average speed, households' ownership in private vehicles, infrastructure development, public transport offer, freight transport demand. But the relation between GDP/cap and transport energy demand per capita differs between countries. This is due obviously to differences in the size of the countries, but also in transport infrastructure (e.g. rail infrastructure in Europe), in urbanization and in energy prices (very low in Middle East and North America, for instance). See Fig. 26.13.

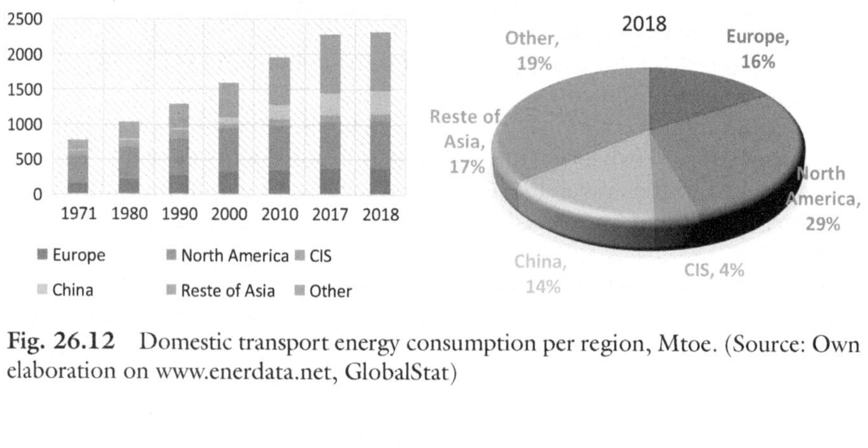

Fig. 26.12 Domestic transport energy consumption per region, Mtoe. (Source: Own elaboration on www.enerdata.net, GlobalStat)

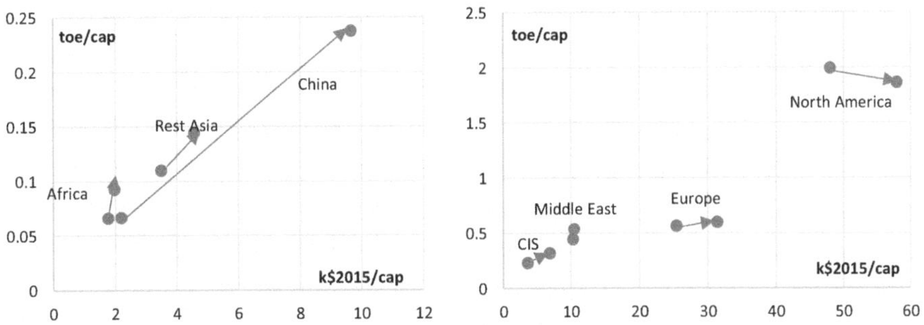

Fig. 26.13 Transport energy consumption versus GDP, from 2000 to 2018. (Source: Own elaboration on www.enerdata.net, GlobalStat)

5 Buildings

From an energy viewpoint, the sector of buildings includes the residential and tertiary sectors of the energy balance. The energy tertiary sector includes the energy demand of the tertiary sector as defined in national accounts, less that accounted for by transport (transport companies), plus everything not accounted for elsewhere: handicraft and very small industries or the informal sector. The residential sector is quite different from the category of households in national economic accounts, as it covers only the energy consumption and expenses related to dwellings.

5.1 *Outlook for Energy Demand in Buildings: Historical Evolution, Structural Aspects*

Buildings account for 30% of the final energy consumed in the world, that is, 3000 Mtoe (2018). This consumption doubled over the last 50 years, as did world population. The increase in fossil fuels consumption has been much slower than total energy consumption: fossil fuels accounted for little more than half of total consumption in 1971, but only 37% in 2018. Biomass consumption has grown faster than that of fossil fuels, but the champion is electricity: its consumption has been multiplied by a factor of almost 7 over the last 50 years, and it accounts today for one third of total consumption, the highest share among energy products. See Fig. 26.14.

5.2 *Overview of Needs and Energy End-Uses in Buildings*

Energy is used in buildings to fulfil three main needs of households and workers: comfort, food and social life. Energy is also used in services buildings for some production activities.

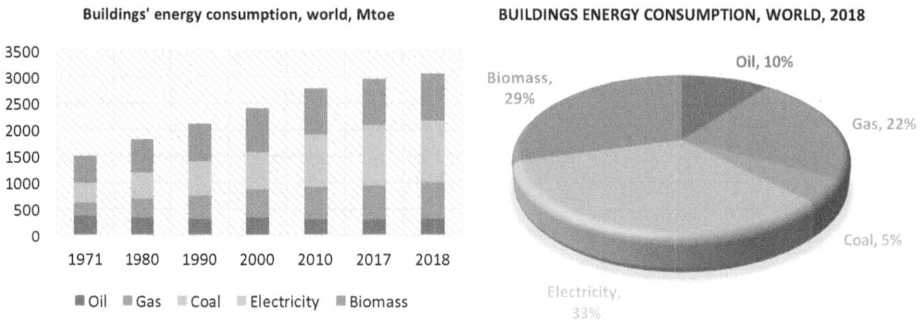

Fig. 26.14 Buildings' energy consumption, World. (Source: Own elaboration on www.enerdata.net, GlobalStat)

5.2.1 *Housing Buildings*

Comfort means space-heating, space-cooling, water-heating, lighting. Except for lighting, the energy involved in these end-uses is in close relation with the climate and the space area of the buildings, either directly (space heating and cooling) or through the number of persons accommodated in the building (hot water). For lighting, energy is mostly related to the number of persons.

Food means food preparation, food conservation and cooking. Energy is required for food preparation and conservation only where electricity and dedicated electrical appliances (e.g. refrigerators) are available, that is, in electrified areas. Energy for cooking is universal. But the expression of the need is very different according to the socio-cultural contexts. In remote rural areas of many developing countries, cooking means open fires usually maintained several hours a day, depending on biomass availability, whatever the number of persons actually fed. And it turns out that the yearly average biomass consumption per household in these areas is three to four times higher than that of gas in a modern kitchen.

Social life involves energy end-uses which are specific to electricity: radio, TV, telephone, computers and so on. These concern only electrified areas, and the expression of the needs is similar everywhere, whatever the socio-cultural context.

Figure 26.15 shows households' energy consumption per end-use and per capita in selected countries.

5.2.2 *Services Buildings*

Depending on their function, the buildings dedicated to services require specific combinations of energy end-uses, and specific space area (m^2) per worker.

Office buildings, either private or public, involve similar end-uses as those of modern urban multi-flats housing buildings, with similar m^2/person.

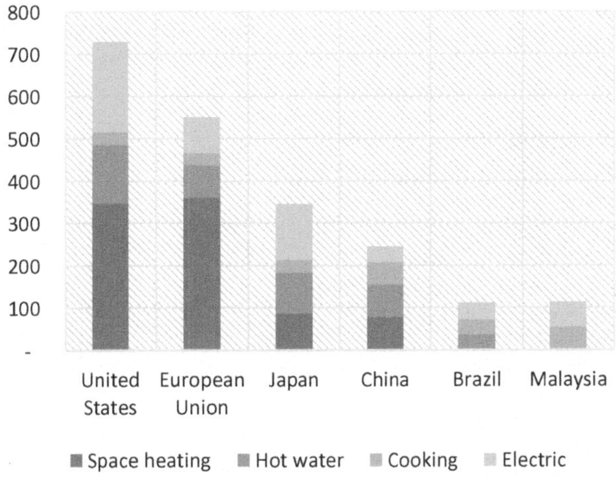

Fig. 26.15 Households' energy consumption per end-use and per capita, selected countries, 2018, koe/cap. (Source: Own elaboration on www.enerdata.net, EnerDemand)

Commercial buildings (groceries, shops, storage facilities, etc.), which accommodate clients from outside, need much larger space area per worker than office buildings. Part of the energy end-uses are similar to those of office buildings, but part is specific to the type of commerce: ovens for bakeries, cooling-freezing-atmosphere for storage, machinery for garages, and so on.

Education, transport and health buildings also accommodate people from outside, and need larger space area per worker. Education buildings involve similar end-uses as those of offices. Health buildings also, but at higher intensity. Health building involves also specific end-uses, mostly related to electricity, for caring: radiology, fluids circulation and so on. Transport buildings (airports, train stations, sea terminals) involve similar end-uses as those of offices plus some others specific: luggage conveying or passengers' information for example.

Figure 26.16 shows the energy consumption of services, per end-use and per capita in selected countries.

5.3 *Socio-economic-Related Drivers*

5.3.1 *Housing Buildings*

The number of occupied dwellings[13] is the first driver of the energy demand. This is a matter of total population and average size of households. The latter

[13] Usually, by definition, one dwelling shelters only one household.

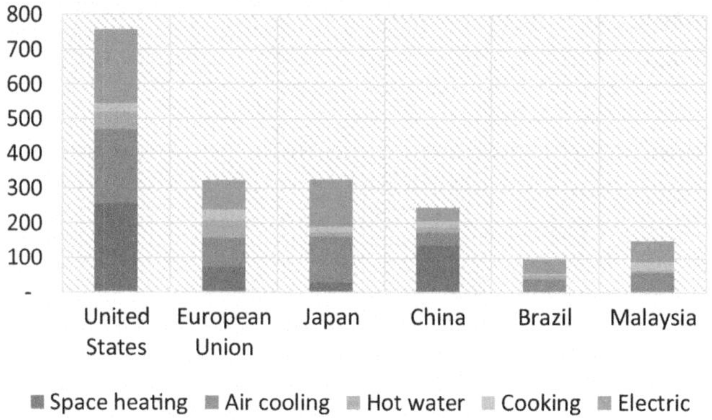

Fig. 26.16 Energy consumption of services, per end-use and per capita, selected countries, 2018, koe/cap. (Source: Own elaboration on www.enerdata.net, EnerDemand)

is driven firstly by the economic development in lower income countries,[14] and secondly by socio-cultural forces specific to each country. Dwellings construction and availability, mostly driven by GDP, play a crucial role in a number of countries: even if they wish to, youngsters and elderly people can live in their own dwellings only to the extent that enough dwellings are available

Income, income distribution and energy prices are the second set of main economic drivers. Indeed, they determine the ability to purchase equipment and energy for each category of households, except those harvesting free energy resources in nature.

Social standards (inside temperature socially considered as comfortable, hygiene practices, etc.) and behaviours (environmental concern for instance) are the last main drivers. Large discrepancies exist between traditional rural areas, and modern urbanized ones. In the latter, technology evolution, imitation from more advanced countries and marketing drive mostly the change of social standards.

5.3.2 *Services Buildings*

In services buildings, the three main economic drivers are the buildings floor area, the employment and production.

Occupied floor areas drive energy demand in space heating and refreshing, and in lighting. Employment drives the energy demand in water heating, cooking, information processing. Production drives the energy demand in specific end-uses directly related to the nature of production (bakeries, data centres, storage, etc.).

[14] This phenomenon, known as "demographic transition," has been observed all over the world, and theorized by demographic experts since the early 1930s (Adolphe Landry, "La Révolution démographique", 1934).

Employment and production are highly correlated to the value-added of the tertiary sector, that is, to the commercial GDP and to the public services.

Occupied floor areas (m^2) are indeed in close relation with employment, but may follow different dynamics, according to sub-sectors and buildings scarcity. Because of the strong inertia of the building stock, new m^2 built are the real driver of the occupied floor areas in most countries. This is driven by the tertiary value-added, public services policy and private services profitability.

5.4 *Technology-Related Drivers*

Technology-related drivers play at two levels: that of buildings and that of energy equipment.

5.4.1 *Buildings*

The size of a building, the materials used for its construction, its architecture, determine its specific useful energy consumption (SEC) per m^2 or per dwelling for a given space heating or space refreshing need: for example, to get 21°C inside all the rooms of a building in winter time as opposed to under the tropics. The size of the building is a matter of floor area and height (number of storeys): ceteris paribus, the higher the building, the lower the SEC per m^2. Architecture involves building shape, orientation and openings, which all determine the communication between natural energy sources (solar, wind) outside and indoor climate. Modern climatic architecture aims at making use of the natural energy sources to improve indoor comfort while decreasing the SEC. Materials used for construction, through their heat transfer properties, may have significant impacts on SECs: the use of insulation materials may reduce by a factor of 2 to 4 the SEC per m^2 for space heating purposes in countries with cold winters.

Existing buildings can be further insulated in order to decrease the SEC and energy cost per m^2 or per dwelling, through retrofitting operations implying appropriate materials for walls, floors, ceilings, roofs and windows. For new building constructions, insulation standards are imposed by national regulations, in most industrialized and emerging countries (Château and Alii 2010). Insulation level is then part of the building concept, as well as its SEC per m^2. For existing buildings, as for new constructions, energy prices and energy efficiency policies are the main drivers of changes in insulation, either as incentives to retrofitting (lowering the investment cost and increasing the energy cost) or as incentives to change the regulations.

Fig. 26.17 shows how insulation has progressed in the housing stock in France and in the EU, since 1990.

5.4.2 *Equipment*

Two kinds of equipment are involved in the fulfilment of the needs: those which directly deliver the services required (cooling, information, lighting), almost entirely powered by electricity; and those providing the useful energy

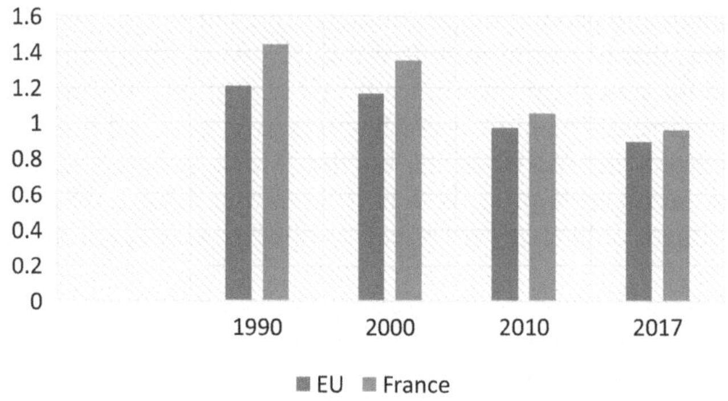

Fig. 26.17 Unit energy consumption per dwelling for space heating, toe/dw. (Source: Own elaboration on www.enerdata.net, ODYSSEE)

required from various alternative energy products (heating or cooling equipment mostly). In the first case, the SEC per dwelling or per person/employee is determined by the size/power and the energy performance of the equipment: for instance, the SEC/dwelling for lighting is determined by the number of light bulbs and the bulb technology (ignition versus LED). In the second case, the energy product used and the equipment performance determine the final energy requirement per unit of useful energy needed.

Innovation, electricity prices, norms and regulations drive the changes of the SEC per person or per dwelling for all kinds of equipment specific to electricity inside the buildings. For each equipment category, norms and regulations set minimum mandatory performances for new appliances sold on the market and make all the performances clear for the clients. They drive the average SEC for that equipment through the replacement of existing appliances by new ones, and through the growth of the stock of appliances. Lifetimes are usually short for this type of equipment (5–15 years), which makes the replacement rhythm rather high.

Electricity prices depend on tariff structure and on taxation, both elements which can be influenced by energy efficiency and environmental policies. Although electricity prices should determine the most cost-effective appliance, marketing and behaviours (for households) drive also the actual choices of the clients among all competing appliances. For example, people can choose a A+++ refrigerator, even if it is not the more cost-effective, just because it is fancier, or because of environmental protection concern.

The same statements could be made for the yields of equipment for space heating, space refreshing, hot water or cooking. For each energy product, only very little differences can be found in yields of new equipment across countries. The average yield per equipment changes therefore because the stock changes, and because the mix of energy products changes.

The heating, hot water and cooling distribution systems have great inertia within existing buildings, because they are usually integrated in the building structure. Their performances can be improved, but in rather small proportions. In new constructions, the energy performances of these systems are usually different (from those in existing buildings), and much better. So, here again, the overall average performances of the heating, hot water and cooling distribution systems on the whole stock of buildings change mostly because of the new constructions and replacement of existing buildings.

5.5 The Main Issues

5.5.1 Building Heritage

In countries with high heating or cooling needs, the dynamics of the demand for fossil fuels and biomass, and to a lesser extent that for electricity, depends strongly on the growth of the stock of buildings and replacement of existing ones, through the specific energy requirement per m^2 or dwelling, and the overall performance of the heat, water and cooling distribution systems. The very long lifetimes of most existing stock of buildings implies very low replacement rates, and this puts high constraints on the evolution of the energy demand. This is particularly true in industrialized countries, where population growth is weak, and which experience limited population migrations inside the country.

5.5.2 Budget Coefficients

It has been observed in many countries all over the world that the share of building-energy expenses of households in their private consumption (the so-called budget coefficient) remains rather constant over time, with limited fluctuations (+/- 25%) due to short-term energy price effects (Fig. 26.18). This means that, at any time, households make trade-offs between their needs' intensities and affordable technology possibilities, according to their income and the prices of energy products. Within the same budget coefficient, more

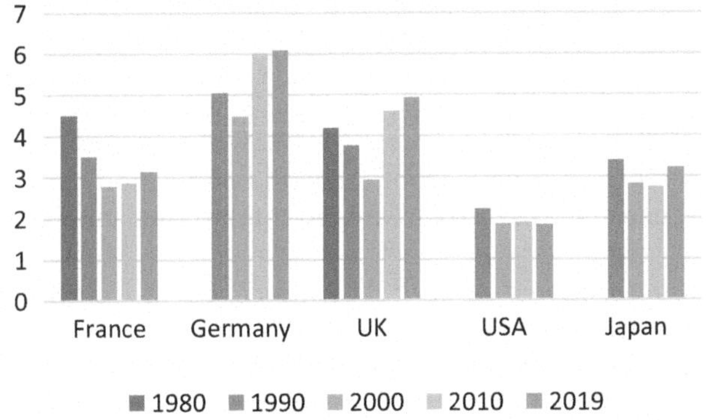

Fig. 26.18 Budget coefficients in dwellings (%). (Source: Own elaboration on www.enerdata.net, GlobalStat)

efficient technologies allow households to maintain their needs intensities despite energy prices increases, and an income increase allows for increased needs intensities or for new modern needs corresponding to new equipment made available by innovation.

5.5.3 *Information Spread and Imitation*

Imitation plays a key role in the dissemination of lifestyles and preferences. Within any country, people tend to adopt lifestyles and equipment of the upper socio-economic classes, as exhibited by the media and social networks, and strongly encouraged by marketing. This is one of the main engines of the growth of final consumption of households. Globalization has enlarged and accelerated this imitation phenomenon worldwide, first through the huge increase in information flows, and second because all consumption opportunities become available everywhere. For example, high- and middle-class Chinese have nowadays lifestyles and consumption patterns much closer to those of the Western countries than to traditional Chinese ones.

5.5.4 *Energy Efficiency and Environment Objectives*

Energy efficiency and environment policies target buildings' energy demand in three ways: buildings' insulation, energy performance of new equipment and individual behaviour. Building insulation depends primarily on norms and regulation for new constructions. Altogether, we can observe worldwide a rapid evolution towards increased efficiency in several fields: lighting, cooling-freezing devices, washing machines, TV and so on. Behaviour is mostly a question of information, education and citizenship. Worldwide, only limited policy implication and success can be observed in this regard. But this may change rapidly in the future along with more severe impacts of climate change.

5.6 *National Versus Global Vision of Energy Demand in Buildings*

5.6.1 *How Energy for Buildings Is Distributed Worldwide?*

Buildings' energy consumption accounts for 30% of the world energy (2018). This share has decreased since the early 1970s (35% in 1971), mostly due to the increase in the share of transport. Europe, North America and CIS, which are countries with cold winters, account for 42% of this consumption (2018), although they represent only 17% of the world population. Asia accounts for 37% of global consumption (2018), with 54% of the population. See Fig. 26.19.

5.6.2 *Buildings' Energy and GDP According to World Regions, and Energy Prices*

Energy demand for buildings is highly dependent on climate. In cold winter countries, up to 80% of the buildings' energy demand can be for space-heating and hot water (Canada, Russia, for instance (Enerdata 2019c)). As shown in Fig. 26.20, the consumption per capita in these countries is less related to GDP

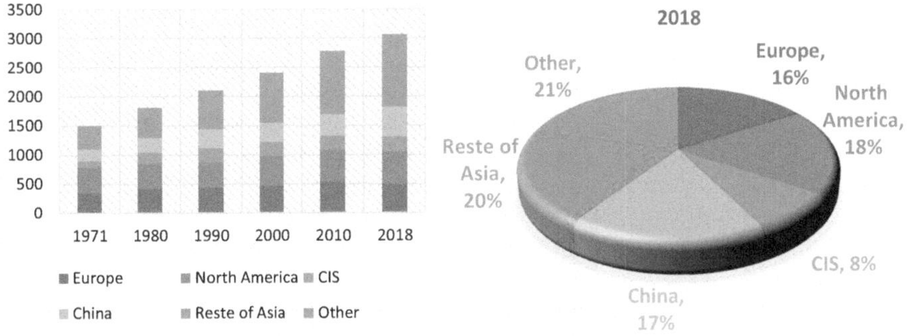

Fig. 26.19 Energy consumption of buildings per world region, Mtoe. (Source: Own elaboration on www.enerdata.net)

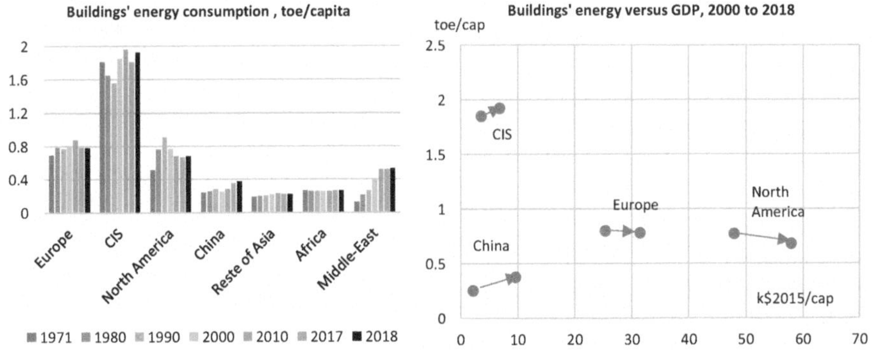

Fig. 26.20 Buildings' energy consumption per capita across the world. (Source: Own elaboration on www.enerdata.net)

or prices, than to other forces, like the building stock. In tropical countries, air cooling may represent up to 60% of the buildings' energy demand (Saudi Arabia (Enerdata 2019c)).

Buildings' electricity demand per capita is much more closely correlated to GDP than overall energy, as shown in Fig. 26.21. But still, Middle East and North America show that, for high GDP/capita, the relation to GDP depends also on additional factors, in particular space cooling requirements.

6 Electricity

Electricity is both an energy product which competes with fossil fuels and renewables in many end-uses of energy, and a captive energy product for other end-uses. The drivers of electricity demand, and of its share in the final energy demand, must be appraised separately in these two cases.

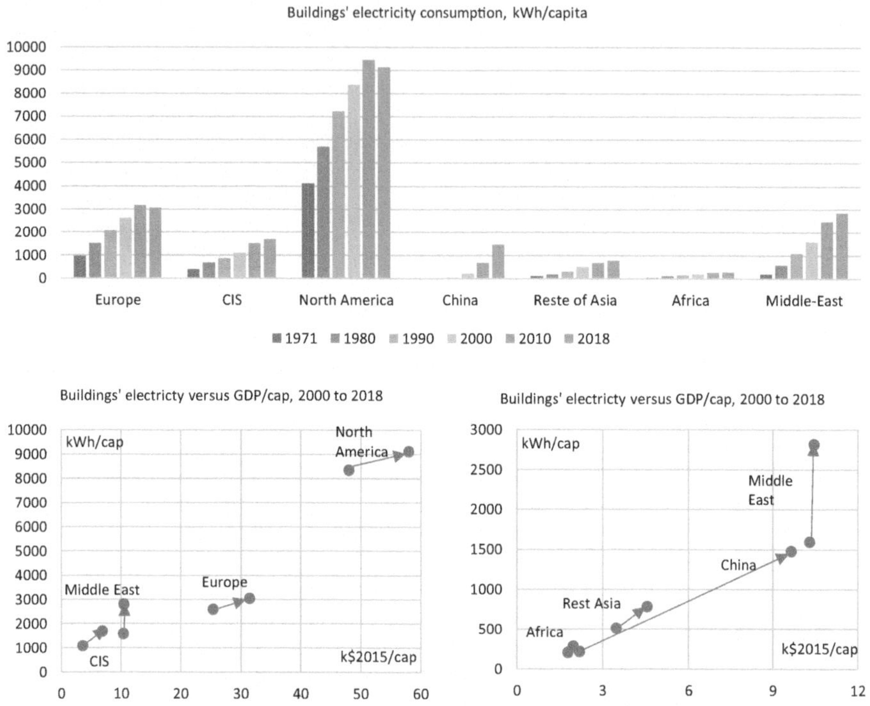

Fig. 26.21 Buildings' electricity consumption per capita across the world. (Source: Own elaboration on www.enerdata.net)

6.1 *Overview*

The share of electricity in world energy demand has roughly doubled during the last 50 years, with a rather steady rate of growth across time. Such penetration of electricity in final energy consumption can be observed all over the world, with some disparities across regions: similar growths in Europe, North America and the rest of Asia, much faster in China, slower in CIS and Africa. See Fig. 26.22.

6.2 *Electricity Substituting for Fossil Fuels*

6.2.1 *Drivers and Limitations*

From a technical viewpoint, electricity can substitute for any other energy product in most thermal end-uses, except those where the chemical content of the energy product makes the difference (blast furnaces, clinker, petrochemicals, etc.). Such a substitution involves generally a change in the whole thermal system, not just in the heat generator. From an economic viewpoint, what drives the substitution is the relative cost, that is, relative energy and equipment prices.

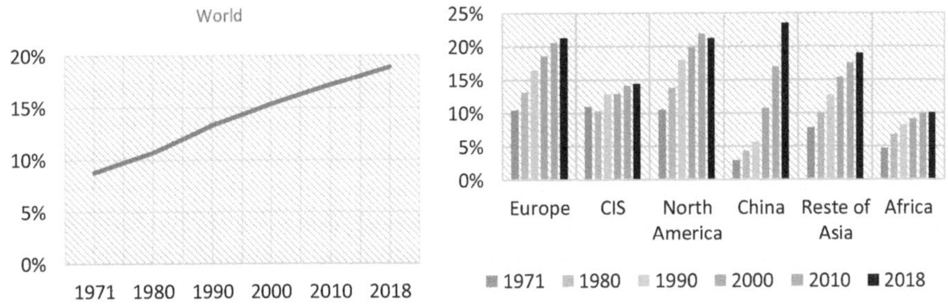

Fig. 26.22 % Electricity in the final energy consumption. (Source: Own elaboration on www.enerdata.net)

When electricity is generated from fossil fuels in thermal plants, the cost of electricity per Joule is at least 2.5 to 3 times higher than the price of the input fuel per Joule, because of the limited efficiency of the power plant (within a range 30%–45%).

For industry, which relies on the same fuels as power plants and at the same prices, this discrepancy between the prices of electricity and fossil fuels remains unchanged. If the price of equipment is similar, electricity becomes competitive only in end-uses where the difference in yields with respect to fossil fuels is roughly of a similar magnitude, that is, for very high temperature furnaces. In some cases, electricity becomes competitive also because it involves a different, more competitive process: for instance, reverse osmosis for desalination.

For buildings, the prices of fossil fuels per joule are higher than those paid by power plants, because of higher quality, distribution costs and taxes. The price of electricity is also higher than the production cost, for similar reasons. Therefore, despite the fact that the price of electric equipment is similar or lower than that using fossil fuels, electricity is not competitive with fossil fuels when generated itself from fossil fuels. Two exceptions nevertheless exist: hot water production and cooking. But the reason is more often lack of alternatives (no gas grid for instance), than competitiveness.

For transport, the price of motor fuels is usually much higher than that of the fuels used by power plants (also because taxes are in general higher), but the performance of the engines is also much lower than that of electric engines, and more than compensate the difference in prices. The key question is therefore the difference in the price of equipment. From this viewpoint, motor fuels have a great advantage over electricity, since they can be stored in the vehicles, at very low cost. Electricity can also be stored in vehicles, but at very high cost. Otherwise, electricity must involve specific electric lines (electric trains, trams) which are also costly, but prove to be cost-effective if the utilization rate is high enough.

When electricity is generated from renewables (hydro, wind, solar) or nuclear rather than fossil fuels, production costs are disconnected from the prices of fossil fuels. In that case, the higher the prices of fossil fuels, the higher the competitiveness of electricity in thermal end-uses. In France, Norway or Quebec, for instance, this has driven very strong development of electric space heating, which, in contrast, almost does not exist in countries where a large share of electricity is generated from fossil fuels.

6.2.2 *Information and Complementarity*

There is another form of substitution of electricity for fossil fuels, through the increase in the performance of fossil fuel equipment. Such an increase occurs generally when improving the management of the equipment. This requires collecting and computing information related to fossil fuel consumption (metering, regulation, etc.). As a result, the fossil fuel demand decreases while that of electricity increases for the same service.

6.2.3 *Impacts on Primary Energy Demand*

When electricity is generated from fossil fuels or nuclear, the amounts of primary energy necessary to generate the electricity exceed that contained in substituted fossil fuels, except for very high temperature furnaces or transport vehicles. In addition, electricity involves transport/distribution losses up to 15%, which is not the case with fossil fuels. In that case, when electricity substitutes for fossil fuels, final energy demand decreases (because electricity is more efficient), but the primary energy input increases, widening the gap between the two. The gap between primary and final energy use increases still more when low efficiency primary fuel (coal, nuclear) substitutes for higher efficiency final fossil fuel (gas for instance) through electricity.

When electricity is generated directly from hydro, solar or wind power, the substitution of electricity for fossil fuels drives the final and primary energy demand downwards at the same speed.

6.3 *Specific/Captive End-Uses of Electricity*

6.3.1 *Information Mastering and Electricity Expansion*

Almost all the new-technology equipment relies on electricity. The main reason is that they rely massively on information technologies: data collection and storage, data processing, data transfer and so on. These are today one of the main engines of the GDP growth worldwide. As a consequence, almost everywhere in the world, the electricity demand grows at a higher speed than demand for fossil fuels.

6.3.2 *Impacts on Primary Energy Demand*

The impact on primary demand depends on the generation mix of electricity. When generated from fossil fuels or nuclear, the primary energy necessary to deliver 1 kwh electricity to final consumers is between 2.5 and 4 times higher than the final energy contained in the kwh. The faster the growth of electricity demand, the wider becomes the gap between final and primary energy demand.

When generated from hydro, wind or solar power, the only difference between primary energy and final energy is due to electricity transport/distribution losses. The closer the generation of electricity to the final consumers (solar panels, windmills), the lower the losses.

6.4 *Main Issues*

Except in countries and areas where electrification is not complete, electricity is now involved in all energy end-uses of all final consumers: either because the end-use requires electricity, or because electricity is used to monitor and pilot the equipment part of the end-use. The progress in intelligence and information control, intimately connected to GDP growth, boosts captive end-uses through innovation and delivery of new services. It also boosts the substitution of fossil fuels with electricity, through energy efficiency improvements. Altogether, this drives a continuous, structural, increase of the share of electricity in final energy demand. It also drives a continuous, structural, decrease of the overall final energy intensity of GDP, which translates into a growing disconnection of final energy demand from GDP (Chen 1992). Depending on how electricity is generated, the primary energy intensity of GDP may follow the same decreasing trend, but at a lower rate, or may even increase in some cases.

The way electricity is generated influences the speed of electrification of final demand. When it is generated from *fossil fuels*, the direct substitution of electricity for fossil fuels is scarcely cost-effective, and plays a very little role in electricity demand growth.

When generated from *nuclear*, because of the huge investment cost involved, the generation cost per kwh decreases when electricity production increases, much faster than in fossil fuels plants. So, there is a threshold in production where the nuclear electricity becomes competitive; passed that threshold, the higher the production, the lower the cost, the stronger the competitiveness and the lower the price to the final consumer. This obviously boosts the substitution of electricity for fossil fuels, but also slows down the progress of efficiency in electrical appliances; and, for households, allows for less constrained electricity consumption. Altogether, this results in faster electrification of energy demand as compared to when electricity is generated from fossil fuels.

Direct renewables (solar, wind, hydro) also have high (but rapidly decreasing) investment costs per kW, with similar consequences as for nuclear. But the main difference is that part of renewable electricity production (wind, solar) has to face physical constraints that do not exist for nuclear, because of intermittency and low spatial densities. It often results in higher costs to meet appropriate stability and safety conditions for electricity delivery (except for hydro), as compared to thermal electricity generated from fossil fuels. This discourages direct substitutions of electricity for fossil fuels, and increases the quest for more efficient electric appliances. For households, because of budget constraints, this results in more constrained electricity consumption. Altogether, in most countries, the higher the share of direct renewables in electricity generation, the lower the rate of electrification of final energy demand, and the lower final energy demand growth. Things are nevertheless different in countries with huge hydropower resources (Quebec, Norway, Brazil): here, the physical constraints do not play, and the situation is very similar to that of the countries with a lot of nuclear.

Bibliography

Agence Internationale de l'Energie (AIE) (2011), *Manuel sur les statistiques de l'énergie.* AIE, Paris

Bagard V. (2005), *Optimisation spatio-temporelle des pratiques de loisirs*, PhD Thesis, Lyon University

Château B. and Alii (2010), PACT Pathways for Carbon transition EC/DG, Research Contract Project 225 503 Final report http://pact-carbon-transition.org

Château B. and Alii (2012), *Enjeux spatiaux, économiques et politiques des scénarios de mobilité durable à l'horizon 2050*, Research contract ADEME/PREDIT N° 0966C0216

Château B. and Alii (2002), *Modelling the dynamics of the needs of energy services in VLEEM*, EC/DG Research Contract ENG2-CT-2000-00441 Final report August 2002

Château B. and Lapillonne B., (1982), *Energy Demand: Facts and Trends. A comparative analysis of industrialized countries.* Springer Verlag, Wien, New York.

Château B. and Lapillonne B., (1977), *la prévision à long terme de la demande d'énergie: propositions méthodologiques.* CNRS, Energie et Société, Paris.

Château B. (2015), *Les besoins d'énergie*, Encyclopédie de l'énergie, www.encyclopedie-energie.org/les-besoins-denergie/

Chen X., (1992), Information et Energie. *Rôle de la maîtrise de l'information dans le rapport entre la croissance économique et la consommation d'énergie.* PhD Thesis, Grenoble University.

Enerdata (2019a), *MedPro model data bases*, www.enerdata.net

Enerdata (2019b), *ODYSSEE data base*, www.enerdata.net

Enerdata (2019c), *EnerDemand*, www.enerdata.net

X. Labandeira, J.M. Labeaga and X. Lopez-Otero (2017), *A meta-analysis on the price elasticity of energy demand.* Energy Policy, March 2017, pp 549–558

Zahavi (1974), *Travel time budgets and mobility in urban area*, Report for the Ministries of Transport of the USA and Germany

CHAPTER 27

Energy Subsidies

Tom Moerenhout

1 Introduction

Energy subsidies are widespread among OECD and non-OECD countries and exist for all energy types. Governments often give noble and legitimate rationales for the introduction and continuation of various energy subsidies. Such reasons include the protection of household welfare, energy access, environmental sustainability, the development of new technologies and the expansion of an industrial base that is able to generate jobs and compete on international markets.

But the reality of energy subsidy policies is nearly always more complex than the stated rationale. A wide spectrum of stakeholders pushes governments to satisfy various policy objectives at once. As a result, governments have tried to balance the energy trilemma by implementing several types of energy subsidies at once. Even when some policy priorities clearly change, the phasing out of existing subsidies may prove politically challenging when powerful vested interest groups exercise their influence over governmental decision-making.

The result of the energy trilemma and the complex political economy of subsidy policies has made energy subsidies rather pervasive. Once implemented, they appear difficult to eliminate. With many governments subsidizing all sorts of energy types, the net impact of a country's energy policy is often unclear and likely suboptimal.

This chapter aims to highlight the pervasiveness of subsidies. It will first introduce the notion of subsidies generally and discuss why energy subsidies

T. Moerenhout (✉)
Columbia University, School of International and Public Affairs, Center on Global Energy Policy, New York, NY, USA
e-mail: tm2794@columbia.edu

M. Hafner, G. Luciani (eds.), *The Palgrave Handbook of International Energy Economics*, https://doi.org/10.1007/978-3-030-86884-0_27

are important in the context of the energy trilemma. Then it will discuss the objectives, types, estimates, and politics of fossil fuel consumption subsidies, fossil fuel production subsidies, and renewable electricity subsidies.

2 Subsidies and Energy Subsidies

2.1 Different Types of Subsidies

Subsidies have been defined in many ways and depending on the definition, one measure can constitute a subsidy or not. One of the most commonly accepted definitions is the one found in the Agreement on Subsidies and Countervailing Measures (ASCM) of the World Trade Organization (WTO). At the time of writing, the WTO has 164 members and covers both energy importing and exporting countries.

The ASCM stipulates that a subsidy exists if a policy measure confers a benefit and constitutes a financial contribution or provides price or income support. The ASCM does not include an exhaustive list of subsidy types but references a number of general subsidy types such as: (1) direct and indirect transfer of funds and liabilities (including direct spending and credit support); (2) government revenue foregone (including tax expenditures and excise taxes); (3) provision of goods or services below market value; (4) income or price support.

Beyond these well-accepted subsidy types, some other categories have often been considered as potential subsidies. Examples include the exclusion of social and environmental externalities, or forms of market price support such as tariff policies. An easy visual representation of the complexity of defining subsidies is a Russian nesting doll. In Fig. 27.1, the inner layers are generally accepted as subsidies, whereas the outer two are more contentious, with especially the underpricing of externalities normally not considered as a subsidy.

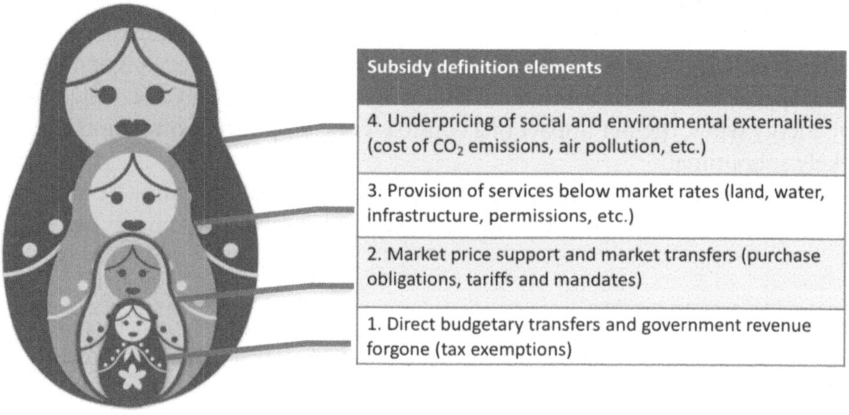

Fig. 27.1 Russian nesting doll of subsidy types. (Source: Own elaboration based on Gerasimchuk et al. 2012)

2.2 Categorizing Energy Subsidies

Because defining exact subsidy types is so difficult, energy subsidies have often been first categorized by energy resource. These include broad categories such as fossil fuel subsidies and renewable energy subsidies. In theory, fossil fuel subsidies should include subsidies to oil, gas, coal, and nuclear consumption and production. In reality, however, the term "fossil fuel subsidies" is mostly used for policy measures affecting the consumption and production of oil, gas, and coal. They also include electricity subsidies in so far as the electricity consumed relies on the use of aforementioned resources in power production. Similarly, renewable energy subsidies should theoretically include biofuel subsidies but instead mainly refers to renewable electricity subsidies such as those to wind, solar, and biomass (Table 27.1).

Only in a second step is the exact type of financial contribution and benefit assessed. Here there are, like with the general subsidy definition, different conceptions of what constitutes an energy subsidy. Generally, there is no disagreement over the inner cores of the Russian nesting doll. There is also the agreement that subsidies exist in all parts of the value chain such as R&D, extraction, transport, storage, production, refining, distribution, consumption, and decommissioning. Other than that, the approaches of international organizations diverge considerably.

The International Energy Agency has defined energy subsidies broadly as "any government action that lowers the cost of energy production, raises the price received by energy producers or lowers the price paid by consumers" (IEA 2006). The IMF on the other hand adopts a wider approach and includes the underpricing of social and environmental externalities in its subsidy

Table 27.1 Taxonomy of energy subsidies

	CO_2 intensity	*Taxonomy*	*Examples of subsidy and support types*
Finite resources	High	Fossil fuel subsidies (Oil, gas, coal)	Retail price support; consumption tax reductions (value-added tax, general sales tax, excise tax on consumption); producer tax reductions; government provided goods and services below market rates; SOE investment
	Low	Nuclear energy subsidies	Capital cost subsidies; production and investment tax credits; feed-in tariffs; combined legacy subsidies
Renewable resources	Variable	Biofuel subsidies	Excise tax reductions; blending mandates; tariff policies; agricultural subsidies for feedstock production
	Low	Renewable electricity subsidies (wind, solar, biomass)	Feed-in tariffs; renewable portfolio standards; tendering; production tax credits; investment tax credits; net-metering and billing

Source: Author

definition and calculation. The OECD, though, has been much more prudent and explicitly refers to "support" rather than "subsidy" when discussing policy measures that provide a benefit to energy producers or consumers.

3 Fossil Fuel Consumption Subsidies

3.1 *Subsidy Objectives*

Fossil fuel consumption subsidies are the largest category of energy subsidies worldwide. They are primarily intended to reduce the price of energy consumption by end users. Formal objectives of these types of pricing policies vary according to the consumers.

For households, consumption subsidies are legitimized as energy has no close substitute, but unquestionably provides essential functions to human life. Especially in developing countries, governments keep the price of energy products low, thereby often providing subsidies. Low energy prices are intended to alleviate poverty by safeguarding commodity prices, keeping inflation in check and sheltering consumers from the volatility of international commodity prices. In short, fuel consumption subsidies are a method to preserve welfare or, at least, provide some form of social safety net.

For firms, fuel consumption subsidies have been used to promote economic development by supporting factors of production in general and competitiveness for international trade in particular. As such, low prices have been used as a part of industrial policy with the explicit goal of supporting export competitiveness. Resource-rich countries in particular have used their domestic endowment to incentivize energy-intensive industrialization (though low prices in this case do not always constitute subsidies in the economic sense of the word—see below).

Besides such stated objectives, many fossil fuel consumption subsidies also serve hidden interests. Fuel consumption subsidies are often considered as an instrument to stay in power and control political stakeholders. Governments use them to direct (financial) benefits to key political stakeholders. Businessmen are often politically connected and able to influence decision-makers directly. To make things even more complicated, underpricing energy has led to the establishment of black markets and smuggling practices, often with the involvement of political stakeholders.

3.2 *Subsidy Types*

Most fossil consumption subsidies are implemented via pricing mechanisms in which consumers are charged a price which is below the cost-reflective level. There are two critical debates among experts and practitioners on what constitutes a fossil fuel consumption subsidy. A first debate is about whether or not to include environmental externalities into the subsidy calculation. The second is about what constitutes a subsidy in countries that are fossil fuel producers. These two questions are intrinsically linked to the subsidy type and definition.

In general, the optimal price of a product is often considered to be equal to the marginal cost, which is the cost of bringing an additional unit of capacity on the market (i.e., including production, operation, and maintenance costs). Since fossil fuels are depletable resources, it is often expected that the long-run marginal cost will go up and therefore the highest unit under current production is used as a proxy. Many however also believe that the marginal value of energy should not simply be determined by supply, but also by the social value of energy, which includes pricing externalities linked to environmental and health considerations.

Externalities aside, it is economically intuitive that producing countries have consumption subsidies when the retail price levels are below the production cost at which they produce the unit of energy. Importing countries, on the other hand, have subsidies when retail prices are below the import cost of fossil fuels, adjusted for transportation costs. In the case of petroleum products, this is often an international price. In the case of gas, prices have more regional variation.

Many analysts, however, have also used international (and regional) market prices for petroleum (and gas) as the benchmark to assess whether a producing country has fossil fuel consumption subsidies. It is clear, however, that the production cost of producers and international market prices of their products are often not the same. As a result, in economic terms, there are price levels at which producers do not have a subsidy, but importers do. These end-user price levels do constitute an opportunity cost for producers: they could earn more money by selling their produced fuel on the international market, as the price level is higher than the domestic end-user market. This is why sometimes this particular category is described as "opportunity cost subsidies" (Fig. 27.2).

3.3 Subsidy Estimates

Fossil fuel consumption subsidies have mostly been calculated using a price gap approach in which the value of a country's subsidy is considered as the difference between their end-user price and a benchmark price, multiplied by the amount of fuel consumed.

The below estimates should be taken with a heavy grain of salt since the benchmark prices used by the International Energy Agency and International Monetary Fund are international market prices. This means that they include producing countries that sell fuel at a price above production costs but below international market prices. As mentioned, this is economically speaking not a subsidy but an opportunity cost. For example, in 2018, the top fuel consumption subsidizing countries included producers such as Iran, Saudi Arabia, Russia, Venezuela, and Algeria. In many of these countries, however, retail prices of energy product lie above domestic production costs. For example, Russia produces gas at a very low price, Saudi Arabia produces petroleum

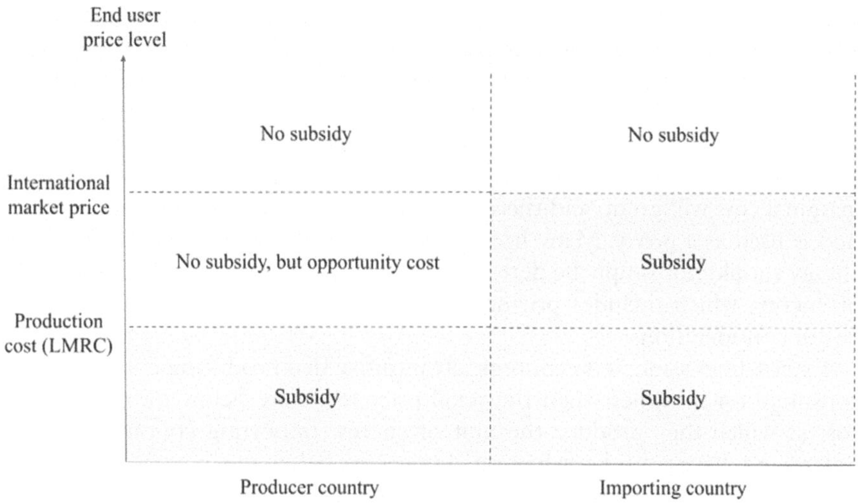

Fig. 27.2 Energy consumption subsidies in producer versus importing countries. (Source: Author)

products at a low cost, and so on. All of this represents an opportunity cost, but not always an economic subsidy.

The absolute value of fossil fuel consumption subsidies has, logically, followed the path of the price of crude oil. During the 2010s, the total value of fuel consumption subsidies hovered roughly US$ 200 and 500 billion, depending on the oil price. Fuel consumption subsidies are the sum of subsidies to oil products, gas products, coal, and electricity. Between 2009 and 2016, subsidies to oil products covered about half of total fuel consumption subsidies. Over time, the electrification of energy provision has meant that electricity subsidies have become relatively larger. When the oil price plummeted in 2015 and 2016, electricity subsidies shortly became the largest category of consumption subsidies. This changed again when the oil price increased (Figs. 27.3 and 27.4).

When including externalities, the absolute value of fossil fuel subsidies changes considerably. The IMF first produces "pre-tax subsidies," which are reliant on a conventional price gap approach that measures the difference between end-user price levels and international market prices (they also include OECD producer support estimates, see below). They then also calculate a broader measure which they call "post-tax subsidies," which reflect the difference between the end-user price and a theoretical price that end users should pay if the price were to reflect supply costs, environmental costs, and revenue requirements. Since this price adjustment would be done by utilizing taxes, they coined the broader subsidy definition "post-tax subsidies."

While pre-tax subsidies fall in the hundreds of millions and are often between 0.3% and 0.7% of world GDP (depending on the oil price), post-tax subsidies are around US$ 5 trillion or closer to 6% of world GDP. The huge difference

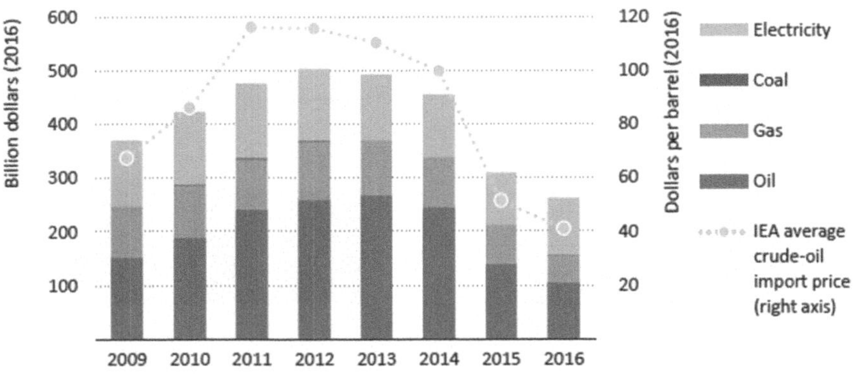

Fig. 27.3 Distribution of FFCS over fuel. (Source: IEA 2017, 84)

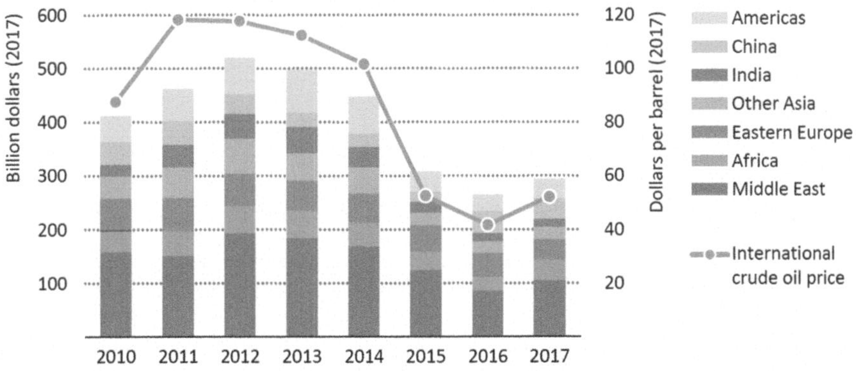

Fig. 27.4 Geographical distribution of FFCS. (Source: IEA 2018, 112)

is mainly explained by accounting for negative externalities related to the emission of carbon dioxide and other pollutants. The single largest form of externality is related to local air pollution, which impacts human health. The second largest source of externalities is found in the contribution of emissions to global warming. Because of these two, coal subsidies become the largest category of post-tax subsidies, while its absolute value was almost negligible when considering pre-tax subsidies. The main lessons learned from including externalities is exactly how polluting coal subsidies are and how relatively cleaner natural gas is (Figs. 27.5 and 27.6).

3.4 The Politics of Fossil Fuel Consumption Subsidies

3.4.1 The Drivers of Fossil Fuel Consumption Subsidy Reform

Fossil fuel consumption subsidies are problematic for a number of reasons linked to government budgets and governance, the misallocation of resources

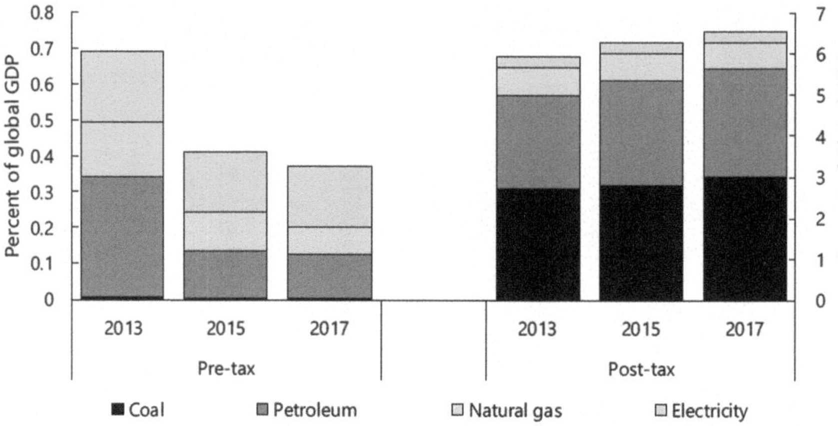

Fig. 27.5 Energy subsidies by product. (Source: IMF 2019, 21)

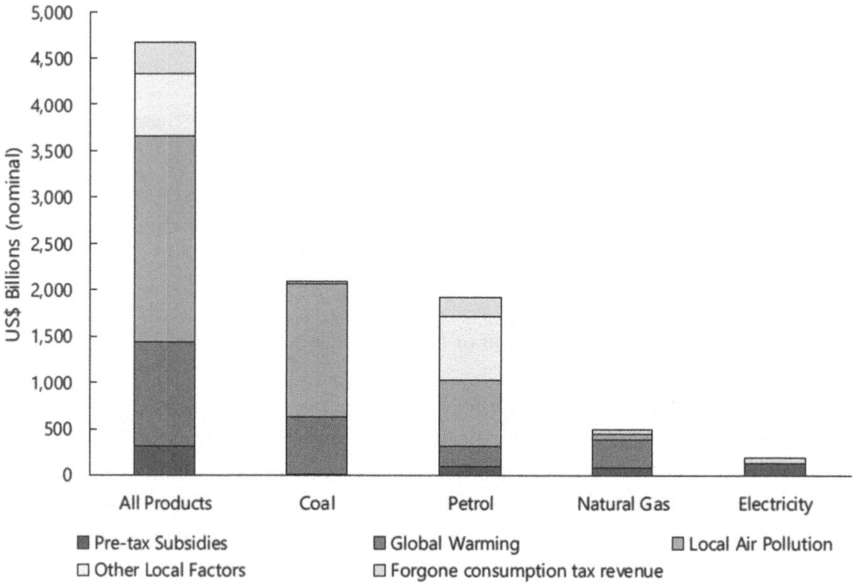

Fig. 27.6 Energy subsidies by product and component. (Source: IMF 2019, 21)

in the economy, the operation of energy sectors, excess consumption, and the environment (Table 27.2).

Intuitively, fuel subsidies may thus seem like a bad idea. They cause excess consumption linked to air pollution and carbon emissions. They cause corruption and the loss of fiscal revenue. They cause inefficiencies in the economy and the energy sector. And they, in absolute terms, mainly benefit the wealthy. While the distribution of benefits is country and fuel specific, in many

Table 27.2 Impacts of fossil fuel consumption subsidies

Impact dimension	*Specific impacts*
Government	Fiscal costs and opportunity costs
	Corruption
Misallocation of resource	Incentivize resource inefficient sectors
	Relative or absolute rise of resource intensity of GDP
	Resource overexploitation
Energy sectors	Harming competitiveness of alternative forms of energy
	Cost-recovery problems for utilities and other service providers
	Threats to infrastructure, quality, and supply
	Fuel smuggling and adulteration
Excess consumption	Negatively affects trade balance
	Inequitable distribution of benefits
Environment	Carbon emissions
	Air pollution

Source: Author

developing countries the share of benefits for the poorest 40% is between 15% and 25% of the total value of consumer subsidies (Coady et al. 2006; Diop 2014), while the top quintile often received more than 40% (del Granado et al. 2010; IMF 2013). The logic is clear: rich people consume more energy, so universal price subsidies benefit them the most, at least in absolute terms.

As a result of those various negative consequences from fossil fuel subsidies, many international organizations started putting their institutional weight behind energy pricing reform. The G-20 and APEC both committed to fuel subsidy reform in 2009. In 2015, countries re-emphasized their commitment to fossil fuel subsidy reform in the Financing for Development Addis Ababa Action Agenda. Eventually, "Rationalizing inefficient fossil-fuel subsidies that encourage wasteful consumption by removing market distortions" was also included as a target of the Sustainable Development Goals under SDG 12.c.

Perhaps more important than international norm creation is the inclusion of pricing reform under IMF and World Bank loan conditions. While this is nothing new—in fact they have conditioned loans on such fiscal reforms for decades—it became more pronounced throughout the 2000s and 2010s as increasing international oil prices caused fiscal crises for many (importing) governments. By the time financing institutions such as the IMF and World Bank are requested for assistance, there are often few options but consumption subsidy reform to strengthen a country's fiscal position. Governments, however, remain wary of implementing reforms fast, frightened by some notable examples of political instability peaking after fuel subsidy reforms as has been the case in, among others, Yemen, Indonesia, Bolivia, and Egypt.

3.4.2 The Drivers of Fossil Fuel Consumption Subsidies

Despite rational arguments in favor of, and international pressure for, consumption fuel subsidy reform, such subsidies remain pervasive for three main reasons: first, there is a social rationale for maintaining subsidies. Many governments rely on price subsidies to protect the social welfare of citizens. Contrary to advanced social protection mechanisms, fuel consumption subsidies are administratively easy and do not require advanced methods of social data collection and subsidy targeting. In some countries, citizens have also become accustomed to low prices, and consider it their right. Increasing energy prices does not only lead to direct price increases; it also impacts households indirectly via inflationary shocks that accompany upward price shocks.

In so-called allocation states low energy prices are often considered as part of an implicit social contract, in which citizens acquiesce to the ruling elite in exchange for the distribution of welfare, among others through the provision of low-priced energy. Whenever governments have decided to increase prices without mitigation measures (such as cash transfers), citizens have often voted them out of office or, in the case of authoritarian regimes, have taken to the street to protest.

Second, there is an economic rationale to maintain consumption subsidies. Many states have used low prices to promote economic development by supporting factors of production in general and competitiveness for international trade in particular. Low prices have thus been part of an industrial policy with the explicit goal of supporting export-competitiveness. Adjusting prices upward too fast may cause those industries to close down or relocate since they affect firms directly by increasing their energy input and indirectly via the effects of price increases on the price of intermediary goods or services. The sectors that suffer the most are logically energy-intensive industries such as heavy manufacturing, transport, petrochemicals, cement, aluminum, and steel.

Third but not least, there are political reasons to maintain consumption subsidies. Given the potential social and economic impacts of pricing reform, it is no surprise that implementing price increases is politically costly and can even threaten political stability. It is now uniformly recognized that political economy factors are the primary barriers to reforming energy prices. Low energy prices and subsidies are also often used as an instrument to stay in power and control political stakeholders. Governments use them to direct (financial) benefits to key political stakeholders, thereby consolidating power. As a result, low energy prices create interest groups that then lobby to maintain them low in the long run. Such lobby groups push for asymmetric decision-making that favor their own interests over a country-wide development plan, and it has been observed time and again that these groups have played a key role in solidifying energy subsidies.

4 Fossil Fuel Production Subsidies

4.1 Subsidy Objectives

Governments have used fossil fuel production subsidies for various reasons, and the main reasons to do so vary according to a country's economic and political context, and whether they are already strong fossil fuel producers or not yet. A similar economic objective involves the ambition to develop and protect an energy-based industrial policy. Fossil fuels are among the largest traded commodities worldwide and owning them can grant governments many benefits. Oil, gas, and coal extraction and production can be an important source of fiscal revenue or a method to assist the diversification of national economies or a country's energy system. For example, switching from coal to natural gas involves a huge amount of investment, which might not occur in the absence of government support.

Perhaps the most important reason for many countries with fewer domestic resource capacity is the quest for more energy security. A negative fossil fuel trade balance implies a relatively heavier reliance on external suppliers. This weakens a country's geo-political position. Heavy importers are also more exposed to commodity price fluctuation, especially in the case of oil. When a country is a producer, however, they have some protection against inflationary impacts from price volatilities. They may also wish to subsidize fossil fuels to step up their geopolitical power.

Fossil fuel producer subsidies, however, often have much stronger and less pronounced policy objectives. On the one hand they can be used to foster governmental legitimacy with the wider public. There are many jobs in fossil fuel extraction and production, and jobs mean votes or, at least, political support. On the other hand, fuel subsidies might be granted for political patronage. Often, fossil fuel extraction and production companies have direct access to politicians, via the existence of cronies and/or campaign financing tactics in exchange for increased profits after taxes.

4.2 *Subsidy Types*

"Fossil fuel production subsidies" is a generic term used to refer to various support measures to exploration, extraction, transport, processing, and distribution and decommissioning of oil, gas, and coal resources, as well as to associated infrastructure.

Linked to the WTO definition above, there are two general categories of subsidies. A first includes national and subnational fiscal support. Such production subsidies can include direct budgetary transfers such as research and development grants, tariff policies, and tax expenditures. Of current reported estimates, tax expenditures cover about two thirds of fossil fuel production support measures. Such tax measures include tax exemptions or tax reductions for fossil fuel producers, for example on corporate income or on royalties they pay.

A second set of potential support measures includes public finance through which governments provide financial services to fossil fuel producers via state-owned financial institutions (i.e., institutions in which the government holds at least a 50% ownership). Such financing support can come in the form of loans, equity, insurance, and guarantees. These types of support measures are more difficult to gauge since they involve estimating risk transfers and foregone revenue by quantifying a specific subsidy fraction of credit assistance. Such credit assistance can come from multilateral finance institutions, export credit agencies, or state-owned enterprises.

4.3 *Subsidy Estimates*

Fossil fuel producer subsidy estimates cannot be attained with a simple formula like the price gap approach and have to be constructed bottom-up through an inventory approach. This makes producer subsidy estimates more time-consuming and, therefore, less holistic. It also means that transparent countries might score higher in subsidy figures than those that hide support in more complicated or subnational tax codes. Furthermore, it is more difficult to compare countries, especially with regard to tax expenditure. Estimating the subsidy value of a tax expenditure relies on a country's benchmark tax regime, and tax regimes vary widely between and even within countries.

The OECD compiles estimates of direct budgetary transfers and tax expenditures, and currently explores a new methodology to quantify the support estimate of government credit assistance. It does so for the 36 OECD economies and 8 partner countries (Argentina, Brazil, China, Colombia, India, Indonesia, Russia, and South Africa). Between 2009 and 2017, total direct budgetary support and tax expenditure to fossil fuel producers hovered between around USD 20 and 56 billion. In recent years, this support has declined from USD 56 billion in 2013 to USD 24 billion in 2017. This decline has mainly been driven by Western Europe's hard coal phase out and fiscal tightening in Indonesia and Argentina (IEA & OECD 2019). At the same time, new measures have been introduced to foster the production of unconventional oil and gas resources. Among the largest "subsidizers" on record are Russia and the US, followed by the UK, Australia, Brazil, and China (OECD 2019).

Besides budgetary transfers and tax expenditures, the Overseas Development Institute (ODI) has focused attention on SOEs and public financing. However, because of a lack of information, ODI could only estimate the total investment by SOEs in fossil fuel production, rather than the specific sub-components that can qualify as a subsidy. With this crude metric, they showed that China has the largest fossil fuel production through SOEs (about USD 77 billion in 2013 and 2014), followed by Russia and Brazil (respectively USD 50 billion and USD 42 billion per year during the same time frame), and Indonesia and Saudi Arabia. ODI has done a similar exercise with public finance, again without the possibility of identifying the subcomponent of public finance that constitutes a subsidy. They found that Japan and China had the largest public financing of fossil fuels in 2013 and 2014 (USD 19 billion and USD 17 billion respectively), followed by Korea (USD 10 billion). Most emerging economies within the G-20 relied on domestic public financing, whereas most public finance from other G-20 countries was aimed at fossil fuel production abroad (Bast et al. 2015).

Overall, fossil fuel production subsidy estimates are severely incomplete and more difficult to attain than consumption subsidy estimates. As a result, various specialized NGOs such as the Global Subsidies Initiative have complemented OECD data by using an inventory approach to study national and subnational fossil fuel production subsidies of various countries. In the context of the G-20 and APEC commitments to phase out inefficient fossil fuel subsidies, various countries have started voluntary peer reviews. The OECD chairs such reviews for the G-20. Starting in 2016 with the US and China, peer reviews had been completed for Germany, Indonesia, Italy, and Mexico by 2019 with Argentina and Canada under way.

4.4 The Politics of Fossil Fuel Production Subsidies

Fossil fuel production subsidies remain difficult to reform because their most notable beneficiaries are large, powerful, and politically connected companies. For example, in the US, the Obama administration submitted proposals to eliminate some of the most abhorrent oil and gas production subsidies from the budget every year. Congress, on the other hand, has refused to consider this measure, given that the majority of its members rely on campaign financing from the fossil fuel industry. In other large producing countries, such as Russia, Saudi Arabia, and Nigeria, many oil and gas companies are also often directly linked to the ruling elite and, as mentioned above, subsidies are used as a rent to keep clients in check.

In addition to beneficiaries, there is also a lack of transparency about various producer subsidies, and a lack of public understanding of those subsidies that we do know. Understanding a price-gap whereby the government is directly funding oil and gas consumption is more intuitive than a tax reduction which constitutes foregone revenue. When such subsidies are linked to clear and legitimate policy rationales such as strengthening the trade balance by reducing a country's reliance on foreign imports, then maintaining such subsidies seems reasonable, even if some of them simply result in windfall profits for producers. In both democratic and authoritarian countries, certain large media corporations often play a critical role in keeping public knowledge about subsidies limited, further deteriorating potential public pressure for their reform.

Internationally, the push for production subsidy reform has been ambivalent, at best. While G-20 and APEC countries committed to fossil fuel subsidy reform in 2009, country reports on their progress were meager, with some countries like Saudi Arabia initially even arguing they had no "inefficient fossil fuel subsidies" at all. As a result of the discussions over definitions and the lack of transparency, the G-20 set up country peer-reviews of each other's fossil fuel subsidies. While the set-up of the system took some time, these peer reviews have given a more holistic and detailed overview of producer subsidies than individual country progress reports on their G-20 and APEC commitments (IEA & OECD 2019). Besides these international commitments, the WTO could have also theoretically played a role in guiding fuel subsidy reform. While many oil and gas subsidies include local content requirements—a prohibited subsidy under WTO law—not one single oil and gas producing country has brought a complaint against another about fossil fuel production subsidies.

Box X: Nuclear Energy Subsidies
Nuclear energy subsidies are found in all parts of the nuclear fuel cycle. As the largest cost component of nuclear energy is the capital costs associated to reactor construction, a lot of subsidies try to reduce those costs. In addition, nuclear energy developers have also often benefited from shifting the economic value of long-term risks (such as waste management, accident risk insurance, security management, and decommissioning costs) to the government.

In the absence of such burden-sharing, the nuclear industry would face potentially prohibitive costs. For example, while the chances for an accident are small, the consequential costs would be of huge magnitude, and if this would have to be covered by private insurance, nuclear energy's levelized cost of electricity would increase substantially.

One notable example of a recent nuclear subsidy was to the UK's development of Hinkley Point C. Here, the government promised a feed-in tariff (see below) of GBP 92.5/MWh for a guaranteed period of 35 years. This subsidy was "out of the roof" for an allegedly mature technology (in comparison, the global average levelized cost of electricity of solar PV in 2018 was around GBP 72/MWh). The nuclear subsidy is large even in comparison with emerging technologies such as wind and solar PV in the 2010s. In addition to the feed-in tariff, the government also employed loan guarantees to transfer project risk, including the risk of cost overruns and delays (which are very common in the construction of new reactors). And a third subsidy was related to waste disposal, promising the developer that any costs above GBP 5 billion would be carried in full by the government.

5 Renewable Electricity Subsidies

5.1 *Subsidy Objectives*

Renewable electricity subsidies, which mostly focus on the deployment of renewable electricity, have three main objectives, all covering facets of the energy trilemma. First, but not always foremost, there are two environmental objectives. On the one hand, governments subsidize renewables to decarbonize the power sector and mitigate carbon emissions that cause climate change. On the other hand, various governments also seek accelerated deployment to reduce air pollution. Especially the latter is becoming a key reason for subsidizing renewables in rapidly growing Asian countries with metropolitan centers.

Second, governments use renewable energy subsidies to achieve social and economic goals. They often try to link deployment subsidies to the creation of long-term and short-term construction jobs. They have also often used such subsidies as an industrial policy tool, trying to achieve a comparative advantage in emerging technologies so that their producers can compete at home and abroad. It has not been uncommon for renewable electricity subsidies to have been linked to local content requirements. This strategy serves the dual purpose of job-creation and fostering other, supportive industries, such as the steel industry in the case of wind turbine towers or the module manufacturing industry in the case of solar PV.

Third, renewable energy subsidies have been used to foster energy security and access. From one side, more renewables can imply a relatively lower dependence on foreign resources. From the other side, renewables can be installed in remote areas to foster electricity access there.

5.2 *Subsidy Types*

There are five main types of renewable energy subsidies, aimed at different types of stakeholders and projects: (1) quotas and certificates, (2) feed-in tariffs and premiums, (3) auctions, (4) net metering and billing, and (5) investment and production tax credits (Fig. 27.7).

First, quotas and mandates (also often called renewable portfolio standards or renewable purchase obligations) mandate utilities to source a certain percentage of distributed electricity from renewable sources. They are used in around 100 jurisdictions in 2016. Governments often increase that rate over time to encourage a gradual uptake of renewable electricity. The advantages of this system are that it theoretically guarantees that a certain amount of

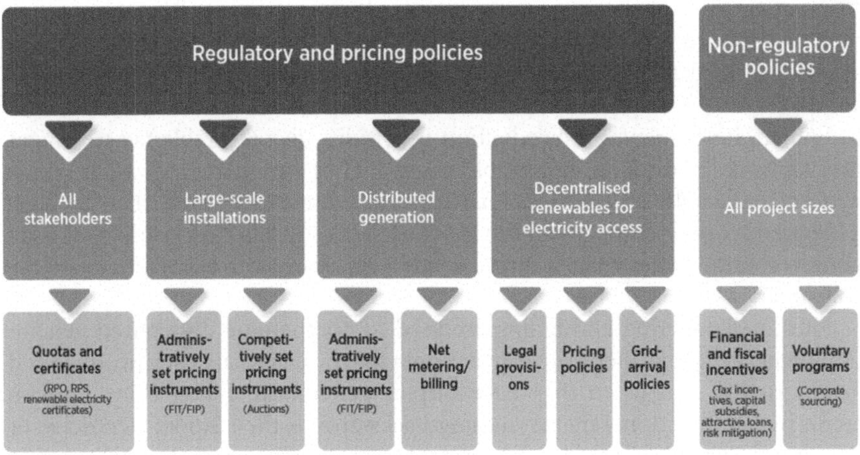

Fig. 27.7 Classification of power sector policies

renewable electricity is used, and that this amount is generated at the lowest cost. To foster compliance, this system is often linked to a trading system of renewable electricity certificates in which each MWh of renewable electricity is granted a certificate, which can then be traded from those with a surplus to utilities that do not reach the quota.

Second, feed-in tariffs (FIT) or premiums (FIP) consist of administratively set tariffs and premiums in which utilities are obliged to purchase electricity from developers at a certain fixed price (FIT) or at the variable market price plus a premium (FIP). FITs and FIPs are used in about 80 countries in 2017. The costs for FITs and FIPs are mostly incurred by utilities, which then mostly pass on that cost to consumers (in the case of liberalized markets) or the government (in the case of government-owned utilities). Feed-in tariff or premium policies can also include a "degression" rate, that lowers the FIT and FIP every year as to foster innovation and technology cost reduction. This system has been hailed as the most successful system for subsidizing renewables. Besides it being easy to differentiate the rates between various technologies, FITs and FIPs have also been most preferred by investors as it guarantees a certain price or premium over a longer term. It can also reduce capital costs by driving down the interest rates on lending.

Third, auctioning (also often called tendering or bidding) is a system in which governments write out auctions to invite companies to submit bids for a long-term contract to install a certain amount of renewable electricity capacity and supply electricity therefrom. Governments can tailor auctions to their demands in terms of policy or technology objectives. Bids subsequently compete over the lowest cost at which they could provide electricity. The winning bid then receives a subsidy equal to the difference between the market price for electricity and the winning bid price. Auctions have been used in 70 countries around the world by 2016, of which 34 had auctions in 2016 alone. In recent years, auctions have become more popular because various RE technologies such as onshore wind and solar have become more cost-competitive. It also avoids the need for regulators to set prices themselves (as is the case in FITs and FIPs).

Fourth, investment and production tax credits give favorable tax treatment to owners or investors in renewable energy. They can give them a partial tax write-off, generally or linked to a particular amount of electricity that has been generated by their company in the last year. This subsidy thus consists of foregone revenue, rather than a direct burden on either the government or the consumer.

Fifth, net-metering and billing are used to compensate distributed generation owners (i.e., smaller scale installations) for the electricity they produce and export to the grid when they have surplus generation. Either they can earn credit by a bidirectional meter running backwards as they export electricity, or they can receive credit measured on a net export meter and then adjusted in their billing cycle through the distribution company.

5.3 *Subsidy Estimates*

In total, subsidies to renewables and electric vehicles were estimated at about USD 150 billion in 2018, up from about USD 50 billion in 2010. While growing in absolute terms, their relative importance has declined since two of the largest technologies—onshore wind and solar PV—have seen drastic cost reductions. As a result of this and the growing use of auctions, the price-differential between the market price and winning bid price is expected to drop further.

Even though the methods to estimate the two most used renewable energy subsidies are not that complicated, there is not yet a systematic overview (in 2019) of the value of different types of renewable electricity subsidies. FITs, FIPs, and auctions are pricing policies, so an estimation of their net subsidy value requires an assumption of the evolution of the market power price over the period that grid operators are mandated to purchase the renewable electricity. The difference between the market price and the feed-in tariff or winning bid tariff is then the per unit subsidy. The total value can then be calculated by multiplying it by the total amount of kWh produced in a given year or, when calculating ahead, an estimated amount of generation including inflation.

For the other subsidies, renewable purchase obligations can be estimated more easily when there is a market for renewable energy certificates. A subsidy estimate can then be reached by taking the net-value of such certificates and multiplying it by the amount of electricity produced. Tax credits need a benchmark tax rate against which the subsidy value is calculated. Estimating the subsidy value of net-billing and net-metering requires knowing the per unit economic value of electricity exported or the rate at which the meter runs backward.

Toward the end of the 2010s, subsidies for solar and wind were being phased out in some countries around the world since the technologies were nearly cost-competitive. Initially, Spain was leading in solar deployment without subsidies, but generally across the world there has been a move to accept shorter term power purchase contracts. While initially they were about 20 to 25 years long, many developers now accept PPAs of 15 years or less (Chediak and Eckhouse 2019).

5.4 *The Politics of Renewable Electricity Subsidies*

As renewable electricity subsidies are relatively new, so are the politics that accompany them. Both domestically and internationally, fierce discussions have complicated subsidy design and implementation.

On a domestic level, every type of subsidy has certain disadvantages that welcome criticism. Perhaps most discussed is the disadvantage of feed-in tariffs and premiums. With FITs and FIPs, the information asymmetry between the regulator and the renewable electricity industry can lead to either overly high prices that create windfall profits for developers but large pains for consumers and government budgets, or overly low prices that prohibit investment altogether. This asymmetry has led, in a few instances, to the retro-active adjustment of feed-in tariffs, destroying investor confidence altogether and often leading to investment arbitration. For example, in Spain, the solar energy FIT was so generous and without degression rate that deployment boomed from 103 MW in 2006 to 2708 MW in 2008. As a result, the government changed FIT policies in 2008 and ultimately abandoned the whole FIT program in 2012. In 2013, they shocked the industry by announcing that the statutorily guaranteed FIT for earlier installations would be reduced with retroactive effect, spurring several lawsuits against the government.

Besides FITs and FIPs, other subsidy types also have considerable disadvantages. The drawback of quotas and mandates is that it is difficult to decide on the exact size of the penalty. Tradable certificates may also lock in existing asymmetries between regions with existing capacity in renewables and those without. Even regions with potential might find it difficult to explore that potential while satisfying quotas at the same time. The disadvantage of auctions, from its side, is that bids have not always been realized because the bidding price was set unrealistically low just to win the project. In some countries, bids have also been tailored to favor specific companies, adding to corruption concerns. And finally, bids bring less certainty for investors than FITs and FIPs, especially when there is not a lot of certainty about when the next bidding round will arrive.

Importantly, several renewable energy subsidies to both large-scale producers and distributed generation are met with skepticism from stakeholders that fear the system's flexibility for short-term large-scale uptake, as well as the impact on operations of distribution companies that are all of a sudden confronted with power purchasing agreements and distributed generation that might conflict with existing contracts and business models.

On an international level, renewable energy subsidies have been followed by various lawsuits, undermining the confidence investors can have in them. On the one hand, various WTO cases have focused on local content requirements attached to renewable electricity subsidies. For example, Ontario, China, India, and US states have seen cases initiated against their renewable energy subsidies. On the other hand, various companies have also sued states through investor-state dispute settlements whenever they believed legislative changes countered their legitimate expectations. Case in point is Spain, where several investors have sued the government after their retroactive change in FIT rates.

Box X: Biofuel Subsidies

There are three main types of biofuel subsidies around the world. A first type consists of blending mandates that set targets to have a certain amount of ethanol and biodiesel as part of the fuel mix. These are a form of market price support, as they guarantee a market for biofuels and

(*continued*)

(continued)

enhance market predictability for investors. A second type comprises excise tax exemptions in which biofuels are granted tax exemptions or reductions compared to the excise taxes lifted on conventional petrol and diesel. A third type includes trade policies such as import duties or anti-dumping measures which aim at protecting domestic markets from foreign competition of either ethanol, biodiesel, or the feedstock needed to produce either.

Biofuel subsidies have been surrounded by political controversy. On the one hand, first-generation biodiesel is not carbon-reducing when integrating indirect land use change (ILUC) effects. In some cases, depending on feedstock, it accounts for even higher emissions than conventional diesel. ILUC takes into account the effect that a heightened demand for vegetable oils as a feedstock for biodiesel has on agricultural expansion and the conversion of natural land, either domestic or abroad. One specific example was the importation into the EU of oil palm that originated from converting high carbon stock lands in Indonesia and Malaysia, or of soy from savannah and rainforest lands in South America. On the other hand, first-generation ethanol, while having a positive carbon reduction impact compared to conventional petrol, was found to impact local and global food prices.

The fact biofuel subsidies were and still are pervasive, even when negative developmental impacts became increasingly evident, was and still is linked to their primary policy objective. Rather than supporting "renewable" energy in transport fuels, biofuel support policies have been used as an indirect agricultural subsidy. By increasing demand for agricultural products, governments have used biofuel support to lift the prices of agricultural commodities, thereby supporting domestic farmers. In the EU, the blending mandate was pushed for by the agricultural directorate during a reform of agricultural subsidies, all while the climate directorate and the joint research center (the European Commission's scientific advisory body) expressed caution and even concern about first-generation biofuels. In the US, ethanol subsidies have been used to support farmers in politically important states. For example, former Vice-President Al Gore has admitted in 2010 that "first generation ethanol I think was a mistake… One of the reasons I made that mistake is that I paid particular attention to the farmers in my home state of Tennessee, and I had a certain fondness for the farmers in the state of Iowa because I was about to run for president." Both the EU and the US have attempted to reform subsidies but have far from eliminated them.

6 Conclusion: Energy Subsidies and the Politics of Reform

Energy subsidies are pervasive, for two reasons. On the one hand, no single energy subsidy can resolve the contradictions of the energy trilemma. Governments cannot simultaneously support the affordability of energy, energy security, and environmental sustainability. Rather, they are required to implement various types of subsidies to various energy types to try and reach an elusive balance of those three policy objectives.

What objectives weigh more heavily in decision-making depends on a country's developmental context, its politics, and its current energy infrastructure. It is however safe to say that all three objectives are becoming ever more pronounced in many countries. This is a direct result of various simultaneous drivers such as population growth and associated demand for energy, a deepening of socio-economic inequalities, the increase in air pollution and global climatic change, and the quest for economic competitiveness to manage the turmoil of economic globalization.

On the other hand, energy subsidies are also pervasive because of whom they benefit. Once installed, domestic interest groups form around the subsidies' beneficiaries and make their reform politically costly. As shown, these beneficiaries are not only energy companies, but can also include, among others, households, farmers, and politicians that directly collect rents from maintaining those subsidies. These vested interests have put the political economy of subsidies and subsidy reform at the forefront of debates on fiscal policy in the field of energy. Likewise, they will also determine what level of progress can be made against the several sustainable development goals linked to affordable and clean energy, the phasing out of fossil fuel subsidies, and global climate change.

References

Agreement on Subsidies and Countervailing Measures, Adopted 15 April 1994, Marrakesh Agreement Establishing the World Trade Organization, Annex 1A, 1869 U.N.T.S. 186.

Bast, Elizabeth, Alex Doukas, Sam Pickard, Laurie van der Burg, and Shelagh Whitley. "Empty Promises: G20 Subsidies to Oil, Gas and Coal Production." ODI & OCI, 2015. https://www.odi.org/sites/odi.org.uk/files/odi-assets/publications-opinion-files/9957.pdf.

Chediak, Mark, and Brian Eckhouse. "Solar and Wind Power So Cheap They're Outgrowing Subsidies." *Bloomberg.Com*, September 19, 2019. https://www.bloomberg.com/news/features/2019-09-19/solar-and-wind-power-so-cheap-they-re-outgrowing-subsidies.

Coady, David, Moataz El-Said, Robert Gillingham, Kangni Kpodar, Paulo Medas, and David Newhouse. "The Magnitude and Distribution of Fuel Subsidies: Evidence from Bolivia, Ghana, Jordan, Mali, and Sri Lanka." IMF, 2006. https://www.imf.org/external/pubs/ft/wp/2006/wp06247.pdf.

Diop, Ndiame. "Why Is Reducing Energy Subsidies a Prudent, Fair, and Transformative Policy for Indonesia?" Economic Premise Number 136. The World Bank, 2014.

Gerasimchuk, Ivetta, Richard Bridle, Christopher Beaton, and Chris Charles. "State of Play on Biofuel Subsidies: Are Policies Ready to Shift?" International Institute for Sustainable Development, 2012. https://www.iisd.org/gsi/sites/default/files/bf_stateplay_2012.pdf.

del Granado, Javier Arze, David Coady, and Robert Gillingham. "The Unequal Benefits of Fuel Subsidies: A Review of Evidence for Developing Countries." IMF, 2010. http://www.imf.org/external/pubs/ft/wp/2010/wp10202.pdf.

IEA. "Carrots and Sticks: Taxing and Subsidising Energy." Paris: International Energy Agency, 2006. https://www.iea.org/publications/freepublications/publication/oil_subsidies.pdf.

IEA & OECD. "Update on Recent Progress in Reform of Inefficient Fossil-Fuel Subsidies That Encourage Wasteful Consumption." In *Contribution by the International Energy Agency (IEA) and the Organisation for Economic Co-Operation and Development (OECD) to the G20 Energy Transitions Working Group in Consultation with: International Energy Forum (IEF), Organization of Petroleum Exporting Countries (OPEC) and the World Bank*, 44. Toyama, 2019. http://www.oecd.org/fossil-fuels/publication/OECD-IEA-G20-Fossil-Fuel-Subsidies-Reform-Update-2019.pdf.

IMF. "Energy Subsidy Reform: Lessons and Implications." IMF, 2013. http://www.imf.org/external/np/pp/eng/2013/012813.pdf.

———. "Global Fossil Fuel Subsidies Remain Large: An Update Based on Country-Level Estimates." IMF, 2019. https://www.imf.org/en/Publications/WP/Issues/2019/05/02/Global-Fossil-Fuel-Subsidies-Remain-Large-An-Update-Based-on-Country-Level-Estimates-46509.

International Energy Agency. *World Energy Outlook 2017*. OECD/IEA, 2017.

———. *World Energy Outlook 2018*. OECD/IEA, 2018.

OECD. "OECD Analysis of Budgetary Support and Tax Expenditures," 2019. http://www.oecd.org/fossil-fuels/data/.

CHAPTER 28

Economics of Access to Energy

Giacomo Falchetta and Simone Tagliapietra

1 Energy Access: Fundamentally an Economic Problem

Energy is a key enabler of human activities. The provision of energy services underpins the socio-economic development of nations and their growing prosperity (Fouquet 2016). Not only is energy required by all industrial activities, but it is also essential for the provision of clean water, sanitation and healthcare, as well as efficient lighting, cooling, cooking, use of mechanical power, transportation, and telecommunication services (McCollum et al. 2018; Nerini et al. 2018). Thus, providing access to affordable modern energy services represents a key requirement for eradicating poverty and reducing inequalities. This is the reason why the United Nations (2015) included the achievement of universal access to affordable, reliable, sustainable, and modern energy among the Sustainable Development Goals at the core of its 2030 Agenda for Sustainable Development.

The concept of energy access does not have a unique, widely agreed definition (International Energy Agency 2017). Generally, it is referred to as household access to minimum levels of modern energy, for both electric appliances and clean cooking needs. However, a heated debate over the quantification of those minimum levels and their measurement is ongoing (Bhatia and Angelou 2015; Nussbaumer et al. 2012; Pachauri 2011). The most widespread metric

G. Falchetta (✉)
International Institute for Applied Systems Analysis (IIASA), Vienna, Austria

Fondazione Eni Enrico Mattei (FEEM), Milan, Italy
e-mail: falchetta@iiasa.ac.at

S. Tagliapietra
Bruegel, Brussels, Belgium

Universita Cattolica del Sacro Cuore, Milan, Italy

M. Hafner, G. Luciani (eds.), *The Palgrave Handbook of International Energy Economics*, https://doi.org/10.1007/978-3-030-86884-0_28

of access to electricity and clean cooking solutions is the share of a country's population that benefits from each energy service. However, much criticism has been raised about this measurement approach, because it is inherently limited by a strong aggregation and mono-dimensionality. This approach disregards crucial questions such as reliability of supply, and the effective use beyond nominal access provision (Falchetta et al. 2020). These discussions have spurred the establishment of measurement schemes, such as the World Bank Multi-Tier Framework, suitable for providing a multi-dimensional indicator of energy access (Bhatia and Angelou 2015). One of the crucial arguments emerging from these frameworks is that energy access and energy poverty are not mutually exclusive. At the same time, energy access is not a static concept, but should be considered a dynamic process following a 'ladder' (Bensch et al. 2017; Chattopadhyay et al. 2015; Grimm et al. 2016; Monyei et al. 2018). In this process, different technologies and solutions gradually replace the previous ones, providing greater power and supporting more appliances and uses. Nevertheless, since measures of country-wide access level are widely used, in this chapter we refer to them extensively. Yet, while we are aware of their intrinsic limitations, concepts and metrics that better characterise the multi-dimensionality of energy access are at the core of the discussion.

Eight hundred and forty million people across the world continue to lack access to electricity, while 2.9 billion people do not have access to clean cooking facilities. Substantial efforts have been made over the last decade in this area, with the global electrification level growing from 83% in 2010 to 89% in 2017. As highlighted by the International Energy Agency, the International Renewable Energy Agency, and the United Nations Statistics Division (2019), electrification efforts have been particularly successful in Central and Southern Asia, where 91% of the population had access to electricity in 2017. Access levels in Latin America and the Caribbean, as well as Eastern and Southeast Asia, climbed to 98%. Among the 20 countries with the largest populations lacking access to electricity, India, Bangladesh, Kenya, and Myanmar have made the most significant progress. Sub-Saharan Africa remains the region with the largest access deficit: here, about 570 million people—more than one in two—lack access to electricity. The continent is home to 15 out of the 20 countries with the lowest electrification levels (Fig. 28.1).

Progress towards universal clean cooking has hitherto been slower than the rollout of electrification. The share of global population with access to clean cooking fuels and technologies increased from 57% in 2010 to 61% in 2017. Sub-Saharan Africa, Central and Southern Asia, and Eastern and Southeast Asia account for the majority of the population lacking access (Fig. 28.2). In sub-Saharan Africa, the number of people without access to clean cooking has been rising as a result of strong demographic dynamics outpacing clean cooking access progress. Throughout the continent, the population lacking access increased from less than 750 million in 2010 to around 900 million in 2017 (International Energy Agency et al. 2019). Over the same period of time, Asia showed instead substantial progress relative to population growth. This result

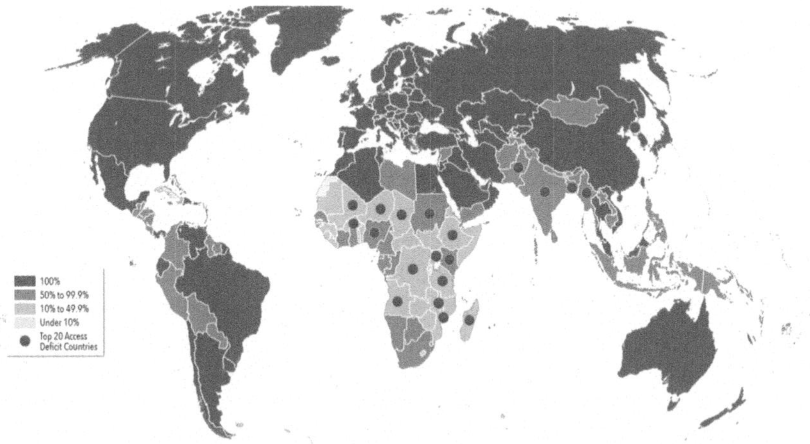

Fig. 28.1 Share of population with access to electricity in 2017. (Source: International Energy Agency et al., Tracking SDG 7: The Energy Progress Report 2019. All rights reserved)

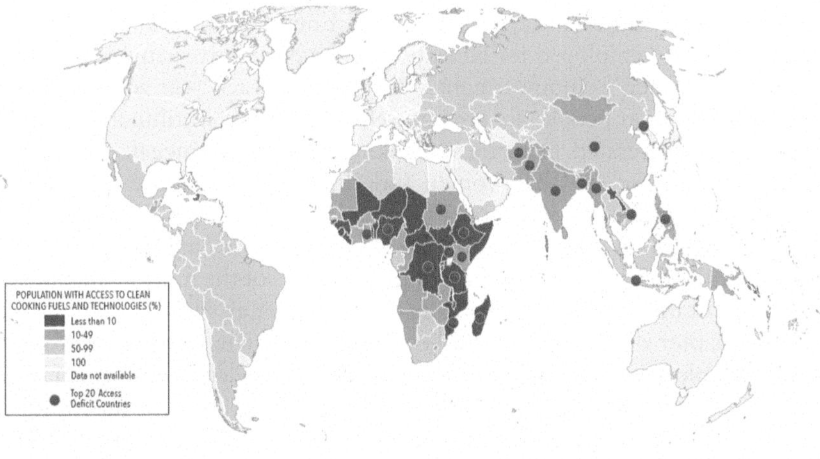

Fig. 28.2 Share of population with access to clean cooking fuels and technologies in 2017. (Source: International Energy Agency et al., Tracking SDG 7: The Energy Progress Report 2019. All rights reserved)

was achieved through a variety of strategies depending on the national context (e.g. the diffusion of liquid petroleum gas (LPG) in India, or the construction of natural gas pipelines in China). Globally, a strong urban–rural divide characterises this challenge: the level of access to clean cooking fuels and technologies stands at 83% in urban areas, while it remains at a low of 34% in rural areas.

Providing universal access to electricity and clean cooking would greatly enhance the living standards as well as the economic prospects of the people currently lacking access. The case of electrification is illustrative of how the lack of energy access represents a major stumbling block for socio-economic development. Any developed country has among its key priorities secure access to electricity to foster its economic development. Electricity access is key to improving health conditions, increasing productivity, enhancing overall economic competitiveness, and ultimately promoting economic growth and poverty reduction. Empirical studies have shown that expanding electricity access indeed increases time spent on income-generating activities (Bernard 2010; Bos et al. 2018; Rathi and Vermaak 2017; Van de Walle et al. 2013), especially outside of the agricultural sector. Electrification also increases the number of manufacturing firms, their productivity, and revenues (Bonan et al. 2017). Moreover, the significance of electricity access for adaptation purposes—including cooling and irrigation—is increasing since coincidentally the regions lacking access are also those forecasted to undergo the greatest temperature increases in the coming decades as a result of anthropogenic climate change (Byers et al. 2018).

The case of clean cooking is illustrative of the social character of the challenge of energy access. In developing countries, women and children are often in charge of collecting firewood, an activity that is estimated to require an average hour and a half each day (International Energy Agency 2017). This time could instead be employed for education or for productive activities, as well as to support women's empowerment. Furthermore, each year across the globe around 3.8 million people die prematurely from illness attributable to indoor air pollution generated from these cooking practices (Amegah and Jaakkola 2016). Due to the fact that women and children spend more time indoors, they are the first victims of this phenomenon (Rumchev et al. 2007). Empirical studies clearly show that expanding access to clean cooking would lower this premature death toll, enhance the living conditions of the most vulnerable, and bring significant economic co-benefits (Rosenthal et al. 2018).

This chapter discusses why the key obstacles that have so far prevented 1 billion people worldwide from having access to modern commercial energy share a fundamentally economic nature. In turn, it explores the different roots tying energy access to technological, governance, and financing aspects. While the lack of either electricity or clean cooking solutions has several common causes, we discuss them separately to highlight the specific techno-economic issues underlying each service. This is beneficial to a tailored discussion of the key economic policy instruments and financing approaches necessary to achieve universal access to modern energy.

2 Access to Electricity: Economic Issues and Policy Instruments

2.1 *Generation, Transmission, and Distribution Infrastructure Expansion*

In countries with electricity access gaps, power generation capacity is often limited. The operational power plants also face recurrent maintenance and fuel provisioning security issues. As a result, a share of the national demand remains unmet and electricity distribution utilities are forced to adopt load-shedding policies. These dynamics determine recurrent supply reliability issues for grid-connected consumers. For instance, the World Bank reports that in sub-Saharan Africa firms faced an average of 9 outages per month in 2018. This implies that even households and businesses considered electrified are not benefitting from secure access to energy. The bottom line is that electricity access planners face significant constraints to broadening the consumer base (and therefore the domestic demand) without ramping up the sources of supply.

Concurrently, the national transmission and distribution networks have a limited extent and coverage. The existing infrastructure often connects power plants to the main urban areas, while the bulk of rural settlements, where most of the population is concentrated, remain far-off from the network. The infrastructure supply inequality determines a situation of strongly unbalanced electricity access levels in urban and rural areas (International Energy Agency et al. 2019). This suggests that commonly reported national electrification levels are hiding wide disparities, especially considering that the bulk of the population of developing countries lives in rural areas (World Bank 2018). It is worth underlining that the unequal expansion of energy access, with both urban–rural and across-province inequalities within each country (Falchetta et al. 2020), is the product of explicit political choices to target investment and infrastructure expansion in determined areas, which do not necessarily respond to an efficiency criterion. A broad stream of literature (Onyeji et al. 2012; Trotter 2016) has highlighted the role of political factors and local institutions in determining electrification pathways, and in particular the inequality in access within regions of the same country. Moreover, as a result of the ongoing rapid urbanisation trends, significant hotspots of people without access are emerging in peri-urban areas surrounding cities. In those areas the local distribution network is sometimes lacking despite the geographical proximity to existing electric substations, or the dwellers simply cannot afford to pay for grid connection charges.

The main economic roots behind the insufficient or poorly maintained generation capacity and the limited extent of grid networks include:

(i). The considerable upfront investment requirements and operation costs of power generation facilities. According to Enerdata (2016), the costs of new power plants in Africa are: (i) 2,000/kW for hydropower; (ii) 1,112 and 1,290 USD/kW for open and combined-cycle gas-fired turbines, respectively; (iii) 2,153 USD/kW for coal-fired plants; (iv) 2,011 USD/kW for utility-scale solar photovoltaic (PV) plants; (v) 11,300 USD/kW for solar concentrated power plants; and (vi) 2,450 USD/kW for wind power plants below 100 MW in size. A steeply growing demand for power as a result of both economic development (e.g. 2.4% and 6.8% on average in Africa and South Asia in 2018) and population growth (2.7% and 1.2% on average in Africa and South Asia in 2018) implies large capacity addition requirements. These, in turn, necessitate substantial investment that in past decades has not been adequately channelled due to the reasons discussed below.

(ii). The key role of running costs. The lack of maintenance and ageing of power plants has led to a situation where 25% of the installed capacity is unavailable in sub-Saharan Africa (Findt et al. 2014). The supply security of the fuels necessary to power existing plants is another issue. For instance, the installed capacity in Nigeria (above 10 GW, USAID 2019) is technically adequate to satisfy the current national demand, and yet supply disruptions due to damage to the pipelines, geopolitical issues, or price volatility have led to their under-exploitation and thus to issues in guaranteeing a secure supply of electricity to grid-connected consumers (e.g. see Occhiali and Falchetta 2018). Hydropower plants—which are the main source of power supply in many countries with electricity access gaps—are also constrained by increasingly frequent and prolonged drought periods which force utilities to suspend generation or limit the operational capacity (Falchetta et al. 2019). Countries heavily relying on coal—such as South Africa, India, and China—are facing substantial socio-economic pressures. For instance, South Africa is water-scarce and faces recurrent droughts, which requires the Government to curtail residential water use. This is also due to the very large cooling water requirements of coal-fired plants (van Vliet et al. 2016). In Asia, burning coal is perceived as increasingly costly for the social impact it has been exerting on public health.

(iii). The high expansion costs of the grid, ranging from 3000 USD per km of low-voltage distribution line to 30,000 USD per km of high-voltage transmission line, which in turn imply an average of 1500 USD for each new household connected to the national grid (Rosnes and Vennemo 2009). These costs are even more difficult to bear considering that the central planner is facing high discount rates (medium-term government bonds average a 15% yield in sub-Saharan Africa), and thus the cost of capital is high. This, of course, discourages long-term infrastructure investment.

(iv). The dispersion of the population—particularly in rural areas—which results in low population densities (e.g. the average for sub-Saharan Africa is 51 inhabitants/km^2 against 455 inhabitants/km^2 in India, where most connections have been achieved through direct connection to the national grid). The low population density often renders the investment not economically profitable.

(v). The low ability-to-pay and low short-term consumption of new customers (Blimpo and Cosgrove-Davies 2019; Jacome et al. 2019; Taneja 2018), which, together, do not allow the national utility to recoup the large upfront investment needed to connect new households to the national grid.

In recent years, a number of decision support tools have been developed to optimise electricity access planning and quantify the required investments, as well as to identify the optimal technological solutions to bring access to each specific settlement. These tools exploit geospatial data of population settlements, existing energy infrastructure, and electricity supply options' potential and costs. In general, least-cost electrification tools optimise each settlement, that is, they look for the technology with the minimum local power supply cost, subject to the local demography, infrastructure, geography, electricity demand sources, and power generation potential factors. Electrification modelling instruments are particularly insightful because they are able to represent and visualise the techno-economic boundary separating areas where grid-based or decentralised solutions are more efficient to reach the access targets defined by the policymakers. Figure 28.3 illustrates an example of the output of the OnSSET geospatial electrification tool for sub-Saharan Africa (Mentis et al. 2017), where colours identify the most efficient technology in each area and

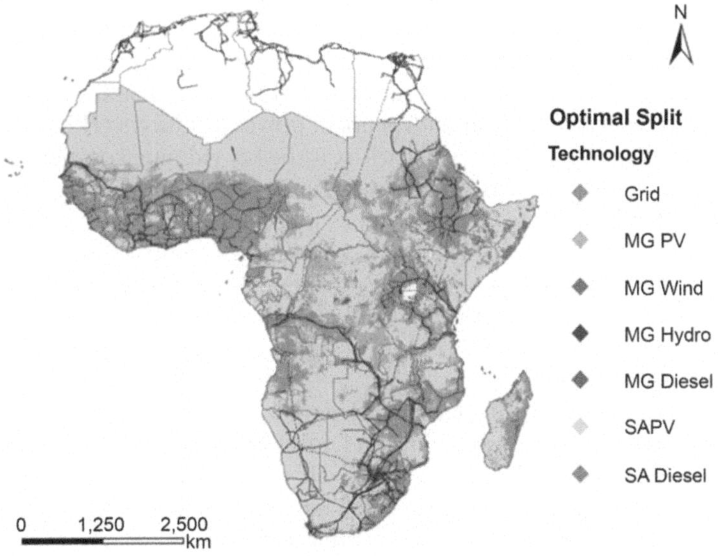

Fig. 28.3 Example of the output of a geospatial electrification model. (Source: Mentis et al. 2017)

black lines represent the current transmission network. The results show, for instance, that in most areas remote from the grid, solar PV-based solutions are the least-cost electrification option, and that different areas are more efficiently electrified either through the development of mini-grids or with the installation of household-level infrastructure. Thus, when provided with reliable data on the potential demand from both the residential sector and productive uses, electrification tools can inform policymakers on the local techno-economic aspects of the design and implementation of electrification plans.

2.2 Budgetary Deficit of National Utilities and Subsidy Reforms

Among the plethora of economic policy measures adopted by utilities to foster the electrification process, two aspects have emerged as crucial: the pricing (Kojima and Trimble 2016) and subsidisation schemes (IMF 2013; Vagliasindi 2012).

Pricing schemes determine the relationship between (i) disposable income at the household level, (ii) the ability to afford electricity, and (iii) the capacity of utilities to recoup their costs and attain a positive budget balance. Historically, electricity pricing is divided into (a) an upfront connection charge, (b) a yearly service charge, and (c) a per-unit (marginal) cost of electricity consumed. Clearly, components (a) and (b) are the greatest household-side upfront barriers to the increase of the local electricity access level. Credit-constrained households necessitate options to pay for those initial charges in instalments or have them waived through appropriate subsidisation.

Traditionally, electricity systems are developed through investments made by national utilities, which allow the achievement of strong balance sheets through the sale of electricity produced at large-scale power plants. Earnings serve as the primary financing source for grid infrastructure expansion and strengthening, and new capacity additions, and, in many markets, they allow utilities purchasing power from independent power producers (IPPs).

Crucially, the marginal cost of electricity is the key running cost determining the final household use of electricity over time. For this reason, utilities have aimed at keeping their electricity prices as low as possible, with the result of running large budget deficits. Figure 28.4 illustrates a comparison of electricity supply costs (capital and operational) with cash collected by the national electric utilities of sub-Saharan Africa. It reveals that most utilities require yearly financial support from the Government and thus steadily contribute to the increase of national debts.

Key reasons behind the deficit include significant transmission, distribution and bill collection losses, overstaffing, and, most crucially, poorly designed customer subsidisation, which leads to excessively low electricity prices. In particular, the universal nature of pricing subsidies has implied large public expenditure to sustain the consumption of all grid-connected households, even those that are not credit-constrained. Universal energy subsidies—which for decades have prevailed in developing countries—are inequitable, as they mostly benefit

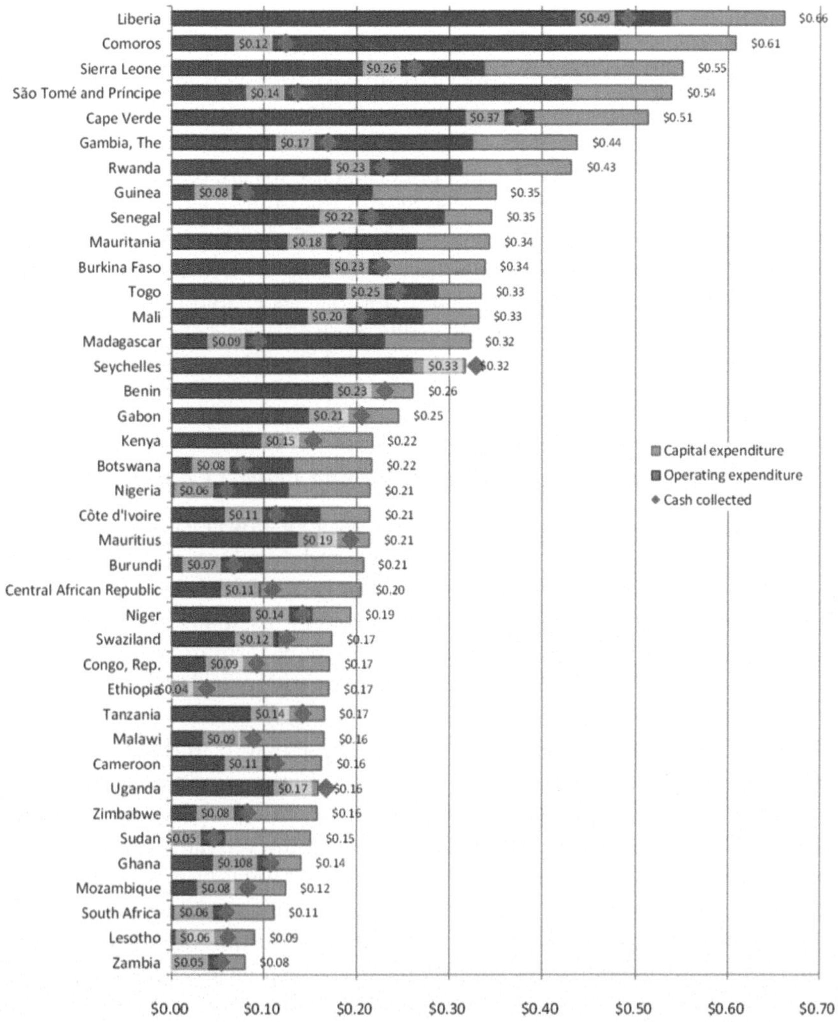

Fig. 28.4 National utilities of sub-Saharan Africa: comparison of electric supply costs with cash collected in 2014 ($/kWh billed). (Source: Kojima and Trimble 2016)

higher-income groups that consume the most (Vagliasindi 2012). These types of subsidies are also regressive, because access to electricity through the national grid is highly skewed towards higher-income groups. Second, universal electric energy subsidies are profoundly detrimental for the development of energy systems. In fact, they create a disincentive for maintenance and investment in the energy sector, perpetuating energy shortages and low levels of access. Subsidies are only efficiently designed if they target reducing connection charges and stimulating new connections to the national grid, rather than reducing the marginal prices of electricity consumption for customers. Large budget deficits have in turn the perverse effect of diminishing the ability of utilities to invest in new infrastructure and connections to improve access to electricity. Together, budgetary deficit-related factors represent an important concurrent cause of the limited expansion of the national grid, and thus the lack of electricity access.

Today, new, 'smarter', pricing and policy paradigms are revealing successful alternatives to the traditional model of subsidisation. Digital technologies enable an automatic, near-real-time monitoring of consumption levels at each customer. This allows the differentiation of pricing structures among households and their consumption tier. These approaches enable both an effective cross-subsidisation through substantially higher prices for non-income-constrained, higher-consuming households, and the rebalancing of the deficit of utilities.

2.3 *Investment Attractiveness and Private Capital*

Historically, the fundamental cause for the lack of power supply infrastructure—both installed capacity and transmission and distribution grid—has been the insufficient private investment in the power sector of developing countries. Because of macroeconomic, political, and monetary instability, the cost of borrowing local capital is extremely high, with medium-term government bonds often yielding more than 15%, compared to, for instance, 1.8% in the US or even 0.3% in Germany as of 2020.

Independent power producers (IPPs) are crucial players in the development of the power sector of emerging countries, because they complement and—on the road towards a competitive power supply market—gradually substitute the national utilities in their role. This is because of the uneven nature of electrification investment, requiring significant amounts of capital upfront—which the public funds of a developing country cannot afford due to the large number of additional priorities to be met under tight budget constraints. A broad stream of literature has highlighted that countries whose policies, institutions, and general investment environment attract IPPs also exhibited the steepest improvement in electricity access levels (Eberhard et al. 2017b, 2018; Eberhard and Gratwick 2011). Kenya and South Africa are the two most prominent examples for the last decade.

On the other hand, countries classified as insecure by investors and lacking a regulatory framework for private power and infrastructure suppliers (a good reference is provided by the Regulatory Indicators for Sustainable Energy database, RISE (2017)) have historically struggled to expand access and domestic supply capacity. More recently, international donors, financial banks, and, pivotally, state-owned enterprises from China have supplied significant investment even to these countries, albeit to a lesser extent than to countries with a more suitable regulatory framework. As shown in Fig. 28.5, China plays a major role. Over the last decade, the country has become the first source of investment in power-generating infrastructure in sub-Saharan Africa (Eberhard et al. 2017a).

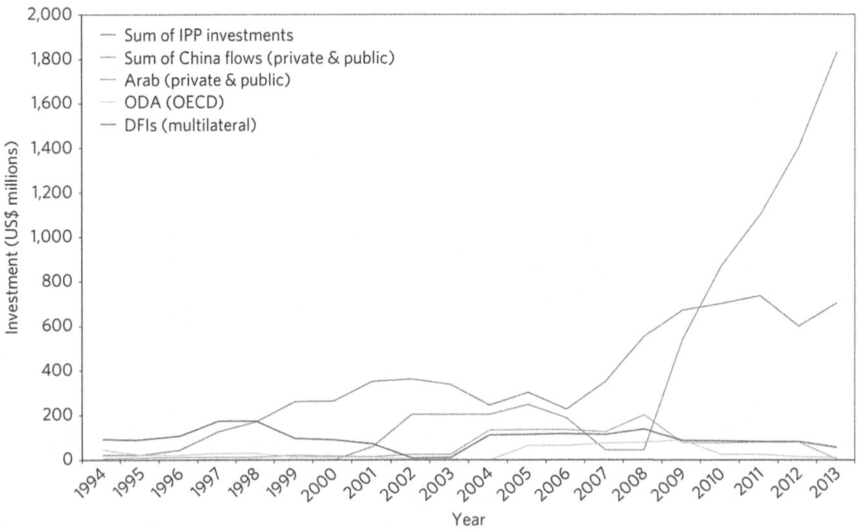

Fig. 28.5 Investment flows in power generation infrastructure in sub-Saharan Africa. (Source: Eberhard et al. 2017a)

According to the International Energy Agency (2016), Chinese companies (90% of which are state-owned) were responsible for 30% of new power capacity additions in sub-Saharan Africa between 2010 and 2015—with a total investment of around USD 13 bn over the quinquennium. Chinese contractors have built or are contracted to build 17 GW of power generation capacity in sub-Saharan Africa from 2010 to 2020, equivalent to 10% of existing installed capacity. These projects have hitherto targeted at least 37 countries out of 54 in the region.

2.4 *The Ability-to-Pay of Households, Connection Charges, and New Payment Schemes*

Roadblocks to electricity access are not only originated from the supply side, but they also relate to the inability to pay by income-constrained households. The issue involves several dimensions, all of which can be tackled by an appropriate policy design.

(i). The first issue concerns the charges levied by national utilities for new connections to the central national grid, which traditionally have been levied in a lump sum of an amount higher than the monthly income of most households (refer to Table 28.1).

(ii). The second aspect concerns the running costs, that is, the price of electricity, and the capacity of the national utility to enforce its regular collection.

Table 28.1 Connection charges and electricity access levels in selected countries

Country	*Connection charge per household*	*Electricity access level*
Kenya	145 USD	73%
Rwanda	350 USD	43%
Tanzania	300 USD	33%
Zambia	200 USD	33%
Ghana	35 USD	84%
Ethiopia	75 USD	45%
Uganda	125 USD	20%
India	25 USD	88%
Bangladesh	25 USD	80%
Laos	100 USD	94%

Sources: Golumbeanu and Barnes (2013), International Energy Agency (2018)

(iii). A third aspect is related to the reliability of the electricity provision from the national grid. An unreliable supply with frequent outages may induce households and, particularly, small business enterprises, hospitals, and schools to purchase a back-up generator, which determines a double cost borne by the consumer for benefitting from the electricity service, or even the decision not to connect to the grid. For instance, wide disparities in electricity consumption levels exist between populations with access to electricity in sub-Saharan Africa and in other regions of the world. As an example, in Nigeria the average person consumes 140 kWh per year of electricity. This is in comparison to 4300 kWh/year for the average Chinese, 6000 kWh/year for the average European, and 13,000 kWh/year for the average American. To put it even more clearly, in many sub-Saharan African countries an average person consumes 10 times less electricity than a refrigerator cooling coke bottles in a typical kitchen in the United States each year.

Expanding off-grid electrification might pose even higher financing challenges than on-grid electricity systems. Investing in on-grid, utility-scale projects is more comfortable for energy companies and investors, as high density of electricity demand guarantees more stable revenue streams. Should sound reforms of electricity utilities and energy subsidies be enacted, there should be no major problem in the future in ensuring the bankability of on-grid electricity infrastructure expansion. Far more problematic will be to ensure the development of small-grid and off-grid solutions needed to bring electricity to populations living in rural areas, which cannot be reached by the national grid, due to either geographical constraints or lack of a business case for grid expansion.

A recent trend has been observed in the diffusion of standalone generation solutions, in particular for household-scale photovoltaic modules running on pay-as-you-go business models (Mazzoni 2019). Several companies—initially in Western and Eastern Africa—have been shifting their business model to mobile-enabled payments, particularly suited for those potential customers who cannot afford a cash-paid system or grid connection charges (Bensch et al. 2018; Muchunku et al. 2018). With an initial payment, customers take their system home and make small periodical payments in order to keep it working, and eventually become owners of the equipment after a certain amount of time (Table 28.2). Solar Home Systems comprise a solar panel, a charge controller with a battery inside, a mobile charger, several DC ports for other appliances, and several light points. Their recent development enables the possibility to connect larger and larger DC appliances, such as refrigerators, fans, TVs, laptops, small-business and agro-processing machines, or even solar pumps (International Energy Agency 2017). Figure 28.6 illustrates a roadmap of the expected technological and service breakthroughs in the electricity access sector thanks to the emerging digitalisation trends. The timeline is divided into three dimensions, that is, by the type of access solution (national grid, mini-grids, or standalone solar home systems).

Table 28.2 Cost of pay-as-you-go solar home systems for major companies operating in sub-Saharan Africa

Company	*Power of systems provided*	*Upfront payment*	*Daily instalments*
M-KOPA	8 W–20 W	30–60 USD	0.5–1 USD
Mobisol	80 W–200 W	63–126 USD	1–2 USD
Fenix Intl.	10 W–34 W	5–37 USD	0.2–0.75 USD

Source: Company websites, accessed in September 2019

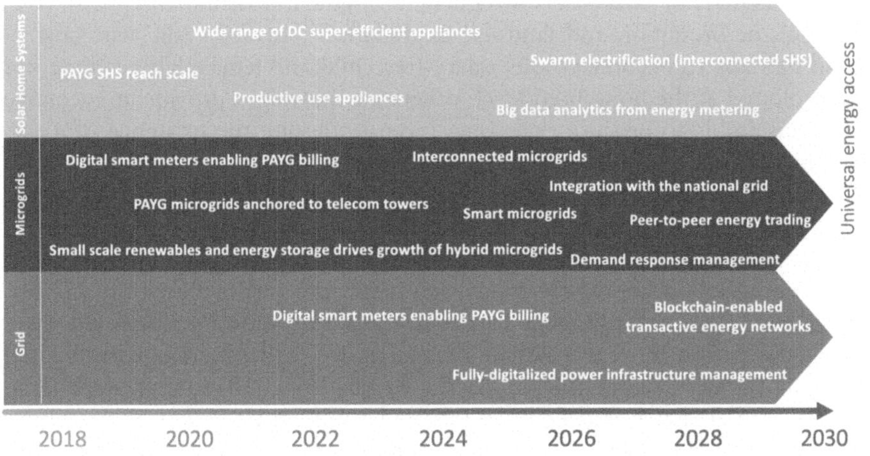

Fig. 28.6 Several developments are expected to bring about a 'leapfrogging' digital transformation of the electricity sector. (Source: Mazzoni 2019)

3 Access to Clean Cooking: Economic Issues and Policy Instruments

3.1 Modern Cooking Fuels: Lack of Infrastructure and Economic Incentive

A key difference between the clean cooking challenge and electricity access is that people cannot live without cooking, while they do not, strictly speaking, need electricity access for survival. Thus, populations without access to modern energy services revert to traditional options to cook food. There are 30 countries in the world where 90% of the population relies on solid biomass for daily cooking activities, 23 of which are located in sub-Saharan Africa (International Energy Agency 2017). Globally, at least 2.8 billion people (Bonjour et al. 2013), that is, almost four in ten, live in these conditions.

Solid biomass consists of firewood—sometimes converted into charcoal—and agricultural residues. These fuels are collected, bought, and burnt daily by the bulk of the population without clean cooking solutions. The main economic issue related to solid biomass is that—where collected at the household or community level—it presents very high non-marketed (thus, shadow) costs. These include (i) the opportunity cost of the time spent collecting wood, (ii) the environmental and resource value of the trees logged to obtain the fuel, and (iii) adverse health effects (Karekezi et al. 2006). Thus, while a shadow price for solid biomass exists, this is often not explicitly stated or found in a market, and this makes it difficult for individuals to compare it with the market price of clean cooking solutions. In this sense, the establishment and regulation of local charcoal and firewood markets can contribute to providing a signal of the true cost of solid biomass. This is, however, only possible where the production activity of wholesalers is regulated to reduce environmental harm (e.g. through deforestation and land-use degradation). Also, for the true cost of solid biomass to become visible, salary-free child and female labour must not be exploited at the household level, otherwise this might provide an incentive for households to procure their own biomass despite the existence of a formal market.

Transitioning towards modern cooking fuels is an even greater economic challenge than electrification, because the marginal transportation costs of modern cooking fuels are substantially higher than those for the provision of basic household access to electricity, no matter the fuel or the vector considered. For instance, developing a natural gas transmission network—the most popular solution in large parts of Europe and North America—is estimated (Agency for the Cooperation of Energy Regulators 2015) to cost, depending on the pipe diameter, between 350,000 and 1 million USD/km. For instance, the LL2 210 km pipeline, bringing natural gas from Mozambique to South Africa, costs 1.65 million USD/km (SASOL 2015), against the 30,000 USD/km of a high-voltage power transmission grid (Rosnes and Vennemo 2009).

The bulk of the global populations without access to clean cooking are concentrated in regions with a warm climate where there is no need for residential heating, which in non-equatorial countries is the first source of household gas consumption, and thus of revenue for utilities. At the same time, households that cook with solid biomass belong to the most income-constrained sections of the population. Even in urban and peri-urban areas, the horizontal and often informal expansion of most urban agglomerates makes the development of a gas distribution pipeline costly, and risky. Thus, it is clear that the economic incentives for such large-scale fixed infrastructure investment are lacking, at least over the medium term.

As a result, alternative paradigms to piped natural gas must be considered. The option which is most frequently considered and—at least in some countries—being implemented is the development of a liquefied petroleum gas (LPG) distribution network, with trucks transporting tanks towards capillary-distributed withdrawal points, where households can buy retail-scale quantities of fuel. Notably, LPG is among the few cooking fuels that can meet the indoor pollution standards set by the World Health Organization, and several studies point to its suitability for cooking in the developing world. The International Energy Agency estimates that about 90% of those who will shift away from solid biomass by 2030 will move to LPG.

Nevertheless, particularly for rural customers, difficulties of distribution due to poor road infrastructure and populations living in remote, low-density rural areas will likely remain a major barrier to a wider uptake (Van Leeuwen et al. 2017). The distribution of LPG from production sites or import stations to individual users requires careful handling, storage, and transport of pressurised gas. Clearly, this type of supply chain cannot be improvised for safety reasons, such as the handling of pressurised cylinders by untrained people.

Despite the energy unit cost of LPG being lower than traditional cooking fuels, the upfront cost of the first cylinder and LPG stove represents a strong entry barrier. Consumers willing to switch away from solid biomass or kerosene often lack sufficient disposable cash. Transportation is often an additional issue: moving heavy cylinders is challenging for rural households living far from the distribution sites. This is due to poor distribution networks in remote areas, and even in some urban centres. Another barrier is the absence of governmental subsidies that, together with lack of an appropriate supply chain, is hampering factors for the uptake of LPG. From an economic point of view, the policy design is also crucial in the transition to cleaner cooking fuels. The experience of Senegal with LPG is emblematic: thanks to an initial high subsidy-based strategy, LPG reached a share of about 70% of urban users. Yet, as soon as the government decided to remove subsidies, there was a massive drop in consumption. The next section elaborates on some of the economic reasons behind this reversal. A related trend was observed in India, where more than 70 million poor women have received free LPG stoves under a government programme. Yet, this has not been matched by an increase in LPG sales, suggesting that LPG access has not induced a full transition away from the use of polluting solid fuels as a result of inadequate incentives accompanying the deployment of the programme (Kar et al. 2019).

3.2 *Complementary Cooking Solutions for the Short and Longer Term*

If the aim is to also bring LPG cooking to rural users, the most critical elements of success will be the existence of far-reaching LPG value chains on the one hand and the effectiveness of targeted pro-poor cross-subsidisation on the other. It is still possible that smarter payment methods could also help in accelerating access to LPG distribution (in the same way this is happening with solar lanterns)—either as a purely market-driven solution or in combination with subsidies. So far, however, the accumulated experience of this solution is still limited (International Energy Agency 2017).

Despite these issues, there is substantial evidence that—once available and affordable—LPG responds to the needs of customers, which is not trivial. For instance, the experience of South Africa shows that (subsidised) LPG cooking can take root even where electrical cooking is available and cheap (Kimemia and Annegarn 2016). At the same time in India—where the use of solid biomass is also widespread—LPG seems to be responsible of the first signs of reduction in solid biomass consumption after decades of promotion of improved biomass stoves, which ended up delivering poor results (International Energy Agency 2017).

Despite the emergence of the market for LPG, estimates (International Energy Agency 2017) show that solid biomass cooking will continue to be the main cooking fuel for several decades. This is due to both the capillary infrastructure and market development necessary to reach remote communities, but also due to behavioural factors linked to local tradition and recipes. Therefore, solutions that allow increasing cooking efficiency and minimising exposure to harm are necessary over the short and medium term. The most viable and commonly supported solution is improved biomass cookstoves, which allow for substantial improvement in fuel efficiency (Mehetre et al. 2017). A number of protocols are adopted to identify the efficiency of cookstoves, in particular exploiting exergy analysis (Colpan 2012).

The adoption of improved cookstoves is strongly influenced by household income, but also by the robustness of supply chains and the type of devices available on local markets (Pattanayak et al. 2019). Empirical evidence shows high technology rejection rates in the lack of specific policy targeting sociocultural aspects that hinder adoption (Okuthe and Akotsi 2014). From an economic point of view, improved cookstoves present significant monetary benefits (less biomass is required to cook the same amount of food) and non-marketed economic gains—both at a local and a global scale. These include health benefits, due to the inferior exposure to indoor air pollution; less time spent collecting or purchasing biomass, less deforestation, and lower greenhouse gas emissions. Empirical evidence has shown that replacement of traditional cookstoves can have a discounted (at 12%) payback period of as little as 5 months (Rubab and Kandpal 1996; Suvarnakuta and Suwannakuta 2006), and substantial fuel cost savings emerge thereafter. Thus, the greatest economic barrier is the upfront cost component that must be abated by ad-hoc business models and subsidisation strategies. At the same time, ensuring sustained use after the initial adoption requires tackling social and community-level barriers (Ruiz-Mercado et al. 2011).

Another clean cooking option is electricity. For instance, electricity is already widely used for cooking purposes in urban areas in South Africa, and, assuming sufficient affordability, it could become a key vector in the future cooking mix of other developing countries. Of course, compared to other basic household uses of electricity, cooking requires substantially more power (Bhatia and Angelou 2015), and a reliable supply. Nevertheless, the declining cost of solar PV modules and of battery storage over recent years is bringing significantly closer the possibility to promote solar electric cooking as the least-cost option for large shares of the population currently cooking with solid biomass (Batchelor et al. 2018).

In fact, similar to what has been observed in recent years for solar-home-systems, the clean cooking market is also—although at a slower pace—moving towards more innovative and private-based business models. Companies offering pay-as-you-go smart LPG valves are already operating in some countries (such as Kenya and Tanzania). These use M2M-connected smart metres on top of gas cylinders to provide an affordable supply of LPG for cooking, and monitor and enable its consumption. The model allows for a lowering of entry barriers thanks to leasing or instalment-based payments for the equipment.

Figure 28.7 shows the timeline of the projected market breakthroughs of smart cleaning solutions, with electric cooking still lagging behind but bound to emerge in the coming decades also thanks to its strong complementarity with the development of electricity access solutions, both standalone and through connection to mini-grids, or even to the national grid.

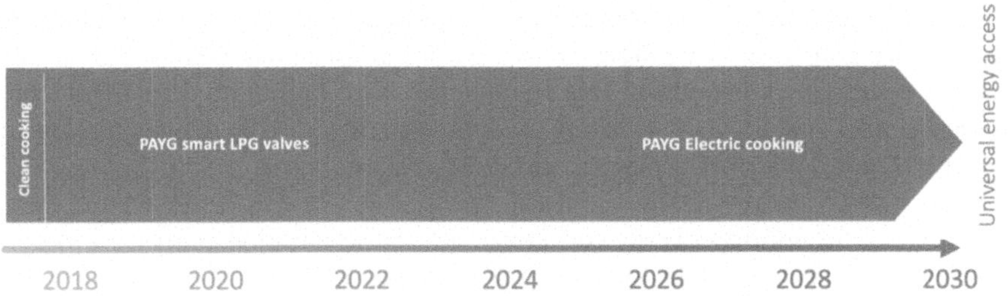

Fig. 28.7 Several developments are expected to bring about a 'leapfrogging' digital transformation of access to clean cooking. (Source: Mazzoni 2019)

3.3 Fuel Choice and Behavioural Barriers

Finally, when examining the household decision as to cooking fuels (Poblete-Cazenave and Pachauri 2018), policymakers must consider that this is not necessarily an explicit, frictionless, cost-minimising decision, because behavioural factors are at play (Lewis Jessica J. and Pattanayak Subhrendu K. 2012; Sunil Malla Govinda and R Timilsina 2014). These relate to traditional cooking habits and recipes, as well as to the socio-cultural dynamics involved, and—from an economic point of view—they suggest that the most appropriate approach to frame the problem is that of an imperfectly rational choice (Vigolo et al. 2018; Akintan et al. 2018).

Thus, energy policy design targeted at expanding access to modern cooking fuel must necessarily assume that a price signal might not be enough to trigger a switch from solid biomass to alternative cooking fuel. Supporting measures targeting communities as a whole (Vulturius and Wanjiru 2017), and in particular linked to education, is an important example.

Irrespective of the technology considered, similar barriers are found, namely the lack of infrastructure and of suitable policy to enable its development. Hitherto, policies aimed at modernising access to clean cooking have proved largely insufficient, and the challenge of universal access to clean cooking still receives less attention than that of electrification. One of the reasons for this is that there has not yet been a real market breakthrough of innovative stand-alone technologies (e.g. solar or biogas cookers), and the alternatives to traditional cooking today are more or less the same as decades ago, most importantly petroleum-based fuels and electricity. In other words, the main challenge of clean cooking remains that of improving the logistics and increasing the affordability and cultural acceptance of alternative solutions to rudimentary stoves.

4 Conclusion: Enabling Energy Access

4.1 Economic Issues of Energy Access

Meeting the SDG7's goal of ensuring universal access to modern energy for all by 2030 requires an intensification of efforts at different scales. In particular, tackling the economic roots of the lack of energy access represents a fundamental requirement to unleash developing countries' social development and economic potential. Throughout this chapter, we have highlighted that the main barriers that still prevent 1 billion people worldwide from having access to electricity are both infrastructural and policy-related.

- First, the limited extent and coverage of the national transmission and distribution network determines a situation of strongly unbalanced electricity access levels in urban and rural areas. This comes in combination with insufficient generation capacity, which renders it both challenging to broaden the consumer basin by establishing new connections for which there is a lack of power and to guarantee a reliable supply of electric energy to already electrified households and businesses. The situation is the result of large capacity and network expansion costs coupled with the high discount rates faced by investors, but also the high degree of dispersion of the populations in sub-Saharan Africa—the main region affected by electricity access deficits, which renders the investment not economically profitable. Finally, there is the low ability-to-pay and low short-term consumption of new customers, which together do not allow the national utility to recoup the large upfront investment borne to connect new households to the national grid.

- Second, there is the issue relating to the budgetary deficit on which energy utilities in most developing countries are running. The key reasons behind the deficit include the significant transmission, distribution, and bill collection losses, overstaffing, and, most crucially, poorly designed customer subsidisation (e.g. universal energy subsidies), which leads to excessively low electricity prices.
- Third, there is the issue of the difficulty in attracting investment, in particular private (IPPs) and foreign sources, which could strongly contribute to boosting generation, transmission, and distribution capacity and thus expanding electricity access and increasing its use. The unattractiveness is the result of macroeconomic, political, and monetary instability, which implies an extremely high cost of local capital.
- Fourth, there are questions related to the ability-to-pay of potential customers and the related upfront barriers, such as grid connection charges, which traditionally have been levied in a lump sum of an amount higher than the monthly income of most households. Other barriers include the running costs, that is, the price of electricity, and the capacity of the national utility to enforce its regular collection, as well as the reliability of the electricity provision from the national grid, which discourages new grid connections when the law forces small business enterprises, hospitals, and schools to purchase a back-up generator.
- Fifth, there is the acknowledgement that a relevant political-economic dimension exists, which depends on the role of political factors and local institutions in determining electrification pathways.

With regard to the challenge of guaranteeing universal access to clean cooking solutions, this is even greater due to both the structural difficulty of replacing solid biomass among remote communities and the behavioural aspects involved.

- First, the lack of an infrastructure that can enable the diffusion of clean cooking solutions has as its underlying cause the lack of an economic incentive, at least if the traditional model followed in Europe and North America is taken as the reference. Setting up a capillary natural gas transmission network is very capital intensive and simply not profitable if the only source of demand for it is cooking, with no heating demand and little industrial consumption.

- Second, the shadow and opportunity costs of solid biomass are still implicit. Households too often disregard the opportunity cost of the time spent collecting wood, the environmental and resource value of the trees logged to obtain the fuel, and the adverse health effects.
- Third, the behavioural barriers relating to the traditional cooking habits and recipes, as well as to the socio-cultural dynamics involved, render the fuel choice problem one of an imperfectly rational choice, where friction prevents the economically optimal solution from being adopted.

4.2 Coordinated Policy Actions to Enable Energy Access

Overall, a set of coordinated policy actions is required to unlock synergetic actions for electricity and clean cooking action (Hafner et al. 2018). A comprehensive policy action aimed at achieving universal energy access by 2030 notably needs to entail: (i) a mix of technological solutions; (ii) pricing and subsidies reform; (iii) digitalisation and smart payment schemes; (iv) a strong role of international organisation in unlocking international investments; and (v) appreciating the synergy of energy access with other sustainable development targets. Let us review these in detail.

(i). A mix of technological solutions is needed to achieve universal energy access by 2030. Electricity planning encompasses the decision around the development of national grid connections, the development of mini-grids, or the installation of standalone off-grid solutions. In a similar fashion, cooking encompasses piped natural gas (mostly in urban districts characterised by a high demand density, e.g. from the industry sector), tanked LPG, eCook (in synergy with electricity access), or—where none of these solutions is viable over the medium term—improved biomass cookstoves. In both cases, modelling tools to assess the optimal technological mix at each settlement is of crucial importance to inform policymakers and private parties in their decision.

(ii). Pricing and subsides reform is a key enabling condition for both electricity and clean cooking solutions access. Subsidies are a potentially very effective policy instrument to overcome energy access barriers. However, policymakers must make the most of today's data collection and analysis capability to target them as precisely as possible, exclusively to those household who need them and would not have the means to afford energy access otherwise. Every dollar spent subsidising the wrong household is a dollar taken away from energy access investment. In a very similar way, pricing schemes must recognise the heterogeneity of customers within countries and be designed to match the ability and willingness to pay of different income groups. If pricing reform is effectively implemented, energy utilities can offer electricity and clean cooking solutions at prices that are below costs to specific customer groups while keeping a positive balance sheet.

(iii). Digitalisation and smart payment schemes are starting to play a greater role as enablers of new business schemes, which enable customers by lowering upfront cost barriers while at the same time ensuring solvency for the businesses for the service provided and eliminating transaction costs. Data collection and analytics, for example on energy use habits and payment patterns, can become much more pervasive, and thus improve planning. A necessary condition that must be met is that this information is shared among public and private parties.

(iv). International organisations play a key role in unlocking international capital towards the energy sectors of developing countries. Where a country's financial sector is not deemed stable enough to attract the required investment under market conditions, the role of development and assistance banks is to provide sufficient guaranties to private investors. This is achieved by negotiations with national governments and conditionality approaches in the financing of public infrastructure.

(v). The cost-benefit analysis of energy access projects is in all instances likely to be downward-biased, as energy access investment presents strong interconnections with the achievement of other development objectives (Bos et al. 2018; McCollum et al. 2018; Nerini et al. 2018). One of the most crucial of these aspects is the synergy between energy access and climate change mitigation and adaptation goals (Dagnachew et al. 2018). In particular, providing universal electricity access has been shown to exert little impact on global CO_2 emissions (Calvin et al. 2016), while switching to universal clean cooking would even imply a reduction in emissions and energy demand due to strong efficiency gains (e.g. see Rosenthal et al. 2018; Singh et al. 2017). At the same time, providing energy access allows for a steeply increased adaptation capability by enabling air cooling and telecommunications, for example. Finally, also from a governance and financing point of view, synergetic initiatives targeting both climate change adaptation and energy access can bring co-benefits (refer to Chirambo 2018).

But how to intervene in practice with policy actions in the energy access space? Operationally, it is sensible to differentiate two levels of intervention: (i) macro-scale reforms to unlock investment and (ii) micro-scale interventions to enable the uptake of access solutions.

At the *macro-level*, large-scale investment is the main responsibility of national and international policymakers involved with the electrification process. To do so, several coordinated options are necessary. These include:

(i). Ensuring macro-economic, exchange rate, and political stability. These are first-order, necessary conditions to allow a country to be perceived as a favourable environment for private capital—including foreign capital—to flow into long-term infrastructure projects (Sweerts et al. 2019).

(ii). Channelling infrastructure investment through competitive processes, rather than with direct negotiations (Ackah et al. 2017). Auctions and tendering procedures have proven particularly effective in attracting IPPs, which can become the real drivers of generation capacity expansions (Ackah et al. 2017; Kruger and Eberhard 2018), letting utilities focus on the management of the natural monopoly of the transmission and distribution grid, while governments act on sector governance.

(iii). When designing subsidies, ensuring that these are neither universal (i.e. they target a population group which is too broad) nor regressive (i.e. they have the perverse effect of supporting the rich more than the poor because the rich are more likely to be grid-connected customers and consume more electricity), and that a clear long-term financing strategy exists. The latter point is particularly crucial to avoid. Consider, for instance, the precedent of the LPG subsidisation scheme in Senegal, where an initial skyrocketing of LPG clean cooking was followed by a dramatic return to solid biomass combustion as soon as public subsidisation came to an end.

(iv). Ensuring that synergies among socio-economic objectives are fully exploited. With regard to energy access planning, synergetic financing and subsidisation of electricity access with eCook capability is a relevant example (Pachauri et al. 2013).

(v). Given the order of magnitude of the challenge, only a joint effort of interested countries and international public and private players (known as PPPs, public–private partnerships) could provide a comprehensive solution. This is already being demonstrated by a number of initiatives currently under way across the developing world (Sovacool 2013). PPPs also encompass data exchange between public and private parties involved in the energy access sector, that is, between companies installing mini-grids and rural electrification agencies, so that an optimal synergetic planning is achieved. International organisations can play an important role by ensuring financing and capacity building conditional on these public-private partnerships being exploited.

At the *micro-level* (or local level), policies should be flexible enough to accommodate heterogeneous necessities and roadblocks. As highlighted in the chapter, some of the most important issues are:

(i). The need to lower entry barriers on both the demand and supply side, that is, simultaneously mitigating connection charges for households and ensuring private companies promoting energy access solutions large flexibility in the business model and implementation strategy they adopt.

(ii). This means fully exploiting the potential of digital technologies, including pay-as-you-go business schemes (which mostly work through the use of mobile e-banking, which thus presents strong synergies with energy access).

(iii). At the same time, behavioural campaigns on the switch away from solid biomass can be particularly effective if they present sound evidence on the monetary and health-related benefits. Specific groups, such as women, should be targeted. These campaigns should, however, be able to recognise the role of traditions (recipes and tastes), otherwise they may be counterproductive.

(iv). Solid biomass cooking issues have no silver-bullet solution. While modelling scenarios agree on the fact that a universal switch to either LPG or eCook cannot be achieved by 2030 (International Energy Agency 2017), an efficient mix of improved biomass cookstoves, LPG, and eCook can be extremely effective over the medium term as a joint strategy to drastically decrease indoor air pollution, reduce deforestation, and prevent households from collecting fuelwood autonomously.

(v). Data collection and analysis at the local scale is necessary to gauge energy access solutions correctly. Accounting for the energy demand components stemming from the productive sectors such as agricultural and entrepreneurial businesses is important because—if provided with sufficient energy supply—these can boost local socio-economic development and employment. Disregarding these energy demand sources might bring an only partial solution of the energy access problem, with persistent energy poverty.

References

Ackah, I., Opoku, F. A., & Suleman, S. (2017). *To Toss a Coin or Shake a Hand: An Overview of Renewable Energy Interventions and Procurement in selected African Countries.* MPRA Paper 77489

Agency for the Cooperation of Energy Regulators. (2015). *Report on unit investment cost indicators and corresponding reference values for electricity and gas infrastructure: Electricity infrastructure.* http://www.acer.europa.eu/Official_documents/Acts_of_the_Agency/Publication/UICReport-Electricityinfrastructure.pdf

Akintan, O., Jewitt, S., & Clifford, M. (2018). Culture, tradition, and taboo: Understanding the social shaping of fuel choices and cooking practices in Nigeria. *Energy Research & Social Science, 40*, 14–22.

Amegah, A. K., & Jaakkola, J. J. (2016). Household air pollution and the sustainable development goals. *Bulletin of the World Health Organization, 94*(3), 215.

Batchelor, S., Brown, E., Leary, J., Scott, N., Alsop, A., & Leach, M. (2018). Solar electric cooking in Africa: Where will the transition happen first? *Energy Research & Social Science, 40*, 257–272. https://doi.org/10.1016/j.erss.2018.01.019

Bensch, G., Grimm, M., Huppertz, M., Langbein, J., & Peters, J. (2018). Are promotion programs needed to establish off-grid solar energy markets? Evidence from rural Burkina Faso. *Renewable and Sustainable Energy Reviews, 90*, 1060–1068.

Bensch, G., Peters, J., & Sievert, M. (2017). The lighting transition in rural Africa—From kerosene to battery-powered LED and the emerging disposal problem. *Energy for Sustainable Development, 39*, 13–20.

Bernard, T. (2010). Impact analysis of rural electrification projects in Sub-Saharan Africa. *The World Bank Research Observer, 27*(1 (February 2012)), 33–51.

Bhatia, M., & Angelou, N. (2015). *Beyond connections: Energy access redefined.* World Bank.

Blimpo, M. P., & Cosgrove-Davies, M. (2019). *Electricity Access in Sub-Saharan Africa: Uptake, Reliability, and Complementary Factors for Economic Impact.* World Bank Publications.

Bonan, J., Pareglio, S., & Tavoni, M. (2017). Access to modern energy: A review of barriers, drivers and impacts. *Environment and Development Economics, 22*(5), 491–516.

Bonjour, S., Adair-Rohani, H., Wolf, J., Bruce, N. G., Mehta, S., Prüss-Ustün, A., Lahiff, M., Rehfuess, E. A., Mishra, V., & Smith, K. R. (2013). Solid fuel use for household cooking: Country and regional estimates for 1980–2010. *Environmental Health Perspectives, 121*(7), 784–790.

Bos, K., Chaplin, D., & Mamun, A. (2018). Benefits and challenges of expanding grid electricity in Africa: A review of rigorous evidence on household impacts in developing countries. *Energy for Sustainable Development, 44*, 64–77.

Byers, E., Gidden, M., Leclère, D., Balkovic, J., Burek, P., Ebi, K., Greve, P., Grey, D., Havlik, P., Hillers, A., & others. (2018). Global exposure and vulnerability to multi-sector development and climate change hotspots. *Environmental Research Letters, 13*(5), 055012.

Calvin, K., Pachauri, S., De Cian, E., & Mouratiadou, I. (2016). The effect of African growth on future global energy, emissions, and regional development. *Climatic Change, 136*(1), 109–125. https://doi.org/10.1007/s10584-013-0964-4

Chattopadhyay, D., Bazilian, M., & Lilienthal, P. (2015). More power, less cost: Transitioning up the solar energy ladder from home systems to mini-grids. *The Electricity Journal, 28*(3), 41–50.

Chirambo, D. (2018). Towards the achievement of SDG 7 in sub-Saharan Africa: Creating synergies between Power Africa, Sustainable Energy for All and climate finance in-order to achieve universal energy access before 2030. *Renewable and Sustainable Energy Reviews, 94*, 600–608.

Colpan, C. O. (2012). Exergy analysis of an integrated two–stage biomass gasifier and Solid Oxide Fuel Cell system. *International Journal of Exergy, 10*(1), 61–76.

Dagnachew, A. G., Lucas, P. L., Hof, A. F., & van Vuuren, D. P. (2018). Trade-offs and synergies between universal electricity access and climate change mitigation in Sub-Saharan Africa. *Energy Policy, 114*, 355–366. https://doi.org/10.1016/j.enpol.2017.12.023

Eberhard, A., Gratwick, K., & Kariuki, L. (2018). Kenya's lessons from two decades of experience with independent power producers. *Utilities Policy, 52*, 37–49.

Eberhard, A., Gratwick, K., Morella, E., & Antmann, P. (2017a). Accelerating investments in power in sub-Saharan Africa. *Nature Energy, 2*, 17005.

Eberhard, A., Gratwick, K., Morella, E., & Antmann, P. (2017b). Independent Power Projects in Sub-Saharan Africa: Investment trends and policy lessons. *Energy Policy, 108*, 390–424.

Eberhard, A., & Gratwick, K. N. (2011). IPPs in Sub-Saharan Africa: Determinants of success. *Energy Policy, 39*(9), 5541–5549.

Enerdata. (2016). *Study of the Cost of Electricity Projects in Africa For the African Development Bank.*

Falchetta, G., Gernaat, D. E. H. J., Hunt, J., & Sterl, S. (2019). Hydropower dependency and climate change in sub-Saharan Africa: A nexus framework and evidence-based review. *Journal of Cleaner Production*, *231*, 1399–1417. https://doi.org/10.1016/j.jclepro.2019.05.263

Falchetta, G., Pachauri, S., Byers, Edward, Danylo, Olha, & Parkinson, Simon. (2020). Satellite observations reveal inequalities in the progress and effectiveness of recent electrification in sub-Saharan Africa. *One Earth*.

Findt, K., Scott, D. B., & Lindfeld, C. (2014). *Sub-Saharan Africa Power Outlook 2014.* KPMG Africa.

Fouquet, R. (2016). Path dependence in energy systems and economic development. *Nature Energy*, *1*, 16098.

Golumbeanu, R., & Barnes, D. (2013). *Connection charges and electricity access in sub-Saharan Africa*. The World Bank.

Grimm, M., Munyehirwe, A., Peters, J., & Sievert, M. (2016). *A first step up the energy ladder? Low cost solar kits and household's welfare in rural Rwanda*. The World Bank.

Hafner, M., Tagliapietra, S., & de Strasser, L. (2018). Energy Investments for Africa's Energy Transition. In *Energy in Africa* (pp. 77–96). Springer.

IEA. (2017). *WEO 2017 Special Report: Energy Access Outlook.* International Energy Agency. https://www.iea.org/publications/freepublications/publication/weo-2017-special-report-energy-access-outlook.html

IEA. (2018). *World Energy Outlook 2018.* https://www.iea.org/weo2018/

IEA, IRENA, & United Nations Statistics Division. (2019). *Tracking SDG7: The Energy Progress Report 2019.*

IMF. (2013, May 13). *Reforming Energy Subsidies is Critical for Realizing Africa's Growth Potential.* ID4D. https://ideas4development.org/en/reforming-energy-subsidies-is-critical-for-realizing-africas-growth-potential/

International Energy Agency. (2016). *Boosting the Power Sector in Sub-Saharan Africa.* https://www.oecd-ilibrary.org/content/publication/9789264262706-en

International Energy Agency. (2017). *Energy Access Outlook (World Energy Outlook Special Report).* https://www.iea.org/publications/freepublications/publication/weo-2017-special-report-energy-access-outlook.html

Jacome, V., Klugman, N., Wolfram, C., Grunfeld, B., Callaway, D., & Ray, I. (2019). Power quality and modern energy for all. *Proceedings of the National Academy of Sciences*, *116*(33), 16308–16313.

Kar, A., Pachauri, S., Bailis, R., & Zerriffi, H. (2019). Using sales data to assess cooking gas adoption and the impact of India's Ujjwala programme in rural Karnataka. *Nature Energy*, *4*(9), 806–814.

Karekezi, S., Lata, K., & Coelho, S. T. (2006). Traditional biomass energy: Improving its use and moving to modern energy use. *Renewable Energy—A Global Review of Technologies, Policies and Markets*, *1*, 231–261.

Kimemia, D., & Annegarn, H. (2016). Domestic LPG interventions in South Africa: Challenges and lessons. *Energy Policy*, *93*, 150–156.

Kojima, M., & Trimble, C. (2016). *Making power affordable for Africa and viable for its utilities.* World Bank, Washington, DC. https://openknowledge.worldbank.org/handle/10986/25091

Kruger, W., & Eberhard, A. (2018). Renewable energy auctions in sub-Saharan Africa: Comparing the South African, Ugandan, and Zambian Programs. *Wiley Interdisciplinary Reviews: Energy and Environment*, *7*(4), e295.

Lewis Jessica J., & Pattanayak Subhrendu K. (2012). Who Adopts Improved Fuels and Cookstoves? A Systematic Review. *Environmental Health Perspectives, 120*(5), 637–645. https://doi.org/10.1289/ehp.1104194

Mazzoni, D. (2019). *Digitalization for Energy Access in Sub-Saharan Africa: Challenges, Opportunities and Potential Business Models. 2198-2019–1357*, 61.

McCollum, D. L., Echeverri, L. G., Busch, S., Pachauri, S., Parkinson, S., Rogelj, J., Krey, V., Minx, J. C., Nilsson, M. and, Stevance, A.-S., & others. (2018). Connecting the sustainable development goals by their energy inter-linkages. *Environmental Research Letters, 13*(3), 033006.

Mehetre, S. A., Panwar, N. L., Sharma, D., & Kumar, H. (2017). Improved biomass cookstoves for sustainable development: A review. *Renewable and Sustainable Energy Reviews, 73*, 672–687. https://doi.org/10.1016/j.rser.2017.01.150

Mentis, D., Howells, M., Rogner, H., Korkovelos, A., Arderne, C., Zepeda, E., Siyal, S., Taliotis, C., Bazilian, M., & de Roo, A. (2017). Lighting the World: The first application of an open source, spatial electrification tool (OnSSET) on Sub-Saharan Africa. *Environmental Research Letters, 12*(8), 085003.

Monyei, C. G., Jenkins, K., Serestina, V., & Adewumi, A. O. (2018). Examining energy sufficiency and energy mobility in the global south through the energy justice framework. *Energy Policy, 119*, 68–76.

Muchunku, C., Ulsrud, K., Palit, D., & Jonker-Klunne, W. (2018). Diffusion of solar PV in East Africa: What can be learned from private sector delivery models? *Wiley Interdisciplinary Reviews: Energy and Environment, 7*(3), e282. https://doi.org/10.1002/wene.282

Nerini, F. F., Tomei, J., To, L. S., Bisaga, I., Parikh, P., Black, M., Borrion, A., Spataru, C., Broto, V. C., & Anandarajah, G. (2018). Mapping synergies and trade-offs between energy and the Sustainable Development Goals. *Nature Energy, 3*(1), 10.

Nussbaumer, P., Bazilian, M., & Modi, V. (2012). Measuring energy poverty: Focusing on what matters. *Renewable and Sustainable Energy Reviews, 16*(1), 231–243.

Occhiali, G., & Falchetta, G. (2018). The Changing Role of Natural Gas in Nigeria. *FEEM Working Paper.*

Okuthe, I. K., & Akotsi, E. N. (2014). Adoptions of improved biomass cook stoves by households: An example from Homabay County. *International Journal of Humanities and Social Science, 4*(9 (1)), 191–206.

Onyeji, I., Bazilian, M., & Nussbaumer, P. (2012). Contextualizing electricity access in sub-Saharan Africa. *Energy for Sustainable Development, 16*(4), 520–527.

Pachauri, S. (2011). Reaching an international consensus on defining modern energy access. *Current Opinion in Environmental Sustainability, 3*(4), 235–240.

Pachauri, S., van Ruijven, B. J., Nagai, Y., Riahi, K., van Vuuren, D. P., Brew-Hammond, A., & Nakicenovic, N. (2013). Pathways to achieve universal household access to modern energy by 2030. *Environmental Research Letters, 8*(2), 024015.

Pattanayak, S. K., Jeuland, M., Lewis, J. J., Usmani, F., Brooks, N., Bhojvaid, V., Kar, A., Lipinski, L., Morrison, L., Patange, O., Ramanathan, N., Rehman, I. H., Thadani, R., Vora, M., & Ramanathan, V. (2019). Experimental evidence on promotion of electric and improved biomass cookstoves. *Proceedings of the National Academy of Sciences, 116*(27), 13282–13287. https://doi.org/10.1073/pnas.1808827116

Poblete-Cazenave, M., & Pachauri, S. (2018). A structural model of cooking fuel choices in developing countries. *Energy Economics, 75*, 449–463. https://doi.org/10.1016/j.eneco.2018.09.003

Rathi, S. S., & Vermaak, C. (2017). The impacts of rural electrification on labour market outcomes in developing countries: Evidence from India and South Africa. *Paper Presented at the ESSA 2017 BIENNIAL CONFERENCE, RHODES UNIVERSITY, GRAHAMSTOWN*. https://2017.essa.org.za/fullpaper/essa_3565.pdf

RISE. (2017). *RISE Renewable Indicators for Sustainable Energy*. http://rise.esmap.org/

Rosenthal, J., Quinn, A., Grieshop, A. P., Pillarisetti, A., & Glass, R. I. (2018). Clean cooking and the SDGs: Integrated analytical approaches to guide energy interventions for health and environment goals. *Energy for Sustainable Development, 42*, 152–159. https://doi.org/10.1016/j.esd.2017.11.003

Rosnes, O., & Vennemo, H. (2009). *Powering up: Costing power infrastructure spending needs in Sub-Saharan Africa*. World Bank.

Rubab, S., & Kandpal, T. C. (1996). Biofuel mix for cooking in rural areas: Implications for financial viability of improved cookstoves. *Bioresource Technology, 56*(2–3), 169–178.

Ruiz-Mercado, I., Masera, O., Zamora, H., & Smith, K. R. (2011). Adoption and sustained use of improved cookstoves. *Energy Policy, 39*(12), 7557–7566.

Rumchev, K., Spickett, J. T., Brown, H. L., & Mkhweli, B. (2007). Indoor air pollution from biomass combustion and respiratory symptoms of women and children in a Zimbabwean village. *Indoor Air, 17*(6), 468–474.

SASOL. (2015). *Mozambique Gas Pipeline In US$210 Million Expansion*. https://www.sasol.com/media-centre/media-releases/mozambique-gas-pipeline-us210-million-expansion

Singh, D., Pachauri, S., & Zerriffi, H. (2017). Environmental payoffs of LPG cooking in India. *Environmental Research Letters, 12*(11), 115003.

Sovacool, B. K. (2013). Expanding renewable energy access with pro-poor public private partnerships in the developing world. *Energy Strategy Reviews, 1*(3), 181–192.

Sunil Malla Govinda R Timilsina. (2014). *Household Cooking Fuel Choice and Adoption of Improved Cookstoves in Developing Countries: A Review*. The World Bank. https://doi.org/10.1596/1813-9450-6903

Suvarnakuta, P., & Suwannakuta, P. (2006). Biomass cooking stove for sustainable energy and environment. *The 2nd Joint International Conference on "Sustainable Energy and Environment (SEE 2006)", Bangkok, Thailand.*

Sweerts, B., Dalla Longa, F., & van der Zwaan, B. (2019). Financial de-risking to unlock Africa's renewable energy potential. *Renewable and Sustainable Energy Reviews, 102*, 75–82.

Taneja, J. (2018). If You Build It, Will They Consume? Key Challenges for Universal, Reliable, and Low-Cost Electricity Delivery in Kenya. *Center for Global Development Working Paper, 491.*

Trotter, P. A. (2016). Rural electrification, electrification inequality and democratic institutions in sub-Saharan Africa. *Energy for Sustainable Development, 34*, 111–129.

The General Assembly (2015). Resolution adopted by the General Assembly on 25 September 2015: Transforming our world: The 2030 Agenda for Sustainable Development.

United Nations. (2015). Resolution adopted by the General Assembly on 25 September 2015. https://www.un.org/en/development/desa/population/migration/generalassembly/docs/globalcompact/A_RES_70_1_E.pdf

USAID. (2019). Nigeria Power Africa Fact Sheet. https://www.usaid.gov/powerafrica/nigeria#Energy%20Sector

Vagliasindi, M. (2012). *Implementing energy subsidy reforms: An overview of the key issues*. The World Bank.
Van de Walle, D. P., Ravallion, M., Mendiratta, V., & Koolwal, G. B. (2013). *Long-term impacts of household electrification in rural India*. No 6527, Policy Research Working Paper Series
Van Leeuwen, R., Evans, A., & Hyseni, B. (2017). *Increasing the use of liquefied petroleum gas in cooking in developing countries*. World Bank. https://openknowledge.worldbank.org/bitstream/handle/10986/26569/114846-BRI-PUBLIC-add-series-VC-LWLJfinOKR.pdf?sequence=5&isAllowed=y
van Vliet, M. T. H., van Beek, L. P. H., Eisner, S., Flörke, M., Wada, Y., & Bierkens, M. F. P. (2016). Multi-model assessment of global hydropower and cooling water discharge potential under climate change. *Global Environmental Change*, *40*, 156–170. https://doi.org/10.1016/j.gloenvcha.2016.07.007
Vigolo, V., Sallaku, R., & Testa, F. (2018). Drivers and barriers to clean cooking: A systematic literature review from a consumer behavior perspective. *Sustainability*, *10*(11), 4322.
Vulturius, G., & Wanjiru, H. (2017). *Role of social relations in the adoption of improved cookstoves*. Stockholm Environment Institute.
World Bank. (2018). *World Bank Data*. https://data.worldbank.org/

CHAPTER 29

Disruptive Technologies

Fabio Genoese

1 Introduction

Disruption denotes an action that completely overhauls the traditional way an industry is working, for instance by introducing a new technology or new standards. The shorter the transition, the more disruptive the event is considered.

A well-known example is the telecommunications industry: for decades, the industry was mainly offering landline telephony based on copper wire networking, with great success. In the 1960s, 6 out of 100 people had a fixed-line subscription in the European Union (see World Bank 2019). By the early 2000s, this number had grown to almost 50 out of 100, reaching its historical peak. Just eight years later, in 2018, the share of people with a fixed-line subscription shrank to 40 out of 100, largely caused by the introduction and massive success of cellular phones—a technological disruption. Meanwhile, the telecommunications industry was dramatically adapting their business models in a very short time frame, by starting to offer mobile information as well as media services. And while the landline might have a future, it will surely not be copper-based, but rather use optic fibre cables, which are able to transmit large amounts of data at much higher speed.

Energy is, of course, not telecoms—despite some similarities, the most obvious one being that both industries are network industries. Yet, energy is considered far more complex in many ways, for instance because various energy carriers co-exist and have been co-existing for decades: oil, gas, coal and electricity being the most widely recognised ones. Moreover, energy is at the forefront of the battle against climate change, because energy-related emissions account for the largest share of global greenhouse gas (GHG) emissions. It is

F. Genoese (✉)
Former Visiting Professor at SciencesPo, Paris, France
e-mail: fabio@genoese.eu

M. Hafner, G. Luciani (eds.), *The Palgrave Handbook of International Energy Economics*, https://doi.org/10.1007/978-3-030-86884-0_29

generally acknowledged that it is far easier to avoid energy-related GHG emissions than those related to land-use, for example in agriculture (see Umweltbundesamt 2018). For this reason, extensive policy efforts have been put in place, the best known being the push for renewables in the electricity sector, a measure adopted in many countries around the globe. Nonetheless, at least so far, historical patterns of energy consumption have proven to be surprisingly stable, despite technology advancements and policy efforts.

In the following, we aim at identifying energy technologies and energy uses that have the potential to become disruptive. To this end, the chapter is structured as follows. First, we will define suitable metrics to track significant changes in the energy system and try to understand existing patterns, analysing why some of them have been stable for decades. In the second section, we will learn more about major change events in the past and whether these can be classified as "disruptive". This is followed by a screening section of potential technology candidates that could be disruptive in the forthcoming decades. Finally, an outlook and conclusions are provided.

2 Monitoring Changes in Energy

In order to assess disruption, it is useful to define a metric that can be used to track and assess a significant change in the energy industry. To this end, we define **three main indicators** to measure structural changes in the energy sector:

1. A reduction in energy demand;
2. A change in the share of final energy carriers;
3. A change in the generation mix of final energy carriers.

The **first indicator**, a **reduction in energy demand**, is widely acknowledged as a key measure to reach long-term climate targets. In general, this can be achieved by making an existing process more efficient (e.g. for power plants by installing a new turbine with a higher conversion efficiency) or by reducing the primary needs (e.g. for houses by increasing insulation). Typically, these processes are not immediate across the whole sector, because the technical lifetime of installations in the energy sector can reach several decades. This makes the diffusion of new appliances a long process. Moreover, given the strong correlation between economic activity and energy consumption, at least until now, economic growth has always been accompanied by an increase in energy demand. To be able to measure efficiency effects, it is therefore useful to compare the evolution of energy demand to a counterfactual scenario (typically called "Business-as-Usual") without any efficiency improvements. This requires a deep-dive into technologies and energy carriers.

For this reason, the **second indicator focuses on what energy statisticians call *final energy consumption***, that is, the energy consumed by households, industries and services. Eurostat defines it as "the energy which reaches the final consumer's door and excludes that which is used by the energy sector itself". One might add that it excludes energy used by the energy sector itself for conversion, for example when transforming crude oil into oil products such as gasoline. Moreover, it is useful to decompose the total final energy consumption, both by energy carrier—oil, gas, coal, electricity—and by sector in which the energy is used, typically distinguishing between transport, households, industry and services. In other words, we are interested in the market share for different competitors (energy carriers) and different product categories (energy sectors) at the same time. This is of particular interest for consumer goods (e.g. passenger cars, boilers), first, because they are renewed more frequently than, say, housing facades, and second, because purchasing decisions are not only guided by economic principles.

The result is illustrated for Germany in Fig. 29.1 (2018 data). Despite not being 100% representative for all countries, the German case provides insight into patterns that can be observed throughout most OECD countries. Looking at this decomposition of total final energy consumption (TFC) one can note that there are **three main energy carriers: oil, gas and electricity**. In 2018, 36% of TFC was covered by oil and oil products, followed by gas (25%) and electricity (21%). The **share of electricity in final energy consumption** is also known as **degree of electrification**. Electricity is a very valuable form of energy, because it can be converted into so-called useful work (e.g. traction) at very high conversion efficiency. By contrast, the conversion efficiency is significantly lower in a combustion process, because thermal energy faces thermodynamic limits when transformed into work. For this reason, switching end-uses to electricity ("electrification") also reduces primary energy needs and contributes to increasing energy efficiency.

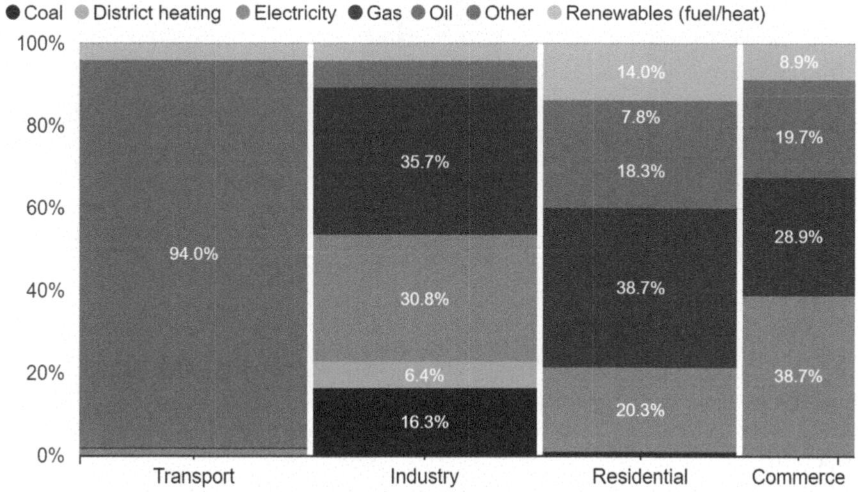

Fig. 29.1 Final energy demand by energy carrier and sector in Germany (2018). (Source: own elaboration on German Federal Energy Ministry data [2020])

Figure 29.1 also shows that significant differences across the various sectors exist. It is the **industry sector** where **coal still has a relevant share** in final energy consumption,[1] for example in primary **steelmaking** from ores. In the so-called *blast furnace route*, coke coal is needed to reduce iron ore, thereby creating molten iron, which is then refined to crude steel. In this process, carbon dioxide is emitted. An alternative is the *electric arc furnace route*, which is less diffused in Germany and most other steelmaking countries. Its main advantage is that scrap metal can be used as feedstock, which is heated up to 1800 °C through an electric arc to produce steel. The process does not generate any direct CO_2 emissions and is generally less energy-demanding than the blast furnace route, as it "recycles" end-of-life products made from steel. It is, however, a **secondary** steelmaking route, which cannot entirely replace primary steelmaking.

When looking specifically at the **transport sector**, it becomes clear that there is an elephant in the room, which is oil and oil products, which covered 94% of the transport demand in 2018. Moreover, this share has remained virtually unchanged in the last 30 years (see Fig. 29.2), when considering the combined contribution of oil products and biofuels (which made up 4% in 2018). So far, the **transport sector has proven to be resistant to disruption**, as no appropriate (and convenient) substitute for (fossil) liquid fuels in transport has yet been found. The introduction of biofuels has mainly been policy-driven and has had a limited impact, as the potential to produce additional biofuels is neither economically attractive (hence the need for continued policy support) nor

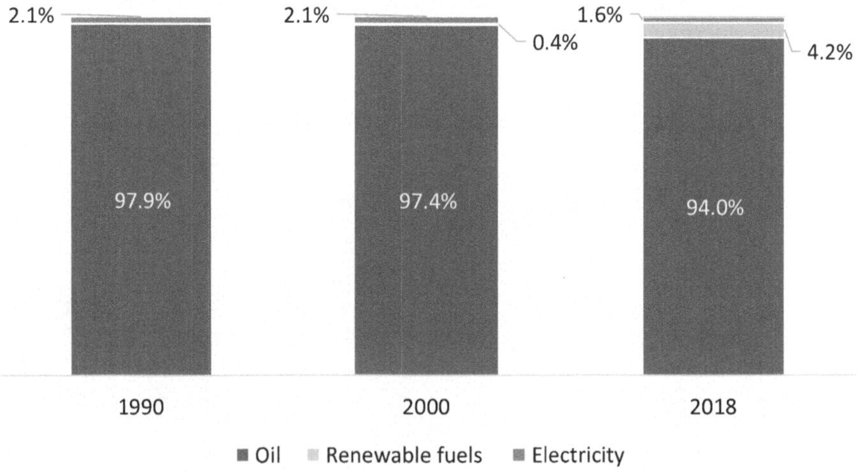

Fig. 29.2 Final energy demand of transport sector by energy carrier in Germany (1990–2018). (Source: own elaboration on German Federal Energy Ministry data [2020])

[1] Coal is also used to generate electricity. In that case, however, it is not considered a *final* energy carrier (see third indicator, generation mix of an energy carrier).

considered particularly sustainable when food crops[2] (e.g. corn or edible vegetable oil) are used as feedstock for biofuels (see FAO 2013). Nevertheless, a key open question for the future is: **Is it possible to disrupt the dominance of oil in transport?**

The other two sectors show a more balanced mix between the three main energy carriers. For example, many households use gas for heating purposes, be it for space heating or hot water, while others rely more on electricity. As mentioned, similar patterns can be found in most OECD countries but reflecting national specificities. In fact, the French version of this graph would show a higher share of electricity in residential consumption, because of a more widespread use of direct electric heaters.

The **third indicator** refers to the **generation mix of an energy carrier**. This concept is well-known for electricity, because electricity is not an energy carrier that occurs in nature, as opposed to oil and gas that are waiting to be extracted from underground reservoirs. Instead, electricity must first be generated from other (primary) energy carriers, which can range from traditional sources (such as solid, gaseous and liquid fuels but also nuclear and hydro energy) to modern ones (like wind and solar energy). A switch from carbon-intensive fossil fuels to renewable energy sources is widely regarded as a key measure to enable a transition to a climate-neutral energy system. In fact, 38% of the electricity consumed in Germany was generated from renewable energy sources in 2018, up from 9% in 2004 and six percentage points above the average of the European Union in that year.

This concept of analysing the generation mix can be applied to all energy carriers, when aggregating energy carriers with similar characteristics. For example, let us consider oil and liquid biofuels as members of a larger energy carrier family named "liquid fuels" and calculate the overall share of renewables in this energy carrier family. For liquid fuels, the share of renewables amounted to 3% in Germany, significantly below the share of renewables in the power sector (see Fig. 29.3). Since the energy transition has primarily been focused on the electricity sector so far, it is not surprising that the share of renewables is higher in electricity than in liquid or gaseous[3] fuels.

It goes without saying that for liquid and gaseous fuels the risk of a *policy-driven* disruption is higher than ever. Policymakers could intervene if liquid and gaseous fuels continued to fail in keeping pace with electricity and in becoming greener over time. Already today it is generally acknowledged that replacing liquid and gaseous fuels with electricity is a key measure to reach climate-neutrality. To understand the feasibility of such a massive switch from one energy carrier to another—which would indeed represent a disruption—it is useful to look at previous change events in the energy industry.

[2] To avoid this type of competition ("food vs fuel"), it has been proposed that only non-food crops such as forest residues from pulp mills be used as feedstock for biofuels. However, the economically viable potential remains limited.

[3] For gaseous fuels, biomethane is considered a renewable energy carrier. However, its share was irrelevant in the German gas mix of 2018.

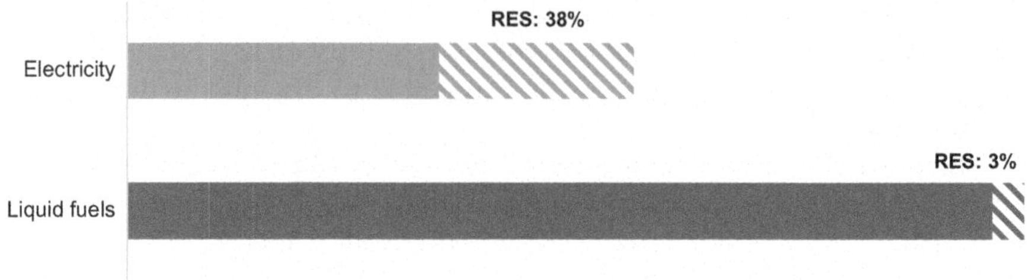

Fig. 29.3 Share of renewables in electricity and liquid fuels (Germany, 2018). (Source: own elaboration on German Federal Energy Ministry data [2020])

3 Past Disruptions in the Energy Industry

In the previous section we introduced three indicators that can be used to disclose disruptions: a reduction in energy demand, a change in the share of final energy carriers and a change in the generation mix of final energy carriers. In the following, we will apply the latter two indicators to past transitions in the energy industry and evaluate their degree of disruption.

3.1 Residential Heating in Germany: The End of Coal in the 1990s

In contrast to the transport sector that has remained virtually the same over the last thirty years, the final energy carrier mix in the residential sector has changed notably over the past two decades. Sticking to the German case (see previous section), a concrete example is the way heating of households changed in just ten years from 1990 to 2000 (see Fig. 29.4). Coal covered merely 2% of residential TFC in 2000, down from 16% in 1990. At that time, solid fuel stoves burning lignite briquettes were still widespread (especially in Eastern Germany) but were quickly replaced in the 1990s. The big winner was natural gas, responsible for more than two thirds of the loss in market share of coal, the other winners being biomass and electricity.

While substituting coal with biomass can be considered a simple "fuel switching" process, meaning that the stove was kept but only a different solid fuel is being burned, choosing natural gas and electricity required customers to install new heating devices like gas boilers—a technology disruption. Data indicates that a similar destiny awaits oil-fired heating devices, as the share of oil in German residential TFC almost halved to 18% from 1990 to 2018. Nevertheless, oil-fired central heating boilers remain fairly widespread. They function in a similar way to gas-condensing boilers but (as their name suggests) rely on oil instead of natural gas as fuel supply, which is of particular interest for households that are not connected to the gas grid. This is not uncommon: while almost every household in modern economies has access to the electricity grid, this is not the case for gas, even in OECD countries with considerable gas consumption such as Italy or Germany. A prominent example is Sardinia: despite being the second-largest island in the Mediterranean Sea, Sardinia is not

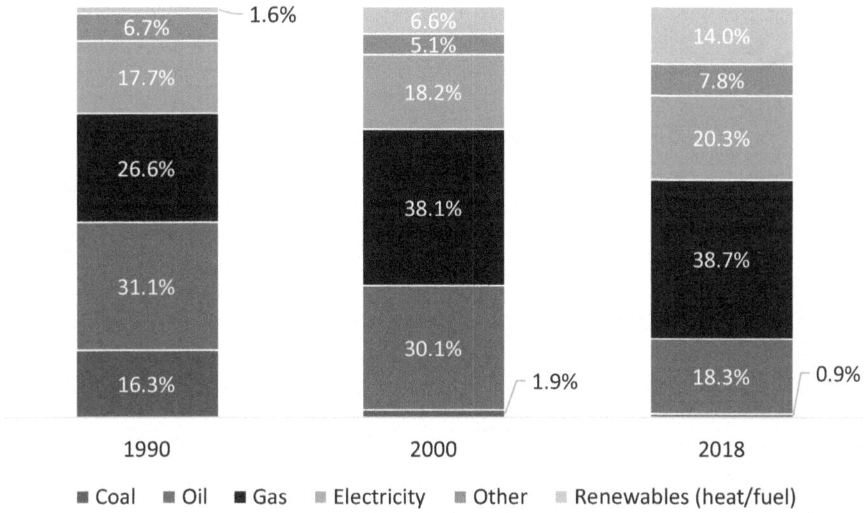

Fig. 29.4 Final energy demand of households by energy carrier in Germany (1990–2018). (Source: own elaboration on German Federal Energy Ministry data [2020])

attached to the Italian natural gas grid. As an alternative fuel, liquefied petroleum gas can be used, which is an oil product that becomes liquid at a pressure of 8 bar and ambient temperature, a physical characteristic that allows for relatively safe on-site storage in an external tank. Looking forward, many oil-fired boilers are bound to reach the end of their lifetime in the next decade. Hence, a key open question for the future is: **Which energy carrier will be able to capture oil's market share in residential heating?**

3.2 *Electricity Generation in the US: Gas Overtaking Coal*

Another example of technology disruption, well-known and thoroughly studied, is the shale gas revolution in the US (see Bellelli 2013). Shale gas (more generally: unconventional gas) is fossil natural gas that is obtained through an extraction process that was considered to be new and different in the past, because it involved hydraulic fracking and horizontal drilling. It is considered a revolution because it enabled the US to massively increase its natural gas production. The abundance of low-cost natural gas had a downward effect on US gas prices and reshuffled many markets, among which was the US power market. Electricity generation in the US had long been dominated by coal-fired power plants. In 2008, coal had a 48% share in electricity generation, with gas covering 21% (see Fig. 29.5). The shale gas revolution resulted in gas-fired production overtaking coal-fired production in 2016, merely five years after the beginning of the shale revolution.

The US case offers two insights. First, there can be quick wins even in the energy industry, despite the long technical lifetime of its assets. Driven by price

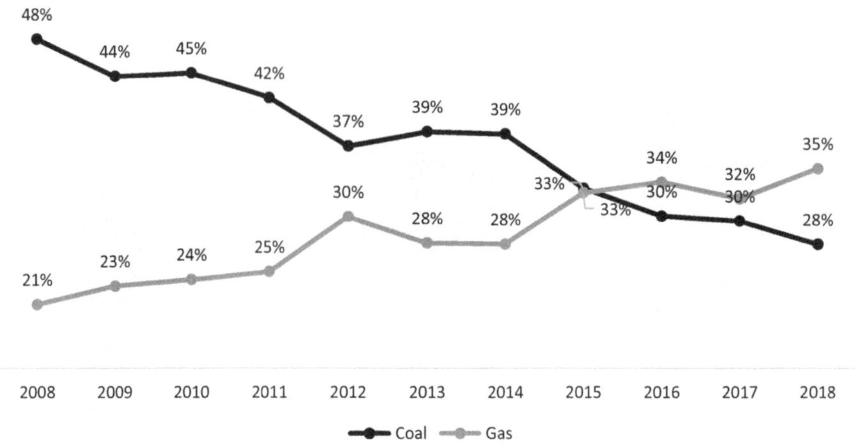

Fig. 29.5 Share of coal and gas in the US electricity generation mix (2008–2018). (Source: own elaboration on EIA data [2020])

signals, it was simply the utilisation of existing assets that was inverted, without a need to deploy new power plants. Therefore, the disruption process quickly slowed down—gas has not reached the market share coal had in 2008. This is the second insight: unless replacement capacity is built, some coal will continue to operate, despite gas being less expensive in terms of variable production costs. However, new capacity will only be built if an investor is confident about recouping total fixed costs (investment, capital and fixed maintenance costs). For existing assets, the main relevant fixed cost component is annual maintenance. Consequently, coal-fired power plants will only be closed if gross profits from annual electricity sales fail to cover these fixed costs. This decommissioning process can be slow if new-builds are rare—a quite common scenario given that investors are risk-averse and postpone their decisions to build new large-scale power plants, which typically cost more than one billion € per gigawatt of production capacity.

It goes without saying that such purely financial considerations do not apply in the same way for consumer goods, because purchasing decisions for these goods are not only guided by economic principles, especially when their price falls below a certain threshold. Thus, a key open question for the future is: **Can electricity generation assets become affordable for the masses and follow the dynamics of consumer goods?**

3.3 Electrification of OECD Countries: The Rise of Electricity

Another interesting but rather silent disruption in the energy industry was the process of massive electrification of modern economies (OECD countries). It can be considered silent because there were no losers: final electricity consumption simply kept increasing over the decades, that is, from 320 Mtoe in 1973

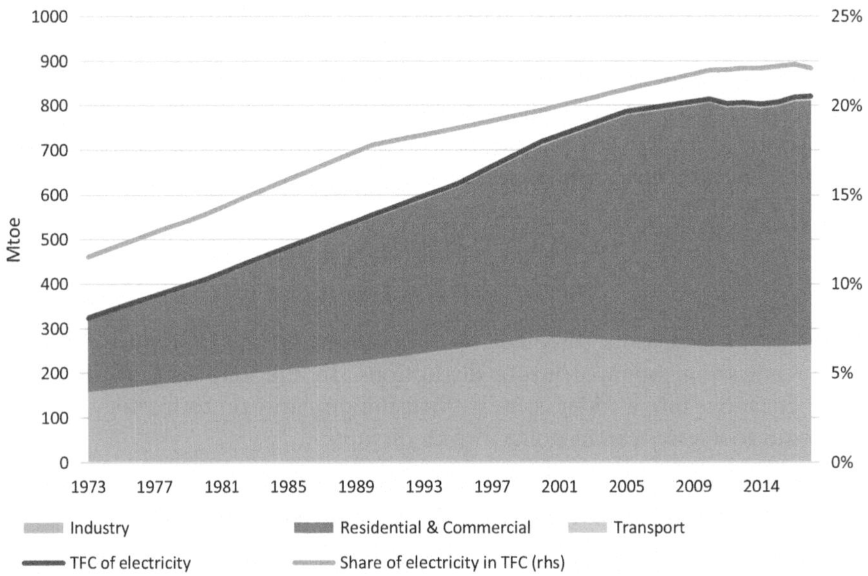

Fig. 29.6 Final consumption of electricity by sector and share in TFC (OECD countries 1973–2017). (Source: own elaboration on International Energy Agency (IEA) data [2019])

to 820 Mtoe in 2018, mostly without displacing other energy carriers but by creating new energy needs, for example due to a rising diffusion of household appliances such as fridges, TVs, washing machines, dishwashers and air conditioners (see Fig. 29.6). Data also shows that the transport sector never gained significant rates of electrification, rail transport being the only notable exception.

Massive electrification in the residential and commercial sectors was a result of technology advancements that allowed for low-cost production of household appliances but also for an ever-decreasing cost of producing, transmitting and distributing electricity. In parallel, household income and household spending in OECD countries grew at an impressive pace, for example at a compound annual growth rate of 8.3% between 1970 and 1990 for the case of Germany and almost 9% in the US (OECD 2020). As a result, household appliances became affordable for most consumers: a mass-market was created.

The latest IEA data shows that electricity has a share of 22% in total final energy consumption in OECD countries, up from 12% in 1973, and in line with German numbers shown in the previous section. What is remarkable is that this share has remained mostly stable over the last ten years. There are two possible reasons for this. First, many households in OECD countries already have a fridge, a TV, a washing machine, a dishwasher and an air conditioner. The market appears to be saturated and driven by replacement purchases, for example to substitute old or malfunctioning appliances. Second, the efficiency of new appliances appears to be increasing, because residential energy demand is not increasing, despite bullish drivers such as the increasing number of one-person households in modern economies, which—ceteris paribus—increases the number of household appliances required.

A key open question for the future is: **Will a second wave of electrification follow, if new electric appliances, affordable for the masses, are launched?**

4 Potential Future Disruptions in the Energy Industry

In the previous section, three key open questions for the future were formulated, indicating potential future disruptions. In the following, we will put these questions into a wider context, focusing primarily on technology disruptions and to a lesser extent policy-driven disruption.

4.1 Towards a Mass Market for Electricity Generation

It is generally acknowledged that electricity is a key energy carrier for energy transition, due to its intrinsic efficiency advantages and the fact that power already has a much higher share of renewables when compared to liquid and gaseous fuels (see Fig. 29.3). Costs for solar and wind, two major green electricity technologies, have declined significantly over the past decade, making them competitive vis-à-vis conventional power generation sources such as coal and gas in geographical areas where meteorological conditions (solar irradiation, wind speeds) are favourable and/or where CO_2 emissions have a price tag.

It goes without saying that policy instruments will remain key in pushing the growth of these alternative energy sources. These policy instruments certainly include CO_2 pricing but also long-term contracts, awarded by competitive bidding procedures that are organised by regulated parties such as governmental agencies.

These developments can be summarised as **regulated or policy-driven disruption**: polluting power production facilities will eventually be phased out, because they are not competitive with green electricity sources that own a long-term contract. Regulated long-term contracts will be increasingly complemented by long-term corporate power purchase agreements. These allow businesses to purchase electricity directly from renewable energy generators without being co-located. In 2018, "121 corporations purchased 13.4 GW of clean power directly from generators", up from 6.1 GW for 2017 (Bird & Bird 2019). However, **most of these new projects tend to be large-scale assets** with an installed capacity ranging from tens to hundreds of megawatts, meaning that a typical wind or solar farm will not only cost between ten and one hundred million euros but will also **require site development and permitting procedures**. Consequently, the **development speed** will remain **by and large predictable** and manageable.

Let us also **consider a more disruptive scenario**, a complementary development, in which small-scale electricity generation assets such as rooftop solar panels would be widely installed. Already in 2018 almost half of Europe's cumulative solar PV capacity was installed on residential rooftops or commercial roofs (SolarPower Europe 2019), a result of generous feed-in tariffs that especially Germany and Italy were granting between 2008 and 2012. This period, despite being policy-driven, shows the potential dynamics of consumer-driven choices: millions of solar panels with an average size of 3 to 5 kilowatts were deployed in just a few years.

A **new disruptive wave**, this time technology-driven, would entail that **solar panels become more affordable, easier to install and fully connectable** to other digital devices. We are not far away from such circumstances. Today, solar panels for residential rooftops cost below 10,000 €, less than a passenger car. Connectivity has become a standard feature for most modern household appliances and is greatly facilitated by smartphones, because they can be used to configure appliances and how they connect to the home WiFi via dedicated apps while standing next to the appliance. The last barrier appears to be the physical installation itself, which remains labour-intensive and far from trivial, because trained workers are required to mount the panels, wire them and connect them to a power inverter. **A disruptive technology breakthrough** would therefore not be triggered by a cost reduction of the solar panels themselves but rather by the development of **do-it-yourself solar kits**.

Another aspect that could accelerate the disruption speed of solar is linked to the **efficiency of panels**, because **more electricity can be produced with the same roof area**. Technically, this can be achieved by so-called **multi-junction cells**. The efficiency limit of single-junction cells is around 33%, largely determined by spectrum losses, that is, not all the solar energy carried by solar particles (photons) can be absorbed by the cell. Any semiconductor material is characterised by a certain energy band gap—that is, the minimum amount of energy required to break free electrons of their bound state and trigger a current. When a photon does not carry enough energy to cross the band gap, it will pass through the material and its energy will remain unused. An efficiency loss can occur even when a photon carries enough energy to cross the band gap, because the amount of energy extracted will be equal to the band gap. All additional energy is lost. When picking a single band gap (as is the case for single-junction cells), there is a trade-off between extracting more energy from fewer photons and extracting less energy from more photons. The latest technology advancements show that multi-junction cells can reach an efficiency of almost 50%. The diffusion of this technology has remained limited so far, due to technical reasons (e.g. complexity of production process, lifetime) and economic competitiveness (higher cost of materials).

Instead, what appears to be a **highly unlikely scenario** is what is typically referred to as an **off-grid revolution**, that is, that consumers would massively disconnect from the grid altogether. On the one hand, it is true that the cost reduction of solar panels has been significant, insofar as auto-consumption (directly consuming the self-produced electricity rather than withdrawing electricity from the grid) already pays for many consumers, albeit at low economic returns (long payback periods). On the other hand, the limited rooftop surface and the limited energy density of batteries make it **nearly impossible to reach 100% self-sufficiency**. Therefore, people will not want to disconnect from the grid unless they are prepared to sit in the dark after two successive cloudy winter days. A minority of consumers might aim for 100% self-sufficiency by installing multiple batteries and oversizing the solar array, but this would require investments above 100,000 € per household and would therefore be unlikely to attract a mass market (see Genoese 2015).

4.2 Hydrogen and Green Gas, a Way to Keep Gas in the Game

So far, gaseous and liquid fuels have remained mostly fossil-based and thus CO_2-emitting, which is incompatible with a climate-neutral energy system. Future energy scenarios therefore indicate a rising importance of green gas and synthetic fuels in general to reach climate-neutrality. Both green gas and synthetic fuels have a common starting point: hydrogen. The molecule is highly versatile and can serve as the basis to create all sorts of synthetic hydrocarbons including jet fuel for aviation.

Like electricity, **hydrogen is not an energy carrier that occurs in nature**. Instead, hydrogen must first be generated from other (primary) energy carriers. There are several ways to produce hydrogen, the most relevant for future scenarios being water electrolysis and steam methane reforming. The former process makes use of electrical energy to split water (H_2O) into its constituent elements: hydrogen (H_2) and oxygen (O_2). Its conversion efficiency currently stands between 60 and 70%, making **water electrolysis a highly electro-intensive process**. The second production technology (steam reforming) uses methane (CH_4) as feedstock to produce hydrogen, emitting CO_2 as by-product. Hence, steam reforming needs to be accompanied by Carbon-Capture-and-Storage technologies to become climate-neutral ("blue hydrogen"), whereas hydrogen from water electrolysis is considered green, if renewable electricity is used as feedstock. Blue and green hydrogen could be highly relevant in future, as indicated in various climate-neutral future energy scenarios (e.g. European Commission 2018).

It is important to point out that already today there is demand for hydrogen as feedstock, for example in the oil industry (hydrocracking) or the ammonia industry. However, **hydrogen is not a relevant carrier for energy end-uses (e.g. heating, transport) today**: there are no H_2 boilers for space heating or hot water, and while hydrogen-fuelled passenger cars exist (known as fuel cell electric vehicles), they are not as affordable as cars with an internal combustion engine and not as mature as battery electric vehicles. In general, **hydrogen is not a cost-competitive energy carrier today**. This is not surprising given that the production of hydrogen comes at an additional cost, as it requires both costly hardware and feedstock:

- Producing H_2 from steam reforming implies H_2 having a higher cost than natural gas
- Producing H_2 from water electrolysis implies H_2 having a higher cost than electricity

At very low electricity prices and with decreasing investment costs for electrolysers, green hydrogen could at some point become less expensive than natural gas. To put it differently, one would first need further cost decreases and efficiency improvements in renewable electricity generation (solar panels, wind turbines), followed by significant cost decreases and efficiency improvements of water electrolysers. It is unlikely that both of these technology improvements will happen fast enough to represent a disruption.

Instead, the **uptake of hydrogen will depend heavily on policy choices**. Aggressive CO_2 pricing and/or regulatory decisions that require a certain share of green gas in the existing natural gas mix will trigger the deployment of hydrogen production facilities. Consequently, the **development speed** will remain **by and large predictable** and manageable.

Nevertheless, **hydrogen is a strategic energy carrier for energy transition**. Already today, green or blue hydrogen could be used as feedstock in order to **produce climate-neutral ammonia and fertilisers**. Another key industry is steelmaking. Dominated by coke coal today (blast furnace route), in the future hydrogen could be used for the direct reduction of iron ore, producing sponge iron, which can be refined to crude steel. Major global steel producers have announced the intention to build demonstration plants.

While we progressively decarbonise the energy system, the use of unabated fossil fuels such as oil, gas and coal will necessarily have to decrease, giving blue and green hydrogen a chance to move from their niche role as climate-neutral feedstock towards climate-neutral energy carriers for end-uses. Their role will be **especially relevant in sectors that require fuels with high energy density**, such as aviation, maritime and long-haul road transport. For other end-uses, such as passenger cars as well as heating and cooling of buildings, alternative decarbonisation measures exist, which fall into the broad category of electrification and are the focus of the next and final section on potential future disruptions in the energy industry running on hydrogen.

4.3 Electrification Phase Two: Transport and Heating

The rate of electrification in OECD countries has been relatively stable in the last 10 years, hovering around 22% of total final energy consumption, indicating that no major energy end-uses have been electrified in the last decade. The **next phase of electrification** consists of capturing a higher "market" share in the **transport and heating** sector, two promising developments, given the advancing technological maturity and increasing affordability of battery electric vehicles (BEVs) and electric heat pumps. Moreover, there is a **remarkable efficiency advantage of a factor of three**, as is illustrated for the case of

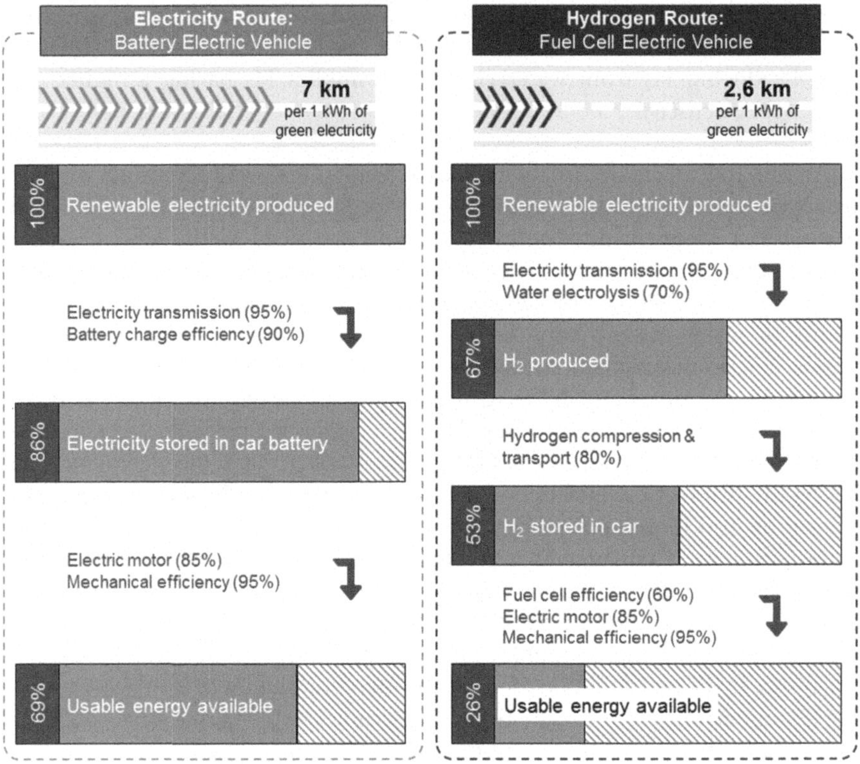

Fig. 29.7 Efficiency comparison between electricity and hydrogen in passenger cars. (Source: own elaboration based on Frontier Economics [2018])

passenger cars in Fig. 29.7. With one kilowatt-hour of electricity produced by a renewable energy plant, a BEV can drive for seven kilometres, whereas the hydrogen route would only allow for a travel distance of 2.6 kilometres. This fundamental efficiency advantage has also been recognised by major car companies such as Volkswagen and Daimler, which decided to abandon the hydrogen route for passenger cars in 2020.

In the case of heating, the efficiency advantage is even higher, because heat pumps are devices that produce heat from both ambient energy and electricity. In fact, for each kilowatt-hour of electricity consumed by a heat pump, between 3 and 5 kilowatt-hours of heat energy are produced. Modern gas-condensing boilers reach a conversion efficiency of 95%, that is, one kilowatt-hour of natural gas can be converted to 0.95 kilowatt-hours of heat energy. Heat pumps are therefore 3–5 times more efficient than gas boilers, even before considering that the production of climate-neutral gas involves additional conversion losses.

For these technological reasons and in view of the stringent EU emission standards for **new cars** and **new or heavily renovated buildings**, an uptake of demand for electric vehicles and electric heat pumps should be considered a baseline scenario in Europe. Car replacement rates range between 5 and 10%, depending on the country (see ACEA 2020), whereas less than 1% of European buildings are renovated each year. Consequently, **adoption speed** (and potential disruption) will be **much higher in passenger transport than in residential heating**, unless governments decide to incentivise the renovation of houses. Nevertheless, in view of the replacement wave of obsolete oil-fired boilers, further electrification in heating should not be underestimated. Rural areas without access to gas distribution networks today are unlikely to be served by natural gas in the future, in view of the more stringent building insulation requirements, which have a bearish effect on gas demand. Without access to gas networks, there is a limited number of technology alternatives once oil-fired boilers have to be replaced, facilitating the diffusion of electric heat pumps.

Further electrification in freight and maritime transport or aviation is less likely in the medium term. While electricity could offer tangible efficiency advantages in these transport segments, it is also true that electricity is hard to store. Current electrochemical batteries have a lower energy density than liquid fuels, too low to power airplanes, ships or trucks. The solid-state battery technology could triple energy density, making electrochemical batteries more attractive at least for long-haul road transport (trucks) but still insufficient for airplanes and ships. The technology uses a solid electrolyte, instead of the liquid electrolytes found in traditional lithium polymer batteries, which currently comes at the cost of a reduced durability and lifetime. Therefore, the solid-state technology has not been deployed at large scale, yet.

5 Summary and Conclusions

History shows that sudden disruptions are very rare in the energy industry, due to the relatively slow diffusion process of new technologies. Technological change is always ongoing but has remained manageable and predictable so far, given the long technical lifetime of assets in the energy industry.

However, in some energy sectors disruption could be imminent, largely driven by consumers, because their purchasing decisions are not only guided by economic principles. **Rooftop solar has already demonstrated its disruptive potential** between 2008 and 2012, mainly triggered by generous government incentives at that time. In the forthcoming decade, a new disruptive wave could be triggered by **easy-to-install solar kits and affordable multi-junction cells**, which increase the amount of solar energy per square metre that a panel can harvest. This will accelerate the already ongoing trend of load defection, that is, that consumers will withdraw less energy from the centralised grid. Nevertheless, people will not want to disconnect from the grid altogether, because this entails the risk to sit in the dark without electricity after two consecutive cloudy winter days.

Transport is another sector ripe for disruption: given stricter emission limits and the efficiency advantages of the electric vector, it is widely expected that **electric vehicles will capture an ever-increasing share in new passenger car registrations**, especially in the European Union, where internal combustion engine cars can no longer comply with new emission standards. Nevertheless, it is important to recall that the transport sector is much broader than just passenger cars. In fact, the passenger vehicle sector represents about a quarter of global oil demand (see IEA 2019b), while freight and maritime transport as well as aviation combined constitute about 30% of global oil demand. There is currently no viable electric alternative on the horizon for these transport means. Hence, the development of climate-neutral liquid and gaseous fuels will also be necessary to combat climate change. In this context, **hydrogen** (green or blue) could become a strategic energy carrier, being a **key measure to decarbonise the steel and ammonia industry**, as well as aviation and maritime transport. If new electrochemical battery technologies such as solid-state batteries matured, these could compete with hydrogen in long-haul transport but would still not have a sufficiently high energy density to run airplanes or ships.

After a decade of stagnation, current technology trends indicate that a **second wave of electrification is imminent**. This by itself would constitute a disruption of the energy industry. Whether hydrogen could also give rise to a disruption will mainly depend on energy policy and how seriously the fight against global warming is pursued.

Acknowledgements The author would like to express his sincere gratitude to Chiara Alvaro, Giovanni Giansiracusa, Nunzia Riccio and Giacomo Luciani for their comments and remarks.

References

ACEA (2020). New registrations in European Union and EFTA. Statistics Report.

Bellelli 2013: The Shale gas 'revolution' in the United States: Global implications, options for the EU. Report.

Bird & Bird (2019): International Corporate PPA Report.

EIA 2020: Electric Power Annual. Statistics Report.

European Commission 2018: A European strategic long-term vision for a prosperous, modern, competitive and climate neutral economy. Report.

Frontier Economics (2018): The Future Cost of Electricity-Based Synthetic Fuels. Report.

Genoese 2015: Low-cost batteries will not disrupt (all) energy utilities. CEPS Commentary.

German Federal Energy Ministry 2020: Energiedaten—Gesamtausgabe. Report.

FAO 2013: Biofuels and the sustainability challenge. A global assessment of sustainability issues, trends and policies for biofuels and related feedstocks. Report.

IEA 2019: World Energy Balances 2019. Report.

IEA 2019b: World Energy Outlook 2020. Report.

OECD 2020: Household spending (indicator). https://doi.org/10.1787/b5f46047-en.

SolarPower Europe (2019): Global Market Outlook for Solar Power 2019–2023. Report.

World Bank 2019: Fixed telephone subscriptions per capita in Europe. World Bank Open Data.

Umweltbundesamt 2018: Strategy for long-term EU greenhouse gas emissions reductions. Report.

CHAPTER 30

The Impact of Digitalization

Stephen Woodhouse and Mostyn Brown

1 Introduction

The energy industry tends to undergo periods of slow and steady efficiency improvements, punctuated by periods of step-changes in productivity when new technologies make a breakthrough, such as the switch from coal to gas generation from the 1990s. Digitalization has the power to facilitate such a step-change without introducing a new energy source, improving outcomes for electricity producers, end consumers and the environment.

This chapter explores the concept of digitalization and how it will impact the energy industry. It is mapped out in Fig. 30.1 and is structured as follows:

- Section 2 defines what we mean by the term 'digitalization';
- Section 3 looks at how digitalization will result in business-as-usual efficiency gains impacting the provision of energy to customers;
- Section 4 explains how digitalization can create a truly transformational integrated, customer-centric power system; and
- Section 5 explores wider issues concerning the risks, costs and threats of digitalization, followed by the chapter's conclusions.

2 Digitalization in the Context of the Energy Sector

Digitalization (defined in Box 30.1) is transforming businesses in many sectors, from banking to telecommunications, from entertainment to publishing. But digitalization is not simply the process of moving from analogue to digital, from print to electronic or wireless delivery, or even the use of improved tools

S. Woodhouse (✉) • M. Brown
AFRY Management Consulting, Oxford, UK
e-mail: stephen.woodhouse@afry.com

M. Hafner, G. Luciani (eds.), *The Palgrave Handbook of International Energy Economics*, https://doi.org/10.1007/978-3-030-86884-0_30

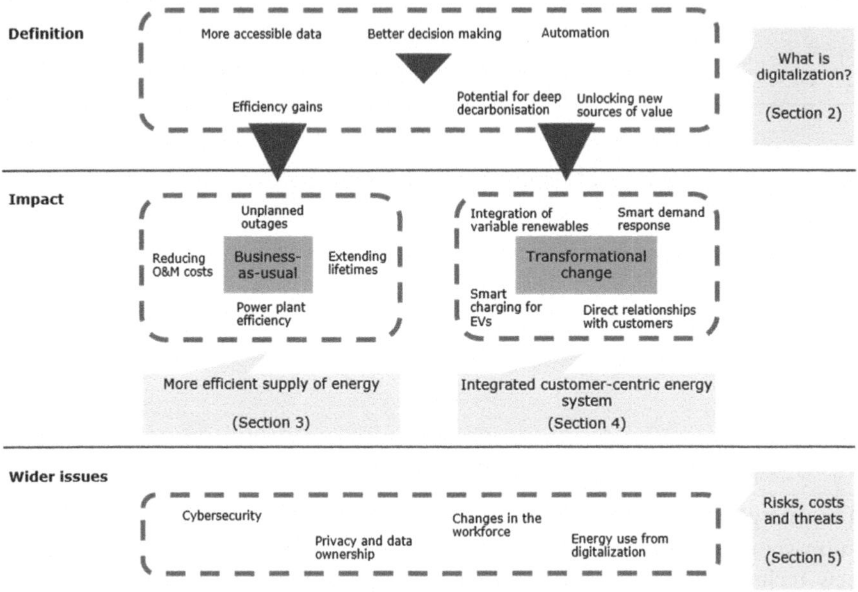

Fig. 30.1 Structure of this chapter looking at the impact of digitalization on energy. (Source: AFRY Management Consulting)

to achieve efficiency gains. Digitalization only realizes its full potential when digital tools (Annex) are allowed to change the underlying business model and the end-to-end processes within the supply chain.

Take publishing, for example: the traditional business model is being eroded by new models—electronic publications are sold online, leased through subscription, or provided for free in return for exposing the reader to advertising. This is a response to two related developments catalysed by digitalization: near zero marginal-cost supply for digitally delivered content, and a proliferation of new ways that authors (supply) and readers (demand) can connect with one another.

We are starting to observe similar developments in the energy industry. In the power sector, homes and businesses are increasingly supplied by essentially zero marginal-cost renewables from distributed plants, with millions of small-scale generators feeding into the network rather than a few central power plants. In the transport sector, electrification is making the variable cost component of driving vanishingly small (when compared to conventional petrol-fuelled cars, and allowing for transitional differences in taxation), and ride-sharing apps are starting to blur the lines between private and public transport and ownership. Advances in autonomous vehicles will push this trend further, where journeys can be optimized to radically improve the efficiency of transporting people and goods. In the heat sector (currently responsible for about 50% of final energy consumption in the EU), smarter temperature control solutions are emerging, some with voice-activated home assistants such as Amazon's Echo or Google Home, which are competing to be the single interface for domestic energy systems.

Digitalization is not new. It started before most of us were even born and has been used to incrementally capture efficiency gains within value chains, for example going from manual to electric typewriters and then word processors, from paper to calculators to spreadsheets. This process continues to deliver incremental efficiency gains in the supply of energy (Sect. 3). But from time to time something more transformational allows the value chain to shift. The transformational impact of digitalization in energy has the potential to enable the creation of an integrated, customer-centric power system using zero carbon sources (Sect. 4).

Box 30.1 What is 'Digitalization'?

Digitalization projects consist of at least two of the following three characteristics:

1. **More accessible data**, due to the collapsing cost and exponentially increasing capacity and availability of communications technologies, data storage, internet, satellite including geo-positioning, solid state electronics and so on, which leads to:
2. **Better decision-making** or optimization on the basis of the better data. This is where the first-tier efficiency benefits come from, although indirect benefits might come from other sectors, for example advertising for appliance sales on the basis of electricity meter readings); and potentially:
3. **Automation** of the results of the decisions. Analogous to self-driving cars, this could involve automation of heating or battery charging to balance renewable energy production or to deal with network faults, reducing the need for human intervention such as dispatch instructions from system operators to generation plant operators.

   Automation is not required in all cases—some digitalization benefits arise from manual decision-making, for example better forecasting underpinning investment decisions, but as consumer-owned sources of flexibility become prevalent, automation of system control becomes inevitable.

   Examples of the various digitalization technologies for energy are shown in Fig. 30.2.

The future digitalized system will allow decisions to be taken and executed autonomously based on a wide range of uncontrolled data sources. Cybersecurity protocols must adapt to this new decentralized and autonomous reality. Digitalization also allows companies to interact directly with people through social media, assessing people's real needs and preferences—potentially influencing their preferences, which in turn raises privacy concerns.

Collectively, digitalization of the energy sectors leads to efficiency and value gains and offers the potential for deep decarbonization through new models of customer engagement which unlock flexibility and enable renewable generation technologies to energise our economies.

Fig. 30.2 Digital technologies in the energy industry. (Source: AFRY Management Consulting)

3 Impact of Digitalization on the Supply of Energy

This section deals with how digitalization will result in business-as-usual efficiency gains, leading to reductions in the cost of energy extraction and the supply of electricity.

3.1 Impact of Digitalization on the Extraction of Fossil Fuels

Although many observers associate digitalization with cleantech and smart energy use, it has been used for years to increase the recovery of fossil fuels, reduce costs and improve safety. The upstream oil and gas sector, for instance, has established protocols for processing large datasets from seismic surveys to help optimize drilling strategies. Other examples include the real-time, dynamic steering of drill bits from remote operations centres, or the use of highly sophisticated sensors to optimize wellbore locations. Future developments will build on these applications, for instance to automate drilling rigs and to use robots to inspect and repair subsea infrastructure.

In the coal sector, efficiency gains in all aspects of fuel transport (shipping/trains/road) have improved dramatically over the last couple of decades due to real-time GPS trackers and instant updates on bottlenecks at ports or rail lines. Digitalization is also improving modelling of geological datasets to optimize mine design, automation and predictive maintenance. One of the main advantages of this is improved worker health and safety, which urgently needs addressing as the mortality rate dwarfs that of the oil, gas and hydro sectors. The ability of the coal sector to attract investment or digital talent is an open question as societal attitudes harden towards the traditional fossil fuel sectors.

3.2 *Impact of Digitalization on the Supply of Electricity*

Progress on the digitalization of the power sector to date has mostly focused on more efficient, secure and sustainable electricity systems. The resulting benefits have helped reduce operations and maintenance costs, improved efficiencies, increased reliability, and led to the extension of operational lifetimes of critical assets.

Further digitalization opportunities are spread across the value chain, as illustrated in Fig. 30.3.

The most significant impacts of digitalization on the various parts of the electricity value chain are described below:

- Advances in the management of generation assets mainly focused on the optimization of plant dispatch, maintenance, fuel and spare parts. Technologies used may include remote sensing and digital monitors, new control systems with automatic predictive and remote maintenance/control—perhaps linked to projected market conditions to plan maintenance periods—augmented intelligence for decision-making, and machine learning for better short-term forecasts for balancing and trading;

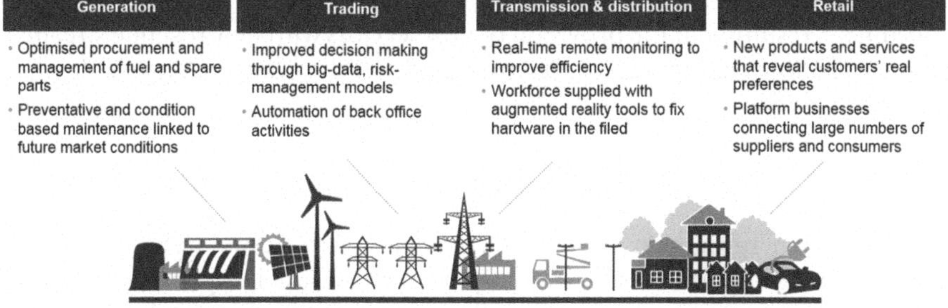

Fig. 30.3 Digitalization opportunities across the power sector value chain. (Source: AFRY Management Consulting)

- Decision-making in trading and scheduling of generation could be improved by digitalization by utilizing strategies based on big data, new risk-management models and new risk-management trading products, based on more rapid decision-making and algo-trading including optimization of short-term generation operations;
- Lower labour costs and electricity losses and predictive maintenance in networks (both transmission and distribution) through real-time remote monitoring, real-time sensor data to aid forecasting, at data hubs compiling smart meter data, and augmented intelligence for network management. In addition, digitalization and smart switching at lower voltage networks can facilitate deferred/avoided network investment and the transition to active distribution network management. Novel regulatory approaches could emerge based on shared data, which could narrow the information asymmetry between companies and regulators;
- Finally, digitalization of the retail sector, where the truly transformative aspects of digitalization are enabled, as described in the next section. Establishing direct relationships with customers and even their appliances will lead to provision of new products and services, lower prices, more customer differentiation through digital marketing, electronic billing/settlement, charging for access to the grid, bundling of other services with energy and/or its delivery, peer-to-peer trading and so on. By unlocking flexibility—potentially of individual appliances—the challenges of fuelling our grids with weather-dependent renewable energy will be mitigated.

In addition to impacting the linear value chain as described above, digitalization will also facilitate the move to a more integrated, highly flexible, customer-centric energy system, as described in the next section.

4 Towards an Integrated Customer-Centric Energy System

This section deals with how digitalization can transform the energy system, firstly by breaking down barriers across energy sectors to create an interconnected energy system, and secondly by establishing direct relationships with consumers, resulting in the provision of new services with new revenue streams, which will allow energy needs to be met from weather-variable renewable production sources.

4.1 An Interconnected and Responsive Energy System

Our current energy system is evolving from being 'very dumb' to 'quite dumb'. The traditional power, heat and transport sectors largely operated independently from one another and energy flowed in one direction only, from distributors of fossil fuel to end customers. The guiding philosophy has been to centrally predict and provide for all of customers' needs and preferences. Many

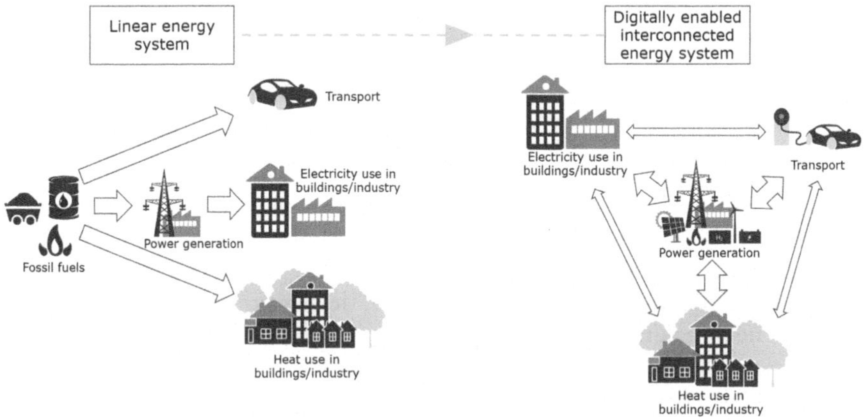

Fig. 30.4 Digitalization will facilitate the transition from a linear energy system to an interconnected one. (Source: AFRY Management Consulting)

European markets have now progressed to a stage where new technologies are enabling electricity to be generated and stored close to demand. Meanwhile, smart meter technology allows domestic customers to have access to time-of-use pricing. In today's electricity system, although energy does flow both ways, fully integrating distributed generation into a system coordinated by top-down centralized system operators is proving difficult.

Digitalization is enabling a third phase of development where these distributed sources of demand, generation and storage can be utilized to benefit the system as a whole rather than running entirely autonomously. In this integrated system, information and energy will flow in both directions and across energy sectors, controlled by multiple operators, for example the coordinated charging of electric vehicle (EV) batteries at times of high renewable output or platforms that optimize thousands of domestic battery systems to manage network congestion.

We envisage a future where these trends accelerate, creating an integrated energy system with renewable power generation at its core (Fig. 30.4). Part of this shift will also see power demand responding to supply, rather than the other way around. The International Energy Agency (IEA, 2017) characterizes three inter-related elements that digitalization can make possible, notably smart demand response, the integration of variable renewables and smart charging for electric vehicles (EVs). These key developments are described elsewhere in this book.

With today's expectations that zero-carbon generation comes predominantly from weather-dependent renewables, electrification is only compatible with decarbonization if we embed flexibility in the newly electrified demand; that is, through sector integration. Existing demand is less important, as much of the existing load is relatively inflexible: true flexibility needs to be baked in at the design stage. Aside from vehicle charging, space heating and cooling and water heating offer the largest achievable potential demand response opportunities without compromising customers' needs in the commercial and domestic sector.

4.2 A Customer-Focused Power Sector

Transformative benefits of digitalization can be achieved by organizations who will manage to establish direct digital relationships with customers, leading to new service offerings and revenues while capturing the inherent flexibility of the customers' energy needs (Brown et al. 2019). Most electricity retailers are currently ignorant about their customers' deeper preferences, but digitalization is now making it possible to offer more bespoke services and establish direct relationships. Conversely, customers are used to 'on-demand' provision of all of their energy needs without compromise. Unlocking a renewable electricity system means separating different needs for continuous supply: for example, most heating and cooling loads are inherently flexible, if the right monitoring and controls can be put in place. Over time, through interaction with the customers, energy companies could, for example, know which rooms and appliances customers use the most and detect when the customer is not home or on holiday.

New relationships could reveal different degrees of 'willingness-to-pay' for what are perceived as premium value services or combinations of services. Customization could enable retailers to offer a wider range of quality and brand differentiators. For instance, customers could choose their own level of service reliability (for different types of appliance), engage in peer-to-peer trading, manage the operation of their 'virtual battery' and possibly select other, non-energy products to be bundled with their energy supply. This requires the customers to change their perceptions and attitudes on how they buy energy and how they interact with their energy supplier.

There is evidence of product differentiation in the prosumer market, resulting in a proliferation of behind-the-meter gadgets. As the cost of solar photovoltaics and distributed batteries continues to decrease (Green 2019), more consumers can produce and manage their own energy supply independently from the electricity retailers. The underlying motivation for consumers to go 'off-grid' is largely driven by a desire to be independent, and the relative affordability of off-grid solutions is improving. These customers may be willing to invest in assets at low or even negative rates of return for reasons that may be hard to justify economically.[1]

This line of reasoning also applies to branded electricity, if it can be been as suitably differentiated from competitors. For instance, market stakeholder research conducted by AFRY in 2017 revealed that about 40% of participants said they would be willing to pay a small (10%) premium for electricity that was from a local and/or renewable source.

[1] Care must be taken to ensure that less enabled customers do not shoulder the residual burden of the centralized grid costs.

Those that doubt the ability of firms to create brands around a homogeneous, undifferentiated, commodity product like electricity should note the success of bottled water brands where sales have now surpassed carbonated soft drinks to become the largest beverage category by volume in the US. Rather than relying on a standard commodity that comes down a pipe or wire, consumers are apparently willing to pay more for something they believe is superior. Digitalization already provides the means to track renewable or locally generated electricity at a much more granular level than was possible before, to allow real product differentiation. As an example, Vattenfall and Microsoft are trialling a 24/7 renewable energy matching service, making it possible to go from year-based data to hour-based data on source of origin. Furthermore, through peer-to-peer trading, digitalization will allow communities of prosumers to manage the supply and demand of their own electricity. Some companies are now basing their consumption decisions on calculations of 'locational marginal emissions' which calculate the exact emission impact of demand at a time and place.

Traditionally, energy utilities have made money primarily, if not exclusively, by investing in assets, which in turn achieve a reasonable rate of return by the regulator or the marketplace. If energy sales flatten or decrease due to the rise of prosumers and prosumagers,[2] and utilities no longer own many (or any) generation or network assets, then how will they survive, or what new forms and organizations will they evolve into? How fast will 'customer focus' translate into increased willingness-to-pay by customers, and will they ever be willing to pay more to traditional energy companies (as opposed to other companies who bundle energy services with more appealing products)? These are open questions that companies are desperately trying to resolve.

5 Wider Issues Concerning the Risks, Costs and Threats of Digitalization

Most of this chapter has dealt with the potential positive impacts of the digitalization of the energy sector. In contrast, this section examines the threats that digitalization brings, including issues around cybersecurity, privacy and data ownership, direct energy use arising from digitalization, and potential changes to the workforce. These digitalization issues stretch beyond energy and shape society at large.

5.1 Cybersecurity

To date, the impact of cyberattacks affecting energy infrastructure has been small compared to other sources of disruption such as mechanical equipment failures or geopolitical disruptions to oil and gas supply. But the frequency and

[2] A prosumager is a 'prosumer' who has made additional investments in distributed storage, usually in the form of batteries.

severity of cyber incidents in the power sector are increasing (World Energy Council 2019), and there is a concern that industry may be unprepared to deal with novel threats. As the entire system becomes increasingly reliant on digital control, cyber-risks have increased significance.

As a concept, cybersecurity risks are not unique to energy; however, the challenge is exacerbated by several factors:

- strong growth in integration of ICT within the power system;
- strong reliance on digital systems for system-critical tasks;
- increased use of public networks and internet-based technologies;
- connection of many different types of Internet of Things (IoT) devices, with reliance on a wider set of data sources;
- increased number of parties connected to the digital grid (i.e. consumers, market agents); and
- greater requirements for transparency of system design and so on, to enable collaboration.

This increased connectivity has resulted in an increase in the 'cyberattack surface', making the risk of potential attacks more likely, and increasing the severity of attack when they do. This is in the context of an interconnected grid which is designed to operate as a whole, with common system frequency shared by all users.

To help minimize the risk and impact of cyberattacks, companies and countries are encouraged to adopt security around three concepts: resilience, basic cyber hygiene (adhering to good practices and so on), and incorporation of security objectives and standards as a core part of the research and design process. Ultimately cyber-risk is a war, not something that can be solved by adhering to standards, and there will be trade-offs between security, cost and inclusivity. The distributed and digitalized energy system offers the prospect of microgrids which could operate independently, increasing resilience and reducing the impact of cyber-threats, but the current grid design of common system frequency and a single system remains pervasive for now.

5.2 *Privacy and Data Ownership*

The interconnected energy system described in Sect. 4.1 relies on a willingness and ability to share customer data with third parties. This creates a tension for policy makers with consumers' privacy concerns on the one hand, and the promise of innovation and operational efficiencies on the other. Where this balance lies will be different for different regulators, but they will need to continue to refine interoperability standards, protocols to protect (and possibly anonymize) customer information, and provisions for consumers to give informed consent prior to any release of usage data. This is new territory for everyone concerned and opens up new questions. For instance, if energy becomes a bundled service offered by appliance manufacturers or tech companies, what is the basis for regulation of the industry?

5.3 *Energy Use from Digitalization*

As of 2019, Bitcoin consumes 66.7TWh per year (comparable to the total energy consumption of the Czech Republic, a country of 10.6 million people). Clearly, emerging technologies driving forward digitalization also require power.

Whilst Bitcoin's electricity consumption is large and growing, the major ICT electricity consumers are data centres (~200 TWh globally in 2014), data transmission networks (~185 TWh globally in 2015, of which mobile networks make up two thirds) and the rapid proliferation of connected devices.

How this electricity use will evolve is highly uncertain. Large data demand growth is a given; the key uncertainty is whether efficiency gains will continue, or whether they will slow or stall. As much of this new load is for cooling, it has the potential to be partnered with synergistic loads such as district heating systems or to offer flexibility to the power system. The tech companies themselves are very conscious of this growing environmental footprint and are among the most pro-active buyers of renewable energy through long-term PPAs, and are behind as more ambitious initiatives including 24/7 renewable energy matching and locational marginal emissions.

5.4 *Changes in the Workforce*

Jobs which are composed of a high degree of automatable tasks (e.g. repetitive physical activities and/or the collection and processing of data) are at higher risk from replacement by automation than those involving less routine or more creative activities. This looming 'great crew change' is creating a considerable source of anxiety for companies and workers alike, and it is becoming more difficult than ever for companies to retain critical knowledge and experience within their organizational memory.

But these are not the only changes afoot. Jobs created by digitalization tend to require a degree of analytical reasoning and are typically served by highly educated workers. These workers, particularly the younger generation, are increasingly blurring the borders between work and life. Work styles are transforming to include teleworking, flexible work schedules and more agile organizational structures, and the energy business needs to attract talent which has opportunities in many other sectors.

6 Conclusions

Digitalization will have far-reaching consequences for the energy system. It will cut costs of energy extraction and electricity supply, but this alone will not be a game changer. The step-change from digitalization will come from:

- the development of an integrated energy system where energy and data can flow in multiple directions across heat, transport and electricity sectors; enabling flexibility to match demand to renewable production; and

- the ability of companies to forge direct customer relationships to create new products/services and reap new revenues.

This brave interdependent new world does not come without its risks, of which cybersecurity presents the greatest threat, and changes to the workforce are likely to be the most wide-reaching.

The digitalization of energy will not occur in isolation. Yes, gains made in the digitalization of energy described in this chapter will be critical to have any hope of reaching net-zero emissions. But it may be the wider set of digitalization initiatives affecting how we organize ourselves as a global society, from cryptocurrencies to social media, that dictates the time it takes to get us there.

Annex: Glossary of Digital Technologies

Below we give a short description of the key digital tools and technologies that are impacting energy.

Existing and New Data Sources

5G	This is the fifth generation of wireless networking technology. The promise is that 5G will bring speeds of around 10 gigabits per second to mobile devices (600× faster than the typical 4G speeds today), enabling access to a far greater volume of real-time operational data.
Sensor data	The volume of sensor data may soon dwarf the amount of data that social media is currently producing. Gathered from cell phones, vehicles, appliances, buildings, meters, machinery, medical equipment and many other machines, sensor data will likely completely transform the way organizations collect information and process business intelligence.
Social media	Interactive technologies accessed by smartphone or computer that facilitate the creation and/or sharing of information, ideas, stories and so on via virtual communities and networks.
Smart meters	Meters that record electricity consumption in intervals of an hour or less, and communicate that information at least daily back to the utility for monitoring and billing purposes. Smart meter functionality includes remote reading, two-way communication, support for advanced tariff and payment systems, and remote disablement and enablement of supply.
GIS	A Geographic Information System (GIS) is an ensemble of hardware, software and geographic data for capturing, managing, analysing and displaying forms of geographically referenced information.

Drone	Also referred to as an Unmanned Aerial Vehicle, a drone can either be piloted remotely by a human or else can be a fully autonomous vehicle, allowing visual and sensor data to be gathered rapidly from remote or dangerous locations.
GPS	The Global Positioning System (GPS) was developed by the US in the mid-1990s. It permits the position of a mobile device to be determined. The GPS uses from two to six of its 24 satellites to a high level of accuracy.
Mobile apps	A mobile application, often referred to as an app, is a type of application software designed to run on a mobile device, such as a smartphone or tablet computer. It is an enabler of new ways of interacting with customers (and their appliances).
IT system data	This refers to databases and data warehouses that contains information that an organization needs to function.
ERP	Enterprise Resource Planning refers to business process management software that allows organizations to use a system of integrated applications to manage the business and automate many back-office functions related to technology, services and human resources.
Blockchain	One of several distributed ledger technologies that allow data to be stored and validated in a decentralized way. Digital records of events (such as a transaction) are collected and linked by cryptography into a time-stamped 'block' together with other events. It can enable decentralized business models: information can be validated and updated without relying on a central authority.
Cloud apps	A cloud application, or cloud app, is a program where cloud-based and local components work together, relying on remote servers for processing logic that is accessed through a web browser with a continual internet connection.
Critical infra data	Historically, the concept of critical infrastructure (to describe assets that are essential for the functioning of a society and economy) has been confined to physical assets, but now data is also included.

Data Visualization, Analysis and Evaluation

Virtual reality	Provides a computer-generated 3D environment that surrounds a user and responds to an individual's actions in a natural way, usually through immersive head-mounted displays.

Augmented reality	The real-time use of information (such as text, graphics, audio and other virtual enhancements) integrated with real-world objects. Augmented reality enhances the user's interaction with the real world (rather than being a simulation).
Digital twin	A replica of a physical asset that can be used to simulate and optimize the functioning of the asset.
Artificial intelligence	Refers to advanced analysis and logic-based techniques, including machine learning, to interpret events, support and automate decisions, and take actions.
Cognitive intelligence	At present, there is no widely agreed upon definition, but in general this refers to software that mimics the function of the human brain.
Cloud computing	Provision of computing services (such as servers, storage, databases, networking, software, analytics and intelligence) over the internet. It allows scalable data processing by companies without needing to buy or manage their own hardware.
Edge computing	Computing that is done at or near the source of the data. Edge computing operates on 'instant data' that is real-time data generated by sensors or users.

Control and Automation

Algo-trading	Automated buying and selling of products like crude oil, gas, electricity and wind power in an electronic trading environment.
Remote switching	An electrical switch that can be controlled remotely. Networks of these switches form the bedrock of remotely operated assets, and this simple technology is a critical enabler of balancing a renewable fuelled electricity using decentralized resources.
Automated operation	Technology by which a process or procedure is performed without human input.
Automated scheduling of maintenance rosters	Automation capabilities applied to workforce management software.
Inventory management	The supervision of non-capitalized assets (inventory) and stock items to ensure the smooth flow of goods from production to point of sale.

Bibliography

Brown, M., Woodhouse, S., and Sioshansi, F. (2019). Digitalization of Energy. In F. Sioshansi, *Consumer, Prosumer, Prosumager* (p. 550). Elsevier AP Academic Press.

Green, M. (2019). How Did Solar Cells Get So Cheap? *Joule, 3*, 631.

IEA. (2017). *Digitalization & Energy.*

World Energy Council. (2019). *Cyber Challenges to the Energy Transition.* World Energy Council.

PART IV

Energy and the Economy

CHAPTER 31

Energy and the Economy in China

Michal Meidan

Since China's reform and opening up in 1978, the country has undergone a profound transformation: the Chinese economy in 1978, as measured in Gross Domestic Production (GDP), stood at $150 billion (current US$ according to the World Bank (World Bank 2019)), and was half the size the Italian economy. Three decades later, China's economy is the second largest in the world and its per capita GDP grew by nearly 24 times from 1978 to 2017. The country has all but eradicated extreme poverty, with the share of China's population living in extreme poverty (according to the World Bank definition) plummeting from 90% in 1971 to less than 2% by 2013.

Urbanisation has been a defining feature of China's economic transformation, with the rural population, which accounted for roughly 85% of China's population on the eve of China's reform and opening up, now down to around 40% (World Bank 2019). Over the course of its economic transformation, China has also reached 100% electrification, meaning that its entire population, both rural and urban, has access to electricity.

Fuelling the country's rapid industrialisation and urbanisation process is a voracious appetite for energy, with primary energy consumption increasing seven-fold, from just under 400 million tonnes oil equivalent (toe) in 1978 (BP 2019), to 3.27 billion toe in 2018, or one quarter of global energy use. Domestically produced coal accounted for 70% of the energy mix in 1978, alongside oil, which accounted for another 23%. In the late 1970s, China consumed a mere 17% of global coal (BP 2019), but by 2018 China burned 1.9 billion toe of coal, half of the coal used worldwide (Fig. 31.1). In light of China's heavy reliance on coal, the country has since 2006 become the world's largest emitter of carbon dioxide (CO_2). In 2018, according to the BP

M. Meidan (✉)
Oxford Institute for Energy Studies, Oxford, UK
e-mail: michal.meidan@oxfordenergy.org

M. Hafner, G. Luciani (eds.), *The Palgrave Handbook of International Energy Economics*, https://doi.org/10.1007/978-3-030-86884-0_31

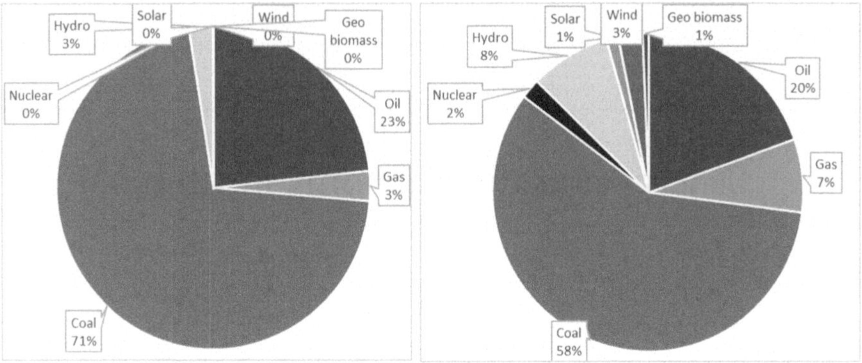

Fig. 31.1 China's energy mix, 1978, 2018. (Source: own elaboration on BP)

Statistical Review (BP 2019), the country accounted for 28% of global CO2 emissions—more than the US and the EU combined, with coal accounting for an estimated 70% of energy-related CO2 emissions (Myllyvirta 2019).

1 An Energy System Dominated by Industrial Use

Indeed, while the country's economic structure has changed significantly since reform and opening up, shifting from a predominantly agricultural economy to one dominated by industry and increasingly services, the industrial sector rapidly became, and remained, the largest consumer of energy.

In 1980, agriculture was a larger part of the Chinese economy than industry and services, but in the early 1980s the Chinese government began to gradually ease central planning and increase the autonomy of farming collectives. Rural residents then found themselves with new-found wealth to invest in labour-intensive light manufacturing enterprises, which, in turn, became the engine of China's economic growth. At the same time, the reform era led to changes within heavy industry, which had become tremendously inefficient under the planned economy. As economic incentives were introduced alongside the traditional planned targets, the growing awareness of profitability combined with the availability of energy-efficient technologies led to a dramatic improvement in the country's energy intensity (Yang et al. 1995). By 2000, Chinese economic activity required two-thirds less energy per unit of output than in 1978 (Rosen and Houser 2007).

By then, China was on the path of gradual economic liberalisation, anchored firmly by its decision to join the World Trade Organization. The country's planners were expecting strong GDP growth while maintaining the gains seen in energy efficiency as the country's economy would transition from energy-intensive heavy industry towards light industry. But over the course of the following decade, the economy grew faster than expected, while energy intensity (energy consumption per unit of GDP) tripled (Zhou and Levine 2003). The surge in economic activity and the ensuing need for energy meant that even as the economic reform agenda, of liberalisation and decentralisation, gathered momentum, similar changes in the energy sector were slower. Yet despite rising energy demand from consumers, industry has remained the largest end-user of energy (Kahrl and Roland-Holst 2009; Rosen and Houser 2007).

In absolute terms, according to China's National Bureau of Statistics (NBS), industrial energy use increased three-fold between 2000 and 2017, while its share of total energy consumption has dropped only slightly, from 70% in 2000 to 66% in 2017. Over that same period, residential and transport use increased from 11% and 8% respectively, to 13% and 9%, while the share of agricultural demand in total energy use has dropped by 1 percentage point (Fig. 31.2).

Within industrial energy demand, the biggest consumer over the past two decades has been the manufacturing industry, where energy demand has not only increased in overall volumes, but has grown to capture a larger share of total industrial consumption (from 77% of industrial energy use in 2000 to 83% in 2017). When looking further into the various subsectors in manufacturing, energy use in sectors such as textile manufacturing and paper products doubled between 2000 and 2017, but the total energy consumed by these sectors still pales in comparison with heavy industry. Chemicals production, which accounted for 14% of total industrial energy use in 2000, consumed 17% of the total in 2017, while smelting of ferrous and non-ferrous metals, which accounted for 22% of industrial energy demand in 2000, represented 28% of consumption in 2017.

The dominance of industry in energy demand reflects the outsized role that heavy industry has played in China's economic development, as well as the political significance of energy-intensive industries such as steel, aluminium, chemicals and cement. Not only has the country's economic growth been led by an investment boom in manufacturing and the associated infrastructure, but

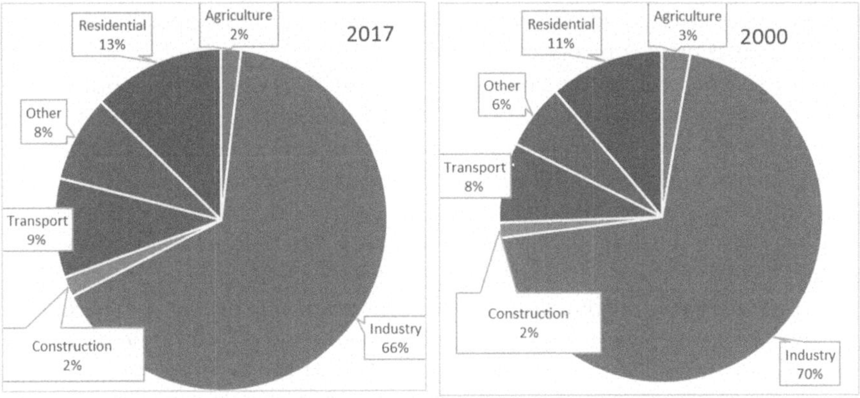

Fig. 31.2 Energy demand by sector, 2000 and 2017. (Source: own elaboration on National Bureau of Statistics)

the country has also sought to localise production of the energy-intensive basic products used to construct roads, factories and buildings. Moreover, since many of these heavy industries are dominated by state-owned companies that benefit from access to cheap capital—through the country's state-owned banks—as well as cheap labour and land, they have been able to reinforce their position as pillars of economic growth and development (Naughton 2007).

2 Supplies and Policy Priorities

With rapid economic growth, especially in the past two decades, energy policy was geared first and foremost towards ensuring supplies: to keep factories churning, to deliver goods from producer hubs to consumer centres, and to keep the rising numbers of urban homes warm in winter and cool in summer. Until 2001, China's economy was able to grow without putting significant strain on energy resources given the abundance of domestic coal, and to a lesser extent domestic supplies of oil and gas. Between 1978 and 2001, demand for fossil fuels grew at an annual average rate of 4% while the economy expanded at an average rate of 9%, allowing the country to produce enough energy to fuel its own development and export the surplus.

After 2001, however, as China's appetite for energy outstripped domestic production, and it outperformed both domestic and international expectations, a number of new challenges emerged: domestic energy shortages became commonplace and deteriorating environmental quality became a social concern, rising in political importance as of 2006, while increased import dependency and price volatility exposed China to the whims of global markets. (Downs 2004; Meidan 2014, Meidan et al. 2009). The Chinese government devised various policy responses to deal with these challenges, although many of them have involved similar methods, including investments in new capacity—adding supplies rather than regulating demand—using government-backed finances and favouring the large state-owned companies, drawing mainly on well-tested administrative instruments (Andrews-Speed and Zhang 2019) such as price controls and subsidies.

With surging energy demand and abundant reserves, coal has dominated China's energy use. Domestic production, for example, more than doubled between 2000 and 2009, from 700 million tonnes oil equivalent (Mtoe) in 2000, to 1,538 Mtoe in 2009, triple the growth rates seen over the previous decade as supplies attempted to catch up with soaring demand (Fig. 31.3). This was made possible by the abundance of China's domestic reserves, estimated at 13% of the world total, compared to 1.5% of oil reserves and 3% of global gas reserves. Indeed, coal has been the backbone of the Chinese energy system, accounting for the overwhelming majority of power generation. Yet throughout the 1980s and 1990s, roughly half of the domestically produced coal was sold directly to industry for use in boilers and coking ovens. An additional fifth was consumed by the power sector and households, each. With rising incomes and increased demand for consumer goods and transport, even

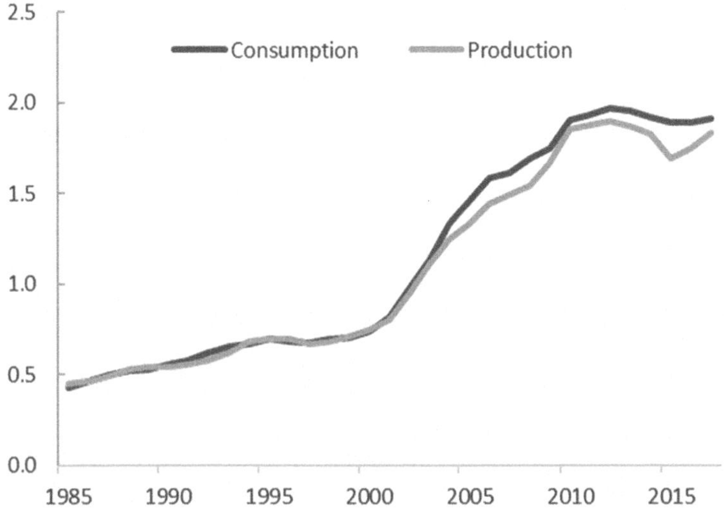

Fig. 31.3 China's coal consumption and production, Mtoe. (Source: own elaboration on BP Statistical Review 2019)

as consumption of oil and gas has increased, demand for coal has not fallen, but shifted from end-use to transformation. This has happened in three main ways. First, China's urbanisation process has fuelled demand for cement and steel for building and infrastructure construction—industries that are heavy coal users. Second, electricity demand, which remains predominantly coal-fired, has risen with home appliance ownership. Finally, overall demand was stimulated by the replacement of rural non-commercial (largely biomass) energy with urban commercial energy services—principally electricity (Aden et al. 2009). In 2000, power generation accounted for 41% of total coal use, but by 2017 its share had increased to 49%, according to China's NBS, just as total coal consumption has more than doubled.

While the abundant coal reserves have allowed China a high degree of resource self-sufficiency, the geographic mismatch between the reserve base (located predominantly in northern China) and the largest consumers in southern coastal areas has created logistical bottlenecks over the years. The variations in coal quality and price differentials between imported coal and domestically produced coal also led to a rise in imports. Even though in relative terms China's import needs at their peak in the mid-2010s accounted for 10% of China's coal demand, in global terms it was roughly the size of Russian coal production. So when China emerged as a large buyer of international coal, this was enough to rattle global coal markets.

While coal has dominated industrial energy use, the rise of Chinese consumers and growing demand for transport has been more closely reflected in oil and gas consumption patterns. Even though the share of oil in the energy mix fell from just under a quarter in 2000 to one-fifth in 2018, absolute demand volumes have skyrocketed, increasing almost three-fold from 4.7 mb/d in 2000 to 13.5 mb/d in 2018 (BP 2019). In 2000, industry accounted for half of the oil consumed in China while transport represented 28% of total demand. By 2017, the share of industrial demand had fallen to a third while transport—including freight transport, private vehicles and aviation—accounted for 38% of total demand. Similarly, the share of residential demand doubled from 6% in 2000 to 12% in 2017. China is the world's eighth largest oil producer, but its soaring demand has overwhelmed domestic resources and the country went from being a net oil exporter in the early 1990s to importing 10 mb/d in 2019 (Fig. 31.4), more than total African oil production.

China's thirst for oil, and the need for large imports, is seen as a strategic vulnerability—given that most of the country's imports are waterborne and could potentially be cut off. China's growing vehicle fleet, both private and commercial, has been a natural outcome of rising incomes and economic development. But it has also been a significant contributor to the country's deteriorating air quality. In 2010, China's passenger vehicle park was estimated at 55 million vehicles, but in 2018, it counted 199 million. Still, in 2018, China was estimated to have 170 vehicles per 1000 persons, compared to around 600 vehicles per 1000 persons in France and Germany, and as the middle class continues to grow wealthier and buy cars, oil demand is set to rise further. Already, however, emissions from 6 million vehicles were responsible for 45% of Beijing's concentration of small, breathable particles known as PM2.5. At the same time, rising demand for freight—powered by diesel—for transporting commodities and goods across the country has also contributed to worsening air

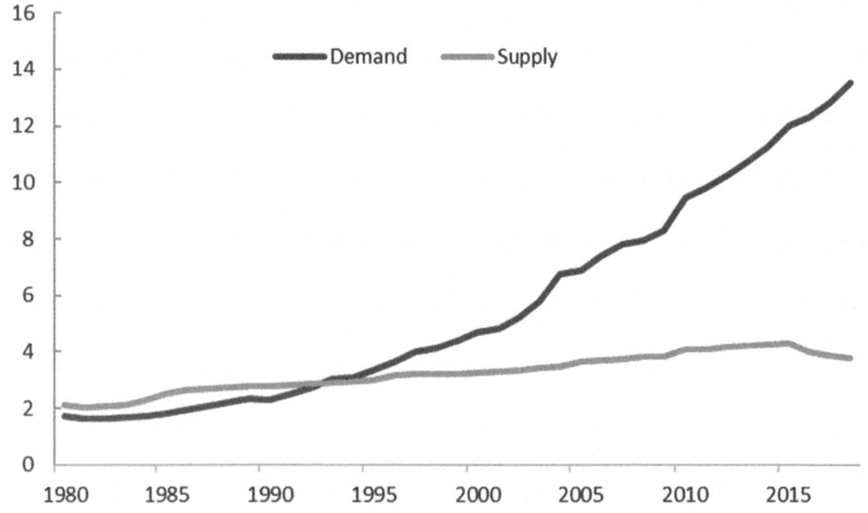

Fig. 31.4 China's crude oil supply and demand, mb/d. (Source: own elaboration on BP Statistical Review 2019)

pollution. According to China's environment ministry, in 2019 diesel trucks accounted for just 7.8% of China's total vehicles, but they contributed more than 57% of total nitrogen dioxide emissions and more than three-quarters of airborne particulate matter.

3 An Economic Transition and Environmental Awakening

In the early 2000s, as China's leaders were struggling to match energy supplies with demand, they were also confronted with a growing need to mitigate the negative environmental impacts of surging energy use. The economic toll of environmental degradation was also becoming increasingly clear, as China is home to around 20% of the world's population but has 5 to 7% of freshwater resources and under 10% of the world's arable land (Ely et al. 2019). China's mega deltas are particularly vulnerable to rising sea levels, while hazardous smog in densely populated cities—from industrial activities and road transport—is driving demand for the government to tackle air pollution (Ramaswami et al. 2017).

But while gearing up for another decade of strong demand growth, economic activity and energy demand growth moderated sharply following the global financial crisis. In response, the Chinese government introduced a massive economic stimulus package, which led to an over-investment in industrial capacity and, in turn, to an oversupply of a wide range of commodities including coal, steel and chemicals but also solar photovoltaic (PV) panels.

That said, following exceptionally strong increases in energy intensity between 2001 and 2005, the 11th Five Year Plan (2006–2010) contained provisions for reducing energy intensity by 20% from 2005 levels by 2010. While plans in the 1980s and 1990s included energy intensity goals, the severity of targets as well as government resources spent to support meeting them were now dramatically increased. Subsequent plans also contained mandatory targets to cut energy intensity using annual, national-level targets, as well as provincial goals. The latter were then incorporated in the assessment metrics for local officials' job performance. A number of regulations and standards were also issued with the aim of promoting efficiencies in the power sector (mainly in requiring that coal-fired power plants be upgraded to use supercritical or ultra-supercritical technology), in appliances as well as in building standards. Finally, the central government also made spending programmes available for energy-efficient equipment, upgrading coal-fired boilers, recovering waste heat and implementing energy managements systems.

Still, China's new leaders, President Xi Jinping and Premier Li Keqiang, came to power in 2012–2013 in the context of a slowing economy and an oversupply of industrial capacity, alongside worsening air pollution. The new administration was keen to rectify what former Premier Wen Jiabao, already in 2007, described as an 'unstable, unbalanced, uncoordinated and unsustainable' growth model.

Policy support and technological gains were set to help improve China's energy efficiency, alongside ongoing structural shifts in the economy away from manufacturing and towards services. Indeed, this rebalancing of China's economic model was a key tenant of the reform agenda and was expected to entail a moderation of economic growth to levels of 6–8% and a greater role for the service sector at the expense of heavy industry. In addition, policy priorities included enhancing the role of market forces in resource allocation, increasing the role of the private sector in industry and in financing and incorporating environmental protection more systematically into leaders' policy priorities.

Yet unlike many developed economies that began to regulate air pollution after their de-industrialisation was under way, the Chinese economy continues to grow and industrialise, leaving the government to grapple with the need to protect its environment while also ensuring affordable and secure sources of energy. The need to diversify the domestic energy mix and ensure more sustainable fuels for growth has coincided with a broader desire to shift the country's economic structure away from industrial-led growth towards a consumption-driven development path. Environmental protection, which was once seen as a costly impediment to growth, became both a social necessity and an industrial opportunity.

This change in priorities was reflected in the 12th Five Year Plan (12th FYP, spanning 2011–2015), in which the government set out for the first time binding targets for a 16% reduction in energy consumption per unit of GDP, an 8% reduction in sulphur dioxide (SO2) emissions and a 10% reduction in nitrogen oxide (NOx) emissions by 2015, from 2010 levels. As a result, PM2.5 monitoring efforts intensified, with the government setting more stringent targets for heavily polluted regions. The 12th FYP also incorporated a number of specific measures to shut down heavily polluting industrial facilities and expand the use of clean energy, including natural gas. Against this backdrop, China introduced its first 'Airborne Pollution Prevention and Control Action Plan' in 2013 (Action Plan 2013), which recognised coal as a key driver of air pollution and sought to limit its use.

The Action Plan 2013 established mid- to long-term targets for reducing total coal consumption and cutting China's share of the energy mix (Miyamoto and Ishiguro 2018), replacing industrial coal furnaces with natural gas. Gas demand, which has long played second fiddle to both the coal and oil industries, began to surge on the back of the coal to gas switch. Even though China has the world's seventh largest proved gas reserves, natural gas has accounted for a small share of China's energy mix. In the early 2000s, natural gas consumption totalled a modest 25 bcm, compared to 100 bcm consumed in the UK or 629 bcm in the US. At the time, it was largely used as feedstock in industry and only played a marginal role in the power sector, where coal remains the dominant fuel. Even within these small volumes, however, industrial use accounted for two-thirds of total consumption. But the environmental push, combined with the prospects of abundant unconventional resources within China, has led to accelerated efforts to develop the sector. With increased penetration in household consumption and commercial use, the share of industry in total gas demand dropped to 44% in 2019, while national gas consumption increased more than ten-fold, to just over 300 bcm that year. Transport demand rose from 4% to over 10% while residential use in 2019 accounted for one-fifth of overall consumption. Natural gas use in the power sector has also been increasing rapidly but, overall, gas remains a marginal fuel in the power stack, accounting for under 5% of installed generation capacity.

Much like with crude oil, natural gas demand rose at a staggering pace between 2000 and 2014 (annual average 16%), but domestic gas production failed to keep up with demand (Fig. 31.5), as the reservoirs are more difficult to access than those in gas-rich countries such as Russia, Venezuela and Qatar. And with limited domestic expertise, infrastructure and technology in the sector, production and exploration growth has been more subdued than demand. China's erstwhile self-sufficiency for gas turned into a growing reliance on imports, although Chinese buyers sought to secure both pipeline gas and LNG imports, to limit their exposure to waterborne supplies.

At the same time, the rise of unconventional gas and its profound impact on the US's energy sector and economy raised considerable interest in China, especially given estimates that China has the largest unconventional reserves outside of the US. Moreover, the technological gains from the development of resources including tight gas, coal bed methane and shale gas in the US meant vast cost reductions, generating greater optimism in China about the feasibility of extracting unconventional gas. Promoting these resources would not only allow China to mitigate its import dependency but would also support the

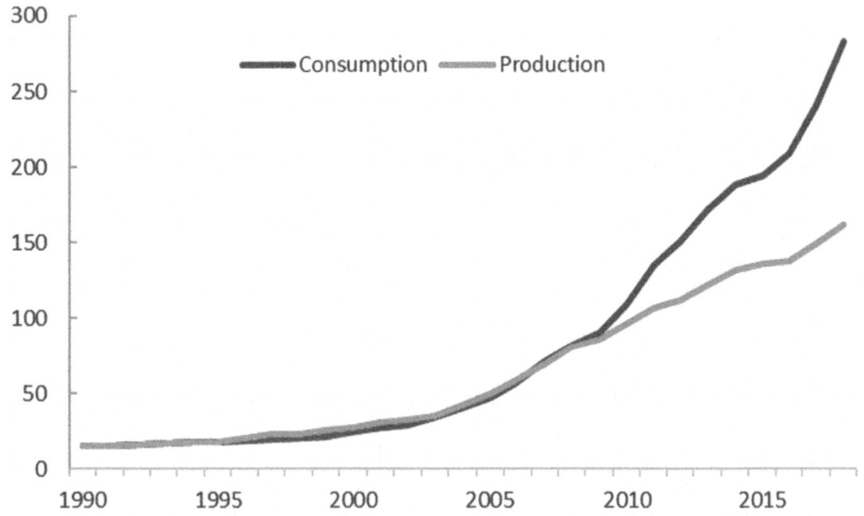

Fig. 31.5 China's natural gas supply and demand, bcm. (Source: own elaboration on BP Statistical Review 2019)

energy manufacturing industry in its quest to become more globally competitive. But despite the government's lofty ambitions, shale gas development has been slower than hoped. In 2012, Beijing set a target to produce 60–100 bcm of shale gas by 2020, which it later revised down to 30 bcm. And while there has been strong growth in a sector that only began drilling in earnest in 2010, output from shale is unlikely to exceed 20 bcm in 2020.

Even though the most conservative estimates of China's technically recoverable shale reserves peg them at half of Qatar's North Field, tapping their potential is harder than in the US. This is due to a combination of above- and below-ground factors: The quality of the reservoir is uncertain, but seems to be more complex than US basins, while the domestic technology and shale drilling expertise are nascent. Moreover, until 2019, the upstream was tightly controlled by the state-owned majors, with limited access to foreign companies. Finally, drilling for shale is complicated by murky ownership structures of subsurface rights, the availability of water for use in hydraulic fracturing, and the availability of pipelines for gathering and transportation, among other factors.

4 Energy and Industry 2.0

The early 2010s therefore saw the convergence of China's industrial upgrade plan and its energy priorities. In mid-2014, the country announced an 'energy revolution', which was later formalised in a publicly released policy paper setting out the main overall targets and strategies for China's energy sector through 2030 (NDRC 2016). The 'energy revolution' includes efforts to limit energy consumption growth, by mandating demand-side management for industry and changing consumer habits; it calls for improving efficiencies in and reducing emissions from China's energy infrastructure while also highlighting the importance of energy technology. Indeed, the 'energy revolution' also includes an effort to develop, commercialise and diffuse next generation energy technologies through innovation and international co-operation.

In the context of China's industrial programme, climate change mitigation became an opportunity for underpinning China's economic transition and a potential means of advancing China's bid for global technology leadership (Geall 2017). And given the country's scale and strong ability to incentivise industrial outcomes, it has proven capable of rapidly driving change. The 12th FYP highlighted seven strategic emerging industries that would receive preferential support, including renewable energy technologies and electric cars. The subsequent plan, the 13th Five-Year Plan (13th FYP; 2016–2020), continues the emphasis on clean technologies, although it aims to give the market, rather than state subsidies, a determining role in selecting the most competitive green industries and technology leaders (Geall 2017).

China has since become the global leader in renewables. In 2012, China's installed capacity of wind and solar power was 61GW and 3.4GW respectively, while the annual electricity generated by renewables was only 2.1% of China's total consumption. By 2017, China's wind and solar power capacity had increased to 168.5 GW and 130.06 GW respectively, and renewables were generating 5.3% of China's electricity supply. Installed solar capacity has outstripped the 110 GW targeted in the 13th FYP, with 186 GW installed in June 2019. Similarly, wind capacity is largely on track to meet its 13th FYP target of 210 GW of installed capacity, having reaching 193 GW in June 2019.

On the back of increased manufacturing capabilities, the average price of global PV modules decreased by 79% from 2010 to 2017. At the same time, the subsidy programme was draining central government coffers, with the total amount of wind and PV subsidies in 2017 estimated at about 170 billion yuan (Lin 2018) and becoming a source of global trade friction, as Chinese manufactured solar PV modules were the target of anti-dumping measures. But ultimately, Chinese companies' ability to reduce costs and support investments globally in the 'low carbon' economy has supported wider efforts to tackle climate change (Goron 2018).

China has therefore been driving global renewables consumption growth, both by installing capacity at home and exporting solar panels and wind turbines. As such, China's decarbonisation goals and commitment to the UN climate process are consistent with and supportive of its key economic and technological ambitions, namely the domestic economic rebalancing away from energy-intensive heavy industries towards innovation and services.

Nonetheless, despite the strong increase in installed capacity and falling costs, the level of curtailment—or energy that is generated but not purchased because it cannot be absorbed by the electricity grid—remains high. This is due to the fact that renewable resources are developed in provinces in China's northwest, far away from consumer bases, with limited coordination with the grid. Moreover, historically coal plant operators in China have preferential access to the grid through contracts that guarantee a minimum number of hours of dispatch per year. This is set to change as power sector reforms include incentives for interprovincial trading of electricity and pilot programs for dispatching electricity on the basis of the lowest marginal cost, but power sector reforms have been slow. Moreover, local governments have been intervening in the bilateral transactions between generators and industrial consumers, ignoring the agreed transmission and distribution tariffs in order to protect their local power generators. Meanwhile, the state-owned grid companies use their strong market position to distort any emerging competition in distribution and retail by demanding a controlling share of new distribution projects as a condition of providing access to the transmission infrastructure.

As China's policy makers considers the country's future energy priorities, in the context of rising geopolitical tensions with the US and a looming global recession in 2020, it is important to note that China's 'energy revolution' emphasises air quality, rather than carbon mitigation, with mandatory targets to reduce air pollutants such as SO2 and NOx and less emphasis on greenhouse gas emissions more broadly. China's domestic plans resonate with its climate change commitments undertaken in the Paris framework in 2015, to peak CO_2 emissions around 2030 or earlier, and to reduce carbon emission per unit of GDP by 60–65% compared to 2005, without, however, setting an absolute cap for carbon emissions. Put simply, China's air quality and climate policies have been developing relatively autonomously from each other, with air pollution the main source of concern for the Chinese government. Air pollution is perceived as an environmental problem, while climate change has been framed as a development issue, and until March 2018 each policy was under the supervision of different parts of the state administration (Yamineva and Liu 2019).

In addition, China's energy transition is at the intersection of a number of policy priorities whose relative importance for decision makers can fluctuate. In 2019, for example, given the decelerating economy and a weak industrial complex, air pollution woes were falling slightly in importance, in large part because the largest polluters are impacted by economic moderation. Thus, costly efforts to mitigate air pollution, such as the coal to gas switch, slowed due to concerns about the cost and availability of natural gas supplies. At the same time, given the ongoing trade war with the US, concerns about supply security and import dependence are resurfacing, leading China's decision makers to review the role of coal in the energy mix.

This comes at a critical time, as China is drafting its next Five Year Plan, which starts in 2021. Yet since 2018, the Chinese government has eased restrictions on new coal-fired power plants, opening the door for more regions to build coal power from 2021 to 2023 even though coal companies are losing money and utilisation rates are low. Beijing's support for the coal sector, however, is due to a number of reasons. First, the coal industry is a huge employer and in the current economic downturn both local and central officials will be reluctant to create unemployment among workers who have few transferrable skills. Second, the coal-fired power fleet is not at the heart of China's air pollution problem, given that the vast majority of the fleet is equipped with pollution abatement equipment and the government's focus is on local pollutants rather than carbon emissions. Indeed, industrial and residential coal use are the key sources of local air pollution and are at the heart of a number of fuel-switching policies. The cost competitiveness of renewables and development of power markets will gradually raise the share of renewables in the energy mix and the power sector, but in light of China's broader employment and security concerns, China's energy transition away from coal could slow in the near term.

5 The Energy Sector: Stranded between the Plan and the Market

China's energy demand has clearly been driven by the needs of its growing economy, but policy and politics have played a large role in shaping the energy mix, at times defying economic calculus. Over the course of China's reform and opening up, while large swaths of the economy underwent waves of liberalisation, the energy sector lagged behind. Hence, the fact that China's energy sector today remains torn between the plan and the market has profound implications for policy choices.

It is easy to forget that China's sophisticated corporations and energy traders today were ministries up until the 1980s. In the 1990s, as the government sought to improve the efficiency of energy production and allocation, it introduced a series of reforms, first in oil and gas and then in coal and power, converting government energy ministries into state-owned enterprises (Yang et al. 1995). Prices were partially liberalised, incentives were gradually introduced and competition was allowed in certain areas. Decision were no longer made by bureaucrats based on political considerations alone, but began to reflect an opaque mix of investment decisions based on markets as well as social and political mandates.

Competition was introduced into some parts of the energy value chain (such as coal extraction and power generation) but state-owned monopolies remained dominant in most others (including power distribution and most of the oil and gas sectors, with signs of change coming in 2019–2020). Upstream prices have been increasingly liberalised, but downstream prices remain under the state's oversight. Bureaucrats have been trying to plan supplies even as markets are determining demand, leading to cycles of under- and over-investment. This was apparent in the 2000s when the reality of China's economic and energy growth defied predictions and strained Chinese and global commodity markets. This, in turn, informed investment decisions both within China and globally, predicated on an expectation that China's appetite for energy would not wane.

Within China, Beijing's concerns about supply shortages led to waves of liberalisation. Following recurring shortages at state-owned coal mines in the 1970s and 1980s, Beijing encouraged coal production from small, private mines, which became the backbone of China's incremental coal production through the mid-1990s. Gradually, however, it became clear that output from these small mines entailed considerable wastage of resources; they had low extraction rates due to limited technological gains, and the high casualty rates among miners alongside rising environmental damage (Andrews-Speed et al. 2003) were becoming social concerns. This prompted the central government to mandate the closure of small mines, only to relax its guidelines when supplies tightened (Aden et al. 2009). When private mines were conducive to supply security, they were encouraged, but as their social cost outweighed the benefits, they were shuttered.

A similar trend was visible in the oil market where independent refineries grew in capacity and market share during the 2000s. Located for the most part in Shandong province, they have traditionally been small, inefficient and unsophisticated—earning them their nickname 'teapots'. Given the oil sector's contribution to environmental degradation and the independent refiners' penchant for tax evasion, the central government issued several mandates to shutter the smaller plants, but the 'teapots' survived, in large part due to local government support, but also by becoming important swing suppliers throughout the

2000s, when China's oil demand growth was surging and refining capacity could not keep up. During the fuel shortages of 2007–2008 and then again in 2010, teapot refiners ramped up their output and eased supply shortages in eastern and central China, highlighting their contribution to supply security (Meidan 2017, Downs 2017). The 'teapots' were able to grow in size and sophistication, and came to international attention in 2015, when the central government relaxed crude import rules and allowed them to source oil directly from international markets, a move that also coincided with widespread corruption investigations that paralysed the state-owned oil majors. By allowing independent refiners to compete in the state-owned monopoly, the central government sought to ensure supply security while also promoting liberalisation. But the unintended consequence of this has been a surge in crude imports, which has far outweighed the country's needs, and an oversupply of refined products.

State-set prices are another case in point. Throughout the 2000s, for example, China's electricity prices were capped by the government to avoid stoking inflation, despite rising coal prices. Within provinces, prices were managed by user categories but the disparity between state-controlled end-user prices, combined with market-oriented coal prices (following gradual price reforms), created incentives for generators to maintain low coal inventories, or even export coal, which in turn made them vulnerable to supply disruptions, and to the government's ire.

A similar phenomenon happened in oil when the surge in domestic demand in the early 2000s led to a spike in global oil prices. As these were not reflected in the domestic pricing mechanism, refiners exported products in order to capitalise on strong margins, creating domestic shortages. Such moves by the state-owned incumbents have often led to tweaks to pricing mechanisms or some form of compensation for losses, but they have also strengthened the government's resolve to weaken the state-owned majors' monopoly over the domestic energy sector. Indeed, China's state-owned energy giants are also constantly assessing their policy goals and the trade-offs between their need to maximise profits for their largest shareholder (the state) and maintaining social stability through employment and ensure energy security.

Beyond these ever-changing policy mandates, China's decentralised governance structure offers a number of advantages, but can also present disadvantages. China's reform process has been marked by an experimental policy design, whereby different localities have been able to pursue development strategies that suit their local conditions. This has also allowed the central government to carry out localised policy experiments before deciding if and how to roll them out nationally.

At the same time, local governments have considerable influence over policy implementation as they regulate tax collection, service standards, product quality, as well as environmental and safety performance in a way that suits local needs (Andrews-Speed and Zhang 2019). This gives local officials significant capacity to enforce or distort policy. In the power sector, for example, local regulators approved the construction of a large number of coal-fired power stations between 2013 and 2016 and the curtailment of renewable energy in favour of thermal power plants over the same period. Both actions undercut the central government's policy to promote clean sources of electricity but supported local growth and employment.

Four decades of reform and opening up have led to profound transformations in the Chinese economy, including a structural shift away from agriculture and heavy industry towards manufacturing and services, and a proliferation of non-state actors. Yet in the energy sector, the state has remained dominant. While market reforms have been introduced gradually, the leadership has chosen to keep major energy companies under state ownership so that they can help it deliver non-commercial policy objectives. At the same time, the government has been keen to expose the energy majors to some market discipline through liberalised pricing and increased competition from non-state actors. This state of affairs has given the government flexibility to alter its policy agenda, but has also exposed it to powerful interest groups capable of distorting policy implementation.

The overarching priorities, however, have seen little change. With rapid economic growth, especially in the past two decades, energy policy has been geared first and foremost towards ensuring supplies, with a preference for domestic resources that also limit import dependency. And the negative environmental impact of China's energy choices has now become a social concern, as well as an industrial opportunity. Developing energy efficiency technologies, delivering innovation in new energy and producing renewable energy equipment have been ways to bolster China's economic, industrial and energy transformation, while also allowing it to take a global leadership role. Furthermore, the availability of renewables in China and their falling cost suggest they will account for a growing share of domestic energy consumption.

But the path there will not be smooth. China's commitment to pursuing its market reforms will be tested by a slowing economy, concerns about surging unemployment and a deteriorating external environment as US–China strategic tensions deepen.

References:

Action Plan (2013), Circular of the State Council on Air Pollution Prevention and Control Action Plan, Guo Fa no 37, 2013, http://www.gov.cn/zwgk/2013-09/12/content_2486773.htm

Philip Andrews-Speed et al., 2003, "The regulation of China's township and village coal mines: a study of complexity and ineffectiveness", Journal of Cleaner Production 11 (2003) 185–196

Philip Andrews-Speed, Sufang Zhang, 2019, *China as a Global Clean Energy Champion: Lifting the Veil*, Palgrave Macmillan: Singapore, 2019

Nathaniel Aden, David Fridley, Nina Zheng, "China's Coal: Demand, Constraints, and Externalities", *Environmental Energy Technologies Division, LBNL*, July 2009

BP Statistical Review of World Energy 2019, https://www.bp.com/en/global/corporate/energy-economics/statistical-review-of-world-energy.html, last accessed 28 October 2019

Erica Downs, 2004, "The Chinese Energy Security Debate", *The China Quarterly*, no. 177.

Erica Downs, 2017, The Rise of China's Independent Refiners, Center on Global Energy Policy working paper, September 2017, https://energypolicy.columbia.edu/sites/default/files/CGEPTheRiseofChinasIndependentRefineries917.pdf

Ely, Adrian, Geall, Sam and Dai, Yixin, 2019, "Low carbon China: emerging phenomena and implications for innovation governance—introduction to the special section of environmental innovation and societal transitions", *Journal of Environmental Innovation & Societal Transitions*, 30. pp. 1–5

Sam Geall, 2017, "Clear Waters and Green Mountains: Will Xi Jinping Take the Lead on Climate Change?", *Lowy Institute Analysis Paper*, https://www.lowyinstitute.org/publications/clear-waters-and-green-mountains-will-xi-jinping-take-lead-climate-change, accessed 10 September 2019

Coraline Goron, 2018, "Fighting against climate change and for fair trade: finding the EU's interest in the solar panels dispute with China", *China-EU Law Journal*, Volume 6, issue 1–2, pp. 103–125.

Kahrl F, Roland-Holst D, 2009, "Growth and structural change in China's energy economy", *Energy*, July 2009, 34(7):894–903

Michal Meidan 2014, "The Implications of China's Energy-Import Boom", *Survival*, Volume 56. Issue 3, pp. 179–200

Michal Meidan, 2017, China's Independent Refiners: A New Force Shaping Global Oil Markets, OIES Energy Insight, May 2017, https://www.oxfordenergy.org/wpcms/wp-content/uploads/2017/05/Chinas-Independent-Refiners-A-New-Force-Shaping-Global-Oil-Markets-OIES-Energy-Insight.pdf

Meidan M, Andrews-Speed P, Xin Ma, 2009, "Shaping China's Energy Policy: actors and processes", Journal of Contemporary China, 18: 61, 591—616, Shaping China's Energy Policy: actors and processes. Available from: https://www.researchgate.net/publication/248999566_Shaping_China's_Energy_Policy_actors_and_processes. [accessed Oct 28 2019]

Akira Miyamoto, Chikako Ishiguro, 2018, "The Outlook for Natural Gas and LNG in China in the War against Air Pollution", OIES Paper, NG 139, https://www.oxfordenergy.org/wpcms/wp-content/uploads/2018/12/The-Outlook-for-Natural-Gas-and-LNG-in-China-in-the-War-against-Air-Pollution-NG139.pdf?v=79cba1185463, accessed October 2019

Lauri Myllyvirta, 2019, "Why China's CO2 emissions grew 4 percent during first half of 2019", Carbon Brief, 5 September, available at https://www.carbonbrief.org/guest-post-why-chinas-co2-emissions-grew-4-during-first-half-of-2019, last accessed Oct 28, 2019

Naughton, Barry, *The Chinese Economy. Transitions and Growth*, Cambridge, MA: MIT Press, 2007

NDRC 2016, 能源生产和消费革命战略 (Energy Supply and Consumption Revolution Strategy (2016–2030), available at http://www.ndrc.gov.cn/gzdt/201704/W020170425548780357458.pdf, last accessed 10 October 2019.

Anu Ramaswami, Kangkang Tong, Andrew Fang, Raj M. Lal, Ajay Singh Nagpure, Yang Li, Huajun Yu, Daqian Jiang, Armistead G. Russell, Lei Shi, Marian Chertow, Yangjun Wang and Shuxiao Wang, 2017, "Urban cross-sector actions for carbon mitigation with local health co-benefits in China", Nature Climate Change volume 7, pages 736–742

Dan Rosen, Trevor Houser, 2007, China Energy: A Guide for the Perplexed, Peterson Institute for International Economics, May 2007, https://www.piie.com/publications/papers/rosen0507.pdf

Yulia Yamineva, Zhe Liu, 2019, "Cleaning the air, protecting the climate: Policy, legal and institutional nexus to reduce black carbon emissions in China", *Environmental Science & Policy,* Volume 95, May 2019, Pages 1–10

Fuqiang Yang et al., "A Review of China's Energy Policy," (Lawrence Berkeley National Laboratory, 1995)

World Bank 2019, "Open Data", https://data.worldbank.org/country/china?view=chart

Zhou, Dadi, and Mark D. Levine. 2003. China's Sustainable Energy Future: Scenarios of Energy and Carbon Emissions. Berkeley, CA: Energy Research Institute and Lawrence Berkeley National Laboratory.

CHAPTER 32

Energy and the Economy in Russia

Tatiana Mitrova

1 Introduction

Russia ranks fourth in the world for primary energy consumption and carbon dioxide emissions and maintains its focus on fossil fuels despite enormous renewables potential. Russia is following a "business as usual" strategy, relying on conventional fuels exports which are critical for the state budget, for the key energy companies and for many regions in the country which rely heavily on hydrocarbon revenues. But the changing global environment, Sustainable Development Goals agreed upon in the UN institutions in 2015 and the decarbonization agenda, as well as the wellbeing of the whole economic system in the country, challenge this energy mix.

Despite the fact that Russia signed the Paris Agreement in September 2019, decarbonization of the domestic energy sector was not the agenda until recently, when in the end of 2021 President Putin has announced net zero target to be achieved before 2060. GDP energy intensity remains high, constrained by relatively low energy prices and high capital costs. The share of solar and wind energy in the Russian energy balance is insignificant and, according to official forecasts, is not expected to exceed 1% by 2035.

The challenge for Russia in the coming years is to develop a new strategy for the development of the energy sector (at least for energy exports), in response to increasing global competition, growing technological isolation and financial constraints.

T. Mitrova (✉)
Columbia University, Center on Global Energy Policy, New York, NY, USA

SciencesPo—Paris School of International Affairs, Paris, France
e-mail: tatiana.mitrova@sciencespo.fr

M. Hafner, G. Luciani (eds.), *The Palgrave Handbook of International Energy Economics*, https://doi.org/10.1007/978-3-030-86884-0_32

There are several factors which define Russia's attitude toward all these changes and energy transition:

- Demography and macroeconomics;
- Resources availability;
- The role of energy in the Russian economy (including the role of hydrocarbon revenues for the sustainability of the Russian economic system, speed of economic growth and investment availability, as well as technological and financial sanctions);
- The institutional framework of the energy sector;
- Climate policy;
- Technological policy.

2 Demography and Macroeconomics

2.1 *Demography*

The current population of **the Russian Federation** is approximately **146 million people and it has been stagnating since the 1990s. The decline of the number of Russian citizens is compensated by migrants (primarily from the former Soviet republics), but there is no population growth envisaged in the future.**

2.2 *Macroeconomics*

GDP annual growth rates in the first decade of this century for the country were of the order of 7–8%. But the global financial crisis in 2008–2009, coupled with the slowdown of global energy demand, resulted in economic recession. The situation was aggravated by the dispute with Ukraine in 2014 and sanctions imposed on Russia, followed by oil price decline in 2014–2016. As a result, Russian GDP growth rates went down to 1.5–2.5% per annum, which is rather gloomy for such an emerging economy as Russia's. The severity of the impact of COVID-19 on the Russian economy is still unclear, but obviously 2020–2021 will have negative growth, and hence the recession will be even deeper than expected before 2019.

2.3 *Impact of Demography and Macroeconomics on Domestic Energy Demand*

This situation of stagnant population and economy has significant implications for domestic energy demand—which is stagnating as well. There is no demand for large capacity additions (in fact, the electricity market was oversupplied for the last decade), and together with very limited availability of financing this means that there is no need for massive investment in new assets and capacities.

As a result, the existing asset structure in the energy sector gets "frozen" as there are no incentives (and no money) to change it.

3 Resources Available

3.1 *Energy Resources*

Russia has abundant resources for all types of energy: it ranks #5 among proved oil reserves holders (after Saudi Arabia, Canada, Iran and Iraq—14.7 thousand million tonnes of proved oil reserves or 6.2% of the global oil reserves at the end of 2019); #1 in total proved natural gas reserves (38 trillion cubic meters of proved natural gas reserves or 19.1% of the global gas reserves at the end of 2019); and #2 in total global proved reserves of coal (162,166 tonnes of proved coal reserves or 15.2% of the global coal reserves at the end of 2019) (BP 2020). The country also has the greatest water resources in the world, huge solar energy potential and the largest wind potential in the world, as well as abundant resources for bioenergy, in all its forms—from forestry products and peat to agricultural residues and various forms of organic waste (IRENA 2017).

3.2 *Energy Resource Production and Exports*

Despite the fact that Russia produces only 3% of world GDP and has a population equivalent to 2% of the world population, it is the third largest producer and consumer of energy resources in the world after China and the US, providing 10% of world production and 5% of world energy consumption. With energy production of about 1470 mtoe, Russia exports over half of the primary energy produced, providing 16% of the global cross-regional energy trade, which makes it the absolute world leader in energy exports (SKOLKOVO-ERI RAS 2019).

Not all energy sources are utilized equally: fossil fuels dominate Russian energy production, consumption and exports. Russia consistently ranks first in the world in gas exports, second in oil exports and third in coal exports (SKOLKOVO-ERI RAS 2019), while renewables represent only a negligible share in the country's energy exports and about 20% of the country's total installed power generation capacity (mainly provided by hydropower). Thus, there are enormous opportunities related to renewable energy sources.

3.3 *Domestic Energy Consumption*

The Russian domestic energy balance is strongly dominated by fossil fuels, with natural gas providing 53% of total primary energy demand, coal 18% and oil-based liquid fuels also 18%. Carbon-free sources of energy in Russia are represented primarily by large-scale hydro and nuclear. The total share of renewables (including hydro, solar, wind, biomass and geothermal) in Russian total primary energy consumption is just 3.6%. Only 17% of Russia's electricity is generated from renewables (about 90% of that is from hydropower, a legacy of the Soviet emphasis on huge infrastructure projects). Roughly 68% of Russia's electricity is generated from thermal power and 16% from nuclear power. The government plans to have 4.5% of all electricity generation from renewable sources by 2024 (which seems low in comparison with 17% in the UK or 25% in Germany), while according to the International Renewable Energy Agency (IRENA) 2017 report, Russia has the potential to increase the projected share of renewables up to 11.3% of total final energy consumption by 2030 (IRENA 2017).

4 The Role of Energy in the Russian Economy

4.1 Current Role of Energy in the Russian Economy

Hydrocarbons are the basis of the Russian economic model. Despite the fact that recently oil and gas export revenues have declined from the heights of 2008–2012 under the impact of falling prices for hydrocarbons, nonetheless, oil and gas still provide approximately a quarter of GDP, 40–50% (depending on oil price) of the federal budget revenues, 65–70% of foreign earnings from exports, and almost a quarter of overall investments in the national economy (MINFIN 2020).

At the beginning of the 2000s, Russia managed to dramatically increase energy exports: from 2000 through 2005, they grew by an unprecedented 56% (ERI RAS 2016), exceeding the total energy exports of the USSR, allowing for an incredible acceleration of the national economy and strengthening the country's position in the international arena as an "energy superpower." But as the global financial-economic crises came in 2008, energy exports stopped growing. Post-crisis years of 2011–2014 saw still very high oil prices, but stagnant export volumes. Lack of petro-dollar revenues has resulted in GDP stagnation at an oil price of 110 $/bbl, which was clear evidence of deep structural economic problems (Mitrova and Melnikov 2019).

The global move toward a decarbonization paradigm and rising targets on renewables are regarded in Russia as a significant threat for the sustainability of hydrocarbon export revenues and for Russian economic security (Presidential Decree 2017). But as the global situation is undergoing fundamental transformation, and the role of hydrocarbons will inevitably change during the next two decades, Russia will have to adapt. In fact, some of these trends can be observed already today: after high growth rates (7–8% per annum) in the first decade of this century, during the last decade Russia's GDP performance went down to 1–2% per annum due to the systemic economic crisis, international financial and technological sanctions, and unfavorable investment climate (World Bank 2018). Stagnant economy and stagnant domestic energy demand, frozen domestic regulated prices as well as low investment availability for the new technology deployment—all these factors, which obviously limit the investment capacity, are aggravated by the financial sanctions and weak domestic financial market with very high cost of capital.

4.2 The Future of Russian Energy Exports

Energy transitions globally create new challenges for Russian energy exports: the impact of COVID-19 in the short term and growing share of Renewable energy sources (RES) in the longer term limit global demand growth for fossil fuels, thus resulting in lower than expected export volumes for hydrocarbons. The creation of border carbon adjustments as part of the carbon taxation mechanism might become a long-term source of instability for economies relying on fossil fuels. Moreover, banks and financial institutions are assessing climate risks and becoming more reluctant to provide financing for fossil fuel projects. Together with the existing financial sanctions introduced by the US and EU, this significantly reduces access to the financing of the hydrocarbon projects for the Russian energy companies. Therefore, the longer-term outlook for Russian energy resource exports turns out to be rather pessimistic, peaking in the 2030s and declining afterwards. According to SKOLKOVO-ERI RAS estimations, due to the transformation of the global markets and reduced call on Russian hydrocarbons, the contribution of oil and gas to Russian GDP will fall by approximately half, from 31% in 2015 to 13–17% by 2040 (depending on the scenario) (SKOLKOVO-ERI RAS 2019). Hence, climate-related policies that target a reduction in GHG emissions from hydrocarbons can substantially affect the Russian economy. Summing up, for Russia, as for many other resource-rich and energy-exporting countries, the energy transition creates new long-term challenges, questioning the sustainability of the whole economy, which is highly dependent on hydrocarbon export revenues.

5 Institutional Framework of the Russian Energy Sector

Historically, the Soviet and then Russian energy sector was developed in an extremely centralized way. In the Soviet Union, the economy was managed under complex state development plans (5-year plans) through the hierarchical structure of the energy industries with single transportation, export and storage infrastructure and centralized dispatching. Market reforms and privatization of many energy assets in the 1990s created more competition in the sector, but still today the institutional framework of the Russian energy sector is characterized by high corporate concentration and a lack of market mechanisms. Privatization and decentralization are facing strong resistance from the authorities: they are regarded as a threat to the stability and reliability of the national energy system, as well as to national security.

5.1 Oil Sector

The oil sector has experienced a dramatic transformation in its corporate structure during the last two decades. In the early 1990s the Russian oil sector was privatized and deregulated, and following a very contradictory transitional period, all the key Russian oil production assets found themselves concentrated in the hands of private corporations such as Yukos, Sibneft, Lukoil and Surgutneftegaz—which had become world-class vertically integrated oil companies, while state-controlled Rosneft accounted for less than 5% of the country's oil production. In the 2000s, however, new trends emerged, and the oil sector gradually became increasingly dominated by state-controlled companies (above all by Rosneft). This process started in 2003 with the Yukos case, when the government for the first time showed its increasing interest in controlling oil revenues. Introduction of the "strategic fields" concept in 2008 marked a new era in the Russian oil sector, with state-controlled companies getting priority access to the most attractive hydrocarbon resources. This strategy was strengthened by the personal ambitions of Rosneft's CEO Igor Sechin, who has been consolidating assets in Rosneft since 2004, turning it into Russia's national champion. After a series of acquisitions (initially assets from Yukos, then from TNK–BP), Rosneft's share of total Russian production reached 40% in 2014. Gazprom's oil assets have been consolidated in Gazprom Neft, while following Rosneft's acquisition of TNK–BP, Slavneft may also be considered to have become a completely state-controlled asset, as it is now half owned by state-controlled Rosneft, the other half being owned by state-controlled Gazprom Neft. Moreover, at the end of 2014 the stake of Bashneft, held by Russia's multi-industry holding AFK Sistema, was nationalized. At the same time, the share of the smaller independent oil companies, which are normally the main drivers of innovations, mobility and entrepreneurship in the oil industry, is just 4%. As a result, the proportion of state-controlled production has increased more than 14-fold to 57% in the course of the ten years and remains nearly the same starting from 2014. The increasing level of Russia's oil industry concentration and state involvement is making it more and more reluctant to adapt and develop innovations and competition.

Another key institutional challenge for the Russian oil sector is taxation. Tax reform has been under discussion for at least a decade, as the current system of volume-based taxation creates no incentives at all for modernization and the development of smaller fields, or hard-to-recover and unconventional oil. It was not such a significant issue for several decades, as the Soviet-legacy fields were providing sufficient production volumes and did not require any significant investments in their recovery. But now Russian oil production has reached its peak and its possible decline is becoming more and more plausible.

In 2013–2014 a number of tax incentives were introduced for new fields and difficult-to-extract oil reserves. These tax incentives include special reducing coefficients used in the Mineral Extraction Tax (MET) formula, which reflect the degree of exhaustion of reserves, specific geological location conditions and targeted tax benefits applied directly to specific projects—such as MET "tax holidays" for the fields in Eastern Siberia, fields located north of the polar circle, the Azov Sea, the Black sea, the Okhotsk Sea, the Caspian Sea shelf zones, and the Nenets Autonomous District. MET will be zeroed for oil produced in the Sakha Republic (Yakutia), in the Krasnoyarsk region and the Irkutsk region. This zero rate will also apply to ultra-viscous oil. Because of these measures, production decline has slowed in Western Siberia. However, it applies only to a quite limited group of producing assets, not solving the problem on the large scale. Tax preferences and numerous specific exemptions became a typically Russian administrative way to deal with this problem, but at a certain point it might not be sufficient—in 2018, according to the Energy Ministry, up to 50% of all Russian oil was produced under different tax breaks, and, obviously, this system is becoming unsustainable.

5.2 *Gas Sector*

Differently from the oil industry, the infrastructure-dependent gas industry (regarded as a 'natural monopoly', critical for the energy security of the country) was consolidated in the 1990s into a huge state-controlled holding company, which includes gas exploration and production, pipeline transportation, and gas sales in domestic and external markets—Gazprom—in order to concentrate resources in the painful period of non-payments and investment deficit. The gas industry for a long period remained an island of regulated Soviet-type monopolistic structure, and has demonstrated all the disadvantages and inefficiencies of state monopolistic power. Gazprom was designated the "guaranteeing supplier," responsible for gas supplies to the domestic consumers. Although the law stipulated that the gas transmission and distribution network owner is obliged to grant access to its systems if "there is free capacity available" (RF Government 1997), the access of non-Gazprom producers to the pipeline system was a huge problem in the 1900s and early 2000s, as Gazprom could refuse transportation services for technical reasons and prioritize its own supplies. By that time, Gazprom controlled 94–95% of total Russian gas output. There were several independent gas producers (Itera, Novatek), but their role in the market was insignificant. But, during the last decade, conversely to the trends in the oil industry, the gas sector has started to see increasing competition, which is mainly driven, amazingly, by Rosneft.

The situation began to change after the global financial crisis of 2008–2009, when, with the crises and the United Gas Supply System expansion, capacity constraints were mainly removed, while Gazprom had to limit production volumes due to lower domestic and external demand. Gazprom has had to fundamentally dampen its activities and has gradually started to lose ground to Novatek, Rosneft and other independent producers, who increased their share in Russian gas production from 15% in 2008 to 33% in 2014. There has been huge growth in the number of contracts awarded to non-Gazprom producers by major industrial gas consumers, assisted by their right to sell gas at non-regulated prices. In recent years, these companies have been offering a 3–10% discount on the regulated prices set by the Federal Tariff Service, while Gazprom is obliged to sell gas at regulated prices without any discounts. As a result, already by 2015 non-Gazprom producers controlled nearly half of the domestic gas market supplies, and this situation remains the same to date. Non-Gazprom gas producers are no longer complaining about pipeline access, but mainly about the non-transparency of the tariffs, and access to underground storage and, most importantly for them, to exports.

Currently, due to demand constraints the less profitable domestic market with frozen gas prices is further distorted by gas overproduction. Ambitious upstream plans of non-Gazprom producers and the development of new production by Gazprom (first, the start of the giant Bovanenkovo field in Yamal) resulted in a huge gas bubble on the domestic market, thus increasing tensions between the producers. However, it should be mentioned that this does not necessarily imply the formation of a competitive market—these companies are, in fact, creating regional monopolies. For example, Novatek accounts for nearly 100% of gas supplies to Russia's largest industrial area, the Chelyabinsk region. Rosneft, through its acquisition of Itera, has also secured the position of 100% gas supplier for the Sverdlovsk region.

At present, all gas market reforms seem to be too risky, especially in the current global geopolitical and economic environment, so the government is clearly postponing all profound changes. Moreover, there is a huge fundamental obstacle for any serious transformation as the Russian State itself is the major stakeholder of the national gas industry with an extensive agenda, regarding gas as an important domestic and international political tool. As long as this is the case, the authorities will need a state-controlled company, performing the functions of guarantying supplies to depressed regions and non-paying customers, providing low gas prices, affordable for the industry and for the population, and cross-subsidizing these social functions and geopolitical export-oriented projects with the help of exclusive export revenues. Thus, the real gas market reform is not advancing.

Gas pricing has been one of the most painful regulatory issues of the Russian oil and gas sector—as gas represents 53% of total Russian primary energy consumption, this question plays an enormous role not only for the gas industry's performance, but also for the power sector and for the whole economy, which is very much dependent on low gas prices. From the very beginning of the Russian gas industry, it was established by Russian laws and government regulations that natural gas produced by Gazprom and its affiliates should be sold to domestic consumers at government-regulated prices. As a result, artificially low prices formed on the domestic gas market. Such pricing policy stimulated consumers into maximum use of gas, making gas saving unattractive. In 2002, in the situation of stormy demand and looming gas deficit, the government decided to cancel the price freeze and started applying the "cap price" approach in combination with high indexation of prices (of 20–25% per annum) in order to stimulate investment and energy saving. Moreover, under the agreements reached with the EU on Russia's accession to the WTO, gas prices on the domestic market were to be brought up to a level where they fully covered all costs of the gas producing companies, including the investment component needed for the industry's development.

In late 2006, a strategic decision was made in favor of accelerating growth of domestic gas prices to ensure a phased transition to export netback levels, that is, equal profitability of supplying gas to the domestic market and for exports,[1] ensuring gas price growth at the annual level of 15–25% until it reaches the netback level (as it was estimated at that time—by 2011). With the rise of the oil price this date was later postponed until 2015–2018. But, in 2013, as negative processes such as the deceleration of GDP growth, industrial production and fixed investments became very strong, the Russian government finally decided to freeze gas prices, just indexing them with the rate of inflation. As a result, the initial target date to reach netback parity, 2011, was postponed to 2030–2035 (especially after the ruble depreciation in December 2014, when prices expressed in dollars were divided by two, back to the level observed in 2008). Russia became locked in the framework of low state-regulated domestic gas prices. Such indexation, of course, will rob a significant share of gas producers' revenues on the domestic market and will force them in the longer term to scale back their investment program. The Federal Antimonopoly Service started to promote the switch from regulated prices to spot, referring to the prices of the Saint-Petersburg Gas Exchange, which has been functioning since 2014, though at a very limited scale.

5.3 *Electricity Sector*

After a long-lasting process of reform, the Russian electricity market finally comprises a variety of different companies—state- and private-owned. State-owned companies dominate—in the power generation sector they control about 70% of capacities, and in the transmission sector they own all high-voltage grids in the country (220 kV and more) and almost all distribution grids as well. Thermal power plants provide for about 63% of total Russian electricity generation and are largely based on outdated technologies (just 25% of gas-fueled power plants have gas turbine or combined cycle technology, and just 22% of coal-fired power plants use supercritical technologies). At the same time, the centralized heat supply and CHP (combined heat and power plants) are very well developed in Russia—almost every city in the country has a unified heat supply system (about 50,000 in total in Russia), and CHP plants account for more than 50% of total fossil-fueled installed capacity (Mitrova and Melnikov 2019).

State-controlled companies produce more than 50% of all oil (Mitrova et al. 2018); domestic prices for oil products are de facto regulated through artificial

[1] Export price with duty, transportation and other costs relating to storage and gas sale deducted is the equal netback price for Russia.

"freeze agreements," while the natural gas market is dominated by state-owned Gazprom, with gas prices for both residential and industrial consumers regulated by the government and currently frozen at the level of inflation (Henderson and Mitrova 2017). Three decades since a command economy under the Soviet Union, low prices for energy in Russia are still regarded as a "public good," and any attempt to increase them sparks strong protests from the consumers. Cheap energy does not create incentives either for energy efficiency improvements, or for the modernization of the existing assets with their high specific fuel consumption.

The controversial and complicated institutional design of the Russian energy sector, with strong state regulation and some elements of market competition, is creating unclear signals for the participants. It is associated with high transaction costs, thus becoming one of the major obstacles for the large-scale energy transition in the country.

6 Climate Policy

Decarbonization is the main driver of energy transitions globally. Despite this global trend, the climate agenda and the drive for decarbonization are not yet essential factors for the energy strategy of the Russian Federation. This very cautious approach toward decarbonization is driven by several factors. Skepticism concerning the anthropogenic nature of climate change dominates among stakeholders—senior representatives of the Russian Academy of Sciences as well as many State officials publicly express their doubts on the very concept of anthropogenic climate change. Very often they refer to the achievements made already by the Russian Federation regarding GHG emissions reduction: following the economic downturn and economic restructuring in the 1990s, Russia de facto reduced greenhouse gas emissions sharply. According to United Nations Framework Convention on Climate Change (UNFCCC) data, the GHG emissions by 1998 compared to 1990 fell by 40.6% excluding land use, land-use change and forestry (LULUCF) and by 50.9% including LULUCF.

In 1998–2008 GHG emissions rose much more slowly than GDP—by about 16% in 11 years (UNFCCC 2018; International Energy Agency (IEA) 2018); by 2014 they constituted approximately 70% of the level of 1990, but since 2009 Russian GHG emissions have been increasing again.

Russia's enthusiasm for the climate topic is also slowed down by the fact that, as of 2017, the Russian electricity sector has a lower carbon footprint (in terms of g CO2 per kWh) than, for example, Poland, Germany, Australia, China, India, Kazakhstan, the Arab countries of the Persian Gulf, the USA, Chile and South Africa (Staffell et al. 2018). Around 35% of electricity is generated by carbon-free nuclear power plants and large hydropower plants, and 48% comes from gas (Makarov et al. 2017), with gas gradually displacing petroleum products and coal in the fossil-fueled power plants fuel mix (the share of gas in fossil-fueled electricity generation increased from 69% to 74% in 2006–2017).

This background explains why Russia kept itself separate from the global decarbonization trend for a long time. Its participation in international environmental cooperation has always been determined primarily by foreign policy objectives. In Soviet times, participation in global environmental initiatives was a channel of collaboration with the West. In the 1990s, it was a means of integration into the international community and one of the major areas of cooperation with the US. In the 2000s, Russia used the environmental agenda for gaining trade-offs from Western partners along with attraction of foreign investment. At present, the understanding of possibilities to reap benefits from the country's natural capital is slowly arising among Russian political and business elites, so in the longer term Russia's involvement in international environmental cooperation may arise. Meanwhile, the status quo is as follows: Russia signed the Paris Agreement in 2016, with voluntarily obligations to limit anthropogenic greenhouse gas emissions to 70–75% of 1990 emissions by 2030, provided that the role of forests is taken into account as much as possible. In September 2019 Russia joined the Paris Agreement and will have to develop carbon regulation and submit its NDAs before the end of 2020.

7 Technological Policy

Not paying serious attention to climate policy, Russia at the same time is very sensitive to technological policy. The country's leadership realizes clearly that Russia faces the risk of falling behind in the development of new energy technologies that become standard globally. This is the reason for strict requirements on equipment localization for renewable energy and smart grids, and numerous import substitution programs. At the same time, green technologies are definitely not the main focus of Russian technological policy: in the key state document, defining priorities in this area—the State Program "Energy Development" approved in 2014 and amended in 2019—only "promotion of innovative and digital development of the fuel and energy complex" is mentioned as a target, together with all the new technologies in hydrocarbon production and processing—nothing at all is mentioned concerning low-carbon technologies (MINENERGO 2019).

7.1 Energy Efficiency

Factors related to Russia's cold climate, vast distances, large raw material structure, poor economic organization and marked technological backwardness have resulted in the high energy intensity of its GDP—1.5 times higher than the USA and the world average, and twice that of the leading European countries (ERI RAS 2016). In almost all industrial technologies there is a substantial energy efficiency gap with not only best available technologies but "actual consumption abroad" too. Even with comparatively low fuel and energy prices, the share of fuel and energy costs in the overall production costs in Russia is higher than in the developed and many developing countries (IEA 2011).

Before the 2008–2009 economic crisis, Russia was one of the world leaders in terms of GDP energy intensity reduction rates, and the gap between Russia and developed countries was narrowing dynamically—40% reduction of GDP energy intensity within 10 years was achieved in 1998–2008; however, since 2009 this reduction has slowed down and even reversed. According to I. Bashmakov (Bashmakov 2018), GDP energy intensity in Russia in 2017 was just 10% lower than in 2007 (at the same time, the initial energy efficiency target set in 2008 was to reach 40% decline in GDP energy intensity by 2020). Substantial federal budget subsidies were allocated but very limited change occurred, and as a result the initial target was significantly scaled down.

Obviously for such an energy-intensive economy, issues such as energy efficiency and conservation are key for the "Energy Transition": according to IEA analyses, 30% of primary energy consumption and enormous amounts of hydrocarbons (180 bcm of gas, 600 kb/d of oil and oil products, and more than 50 Mtce of coal per annum) could be saved in Russia if comparable OECD efficiencies were applied (IEA 2011). The main role in reducing the growth of energy consumption could be provided by structural energy conservation (changing the industrial and product structure of the economy), with an increase in the share of non-energy-intensive industries and products. The next most important factor in constraining the growth of energy consumption is technical energy conservation, which can provide a total energy saving of 25 to 40%. However, it will be extremely difficult to close this gap with the OECD countries—it actually widens due to the lack of investment possibilities capable of quickly renewing assets or investing in energy efficiency. If we add to this the continuing administrative barriers and, most importantly, the unavailability of "long money" and of credits for energy efficiency projects for small market participants, coupled with the persistence of relatively low natural gas prices in the long term, Russia remains stuck in a state of high energy intensity. Strong policies are required to change this pattern, accompanied with substantial increase in the energy prices, but potential benefits are also huge.

7.2 *Renewable Energy Sources*

Carbon-free sources of energy in Russia are represented primarily by large-scale hydro and nuclear (which enjoys strong state support). The total share of renewables (including hydro, solar, wind, biomass and geothermal) in the Russian total primary energy consumption was just 3.2% in 2015. By the end of 2015, total installed renewable power generation capacity was 53.5 gigawatts (GW), representing about 20% of Russia's total installed power generation capacity (253 GW), with hydropower providing for nearly all of this capacity (51.5 GW), followed by bioenergy (1.35 GW). Installed capacity for solar and onshore wind by 2015 amounted to 460 MW and 111 MW, respectively (IRENA 2017).

According to the draft Energy Strategy of Russia for the period up to 2035, the share of renewable energy in Russia's total primary energy consumption should increase from 3.2% to 4.9% by 2035. This includes Russia's approved plan to expand its total solar photovoltaics, onshore wind and geothermal capacity to 5.9 GW by the end of 2024. The existing legislation sets out the terms for participation in the country's renewables capacity markets. Under this system, energy developers of projects with an output of at least 5 MW can bid for capacity supply contracts with Russia's Administrator of the Trading System in annual tenders. Winning suppliers are paid both for the capacity they add to the energy system and for the energy they supply, based on long-term 15-year contracts with fixed tariffs. This regulation sets a legal and regulatory environment that allows developers to commercialize capacity as a separate commodity to the power itself, and ensures the economic attractiveness of these projects for the investors. In return, renewables developers are expected to ensure they can provide the promised capacity, along the right timeline and with sufficient localization of the equipment (Power Technology 2018).

Since then annual renewable capacity additions have risen from 57 MW in 2015 up to 376 MW in 2018 (320 MW solar, 56 MW wind). What is more important, a significant decline of CAPEX in the renewables auctions took place during the last two years: by 35% for wind and by 31% for solar, according to the Energy Ministry (Power Technology 2018). This process was not smooth: some capacity auction rounds have struggled to attract bids for a number of reasons, just over 2GW of renewable capacity was awarded in the tenders between 2013 and 2016, while in 2017 the auction resulted in a total of 2.2GW of wind, solar and small hydro awarded in a single round, and in 2018 1.08GW of capacity was allocated between 39 projects.

As technological policy is the main driver of Russia's interest in renewables, the country is first focused on building its own renewables manufacturing capacity. Russia has set a quite high level of local content required to qualify for the highest tariff rates, an essential component of many Russian renewables projects' long-term feasibility. The percentage of Russian-made equipment required to avoid tariff penalties was relatively modest in the early days of the auction system, but has now risen to 65% for wind farms and small hydro, and 70% for solar until 2020, with the long-term target level of localization set by the government at 80%. These high levels have been behind several tenders, especially in wind farm development, for which there has been little to no Russian-made equipment.

The problem is that the current support mechanism for renewables will expire in 2024—Russia's unambitious renewables share targets and ambitious localization targets will almost be fulfilled by this time and an influx of foreign renewables developers might stop if no new incentives for the renewables are created. But in order to create these incentives, the Russian government should first formulate the long-term role of renewables in its energy balance, which is quite difficult to do without a decarbonization agenda. According to IRENA (IRENA 2017), Russia theoretically has the potential to increase the projected share of renewables from 4.9% to 11.3% of total primary energy consumption by 2030. But without a reassessment of the energy strategy priorities and a wider transformation of Russia's energy system this target could hardly be achieved (Mitrova and Melnikov 2019).

7.3 Decentralization and Distributed Energy Resources Potential in Russia's Power System

Historically, the Russian energy system was always developed in an extremely centralized way: Russia has one of the world's largest national centralized power systems with a single dispatch control—as of 2017, the total length of its trunk networks was over 140 thousand km, of distribution networks over 2 million km, and the installed capacity of power plants was 246.9 GW. This energy system was created and historically developed on a hierarchical basis, with centralized long-term planning bodies. For decades, the centralized model has been and still remains the basis of the energy strategy, while distributed energy resources, including microgrids or renewables, are developing slowly and only in remote and isolated areas. The role of distributed generation has historically been significant only in the remote areas of the Far East, Siberia and the Arctic, which are too expensive to connect to the unified national network. However, distributed energy resources (DER) penetration in the centralized system has begun, as is the case elsewhere in the world (Mitrova and Melnikov 2019). Similar to other countries, integration of distributed energy resources into the Russian electricity sector became noticeable in the 2000s, but in the past 17 years it was limited to distributed generation only. The development of this process in Russia is driven not by global climate agenda or energy independency concerns, but by economic considerations of the largest electricity consumers. Almost all Russian large industrial companies (including oil and gas industry leaders like Gazprom, Rosneft, Lukoil, Novatek and Sakhalin Energy) develop their own distributed generation projects in order to obtain more affordable power supply.

Micro-generation using renewables for households in Russia is still largely confined to enthusiasts. There are just a few cases in place in several regions, all of them stimulated almost solely by economic expediency reasons. Non-generation types of DER in Russia are in the very early phase of development. Demand response technologies began to develop in the country in 2016–2017, but only a small proportion of power consumption is affected. Demand response in retail electricity market is in the experimental stage.

However, distributed energy resources have significant potential in Russia. According to the study by SKOLKOVO Energy Centre (Khokhlov et al. 2018), this potential can easily cover over half of needs for generating capacities (about 36 GW by 2035). In order to stimulate the maximum usage of DER technologies systemic changes are necessary in the architecture and policy of the Russian power sector, balancing interests of new players with the existing model.

7.4 *Digitalization of Energy as the Government Priority*

Digitalization of the energy sector as a whole and of the power sector in particular is part of a global trend, which means that rapidly developing digital technologies penetrate the economy. Russian authorities regard the digital transformation of the energy sector as a technological challenge (also having in mind the high level of current import dependence on all high-tech equipment and the potential threat of sanctions, which could create serious risks for national energy security), and this is the reason why digitalization became the main driver of the "Energy Transition" in Russia. In 2018 Vladimir Putin signed a decree establishing a special state program of "Digital Economy," in which energy infrastructure is mentioned as one of the key components. The Energy Ministry has also developed its special project "Digital Energy" (Power Technology 2018) focused primarily on digitalization of regulation, coordination and creation of the whole institutional framework for the massive introduction of digital technologies in the energy sector.

7.5 *Hydrogen*

Russia has huge potential for hydrogen production (grey, blue, green, yellow and turquoise hydrogen production technologies are currently under discussion), but it still remains isolated from the international communities and partnerships developing hydrogen technologies. First, this is explained by the already mentioned fact that the climate change agenda and decarbonization still play a minor role in the energy strategy, which significantly hinders the development of all low-carbon technologies. At the same time, there are abundant resources in Russia to produce hydrogen, and there are some R&D activities in this area (mostly, however, far from commercialization) and prospective domestic demand niches for hydrogen. Currently all their focus is on hydrogen export, because the domestic market does not seem attractive for these technologies. In 2020 the Russian Energy Ministry developed a National Hydrogen Roadmap, which was recently submitted for governmental approval. The major stakeholders of hydrogen development are currently Gazprom and Rosatom, but there is also a list of other actors interested in this area (Rosneft, Novatek, Rosnano, NLMK, Evraz, Roshydro, Gazprom Neft, INK), which also look at different options for how to monetize this hydrogen potential.

8 Prospects of Energy Transition: Challenges and Opportunities

Russia's attitude toward energy transition is quite controversial: trying to introduce some components of this trend in the traditional centralized manner (first, new technologies), the country is basically refusing to accept its main driver, the decarbonization agenda. Existing strategic documents (primarily the "Energy Strategy Up to 2035," approved in June 2020 (MINERGO

2020)) do not take energy transition into account. Nevertheless, at a certain point the country will have to develop a long-term vision for both domestic energy market development and export strategy, in order to adapt to the profound transformation of the global energy system. Generally speaking, Russia has many options to participate in energy transition and even to lead some of its dimensions, namely:

- Energy efficiency
- Renewables (solar, wind, tidal, biomass—biomethane, pellets, small hydro),
- including potential export projects (Arctic wind, Yakutia solar + DC transmission)
- Nuclear (next generation reactors on fast neutrons)
- Natural gas replacing oil in transportation (maritime, road), LNG leadership
- Hydrogen (blue, green, yellow, turquoise?)
- Carbon Capture Utilization and Storage (CCUS) (including for Enhanced Oil Recovery (EOR))
- Offsets (including reforestation/natural sinks investment projects)

But realization of all this potential will depend on the political will and on the overall perception of the decarbonization paradigm in Russia.

References

Bashmakov, I. (2018), What Happens to the Energy Intensity of Russia's GDP?, Ecological Bulletin of Russia, No.7, 8 (2018), (Russian).

BP (2020), Statistical Review of World Energy, June 2020.

ERI RAS (2016), Global and Russian Energy Outlook Up To 2040. ERI RAS and AC RF. Available at: https://www.eriras.ru/files/forecast_2016.pdf.

Henderson J. and Mitrova T. (2017), Natural Gas Pricing in Russia: Between Regulation and Markets. SKOLKOVO Energy Centre, (Russian). Available at: https://energy.skolkovo.ru/downloads/documents/SEneC/research02.pdf.

IEA (2018), Electricity Information, International Energy Agency (IEA)/OECD Publications, Paris.

IEA (2011), World Energy Outlook 2011, International Energy Agency (IEA)/ OECD, Paris.

IRENA (2017), Renewable Energy Prospects for the Russian Federation, REMAP 2030 Working Paper, April 2017. Available at: https://www.irena.org/publications/2017/Apr/Renewable-Energy-Prospects-for-the-Russian-Federation-REmap-working-paper.

Khokhlov, A., Melnikov, Y., Veselov, F., Kholkin, D. and Datsko, K. (2018), Distributed energy resources in Russia: Development Potential, SKOLKOVO Energy Centre. Available at: https://energy.skolkovo.ru/downloads/documents/SEneC/Research/SKOLKOVO_EneC_DER_2018.10.09_Eng.pdf.

Makarov I. A., Chen H. Y. and Paltsev S. (2017), Finding Itself in the Post-Paris World: Russia in the New Global Energy Landscape, MIT CEEPR Working papers. CEEPR. MIT Center for Energy and Environmental Policy Research, 2017. No. WP-2017-022 (2017).

MINERGO (2020), Energy Strategy of the Russian Federation Up to 2035, Energy Ministry of the Russian Federation. Available at: https://minenergo.gov.ru/node/1026. Accessed 21 September 2020.

MINENERGO (2019), State Strategy "Energy Development", Ministry of Energy of Russian Federation, (Russian), Available at: https://minenergo.gov.ru/node/323.

MINFIN (2020), Federal Budget, Brief information about the execution of the federal budget, Available at:https://minfin.gov.ru/ru/statistics/fedbud/execute/?id_65=80041-yezhegodnaya_informatsiya_ob_ispolnenii_federalnogo_byudzhetadannye_s_1_yanvarya_2006_g.#.

Mitrova T. and Melnikov, Y. (2019), Energy transition in Russia. Energy Transition, 73–80 (2019). https://doi.org/10.1007/s41825-019-00016-8.

Mitrova T., Grushevenko E. and Malov A. (2018), The Future of Russian Oil Production: Life Under Sanctions, SKOLKOVO Energy Centre. Available at: https://energy.skolkovo.ru/downloads/documents/SEneC/research04-en.pdf.

Power Technology (2018), Is Russia finally ready to embrace renewable energy? https://www.power-technology.com/features/russia-renewable-energy/. Accessed 22 September 2020.

Presidential Decree (2017), "On the Strategy of Economic Security of the Russian Federation for the Period until 2030", No. 208, May 13, 2017 (Russian). https://www.garant.ru/products/ipo/prime/doc/71572608/ (2017).

RF Government (1997), Regulation "On the Provisions for Access of Independent Enterprises to the Gas Transportation System of JSC Gazprom" approved by the Resolution No. 858 of the RF Government, 14 July 1997.

SKOLKOVO-ERI RAS (2019), Global and Russia Energy Outlook. Available at:https://energy.skolkovo.ru/downloads/documents/SEneC/Research/SKOLKOVO_EneC_Forecast_2019_EN.pdf.

Staffell, I., Jansen, M., Chase, A., Cotton, E. and Lewis, C. (2018), Energy Revolution: Global Outlook. Drax: Selby.

UNFCCC (2018), Summary of GHG Emissions for Russian Federation. Available at: https://di.unfccc.int/ghg_profiles/annexOne/RUS/RUS_ghg_profile.pdf.

World Bank (2018), Modest Growth Ahead. 39 Russia Economic Report, May 2018. Open Knowledge Repository. Available at: https://openknowledge.worldbank.org/bitstream/handle/10986/29913/127254-WP-PUBLIC-ADD-SERIES-JunefinalRussiaEconomicReportENG.pdf?sequence=1&isAllowed=y.

CHAPTER 33

Energy and the Economy in the Middle East and North Africa

Radia Sedaoui

1 Introduction

The Arab region is a large and diverse region that shares a rich geography known for its natural resource wealth as well as its climate vulnerability (UN ESCWA 2017a, 2017b, 2019a, 2019b). It is home to some 400 million people (World Bank 2019a), stretching from the Atlantic coast of North Africa in the West to the Straits of Hormuz in the East, and includes some of the world's wealthiest as well as some of the world's poorest nations.

The ability to harness the pool of natural resources through adequate choices of infrastructure, technology, governance and sustainable management practices will be key in creating economic opportunities for young people and improving their living standards. It is also the main driver for socio-economic development and for the attainment of gender equality, empowerment of women and intergenerational equity, which are also at the heart of driving long-term prosperity in the Arab region.

Ensuring access to affordable, reliable, sustainable and modern energy for all (Sustainable Development Goal 7 (SDG 7) is a key condition for reducing inequalities, poverty eradication, advances in health and education, sustainable economic growth, and the principle of "leaving no one behind". Economic and socio-economic opportunities include local market creation by new technologies and standards, such as energy access, local job creation, and cross-linkages to other core sectors such as water management and agricultural

R. Sedaoui (✉)
United Nations Economic and Social Commission for Western Asia, Beirut, Lebanon
e-mail: sedaoui@un.org

M. Hafner, G. Luciani (eds.), *The Palgrave Handbook of International Energy Economics*, https://doi.org/10.1007/978-3-030-86884-0_33

development; as well as environmental protection, the fight against indoor and outdoor air pollution and climate action.

In the context of the Arab region, sustainable energy entails vast opportunities in a region endowed with significant human, oil and gas, economic and technological resources. Indeed, ensuring that sustainable energy becomes an integral part of Arab governments' policymaking, beyond headline targets and green visions, involves the profound rethinking of institutional setups and capacity building to support genuine national efforts. Designing and implementing effective sustainable energy policies presents special challenges because of the complexity and cross-cutting nature of energy policy. This challenge is compounded by existing institutional weaknesses, lack of adequately skilled staff, as well as institutional structures that have not traditionally evolved to accommodate one-stop national planning for matters related to energy access, energy efficiency, domestic energy supply side management and climate policies. The results are often ambitious national development targets that fail to be supported by sufficient market-oriented policies and, in some cases, by weak enforcement of existing law.

This chapter provides a very brief synopsis on the Arab region economies and energy context. It starts by an overview of the role of energy and policy reforms in Arab countries' economies, followed by a summary of progress in recent years in three main areas that are linked to SDG 7, sustainable energy for all as part of the global Agenda 2030 and then provides key recommendations and policy guidelines.

2 Economic and Demographic Growth

The Arab region's population has grown considerably over the past decades, from around 216 million in 1990 to almost 400 million in 2017 with exceptionally high population increases in individual GCC countries ranging from 100% in Kuwait to over 400% in Qatar and the United Arab Emirates, owing to large-scale labour migration and high birth rates. At the same time, Arab living standards have risen dramatically, alongside high levels of education and health care access, particularly in upper middle- and high-income countries. Since 1990, per capita GDP purchasing power parity (PPP) in Arab countries has risen by 16% in Saudi Arabia, 36% in Jordan, 70% in Lebanon and over 90% in Morocco (Fig. 33.1).

3 Energy in Arab Economies

The Arab region is a rapidly growing market for energy and relies on oil and natural gas for its energy mix more than anywhere else in the world. Over the past 25 years, regional primary energy consumption tripled, from around 150,000 ktoe in 1990 to around 435,000 ktoe by 2016 (Fig. 33.2). The GCC economies—all of them fossil fuel producers with a concentration of energy intensive industrialisation strategies since the 1980s—have seen particularly fast

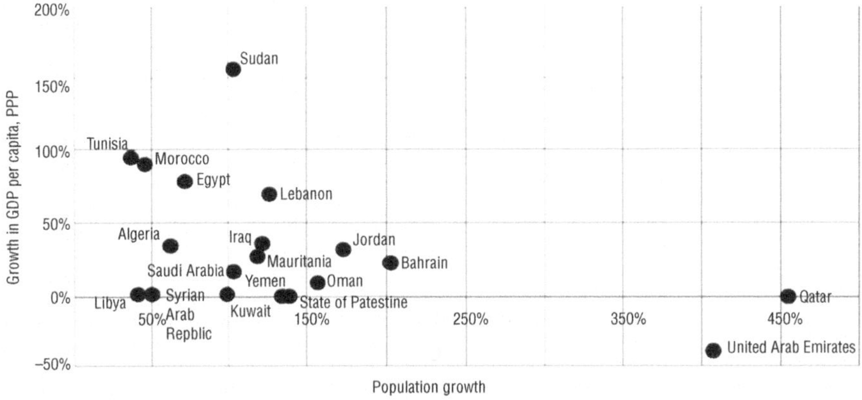

Fig. 33.1 Population and GDP per capita growth in the Arab region, 1990–2017. (Source: World Bank (2019). World Development Indicators. Notes: Not represented due to incomplete data: Kuwait, Libya, Qatar, State of Palestine, Syrian Arab Republic and Yemen)

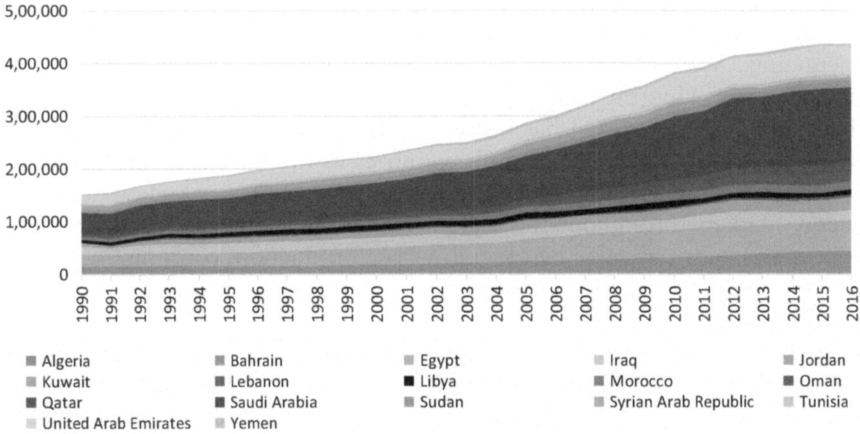

Fig. 33.2 Historical total final energy consumption in the Arab region by country (ktoe), 1990–2016. (Source: IEA (2019a), "World energy balances", IEA World Energy Statistics and Balances (database))

demand growth. In the GCC states alone, total energy consumption quadrupled since 1990, with two countries, the Kingdom of Saudi Arabia and United Arabia accounting for 45%, and countries such as Qatar, Bahrain and Oman having seen particularly fast growth in consumption between 7 and 15% per annum (ESCWA 2019b).

Population growth, economic and industrial expansion and rising living standards have all been contributing to the Arab region's rise in energy consumption. With some of the region's members counting to the world's

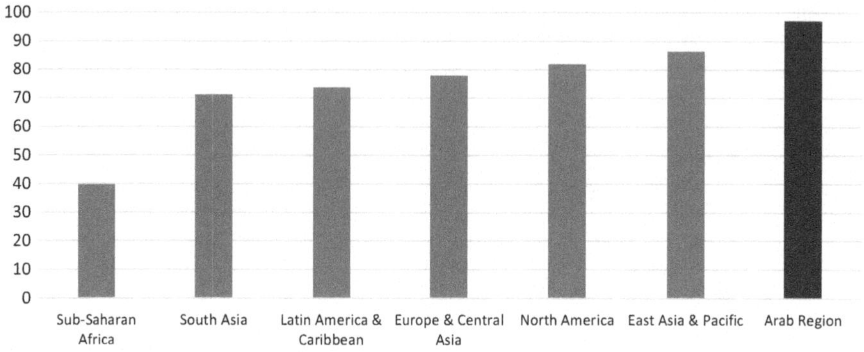

Fig. 33.3 Fossil fuel energy consumption (% of total primary energy supply) by world region, 2014. (Source: World Bank (2018))

wealthiest states on a per capita basis (World Bank 2019a), and most others being middle-income countries, demand for energy is further set to grow over the coming decades, resulting in a further rise in regional energy consumption throughout the period up to 2030.[1]

Fossil fuels have historically been vitally important in the Arab region's energy mix. More than 95% of regional energy supply is derived from oil and natural gas, making the Arab region the most fossil fuel-dependent region in the world (Fig. 33.3). Oil has historically played a key role as a key natural resource asset in a number of Arab countries in the Gulf and the Maghreb, making it both the most important export product and a key fuel on domestic energy markets throughout the region. Natural gas is a second, increasingly important energy resource besides oil, whose production, consumption—particularly in Arab countries' power sectors—and import have risen sharply in recent decades.

Arab countries hold some of the world's most important conventional energy resources, accounting combined for over 40% of globally traded oil alone (OPEC 2018). Yet, fossil fuel resources are unevenly distributed between Arab countries. The GCC economies, Algeria, Egypt, Iraq and Yemen are net exporters of energy, although all of them also import energy such as transport fuel and, in some cases, natural gas. Other countries such as Jordan, Lebanon, Morocco, Sudan, the Syrian Arab Republic and Tunisia are net importers whose domestic energy mix has historically been more diversified, though it remains heavily dependent on imported fossil fuels (Table 33.1).[2]

[1] The IEA uses the Middle East as the basis for their consumption growth projections. Ref IEA WEO.

[2] The Sudan is an exception, as the secession of the South in 2011 removed previous oil resources from the Northern part.

Table 33.1 Energy balances in the Arab region, 2017

	Oil production (ktoe)	*Natural gas production (ktoe)*	*Net oil and gas exports (ktoe)*	*Share in world oil production (%)*	*Share in world natural gas production (%)*
Maghreb					
Algeria	70,953	81,833	-75,909	2	3
Libya	46,371	7433	-44,886	1	0
Morocco	4	62	963	0	0
Tunisia	2119	2139	2242	0	0
Mashreq					
Egypt	32,153	42,876	1132	1	1
Iraq	231,469	7094	-191,070	5	0
Jordan	0	83	6278	0	0
Lebanon	0	0	0	0	0
State of Palestine	n/a	n/a	n/a	n/a	n/a
Syrian Arab Republic	1041	2998	4933	0	0
GCC					
Bahrain	10,390	12,047	3386	0	0
Kuwait	148,226	13,970	-99,910	3	0
Oman	48,881	28,997	-48,406	1	1
Qatar	75,425	149,787	-156,928	2	5
Saudi Arabia	568,727	78,009	-353,804	13	2
United Arab Emirates	178,985	50,263	-111,366	4	2
Arab LDCs					
Mauritania	n/a	n/a	n/a	n/a	n/a
Sudan	5069	0	413	0	0
Yemen	1049	517	–	0	0

Source: IEA (2019b)

Notes: Oil production includes crude, NGL and feedstocks

4 Energy Pricing and Fiscal Policies

Pricing policies are of pivotal importance for the allocation of scarce resources, including energy. In addition to fiscal challenges and losses in income, the unchecked domestic demand in energy- exporting countries of the Arab region reduces their export capacity. Even so, many exporters continue to subsidise the domestic energy markets thereby reinforcing the problem. Energy importers are facing challenges in meeting the fiscal cost of rising levels of energy imports, in particular since domestic energy prices in many Arab countries have historically been unreflective of movements in international import costs (Fattouh and El-Katiri 2012), leading to heightened concerns about their energy security.

Relatively high and rising oil prices during the 2000s up to the early 2010s have since triggered a series of reform efforts throughout Arab countries (Fig. 33.4), including in oil and gas exporting countries. Both groups share a

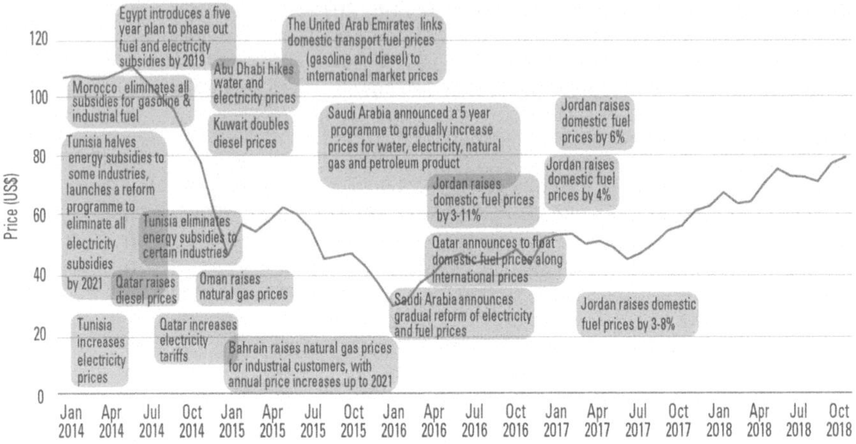

Fig. 33.4 Energy price reform in Arab countries. (Note: Brent price based on BP's annual statistical review 2018)

historically high degree of dependence on fossil fuels, though some progress has been observed in both energy importing and exporting countries that have made diversifying their domestic energy mix a policy priority. Indeed, policy changes have included efforts to adjust domestic energy pricing frameworks and to integrate some elements of energy-efficiency regulation into an increasing number of Arab countries' domestic energy sector policy frameworks (James 2014; UN ESCWA 2017e; Sdralevich et al. 2014; Verme 2016). More recently, increased policy focus has arisen around the promotion of a more diversified range of energy sources, boosting the profile of renewable energy in particular (IRENA 2019; UN ESCWA 2017c, 2018a, 2018b, 2018c, 2018d; World Bank 2016).

Arab oil and gas exporters have been part of this transition, as their economies have significant opportunities to gain from a more sustainable use of energy within their domestic markets. Producers such as Iraq, Kuwait, Libya and Qatar rely for over 80% of their government revenues on fossil fuel export earnings, a proportion that has barely changed over the past decades (UN ESCWA 2019b; IMF 2017a, 2017b). Fossil fuels diverted from international to domestic markets in producing states result in a fiscal opportunity cost that could be minimised through more efficient use of energy—which historically received little priority—and greater reliance on renewable energy, which has grown increasingly cost-effective in recent years (IRENA 2017, 2019a).

The level and depth of reform differ significantly between countries and energy sources, with many price corrections for selected fuels and consumer groups made in an ad hoc manner and few systematic reforms in domestic energy pricing. Ad hoc price corrections simply translate to higher prices for the final consumer groups, whose price remains effectively static after the price increase, irrespective of further price movements for energy products on international markets.

In the case of electricity, prices vary across the Arab region, affecting real as opposed to statistical access. Jordanians, Moroccans, Palestinians and Tunisians pay on average more than 20 times the average bill in the Arab region's lowest cost country (Kuwait); while average incomes are also far below those found in the Arab region's lowest price electricity markets. Domestic energy price reform in a number of Arab countries in most recent years has further increased the financial burden on lower- and middle-income households in particular, affecting disposable household income and, as a result, de facto access to modern energy. Lagging parallel progress in the area of energy-efficiency regulation, poorly insulated existing building stock, and inefficient vehicles imply final consumers in many cases face rising energy and utility bills without the ability to meaningfully adjust consumption behaviour (Fig. 33.5).

Energy price reform that has been progressing in the Arab region is likely to play an important enabling role for more sustainable energy consumption and production patterns. Lack of cost-reflective energy prices is a major disincentive to energy efficiency and distributed renewables. At the time of writing, energy subsidies remain a feature in many Arab energy markets for different user groups, although their size has been falling along with reform progress in some countries, coupled to fluctuating shadow prices on international markets. At the same time, changing energy prices also entail many socio-economic challenges, including the protection of energy access by low- and middle-income households as well as businesses and industries. Integrating energy planning into wider socio-economic development planning will help governments design policies in an inclusive way, for instance by coupling energy price reform to improved other social safety nets, and the redirection of subsidies to investment in sustainable energy technologies.

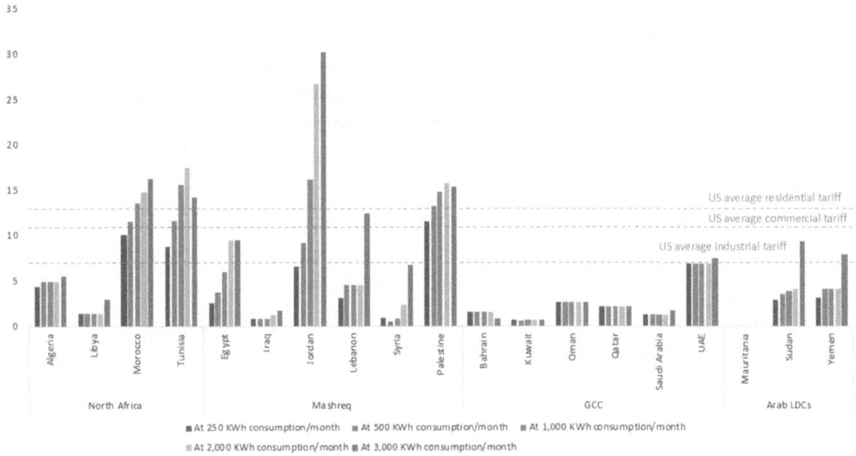

Fig. 33.5 Average domestic electricity tariffs in the Arab region (US$ Cents/KWh/Month), 2016. (Notes: Data for Mauritania not available)

5 Arab Region Progress on SDG 7

Box 33.1 Sustainable Development Goal (SDG) 7

"Ensure access to affordable, reliable, sustainable and modern energy for all"

7.1 By 2030, ensure universal access to affordable, reliable and modern energy services

7.2 By 2030, increase substantially the share of renewable energy in the global energy mix

7.3 By 2030, double the global rate of improvement in energy efficiency

Progress on sustainable energy (SDG 7) differs significantly across the region in reflection of vast socio-economic and geographic differences. While some of the region's countries are amongst the wealthiest on a per capita basis, and striving to improve the productivity of their vast energy resources; Arab LDCs have yet to achieve universal access to modern energy. SDG 7 tracks progress in sustainable energy across three main targets: for (i) access to modern energy—electricity and clean cooking fuels and technologies (CFTs); (ii) renewable energy; and (iii) energy efficiency (Box 33.1).[3] The remainder of this section outlines the region's overall status across these targets.

5.1 *Energy Access*

Access to energy overall is one of the brightest spots in the Arab region's sustainable development agenda.[4] The Arab region's electrification rate stood at 92.5% in 2017, slightly up from 88.4% in 2010, making it the most electrified regional group of countries in the developing world. Highly urbanised populations in all but the Arab LDCs, the availability of low-priced modern fuels and electricity and considerable efforts by most Arab countries since the 1950s to expand their utility sector infrastructure account to a large extent for this success. By 2017, electrification access was virtually universal in all but three Arab countries.

Encouragingly, the decline of the region's access deficit has further been accelerating in recent years as several countries managed to close their access gap to achieve virtually universal access. In the same year, 14 out of 19 countries had access rates for clean cooking fuels and technologies (CFTs) above 95%, reflecting, among other factors, widespread access to electricity and

[3] For a background, please see https://trackingsdg7.esmap.org/about-us.

[4] Access to electricity and to CFTs is the standard current measure for progress in energy access under the inter-institutional tracking framework for SDG 7, *Tracking SDG 7*. For a background, please see https://trackingsdg7.esmap.org/about-us.

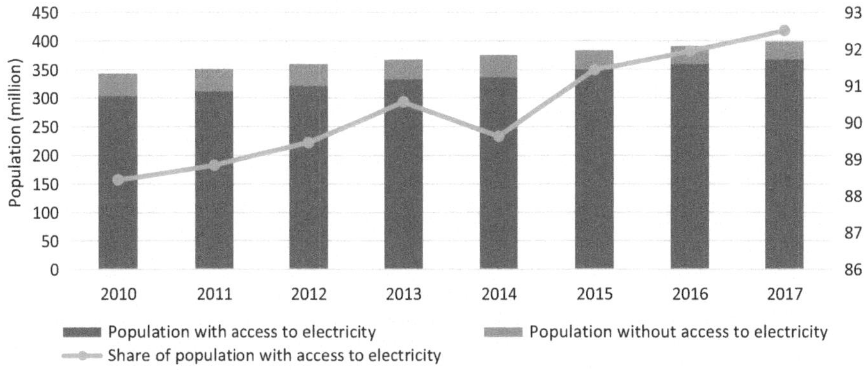

Fig. 33.6 Progress in population with electricity access in the Arab region from 2010 to 2017 (millions of people and share of population with access to electricity). (Source: UN ESCWA (2019d))

Liquefied Petroleum Gas (LPG) for cooking in most urban and many rural households (Fig. 33.6).

The Arab region's population without access to electricity fell from about 40 million in 2010 to around 30 million in 2017. Over 90% of the Arab region's access deficit for electricity, and over 95% for CFTs in 2017 remained concentrated in the three Arab LDCs: Sudan, Yemen and Mauritania. The Sudan accounts for the largest population access deficit in the Arab region with almost 18 million people without formal access to electricity. The rest of the region's access deficit is found in Libya and the Syrian Arab Republic, both conflict-torn countries, with Libya never recovering its 100% electricity access rate since 2000. Libya, the Syrian Arab Republic and Mauritania are the only three countries in which more people lacked access to electricity in 2017 than in 2010.

Rural populations are disproportionally more affected by missing energy access. Eighty-eight per cent of Arab LDCs' urban, but only around 50% of their rural populations had access to electricity in 2017. Many initiatives aimed at increasing electricity access in Arab countries have hence focused on rural areas. In Yemen, 98% of the urban population have access to electricity, versus 69% in rural areas. In the Sudan and Mauritania, these numbers are 82% for urban access, versus 43% rural access in the Sudan and no access at all for rural populations in Mauritania. Access distribution for clean cooking fuels and technologies (CFTs) such as LPG and improved cooking stoves is comparable (Fig. 33.7).

Conflict and instability have had a highly detrimental impact on modern energy access in the region and led to the destruction of significant parts of national and local energy sector infrastructure as well as disruptions to fuel supply routes. Living conditions and level of energy access remain in many cases estimated and likely not reflected in our current data.

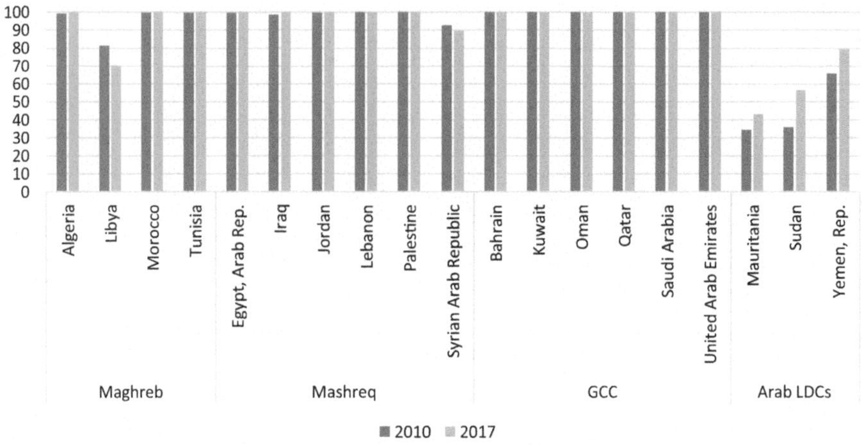

Fig. 33.7 Electrification rates in the Arab region, 2000–2017 (%). (Source: UN ESCWA (2019d))

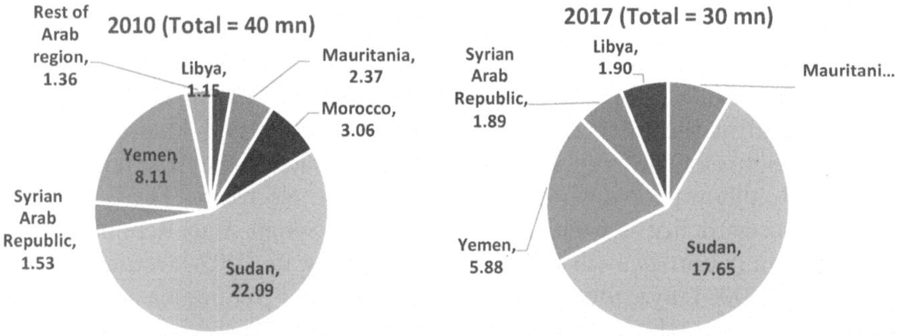

Fig. 33.8 The Arab region's electrification access-deficit in population numbers, 2010 and 2017. (Source: UN ESCWA (2019d))

Conflict-affected countries Libya and Syrian Arab Republic saw declining rates of electricity access (the latter also according to official data), reflecting large-scale destruction of infrastructure that will likely challenge the countries' efforts in providing universal access to electricity to all citizens for many more years to come. Reduced access to electricity has furthermore increased the demand for liquid fuels in countries like Iraq, Libya, the Syrian Arab Republic and Yemen, leading to shortages and surging prices that have placed even liquid fuels out of many households' budget, even where actual fuel supplies have not been interrupted as a result of conflict (Fig. 33.8).

5.1.1 *Electricity Service Quality and Affordability*

While access to electricity is today near universal in most Arab countries outside the Arab LDCs, the quality and cost of service vary significantly across countries. In most recent years, planned and unplanned service disruptions due to insufficient generation capacity and transmission infrastructure have been of particular concern in conflict-affected countries like Iraq, Libya, the Syrian Arab Republic, the occupied Palestinian territory, Yemen; but also, in neighbouring countries like Jordan and in particular Lebanon. Lebanon having itself suffered from chronic utility sector problems long preceding the conflict in the Syrian Arab Republic, saw these problems exacerbated by the dramatic increase in electricity demand by more than a million Syrian refugees who fled to Lebanon during the civil war (Wright 2018; McDowall 2019).

In the conflict-torn Syrian Arab Republic, average electricity services last for around four–six hours per day (UN ESCWA 2019c); in the occupied Palestinian territory, electricity is supplied on average for eight hours per day (UN ESCWA 2019c). Irregular electricity supply is of grave concern for the functioning of basic health services, education, and economic activity, making it a top priority to address electricity provision as a precondition for post-conflict reconstruction and the building of sustainable peace and security in affected Arab countries.

5.2 *Renewable Energy*

Progress in the deployment of modern renewable energy has been far more modest than regional inroads in energy access, although recent years have been encouraging. The share of renewable energy in total final energy consumption has been in slow decline in the Arab region (Fig. 33.9), a historical long-term trend that reflects the high share of traditional biofuel in the region's

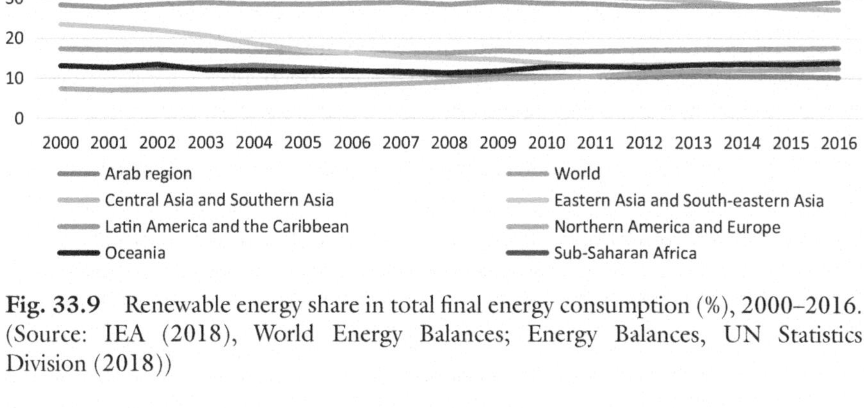

Fig. 33.9 Renewable energy share in total final energy consumption (%), 2000–2016. (Source: IEA (2018), World Energy Balances; Energy Balances, UN Statistics Division (2018))

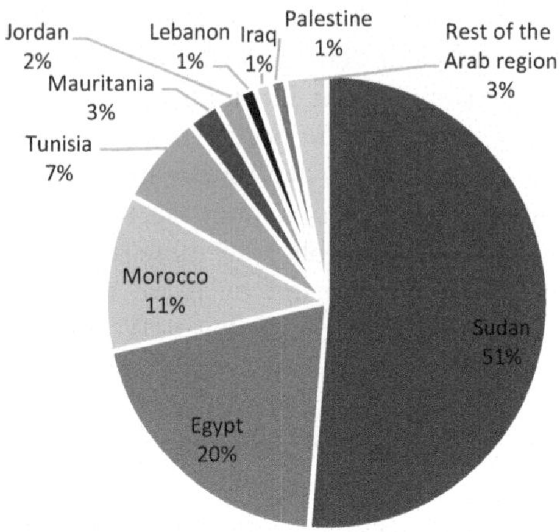

Fig. 33.10 Total Arab renewable energy consumption by country, 2016. (Source: IEA (2018), World Energy Balances; Energy Balances, UN Statistics Division (2018))

renewable energy mix. Falling consumption of traditional biomass in favour of more modern, higher quality liquid fuels and electricity in Arab LDCs and parts of North Africa accounts for virtually all of this trend, indicating a net welfare benefit despite falling overall renewable energy consumption. Three countries—Egypt, Morocco and the Sudan—account for over 85% of the region's total consumption of solid biofuel; the Sudan alone consumes 59% (Fig. 33.10).

The share of renewable energy has been plateauing at around 10.2% of the Arab region's total final energy consumption since 2010; it declined by another 11% between 2014 and 2016. Other, more modern forms of renewable energy such as solar and wind power have historically played a limited role in the Arab region. Hydro power forms an exception, but its deployment is limited in geographical scope, as is its potential for expansion given many important hydro resources are already being utilised. In consequence, encouraging yet slow growth in the deployment of modern renewable energy technologies in the region has not yet been sufficient to halt the region's overall trend of falling renewable energy consumption.

Against the backdrop of relatively long-lasting resistance of Arab energy markets to embrace modern renewable energy, the recent surge in deployment is a significant development, despite comparably small numbers. In 2016, solar, wind and hydro power accounted for 19% of the region's total renewable energy consumption, with slow but consistent growth since the 2000s (Fig. 33.11).

Very few Arab countries rely on renewable energy for a substantial share of their final energy consumption. Excluding solid biofuel consumption, the highest shares of renewable energy consumption as part of the national energy mix are found in Sudan, the occupied Palestinian territories, Jordan and Morocco, based on a mix of hydro, solar and wind resources (Fig. 33.12). If solid biofuel is included, renewable energy contributes above 10% of the

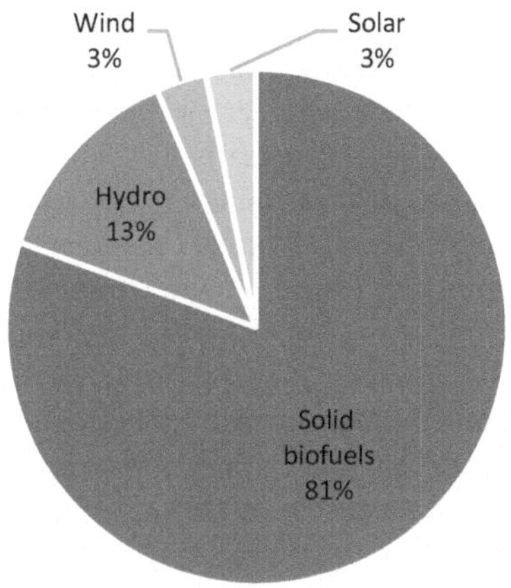

Fig. 33.11 Renewable energy consumption by type of fuel in the Arab region, 2016. (Source: IEA (2018), World Energy Balances; Energy Balances, UN Statistics Division (2018))

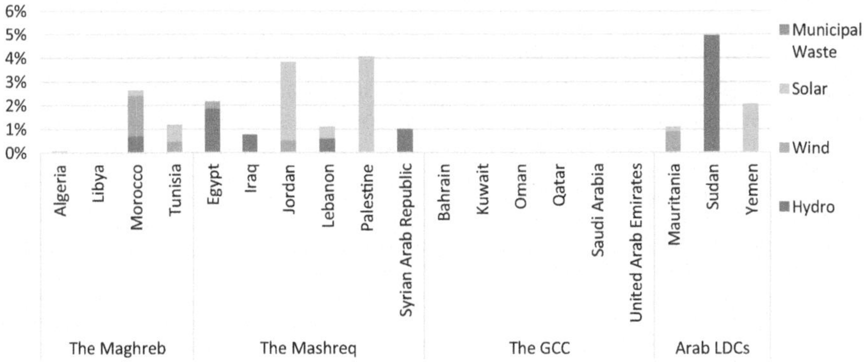

Fig. 33.12 Renewable energy share in TFEC by technology (excluding solid biofuel), 2016. (Source: IEA (2018), World Energy Balances; Energy Balances, UN Statistics Division (2018))

national energy mix in Mauritania, Morocco, the occupied Palestinian territories, the Sudan and Tunisia. Nine Arab countries—including all GCC countries—consumed no or negligible amounts of renewables, basing their energy mix virtually entirely on fossil fuels.

The residential sector remains the dominant end-user of renewable energy. In 2016, it accounted for over 80% of total renewable energy consumption, owing to the large proportion of solid biofuel used for cooking and lighting, in particular in the Arab LDCs. Only 18% of the Arab region's renewable energy consumption is accounted for by electricity generation, once again reflecting limited systematic deployment of renewable energy beyond hydro power in a limited number of Arab countries. Renewable energy has not yet made its way into the transport sector's energy mix in any Arab country, with minor exceptions such as pilot schemes using biofuel (Warshay et al. 2016; SBRC 2018).

5.2.1 *Renewable Energy Announced Targets, National Policies, Projects and Upcoming Capacities*

Falling costs for renewable technologies that have rendered renewables increasingly cost-competitive vis-à-vis fossil fuels have considerably increased the relevance of renewable energy solutions to policy planning in a number of Arab countries. Individual, scene-setting utility-size projects in a number of Arab countries have been elemental in demonstrating the increasing cost-competitiveness of wind and solar technologies (Table 33.2). Added benefits that are seen as increasingly valuable among governments in the region include contributions to national efforts to participate in global climate mitigation, and economic value creation through local job creation (IRENA 2019a).

Consecutive auction rounds for utility-scale projects in the United Arab Emirates and Saudi Arabia that scored world record low price bids for solar PV and CSP technology in 2016, 2017 and 2018 have helped demonstrate the enormous economic potential of solar energy for large-scale power generation. In both countries, solar PV is now cost-competitive with all other conventional fuels, substantially strengthening their business case here and elsewhere in the region (IRENA 2019a). Morocco, Egypt, Tunisia and Jordan have also been investing separately into wind power, which, owing to excellent local resources, has helped generate low-cost electricity (APICORP 2018; The National 2017). These increasingly compelling economic arguments in favour of renewable

Table 33.2 Renewable electricity generation capacity installed in the Arab region, 2017

	Wind	*PV*	*CSP*	*Renewable hydro*	*Other*	*Total renewables*	
	MW	*MW*	*MW*	*MW*	*MW*	*MW*	*%*
Algeria	10	400	25	228		663	3
Bahrain	1	5				6	0.2
Egypt	750	169	20	2851	67	3857	9
Iraq		37		2274		2311	9
Jordan	198	396		12	4	610	14
Kuwait	10	31				41	0
Lebanon	3	26		253	2	284	9
Libya		5				5	0
Mauritania	34	85		48		167	n/a
Morocco	1017	26	180	1306	1	2530	29
Oman		8				8	0.1
State of Palestine		35				35	23
Qatar		5			38	43	0.4
Saudi Arabia	3	89				92	0.2
Sudan		13		1928	190	2131	60
The Syrian Arab Republic	1	1		1571	7	1580	16
Tunisia	245	47		66		358	7
United Arab Emirates	1	255	100		1	357	1
Yemen		400				400	26
Total	2273	2033	325	10,537	310	15,478	6

Source: IRENA (2019c), AUPTDE, Authors

energy should help boost the role of renewable energy technologies in some regional countries' energy mix.

Most Arab countries by now have national renewable energy targets that reflect the growing importance of renewable energy technologies to national energy planning across the region. Increased cost-competitiveness, along with the increased value of renewable energy technologies in areas such as energy independence, natural resource management and climate policy has been reflected in ambitious renewable energy targets set by countries such as Egypt, Jordan, Morocco, Saudi Arabia and the United Arab Emirates. For instance, the Egyptian government's Sustainable Energy Strategy to 2035 confirms the country's target stated in 2009 of 20% of Egypt's electricity generation from renewable sources by 2022, with more recent plans for renewable energy to contribute 42% of electricity generation by 2025 (Bloomberg 2017). Morocco plans to increase the share of renewables including hydro power in its energy mix to 42% by 2020, then rising to 52% (around 10 GW) by 2030 (Le Matin 2018). Endowed with some of the Arab region's best solar as well as excellent wind resources, Jordan launched its new *National Green Growth Plan* in early 2018, aiming to scale up renewables to 10% of the total energy mix by 2020 (Ministry of Water and Irrigation 2015).

Among the GCC countries, which were among the last Arab countries to open their markets to renewable energy, some have in recent years pushed ahead with ambitious renewable energy targets. The United Arab Emirates, so far the GCC's most dynamic renewable energy player, recently launched its first federal "Energy Strategy 2050" that aims to increase the share of clean energy in the country's electricity generation capacity to 50% by 2050 (UAE Government 2018). IRENA in 2019 estimated potential capacity additions in the GCC, excluding most recent plans by Saudi Arabia, to amount to around 7 GW by the early 2020s (IRENA 2019a). In early 2019, Saudi Arabia separately announced ambitious plans for 60 GW of solar and wind generation capacity by 2030 in a bid to diversify its energy mix, which would make it one of the Arab region's largest producer of renewable energy-powered electricity (Renewables Now 2019).

5.3 *Energy Efficiency*

The Arab region is not on track with global energy-efficiency targets. Regional energy intensity rose during the 1990s—contrary to most other regions of the world—and has only started to decline slowly since the beginning of the 2010s. In 2016, aggregate regional energy intensity stood at around 4.7 MJ/ USDPPP2011, a decline of around 3% over the six-year period. The Arab region has the second lowest regional energy intensity rate in global comparison, largely an artefact of its fuel mix based on widespread efficient use of gas. Nonetheless, lacking progress in implementing energy efficiency as a strategic policy priority implies past modest decline in regional energy intensity rates

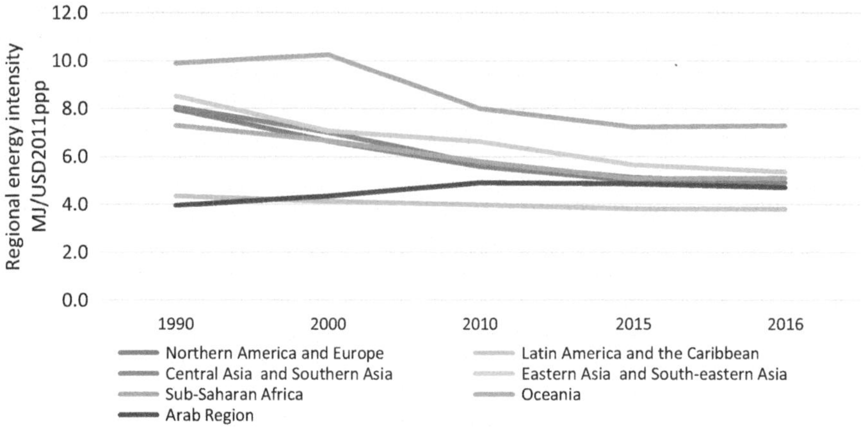

Fig. 33.13 World regional energy intensity trends, 1990–2016. (Source: IEA (2018), World Energy Balances; Energy Balances, UN Statistics Division (2018); World Bank, World Development Indicators)

stays far behind potential, and is not enough to help the region maximise the productive use of its energy resources (Fig. 33.13).

Regional aggregate scores also conceal substantial cross-regional differences in energy intensity dynamics. The Maghreb as a sub-regional aggregate has seen slightly rising rates of energy intensity since the 1990s, with a slight decline over the period 1990 to 2016. Less extensive oil and gas resources have enabled exports and supported increasingly urbanised economies. Industrial productivity has increased and a shift to service-structure economies has been observed, albeit with a remaining important share of agriculture in Morocco and Tunisia in particular.

The Mashreq has seen a slight decline in energy intensity rates in recent years, albeit with individual country exceptions. Conflict and instability have had a strong influence on energy intensity in Iraq and the Syrian Arab Republic, as well as some of their neighbours. Arab LDCs have converged at energy intensities of around 4 MJ/USD. With Mauritania and the Sudan being largely agrarian economies, industrial activity serves domestic or regional markets but is limited in exports. Both the Sudan and Yemen struggle with geopolitical conflict and all three countries face numerous constraints in energy access and services—a key limitation to development and increasingly linked to provision of safe water and food.

Overall energy intensity in the GCC has been rising since the 1990s, albeit with a gradual decline in more recent years. Individual countries have driven the regional trend, with Kuwait, Oman, Saudi Arabia and United Arab Emirates undergoing long-term growth in their energy intensity rates since the 1990s, although from lower starting points. Bahrain and Qatar's energy intensity is far above the rest of the GCC, though with a downward trend. GCC economies

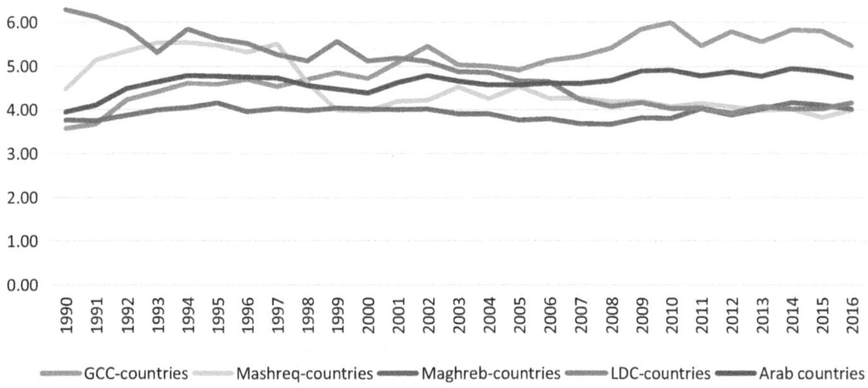

Fig. 33.14 Arab subregion energy intensity trends from 1990. (Source: International Energy Agency 2018; United Nations Statistics Division 2018; World Bank 2019b)

are characterized by their carbon-intensive extractive industries, often with global competitiveness and global export of indigenous oil and gas products, and services. Most have developed downstream value-added products in derived petroleum products and metal processing (Fig. 33.14). High levels of terrestrial water scarcity on the Arabian Peninsula have been driving significant investment in high-efficiency integrated power water systems (see Box 33.1 on trends in energy-efficiency policy).

There are some signs that economic activity is starting to decouple from energy use. Few countries in the region have continued their general trend to increasing energy use as they develop. Primary energy growth in the industrialised GCC countries started to stall, or slightly reverse from 2014 as less energy intensive economic activities have been developed. This is probably due in part to the fall of global oil prices from a record annual average price in 2014 stimulating new economic and budget approaches in oil-exporting countries.

The progress for energy efficiency is often tentative. Most countries in the Arab region still need to transpose energy-efficiency ambitions and plans into largely implemented measures and measurable energy-efficiency progress. Some substantive new policies have emerged, offering evidence that well-designed, implemented policies achieve results (see Box 33.2). Arab countries that are starting to build implementation substance to their energy-efficiency policies will experience a lag as policies take some time to influence investment, operations and behaviour. Robust programmes of policies tend to embed consistent change trends in energy use and increase its value. Whether this change can be sustained remains to be seen, but countries with effective energy-efficiency policies do tend to generate consistent energy intensity improvement trends that flow on to stall energy-use growth.

Box 33.2 Energy-Efficiency Policies in the GCC Countries

Countries such as Kuwait, Oman and the United Arab Emirates have in recent years demonstrated considerable focus on energy-efficiency improvements throughout their economies and have been working on subsequent strategies. Saudi Arabia, the GCC's largest energy market, for instance has in recent years expanded its policies on energy efficiency significantly, including in areas such as standards for air-conditioning units, labelling for consumer appliances and fuel-economy standards for new personal vehicles. Other GCC members such as Qatar and the United Arab Emirates engaged in energy-efficiency (EE) programmes, including substantial new initiatives (labelling and minimum energy performance standards (MEPS), EE financing programmes, among others).

In January 2014 the Saudi government confiscated 40,000 non-compliant air conditioners (ESA 2014). Since 2014, the United Arab Emirates Etihad energy service company (ESCO) funded 200 million dirham (AED) in 2500 building energy-efficiency retrofits (AED 180 million in 2016) (DEWA 2019). The per capita consumption of electric power in Qatar was 15,307 kWh per year in 2014 (Fig. 33.15). This consumption was reduced by 18% during the "Tarsheed" rationalisation programme period (2012–2016) (State of Qatar 2018).

Qatar and the United Arab Emirates both have also comprehensive national energy strategies integrated into their economic long-term plans. Qatar's National Development Strategy 2011–2016 towards Qatar National Vision 2030 covers controls and incentives for water and conservation "in place of today's fragmented system of laws and regulations", including new, green building standards (General Secretariat for Development Planning 2011). The challenge here is undoubtedly the rigidity of ensuing legislation and enforcement thereof. In the United Arab Emirates, Abu Dhabi's Economic Vision 2030 and Dubai's Integrated Energy Strategy 2030 are dedicated plans that include demand-and-supply policies and focus on the development of sustainable ways of providing energy to the next generation.

Source: UN ESCWA (2017c), SDG7 Tracking Report 2019—Arab Region.

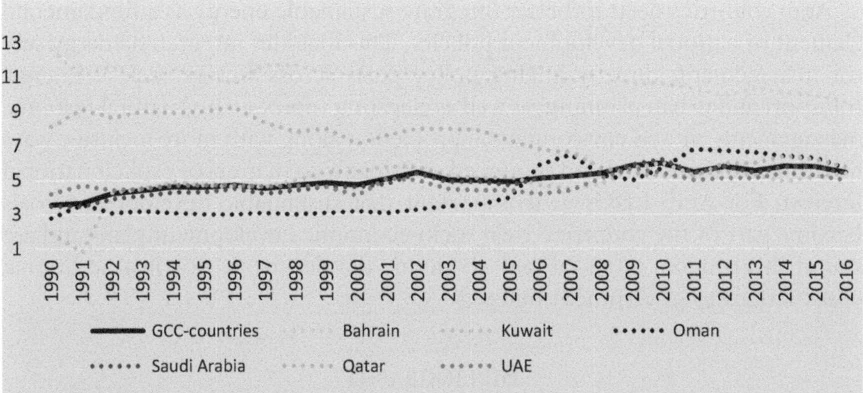

Fig. 33.15 Energy intensity in Gulf Cooperation Council countries. (Source: World Energy Balances IEA (2018); Energy Balances, UN Statistics Division (2018); World Bank, World Development Indicators)

Conflict-affected countries' energy intensity levels are substantially higher than those of neighbouring countries and fluctuate considerably over time. Iraq, Libya, the State of Palestine and the Syrian Arab Republic experienced significant disturbances to their economic activities during the period under study, due to the ongoing geopolitical conflict in this region. Conflict-induced effects on energy intensity include damage to key energy infrastructure including power plants, T&D infrastructure, dams, and conflict-driven constraints to operation and maintenance. This also impacts the region, with neighbouring Lebanon and Jordan each handling large influxes of refugees.

Agriculture and services have seen the deepest fall in energy intensity in the Arab region since 2010. By contrast, the industrial and residential sectors' energy intensity has slightly increased. These trends have been observed across all Arab countries, except for Egypt, Iraq, Morocco and Jordan who also had their industrial sector energy intensity improve. Most of the improvement in energy intensity is probably due to the changes in the economy's structure, moving towards more energy productive activities.

6 Conclusion and Key Policy Recommendations

The Arab region consists of a diverse set of countries with different national contexts, including in the case of energy. However, most countries remain exceptionally reliant on fossil fuels with a highly limited role played by clean energy alternatives, in particular renewable energy; while the region also lags behind other region's progress in energy efficiency. In the Arab LDCs, energy access remains incomplete, severely obstructing socio-economic progress. Making sustainable energy part of Arab countries' policy agenda requires far more systematic efforts than has been the case in the past.

Arab countries need to better integrate sustainable energy as a fundamental element of national development policies. This includes integrated energy sector management; directly linking policy goals across sectors such as energy, transport and urban planning; as well as elevating topics such as natural resource management, air and environmental protection along with more inclusive ways to ensure energy is used and produced sustainably to matters of explicit national interest. For Arab LDCs, it is important that sustainable development goals become part of the countries' own socio-economic development plans and are sound investments in social and economic development, not just additional cost burdens to government budgets.

Bibliography

AFD [Agence Francaise de Developpement] (2013). Le Programme d'électrification rurale global (PERG) au Maroc. Available online at http://www.afd.fr/home/AFD/L-AFD-s-engage/rioplus20/projets-rio20/electrification-maroc (accessedApril 2017).

Al-Soud, Mohammed S., and Eyad S. Hrayshat (2004). "Rural photovoltaic electrification program in Jordan" *Renewable and Sustainable Energy Reviews* 8(6): 593–598.

APICORP (2018). "Renewables in the Arab world: maintaining momentum" *APICORP Energy Research* 3: 8. Available online at http://www.apicorp-arabia.com/Research/EnergyReseach/2018/APICORP_Energy_Research_V03_N08_2018.pdf (accessed August 2018).

Bloomberg (2017). "Egypt to generate 42% of electricity from renewables by 2025", 18 December 2017.

BP (2019). Annual statistical review 2019. Available online at https://www.bp.com/content/dam/bp/business-sites/en/global/corporate/pdfs/energy-economics/statistical-review/bp-stats-review-2019-full-report.pdf

Clancy, J.S., and M. Skutsch (n.d.). The gender—energy-poverty nexus—finding the energy to address gender concerns in development. UK Department for International Development (DFID). https://www.esmap.org/sites/default/files/esmap-files/The%20Gender%20Energy%20Poverty%20Nexus.pdf

DEWA [Dubai Electricity and Water Authority] (2019). "Dubai invests AED 500 million in energy efficiency" 19 July. https://www.dewa.gov.ae/en/about-us/media-publications/latest-news/2018/07/dubai-invests-aed-500-million-in-energy-efficiency

ESA (2014). "40,000 inefficient air-con units confiscated" 16 January. http://www.the-esa.org/news/articles/-/40-000-inefficient-air-con-units-confiscated

Fattouh, B., and L. El-Katiri (2012). Energy subsidies in the Arab World, Arab Human Development Report Research Paper, United Nations Development Programme.

General Secretariat for Development Planning (2011). *Qatar national development strategy 2011–2016*. Doha: General Secretariat for Development Planning. Available online at http://www.mdps.gov.qa/en/knowledge/HomePagePublications/Qatar_NDS_reprint_complete_lowres_16May.pdf (accessed April 2017).

Huenteler, J.T., A. Khanna, S. Badiei, T.M. Matsuo, E. Maier, and E.M. Fernstrom (2017). *Republic of Yemen—restoring and expanding energy access: Power sector reengagement note*. Washington, DC: World Bank Group. Available online at http://

documents.worldbank.org/curated/en/655811496412539032/Republic-of-Yemen-Restoring-and-expanding-energy-access-power-sector-reengagement-note

IEA (2018). World energy statistics and balances database. Available online at https://www.oecd-ilibrary.org/energy/data/iea-world-energy-statistics-and-balances/world-energy-balances_data-00512-en?parentId=http%3A%2F%2Finstance.metastore.ingenta.com%2Fcontent%2Fcollection%2Fenestats-data-en

IEA (2019a). "World energy balances", IEA World Energy Statistics and Balances (database). Available online at https://doi.org/10.1787/data-00512-en (accessed on 15 November 2019).

IEA (2019b). Iraq's energy sector—a roadmap to a brighter future. Available online at https://webstore.iea.org/download/direct/2700?fileName=Iraq_Energy_Outlook.pdf

IMF (2017a). *Algeria 2017 article IV consultation-press release; staff report; and statement by the executive director for Algeria*. IMF Country Report No. 17/141, June 2017.

IMF (2017b). *Iraq: 2017 article IV consultation and second review under the three-year stand-by arrangement-and requests for waivers of nonobservance and applicability of performance criteria, and modification of performance criteria-press release; staff report; and statement by the executive director for Iraq*. Available online at https://www.imf.org/en/Publications/CR/Issues/2017/08/09/Iraq-2017-Article-IV-Consultation-and-Second-Review-under-the-Three-Year-Stand-by-45174 (accessed August 2018).

Inchauste, G., and D.G. Victor (2017). "Introduction" in: Inchauste, G., and D.G. Victor (eds.). *The political economy of energy subsidy reform*. Washington, DC: International Bank for Reconstruction and Development/The World Bank, 1–44.

IRENA (2013). REN21 (Renewable Energy Policy Network for the 21st Century) and UAE MOFA (United Arab Emirates Ministry of Foreign Affairs) (2013), "MENA: Renewables Status Report". Available online at https://www.ren21.net/Portals/0/documents/activities/Regional%20Reports/MENA_2013_lowres.pdf

IRENA (2016a). *Renewable energy in cities*. Abu Dhabi: International Renewable Energy Agency (IRENA). Available online at http://www.irena.org/DocumentDownloads/Publications/IRENA_Renewable_Energy_in_Cities_2016.pdf (accessed April 2017).

IRENA (2016b). *Renewable energy in the Arab region. Overview of developments*. Abu Dhabi: International Renewable Energy Agency.

IRENA (2017). *Renewable energy auctions: Analysing 2016*. Abu Dhabi: IRENA. Available online at https://www.irena.org/-/media/Files/IRENA/Agency/Publication/2017/Jun/IRENA_Renewable_Energy_Auctions_2017.pdf

IRENA (2018). *Renewable energy statistics 2018*. Abu Dhabi. Available online at https://www.irena.org/publications/2018/Jul/Renewable-Energy-Statistics-2018

IRENA (2019a). *Renewable energy market analysis: GCC 2019*. Abu Dhabi. Available online at https://www.irena.org/publications/2019/Jan/Renewable-Energy-Market-Analysis-GCC-2019

IRENA (2019b). *Off-grid renewable energy solutions to expand electricity access: An opportunity not to be missed*. Abu Dhabi: International Renewable Energy Agency (IRENA). Available online at https://www.irena.org/publications/2019/Jan/Off-grid-renewable-energy-solutions-to-expand-electricity-to-access-An-opportunity-not-to-be-missed

IRENA (2019c). *Renewable capacity statistics 2019*. Abu Dhabi: International Renewable Energy Agency (IRENA). Available online at https://www.irena.org/publications/2019/Mar/Renewable-Capacity-Statistics-2019

James, L.M. (2014). "Recent developments in sudan's fuel subsidy reform process" Research Report, The International Institute for Sustainable Development. Available online at http://greenfiscalpolicy.org/wp-content/uploads/2017/04/GSI-2014-FFS-in-Sudan_lessons_learned.pdf (accessed August 2018).

Le Matin (2018). "Développement durable. Nouveaux horizons pour les énergies renouvelables au Maroc et en Afrique", 28 February 2018.

McDowall, A. (2019). "World Bank urges new Lebanese government to reform power sector" *Reuters*, 1 February. Available online at https://www.reuters.com/article/us-lebanon-government-reforms/world-bank-urges-new-lebanese-government-to-reform-power-sector-idUSKCN1PQ4Y1

Ministry of Water and Irrigation (2015) *Energy efficiency and renewable energy policy for the Jordanian water sector*. Available online at http://www.jva.gov.jo/sites/en-us/Hot%20Issues/Energy%20Policy.pdf

OPEC (2018). OPEC data, 2018. Available online at https://www.opec.org/opec_web/en/publications/202.htm

Ramani, K.V., and E. Heijndermans (2003). Energy, poverty, and gender. A synthesis. The International Bank for Reconstruction and Development/THE WORLD BANK. http://documents.worldbank.org/curated/en/441631468140976681/pdf/345390Energy0poverty010gender0synthesis.pdf

Renewables Now (2019) "Saudi Arabia targets 60 GW of renewables by 2030—report" 19 January. Available online at https://renewablesnow.com/news/saudi-arabia-targets-60-gw-of-renewables-by-2030-report-639430/

Saheb-Koussa, D., M. Koussa, M. Haddadi, and M. Belhamel (2011). "Hybrid options analysis for power systems for rural electrification in Algeria" Energy Procedia 6: 750–758.

SBRC (Sustainable Bioenergy Research Consortium) (2018). About us: Overview. Available online at www.sbrc.masdar.ac.ae/index.php/about-us/overview

Sdralevich, C., R. Sab, Y. Zouhar, and G. Albertin (2014). *Subsidy reform in the Middle East and North Africa: Recent progress and challenges ahead*. Washington, DC: International Monetary Fund. Available online at http://www.imf.org/external/pubs/ft/dp/2014/1403mcd.pdf (accessed August 2018).

Stambouli, A.B. (2011). "Algerian renewable energy assessment: The challenge of sustainability" *Energy Policy* 39(8): 4507–4519.

State of Qatar (2018). *Second voluntary national review, 2018 submitted to the high level political forum on sustainable development*. Available online at https://www.psa.gov.qa/en/knowledge/Doc/QNV/Report%20of%20the%20National%20Voluntary%20review%202018%20(Landscape).pdf

Taha, K. (2018). "Renewable energy on rise in resource-poor Jordan" Phys.Org, 28 September. Available online at https://phys.org/news/2018-09-renewable-energy-resource-poor-jordan.html

The National (2017, 2 April). Morocco breaks ground on $220m Noor Ouarzazate IV solar plant.

UAE Government (2018). UAE energy strategy 2050. Available online at www.government.ae/en/about-the-uae/strategies-initiativesand-awards/federal-governments-strategies-and-plans/uaeenergy-strategy-2050

UN ESCWA (2016). *Arab governance report II: Governance and institutional transformations in conflict-affected Arab countries.* Available online at https://www.unescwa.org/publications/arab-governance-Report-2016 (accessed March 2017).

UN ESCWA (2017a). Regional initiative for the assessment of climate change impacts on water resources and socio-economic vulnerability in the Arab region. RICCAR. Arab Climate Change Assessment Report—main report. Available online at https://www.unescwa.org/climate-change-water-resources-arab-region-riccar

UN ESCWA (2017b). Sustainable energy in the Arab region, Energy-related sustainable development goals. Available online at https://www.unescwa.org/sites/www.unescwa.org/files/events/files/sustainable_energy_in_the_arab_region_energy-related_sustainable_development_goals.pdf

UN ESCWA (2017c). *Arab region progress in sustainable energy: Global tracking framework regional report.* Available online at https://www.unescwa.org/sites/www.unescwa.org/files/publications/files/gtf-regional-report-arab-region-progress-sustainable-energy-english_1.pdf

UN ESCWA (2017d). *Sustainable energy in the Arab region. Energy-related sustainable development goals.* Committee on Energy Eleventh session Cairo, 14–16 May 2017. Available online at https://www.unescwa.org/sites/www.unescwa.org/files/events/files/sustainable_energy_in_the_arab_region_energy-related_sustainable_development_goals.pdf

UN ESCWA (2017e). *The social impacts of energy subsidy reform in the Arab Region.* Available online at https://www.unescwa.org/sites/www.unescwa.org/files/page_attachments/social-impacts-energy-subsidy-reform-en.pdf (accessed August 2018).

UN ESCWA (2018a). *Case study on policy reforms to promote renewable energy in Morocco.* Available online at https://www.unescwa.org/sites/www.unescwa.org/files/publications/files/policy-reforms-promote-renewable-energy-morocco-english.pdf (accessed August 2018).

UN ESCWA (2018b). *Case study on policy reforms to promote renewable energy in the United Arab Emirates.* Available online at https://www.unescwa.org/sites/www.unescwa.org/files/publications/files/policy-reforms-promote-renewable-energy-uae-english.pdf (accessed August 2018).

UN ESCWA (2018c). *Case study on policy reforms to promote renewable energy in Jordan.* Available online at https://www.unescwa.org/sites/www.unescwa.org/files/publications/files/policy-reforms-promote-renewable-energy-jordan-english.pdf (accessed August 2018).

UN ESCWA (2018d). *Case study on policy reforms to promote renewable energy in Lebanon.* Available online at https://www.unescwa.org/sites/www.unescwa.org/files/publications/files/policy-reforms-promote-renewable-energy-lebanon-english.pdf (accessed August 2018).

UN ESCWA (2019a, March). *Regional consultation on climate change for the Arab forum on sustainable development and high level political forum.* UNESCWA.

UN ESCWA (2019b). *Energy vulnerability in the Arab Region.* Available online at https://www.unescwa.org/publications/energy-vulnerability-arab-region

UN ESCWA (2019c). Report on the seminar "Monitoring the Implementation of Energy Related SDG Indicators in the Arab Region". Available online at https://www.unescwa.org/events/seminar-monitoring-energy-sdgs-arab-region

UN ESCWA (2019d). Tracking SDG 7: Energy progress report Arab Region 2019. Available online at https://www.unescwa.org/publications/energy-progress-report-arab-region

UN Statistics Division (2018). https://efaidnbmnnnibpcajpcglclefindmkaj/viewer.html?pdfurl=https%3A%2F%2Funstats.un.org%2Funsd%2Fenergystats%2Fpubs%2Fbalance%2F2018%

UNDP (2014). Promoting sustainable mini-grids in mauritanian provinces through hybrid technologies. Available online at https://www.thegef.org/sites/default/files/project_documents/11-11-15_Project_Document_PADpdf_0.pdf (accessed March 2017).

Verme (2016). *Subsidy reforms in the Middle East and North Africa Region: A review.* The World Bank Group. Policy Research Working Paper 7754. Available online at https://openknowledge.worldbank.org/bitstream/handle/10986/24835/Subsidy0reform0ca0Region000a0review.pdf?sequence=1&isAllowed=y

Warshay, B., J. Brown, and S. Sgouridis (2016). "Life cycle assessment of integrated seawater agriculture in the Arabian (Persian) Gulf as a potential food and aviation biofuel resource" *The International Journal of Life Cycle Assessment* 39(6): 409–416. Available online at https://doi.org/10.1007/s11367-016-1215-5

Whitehead, F. (2015). "Water scarcity in Yemen: the country's forgotten conflict" The Guardian, 2 April. Available online at https://www.theguardian.com/global-development-professionals-network/2015/apr/02/water-scarcity-yemen-conflict

World Bank (2005). Household energy supply and use in Yemen, Volume II, Annexes, Report No. 315/05, December.

World Bank (2016). *Delivering energy efficiency in the Middle East and North Africa.* Washington, DC: International Bank for Reconstruction and Development. Available online at https://openknowledge.worldbank.org/ bitstream/handle/10986/25295/109023-WP-P148222-PUBLIC-DeliveringEEinMENAMayEN.pdf?sequence=1&isAllowed=y (accessed March 2017).

World Bank (2018). *Combined project information documents/integrated safeguards datasheet (PID/ISDS).* Yemen Emergency Electricity Access Project. Report No: PIDISDSA24561, 26 March 2018. Available online at http://documents.worldbank.org/curated/en/895191523306712217/pdf/Project-Information-Document-Integrated-Safeguards-Data-Sheet-Yemen-Emergency-Electricity-Access-Project-P163777.pdf

World Bank (2019a). *World development indicators.* Accessible online at http://data.worldbank.org/data-catalog/world-development-indicators

World Bank (2019b). Available online at https://trackingsdg7.esmap.org/data/files/download-documents/2019-Tracking%20SDG7-Full%20Report.pdf

Wright, R. (2018). "The lights are going out in the Middle East" *The New Yorker*, 21 May. Available online at https://www.newyorker.com/news/news-desk/the-lights-are-going-out-in-the-middle-east

CHAPTER 34

Energy and the Economy in Sub-Saharan Africa

Philippe Copinschi

"*Sub-Saharan Africa is rich in energy resources but very poor in energy supply.*" So began the Africa Energy Outlook published by the International Energy Agency (IEA) in 2014, underlying the fact that "*making reliable and affordable energy widely available is critical to the development of the region*". Five years later, in the 2019 edition of the Africa Energy Outlook, this remains globally unchanged: while Sub-Saharan Africa is home to around 15% of the world's population, the region only accounts for 4.3% of the global energy demand and less than 1.75% of the world's electricity consumption (Enerdata 2020).

Sub-Saharan Africa embodies a paradox. On one hand, the region has long attracted the energy industry and represents a significant part of the major international oil and gas companies' activities, thanks to its endowment in natural resources combined with attractive fiscal regimes. On the other hand, the majority of the one billion people lack access to energy, especially electricity, which hinders their economic and social development.

For decades the dominant discourse, from governments as well as international development agencies and economic actors, has considered that the exploitation of its energy resources would prompt the economic growth of the continent by giving the countries the financial means to undertake development strategies. Unfortunately the reality seems more complex. On the contrary most energy producing countries in Sub-Saharan Africa seem to underperform in terms of economic development.

As the process in which the exploitation of energy resources leads to misdevelopment is being better understood, a new approach has emerged which focuses on the development of access to energy for the population. As a

P. Copinschi (✉)
SciencesPo—Paris School of International Affairs, Paris, France
e-mail: Philippe.copisnchi@sciencespo.fr

M. Hafner, G. Luciani (eds.), *The Palgrave Handbook of International Energy Economics*, https://doi.org/10.1007/978-3-030-86884-0_34

consequence all over the continent new national, regional and international initiatives have been put in place to boost access to energy for the local population, eventually acknowledged as a key driver for economic development.

This chapter will start by drawing a quick panorama of the oil and gas scene in Sub-Saharan Africa, which remains the main energy sector in the region. I will then analyse the impact of this industry on the economic situation of the producing countries, and end with a presentation of the new challenges of developing access to reliable and affordable energy for the population.

1 An Energy Scene Dominated by Foreign Actors

1.1 Oil Production and Reserves

Although Sub-Saharan Africa is blessed with natural resources, especially energy, the continent made its appearance on the oil and gas map relatively recently when compared with other hydrocarbon-producing regions like North and Latin America, the Middle East and North Africa. It was only in the 1960s that oil production started, after discoveries were made around the Gulf of Guinea, in Angola (in the Cabinda enclave) in 1955, followed by Nigeria and Gabon in 1956, and Congo-Brazzaville and Cameroon in the early 1970s. The oil production in the region substantially got underway in the 1970s, after the end of the Nigeria Civil War (1967–1970) during which the oil-producing region of Biafra tried to secede.

Production boom was helped by the sharp increase in oil price after the 1973 and 1979 oil shocks and by the wave of nationalisations in OPEC countries. By raising the oil price, the two successive oil shocks opened new exploration and production opportunities everywhere in the world. This was especially so in Sub-Saharan Africa where governments, keen on attracting foreign investors to boost development, offered favourable fiscal regimes to international oil companies who, after having been kicked out of OPEC countries, were very happy to invest in Sub-Saharan Africa in order to diversify their portfolio of activities. Indeed, reflecting on the weakness of the State in Africa, none of the oil-producing countries in Sub-Saharan Africa ever nationalised their oil industry. Although OPEC used to encourage its members to nationalise their oil industry to further their economic independence, Nigeria (which became a member of the cartel in 1971) never took control of operations through its national company; neither did Angola nor Congo ever nationalise the foreign private companies' interests, even after having established Marxist regimes in the 1980s. This explains why Sub-Saharan Africa was one of the oil and gas regions—along with the North Sea, the Gulf of Mexico and Alaska—that benefited the most from the nationalisations in OPEC countries in the 1970s.

The region experienced a second oil boom in the 1990s with a series of huge discoveries made offshore. At the same time, exploration expanded throughout the continent, both offshore and onshore, and new producers appeared, including Equatorial Guinea, Ghana, Chad, Niger, Mauritania, Sudan and so on. As a consequence, Sub-Saharan oil production rose from about 400,000 barrels per day (bpd) in the late 1960s to 2.5 million bpd (Mbpd) in the mid-1970s (essentially from Nigeria), before reaching 4 Mbpd by the late 1990s and 5 Mbpd in 2019 (with Nigeria and Angola contributing about 2.1 and 1.5 Mbpd respectively). During the same period, oil reserves in Sub-Saharan Africa rose from about 10 billion barrels in 1970 to 20 in 1980, 40 in 2000 and more than 60 in 2019 (Enerdata 2020).

Even if some countries, like Cameroon and Gabon, are gradually nearing the end of their oil era as their reserves are rapidly declining and no new discoveries have recently been made, Sub-Saharan Africa is now home to more than a dozen oil producers, although only a few (mainly Nigeria and Angola) do really have a significant production. Several other countries may soon be joining the list as almost all the governments across the continent have granted exploration licenses. Although the Gulf of Guinea remains the central point of focus for oil and gas players in Sub-Saharan Africa, exploration and production have spread out since the 1990s across the whole continent, with discoveries made both offshore (in Mauritania, Ghana, Ivory Coast, Senegal, Sao Tome and Principe, Tanzania, Mozambique, South Africa, etc.) and onshore (Uganda, Niger, Chad, etc.) (Table 34.1).

All together, Sub-Saharan Africa produces about 5 Mbpd of oil. On a global scale, this doesn't seem to account for much: the current production of the continent represents less than 5% of the global oil production and the oil reserves only just 3.5% of the world's total. The importance of the continent is

Table 34.1 Oil production and proved reserves in Sub-Saharan Africa 2020

	Proved Reserves (in Mb)	*Share of global reserves (%)*	*Production (in 000 bpd)*	*Share of global production %)*
Nigeria	36,890	2.13	1743	2.09
Angola	7783	0.45	1220	1.46
Congo-Brazzaville	2882	0.17	310	0.37
Gabon	2000	0.12	216	0.26
Chad[a]	1500	0.09	127	0.15
Sudan[a]	1500	0.09	92	0.11
Equatorial Guinea	1100	0.06	126	0.15
Cameroon[a]	309	0.02	71	0.09
DR Congo[a]	278	0.02	22	0.03
Ivory Coast[a]	154	0.01	38	0.05
Mauritania[a]	154	0.01	2	0.00
Niger[a]	147	0.01	18	0.02
Ghana	23	0.00	195	0.23
South Africa	23	0.00	99	0.12
TOTAL Sub-Saharan Africa	**58,711**	**3.39**	**4883**	**5.85**

Source: Enerdata

[a] Production of 2019

elsewhere: because of it always being very open to foreign investors, Sub-Saharan Africa has generally been viewed by the oil industry as one of the world's hotspots for oil production and exploration and one of the leading deepwater offshore oil production centres. Today, all major energy companies (Shell, BP, Total, ExxonMobil, Chevron, ENI, etc.), as well as many independent and junior companies and even some public (mostly Asian) companies are involved in oil and gas exploration and production in Sub-Saharan Africa, often in cross-partnerships. Far beyond its importance in the global energy production, the region accounts for a quarter to a third of the activities of the major international energy companies.

1.2 Natural Gas Production and Reserves

While Sub-Saharan Africa is key for private international oil and gas companies, the continent also remains dependent on those companies for the development of its hydrocarbon resources, as no country has ever managed (or even attempted) to play a central role in the local oil and gas industry, leaving the entire sector to foreign (mostly private) companies. As a consequence, the development of the oil and gas industry in Sub-Saharan Africa has always depended on the interests of the international oil business, which explains why the gas sector stayed marginal for so long (Copinschi and Smedley 2016).

Until quite recently, international oil companies operating in Sub-Saharan Africa showed no real interest in developing gas production. Very little exploration was targeted specifically at gas, and associated gas (unavoidably extracted with crude oil) has long been considered an unwanted by-product of oil. The gas was (and still is) mostly vented or flared on site (some part being re-injected in the fields to enhance their productivity), despite the serious direct and indirect impacts of flaring on human health, soil, vegetation and the atmosphere. From the companies' point of view, the local markets were too small and the distances to major market centres (Europe, North America and Asia) too great to make gas production and its associated transportation infrastructures (pipelines and liquefaction plants) economically viable. For example, oil fields in Nigeria are generally scattered, and the associated gas collected from these fields must first be piped to a common collection point, compressed and transported to a processing unit before being available for economic purposes, all of which increase production costs.

Long restricted by the lack of infrastructure to monetise natural gas being flared, the Sub-Saharan African natural gas sector eventually emerged in the late 1990s when the first LNG plant came on stream in 1999 in Nigeria, followed by Equatorial Guinea (2007), Angola (2013) and Cameroon (2018), finally connecting the region to the global gas market. In 2019, Nigeria's production accounted for about 7% of globally traded LNG and ranks the country among the world's top five LNG producers behind Qatar, Australia, Malaysia and the United States. In the other oil production countries (Congo,

Gabon, etc.) most of the natural gas production is re-injected into oil fields or flared, with only a small part of it being commercially used, mostly in gas-fuelled power plants.

On the other side of the continent, East Africa has been virtually ignored by international oil and gas players for decades. The presence of gas has been known in Mozambique and Tanzania since the 1960s, but at the time, oil companies were exclusively looking for oil and few geologists believed in the region's potential. A new era began in the late 2000s when some oil companies were awarded exploration blocks in the offshore Rovuma Bassin, straddling the maritime border of Mozambique and Tanzania. From 2009 onwards, a huge series of natural gas discoveries, large enough to support LNG projects, were made and changed the oil and gas industry's interest in the whole region. Given the size of the discoveries (3000 to 5000 billion cubic metres (bcm) in Mozambique, and 1000 to 1700 bcm in Tanzania), licence-holders (ENI, Total, Shell, ExxonMobil, Equinor, etc.) are now moving ahead on plans to build LNG trains, especially in Mozambique where the first LNG production is expected by 2023. As oil companies tend to work by imitation, more offshore exploration was subsequently carried all around the continent, leading to significant discoveries made offshore in Senegal and Mauritania since 2016 (500 to 1000 bcm) and in South Africa in 2019, just to name a few (Table 34.2).

Note: These official figures of the proven reserves don't take into account all the recent giant gas discoveries made offshore Mozambique and Tanzania in East Africa, and in Senegal and Mauritania in West Africa.

Table 34.2 Natural gas production and proved reserves in Sub-Saharan Africa 2020

	Proved Reserves (in bcm)	*Share of global reserves (%)*	*Production (in bcm)*	*Share of global production (%)*
Nigeria	5761	2.82	47.90	1.20
Mozambique[a]	650	0.32	4.21	0.11
Angola	343	0.17	7.28	0.18
Congo-Brazzaville	284	0.14	0.70	0.02
Cameroon[a]	179	0.09	2.38	0.06
Ghana	53	0.03	2.77	0.07
Senegal	52	0.03	0.01	0.00
Mauritania	50	0.02	–	–
Equatorial Guinea	39	0.02	6.19	0.15
Tanzania[a]	35	0.02	0.88	0.02
Gabon	26	0.01	0.48	0.01
Sudan	25	0.01	–	–
Ivory Coast[a]	12	0.01	2.28	0.06
TOTAL Sub-Saharan Africa	**7631**	**3.74**	**74.86**	**1.87**

Source: Enerdata
[a] Production of 2019

2 A Region Plagued by the Resource Curse

Until the COVID-19 pandemic and the collapse of the oil price in early 2020 that obliged the companies to drastically reduce their investments, Sub-Saharan Africa was considered as one of the hottest spots for major oil companies. All of them were carrying out huge projects all around the continent, especially in Mozambique, Nigeria, Angola and Senegal/Mauritania. Although the 2020 slump in world oil and gas prices has led many developers to scale back projects and rein in costs, the resources in the above-mentioned countries are probably important enough to consider that their development is only a matter of time.

The flow of foreign investment into the African oil and gas sector that has been generated over the last three decades, and that is still expected in the future thanks to new projects, is usually presented as a great opportunity for the economic development of poorer countries. Especially since foreign aid to Africa from industrialised countries has been falling and gradually being replaced by an emphasis on trade as a means for African countries to escape poverty, the promise that oil and gas will boost the standard of living of Africans echoes repeatedly throughout the continent, raising popular expectations to sometimes-soaring heights. Today (in Mozambique, Senegal, Mauritania, etc.) like yesterday (in Nigeria, Angola, Congo-Brazzaville, etc.), many think that oil and gas will provide a revenue stream that will break the cycle of poverty that plagues their countries. They believe that oil and gas will bring jobs, food, schools, healthcare, agricultural support and housing.

Unfortunately, the lived experience of Sub-Saharan African oil-producing countries over the past several decades tells a story which differs radically from the promise of petroleum. The dramatic development failures that have characterised most oil-producing countries in the region warn that petrodollars have not helped developing countries to bring economic growth and reduce poverty. In many cases they have actually exacerbated it and more generally have had a very negative impact on the local economies (Ross 2013). Like many oil exporters in other developing regions (with the notable exception of Arab Monarchies), long-time African oil producers such as Nigeria, Angola, Congo-Brazzaville and Gabon, have been largely unable to convert their oil wealth into broad-based poverty reduction. These countries have not been able to diversify their economies or prepare for a post-oil future either. On the contrary, petroleum has become a magnet for conflict and, in some cases, civil war.

African oil-producing countries exhibit all classic oil-related patterns. With the emergence of the oil sector in the 1970s, the so-called Dutch Disease set in. Initially, oil development seems to work—at least for some time. Especially at the beginning, oil exploitation provides positive outcomes as per capita income may rapidly increase: Gabon and Equatorial Guinea, two oil-producers with a tiny population, do have amongst the highest GDP per capita of the continent (as well as very high inequalities in the distribution of these revenues). But these positive outcomes are undermined by greater and greater rent-seeking.

Because profit margins are so huge, the rents generated by oil generally overwhelm all other revenue sources. Even healthy pre-existing economic activities can be quickly disrupted and replaced by the growing reliance on petrodollars. It is easier to import food or consumer goods than to produce it if a government has the cash, and it is far simpler to buy technological know-how than develop it. Thus, the fiscal advantage of petroleum can actually serve as a handicap, hindering the development of other productive activities. When oil windfalls push up the real exchange rate of a country's currency, it tends to render most other exports non-competitive. The decline of the agriculture and manufacturing sectors of oil countries not only makes them more dependent on oil, thereby exacerbating other problems of dependency, but it can also lead to a permanent loss of competitiveness. Meanwhile, the oil sector cannot make up for the shortfall: because oil is an economic enclave and a highly capital-intensive activity, it provides little employment and relatively few linkages with the rest of the economy.

As oil becomes the dominant economic activity of a country and the leading export activity, governments become dependent on oil money. For those governments, oil is the main source of revenue and foreign exchange and, as a consequence, the economic basis of their power. Oil-led development has a strong tendency to concentrate on both production and revenue patterns, and this occurs in countries where economic and political power is often already very concentrated. Only those who control political power can grant the opportunity to make money from oil, and only those who receive this opportunity can provide the revenues to keep regimes in power. This does not occur to the same extent in more diffuse wealth-generating activities based on, say, fertile soil or fisheries, where the barriers to entry are far lower, the actors more numerous and the benefits more dispersed.

This dependence on oil revenues negatively affects the capacity of states and their ability to govern. There is a vicious circle is which the more governments spend, the more they need oil revenues. As a consequence, oil dependence is today overwhelming: in Nigeria (about 200 million inhabitants), petrodollars account for more than 50% of federal government revenue and more than 80% of export earnings, although it only accounts for 10% of GDP (World Bank 2020b). Like Nigeria, Angola's oil dependence is legendary: oil and gas account for about two-third of Angola's government revenue, more than 90% of its export earnings and approximately 30% of its GDP (International Monetary Fund 2019). Although this situation is repeated in a way in many other oil-producing countries around the world (including Venezuela, Russia, etc.), it is particularly putrid in Africa where State institutions are usually weak and unable to tackle the problem in order to broaden its productive base and not fall into the pitfall of the resource curse, as Norway or Dubai managed to do.

The problem is that high vulnerability to oil revenues makes it difficult to plan or project government spending levels. In almost every African oil-producing country various development schemes over the past decades have been launched and then abandoned because of declines in oil revenues due to a sudden drop in the oil price, like in early 2020. The volatility of oil prices—the rapid fluctuation from $20 to $100 per barrel and back—makes planning extremely difficult and undercuts efforts to turn oil wealth into other more permanent forms of sustainable development. Furthermore, volatility has been shown by scholars to be bad for investment, income distribution, educational attainment and poverty alleviation (Humphreys et al. 2007). Everywhere, the result has been painful.

2.1 *The Paradigmatic (and Dramatic) Case of Nigeria*

Nigeria, Sub-Saharan Africa's largest oil and gas producer, is a classic illustration of the oil dependency in Sub-Saharan Africa's oil-producing countries. The country abounds in proven reserves (approximately 37 billion barrels of oil and 5675 bcm of natural gas) and is currently the OPEC's sixth producer (Enerdata 2020). For the last 50 years, Nigeria has earned several dozen billion dollars annually from the oil and gas industry. The earnings depend on the production level and the price of oil: while it was only 20 billion dollars in 2018, it reached nearly 70 billion dollars in 2008 and 2011 when the oil price was at its highest (NEITI 2019). But these oil riches have done little to change the situation of the poor. Nigeria ranks 152nd out of 157 countries in the World Bank's Human Capital Index despite being a lower-middle-income country, reflecting the country's prolonged underinvestment in health, education and nutrition of its citizens. Health outcomes in the country are among the poorest in the world, and there are large regional and socioeconomic inequalities. Life expectancy (53 years in 2016) is particularly low while maternal mortality (576 per 100,000 live births in 2013) and infant mortality (65 per 1000 live births in 2017) are particularly high for a lower-middle-income country. In 2019, 40% of the population lived below the national poverty line (against 28% in 1980), and that rate will most probably increase because of the economic consequences of the COVID-19 pandemic (World Bank 2020b). Nigeria is not an isolated case as Angola, the second largest oil producer in the region, exhibits more or less the same patterns: despite the country's impressive expansion of the economy and the exceptional revenues generated by the oil industry over the last 20 years, the proportion of people living below the US$ 1.90 poverty line showed only a small decline, from about 33% in 2000 to 28% today. Only two-thirds of the Angolan urban population and less than a quarter of the rural population have access to clean drinking water and to basic sanitation, and life expectancy is only just above 60 years. Worldwide, Angola ranks among the last in terms of human resources in the health sector, with only one physician and 23 healthcare workers per 100,000 people; maternal and child mortality rates are about double the average in lower-middle-income countries (World Bank 2020a).

Over the years, the deterioration of the socioeconomic situation in Nigeria has been accompanied by political decay, a rise in oil-related human rights violations and violence, most notably in the Niger Delta where most oil is produced, causing huge environmental degradation resulting in the loss of livelihoods for many residents. For more than 25 years, there has been a cycle of activism, militancy and repression linked to oil (Ariweriokuma 2009). Given the neglect by the local authorities, which are generally highly corrupted,[1] the local population tends to turn straight to the oil companies to obtain the fruits of what they consider to be "their" oil. Since government institutions are practically non-existent on the ground (or at least invisible), the companies are the sole representatives of public authorities that are accessible to the local populations. Although companies pay considerable sums to the federal State in the form of royalties and income taxes, most of the population of the Niger Delta feels completely excluded from the benefits of oil activities and complain about serious environmental damage and human rights violations and hold multinational oil companies responsible. Regularly and in a more and more violent way, young members of these forgotten people demonstrate their hostility to the oil companies and claim better access to positions of power and, more specifically, a redefining of the distribution of oil rent in their favour. Pressure is applied in various ways, ranging from sabotage of pipelines, kidnapping of employees and occupation of installations, including offshore platforms.

The oil companies find themselves caught in a vicious circle, where their activities and the revenues they generate distort political life, increase the tendencies towards the formation of the rent economy and the collapse of political institutions, and create the frustrations of which they are the first victims, while being considered guilty by public opinion in the West. Confronted with this double threat (local instability and accusation at an international level that could impact their reputation), companies are adopting strategies to change this image through programmes which are intended to enable the local populations to benefit directly from the presence and activity of the oil companies. These efforts, not surprisingly, are well publicised by the oil companies. They insist that their investments are not just for extracting oil resources and generating revenues for the governments, but are also used to pay for scholarships, build roads, schools, clinics and housing, to provide job training, to fund small businesses, or even to support the fight against AIDS. Every year companies spend over 100 million dollars on community development projects in the Niger Delta, in an attempt to restore their legitimacy in the eyes of the local population and international observers.

Sometimes oil-company-funded social development projects are well designed, useful, they address an expressed need of the community and really help the local economy. Other times oil company projects can amount to no more than a cash payout to a local leader in order to quell agitated youth activists. But in the long run these actions can actually exacerbate community tensions or other cleavages, without contributing to any sustainable

[1] Nigeria ranks 146 out of 180 in the 2019 Transparency International's Corruption Perceptions Index.

development of the economy (Chukwana 2015). In the Niger Delta region, much of the infrastructure built by the oil companies is usually not operational since there are no public funds to cover the running costs (teacher's salaries, health equipment, maintenance of roads, etc.). Without any lasting impact on local development, due to the lack of partnership with the public authorities (often non-existent), these programmes seem essentially to be a mere response to the critics and to pressure from the local populations and international NGOs.

Companies are not well suited to be development agencies. They are private oil companies: their aim is to do business, not development. While some of the companies' efforts may produce laudable outcomes, corporate philanthropy can not be an answer to the failure of the local and national governments to respond to the needs of their people. In fact, companies find themselves obliged to take the place of the State in order to assure a minimum of public services. Thus they are locked in a vicious circle where, by taking on the role of the State in order to buy short-term social peace, they perpetuate a situation (the weakening of the State and the tendency to rent-seeking) which is the very source of the problems they face.

Africa's trade relationship with the rest of the world is dominated by extractive industries, especially oil, gas and mining. For most African oil-producing countries, notably Nigeria, the failure to develop has been catastrophic. The gap between the promise of petroleum and the perversity of its economic performance in recent times is enormous. Study after study demonstrates that, as a group, countries dependent on oil as their leading export have performed worse than other developing countries on a variety of economic indicators.

But while the record of oil and gas exporters in Sub-Saharan Africa shows that oil-dependence is most often a perilous development path, negative outcomes from oil booms are not inevitable. This has been illustrated by the case of Norway that managed to use the benefits from North Sea petroleum to earn the highest place on the United Nations Development Program's list of best development performers. This means that the underlying development problems around oil and gas are not inherent in the resource itself. Whether countries succeed in turning oil and gas revenues into long-term economic benefits for their people, ultimately depends on the quality of public policies, especially those dedicated to fuel poverty reduction, including access to energy.

3 The Lack of Access to Energy

Long neglected, the issue of access to energy for the population has recently become a priority for the international community as well as for most of African governments. While none of the eight UN Millennium Development Goals (MDGs) in 2000 covered the issue of energy, the UN has since identified access to sustainable energy as a prerequisite for poverty eradication. The UN has made it a specific topic in the 2015 Sustainable Development Goals (SDG) through the SDG 7 which aims, amongst other things, at ensuring universal access to affordable, reliable and modern energy services by 2030, and at substantially increasing the share of renewable energy in the global energy mix.

Energy supports the provision of basic needs (cooking, heating, lighting, access to clean water, transport, social services, etc.), creates productive activities (manufacturing, industry, commerce, agriculture, etc.) and stimulates employment creation. Conversely, the lack of access to reliable, affordable and modern energy services severely impedes social and economic development, especially as the poorest segments of the population often pay the highest price (in money, time and health) for the worst-quality energy services. The lack of access to modern energy also hampers enterprise development, and undermines competitiveness and thus access to regional and global markets for producers. Promoting access to electricity and clean cooking energy is now acknowledged as a key driver for economic development and essential to fostering inclusive growth in view of lifting people out of poverty.

3.1 *The Lowest Electrification Rate in the World*

As for many of the SDG, Sub-Saharan African countries are particularly concerned by the SDG 7. With the exception of South Africa,[2] Sub-Saharan Africa is by far the region on the globe with the lowest electrification rate and where progress towards achieving SDG 7 is the slowest. While the population without access to electricity dropped worldwide from 1.2 billion in 2010 to about 840 million in 2017, the decrease is much slower in Sub-Saharan Africa. In 2017 about 55% of the Sub-Saharan African population (some 573 million people, that is, two-thirds of the world population without electricity) still lacked access to electricity, and that number will probably be about the same in 2030 (whereas everywhere else in the world it will further decrease) (IEA et al. 2019). Based on the relationship between electricity access on one hand and GDP per capita, population growth (given that most Sub-Saharan African countries haven't achieved their demographic transition yet), and urbanisation rate on the other, model projections show that about 515 million people will still lack access to electricity in 2030 (IEA 2019). At the moment Sub-Saharan Africa is clearly not on track to achieve the seventh SDG.

[2] South Africa is an exception in the energy landscape of Sub-Saharan Africa. The country has a long history of industrialisation and inherited an extensive, large capacity centralised system from the apartheid era in 1994. Having been diplomatically and economically isolated for decades because of the apartheid regime, the country was forced to set up its own pathway to ensure the energy supply of its economy: historically, the country relies mostly on its own coal resources, which still provide 90% of its electricity production, as well as on nuclear energy (5% of the electricity generation), of which it is the only producer on the continent (data from Enerdata). However, despite having the largest energy system in Africa, the country is nowadays grappling to ensure an adequate energy supply, especially electricity. The latter along with severe limitations in generation capacity and frequent load shedding have hobbled economic growth for the last two decades, thus bringing South Africa closer, in that aspect, to the rest of the continent.

The average electricity consumption per capita in Sub-Saharan Africa (excluding South Africa) is 175 kilowatt hours (kWh), compared to 2100 kWh in emerging Asian economies, 2855 kWh on average globally, 5100 kWh in Europe, and more than 10,000 kWh in the United States (Pistelli 2018). The energy challenges facing households vary, however, significantly between urban and rural areas. In urban areas, on average, almost three-quarters of the Sub-Saharan African households have access to electricity, whereas in rural areas, where populations are spread over large distances and are usually not connected to a grid, this figure falls to one-quarter. It is expected that in 2030 about 85% of the population without access to electricity will be located in rural areas (Dagnachew et al. 2018).

At about 120,000 MW, the installed power generation capacity in Sub-Saharan Africa is even below that of France, with a population 16 times bigger. Moreover, two-thirds of the Sub-Saharan African countries experience recurrent outages and load shedding, forcing businesses as well as households to rely on back-up generators running on diesel or gasoline at costs that are four times the price of grid power. In other words, not only Sub-Saharan Africa isn't producing enough electricity, but the production costs are generally much higher than in other developing regions. The small scale of most national power systems and the reliance on expensive, oil-based generation make the cost of electricity generation in Africa two to three times higher than the global average (AfDB 2016). Hence modern energy services are not affordable for the poor segments of the Sub-Saharan population as the costs of energy services are generally higher than anywhere else and the up-front costs of connection very high.

Investments in energy generation and transmission are generally inadequate, and regional cooperation to boost energy supply is moving slowly. Indeed, most investment in power generation in Sub-Saharan Africa is geared not towards the basic energy needs of the poor, but towards industrialisation and the rising demands of existing consumers. Approximately half of current electricity consumption in Sub-Saharan Africa is used for industrial activities, mostly mining and refining.

3.2 Limited Access to Clean Cooking Energy and Heavy Reliance on Biomass

Access to clean, non-polluting cooking and heating facilities is even more restricted. Mostly used for cooking, traditional biomass is by far the most widely used energy source across Sub-Saharan Africa, with the exception of South Africa, where the energy mix is coal-heavy. Despite the fact that burning biomass causes serious health hazards that have a major impact, particularly on women and children, biomass' share in the overall Sub-Saharan African energy mix has barely changed over the last 25 years. Biomass continues to dominate the primary energy mix, accounting for 65% of total energy use in the region (if South Africa is excluded, this share increases to almost three-quarters).

According to the IEA nearly four in five people of the population in Sub-Saharan Africa use biomass energy (often used in inefficient and unhealthy forms), compared with 52% in the developing world as a whole (IEA 2019). As a consequence, some 600,000 Africans die each year from the effects of household air pollution. There is no other region in the world that relies so heavily on bioenergy. The high levels of poverty partly explain the heavy reliance on traditional biofuels as an energy source for cooking.

Reliance on traditional biomass (especially charcoal) also encourages deforestation and land degradation. In many areas around major cities, charcoal demand contributes to the degradation of the surrounding woodlands and forests. In addition, foraging for fuel takes time, especially for women and children, who may therefore miss out on opportunities to undertake more productive activities, such as schooling and livelihood activities. In some places climate change and deforestation are compounding the problem of finding suitable biomass for fuel.

Over the last decade, although Africa's global primary energy supply has grown by more than 3% each year, the energy mix has remained substantially unchanged. In 2018, biomass still represented two-thirds of the final energy consumption in Sub-Saharan Africa (and even three-quarters without considering South Africa) while oil accounted for about 20%, as it was ten years ago. As far as power generation is concerned, fossil fuel dominates, accounting for 70% (50% for coal, 12% for natural gas and 7% for oil), and hydroelectricity for 25%. However, as South Africa, which relies mostly on coal (90% of its electricity production), accounts for about half of the whole Sub-Saharan African electricity production, the figures for the region excluding South Africa are slightly different, with hydroelectricity representing half of the electricity generation, natural gas 25% and oil 15%. In any case modern renewable energies (wind, solar, geothermal, etc.), although growing fast, only account for less than 5% of the electricity generation (coming from less than 1% in 2010) (Enerdata 2020).

Despite 15 years of economic growth, Africa's energy systems are still grossly inadequate. Restricted access to electricity, power shortages and dependence on biomass for fuel are undermining efforts to reduce poverty. At the same time energy demand is climbing as cities, populations and economies grow. The lack of access to modern energy is clearly a major factor in the high level of poverty in Sub-Saharan Africa and its slow progress towards the achievement of the SDGs. The energy-sector bottlenecks and power shortages that affect most of the Sub-Saharan countries have a deep economic impact. In practice the lack of reliable and affordable power is one of the biggest constraints when investing on the continent undermining job creation and social development. As African businesses have to wait an average of 130 days to receive an electricity connection, it is estimated that the difficulty to access energy costs between 2 and 4% of GDP annually (AfDB 2019). In rural Africa agricultural production and productivity are constrained by limited access to modern energy services to power water for irrigation, agriculture mechanisation and post-harvest storage and processing. This in turn depresses crop yields, added value and farmers' incomes, thus aggravating food-security problems. Low incomes from agriculture in turn make it difficult for farmers to afford cleaner, modern energy services, thus perpetuating the poverty trap.

4 The Challenges Ahead

4.1 *Harnessing the Resources*

There are enormous power deficits across Africa. The situation seems paradoxical as the continent has huge renewable energy potential as well as abundant natural gas—the cleanest hydrocarbon—which could be combined to deliver stable and relatively environmentally sustainable electricity generation (Hafner et al. 2019).

The continent is indeed reported to have more than half of the world's renewable energy potential. In particular, Africa has the richest solar resources on the planet, although only 5 gigawatts of solar photovoltaics (PV) are installed, accounting for less than 1% of global capacity. If properly harnessed solar could certainly become one of the continent's top energy sources and help meet a significant proportion of energy demand, especially in rural areas (Hafner et al. 2018b). Due to a high irradiation potential (many African countries have daily solar radiation ranging between 5 and 6 kWh/m^2), the falling cost of solar photovoltaic and the limited capital investment required (compared to grid connections), solar home systems could be an attractive solution for the population currently deprived of access to electricity. Even low levels of electrification, especially solar lamps, can bring substantial economic and non-economic benefits (Aevarsdottir et al. 2018).

The second important potential source of renewable energy is hydropower. Although it already accounts for half of the electricity generation in Sub-Saharan Africa, it is estimated that the potential remains substantial as only 7% of it has been harnessed. Similarly, the technical potential of wind and geothermal energy is significant. Using the prevailing technology, the region of the Great Rift Valley has the potential to generate 20,000 MW of electricity from geothermal sources. To date, the exploitation of the resource remains limited to only 150 MW in Kenya and 7.3 MW in Ethiopia, partially because of the significant up-front cost and the specialised expertise required.

With sizeable reserves in much of the region, natural gas, meanwhile, could certainly play a key role in meeting Africa's industrial growing need for reliable electricity supply. Today, however, the share of gas in Sub-Saharan Africa's energy mix is among the lowest in the world. Natural gas accounts for just 12% of Sub-Saharan Africa's on-grid power generation capacity (most of that in Nigeria), against 23% globally.

Although natural gas has a large potential, reserves are often only developed when the production can be exported by LNG. International companies usually don't consider the domestic markets because prices are usually subsidised and thus provide inadequate return on investments, or the off-takers have creditworthiness issues. Even when gas is associated with oil production, flaring is still very common.

The experience in Ghana, the only country in Sub-Saharan Africa in which non-associated gas has been developed in deep water and is entirely dedicated to the domestic market, is a good example of a model that could be more frequently applied. The development of the gas resources was made possible by the negotiation of an innovative payment security structure involving World Bank guarantees amounting to $700 million to secure payments by the state-owned Ghana National Petroleum Corporation for the purchase of gas (Pistelli 2018). As a result, Ghana is today one of the most advanced countries in the region in terms of access to energy, with the electrification rate above 80% (against 44% in 2000), thanks to its natural gas and hydropower resources that account respectively for 52% and 37% of the power generation (Enerdata 2020).

4.2 *Improving the Governance to Attract Investments*

The production and distribution system of electricity in Sub-Saharan Africa is globally a failure: not only the current power systems are inadequate for present day demand for reliable power, but given the projected growth of population, the future expanding demand will result in worsening shortfalls unless radical strategies of expansion and change are implemented.

Sub-Saharan Africa is endowed with important energy resources, including both fossil fuels and renewable sources, that could easily meet the continent's energy demand. However, the lack of access to energy doesn't seem to be related to the availably of energy resource per se but rather to the way these resources are harnessed. The main issue is not the resource endowment, but the difficulty to mobilise or attract investment needed to valorise them, which, ultimately, pertains to the level of governance and the quality of the institutions.

There are three priority tasks for electrifying Sub-Saharan Africa, each of them involving a significant improvement of the governance of the energy sector (Harris 2018). The first one is to expand the output and reliability of existing centralised systems for power generation, transmission and distribution that supply connected consumers through centralised grids. The second one is to connect the unconnected population (mainly rural) with the development of decentralised small systems in which distributed local generation is linked to mini-grids. The third task is to decarbonise the energy mix by substituting coal, biomass and diesel with renewable sources.

Governance of power utilities is indeed one of the key components of Africa's energy crisis. Effective governance and regulatory frameworks in the energy sector are crucial for promoting sound management practices and attracting private investments. By setting up the rules in the sector, regulation increases comfort for the private sector to invest and imposes on utilities cost discipline and quality standards for enhanced efficiency. Regulation also helps maintain a balance between the interests of service providers and the needs of consumers in terms of quality of service, profits and reasonable tariffs.

For a long time, the energy sector in Africa (especially the power sub-sector) was under state ownership and poorly managed because of political interference requiring that utilities play a difficult dual role as commercial entities and implementers of governments' social objectives. The consequences have been inadequate maintenance, poor performance of utilities and low-quality service. In response to these inefficiencies and under the pressure of international donors, many Sub-Saharan African countries initiated a liberalisation process in order to boost performance and energy supply. In practice, African governments spend around $20 billion annually bailing out loss-making utilities and providing subsidies for oil-based products, while these funds could be spent on more productive energy investments, including setting up targeted subsidies for the poorest households within a full cost recovery system.

Establishing robust legal and regulatory frameworks at national and regional levels is critical in order to attract international private investors and improve operating efficiency (Hafner et al. 2018b). However, most African households, especially in rural areas, live on very modest budgets, which constitute a barrier for access to modern energy services in a liberalised market where energy providers rely solely on revenues from sales. In other words, it is very unlikely that the market alone would succeed in achieving universal access to energy in Sub-Saharan Africa. Meeting the energy needs of low-income communities implies finding a balance between the traditional supply-oriented approach and a demand-driven one, which means paying greater attention to the needs of the end-users and their capacity to afford services. This can be done through innovative pricing mechanisms and flexible payment schemes, including targeted subsidies, to reduce the financial burden for consumers, facilitate access and share potential financial risks with investors, all of which, once again, depends on the quality of the governance.

Despite its high level of corruption and ethnic competition and violence, Kenya offers a good example of what can be achieved. Thanks to a well-developed regulatory framework and innovative off-grid solutions (especially in geothermal and micro-hydropower), Kenya has been able to attract domestic and foreign private investments in renewable energy which resulted in an impressive expansion of access to electricity (Gordon 2018). With an electrification rate above 75% (against less than 20% in 2000) both from grid and off-grid solutions, the country now has the highest electricity access rate in East Africa and is projected to achieve universal access before 2030 (IEA et al. 2019).

4.3 Fostering Regional and International Cooperation

The African Development Bank (AfDB) estimates the total investment requirement, in order to reach universal access to reliable and clean electric power in all the countries of the continent by 2030, at an average annual investment of between US$27 billion (assuming a global climate policy) and US$33 billion (assuming no global climate policy) (AfDB 2019). For now these amounts seem totally out of reach and the chances of meeting the SDG7 in Sub-Saharan Africa seem minimal. However, change seems to be happening, as efforts to promote energy access are clearly gaining momentum. For the first time in 2017 the increase in the rate of access to energy in Sub-Saharan Africa outpaced population growth.

Africa's strong economic growth since 2000 has resulted in an increase in demand for energy from the private sector, prompting major investments in power generation and transmission. A considerable push towards cleaner, lower-carbon energy is promoting investment in the Sub-Saharan African energy sectors, strongly supported by international development agencies. Indeed, for the last decade or so, numerous international organisations such as the World Bank Group, the African Development Bank (AfDB, through its New Deal on Energy for Africa), European governments and institutions (Africa-European Union Energy Partnership, AEEP) and the United States government (USAID's Power Africa programme) have launched several ambitious initiatives. These initiatives aim to promote investment in the energy production and distribution infrastructure and establish effective governance systems needed to reach a sustainable and cleaner energy sector that ensures universal access to modern, affordable and reliable energy services for all Africans. Some private initiatives also exist, including the Sustainable Energy for All (SEforAll) initially launched by former UN Secretary-General Ban Ki-moon in 2011, and the Clean Cooking Alliance established in 2010.

All these initiatives from international public donors are important not only for the funds they provide, but also because they help to catalyse private funds. In many cases, the presence of development institutions, providing financing and risk mitigation measures, has been critical to obtain funding (Tagliapietra 2018). In particular, the action of some donors such as the AfDB is also crucial in helping to plan and implement regional cooperation in the energy sector in view of developing infrastructure, especially for electricity generation and distribution, and promoting regional electricity markets. This is illustrated by the establishment of several sub-regional power pools, namely the South African Power Pool (SAPP), West African Power Pool (WAPP), Central African Power Pool (CAPP) and East African Power Pool (EAPP). Although most of them are still fairly embryonic and face challenges such as a lack of funding, political instability and weak cross-border regulations, they could enable countries to develop their energy systems more collaboratively and stimulate cross-border trade of energy resources and services, avoiding the inefficiencies of small national markets and therefore enhancing the security of electricity supply on the continent (Hafner et al. 2018a).

In recent years a high proportion of the foreign investments being made in Sub-Saharan Africa's centralised electricity systems originates from China. Although precise data about China's financial involvement on the continent are lacking, it is estimated that Chinese companies (which are mostly state-owned) are responsible for about a third of new power capacity in Sub-Saharan Africa since 2010. Over the last decade China has completed about 150 projects for new capacity in generation, transmission and distribution all over the continent (Harris 2018). Focusing mostly on large hydropower projects, China has become the largest national source of investment in the electricity sector's expansion and upgrading in Sub-Saharan Africa.

Praised by most African governments, eager to benefit from Chinese funds as they are deemed to be unconditional (in terms of governance)—contrary to those from Western donors—these loans, however, raise questions about their sustainability as well as their political cost. Indeed, by contracting a loan from the Chinese government in order to finance infrastructures, African governments not only are obliged to call in Chinese companies to design and carry out the projects, but also might end up finding themselves caught in a debt trap (Copinschi et al. 2019). Unable to reimburse the loans, African governments could eventually have to give away the property of the infrastructures to Chinese companies, giving them control on key strategic energy assets.

Times are changing in Sub-Saharan Africa. As Africa's population continues to grow at a rapid rate and the continent could number up to four billion people by the end of the century, working for development is more than ever a political and moral imperative. While access to energy is now well identified as a necessary condition for development, it seems less and less acceptable to continue to consider Africa only as a reservoir of energy resources available for supplying the rest of the world. The economic, social and political consequences have become too great, as illustrated by the evolution of Nigeria, a demographic giant and a major oil and gas country, where the mismanagement of oil revenues and the carelessness of the local political class have plunged the country in a spiral of violence that threatens to spill over into its neighbours.

Africa's energy potential is enormous. However, turning this potential into economic growth and development requires more than political will; it is important to put in place the conditions for attracting the investments that are essential to develop these resources for the benefit of the emerging middle classes but also the poor. The experiences of several countries, such as Kenya and Ghana, show that very different strategic choices can lead to positive results. However, there is still a long way to go before these good practices can apply across the continent.

Bibliography

Anna Aevarsdottir, Nicholas Barton and Tessa Bold (2018), "Rural Electrification. The Potential and Limitations of Solar Power", *Oxford Energy Forum*, Issue 115, September 2018, pp. 37–39.

African Development Bank (AfDB) (2016), *The Bank Group's Strategy for The New Deal on Energy for Africa 2016–2025.*

African Development Bank (AfDB) (2019), *Development Effectiveness Review 2019.*

Soala Ariweriokuma (2009), The Political Economy of Oil and Gas in Africa: The Case of Nigeria, Routledge, 354 p.

I. T. Chukwana (2015), "The Resource Curse in Nigeria: Lessons and Policy Options", International Journal of Research in Humanities and Social Studies, Vol. 2, No. 8.

Philippe Copinschi and Mark Smedley (2016), "Sub-Saharan Africa: A Future Global Gas Player?", in Silvia Colombo, Mohamed El Harrak and Nicolò Sartori (eds), The Future of Natural Gas. *Markets and Geopolitics*, Hof van Twente: Lenthe/European Energy Review, pp. 181–205.

Philippe Copinschi, Catherine Locatelli, Manfred Hafner, Raphaël Danino-Perraud, Samuel Carcanague (2019), "La Belt and Road Initiative et la stratégie de sécurisation des approvisionnements énergétiques chinois en Afrique", *Observatoire de la sécurité des flux et des matières énergétiques*, IRIS Enerdata Cassini, 57 pages.

Anteneh G. Dagnachew, Paul L. Lucas, Andries F. Hof and Detlef P. van Vuuren (2018), "Opportunities and Challenges in Achieving Universal Electricity Access in Sub-Saharan Africa", *Oxford Energy Forum*, Issue 115, September 2018, pp. 22–27.

Enerdata (2020), *Global Energy and CO2 Data*, online database.

Mandred Hafner, Philippe Copinschi, Jean-Pierre Favannec and Simone Taglieapietra (2018a), Handbook of Energy in Sub-Saharan Africa, Deventer: Claeys and Casteels.

Manfred Hafner, Simone Tagliapietra and Lucia de Strasser (2018b), Energy in Africa. Challenges and Opportunities, Cham: Springer, 112 pages.

Manfred Hafner, Simone Tagliapietra, Giacomo Falchetta, Giovanni Occhiali (2019), Renewables for Energy Access and Sustainable Development in East Africa, Cham: Springer, 158 pages.

Laurence Harris (2018), "Financing System Challenges for Energy Transformation in Africa", *Oxford Energy Forum*, Issue 115, September 2018, pp. 6–12.

Macartan Humphreys, Jeffrey D. Sachs, Joseph E. Stiglitz (2007), Escaping the Resource Curse, Columbia University Press, 432 p.

Emma Gordon (2018), "The Politics of Renewable Energy in East Africa", Oxford Energy Forum, Issue 115, September 2018, pp. 41–46.

International Energy Agency (IEA) (2019), Africa Energy Outlook, 280 pages.

IEA, IRENA, UNSD, WB, WHO (2019), Tracking SDG 7: The Energy Progress Report 2019, Washington DC.

International Monetary Fund (2019), IMF Country Focus. Angola: Promoting Sustained, Inclusive Growth and Reducing Oil Dependency, December 19, 2019.

Nigeria Extractive Industry Transparency Initiative (NEITI) (2019), *Nigeria Oil and Gas Industry Audit Report 2018*, October 2019.

Lapo Pistelli (2018), "Electrification in Africa. The Need for New Forms of Cooperation", *Oxford Energy Forum*, Issue 115, September 2018, pp. 12–14.

Michael L. Ross, (2013), The Oil Curse: How Petroleum Wealth Shapes the Development of Nations, Princeton: Princeton University Press, 312 pages.

Simone Tagliapietra (2018), "Electrification in Sub-Saharan Africa. The Role of International Institutions", *Oxford Energy Forum*, Issue 115, September 2018, pp. 49–52.

The World Bank (2020a), *Angola Poverty Assessment*, June 2020.

The World Bank (2020b), *Nigeria Development Update. Nigeria in Times of COVID-19: Laying Foundations for a Strong Recovery*, June 2020.

CHAPTER 35

Energy and the Economy in North America

Edward C. Chow and Jorge-Andres Rincon-Romero

1 Introduction

North America is blessed with abundant energy resources. In many ways, 2020 was a pivotal year. U.S. oil production peaked at 13 million barrels per day early in the year. However, momentum behind the unconventional oil and gas revolution (or shale gale) slowed after 15 years. Its remarkable success moderated global oil and gas prices, even as this favorable outcome exposed the shale industry's business model that emphasized growth over profitability. Similarly, lower prices hurt high-cost oil sands production in Canada, while ample U.S. supply limited access for Canadian exports of oil and gas. Lower prices also harmed the prospect of reviving Mexico's petroleum industry either by attracting foreign investment or through organic domestic growth.

Global oil prices plummeted in March 2020, even before the full impact of the COVID-19 pandemic was felt. Worldwide economic recovery accelerated considerably in 2021, given the unprecedently large fiscal and monetary stimuli applied to prevent economic collapse. Consequently, energy prices rose significantly, prompting calls for renewed oil and gas investment and increased exports, and relatively less emphasis on climate policy measures to restrict fossil fuel use. For all three countries in North America—the U.S., Canada, and Mexico—energy development and consumption play a crucial role in their economies.

E. C. Chow (✉)
Center for Strategic and International Studies, Washington, DC, USA

J.-A. Rincon-Romero
Newmont Corporation, Mexico City, Mexico

M. Hafner, G. Luciani (eds.), *The Palgrave Handbook of International Energy Economics*, https://doi.org/10.1007/978-3-030-86884-0_35

2 The U.S.

The U.S. went through a number of transitions that enhanced the country's energy security and slowly decreased its reliance on fossil fuels to meet energy needs. However, current trends for greenhouse gas (GHG) emissions suggest climate change mitigation targets will not be met.

The U.S. is a market economy designed to take advantage of its resource endowment and competitive advantages in technological innovation. These drivers led to the Shale Revolution. The increased production made the U.S. less dependent on energy imports, enabled a transition from coal to natural gas-fired electricity production, and opened the door for substantial U.S. oil and gas exports. Nonetheless, the low social acceptance of oil and gas infrastructure due to environmental and climate change concerns prevent producers from efficiently accessing domestic and international markets.

Simultaneously, the renewable energy (RE) industry experienced a production bonanza. The growing share of wind and solar energy is underpinned by popular policy support for non-emitting sources of energy, technological innovation, and stagnant electricity demand.

For the U.S. to significantly reduce GHG emissions, it will need to accelerate the transition toward a RE-based energy matrix through more favorable policies to meet the needs of its top energy consumers. This will likely involve energy storage solutions that economically and technically overcome intermittency challenges for solar and wind. Additionally, fuel efficiency trends, electric vehicle penetration rates, and the social acceptance of renewable energy (RE) mega projects will play a role in determining the pace of GHG emission reductions.

The U.S. is the world leader of oil and gas production. For instance, in 2018 the U.S. reached historic production levels for both oil and gas products with 11 million barrels per day (mmb/d) of crude oil (EIA 2019a) and around 930 billion cubic meters annually (bcma) of natural gas marketed production (EIA 2019b). This represents a 7 mmb/d production increase for crude oil in the 2008–2018 period (EIA 2019a), and an equally impressive total production increase for marketed natural gas in the U.S. of 332 bcma from 2008 to 2018 (EIA 2019b).

The production boom was fueled by decisive improvements in extraction techniques for unconventional resources combined with favorable investment and operating conditions. On the technology side, innovation around hydraulic fracturing, directional drilling, and information technology enabled the economic extraction of hydrocarbons from shale deposits (US CRS 2018). Moreover, it was the new technologies combined with private mineral rights ownership, availability of geological data, liberalized integrated markets, abundant risk capital, competitive oil and gas service providers, and interconnected infrastructure that made the extraction profitable and massive (CSIS 2019).

Indeed, data indicate shale formations accounted for 70% of natural dry gas production and 60% of crude oil production in December 2018 (EIA 2019c).

Specifically, the shale plays in the Permian region—located in Western Texas and Eastern New Mexico—contributed the most to growth crude oil outputs (EIA 2019d), while the Utica and Marcellus U.S. shale formations in Appalachia accounted for 85% of incremental natural gas production from 2012 to 2015 (US CRS 2018).

The rise in output amid stagnant energy demand produced a state of energy abundance. Data from 2000 to 2018 indicate total annual primary energy consumption stagnated at roughly 100 quadrillion British Thermal Units (BTUs) (EIA 2019e; US CRS 2018). Increased energy efficiencies and a structural shift from a manufacture-driven to a service-led economy account for the 1.5% annual U.S. energy intensity decline from 1957 to 2017 (Saundry 2019).

Contrastingly, U.S. primary energy production increased by 23% in the 2000–2017 period (US CRS 2018) from about 70 quadrillion BTUs in 2000 to almost 90 and estimated at about 95 quadrillion BTUs for 2018 (EIA 2019e). The Shale Revolution enabled oil production to rise by 64% and natural gas production by 42% in that period (US CRS 2018), and as of 2018 energy produced from petroleum and gas products accounts for 36% and 31% of total energy consumed, respectively (EIA 2019e).

Oil and gas products play an important role in the energy demand of the U.S. transport, industrial, residential, and commercial sectors. In fact, petroleum products represent 92% of the 28.3 quadrillion BTUs the U.S. transport sector consumed in 2018 (EIA 2019e). Petroleum and natural gas products respectively provided the industrial sector with 34% and 40% of its energy demand; the residential sector with 8% and 43%; and the commercial sector with 9% and 39% (EIA 2019e). Natural gas also represented the largest source of electricity generation at 35% of total electricity in 2018. Residential and commercial consumers rely on electricity for 45% and 50% of their energy demand, respectively (EIA 2019e).

The Shale Revolution positioned the U.S. to meet domestic need for oil and gas and further integrate the North American oil and gas markets. On the one hand, the increased production of light sweet crude oil from shale deposits reduced the need for oil imports. The net import of crude oil and petroleum products was reduced by 6.5 mmb/d from the 2008–2012 period to the 2016–2018 period (Pirog 2019).[1] However, due to refining configurations—major refineries are optimized to process cheaper heavy crudes (Pirog 2019)—the U.S. is still importing large amounts of crude oil from nearby Canada and to a lesser extent Mexico.

At the same time, abundant natural gas production increased demand for natural gas products as prices declined, while significantly reducing imports to make the U.S. a net gas exporter. This trend is most apparent in the transition from coal to natural gas-based electricity generation. Hence, from 2000 to 2017 total natural gas demand grew by 16%, and by 2018 natural gas demand for electricity generation grew by 80% (US CRS 2018). Contrastingly, coal's

[1] Data for 2018 only include the first ten months of the year.

share of electricity production declined to 30.1% in 2017 from 52% in 2000 (US CRS 2018). The decline was reinforced by the proximity of shale gas production areas to consumers in the northeast U.S. and efficiency gains in combined cycle gas-based power plants (US CRS 2018). Despite the rise in demand, 2017 natural gas imports were 34% less than at 2007 peak levels (US CRS 2018).

The growing contributions of natural gas to the U.S. electricity sector exacerbated the nuclear sectors' challenges. Nuclear energy represented about 20% of U.S. electricity generation for 30 years (Saundry 2019). Yet, the fleet of reactors is nearing retirement age. Permitting challenges for new reactors as well as more cost-competitive gas or renewable electricity will continue to reduce nuclear's role in meeting future electricity demand.

Surplus oil and gas from shale made the U.S. an important exporter of both. For example, refined oil product exports increased from an average of 2.2 mmb/d in the 2008–2012 period to 5.1 mmb/d from 2016 through the first ten months of 2018 (Pirog 2019). Likewise, crude oil exports increased from an average of 45,000 b/d in the 2008–2012 period to 2.2 mmb/d in 2018 after the previous crude oil export ban was lifted starting in 2016 (Pirog 2019). LNG exports started in 2016 and natural gas exports totaled 102 bcma in 2018 (EIA 2019f). When more LNG export terminals come online in 2022, the EIA projects natural gas exports to rise to over 212 bcma by 2030 (EIA 2019g).

Nevertheless, oil and gas firms face market access issues due to insufficient transport infrastructure. U.S. pipeline networks did not keep pace with production increases, and existing nodes do not efficiently connect producers with domestic and international consumers. Public opposition to oil and gas projects prevents those transportation gaps from being filled effectively and expeditiously.

A major driver for the low social acceptance of oil and gas projects is the sector's contribution to climate change through increased GHG emissions. In fact, current trends indicate the U.S. will not meet its Nationally Determined Contribution's emissions targets, despite gradual decreases in emissions and energy intensity. The latest EPA GHG emissions inventory calculates U.S. emissions at 6456 Million Metric Tons (MMT) of CO2e for 2017. Although emissions have decreased by 1% every year since 2005, the 2017 emissions levels are 1.3% higher than in 1990 (EPA 2019).

The highest emitters are also the greatest consumers of energy. Thus, in 2017 the transport sector emitted 1866 MMT of CO2e or about 29% of the total; the power sector 1778 MMT of CO2e or 27.5% of the total; and industry 1436 MMT of CO2e or 22.2% of the total (EPA 2019). There are mixed trends in emissions across sectors, however. For example, emissions in the transport sector have been rising since 2012. In contrast, the power sector has experience declines in GHG emissions since 2005 and industry emissions declined by 14.8% since 1990 (EPA 2019).

The discrepancies in emission trends are partly explained by contrasting gains in energy efficiencies. In fact, 2015 data demonstrate vehicles use 7%

more energy per mile traveled than in 2003—customer preferences for heavy vehicles and the U.S.'s vast territory explain the sector's growing energy intensity (Benoit 2019). This trend contrasts with overall energy and emission intensity improvements in the U.S. For example, from 1957 to 2017 there was an annual average 1.5% decline in U.S. energy intensity due to improved efficiency in the manufacturing and electricity sectors, the offshoring of energy intensive activities, and a structural transition to a service-based economy (Saundry 2019).

If current trends continue, the Climate Action Tracker estimates the U.S. will not meet its 2020 GHG emission target of 6348 MMT of CO2e or its 2025 5760 MMT of CO2e target by 60–90 MMT of CO2e and by about 500–600 MMT of CO2e, respectively (Climate Action Tracker 2019).

Public pressure to reduce GHG emissions through non-emitting sources of energy further explains the decline in U.S. emissions as renewable energy sources increasingly meet more energy needs. The combination of favorable public policies, technological innovation, and large markets for electricity with declining demand rates enabled RE outputs to grow substantially and economically compete with hydrocarbons. The cases of the wind and solar industries underscore these trends.

In response to growing public pressure to decrease GHG emissions and concerns around climate change, federal and state policymakers established favorable investment regimes for wind and solar energy firms. At the federal level, tax incentives for investing in wind and solar energy assets that included accelerated depreciation benefits (US CRS 2018) were introduced through legislation like the Production Tax Credit for wind and the Investment Tax Credit for solar (Deloitte 2019). At the state level, policymakers introduced Renewable Portfolio Standards (RPS) that required minimum annual increments in the capacity installed of RE assets (Saundry 2019).

To date, these policies have had a substantial effect in the primary energy produced through RE sources. For instance, RE contributions to primary energy rose from 5.3% in 2001 to 11.3% in 2017—this trend was intensified in the electricity sector where RE generation grew from 9% to 17% (US CRS 2018). Non-hydroelectric sources drove the growth, with hydro's contribution stagnating at 6–8% of the total. Thus, from 2001 to 2017 wind production grew from 7 to 254 MWh; utility scale solar from 0.6 to 53 MWh; and distributed solar from 129 MWh to 24,000 MWh (US CRS 2018). The success was so great that as of 2016 data wind and solar represent the largest component of new installed capacity added for electric generation since 2014 (US CRS 2018). The RPS play a vital role in this increment, accounting for about half of all non-hydro RE electricity deployed from 2000 to 2016 and for 21% of wind and 59% of large-scale utility solar in 2016 (Saundry 2019). Deloitte anticipates this trend to continue into the future with 96% of new net generation capacity to come from wind and solar energy sources in 2020—about 74 GW (Deloitte 2019).

The favorable investment environment and mass deployments also fueled innovations that resulted in major cost improvements for both wind and solar. From 2009 to 2017 the levelized cost of electricity (LCOE) for wind and solar photovoltaic dropped by 67% and 86%, respectively (Saundry 2019). More recent data indicate further reductions with 10% and 18% costs reductions, respectively, for the LCOE for onshore wind and utility scale solar just in the first half of 2019 (Deloitte 2019).

Stagnate demand for electricity also favored wind and solar energy industries, since even efficient gas-based electricity producers would face unfavorable economic conditions under current demand projections. Renewable energy can produce electricity profitably due to existing tax benefits and escalating efficiency improvements (US CRS 2018).

However, for the U.S. to significantly reduce its GHG emissions more policies are needed to reduce fossil fuel dependency of the transport, electricity, and industrial sectors. To reduce emissions in the transport sector, greater fuel efficiency standards will likely need to be combined with programs that enable the penetration of electric vehicles, such as additional charging infrastructure in urban centers. Current investment patterns may leave 88 of the country's 100 most populous metropolitan areas with less than 50% of the assets needed to meet the charging demand for their regions in 2025 (Nicholas et al. 2019).

Another key factor includes diversifying the electricity sector away from gas and coal to ensure electric vehicles run on non-emitting electricity. This will require technical and economical solutions to the intermittent generation of wind and solar electricity. Potential solutions include energy storage—levelized cost of storage (LCOS) has declined substantially in past years (Deloitte 2019)—where lithium ion batteries are used to store competitively priced wind and/or solar electricity and then discharged to meet demand. These solutions already exist in the form of energy storage assets that discharge electricity for 4 hours during peak time. A recent study by the National Renewable Energy Lab (NREL) indicates these solutions could help mitigate the differences in peak versus baseload demand (Denholm et al. 2019) making the grid more reliable.

3 Canada

As one of the world's large oil and gas producers, Canada holds substantial proven reserves, and the sector is an important contributor to as well as enabler of economic growth. Canada also illustrates the socioeconomic contradictions in a democratic country that relies on the export of hydrocarbons to grow as well as oil and gas to meet domestic energy demand, while remaining committed to achieving ambitious greenhouse gas (GHG) emission reductions due to public and international pressure.

On the one hand, oil and gas investors seek to develop Canada's vast resource potential to profitably meet domestic, U.S. and Asian energy demands. On the other hand, parts of civil society and some provincial governments block those investments to prevent Canada from moving further away from its GHG emissions target. In the middle, the Federal Government struggles to reconcile these contrasting views in a policy framework that secures growth and reduces GHG emissions to levels that would effectively mitigate climate change.

Furthermore, due to inadequate transport infrastructure, Canadian hydrocarbon producers have insufficient access to U.S. and Asian markets despite growing output. This is a challenge for crude oil producers who want to export to the U.S. and for gas producers seeking export markets in Asia to off-set decreasing U.S. demand for imports. Adding to these challenges is that developing Canada's oil sands—the source of output growth—is a high-cost and carbon-intensive process. As future fossil fuel demand growth concentrates in Asia, transportation costs will likely prevent Canadian producers from receiving sufficiently high prices to justify increased investments.

As a country that produced an average of 4.3 mmb/d of crude oil and 167 billion cubic meters annually (bcma) of dry natural gas in 2018, Canada has a robust production base (EIA 2019h). The country's 170 billion barrels of crude oil in established reserves (National Energy Board 2018), 2 trillion cubic meters in proved natural gas reserves, and a refining capacity of 2 mmb/d mean Canada could maintain current output levels for many years (EIA 2019h).

In 2018 Canada exported an average of 3.6 mmb/d of crude oil (Canada Energy Regulator 2019) and 80 bcma of natural gas (Natural Resources Canada 2019a). The sales are highly concentrated with over 96% of Canadian crude oil and gas exports going to the U.S. in 2018 (EIA 2019h) due to logistical links and geographic proximity. These sales valued at US $119 billion are Canada's largest source of export revenues (Cleland and Gattinger 2019). Likewise, the oil and gas sector is responsible for employing over 60,000 people nation-wide, over US $36 billion in capital expenditures, and contributing a yearly average of US $14.8 billion to the Federal and provincial governments through indirect and direct taxes as well as land sales from 2014 to 2018 (Natural Resources Canada 2019b). The employment, investment, and revenue benefits are concentrated in Western Canada's production centers—Alberta and Saskatchewan (Cleland and Gattinger 2019).

Furthermore, the oil and gas sector plays a key role in fueling Canada's energy intensive economy. Fossil fuels enable Canadians to stay warm and operate in the country's cold temperatures and connect its dispersed population across Canada's vast territory (Cleland and Gattinger 2019). For instance, 9% of electricity in Canada is produced using natural gas (Natural Resources Canada 2019b). This share is expected to rise while coal-based electricity—accounting for 9% of the total—decreases as power plants in Alberta, Saskatchewan, and Nova Scotia close or are retrofitted to function on natural gas (Environment and Climate Change Canada 2017). Similarly, 96% of the Canadian transport sector runs on fossil fuels consuming 1.1 mmb/d of oil products and 73,000 barrels of oil equivalent per day of gas in 2016 (Inter-American Development Bank 2019). While the dependency is lower, natural gas products accounted for 34% and 45% of industrial and commercial energy use, respectively, in 2016 (Inter-American Development Bank 2019). Overall, according to the Institut de l'énergie Trottier the energy industry contributes US $188 billion to GDP, representing 9.9% of the total (Langlois-Bertrand et al. 2018).

Canada's oil and gas pipeline network is insufficient to transport surplus supplies to U.S. and Asian markets. While crude oil production increased in Western Canada by 9.8% and by 8% in the first half of 2018 alone, export capacity stagnated at 2016 levels (National Energy Board 2018). This has led to peak levels of crude oil inventories and price discounts between Western Canada Select (WCS)—Canada's leading commercial heavy crude oil benchmark (Oil and Sands Magazine 2017)—and Western Texas Intermediate (WTI)—North America's leading crude oil benchmark. In fact, Alberta's processed oil inventories are double historic levels (Canada Institute 2019) and WCS-WTI price discounts were above US $21 in 2018 (National Energy Board 2018). Price discounts are normal for heavy crudes like WCS that incur transport costs to reach U.S. refineries. However, previous discounts for WCS varied between US $10 and $15 (National Energy Board 2018). The economic losses to Canadian firms intensified despite rising demand for heavy crude oil imports in the U.S. Gulf region as Venezuelan exports declined from 2014 to 2018 due to sociopolitical unrest and were finally prohibited by U.S. sanctions in 2019 (Eaton 2019).

Additionally, natural gas producers face the dual challenge of declining import demand in the U.S., while export infrastructure does not yet exist to meet rising demand for gas products in Asia. U.S. demand for natural gas imports peaked in 2007 at 131 bcma, and by 2018 declined to 82 bcma as the Shale Revolution greatly increased U.S. domestic output, enabling U.S. producers in the Appalachians to meet East Coast demand (EIA 2019f). Equally important, the absence of a liquefied natural gas (LNG) export facility in Canada means natural gas exporters lack the infrastructure to sell to the world's largest LNG importers: China, Japan, and South Korea (EIA 2019i).

To address these challenges investors planned projects to expand the existing oil and gas pipeline infrastructure. Key proposed projects include new pipelines like Keystone XL and Northern Gateway, expansions of existing assets such as the Clipper and the Trans Mountain pipelines, and new LNG terminals near Kitimat, British Columbia.

Nonetheless, many of these projects have been suspended due to low social acceptance and legal challenges rooted in environmental concerns. A contributor to project opposition is that Canada is unlikely to meet the GHG emission commitments of its Nationally Determined Contribution under the Paris Accords due to growing emissions from the transport and oil and gas sectors.

Concerns around higher GHG emissions contributed to public opposition and legal challenges against the Keystone XL (Swift 2019), Northern Gateway (Mackay and Lemiski 2019), Trans Mountain (Mackay and Lemiski 2019), and Clipper (Williams 2017) projects. Considering Canada's latest report to the United Nations Framework Convention on Climate Change (UNFCCC) estimates emissions at 722 megatons of CO_2 equivalent (MtCO2e) (Environment and Climate Change Canada 2017) and policies to achieve the 513 MtCO2e 2030 target have yet to be announced or implemented (Environment and Climate Change Canada 2017), concerns seem justified. In fact, the report shows increased energy consumption in the transport and oil and gas sectors more than off-set emission reductions in the electricity sector (Environment and Climate Change Canada 2017). Moreover, as of 2015 these two sectors account for 50% of Canada's emissions (Environment and Climate Change Canada 2017). Greater demand for internal combustion engine vehicles and oil and natural gas products led to higher GHG emissions. Although transport sector emissions are leveling out, oil and gas production gains will likely further increase emissions, since Canada's oil sands require energy and CO_2 intensive extraction mechanisms (EIA 2015).

While blocking specific oil and gas projects may limit GHG emissions, ad hoc opposition fails to address the systemic challenges of having an economy traditionally designed to respond and benefit from domestic and international demand for oil and gas products. Additionally, ad-hoc opposition reinforces concerns that the multi-billion economic contributions of the oil and gas sector will not be off-set economically to enable a transition toward less GHG emissions. For instance, achieving 50% GHG reductions from 2005 levels by 2050 could require cutting oil and gas exports by 50% and thus losing half of those export revenues as well (Cleland and Gattinger 2019). This is a concern not only for oil and gas investors but also for provincial governments who depend on these sectors to maintain their economies and workforces employed. If these legitimate issues are not addressed, provinces like Alberta and Saskatchewan will continue to challenge the Federal Government's cornerstone project to reduce emissions: the Pan-Canadian Framework on Climate Change (Cleland and Gattinger 2019).

Additional complicating factors are the environmental, social, and technical challenges of energy alternatives to oil and gas products. While most Canadians favor renewable energy alternatives such as hydro, projects continue to face opposition due to their potential impacts to wildlife (Cleland and Gattinger 2019). Moreover, although wind and solar projects have traditionally lower environmental impacts than hydro projects, effectively replacing demand for oil and gas products will require investing in massive assets that can produce the energy equivalent of millions of barrels of oil per day to fuel electric cars and meet the needs of industrial and commercial end-users. As a case in point, the Trottier report estimates that 30–50% GHG reductions from 2005 emission levels will require a total yearly electricity output of over 800 terawatt-hours by 2030 of hydro alone (Langlois-Bertrand et al. 2018). These mega projects will unquestionably have significant environmental impacts. Similarly, expanding the electric infrastructure in Canada's vast and sparsely populated territories will remain a major challenge for investors but would play an important role in facilitating electric vehicle market penetration.

Overall, Canada's future economic success will depend on its ability to effectively address these tensions within the existing political system. Likewise, external intervening variables like the international demand for Canadian oil and gas products will be key in determining the costs of more aggressive climate change measures.

4 Mexico

The case of Mexico illustrates how policies to address pressing energy security needs can also undermine existing programs to reduce GHG emissions. Investments to increase Mexico's energy supply have not kept pace with the rise in energy consumption leading to substantial import dependencies. Ineffective institutions in the hydrocarbon sector as well as rising crime, violence, and low social acceptance for mega projects are the main causes. To address these challenges the government instituted market-oriented reforms that resulted in significant upstream and RE investments.

However, the reforms will likely reinforce GHG emission growth rates underpinned by higher emissions in Mexico's energy, transport, and heavy industries. Moreover, unlike Canada, Mexico has yet to report the aggregate effect of its GHG emission reduction policies, which makes measuring progress and correcting course to meet emission reduction targets in 2030 difficult. Until more pressing problems like energy insecurity are addressed, the government will likely face limited domestic pressures to reinvigorate actions to mitigate the causes of climate change.

For over a decade Mexico's energy demand has outgrown its declining domestic production. The latest National Energy Balance indicates that from 2007 to 2017 energy production in Mexico declined on average by 3.3% annually, with 2017 experiencing the largest year-over-year decline calculated at 8.9%—energy production totaled 7000 petajoules (PJ) (Secretaria de Energia 2018). Meanwhile energy demand rose considerably, reaching 9200 PJ in 2017, from around 8000 PJ in 2007 (Secretaria de Energia 2018). This trend was reinforced in 2017, with a year-on-year increase in total energy demand of 1.2%. The overall growth is underpinned by Mexico's growing energy per-capita consumption which increased at an annual rate of 0.2% from 2007 to 2017 (Secretaria de Energia 2018). The increment is driven by growing demand in the transport and electricity sectors.

The imbalance between domestic energy demand and production has made Mexico increasingly dependent on energy imports. For example, in 2017 consumption was 31.6% higher than total energy production forcing Mexico to import 4400 PJ of energy (Secretaria de Energia 2018) to meet 47.8% of its energy demand (Secretaria de Energia 2018).

The country's highly hydrocarbon-centric demand and declining domestic production drive the import dependency. Hydrocarbons accounted for 84.8% of total primary energy consumed in 2017. Natural gas products accounted for 46.8% of the total—a large proportion compared to the U.S. and Canada—and oil products for 38% (Secretaria de Energia 2018). Yet, despite its importance to domestic energy needs crude oil production fell from the 2004 peak of 3.4 mmb/d in 2004 to less than 2 mmb/d in 2017 (Wood 2018), with a production decrease of 8.9% from 2016 to 2017; similarly, natural gas production fell by 14.7% from 2016 to 2017 (Secretaria de Energia 2018). Accordingly, imports are concentrated into these two energy sources with oil accounting for roughly 25% of total imports and natural gas for about 50% of the total (Secretaria de Energia 2018).

The main consumers of oil and gas products are the transport and industrial sectors, followed by the residential, commercial, and public sectors. Of their total sector energy consumption, oil represents 90% for transport consumers, gas and electricity 66% for industrial consumers, and 66% as well for residential, commercial, and public consumers (Secretaria de Energia 2018).

Most imports—about 85% (Secretaria de Energia 2018)—come from the U.S., due to geographic proximity to refining centers and pipeline infrastructure. A comparative disadvantage in refining capacities—due to technology and logistics—partly explains Mexico's dependence on hydrocarbon imports from the U.S. (EIA 2017). In fact, Mexico mostly produces heavy crude oil that is best suited for U.S. refineries in the Gulf of Mexico (Secretaria de Energia 2018).

Nonetheless, the monopoly on the oil and gas sector by Petroleos Mexicanos (PEMEX), the national oil company, played a greater role in creating Mexico's current oil and gas scarcity. Specifically, PEMEX had insufficient capital to invest in production due to government interference and excessive government take. During the decline PEMEX had full monopoly over oil production, but operated at a loss because the government imposed unsustainable dues and it also controlled its access to external sources of financing. For example, from 1999 to 2008 PEMEX reported net income losses since the government's take exceeded the operational surplus: transfers to the government accounted for 63% of revenue, creating a 6% net income loss after accounting for operating costs (Balza and Espinasa 2015). The dues did not vary with the oil price and PEMEX was forced to go into debt to finance investments into prospective and exiting ventures.

However, in 2006 PEMEX's access to foreign capital markets was restricted to curtail the company's growing debt (Balza and Espinasa 2015). The restriction led PEMEX to severely cut investments into efforts to expand production in existing fields and into exploration ventures (Balza and Espinasa 2015; Wood 2018). The production decline at the Cantarell field, from 2.4 mmb/d of crude oil in 2004 to 228,000 in 2015 (Balza and Espinasa 2015), due to insufficient investments is a case in point (EIA 2017).

Additionally, Mexico's unfavorable operating environment further exacerbated the country's deteriorating oil and gas production. On the one hand, rising criminality has led to substantial oil theft through attacks on transport trucks or illegal taps on the pipeline system (Montero Vieira 2016). These robberies have been increasing in past years: from 102 in 2004 to 4219 in 2014—data suggest extractions in 2014 were equivalent to 7.5 million barrels of oil, further aggravating energy scarcity (Montero Vieira 2016). At the same time, the rising insecurity and low social acceptance of mega projects like oil and gas increase the operating costs for companies like PEMEX, as more resources are needed to protect personnel and assets and to address community concerns.

The government introduced market reforms in 2013 to the hydrocarbon and electricity sectors to increase investments and also to reduce inefficiencies in the energy sector and dependency on fossil fuels through increased renewable energy production. The primary tenets of the reforms were to end the monopoly of state-owned companies on production of oil, gas, and electricity; to allow foreign and private investments into both sectors; and to create auctions where the most cost-competitive bids get the right to develop a deposit or generate electricity (Wood 2018).

The results for both sectors were quite positive. In the oil and gas sector as of January 2019 and after three official rounds of public tenders, 107 contracts with 73 companies were signed to explore and develop resources; the government already received \$1 billion in direct rents; and a discovery of 1 billion barrels of oil was made in the Zama field near Tabasco (Lynch 2019). These contracts could lead to 400,000 b/d in production increases for crude oil with \$6 billion of additional rents for the government and operated at costs below PEMEX's historical performance (Lynch 2019). Mexico's substantial shale potential—sixth in the world in gas and eighth in oil (EY 2019)—suggests that the country could benefit significantly from additional investments.

In the electricity sector, the auctions for long-term contracts of power production resulted in allocations of 4867 MW to solar and 2121 MW to wind producers (Wood 2018). In fact, the third round was so competitive that average prices of solar and wind energy were below the costs of combined cycle gas power production after accounting for carbon taxes (Wood 2018). These renewable energy assets will help decrease Mexico's reliance on hydrocarbons for its consumers.

While these reforms may indeed improve Mexico's energy security, GHG emissions will likely increase and move Mexico further away from its Nationally Determined Contribution's emission targets. Mexico's latest report (Semarnat 2018) to the United Nations Framework Convention on Climate Change (UNFCCC) indicates that GHG emissions grew annually at a 1.8% rate since 1990 and were estimated at around 670 MtCO2e for 2015 (Semarnat 2018). The greatest contributors are the same large energy consumers: the transport, energy, and construction/manufacturing sectors. These consumer groups account for 24.5%, 25.9%, and 9.1% of total emissions, respectively (Semarnat 2018). In fact, growth in emissions in the energy production sector, underpinned by gas production due to rising consumer demand for energy, drove the sector's 117% growth in GHG emissions from 8500 gigagrams of CO2e in 1990 to 85,000 in 2015 (Semarnat 2018).

The reforms will likely accelerate the GHG emission growth trend as more oil and gas is produced, economic growth intensifies, and the Mexican population consumes more energy with higher incomes. The report to the UNFCCC suggests that although the economy is getting less CO_2 intensive (Semarnat 2018), the average citizen in 2015 is emitting 18% more CO_2 than in 1990 (Semarnat 2018). For instance, economic development could accelerate the acquisition of cars for personal use in Mexico and increase GHG emissions from the transport sector—the sector already experienced an 83% increase in emissions from 1990 to 2015 (Semarnat 2018). Indeed, institutions like the Climate Action Tracker estimate that under current conditions Mexico will miss its 2030 GHG emission target of 755 MtCO2e by around 50–90 MtCO2e (Climate Action Tracker 2019).

Moreover, although Mexico developed early on a robust institutional base and ambitious GHG emissions reduction targets (Semarnat 2018), detailed plans to measure aggregate progress toward those targets have yet to follow. For example, while the overall CO2e reductions of some policies are identified as 72 MtCO2e (Semarnat 2018), and the report to the UNFCCC outlines the potential mitigation effects of policies in key sectors like transport and oil and gas (Semarnat 2018), no clear reduction path toward the 2030 target is outlined. A first step in the right direction would be to aggregate the GHG mitigation effects of all measures like Canada did, to identify progress, and to plan according to correct shortcomings.

Overall, as public pressure demands more immediate solutions to Mexico's pressing energy security challenges and ongoing violence crisis, the government will have reduced bandwidth to devote sufficient resources to address climate change. Compounding the challenge is the country's single-term president which reduces policy continuity as a new administration steps into office. Strong public support for a domestically managed oil and gas sector also represents barriers to more market-oriented reforms that may also undermine efforts to reduce GHG emissions, as investments are directed to hydrocarbons and not renewable energy sources.

5 Future Development

After the COVID-19 pandemic, economic recovery will dominate politics and policymaking for all three countries in the medium term. Given their resource endowment, energy development will continue to play an important, if diminished, role in the U.S., Canada, and Mexico. Increased sensitivity to climate concerns and public pressure will lead to increased mandates for reducing GHGs at the federal and state/provincial levels in the U.S. and Canada. Extreme weather conditions, leading to more damaging hurricanes, flooding, sea-level rise, and drought-related forest and brush fires, heighten public concerns in the U.S. In Mexico, economic growth and expanding energy access will continue to take higher priority.

Although the shale boom may be over, along with so-called American "energy dominance," the ability of this resource to surge or reduce production within a short period of time as compared to conventional production will help stabilize global oil and gas prices. Actual and potential U.S. oil and gas exports will also lead to the convergence of prices in the main consuming markets of Europe, East Asia, and North America.

The U.S. will continue to invest heavily in basic research and development and technological innovation in more cost-effective, environmentally, and climate friendly energy production and energy use, with the added impetus of competition against China to be the leader in these fields. Unlike in Europe, the commercial application of new energy technology, particularly disruptive technology, will be driven more by capital markets than by government mandates and subsidies or by incumbent energy companies whose business will be negatively impacted.

Much will depend on political developments in the U.S. and interaction among federal, state, and local authorities as they address rising public concerns over the effects of climate change and other challenges related to fossil fuel use. Government will concentrate on setting the rules of the game in American energy transition and avoid selecting technologies or funding their deployment. The private sector and investors will bear the business and financial risks of energy transition.

The advent of the Biden administration has marked the return of the U.S. to global climate negotiations and greater cooperation and coordination with international partners. There may also be opportunities to optimize new energy development by further integration of North American energy markets among the three countries with additional infrastructure connections. Whether the U.S. will take a leadership role in international energy cooperation, as it did for the 2016 Paris Climate Accords and in the preceding decades since the Arab Oil Embargo of 1973, will depend on evolving politics. Nevertheless, the policy case is clear even as U.S. relative weight in global affairs declines and the need for global cooperation to address the climate challenge, energy transition, and associated trade distortions becomes more acute. The politics will have to catch up.

Bibliography

Balza, Lenin H. and Espinasa, Ramon (2015) *Oil Sector Performance and Institutions.* Washington, DC. Inter-American Development Bank. January 2015.

Benoit, Phillipe (2019), "The U.S. Transport Sector Has Become Less Energy Efficient: Should We Care?". *Center for Strategic and International Studies*, 2019. Accessed November 2019. https://www.csis.org/analysis/us-transport-sector-has-become-less-energy-efficient-should-we-care.

Canada Energy Regulator (2019), "Crude Oil Annual Export Summary". Government of Canada. Accessed December 2019. https://neb-one.gc.ca/nrg/sttstc/crdlndptrlmprdct/stt/crdlsmmr/crdlsmmr-eng.html.

Canada Institute (2019), "Curtailing Alberta Oil: The Right Solution to the Problem?". Wilson Center. January 30, 2019. https://www.wilsoncenter.org/article/curtailing-alberta-oil-the-right-solution-to-the-problem.

Cleland, Michael and Gattinger, Monica (2019), *Canada's Energy Future in an Age of Climate Change.* Ottawa: University of Ottawa, 2019. Accessed October 30th,

2019. https://www.uottawa.ca/positive-energy/sites/www.uottawa.ca.positive-energy/files/canadas_energy_future_design_rd_web.pdf.

Climate Action Tracker (2019), "Home". Climate Action Tracker. Accessed December 15th 2019. https://climateactiontracker.org/.

CSIS (2019), "The Unconventional Oil and Gas Revolution: Why the US?". US: *Center for Strategic and International Relations*, 2019.

Deloitte (2019), *2020 renewable energy industry outlook*. US: Deloitte, 2019. Accessed November 22, 2019. https://www2.deloitte.com/us/en/pages/energy-and-resources/articles/renewable-energy-outlook.html.

Denholm, Paul, Nunemaker, Jacob, Gagnon, Pieter and Wesley, Cole (2019), *The Potential for Battery Energy Storage to Provide Peaking Capacity in the United States. Golden, CO:* National Renewable Energy Laboratory, 2019. Accessed November 22, 2019. https://www.nrel.gov/docs/fy19osti/74184.pdf.

Eaton, Colin (2019) "Canadian crude Gulf Coast exports rise as Venezuelan gap is filled: trade sources". *Reuters*. June 18, 2019. https://www.reuters.com/article/us-usa-crude-exports/canadian-crude-gulf-coast-exports-rise-as-venezuelan-gap-is-filled-trade-sources-idUSKCN1TJ2AC.

EIA (2019a) "Petroleum and other Liquids". US Energy Information Administration, Washington, DC. Accessed December 15th 2019. Available at: https://www.eia.gov/dnav/pet/hist/LeafHandler.ashx?n=pet&s=mcrfpus2&f=a.

EIA (2019b). "Natural Gas". US Energy Information Administration, Washington, DC. Accessed December 15th 2019. Available at: https://www.eia.gov/dnav/ng/hist/n9050us2a.htm.

EIA (2019c). "EIA adds new play production data to shale gas and tight oil reports". US Energy Information Administration, Washington, DC. February 15, 2019. https://www.eia.gov/todayinenergy/detail.php?id=38372.

EIA (2019d). "The U.S. leads global petroleum and natural gas production with record growth in 2018". US Energy Information Administration, Washington, DC. August 2019. https://www.eia.gov/todayinenergy/detail.php?id=40973.

EIA (2019e). "U.S. energy facts explained". US Energy Information Administration, Washington, DC. Accessed December 15th 2019. https://www.eia.gov/energyexplained/us-energy-facts/.

EIA (2019f). "Natural Gas Explained". US Energy Information Administration, Washington, DC. Accessed December 15th 2019. https://www.eia.gov/energyexplained/natural-gas/#:~:text=Natural%20gas%20is%20a%20fossil,gas%20contains%20many%20different%20compounds.&text=Natural%20gas%20also%20contains%20smaller,carbon%20dioxide%20and%20water%20vapor.

EIA (2019g). *Annual Energy Outlook 2019 with projections to 2050*. US Energy Information Administration, Washington, DC, 2019. Accessed November 22, 2019. https://www.eia.gov/outlooks/aeo/.

EIA (2019h). *Country Analysis Executive Summary: Canada*. United States: US Energy Information Administration, 2019. October 2019.

EIA (2019i). *International Energy Outlook*. US Energy Information Administration, Washington, DC. 2019.

EIA (2017). *Country Analysis Brief: Mexico*. US Energy Information Administration, Washington, DC October 2017.

EIA (2015). *Canada: International energy data and analysis*. United States: US Energy Information Administration, 2015. November 2015.

Environment and Climate Change Canada (2017) *Canada's Seventh National Communication on Climate Change and Third Biennial Report.* Gatineau: Government of Canada, 2017. Accessed October 30th, 2019. https://www.canada.ca/en/environment-climate-change/services/climate-change/greenhouse-gas-emissions/seventh-national-communication-third-biennial-report.html.

Environment and Climate Change Canada (2018), *Pan-Canadian Framework on Clean Growth and Climate Change.* Gatineau: Government of Canada, 2018. Accessed October 30th, 2019. https://www.canada.ca/en/environment-climate-change/services/climate-change/pan-canadian-framework-reports/second-annual-report.html.

EPA (2019). *Inventory of US Greenhouse Gas Emissions and Sinks.* Washington, DC: Environmental Protection Agency, 2019. Accessed November 22, 2019. https://www.epa.gov/ghgemissions/inventory-us-greenhouse-gas-emissions-and-sinks.

EY. "Mexico's Shale Potential". EY. Accessed November 2019. https://www.ey.com/Publication/vwLUAssets/ey-mexicos-shale-potential/$FILE/ey-mexicos-shale-potential.pdf

Inter-American Development Bank. "Energy Database". IADB. Accessed November 2019. https://www.iadb.org/en/dataset-energy-database.

Langlois-Bertrand, Simon, Mousseau, Normand and Beaumier, Louis (2018). *Canadian Energy Outlook 2018.* Montreal: Institut de l'énergie Trottier, 2018.

Lynch, Michael (2019). *El Futuro del Petroleo en México:Entendiendo el Valor Económico del Nuevo Modelo Energético.* Energy Policy Research Foundation. January 2019.

Mackay, Paul and Lemiski, Ryan (2019). "Status of pipelines in Canada". JWN Energy. October 2019. https://www.jwnenergy.com/article/2019/10/status-pipelines-canada/.

Montero Vieira, Jose Ignacio (2016). *El robo de combustible en México en el contexto del narcotráfico: Una vía alternativa de financiación.* Instituto Español de Estudios Estratégicos. June 2016. 2.

National Energy Board. *Canada's Energy Future 2018: An Energy Market Assessment.* Canada: National Energy Board, 2018. Accessed October 30th, 2019. https://www.cer-rec.gc.ca/nrg/ntgrtd/ftr/2018/index-eng.html.

Natural Resources Canada (2019a). "Natural Gas Facts". Government of Canada. Accessed November 2019. https://www.nrcan.gc.ca/science-data/data-analysis/energy-data-analysis/energy-facts/natural-gas-facts/20067.

Natural Resources Canada (2019b). "Energy and the Economy". Government of Canada. Accessed November 2019. https://www.nrcan.gc.ca/science-data/data-analysis/energy-data-analysis/energy-facts/energy-and-economy/20062.

Nicholas, Michael; Hall, Dale and Lutsey, Nic (2019). *Quantifying the electric vehicle charging infrastructure gap across US markets.* Washington, DC: International Council on Clean Transportation, 2019.

Oil and Sands Magazine. "Western Canadian Selected Explained". May 3, 2017. Accessed December 6, 2019. https://www.oilsandsmagazine.com/technical/western-canadian-select-wcs.

Pirog, Robert (2019) *US Oil Imports, Exports, and Energy Security.* US: Congressional Research Service, 2019. Accessed November 22, 2019. https://crsreports.congress.gov/product/pdf/IF/IF11095.

Romanieuk, Andrei, Kralovic, Paul, and Asghar, Kaleem (2018). *Competitive Analysis of Canadian LNG.* Calgary: Canadian Energy Research Institute, 2018. Accessed October 30th, 2019. https://ceri.ca/studies/competitive-analysis-of-canadian- lng.

Saundry, Peter D (2019). "Review of the United States energy system in transition". Sustainability and Society: 2019, 9:4. https://doi.org/10.1186/s13705-018-0178-8.
Secretaría de Energía (2018). *Balance Nacional de Energia: 2017*. December 2018.
Semarnat (2018) *Sexta Comunicación Nacional y Segundo Informe Bienal de Actualización ante la Convención Marco de las Naciones Unidas sobre el Cambio Climático*. Ciudad de México, México. Instituto Nacional de Ecología y Cambio Climático. 2018.
Swift, Anthony. "Nebraska Ruling Does Not Clear Path for Keystone XL". NRDC, August 28th 2019. https://www.nrdc.org/experts/anthony-swift/nebraska-ruling-does-not-clear-path-keystone-xl.
US CRS (2018),*21st Century US Energy Sources: A Primer*. Congressional Research Service, Washington, 2018. Accessed November 22, 2019. https://crsreports.congress.gov/product/pdf/R/R44854.
Williams, Nia (2017) "U.S. issues permit to expand Enbridge cross-border oil pipeline". *Reuters*. October 16, 2017. https://www.reuters.com/article/us-enbridge-inc-pipeline-regulations/u-s-issues-permit-to-expand-enbridge-cross-border-oil-pipeline-idUSKBN1CL2UE.
Wood, Duncan (ed.) (2018) *La Nueva Reforma Energetica de Mexico*. Washington, DC. Wilson Center; Mexico Institute. October 2018.

CHAPTER 36

Energy and the Economy in Europe

Manfred Hafner and Pier Paolo Raimondi

1 Introduction

Europe is one of the most important components of the world's economic and energy systems, but the European energy landscape is characterized by great heterogeneity due to important differences in terms of population, economy and energy resources of individual countries. This chapter presents an overview of the energy characteristics of geographical Europe[1] (not just the European Union [EU]). It then focuses in particular on the historical evolution of the European Union energy policy and energy mix and their interaction with the economy. It also discusses the energy evolution in some selected European

[1]According the UN DESA (2019), Europe includes Albania, Andorra, Austria, Belarus, Belgium, Bosnia and Herzegovina, Bulgaria, Channel Islands, Croatia, Czechia, Denmark, Estonia, Faroe Islands, Finland, France, Gibraltar, Germany, Greece, Holy See, Hungary, Iceland, Ireland, Isle of Man, Italy, Latvia, Liechtenstein, Lithuania, Luxemburg, Malta, Moldova, Monaco, Montenegro, the Netherlands, North Macedonia, Norway, Poland, Portugal, Romania, Russian Federation, San Marino, Serbia, Slovakia, Slovenia, Spain, Sweden, Switzerland, Ukraine and the United Kingdom.

M. Hafner (✉)
SciencesPo—Paris School of International Affairs, Paris, France

Johns Hopkins University SAIS Europe, Bologna, Italy

Fondazione Eni Enrico Mattei (FEEM), Milan, Italy
e-mail: manfred.hafner@sciencespo.fr

P. P. Raimondi
Fondazione Eni Enrico Mattei (FEEM), Milan, Italy

Istituto Affari Internazionali (IAI), Rome, Italy

Catholic University of Milan, Milan, Italy

M. Hafner, G. Luciani (eds.), *The Palgrave Handbook of International Energy Economics*, https://doi.org/10.1007/978-3-030-86884-0_36

countries (the United Kingdom [UK], Italy, France, Germany and Poland), taking into account the different resource bases, policy pathways and socio-economic dimensions. Lastly, the chapter presents the "European Green Deal", which aims at reaching carbon-neutrality by 2050. To achieve the climate-neutrality goal, substantial transformation of the EU economy is required, which comes with internal and external frictions.

2 The Heterogeneity of Europe's Energy Sector

Europe is one of the largest economic blocs in the world, with a total population of about 747 million inhabitants in 48 countries (UN DESA 2019). In 2019, the European Union (EU-28) had a population of 513.5 million people,[2] which accounts for 6.9% of total world population, and a GDP[3] of €16.6 trillion, representing 20% of the global economy. This can be compared with the US, which represents about 4% of world's population with 331 million citizens and 22% of world's GDP with a GDP of $18.3 trillion, and China, which represents 19% of world's population with 1.4 billion people and 14% of world's GDP with a GDP of $11.5 trillion.

The European energy landscape by country is characterized by great heterogeneity due to differences in terms of population, economy and energy resources (Table 36.1).

The diversity is reflected also in the energy system, policies and resources of each country. Indeed, there is great disparity across European countries in the energy mix related to both the structure of consumption and of production. The heterogeneity of the energy mix can be largely explained by the availability of different energy sources by country, such as coal, gas, oil, hydropower and other renewable energy potential, as well as differing policies in favor or against specific energy sources (fossil fuels, nuclear or renewables). This heterogeneous energy mix is well-represented in the following figures that show electricity production and total primary energy supply (TPES) in European countries by source in 2019 (Table 36.2).

Fossil fuels still dominate the energy system, with some diversity across the continent (Figs. 36.1 and 36.2). Natural gas is relevant in Northwestern European countries and Italy, due to past domestic production which led to the establishment of a well-developed network of pipelines. Coal still plays an essential role in the energy systems of Central and Eastern European countries (Germany, the Czech Republic and Poland). Other countries, notably France, Norway, Sweden and Switzerland, have a lower carbon energy mix mainly thanks to nuclear and hydro.

[2] Following Brexit in 2020, the EU-27 had a population of 447.7 million inhabitants and a GDP of €13.7 trillion.

[3] Constant 2010 US$.

Table 36.1 Key socio-economic and energy indicators of selected European countries

	Population in 2019 (million)	*GDP in 2019 (constant 2010 US$, billion)*	*GDP per capita in 2019 (constant 2010 US$)*	*Energy consumption per capita in 2019 (toe per capita)*	*Energy intensity in 2017 (koe/1000 US$ (2010 PPP))*	*Carbon intensity in 2016 (kg/1000 2010 US$ of GDP)*
Austria	8.9	449	50,654	4.1	90	144
Belgium	11.5	546	47,540	5.7	120	186
Bulgaria	7.0	63	9026	2.6	150	803
Croatia	4.1	67	16,454	2	100	291
Czech Republic	10.6	254	23,833	3.9	130	451
Finland	5.5	271	49,241	4.8	150	190
France	65.1	2972	44,317	3.6	100	110
Germany	83.5	3959	47,628	3.8	90	198
Hungary	9.6	170	17,466	2.5	110	301
Ireland	4.8	393	79,703	3.3	40	139
Italy	60.5	2147	35,613	2.5	70	157
Netherlands	17.0	965	55,689	5	90	194
Norway	5.3	495	92,556	8	90	104
Poland	37.9	660	17,386	2.7	100	533
Portugal	10.2	252	24,590	2.5	80	201
Romania	19.3	234	12,131	1.7	80	378
Slovakia	5.4	114	21,039	2.9	110	314
Slovenia	2.0	56	27,152	3.3	110	266
Spain	46.7	1570	33,349	2.9	80	171
Sweden	10.0	596	57,975	5.4	110	82
Switzerland	8.5	681	79,409	3.2	50	56
Turkey	83.4	1251	14,998	1.9	80	337
UK	67.5	2920	43,668	2.8	70	157
EU-28	513.5	16,604	37,104	3.3	70	217
EU-27	446	13,684	30,681	3.4	70	230

Until 31.01.2020, the EU was composed of 28 countries, including Austria, Belgium, Bulgaria, Croatia, Cyprus, the Czech Republic, Denmark, Estonia, Finland, France, Germany, Greece, Hungary, Ireland, Italy, Latvia, Lithuania, Luxemburg, Malta, the Netherlands, Poland, Portugal, Romania, Slovak Republic, Slovenia, Spain, Sweden and the United Kingdom. On 31.01.2020, the United Kingdom left the EU which is now EU-27

Sources: Authors' elaboration on UNDESA, World Bank, BP and IEA

Note: EU-28 includes the United Kingdom which left the EU on 31.01.2020; after 31.01.2020, the EU is EU-27; EU energy intensity related to 2015; EU's energy consumption per capita related to 2017

3 Historical Evolution of the EU Energy Policy Framework

Notwithstanding some disparities, energy intensity[4] and carbon intensity[5] have decreased across Europe over the last decades. Between 1990 and 2017, a relative decoupling of gross inland energy consumption from economic growth

[4] Energy intensity is defined as the ratio between the primary energy consumption and gross domestic product (GDP) calculated for a calendar year.

[5] Carbon intensity is defined as the ratio between carbon emission and gross domestic product (GDP).

Table 36.2 Total electricity production and TPES of selected European countries in 2019

	Electricity production (TWh)	*TPES (ktoe)*
Austria	74.2	32.8
Belgium	93.5	55.2
Bulgaria	44.2	19.1
Croatia	12.7	8
Czech Republic	87	43.6
Finland	68.7	32
France	570.8	246.3
Germany	618	303.6
Hungary	34.1	25.6
Ireland	30.3	13.4
Italy	291.7	144.3
Netherlands	121.3	70.7
Norway	134.6	23.7
Poland	163.4	102.6
Portugal	53.1	21.3
Romania	60.1	33.8
Slovakia	27.8	16.3
Slovenia	16.1	6.8
Spain	274.2	121.1
Sweden	168.4	49.2
Switzerland	73.6	24.9
Turkey	304.2	151.8
United Kingdom	323.7	169.5
EU-28	3243.6	1599.7
EU-27	2919.9	1430.2

Source: Authors' elaboration on IEA data

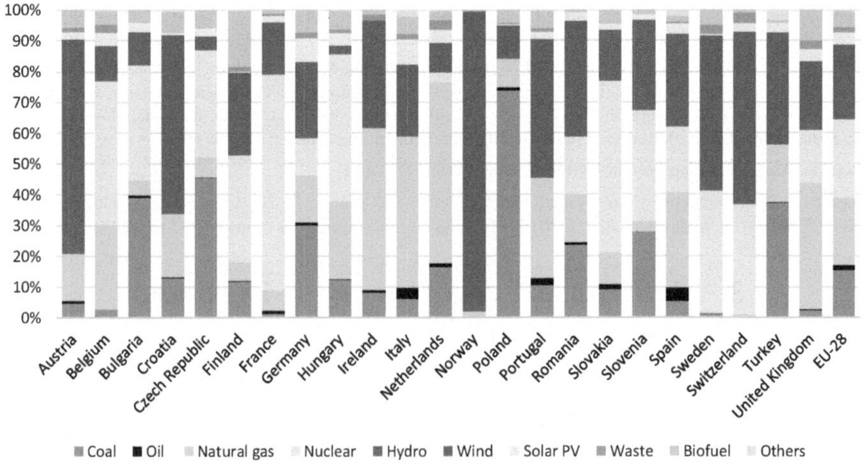

Fig. 36.1 Production share of electricity of key European countries by source, 2019. (Source: Authors' elaboration on IEA data, https://www.iea.org/data-and-statistics?country=WORLD&fuel=Energy%20supply&indicator=ElecGenByFuel)

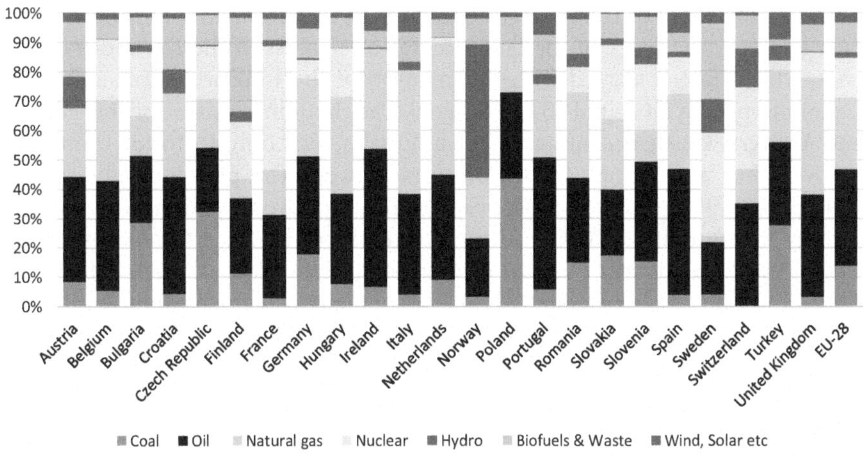

Fig. 36.2 Share of total primary energy supply (TPES) of key European countries by source, 2019. (Source: Authors' elaboration on IEA data, https://www.iea.org/data-and-statistics?country=EU28&fuel=Energy%20supply&indicator=Total%20primary%20energy%20supply%20(TPES)%20by%20source. Note: latest data available for Bulgaria, Croatia and Romania are related to 2018)

occurred in the European Union (EU): while gross inland energy consumption in 2017 was at the same level as in 1990, GDP (measured in 2010 constant prices) grew by 1.7% per year, on average. As a consequence, energy intensity in the EU fell by 37% (1.7% per year on average) during this period (EEA 2019). The improvement of energy intensity in Europe is the result of technological developments, changes in the structure of the economy and energy policies. The change in the structure of the economy refers in particular to the general shift from industry (especially high energy-intensity productions such as iron and steel) toward a service-based economy. Also, delocalization of industrial production outside of Europe plays an important role in reducing energy and carbon intensity, shifting the related energy consumption and carbon emissions to third countries (*carbon leakage*). Currently, the measurement of carbon emissions is based on a production-based approach, which calculates the CO_2 produced within a country's borders and does not fairly represent the reality of carbon intensity. A consumption-based approach, which calculates the emissions related to the production and supply of the goods and services consumed in the concerned country, would be much preferable.

One of the main reasons of energy heterogeneity between EU countries is that energy is a shared competence between Member States and European institutions. For several decades, energy issues remained of purely national competence. Indeed, energy has always been considered a strategic issue; thus, member countries were unwilling to give up any of their sovereignty in this area, and EU energy systems were shaped by national policies. For decades, energy policies struggled between being considered as a national prerogative versus a useful tool of European integration. In the aftermath of World War II, energy was at the heart of the first integration process of the European countries, which indeed started with the creation of the European Coal and Steel Community[6] (ECSC) in 1951. The goal was the joint control of the French and Western German coal and steel industries, not only to foster economic recovery but also to prevent future wars between the two countries and in Europe. In 1957, the same European countries created the European Atomic Energy Community (EAEC) in the aftermath of the Suez Canal crisis. The EAEC was created with the goal of enhancing the uptake of nuclear technology in the European continent while being a main instrument of political integration. Among the three original treaties, EURATOM is the only one still in force, granting the European Commission important responsibilities and powers concerning the nuclear fuel cycle. Despite these positive and coordinated efforts to shape a common energy policy among some European countries, in the 1960s national policies prevailed over further integration. The 1973 oil crisis shocked the European importing countries, showing their vulnerability to external suppliers. The crisis substantially shaped the concept of energy security in the mind of Europeans, as well as globally. Security of supply started to be considered a key theme for European countries, becoming a pillar of the European energy policy.

After the 1973 oil crisis, European countries addressed energy security issues, mostly through national strategies, through development and increase of nuclear energy, domestic reserves and energy conservation policies. At the European Community (the predecessor entity to the European Union) level, there was an attempt to elaborate a common energy policy strategy with the Council Resolution of 17 September 1974.[7] Hence, for almost three decades energy policy focused on issues related to security of supply, for example, mandating the creation of minimum strategic stocks for crude oil and products, but remained mainly dominated by national policies. Indeed, the energy mix was, and still largely is, a prerogative of Member States.

It is only with the conclusion of the Lisbon Treaty in 2005 that a proper common energy policy was defined. Indeed, the Treaty lays down the three pillars, which the EU's energy policy is based on: security of supply, competitiveness (affordable prices) and sustainability (clean energy). These three goals appear to be contradictory, especially in the short term, but are seen as converging in the longer term.

The second pillar of the EU energy policy (competitiveness) had begun to be discussed already in the 1980s and 1990s. Due to the lack of legitimation for a common energy policy at that time, the European institutions leveraged the economic objectives of the EU internal market (liberalization and competitiveness), for which they had a mandate, and applied them to the energy sphere.

[6] Composed of Belgium, France, Italy, Luxemburg, the Netherlands and West Germany.

[7] "Council Resolution concerning a new energy policy strategy for the Community" https://eur-lex.europa.eu/legal-content/EN/TXT/PDF/?uri=CELEX:31975Y0709(01)&from=EN.

Indeed, energy markets in the European countries were traditionally dominated by large vertically integrated companies, national monopolies, and characterized by the strong role of the State. The legal basis of the European Commission's drive to liberalize and foster competition in the energy sector came from the 1957 Treaty of Rome, the 1987 Single European Act, and a later stage, the 1995 Green Paper. European institutions used existing legal frameworks to foster energy competition and liberalization. At the end of the 1990s, two key European directives were approved concerning the electricity and gas markets, in 1996 and 1998, respectively. These directives are driven mostly by economic considerations to make the energy sector more cost-efficient and provide affordable prices to consumers through the introduction of competition between national players. This policy was inspired by the British experience under the government of Margaret Thatcher.

Finally, the third pillar—sustainability—started to appear in the 1990s following the 1992 "Earth Summit" in Rio de Janeiro and the 1997 Kyoto Protocol. Since then, the fight against climate change has gained more and more relevance as the EU set ambitious energy and climate targets for the coming decades. In 2009, the EU launched its 2020 objectives in the "*Green Package—A European strategy for Sustainable, Competitive and Secure Energy*", setting three targets, commonly known as "20-20-20" by 2020, which consist in achieving a 20% greenhouse gas (GHG) emission reduction compared to 1990, 20% market share of renewable energy compared to primary energy demand and 20% energy efficiency compared to a baseline scenario (EUROPA 2006).

The EU Emissions Trading System (ETS) is the cornerstone of Europe's climate policy (see also Chap. 23). Its goal is to tackle climate change reducing greenhouse gas emissions cost-effectively. It was the result of the 1997 Kyoto Protocol, but officially started operating in 2005. It operates in phases and covers all EU countries plus Iceland, Liechtenstein and Norway. It is the largest example of emissions trading in operation, regulating emissions over 11,000 heavy energy-intensive installations as well as for airlines. It covers around 25% of the EU's greenhouse gas emissions. It is based on the "cap and trade" principle, meaning that a "cap" is set on the total amount of certain greenhouse gases that can be emitted by installations covered by the system. The EU creates allowances, each giving the holder the right to emit GHGs equivalent to the global warming potential of 1 ton of CO_2. The cap is designed to decrease annually over time so that total emissions fall in line with the desired objective. Within the cap, companies in selected sectors annually obtain emission allowances, through auctioning or free allocation (reducing the risk of carbon leakage). If a participant has insufficient allowances then it must either take measures to reduce its emissions or buy more allowances on the market. Participants can acquire allowances at auction or from each other. Ideally, as scarcity increases carbon prices are expected to rise correspondingly, supporting more decarbonization options.

Given the relevance of climate change issues and GHG emissions, in 2011 the European Council for the first time mentioned the objective to reduce emissions by 80–95% by 2050 compared to 1990 levels. In 2014, the EU proposed the 2030 Climate and Energy Framework. Under this framework, the European Union committed itself to (a) reduce its GHG emissions by 40% compared to 1990 levels; (b) increase the share of renewable energies in final energy consumption to at least 27% by 2030 and (c) increase the energy efficiency of its economy by 27% compared to a 2007 baseline (EC EUROPA 2014). A further effort was announced in the strategic long-term vision of the Commission in November 2018 called "A Clean Planet for all—A European strategic long-term vision for a prosperous, modern, competitive and climate neutral economy" (EC EUROPA 2018). The aim of this document was to create a prosperous, modern, competitive and climate-neutral economy by 2050. In 2019 and in line with the EU's 2050 long-term strategy, the EU presented also a comprehensive update of its energy policy framework to facilitate the transition away from fossil fuels toward cleaner energy and to deliver on its Paris Agreement commitments for reducing GHG emissions. This new framework is called the "*Clean energy for all Europeans package*", consisting of eight legislative acts (EC EUROPA 2019). In these documents, the EC reconsidered and extended the Renewable Energy Directive, with a binding EU-level target to increase the share of renewable energy in the energy mix to at least 32% by 2030, and updated the Energy Efficiency Directive, with an indicative target at EU level of reduced energy consumption by least 32.5% by 2030 (Consilium 2014). All these targets illustrate the strong political commitment to tackle climate change and the relevance of climate issues on the European energy agenda.

4 Historical Evolution of the EU Energy Mix

Over the last century, the EU energy supply structure underwent a great transformation. Initially, coal was replaced by oil and—later—by gas. In recent years there have been important policy driven investments in the EU in renewable energy sources (RES) which reached a share of 18.0% in gross final energy consumption in 2018.

After World War II, the supremacy of coal in Europe started to decline in favor of oil, thanks to the fast expansion of transport and consumption of goods and services. Nevertheless, coal remained a pivotal source despite its declining share. In 1990, coal provided for almost 41% of the gross energy consumption in the EU-28 Member States and 39% of power generation; while in 2019 it provided only 16% of EU energy consumption and about 24% of the power generation mix. Coal maintained its role especially in countries with significant domestic coal reserves, for example, Germany, Poland, the Czech Republic and other Eastern European countries. In these countries, coal currently accounts for a large share of electricity production. In the Czech

Republic, Bulgaria, Greece and Germany, coal represents a share in power generation of around 40%; in Poland it reaches 80%.

The European natural gas industry effectively began with the discovery of the giant Groningen gas field in the Netherlands in 1959, and later in the 1970s and 1980s (after the first and second oil price shock) with exploration and production activities in the North Sea. Europe's natural gas industry was strongly influenced by the Dutch commercial framework based on oil price indexation and "take-or-pay" contracts.[8] Today's gas demand is mainly concentrated in Northwestern Europe plus Italy and Spain.

Natural gas in the EU witnessed incredible growth between 1990 and 2008. Its market share increased rapidly from less than 10% of TPES in the early 1970s to about 24% in 2009 replacing the use of oil and to a lesser extent coal (it remained stable thereafter). While in the 1970s and 1980s gas demand growth was mainly due to the industrial, commercial and residential sectors, in the 1990s and 2000s the strong growth was mainly driven by power generation due to the development of combined cycle gas turbines (CCGTs). Despite some disparities between countries, natural gas became the fuel of choice for power generation in most European markets. The economic crisis of 2009 significantly halted the growth of gas demand in Europe, which was already slowing down due to its increasingly high prices (because of oil price indexation—see Chap. 20) during the second half of the 2000–2010 decade. In the post-2009 economic context, relatively expensive gas found itself squeezed in the power generation sector between on the one hand strong RES development and, on the other hand, cheap coal combined with a low CO_2 price in the EU ETS, due to the economic crisis.

Indeed, carbon prices fell from 15–17 €/ton of CO_2 in the late second phase of EU ETS (2008–2012) to 4–8 €/ton of CO_2 in its third phase (2013–2020). Only recently, due to strengthened EU regulation and an improved economy, the CO_2 prices soared, hitting an 11-year record in July 2019 (29 €/ton), and then stabilized around 25 €/ton before the coronavirus outbreak in 2020.

4.1 *The Role of Energy Imports and Security Concerns*

The sources of energy supply to each European country vary by country and fuel. In 2018, the production of primary energy in the EU-27[9] totaled 635 million tons of oil equivalent (Mtoe), following constant decline (-9.2%) compared to a decade earlier. The general downward development of domestic

[8] Take-or-pay contracts were created by the Dutch natural gas industry in the 1960s following the discovery of major gas resources in the Netherlands. Commonly, they are used in long-term supply contracts, typically natural gas. They establish that if the buyer is unwilling or unable to "take" the volumes specified in the contract, he must "pay" anyway. The unused gas may normally be taken at a later date. Under these contracts, the buyer bears the market and volume risks, while the seller bears the price risks. Commonly, they are used in long-term natural gas supply contracts.

[9] The EU-27 refers to the EU-28 aggregate with the exclusion of the United Kingdom.

production highlights the need to import significant volumes of energy to meet European gross inland energy consumption (1675 Mtoe in 2017). Therefore, in 2017 the EU produced around 45% of its own energy, while 55% was imported. The EU mainly depends on Russia for imports of crude oil, natural gas and solid fuels, followed by Norway for crude oil and natural gas. Other suppliers are Iraq and Kazakhstan for oil and Algeria and Qatar for natural gas. In the last decades, domestic energy production in the Netherlands, Norway and other countries helped to balance the increasing import dependency elsewhere in the EU.

EU-28 dependency on energy imports increased from 44% of TPES in 1990 to 55% by 2018 (EUROSTAT 2020). The dependency rate is different for each country, but all EU Member States are net importers of energy since 2013 (Fig. 36.3).

Looking in more detail, in 2018 the highest dependency of the EU-27 was recorded for crude oil (94.6%) and for natural gas (83.2%), while the EU-27 was dependent on solid fossil fuels imports for 43.6% (EC EUROPA 2020a).

During the 2020s, the import dependency rate is expected to further increase due to the combination of depletion of domestic production of fossil fuels and implementation of climate policies. Some Member States announced plans for the phasing-out of coal (Italy) and nuclear (Germany) already during the 2020s. Such climate policies will inevitably increase imports especially of natural gas, which is considered a bridge fuel for the energy transition. This trend is moreover enhanced also by the decision of the Dutch government to close the Groeningen gas field, due to social acceptance issues.

High natural gas dependency is often perceived as a security concern. In Europe, the high levels of Russian gas imports have always been considered a

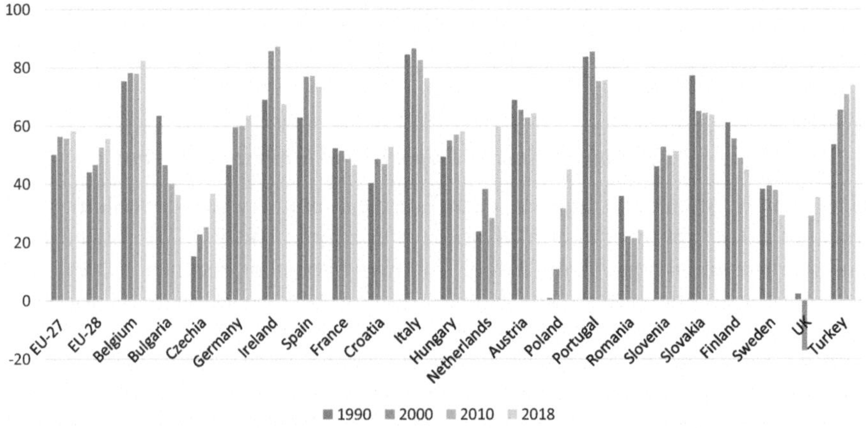

Fig. 36.3 Import dependency rate in 1990, 2000, 2010 and 2018 (%). (Source: Authors' elaboration on EUROSTAT data (nrg_ind_id). Note: EU-28 (2013–2020); EU-27 (from 2020))

Table 36.3 Main origin of primary energy imports, EU-28, 2009–2019 (% of extra EU-28 imports)

	2009	*2010*	*2011*	*2012*	*2013*	*2014*	*2015*	*2016*	*2017*	*2018*	*2019*
Hard coal (based on tonnes)											
Russia	22.9	22.4	21.9	20.2	23.9	25.1	26.4	28.7	35.4	39.5	43.5
USA	13.0	15.3	16.6	20.7	18.5	17.0	12.4	11.9	14.8	17.3	16.8
Australia	7.0	9.6	8.2	8.0	8.8	7.5	11.1	15.3	10.8	11.0	13.1
Colombia	15.1	15.4	18.6	19.1	16.4	17.0	19.3	18.7	15.9	12.6	7.6
S. Africa	15.5	9.6	8.6	7.4	7.1	9.1	7.7	5.1	4.8	2.7	2.7
Canada	1.6	1.9	2.3	1.9	2.1	3.1	1.6	2.3	2.4	2.4	2.2
Kazakhstan	0.2	0.2	0.3	0.3	0.3	0.7	0.5	0.6	0.6	0.9	2.1
Indonesia	7.1	5.5	5.5	5.4	3.9	4.3	4.2	3.2	3.3	3.5	2.1
Mozambique	0.0	0.0	0.1	0.0	0.2	0.3	0.5	0.7	1.2	1.6	1.5
Others	17.6	20.1	17.8	16.9	18.8	15.8	16.2	13.6	10.9	8.4	8.5
Crude oil (based on tonnes)											
Russia	33.7	34.7	35.1	33.9	34.5	31.4	29.7	32.4	30.7	29.6	26.8
Iraq	3.9	3.3	3.7	4.3	3.8	4.8	7.8	8.5	8.4	8.6	8.9
Nigeria	4.1	3.8	5.6	7.2	7.2	8.3	7.7	5.2	5.8	7.0	7.8
Saudi Arabia	5.8	6.0	8.3	9.1	8.7	9.0	7.9	7.7	6.5	7.4	7.7
Kazakhstan	5.4	5.6	5.9	5.3	6.0	6.7	6.8	7.0	7.6	7.1	7.3
Norway	9.5	7.7	7.2	6.8	8.1	9.2	8.4	7.9	7.7	7.2	6.9
Libya	8.8	9.8	2.7	7.9	5.4	3.3	2.5	2.2	4.8	6.1	6.2
USA	0.0	0.0	0.0	0.0	0.0	0.0	0.2	0.6	0.9	2.4	5.2
UK	4.9	5.6	4.5	4.4	4.2	4.2	4.0	4.1	4.1	3.9	4.9
Azerbaijan	4.1	4.5	5.1	4.0	5.0	4.6	5.3	4.6	4.6	4.6	4.5
Others	19.7	19.0	21.8	17.0	17.0	18.5	19.9	19.9	18.8	16.3	13.8
Natural gas (based on terajoule (gross calorific value—GCV))											
Russia	26.9	26.3	27.9	28.4	33.5	30.5	30.8	36.2	34.5	34.4	34.3
Norway	18.5	17.2	17.1	19.4	17.9	19.9	19.8	15.8	15.4	14.9	13.2
Qatar	6.2	9.2	8.8	7.0	6.2	5.5	6.1	5.5	6.8	7.5	8.3
Algeria	14.8	14.5	13.4	13.3	12.5	12.5	10.9	13.5	11.3	11.1	7.7
Nigeria	3.9	6.5	6.5	5.1	2.8	2.3	3.2	3.6	4.4	4.6	5.3
USA	0.0	0.0	0.0	0.0	0.0	0.0	0.0	0.1	0.8	1.1	4.8
UK	2.5	2.8	3.2	2.6	2.3	2.4	3.1	2.3	2.5	1.9	2.1
Trinidad and Tobago	2.7	1.7	1.7	1.4	1.2	1.3	0.8	0.4	0.4	1.1	1.9
Others	24.3	21.8	21.4	22.9	23.7	25.7	25.4	22.5	23.9	23.4	22.4

Source: EUROSTAT, https://ec.europa.eu/eurostat/statistics-explained/index.php?title=File:Main_origin_of_primary_energy_imports,_EU-28,_2007-2017_(%25_of_extra_EU-28_imports).png

potential threat to Europe's energy security. Remarkably, Russia accounts for the largest import volumes not only of natural gas but also of crude oil and coal (Table 36.3) where no security concerns are generally voiced. This is due to the global nature of the market for oil and coal, while gas remains mainly a regional market which is dependent on existing import infrastructure (in the case of Russia-EU gas trade: mainly pipelines).

However, natural gas markets are also becoming more and more globalized, driven by increasing availability of liquefied natural gas (LNG), which is much more flexible than pipelines. The impressive growth of unconventional shale gas production in the US has allowed the country to become an LNG exporter,

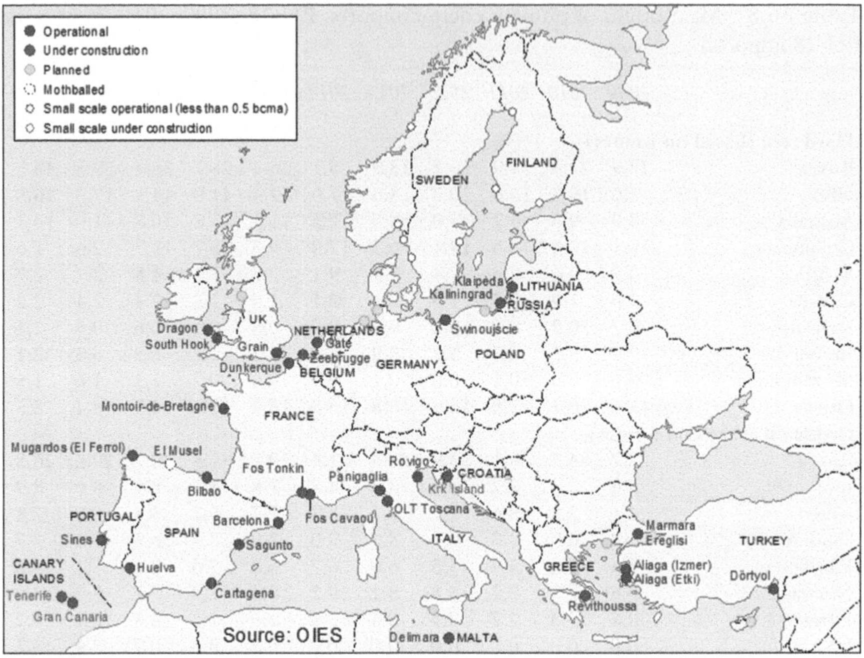

Map 36.1 LNG import terminals in the EU. (Source: K. Yafimava (2020), OIES)

promoting flexibility and diversification of the natural gas market. Thus, Europe has become a battleground between LNG (from US and others) and Russian pipeline gas. LNG allows those countries strongly dependent on a single pipeline supplier—notably Poland, Eastern European and the Baltic countries—to improve their supply security and, at the same time, enhance market competition. As of 2020, in Europe there are 25 large-scale LNG import terminals (Map 36.1) with total regasification capacity of 158 million tons per annum (Mtpa)—or 215 bcma. Theoretically, that capacity could enable LNG to meet around 45% of EU gas demand. However, historically, the average level of utilization of these terminals has been very low; during 2012–2017 it was at just around 20%. Over the last few years LNG deliveries to Europe have strongly grown, driven by the increased availability of competitively priced gas in global LNG markets. In 2019 the average terminal utilization rate reached 48%, with record high volume of LNG imports of 104 bcm (Yafimava 2020).

Import dependency also causes exposure to oil prices volatility. In 2018, the EU "import bill" was estimated to be €330 billion, which corresponds to 2% of EU's GDP (EC EUROPA 2020b). The volatility of oil prices affects the size of the "import bill", which can enlarge considerably when oil prices increase. Oil accounts for 70% of the total EU energy imports and natural gas 17%. The vulnerability to oil price volatility became a pressing issue in the 1970s following the two oil crises of 1973 and 1979. The oil price shock had important

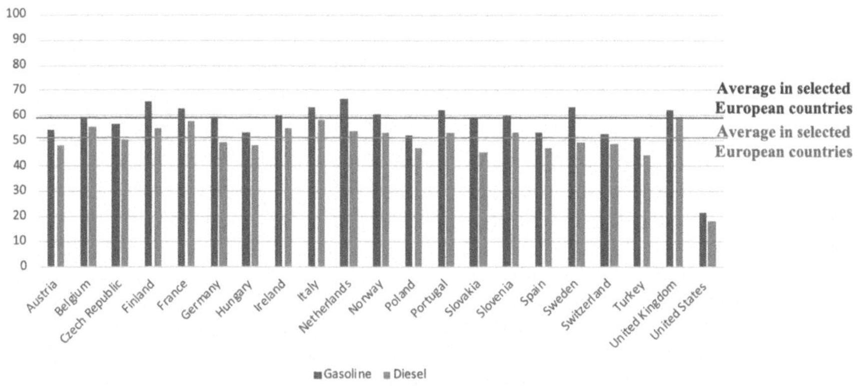

Fig. 36.4 Percentage of taxes on unleaded gasoline and automotive diesel for non-commercial purposes in selected European countries and the US, 4Q 2018. (Source: Authors' elaboration on IEA Energy Prices and Taxes (2019))

effects for the European energy sector, notably the push for improvement of energy conservation in various industries, notably the car industry, which was required to improve fuel efficiency. Due to the increase of oil prices and subsequent economic stagflation, governments relied on increased taxation on transport fuel, which has low short-term demand elasticity. However, a distortion arose from the structure of taxation on fuel for transport: diesel (mainly used at that time for heavy duty vehicles) was generally taxed at a lower rate than gasoline (mainly used for passenger cars) in most of the European countries. This disparity (coupled with improvement on diesel engine technology) led over the last three decades to a significant increase in the share of diesel vehicles (the so-called *dieselization*). Diesel vehicles now account for nearly 40% of the cars on the road. Since the 1970s, the price at the pump is driven to a large degree by tariffs and taxes. On average, over half the cost of fuel at the pump represents taxes. It is interesting to notice the high tax rate of gasoline and diesel in European countries compared to the US (Fig. 36.4). Fuels taxes contribute substantially to Member States' revenues, on average some 7% (FuelsEurope 2019).

5 Case Studies on Selected National Pathways

As mentioned, Europe's energy supply has undergone profound transformation throughout the last decades. This transformation has occurred at a different scale and pace in each country according to political preference and availability of energy sources. Moreover, individual European countries decided to pursue different policies taking into account the energy trilemma (competitiveness, security and sustainability) depending on the time period and national characteristics. This trend is well-illustrated by five case studies: the United Kingdom, Italy, France, Germany and Poland, which underwent transformations at different paces and implemented different policies.

5.1 United Kingdom

Historically, coal mining has been the backbone of the British energy sector since the Industrial Revolution. However, coal consumption has been declining in the UK since it peaked in 1956. In that year, the UK enacted the Clean Air Act, prompted by the great London smog of 1952. With coal's role diminishing, oil and gas increased their relevance in the British energy mix. The turning point was the oil price increases of 1973 which created the economic conditions to start exploration and production activities in the North Sea. Indeed, the combination of high oil prices and availability of new technologies made the operations in that region commercially feasible. Moreover, exploration in most of the Organization of Petroleum Exporting Countries (OPEC) countries was foreclosed because of ramping nationalizations in OPEC countries, so companies redirected their exploration spending, when possible, to the industrial countries of the Western world, for example Canada, Gulf of Mexico, Alaska and the North Sea (Yergin 2009). The British and Norwegian oil and gas sectors of the North Sea thus witnessed rapid development after the 1973 oil crisis.

Due to the different sizes of their population and economy, the development of oil and natural gas sector in Norway and the UK took diverging paths. The UK developed its oil and gas offshore reserves at a fast pace (Fig. 36.5), in order to meet its important energy needs due to its high population (56 million inhabitants in 1980) and size of the economy. This resulted in a fast depletion rate of its reserves. In contrast, Norway developed its North Sea resources at a slower pace (Fig. 36.6), pursuing thus a more sustainable exploitation thanks also to its small population (4 million inhabitants in 1980, less than a tenth of the British population) and thus smaller energy needs (Table 36.4).

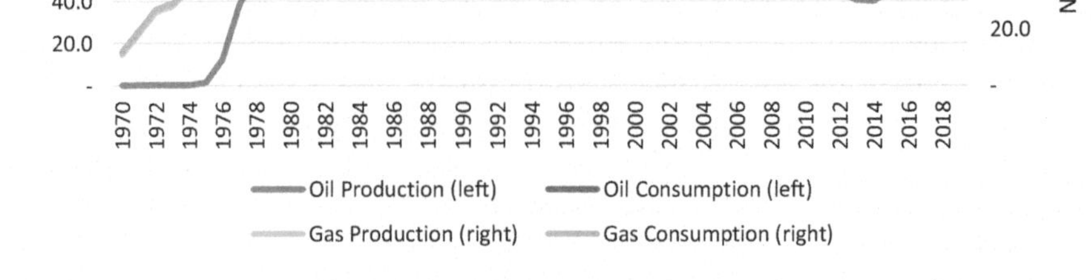

Fig. 36.5 UK's oil and gas production and consumption, 1970–2019. (Source: Authors' elaboration on BP Statistical Review of Energy all data 1965–2019)

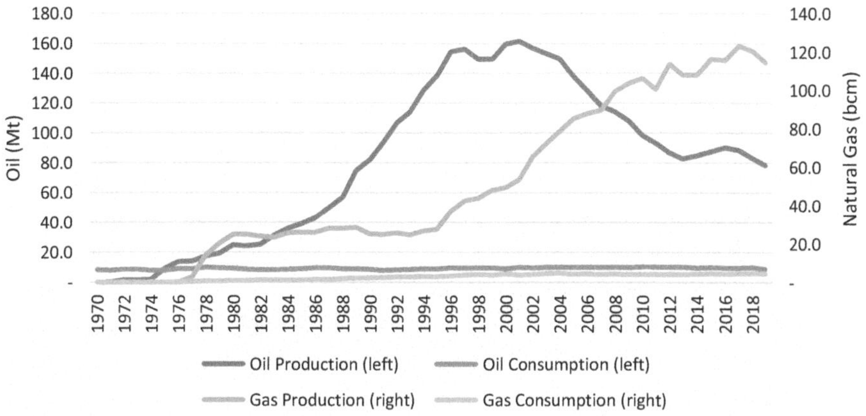

Fig. 36.6 Norway's oil and gas production and consumption, 1970–2019. (Source: Authors' elaboration on BP Statistical Review of Energy all data 1965–2019)

Table 36.4 Norway and United Kingdom population, 1960–2018 (million people)

	1960	*1970*	*1980*	*1990*	*2000*	*2010*	*2018*
Norway	3.5	3.8	4.0	4.2	4.5	4.9	5.3
United Kingdom	52.4	55.6	56.3	57.2	58.8	62.7	66.5

Source: World Bank data

The UK became self-sufficient in oil and a net oil exporter in 1981. However, oil exports peaked in 1985 and production in 1999. A similar trajectory occurred for gas production. The UK discovered and developed vast gas reserves offshore, becoming a net exporter in 1997, but production began to decline in 2000. The fast decline in oil and gas production turned the country into a net importer of oil and gas in 2004, resulting in the UK importing more than 50% of the gas needed to meet domestic demand via pipeline and liquefied natural gas (LNG) starting in 2019 (BEIS 2020).

The growth of the oil and gas sector helped the UK to transform its energy mix away from coal (Fig. 36.7). However, the price of the transition was great social unrest, as shown by the well-known 1984–1985 miners' strike against the economic policies of the then-Prime Minister Margaret Thatcher. A clear motivation of social unrest was the collapse of the employment rate in the coal sector during her term. Indeed, employment in the coal sector dropped from 242,000 miners in 1979 (when Thatcher became prime minister) to 49,000 in 1990 (when she left Downing Street), to only 1000 in 2018 (UK GOV 2019). The British social unrest waged by coal miners provides an important warning on the importance of caring for social justice within the energy transition.

But the most significant transformation of the British energy system occurred in the electricity generation (Fig. 36.8).

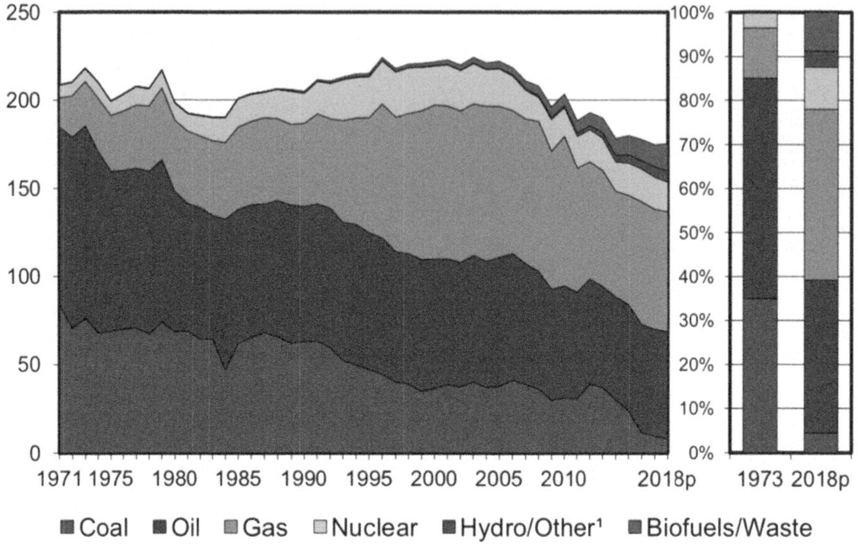

Fig. 36.7 UK's total primary energy supply by source (Mtoe). (Source: IEA World Energy Balances 2019, p. 152)

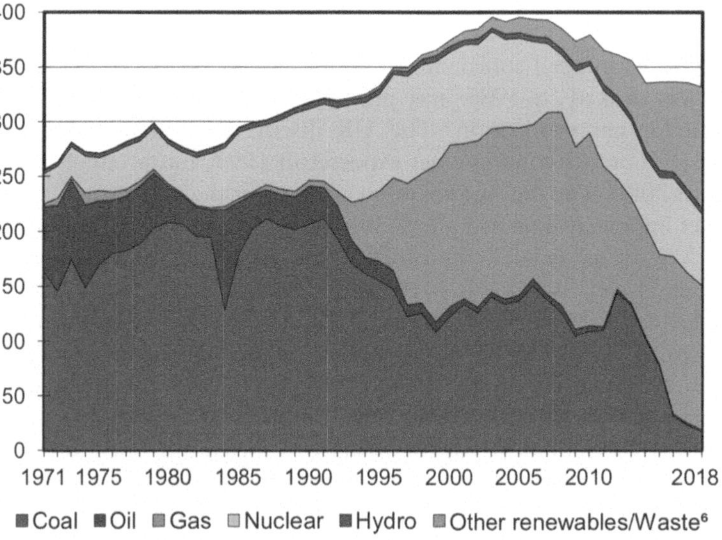

Fig. 36.8 UK's electricity generation by source (TWh). (Source: IEA World Energy Balances 2019, p. 152)

As industrial, railroad and residential use of coal decreased, its consumption in the electric power sector increased, peaking in 1980 (EIA 2018). Since 1990, the power sector witnessed a decline of coal, a rise of gas and, only recently, of renewables. While coal-fired power generation has strongly decreased over the last decades to reach a historical record low of 6.9 TWh in 2019, gas-fired generation has soared from 0.4 TWh in 1990 to 132.5 TWh in 2019 (BP 2020). Along with the increasing role of gas, an even more impressive increase occurred with renewable energy sources (wind and solar especially). Indeed, in less than two decades, the share of renewable energy increased from almost zero to 35% of electricity generation in 2019, with a strong role for wind. Between nuclear (around 20%) and renewables, the share of low-carbon power generation is presently over 50%.

The recent phasing-out of coal, and the consequent coal-to-gas shift, in the British power sector was achieved thanks to the implementation of the U.K. Carbon Price Floor (CPF) in 2013. It was introduced in 2013 at the rate of GBP 16 per ton of carbon dioxide-equivalent (tCO_2e) to be increased to GBP 30/tCO_2e, increasing the cost of carbon emissions for electric generators. The UK's CPF works in combination with the EU's Emissions Trading System (ETS). If the EU ETS carbon price is lower than the UK CPF, electric generators have to buy credits from the UK Treasury to make up the difference. The CPF applies to both generators that produce electricity for the grid and companies that produce electricity for their own use.

5.2 *Italy*

Italy is heavily dependent on imported fossil fuels, due to its low coal supply and the absence of nuclear power plants. In the aftermath of World War II, Italy witnessed strong economic growth, which required increasing energy supply, mainly met with imported oil.

Like for other countries, the 1973 oil crisis deeply affected the Italian economy, highlighting the need of an adequate energy security strategy. To achieve that, Italy had to diversify its energy mix, reducing the share of oil imports. Since 1973, the share of natural gas has increased and recently displaced oil as the largest contributor to TPES (Fig. 36.9). Oil's share has fallen from 76% in 1973 to 34% of the TPES in 2019. Natural gas share was 42% of TPES in 2019 (IEA 2016, 2020a). This strong increase of gas' share in TPES has been achieved thanks to large-scale development of gas pipeline import infrastructures. The main import sources became Russia, Algeria, Northern Europe, later Libya and very recently Azerbaijan. Also, some LNG facilities were built.

A further transformation of Italy's energy mix occurred since the beginning of the second millennium, with the rise of renewable energy sources (Fig. 36.10). While in 2000, fossil fuels covered about 88% of total Italian energy demand (oil accounted for 50%), this share fell to 74% in 2018. At the same time Italy has been able to boost its renewable energy contribution from

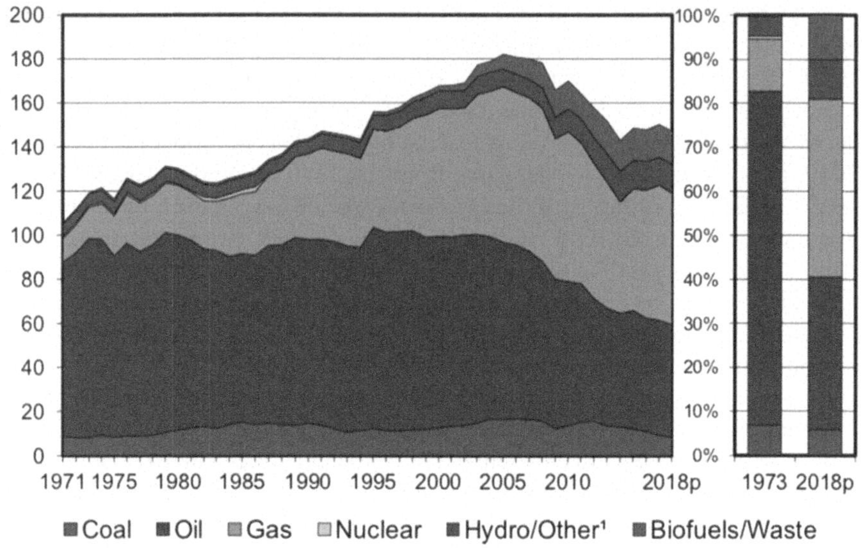

Fig. 36.9 Italy's total primary energy supply by source (Mtoe). (Source: IEA World Energy Balances 2019, p. 98)

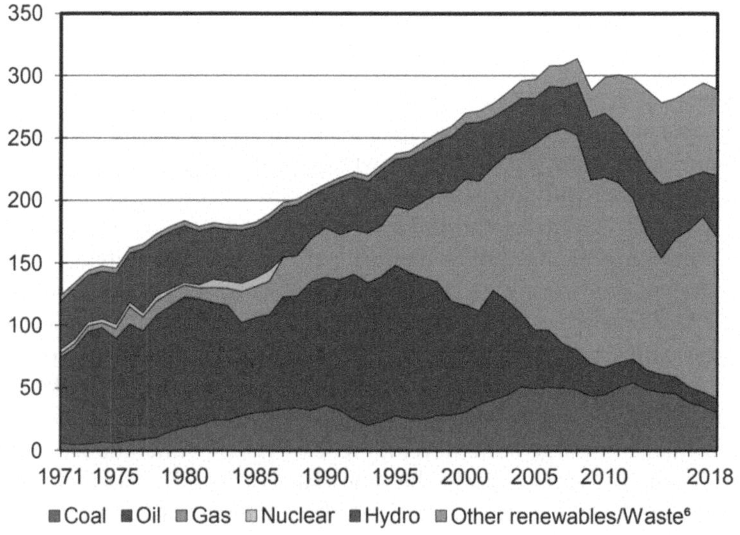

Fig. 36.10 Italy's electricity generation by source (TWh). (Source: IEA World Energy Balances 2019, p. 98)

7% in 2000 to 20% of the total in 2018 (CDP et al. 2019). This increase was mostly driven by solar PV development.

Moreover, in its efforts to decarbonize its energy system, Italy decided to phase out coal for electricity generation by 2025.

An important earlier development was Italy's decision to abandon its nuclear power development plans. The 1986 Chernobyl nuclear accident in Ukraine sparked an enormous and general debate on the implications of the use of nuclear energy in Italy. The debate resulted in a referendum in 1987, which stopped all activities in the nuclear sector. In 2009, the Italian government tried to restart an ambitious nuclear power program; this attempt was stopped in 2011, following a second popular referendum which was affected also by the 2011 Fukushima nuclear accident in Japan. In two decades, two successive generations decided to stop the development of a nuclear sector in Italy.

5.3 *France*

France took a completely opposite path. The country has today one of the least carbon intensive energy mixes thanks to its highly developed nuclear sector. Only 46% of TPES came from fossil fuels in 2019, whereas the share of nuclear energy made up 46% in the energy mix and 78% of electricity generation—the highest share worldwide (Figs. 36.11 and 36.12). The decision to develop the nuclear sector was supported by the 1973 oil crisis. That episode highlighted the risk of oil dependency and thus the political establishment decided to strongly pursue civil nuclear power development as a tool for energy

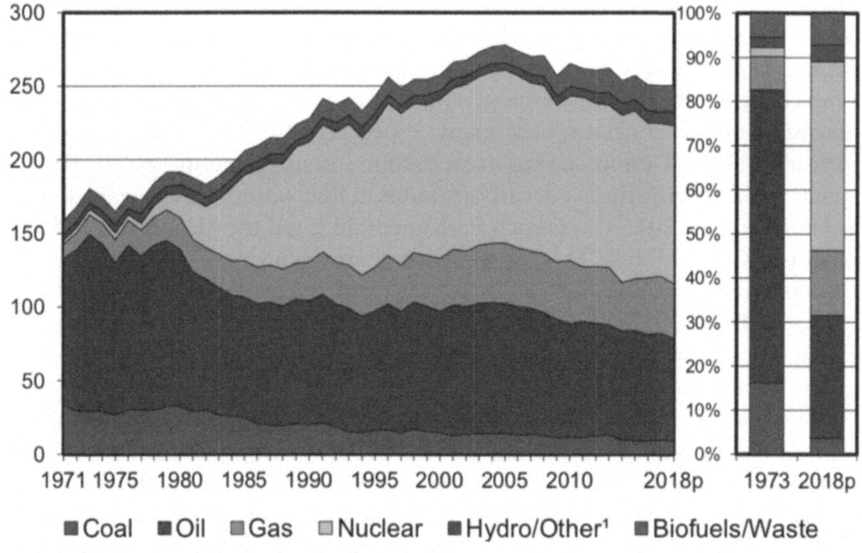

Fig. 36.11 France's total primary energy supply by source (Mtoe). (Source: IEA World Energy Balances 2019, p. 77)

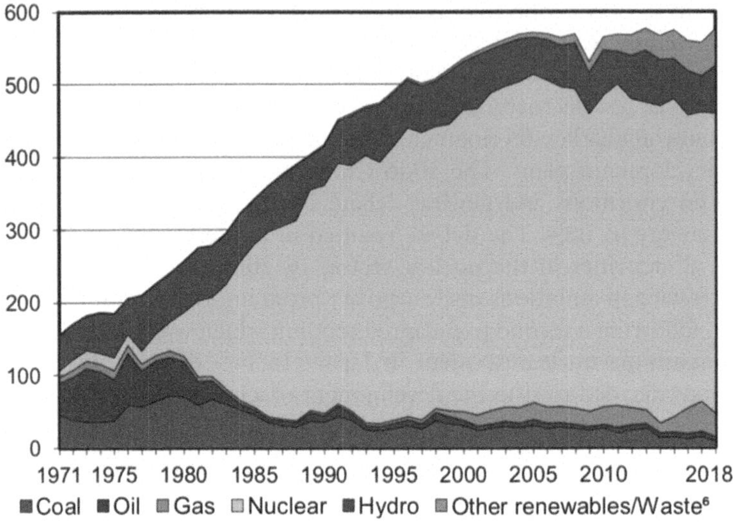

Fig. 36.12 France's electricity generation by source (TWh). (Source: IEA World Energy Balances 2019, p. 77)

independence and security. The share of oil in France's TPES has declined markedly since the early 1970s, from 66.5% in 1973 to 28% in 2019 (IEA 2017, 2020a). Nevertheless, oil is still the second-largest energy source given its strong role in transport and industry.

France comes second only to the US for installed nuclear power capacity (61 GW vs. 98 GW in 2020), however, with only one-fifth of the US population. France has not only the highest share of nuclear power generation in the world but also became the largest net exporter of electricity. Yet, France must address some challenges to its well-developed nuclear sector: an aging nuclear fleet and increasing public concerns over safety, especially after the 2011 Fukushima nuclear accident. Despite having a low-carbon intensive energy system, France decided to further foster its decarbonization in line with the European climate commitment. In 2015 the French Parliament adopted the "Energy Transition for Green Growth" bill. This bill sets several environmental and energy goals, including reducing the nuclear share of electricity production from 78% in 2015 to 50% by 2025 (IEA 2017). Additionally, it caps nuclear power generation at the current capacity level of 63.2 GW. In 2018, the government presented the Multiannual Energy Program, revising its objective to diversify the energy mix and reduce nuclear energy to 50% by 2035. In order to do so, France plans to shut down 14 reactors by 2035, which represent a quarter of reactors in operation in 2018 (GOUVERNEMENT FR 2018). However, following the 2021 energy price crisis, President Macron unveiled a "France 2030" investment plan restoring a primary role for France's nuclear sector—with a particular interest for small-scale nuclear reactors—through a €1 billion investment plan by the end of the decade. Moreover, the 2021 energy price crisis induced France along with some Eastern European countries to require nuclear energy to be labeled as "green" in the upcoming EU taxonomy that determines which economic activities can benefit from a "sustainable finance" label.

Within its decarbonization efforts, France decided to establish a new fuel tax in 2019. This was designed to discourage consumers from using diesel cars and raise additional revenue for funding renewable energies. However, the new tax set off a massive protest movement called *Gilets Jaunes* ("Yellow Vests"), accusing the government of widening social inequality. The social unrest in France highlighted the need to develop and implement just and inclusive climate policies.

5.4 *Germany*

In the last four decades, Germany's energy mix has shifted from a clear dominance of coal and oil to greater diversification. Yet, fossil fuels still dominate the energy supply, mainly due to domestic coal production and significant imports of oil and gas.

In 2018, fossil fuels accounted for 80% of TPES (oil for 33%, natural gas for 24% and coal for 23%), while low-carbon energy sources accounted for 22% (Fig. 36.13). Among these sources, nuclear energy, which was introduced in the 1970s in the aftermath of oil crisis, accounted for 13% of TPES (IEA 2020b).

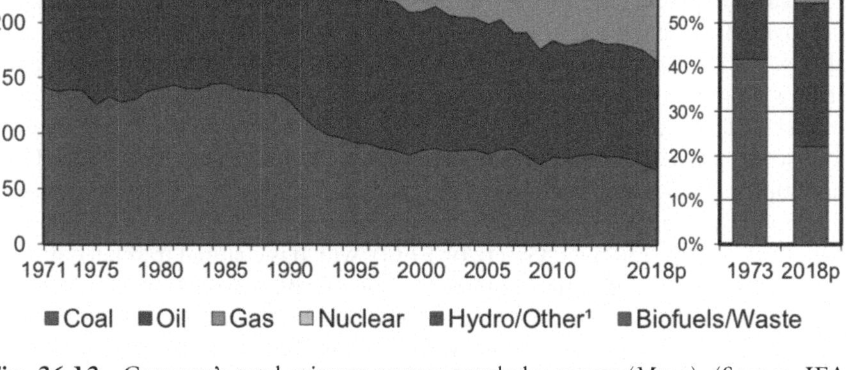

Fig. 36.13 Germany's total primary energy supply by source (Mtoe). (Source: IEA World Energy Balances 2019, p. 80)

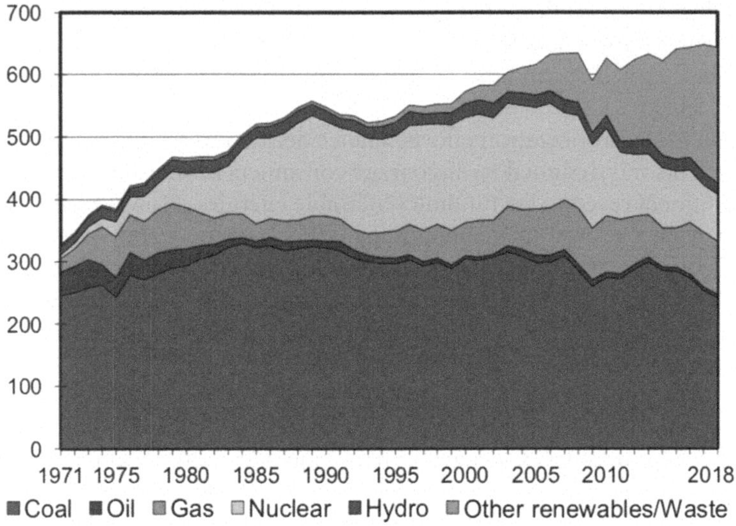

Fig. 36.14 Germany's electricity generation by source (TWh). (Source: IEA World Energy Balances 2019, p. 80)

Being so much reliant on fossil fuels and with the pressing issue of decarbonization, in 2010 Germany launched its energy transition plan (*Energiewende*) in order to promote energy efficiency and renewable energy sources. In 2011, following the Fukushima accident, the German government announced the decision to completely phase out nuclear from electricity generation by 2022, responding to popular concerns over nuclear safety. The decision to phase out nuclear has made the ambition to create a low-carbon energy system by 2050 more challenging, especially in the short term. Germany has set long-term targets for the share of renewables in electricity to at least 50% by 2030, 65% by 2040 and 80% by 2050. In the 2018, this share was approximately 38% (Fig. 36.14) (IEA 2020b).

To achieve these targets, since 2000 Germany has successfully promoted the deployment of renewables—especially wind turbines in Northern regions, but also solar PV for power generation—through feed-in tariffs. However, the strong support for renewables through feed-in tariffs generated an oxymoron: higher retail electricity prices for consumers (households and small and medium industry), while wholesale prices witnessed a sharp decline (to the benefit of distributors and large-scale industry that can access the wholesale market directly). Indeed, the feed-in tariff scheme is funded through an ad hoc levy (the Erneuerbare Energien Gesetz or EEG), which is charged to retail consumers and can be particularly harmful for low-income households. Today, Germany has one of the highest electricity prices for households in the EU (Fig. 36.15).

Since 2000, the growth of renewable energy has mainly compensated the partial withdrawal of nuclear power. In 2018, coal and natural gas still accounted

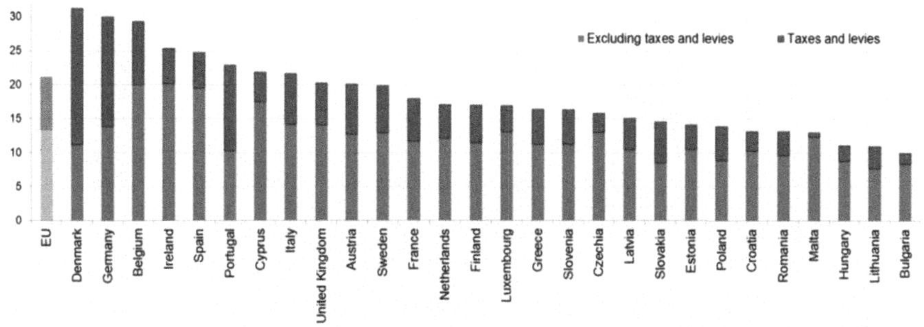

Fig. 36.15 Average electricity price for households per 100 kWh in 2H 2018 (€). (Source: EUROSTAT)

for 52% of total power generation. With a market share of 38%, coal is still the major source of power generation, down from about 50% a decade earlier (IEA 2020b). However, in line with its political commitment to foster decarbonization, Germany has started to plan the phase out of coal by 2038.

5.5 *Poland*

The political pressure and momentum against the use of coal in the European energy mix by the European Commission and its major Western Member States are at odds with the realities of some Central and Eastern European Member States, which are still highly dependent on coal. As shown in Fig. 36.2, the market share of coal in TPES in 2019 represents 44% for Poland, 32% for the Czech Republic and 29% for Bulgaria.

Poland in particular is strongly dependent on coal and fossil fuels. Besides having significant coal reserves, coal has been essential also in order to counterbalance its almost-entire dependence to Russian oil and gas, given the animosity between the two countries. In this effort, Poland started importing US LNG in order to reduce its vulnerability to Russian gas. Currently, coal accounts for almost 50% of TPES and 80% of the electricity generation (Figs. 36.16 and 36.17). Though in relative terms natural gas and renewables did replace part of coal's share in the fuel mix between 1990 and 2017, in absolute terms, coal remained exactly stable (Rentier et al. 2019).

Although coal production grew steadily until the late 1970s, the sector and related industries became dysfunctional. In 1979, production reached its peak of 201 million tons. However, the relevance of coal in the energy mix also has social and employment implications. Poland's coal sector employs around 100,000 workers. However, in the last decades coal in Poland has become uncompetitive and unprofitable on the international markets, facing competition from extra-EU coal producers and international climate pressure. Therefore, subsequent governments have provided financial aids and subsidies to the sector. It is estimated that between 2013 and 2018, Poland spent as

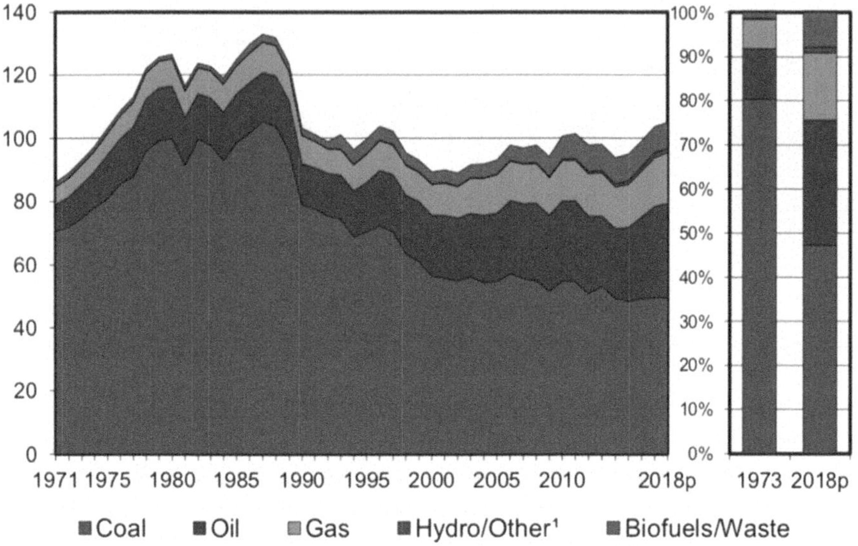

Fig. 36.16 Poland's total primary energy supply by source (Mtoe). (Source: IEA World Energy Balances 2019, p. 128)

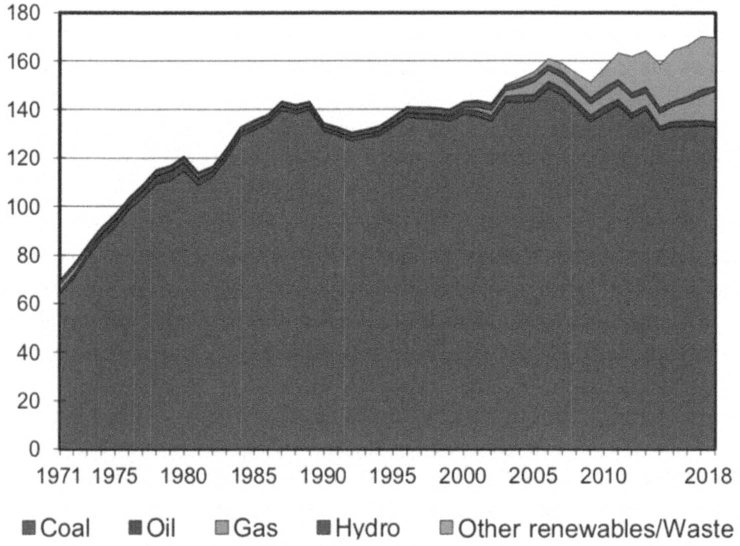

Fig. 36.17 Poland's electricity generation by source (TWh). (Source: IEA World Energy Balances 2019, p. 128)

much as €6.8 billion on bailouts of the country's coal sector energy sector (DW 2020).

The Polish government started to reflect on some major transformations for its energy sector. Such considerations are driven by (i) the economic disadvantages to keep producing coal in Poland, (ii) the pressure of expected increasing costs under the EU ETS and (iii) political pressure from European institutions for decarbonization (POLITICO 2020). To do so, Poland considers the development of a nuclear sector and renewable energy (especially offshore wind). In 2020, Poland presented a $40 billion plan to build its first nuclear power plants, while setting out its new energy strategy for 2040 (FT 2020). Poland wants to build 6–9 GW of nuclear capacity and its first nuclear unit should come on line in 2033. In 2021, Poland announced a new scheme to support offshore wind farms for €22.5 billion until 2030.

6 The Green Deal: Toward a Carbon-Neutral EU in 2050

As mentioned before, climate issues and decarbonization efforts have been the top priority of the EU energy policy during the last decades. The political commitment of the EU on climate change was reaffirmed in 2019 by the new Commission President Ursula von der Leyen. She launched an ambitious and comprehensive policy program, called "European Green Deal". The main goal of this plan is to transform the European society into a resource-efficient and competitive economy, making the EU a net-zero GHG emissions society by 2050. To do so, it is necessary to further decouple economic growth from resource use and decarbonize energy. To achieve the climate-neutrality goal, substantial transformation of the EU economy is required.

Over the last decades, EU decarbonization strategies have mainly focused on the power sector as it is by far the easiest sector to decarbonize, even though it is not an easy task. To reach carbon-neutrality, the EU needs not only to step up its efforts to decarbonize the power sector but also to address all other sectors including those which are difficult to decarbonize like buildings, industry and transport. Figure 36.18 presents the share GHG emissions by sector.

In 2020 the European economies experienced an unprecedented health crisis (the COVID-19 pandemic) that quickly became an economic and social one. The European governments and the European Union needed to plan economic and social recovery. The initial recovery phase saw a return of the role of the State in the economy, with significant amounts of public debts and investments.

After long and difficult negotiations, the European Member States managed to agree on a €750 billion recovery plan, the Next Generation EU. The Recovery package consists of €390 billion of grants and €360 billion of loans to be directed to European economies. Through Next Generation EU, the European leaders seek to reshape the economic model, promoting a cleaner,

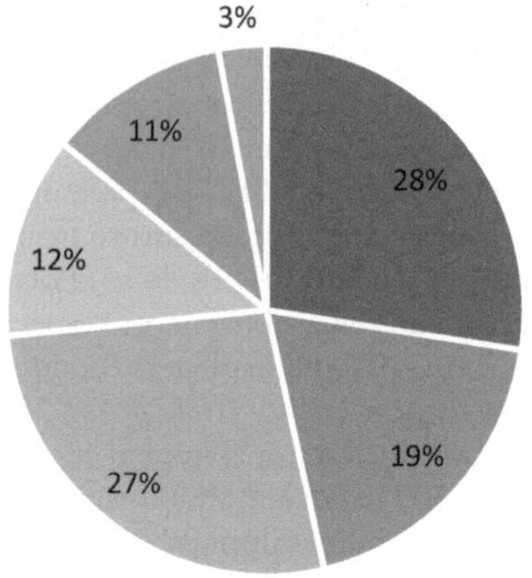

Fig. 36.18 EU-28 GHG emissions by aggregated sector in 2017. (Source: EEA https://www.eea.europa.eu/data-and-maps/daviz/ghg-emissions-by-aggregated-sector-5#tab-dashboard-02. Note: Transport includes international aviation and shipping)

more sustainable and digital society, while addressing some of the major issues generated by the 2020 health and economic crisis.

Thus, in light of the need of economic recovery, the EU not only maintained its commitment to decarbonization but further proposed to step up Europe's 2030 climate ambition by reducing GHG emission by at least 55% below 1990 levels (Fig. 36.19). Moreover, in July 2021, the European Commission released its "Fit for 55" package, which is set to facilitate a GHG emissions reduction of 55% by 2030 compared to 1990. Although its approval and implementation will not be an easy task, the package would deepen and broaden the decarbonization of Europe's economy and society in the 2020s in order to be on track to achieving climate-neutrality by 2050. The package contains several legislative proposals. Some proposals are the evolution of existing climate and energy policies and targets, such as the upgrading of renewable energy (from at least 32% to 40%) and energy efficiency (from at least 32.5% to 36%) or a profound restructuring of European energy taxation. On the other hand, other legislative proposals envisage the creation of new and ambitions climate tools. For example, the creation of a new EU ETS for buildings and road transport or the revision of CO_2 emissions standards for new cars—emissions should be cut by 55% by 2030 and by 100% by 2035.

In order to achieve the envisaged energy transition, the EU economy will need to adjust and adapt in order to remain competitive. To this end, the Commission has launched several initiatives: the European Battery Alliance,

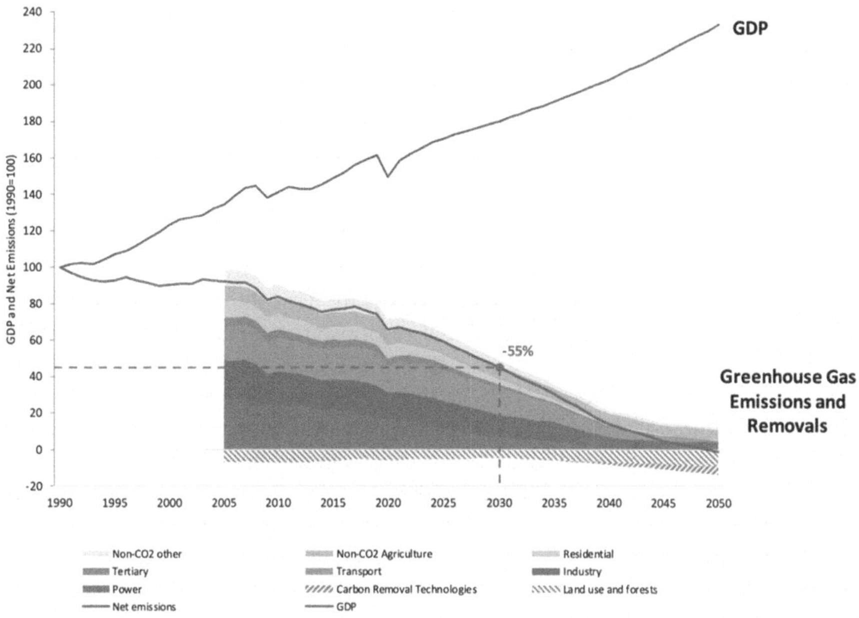

Fig. 36.19 EU's GHG emissions targets by 2030 and carbon-neutrality by 2050. (Source: European Commission 2020c)

the European Clean Hydrogen Alliance and the European Raw Materials Alliance. These initiatives are expected to develop value chains in order to maintain Europe's industry competitive as well as create new jobs preparing tomorrow's low-carbon economy. With electrification conquering tomorrow's automotive sector, the EU needs to transform its leading position in internal combustion engine technologies toward electric vehicles. The European Battery Alliance represents an example of this effort to avoid being left behind by other major technological hubs, notably China. Moreover, such initiatives are also motivated by energy security considerations, as technological know-how and access to rare earths are both needed for the transition.

The transformation of the European economy will cause profound socio-economic consequences. The EU must avoid negative distributive effects and minimize the burden of the transition. In 2019, the EU created the Just Transition Fund (JTF) to support the economic diversification and reconversion in areas negatively affected by the energy transition.

Although the EU decided to allocate funds to reduce the burden of the energy transition, the road toward carbon-neutrality is not exempt from challenges and opposition both among Member States and within Member States, especially in an increasingly polarized society. The EU is facing multiple divisions between East and West European countries as well as within its own societies between nationalism and Europeanism. At the national level, popular protests—like the French Yellow Vests—might erupt in the future because of the burden of additional costs of the transition and the loss of previous privileges, benefits and jobs, especially for the low- and middle-income classes. At the European level, some Member States are against a strong decarbonization due to their socio-economic characteristics and energy mix. For example, the Central and Eastern European countries regularly express their skepticism toward a full decarbonization because of the relevant role of coal in their economy.

Besides the internal European dimensions, the energy transition also includes external dimensions. The EU needs to cooperate with third countries to intensify the pursuit of a common and global response to climate change. In 2019, the EU accounted for about 9.5% of world's CO_2 emissions, while China accounted for 28.8%, the US 14.5%, India 7.3% and Russia 4.5%. Thus, the participation and collaboration of other major world economies and emitters is crucial for achieving a global decarbonization and tackling climate change successfully. To do so, the EU engages with other countries pursuing a so-called climate diplomacy.

The EU also considers to implement a carbon border adjustment mechanism (CBAM) for certain sectors, in order to prevent potential reallocation of activities outside the EU (*carbon leakage*). The potential reallocation would be motivated by the need to avoid European climate policies and higher CO_2 prices. With a CBAM the price of imports would reflect more accurately their carbon content, ensuring that EU green targets are not undermined by producing goods in countries with less ambitious climate policies. However, the proposed mechanism encounters both legal and political obstacles. From the legal point of view, the EU must set a mechanism in line with WTO rules. Politically, such a mechanism encounters significant opposition from some major economies, notably the US, China and Russia. Despite the political controversy, the Commission included in its "Fit for 55" package a legislative proposal for the implementation of a CBAM, envisaging a transitional period until 2026 and for a limited set of goods.

In 2020, several major economies and emitters[10] have pledged to reach carbon-neutrality by mid-century. The EU could benefit from the growing political commitment to carbon-neutrality worldwide. It will need to cooperate with those countries—and others which will commit in the future—to enhance the global effort to reach decarbonization and tackle climate change.

7 Conclusions

The EU energy mix has experienced successive transformations since World War II, driven by multiple goals (energy security, competitiveness and sustainability). As climate policies became more and more relevant over the last two decades, the EU strengthened its political commitment to reach

[10] Among others, Japan by 2050; South Korea by 2050; China by 2060.

carbon-neutrality by 2050. To achieve this goal, the EU must decarbonize all sectors, while developing all possible ways to offset remaining emissions. In this major effort, the EU has put in place several industrial policies in order to adjust and adapt its economy and remain competitive compared to other major economies and leading technological hubs, notably China.

However, the energy transition is not an easy path neither within the EU nor globally. Domestically, the energy transition could meet opposition both from specific population segments and from some Member States. Therefore, the EU seeks to avoid negative distributive effects reducing the burden of the transition for specific population segments as well as the most affected regions. Globally, the EU is engaging with other major economies and emitters in order to successfully tackle climate change and make sure that decarbonization gets implemented globally.

Bibliography

BEIS (2020), Natural Gas, in: *Digest of United Kingdom Energy Statistics 2020*. Available at: https://assets.publishing.service.gov.uk/government/uploads/system/uploads/attachment_data/file/924591/DUKES_2020_MASTER.pdf

BP (2020), Statistical Review of World Energy 2020.

CDP, SNAM, Terna, and The European House Ambrosetti (2019), The Energy Transition in Italy and The Role of the Gas and Power Sectors. Available at: https://download.terna.it/terna/Transizione_Energetica_8d75215ad40fffa.pdf

Consilium (2014), The 2030 Climate and Energy Framework. Available at: https://www.consilium.europa.eu/en/policies/climate-change/2030-climate-and-energy-framework/

DW (2020), Poland Shelves Major Coal Sector Restructuring Plans, 29 July 2020. Available at: https://www.dw.com/en/poland-shelves-major-coal-sector-restructuring-plans/a-54363275

EC EUROPA (2014), European 2030 Climate & Energy Framework. Available at: https://ec.europa.eu/clima/policies/strategies/2030_en

EC EUROPA (2018), A Clean Planet for All a European Strategic Long-Term Vision for a Prosperous, Modern, Competitive and Climate Neutral Economy, COM(2018) 773 final. *Access on October 2020*. Available at: https://eur-lex.europa.eu/legal-content/EN/TXT/PDF/?uri=CELEX:52018DC0773&from=EN

EC EUROPA (2019), Clean energy for all Europeans Package. Available at: https://ec.europa.eu/energy/topics/energy-strategy/clean-energy-all-europeans_en

EC EUROPA (2020a), Energy Production and Imports. *Access on October 2020*. Available at: https://ec.europa.eu/eurostat/statistics-explained/index.php/Energy_production_and_imports#The_EU_and_its_Member_States_are_all_net_importers_of_energy

EC EUROPA (2020b), Energy Prices and Costs in Europe, COM(2020) 951 final. *Access on October 2020*. Available at: https://eur-lex.europa.eu/legal-content/EN/TXT/PDF/?uri=CELEX:52020DC0951&from=EN

EC EUROPA (2020c), Stepping up Europe's 2030 climate ambition, COM(2020) 562 final. *Access on 17 September 2020*. Brussels.

EEA (2019), Energy Intensity, Available at: https://www.eea.europa.eu/data-and-maps/indicators/total-primary-energy-intensity-4/assessment-1
EIA (2018), Coal Power Generation Declines in United Kingdom as Natural Gas, Renewables Grow, 24 April 2018. Available at: https://www.eia.gov/todayinenergy/detail.php?id=35912
EUROPA (2006), Green Paper. A European Strategy for Sustainable, Competitive and Secure Energy, COM(2006) 105 final, Brussels, 8.3.2006. Available at: https://europa.eu/documents/comm/green_papers/pdf/com2006_105_en.pdf
EUROSTAT (2020), Energy Production and Imports. *Access on April 2020.* Available at: https://ec.europa.eu/eurostat/statistics-explained/index.php/Energy_production_and_imports#The_EU_and_its_Member_States_are_all_net_importers_of_energy
FT (2020), Poland Plans $40bn Nuclear Push to Cut Reliance on Coal, September 8, 2020. Available at: https://www.ft.com/content/1ed55036-24b0-4734-9901-76133cfd3c3b
FuelsEurope (2019), Statistical Report 2019. Available at: https://www.fuelseurope.eu/wp-content/uploads/FuelsEurope-Statistical-Report-2019-2.pdf
GOUVERNEMENT FR (2018), Multiannual Energy Programme: Its Aims, 28 November 2018. Available at: https://www.gouvernement.fr/en/multiannual-energy-programme-its-aims
IEA (2016), Italy Review 2016, Energy Policies of IEA Countries.
IEA (2017), France Review 2016, Energy Policies of IEA Countries.
IEA (2019), Energy Intensity, Available at: https://www.iea.org/reports/sdg7-data-and-projections/energy-intensity, in: IEA "SDG7: Data and Projections", IEA, Paris.
IEA (2020a), Energy Data and Statistics. *Access on October 2020.* Available at: https://www.iea.org/data-and-statistics?country=WORLD&fuel=Energy%20supply&indicator=TPESbySource
IEA (2020b), Germany Review 2020, Energy Policies of IEA Countries.
POLITICO (2020), Coal-Dependent Poland Pivots Toward Green Energy, September 25, 2020. Available at: https://www.politico.eu/article/coal-dependent-poland-green-energy-pivot/
Rentier, G., Lelieveldt, H., and Kraner, G.J. (2019), Varieties of Coal-Fired Power Phase-Out Across Europe, Energy Policy, Volume 132, pp. 602–632. Available at: https://www.sciencedirect.com/science/article/pii/S0301421519303465
UN DESA (2019), World Population Prospects 2019, UN Population Division, Department of Economic and Social Affairs.
UK GOV (2019), Historical Coal Data: Coal Production, Availability and Consumption. Available at: https://www.gov.uk/government/statistical-data-sets/historical-coal-data-coal-production-availability-and-consumption
Yafimava, K. (2020), 'Finding a Home' for Global LNG in Europe: Understanding the Complexity of Access Rules for EU Import Terminals, The Oxford Institute of Energy Studies, OIES Paper NG 157, January 2020. Available at: https://www.oxfordenergy.org/wpcms/wp-content/uploads/2020/01/Finding-a-home-for-global-LNG-in-Europe-NG-157.pdf
Yergin, D. (2009), The Prize—The Epic Quest for Oil, Money & Power, Free Press.

Energy Units Conversion Tables

Units

1 metric tonne	= 2204.62lb	= 1.1023 short tonnes
1 kilolitre	= 6.2898 barrels	
1 kilolitre	= 1 cubic metre	
1 kilocalorie (kcal)	= 4.1868 kJ	= 3.968 Btu
1 kilojoule (kJ)	= 0.239 kcal	= 0.948 Btu
1 petajoule (Pj)	= 1 quadrillion joules (1×10^{15})	
1 exajoule (EJ)	= 1 quadrillion joules (1×10^{18})	
1 British thermal unit (Btu)	= 0.252 kcal	= 1.055 kJ
1 tonne of oil equivalent (toe)	= 39.683 million Btu	
1 tonne of oil equivalent (toe)	= 41.868 million kJ	
1 barrel of oil equivalent (boe)	= 5.8 million Btu	= 6.119 million kJ
1 kilowatt-hour (kWh)	= 860 kcal	= 3600 kJ = 3412 Btu

Source: BP Statistical Review of World Energy 2019 & 2020

Crude oil (based on the worldwide average gravity)

From	*To convert*				
	tonnes (metric)	*Kilolitres*	*Barrels*	*US gallons*	*Tonnes/year*
Tonnes (metric)	1	1.165	7.33	307.86	–
Kilolitres	0.8581	1	6.2898	264.17	–
Barrels	0.1364	0.159	1	42	–
US gallons	0.00325	0.0038	0.0238	1	–
Barrels/day	–	–	–	–	49.8

Source: BP Statistical Review of World Energy 2019 & 2020

M. Hafner, G. Luciani (eds.), *The Palgrave Handbook of International Energy Economics*, https://doi.org/10.1007/978-3-030-86884-0

Petroleum products

From	To convert					
	barrels to tonnes	*Tonnes to barrels*	*Kilolitres to tonnes*	*Tonnes to kilolitres*	*Tonnes to gigajoules*	*Tonnes to barrels oil equivalent*
Ethane	0.059	16.850	0.373	2.679	49.400	8.073
Liquefied petroleum gas (LPG)	0.086	11.60	0.541	1.849	46.150	7.542
Gasoline	0.120	8.35	0.753	1.328	44.750	7.313
Kerosene	0.127	7.88	0.798	1.253	43.920	7.177
Gas oil/diesel	0.134	7.46	0.843	1.186	43.380	7.089
Residual fuel oil	0.157	6.35	0.991	1.010	41.750	6.793
Product basket	0.124	8.058	0.781	1.281	43.076	7.039

Source: BP Statistical Review of World Energy 2019 & 2020

Natural gas and LNG

From	To convert						
	billion cubic metres NG	*Billion cubic feet NG*	*Petajoules NG*	*Million tonnes oil equivalent*	*Million tonnes LNG*	*Trillion British thermal units*	*Million barrels oil equivalent*
1 billion cubic metres NG	1.000	35.315	36.000	0.860	0.735	34.121	5.883
1 billion cubic feet NG	0.028	1.000	1.019	0.024	0.021	0.966	0.167
1 petajoule NG	0.028	0.981	1.000	0.024	0.021	0.952	0.164
1 million tonnes oil equivalent	1.163	41.071	41.868	1.000	0.855	39.683	6.842
1 million tonnes LNG	1.360	48.028	48.747	1.169	1.000	46.405	8.001
1 trillion British thermal units	0.029	1.035	1.050	0.025	0.022	1.000	0.172
1 million barrels oil equivalent	0.170	6.003	6.093	0.146	0.125	5.800	1.000

Source: BP Statistical Review of World Energy 2019 & 2020

Calorific equivalents

One exajoule equals approximately	
Heat units	• 239 trillion kilocalories
	• 948 trillion Btu
Solid fuels	• 40 tonnes of hard coal
	• 95 tonnes of lignite and sub-bituminous coal
Gaseous fuels	• See natural gas and LNG table
Electricity	• 278 terawatt-hours

All fuel energy content is net or lower heating value (i.e., net of heat of vaporization of water generated from combustion)	
1 tonne of ethanol	= 0.68 tonne of oil equivalent
1 tonne biodiesel	= 0.88 tonne of oil equivalent
1 barrel of ethanol	= 0.58 barrels of oil equivalent
1 barrel of biodiesel	= 0.86 barrels of oil equivalent

One tonne of oil equivalent equals approximately	
Heat units	• 10 million kilocalories
	• 42 gigajoules
	• 40 million Btu
Solid fuels	• 1.5 tonnes of hard coal
	• 3 tonnes of lignite and sub-bituminous coal
Gaseous fuels	• See natural gas and LNG table
Electricity	• 12 mega watt-hours

One million tonnes of oil produces about 4400 gigawatt-hours (= 4.4 terawatt-hours) of electricity in a modern power station	
1 tonne of ethanol	= 0.68 tonne of oil equivalent
1 tonne biodiesel	= 0.88 tonne of oil equivalent
1 barrel of ethanol	= 0.58 barrels of oil equivalent
1 barrel of biodiesel	= 0.86 barrels of oil equivalent

Source: BP Statistical Review of World Energy 2019 & 2020

Index[1]

[1] Note: Page numbers followed by ‘n’ refer to notes.

M. Hafner, G. Luciani (eds.), *The Palgrave Handbook of International Energy Economics*, https://doi.org/10.1007/978-3-030-86884-0

F

G

H

I

The manufacturer's authorised representative in the EU is Springer Nature Customer Service Centre GmbH, Europaplatz 3, 69115 Heidelberg, Germany. If you have any concerns regarding our products, please contact ProductSafety@springernature.com

Printed and bound by CPI Group (UK) Ltd, Croydon, CR0 4YY
30/09/2026
02225704-0013